PUBLIC LAW

Public Law

DR MARK ELLIOTT

University of Cambridge

DR ROBERT THOMAS

University of Manchester

OXFORD

UNIVERSITY PRESS

OXFORD
UNIVERSITY PRESS

Great Clarendon Street, Oxford OX2 6DP

Oxford University Press is a department of the University of Oxford.
It furthers the University's objective of excellence in research, scholarship,
and education by publishing worldwide in

Oxford New York

Auckland Cape Town Dar es Salaam Hong Kong Karachi
Kuala Lumpur Madrid Melbourne Mexico City Nairobi
New Delhi Shanghai Taipei Toronto

With offices in

Argentina Austria Brazil Chile Czech Republic France Greece
Guatemala Hungary Italy Japan Poland Portugal Singapore
South Korea Switzerland Thailand Turkey Ukraine Vietnam

Oxford is a registered trade mark of Oxford University Press
in the UK and in certain other countries

Published in the United States
by Oxford University Press Inc., New York

British Library Cataloguing-in-Publication Data
Data available

Library of Congress Cataloging in Publication Data
Data available

Typeset by Newgen Imaging Systems (P) Ltd, Chennai, India
Printed and bound by
CPI Group (UK) Ltd,
Croydon, CR0 4YY

ISBN 978–0–19–923710–4

5 7 9 10 8 6 4

About the Online Resource Centre

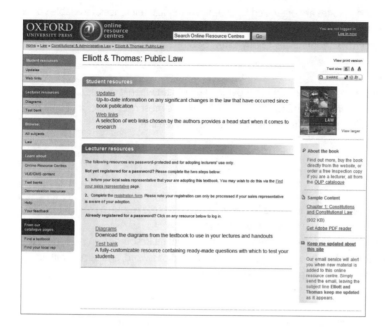

Public Law is complemented by an Online Resource Centre that provides a range of features that are of use to students and lecturers.

www.oxfordtextbooks.co.uk/orc/elliott_thomas/

For Students

Updates

Updates are an indispensable resource that will allow you to access up-to-date information on any significant changes in the law that have occurred since publication of the book. The website is regularly updated, and updates are organized by chapter, with page references, to enable you to easily identify any material that has been superseded or supplemented. They allow you to keep up to date with developments without having to buy a new book.

Annotated web links

A selection of web links chosen by the authors provides a head start when it comes to research. The additional annotation will help you to identify which links are most relevant to your area of study and they are checked regularly to make sure that they remain live.

For Lecturers

Password protected to ensure only adopting lecturers can access these resources - each registration is personally checked to ensure the security of the site.

Registering is easy: click on the 'Lecturer Resources' on the Online Resource Centre, complete a simple registration form which allows you to choose your own password, and access will be granted within three working days (subject to verification).

Test bank

Test banks are a fully customizable resource containing ready-made assessments with which to test your students. There are over 200 questions that apply to the material in the book and the provision of instant feedback allows students to understand the reasons for the correct answers.

Diagrams

All of the diagrams in the book are provided electronically and are available to download for use in lectures and seminars to aid student understanding. There are over 50 diagrams in this textbook and each one has been designed to help students visualise the topics in more detail.

Brief Contents

Part V Administrative Justice

Part VI Human Rights

Contents

Preface

Of all the subjects that law students study, public law—at least at the moment—is surely one of the most dynamic, fast-moving, and obviously relevant. From the recent formation of a coalition government to its proposals for wide-ranging political and constitutional reform, and from the so-called 'war on terror' to the now-ubiquitous talk of human rights, very few of the big issues of the day lack a public law dimension of some sort. In writing this book, one of our central aims has been to underline the contemporary significance of public law, and to highlight its importance to so many of the issues that have dominated public and political discourse in recent years, and which continue to do so today. An early and obvious way in which this approach is evident is through our use of case studies in Chapter 1, which make plain the sweep of issues to which public law is relevant, the range of matters with which students must grapple if they are to make sense of the law, and the interconnected and contested nature of many of those issues.

Public law is, then, an endlessly fascinating area of legal study—yet it is also a challenging subject. Like most branches of law, public law is, at one level, a complicated, technical, and difficult subject; and this book embraces and deals with the complexity of public law. However, it also emphasises the nature and importance of the political, theoretical and social context within which the black-letter legal rules exist. In this way, we show that public law both shapes and is shaped by the wider environment within which politics, governance, and public life are conducted today. Far from being a collection of dry legal rules, public law is intimately connected with fundamental issues such as the legitimacy of government, the institutions of the state, and the control and oversight of governmental power. To appreciate the nature of public law, such issues must necessarily be examined against the broader backdrop of themes such as the exercise of public power in a modern liberal democracy; the relationship between the individual and the state; and the shifting nature of governmental power in the context of the global economy, and the establishment and development of governmental structures, such as the European Union, at the level above that of the nation state. We therefore also approach public law from the standpoint of relevant principles, issues, debates, and ideas, presenting the technical detail of the subject in the light of those forces that drive its evolution.

Consistently with our general approach to the subject, our treatment of it is informed by three key themes, which distil the main challenges faced by public law today. These three themes provide a narrative structure for the book by reference to which the development of the UK constitution and public law more generally are analysed. It is therefore appropriate to identify, albeit briefly, these three themes right at the outset. The first concerns the particularly powerful position of the executive branch with the United Kingdom's system of government, and the resulting challenges that this poses in respect of such matters as accountability and the responsible use of power. The second theme that runs throughout the book is the relationship between political and legal modes of constitutionalism, and the growing emphasis placed within the UK upon the latter. Our third theme is the increasingly multilayered nature of governance within the UK and its impact upon traditional pillars of British constitutionalism such as parliamentary sovereignty.

Our overriding objective in writing this book has been to provide an account of the UK constitution, and of public law more generally, that is scholarly and accurate, but also accessible and interesting. Although there is an apparently never-ending stream of major legal and political developments in this area—many, such as proposed reforms to the voting system and the House of Lords are ongoing at the time of writing—this book was completed and largely written after the implementation of the unusually extensive and far-reaching constitutional changes introduced by the 1997–2010 Labour administrations. This has made it possible to organise the book and approach the material in a way that reflects the ground-breaking reforms of the last decade or so, and which captures the full extent to which public law in the UK has changed in recent years. Of course, it remains to be seen what future constitutional developments wait in store.

While we have been writing this book, we have received help, in the form of comments, feedback, suggestions, and advice, from several colleagues. In particular, we wish to thank Albertina Albors-Llorens, Catherine Barnard, John Bell, David Feldman, and Jason Varuhas; we also thank the anonymous reviewers who commented on individual chapters as our writing progressed. We are grateful too to those at Oxford University Press who have been involved in various capacities in this project. We particularly thank Kate Whetter, for commissioning this book; John Carroll, Francesca Griffin, and Gareth Malna, who consecutively served as the book's development editors; and Anya Aghdam, Philip Moore, and Tom Young for their help during the production phase. Finally, but most importantly, we are immensely grateful to our respective families—in Mark's case, to his wife, Vicky, and their daughter, Maisie; in Robert's case, to his wife Nicola, and their children, Penelope, Rosamund, Constanza, Edward, and Gwendolyn—for their love and support throughout the course of this project.

Mark Elliott, Cambridge
Robert Thomas, Manchester
27 October 2010

Table of Cases

Table of UK Legislation

Secondary Legislation

Table of European Legislation

Table of Legislation from other Jurisdictions

Table of other International Instruments

PART I

Introduction to Public Law

1 Constitutions and Constitutional Law

1. Introduction

People often say that the United Kingdom does not have a constitution. They are wrong. It may not have a *written* constitution, in the sense of a single document entitled 'The Constitution', but it undoubtedly has a constitution.

No organisation can work effectively without ground rules setting out who is responsible for doing particular things, how they should do them, and what is to be done if things go wrong. This is true of companies, schools and universities, and even of sporting clubs and debating societies. Does the head teacher have the authority to compel science teachers to teach creationism? (And, if she has no such authority, but tries to do so anyway, what can be done?) Who gets a say in appointing the head of a university? Can the chair of the debating society be removed if she tries to stifle open discussion and, if so, how? In the absence of rules providing for eventualities such as these, a number of risks arise. A dictatorial leader may be able to carry on unchecked, in the absence of an effective mechanism for bringing him into line or getting rid of him. Chaos might reign if there is no accepted way of deciding who should be in charge and what should be done if she misbehaves. And people might end up being treated in ways that are widely considered to be unacceptable if the authority of those in power is not subject to appropriate and effective limits.

Such circumstances are undesirable in most walks of life, but they are particularly undesirable when it comes to the running of a country. If someone dislikes how his company or club or university is governed, there are at least the options—albeit ones that might be practically difficult to take—of walking away or of joining another organisation. But, short of emigration, people do not have that option if the country is governed badly or corruptly. For that reason (and, as we will see, many others), it is especially important that transparent, widely accepted rules exist concerning the arrangements for governing the country and for changing how it is run—and by whom—if a particular government, or an aspect of the system of government, is felt to be deficient. How is the Prime Minister chosen? How often must elections be held? What happens if no political party wins a clear majority in an election—who decides, and according to what principles, which party should form the next government? Can the government sack the judges if the courts give Ministers a hard time? To what extent is the government allowed to intervene in people's lives in order to promote (what it regards as) the common good?

For example, can it put people in prison because it thinks that they are at risk of committing serious criminal offences, or torture people to extract confessions, or are people entitled not to be treated in such ways? Questions like these raise issues relating to how the country is run, the powers of those in government, and the rights of those of us who are governed. These issues are fundamental. They are the concern of public law—and they are the sort of questions with which we will engage in this book.

2. Constitutions

'Public law' is a broad term. Some people prefer instead to talk of 'constitutional law' and 'administrative law', the former being concerned with the basic ground rules determining the powers of the government and the fundamental rights of individuals, the latter being to do with the more detailed rules with which the government is required to comply. This distinction makes some sense in countries with written constitutions, in which 'constitutional law' is primarily about the meaning and application of a single constitutional text. In the UK, however, the absence of a written constitution makes the dividing line between constitutional and administrative law hard to locate and somewhat artificial. There is little practical, or even academic, merit in trying to draw that line in relation to the UK, and we do not propose to do so. But that does not change the fact that the UK has certain ground rules that would, in most countries, be found in a constitutional text. An important part of the purpose of this book is to explain what those ground rules are and to assess them critically. And if we are to do that, we must begin by explaining what constitutions are *for*.

At a very basic level, a constitution serves the same purpose as any other set of rules: it anticipates issues that may arise—the resignation of a Prime Minister, an attempt by the government to suppress freedom of speech, a row between central and local government about who is responsible for doing what—and prescribes what should happen when they do, or at least provides mechanisms by which such matters might be resolved. But constitutions also serve a number of specific functions and possess a number of particular characteristics that distinguish them from ordinary rules and laws.[1] In the following sections, we examine these functions and characteristics in general terms—thinking of what the constitutions of Western democratic countries are typically like—rather than with particular reference to the UK. Later in the chapter, we consider how the UK's constitutional arrangements measure up.

2.1 Power allocation

Many legal rules are concerned with regulating the conduct of *private parties*: individuals, companies, and so on. For example, the criminal law stipulates that

---

[1] See, eg Feldman, 'None, One or Several? Perspectives on the UK's Constitution(s)' [2005] CLJ 329.

certain things—such as intentionally killing someone—may generally not be lawfully done, and specifies what punishment may be applied to offenders. And the law of tort says that people must take reasonable care to avoid causing foreseeable harm to those liable to be affected by their actions, otherwise they may have to pay compensation. In contrast, the pre-eminent function of a constitution is to allocate *state* power—that is, the power to do things such as make laws (such as legislation), exercise governmental power (such as administer government programmes), and determine disputes between people (through the judicial process). These are things that ordinary people cannot do, either for practical reasons (if you were to say that you had made a 'law', everyone would ignore it) or because it would be unlawful if they did (if you were to lock someone in your cellar because they had stolen from you, you would be acting unlawfully). In contrast, the state has both the legal power (because it is given such power by the constitution) and the practical wherewithal to do such things. If the state body responsible for making law says that something is illegal and, if committed, is punishable by several years' imprisonment, most people will sit up and take notice.

So one of the functions of constitutions is to allocate state power—that is, they determine what the government can and cannot do. Three points should be noted in this regard.

First, constitutions generally *divide powers among different institutions of government*. These divisions are usually along functional lines; thus, in most systems, there is a legislative branch that is authorised to make law, an executive branch that is empowered to implement the law, and a judicial branch that is responsible for rendering authoritative resolutions to disputes concerning the interpretation and application of the law. It is, as we will see, the function of the constitution to determine precisely where these dividing lines should be situated, how rigidly they should be enforced, and what should happen if they are crossed.

Second, along with these 'vertical' dividing lines (so-called for reasons that Figure 1.1 makes apparent),[2] constitutions generally also *divide power horizontally*—that is, they allocate power to different tiers of government. For example, in the UK, government power is shared between the European Union (EU), the UK government, the governments of the devolved nations, and local councils.

Third, a key function of most constitutions is to lay down not only the internal divisions of power within government, but also to determine *where government power stops and individual freedom begins*. There are a number of ways of thinking about this matter.

We might say that what government can do is limited by *fundamental constitutional principles* (or what are sometimes referred to as the principles of 'the rule of law'). An example will help to illustrate this point. Assume that, on 1 February 2011, a woman

---

[2] Vertical dividing lines are shown in Figure 1.1 only in respect of central government. Although some such dividing lines exist in relation to other levels of government, they tend to be drawn in rather different ways, as we explain in Chapters 7 and 8, in which we deal with the European Union, devolution, and local government.

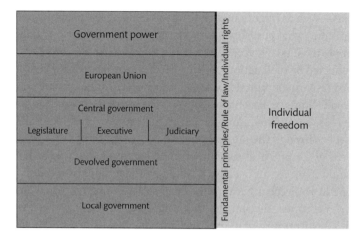

Figure 1.1 Government power and individual freedom

has sex with a married man. On 1 March 2011, a new government is elected and immediately enacts a law that makes adultery a criminal offence *with retrospective effect*: in other words, even people, like those in our example, who engaged in adultery *before* the new law was enacted will be guilty of a criminal offence. This type of law, known as 'retroactive criminal legislation', is unconstitutional in many countries—that is, the legislature is not constitutionally authorised to enact such legislation. Why? Because it offends against the fundamental principle of legal certainty, which says that people should have the opportunity to know what the law is so that they can make informed choices about whether to conform to it and thus avoid legal liability. In many countries, denying people that sort of choice is regarded as so unfair that the constitution prohibits the enactment of legislation that would have such an effect. There are many other principles that might, and in many countries do, similarly limit government power. What those principles are is presently unimportant;[3] the point, for now, is simply that constitutions often restrict what the state can do by denying government the power to infringe such principles.

Alternatively, or additionally, the constitutional limits of government authority may be characterised in terms of *individuals' rights*. In many legal systems, the constitution confers fundamental human rights on people and provides that the government must not interfere with those rights. For example, the constitution might give people a right to free speech—the corollary of which will be that the government is denied constitutional authority to make laws (or do other things) criminalising (or otherwise limiting) free speech.[4] In this sense, the fundamental rights of the individual limit the scope of government power: they determine the position of the line dividing areas in

---

[3] We discuss such principles in Chapter 2.

[4] Of course, this depends on what is contained within the right to free speech and whether it is subject to any limits—see Chapter 20 below.

which the government has the constitutional power to act and those in which individuals are free to do as they please.

2.2 **Accountability**

It has been said that 'Power tends to corrupt, and absolute power corrupts absolutely'.[5] There is more than a grain of truth in this. If someone is given extensive power to do as he wishes, he might exercise it wisely and selflessly; alternatively, he might—because he is incompetent, badly advised, or downright corrupt—make imprudent or self-serving decisions. An employer fearful of such conduct on the part of employees will seek to guard against it by carefully vetting people before appointing them; she will, however, almost certainly monitor their performance once they have been appointed, requiring them to account for how they are spending their time and checking to see whether their work is of an acceptable standard.

Those who are in charge of government go through a very public form of vetting procedure in the form of elections, and their jobs are not secure—they must submit themselves to re-election periodically. But the sheer amount of power wielded by government, and the importance of the tasks with which it is entrusted, are such that it would be extremely unwise to leave politicians to their own devices for the periods of several years that normally elapse between elections. If, for example, a government were to use its armed forces to invade another country in breach of international law,[6] or introduce a new benefits system the flawed design and implementation of which resulted in erroneous payments running to several billions of pounds,[7] most people would consider it desirable, if not imperative, to have systems in place enabling those responsible to be identified, making them explain themselves, requiring them to put things right (where possible), enabling them to learn lessons for the future, and providing redress in the event of unlawful, as opposed to merely unwise, government action. All of these enterprises fall under the broad heading of *accountability*, and a key purpose of a constitution is to ensure that those entrusted with power are required to exercise it responsibly and called to account when they do not.

2.3 **Legitimacy and consensus**

The fact that a country has a system of *constitutional* government does not necessarily mean that it has a *good* system of government. A constitution might, for example, ascribe very broad powers to the government, and accord very few rights to individuals, making the state capable of lawfully doing things that most people in the country concerned would consider unacceptable. There are, of course, many such constitutions to be found around the world. But within the democratic tradition, the purpose of a

---

[5] Acton, Letter to Bishop Mandell Creighton, 3 April 1887.

[6] As has been said to be the case in respect of the invasion of Iraq in 2003.

[7] As in the case of the tax credits system: see House of Commons Public Accounts Committee, *HM Revenue and Customs: Tax Credits and Income Tax* (HC 311 2008–09).

constitution is not only to allocate power; it is also to allocate power *in a manner that is regarded as morally acceptable.*

This view of the purpose of constitutions conceals a number of important value judgements. Key amongst them, however, is that people are not objects to be governed by those lucky or brutish enough to seize the reins of power; rather, each individual is to be recognised as an autonomous, morally valuable being, whose views are worthy of respect (or at least of being heard). In practice, the principle of individual autonomy cannot, and should not, mean that everyone can do as they wish: people's desires inevitably conflict (one person may like to play very loud music at 2.00 am; her neighbour may like a good night's sleep), and so law is used as a means of ensuring that the exercise of a given person's autonomy does not unreasonably impact on others. Such laws are legitimate not because everyone necessarily agrees with them, but because those responsible for making, implementing, and adjudicating on such laws have been authorised to do so via a democratic process.[8]

Viewed thus, one of the main purposes of a constitution is to put in place a set of arrangements that enjoys popular legitimacy, which enables the people of a given country to be governed in a way that they regard as acceptable, and which thereby renders legitimate the exercise of power by the institutions of government. There are a number of practical ways in which a constitution may be imbued with this sort of legitimacy. The most obvious and transparent way is to have a genuinely inclusive national debate about what the constitution should say and then to hold a referendum on the terms of the new constitution. A process of this nature[9] was followed in South Africa in the 1990s as it emerged from the shadow of apartheid.

Constitutions thus derive legitimacy from the fact that they reflect some sort of consensus about how the country should be governed, and about where the line should be drawn between the powers of the government and the autonomy of the individual. But surely such consensus is, in practice, impossible to achieve? Within most societies, there will be sharp divisions of opinion about what the government should do and how it should do it. Should the state should provide health care that is funded from general taxation and free at the point of access, or should people pay for their own health insurance? Should the main purpose of the criminal justice system be deterring criminality through harsh punishment or rehabilitating offenders by helping them to rebuild their lives? Democratic politics is premised on the assumption that disagreements like these exist, and on the resulting need to make provision for choosing between competing visions of how the country should be governed. So if consensus is generally so hard to achieve, how is it attained in relation to constitutions (in which context, we have noted, consensus is all-important)? Here, two crucial features of constitutions need to be considered: their *generality* and their *fundamentality*. We address each in turn.

---

[8] Democracy itself is a complex and contested notion. We explore its different possible meanings in Chapter 5.

[9] Albeit involving endorsement by the South African Parliament rather than by the people generally in a referendum.

First, constitutions tend to be drafted in general, lofty, unspecific terms, *raising* diffi-cult questions without *answering* them. For example, a constitution may say that 'every-one has the right to life'—but does this mean that people have a right to choose when and how their life should be ended, meaning that the government is not allowed to enact laws criminalising euthanasia? If, as is often the case, constitutions themselves dodge such hard questions, they ought at least to make provision for them to be answered in some way. This, in turn, raises a very thorny issue: if the constitution is unclear and its meaning disputed, who should be responsible for deciding what it means? In particular, should courts have the last word (constitutions are legal texts, so judges are surely best placed to interpret them) or does democracy require that this should be left to politi-cians (it being arguable that elected representatives have a more legitimate claim to decide upon controversial social issues)? Many constitutions fail even to address this question. Although the former position applies in the USA (courts are able to strike down unconstitutional laws), its Constitution does not explicitly address this point. It fell to the US Supreme Court, shortly after the adoption of the US Constitution at the turn of the nineteenth century, to assert a strike-down power—an assertion that proved controversial, given the absence of any express constitutional basis for it.[10]

Second, constitutions often secure consensus not only by avoiding difficult ques-tions, but also by focusing on fundamental matters on which a *natural* consensus exists. Many of the matters with which constitutions deal are genuinely uncontrover-sial because they reflect views that are both deeply and widely held. For example, few people would dissent from the propositions that criminal liability and punishment should not be imposed upon someone unless he has received a fair trial before an inde-pendent court, or that legislators and members of the executive government should hold office only for limited periods, after which they are required to submit themselves to re-election if they wish to continue. This is not to deny that difficult questions arise even in relation to the most fundamental matters. (Is the constitutional requirement of a fair trial met if the government, citing national security concerns, refuses to let the defendant adduce potentially helpful evidence? Must the government be dissolved and an election held on the constitutionally appointed date even if large swathes of the country are ravaged by a natural disaster the week before, such that many people would be unable to exercise their right to vote?) Nevertheless, some principles—even though they may have to be applied in unforeseen circumstances that raise hard ques-tions—are regarded as sufficiently fundamental to be the subject of genuine consensus and, as such, they find a natural home in the constitution.

2.4 **Permanency—amendment and interpretation**

This leads on to a final, closely related point. If constitutional principles are in this sense fundamental, then they are also, in a sense, timeless. Many of the laws that the

---

[10] *Marbury v Madison* 5 US 137 (1803).

legislature enacts remain on the statute book for only a few years, to be replaced by a new set of laws enacted by different—or even the same—legislators, convinced that they have found a better, cheaper, or more palatable solution to a given problem. But if constitutions are repositories of fundamental principles, should they be capable of being amended with the same ease as regular law? Few, if any, people would argue that constitutions should be set in stone, that they should be incapable of amendment, such that societies should be made to live in thrall to the past, enslaved by the values of earlier, perhaps less enlightened, generations. But most constitution-drafters across the world have—rightly—taken the view that constitutions should not be easy to amend. If their purpose is to reflect genuinely fundamental principles that represent a deep-seated consensus that limits the power of the government and protects the rights of the individual, they should not be capable of being amended casually and thoughtlessly as a knee-jerk reaction to some passing fashion or crisis. Constitutions therefore often prescribe an amendment process that demands a broad consensus, such that they cannot easily be altered. For example, to change the US Constitution, an amendment must be proposed by a two-thirds' majority of both chambers of the national legislature and then approved by three-quarters of the individual states' legislatures.[11]

But just as there are risks in making constitutions too easy to change, problems are also likely to arise if amendment is too difficult. However hard constitution-drafters try to include only fundamental principles, it is inevitable that a constitution will, to some extent, reflect the views, attitudes, and circumstances prevailing in the country at the particular time when the constitution is adopted. If the constitution is very difficult to amend, then courts may have to be relied upon to reinterpret provisions that are regarded as out of date.[12] This, in turn, places immense powers in judicial hands. Take, for example, the Second Amendment to the US Constitution, which says that 'A well regulated Militia, being necessary to the security of a free State, the right of the people to keep and bear Arms, shall not be infringed'. Does this mean that everyone is entitled to own a handgun such that gun-control legislation would be unconstitutional? The anti-gun lobby argues that it does not, pointing out that the Second Amendment was adopted at a time when the USA, lacking professional armed military and police forces, sometimes had to rely on groups of armed citizens—'militia'—to undertake law-enforcement duties. Viewed in this way, it is said that the right to bear arms conferred by the Second Amendment is contingent on a need for citizen militia—and that, since that need does not arise today, regular citizens are no longer constitutionally entitled to own handguns. However, the US Supreme Court has refused to accede to this argument. Striking down gun-control

---

[11] US Constitution, art 5. (There is an alternative process that is even harder to comply with, but which has never been successfully used.)

[12] Not everyone agrees that such reinterpretation is legitimate. While some courts and commentators take the view that constitutional texts are 'living instruments' to be interpreted according to contemporary circumstances, the school of thought known as 'originalism' holds that courts are simply required to ascertain and implement the original intention of those who drafted the constitution, however long ago that was. See generally Goldsworthy (ed), *Interpreting Constitutions: A Comparative Study* (Oxford 2006).

legislation in 2008, it ruled that the right to bear arms is 'unconnected with service in a militia'.[13] Unless a future Court adopts a different view, the only solution (from the standpoint of those who regard the present position as problematic) lies in amending the Constitution—which is no easy task.

We can take two points from this discussion. First, the easier it is to amend a constitution, the less point there is in having it in the first place: if a constitution can be amended or overridden with ease, it ceases to be a constitution in any meaningful sense and becomes akin to any other law. Second, however, if a constitution is very hard to amend, the risk arises that, unless judges can be persuaded to reinterpret the constitution, lawmakers may find that their hands are tied by principles that were adopted centuries earlier in radically different social circumstances and which are arguably inappropriate today. Getting that balance right is one of the hardest tasks faced by those who have to draft constitutions.

2.5 **What about the UK?**

Of course, those difficulties have never had to be faced in the UK—because it does not have, and has never had, a written codified constitution. So far, we have said little about the UK, referring instead to the functions and characteristics of constitutions *generally*. It is the purpose of this book as a whole to address the specific constitutional arrangements that apply in the UK, and it would be counterproductive to attempt a detailed critique of those arrangements in an introductory chapter. It is, however, appropriate to say something at this point about how the UK's arrangements measure up against what has been said thus far.

There are a number of respects in which the UK constitution is consistent with what has been said of constitutions generally. Power is divided vertically (albeit, as we will see, in a rather incomplete fashion) between three branches of central government (legislature, executive, and judiciary), as well as horizontally between several tiers of government (European, UK, devolved nations, and local). Provision is made for holding the government to account both politically and legally. People are said to possess constitutional and human rights, and fundamental constitutional (or 'rule of law') principles are recognised. And all of these arrangements enjoy a form of consensus-based legitimacy: although they have never been endorsed in a referendum or subjected to the sort of national conversation that preceded the adoption of the South African Constitution, some of the UK's arrangements have been put in place by a democratic institution in the form of the UK Parliament. Meanwhile, those that have not (such as those aspects of the constitution that pre-date the existence of genuine democracy in the UK) can be replaced by Parliament if it wishes, meaning that such arrangements enjoy a sort of indirect democratic legitimacy: the fact that they remain in place implies that they are deemed to be acceptable.

---

[13] *District of Columbia v Heller* 128 S Ct 2783 (2008). See also *McDonald v City of Chicago* (US Sup Ct, 28 June 2010).

But whatever the similarities, there is an important difference between the constitution of the UK and the constitutions of most other countries. That the UK's constitution is not 'written' is the most obvious difference—but it is not the *crucial* difference. The key point of distinction is that the UK's constitutional arrangements have *no special legal status*.[14] These two things—the existence of a written constitution, on the one hand, and the attribution of special status to the constitution, on the other—often, but do not have to, go hand in hand.[15] It is the latter factor—assigning special status to constitutional law—to which many of the typical characteristics of constitutions considered earlier in this chapter are attributable. When such status is given to constitutional law, several things are likely to follow. First, the constitution will enjoy a degree of *permanence*—that is, it will be capable of amendment only if the appropriate constitutional process is fulfilled. Second, other law will exist *in the shadow of the constitution*—that is, it will be valid only if it is consistent with the constitution. Third, as a result, *fundamental constitutional values*[16] will constitute an absolute brake on government—that is, it will be unauthorised to act contrary to them, even through the medium of democratically enacted legislation, and, if it tries to do so, the courts will be able to intervene.

In the UK, none of these things is true. First, because there is no legally distinct (and superior) category of constitutional law, *the law dealing with constitutional matters has the same status as all other law*. This means that any aspect of the constitution can be changed as easily as any regular law can be changed. Second, it follows that *'regular' law does not exist in the shadow of 'constitutional' law*—because no such distinction exists. The validity of any given law therefore cannot be called into question on the ground that it is inconsistent with the constitution. Third, as a result, *fundamental constitutional values and human rights cannot exist in the UK in the sense that they exist in many legal systems*. They cannot operate as an absolute brake on government power, precisely because there is no body of constitutional law or principle that is hierarchically superior to ordinary law. The government can therefore, by causing legislation to be passed, do anything—even if that involves contradicting long-established constitutional principles or rights that people regard as fundamental.

The foregoing is—necessarily at this stage of the book—a sketch of the UK's constitutional arrangements. All of the issues just mentioned are addressed in detail in subsequent chapters. But it is immediately necessary to enter three qualifications, not

---

[14] We note in Chapter 5 that one judge has suggested that courts should only be willing to accept that Parliament has interfered with certain pieces of constitutionally important legislation if it specifically says that this is its intention. However, even if this suggestion were to come to be widely accepted, it would result in constitutional law enjoying a superior status to regular law only in a very limited sense.

[15] For example, in 2009, the then Justice Secretary, Jack Straw, said that he was in favour of a written constitution drawing together existing constitution laws, but that he would not want it to have special legal status. See House of Commons Justice Committee, *Constitutional Reform and Renewal* (HC 923 2008–09), [61].

[16] Or 'rule of law principles', or 'fundamental human rights'—the terminology is, for the time being, unimportant.

because they contradict what has been said, but because it is necessary to give a rather fuller picture—not least in order to explain why, its unusual constitutional arrangements notwithstanding, the UK is a country in which fundamental principles and rights are (generally) respected.

First, the fact that important principles in the UK are not written into laws that have special, higher constitutional status *does not mean that there are no such principles*. In many countries, lawmakers respect fundamental rights and principles because they are legally impotent to do otherwise: retroactive criminal laws (which would offend legal certainty) and laws criminalising criticism of the government (which would contradict free speech) remain unenacted because the constitution denies the legislature any power to make such laws. In the UK, such rights and principles are also regarded as important: criticising the government has not been made into a criminal offence; and criminal law does not normally have retroactive effect. The difference is that in the UK lawmakers are legally *capable* of enacting legislation that conflicts with fundamental principles and rights—yet they generally *choose* not to. There are several reasons for this: legislators hopefully do not usually wish to make such laws; and if they are tempted to do so, they may fear adverse consequences at the next election. Fundamental constitutional principles therefore exist in the UK at least in a political sense: it is generally recognised by those involved in legislating and governing that it is wrong or at least inexpedient to do things that conflict with such principles.

> **Q** Is it acceptable that, in the UK, basic rights and fundamental constitutional principles rely, for their ongoing existence, upon lawmakers choosing not to interfere with them, rather than being legally incapable of doing so?

Second, the fact that lawmakers can, if they are determined to do so, pass laws that conflict with fundamental constitutional principles *does not mean that such principles are without any legal significance*. When, in this chapter, we refer to 'lawmakers' and 'legislation', we mean the UK Parliament and the laws that it enacts. Acts of the UK Parliament are the highest form of law within the UK constitution and, as such, cannot be struck down by courts if they conflict with fundamental constitutional principles. However, *other lawmakers*, such as the legislatures of the devolved nations, and *other parts of the government*, such as Ministers and local authorities, do not wield the sort of power that the UK Parliament possesses. We will see that, in relation to such lawmakers and parts of the government, it often *is* possible for the courts to police their conduct—overturning things that they have done, where appropriate—in order to ensure compliance with fundamental constitutional principles. In this sense, then, such principles *do* have legal significance: they are often enforceable against a broad range of legislators and parts of the government, albeit that the UK Parliament itself can, if it is determined to do so, lawfully act contrary to such principles.

Third, *the orthodox view of the British constitution presented here is not a universally accepted one*. While the view that constitutional principles do not have a special, higher legal status in the UK remains the dominant one, that view is increasingly being questioned by constitutional lawyers and judges. Indeed, three very senior judges indicated in 2005 that if laws were enacted that offended against the most fundamental constitutional principles, the courts might consider themselves capable of striking down, or refusing to apply, such laws[17]—a view that was echoed by the President of the UK Supreme Court in a media interview in 2010.[18] Whether such statements are anything more than empty threats is a question that is beyond the scope of this introductory chapter. However, we note that, if the UK courts were to adopt such a position, it would imply that the UK *does* have a body of constitutional principles that is superior to all other law—and would therefore entail removing the principal factor that distinguishes the UK's constitutional arrangements from those that apply in many comparable countries.

3. Case studies

One of the difficulties involved in studying public law is that its many different aspects are interconnected: it is hard to grasp any given topic without knowing something about other parts of the subject. We therefore conclude this introductory chapter with three case studies that—without attempting the impossible task of explaining the entire subject in a few pages—aim to provide a sense of how the different topics to be considered in this book relate to one another. The case studies are also intended to convey a flavour of the type—and importance—of the issues with which public law is concerned.

3.1 Terrorism and public law

When Al-Qaeda terrorists killed around 3,000 people by flying aircraft into prominent landmarks in the USA—most notably the World Trade Centre in New York—on 11 September 2001 ('9/11'), the geopolitical consequences were immeasurable. The most obvious such consequence was the decision of the US and UK governments, only weeks after the 9/11 attacks, to invade Afghanistan, Al-Qaeda's main stronghold, and to overthrow its Taliban-led government, which was supportive of Al-Qaeda. Domestically, the US and UK governments took other drastic steps. Most notoriously, the US government established an enormously controversial detention camp at a US military base at Guantánamo Bay, Cuba, where 'enemy combatants' were held. Most were never charged with or convicted of any criminal offence, and received no recognisable form of due process. A form of torture known as 'waterboarding', involving simulated drowning, was practised there.

---

[17] See the speeches of Lord Hope, Lord Steyn, and Baroness Hale in *R (Jackson) v Attorney General* [2005] UKHL 56, [2006] 1 AC 262.   [18] Lord Phillips, BBC *Today* programme, 2 August 2010.

The UK's domestic response was different from that of the USA, but was, at least in some respects, no less draconian. The centrepiece of that response was the Anti-terrorism, Crime and Security Act 2001. The Act dealt with a wide range of matters,[19] but we are concerned with one particular aspect. In the wake of 9/11, the government perceived that a major threat to the security of the UK was posed by foreign Islamic extremists.[20] Ordinarily, that perceived threat could have been dealt with in one of two ways: by instituting criminal proceedings or by deporting the suspects to their countries of origin. However, the government was unable or unwilling to adopt either of those courses of action. On the one hand, criminal proceedings (for example, for conspiracy) could not be brought because, it was asserted, securing convictions would involve revealing to the court evidence that would compromise national security. On the other hand, physically removing such people from the UK by deporting them to their home countries was not legally possible. This is because the European Convention on Human Rights (ECHR)—which, as a matter of international law, is binding upon the UK[21]—prohibits deportation if there is a real risk that the person concerned will be tortured or otherwise ill-treated on return to his home country. Many of the people about whom the UK government was concerned came from countries in which precisely that risk would arise. Taking the view that neither deportation nor criminal proceedings were viable, the government instead invited Parliament to pass the 2001 Act.

As Figure 1.2 shows, the effect of Pt 4 of the Act was to allow the government to imprison (notwithstanding the absence of any criminal charge or trial) suspected foreign terrorists who could not be deported. This involved depriving (an admittedly small number of) people of their liberty on the say-so not of an independent court, but of the executive government, and not on the basis of criminal charges proven beyond reasonable doubt, but on the basis of suspicion—reasonable belief—that the person concerned was a threat to national security and involved in terrorism. Although detainees could appeal to a specialist judicial tribunal (the Special Immigration Appeals Commission), they could not, for national security reasons, know the case against them or the evidence on which the decision to detain them was made; they could, however, be represented by a security-cleared lawyer (a Special Advocate).

This regime proved to be highly controversial. Some people deplore a situation in which the government cannot remove from its territory foreign nationals who are suspected of posing a threat to national security; other people abhor a situation in which the government is able to detain people without trial. After all, the ordinary situation is that individual liberty is a fundamental right that can be curtailed only in very limited circumstances (such as conviction of a criminal offence, not ministerial suspicion), and then only following due process before an independent and

---

[19] For a concise, critical overview, see Tomkins, 'Legislating against Terror: The Anti-terrorism, Crime and Security Act 2001' [2002] PL 205.

[20] We note in passing that the terrorist attacks on the London transport network on 7 July 2005 were carried out by British citizens.   [21] Because the UK chose to become bound by it.

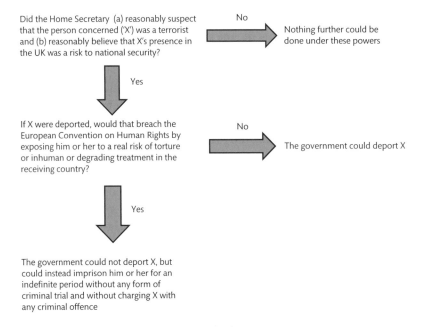

Figure 1.2 Part 4 of the Anti-terrorism, Crime and Security Act 2001

impartial court. This episode tells us a great deal about the UK constitution. In the remainder of this section, we focus on three key aspects of the story: the relative ease with which the legislation could be enacted, the involvement of the courts and the use of human rights law to challenge the legislation, and the aftermath of the legal process.

3.1.1 The enactment of the legislation

How and why was the executive branch of government able to get Parliament to confer these extraordinary powers upon it? The answer lies in three interlocking features of the UK constitution.

First, in the UK, the political party (or coalition of political parties) with a majority of seats in the *House of Commons* is asked by the Queen to form the executive government. The House of Commons is one of the two chambers of the UK Parliament, the other being the House of Lords. Because the government has a majority in the House of Commons, it can almost always rely on the Commons approving its proposals for new legislation: members of each political party usually vote as instructed by the party's leadership. But the House of Commons was even more supine than usual when it came to passing the 2001 Act. In a climate of genuine fear created by the 9/11 attacks in the USA, politicians were falling over themselves to be seen as tough on terrorism. Many opposition, as well as government, MPs were therefore willing to support the legislation, and it received almost no genuine scrutiny: a parliamentary committee later observed that 'many important elements of the [legislation] were not considered at all in the House of Commons, which had only 16 hours to deal with 126 clauses and eight Schedules'.[22]

Second, it is not normally sufficient for the House of Commons to support proposed legislation: in most circumstances, the approval of the *House of Lords* is also required. It is fair to say that the House of Lords—most of the members of which are appointed on the recommendation of the leaders of the main political parties, and none of whom is elected[23]—looked much more critically and carefully at the legislation. But although grave concerns were expressed by some of its members, the House of Lords eventually approved the legislation. In part, this reflects the House of Lords' consciousness that if it asserts itself too vigorously, it lays itself open to the charge that it is an undemocratic institution with no right to frustrate the will of the elected House of Commons. It is also significant that, partly in recognition of its lack of democratic legitimacy, the House of Lords has limited powers: the most that it can normally do is to delay the enactment of legislation for one year. That power can be, and sometimes is, used to significant effect if a government is desperate to get legislation through quickly, and indeed the government did agree to some significant amendments in order to appease the House of Lords. Ultimately, however, the Lords did not exercise its power to delay the enactment of the legislation, no doubt accepting that it would have been inappropriate to block measures regarded by the elected branches of the constitution as imperative to national security.

So far, we have seen that the executive branch of government faces little serious opposition when it is determined to push legislation through Parliament, because of its effective control of the House of Commons and the subservient position of the House of Lords. But a third, crucially important, point must not be overlooked—that is, that, as we have already seen, *the UK constitution imposes no absolute limits upon the authority of lawmakers*. Because there is no body of constitutional law or principle that has a special, higher legal status, even fundamental principles—such as the liberty of the individual—can be abolished or limited provided that the government can persuade Parliament to enact legislation having such an effect. This means that the executive branch of government is in effective control of a legislature that has unlimited constitutional authority to make law. It would be a gross oversimplification to say that this means the government can do whatever it wants—but the 9/11 experience shows that, at least in some circumstances, it is in an extraordinarily powerful position.

3.1.2 The *Belmarsh* case

We have not yet mentioned the role of the courts in relation to the legislation passed following 9/11. The reason may seem obvious: if Parliament has unlimited constitutional authority to make law, surely there can be no scope for a legal challenge

---

[22] Joint Committee on Human Rights, *Anti-terrorism, Crime and Security Bill: Further Report* (HL 51 HC 420 2001–02), [2].

[23] Although this may change: see Chapter 5, section 2.3, below on proposed reforms to the House of Lords.

to the laws it makes? The true position, however, is more subtle than this. As we noted above, the fact that the UK constitution does not occupy a higher legal stratum than regular law does not mean that fundamental constitutional principles and rights are not recognised. Lawmakers who are determined to do so can enact legislation that overrides such values, and courts *cannot* strike such legislation down. There are, however, two things that they *can* do when faced with law that appears to conflict with fundamental constitutional values.

First, the courts adopt as their starting point the assumption that lawmakers do not wish to enact legislation that offends basic constitutional principles or cuts across fundamental human rights. The courts therefore generally attempt to find an interpretation of the law that is consistent with such rights and principles. But of course this approach can only work—in the sense of yielding an outcome that is consistent with constitutional principles—if it is possible to interpret the legislation in question in such a way. If lawmakers have made their intention to override basic rights sufficiently clear—as they doubtless did when, in passing the Anti-terrorism Act, they authorised the government to deprive people of their liberty without charge or trial—then this approach cannot bear fruit: the law is clear and the courts have to apply it.[24]

However, the courts have a second string to their bow. In 1998, Parliament enacted the Human Rights Act 1998 (HRA). This Act authorises the courts, in appropriate cases, to consider whether legislation is compatible with certain human rights—and, if it is not, to issue a 'declaration of incompatibility': a formal statement from the court that the legislation concerned breaches human rights standards, even though it remains valid until amended. This is precisely what happened in relation to the Anti-terrorism Act. In 2004, in the *Belmarsh* case[25]—so-called because the people detained under the Act were held in Belmarsh high-security prison—a number of detainees asked the court to rule on whether the Anti-terrorism Act breached their right to liberty, which is one of the rights protected by the HRA. Superficially, the answer to this question seems obvious: the detainees were being deprived of their liberty, and none of the circumstances in which the right to liberty can validly be restricted—such as detention following conviction and sentencing by a criminal court—applied. However, there was a complication. Under the HRA, it is possible to suspend certain rights—including the right to liberty—if, and to the extent that, a war or a public emergency threatening the life of the nation makes it necessary to do so. The court therefore had to decide whether those conditions were satisfied. If they were, it would not be possible (as the detainees wished the court to do) to declare that the Anti-terrorism Act was incompatible with the detainees' right to liberty—because their right to liberty would have been lawfully suspended. But if those conditions were not met, the court would be able to issue such a declaration, because the right to liberty would remain in force. The court held that the conditions were *not* satisfied. Although most of the judges

---

[24] This is the orthodox view. It is not universally shared, as we explain in Chapter 5.
[25] *A v Secretary of State for the Home Department* [2004] UKHL 56, [2005] 2 AC 68.

refused to overrule the government's view that, following 9/11, the risk posed by terrorism constituted a public emergency threatening the life of the nation, the majority held that the government had not shown that it was necessary to detain foreign suspects without charge or trial. They noted that the government had not taken any steps to detain *British* suspects, and said that 'if it is not necessary to lock up the nationals it cannot be necessary to lock up the foreigners'.[26] The right to liberty had therefore not been validly suspended, and the court declared that the relevant provisions of the Anti-terrorism Act were incompatible with it.

3.1.3 **The aftermath**

The obvious question that this invites is: 'So what?' We already know that UK courts cannot strike down legislation that is incompatible with fundamental constitutional principles and rights, because such things do not have a higher constitutional status such that they tie lawmakers' hands. What, then, was the point of obtaining a mere *declaration* that the detainees' right to liberty was infringed by their incarceration under the Anti-terrorism Act? This question throws into sharp relief a fundamental aspect of the UK constitution that we have so far only addressed in passing—that is, that while there are no *legal* limits that confine lawmakers' powers, there are considerable *political* limits upon the exercise of such powers. We mentioned above that, the absence of legal limits notwithstanding, there are several reasons explaining why—in general—UK legislators do not enact oppressive laws. One of the most important such reasons is that, even if they are tempted to do so, elected legislators will be sensitive to public opinion: there may be public protests or hostile media comment in response to oppressive laws, and MPs may fear losing their seats in the House of Commons at the next election if they vote in favour of legislation that is despised by a sufficient number of people. Thus, in practice, the political process provides a brake on the exercise of lawmaking power. Against this background, a declaration by the highest court in the land—and one accompanied by excoriating criticism by several senior judges—that UK law is inconsistent with basic human rights has a good deal of significance. It does not, for reasons that we have already mentioned, amount to the court striking down the legislation: as one of the *Belmarsh* judges put it, the impact of a declaration of incompatibility 'is political not legal'.[27] But its political significance should not be underestimated: it will be grist to the mill of those inside and outside Parliament who wish to see the legislation repealed.

The declaration issued in the *Belmarsh* case had precisely that effect: the government found itself under irresistible pressure to repeal Pt 4 of the Anti-terrorism Act. The then Home Secretary told the House of Commons that he 'accept[ed] the [court's] declaration of incompatibility' and its 'judgment that new legislative measures must apply equally to nationals as well as to non-nationals',[28] and later stated,

---

[26] *A* at [231], *per* Baroness Hale.
[27] *A* at [142].   [28] HC Deb, 26 January 2005, col 306.

when seeking Parliament's approval of fresh legislation,[29] that it had been 'designed to meet the [court's] criticism that the previous legislation was both disproportionate and discriminatory'.[30] What we see here, then, is an example of the *legal* process, which resulted in a declaration that the Anti-terrorism Act was incompatible with fundamental constitutional principles, triggering a *political* process that resulted in those principles being upheld. In turn, this phenomenon raises the ideas of *legal constitutionalism* and *political constitutionalism*. We address these matters in the next chapter—indeed, we argue that the relationship between them is key to understanding how the modern British constitution works—but for now we need simply say that they reflect two different views of how fundamental constitutional values should be upheld. The former puts its faith in the courts; the latter relies on the political process. Quite sensibly, few countries put all of their eggs in one basket—but, as we explain in more detail in the next chapter, the absence in the UK of a body of constitutional law that ties the hands of lawmakers means that unusually heavy reliance has to be placed upon the safeguards afforded by the political process. Whether those safeguards are adequate is another matter—and one that we explore in a later part of this book.

3.1.4 Conclusions

What, then, does this episode tell us about the UK constitution? Without rehearsing all that has been said so far, three points should be emphasised. First, it underlines *the pivotal position occupied by the executive government*. It wields enormous power because of its capacity to get legislation enacted—a capacity that is attributable to its control of the House of Commons and the constitutionally inferior position of the House of Lords. Second, the power of the executive is augmented by the fact that the Parliament it dominates is *not subject to any absolute constitutional limits*: there being no hierarchically superior body of constitutional law in the UK, Parliament is legally free to do as it wishes. Third, however, we have seen that this does not mean that *fundamental constitutional principles* are irrelevant. The principle at stake in the *Belmarsh* case, concerning the liberty of the individual, was ultimately upheld through the combined effect of the legal and political processes. While lacking the power to strike down the offending provisions of the Anti-terrorism Act, the court's declaration that it conflicted with the right to liberty proved to be of enormous political significance, prompting the executive government to ask Parliament to repeal Pt 4 of the Act. As we embark on our study of public law, this episode therefore serves as an important reminder that it will be crucial to aim to understand the nature of, and the relationship between, the legal and political systems that exist for holding government to account.

---

[29] The Anti-terrorism Act was replaced by the Prevention of Terrorism Act 2005. It provides for the imposition of 'control orders' on suspected terrorists (both British and foreign), but stops short of giving the executive branch of government the authority to imprison suspected terrorists without reference to the courts.

[30] HC Deb, 22 February 2005, col 151.

3.2 **Prisons**

We can now turn to consider our second case-study: the operation and accountability of the prisons system. Individuals who have broken the criminal law and been convicted of an imprisonable offence by a criminal court can be subjected to a prison sentence for a certain period of time. Prisons detain criminal offenders by depriving them of their personal liberty.

At first glance, it might be assumed that the prisons system has more to do with criminal law and justice than with public law, but this would be incorrect for several reasons. The prisons system comprises a large administrative apparatus that is run, managed, and financed by the government. It is the means by which key policy goals are pursued: the punishment of offenders, the protection of the public from offenders, the reduction of future reoffending, and the rehabilitation of offenders. The prisons system is also a large-scale area of government. There are over 140 prisons with some 85,000 prisoners. Some 26,000 prison officers work within HM Prison Service, the government agency that manages and runs the prisons system. In 2007–08, the total cost of the prison estate was £3.8 billion. There is also a government Minister who is answerable to Parliament on matters concerning prisons.

To operate the prisons system, it is necessary that the government has the appropriate legal powers. These are provided by the Prison Act 1952, which gives the power to the government to confine and treat prisoners. However, while this Act provides the legal basis for the prisons system, it is by itself an incomplete statement of the law concerning prisons. This is partly because that legislation is now over half a century old and successive governments have come into power with different ideas as to how prisons should be run and organised. It is also partly because the challenges facing prisons have changed over time. For example, the 1952 Act said nothing about testing prisoners for drugs: provision for this was introduced by subsequent Acts of Parliament. But there is another reason why the 1952 Act is an incomplete statement of the law governing prisons: much of the detailed rules governing the regulation and management of prisons are set down not in 'primary legislation'—that is, an Act of Parliament—but in statutory instrument—that is, a piece of 'delegated' or 'secondary legislation'. Such legislation, which is commonplace, is enacted by the government under powers conferred by an Act of Parliament. So, in the context of prisons, the 1952 Act authorises the government to make rules concerning the regulation and management of prisons. These rules—the Prison Rules—govern matters such as prisoners' physical welfare and work, their communications with people outside prison, and the ability of prison officers to search prisoners' property. These are the detailed rules that are administered by prison officers on a daily basis.

3.2.1 **Public administration and administrative law**

Against this background, three general points might be made. The first is that the constitution is not inhabited only by Parliament, government Ministers, and the courts, but also by many other public bodies, called *administrative agencies*, of which HM Prison

Service is but one. Such agencies shoulder much of the responsibility for providing front-line services. For example, the Highways Agency is responsible for operating, maintaining, and improving the strategic road network in England; HM Revenue and Customs collects the taxes that fund public services; the Environment Agency is charged with addressing climate change, and improving air and water quality. These are only a few examples of the many government agencies that form part of the larger governmental machine. As we shall see, such administrative agencies are accompanied by a whole host of other bodies, such as regulators, tribunals, and ombudsmen.

Why do we have such bodies? In the modern state, government exercises many different policy functions; it is responsible for a large number of areas of social life, and often the only way of managing and implementing policy is through public administration. When government acts, it is usually through the medium of some administrative agency or other. In the case of prisons, it is HM Prison Service that manages and governs prisons, and this agency is staffed by permanent officials who are appointed and not elected. Elected politicians perform very few, if any, of the basic operational tasks of government; this is the responsibility of public officials and civil servants who work in administrative agencies. While the Prime Minister is the head of the UK government, he does not personally deliver public services; the task of the Prime Minister and other government Ministers is to oversee and direct the work of government agencies rather than to perform governmental functions themselves. In the context of prisons, it is prison governors and officers who actually run and manage prisons.

A second point is that the development and growth of administrative agencies has gone hand in hand with the development of a particular type of law. Consider the Prison Act 1952, for example. This is what might be labelled *administrative legislation*—that is, legislation that does not impose duties upon or confer rights on private individuals, but which lays down the legal rules as to how a particular part of government is to operate and be organised. Such legislation will typically confer legal powers and obligations on administrative agencies, which are needed so that they can perform their public functions. Virtually all contemporary legislation is of this character and this has been the case for some time. As long ago as 1901, it was noted that 'the substantial business of Parliament as a legislature is to keep the machinery of the state in working order' and that the net result of Parliament's legislative activity 'has been the building up piecemeal of an administrative machine of great complexity, which stands in constant need of repair, renewal, reconstruction, and adaptation to new requirements'.[31] Parliament keeps the governmental machine—the administrative state—in working order by enacting administrative legislation. In order to manage the myriad policy programmes for which government is now responsible—managing the economy, policing, taxation, welfare, planning, immigration, transport, environment, climate change, and so on—it is necessary to have legislation setting out the legal powers, duties, and organisation of government agencies and bodies. Furthermore, as

---

[31] Ilbert, *Legislative Methods and Forms* (Oxford 1901), pp 210, 212, and 213.

the government of the day dominates Parliament, it usually has little, if any, difficulty in getting its proposals enacted as legislation.

A third point is that while much of this legislation is detailed and complex, it is often only a *partial statement of the law*. As we have noted, the Prison Act 1952 is supplemented by delegated legislation in the form of the Prison Rules. Today, the volume of such delegated legislation far outstrips that of primary legislation. In 2008, Parliament enacted 22 Acts of Parliament, while there were some 3,500 statutory instruments made by the government. Delegated legislation is an essential tool by which government implements its policies. Given the increasing complexity of administration, it has been necessary for Parliament to delegate extensive legislative power to government agencies. Both Parliament and government would grind to a halt if there were no adequate system of delegated legislation. As a parliamentary select committee has noted, 'secondary legislation makes up the majority of the law of this country. When implemented it affects every sphere of activity'.[32]

All of the above points could be applied to any area of government. Modern government is a very large and complex organisation. It is regulated by a particular type of law—administrative law. One purpose of administrative law, as we have seen, is to lay down the detailed rules and regulations concerning how government is to operate in the particular area concerned. However, setting out the responsibility and powers of government is only one side of the coin: the other concerns holding government to account for the exercise of its powers.

3.2.2 Government accountability

In 2006, it was publicly disclosed that over 1,000 foreign national prisoners had been released from prison by HM Prison Service without first being considered for deportation to their country of origin by the Immigration and Nationality Directorate, as should have happened. Both HM Prison Service and the Immigration and Nationality Directorate were administrative agencies within the same parent government department, the Home Office. The release of the foreign national prisoners was a major failure within government to coordinate the activities of these two agencies and to protect the public. As a consequence, the then Home Secretary, Charles Clarke, was dismissed from the government by the Prime Minister.

Following this, in 2007, there was an important reorganisation within government—a 'machinery of government' change, which is a structural reorganisation of the responsibilities of different government agencies. To enable the Home Office to focus on its core mission of protecting the public, it was decided by the government to reduce its size by transferring HM Prison Service from its traditional location within the Home Office to a new government department, the Ministry of Justice, responsible for the administration of justice. This was a major change in the organisation of executive government, and the decision had various ramifications as regards the funding

---

[32] House of Lords Merits of Statutory Instruments Committee, *What Happened Next? A Study of Post-Implementation Reviews of Secondary Legislation* (HL 180 2008–09), [1].

of government and the relationship between the executive and the judiciary. This decision was, however, simply announced by the then Prime Minister, Tony Blair, to Parliament not by way of an oral statement to the House of Commons, but through a written ministerial statement. MPs in the House of Commons regretted that there had been no opportunity for detailed parliamentary scrutiny of this significant change to the machinery of government.

These two episodes each raise a number of questions. Why was the Home Secretary dismissed when the failure had been that of the two agencies within his government department to coordinate their activities? Who is responsible for the overall organisation of the executive government? What role is there for Parliament to scrutinise the government, whether in relation to specific issues such as the failure to consider deporting foreign prisoners or big-picture questions such as changes in the organisation of central government? All of these questions are, at root, about accountability. In any area of government activity, it is imperative that there should be systems for ensuring that power is being exercised responsibly, that decisions are being taken conscientiously and fairly, and that corrective action can be taken if these standards are fallen short of. Taking the prisons system as an example, how should, and how can, those responsible for its operation be held to account?

First, given the importance of the functions performed by the prisons system, it is important that Parliament is able to scrutinise policy and administration in this area of government. This can be done by asking questions of relevant Ministers in Parliament or by holding parliamentary debates on policy issues pertaining to the prisons system. Moreover, in the UK, each government department is overseen by a parliamentary select committee made up of MPs from the House of Commons. As the prisons system is an area of responsibility within the Ministry of Justice, it is overseen by the House of Commons Justice Committee, which conducts inquiries and publishes reports into the prisons system.

Second, the prisons system is funded by government—meaning that it is paid for by taxpayers. An essential attribute of a good government is that it does not waste public money, but spends it wisely. Given the cost of the prisons system, it is important that there are effective mechanisms for overseeing how money is spent within it and whether such money could be spent more efficiently. The public needs to know that government is delivering value for money—in other words, it is necessary to have financial accountability. This raises issues that are peculiar to government. If a given company is inefficient, customers will flock to better, cheaper providers. But if people do not think that government is providing value for money, they cannot go elsewhere. In the absence of the sort of discipline normally supplied by market economics, distinctive audit bodies are needed to oversee how government spends public money. In the UK, the principal audit body is the National Audit Office; it reviews government agencies to assess whether or not they are delivering value for money and then reports its findings to Parliament.

Third, the prisons system makes decisions that adversely affect the lives and rights of individuals. It is therefore important that such individuals whose rights and interests have been affected are able to challenge such decisions. Public law provides a variety of different mechanisms by which individuals can seek to challenge administrative decisions. One such mechanism is for the individual concerned to take the government agency concerned to a court in order to test the lawfulness of its decision. This court process is known as 'judicial review' and it is the principal mechanism by which individuals can challenge the legality of public decisions.

Indeed, legal challenges against prison decisions are a major area of judicial review. The courts have recognised that 'under English law, a convicted prisoner, in spite of his imprisonment, retains all civil rights which are not taken away expressly or by necessary implication'.[33] Consequently, if a decision by the prison authorities infringes the rights of a prisoner, then the prisoner is able to take the prison authorities to court in order to protect her rights. For example, in the case of *Daly*, a prisoner challenged a Prison Service policy whereby prisoners could be excluded from their cells while their cells were being searched, even if this meant that their legally privileged correspondence—for example, letters to or from their lawyer—would be examined in their absence. Allowing the challenge, the court recognised that, under the common law, there is a fundamental right to confidential communication with a legal adviser for the purpose of obtaining legal advice.[34] The Prison Service policy, it was held, unlawfully interfered with this right: while it would be justifiable to exclude some prisoners (for example, those prone to violence) during cell searches, it was not necessary to have a blanket rule excluding *all* prisoners. Judicial review therefore went to correct an administrative policy that disproportionately interfered with prisoners' rights.

While important, judicial review is not the only mechanism that individuals are able to access to challenge decisions by government bodies. There are a range of non-court processes that, together, comprise the administrative justice system. We can illustrate here two such mechanisms that operate in the general context of prisons and criminal justice.

First, there are mechanisms through which to investigate complaints that individuals make against government bodies. Such complaints may be investigated by an 'ombudsman' or another specialist complaint-handling body. For example, the Prisons and Probation Ombudsman investigates complaints from prisoners about their treatment by prisons. An effective complaint mechanism for prisoners is an important safeguard against the abuse of power by prison officers. Furthermore, if prisoners were to have no such mechanism of addressing their legitimate grievances, then the already difficult challenges in managing prisons effectively would be rendered more problematic. (We examine ombudsmen in detail in Chapter 16.)

Second, there are other mechanisms—tribunals—that enable individuals who have received a negative decision from a government body to appeal against that decision. For example, the UK government has long-established policy of providing money

---

[33] *Raymond v Honey* [1983] 1 AC 1, 10.
[34] *R (Daly) v Secretary of State for the Home Department* [2001] 2 AC 532.

(compensation) to people who have been physically or mentally injured because they were the blameless victim of a violent crime. This policy is administered by a government body, the Criminal Injuries Compensation Authority, but what if someone thinks that her application has been wrongly refused by the authority? In such cases, the person concerned can appeal against the authority's decision to an independent judicial tribunal.[35] It adjudicates upon such disputes and is able to substitute its own decision for that of the Criminal Injuries Compensation Authority. (We examine tribunals in detail in Chapter 17.)

3.2.3 Conclusions

What does all of this tell us about government accountability? First, there are a whole range of different institutions that oversee the work of government and scrutinise its activities. The work of administrative agencies is so varied and diverse that there has to be a range of different institutions to hold such agencies to account. Political accountability is effected through mechanisms such as general elections, scrutiny by MPs and peers in Parliament, and by parliamentary select committees. Financial accountability and audit is provided by specialist audit bodies such as the National Audit Office. Legal accountability is provided by courts and tribunals. Administrative accountability is provided by bodies such as ombudsmen and specialist complaint-handling bodies that investigate complaints of maladministration—that is, bad administrative practices.

Second, it is fundamentally important that the exercise of governmental power is subject to effective and searching scrutiny. However, the institutions that scrutinise government are looking for somewhat different things from it. The above institutions are looking at the same public body, but are each, in turn, exposing it to scrutiny against different, yet complementary, standards of accountability. This serves as a useful reminder, as we embark upon our study of public law, that government is a large and complex enterprise, and that the different accountability processes that oversee government operations do not operate in isolation from each other, but together comprise a wide-ranging system for holding government to account. Whether or not those institutions, individually or collectively, provide wholly adequate scrutiny is an important question—but one that we can tackle only in subsequent chapters, as we look at each area in detail.

3.3 Post-1997 constitutional reforms

The Labour governments of 1997–2010 implemented a far-reaching set of constitutional reforms.[36] They include 'devolution' (that is, the creation of new governments and legislatures in Northern Ireland, Scotland, and Wales); the introduction of new

---

[35] Known as the 'First-tier Tribunal (Criminal Injuries Compensation)'.

[36] See generally Bogdanor, 'Our New Constitution' (2004) 120 LQR 242; Bogdanor, *The New British Constitution* (Oxford 2009).

voting arrangements for elections to the devolved legislatures; the creation of a city-wide system of government in, and an elected mayor for, London; significant changes to local government; the enactment of freedom of information and human rights legislation; the removal from the House of Lords of most members who inherited their seats; the near-abolition of the ancient office of Lord Chancellor; the abolition of the judicial functions of the House of Lords; the creation of the UK Supreme Court; and the creation of a statutory body responsible for dealing with MPs' pay and allowances. By any measure, this is a significant set of changes to the country's constitutional arrangements. And the pace of change shows no sign of slowing. The coalition government formed in the wake of the 2010 general election has announced a further raft of changes, including fixed-term Parliaments, a referendum on changing the voting system and further House of Lords' reform. It is not our purpose here to address the individual or collective significance of these changes, actual or proposed (although many are examined in detail in subsequent chapters); rather, our present concern is with the way in which constitutional reform is undertaken in the UK.[37]

In most countries, constitutional reform is a big deal. Changing constitutions is usually hard: a wide consensus is normally needed in order to secure compliance with the constitutionally prescribed amendment process. Politicians (who are usually the initiative-takers in such matters) therefore do not casually seek the amendment of constitutions. The possibility is only mooted if the matter is of grave importance, and, even then, only if it is felt that the proposed change would withstand the intense scrutiny that it would be likely to attract and stand a good chance of commanding the necessary support. We noted above that there are good reasons for making constitutions difficult to amend: they are supposed to represent a brake on government power, a guarantee of individuals' rights, and a repository of fundamental principles that should not be allowed to yield just because a government can muster a bare majority in the legislature. Unusually, of course, the UK constitution is capable of being amended in precisely such circumstances: constitutional law having no higher legal status, everything is up for grabs provided that the government can persuade Parliament to enact the necessary legislation. This simple fact of constitutional life in the UK has profoundly important implications for the approach taken by governments to constitutional reform. It strips it of the difficulty, formality, and momentousness that usually attends attempts to change constitutions, making it possible to do so relatively easily, even casually. And these are not mere possibilities. The post-1997 constitutional reforms were practically influenced in a number of ways—several of which we highlight in the following paragraphs—by the relative ease with which they could be accomplished.

3.3.1 Piecemeal reform

First, human nature is such that, generally speaking, the harder something is to do, the less keen people will be to do it. If you live a long walk from the nearest water source,

---

[37] See generally Baker, 'Our Unwritten Constitution' (2010) 167 Proceedings of the British Academy 91; Beatson, 'Reforming an Unwritten Constitution' (2010) 126 LQR 48.

you will take the biggest container you can carry and fill it up before returning home, rather than making several daily trips to fill 500ml bottles. And if constitutions are hard to amend, governments (or anyone else putting forward proposals) will be inclined to think long and hard before suggesting changes: repeatedly going through a protracted constitutional amendment process is likely to be unattractive. Attaching a degree of difficulty to constitutional amendment is therefore a disincentive to the presentation of ill-thought-through, disjointed, piecemeal proposals. Since the converse is also true, it is unsurprising that the post-1997 constitutional changes cannot be said to amount to a *programme* of reform in the sense of being a coherent package. The myriad Acts of Parliament that effected the reforms were introduced over a period of several years; the first reforms were thus drafted and implemented many years before not only the shape of later reforms was known, but before such reforms had even been contemplated. As a result, difficult questions were simply brushed aside or postponed (perhaps indefinitely). Reviewing the general approach to constitutional reform in the UK, a parliamentary committee noted in 2009 that '"unfinished business" has been the enduring motif of many of the strands of constitutional renewal'.[38]

As we will see in Chapter 7, shortly after it was elected in 1997, the Blair government introduced devolution in Scotland, Wales, and Northern Ireland.[39] It did so, however, without any clearly worked-out plan in relation to England, which, in the absence of devolution, continues to be governed and legislated for by the UK executive and Parliament. One of the strangest results of this is the so-called West Lothian question,[40] which, briefly, asks why it is legitimate for MPs representing the devolved nations to be allowed to vote on laws affecting only England, now that English MPs cannot vote on laws affecting only the devolved nations (because the latter are enacted by devolved legislatures in which English MPs do not sit). Lord Irvine, the cabinet Minister responsible for driving through many of the post-1997 reforms, famously said: 'Now that we have devolution up and running, I think the best thing to do about the West Lothian question is to stop asking it.'[41] The coalition government that took office in 2010 disagreed, and has announced its intention to find a solution to this issue. What that solution might be is a question for a later chapter; for now, the point is simply that the government that introduced devolution clearly felt no obligation to present a cohesive package of proposals that addressed the West Lothian question.

The sometimes piecemeal nature of constitutional reform in the UK is a phenomenon that is not confined to the post-1997 changes. We will see in Chapter 5 that the democratic credentials of the House of Commons are a fairly recent innovation: it is less than 100 years since all adult men and women were given the right

---

[38] House of Commons Justice Committee, *Constitutional Reform and Renewal* (HC 923 2008–09), [1].

[39] The position in Northern Ireland was complicated by its unusual political circumstances and the need to broker a deal that would facilitate an end to terrorist violence; as such, it was something of a special case. See further Chapter 7.

[40] Named after Tam Dalyell, who, when MP for West Lothian, drew public attention to this issue.

[41] HL Deb, 25 June 1999, col 1201.

to vote in elections to the Commons. But as the democratisation of the Commons proceeded, the view developed, unsurprisingly, that it was anomalous to have a wholly unelected House of Lords. In 1909–11, in circumstances that we relate later in the book, legislation was enacted to curtail the powers of the Lords, eliminating its involvement in financial legislation and giving it a power only to delay, rather than block, other legislation. The preamble to the Parliament Act 1911—the Act that imposed those limits on the House of Lords—explicitly stated that it was a temporary measure, pending the replacement of the House of Lords with 'a Second Chamber constituted on a popular instead of hereditary basis'. A century later, that has not yet happened. However, one of the first elements of the post-1997 reforms to be implemented was the removal from the House of Lords of 'hereditary peers'—that is, those who had inherited the right to sit in the upper chamber.[42] This change was introduced before a Royal Commission established by the government had made its recommendations about full reform of the House of Lords, and was intended to be a stopgap measure pending such reform. But, as with the 1909–11 reforms, this one has not (yet) been completed—although, at the time of writing, a government commission, appointed to make recommendations on final reform of the House of Lords, is due to report.

3.3.2 Constitutional reform on the hoof

The first consequence, then, of the relative ease with which constitutional reform can be accomplished in the UK is that it is sometimes piecemeal in nature. A second (related) consequence is that it can be undertaken in a relatively informal way that is not attended by the sort of consultation and forethought that is likely to be exhibited in systems in which reform is a more difficult business. There can be no clearer example of this than the way in which the constitutional changes effected through what became the Constitutional Reform Act 2005 were introduced.

On 12 June 2003, a government press release was issued stating that the office of Lord Chancellor (who was head of the judiciary, a senior government Minister, and speaker[43] of the House of Lords) was to be abolished; a new post (and a new department to go along with it) of Secretary of State for Constitutional Affairs was to be created, a new way of appointing judges in England and Wales was to be established, and the Appellate Committee of the House of Lords, which had served as the court of final appeal for most matters in the UK, was to be abolished and replaced with a Supreme Court.[44] These announcements concerned constitutional changes of momentous significance, going to the heart of the legal system, the principle of judicial independence, and the relationship between the courts and the government. Yet they were announced without any consultation: even the senior judiciary, including those directly affected by the proposals, knew nothing of them until the day on which they were announced.

---

[42] House of Lords Act 1999.   [43] That is, the presiding officer.
[44] Le Sueur, 'The Conception of the UK's New Supreme Court', in Le Sueur (ed), *Building the UK's New Supreme Court* (Oxford 2004), p 4.

And all of this happened in the middle of a Cabinet reshuffle in which the then Lord Chancellor, Lord Irvine, left the government, giving rise to strong suspicions that these major changes were as much about personality as about constitutional reform. One commentator has said that 'it is difficult to resist the conclusion that the reforms were the product of policy making on the hoof', not least because they directly contradicted things that the government had said shortly before the announcements were made.[45] Thus the new Supreme Court has been characterised as one 'born of secret ministerial cabal and a press release'.[46]

Succour is given to this view by a paper submitted by Lord Irvine—who had maintained a dignified silence since leaving the government in 2003—to the House of Lords Constitution Committee in November 2009.[47] In it, he says that he only learned of the proposals a week before they were announced, and that, upon doing so, he asked the then Prime Minister, Tony Blair

> how a decision of this magnitude could be made without prior consultation with me, with…my Permanent Secretary [that is, the most senior civil servant in his department], within government, with the judiciary, with the authorities of the House of Lords which would lose its Speaker and with [Buckingham] Palace.

Blair, according to Irvine, 'appeared mystified and said that these machinery of government changes always had to be carried into effect in a way that precluded discussion because of the risk of leaks'.

Taken at face value, this is an extraordinary view that treats fundamental changes to the architecture of the constitution as akin to such commonplace phenomena as the rebranding of government departments and the transfer of responsibilities between them. So poorly thought-through were the government's initial proposals that those involved appeared ignorant of the fact that the 700-year-old office of Lord Chancellor—to which there were over 5,000 statutory references—could be abolished only through the enactment of complex primary legislation. In fact, as we relate in Chapter 6, the office of Lord Chancellor still remains today, albeit that the Constitutional Reform Act 2005 drastically reshaped it. The purpose of this discussion is not to consider the substantive merits of the reforms introduced by that Act. There were, as we will see later in the book, strong—perhaps even compelling—arguments for many or all of the changes that it ushered in. But even those who support the *effects* of the Act have expressed concern about the *process* (or rather lack of process) that preceded it. Indeed, Blair himself concedes that the process was 'bumpy' and 'messy', and that questions of detail were only addressed at the 'last minute'—but, he maintains, 'the outcome was right', the implication being that this is what really matters.[48]

---

[45] Le Sueur, p 4.   [46] Le Sueur, p 5.

[47] House of Lords Committee on the Constitution, *The Cabinet Office and the Centre of Government* (HL 30 2009–10), Ev 81–4.

[48] House of Lords Committee on the Constitution, HL 30, Ev 86–7.

3.3.3 **Constitutional reform as an ongoing process**

The third and (for the purposes of this discussion) final implication of the ease with which the UK constitution can be changed is that it allows constitutional reform to be, in effect, a rolling process that lacks finality. This has important implications. Some might be regarded as advantages. Treating the constitution as a 'work in progress' makes it possible to keep it under review, and to react quickly when it is felt that things are not working well or that established arrangements need to be updated. For example, the systems of devolution introduced in Scotland and Wales have been reviewed since their introduction in 1999. Several shortcomings were identified in relation to the Welsh system that changes implemented in 2007 sought to correct.[49] And in 2009, the Commission on Scottish Devolution—a body set up by the Scottish Parliament and the UK government to review Scottish devolution—concluded that the Scottish institutions of government should be given additional powers.[50] Meanwhile, notwithstanding the extensive nature of the post-1997 reforms, the Brown government, in 2009—responding, it seems, to public disaffection with politics and government following a scandal concerning MPs' expenses—mooted the possibility of a new swathe of changes, perhaps even including a written constitution.[51] And, as noted earlier, the change of government wrought by the 2010 election has not put an end to constitutional reform. Far from it: one of the conditions underpinning the formation of the coalition government was the implementation of further far-reaching changes to the constitution, including fixed-term Parliaments and a referendum on changing the voting system.

All of this, it might be said, illustrates the greatest strength of the UK's constitutional arrangements: their immense flexibility—that is, their capacity to adapt to changing needs and circumstances. It is, of course, hard to argue against the proposition that it should be possible, without undue difficulty, to improve constitutional arrangements that prove to be defective or outmoded. But it is important, in thinking about this matter, to make sure that two conceptually distinct matters are not confused with one another. The fact that *some issues, such as detailed, technical arrangements*, should be capable of being amended with relative ease does not mean that *all constitutional arrangements, including those pertaining to fundamental principles*, should be amenable to equally casual amendment. After all, one of the main points of enshrining such principles in constitutional law is to ensure that they cannot be discarded whenever they prove inconvenient to the government of the day. This distinction is one that is, or at least can be, well served by legal systems with hard-to-amend written constitutions: matters of the latter type can be reflected in the constitutional text itself; while

---

[49] The arrangements introduced in 2007 provided for more far-reaching changes to Welsh devolution if supported in a referendum. At the time of writing, such a referendum is anticipated—see further Chapter 7.

[50] *Serving Scotland Better: Scotland and the United Kingdom in the 21st Century* (Edinburgh 2009). At the time of writing, it is anticipated that the UK Parliament will enact legislation implementing the Commission's recommendations.

[51] Prime Minister's Office, *Building Britain's Future* (Cm 7654 2009), ch 1.

matters of detail can be dealt with in regular law, which (subject to the limits imposed by the constitution) can be amended with relative ease as circumstances change and experience develops. The difficulty is that, in the UK, this distinction does not exist in formal terms: while it might be possible to say that arrangement 'X' is fundamental and should not be interfered with readily, but that matter 'Y' is a mere point of detail that should be more readily capable of amendment, no such distinction is reflected in *law*. The result is that even constitutional arrangements concerning indisputably fundamental principles remain exposed to the chill winds of party politics. A good illustration of this is the way in which the HRA, has been kicked around by the main parties as if it were a political football.

The effect of the HRA is considered in outline in Chapter 2 and in detail in Chapter 19. For now, it suffices to say that it gives effect in UK law to certain fundamental human rights, such as the right not to be tortured, the right to a fair trial, and the right to free speech. In many countries, such rights enjoy constitutional status—that is, they are recognised by the written constitutional text and thus limit the powers of the executive government and the legislature. Within such a system, constitutional rights can be removed or otherwise interfered with only by amending the constitution itself—which, as we know, is likely to be difficult. The UK, lacking such a higher body of constitutional law, could not adopt that sort of approach to the legal protection of human rights and so the HRA was enacted. Being a regular law (there being no other type), the Act is capable of being amended or even repealed, just like any other such law. This fact has not evaded the notice of politicians from both of the main parties. One of the great ironies of the Act is that the government that caused it to be enacted subsequently complained bitterly when judges applied it (quite properly) in ways that stopped Ministers from doing things that they wanted to do. We saw earlier that, to its credit, the Blair government accepted the historic ruling in the *Belmarsh* case, but the courts' judgments in human rights cases have not always been so meekly received by government.

In one notable incident in 2003, the then Home Secretary, David Blunkett, reacted furiously to a decision by Collins J in the Administrative Court holding, in a case to which the HRA was relevant, that Blunkett's department had treated certain asylum seekers unlawfully. In a radio interview, Blunkett said that he was 'fed up with having to deal with a situation where Parliament debates issues and the judges then overturn them', that he did not 'accept what Justice Collins has said', and that 'We will continue operating a policy which we think is perfectly reasonable and fair'.[52] Writing shortly after these comments were made, one commentator observed that Blunkett's 'outburst appears to have fuelled an unusual and extreme personal onslaught on Collins J in much of the daily and weekly press, that was linked with an expression of dissatisfaction with judges in general'.[53] Subsequently, the then Prime Minister criticised the

---

[52] Quoted by Bradley, 'Judicial Independence under Attack' [2003] PL 397, 400.

[53] Bradley at 400. Labour Home Secretaries do not have a monopoly on confrontation with the judiciary: Michael Howard, Home Secretary in the Major government in the 1990s, had run-ins with the judges.

HRA. In the wake of the terrorist attacks on the London transport network in July 2005, Tony Blair said that he would consider seeking the amendment of the Act if it were to turn out that it would stop the government from effectively fighting the so-called 'war on terror'.[54] And in 2009, responding, it would seem, to the view expressed strongly in certain sections of the media that the HRA gives undue weight to the interests of criminals and asylum seekers at the expense of the so-called law-abiding majority, the Brown government proposed replacing or supplementing the Act with a 'Bill of Rights and Responsibilities'.[55] Meanwhile, the Conservative Party undertook, in its 2010 election manifesto, to repeal the HRA, replacing it with a 'British Bill of Rights'.[56] At the time of writing, a government commission is expected to review the Act.

This is not the place in which to consider the merits or otherwise either of the HRA itself or of possible reforms in this area (matters that are addressed in Chapter 19); rather, our point is simply that the fact that the HRA—the closest thing that the UK has to a constitutional Bill of Rights—is perceived as fair game by politicians tells us something important about the UK constitution. It tells us that, ultimately, very little is sacrosanct and that, in the UK, at least to some extent, the normal principles of constitutionalism are turned on their head. In most countries, the constitution is hierarchically at the top of the system of law and government: everything else has to fit around it. In the UK, the constitution, such as it is, is malleable. If existing constitutional arrangements prove to be an obstacle to what the government regards as the efficient processing of asylum seekers, the effective prosecution of the 'war on terror', or the avoidance of critical comment in the tabloid press, then they can, if the political will can be mustered, be changed or done away with.

> **Q** Is this a good or a bad thing? Might it be argued that the British approach is democratic, in the sense that politicians are able to do whatever the people want? What might be the disadvantages of such a system? In particular, why might the British approach serve the interests of minorities—especially of unpopular minorities, such as asylum seekers and suspected terrorists—poorly?

4. Conclusions

In this chapter, we have looked at the sort of things that constitutions generally do and (in a necessarily introductory fashion) at whether, and if so how, the UK's constitution does those things. We have seen that the main factor that distinguishes

---

[54] Downing Street press conference, 5 August 2005.

[55] Ministry of Justice, *Rights and Responsibilities: Developing Our Constitutional Framework* (Cm 7577 2009). The proposal was tentative and the relationship of the proposed Bill of Rights and Responsibilities with the HRA was unclear.

[56] Conservative Party, *An Invitation to Join the Government of Britain* (London 2010), 79.

the UK's arrangements is that none of them is laid down in a body of law that has a status higher than regular law. The net results of this idiosyncrasy of the UK system are twofold. First, those laws that deal with constitutional matters can, in principle, be amended as easily as any other law. This means that the UK constitution does not legally restrict the powers of government to the same extent as constitutions that do have a higher legal status and which can be changed only by going through a hard-to-comply-with amendment process. Second, it follows that, if arbitrary government is to be avoided in the UK, greater faith must be placed in the capacity of the political process to guard against the misuse of public power and the enactment of oppressive legislation. Public opinion is a powerful deterrent against such conduct, although we will see later in the book that the constitution supplies a wealth of more sophisticated mechanisms that seek to guard against, and correct, abuses of power by those in authority.

However, this brief portrait of the UK constitution is incomplete. Although it is sometimes said that, for the reasons set out in the last paragraph, the UK has a 'political constitution' rather than a 'legal constitution', it is clear that today there is far more constitutional law in the UK than ever before—thanks in large part to the post-1997 reforms. As a result, people have a wider array of legal rights that they can enforce against the government: rights of access to information under freedom-of-information legislation; and fundamental civil and political rights—to free speech, to respect for private life, to freedom of religion, and so on—under human rights law. In this sense, the UK now has a 'legal constitution' to a greater extent than it ever has done.

This does not detract from the fact that the UK's constitution is still a political one in the sense that it is politics and not law that is the ultimate safeguard against abuse of power. On any traditional analysis, if the political process were to fail to deter such a step from being taken, Parliament could take away any of the legal rights that people currently enjoy and the courts ultimately would be powerless to do anything about it.[57] However, what must not be overlooked is the way in which the legal and the political dimensions of the constitution relate to one another. Once legal arrangements concerning fundamental constitutional matters are put in place—for example, entitling the people of Scotland, Wales, and Northern Ireland to run their own affairs, or giving people enforceable human rights—it may not be easy for politicians, at a stroke of the legislative pen, to get rid of or override them, even though, in theory, they have the power to do so. (Think back to the *Belmarsh* case: the court lacked power to strike down the offending law, but the government felt obliged to ask Parliament to repeal it once the judges had said that it infringed human rights standards.) Once the genie is out of the bottle, it is hard to get it back in. In this way, the legal aspects of the constitution, while not technically immutable, may well shape the political landscape—and those

---

[57] We noted above that this traditional analysis is increasingly contested. We assess criticisms of it in Chapter 5 below.

aspects of the constitution that are highly valued by people generally may become so ingrained as to become, in practice, constitutional limits as real as any laid down in a written constitution.

The UK constitution is idiosyncratic and messy; it has strengths and weaknesses; certainly, no one sitting down with a blank sheet of paper would design such a constitution. But constitutions that are designed from scratch are not perfect either: they have their own difficulties and complications. We should keep this in mind as we embark, in the following chapters, upon a detailed exploration of the UK's constitutional arrangements and as we try to work out whether they are merely eccentric or genuinely inadequate.

Further reading

BOGDANOR, *The New British Constitution* (Oxford 2009)

FELDMAN, 'None, One or Several? Perspectives on the UK's Constitution(s)' [2005] CLJ 329

2 Themes, Sources, and Principles

1. Introduction

We saw in Chapter 1 that constitutions tend to perform a number of different functions and to have certain characteristics. We also looked briefly, against that background, at the United Kingdom's constitutional arrangements. In this chapter, our focus switches more fully to those arrangements. In particular, we consider four important matters concerning the UK constitution of which it is necessary to be aware at the outset.

First, we set out the *three key themes* that, in our view, emerge from the study of contemporary UK public law. These themes reflect the dominant characteristics of and challenges faced by public law in the UK today. Being aware of them right at the beginning of our study of the subject will help their significance to be appreciated as relevant material is addressed during the course of the book. It will also, we hope, help to illustrate that while public law, like any branch of the law, consists of a good deal of technical, detailed material, it is also an area in which big ideas and broad narratives are to be found. Public law is also a subject that invites debate and disagreement—much of which, as we will see, centres upon the themes around which this book is based.

Second, we examine the *sources of the UK constitution*. We have already said that the UK does not have a 'written constitution', in the sense of a constitutional text with superior legal status. Where, then, do we look if we wish to ascertain the constitutional arrangements applicable in the UK? As we will see, the UK's constitution is to be found in a range of sources—written, unwritten, legal, and political.

Third, we address a number of *principles* that occupy a central role in UK public law. Many of these principles are considered in greater detail in subsequent chapters, but it is necessary to be aware of them, at least in outline, at the outset, because of their pervasive relevance to the matters considered in this book.

Finally, and by way of conclusion, we consider whether the UK should adopt a written, or *codified*, constitution.

Before turning to those matters, it is necessary to address a preliminary issue that is technical, but important. It concerns the structure of the UK and the terminology used to describe its constituent parts. The UK consists of Great Britain—England, Scotland, and Wales—and Northern Ireland. Some law, including much constitutional law, applies throughout the UK, but in some instances, different laws apply in the different parts of the UK. Where this is the case, our primary focus will be on the laws applicable in England and Wales—'English law', for short.

2. Three key themes

Determining what the key themes in modern UK public law are is, to some extent at least, a subjective matter: certainly, not all public lawyers would agree upon the same themes as those identified here. We have, however, sought to identify three key matters that provide a means by which to understand the big questions with which public law is (or ought to be) grappling, and its direction of travel as it attempts to do so.

2.1 The role of the executive and the importance of accountability

Our first theme concerns the central role occupied in the UK constitution by the executive branch of government, and the fundamental importance of ensuring that the executive is effectively held to account. We saw in Chapter 1 that Parliament is all-powerful, in that it can enact any law that it wishes, but it is nevertheless the executive branch of central government—the Prime Minister, other Ministers, their government departments, and civil servants—that is in the driving seat. It is the executive branch that formulates a programme for government and then seeks to implement it. One of the ways in which it does so is by getting Parliament to enact legislation—and the executive nearly always gets its way in this regard, bearing in mind that it will almost inevitably have a majority in the House of Commons and that the House of Lords ultimately lacks the power to block legislation.

It follows that, because the courts are subservient to Parliament (in that they cannot strike down the laws that it enacts) and because Parliament is, in practice, subservient to the executive (for the reasons just given), the executive finds itself in an extremely powerful position. In the UK, the executive government is by far the largest, most complex, and most powerful branch of the state. It has the basic responsibility for running the country and for delivering public services. Each year, the government spends hundreds of billions of pounds of taxpayers' money. It also has extensive legal powers that can radically affect people's lives for good or ill. The very considerable strength of UK governments derives from the basic political fact that they control the parliamentary and legislative process; they also control the administrative machinery of central and local government. This, in turn, means that one of the central challenges that arises in relation to the UK constitution is to make sure that the executive is properly held to account for its actions and decisions, and its policies and their implementation.

We explore the concept of accountability in detail in Chapter 10; for the time being, it suffices to say that holding the government to account involves requiring it to explain and justify what it is doing and why, particularly when things have gone wrong, and, where appropriate, providing the means by which corrective or punitive action may be taken against those guilty of wrongdoing or bad judgement. Being able to hold government to account is an essential feature of democratic government. In a democracy, government is supposed to act as the servant, as opposed to the master, of the people. To perform the many tasks deemed necessary in modern society, the people collectively delegate their power to government so that it can act on their behalf. However, human nature being what it is, there is always the risk that government may exceed the limits of its powers, betray the trust of the people, or be incompetent. It is therefore necessary for the people to be able to call the government to account. Holding government to account has a number of purposes: to make sure that government is responsive to what the people want, to ensure that government is effective, and to guard against abuse of power and incompetence. An effective system of accountability is an essential adjunct of a healthy democracy: voters—the electorate—must be able to ascertain how the government is performing, so as to be able to make informed choices at the next election. But accountability is about more than simply enabling elections to be conducted in an informed way. Ultimately, although important, elections are a blunt instrument of accountability. They enable the electorate to render a single judgement on the government's overall performance—but given the enormous amount and diversity of the tasks undertaken by governments, there is a clear need for a more granular form of scrutiny and oversight. Elections therefore have to be supplemented by other accountability processes. It is crucial that such processes work effectively. Whether they do so is one of the main questions that falls to be examined in this book.

2.2 **Legal and political constitutionalism**

The second of our key themes is connected to the first. It concerns the *shift from a more political to a more legal form of constitutionalism* in the UK. Before we say anything about the nature and significance of this shift, we need to explain what, in the first place, is meant by 'legal constitutionalism' and 'political constitutionalism'—and indeed by 'constitutionalism' itself.

If a constitution is to amount to more than empty words, provision must be made for ensuring that the relevant parties—most obviously, the government in its various guises—behave as the constitution requires them to, and for dealing with situations in which they fail to do so. To put the matter in terms that recall our first theme, the question is about precisely how the government should be held to account. It is in relation to this question that the distinction between legal and political constitutionalism emerges: each is a theory—a set of views—concerning how, in practice, constitutional behaviour should be promoted and unconstitutional conduct dealt with.

Advocates of political constitutionalism put their faith in the political process. They argue that, in a democracy, that process guards against unconstitutional behaviour by those in authority—and that, even if, exceptionally, it fails to deter such conduct, it is the means by which corrective action may be taken. For example, in a celebrated essay entitled 'The Political Constitution', Griffith argued that at the heart of the British constitution lies the recognition that governments of the UK may take any action necessary for the furtherance of the public interest and the proper government of the UK.[1] This position seems to give the government virtually untrammelled power to do as it pleases, but the government is subject to some limitations. The first is that the government of the day continues in office only for so long as it can maintain the majority support of the House of Commons. The second is that the government can only act within the law as laid down by statute and common law. The first limitation is undoubtedly a political one: governments acquire their majority by virtue of general elections, which are political events designed to determine the political preferences of the electorate. The second limitation—that government can only act within the limits of the law as laid down by statute and common law—may seem to be a legal limitation. However, as we saw in Chapter 1, the executive government is generally able to legislate as it wishes thanks to its control of Parliament—and the courts, because of parliamentary sovereignty, cannot ultimately strike down Acts of Parliament. This means that the government may modify or discard legal limitations to which it is subject, provided that it has the political strength to cause the enactment of the necessary legislation.[2] From the perspective of political constitutionalism, there are (and should be) no overriding legal constraints whatsoever upon the government; the only constraints are (and should be) political.

According to political constitutionalists, the political process deters politicians from doing unconstitutional things (because Parliament or the people might think badly of this and might therefore refuse to support the government in a vote in the Commons or at a general election) and provides a corrective if such things are done (because the people can vote for a different party, which might govern in a more constitutionally acceptable manner). It would be wrong to give the impression that political constitutionalists see votes in the House of Commons and in general elections as the only ways in which the government should be held to account and constitutional values upheld. Political constitutionalism also embraces more nuanced devices, such as public inquiries and investigations by parliamentary committees, by which the work of the executive (and its adherence or otherwise to principles of constitutional government) can be examined and evaluated. Importantly, however, the underlying purpose of such devices, within the tradition of political constitutionalism, is to place parliamentarians and the public in the best possible position to judge whether the government is behaving acceptably; the ultimate focus, therefore, remains on the ballot box.

Unsurprisingly, the emphasis of those who advocate legal constitutionalism is rather different. They prefer to put their faith in the judicial, not the political, system. Both philosophical and pragmatic arguments underpin this view. In philosophical terms, it is said that there are certain moral principles—principles of 'natural law' or 'higher law'—that are so fundamental as to be immutable. A 'law' that contradicts

---

[1] (1979) 42 MLR 1, 15. See also Foley, *The Politics of the British Constitution* (Manchester 1999).

[2] For reasons considered in Chapters 8 and 19, the picture today is rather more complicated because of EU law and the Human Rights Act 1998, but the position set out here remains generally accurate.

such principles cannot be a genuine law at all and should not be enforced by courts—a view that means that, in practice, courts have the task of ensuring that politicians do not overstep the mark. There are also practical reasons why it might be thought that courts should have such a role in the UK. The most obvious is that the executive's effective control over Parliament means that there is, in practice, a fusion of power between the legislature and executive—a phenomenon that leads some to argue that there must be an *external* body, such as the judiciary, capable of ensuring that the political branches of government act constitutionally.[3] For reasons that we explain in Chapter 3, confidence in the ability of the political branches to regulate themselves and each other has declined in recent years, adding impetus to the view that courts should be able to step in when things go wrong.

A further argument (according to its proponents) in favour of legal constitutionalism is that while reliance on the political process is likely to result in the interests of the majority being adequately looked after, the same might not be true of minorities of various sorts. The majority, acting through political institutions such as Parliament, might be inclined to do things—such as locking up suspected foreign terrorists without charge or trial[4]—that serve their own interests at the expense of unpopular, marginalised groups. And in order to prevent this from happening, it might be necessary to empower judges—whose independence allows them to be uninfluenced by public opinion—to protect the constitutional rights of *everyone*, even if that means curbing the self-serving instincts of the majority. To this suggestion, political constitutionalists retort that giving judges such power overlooks the fact that 'law is not and cannot be a substitute for politics'.[5] Thus Waldron, a leading American critic of judges being allowed to strike down unconstitutional legislation, argues that giving judges such powers 'disenfranchises ordinary citizens and brushes aside cherished principles of representation and political equality in the final resolution of issues about rights'.[6] And the argument against giving judges extensive powers of this nature may be thought to be stronger still in the UK, given that no popularly endorsed text lays down what the fundamental principles of the constitution are. Giving judges such powers, it has been said, 'would arguably be tantamount to the abdication of democracy in favour of a system of democracy layered with aristocracy (the decisions of the elite)'.[7]

Although it is helpful to be aware of the broad distinctions (set out above) between legal and political constitutionalism, in truth, neither is a monolithic concept—there are many different views about precisely what each concept should mean—and it is artificial to suppose that a given constitutional system must opt for one or other of

---

[3] This argument is put forward by several commentators in different ways and with different emphases. For leading examples, see: Allan, *Constitutional Justice* (Oxford 2001); Woolf, '*Droit Public*: English Style' [1995] PL 57; Laws, 'Law and Democracy' [1995] PL 72.   [4] See Chapter 1, section 3.1, above.

[5] Griffith (1979) 42 MLR 1, 16.

[6] 'The Core of the Case against Judicial Review' (2006) 115 Yale Law Journal 1346, 1353.

[7] Poole, 'Dogmatic Liberalism? TRS Allan and the Common Law Constitution' (2002) 65 MLR 463, 475. See further Poole, 'Questioning Common Law Constitutionalism' (2002) 25 LS 142.

those two models. The UK constitution, like all developed constitutions, relies upon both legal and political processes for the purpose of encouraging and enforcing compliance with constitutional principles. The question, therefore, is not whether we should put our faith in the legal or political process; rather, the important issue concerns the extent to, and the ways in, which each of those systems should be relied upon in order to ensure that those in authority behave in a manner that respects the principles of the constitution. The UK constitution has come in recent years to rely to a lesser extent than it has traditionally done on political forms of control, and to a greater extent on legal forms of control (albeit that UK courts have not—yet—unequivocally asserted authority to disregard Acts of Parliament that conflict with fundamental constitutional principles). Recent legislation—in particular the Human Rights Act 1998 (HRA)—has been a major driver of this trend as Parliament has conferred power on the courts to review government decisions on human rights grounds. Thus the second of our three key themes is that the UK has shifted (and is arguably continuing to shift further) from a more political to a more legal form of constitutionalism. We will see several examples of this phenomenon throughout the book and, as we encounter them, we will need to think critically about whether it is wise to place growing reliance on the legal system in this regard. One prominent critic of this trend, for example, has argued that, to the extent that such reliance is motivated by dissatisfaction with the political process, strengthening that process would be preferable to leaving it to courts to step in.[8]

> **Q** Which of the two schools of thought outlined above—'legal constitutionalism' and 'political constitutionalism'—do you find more appealing? Do you agree that each has strengths and weaknesses, and, if so, can you think of ways in which the best features of the two systems might be combined?

2.3 The multilayered nature of the modern UK constitution

The UK has traditionally been a highly centralised state. Executive and legislative power was, until comparatively recently, largely concentrated at the centre: the UK executive government was responsible for the running of the whole country, while the UK Parliament made law for the whole of the UK. Although local government has long existed alongside central government, and although local government fulfils many important functions, it only has the powers given to it via law made by the UK Parliament. Over recent decades, central government has legislated to restrict and confine local government, which, in turn, has often come to be seen, to some extent, as an offshoot of central government—an implementer of the latter's policies—rather than a constitutionally separate branch of government with its own independent area of authority.[9]

---

[8] Tomkins, *Our Republican Constitution* (Oxford 2005), ch 4.   [9] See further Chapter 7.

But this picture—of a system in which central government has a monopoly of real power—has changed markedly in recent years. There has been a clear shift from a system in which power is concentrated in central government to one in which power is shared by a number of different levels of government. This shift to a system of *multi-layered governance* is the third of our three key themes. The drivers of this change have been twofold: the UK's membership of the European Union (EU); and the devolution of power to Scotland, Wales, and Northern Ireland.[10] Since becoming a member State of the EU in 1973, the UK has seen swathes of government power transferred upwards to the institutions of the EU. Likewise, since the introduction of devolution in 1999, the UK executive and Parliament have, in practice, ceded considerable authority downwards to new governments in Scotland, Wales, and Northern Ireland.

The significance of these changes has been, and will continue to be, considerable. Short of some major political change, it is highly unlikely that the UK will leave the EU; equally, it is hard to imagine circumstances in which devolution would be abolished. The emergence of multilayered governance forces us to confront questions that previously simply did not arise and to reassess established ways of thinking. For example, once power is shared between different levels of government, questions of demarcation inevitably arise. Does a given function fall to be performed at the local, devolved, national, or European level? What are the powers of the different governments in relation to one another? Who has the last word in the event of a disagreement? What should be the role of the courts in attempting to resolve such disputes? And once we start to think about issues of this nature, we are also forced to consider whether certain long-established constitutional principles remain relevant. Most obviously, as we saw in Chapter 1, the orthodox principle is that the UK Parliament can make any law that it wishes. But can this still be the case now that the UK tier of government has, in effect, given away power to the EU and the devolved governments? Is the UK Parliament, in spite of this, free to make laws that, for example, cut across the powers of those new institutions—could it, for example, repeal a Scottish law with which it disagreed, or are the new legislatures free to do whatever they wish without interference by the UK Parliament? These are questions that we will confront in the relevant parts of the book; for the time being, it is simply necessary to be aware of the fact that the shift to multi-layered governance makes it necessary to address such matters.

2.4 Conclusion

As we said at the beginning of this section, it would be misleading to suggest that the whole of the subject matter of this book could be organised meaningfully around these three key themes. But that is not the point of identifying those themes; rather, the point is that they reflect three of the major characteristics of, and issues faced by, UK public law today. It is in relation to our three key themes—the need effectively

---

[10] See Chapters 8 and 7 respectively.

to hold the executive to account, the balance between legal and political forms of constitutionalism, and the implications of distributing power among several tiers of government—that many of the most important, difficult, and pressing questions in modern UK public law arise. We will need to pay particularly close attention to them in the course of our exploration of the subject.

3. **Sources of the constitution**

3.1 **Introduction**

No constitution is to be found in a single document; even 'written constitutions' are only a starting point. For reasons considered in Chapter 1, such documents are likely to contain only a statement of the most fundamental principles—which might well be expressed in vague language that leaves many questions unanswered. In systems based on written constitutions, such texts must therefore be supplemented and fleshed out. This is likely to happen in three ways.

First, *ordinary legislation* will make detailed provision in relation to matters referred to in the constitution. For example, the constitutional text might say that free and fair elections to the national legislature must be held at reasonable intervals, while leaving the detailed arrangements—exactly how regularly must elections be held, who is entitled to vote, and so on—to be set out in a statute.

Second, it will often be necessary for courts to interpret the constitutional text; in this way, a body of *judicial precedent* will develop that itself can properly be regarded as a source of constitutional law. For example, if the constitution says that elections must be held 'at reasonable intervals', and the legislature passes a law providing for elections every ten years, a court might well be called upon to decide whether such relatively infrequent elections meet the constitutional requirement that they be held at reasonable intervals.

Third, there may be certain matters in relation to which no provision is made, either in the constitutional text itself or in ordinary legislation. When issues arise that have not been anticipated by any law, one possibility is that the parties concerned may arrive at an informal resolution. If it proves satisfactory, and the relevant parties appear willing to adhere to it, it might be felt that there is no need to enshrine it in law; rather, a *political precedent* or *constitutional convention* with which future parties will be expected to comply will arise. Several examples of such conventions are given in Figure 2.1 below.[11]

Except for the absence of a written constitution, the position in the UK is essentially the same as that which is set out above. The sources of the UK's constitutional arrangements are therefore to be found in a combination of ordinary law (including

---

[11] See section 3.5.2 below.

Convention	Precedent	Evidence that relevant parties feel bound	Constitutional reason
Legally, a Bill approved by Parliament can become law only if the Queen assents to it, and the Queen is under no legal duty to do so. However, by convention, the Queen always assents.	No monarch has withheld royal assent to a Bill for over 300 years.	It is highly unlikely that every monarch since the early 1700s has agreed with every Bill. This strongly suggests that monarchs feel obliged to grant assent whatever their personal views.	Today, Parliament is a democratic institution. It would be fundamentally undemocratic for an unelected monarch to thwart the wishes of the elected legislature.
On being appointed, judges sever any ties that they have had with political parties.	Appointees who are affiliated to political parties habitually end such affiliations upon appointment.	The Judges' Council, the judges' representative body, accepts and stipulates that political ties must be severed.	The law must be applied by independent and impartial judges without reference (or the appearance of reference) to extrinsic factors such as party politics.
The Prime Minister and other Ministers regularly appear in Parliament to answer questions from MPs or peers (depending on which chamber they belong to).	The Prime Minister and Ministers habitually do this.	There are often occasions (eg when a Minister is embroiled in personal or political controversy) on which it may be advantageous to the Minister not to appear in Parliament, but Ministers do appear in such circumstances.	It is important that the government is held to account for its policies and their implementation; this is a way of doing so.
The monarch retains certain 'prerogative' powers (eg to declare war and to sign international treaties) but only, and always, exercises them on the advice of the government.	There are no modern examples of monarchs exercising these powers of their own accord, or of refusing to exercise them when advised to do so by the government.	Consistent compliance with the convention implies that monarchs accept that their only role in this area is to do as the government advises.	In a democracy, it would be inappropriate for major policy decisions to be taken by an unelected head of state.
Although senior Ministers can be members of the House of Lords, the Queen will only appoint as Prime Minister someone who is a member of the House of Commons.	It is more than 100 years since a Prime Minister served without being or becoming a member of the House of Commons.	When Alexander Douglas-Home was appointed Prime Minister in 1963, he renounced his peerage and became a member of the House of Commons by winning a by-election.	As the most senior member of the government, it would be undemocratic for the Prime Minister not to be a member of, and directly accountable to, the elected chamber.
Under the 'Sewel convention', the UK Parliament will not normally legislate for parts of the country with devolved governments on matters within the competence of the latter without the prior consent of the relevant devolved legislature.	This convention has been respected since devolution, but because devolution only began in 1999, there is not a long precedent.	The UK government has publicly stated that it accepts this convention.	Underlying devolution is acceptance of the principle that certain parts of the country should, within certain limits, be able to govern themselves. Unwanted interference by the UK legislature would contravene that principle.
According to the 'Salisbury convention', the House of Lords will not vote against a Bill implementing a commitment contained in the governing party's election manifesto.	The convention has generally been respected since it was first articulated in 1945.	In circumstances in which the convention applies, opposition peers in the House of Lords have desisted from blocking government Bills notwithstanding personal opposition to them.	It would be undemocratic for the unelected chamber to prevent the implementation of policies for which the government can claim an electoral mandate.

Figure 2.1 Constitutional conventions

legislation, international treaties, and common law),[12] judicial precedent (for example, concerning the interpretation of legislation), and political precedent.

3.2 Legislation

A great deal of constitutional legislation—that is, legislation dealing with constitutional matters—exists. Indeed, there is so much such legislation that it could be argued that it is misleading to say that the UK lacks a *written* constitution: a large proportion of its constitutional arrangements are laid down in statutes; it is just that those arrangements (or at least the fundamental principles underpinning them) have not been codified into a single text called 'The Constitution'.[13] Precisely because statutory constitutional law is to be found in regular legislation rather than in a separate constitutional text, there is no straightforward, formal way of identifying such legislation; rather, it can be identified only by reference to its subject matter—constitutional legislation is that legislation which deals with constitutional matters. It is helpful, in this regard, to distinguish between the two principal types of such matters.

First, constitutional law is concerned with the *organisation of, and the allocation of power to, the institutions of government*. A good deal of legislation deals with such matters.[14] Prominent examples include the legislation devolving executive and legislative power to the Scottish, Welsh, and Northern Irish governments.[15] Similarly, legislation was enacted when the UK joined the EU in order to make provision for (among other things) EU law to take effect in the UK and to be enforceable by national courts.[16] And a great deal of legislation exists concerning the role and functions of local government and its relationship with central government.[17] Meanwhile, important issues concerning the UK Parliament itself—including the limitation of the powers of the House of Lords,[18] eligibility for membership of Parliament,[19] and elections to the House of Commons[20]—are dealt with by legislation. There is also legislation concerning the judicial system:[21] the new UK Supreme Court was, for example, created by an Act of Parliament.[22] Indeed the creation of the United Kingdom itself is attributable in part

---

[12] Including the so-called royal prerogative, on which, see section 3.3 below.

[13] See, eg Bogdanor, *The New British Constitution* (Oxford 2009), pp 8–9. But this point should not be overstated. However much constitutional legislation there is in the UK, it is still only legislation: it is not constitutional law that has a higher legal status in the sense discussed in Chapter 1.

[14] All of the following legislation is considered in detail in the relevant chapters below.

[15] Scotland Act 1998, Government of Wales Act 2006, Northern Ireland Act 1998.

[16] European Communities Act 1972.

[17] See, in particular: Local Government Act 1972, Local Government Act 2000, Local Government and Public Involvement in Health Act 2007.   [18] Parliament Acts 1911–49.

[19] House of Lords Act 1999, House of Commons Disqualification Act 1975.

[20] For example, Representation of the People Act 1983.

[21] For example, Senior Courts Act 1981; Tribunals, Courts and Enforcement Act 2007.

[22] Constitutional Reform Act 2005.

to legislation: the joining of England and Wales with Scotland and Ireland was effected by statute.[23]

Second, there is a good deal of legislation concerning the other main aspect of constitutional law: *the regulation of the relationship between the individual and the state*. Formal statements setting out important rights and interests to be respected by the state are not a modern innovation. Consider, for example, Magna Carta 1215, which (among other things) made provision concerning the liberty of the individual and the right to trial by jury. Also noteworthy is the Bill of Rights 1689, parts of which remain in force today: art 9, for example, lays down the principle of parliamentary privilege, whereby things said in Parliament cannot be the subject of legal proceedings (for example, for defamation), thus ensuring that parliamentarians are free to express their views uninhibited by the threat of litigation. Today, however, the most obviously significant legislation concerning the rights of the individual vis-à-vis the state is the HRA.[24]

As we noted above and in Chapter 1, even legislation dealing with fundamental constitutional matters is, ultimately, still only regular legislation; it can therefore be amended or even repealed simply by enacting a further piece of such legislation. This absence of hierarchy in UK statutory law—the notion that all laws are equal—was vividly captured by the (once) influential Victorian scholar Dicey, who remarked that 'neither the Act of Union with Scotland nor the Dentists Act 1878 has more claim than the other to be considered a supreme law'.[25] It is, however, worth noting that this view has been questioned. In *Thoburn v Sunderland City Council*, it was suggested by Laws LJ that '[w]e should recognise a hierarchy of Acts of Parliament: as it were "ordinary" statutes and "constitutional" statutes'.[26] The latter category, he said, included legislation that 'conditions the legal relationship between citizen and state in some general, overarching manner' or which affects individuals' fundamental rights.[27] Importantly, Laws LJ's argument was that this distinction should be one to which legal significance attaches. The general principle, as we will see in Chapter 5, is that whenever two pieces of legislation conflict, the courts will prioritise the more recent one: even if the later Act does not explicitly say that it is overriding the earlier one, it will have that effect. However, Laws LJ said that this doctrine of 'implied repeal' should not apply to *constitutional* statutes. On this view, legislation dealing with constitutional matters can still be repealed or amended simply by Parliament enacting another piece of legislation— but only if, in that legislation, Parliament specifically says that it intends to override an earlier piece of constitutional legislation.

These comments were contained in *obiter dicta*—that is, they did not form part of the binding element of the judgment. But even if Laws LJ's view is followed in other

---

[23] Union with Scotland Act 1706, Union with Ireland Act 1800.   [24] See section 4.5 below.

[25] Dicey, *An Introduction to the Study of the Law of the Constitution* (London 1959), p 145.

[26] [2002] EWHC 195 (Admin), [2003] QB 151, [62].

[27] *Thoburn* at [62]. Much, or even all, of the legislation mentioned above would fall into the category of 'constitutional legislation'.

cases, it is a relatively modest one. Technically, it suggests that there is now a special category of *harder*-to-amend constitutional legislation in the UK—but yet such legislation is not *hard* to amend, given that all that is needed is express words of repeal. It therefore remains the case that the UK lacks any meaningful hierarchy of statutory law that enables fundamental constitutional arrangements to be given a degree of legal permanence.

Q Do you agree that constitutional law should be more difficult to amend than other forms of law? If so, how difficult? If not, why not?

3.3 Judge-made law and common law

The principal role of courts is to decide disputes between litigants by resolving disagreements about the facts and then applying the law to the facts. It may be thought that this is a mechanical process whereby the court simply decides whether the facts fit whatever test is laid down in the statute. The reality, however, is more complex, and in many situations, courts end up *making* law—and, in cases with a constitutional dimension to them, making *public law*. It follows that judicial precedent—that is, the body of decisions made by courts when deciding cases—itself constitutes an important source of public law. This is so in three senses.

The first is concerned with the *interpretation of constitutional legislation*. Such legislation may be—and indeed often is—unclear or unspecific, capable of being interpreted in different ways, each of which would produce a different practical outcome for the parties. In this sense, courts augment legislation by interpreting it: they put flesh on the bones by giving it the more precise meaning that it turns out to require once it falls to be applied in real cases. For example, the HRA only explicitly obliges 'public authorities' to respect the rights protected by the Act.[28] But what does this mean? If a local council (which is itself a public authority) that is legally required to arrange care and accommodation for vulnerable people chooses to discharge that obligation by paying a commercial organisation to provide the relevant services, is the latter a public authority that can be sued by residents if their human rights are breached?[29] In the leading case on this point, one of the judges candidly admitted that the words used in the Act are 'so imprecise in their meaning' that the court has to try to work out the policy underlying them: in other words, the statute has to be interpreted by reference to extrinsic considerations about what the judge thinks Parliament was trying to achieve.[30] And the judge went on to admit that the 'identification of the policy is almost inevitably governed, at least to some extent, by one's notions of what the policy

---

[28] Section 6(1).

[29] For the answer to this question, see Chapter 19, section 3.5.2, below. The point for present purposes is simply that the answer is not provided by the Act.

[30] *YL v Birmingham City Council* [2007] UKHL 27, [2008] 1 AC 95, [128], *per* Lord Neuberger.

should be'.[31] There are therefore clearly occasions on which, in interpreting legislation dealing with constitutional matters, courts make law by filling gaps in the statute or giving precise meaning to statutory language that is, taken in isolation, so vague as to be almost meaningless. Furthermore, the views of the courts as to what the law actually is will, to some degree, be inevitably influenced by their views as to what the law ought to be.

Second, the principal hallmark of a *common law* system is that the lawmaking role of courts extends beyond the interpretation of legislation. The common law is a body of law that is unambiguously judge-made. Large areas of private law, such as much of the law of tort, are based on common law—that is, on legal principles articulated and refined by judges on a case-by-case basis. Important parts of public law, too, consist of judge-made common law rules. For example, when public bodies, such as government Ministers, exercise discretionary powers—say, to decide whether someone should be granted British citizenship or whether permission should be given for a new runway at an airport—they are required to act in accordance with certain legal principles of good administration. Public bodies must, for example, give the parties concerned a fair hearing. They also must make decisions that are neither irrational nor unreasonable. These public law principles have been developed by the courts, in accordance with the common law method, in much the same way as the law of tort has been developed. Furthermore, they are general principles that apply across the board to the decisions of all public bodies. Thus it can be said that the common law is a significant source of public law. Today, judicial review—whereby the sorts of principles referred to above are enforced—comprises one of the most important areas of public law; this is why we devote a whole part of this book to examining it.[32]

Third, judge-made law is a source of public law in which there exists a set of *common law constitutional principles*. These principles are distinct from straightforward common law rules. If the latter are breached, the person concerned may sue the perpetrator. This is true in private law (if X acts negligently and causes foreseeable harm to you, you can sue her) and in public law (if Minister Y decides to deport you without first giving you a fair hearing, you can take legal action against him). The legal relevance of common law constitutional principles, on the other hand, is more subtle: such *principles* influence how courts interpret and apply existing legal *rules*. We explore these issues towards the end of the chapter. For the time being, a brief example will suffice. In Chapter 1, we noted that the principle of legal certainty is recognised in many countries, including the UK, as a fundamentally important one. The principle means, among other things, that people should be able to know what the law is in order that they can (if they wish) regulate their conduct so as to stay on the right side of it. In the UK, this principle is regarded as a common law constitutional principle. It is not, of course, recorded in a written constitution—and it is, of course, possible for the UK Parliament to override it. But this does not rob it of any practical significance.

---

[31] *YL* at [128].   [32] See Chapters 12–15 below.

First, fundamental constitutional principles have a *political* relevance: a government that wishes to do something that flies in the face of such a principle is likely to face considerable opposition. The existence of fundamental constitutional principles thus helps to shape public debate, and to determine what it is politically possible for governments to do. Second, and perhaps more concretely, courts will strive to interpret legislation and to develop the common law in ways that respect common law constitutional principles. Thus, for example, if the wording of a statute were unclear, such that it could be interpreted as either creating or not creating criminal liability in respect of acts committed before its enactment, the court would adopt the latter interpretation, so as to render the legislation compatible with the principle of legal certainty. An important question that this raises is just how far courts can go: if the statute is crystal clear, do they have to enforce it even if it fundamentally conflicts with an important constitutional principle? The traditional answer to this question is that, because Parliament is sovereign, the court would have to apply the legislation however repugnant it was to such a principle—but, as we explain in Chapter 5, this view is increasingly challenged.

Finally in this section, mention should be made of the royal prerogative. This is considered in more detail in Chapter 4. For now, it is sufficient to say that the prerogative is generally regarded as part of the common law that, *inter alia*, authorises (in practice) the executive branch of government to do certain things such as declaring war and granting honours. The prerogative is an historical anachronism that reflects the fact that government used to be carried on by or under the direction of the monarch exercising the prerogative powers. Most vestiges of the prerogative have by now been swept away by legislation, upon which the vast majority of executive authority depends, but pockets of prerogative power remain. Although formally belonging to the monarch, such powers are generally exercised on her behalf by government Ministers.

3.4 **International law**

International law is an important influence upon, and in some senses a source of, UK constitutional law. This is so in two main ways.[33]

First, when the UK becomes party to a treaty—that is, an agreement with one or more other states that is binding in international law—it is often given effect in national law through the enactment of legislation. For example, the treaties concerning the EU are given domestic legal effect by the European Communities Act 1972, while a separate treaty, the European Convention on Human Rights (ECHR), is given effect by the HRA. As we explain later in the book, the EU treaties and the ECHR—through the domestic legislation giving them effect in UK law—have an immense impact on the UK's constitutional arrangements.

---

[33] See further Brownlie, *Principles of International Law* (Oxford 2008), ch 2.

Second, even if legislation is not enacted so as to give domestic effect to a treaty, there is a well-established principle that national law should be interpreted, where possible, in conformity with treaties to which the UK is a party.[34] Thus, for example, prior to the enactment of the HRA, the ECHR was not ignored by UK courts; rather, it was, at the very least, used as an aid to interpretation when the meaning of national law was unclear.[35]

3.5 Conventions and political practice

3.5.1 Introduction

Although, as we have seen, law is an important source of constitutional rules, many aspects of the constitution are not regulated by strict rules of law.[36] There are many crucial constitutional matters for which no relevant law exists. Assume, for example, that there is a Labour government, that a general election is held, and that the Conservative Party wins a majority of the seats in the House of Commons. The relevant convention here concerns the formation of governments and is the most important convention in the UK constitution. The convention is that a government or Prime Minister who cannot command the confidence of the House of Commons is required to resign; if a general election results in a clear majority for a different political party, then the Queen must invite the leader of that party to form a new government. Applying this convention to our scenario, we would expect the Labour Prime Minister to resign, and the Queen to invite the leader of the Conservative Party to become Prime Minister and to form a new government. It would be surprising—unthinkable, even—if these things did not happen. Even so, no law requires that they take place. No legal wrong would be committed if a Prime Minister were to refuse to resign after his party lost its majority at a general election, and no legal wrong would be committed if the Queen were to invite the leader of a party other than that which had secured a majority to form a government. In such circumstances, neither the Prime Minister nor the Queen would be open to any legal action.

But the fact that the *law* does not regulate such matters does not mean that the relevant people are, in practice, free to do as they please. This is because, in relation to many constitutional matters, *legal freedom* is often constrained by *political precedent*. For example, while the Queen is *legally* free to ask someone other than the leader of the majority party to form a government, there is a long-standing *political* precedent—or 'constitutional convention'—to the effect that she will ask that person to become Prime Minister. These sorts of political rule are not found uniquely in systems, such as that of

---

[34] *Garland v British Rail Engineering Ltd* [1983] 2 AC 751, 771.

[35] *R v Secretary of State for the Home Department, ex p Brind* [1991] 1 AC 696. See further Hunt, *Using Human Rights Law in English Courts* (Oxford 1997).

[36] See generally Brazier, *Constitutional Practice* (Oxford 1994), and Marshall, *Constitutional Conventions* (Oxford 1984), for discussion of a range of constitutional matters governed largely by political practice as distinct from legal rules.

the UK, lacking a written constitution. They might equally well play a role in augmenting a constitutional text. For example, it used to be the case that the US Constitution imposed no limit on the number of terms of office for which a President could serve. Although the Constitution was amended in 1951 to stipulate a maximum of two four-year terms,[37] it was widely accepted *before* the law was changed in that way that it was improper for anyone to seek a third term of office. In other words, there was a constitutional convention—a political, rather than a legal, rule—to that effect.

Such conventions are akin to the 'unwritten rules of the game'; they are the accepted practices by which all parties implicitly agree to abide. They have developed through usage and habitual or customary practices within government. Conventions have not, therefore, traditionally been written down or codified. However, over recent years, even these 'unwritten' conventions have increasingly come to be codified and formalised in a piecemeal fashion. Let us consider two examples: the Ministerial Code and guidance concerning 'hung' Parliaments—that is, the situation in which a general election does not result in a clear majority for a single political party.

The standards of conduct for government Ministers used to be entirely unwritten. It was simply assumed that Ministers would both know and adhere to accepted standards of propriety appropriate to their position in public life. It was also a convention that government Ministers would be responsible—that is, they were obliged to account to Parliament for the policies, decisions, and actions of their government departments and agencies. However, unwritten conventions are likely to be both vague and ambiguous, which renders them liable to exploitation and manipulation by the unscrupulous. Following well-publicised lapses of ministerial propriety in the 1990s, successive Prime Ministers have published a formal code—the Ministerial Code—that sets out the principles and standards expected of Ministers.[38] Each time a Prime Minister assumes office, a new version of the Ministerial Code is published. As we shall see in later chapters, there are many issues surrounding the operation of the Code in practice (such as whether or not there ought to be an independent investigator into ministerial conduct). There are also perennial questions raised as to whether or not, despite the code, government Ministers are properly held to account by Parliament. However, for present purposes, the point is that unwritten conventions have transmuted into a formal code.

A similar process is also evident in relation to the constitutional position when no political party wins an overall majority in a general election, such that Parliament is 'hung'. Before the UK general election in 2010, the Cabinet Secretary, the most senior civil servant in the UK government, disclosed draft guidance to a parliamentary select committee on the applicable conventions in the event of a hung Parliament.[39] When the 2010 election produced precisely such a situation, the draft guidance provided

---

[37] US Constitution, 22nd amendment.   [38] Cabinet Office, *Ministerial Code* (2010).

[39] This guidance was presented by the Cabinet Secretary to the House of Commons Justice Committee. See House of Commons Justice Committee, *Constitutional Processes Following a General Election* (HC 296 2009–10).

certainty as to the constitutional position, and the coalition formed between the Conservative Party and Liberal Democrats took place against a clear understanding of the relevant constitutional position—namely, that any coalition would have to be able to command a majority in the House of Commons to have the authority to govern.

But even when formally written down, constitutional conventions remain binding only in a political sense. The distinction between those areas of the constitution that are regulated by conventions—whether codified or not—and those areas to which legal regulation applies is therefore relevant to the difference, considered earlier in this chapter, between legal and political constitutionalism. Those areas that are governed by convention fall within the realm of the political constitution: to the extent that people are obliged to respect (or in any event actually respect) the norms underlying constitutional conventions, they do so for reasons unconnected with legal coercion. Because conventions are (at least on a traditional view) legally unenforceable, their enforceability, such as it is, derives from the political process.

In the remainder of this section, we examine three key issues concerning constitutional conventions. First, how do such conventions arise—and how do we know when something counts as a constitutional convention? Second, what exactly is the relevance of conventions? In particular, what might be the consequences of behaving contrary to established political precedent? Third, is the traditional view alluded to above, that conventions are legally unenforceable, accurate? And, even if it is accurate, is it sensible?

3.5.2 What counts as a convention—and does it matter?

There is no shortage of definitions of constitutional conventions.[40] Dicey said that they form the 'morality' of the constitution, defining them as 'understandings, habits, or practices' that 'regulate the conduct of the several members of the sovereign power, of the Ministry, or of other officials'.[41] Other writers have characterised conventions as the 'flesh which clothes the dry bones of the law'[42] and as 'rules of constitutional behaviour which are considered to be binding by and upon those who operate the constitution'.[43] From these various definitions, or descriptions of the role of, conventions, we can deduce the following.

First, constitutional conventions are concerned, unsurprisingly, with *constitutional matters*; they are therefore different, in that sense at least, from mere *social* conventions (for example, that people generally hold the door open for the person immediately behind them rather than allowing it to slam in their face). Second, they operate in a manner that is *supplementary to law*: as we have already seen, convention may operate so as to constrain the exercise of a legal power or freedom—a constitutional actor who is legally free to do something may be constrained from doing so by convention.

---

[40] See generally Jaconelli, 'The Nature of Constitutional Convention' (1999) 19 LS 24.
[41] Dicey, *An Introduction to the Study of the Law of the Constitution* (London 1959), p 24.
[42] Jennings, *The Law and the Constitution* (London 1959), p 81.
[43] Marshall and Moodie, *Some Problems of the Constitution* (London 1967), p 26.

Third, the people at whom conventions are directed regard themselves as *bound* by them—that is, they feel obligated in some sense (albeit not a legal one) to do as the convention says. Fourth, Dicey's reference to 'habits' and 'practices' implies that there must be some sort of *track record* of—or precedent for—doing things in the way concerned. This suggests that conventions are not created, but rather that they crystallise over a period of time. And fifth, if conventions represent the 'morality' of the constitution, they must have some sort of basis in morality—not necessarily in morality as traditionally conceived, but in *constitutional morality*. In other words, conventions, on this view, constitute rules that give effect to underlying constitutional principles. For example, the convention that requires the Queen to invite the party best able to command a majority in the House of Commons to form a government is underpinned by a fundamental constitutional principle—namely, democracy. In the absence of any law determining how the government is appointed, it ensures that the wishes of the people are reflected when a government is formed.

Many of these ideas are helpfully reflected in the so-called Jennings test, the purpose of which is to determine whether any given form of political practice or rule can properly be regarded as a constitutional convention. According to this test: 'We have to ask ourselves three questions: first, what are the precedents; secondly, did the actors in the precedents believe that they were bound by a rule; and thirdly, is there a reason for the rule?'[44] Applying these criteria, it is easy to see why many accepted constitutional conventions are so regarded. The table in Figure 2.1 lists a number of prominent conventions, indicating how the Jennings criteria apply to them.

For a more detailed example of the Jennings test in action, it is helpful to turn to events that occurred in Canada several decades ago. Once part of the British Empire, Canada was, by the mid-twentieth century, to most intents and purposes a separate country wholly independent of the UK. However, one vestige of its colonial past remained: the Canadian constitution was based on a piece of UK legislation—the British North America Act 1867. And although a number of steps had been taken over the years to transfer to Canada greater control over its own affairs, certain matters were still governed by the 1867 Act, meaning that when Canada wanted to make changes in respect of such matters, it had to ask the UK government to procure UK legislation amending the 1867 Act. By 1980, the Canadian government felt that this arrangement was no longer appropriate, and took steps to 'patriate' the Canadian constitution—that is, it asked the UK government to get the UK Parliament to pass legislation severing the legal connection between the UK and Canada once and for all, giving Canada control over its own constitutional arrangements.

However, the Canadian government's proposals were not uniformly warmly received within Canada. The system of government in Canada was (and is) a federal one: the constitution divides power between a national (federal) government and regional (provincial) governments. The provincial governments were concerned

---

[44] Jennings, p 136.

that the federal government's proposals would affect the balance of power between the two tiers of government in a manner adverse to the former. Only two of the ten provinces supported the proposal—and the other provinces argued that the federal government, by pressing on in spite of their opposition, was acting in breach of a constitutional convention that stipulated that UK legislation amending the Canadian constitution should be sought only with the support of the majority of the provinces. They therefore took the unusual step of seeking an injunction—a legal remedy prohibiting the federal government from asking the UK to enact the necessary legislation.[45]

This required the Canadian Supreme Court to decide, in the first place, whether the convention asserted by the provinces existed. The Court concluded that the convention did exist—and came to that view by applying the Jennings test.[46] First, then, it asked whether there was a *precedent*: historically, had the assent of the provinces been sought and obtained by the federal government before it asked the UK to enact constitutional changes? It certainly had. The majority observed that 'no amendment changing provincial legislative powers has been made . . . when agreement of a province whose legislative powers would have been changed was withheld. There are no exceptions'.[47] Moreover, the judges noted that when, in 1951, a proposal that would have affected the provinces' powers did not meet with the approval of certain provinces, it was dropped.[48]

Second, had the federal government sought the provinces' consent in such cases *because it felt bound to do so*? Yes. In fact, the federal government had said as much: in an official document—which, the Court noted, was a 'carefully drafted document', not a 'casual utterance'—it had accepted that 'the Canadian Parliament will not request an amendment directly affecting federal–provincial relationships without prior consultation and agreement with the provinces'.[49]

Third, was there a constitutional reason for the rule? Clearly, there was. As we explain in Chapter 7, the essence of a federal system of government is that there is a carefully defined balance of power between the central and regional levels of government. Such a system demands that neither tier of government can unilaterally change the balance of power to the other's disadvantage. It follows that allowing the Canadian federal government, acting without provincial consent, to get the UK to amend the constitution in ways that were detrimental to the provinces' powers would have been directly contrary to the federal principle.

So, having applied the Jennings test, the Canadian Supreme Court came to the conclusion that there was, as the provinces asserted, a clear constitutional convention—to which, by asking the UK to change the constitution without the provinces' support,

---

45 *Re Resolution to amend the Constitution* [1981] 1 SCR 753.
46 *Re Resolution to amend the Constitution* at 888.
47 *Re Resolution to amend the Constitution* at 893.
48 *Re Resolution to amend the Constitution* at 893.
49 *Re Resolution to amend the Constitution* at 899–900.

the federal government was acting contrary. But if (as we will see when we return to this case later in the chapter) the general position is that breaches of convention do not give rise to any form of *legal* liability, an obvious question is begged: why does it matter whether something passes the Jennings test (such that it counts as a convention) or fails it (such that it counts not as a convention, but merely as something falling short of that status—a 'tradition', say)?

Figure 2.2 may help us to think about this question. The solid vertical line represents the distinction between legal and non-legal constitutional rules. If the former are enforceable by courts, but the latter are not, this dividing line is clearly a significant one: knowing on which side of it a given rule falls is important, because that will determine how, if at all, it can be enforced. But the Jennings test implies that it makes sense to draw a *further* distinction, represented in the figure by the broken vertical line, between non-legal rules that qualify as conventions and those that do not. Yet if all of these non-legal rules are legally unenforceable, why bother with this further distinction—surely nothing practical turns on it? In other words, while it is important whether a given rule occupies position 4 or 5 in the figure, because those positions fall on either side of the law/non-law distinction, it is hard to see what turns on whether a given rule occupies position 2 or 3: does it really matter whether we call it a convention or something else (for example, a tradition)?

On one view, it does: categorising a rule as a convention may confer rhetorical force upon it, making those to whom it is addressed feel a greater sense of compulsion to

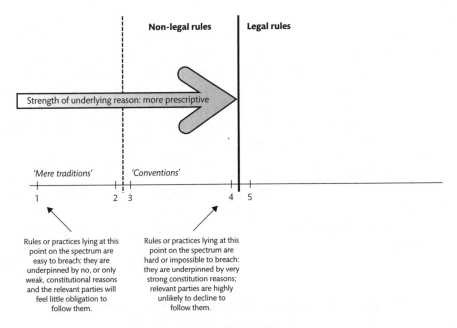

Figure 2.2 Law, convention, and tradition—dividing lines

follow it.[50] But a different view is to be preferred. In reality, the convention/tradition line is largely irrelevant and, once we accept this, we can appreciate that the Jennings test asks the wrong questions—or, more accurately, that it asks the right questions in the wrong way.[51] The issues are not *whether* there is a precedent, *whether* the actors feel bound, and *whether* there is a reason for the rule; rather, the more relevant questions are *how strong* is the precedent, *to what extent* do the actors feel bound by it, and *how good* is the reason for it? Once it is recognised that the real questions are ones of degree, their purpose can better be appreciated: while the *side of the tradition/convention line* on which a given rule falls is unimportant, *where the rule lies on the non-legal part of the spectrum is much more significant*. In other words, while it is relatively unimportant whether a given rule occupies position 2 or position 3 in Figure 2.2, more turns on whether it occupies position 1 (barely scraping into the category of mere tradition) or position 4 (a rule that, although a convention, lies close to the boundary between conventional and political rules).

The reason for this lies in the underlying factors that, in the first place, determine where on the spectrum a given rule lies. What, then, are those factors? We have already said that they consist of the matters identified in the Jennings test, albeit posed as questions of degree, but some further consideration of this matter is needed. The three Jennings criteria—precedent, sense of obligation, and reason—are not co-equal. In reality, it is the second of those criteria that is of principal practical relevance—how obliged the actors feel will determine how seriously the convention is taken, how easy it is to breach it, and whether anyone will care if it is breached—while the first and third criteria determine or reflect, in the first place, the extent to which a sense of obligation exists. Thus the stronger the precedent, the greater will be the expectation that the relevant actors will continue to behave in accordance with the rule: in this, as in most contexts, long-established practices are harder to deviate from than those that have only existed for a very short time. But Jennings conceded that the absence of a long-standing precedent is not necessarily of decisive importance.[52] The main determinant of the practical importance of a given non-legal rule is therefore the strength of the reason underlying it: the stronger the constitutional reason for the rule, the greater will be the extent to which those to whom it is addressed feel obliged to abide by it—and the more dire the likely consequences if they do not.

Some examples will help to illustrate these points. Since 1961, it has been the practice of the Prime Minister personally to answer questions in the House of Commons. The practice of successive Prime Ministers was to spend 15 minutes in the House of Commons on Tuesdays and Thursdays answering MPs' questions. However, when he became Prime Minister in 1997, Tony Blair changed the arrangements for Prime Minister's questions, choosing to attend one weekly 30-minute session every Wednesday. While there were mutterings in some quarters that Blair was guilty of a

---

[50] See Jaconelli, 'The Nature of Constitutional Convention' (1999) 19 LS 24, 27.
[51] Munro, *Studies in Constitutional Law* (London 1999), pp 86–7.
[52] Jennings, *The Law and the Constitution* (London 1959), p 136.

breach of convention, he clearly felt, and in fact was, perfectly free to make this change. The reason, it would appear, is that the original practice, involving twice-weekly questions, was not an important convention—it was a practice occupying a position nearer to position 1 than to position 4 in Figure 2.2—because no strong constitutional reason required the Prime Minister to answer questions *on Tuesdays and Thursdays*. The absence of any such reason presumably accounts for why Blair felt free to dispense with that practice—and for why there was no great outcry when he did so.

Q Would the position be different if a Prime Minister were to decide not to attend the House of Commons to answer questions *at all* (rather than simply, as Blair did, to change the detailed arrangements for such attendance)? (When thinking about this question, consider what constitutional reason underlies the practice whereby the Prime Minister periodically attends the House of Commons to answer MPs' questions.)

This may be contrasted with the conventions set out in Figure 2.1. All of these are important conventions—that is, they are not mere traditions that can be flouted with ease; rather, they are rules that are taken with the utmost seriousness and which, in many cases, no one would dare to breach. It is highly unlikely that such conventions will be broken because the political reasons underlying them are so strong. If, for example, the Queen were to withhold royal assent from a Bill that had been passed by Parliament because she personally disagreed with it, she would be undermining the democratic nature of governance in the UK. Similarly, if a judge were to retain political links (such as affiliations with political parties) following appointment to judicial office, then the independence of the judiciary would be called into question—along with public confidence in the court system and adherence to fundamental constitutional principles that require the law to be interpreted and applied by judges who are independent of the government and thus able to act objectively. We develop this point in the next section, but for now we will confine ourselves to saying that it stands to reason that, even if legal sanctions are unavailable, people are less likely to disrespect rules that are underpinned by a strong reason.

This accounts for Jennings's view that lack of precedent need not be decisive: in other words, that a given rule might constitute a strong convention—one that lies near the law/convention borderline and that is taken very seriously by those to whom it is addressed—notwithstanding the absence of much, if anything, by way of precedent. A good example is provided by the 'Sewel convention', which holds that the UK Parliament will not normally legislate for parts of the UK—Scotland, Wales, and Northern Ireland—with devolved governments on matters within the competence of the latter without the prior consent of the relevant devolved legislature. Unlike most conventions, which *emerge* over a period of time and which thus have a degree of precedent behind them by the time they are acknowledged to be conventions, the Sewel convention was, in effect, *created*. The UK government accepted, when devolution was instituted, that unwanted interference by the UK Parliament in devolved affairs would be improper, and entered into a political agreement with the devolved administrations undertaking that it would respect this principle. The initial lack of precedent notwithstanding, it was (and still is) widely accepted that a convention to this effect exists. The absence of precedent was more than compensated for by the fact that a strong constitutional principle underlies the Sewel convention: the existence of devolved governments reflects widespread acceptance of the principle that certain parts of the country should enjoy a degree of self-government, and unwanted interference by the Westminster Parliament in devolved matters would fly in the face of that principle.[53] This is not to say that precedent is unimportant, since the longer the period during which the convention (and thus the underlying constitutional principle) is respected, the more difficult in practice it will become to act contrary to it. It would, however, be mistaken to think that a long track record of compliance is a condition precedent to the existence of a convention.

3.5.3 Why are conventions obeyed—and what if they are not?

If—as traditional theory would have us believe—conventions are unenforceable by courts, how, if at all, are they enforceable? One way of thinking about this question is to ask why rules that *are* legally enforceable are respected. Clearly, one reason for obeying legal rules is to avoid legal liability: people will generally try to avoid acting carelessly because harm caused by careless conduct may result in civil liability, and a requirement to pay damages, under the law of tort. Equally, one individual might desist from deliberately killing another person because she fears that she may be caught and punished for the crime of murder. But there are undoubtedly other reasons why most people try to stay on the right side of the law.

First, many aspects of the law reflect most people's *personal sense of morality*. For example, most people's primary reason for not deliberately killing others is not a desire to avoid punishment, but rather a personal moral conviction that killing others is wrong. Second, even if a given law fails to coincide with a particular person's own sense of morality, that person may nevertheless choose (irrespective of the possibility of punishment) to obey the law in question because they accept that, *in civilised society, people have a duty to abide by whatever system of rules commands the respect of the majority of people* and is thus institutionalised in law. For example, someone might hold the view that adults should be allowed to take whatever drugs they like in private, but may desist from doing so because he accepts the legitimacy of the proscriptions that society has laid down through law. Third, in practical terms, even if breach of the law were not to result in adverse consequences such as imprisonment or a requirement to pay a fine or damages, some people would still choose to abide by the law in order to avoid the *potentially stigmatising effect of being seen to reject society's accepted norms*.

These three reasons that help to explain why—quite apart from the possibility of legal liability—many people choose to obey the law also help us to understand

---

[53] This convention is considered in more detail in Chapter 7.

why constitutional actors generally obey conventions. First, as we have seen, many conventions—indeed *all* important conventions—are simply particular practical applications of underlying fundamental constitutional principles. By definition, such principles are widely accepted and deeply rooted: most judges, for example, would personally agree that it is wholly improper for people to retain political affiliations following appointment to judicial office. Thus many conventions are respected because those at whom they are addressed have no desire to breach them in any event.

Second, even if a given constitutional actor does not personally *agree* with the principle underlying a given convention, they may nevertheless feel personally inclined to *respect* it because they recognise that it reflects a widely shared sense of constitutional morality. For example, an opposition peer in the House of Lords might personally think that there is nothing wrong in the unelected chamber using its legal power to delay Bills implementing government manifesto commitments, but might nevertheless desist from opposing such Bills because he accepts the moral authority of the Salisbury convention (see Figure 2.1).

Third, even if these largely moral arguments are not regarded by a given individual as decisive, she might nevertheless go along with the convention for self-serving reasons. Even though legal liability need not result from breaching a convention, plenty of other unpleasant consequences might. For example, a hypothetical monarch might personally think that democracy is hugely overrated, that he knows best, and that he should be able to withhold royal assent from Bills as he sees fit. Yet he might decide, for practical reasons, to respect the convention that says monarchs should grant assent as a matter of course, recognising that any other approach would be so undemocratic as to risk, at worst, popular uprising or, at best, the invigoration of campaigns for the abolition of the monarchy. A variant of this argument from self-serving reasons is that politicians in government might choose to play by the conventional rules for fear that their failure to do so might incline opposition politicians—when they are in government at some point in the future—to do likewise.[54]

It follows from all of this that, their legal unenforceability notwithstanding, constitutional conventions (or at least those that are underpinned by strong constitutional reasons) are not merely *descriptive*—that is, they do not simply distil current and historical practice in a morally neutral way; rather, conventions can be *prescriptive*, in the sense of directing how things *should* be done. That prescriptiveness—in other words, the sense of obligation under which the relevant actors find themselves—derives not from legal enforceability, but from the combined effect of the other matters considered above. However, it is, of course, nevertheless the case that conventional rules—like their legal counterparts—may not *always* be respected. In such circumstances, one of three situations is likely to arise.

---

[54] See further Jaconelli, 'Do Constitutional Conventions Bind?' [2005] CLJ 149.

First, a convention may be breached *without any significant consequences*. If this happens, it suggests either that the convention was an unimportant one or that it admits of a hitherto unacknowledged exception. We have seen, for example, that the apparent convention regarding the twice-weekly attendance at the House of Commons of the Prime Minister to answer MPs' questions was dispensed with (in favour of a different, but substantially similar, practice) by Tony Blair with little difficulty in 1997. This simply reflects the fact that the *specific* arrangements that had previously obtained (as distinct from the *general* requirement that the Prime Minister answers MPs' questions) were not dictated by any important constitutional principle—meaning that the detailed arrangements could be changed without affronting any such principle, and hence without attracting serious criticism.

Second, and conversely, a breach of convention may result in *significant practical consequences*. As noted above, a monarch's refusal to assent to a Bill approved by Parliament would most likely call the future of the monarch, possibly also the monarchy, into question. Similarly, if an individual government Minister were to refuse to abide by an important convention, his colleagues, or the public, might expect him to resign, and his position might become untenable. And if a whole government were to be tainted with unconstitutional behaviour—by virtue, for example, of collective ministerial action in breach of key conventions—it might face dire consequences at the following general election. If, for example, the UK government were to push a Bill through the Westminster Parliament undoing popular legislation enacted by the Scottish Parliament, the Scottish people might take a dim view of such behaviour come the next election. A further point that should be borne in mind is that if a given party refuses to abide by convention, other relevant parties may do likewise, on the basis that the party in default has sacrificed any right to expect others to observe the established rules of the game. For example, when Canada's federal government, in breach of a Canadian convention, asked the UK to enact legislation,[55] the UK government refused to treat itself as bound by its own convention under which it would normally accede automatically to such requests.

Third, even though conventions are not *themselves* generally regarded as legally enforceable, there is always the possibility that they may be *turned into laws* through the enactment of legislation. Taking such a step should be necessary only rarely: if the underlying principle is so important as to warrant legal protection, breaches of the convention in question should, for the reasons considered above, be extremely unlikely in the first place. However, in some circumstances, it may be practically desirable—or politically expedient—to place a given convention on a legal footing. A prominent example arises from the constitutional crisis of 1909–11, in which the House of Lords (which was dominated by Conservative peers) refused to pass a finance Bill that had been endorsed by the House of Commons, thus preventing the Liberal government from implementing key aspects of its programme. So grave was

---

[55] See section 3.5.2 above.

the situation, and so serious were its consequences, that legislation was subsequently enacted that denied the House of Lords any real role in the enactment of financial legislation.[56]

> **Q** When do you think it is appropriate to legislate so as to turn conventions into laws? Should all conventions be made into laws in this way?

3.5.4 Are conventions legally irrelevant?

The general view, as we have noted, is that conventions are legally unenforceable. This view has been advanced by commentators[57] and has often been endorsed by courts. The case concerning the patriation of the Canadian constitution, considered above, is a good example. The Canadian Supreme Court—having held that the federal government, if it proceeded in spite of most provinces' objections, would be acting 'unconstitutional[ly] in the conventional sense'[58]—nevertheless went on to conclude that no *law* prevented the government from proceeding with its attempt to reform the constitution against the provinces' wishes. The Court was therefore unable to grant any remedy against the federal government.[59] UK courts have also been unreceptive to the argument that conventions can be legally enforced. For example, in *Madzimbamuto v Lardner-Burke*,[60] it was argued that the UK Parliament had acted improperly by enacting legislation in circumstances that breached a clear convention. This argument, however, was given short shrift. Even if it was 'unconstitutional' for Parliament to legislate thus—for example, if people would have thought there to be 'moral', 'political', or 'other reasons', making it 'highly improper' for Parliament to act as it had done—the court, 'in declaring the law', was 'not concerned with these matters'.[61] It must be borne in mind, however, that this case concerned a challenge to the constitutionality of an Act of Parliament: the fact that the court was unwilling to entertain such a challenge is unsurprising, given that Parliament is said to have unlimited lawmaking power.

That said, there is no clear authority supporting the proposition that conventions are *straightforwardly enforceable*, but certain case law does suggest that conventions are *not wholly legally irrelevant*. In considering this matter further, it is helpful to

---

56 Parliament Act 1911. See further Chapter 5.

57 See, eg Dicey, *An Introduction to the Study of the Law of the Constitution* (London 1959), p cxlv; Marshall and Moodie, *Some Problems of the Constitution* (London 1967), pp 12–17. However, not all commentators share this view. Allan, *Law, Liberty and Justice* (Oxford 1993), ch 10, and Jennings, *The Law of the Constitution* (London 1967), disavow any rigid distinction between law and convention.

58 *Re Resolution to amend the Constitution* [1981] 1 SCR 753, 909.

59 However, as noted above, the UK took the view that it did not have to accede to a request made by the Canadian federal government in breach of constitutional convention. As a result, the Canadian government changed the proposals, casting them in terms more palatable to the provinces. They were later enacted in that revised form: see Canada Act 1982 (UK).   60 [1969] 1 AC 645.

61 *Madzimbamuto* at 723, *per* Lord Reid, speaking for the majority of the Judicial Committee of the Privy Council. On the nature and role of that body, see Chapter 6.

distinguish between two forms of significance that conventions might have, concerning, respectively, the *application of the law to the facts*, and the *content of the law itself.*

First, it is hard to deny that convention can influence, and on occasion has influenced, the application of the law to the facts of cases. Consider, for example, the convention of 'collective responsibility', which, among other things, requires Cabinet Ministers to treat Cabinet discussions—including disagreements voiced during the course of such meetings—confidentially. In *Attorney General v Jonathan Cape Ltd,*[62] the government sought a remedy to prevent publication of a former Cabinet Minister's memoirs, on the ground that they contained information concerning discussions in Cabinet meetings; publication would therefore breach the convention. The court refused to grant a remedy because the meetings concerned had taken place many years ago and no useful purpose would have been served by prohibiting publication. Importantly, however, the court said that, but for that fact, it could have restrained publication. This did not amount to the court asserting a power to *enforce* the convention requiring secrecy in relation to Cabinet meetings, but the court did indicate that the convention could be *taken into account.* The *law* concerning breach of confidence[63] made it impermissible to disclose information received in circumstances under which it was understood to be confidential—and the fact that there was a widely accepted *convention* concerning confidentiality could therefore be treated by the court as evidence that the legal requirement, of an understanding that the material was confidential, was satisfied.

A further way in which conventions may influence the application of the law to the facts of a case is through the doctrine of legitimate expectation. This legal principle is considered in detail in Chapter 13; for now, we need only say that it allows claimants, in certain circumstances, to obtain a remedy if a public body fails to do that which it has led the claimant to expect, whether through an express promise or through consistent past practice. For example, in the *GCHQ* case, the relevant Minister had habitually consulted trade unions before changing employment conditions at the government's communications headquarters.[64] The court in *GCHQ* accepted that this established practice—which, it has been suggested, amounted to a convention[65]—had given rise to a legitimate expectation. The court would therefore have been willing to strike down the Minister's decision to change important employment conditions *without* consultation had it not been for other considerations[66] that are presently irrelevant.

3.5.5 Some conclusions—and the distinction between legal and political constitutionalism

Cases such as *Jonathan Cape* and *GCHQ* show that conventions are not legally irrelevant: they can at least constitute, in effect, *factual evidence* that may trigger the

---

[62] [1976] QB 752.   [63] On which, see Chapter 20.

[64] *Council of Civil Service Unions v Minister for the Civil Service* [1985] AC 374.

[65] See, eg Allan, *Law, Liberty and Justice* (Oxford 1993), p 242.

[66] Namely, the national security implications of the case.

application of legal principles such as confidentiality or legitimate expectation. But will the courts go further? Can—and should—conventions be enforced *as if they were themselves laws*? Doing so would dissolve the distinction between convention and law, given that that distinction consists pre-eminently in legal enforceability of law but not of convention. The very idea of convention is of a body of *political* practice that supplements the legal rules of the constitution, and conferring full legal enforceability upon conventions would rob them of their distinctive character. But this simply begs the question whether that distinctiveness is worth preserving: is the legal unenforceability of conventions a strength or a weakness?

In many senses it is arguably a strength. This case can be made in two ways. First, a *negative argument* that might be made against conventions—that their legal unenforceability renders them futile—can be dismissed. This is because, as we have seen, conventions exert real influence over constitutional actors even if they cannot ultimately be enforced by courts. Second, a *positive argument* can be made to the effect that the legal unenforceability of conventions is a good thing. The enforcement of constitutional rules by courts is undoubtedly important—but it is not a panacea. A healthy constitution will—alongside appropriate judicial oversight of government (for example, in cases in which legal rights are at stake)—incorporate a political system whereby those in positions of authority can be held to account for what they do. Many constitutional conventions deal with the sort of political matters that, for reasons we explore in Chapter 14, are generally unsuitable for adjudication by courts. If a Minister refuses to submit to being questioned by MPs in the House of Commons or if the House of Lords exercises its muscle by blocking a Bill notwithstanding the government's view that the Bill would implement a manifesto commitment, it is strongly arguable that such matters should be resolved by the political, not the legal, system. Viewed in this way, the existence of a body of political constitutional norms, in the form of conventions, is entirely appropriate, because some matters are more properly dealt with by the political process.

This argument ultimately reduces to the proposition that legal and political forms of constitutionalism are mutually complementary, and that the constitution's recognition of a distinction between legal and conventional rules is therefore entirely appropriate. However, there is a danger inherent in this analysis. While it is important to recognise the distinction between, and the appropriate spheres of operation of, legal and political forms of constitutionalism, that distinction should not be overstated. In particular, it should not be permitted to obscure the fact that, in this area, both legal and political rules are underpinned by constitutional principles—and that any given principle might be upheld by a combination of convention and law.[67] It follows that even if it is inappropriate for courts straightforwardly to enforce conventions, this does not mean that they should close their eyes to them when developing or seeking to ascertain the meaning of the law.

---

[67] See generally Allan, ch 10.

An example will help to illustrate the argument. Consider the Sewel convention, which holds that the UK Parliament should not normally legislate on devolved matters without the consent of the relevant devolved legislature. This rule of political practice, being a convention, cannot be directly enforced by the courts: it would, for example, be impossible to obtain an injunction preventing the enforcement of legislation enacted in breach of the Sewel convention. But this does not mean that courts, in appropriate cases, should ignore the principle underlying it. The principle underpinning the convention is that the constitutional right of the devolved nations to govern themselves (within the confines of the devolution settlements) should be respected. If, then, a court were to be faced with a piece of UK legislation that appeared to have been enacted in breach of the Sewel convention, it would be perfectly entitled—taking account of the principle underlying the convention, just as courts take account of other important constitutional principles—to attempt to interpret the legislation in a way that confined its operation to England, or to those devolved nations the legislatures of which had consented to its enactment. This is not the same as saying that conventions are, or should be, enforceable by courts; it simply recognises that a single body of principle underlies legal and conventional systems of constitutional rules, and that just because a given principle is primarily upheld by one of those systems does not render it irrelevant to the operation of the other.

Q Would it be appropriate to go further? Should courts directly enforce conventions?

One final point needs to be made about conventions. It is apparent from what has been said so far that anyone who knew only about UK constitutional law and nothing about conventions would have a very inaccurate picture of the contemporary UK constitution. She would, among other things, expect there to be a monarch with absolute power to veto legislation and capable of exercising significant legal powers without reference to the democratic parts of government, an unelected House of Lords free to block (at least within the limits prescribed by the Parliament Acts) legislation implementing election promises, and a government free to continue in office after losing a general election. Of course, none of these things is true. This demonstrates that, in order to understand how the UK system really works, constitutional law has to be overlaid with convention; once this is done, the picture changes markedly. Powers and freedoms that exist as a matter of law turn out to be meaningless, because convention prevents them from being exercised, or prescribes how they are to be exercised. In this way, it is often left to convention to ensure that the constitution operates in accordance with contemporary principles such as democracy.

We might say, then, that convention bridges the gap between a legal constitution that is, in some respects, outdated—few people would think it appropriate to allow the monarch to veto Bills today—and a 'real' constitution within which anachronistic laws are neutralised or otherwise rendered acceptable through the operation of convention. To the traditional British mindset, this facilitates a pleasing form of doublethink. Contemporary principles of constitutionalism can be embraced, but beneath a dignified veneer of historical continuity—thus we encounter phenomena such as an all-powerful monarch who turns out to be largely powerless. But is this approach satisfactory? Why not get rid of outdated legal arrangements, rather than simply, in effect, agree to ignore them? The greater the gap between the legal and real constitutions, the greater the traction of this sort of argument—on the grounds of promoting public understanding of the constitution, if nothing else.

4. Constitutional principles

We have mentioned 'constitutional principles' on several occasions in passing; we now need to consider both their role and their nature in more detail.

4.1 The role of constitutional principles

By constitutional principles, we mean fundamentally important values that are relevant in at least one (and often all) of several ways.

First, constitutional principles help us to *make sense of the constitution as it is*: they enable us to understand why certain arrangements obtain, why certain rules, whether legal or conventional, exist, and how the constitution operates.

Second, constitutional principles have a *real, practical impact*. On a political level, they are, as we have seen, given effect via conventions that influence how constitutional actors behave. Meanwhile, on the legal plane, constitutional principles shape the interpretation and development of the law. Courts, as we will see, habitually attempt to interpret and apply the law in a way that makes it consistent with fundamental values. Such values also exert influence over legislators: a government seeking to procure the enactment of legislation that conflicts with very basic constitutional principles is likely to face considerable opposition, both within Parliament and from the wider public.

Third, constitutional principles serve an *evaluative function* that has both political and legal dimensions. The *political dimension* is an extension of the immediately preceding point: whether or not a given form of conduct—whether the enactment of a particular piece of legislation, a government policy, or decision taken by a Minister—is legitimate and acceptable falls to be judged (by the public, MPs, and so on) by reference to a number of factors, prominent among which will be the fundamental principles of the constitution. In turn, the extent to which a government has complied with such principles will inform people's assessments of it, and may influence how they vote at the following election. For example, the Blair government's decision to invade Iraq in circumstances involving (in the view of many leading authorities) a breach of international law arguably showed disregard for the fundamental constitutional principle of 'legality', or the 'rule of law'. This, in turn, resulted in substantial criticism and loss of popularity. The evaluative function of constitutional principles also possesses a *legal dimension*: subject to one important exception, legislative and government action taken in breach of relevant constitutional principles can be struck down by courts as unlawful.

4.2 **Democracy and parliamentary sovereignty**

The exception mentioned in the previous sentence relates to the first key constitutional principle, to which we now turn. The principle in question is often said to be *parliamentary sovereignty*, although in truth that concept is merely one way of implementing a deeper underlying principle—*democracy*. At a basic level, the notion of democracy is straightforward, being based on the idea that people should be allowed to have a say in how they are governed. However, there are different views both as to what exactly constitutes the principle of democracy and how that principle should be implemented in practical terms. In the UK, democracy is ultimately understood as meaning that the wishes of the majority should prevail—a view that is given concrete effect through the principle of parliamentary sovereignty. The exact meaning of that principle—like that of the underlying notion of democracy—is the subject of some disagreement, but, in essence, it means that an Act of the UK Parliament is the highest form of law in the UK. It follows that no court can refuse to apply such law and that other law (for example, judge-made common law and legislation enacted by other bodies) is invalid if found inconsistent with parliamentary legislation. In this way, the majority view in the country can always be translated into law by the representative legislature.

We consider parliamentary sovereignty in detail in Chapter 5. For the time being, we simply note that its influence is substantial. Indeed, it shapes the UK constitution at a fundamental level. In particular, it accounts for the key characteristic, considered in Chapter 1, whereby no special category of constitutional law exists. If Parliament is sovereign, such that it can make, amend, or repeal any law, this removes the possibility of there being any higher body of constitutional law that is binding upon legislators. It follows that all other constitutional principles exist in the shadow of parliamentary sovereignty: as a matter of strict law, they exist only to the extent that Parliament chooses not to override them. This, in turn, means that Parliament is in ultimate legal control of the constitution, such that the UK constitution is, and will remain, a significantly political one. While, on this orthodox view, the *law* cannot ultimately vouchsafe any set of constitutional values or arrangements (because they are always vulnerable to being changed or revoked by the sovereign Parliament), *political* considerations may dissuade lawmakers from overriding established arrangements, particularly when this would affront some fundamental principle. However, we will see, when we consider these matters in detail in Chapter 5, that not everyone shares the orthodox view that Parliament is legally free to do anything that it likes.

4.3 **Responsible government and the separation of powers**

A second key constitutional principle is that of the *separation of powers*. But, like parliamentary sovereignty, separation of powers is really just a particular way of securing an underlying objective—in this case, *responsible government*. Human nature being what it is, there is a real possibility—one that is realised on a grand scale and on a daily basis in many countries—that those in authority will exercise their power in arbitrary, abusive, unwise, or corrupt ways. Such conduct is the antithesis of responsible government—a paradigm within which authority is used fairly and wisely to advance the public good. Many practical measures can be taken to minimise the chances of abuse of government power. The separation of powers is such a measure, and one that operates at a fundamental—architectural—level.

In systems that embrace a strict doctrine of separation of powers, the three principal functions of government are allocated to three wholly distinct bodies: lawmaking is the preserve of the legislature, the judiciary resolves disputes about the meaning and application of the law, and the executive branch is responsible for the administration of the country. We consider these matters in Chapter 3, and will see that, in the UK, while there are three largely distinct branches of government performing three largely distinct functions, the separation of powers is not rigorously adhered to. It nevertheless serves several of the functions, mentioned above, which are associated with constitutional principles. For example, until recently, an appellate committee of the House of Lords acted as the UK's court of final appeal on many matters; the decision to transfer that role to a newly created Supreme Court, wholly separate from the other branches of government, was plainly influenced by the fact that such an arrangement would better comply with the separation of powers principle. Moreover, we will see that the principle is an important influence on the courts. For example, legislation used to allow Ministers to decide on the length of sentences to be served by convicted murderers. This involved a breach of the separation of powers in that it entailed members of the executive branch exercising a classically judicial function. Since the sovereign Parliament had decreed that this should be so, the courts could not remove that function from Ministers—but they did insist that if Ministers were to exercise a judicial function, they had to act as if they were judges; thus the courts required Ministers to make decisions based on the seriousness of the offence and to ignore extrinsic factors such as public opinion.[68]

4.4 **Legality and the rule of law**

4.4.1 **Introduction**

The *rule of law* is, in many senses, the most elusive of the main constitutional principles. Indeed, it is not really a principle at all; rather, it is a term that is used as a wrapper that is placed around a bundle of more specific principles.[69] One of the many oddities of the rule of law is that most people agree that it is a good thing while disagreeing

---

[68] *R v Secretary of State for the Home Department, ex p Venables* [1998] AC 407.

[69] For example, Bingham, 'The Rule of Law' [2007] CLJ 67, argues that the rule of law consists of eight 'sub-rules'.

sharply about what it means.[70] In order to understand the importance of the rule of law as it relates to the UK constitution, it is necessary to address two distinct, but related, issues. First, *what does it mean?* What are the specific principles that we find when we peel back the 'rule of law' wrapper? Second, *what does it do?* What, in other words, is the practical relevance, if any, of the rule of law?

It is important, at the outset, to realise that these two sets of questions cannot be considered in isolation. The horizontal axis of the diagram in Figure 2.3 sets out three views ascribing different—and, as we progress along the axis, increasingly practically important—roles to the rule of law. At one extreme, it is simply a political philosophy: a set of opinions about what the characteristics of the law ought to be. Understood thus, the rule of law is little more than a rhetorical device: someone might seek to add gravitas to their support for or criticism of a given legal provision by saying that it does or does not comply with the rule of law, but that is as far as it goes. When the *role* of the rule of law is conceived of in such a limited way, its *content* is relatively unimportant: if we disagree about it, then that might be philosophically interesting, but it will be practically insignificant. But at the other extreme, some people argue that the rule of law determines the *validity* of law: that laws that conflict with the principles of the rule of law are invalid. If this is so, then the content of the rule of law is dramatically more important—it is something that is really worth arguing about—because it constrains lawmakers' power: courts, within this model, are entitled to refuse to enforce 'laws' that conflict with the rule of law, because such measures are not, in the first place, truly entitled to be treated as law.

What, then, is the position in the UK? The rule of law is certainly treated as an important political principle in the sense that it informs political discourse: proposals for new laws might, for example, be criticised on the ground that they affront this or that aspect of the rule of law. However, when used in this way, the term 'rule of law' proves to be a highly elastic one: one commentator has suggested that it has become nothing more than 'one of those self-congratulatory rhetorical devices that grace the public utterances of Anglo-American politicians'.[71] But, as it is understood in relation to the UK's constitution, the rule of law is more than a political philosophy: it is also a legal principle of more precise meaning.[72] It produces legal effects in two main ways. First, *it influences the courts when they interpret legislation*: whenever possible, courts interpret legislation in a way that gives effect to rule of law principles. Second, the rule of law *determines the validity of government action and some legislation*. If a government Minister makes a decision that affronts rule of law principles, the courts will have no hesitation in striking it down. And the same goes for legislation enacted by almost any lawmaking body[73] (for example, a local authority or a devolved legislature).

---

[70] Section 1 of the Constitutional Reform Act 2005 explicitly recognises the 'constitutional principle of the rule of law', but says nothing about its meaning.

[71] Shklar, 'Political Theory and the Rule of Law', in Hutchinson and Monahan (eds), *The Rule of Law: Ideal or Ideology* (Toronto 1987), p 1.   [72] We examine what that meaning is below.

[73] Unless such a body has been specifically authorised by an Act of the UK Parliament to pass legislation in contravention of rule of law principles.

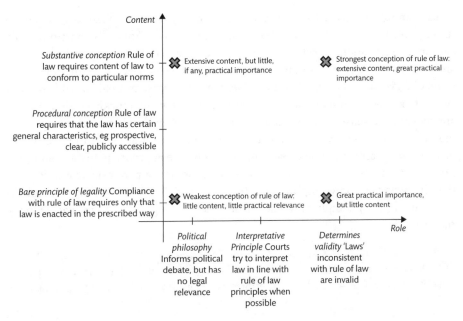

Figure 2.3 The contested content and role of the rule of law

The UK Parliament, however, is sovereign (at least in orthodox theory), in which case it must be capable of making laws that affront rule of law principles. Whether that view is a desirable or even accurate one today is a question we return to briefly at the end of this section and in more depth in Chapter 5.

These preliminary conclusions help to focus the terms of our inquiry. If there is a set of principles collectively known as the rule of law upon which courts will rely in the ways described above, we need to know what those principles are. But in order to place in context discussion of what the rule of law *actually means* in UK law, it is necessary to say something about the range of views that exist about what the rule of law *ought to mean*.[74]

4.4.2 **Legality**

The vertical axis of the diagram in Figure 2.3 sets out three (increasingly extensive) views concerning the latter point. The most modest way in which the rule of law can be conceived is as a *bare principle of legality*. This simply holds that if something is to be regarded as a law, it must be enacted in whatever way the relevant legal system prescribes. For example, in UK law, the rule is that something will count as an Act of Parliament if it is approved by both Houses of Parliament and by the Queen. A measure that has not, for example, been approved by the House of Commons or the

---

[74] This debate is normally conducted on the assumption that the rule of law determines the validity of law, in that laws that breach rule of law principles are invalid and can be struck down by courts.

Queen cannot be regarded as a law because there will have been a failure to adhere to the required process.[75] The principle of legality thus ensures that only constitutionally authorised institutions are able to make law—and then only if they play by whatever are the established rules for doing so. This very limited conception of the rule of law is uncontroversial; indeed, it is imperative if law is to exist as an identifiable body of rules. If anyone could make law in any way, then law would quickly cease to exist in any meaningful sense. The key point, however, is that the bare principle of legality is morally neutral: *any* law, whatever its content, will pass muster with respect to the principle of legality, provided that it is enacted by the appropriate institution in the prescribed way. If the rule of law is coextensive with the bare principle of legality, then heinous laws providing for such things as racial segregation, slavery, and the like would be fully compliant with the rule of law, as long as they were enacted in the right way.

> **Q** Do you think that the rule of law should be defined as narrowly as this? If not, before reading on, consider what additional principles you would wish to see as part of the rule of law.

4.4.3 Formal conceptions of the rule of law

However, many writers argue that the bare principle of legality is only one component of the rule of law—that, properly understood, the rule of law encompasses other principles too. On this view, enactment by the authorised body in the required way is a necessary, but not sufficient, condition for a measure to comply with the rule of law. What, then, are the additional requirements laid down by the rule of law? Here, we encounter a sharp division of opinion between those who favour *formal* and *substantive* conceptions of the rule of law.[76] The nature of that distinction is contested. However, the essential point is that adherents to the former view contend that the rule of law should prescribe certain general characteristics that are morally neutral as to the content of the law: as Allan puts it, on this view, 'Like a sharp knife, the rule of law is morally neutral—[law is therefore] an efficient instrument for good purposes, or wicked'.[77] In contrast, those who favour a substantive conception of the rule of law argue that it does lay down requirements as to its content; thus the rule of law amounts to the rule of *good* law.

The distinction between the formal and substantive views of the rule of law can best be appreciated by reference to some practical examples—which will also show how hard it is to draw the distinction cleanly. One of the leading proponents of the formal

---

[75] In limited circumstances, an Act of Parliament can be passed without the approval of the House of Lords: see Chapter 5.

[76] See, eg Craig, 'Formal and Substantive Conceptions of the Rule of Law: An Analytical Framework' [1997] PL 467.   [77] Allan, *Law, Liberty and Justice* (Oxford 1993), p 23.

conception of the rule of law is Raz.[78] He argues that the primary function of the rule of law is to ensure that 'the law should conform to standards designed to enable it effectively to guide action'.[79] This means, among other things, that the law should be publicly and clearly stated, that it should not have retroactive effect,[80] and that the law should not change too often.[81] If the law has these characteristics, people will be able to know where they stand: they will be able to plan their lives and make informed choices about their actions in full knowledge of the constraints imposed by the law.

Raz then goes on to argue that there must be practical arrangements capable of ensuring that these principles are actually observed. In particular, people must have access to courts the independence of which equips them to resolve disputes objectively in accordance with legal principles. If this task were entrusted to other bodies that might make decisions by reference to considerations other than law, then the potential of clear, public, non-retroactive legal rules to bring about certainty would remain unrealised: decisions in particular cases might be made for all sorts of reasons—political, moral, social, financial—and people would be unable to rely on the practical application of the law.[82] A related point is that if the law gives the authorities very wide discretionary powers (for example, 'the Home Secretary may detain anyone whom he believes to be a terrorist'), this may undermine the rule of law because it introduces a degree of unpredictability that makes it hard for people to plan their lives.[83] Thus Dicey famously said that 'government based on the exercise by persons in authority of wide, arbitrary, or discretionary powers of constraint' would be contrary to the rule of law.[84] However, as Raz correctly points out, the existence of such government powers—which is commonplace today, including in the UK—is not per se problematic provided that there is an adequate framework of law governing how such powers are to be exercised.[85]

4.4.4 Should the rule of law be confined to formal matters?

Writers like Raz argue for a formal—and *only* a formal—conception of the rule of law for two reasons. The first argument is a *positive one* that seeks to justify including within the rule of law the sort of things mentioned in the previous paragraph. It is ultimately a moral argument. Of course, the formal model does not bring moral considerations into play in the sense that it seeks to deny lawmakers the capacity to pursue particular policies: Raz concedes that a legal system based on the denial of human rights or on racial, gender, or religious discrimination could still conform to his version of the rule of law.[86] But Raz's argument is nevertheless not a morally neutral one. The importance that he attaches to legal certainty is itself based on his underlying conviction that 'human dignity' should be respected—which means 'treating human beings as persons capable of planning and plotting their future'.[87] If the system allows people to be caught

---

[78] Raz, *The Authority of Law* (Oxford 1979), ch 11.
[79] Raz, p 218.   [80] See Chapter 1, section 2.1, above on the meaning of this concept.
[81] Raz, pp 214–15.   [82] Raz, pp 216–18.   [83] Raz, p 216.
[84] Dicey, *An Introduction to the Study of the Law of the Constitution* (London 1959), p 188.
[85] Raz, *The Authority of Law* (Oxford 1979), p 216.   [86] Raz, p 211.   [87] Raz, p 221.

out by, and punished pursuant to, laws about which they could never reasonably have known—retroactive laws being the prime example of such measures—there is a basic failure to respect their dignity and autonomy as individuals.

The second argument is a *negative one*: it holds that, while the moral principles underlying the formal conception of the rule of law are modest and uncontentious, taking the rule of law further would transform it into nothing more than a contestable political theory. In service of this argument, Raz cites a 1959 report of the International Committee of Jurists that adopted a substantive view of the rule of law, according to which the principle encompasses 'civil and political rights' and requires 'social, educational and cultural conditions which are essential to the full development of [each person's] personality'. Raz retorts that, 'If the rule of law is the rule of the good law then to explain its nature is to propound a complete social philosophy'.[88] There is, however, an obvious difficulty with this argument. As we have already noted, the formal conception of the rule of law is not itself morally neutral; rather, it is premised on the importance of respecting the autonomy and dignity of the individual. Requiring legal certainty via the principles advocated by Raz is *one* way of securing such respect, but if we accept that respect for individual autonomy and dignity is our starting point, do not other conclusions follow from this—for example, that it would be improper for the state to enact laws (however clear and prospective) making provision for torture, which on any view must be incompatible with respecting victims' dignity? Should we, then, not embrace a fully substantive account of the rule of law? There is no shortage of such accounts in the literature,[89] and they differ from one another in important respects, but they often place under the rule of law rubric such matters as respect for freedom of expression and principles of equality (such as non-discrimination on racial, religious, and gender grounds).[90] Even a view of the rule of law as extensive as this can be traced back to foundational concerns about the autonomy and dignity of the individual, which considerations suggest that people should be free to express themselves and that it is improper (because it is a denial of dignity) to treat people less favourably because of their gender, race, or religion.

Two points should be made in conclusion to this part of our discussion. First, although it is, as we have just seen, difficult to draw a fully principled distinction between formal and substantive conceptions of the rule of law, this does not mean that there is no difference. What is clear is that as we move further along the continuum from procedural to substantive principles, the scope for disagreement increases. Few

---

[88] Raz, p 211.

[89] For examples, see Allan, *Constitutional Justice* (Oxford 2001); Laws, 'The Constitution: Morals and Rights' [1996] PL 622; Bingham, 'The Rule of Law' [2007] CLJ 67.

[90] This form of equality is to be distinguished from the much more modest argument advanced by Dicey that the rule of law requires 'equality before the law'. By this, he meant that no one—and here he specifically had in mind government officials—should be above the law. This fits with a substantive conception of the rule of law (because he was arguing that the *content* of the law should not provide special exemption for officials), but it is a more limited proposition than one that holds that the rule of law demands substantive equality on gender etc grounds.

people would disagree that it is improper to punish someone for breaching a retroactive law that did not exist at the time the conduct in question occurred. But the scope for disagreement is comparatively great in relation to (for example) the proposition that everyone should have a right to strike or a right to a high standard of living. There is certainly an argument for restricting the rule of law to that body of principles which, within a given country, are regarded as sufficiently fundamental as to be relatively uncontroversial. Whether the dividing line thereby entailed coincides with that which separates the formal and substantive conceptions of the rule of law is another matter.

Second, it does not follow that those who are sceptical about conceiving of the rule of law in broad, substantive terms are in favour of such things as arbitrary discrimination and the suppression of freedoms. What they are questioning is not the proposition that such things are objectionable, but the proposition that they should be incorporated within the 'rule of law' concept.

4.4.5 The rule of law, legitimacy, and the unwritten constitution

We said at the beginning of this section that questions about the *content* of the rule of law cannot be divorced from questions about its *role*, and it is time that we reminded ourselves of that fact. The more extensive—the more *substantive*—the operative conception of the rule of law, the more likely people are to disagree about it, and the less comfortable they are likely to be with ascribing a decisive practical role to it (such as determining the validity of legislation). But all of this begs a question that we have not so far explicitly addressed: if the rule of law is to have practical, legal force (as opposed simply to being a point of philosophical discussion), *who ultimately decides what it means?*

As a preface to answering this question, it is important to note that, in many legal systems, some or all of the matters considered above would be dealt with in a written constitution. Constitutions typically flesh out the principle of legality by determining which bodies are allowed to legislate and pursuant to what procedures, and lay down what constraints—whether formal or substantive—the legislature is under. Many constitutions, for example, enshrine certain human rights, such as free speech and non-discrimination, explicitly depriving legislators of any authority to make laws inconsistent with such rights. Although this does not mean that the rule of law is irrelevant in such systems—underlying principles of the type that might fall within the rule of law rubric will often have to be relied upon in giving concrete meaning to vague constitutional provisions—it is undeniable that it assumes greater importance in a system such as that of the UK. Here, the absence of a written constitution makes a concept such as the rule of law all the more significant.

So who decides what it means? The answer is 'the judges'. As we will see shortly, the main vehicle through which the principles comprising the rule of law are articulated in the UK is judicial interpretation of legislation and judicial evaluation of the legality of government action. This is the anvil on which the rule of law has been refined in the UK as a legal concept, and it necessarily follows that it is the courts that have been responsible for undertaking that task. Judges have generally recognised that formal and procedural principles have what Laws has called 'a settled, overarching quality'.[91] They are more likely to be the subject of the sort of consensus referred to above than are more substantive principles. This, in turn, has meant that judges have felt themselves to be on safer ground—in terms of the perceived legitimacy of their articulation of the rule of law—in relation to more formal principles.

4.4.6 The rule of law as a constitutional principle in the UK

Against this background, we turn to consider what the rule of law means as a constitutional principle in the UK. In doing so, it is helpful—subject to the already entered health warning that clear dividing lines are hard to draw—to distinguish between the three senses of the rule of law shown in Figure 2.3.

4.4.7 The bare principle of legality

First, the most modest aspect of the rule of law—*the bare principle of legality*—is undoubtedly recognised in UK law. This is exemplified by the *Jackson* case, in which it was argued that an Act of Parliament was invalid because it had not been enacted in conformity with the relevant procedure.[92] As we have seen, the principle of parliamentary sovereignty means that courts cannot (at least on a traditional reading of that principle) refuse to apply Acts of Parliament, the question in *Jackson* was whether the measure in question was truly such an Act. Although, in the end, the House of Lords held that it was, the fact that the question was asked indicates that the principle of legality was applied: the Lords accepted that the measure concerned would only count as a law if, when it was enacted, the relevant requirements for making an Act of Parliament had been complied with.

The same principle is at stake when courts strike down legislation enacted by bodies other than Parliament. For example, in *Witham*, a government Minister had been given a limited power to make certain rules.[93] The claimant (to whom the application of the rules would have caused hardship) argued that the Minister had exceeded his power—that he had, in effect, made rules that he had not been authorised by Parliament to make. The court agreed, striking down the rule and upholding the principle of legality in doing so. The Minister could only make rules that were within the parameters stipulated by Parliament; by exceeding those parameters, he had acted without lawful authority and so in breach of the principle of legality.

Finally, on this point, note the celebrated case of *Entick v Carrington*.[94] A government Minister issued a warrant that purported to authorise state agents to break into the claimant's house and seize his papers, in clear breach of the claimant's property rights. But the Minister could point to no law enabling him to issue such warrants—and so the warrant was ineffective and the agents had acted unlawfully. This decision

---

[91] 'The Limitations of Human Rights' [1998] PL 254, 260.

[92] *R (Jackson) v Attorney General* [2005] UKHL 56, [2006] 1 AC 262. This case is discussed in more detail in Chapter 5.   [93] *R v Lord Chancellor, ex p Witham* [1998] QB 575.

[94] (1765) 19 St Tr 1030.

was clearly animated by the principle of legality: the state could not lawfully override individuals' property rights in the absence of legal authorisation. However, the limits of this principle were demonstrated in the *Malone* case, in which it was held that the government had not acted unlawfully by listening in to the claimant's telephone conversations.[95] At the time that the case was decided, no right to privacy was recognised in English law, no law prevented the interception of telephone calls, and no physical trespass (in breach of recognised property rights) had been committed.[96] What this case shows, then, is that the principle of legality does not require positive legal authorisation for government action when such action will not affect others' recognised legal rights.[97]

4.4.8 A formal conception of the rule of law

There is also plenty of evidence showing judicial recognition of a *formal conception of the rule of law*.

First, we saw above that a key component of that view of the concept is the principle of legal certainty—which means, among other things, that people should be able to know where they stand. This principle was strongly endorsed in *Anufrijeva*.[98] The claimant was an asylum seeker whose benefit payments were stopped. Under the relevant legislation, her entitlement to such payments ceased when her claim had been 'determined'—a condition that the government said had been fulfilled because it had decided that her asylum claim should be turned down. Crucially, however, the claimant was not told of this—and the House of Lords agreed with her that until she was told, her entitlement to benefits continued. In reaching this conclusion, Lord Steyn explicitly invoked the rule of law, saying that it

> requires that a constitutional state must accord to individuals the right to know of a decision before their rights can be adversely affected. The antithesis of such a state was described by Kafka:[99] a state where the rights of individuals are overridden by hole in the corner decisions or knocks on doors in the early hours. That is not our system.[100]

Second, a related aspect of the principle of legal certainty is that laws should not have retroactive effect—an axiom that is clearly regarded as an aspect of the rule of law in the UK. This is illustrated by *Pierson*,[101] in which the Home Secretary, under a misapprehension as to the circumstances in which the claimant had committed a

---

[95] *Malone v Metropolitan Police Commissioner* [1979] Ch 344.

[96] The position is now different: the Regulation of Investigatory Powers Act 2000 regulates the interception of communications and a (limited) common law right to privacy is recognised (on which, see Chapter 19 below).

[97] See further *Shrewsbury and Atcham Borough Council v Secretary of State for Communities and Local Government* [2008] EWCA Civ 148, [44], *per* Carnwath LJ.

[98] *R (Anufrijeva) v Secretary of State for the Home Department* [2003] UKHL 36, [2004] 1 AC 604.

[99] In Franz Kafka's dystopian novel *The Trial* (1925), the protagonist is accused of and punished for a crime, the nature of which is never disclosed to him.   [100] *Anufrijeva* at [28].

[101] *R v Secretary of State for the Home Department, ex p Pierson* [1998] AC 539.

double murder, decided that he should spend at least 20 years in prison.[102] However, on established principles and a correct understanding of the circumstances, 15 years' detention would have been the norm. The Home Secretary later accepted that he had been under a misapprehension, but confirmed his decision that the claimant should serve at least 20 years. By doing so, the Home Secretary had, in effect, subjected the claimant to a harsher punishment than that which would have been imposed had the original decision been taken on a correct basis. This, said the court, was unlawful: it was contrary to 'the fundamental principle that a sentence lawfully passed should not retrospectively be increased'.[103]

Third, we saw above that, for writers such as Raz, a formal conception of the rule of law does not rule out conferring broad discretionary powers on (for example) government Ministers. But we also saw that it requires the existence of a legal framework that serves to constrain such discretion such that its operation is rendered predictable enough to meet the requirements of legal certainty. Such a framework undoubtedly exists in English law. For example, if legislation permits Ministers to exercise a given power for a given purpose, the courts will not permit Minsters to use that power for other purposes that could not have been deduced from the wording of the legislation.[104] Equally, if the government announces that it will exercise a given power in accordance with a stated policy—for example, that it will not deport asylum seekers in stated circumstances—the courts will generally hold that it is unlawful for the government to refuse to honour such pledges unless it has good reason not to do so.[105] In these ways, the exercise of discretionary powers is rendered more predictable—and so the existence of such powers is reconciled with the principle of legal certainty.

Fourth, a formal conception of the rule of law requires, for the reasons considered above, that people must be able (if they so wish) to have legal disputes resolved by independent courts. The principle of access to courts is a well-established one in English law. In the *Witham* case, mentioned above,[106] the rules in question had the effect of substantially increasing the fees to be paid by people wishing to initiate litigation. The claimant successfully argued that the rules contravened the principle of access to court by, in effect, preventing people on low incomes from making legal claims—and on this basis, the court held that the rules were unlawful. More dramatically, in *Anisminic*, when faced with legislation stipulating that no decisions taken by a body established by the government could 'be called in question in any court of law', the House of Lords[107] refused to accept that Parliament had meant entirely to preclude judicial review of such decisions.[108]

---

[102] Neither the Home Secretary nor any other government Minister is today involved in making decisions of this nature. However, the principle illustrated by this case remains relevant.

[103] *Pierson* at 591, *per* Lord Steyn.   [104] *Municipal Council of Sydney v Campbell* [1925] AC 339.

[105] *R (Rashid) v Home Secretary* [2005] EWCA Civ 744.

[106] *R v Lord Chancellor, ex p Witham* [1998] QB 575.

[107] Acting in its now-abolished judicial capacity.

[108] *Anisminic Ltd v Foreign Compensation Commission* [1969] 2 AC 147.

4.4.9 A substantive conception of the rule of law?

There is, then, no doubt that a formal conception of the rule of law is recognised. But does English law go further? It certainly recognises some rule of law principles that cannot easily be characterised as merely formal. For example, many of the principles of judicial review—that is, the principles that courts use to determine whether government action is lawful—reflect a substantive conception of the rule of law. Thus courts will strive to read legislation compatibly with, and will strike down executive action that conflicts with, such principles as the right to a fair hearing,[109] the right to freedom of expression,[110] and the right to confidential legal advice.[111] The courts' willingness and capacity to uphold such principles is now augmented by the HRA, but it is clear[112] that such principles are recognised by English law independently of that Act. For example, in *Daly*, a government policy was held to be unlawful because it conflicted with the right to communicate confidentially with one's lawyer. Although the 1998 Act was in force when the case was decided, Lord Bingham emphasised that he had reached his decision through 'orthodox application of common law principles'.[113] And Lord Cooke said that 'some rights [such as the one at stake in *Daly*] are inherent and fundamental to democratic civilised society. Conventions, constitutions, bills of rights and the like respond by recognising rather than creating them'.[114]

It is also clear that the courts recognise the principle of equality as an aspect of the rule of law. Here, too, the picture is complicated by the existence of legislation: statute provides extensive protection against discrimination on grounds such as gender, race, and sexual orientation—but the fundamental principle of equality is recognised, independently of such legislation, as an aspect of the rule of law. *Entick v Carrington*, considered above, illustrates this point. It would have been unlawful for an ordinary individual to break into someone's house and steal his papers—and, absent any statutory authority, it was just as unlawful for a government Minister or his agents to do so. The latter were therefore to be treated no more favourably than a regular citizen. This point is underlined by *Re M*,[115] in which, in clear breach of a court order, the Home Secretary instructed that an asylum seeker should be deported. If an ordinary individual breaches a court order, she may be convicted of the criminal offence of contempt of court and punished by fine or imprisonment. And despite the Home Secretary's protestations to the contrary, it was held that the same rule applied to government Ministers. Lord Templeman noted that the Home Secretary's argument 'would, if upheld, establish the proposition that the executive obey the law as a matter of grace and not as a matter of necessity, a proposition which would reverse the result of the Civil War'.[116]

---

[109] *Ridge v Baldwin* [1964] AC 40.

[110] *R v Secretary of State for the Home Department, ex p Simms* [2000] 2 AC 115.

[111] *R (Daly) v Secretary of State for the Home Department* [2001] UKHL 26, [2001] 2 AC 532.

[112] Including from the cases cited in *Ridge* and *Daly*, which were decided before the Act came into force.

[113] *Daly* at [23].   [114] *Daly* at [30].   [115] [1994] 1 AC 377.   [116] *M* at 395.

4.4.10 Last word

We conclude this discussion of the rule of law with the point with which it began—that the *meaning* of the concept cannot be addressed without reference to its *practical effect*. In English law, the main practical effects of the rule of law are threefold: courts try, whenever possible, to give legislation a meaning that is compatible with it; if that is not possible, courts will hold most legislation[117] to be invalid; and courts will strike down government action that is inconsistent with the rule of law. But all of this is subject to the longstop that, in orthodox theory at least, the UK Parliament is sovereign: it can therefore legislate contrary to the rule of law—including by authorising others, such as government Ministers, to breach the rule of law—if it so desires. The upshot is that while the rule of law—and hence the meaning of that concept—is important, it is not decisively important: for as long as Parliament is sovereign, legislation enacted by it can trump rule of law principles.

But, as we have already intimated, not everyone takes that view. There is a growing school of thought that holds that certain fundamental principles are so important that they should be (and, some argue, *are*) beyond interference even by Parliament. This introductory chapter is not the appropriate point at which to consider these views in any detail—we do that in Chapter 5 below—but we mention them here simply to indicate that there is disagreement about the very fundamentals of the UK constitution, and that the meaning and status of the rule of law are central to that disagreement.

4.5 The Human Rights Act 1998

We indicated above that there is an overlap between the concepts of the rule of law and human rights, particularly if the former is conceived of in more than purely formal terms. Detailed consideration of human rights matters, including the HRA, can be found in the final part of this book.[118] But the relevance and influence of human rights and the HRA is pervasive. Relevant aspects of the HRA will need to be considered at various points in subsequent chapters, and so we provide in this introductory chapter an overview of the main features of the Act. The purpose of what follows is not to explain those features in detail; rather, it is to highlight points that will need to be considered in context in later parts of the book. With that in mind, six key points should be noted.

First, the HRA *gives effect in UK law* to the European Convention on Human Rights (ECHR), an international treaty that, irrespective of the existence of the HRA, is binding upon the UK as a matter of international law. The main point of the HRA, however, was to enable people to enforce their ECHR rights in UK courts, rather than being able to do so only, or at least mainly, in the European Court of Human Rights (ECtHR) in Strasbourg.

Second, although, as noted above, English law itself recognises—and through the medium of the rule of law confers some protection on—some human rights, the HRA

---

[117] But not legislation enacted by the UK Parliament.   [118] See Chapters 19–21 below.

clarifies and expands the range of rights that can be protected by UK courts. The rights that can be protected under the HRA—known as the 'Convention rights'[119]—are set out in Figure 19.2 below.[120]

Third, the HRA authorises courts to *strike down decisions and rules made by public bodies* if they are incompatible with any of the Convention rights.[121] As we explain in Chapter 13, this has resulted in UK courts scrutinising government action more rigorously than in the past, which, in turn, raises questions about the balance of power, under the separation of powers doctrine, between the courts and the executive.

Fourth, the HRA places courts under a *duty to interpret legislation, including Acts of Parliament, compatibly with the Convention rights* if it is possible to do so.[122] We will see in Chapter 19 that, in practice, this gives the courts extensive powers to mould legislation so as to render it consistent with the ECHR, even if this means inserting words into the legislation or departing from the intention that lay behind it when it was enacted.

Fifth, the HRA *does not empower courts to strike down Acts of Parliament*. The HRA is therefore, at least formally, consistent with the doctrine of parliamentary sovereignty. But the HRA does authorise courts to *declare that an Act of Parliament is inconsistent with Convention rights*.[123] Such a declaration does not affect the validity of the legislation; rather, it is left to the executive and Parliament to decide whether, and if so how, to reform the law so as to render it consistent with the ECHR.

Sixth, and finally, *the discussion of the rule of law above must be read in the light of the HRA's implications*. The HRA certainly does not make the rule of law irrelevant: the Convention rights and the principles upheld under the colour of the rule of law may overlap, but the two categories are not precisely coterminous. Moreover, the HRA, being a mere Act of Parliament, is not necessarily a permanent feature of the constitution: like any other Act, it can be repealed. However, in two senses, the HRA and the rule of law do work in tandem. To the extent that the Convention rights coincide with rule of law principles, the HRA endorses, and lends a form of democratic legitimacy to, the courts' pre-existing tendency to attempt to interpret legislation compatibly with such principles. Moreover, the fact that courts now have at their disposal the option of issuing a declaration of incompatibility removes some of the heat from the debate about whether courts should be able to strike down provisions in Acts of Parliament that conflict with the rule of law. Although a declaration of incompatibility is not, in law, the same as a strike-down power, it is (as we explain in Chapter 19) a very significant power, and one that makes a formal strike-down power less practically important.

As explained above, the foregoing points are made only in a preliminary fashion at this stage. All of them will be considered in the relevant chapters.

---

[119] HRA, s 1.   [120] See Chapter 20, section 3.3.1, below.   [121] HRA, s 6.
[122] HRA, s 3.   [123] HRA, s 4.

5. Codification and the constitution

It is appropriate, at the end of this introductory part of the book, to take stock of the uncodified nature of the British constitution. We have already noted that, despite its uncodified nature, the British constitution has numerous rules and principles governing the allocation and exercise of public power. The uncodified nature of the UK constitution is certainly unusual. It is not, however, unique: two other democracies—Israel and New Zealand—are in a similar position. And over recent years, the UK's constitutional arrangements have certainly become more formalised. Important conventions have been codified, and much legislation on issues such as human rights and devolution has been enacted. As we shall see throughout this book, one consequence of this has been a shift from a political to a more legal form of constitutionalism. Two questions arise from this. First, why has the constitution taken the form it has? Second, should the UK now take the next step and adopt a fully codified constitution?

5.1 Why no codified constitution?

There are various explanations as to why the British constitution has never been codified into a single document called 'The Constitution'.

One explanation is *historical*. Codified constitutions tend to come about after there has been a severe rupture in the political system of the country concerned—as a result of, for example, revolution, civil war, the ending of dominance by another country,[124] or a fundamental reordering of society.[125] In such circumstances, adopting a new constitution facilitates and underlines the country's 'fresh start'. But Britain has not—at least not since the English civil war in the seventeenth century—experienced any of these cataclysmic events. There has never been a 'constitutional moment' at which the fundamental rules required clarification and laying down in a single document; instead, there has been an unusual degree of continuity in the governing institutions. Of course, over the centuries, those institutions have changed beyond all recognition—no one now believes in the divine right of kings, and the powers of the Crown are no longer personally exercised by the monarch—but the changes have been gradual.

A second reason for the absence of a codified constitution is *conceptual*: in the absence of a codified constitution, the dominant constitutional principle has been parliamentary sovereignty. On the orthodox view, Parliament may enact whatever law it wishes and there are no legal limitations on Parliament's lawmaking role. If an Act of Parliament is the highest form of law, there can be no higher law such as a codified constitution. The doctrine of parliamentary sovereignty is thus incompatible with the idea of an entrenched codified constitution.

---

[124] For example, the grant of independence to a colony or the end of Soviet domination of eastern European countries in the early 1990s.

[125] For example, the ending of apartheid in South Africa in the early 1990s.

A third explanation is *practical*: there has never been much public desire for the UK to have a codified constitution. Indeed, the British people have sometimes assumed—whether rightly or not—that the distinctive nature of their unwritten constitution has provided them with superior protection of their rights and liberties, and that 'paper rights' count for little. Furthermore, it has long been thought that an uncodified constitution provides a degree of flexibility in constitutional arrangements that is preferable to the rigidity of a codified constitution—although we saw in Chapter 1 that a highly flexible constitution, like that of the UK, is arguably a contradiction in terms, given that constitutions are generally regarded as repositories of fundamental, enduring values.

Whatever happens as regards future reform of the constitution, it is important to recognise that various consequences flow from the uncodified nature of the British constitution, which can help us to understand it better.

First, the UK constitution cannot be said to be the product of a conscious and deliberate constitutional design. No group of people ever sat down together to design the UK constitution; rather, it has simply evolved over time. This in turn suggests a particular approach toward constitutional issues. The British constitutional mindset is, then, one that eschews a rationalistic, comprehensive approach—that is, an approach that would seek to settle all important issues at the outset. On the contrary; the approach in the UK has always been an incremental, ad hoc one, whereby the constitution develops piecemeal over time. As we saw in Chapter 1, this approach was evident in the fact that the major constitutional reforms undertaken since 1997 have taken the form of a rolling, sometimes disjointed, programme rather than a coherent package.

A second consequence is that it can often be highly debatable as to what the constitution actually means at any one particular time. Constitutional debate and disagreement often arise because, as we have already noted, constitutional lawyers hold different views as to what the constitution ought to be. Given the nature of the UK constitution, it can often be difficult to separate out description of the constitution and its evaluation. As noted above, such debates are an inherent feature of most constitutions, but in an uncodified constitution they can be accentuated.

Third, although it does not necessarily follow that an uncodified constitution will be an unentrenched one—that is, one that lacks special legal status and is therefore harder than normal law to amend—the latter characteristic, in practice, tends to follow from the former. And so it is in the UK—with the result, as we saw in Chapter 1, that nothing in the constitution (except the principle of parliamentary sovereignty) is fixed.[126]

5.2 **To codify or not to codify?**

Given the unusual nature of the British constitution, it is worth asking whether the UK should codify its constitutional arrangements by adopting a single constitutional

---

[126] This presupposes that Parliament is, in the first place, sovereign. Criticism of this view is considered in Chapter 5.

document. Arguments in favour of codification tend to be based on one (or both) of two underlying concerns.

First, it is said by some writers that codification would provide a *clearer and more accessible* set of fundamental rules and principles governing the constitution of the state. Proponents of this view are thus centrally concerned with formal considerations rather than with substantive constitutional reform. Emphasis is therefore placed on the potentially educative effect of codification: collecting together the fundamental constitutional rules in a single place might make it easier for people to understand the constitution.[127]

Second, however, those who advocate codification often do so as part of a *broader argument encompassing substantive reform*.[128] Codification, on this view, represents an unprecedented opportunity for major constitutional reform. This argument is often animated by the view that the power of the executive government in the UK is excessive, and the methods of controlling the executive and calling it to account are too weak. Other areas of concern that have spurred people to argue for a new, codified constitution include the role and composition of the House of Lords, the voting system, the limited role of the judiciary, and the lack of entrenched protection for human rights. Those who advocate major change in such areas tend to favour codification for two connected reasons. First, fundamental change in one area may have knock-on consequences for other parts of the constitution (thus making a holistic approach more attractive). Second, the creation of an entrenched constitution—an enterprise that would necessarily involve codification—would be imperative if reform in some of the areas mentioned above were to be secured.

The arguments for codification may seem compelling, but they need to be weighed up against the arguments against, and potential problems with, codification. Five issues need to be considered.

First, it is far from universally accepted that codification is *necessary or desirable*. It can be argued that the UK constitution has worked reasonably well, enabling the UK to balance the needs of continuity with the past and change in light of present circumstances. And, as we saw in Chapter 1, when change is felt necessary, reform can be undertaken in individual areas rather than via wholesale codification. Indeed, it is arguable that problems are more likely to be successfully resolved by way of smaller-scale constitutional reform projects focusing upon particular issues. It would be naive to assume that a codified constitution would be some universal cure for all constitutional problems.[129] The counter-argument, of course, is that codification would force

---

[127] For one attempt to draft a codified constitution without substantive constitutional reform, see Bogdanor, Khaitan, and Vogenauer, 'Should Britain Have a Written Constitution?' (2007) 78 Political Quarterly 499, 506–17.

[128] For examples of draft constitutions, see Institute for Public Policy Research, *The Constitution for the United Kingdom* (London 1991); Gordon, *Repairing British Politics: A Blueprint for Constitutional Change* (Oxford 2010).   [129] Barber, 'Against a Written Constitution' [2008] PL 11.

the sort of joined-up thinking about constitutional reform that, as we saw in Chapter 1, has arguably been lacking in recent years.

Second, there is no clear evidence of *public support* for codification. Realistically, no government is likely to invest the necessary time, resources, and political capital if there is little public clamour to satisfy. The lack of public opinion in favour of codification is not necessarily an insuperable impediment. A government intent upon codification could hope to use it as a means of raising public awareness and interest, and of engaging with the public. It is, though, important to recognise that governments typically respond to public opinion and, in this way, constitutional issues are no different from other political issues.

Third, adopting a codified constitution would *require hard questions to be confronted*. Just as there is no consensus on whether a codified constitution is necessary, so there is no consensus about what the content of such a constitution, if adopted, should be. How detailed would the constitution be? Would it be a relatively short document containing a statement of general principles, values, and aspirations, or a long, detailed document setting out all of the respective legal powers of the legislature, executive, and judiciary? Would conventions be included? Would they be made legally enforceable? And which conventions would be included? Would the constitution make detailed provision about such matters as the voting system for the House of Commons and whether the second chamber should be wholly or mainly elected? Would it entrench the constitutional position of local government? Would the constitution have entrenched protection for human rights with a constitutional court to review the constitutionality of legislation? Would the constitution include a special procedure for amending it? If so, then what would that procedure be?

Fourth, the fact that questions such as those mentioned above would have to be confronted suggests that producing a codified constitution would require the adoption of a complex *process* that would be lengthy and potentially costly. It would be foolhardy to attempt to codify the constitution by way of an ordinary statute enacted by Parliament in the usual way. To effect such a major change, the whole enterprise would need to follow a special, distinctive procedure capable of generating consensus and thereby conferring legitimacy on the resulting constitutional document. As the Labour government noted in 2007, a codified constitution could not come into being except over an extended period of time, through extensive and wide public consultation, in order to secure broad agreement upon the values, rights, and responsibilities to be enshrined in the constitution.[130] It would be necessary to establish a constitutional commission comprised of appropriate people to undertake the task of codification. Such a commission would hold public evidence sessions, consult with the public, and produce a draft constitution. Any such draft would then have to be both approved by Parliament and by the people in a national referendum. However, while this sort of process would stand the best chance of producing a successful outcome, this could not

---

[130] HM Government, *The Governance of Britain* (Cm 7170 2007), [213].

be taken for granted. As King has argued, 'holding a constitutional convention, and then debating the outcome, would be bound to divide the country rather than unite it'.[131] Codification would, then, be a dauntingly large and difficult enterprise, and there could be no guarantee that it would succeed.[132]

Fifth, *technical issues* would have to be confronted. In particular, would the codified constitution be entrenched—in other words, given a special legal status, meaning that it could not be altered as easily as other laws? If not, then its meaning would always been open to future amendment by way of legislation enacted in the ordinary way. Yet this would risk bringing the whole notion of a codified constitution into disrepute: why go to all the trouble of adopting such a constitution if it is to be vulnerable to being casually overridden whenever Parliament pleases? Alternatively, the constitution could seek to attain an entrenched status. After all, virtually all constitutions allow for amendment only through the use of special procedures, such as a specified majority of votes. Yet the traditional view of parliamentary sovereignty would preclude this. This is not necessarily an insuperable obstacle: not everyone agrees that Parliament really is sovereign, and even those who think it is accept that there may be ways in which parliamentary sovereignty may be manipulated by legal means or extinguished by political ones. These are deep waters that we are not yet in a position to navigate;[133] the point, for now, is simply that there *are* difficult issues that would necessarily complicate any attempt to adopt an entrenched constitution.

5.3 **The future**

What is the likelihood that the constitution may be codified at some stage in the future? While the problems with codification are real, they are not insurmountable. If the necessary political will were to exist, then it would be possible to overcome such obstacles. If public opinion were strongly in favour of codification, then any government would feel compelled to respond accordingly. However, it is the absence of such public opinion that is perhaps the biggest stumbling block. At the moment, there is no groundswell of public feeling in favour of codifying the constitution; other concerns, such as the economy, taxation, public spending, and employment, are regarded as far more pressing. And yet it is quite possible to envisage circumstances in which codification of the constitution moves up the political agenda. The crisis over MPs' expenses engulfed the House of Commons in 2009 and tarnished its reputation. Politicians felt compelled to respond by seeking to restore public confidence in Parliament, resulting in a series of significant, but largely self-contained, constitutional reforms. It is entirely possible that, at some point in the future, an event, or a combination of events, will illustrate some of the fundamental shortcomings of

---

[131] *The British Constitution* (Oxford 2008), p 363.
[132] Bogdanor and Vogenauer, 'Enacting a British Constitution: Some Problems' [2008] PL 38.
[133] We address these questions in Chapter 5.

the British constitution in a way that generates widespread public concern, thereby triggering demands for wholesale reform, including codification.

We also have to recognise that politicians do not merely react to public opinion; the political class is also often able to shape public opinion, persuading the people of the wisdom of policies for which there is, at least to begin with, no great public appetite. Against that background, it is noteworthy that there has been particular receptiveness amongst two of the main political parties in the UK toward the notion of codification. During the 2010 general election campaign, both the Labour and Liberal Democrat parties pledged to establish a constitutional commission or convention to draft a written constitution for the UK as a whole. The Liberal Democrats have long been committed to both constitutional reform and codification. It remains to be seen whether this will continue to be the policy of the Labour Party. By contrast, the Conservative Party—which has traditionally been unenthusiastic about the issue—made no such pledge. In the event, the general election resulted in no overall majority for any single political party. The Liberal Democrat–Conservative coalition agreed on various political reforms—including a referendum on electoral reform, a commission on reform of the House of Lords, and five-year fixed-term Parliaments—but not upon the introduction of a codified constitution.[134] Coalition governments in the UK are relatively unusual; this was the first for some 70 years. But it can be seen that this approach to constitutional reform is wholly in keeping with tradition, with incremental reform of particular parts of the constitution rather than comprehensive reform of the whole constitution.

> **Q** In your opinion, should the UK have a fully codified constitution? If so, then how might it be possible to overcome the obstacles mentioned above?

6. Concluding remarks

In this chapter, we have seen that, in the absence of a 'written constitution', the UK's constitution is to be found in a number of places. Having examined the range of sources from which the UK constitution is drawn, it can be said that they are of three main types. First, there are *rules that are straightforwardly legal in nature*. Such rules are either set down in legislation or are the result of judicial development of the common

---

[134] In June 2010, in response to a parliamentary question asking whether the government had any plans to bring forward proposals for the adoption of a written constitution, the government stated:

The British constitution is not, as it is in many countries, codified in a single document, although much of it is already written. It is made up of a complex web of statutes, conventions, and a corpus of common and other law. It is also informed by an interweaving of history and more modern democratic principles. There are no current plans to bring forward proposals for the adoption of a codified constitution for the United Kingdom. (Hansard HC Debs, vol 511, col 519W, 17 June 2010)

law. Second, there are *principles that find expression principally as constitutional conventions*. As we have seen, such conventions (or at least a subset of sufficiently important ones) are binding in a political sense, but are of limited legal relevance; they are generally thought not to be directly enforceable by courts. Third, there are *the fundamental principles of the constitution*. The relevance of such principles is both legal and political. Principles such as parliamentary sovereignty, the separation of powers, and the rule of law are of undoubted legal significance: courts apply Acts of Parliament as the law because the doctrine of parliamentary sovereignty ascribes lawmaking power to Parliament; and courts are prepared to strike down administrative action and to adopt particular interpretations of legislation in order to uphold such principles. But such principles also have a broader, political significance: they form an important part of the set of benchmarks against which people—individuals, the media, opposition politicians—will evaluate the legitimacy of government action and proposals for legislation.

It therefore becomes apparent that the UK constitution is both a political and a legal constitution: both law and politics supply the norms that determine how the constitution works, how those in charge are judged, and how they are held to account. As we explained at the beginning of the chapter, the relationship between legal and political approaches to constitutionalism is one of the key themes of this book, the others being the power of the executive branch and the importance of holding it to account, and the growing diffusion of government power as the UK shifts to a multilayered form of constitutionalism. Those three themes will be to the fore as we commence, in the next chapter, our study of the three main branches of government.

Further reading

ALLAN, *Law, Liberty and Justice* (Oxford 1993), ch 10

BARBER, 'Laws and Constitutional Conventions' (2009) 125 LQR 294

BINGHAM, 'The rule of law' [2007] CLJ 67

CRAIG, 'Formal and Substantive Conceptions of the Rule of Law: An Analytical Framework' [1997] PL 467

LAWS, 'The Constitution: Morals and Rights' [1996] PL 622

JACONELLI, 'The Nature of Constitutional Convention' (1999) 19 LS 24

TOMKINS, *Our Republican Constitution* (Oxford 2005)

PART II

The Constitution— Institutions and Principles

3 Separation of Powers—An Introduction

1. The basic idea

This part of the book is concerned with the main institutions that, together, comprise the British constitution: the executive, the legislature, and the judiciary. One part of our concern will be with the responsibilities of these institutions—that is, what they do—but our attention will not be confined to this. We will also consider how these institutions fit into the constitutional system and how they relate to one another. In doing so, we will refer regularly to the three key themes of the book set out in Chapter 2. We will therefore consider how the institutions of government are held *accountable* for the exercise of the powers that they each wield. We will examine where the various institutions of government sit within today's *multilayered constitution*; this will include looking at institutions at different levels of government—local, devolved, national, and European—and at how their powers and responsibilities fit together. In that way, we can build up a picture of where authority for different matters lies within a constitution characterised by overlapping and interlocking seats of power. And, as part of our inquiry into the differences and relationship between *political and legal constitutionalism*, we will look at both the political and legal norms that constitute the framework within which government operates.

Before proceeding further, it is necessary to consider the basic set of arrangements that characterise modern constitutions. The constitutions of most countries share and distribute public power among three principal branches of government. First, there is usually a *legislative branch*. The principal role of the legislature is to represent the views of the people and to make legislation. The primary responsibility for enacting United Kingdom legislation rests with the UK Parliament (often known simply as 'Westminster'), although, as we will see, the picture is more complex than this because there are other legislatures (for example, the Scottish Parliament) and institutions that exercise legislative power. Parliament also has the basic responsibility for holding the executive to account.

Second, there is the *judicial branch*—that is, the system of courts that is responsible for both interpreting the law and adjudicating upon legal disputes. In the UK, the court system contains many different types of court and tribunal, with the Supreme Court at its apex.

Third, there is the *executive* or *administrative branch* (often referred to colloquially simply as 'the government'). The executive is responsible for making public policy and implementing the laws enacted by the legislature. In the UK, the executive branch exists and operates at different levels. So, UK central government consists, *inter alia*, of the departments of state (the Home Office, the Treasury, and so on) and the Cabinet, all under the leadership of the Prime Minister.[1] Above this level of government, executive power is also exercised within the European Union (EU); below it, executive power is exercised by the devolved administrations in Scotland, Wales, and Northern Ireland, and by local government also.

There are many specific issues in relation to individual institutions that we need to address, but it is necessary to begin our examination of the institutions of government by thinking about how they relate to one another—and also how these institutions *ought* to relate to each other. We will spend much of this part of the book considering the former matter in relation to the UK. However, at the outset, it is important to consider the latter point. How should a system of government be designed? What should be the respective powers and functions of the different branches? And should they be independent of or interconnected with one another?

There are no straightforward answers to these questions. Any answers will necessarily depend on what one is trying to achieve. A dictator would plainly design a system of government in such a way as to enable him to do as he wished without interference by others; he would not, for example, want to be troubled by an independent judiciary liable to tell him that the law prevented him from doing certain things. He might therefore (if he had to tolerate the existence of a judiciary at all) design the system so that he could appoint tame judges who would be unlikely to challenge him, and dismiss them if they did.

Thankfully, most systems of government, at least formally, are not designed in such a way; rather, there is a broad consensus that government should be organised according to the separation of powers doctrine. The tripartite system of government briefly described above reflects the separation of powers doctrine, in that it distinguishes between judicial, executive, and legislative branches. That doctrine has been described as one of the two 'great pillar[s] of Western political thought' that underpin the notion of 'constitutional' government (the other being representative democracy).[2] That there should be three branches, and that they should be distinct from one another, is the central tenet of the separation of powers doctrine, at least according to its classical definition.[3] However, beyond this very rudimentary outline of the doctrine, there is no uniform view as to what the precise relationships between the legislative, executive, and

---

[1] The executive's role is the hardest to define concisely. It may, most straightforwardly, be described as the branch of government that runs the country, in that it is the executive's job to take the initiative in proposing new laws, responding to events, and so on. For more detailed discussion of the roles of the three branches of government in the UK, see Chapters 4–6 below.

[2] Vile, *Constitutionalism and the Separation of Powers* (Oxford 1967), p 2.

[3] Montesquieu, *The Spirit of the Laws* [1748] (Cambridge 1989), Book XI, ch 6.

judicial branches should be. A strict formulation of the doctrine would require that no branch should be capable of exercising power *over* another branch, that none should be able to exercise the powers *of* another, and that no individual person should be a *member* of more than one branch. This is not the only interpretation of the doctrine, although we will use it, for the time being, as our working definition. However, as we will see later, this view of the doctrine may be regarded, as one commentator put it, as an 'extreme' formulation.[4] There are other, arguably better, interpretations of the doctrine.

It is important, at the outset, to be clear about the status of the separation of powers doctrine: what it is, and what it is not. It is, ultimately, merely an idea—a model, or template, that prescribes how some people think both the system and institutions of government ought to be organised. It is not the only way in which government *may be* organised, it is not the only way in which government *is* organised, and it is not—at least in the strict form set out in the previous paragraph—the way in which government is organised *in the UK*. This is not to suggest that the separation of powers is unimportant. It is an influential idea with a long historical pedigree.[5] Down the ages, the doctrine of the separation of powers has been regarded by many constitutional writers as representing the ideal governmental structure, and it is reflected in the constitutions of many countries—including, to a limited extent, the UK. Indeed, Montesquieu, one of the writers most closely associated with the separation-of-powers doctrine, based his elaboration of it on his perceptions of the constitution of eighteenth-century England (although it is generally held that he was labouring under a misapprehension to the extent that he thought that that constitution adhered to a strict separation of powers).[6]

In any event, it is necessary to appreciate that the view that government should be organised in line with the separation of powers doctrine is not one that is universally held, and that the failure of a country fully to implement the doctrine is not *necessarily* a bad thing. Whether one thinks that such failure is *actually* a bad thing depends on whether one agrees with the assumptions that underlie the separation of powers doctrine. In the next section, therefore, we critically examine those assumptions—that is, we ask why it is that the separation of powers is perceived by many to be a *good* thing, and whether they are right to think so.

2. Why embrace the separation of powers?

One way of addressing this question is to consider what might happen in a constitutional system *without* any recognisable separation of powers. Let us imagine what such a system might look like. Even if there were not a separate legislature, executive, and

---

[4] Vile, p 13.   [5] Vile, ch 2; Munro, *Studies in Constitutional Law* (London 1999), pp 295–302.
[6] Montesquieu.

judiciary, many of the functions that would, in most countries, be carried out by those three institutions would still somehow have to be performed. Laws would have to be made, implemented, and adjudicated upon.[7] In the absence of distinct institutions, therefore, it would presumably fall to a single institution—let us call it simply the 'government'—to perform all such functions.

Q Against that background, consider the following hypothetical scenario.

In a system with no separation of powers, the government decides that it wants to be able to expel from its territory foreign nationals who are likely to pose a security threat. The government therefore drafts and enacts legislation that gives government Ministers the power to expel from its territory 'any foreign national who, in the opinion of any Minister, may pose a threat to national security'. Government Ministers subsequently expel certain persons who are critical of the government, but who, most right-thinking people believe, pose no threat to national security. Those persons appeal to Ministers asking them to reverse their decisions, but Ministers refuse to do so.

Why might the scenario described above be regarded as an example of abuse of power? What forms does that abuse take? To what extent does the absence of a separation of powers enable (or make easier) such abuse? Would the existence of a separation of powers necessarily mean that such abuse would not occur?

It is highly unlikely that the situation described above could come about in a constitutional system based upon the separation of powers doctrine. In such a system, if Ministers—that is, members of the executive branch—were to desire legal powers to do certain things, then they would, in general, have to ask the legislature to confer such powers upon them. The legislature, as a separate and independent institution, might accede to the request—but it might decline the request outright, or it might agree to provide the requested powers, but only on terms different from those proposed by the executive. For example, if the executive were to request (as in the example above) a power to expel 'any foreign national who, in the opinion of any Minister, may pose a threat to national security', the legislature might take the view that while it is appropriate for the executive to have powers to exclude or expel dangerous individuals, it should not have a power to expel anyone who Ministers *think* is or *may be* dangerous. The legislature may therefore respond by granting Ministers a power to expel any foreign national who is *reasonably* believed by a Minister to pose a *serious* threat to national security—a much narrower power than the one desired by Ministers. Moreover, the existence, in a system that embraces the separation of powers, of an independent judiciary would provide a forum in which Ministers' exercises of the power could be challenged. Excluded individuals could, for example, ask courts to overturn Ministers' decisions if Ministers were unable to identify objective grounds

---

[7] This assumes (which, for present purposes, we do) that the country concerned is governed in a way that is based on some form of law, rather than, say, on brute force.

demonstrating the reasonableness of their belief, or if the evidence did not establish a serious—as opposed to a fanciful—risk to national security.

It should be apparent from the scenario sketched above that, within a constitutional system without any vestige of the separation of powers, there is a very serious risk—if not an inevitability—of the *abuse of power*. Lord Acton's famous statement that 'Power tends to corrupt and absolute power corrupts absolutely' is obviously a generalisation, but it certainly contains a kernel of truth.[8] Acton went on to explain his view by saying that '[g]reat men'—he was writing at a time when only men tended to be great in the sense of wielding power and when government Ministers were all men—'are almost always bad men'.[9] This is perhaps going too far, but it is clearly prudent to seek to design a system of government in a way that guards against the abuse of power by ensuring that the bad—as well as the merely well-intentioned, but incompetent or misguided—cannot do precisely as they please. That is precisely what the separation-of-powers doctrine seeks to do: it provides a model of government in which the risks of the abuse of power are reduced, and it does so by taking to heart Lord Acton's aphorism and by advocating a constitutional architecture in which power is divided rather than concentrated in one institution or one set of hands. Of course, the separation of powers does not guarantee that power will not be abused—all three branches might be prepared to collude in the abuse of public power—but it certainly makes the abuse of power far less likely.

Q Why is abuse of power less likely in a system of government characterised by the separation of powers? If separation of powers cannot guarantee that power will not be abused, what other safeguards might be necessary?

It follows that organising government according to the separation of powers principle is not something that should be pursued for its own sake. In other words, the separation of powers is not an end in itself; rather, it is a means to an end. The end is often said to be preventing abuse of power. As James Madison—the fourth US President and a key architect of its Constitution—put it: 'The accumulation of all powers, legislative, executive, and judiciary, in the same hands, whether of one, a few, or many, and whether hereditary, self-appointed, or elective, may justly be pronounced the very definition of tyranny.'[10] Similarly, Montesquieu feared the use of power in a 'tyrannical manner' if it was not divided among legislative, executive, and judicial branches.[11] It has been noted that placing the prevention of abuse of power centre-stage implies a set of assumptions—in particular, that preserving the liberty of the individual against inappropriate governmental interference is all-important.[12] Those who place greater faith in the capacity of government, through

---

[8] Letter to Bishop Mandell Creighton, 3 April 1887.   [9] Letter to Bishop Mandell Creighton.

[10] Hamilton, Madison, and Jay, *The Federalist* [1787–88] (Washington DC 1992), no 47.

[11] Montesquieu, *The Spirit of the Laws*.   [12] Vile, p 14.

the pursuit of collectivist policies, to secure the public good might approach the matter differently. In particular, they would be inclined to characterise the primary purpose of the separation of powers not as preventing the government from doing bad things, but as helping it to do beneficial things, such as securing the liberty of the individual and of the community as a whole, by ensuring that any given function is allocated to the institution best capable of discharging it.[13] Of course, these two objectives—the prevention of tyranny and the facilitation of socially useful conduct by government—are not mutually exclusive; it might, for example, be desirable to strike a balance between a government so powerful as to be liable to act tyrannically and one so weak as to be unable to do anything useful. In any event, both views fit our notion of the separation of powers as a means to an end. Viewed thus, the separation of powers is a methodology. It is a way of organising things so as to secure or prevent particular outcomes.

It is also a methodology that works hand in hand with democracy. It is, of course, possible to conceive of constitutional systems that are democratic, but which entail no separation of powers, or that subscribe to the separation of powers, but which embody no recognisable form of democracy. Nonetheless, the separation of powers doctrine and democracy are often found together. Indeed, the two ideas might be said to be mutually reinforcing. On the one hand, democracy is likely to assist with attaining goals (such as preventing abuse of power) that are the objective of separation of powers, the prospect of having to submit to re-election being a powerful—but not necessarily sufficient[14]—incentive against such abuse. On the other hand, the separation of powers is liable to bolster democracy: by requiring the legislative function to be performed by the legislature, the separation of powers helps to ensure that the most significant changes to law and policy can be made only with the approval of the branch that is the most representative of the people.

3. Different conceptions of the separation of powers

That the doctrine of the separation of powers is not an end in itself is an important insight, because it helps us to think more carefully about how systems of government should be designed and to evaluate critically existing constitutional arrangements, including those of the UK. In particular, conceiving of the separation of powers in this way should caution us against thinking of the doctrine as laying down a set of prescriptive rules any infraction of which is necessarily a bad thing.

---

[13] See, eg Barber, 'Prelude to the Separation of Powers' [2001] CLJ 59.

[14] Thomas Jefferson, the third US President, thought democracy without separation of powers to be far from ideal. It risked 'elective despotism' in that the government, once elected, was free to do as it wished due to an overconcentration of power in its hands. See 'Notes on the State of Virginia', quoted in *The Federalist*, no 48.

> **Q** Consider each of the following provisions of an imaginary constitution. Before reading further, think about any senses in which they disclose a breach of the separation of powers doctrine. To the extent that the following situations disclose such breaches, are they necessarily problematic?
>
> (i) Senior members of the executive may dismiss judges at will.
>
> (ii) The executive can enact any legislation that it chooses without needing to obtain the consent of the legislature.
>
> (iii) Judges may strike down legislation that is inconsistent with a constitutional Bill of Rights.
>
> (iv) The president may veto legislation passed by the legislature (unless the legislature overrides the president by a two-thirds majority).

All of the above situations involve one branch of government being capable of interfering with, or undertaking, the business of another. If the separation of powers were conceived of as an end in itself, any breach—and hence all of those set out above—would be problematic. That view of the doctrine has been referred to as the *pure version* of the separation of powers because it conceives of it in absolute terms: the dividing lines between the legislature, executive, and judiciary must be crystal clear, and must not be crossed in any circumstances.[15]

This may be contrasted with the *partial version* of the separation of powers doctrine.[16] On this view, arrangements that would be regarded as breaches of the pure version are not regarded as either inherently problematic or illegitimate; rather, the acceptability of any such 'breach' depends on whether, and if so to what extent, it compromises achievement of the ultimate objective that the separation of powers doctrine pursues. Indeed, we can go further than this by observing that a paradox lies at the heart of the separation of powers doctrine. On the one hand, its ultimate objective is (for many commentators) to guard against the abuse of power; yet, on the other hand, the achievement of that objective is likely to be fundamentally compromised by the sort of literal implementation of the doctrine envisaged under the pure version. If each branch of government is truly independent and free from any sort of control, interference, or oversight by the others, then the abuse of power by each branch remains a distinct possibility.

This was a major influence on the framers of the US Constitution, who thought that it would be unwise simply to lay down in a constitutional text the boundaries of the three branches' powers and to 'trust [such] parchment barriers against the encroaching spirit of power'.[17] Thus, they said, it was necessary to design 'the interior structure of government [such] that its several constituent parts may, by their mutual relations, be the means of keeping each other in their proper places'.[18] This meant striking a

---

[15] Vile, *Constitutionalism and the Separation of Powers* (Oxford 1967), ch 1.

[16] Vile, ch 1; Barendt, 'Separation of Powers and Constitutional Government' [1995] PL 599.

[17] *The Federalist*, no 48.   [18] *The Federalist*, no 51.

balance between, on the one hand, keeping the three branches as distinct as possible in order to avoid the risk of tyranny created by overconcentration of power, and, on the other hand, enabling the institutions of government to regulate one another and to keep one another in check.

It follows that within this partial, or 'checks and balances', conception of the separation of powers, the ability of one branch to involve itself in matters that are the primary concern of another branch is not necessarily a bad thing—and may indeed be regarded as entirely positive. It is therefore necessary, once this more nuanced view of the separation of powers is embraced, to distinguish between constructive 'breaches' (that is, situations in which one branch is somewhat involved in the work of another) and destructive breaches. The former are to be welcomed, because they contribute to the attainment of the overall goal of preventing tyranny, while the latter are to be deplored, because they make the attainment of that goal less likely. The example given above of a presidential power of legislative override subject to the possibility of reversal by a legislative super-majority may be regarded as a constructive breach of the separation of powers: it creates a balance of power between the executive and legislative branches, making it harder, but not impossible, for the legislature to do something to which the executive is opposed, while preserving the supremacy of the former in matters of law-making. In contrast, an executive power to dismiss judges at will or to enact legislation without the consent of the legislature may be regarded as problematic breaches of the separation of powers: they effectively make the executive dominant over the other two branches and serve to create not a balance of power, but an overconcentration of power in executive hands. Such arrangements do not contribute to the important task of the various branches keeping one another in their 'proper places'.

> **Q** Look again at situation (iii) above. Under a partial conception of the separation of powers, would a judicial power to strike down legislation as unconstitutional be regarded in positive or negative terms?

This view of the separation of powers also fits better with the reality of modern government.[19] For example, over the last 200 years, many countries with constitutions based upon the separation of powers have witnessed the development of administrative agencies that undertake many of the day-to-day tasks of government. However, these agencies cannot comfortably be slotted into only one of the three traditional categories (that is, legislative, executive, or judicial). It has been noted that it is commonplace in the USA for administrative agencies to 'engage in [lawmaking], to formulate and apply policies, and to take individual decisions, often after a formal hearing'.[20] Such agencies

---

[19] Vile, p 319, goes further by arguing that it is simply impossible to draw clean distinctions (such as would allow their allocation to different institutions) between 'rule-making, rule-application and rule-adjudication': 'most operations of government are much too complex, requiring a whole stream of decisions to be taken, such that it is impossible to divide them up' in this way.

[20] Barendt, 'Separation of Powers and Constitutional Government' [1995] PL 599, 607.

constitute a 'one-stop shop' that deals with many aspects—legislative, executive, and judicial—of a particular subject matter. The US Food and Drug Administration, which exists, among other things, to ensure the safety of medicines and food, is an example of such a body. We will see later that the UK also possesses governmental bodies, some of which are headed by government Ministers and others of which are not, which cannot be neatly characterised as performing only executive, legislative, or judicial functions. A pure conception of separation of powers would demand that such bodies did not exist: the blurring of the lines between the three branches would be unacceptable. In contrast, the partial version of the separation of powers doctrine holds that such agencies are not per se objectionable; rather, the question is whether they threaten the objective(s) that the doctrine exists to serve.

Barendt, for example, argues that the existence of administrative agencies that span the three branches of government is unobjectionable provided that they can be held adequately to account for their actions (for example, via political accountability to the legislature and through the possibility of judicial review).[21] Barber goes as far as to suggest that the traditional 'tripartite vision of the state' is a distraction. The existence of the type of agencies described above and of multilayered governance arrangements means that it is no longer—if it ever was—the case that the state consists of 'three great monoliths': a legislature, an executive, and a judiciary.[22] He therefore concludes that the proper concern of the separation of powers cannot be the preservation of clear dividing lines between (what are, for him at least) chimerical institutions, but rather the allocation of power in the way most likely to realise the objective underlying the separation of powers.[23] Of course, this might well still entail that a given agency should be unable to wield overweening power and marginalise other institutions of government—but, for Barber, there is no particular need to carve government up along rigid lines demarcating legislative, executive, and judicial functions.

In conclusion on this point, it is worth noting that while few countries stick rigidly to a pure version of the separation of powers doctrine, most constitutional systems do embody a recognisable partial separation of powers in which a genuine attempt is made to demarcate legislative, executive, and judicial functions, allocating them to institutionally distinct branches of government. This is combined with the insertion of appropriate checks and balances to ensure that each branch is subject to oversight, or is counterbalanced, by another. But that is not to say that Barber's and Barendt's points are without force. Not every government body can neatly be assigned to one of the three standard categories; whether or not that is a problem from a separation-of-powers standpoint depends on whether such bodies threaten the underlying purposes of the doctrine and whether adequate arrangements exist for minimising the possibility of their doing so.

---

21 Barendt at 607.   22 Barber, 'Prelude to the Separation of Powers' [2001] CLJ 59, 70–1.

23 For Barber, the principal objective of the separation of powers is the protection of liberty. His argument, however, is equally relevant if the main purpose of the doctrine is regarded as the prevention of tyranny.

4. The separation of powers in the UK

Adherence to the pure doctrine of the separation of powers in most constitutions is rare. What then is the status of the doctrine in the UK constitution? This is not an easy question to answer simply because there is no consensus over whether the doctrine either is or should be a fundamental feature of the UK constitution. There are even different views as to whether the doctrine exists in any meaningful form in the UK constitution. Lord Diplock, for one, thought that it did. He felt confident that 'the basic concept of separation of legislative, executive and judicial power ... had been developed in the unwritten constitution of the United Kingdom'[24] such that that constitution was 'firmly based upon the separation of powers'.[25] Others, however, have differed. For example, the nineteenth-century constitutional writer and journalist Bagehot noted that the 'efficient secret of the English Constitution may be described by the close union, the nearly complete fusion, of the executive and legislative powers'.[26] In other words, in the UK, there is a substantial overlap between the executive and Parliament, with the executive exerting a powerful influence over the work of Parliament. We will see in the following two chapters that this is indeed the case—and we will encounter, in the rest of this part of the book, many other ways in which the UK's constitution fails to adhere to a pure conception of the separation of powers. Indeed, the extent to which the British constitution falls short of adherence to that version of the doctrine has led some writers to contend that it does not adhere to the separation of powers *at all*. Influential commentators have characterised it as a 'myth',[27] and as 'an irrelevant distraction for the English law student and his teachers'.[28]

Those views were proffered some time ago and, as we will see, the UK constitution has changed significantly in the meantime. That point aside, however, such views—based as they are on examples of technical breaches of the separation of powers doctrine[29]—rather miss the point. Indeed, to suppose that a constitution must either exhibit *separation* of powers or, as Bagehot put it, *fusion* of powers[30] is to postulate a false dichotomy.[31] Our discussion so far shows that the pure version of the doctrine is unrealistic (few, if any, countries adhere to it) and even undesirable (because it precludes measures, such as checks and balances, which are likely to promote the overall objective of preventing tyranny). The important question, therefore, is not whether the UK adheres to a pure conception of the separation of powers (it manifestly does not), but whether its institutions of government are organised in such a way as to guard

---

[24] *Hinds v The Queen* [1977] AC 195, 212.   [25] *Duport Steels Ltd v Sirs* [1980] 1 WLR 142, 157.
[26] *The English Constitution* (London 1867), p 12.
[27] Hood Phillips, 'A Constitutional Myth: Separation of Powers' (1977) 93 LQR 11.
[28] De Smith, 'The Separation of Powers in New Dress' (1966–67) 12 McGill Law Journal 491.
[29] Hood Phillips at 12.
[30] *The English Constitution* (London 1867), p 12.
[31] Vile, *Constitutionalism and the Separation of Powers* (Oxford 1967), pp 213–14.

satisfactorily against the abuse of power. As we address that question during our study in the following three chapters of Parliament, the legislature, and the executive, we will find that the position is complex. We will encounter instances in which one institution has so much power over another branch as to create precisely the sort of over-concentration of power that enhances the risk of its abuse; the extent to which the executive branch is able to dominate and control proceedings in Parliament is perhaps the most obvious example of such a phenomenon.[32] On the other hand, we will find many situations in which a strict separation of powers *is* adhered to, the independence of the judiciary being a clear example of such a situation.[33] And we will confront situations in which the absence of strict separation actually serves to guard against abuse of power, an example being the courts' power to review the legality of executive action and to strike down any such action that is unlawful.[34]

Critically assessing the British constitution from a separation of powers standpoint—as we attempt to do in the next three chapters—is not therefore a straightforward task. This is so for two principal reasons. First, it does not involve the asking of a binary question: we will not, by the end of our inquiry, be in a position to say that the UK constitution either does or does not adhere to the doctrine; rather, the question that falls to be asked is one of degree. To what extent does the UK constitution adhere to the separation of powers? Or, to put the question in slightly different terms, does the UK constitution fulfil the ideal of the separation of powers to the extent necessary to keep the risk of abuse of power within acceptable limits? Whatever the answer to that question might be, it is clear at the outset that the British constitution should not be condemned as faulty merely because it does not embody the sort of rigid distinctions inherent in the pure conception of the separation of powers.[35]

This leads on to a second difficulty. The partial conception of the separation of powers necessarily calls for the striking of a balance between, on the one hand, the separateness of government institutions (so as to avoid overconcentration of power) and, on the other hand, the existence of relationships between them (in order that they may keep one another in their 'proper places'). Unsurprisingly, what constitutes the 'right' balance is not something on which everyone agrees.

The division of opinion amongst the Law Lords in the *Fire Brigades Union* case is a good example of this.[36] In this case, the Home Secretary had refused to exercise his power under s 171(1) of the Criminal Justice Act 1988 to bring into force a new scheme (contained elsewhere in the statute) for compensating victims of crime. The Home Secretary had also indicated that he had no intention of bringing the statutory scheme into force. This was tantamount to repeal of the relevant parts of the 1988 Act. The case therefore raised important questions as to whether, under the separation of powers, it was appropriate for a government Minister to be allowed, in effect, to repeal an Act of

---

[32] See Chapters 4 and 5 below.   [33] See Chapter 6 below.   [34] See Chapters 12–15 below.

[35] See further Munro, *Studies in Constitutional Law* (London 1999), ch 9, and Munro, 'The Separation of Powers: Not Such a Myth' [1981] PL 19.

[36] *R v Secretary of State for the Home Department, ex p Fire Brigades Union* [1995] 2 AC 513.

Parliament—something that, it might be thought, should be done only by Parliament itself—and, if not, whether it was appropriate for the court to intervene.

By a three–two majority, the House of Lords held that the Home Secretary had exceeded his powers. What is striking is that all of the judges sought to justify their conclusions by reference to the separation of powers doctrine, even though they arrived at completely different conclusions. The majority concluded that the Home Secretary had acted unlawfully by breaching the duty to keep under active consideration the implementation of the statutory compensation scheme that was held to be implicit in the s 171(1) discretion. The majority was therefore willing to intervene in order to prevent executive usurpation of a legislative function. The dissentients, however, considered it inappropriate for a court to intervene in such a matter because it concerned legislation that was not yet fully in force, thereby making the issue a political one, which should have been resolved by Parliament and the executive. They were concerned that judicial intervention would entail the *courts* contravening the separation of powers by interfering in a matter outside their area of constitutional responsibility. This nicely illustrates how views can differ about how to strike the balance between the separateness of government institutions and the pursuit of relationships between them, within which checks and balances may be provided. The minority considered the separateness of the judiciary—in the sense of remaining outside the political arena—to be of overriding importance, thereby rendering inappropriate any intervention by the court. In contrast, the majority emphasised the importance of checks and balances; judicial intervention in the affairs of the other branches was a price worth paying in order to ensure that the executive could not arrogate to itself powers of repealing legislation that should belong exclusively to the legislature.

Q Which of the two views adopted in *Fire Brigades Union* do you find more persuasive? Why?

5. Conclusions

We have seen in this chapter that the separation of powers doctrine, although capable of being stated in relatively simple terms, is far from straightforward. Once we recognise that distinguishing between legislative, executive, and judicial functions, and allocating each to a different institution, is merely a means to an end, the extent to which any constitutional system precisely adheres to the doctrine, thus stated, becomes insignificant; rather, the important matter is whether the system is designed so as to be capable of adequately guarding against the misuse of power. As we have seen, this is likely to involve striking a balance between, on the one hand, the need to avoid an overconcentration of power by allocating different functions to different institutions and, on the other hand, the need to ensure that the various branches relate to one another in constructive ways that allow for sufficient checks and balances. Viewed thus, it becomes apparent that the separation of powers doctrine is closely related to—indeed, is a way of pursuing—the concept of accountability. The importance of ensuring that those who exercise public power are properly held to account is one of the key themes of this book, and we have already noted, in Chapters 1 and 2, that there are various ways, political and legal, in which those who wield power may be held to account. Accountability, like the separation of powers, is ultimately a means to an end, rather than an end in itself: both concepts may assist in ensuring that governmental power is used responsibly, for the public good, rather than abused. The separation-of-powers doctrine represents a particular way in which the constitutional architecture might be arranged in order to guard against the abuse of power—both by avoiding its overconcentration and by embedding each institution of government within a network of relationships through which others may hold it to account for the use of such powers as it has. In the rest of this part of the book, we will consider (among other things) the extent to which the UK's constitutional arrangements live up to this ideal.

Further reading

BARBER, 'Prelude to the Separation of Powers' [2001] CLJ 59

BARENDT, 'Separation of Powers and Constitutional Government' [1995] PL 599

HAMILTON, MADISON, AND JAY, *The Federalist*, nos 47–51, available online at **http://thomas .loc.gov/home/histdox/fedpapers.html**

MUNRO, *Studies in Constitutional Law* (London 1999), ch 9

VILE, *Constitutionalism and the Separation of Powers* (Oxford 1967)

4 The Executive

1. Introduction

As we saw in Chapter 3, the separation of powers doctrine requires that the government is divided into three branches: the judiciary, the legislature, and the executive. It is with the latter that we are primarily concerned in this chapter. However, at the outset, it is worth entering three caveats about the scope of this chapter.

First, it would be futile to attempt to explain the role of the executive without considering how it relates to, differs from, and—perhaps most importantly—impinges upon the other two branches. Indeed, it is when we consider the position of the executive—and, in particular, its relationship with the legislature—that we encounter in its starkest form the somewhat cavalier approach to the separation of powers that prevails in the United Kingdom and which we noted, by way of introduction, in the previous chapter.

Second, precisely because we endeavour in this chapter to consider the executive not in isolation, but by reference to its place within the wider network of constitutional arrangements via which the UK is governed, it is necessary to look ahead to a number of matters that are considered in more detail in later parts of the book. This is an unavoidable consequence of the centrality of the executive's role within the British constitution, and of the fact that its role can be properly understood only by setting our analysis of it within a wider context.

Third, we will see in Chapter 7 that Scotland, Northern Ireland, and Wales each have their own institutions that perform executive functions within those policy areas that have been devolved to them, and that local government also has important executive responsibilities. The primary focus of this chapter, however, is the executive branch of the UK government.

With those caveats in mind, the purpose of this chapter is to explore what the executive is, and what it does; how it relates to other branches of government—with particular reference to its relationship with Parliament; how it is held to account, both politically and legally;[1] the institutions and constitutional actors that make up the modern UK executive; and the considerable powers that it has at its disposal. In this

---

[1] See further Chapters 9–18.

way, we will show that the executive plays a pivotal role in the British constitution today, and that there are real concerns about whether it enjoys too much power—and about whether that power is subject to adequate oversight and control. An appreciation of the executive is therefore central to any understanding of the contemporary UK constitution.

2. The modern executive and its constitutional position

2.1 What is the executive?

The executive (or the 'government', or 'administration') is the governing body of the state. At its most basic level, the purpose of the executive is to make and implement public policy across the range of areas for which it is responsible. The executive is that branch of the state responsible for executing and administering laws drawn up by the legislature. The legislature produces legislation and scrutinises the actions of the executive. By contrast, the purpose of the judiciary is primarily to adjudicate upon and resolve legal disputes. The executive and the legislature are then the most political branches of the state. Their actions and the laws that they enact are directly guided by political factors, whereas the judiciary is non-political: it merely interprets the laws as laid down by the legislature and develops general legal principles when called upon to resolve disputes.[2]

The respective roles of the legislature and the judiciary can be defined quite straightforwardly by reference to what they do: the former makes the law; the latter interprets and applies it in individual cases. By contrast, the executive is not principally responsible for either of those tasks. It is therefore possible to think of the role of the executive in residual terms: it is responsible for those aspects of the business of government that do not fall within the purview of the legislature or the judiciary.[3] However, defining the executive by reference to what it does *not* do is hardly satisfactory. If we are to study the executive, we need to know for what it *is* responsible. Although it will take the entire chapter to answer that question properly, it is helpful, at least as a starting point, to note that the executive's role is distinctive in two senses.

First, it is the lead branch of government in terms of *running the country*.[4] Of course, this is a very imprecise notion, but it reflects the idea that it is the executive that is responsible for doing things as diverse as running the National Health Service (NHS),

---

[2] We explain in Chapter 6 that, in fact, judges do sometimes—perhaps often—have to make choices about policy. Nevertheless, the general distinction set out here, between the judiciary and the other, political, branches remains valid.

[3] This statement is qualified below, in light of the substantial overlap between the executive and the other branches with respect to certain functions.

[4] See, eg *R v Secretary of State for the Home Department, ex p Fire Brigades Union* [1995] 2 AC 513, 567–8.

detaining certain convicted criminals in prison, controlling immigration, making sure that the country's energy needs are met, conducting relations with other states and with international bodies such as the European Union (EU), ensuring that the UK meets its obligations under international treaties in areas ranging from human rights to climate change, collecting taxes, distributing welfare payments, regulating myriad forms of activity such as the conduct of financial institutions and utility companies, and even fighting wars.

Second, the executive is the only branch of government that can fairly be described as an *initiative-taker*. The role of the courts is limited by their *modus operandi*. They make decisions in whatever cases come before them, and although such decisions may have far-reaching implications—even going as far, in exceptional circumstances, as to create new forms of criminal liability[5]—courts cannot act unilaterally. For example, while, as we will see in Chapters 12–15, courts can strike down unlawful government decisions, they can only do so if, in the first place, an appropriate party institutes legal proceedings against the relevant public body; judges cannot simply strike down unlawful government actions that they happen to read about in a newspaper. Equally, Parliament is not generally in a position to take the initiative. The reasons for this are explored below; for the time being, it is sufficient to note that Parliament is not set up in such a way as to enable its members, acting collectively, to think up and implement new legislation. In reality, Parliament's role is limited to scrutinising and enacting legislation that is thought up and proposed by the executive branch: its approval is required before a Bill can become law, but law is made, in the sense of being 'formulated in a coherent form', by the executive.[6] Thus, it has been pointed out, the executive is 'the dominant institution to which the other two institutions react'.[7]

It therefore falls to the executive branch, in two ways, to take the initiative. On the one hand, it is the executive that develops and designs planned changes in public policy. Changes as major as the creation of the NHS, the conferral of independence upon the Bank of England, and entry into the EU, and as (comparatively) minor as the banning of smoking in public places and the introduction of free bus travel for pensioners all came about because the executive thought of them, designed them, and made arrangements—including, where necessary, the enactment by Parliament of legislation—for their implementation. On the other hand, it is also the executive, as initiative-taker, to which the task of reacting to sudden, unforeseeable (or at least unforeseen) events falls.

It is important to recognise that the scope of executive action, the areas of social life for which it has assumed responsibility, is neither fixed nor static, but constantly

---

[5] *R v R (Rape: Marital Exemption)* [1992] 1 AC 599.

[6] Norton, 'Parliament and Legislative Scrutiny: An Overview of Issues in the Legislative Process', in Brazier (ed), *Parliament, Politics and Law Making: Issues and Developments in the Legislative Process* (London 2004), p 5.

[7] Griffith, 'The Common Law and the Political Constitution' (2001) 117 LQR 42, 49.

changing and often a contentious area of political debate. In earlier centuries, the executive had comparatively few areas of responsibility. For example, in medieval times, government was under the personal influence of the monarch of the day, the Crown, and possessed very little responsibility other than for the defence of the realm. If the country were being invaded or if the monarch were to wish to conquer other countries, then the monarch could personally decide whether or not to go to war. During the nineteenth century, however, with the Industrial Revolution, government began to assume new functions, such as maintaining law and order, and the regulation of trade and industry. Government was still limited—the pervasive ethos was that of laissez-faire: state intervention was relatively slight—but its role was growing.

Now let us compare that with modern government. Today, government assumes responsibility for a bewildering variety and seemingly endless number of public tasks, such as managing the economy; protecting the public from terrorism; administering the welfare state; regulating the media and financial services; maintaining immigration control; delivering public services, such as education, health care, policing, and transport; protecting the environment; securing energy supplies; promoting the arts and culture; regulating food production; and promoting (*inter alia*) sex and race equality. The daily influence of government on all of our lives is so pervasive that often we do not even realise it.[8] In terms of its size and complexity, modern government is without precedent and dwarfs anything attempted by the largest global corporations. The basic point is that modern government is an enormous and highly complex organisation that exerts influence over many aspects of our lives.

The growth of government has been driven, *inter alia*, by the increasing complexity and interconnectedness of modern life (simple, primitive societies generally require less regulation), as well as by people's changing expectations of government. Today, when citizens want something done—whether it is reducing childhood obesity or carbon emissions, building eco-towns, ensuring animal health and welfare, improving public transport, or ensuring food is safe to eat—it is often the executive to which they turn in order make and implement policy. When major catastrophe looms or occurs—a public health scare or a financial crisis, for example—it is the executive branch that has to respond, whether, as in 2001, by arranging for the destruction of several million animals potentially infected with foot-and-mouth disease or, as in 2007–08, by committing hundreds of billions of pounds of public money to shore up the banking system during the global financial crisis. Given that the executive now has responsibility for so many different public functions, it is unsurprising that it has been transformed over the last century. While globalisation has, to some extent, limited the abilities of national governments to deal with worldwide problems (think, for example, of the international action needed to combat climate change or third world debt), at the national level, the executive is the most powerful institution of the state.

---

[8] Just think, for example, of how the government regulates simple activities such as driving a car: you will need a driving licence and to pay car tax, the car will need an MOT, speed cameras will monitor compliance with speed limits, and you must obey the Highway Code and, in London, pay the congestion charge.

As people's expectations of government have increased, so has the scale and complexity of modern government. This, in turn, has resulted in a more powerful executive branch, and in a greater need for government to be held to account.

2.2 **The modern executive in the UK**

What then of the executive in the UK? If we think of the UK executive, then what images are generated in our minds? Initially, we might think of the personnel at the very centre of the governmental machine, such as the Prime Minister stepping out of the door of No 10 Downing Street to attend the weekly session of Prime Minister's questions in the House of Commons or to attend an international meeting with the leaders of other national governments. This surely is where executive power resides. In the UK, the most important politician is the Prime Minister, who exercises considerable political power as to how the country is run. The Prime Minister is the head of the government, ultimately responsible both to Parliament and the public for its success or failure, and the electorate, if unimpressed by a particular Prime Minister, can always vote for another political party at the next general election.

But the Prime Minister, while undoubtedly powerful, is only one person; no large-scale organisation, such as the modern executive, could ever be solely operated or even directed by a single individual. We might then think of the top-level government Ministers, known as Secretaries of State, for example, announcing a new government policy or initiative, or answering questions in Parliament or before a parliamentary select committee, or on the front pages of the newspapers as they seek to handle the latest crisis. Each of these Ministers has his or her own portfolio of government responsibilities. For example, the Home Secretary is responsible for the conduct of internal affairs, while the Foreign Secretary is responsible for foreign affairs. Together with the Prime Minister, these personnel are perhaps the most visible manifestations of the executive. Together, they form the Cabinet, the committee of senior Ministers responsible for controlling government policy—the supreme decision-making body in the UK government.

But again, while important, government Ministers form only a relatively small group of people. They might have considerable power in deciding what government policy is, but they are not primarily responsible for administering that policy. We might then think of the large administrative organisations, the central government departments, overseen by Ministers and responsible for much of policymaking and its implementation or 'delivery'—that is, exercising governmental power by making the millions of administrative decisions by which policy is put into practice. These central government departments include, amongst others, the Home Office, the Foreign and Commonwealth Office, the Department for Communities and Local Government, the Department of Health, and so on, and are known collectively as 'Whitehall', after that area of central London in which most government departments are located. Each central government department is headed by a Secretary of State, but populated by many civil servants, the administrators, who undertake much of the day-to-day work of government. For example, the Secretary of State for Work and Pensions heads up the largest government department, the Department for Work and Pensions, which has a workforce of over 100,000 people and an annual budget in the region of £150 billion. Civil servants are expected to be politically neutral and to provide impartial advice to Ministers in addition to carrying out much of the routine work of government. So, in considering the constitutional position of the executive, we will need to examine the nature of the relationships between Ministers and civil servants. Furthermore, Ministers are nowadays also assisted by special advisers, who provide assistance from a perspective that is more political than that which civil servants can properly adopt. We will therefore also need to consider the nature of the relationships between Ministers and their special advisers.

Again, at a level further removed from the centre of government, we might think of other public bodies responsible for the delivery of public services that operate at 'arm's length' from Ministers: for example, HM Prison Service, NHS Trusts, and the Environment Agency—bodies that have been established in order to deliver public services. Alternatively, we might think of the different levels of government that operate in the UK's 'multilayered' constitution: the cooperation of the UK government with those of other member States of the EU to make EU law that binds national governments; the devolved executives in Scotland, Wales, and Northern Ireland that exercise powers within their devolved responsibilities; and local government.[9]

The early twenty-first-century executive is thus a large and highly complex organisation. Whether we like it or not, it governs us all. It comprises the government Ministers who act as our political leaders, and the many civil servants who implement and administer policy. It is the executive that, for the most part, makes the decisions by which society is governed. To this end, the executive has a number of different tools at its disposal, including, as we will see, the use of coercive powers, and the collection and distribution of wealth and resources.

2.3 **The executive and public law**

That the UK has a large and powerful executive is, then, indisputable. What, though, is its constitutional and legal position? Curiously, in formal terms, the executive is not recognised by public law; indeed, the term 'the executive' is 'barely known to the law'.[10] As Maitland noted, in the UK, the executive is not a legal organisation; this does not mean that it is an illegal organization, but that it is an 'extra-legal organization; the law does not condemn it; but it does not recognize it—knows nothing about it'.[11] In strictly legal terms, it is only the constituent parts of the executive that exist. It

---

[9] See Chapters 7 and 8.

[10] *Town Investments Ltd v Department of the Environment* [1978] AC 359, 398, *per* Lord Simon.

[11] Maitland, *The Constitutional History of England* (Cambridge 1908), p 387.

follows, for example, that when Parliament wishes to grant powers to the executive branch, it actually confers them not upon the executive as a whole, but upon Ministers (and thus, in practice, upon the departments of which they are in charge). Therefore, the 'executive' is merely convenient shorthand for the collection of Ministers and departments that *are* recognised in legal terms. UK public law's failure to recognise the executive as a legal entity is of a piece with its failure to recognise any concept of the 'state': like the executive, '[t]he state is not an entity recognised by English public law in its present stage of development'.[12]

At first sight, the lack of recognition given by public law to the vast entity of the modern executive or the state might seem bizarre. How can public law achieve one of its principal purposes—that of holding the executive to account—if it does not even formally recognise the existence of either the executive or the state? The problem is curious and mainly arises for historical reasons. By virtue of the historical development of their constitution and its unwritten nature, the British people have continued to use the concept of the Crown to signify an executive rather than to recognise a separate concept of the executive or the state. This is one reason for the non-recognition of the executive by public law.

Another is that long-established practice largely obviates the difficulties that failing to recognise the executive might be expected to create. As noted above, the functions and powers of modern government are conferred not on the executive as a whole, because in legal terms it does not exist, but on individual Ministers, public officers, and public authorities. When public power is delegated by Parliament to the executive, it is habitually conferred on 'the Secretary of State', meaning a senior government Minister. The office of the Secretary of State is supposed to be a single, unitary office, but in fact many Secretaries of State exist and it is possible for powers conferred on one Secretary of State to be transferred to another under the Ministers of the Crown Act 1975. Furthermore, the exercise of most powers allocated to the Secretary of State will (unless the relevant legislation provides otherwise) often be delegated to civil servants who make decisions in the name of the Secretary of State. For example, the Home Secretary has responsibility for administering immigration control and has a statutory power to allow foreign nationals to enter the UK. In practical terms, it would be impossible for one individual to make the very many decisions required; the vast majority of decisions are therefore made not by the Home Secretary personally, but by officials acting on his behalf.

Q The executive clearly exists, even though it is not legally recognised as such. Why, in this, as in so many other areas, does the formal, legal constitution of the UK fail fully to reflect political reality? Should this phenomenon be regarded as a weakness of UK current constitutional arrangements and, if so, how might it be remedied?

---

[12] *R (K) v Camden and Islington Heath Authority* [2001] 3 WLR 553, 586, *per* Sedley LJ.

2.4 **The Crown**

Consider the following phrases of British constitutionalism: the 'Crown in Parliament', 'Her Majesty's government', 'Ministers of the Crown', the 'Royal Courts of Justice'. The pervasive references to the Crown might appear to indicate that it is the Queen personally who runs the country rather than her government. In formal, constitutional terms, the Queen does indeed possess executive powers to appoint Ministers, to dissolve Parliament, and to grant royal assent to legislation. However, in practice, such powers are exercised not by the monarch personally, but by elected politicians. Again, legal theory does not correspond with political reality.

What then does the concept of 'the Crown' actually mean? In one sense, the Crown is merely 'an object of jewelled headgear under guard at the Tower of London'.[13] In another sense, the Crown is an important symbol of continuity and change in the British constitution. As a symbol of royal authority, 'the Crown' was used in pre-modern, medieval times to refer to the monarch when doing acts of government as opposed to acts undertaken by the monarch in his or her personal capacity. To preserve continuity with the past, the concept of the Crown has been retained, although in practice governmental power is now exercised by both elected politicians and their administrators in the name of the Crown rather than by the monarch personally.

In other words, the language of public law has not kept pace with the evolution of modern executive power in democratic times. As Maitland put it, the concept of the Crown is a 'convenient cover for ignorance'.[14] Real executive power is not exercised by the Crown through its inherent powers of government; rather, much—although not all—executive power has been granted by Parliament to the Secretary of State, meaning the government of the day. As Lord Diplock commented, it would be better, instead of speaking of the Crown, to speak of the 'government'—'a term appropriate to embrace both collectively and individually all the ministers of the Crown and parliamentary secretaries under whose direction the administrative work of government is carried on by the civil servants employed in the various government departments'.[15] In short, for all practical purposes, 'the Crown' now simply means 'the government'. Thus, as Lord Rodger recently put it, the 'executive power of the Crown is, in practice, exercised by a single body of ministers, making up Her Majesty's government'.[16]

2.5 **Executive–legislative relations: an 'elective dictatorship'?**

The relationship between the executive and the Crown is not, however, the only relationship that we must consider in order to appreciate the constitutional position of the executive in the UK. What of the relationships between the UK government and

---

[13] *Town Investments* at 397.

[14] Maitland, p 418. See generally Sunkin and Payne (eds), *The Nature of the Crown: A Legal and Political Analysis* (Oxford 1999).   [15] Maitland, p 381.

[16] *R (BAPIO Action Ltd) v Secretary of State for the Home Department* [2008] UKHL 27, [2008] 1 AC 1003, [33].

Parliament, and between the government and the judiciary? These relationships are central to how the constitution seeks to promote and sustain effective, accountable, and lawful executive action. Much of this book is concerned with considering these particular and complex relationships in more detail. For the moment, though, we only need to consider the basic aspects of those relationships.

First, let us consider the relationship between the executive (the government) and the legislature (Parliament). Central to this relationship is the fact that, in the UK, the composition of Parliament determines the political complexion of the executive. As we explain in more detail in Chapter 5,[17] general elections in the UK are *directly* concerned only with membership of the House of Commons: the executive is only *indirectly* elected, in the sense that, following an election, the Queen asks the leader of the political party most likely to able to command the confidence of the House of Commons—that is, to secure a majority in it—to form a government.[18] Normally, this will be the leader of the party with an overall majority (that is, over half of the MPs).[19] Very occasionally, an election produces no party with such a majority. For example, in 2010, the Conservative Party won more seats than any other, but fewer than half of the total; the leader of that party, David Cameron, was nevertheless asked to form a government when it became clear that he was best placed to command the confidence of the Commons by entering into a coalition arrangement with another party, the Liberal Democrats.

Whether the government consists of a single party or a coalition, it is the function of Parliament to hold the government to account. Most of the important government Ministers will be MPs drawn from the party or parties that form the government, while some Ministers will be members of the unelected chamber, the House of Lords. The government's majority of MPs in the House of Commons exists in order to sustain the government in power by enabling it to have the votes to support its policies and legislation. At the same time, it is the purpose of the opposition parties to hold the government to account, to criticise and oppose it in the hope that they might either overthrow the government or win the next general election. Parliament's function in providing the government of the day with the authority to govern is complemented by Parliament's role in holding the government to account and scrutinising its actions. In summary, Parliament therefore serves a dual purpose with regard to the government: to sustain the government in power, while at the same time scrutinising what it does whilst in power.

In order to understand what all of this means in practice, consider the process, sketched in Figure 4.1, whereby an idea for a new policy or a change to existing policy may take practical effect. Assume, for example, that, in the interests of fairness (as it perceives it), the executive wishes to abolish the policy that health care should be free at the point of access, replacing it with a sliding scale of charges such that the

---

[17] See Chapter 5, section 2.2, below.   [18] Draft Cabinet Office Manual (February 2010), ch 6.
[19] The terms 'MP' and 'member of Parliament' refer to members of the House of Commons.

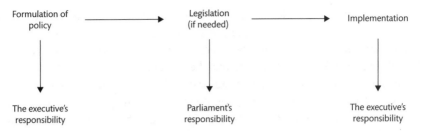

Figure 4.1 How policy changes are effected

unemployed and those on low incomes would pay nothing, while those earning at higher levels would pay for treatment; the fees to be paid by any given individual being related to his income.

If it wishes to see such measures implemented, then the executive's first task is to *formulate the policy* in terms that are specific enough to be capable of being turned into legislation. (At what income level would charges begin to be levied? Would people on higher incomes ever be exempt from charges—for example, if they were to have a very serious or chronic illness? How high should the charges be? Should the charges be prescribed centrally, or should hospitals be allowed to set their own charges, thus introducing competition?)

The *enactment of the legislation* would then be a matter for Parliament: the executive would put its proposals to Parliament in the form of a Bill, but it would be for Parliament to decide whether to enact it as proposed, to insist upon amendments, or to refuse to enact it at all.[20]

If enacted, the *implementation* of the new legislation would be a matter for the executive. For example, it would be for the executive to put in place whatever practical arrangements the legislation stipulated for setting and collecting fees, determining the fee level applicable to individual patients, deciding whether a given patient qualified for exemption from the requirement to pay fees, and so on.

This scheme implies an important division of labour. Although it is for the executive to come up with proposals—and, eventually, to implement whatever arrangements are enshrined in law—the process is punctuated by the involvement of Parliament at the legislative stage. On the face of it, therefore, the executive's ability to get its own way is constrained by the need to obtain parliamentary approval. It is one thing for the executive to propose that legislation along the lines described above is enacted; whether Parliament agrees and is prepared to do as the executive wishes is (it might be thought) a different matter entirely. Parliament might, for example, disagree fundamentally with the executive's suggestion, preferring to retain the principle that health care should be provided free of charge at the point of access; or it might agree with the general policy, but prefer to make everyone pay something, rather than providing free

---

[20] For detailed discussion of how Bills are enacted, see Chapter 5, section 3, below.

health care for certain people; or it might be willing to enact the government's proposals provided that there are safeguards exempting people with chronic illnesses.

The important point is that where the executive needs parliamentary legislation to be enacted in order that its policy may be implemented,[21] Parliament's involvement means that the executive cannot automatically have its way: it has to convince Parliament that its ideas make sense, and it may have to negotiate and make certain compromises in order to persuade Parliament to enact the proposals in some form. While such arrangements are, in a sense, inefficient, in that they prevent the executive from quickly and easily implementing new policies, they reflect the idea that we encountered in the previous chapter that state power must be distributed between different branches of government so as to avoid the hegemony of one branch, thereby guarding against abuse of power.

So much for the theory; the reality is rather different. The British system of parliamentary government means that the executive and legislative branches are, to a significant extent, intertwined in such a way as to place the former in a very powerful position—so powerful that Lord Hailsham, a former Lord Chancellor, argued that the UK's constitutional arrangements reduce to an 'elective dictatorship'.[22] Three interlocking points, all of which we explore more fully in subsequent chapters, are particularly important in terms of understanding why the executive finds itself in such a powerful position.

The first point is that, as noted above, the executive is not directly elected; rather, by convention, the monarch invites the party leader best able to command the confidence of the House of Commons to become (or remain) Prime Minister and form a government. The composition of the *executive* is therefore determined by the outcome of elections to the *legislature*.[23] All members of the executive branch—that is, the Prime Minister, Cabinet Ministers, and junior Ministers—are drawn from Parliament, and since, by convention, most Ministers are members of the House of Commons (rather than the House of Lords), this means that members of the government account for around one sixth of the total membership of the Commons.[24] Second, the party from which the executive is drawn will normally account for more than half of the MPs in the Commons. In the event of a coalition, the governing parties between them will normally have more than half of the MPs.

Third, the government's numerical dominance of the Commons would be unimportant if it were not for the fact that government MPs can generally be relied upon

---

[21] An Act of Parliament is only needed for the implementation of a new policy if the government does not already have the necessary legal powers. However, the general principle that health care must be provided free of charge is enshrined in s 1(3) of the National Health Service Act 2006; the proposals described above could therefore only be implemented if that provision were repealed or amended. We will assume for the time being that this would require an Act of Parliament, but see section 4.2.2 below on 'Henry VIII clauses'.   [22] Lord Hailsham, *The Dilemma of Democracy* (London 1978), ch 20.

[23] See Chapter 5, section 2.2, below on elections.

[24] Up to 95 government Ministers are drawn from the House of Commons (the remainder being members of the Lords): see House of Commons Disqualification Act 1975, s 2. There are 649 MPs in the Commons.

to do as the government wishes. Ministers are required to support government Bills, and although other MPs belonging to the governing party or parties are technically free to vote as they wish, in practice the vast majority tend to support the government. This might be because they agree with it, but might also be because they wish to appear loyal so as to bolster their chances—which are ultimately dependent upon whether they find favour with senior Ministers—of embarking upon a ministerial career. It follows, therefore, that the lack of any clear distinction between the legislative and executive branches within the UK constitution means that there is, in effect, a career ladder leading from the former to the latter that incentivises MPs of the governing party or parties to vote according to the wishes of the government.[25] This, in turn, means that the government can be confident that its Bills will usually get through the House of Commons.[26]

Of course, this does not always happen. For example, government MPs may be willing to rebel if the executive attempts to push through legislation that is especially controversial and that attempts to do things that are felt to be so objectionable as to override MPs' sense of loyalty (self-serving or otherwise). Moreover, the extent to which the government can be certain of getting its own way is heavily dependent upon the size of its majority in the Commons. Historically, the voting system used for UK general elections has often delivered a large overall majority for a single party. For example, in both 1997 and 2001, Labour had 63 per cent of the seats. In contrast, after the 1992 election, the Conservative government had only 52 per cent of the seats: it took only a small number of 'rebel' MPs to side with the opposition parties for a government Bill to be placed in jeopardy. The picture is further complicated if the government takes the form of a coalition between two (or more) parties. Although a coalition government is likely to consist of parties that, between them, account for more than half of the MPs in the Commons (the 2010 Conservative–Liberal Democrat coalition accounts for 56 per cent of the seats), the exercise of control over MPs may be more difficult. This is so not least because partners in coalition governments have to compromise, enhancing the likelihood that the governing parties' 'backbench' MPs (that is, those who are not Ministers) may rebel.

In reality, few government Bills emerge from the parliamentary process unscathed; most are subject to amendments, many of which will be suggested by opposition parties in the House of Commons and also the House of Lords. The key point, however, is that, for the reasons outlined above and explored more fully in subsequent chapters, 'the amendments that survive will with rare exceptions be those promoted or accepted by ministers, sometimes as compromises'.[27] The executive branch is therefore firmly in the driving seat when it comes to enacting legislation, such that it has effective control

---

[25] See further Liaison Committee, *Shifting the Balance: Select Committees and the Executive* (HC 300 1999–2000), [29]–[34].

[26] As we explain in Chapter 5, section 2.3.3, below, although the approval of the House of Lords is also generally needed, this requirement can, in certain circumstances, be dispensed with.

[27] Griffith, 'The Common Law and the Political Constitution' (2001) 117 LQR 42, 54.

of all three parts of the process, outlined in Figure 4.1, whereby policy ideas become practical reality.

> **Q** Do you regard the nature of the relationship, as described above, between the executive and legislative branches as either a strength or a weakness of the UK constitution? Why?

2.6 Executive–judicial relations

What then is the relationship between the government and the judiciary? The first point to note is that while there is a substantial overlap between the government and Parliament, with the government dominating Parliament, there is a strict separation between the government and the judiciary. In order to maintain the integrity of the administration of justice and public confidence, the judiciary must be wholly independent of the government.

Second, while it is the task of the government to govern, it is the role of the judiciary to adjudicate on legal disputes and to provide legally authoritative rulings. Sometimes, these rulings will concern challenges (for example, under the Human Rights Act 1998) to the legality of government decisions. The government is expected to respect the judiciary's rulings and in this way to ensure that government acts in compliance with the rule of law. At the same time, since the courts are themselves bound by the doctrine of parliamentary sovereignty to respect primary legislation, their role is one of interpreting and giving effect to legislation. As the government tends to exert much influence over the content of legislation, it will also exert a degree of influence over how the courts interpret it. So while the government must respect judicial interpretations of legislation, it is always possible for the government to bring forward new proposals to amend legislation in order to reverse a particular judicial decision.[28] It follows that although the judiciary is independent of the government, and although the government must comply with court rulings, the government's influence over the *legislature* renders its relationship with the *judiciary* more subtle and more complex than it might otherwise be.

2.7 The executive in a political constitution

In order to appreciate the constitutional position of the executive, we need to understand the nature of its relationships with the other branches of government; we also need to recognise the political realities that exist underneath constitutional principles such as parliamentary sovereignty and the rule of law. From the executive's perspective, its constitutional role is not necessarily governed by constitutional or legal principles, but by the political imperative to run and manage the country in accordance with

---

[28] We are assuming, for the time being, that Parliament is sovereign in the orthodox sense. For further discussion, see Chapter 5.

the wishes of the electorate. On this approach, at the heart of the British constitution lies the recognition that the government of the day may take any action necessary for the furtherance of the public interest subject to the following caveats.[29] First, the government may not infringe the legal rights of others unless expressly legally authorised to do so. Second, if the government should wish to change the law, whether by adding to its existing legal powers or otherwise, then it must attain the assent of Parliament. Third, any governmental action must comply with applicable EU law and the Human Rights Act 1998.

If this seems to be an unorthodox way of viewing the constitution, that is because it is. This approach places the executive, rather than the courts or Parliament, at the centre of the British constitution. Given the centrality of the executive's role and place within the constitution, this approach might be said to offer a more realistic perspective on what really happens within the constitution. Furthermore, we need to recognise that there is a fundamental difference of approach in how the nature of the British constitution is both understood and conceptualised: is the nature of the constitution fundamentally based on law or politics? Is it a legal or a political constitution? This is a question that often divides constitutional scholars and to which there is no objectively right or wrong answer. Some argue that the constitution is firmly based on legal principles, whereas others argue that it is pre-eminently based on politics and the political relationships between different institutions and actors in the constitution. For the moment, we can note that those who emphasise the role of the courts and Parliament as the pre-eminent actors within the constitution often argue that the constitution is fundamentally based upon legal principles such as the rule of law and parliamentary sovereignty. By contrast, those who emphasise the role of the executive tend to emphasise that the British constitution is, above all, a political constitution—one that is shaped and reshaped by changing political circumstances, and therefore continually on the move.

2.8 **Political and legal accountability of the executive**

Whatever approach is preferred, the centrality of the executive within the constitution, and the power that it possesses, highlights one of the key themes of this book—namely, the importance of holding the executive to account. Governmental effectiveness in making and implementing policy—essentially, getting things done—is, of course, important. But, at the same time, government must be accountable for the exercise of its powers.

Broadly speaking, there are two ways in which the executive can be held to account: legally, by the courts; and politically, by Parliament. The former means that individual claimants may, by issuing judicial review proceedings against government departments, require Ministers to justify their policies, decisions, and actions by reference

---

[29] Griffith, 'The Political Constitution' (1979) 42 MLR 1, 15. See also Foley, *The Politics of the British Constitution* (Manchester 1999).

to the principles of law that courts have developed for the purpose of ensuring good standards of governance. Meanwhile, political accountability might, for example, involve Ministers, including the Prime Minister, being required to submit to questioning by MPs, justify their actions, explain why problems have arisen, and set out how past mistakes will be learned from rather than repeated.

However, the notion that Ministers are accountable for their actions to Parliament raises an obvious paradox. We have already seen that the executive is, at least to a considerable extent, in control of the legislature (or at least of the House of Commons) by virtue of its numerical dominance and the general willingness of government MPs to comply with the wishes of the leaders of the governing party or parties. The precise nature of the difficulties that arise as a result fall to be considered elsewhere,[30] but even leaving the details to one side for now, it is clear that Parliament's capacity to hold the executive to account is necessarily compromised by the dominance of the latter.

This, in turn, raises another of our key themes—namely, the relationship and balance between legal and political notions of constitutionalism.[31] While few people would argue that the executive should be held to account solely by legal, or solely by political, means, there is considerable debate about the extent to which each of these mechanisms should be relied upon. There has been a tendency in recent decades to look increasingly to the courts in order that, by holding the executive legally to account, they may plug the gap that arises as a result of Parliament's limited ability to enforce political accountability. This implies a drift towards a more court-centred approach—something that is not universally welcomed as a positive development. As we explain in Chapter 12, while it is relatively uncontroversial that it is appropriate for courts to rule on obviously legal questions such as whether Ministers have contravened the terms of the legislation under which they purport to be acting, it is not immediately apparent that judges are the right people to decide whether the government is correct to prefer one policy option over another. While unelected and (therefore) independent judges are well placed to make decisions about the propriety of government conduct where there is an objective yardstick by which to measure it, it is arguable that it is ultimately for elected politicians to evaluate the wisdom of what the government is doing where this essentially reduces to making value judgements about the merits of one approach over another.[32] This suggests that political and legal mechanisms for holding the executive to account complement one another, such that both are required within a healthy system of governance.

We explore all of these issues in depth in Chapters 9–18. For the time being, the important points to bear in mind are that the existence of effective ways of holding

---

[30] See Chapter 10 below.   [31] See generally Chapter 2.

[32] For example, in the example given above, it would clearly be appropriate for a court to decide whether a Minister had contravened the new legislation by insisting on payment of fees by a person who, according to the Act, was exempt from the requirement to pay fees. On the other hand, whether, in the first place, it is a good idea to make people pay for health care rather than to fund it out of general taxation is not an objective legal question; rather, it is a policy question—and scrutiny of the position adopted by the government in relation to it is therefore more obviously a matter for political, as distinct from legal, oversight.

the executive to account is imperative, not least because of the uniquely powerful position that it occupies within the UK's constitutional arrangements; that such accountability can be secured via both political and legal means; and that appropriate reliance upon both such forms of accountability is necessary. Thus two of our key themes—the importance of holding the executive to account, and the relationship between legal and political notions of constitutionalism—intersect in this area; exploring the nature and implications of their interaction is something to which we will have to return in a number of contexts.

3. Central government

Having considered the nature of executive power and the constitutional position of the executive in the UK, we now need to analyse in more detail the component parts of the executive. An important theme here concerns the nature of the constitutional rules governing the relationships between the different office-holders. In this respect, much has traditionally been governed by constitutional conventions rather than by legal rules laid down in legislation. In considering the constitutional aspects of the different parts of the executive, we therefore need to recognise that the executive largely inhabits the world of the political constitution, the rules governing the operation of the executive and its relationship with other branches being largely shaped and reshaped by political understandings.[33] For example, the office of Prime Minister is virtually nowhere recognised by legislation; it is almost entirely a creature of convention. So, too, is the Cabinet. However, the fact that the relationships are a product of the political constitution does not mean that conventions are necessarily unwritten or readily dispensable. Indeed, over recent years, it has become increasingly common for conventions to be set down in codes—some of which will be considered below—that are produced and published by the government itself. Furthermore, conventions can only be understood against the political context in which they develop and operate; there can be no better illustration of this than the convention governing the exercise of the monarch's prerogatives.

3.1 The monarch's personal prerogatives

We have already considered the significance of the concept of the Crown, noting that most of the monarch's prerogative powers are actually exercised by, or on the advice of, the executive. But what of the monarch's so-called personal prerogatives? In formal, constitutional terms, the Queen has a number of important constitutional powers that are exercised under the prerogative: for example, the sovereign may

---

[33] On conventions, see generally Chapter 2, section 3.5, above.

appoint anyone to be her Prime Minister, and may appoint and dismiss government Ministers.[34] To what extent does the Queen personally exercise such powers? If, as we have seen above, the concept of the Crown is synonymous with the government of the day, what, if any, power is actually exercised personally by the sovereign? The answer is that the relationship between the Queen and her government, and the exercise of these powers, is governed by the convention that the Queen does not personally command her Ministers; instead, she acts on their advice. In this way, the exercise of such powers supports the symbolism of the monarchy while at the same time ensuring that political power, and with it, responsibility for the exercise of such power, resides with the government.

Consider, for example, the principles concerning the formation of governments. Bearing in mind the possibility (that eventuated) of a 'hung Parliament' in which no party had an overall majority, there was particular focus in the run-up to the 2010 general election on the monarch's role in appointing a Prime Minister. As a result, the conventions in this area were published by the Cabinet Secretary—the most senior civil servant in the country.[35] According to this guidance: 'When a Government or Prime Minister resigns it is for the Monarch to invite the person whom it appears is most likely to be able to command the confidence of the House of Commons to serve as Prime Minister and to form a Government.'[36] It is also emphasised that, in the event of a hung Parliament, 'the expectation is that discussions will take place between political parties on who should form the next Government', but that '[t]he Monarch would not expect to become involved in such discussions'.[37] The value of these conventions lies in ensuring both that government is democratically elected and accountable to Parliament, and that the Queen does not exercise, or even appear to exercise, any political influence. Similarly, the appointment and dismissal of government Ministers is, in practice, a matter purely for the Prime Minister. To adopt Bagehot's famous analysis, the constitution may be divided into two general parts: those dignified parts 'which excite and preserve the reverence of the population'; and the efficient parts—'those by which it, in fact, works and rules'.[38] If so, then the sovereign belongs to the dignified parts, whereas the Prime Minister clearly belongs to its efficient parts.

It is because the conventions or political understandings have been accepted by all concerned that this system of governance has operated so smoothly.[39] If, however, the parties concerned were to decide that they no longer wished to adhere to the conventions—for example, suppose that the Queen did not decide to appoint as Prime Minister the leader of the political party best able to command the confidence of the

---

[34] The monarch has also traditionally been legally free to dissolve Parliament, although this power will be removed if the Fixed-term Parliaments Bill, which is before Parliament at the time of writing, is enacted.

[35] Draft Cabinet Office Manual (London 2010), ch 6.   [36] Draft Cabinet Office Manual, [14].

[37] Draft Cabinet Office Manual, [17].

[38] Bagehot, *The English Constitution* [1867] (Fontana 1993), p 63.

[39] See Bogdanor, *The Monarchy and the Constitution* (Oxford 1995).

House of Commons—then the relationships would break down. Constitutional crisis would ensue, firmer and clearer constitutional rules would be demanded, and there might even be calls for reform of the monarchy itself.

> **Q** Do you regard it as acceptable for the monarch to retain legal powers such as those described in this section? Is the fact that she only exercises them in line with constitutional convention an adequate response to the charge that it is undemocratic for the Queen to be legally empowered to influence such matters as the identity of the Prime Minister?

3.2 **The Prime Minister**

We have already noted that the Prime Minister, as the leader of the government of the day, is the most important politician in the UK. By convention, the Prime Minister is also a member of the House of Commons and the person best able to command the confidence of that House. As the head of the UK government, the Prime Minister is ultimately responsible for its policies and decisions. The Prime Minister also oversees the operation of the civil service and government agencies, appoints members of the government, and is the principal government figure in the House of Commons. The Prime Minister also chairs the Cabinet, selects and dismisses Ministers, and is responsible for the overall organisation of the executive. The office of Prime Minister is almost solely one of convention and political practice. The Prime Minister has few formal legal powers and is only occasionally mentioned specifically in legislation.[40] However, for the most part, the power exercised by the Prime Minister results not from legislation, but from the political influence that the office-holder is able to exert. In other words, the power of the Prime Minister is usually in terms of directing and influencing other Ministers to make decisions and policies in accordance with his wishes.

As the roles and powers of the Prime Minister are not precisely defined in legislation or elsewhere, the post is often what the particular individual who holds it makes of it. It should come as no surprise that being Prime Minister is an exceptionally demanding job. Some previous Prime Ministers, such as Margaret Thatcher (1979–90) and Tony Blair (1997–2007), gained reputations for being strong, dominant Prime Ministers, for not welcoming or accepting dissension from their own views, and for not paying due regard to discussions over policy within the Cabinet. For example, Margaret Thatcher considered herself to be a 'conviction' politician and was not accustomed to yielding to the views of Cabinet colleagues. Such an approach can, of course, raise concerns. As one commentator has noted, during the Thatcher governments, Cabinet members had 'allowed the usual forms of Cabinet government to be displaced by imperious prime

---

[40] For a rare example, see Regulation of Investigatory Powers Act 2000, ss 57 and 59, which authorises the Prime Minister to appoint the Interception of Communications and Intelligence Services Commissioners (on which, see Chapter 10, section 8.3, below).

ministerial rule'.[41] Equally, Tony Blair's prime ministerial style has been characterised as one of 'command and control', with some important governmental decisions
being taken outside of the Cabinet by cliques of senior Ministers and their special
advisers—a feature occasionally described as 'sofa government'.[42] The personal style
of individual Prime Ministers has prompted debate over the extent to which 'prime
ministerial' government has taken over, or even the extent to which there has been
a move toward a British presidency, but without the necessary checks and balances
to constrain such power.[43] Those concerned about such matters will not have taken
comfort from the presidential-style televised debates between the main party leaders
that took place, for the first time in the UK, during the 2010 general election campaign.
On the other hand, other Prime Ministers have gained a reputation for operating in a
more consensual way and for taking more account of Cabinet discussions.

To a large extent, the style adopted by any individual Prime Minister is influenced
not only by the personality of the individual officer-holder, but also by the political
authority of the Prime Minister. This is largely dependent upon the size of the government's majority in the House of Commons: the larger that majority is, and the more
disciplined it is, then the greater the likely authority of the Prime Minister. Conversely,
the smaller the government's Commons majority, then the greater may be the need for
the Prime Minister to adopt a more consensual style of governing. This point applies
more acutely and obviously when the government consists of a coalition between two
or more parties. For example, the Conservative–Liberal Democrat coalition formed
after the 2010 general election adopted a formal protocol under which the Prime
Minister's powers are, in practice, more limited than usual: for example, the appointment of Ministers is the shared responsibility of the Conservative Prime Minister and
the Liberal Democrat Deputy Prime Minster.[44]

In one sense, the debate over the role and power of the Prime Minister is central to
our constitutional arrangements. The Prime Minister has enormous political power
to influence policy, public appointments, the management of the civil service, and
so on. Should the Prime Minister be able to exert so much power? If the office of
Prime Minister has developed into a *de facto* presidency, then there should be appropriate checks and balances. At the same time, the nature of governing has changed
radically over the last hundred years; new challenges have arisen from the complexity of governmental action in the modern age and the pressure on governments to
deliver public services. The basic deal upon which our system of government is based
is that the public elects MPs to the House of Commons, thereby determining who is
the Prime Minister, and which party (or parties) forms the government. The Prime

---

[41] Brazier, 'The Downfall of Margaret Thatcher' (1991) 54 MLR 471, 476.

[42] Hennessy, *The Prime Minister: The Office and Its Holders Since 1945* (London 2000), ch 18.

[43] Foley, *The British Presidency* (Manchester 2000); Allen, *The Last Prime Minister: Being Honest About the UK Presidency* (Thorverton 2003). See also Blick and Jones, *Premiership: The Development, Nature and Power of the Office of the British Prime Minister* (Exeter 2010).

[44] HM Government, *Coalition Agreement for Stability and Reform* (London 2010).

Minister is then able to exercise considerable power for up to five years, albeit that, for two reasons, he is not invulnerable. First, a Prime Minister may fall for internal party reasons. For example, in 1990, Margaret Thatcher was forced to resign as Prime Minister when she lost the support of many of her MPs, and was replaced by another Conservative politician, John Major. Meanwhile, in 2007, Tony Blair stood down as Prime Minister against the background of internal divisions within the Labour Party, and was succeeded by Gordon Brown. Second, there is a long-standing convention that if the government loses a vote of confidence in the Commons, the Prime Minister should resign and a general election should be held. If enacted, the Fixed-term Parliaments Bill[45] will modify this position somewhat: an election will be triggered only if a new government capable of commanding the confidence of the House of Commons cannot be formed within 14 days of a vote of no confidence in the previous administration.[46]

Of course, to say that the Prime Minister exercises considerable power does not imply that he is not personally subject to various accountability processes. The Prime Minister is accountable to the public through general elections and constant media scrutiny and to Parliament through the weekly Prime Minister's questions in the House of Commons; since 2002, the House of Commons Liaison Committee (comprising the chairs of the House's select committees) has regularly heard evidence from the Prime Minister on matters of public policy. Furthermore, while the Prime Minister appoints Cabinet members, it is clear that, on occasion, the Cabinet may hold in check a Prime Minister. However, the effectiveness of some of these methods for holding the Prime Minister to account politically might readily be questioned. The relative infrequency of general elections means that accountability must also attach to the actions of the Prime Minister *during* his term of office. While, in formal terms, Prime Minister's questions in the House of Commons is an exercise in holding the Prime Minister to account, in practice, it has often been described as a 'Punch and Judy' show in which the opposition leaders and other MPs attack the Prime Minister, prompting him to retaliate with the support of his MPs. Furthermore, while the Prime Minister attends meetings of the Liaison Committee, this only occurs on a comparatively infrequent basis.

Q Watch Prime Minister's questions in the House of Commons (it occurs every Wednesday at noon when Parliament is in session and can be viewed online at **http:// www.parliament.uk**). Do you think that it provides an effective forum for holding the Prime Minister to account? Is it desirable for there to be more effective control over the exercise of prime ministerial power? If so, then how could this be achieved?

---

[45] Which is before Parliament at the time of writing.

[46] The Bill also provides that (irrespective of any vote of no confidence) an earlier-than-usual election would also be triggered if two-thirds of MPs were to support a motion to that effect. See further Chapter 5, section 2.2.2, below.

3.3 **Ministers**

According to the Ministers of the Crown Act 1975, the term 'Minister of the Crown' means 'the holder of any office in Her Majesty's government in the United Kingdom, and includes the Treasury...and Defence Council'.[47] Ministers of the Crown are those Ministers who are members of the governing political party and who have been appointed to a political office in the government.

While, formally, Ministers are appointed by the Crown on advice of the Prime Minister, in terms of political practice, the Prime Minister has the ultimate say on who is appointed as a Minister. A strong Prime Minister may be able to decide unilaterally on ministerial appointments, while a weak Prime Minister may have to appease factions within his own party; one who leads a coalition, as noted above, will have to operate collaboratively with the leader of the other party or parties involved when making appointments.

By convention, Ministers are members of either House of Parliament; most are members of the Commons. That Ministers are members of either House of Parliament is important in terms of ministerial responsibility to Parliament; Ministers exercise public power and constitutional convention demands that they are accountable to Parliament for the exercise of such power. By statute, there can be no more than 95 holders of ministerial office in the House of Commons; this rule is designed to prevent the executive from unduly dominating the House of Commons.[48]

There is a clear hierarchy of governmental positions. Ministers are graded in terms of their importance and areas of responsibility. Each of the principal Secretaries of State heads up a government department, sits in the Cabinet, and also in Cabinet committees. The Minister in charge of a department is accountable to Parliament for the exercise of the powers on which the administration of that department depends. For example, the Secretary of State for Health is the senior Minister responsible for health policy. In practice, though, no individual Minister could ever assume sole responsibility for managing and running a large organisation such as a central government department. The basic task of the Secretary of State is to provide political leadership to his department and to be responsible to Parliament and the public for its policy and performance. According to the Ministerial Code, it is desirable that Ministers in charge should devolve to their junior Ministers responsibility for a defined range of departmental work, particularly in relation to Parliament.[49] The legal powers of the Secretary of State are then often delegated to a Minister of State, a Parliamentary Under Secretary, or, as happens far more often, to civil servants. So, for example, the Home Secretary is responsible for the overall work of the Home Office, but there are also three Ministers of State (respectively responsible for security, immigration, and policing) and a Parliamentary Under Secretary of State

---

[47] Ministers of the Crown Act 1975, s 8(1). See generally Brazier, *Ministers of the Crown* (Oxford 1997).

[48] House of Commons Disqualification Act 1975, s 2(1).

[49] Cabinet Office, *Ministerial Code* (2010), [4.6].

(responsible for equalities). In practice, most governmental powers are exercised by civil servants.

In some governments, there is also a *Deputy Prime Minister*. There is no legal or constitutional requirement for such a post, but its existence is sometimes politically expedient. For example, throughout Tony Blair's time as Prime Minister, John Prescott was Deputy Prime Minister, the thinking being that Prescott would be able to command the support of traditional elements of the Labour Party that Blair, on his own, may not have been able to. Meanwhile, in the coalition government formed in 2010, the leader of the Liberal Democrats—the smaller of the two parties involved in the government—was appointed Deputy Prime Minister in recognition of the partnership between that party and the Conservative Party. The powers and responsibilities of the Deputy Prime Minister are not fixed: the role of any particular holder of that office will depend upon the political reasons for appointing a Deputy Prime Minister. For example, as part of the coalition deal entered into following the 2010 election, the Deputy Prime Minister was given particular responsibility for reform of the political system.

Next, we turn to the *whips*. Their role is to ensure, wherever possible, that the government wins votes in the Commons and the Lords. They do this by 'encouraging' MPs and peers who are members of the governing party or parties to vote with the government. If a parliamentary vote is subject to a 'three-line whip', then backbench MPs must vote with the government or else risk expulsion from the governing political party or parties.

Special mention might be made of the constitutional position of the *Lord Chancellor*. For centuries, the office of the Lord Chancellor occupied a unique place in the constitution. The Lord Chancellor was a member of the government and in charge of the Lord Chancellor's Department, speaker of the House of Lords, and head of the judiciary. The Lord Chancellor could also sit as a member of the Appellate Committee of the House of Lords and give opinions as a Law Lord. By convention, it was assumed that the post was not to be occupied by a 'career politician' in search of political advancement, but by an individual with a legal background who would know how to balance the several different roles of an office that, in formal terms, appeared to offend the principle of the separation of powers. However, in the Constitutional Reform Act 2005, Parliament legislated to change this position in order to establish a clearer separation of powers. The Lord Chancellor is no longer the head of the judiciary and can no longer sit as a judge. Unusually for appointment as a Minister, there is, under s 2 of the 2005 Act, a statutory qualification for appointment to the office of Lord Chancellor: a prospective office-holder cannot be recommended for appointment unless he appears to the Prime Minister to be qualified by experience either as a Minister of the Crown, a member of either House of Parliament, a qualifying practitioner, a teacher of law in a university, or other experience that the Prime Minister considers relevant.[50] The

---

[50] See further Lord Windlesham, 'The Constitutional Reform Act 2005: Ministers, Judges and Constitutional change' [2005] PL 806 and 'The Constitutional Reform Act 2005: The Politics of Constitutional Reform' [2006] PL 35.

principal role of the Lord Chancellor is now heading up the Ministry of Justice, which he does in his capacity as Secretary of State for Justice.

Another Minister of whom mention ought to be made is the *Attorney-General*. The Attorney-General has three main functions: as the government's chief legal adviser; as responsible for the criminal justice system, such as superintending the Crown Prosecution Service and Serious Fraud Office; and as the guardian of the public interest. As regards the provision of legal advice, the Law Officers (the Attorney-General and the Solicitor-General) must be consulted in good time before the government is committed to critical decisions involving legal considerations.[51] At the same time, the Attorney-General is a member of the government who takes the party whip and attends, but is not a member of, the Cabinet. The office therefore combines both legal and political responsibilities, which can sometimes conflict. For example, recent controversies have concerned the Attorney-General's legal advice to the government as to the legality of the invasion of Iraq (was the Attorney-General placed under political pressure to produce legal advice favourable to the government's intention of invading Iraq?) and the Attorney-General's decision to halt a criminal investigation by the Serious Fraud Office into whether Saudi officials were bribed in order to win an order for British arms (did the Attorney-General drop the investigation because of political pressure from the Prime Minister? If so, then what of the rule of law?).[52] Controversies such as these have raised concerns as to political bias and lack of independence, and prompted calls for reform of the office by, for example, dividing up responsibility for the Attorney-General's various functions.[53]

3.4 **Ministerial standards**

It is clear from what has been said so far that Ministers find themselves in positions of great power and influence. It stands to reason that those in such positions should be required to adhere to certain standards of probity in order to ensure that the business of government is conducted in a way that is transparently fair and in the public interest. Such standards are contained in the Ministerial Code issued by the Prime Minister. Since 1997, the Code has been updated regularly, the current version having been issued following the 2010 election.[54] The Code is intended as a helpful guide to the principles and practices underpinning the way in which Ministers should discharge their duties. The Code is not therefore a set of legally binding rules possessing the force of law. Nevertheless, Ministers are clearly expected to follow the Code fully. The Code is then a government, rather than a parliamentary, document and is therefore capable of subsequent amendment by the government. At the same time, some aspects

---

[51] *Ministerial Code*, [2.10].

[52] The latter decision was unsuccessfully challenged by way of judicial review: *R (Corner House Research) v Director of the Serious Fraud Office* [2008] UKHL 60, [2009] 1 AC 756.

[53] House of Commons Constitutional Affairs Committee, *Constitutional Role of the Attorney-General* (HC 306 2006–07).   [54] *Ministerial Code*.

of the Code—particularly those parts of it concerning ministerial accountability to Parliament—have been approved by a resolution of Parliament.

According to the Ministerial Code, Ministers are expected to behave in a way that upholds the highest standards of propriety. The Code is to be read against the background of the overarching duty on Ministers to comply with the law, including international law, and to uphold the administration of justice and to protect the integrity of public life. Ministers are expected to observe the seven principles of public life: selflessness, integrity, objectivity, accountability, openness, honesty, and leadership.

The most important principles of ministerial conduct to which the Code requires adherence relate to the doctrine of ministerial responsibility to Parliament.[55] Earlier in this chapter, we explained the meaning of this concept in outline, and we examine it in detail in Chapter 10. However, the Ministerial Code also specifies other standards. Ministers must ensure that no conflict arises, or appears to arise, between their public duties and their private interests. They should not accept any gift or hospitality that might, or might reasonably appear to, compromise their judgement or place them under an improper obligation. Ministers in the House of Commons must keep separate their roles as Minister and constituency member. Ministers must not use government resources for party-political purposes. Ministers must also uphold the political impartiality of the Civil Service and not ask civil servants to act in any way that would conflict with the Civil Service Code.[56] In more detailed provisions, the Code elaborates on these general principles.

One particular issue as to the operation of the Ministerial Code concerns the question of investigating alleged breaches of the Code by Ministers and of its enforcement—both of which are ultimately matters for the Prime Minister. But if the public is to have confidence that Ministers adhere to the standards of propriety contained in the Code, then should there not also be a mechanism for investigating alleged infringements of the Code that is itself manifestly independent of the government? On the other hand, it is said that the Prime Minister must be the ultimate judge of the standards of behaviour expected of Ministers and the appropriate consequences of a breach of those standards: Ministers only remain in office for as long as they retain the confidence of the Prime Minister. Furthermore, the Prime Minister is ultimately accountable to Parliament. To introduce an independent investigatory mechanism to determine breaches of the Code and any sanction would weaken this core principle. It would also constrain the Prime Minister's ability to make what are ultimately political judgements about the conduct of Ministers by introducing a quasi-judicial element into what are essentially matters of political practice. Nevertheless, if there is no independent investigatory mechanism, the risk is that the news media, with its voracious appetite for stories of political impropriety, may replace ordinary due process and place Ministers against whom allegations have been made, but not proved, either

---

[55] *Collective* responsibility is discussed in the next section.

[56] And that Code must itself require civil servants to act in a politically neutral manner: Constitutional Reform and Governance Act 2010, s 7(2).

under pressure to resign or make their discharge of their governmental duties acutely difficult.

Such arguments culminated in the recognition that a mechanism was needed whereby complaints could be independently investigated, in order to promote public confidence, but without undermining the Prime Minister's right to decide whether a Minister has breached the Code.[57] In 2006, the Prime Minister therefore created the post of Independent Adviser on Ministers' Interests. The post-holder has two responsibilities: first, to provide an independent check and source of advice to government Ministers on the handling of their private interests, in order to avoid conflict between those interests and their ministerial responsibilities; second, to investigate—when the Prime Minister, advised by the Cabinet Secretary, so decides—allegations that individual Ministers may have breached the Code. This has been welcomed as a positive step forward, as it enables an independent person with appropriate expertise both to advise Ministers and to investigate their conduct. However, at the same time, the post also has some limitations. The Independent Adviser is not free to instigate his own investigations, but may only act if invited to do so by the Prime Minister. Findings of investigations will not necessarily be published. Furthermore, as the Independent Adviser is appointed by the Prime Minister and dependent on the government for staff and assistance, the post cannot be described as being fully independent.[58]

Q Is it appropriate for the standards that Ministers are expected to observe to be set by the Prime Minister? Should there be a fully independent office to investigate alleged breaches of the Ministerial Code?

3.5 The Cabinet

The Cabinet is the supreme directing authority of British government, which works by integrating what would otherwise be 'a heterogeneous collection of ministers, officers and authorities exercising a mass of apparently unrelated miscellaneous functions'.[59] In other words, in a plural executive consisting of various different departments, the Cabinet, as the supreme decision-making body, is a force for ensuring unity within government. Like the executive, the Cabinet is unknown to the law and extra-constitutional; it is, again, a creature of convention. So, the Cabinet itself has no legal powers: they are held by Secretaries of State. However, a key doctrine or constitutional norm is that members of the Cabinet have collective responsibility to Parliament, so all members are bound to support Cabinet decisions.

The Cabinet normally meets once a week and is chaired by the Prime Minister. The principal business of the Cabinet consists of resolving questions that significantly

---

[57] House of Commons Public Administration Select Committee, *The Ministerial Code: The Case for Independent Investigation* (HC 1457 2005–06).

[58] House of Commons Public Administration Select Committee, *Investigating the Conduct of Ministers* (HC 381 2007–08).   [59] Jennings, *Cabinet Government* (Cambridge 1959), p 90.

engage the collective responsibility of the government, because they raise major issues of policy or because they are of critical importance to the public, and questions on which there is an unresolved argument between government departments.[60] Matters wholly within the responsibility of a single Minister and which do not significantly engage collective responsibility need not be brought before the Cabinet or to a ministerial Committee unless the Minister wishes to inform his colleagues or to have their advice.[61] The role of the Cabinet is, then, to make the most important policy decisions and to resolve differences within government. The whole premise of the Cabinet system is that of collective responsibility. This means that while Ministers are able to discuss policy options in the Cabinet, once a decision has been made, all Ministers must then agree to that decision and defend it irrespective of their personal views. As the Ministerial Code explains, collective responsibility, when it applies

> requires that Ministers should be able to express their views frankly in the expectation that they can argue freely in private while maintaining a united front when decisions have been reached. This in turn requires that the privacy of opinions expressed in Cabinet and ministerial Committees, including correspondence, should be maintained.[62]

If a Minister is unable to agree to a decision made by the Cabinet, then he should resign from the government. For example, when the Blair government decided to invade Iraq in 2003, Robin Cook, then leader of the House of Commons, decided to resign from the government because he did not agree with this policy.[63] Alternatively, Ministers may simply hold their tongue and leak their disagreement to the media, ensuring that it is anonymously reported.

Like all conventions, however, collective responsibility is not rigid. Although the coalition government formed after the 2010 general election has made it clear that the principle of collective responsibility applies to it,[64] it has always been the case that the doctrine can be suspended in relation to specific issues. For example, the coalition agreement left it open for the Conservatives and the Liberal Democrats to adopt conflicting public positions on electoral reform.[65] It also made specific provision for the government to put forward proposals for a new nuclear energy programme, but for Liberal Democrat MPs to abstain and for a Liberal Democrat member of the coalition to speak against the proposal.[66]

Whether the Cabinet really does possess the decision-making power that is normally attributed to it has been widely questioned. With the growth in prime ministerial power, concerns have commonly been expressed that Cabinet may often operate as a 'rubber stamp' to approve important decisions already made elsewhere. For example, during the Blair government, Cabinet meetings were brief and took few real decisions,

---

[60] *Ministerial Code*, [2.2].   [61] *Ministerial Code*, [2.4].   [62] *Ministerial Code*, [2.1].

[63] Cook, *The Point of Departure* (London 2003).

[64] HM Government, *Coalition Agreement for Stability and Reform* (London 2010), [2.1].

[65] HM Government, *The Coalition: Our Programme for Government* (London 2010), p 27.

[66] *The Coalition: Our Programme for Government*, p 17.

because the Prime Minister's practice had been to take important decisions before-hand that were then announced to the Cabinet.[67] In effect, the role of the Cabinet is inseparable from the style adopted by the Prime Minister. It follows that if the Prime Minister is weak (for example, due to a small majority) or if there is a coalition government (which demands a more collaborative approach), the Cabinet is likely to assume a more prominent role.

However, there are other reasons for the declining importance of Cabinet. One is the development of ministerial committees and subcommittees. Given the mass of decisions for which government is responsible, it is simply not practicable to expect a single Cabinet to make all policy decisions. In practice, it is necessary to have a number of other bodies that have responsibility for particular policy areas. There are currently 15 ministerial committees and subcommittees.[68] Prominent among these are the National Security Council, which coordinates security policy, and the Coalition Committee. The latter meets 'weekly, or as required, to manage the business and priorities of the Government and the implementation and operation of the Coalition agreement'.[69] Ministerial committees and subcommittees clearly have an important role to play: they relieve pressure on the Cabinet by settling as much government business as possible at a lower level or by clarifying the issues and defining points of disagreement. They also support the principle of collective responsibility by ensuring that, while an important issue may not reach Cabinet itself, the decision made will be considered in a way that makes sure that the government as a whole can properly be expected to accept responsibility for it.

3.6 Government departments

We have seen that the executive does not exist as a single legal entity, but there are also many practical senses in which it does not function as a single organisation. It is arguably best thought of as a federation of central government departments, each of which has its particular responsibilities.[70] In other words, the executive is plural rather than unitary: far from being monolithic, it is made up of a number of large governmental organisations—government departments—each administering their own areas of policy. As Mount has observed: '[T]he loose-baronial nature of the system is not something accidental or fleeting; it is inherent. This is the reality of day-to-day executive power.'[71] Furthermore, each department itself will comprise a number of different internal organisations, such as front-line delivery agencies or other agencies that operate at 'arm's length' from Ministers. In short, the British government consists of a complex and changing Byzantine structure through which few can pick their way with any certainty.

---

67 See Foster, 'Cabinet Government in the Twentieth Century' (2004) 67 MLR 753, 766.
68 Cabinet Office, *Cabinet Committee System* (London 2010).   69 *Cabinet Committee System*.
70 Sir William Armstrong quoted in Hennessy, *Whitehall* (London 2001), p 380.
71 Mount, *The British Constitution Now* (London 1992), p 156.

The arcane and pragmatic nature of the governmental system is illustrated by the fact that there is, in law, no definition of the term 'government department'. Government departments owe their establishment, organisation, and powers to two principal sources of law: legislation and the prerogative. There is no overarching constitutional framework for government departments. In constitutional terms, government departments do not generally seem to exist as distinct entities in their own right because statutory and prerogative powers are usually conferred upon the Secretary of State rather than the department itself. Instead, departments have developed on an ad hoc basis over time. The upshot of this is that there is no overall coherent pattern of government departments; instead, the constitutional and legal position of government departments is characterised by pragmatic arrangements rather than consistent principle.[72]

The departments of state headed up by Cabinet Ministers may be classified in a number of different ways.[73] First, there are what might be termed 'central' government departments (central not in the sense that they are part of central as opposed to local government, but in the sense that they affect all government action in one way or another). Key among these is HM Treasury, which is responsible for formulating and implementing the government's financial and economic policy. As such, it determines matters such as taxation, public borrowing, and public spending, and is thus the most powerful government department. As a former Prime Minister, Harold Wilson, once noted: 'Whichever party is in office, the Treasury is in power'.[74] Why is this the case? It is simply because virtually all governmental action requires resources, which the Treasury controls. The Minister responsible for the Treasury, the Chancellor of the Exchequer, is often regarded as second in importance only to the Prime Minister.[75] From 1998 to 2010, the Treasury's influence was augmented through its establishment of public service agreements with individual departments, setting out targets for the delivery of public services.[76]

The other principal central department is the Cabinet Office, which, with the Treasury, constitutes the 'head office' of government. The Cabinet Office was formed in 1916 to record Cabinet proceedings and to transmit decisions to relevant government departments. However, given the pressure on modern governments and the complexity of public business, the Cabinet Office now sits at the centre of government in the middle of an extensive and intricate web of other government agencies.[77] The stated aims of the Cabinet Office are to 'support the Prime Minister and the Cabinet'; to help to ensure 'effective development, coordination and implementation of policy and operations across all government departments'; and to 'ensure the Civil Service

---

[72] See Jordan, *The British Administrative System: Principles Versus Practice* (London 1994).

[73] Hennessy, p 381.   [74] Quoted in Sampson, *The Changing Anatomy of Britain* (London 1982).

[75] This was certainly so when Gordon Brown was Chancellor in Tony Blair's administration, the existence of a Deputy Prime Minister notwithstanding.   [76] See further Chapter 11, section 3.2, below.

[77] See House of Lords Select Committee on the Constitution, *The Cabinet Office and the Centre of Government* (HL 30 2009–10).

provides the most effective and efficient support to Government to help it meet its objectives'.[78]

Second, there are those departments that deal with policy concerning overseas and defence matters: the Foreign and Commonwealth Office, the Department for International Development, and the Ministry of Defence. Third, other departments concern social policy—the Departments for Work and Pensions; Health; Communities and Local Government; Education; Culture, Media and Sport; and the Government Equalities Office. Fourth, there are departments for economic policy—the Departments for Business, Innovation and Skills; Transport; Environment, Food and Rural Affairs; and Energy and Climate Change. Fifth, there are the territorial departments: the Northern Ireland Office, the Scotland Office, and the Wales Office. Finally, the Home Office, the Ministry of Justice, and the Attorney-General's Office have responsibility for internal affairs, the legal system, and the administration of justice.

While Ministers head up government departments, the actual management of the department is entrusted to its Permanent Secretary, the most senior civil servant in the department. Ministers decide on policies, and set strategic objectives and priorities, while the Permanent Secretary chairs the department's board to ensure that the department delivers those objectives. The Permanent Secretary is, as the department's accounting officer, accountable to Ministers for the department's performance, organisation, and delivery; and to Parliament for the effectiveness, efficiency, and propriety of spending by the department.[79] Below the level of Permanent Secretary, various grades of civil servant undertake the vast majority of the work within a government department.

Ensuring the effective government of a country is a highly problematic enterprise. In the UK, one particular challenge has always been to ensure that different government departments work together effectively. However, the 'departmental cultures' of different government departments can become very deeply engrained and this can sometimes lead to difficulties when the government needs to deal with policy issues that cut across several departments' areas of responsibility: individual departments may not necessarily agree on how that issue should be handled or which department should bear the cost of dealing with it. Indeed, it is not unknown for different units within the *same* government departments to fail to cooperate with each other; as an example, consider the failure of the Home Office to deport foreign national prisoners in 2006. This major operational failure arose because of a lack of coordination between two Home Office agencies—one responsible for immigration and the other for prisons—and led to the resignation of the then Home Secretary.[80] This episode illustrates an important aspect of how government actually operates. It has become customary, from one perspective, to view the executive and the office of the Prime

---

[78] http://www.cabinetoffice.gov.uk

[79] HM Treasury, *Managing Public Money* (London 2007), ch 3.

[80] House of Commons Home Affairs Committee, *Immigration Control* (HC 775 2005–06).

Minister as a bastion of enormous executive power. However, from another perspective, one of the major challenges for the Prime Minister, and the government as a whole, is to ensure that government departments work together to ensure that policy is implemented effectively. In short, while government should be held to account for its actions, it is important not to lose sight of the fact that effective governance is, at the best of times, a highly elusive endeavour.

3.7 **Machinery of government changes**

One important issue concerns 'machinery of government' changes—the allocation and reallocation of functions between departments—and the degree of public scrutiny attached to such changes. As the Prime Minister is responsible for the overall organisation of the executive and the allocation of functions between Ministers, he is responsible for machinery of government changes.[81] Such changes typically involve the reallocation of responsibilities between departments; they may also involve creating new departments and abolishing or rebranding existing ones. There are many reasons why such things might be done. First, it may simply be that existing structures are not considered to be fit for purpose. For example, following the Home Office's difficulties in deporting foreign national prisoners in 2006, the Prime Minister in 2007 decided to strip the Home Office of responsibility for the Prison Service, giving that function to the Ministry of Justice.[82] A reduced Home Office, meanwhile, would focus on its core functions of crime, terrorism, and immigration. Second, the reprioritisation of particular policy areas may be felt to necessitate departmental reorganisation—for example, to provide (or at least to give the impression of) greater institutional focus on pressing issues. For example, in 2008, a new government department, the Department of Energy and Climate Change, was created. Third, machinery of government changes may be driven by political considerations such as the need to provide given individuals with appropriate portfolios. This may have been a reason for the creation in 1997 of a new 'super-department' (since disbanded) known as the Department of the Environment, Transport, and Regions, overall responsibility for which was given to the then Deputy Prime Minister.

In law, changes of this nature are relatively easy to accomplish. Functions conferred on 'the Secretary of State' can be exercised by any Secretary of State, and the Prime Minister can redistribute the responsibility for exercising them from one Secretary of State to another administratively. In order to make related, consequential changes, the Ministers of the Crown Act 1975 also gives the Queen in Council statutory authority to make changes in relation to Secretaries of State by Transfer of Functions Orders made under that Act. The government can transfer to any Minister any functions previously exercisable by another; dissolve a government department and transfer its functions to any Minister; and direct that functions of any Minister of the Crown

---

[81] *Ministerial Code*, [4.1].   [82] Formerly the Department for Constitutional Affairs.

shall be exercisable concurrently with another Minister of the Crown, or shall cease to be so exercisable.[83] When the Prime Minister wishes to reallocate governmental functions between different Ministers, a Transfer of Functions Order is laid before Parliament and enacted in order to give effect to the necessary changes in the government machinery.

The advantage of this is that any changes can be made quickly; the procedure is designed to combine flexibility and speed. However, at the same time, the Prime Minister can effectively make almost any change to the overall structure of government at will with little scrutiny by Parliament. This is concerning, since such changes are not unimportant: the departmental structure of government necessarily affects its capacity to operate effectively and efficiently. Furthermore, structural changes are not cost-free—they may involve considerable disruption to normal business, for one thing. It has been reported that, between 2005 and 2009, there were over 90 reorganisations of central government departments and their associated agencies at a cost of just under £200 million a year.[84]

Against this background, the Public Administration Select Committee has argued that machinery of government changes under the Ministers of the Crown Act 1975 do not allow for sufficient political scrutiny, because there is no need for a parliamentary vote or even a debate over the merits of a proposed change. There have been no parliamentary debates or votes on such orders since 1982. Furthermore, such orders are normally laid some time after the changes come into effect. A machinery of government change will be accompanied by a ministerial written statement to Parliament, but this is merely to inform Parliament of the change and does not allow for meaningful scrutiny of the merits or otherwise of the change.[85] As a former Home Secretary has noted, it 'has never been the practice of Administrations to make oral statements on the machinery of government'.[86]

Given the lack of parliamentary scrutiny of such decisions, the Public Administration Select Committee has recommended that Parliament ought to have the opportunity to debate and vote on machinery of government changes.[87] If Parliament had a greater role in scrutinising such changes, then it could have some input into assessing whether or not any proposed change was desirable; it would also require government both to explain and justify proposed changes. However, the government resisted any alteration to the procedure by which such changes are effected, one of its principal concerns being that, constitutionally and legally, the organisation and functions of a government department are fundamentally a reflection of the responsibilities of the Minister in

---

[83] Ministers of the Crown Act 1975, s 1.

[84] National Audit Office, *Reorganising Central Government* (HC 452 2009–10).

[85] House of Commons Public Administration Select Committee, *Machinery of Government Changes* (HC 672 2006–07). See also House of Commons Public Administration Select Committee, *Machinery of Government Changes: A Follow-up Report* (HC 160 2007–08) and (HC 514 2007–08).

[86] Hansard HC Debs, vol 458, col 1641, 29 March 2007 (Dr John Reid).

[87] House of Commons Public Administration Select Committee, *Machinery of Government Changes* (HC 672 2006–07).

charge of the department. As the Prime Minister is responsible for the overall organisation of the executive and for appointing Cabinet members, greater parliamentary control over the organisation of government could then effectively mean parliamentary control over the organisation of the Cabinet. While the government resisted allowing Parliament to veto such changes, it did commit itself to facilitating greater parliamentary scrutiny by making Ministers available to answer questions by Parliament on such changes *after* they have taken place.[88] The government, via the Cabinet Office, has also produced 'best practice' guidance. While this does not limit the Prime Minister's freedom in this sphere, it does acknowledge that such changes should not be undertaken lightly and that 'making existing mechanisms work should be a first priority'.[89]

> **Q** Should Parliament have a greater role in scrutinising machinery of government changes? Does the current system promote effective parliamentary scrutiny of such changes?

3.8 Civil servants

Civil servants are the permanent administrators who implement government policy; without them, it would be impossible for government to operate. Understandably, given the scale and complexity of government, there are different grades of civil servant. The most senior civil servant, the Cabinet Secretary, has overall responsibility for ensuring that the Civil Service provides effective and efficient support to the Prime Minister and the government, and is also Permanent Secretary of the Cabinet Office whose overarching purpose is 'making government work better'.[90] Each government department has a Permanent Secretary—a senior civil servant responsible for its management. Beneath them, there are many grades of civil servant going down to the 'front-line' officials. There are currently around half a million civil servants (in addition to the many other public sector workers, such as teachers and nurses).

Constitutionally, civil servants are servants of the Crown. However, as we have seen, the Crown's executive powers are exercised by the government of the day. This means that the core function of the Civil Service is implementing the policies of the government. The constitutional line of accountability works as follows: the electorate elects MPs to the House of Commons, the political composition of the Commons determines who forms the government, the government is then assisted by the Civil Service, Ministers are accountable to Parliament and civil servants are accountable to Ministers. As the Civil Service Code explains:

> The Civil Service is an integral and key part of the government of the United Kingdom. It supports the government of the day in developing and implementing its policies, and

---

[88] House of Commons Public Administration Select Committee, *Machinery of Government Changes: Government Response to the Committee's Seventh Report of 2006–07* (HC 90 2007–08).

[89] Cabinet Office, *Machinery of Government Changes: Best Practice Handbook* (London 2010), p 7.

[90] http://www.cabinetoffice.gov.uk

in delivering public services. Civil servants are accountable to Ministers, who in turn are accountable to Parliament.[91]

The Civil Service is a largely permanent service in which civil servants are expected to serve whichever political party forms the government of the day. The tradition of a permanent, independent, and politically neutral civil service in which appointments are made on merit rather than as political patronage dates back to the Northcote Trevelyan Report on the civil service published in 1854.[92]

The core values of the Civil Service are now prescribed by statute[93] and reflected in the Civil Service Code.[94] These are integrity (putting the obligations of public service above personal interests), honesty (being truthful and open) objectivity (basing advice and decisions on rigorous analysis of the evidence), and impartiality (acting solely according to the merits of the case and serving equally well governments of different political persuasions).

However, it is questionable whether the role of civil servants is really limited to merely implementing their Minister's wishes. On the one hand, the traditional role of the Civil Service is that of 'speaking truth unto power'—that is, telling Ministers what can and cannot be delivered. On the other hand, in reality, the Civil Service may often possess considerable power both to make and implement policy. For example, a former Home Secretary, David Blunkett, observes that senior civil servants have frequently told Ministers that 'Department policy is this' rather than that 'Department policy is what Ministers, on behalf of the government, say it is so long as it is in line with legislation, the stated government policy and/or the party manifesto'.[95] Furthermore, the reality is that civil servants, even middle-ranking ones, are heavily involved in policy-making over which there may be little, if any, ministerial supervision. Therefore, the chain linking Parliament, Ministers, and civil servants, upon which the doctrine of ministerial responsibility is based, may often be rather weak. The reality behind the fiction is that civil servants do make policy over which there may be little ministerial supervision and for which Ministers may not be held responsible in Parliament.

Ministers may be said to form the 'temporary' government—they come and go (sometimes very often); by contrast, the Civil Service is part of the 'permanent' government. It is therefore perhaps not really surprising if civil servants often possess some degree of power in both making and implementing policy. In practice, no Minister ever exercises full control over every aspect of work going on within a governmental department—government is just too large and too complex. The Minister's role is then normally to provide political leadership—to define the general course of action, while the civil servants consider the most appropriate and effective means of giving effect to policy. For example, it has been argued that civil servants work under the

---

[91] Civil Service Code, [1].   [92] *Report on the Organisation of the Permanent Civil Service* (1854).
[93] Constitutional Reform and Governance Act 2010, s 7(4).   [94] Civil Service Code, [2].
[95] House of Commons Public Administration Select Committee, *Politics and Administration: Ministers and Civil Servants* (HC 122 2006–07), [36].

twin principles of 'improvised expertise' and 'invited authority'.[96] Improvised expertise means that, in a generalist Civil Service, in which officials often change to different types of work, officials are usually good at acquiring quickly an expertise in the particular policy area to which they have been moved. Meanwhile, invited authority implies that Ministers usually have little time to think through how to turn desirable, although vague, goals into concrete administrative programmes; civil servants inevitably have to do much policy work in giving effect to the wishes of politicians.

This is, of course, not to imply that the Civil Service is always effective in implementing policy. Consider, again, the Home Office's failure in 2006 to consider for deportation foreign national prisoners. An important reason for this failure was significant weaknesses in departmental management within the Home Office; the Home Secretary subsequently declared that the department was 'not fit for purpose'.[97]

Some important lessons can be learned from this and other episodes of governmental failure. First, the nature of the relationship between Ministers and civil servants has traditionally been unwritten. However, it is apparent that, during the foreign national prisoner episode, relations between Ministers and civil servants, had, to some extent, broken down. This, together with the importance of the tasks entrusted to the Home Office, highlighted the need for a clearer demarcation of the respective responsibilities of Ministers and civil servants. As a result, the Home Office issued a 'compact' between Ministers and the Home Office Board that provides that Ministers are responsible for overall strategy and policy, while officials are responsible for the delivery of that strategy and policies.[98] Governmental failure and a breakdown of Minister–civil servant relations thus produced a more formal agreement concerning the nature of those relations—albeit one that remains at the level of formal written convention, rather than legally binding rules enacted by statute. In that sense, it reflects the more general trend that we have detected in this section: the codification or formalisation of conventions previously unwritten—a trend also illustrated by the Ministerial Code and the Draft Cabinet Office Manual.

Second, what of the accountability of the Civil Service? Is this adequately ensured by virtue of the facts that civil servants are accountable to Ministers, who in turn are accountable to Parliament? Partly because of failures such as that described above and partly because of Ministers' desires that the Civil Service be able to deliver public services effectively, the Cabinet Secretary in 2005 announced a new process by which departments would be held to account—known as 'capability reviews'.[99] Such reviews have been undertaken not by Parliament or Ministers, but by review teams comprising individuals from the business and public sectors with experience in managing large

---

[96] Page and Jenkins, *Policy Bureaucracy: Government with a Cast of Thousands* (Oxford 2005).

[97] House of Commons Home Affairs Committee, *Immigration Control* (HC 775 2005–06), [4]. Similar problems have been evident in other government agencies such as the Child Support Agency and the Rural Payments Agency. See House of Commons Environment, Food and Rural Affairs Select Committee, *The Rural Payments Agency and the Implementation of the Single Payment Scheme* (HC 107 2006–07).

[98] See Home Office, *Home Office Departmental Framework* (London 2007), annex B.

[99] Cabinet Secretary, *Capability Reviews: Refreshing the Model of Accountability* (London 2009).

organisations. They have examined the effectiveness and capability of the Civil Service to deliver pubic services, the overarching aim being to achieve a Civil Service that is better at delivery. An important point arises here in terms of one of our principal themes—the processes through which government is held to account. We distinguished above between political and legal accountability, but capability reviews cannot be classified as belonging to either category; rather, we might understand them as a form of administrative accountability focusing not upon the desirability of political judgements or the legality of public decisions, but upon the effectiveness of the government machine in delivering public services. A related point is that as the challenges facing government have changed, so too has it become necessary to institute different forms of accountability. The traditional form of political accountability—Ministers being responsible to Parliament—is insufficient by itself, given the size and complexity of modern government, and so must be supplemented by other accountability processes.

Since its inception, the Civil Service has been managed by the government under the royal prerogative—this despite the original recommendation of the Northcote Trevelyan Report in 1854 that the Civil Service should have a statutory basis, not least in order that its core principles and values may be enshrined in law. This has now finally been done.[100] The Constitutional Reform and Governance Act 2010 places the Civil Service on a statutory footing. Among other things, the legislation requires the Civil Service Code to be laid before Parliament, and to provide for civil servants to act with integrity, honesty, objectivity, and impartiality.[101]

3.9 **Special advisers**

Special advisers are employed to help Ministers on matters in relation to which the work of government and the work of the governing party or parties overlap—an area in which it would be inappropriate for permanent civil servants to become involved. The Code of Conduct for special advisers explains that the rationale for such advisers is that they provide an additional source of advice for the Minister, from a standpoint that is more politically committed and politically aware than that which a civil servant could provide.[102] Special advisers provide assistance to Ministers on the development of government policy and its presentation.[103] They are also able to represent Ministers' views on government policy to the media with a degree of political commitment that would not be possible for the permanent Civil Service.[104] In recognition of their political allegiance to the governing party or parties, special advisers are exempt from the normal requirements to behave impartially and objectively.[105]

---

[100] For background, see Ministry of Justice, *The Governance of Britain* (Cm 7170 2007), [40]–[48]; House of Commons Public Administration Select Committee, *A Draft Civil Service Bill: Completing the Reform* (HC 128 2003–04).   [101] Section 7(4).

[102] Cabinet Office, *Code of Conduct for Special Advisers* (London 2010), [2].

[103] *Code of Conduct for Special Advisers*, [13].   [104] *Code of Conduct for Special Advisers*, [16].

[105] Constitutional Reform and Governance Act 2010, s 7(5).

Under the Ministerial Code, with the exception of the Prime Minister (who has 18 special advisers)[106] and Deputy Prime Minister (who has four), Cabinet Ministers may each appoint up to two special advisers. The Prime Minister may also authorise the appointment of one special adviser by Ministers who are not Cabinet Ministers as such, but who regularly attend Cabinet meetings.[107] Legally, special advisers may now only be appointed with the prior written approval of the Prime Minister.[108] Their appointment ends when the Minister who appointed them ceases to hold the minister-ial office to which the appointment related or, if earlier, the day after the first general election following the appointment.[109]

In 2000, the Committee on Standards in Public Life concluded that special advisers perform a valuable function within government, but that they should be required to observe a code of conduct drafted to reflect their special position.[110] The Public Administration Committee also concluded that special advisers can make a posi-tive contribution to good government by broadening the range of policy advice upon which Ministers can draw, but that they should be subject to a code of conduct.[111] In 2001, the government published a Code of Conduct for Special Advisers that governs their behaviour and which was last updated in 2010.[112] The existence of such a code is now statutorily required.[113] Because special advisers are civil servants, they are bound by the normal obligation to act with honesty and integrity.[114] In addition, the Code of Conduct for Special Advisers states that they should not deceive or knowingly mislead Parliament or the public; neither should they misuse their official position or informa-tion acquired in the course of their official duties to further their private interests or the private interests of others.[115]

Two controversial issues as to the role of special advisers should be noted. The first concerns their function in the presentation and media management of governmental policy. During the Blair government (1997–2007), special advisers gained a reputation for their involvement in 'spin'—that is, the presentation of information and of stories in the media in order to show the government in its best light. The most notorious episode occurred when, shortly after the terrorist attacks in the USA on 11 September 2001 ('9/11'), the special adviser to the Transport Secretary sent an email noting that it was 'a very good day to get out anything we want to bury'. In other words, because the world's attention would be on the terrorist attacks, the government could make use of the opportunity to disclose adverse information (such as statistics concerning train

---

[106] Written ministerial Statement on Special Adviser numbers, costs, and revised model contract and code of conduct, 11 June 2010.   [107] *Ministerial Code*, [3.2].

[108] Constitutional Reform and Governance Act 2010, s 15.

[109] Constitutional Reform and Governance Act 2010, s 15.

[110] Committee on Standards in Public Life, *Sixth Report: Reinforcing Standards* (Cm 4557 2000), [6.26].

[111] House of Commons Public Administration Committee, *Special Advisers: Boon or Bane?* (HC 293 2000–01), [81].   [112] Cabinet Office, *Code of Conduct for Special Advisers* (London 2010).

[113] Constitutional Reform and Governance Act 2010, s 8(1).

[114] Constitutional Reform and Governance Act 2010, s 7(4).

[115] Cabinet Office, *Code of Conduct for Special Advisers* (London 2010), [5].

delays). The special adviser concerned was reprimanded, but not dismissed, although she subsequently resigned. Under the Code of Conduct, special advisers may represent to the media the views (including party-political views) of their Minister, provided that they have been authorised by the Minister to do so. All contacts with the news media should be authorised by the appointing Minister and be conducted in accordance with government guidelines on communications. However, special advisers must 'observe discretion and express comment with moderation, avoiding personal attacks'.[116]

Second, some unease has been expressed that the proliferation of special advisers could undermine the neutrality of the Civil Service. The concern is that because special advisers are essentially political advisers to Ministers, their role may at times undermine the non-political and impartial advice given by civil servants. In 1997, Tony Blair authorised his three special advisers to issue instructions to civil servants.[117] However, this authorisation was removed when Gordon Brown became Prime Minister in 2007,[118] and primary legislation now states that special advisers may not exercise 'any power in relation to the management of any part of the civil service' except in relation to other special advisers.[119]

3.10 **Other public agencies**

We now need to consider a final part of the executive: those public bodies and agencies that operate at 'arm's length' from Ministers and government departments. These agencies fall into three categories: non-ministerial departments, non-departmental public bodies (NDPB), and executive agencies. Such agencies and public bodies proliferate because of the range of tasks undertaken by government and the need for such functions to be performed at one level removed from Ministers at the centre of the government machine.

First, non-ministerial departments are those departments created, often by statute, in order to discharge a particular public function. They exercise their functions on behalf of the Crown, and their separation from central government and Ministers is normally introduced in order to confer a degree of independence upon them. For example, the Charity Commission is the independent regulator of charitable activity and is not subject to the direction or control of any Minister of the Crown or other government department.[120] Having said that, Ministers may have the power to appoint members of such departments and to provide oversight. For example, HM Revenue and Customs (HMRC) is the agency responsible for collecting tax revenues. The Commissioners of the HMRC are to be treated as if they were Ministers of the

[116] *Code of Conduct for Special Advisers*, [10]–[12].
[117] The Civil Service (Amendment) Order in Council 1997.
[118] The Civil Service (Amendment) (No 2) Order in Council 2007.
[119] Constitutional Reform and Governance Act 2010, s 8(5) and (6).
[120] Charities Act 2006, s 6.

Crown and must comply with any directions of a general nature given to them by the Treasury.[121]

Second, there are NDPBs. These are bodies that have a role in the processes of national government, but are not government departments or part of one, and which accordingly operate to a greater or lesser extent at arm's length from Ministers.[122] In March 2009, there were 766 such bodies.[123] They fall into four categories:

(i) Bodies with executive powers (for example, the Environment Agency).

(ii) Advisory bodies that are set up by Ministers in order to advise them and their departments on matters within their area of responsibility (for example, the Social Security Advisory Committee provides advice to the Department for Work and Pensions).

(iii) Tribunals, which perform judicial functions to determine the rights and obligations of individuals in relation to each other or in relation to a government department.

(iv) Independent monitoring boards (for example, the independent monitoring boards of prisons act as independent 'watchdogs' for overseeing prisons, their administration, and treatment of prisoners).

That such functions are conferred on NDPBs means that there is recognition that they have a degree of independence from Ministers in carrying out those functions. At the same time, Ministers are accountable to Parliament for such bodies, their usefulness as an instrument of government policy, and their overall effectiveness and efficiency. NDPBs have recently fallen out of favour with central government, not least on the ground that they are perceived to be expensive. If enacted, the Public Bodies (Reform) Bill (announced in the 2010 Queen's Speech) will authorise Ministers to abolish such bodies. The thinking seems to be that such bodies' functions should be transferred back to government departments unless there is a clear need for those functions to be carried out at arm's length from central government.

Third, there are executive agencies. In 1988, the Thatcher government decided to establish executive agencies as a means of securing better managed and more efficient public services. The essential idea was that the executive and operational functions of government would be carried out within distinct agencies, while policy advice to Ministers would be provided by civil servants within the central government department. Many aspects of the work of government departments were then 'hived off' to executive agencies. Each executive agency is headed not by a Minister who is directly accountable to Parliament, but by an official—a chief executive. The relationship between executive agencies and their 'parent' government departments are formally set out in framework agreements. The executive agency works to performance targets set down by the parent department and is also funded by it. For

---

[121] Commissioners for Revenue and Customs Act 2005, ss 8 and 11.
[122] Cabinet Office, *Public Bodies 2009* (London 2009), p 5.   [123] *Public Bodies 2009*, p 10.

example, the Driver and Vehicle Licensing Agency, the parent department of which is the Department for Transport, issues driving and vehicle licences; meanwhile, the National Offender Management Service, an executive agency of the Ministry of Justice, is responsible for adult offender management services and the delivery of prison services.

The establishment of executive agencies provides another example of how the executive in the UK is able to reorganise itself without the need for any recourse to legislation. Executive agencies have been established without any parliamentary approval or oversight because none was required. Framework agreements governing the relationship between parent departments and executive agencies are not formally, legally binding. It is, though, government policy to review periodically the work and status of executive agencies.

For the most part, executive agencies operate in order to deliver public services more efficiently and effectively. However, problems can arise in relation to the accountability of such agencies. We can see that the responsibility chain has become lengthened—the Minister is responsible to Parliament, but the executive agency is responsible to the Minister—so can Parliament effectively hold the executive agency to account? In practical terms, parliamentary select committees can hear evidence from the chief executives of executive agencies, meaning that chief executives are increasingly responsible for operational matters while Ministers remain responsible for policy matters. But what is the precise difference between policy and operations?

The classic example of how difficult it is to draw that distinction, and of how Ministers might be tempted deliberately to manipulate this ambiguity in order to evade accountability, is provided by the 'Howard–Lewis' affair that occurred in 1995. Michael Howard was the Home Secretary and Derek Lewis was the chief executive of the Prison Service. Following a number of prison escapes, Howard demanded Lewis's resignation because of operational failures; by contrast, Lewis argued that the Home Secretary had interfered in operational matters, while simultaneously wishing to escape responsibility for a failure for which he was ultimately accountable to Parliament.[124] The obvious concern is that the principle of ministerial responsibility has been weakened or even manipulated to the benefit of Ministers and the detriment of officials. As Drewry has argued more generally, the largely fictional character of ministerial responsibility in an era of large-scale government and huge public bureaucracies has been increasingly apparent since the latter part of the nineteenth century—even though much of the fiction has been preserved, largely for the convenience of Ministers who are happy to accept the credit for successful initiatives, but quick to pass the buck to their officials when things go wrong.[125]

---

[124] Barker, 'Political Responsibility for UK Prison Security: Ministers Escape Again' (1998) 76 Public Administration 1.

[125] Drewry, 'The Executive: Towards Accountable Government and Effective Governance?', in Jowell and Oliver (eds), *The Changing Constitution* (Oxford 2007), p 205. These issues are explored more fully in Chapter 10.

4. **The powers of the executive**

Having looked at the position of the executive branch within the UK's constitutional arrangements and at the different institutions and constitutional actors of which it is comprised, it remains to consider the powers of the executive. How does the executive actually govern? By what legal (and other) means does it get things done and, more generally, project influence?

4.1 **Statutory powers generally**

Most obviously, the executive has at its disposal a vast array of statutory powers given to it by Parliament. This, in turn, begs the question: why does Parliament grant statutory powers to Ministers (and others)?[126] The most obvious answer to this question is that Parliament simply cannot legislate for every eventuality. The work of government is far too extensive for this to happen. Furthermore, on many issues, Parliament is not competent to undertake the detailed decision-making required; rather, its role is limited to resolving general policy questions. Consider, for example, the Inquiries Act 2005, which makes provision for the holding of inquiries into matters of public concern.[127] In theory, every time an event occurs that caused such concern, it would be possible for Parliament to legislate in order to establish an inquiry, set out the matters that should be investigated, appoint people to carry out the inquiry, and so on. But this would not be a sensible use of Parliament's time. For that reason, the Inquiries Act 2005 confers statutory powers upon Ministers to set up inquiries, decide who should chair them, determine their terms of reference, and so on. Of course, the legislation only authorises Ministers to act within certain parameters: for example, they cannot appoint people to run inquiries who appear to have vested interests, and they must inform Parliament that an inquiry is being established. In this way, the Inquiries Act, like all Acts that grant statutory powers to Ministers, reflects a division of labour between executive and legislature. The latter lays down the ground rules and general principles, while the more detailed decision-making required by the administration of policy is left to the former.

However, leaving certain matters for ministerial decision is not simply a necessary evil that must be endured because Parliament cannot do everything. There are also a number of positive reasons for leaving certain matters to the executive branch. It is generally appropriate for decisions concerning particular individuals or sensitive issues, or requiring detailed consideration of specific facts, to be taken otherwise than by Parliament. Government departments may well have greater expertise, and may be able to adopt a more appropriate style of decision-making: it may, for example, be necessary or desirable to take detailed evidence from individuals liable to be affected by

---

[126] For example, non-departmental public bodies, local authorities, and so on. Our focus here, however, is on the powers of central government ministerial departments.   [127] See further Chapter 18.

the decision, perhaps even affording certain such individuals some form of fair hearing. It is abundantly clear that Parliament is not institutionally well placed to carry out such tasks. It is equally clear that the executive branch may need to be authorised in certain contexts to take urgent decisions, bearing in mind that it is far better equipped than Parliament to respond quickly to events.[128] For reasons such as these, it is the executive, rather than Parliament, that can, *inter alia*, decide that a foreign national should be deported on the ground that his presence in the UK is not conducive to the public good,[129] decide whether the go-ahead should be given to major infrastructure projects of regional or national importance,[130] and introduce emergency measures when this is necessary to deal with matters that threaten serious damage to human welfare, the environment, or national security.[131]

Q What general principles would you wish to see applied by Parliament when determining whether a particular matter should be left to the executive branch to decide under statutory powers or determined by Parliament itself by means of primary legislation?

The amount of statutory power conferred by Parliament increased dramatically during the last century. This is hardly surprising. Over that period, the government took on a much broader range of responsibilities—and therefore needed the powers necessary to discharge them. As Wade and Forsyth have pointed out, if the state is to 'care for its citizens from the cradle to the grave'—providing education, training, health care, social security, and so on—then 'it needs a huge administrative apparatus'.[132] This throws into especially sharp relief questions about the accountability of the executive in its use of statutory powers. The existence of adequate mechanisms for ensuring the accountable use of such power is self-evidently important, but all the more so given the sheer scale of the powers at the disposal of today's executive branch. In this sphere, we therefore encounter a clear example of the phenomenon mentioned at the beginning of this chapter—namely, the intersection of our two key themes of holding the executive to account, and the relationship between legal and political forms of constitutionalism. It might be thought that the task of ensuring the responsible use of statutory power ought to fall to the institution—Parliament—that confers it in the first place. However, for reasons that we outlined at the outset of this chapter, and which we explore in more depth in Chapter 5, Parliament is, in fact, poorly situated to discharge this function. As a result, the extent to which the executive is politically accountable to the legislature for the exercise of statutory powers is today eclipsed in some respects by the former's legal accountability to the courts, which have assumed primary responsibility for ensuring that the government does not misuse its legal

---

[128] Not least because Parliament is in 'recess'—ie does not sit—for a substantial proportion of each year.
[129] Immigration Act 1971, s 3(5).   [130] Town and Country Planning Act 1990, s 76A.
[131] Civil Contingencies Act 2004, Pt 2.   [132] *Administrative Law* (Oxford 2009), p 4.

powers. We consider the means—known as 'judicial review'—by which the courts discharge this responsibility in Chapters 12–15.

Finally, it is worth bearing in mind the implications for the present context of the matters considered earlier in this chapter concerning the nature of the relationship between the legislature and the executive. The executive only has the statutory powers that Parliament gives to it; and those statutory powers that it does have are granted on whatever terms, and subject to whatever restrictions, Parliament chooses to impose. It might therefore be anticipated that Parliament would normally frame statutory powers in relatively narrow terms, in order to ensure that those permitted to exercise them may do so only for the specific purposes and in the particular way intended by Parliament. In practice, however, statutory powers are often granted in very broad terms, thus affording the executive a wide degree of latitude vis-à-vis the uses to which such powers may be put and the manner of their exercise.[133] It is not hard to work out why this tends to happen. We explained at the beginning of the chapter that the reality of Parliament's relationship with the executive is that the latter is in a strong position to secure the enactment of legislation by the former. It follows that although, in strictly technical terms, it is for Parliament to decide what powers to confer on the executive, and on what terms, the actual position is that the executive is strongly placed to get Parliament to confer upon it the powers that it wants on the terms that it wants them.

4.2 **Statutory powers to make delegated legislation**

The sort of statutory powers thus far considered concern the making of decisions in individual cases within the framework of rules laid down by Parliament in the relevant statute. However, it is very common for Parliament to authorise the executive not only to make decisions of that nature, but also to make some of the legal rules itself. Such rules are known as *delegated legislation*.[134]

4.2.1 **The use of delegated legislation**

The reasons for allowing the use of delegated legislation are similar to those that militate in favour of permitting the executive to use statutory powers generally. The sheer volume of legislation that is felt to be necessary today means that Parliament does not have the capacity to enact all of it. In effect, therefore, Parliament has to contract out to the executive branch the enactment of a good deal of legislation. This is clearly inconsistent with a rigid notion of the separation of powers, but it is now simply a fact of life. The focus of concern in this area is not whether the executive should have legislative powers—that is now accepted; rather, the issues are whether those powers are subject to adequate controls and safeguards, and whether the extent of the modern

---

[133] Without prejudice to this point, it is important not to overstate the degree of the executive's freedom in this regard, not least because, as we explain in Chapter 13, if the exercise of statutory powers is challenged legally, courts are often prepared to read restrictions into broadly worded legislation.

[134] The terms 'secondary', 'subordinate', 'executive', and 'administrative' legislation are also used.

executive's lawmaking powers is appropriate.[135] For example, it has been argued that there is 'too great a readiness in Parliament to delegate wide legislative powers to Ministers, and no lack of enthusiasm on their part to take such powers', resulting in 'an excessive volume of delegated legislation'.[136]

4.2.2 Henry VIII powers

It is important to be aware of the *types of lawmaking power* that the executive can exercise. Most straightforwardly, the executive may be allowed to fill in the details of a statutory scheme. For example, s 19 of the London Olympic Games and Paralympic Games Act 2006[137] says that 'The Secretary of State shall make regulations about advertising in the vicinity of London Olympic events'. It is clear[138] that Parliament's intention was that legal rules should be put in place to regulate advertising near Olympic venues in order to ensure compliance with the International Olympic Committee's strict requirements on this subject[139]—but rather than lay down detailed rules, Parliament left this task to the Minister.

However, it has been observed that there is 'an increasing tendency for governments to use delegated legislation as a means of dealing with matters of principle and policy rather than [just] with detail'.[140] Particular concerns have been expressed in relation to 'Henry VIII powers',[141] which, as Figure 4.2 shows, authorise Ministers to make secondary legislation amending or even repealing Acts of Parliament. Indeed, s 19 of the Olympics Act can be deployed in such a way: it can be used to 'disapply or modify specified enactments relating to planning or the control of advertising'.[142] This ensures that the Secretary of State is not hampered by existing legislation, which may be at odds with the requirements of the International Olympic Committee, in her attempt to establish a regulatory regime that fulfils those requirements. However, this is a relatively modest example of a Henry VIII power, in that it allows only certain Acts of Parliament to be modified or disapplied only for as long as is necessary to secure compliance with Committee requirements.[143]

In contrast, the Civil Contingencies Act 2004 illustrates just how broad executive powers to legislate can be. It allows certain Ministers to make 'emergency regulations' if it is considered that it is urgently necessary to do so in order to make provision to prevent, control, or mitigate an aspect or effect of an emergency that has occurred, is

---

[135] The use of some types of delegated legislation grew by 100 per cent between 1981 and 1996: House of Commons Select Committee on Procedure, *Delegated Legislation* (HC 152 1995–96), [41].

[136] House of Commons Select Committee on Procedure, HC 152, [14]. These comments were endorsed more recently by the same select committee: see House of Commons Select Committee on Procedure, *Delegated Legislation* (HC 48 1999–2000), [26].   [137] The 'Olympics Act'.

[138] London Olympic Games and Paralympic Games Act 2006, s 19(2).

[139] See International Olympic Committee, *Olympic Charter* (2007), r 51.

[140] Page, *Governing by Numbers* (Oxford 2001), p 25.

[141] So-called because of King Henry VIII's arrogation to himself of powers to enact measures having the same force as statutes. See further Barber and Young, 'The Rise of Prospective Henry VIII Clauses and their Implications for Sovereignty' [2003] PL 112, 113.   [142] Section 20(1)(a).

[143] Section 19(6).

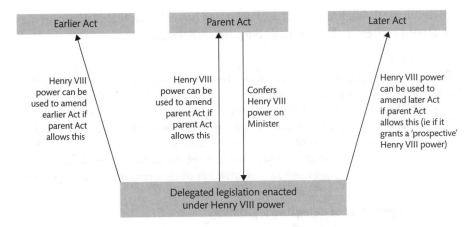

Figure 4.2 Henry VIII powers

occurring, or is about to occur, and if the urgency of the situation is such that more cumbersome legislative procedures cannot practically be used.[144] The breadth of what can be accomplished under these powers is immense: emergency regulations can, *inter alia*, 'provide for...the destruction of property, animal life or plant life (with or without compensation)',[145] 'prohibit...travel at specified times', and 'prohibit'[146] or 'require...movement to or from a specified place'.[147] Moreover, the Act makes clear that emergency regulations 'may make provision of any kind that could be made by Act of Parliament',[148] including the disapplication and modification of primary legislation.[149] The power to make emergency regulations is therefore a particularly broad form of Henry VIII power, since it can potentially be used in relation to any Act of Parliament for any of a very wide range of purposes.[150] Barber and Young argue that Henry VIII clauses of this type, which can be used in relation to all primary legislation whether enacted before or after the Act conferring the power, are objectionable in constitutional terms. The essence of their argument is that when Parliament confers a 'prospective' Henry VIII power—that is, one that can be used in relation to legislation not yet on the statute book—it cannot fully appreciate the uses to which it might be put, because those uses include the amendment or repeal of primary legislation not yet enacted. They point out that this creates 'the risk that as yet unthought of statutes will

---

144 Civil Contingencies Act 2004, s 20(2). By s 19(1):

> An 'emergency' is, for these purposes, an event or situation which threatens serious damage to human welfare in the United Kingdom or in a Part or region; an event or situation which threatens serious damage to the environment of the United Kingdom or of a Part or region; or war, or terrorism, which threatens serious damage to the security of the United Kingdom.

145 Civil Contingencies Act 2004, s 22(3)(c).   146 Civil Contingencies Act 2004, s 22(3)(g).
147 Civil Contingencies Act 2004, s 22(3)(d) and (e).   148 Civil Contingencies Act 2004, s 22(3).
149 Civil Contingencies Act 2004, s 22(3)(j).
150 Provided that they are considered by the Minister to be necessary for preventing, controlling, or mitigating an aspect or effect of the emergency in question: Civil Contingencies Act 2004, s 22(1).

be overturned through the exercise of delegated power', such that 'Parliament must put its trust entirely in the body to whom power is delegated'.[151]

> **Q** Barber and Young go on to argue that such Henry VIII clauses 'constitute a fetter on the power of future Parliaments', meaning that they enable the executive to thwart the wishes of such Parliaments by undoing by means of secondary legislation what such Parliaments have accomplished by passing enactments. Given that it would, in principle, be open to a future Parliament to cut down or remove such a Henry VIII power, do you agree with Barber and Young? How might our discussion, at the beginning of this chapter, of the relationship between the legislative and executive branches be relevant to their argument?

4.2.3 The legal effect of delegated legislation

In many instances, the legal effect of delegated legislation is clear. For example, the Olympics Act says that '[a] person commits an offence if he contravenes regulations [made] under section 19' and that such an offence is punishable by a fine. The legal status of s 19 regulations is thus clear—they form part of the criminal law—as are the consequences of their breach.

However, the position is not always as simple. Particular difficulties arise where the executive is authorised by statute—or takes it upon itself—to issue guidance, rules, regulations, and the suchlike, the legal status of which is not made clear by the parent Act or otherwise. For example, s 38(7) of the Road Traffic Act 1998 stipulates that while breach of the Highway Code is not in itself a criminal offence, such a breach may be relied upon in criminal or civil proceedings 'as tending to establish or negative any liability which is in question in those proceedings'. So while a breach of the Highway Code is not actionable in itself, its contravention by a defendant may help the claimant to establish liability for negligence.[152] Similarly, under s 118(1) of the Mental Health Act 1983, the Secretary of State is required to issue a 'code of practice' concerning, *inter alia*, the treatment of patients suffering from mental disorders. The House of Lords concluded in the *Munjaz* case that such a code of practice could not be regarded as having the binding force of law.[153] It followed that when the defendant hospital departed from it, by operating a regime for supervising patients confined to their rooms that was less rigorous than that required under the code, this was not unlawful per se. However, their Lordships did hold that the code of practice—and the fact that the hospital had departed from it—was not wholly irrelevant to determining whether the hospital had acted lawfully according to the normal principles governing the use of statutory powers. What this meant, in effect, was that the hospital had to show that its refusal to apply the code was not unreasonable—a burden that it discharged by

---

[151] Barber and Young at 114.

[152] *Russell v Smith* [2003] EWHC 2060 (Admin), (2003) 147 SJLB 1118. See further *Odelola v Secretary of State for the Home Department* [2009] UKHL 25, [2009] 1 WLR 1230 and *Secretary of State for the Home Department v Pankina* [2010] EWCA Civ 719 for discussion of the legal status of the Immigration Rules.

[153] *R (Munjaz) v Mersey Care NHS Trust* [2005] UKHL 58, [2006] 2 AC 148.

virtue of the fact that it cared for an unusually high number of unusually dangerous patients.

It is therefore appropriate to think of the various sorts of measure that the executive enacts as existing on a spectrum, as shown in Figure 4.3. At one end, we find such things as the regulations made under s 19 of the Olympics Act: those regulations can self-evidently be regarded as 'law', in the sense that they are directly legally enforceable, and here the term 'delegated legislation' is manifestly appropriate. However, as we move along the spectrum, we enter the realm of so-called 'soft law', or quasi-legislation—measures that may have some, less direct legal relevance, but which cannot straightforwardly be regarded as laws in the sense of being directly enforceable in legal proceedings.[154]

4.2.4 Publication

The idea that law should be published is central to the notion of the rule of law. Individuals can only plan their lives and choose to behave in a way that is lawful if they can know what the law is; that, in turn, is possible only if all legal rules are publicly available. As Lord Steyn pointed out in *Anufrijeva*, speaking in an analogous context, a situation in which 'the rights of individuals are overridden by hole in the corner decisions or knocks on doors in the early hours' is antithetical to the British tradition of the rule of law. He continued: 'That is not our system. ... In our system of law surprise is regarded as the enemy of justice.'[155] It is therefore unsurprising that the Statutory Instruments Act 1946, s 2(1), provides that 'statutory instruments' must be published.[156] However, two issues arise.

First, delegated legislation only constitutes a statutory instrument if the parent Act, in conferring the power to make delegated legislation, stipulates that it must be made in the form of statutory instrument. Where that is not the case, the publication requirement in the 1946 Act does not apply. In such circumstances, as Scott LJ pointed out in *Blackpool Corporation v Locker*, individuals may remain 'in complete ignorance' of the law, meaning that, '[f]or practical purposes, the rule of law, of which the nation is so justly proud, breaks down'.[157] However, some other publication requirement may apply: for example, the Act conferring the power to enact the delegated legislation in question may insist upon publication[158] or the Freedom of Information Act 2000[159] may require publication.

Second, in light of the importance—from a rule of law perspective—of publication, it might be thought that failure to publish delegated legislation (where this is

---

[154] See further Ganz, *Quasi-Legislation: Recent Developments in Secondary Legislation* (London 1987).

[155] *R (Anufrijeva) v Secretary of State for the Home Department* [2003] UKHL 36, [2004] 1 AC 604, [28]–[30].

[156] For certain exceptions to this requirement, see the Statutory Instruments Regulations 1947, SI 1948/1.　　　　　　　　　　　　　　　　　　[157] [1948] 1 KB 349, 362.

[158] Indeed, courts may be willing to read an implied obligation to that effect into the parent Act. See (in an analogous context) *Salih v Secretary of State for the Home Department* [2003] EWHC 2273 (Admin).

[159] See Chapter 10.

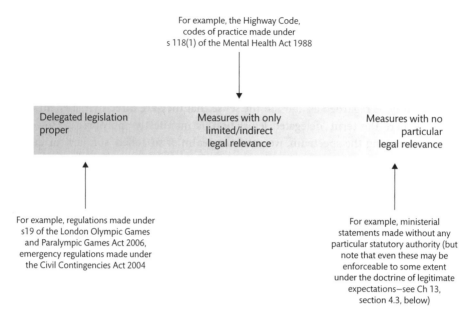

Figure 4.3 Delegated legislation and 'soft law'

legally required) should result in its invalidity (or at least unenforceability pending publication). However, it appears that this is not so, and that delegated legislation remains valid and enforceable even if it is not published[160]—although it is, subject to certain exceptions, a defence to a *criminal* charge of contravening a statutory instrument to prove that the legislation had not been published at the date of the alleged contravention.[161]

4.2.5 **Consultation**

We will see in Chapter 13 that when the executive branch makes decisions under statutory powers of the type considered in the previous section, it is generally required to act fairly. An important aspect of acting fairly in this sense is allowing those likely to be affected by the decision to have their say *before* any decision is made. There are many different ways in which this can be done; such practices, depending on the context, may be referred to as providing a fair hearing or consulting interested parties. When the executive enacts delegated legislation (as opposed simply to making decisions) under statutory powers, the relevant legislation may require consultation; when it does not, there is generally no common law duty to consult or otherwise to treat fairly those liable to be affected.[162] More recently, however, in the *BAPIO* case, Sedley LJ said that 'the common law could recognise a general duty of consultation

---

[160] *R v Sheer Metalcraft Ltd* [1954] 1 QB 586, 590, *per* Streatfield J.
[161] Statutory Instruments Act 1946, s 3(2).
[162] *Bates v Lord Hailsham of St Marylebone* [1972] 1 WLR 1373.

in relation to proposed measures which are going adversely to affect an identifiable interest group or sector of society', but went on to conclude that it would often be inappropriate, in the absence of a statutory duty to consult, for the courts to impose one: doing so, he said, may require the court to adopt the position of a legislator.[163] Meanwhile, Maurice Kay LJ, with whom Rimer LJ agreed, pointed out that if (as is often the case, as we explain below) the parent Act were to make Parliament responsible for scrutinising the executive legislation in question, it would be inappropriate for the court to superimpose a common law duty to consult.[164] For some commentators, the general absence of any requirement to consult prior to enacting secondary legislation is a source of concern: Page calls executive lawmaking 'the politics of seclusion', the (pejorative) implication being that it is an activity that takes place in a way that lacks adequate transparency.[165]

While there is no general legal duty for the executive to consult on delegated legislation, this does not, of course, preclude such consultation. It should not be assumed that the executive is generally unwilling to consult. On the contrary, the government has published a general policy on consultation—the Code of Practice on Consultation—which recognises that ongoing dialogue between government and stakeholders is an important part of policymaking.[166]

4.2.6 The role of Parliament

There is something paradoxical in addressing Parliament's role in relation to delegated legislation. After all, an important part of the purpose behind granting to the executive powers to make such legislation is Parliament's inability to cope with the volume of lawmaking that is deemed necessary today. However, it is inevitable that Parliament must, in the first place, be involved in *conferring powers* on the executive to enact delegated legislation—and it is desirable that Parliament should be involved in *overseeing the exercise of such powers*.

As to the former, it is clearly for Parliament to decide whether it wishes to confer upon the executive powers to enact legislation in relation to any given matter—and, if it does, on what terms. However, here, we encounter the by-now-familiar point that all is not as it seems as regards the relationship between the executive and the legislature. The reality, as we now know, is that the former is well situated to get the latter to do as it wishes. It is therefore unsurprising that, as noted above, both the amount and scope of the contemporary executive's lawmaking powers are very considerable indeed. Having said that, it is worth noting that systematic scrutiny of the appropriateness of granting legislative powers to the executive is provided by the House of Lords Select Committee on Delegated Powers and Regulatory Reform, which has a good track record of getting

---

[163] *R (BAPIO Action Ltd) v Secretary of State for the Home Department* [2007] EWCA Civ 1139, [47] (decided on other grounds by the House of Lords: [2008] UKHL 27, [2008] 1 AC 1003). Sedley LJ had in mind the fact that the court would have to make a series of detailed decisions about the nature of the required consultation exercise.   [164] *BAPIO Action Ltd* at [58].

[165] Page, *Governing by Numbers* (Oxford 2001), ch 1.

[166] HM Government, *Code of Practice on Consultation* (London 2008).

the government to amend Bills that it thinks would, if enacted, confer unduly wide or otherwise inappropriate powers on the executive branch.

Objections on separation of powers grounds to the executive holding legislative power are less compelling if there is an effective oversight mechanism: after all, as we saw in Chapter 3, the doctrine does not necessarily demand rigid separation between the institutions of government such that none may exercise functions that fall principally within the purview of another. In some versions of the doctrine, particular emphasis is placed on checks and balances—that is, on ensuring that each branch is subject to adequate scrutiny and control supplied by one or more of the other branches. If, as discussed in Chapter 3, the overarching purpose of the separation of powers is to guard against (and, failing that, to deal effectively with) abuse of power, the key question is not whether it is improper for the executive to exercise any measure of lawmaking power, but whether it is subject to sufficient oversight when it uses such powers. An important aspect of such oversight consists of judicial review, which we consider in Chapters 12–15, but there is also a strong case for saying that Parliament should oversee the exercise of the legislative powers that it grants to the executive. Whereas the courts are able to intervene when the executive exceeds its legal powers, Parliament is, at least in theory, capable of supplying a broader, more political form of scrutiny, by asking not only whether, in a technical, legal sense, the executive is allowed to use its powers in a given way, but also whether putting them to such a use is appropriate by reference to a wider range of political, social, moral, and economic criteria.

Parliamentary scrutiny of delegated legislation takes two main forms. *Technical scrutiny* is provided by the Joint Committee on Statutory Instruments.[167] It is concerned with matters such as whether proposed delegated legislation is poorly drafted and whether it relates to matters that may be outside the powers under which it is being made. In a sense, the work of the Committee anticipates the sort of issues that might otherwise be the subject of litigation—and, perhaps for that reason, the executive tends to acquiesce when the Committee is of the view that proposed legislation needs to be changed before being finalised.[168]

Meanwhile, *policy scrutiny* of delegated legislation is patchy at best. It is clear that Parliament cannot debate at length every governmental proposal for such legislation: such an approach would be self-defeating, given that the executive is, in the first place, authorised to make law due to limited parliamentary time. Although some delegated legislation—known as 'affirmative instruments'—must be approved by Parliament before taking effect,[169] most secondary legislation—so-called 'negative instruments'—takes effect unless Parliament takes steps to disapprove it. Affirmative instruments receive some policy scrutiny as a matter of course, since they must be debated in committee, but negative instruments are only rarely debated. *Prima facie*, this system represents a sensible use of scarce parliamentary time and resources: some delegated

---

[167] See generally Wallington and Hayhurst, 'The Parliamentary Scrutiny of Delegated Legislation' [1988] PL 547.   [168] See further Page, pp 161–8.

[169] Albeit that they may have interim effect pending approval.

legislation—presumably that which is the most important or contentious—is subject to debate, whereas the rest is not. The difficulty, however, is that the distinction between affirmative and negative instruments is often not aligned with the distinction between delegated legislation that is worthy of debate and that which it is appropriate to subject to less (or no) scrutiny. As a result, it was suggested that Parliament should create a system of triage—a 'sifting committee'— in order to identify at an early stage which pieces of delegated legislation need close scrutiny and which do not.[170] The suggestion that a joint committee of both Houses should be formed for this purpose was rejected by the government,[171] but the House of Lords has now created its own sifting committee—the House of Lords Merits of Statutory Instruments Committee—which aims to identify which pieces of delegated legislation should be the subject of closer scrutiny by the Upper House.[172]

4.2.7 Judicial review

As noted above, the courts are able to intervene (provided that a litigant pursues the matter) if executive lawmakers exceed the powers granted to them by Parliament. Most obviously, courts can step in if the executive, when making secondary legislation, fails to do things that Parliament has indicated must be done if the legislation is to be valid (or at least enforceable). For example, when, in the *Aylesbury Mushrooms* case, the government failed to comply with a statutory duty to consult a particular interest group before making a piece of delegated legislation, the court ruled that the legislation could not be enforced against the members of that group.[173] Courts are also willing to go beyond the plain words of the parent Act by reading implied restrictions into provisions conferring lawmaking powers upon the executive. For example, when the Home Secretary attempted to use a statutory power to make delegated legislation precluding subsistence payments to certain categories of asylum seeker, it was held that he had exceeded his powers: Simon Brown LJ, in the *JCWI* case, said that the secondary legislation in question, if it were allowed to stand, would reduce the asylum seekers to whom it applied to 'a life so destitute that to my mind no civilised nation can tolerate it'.[174] Parliament, said his Lordship, must be assumed not to have intended to authorise Ministers to make secondary legislation that would bring about such a state of affairs. Similarly, it was held in *Witham* that Parliament could not be assumed

---

[170] See House of Commons Select Committee on Procedure, *Delegated Legislation* (HC 152 1995–96) and *Delegated Legislation: Proposals for a Sifting Committee* (HC 501 2002–03); Royal Commission on the Reform of the House of Lords, *A House for the Future* (Cm 4534 2000), p 74.

[171] House of Commons Select Committee on Procedure, *Delegated Legislation: Proposals for a Sifting Committee: The Government's Response to the Committee's First Report* (HC 684 2002–03).

[172] See House of Commons Select Committee on the Merits of Statutory Instruments, *Special Report: Inquiry into Methods of Working* (HL18 2003–04).

[173] *Agricultural, Horticultural and Forestry Industrial Training Board v Aylesbury Mushrooms Ltd* [1972] 1 WLR 190.

[174] *R v Secretary of State for Social Security, ex p Joint Council for the Welfare of Immigrants* [1997] 1 WLR 275, 292. In fact, this decision was, to a substantial effect, reversed by Parliament: see Nationality, Immigration and Asylum Act 2002, s 55.

to have intended to authorise the making of secondary legislation the effect of which would have been to set court fees in a way and at a level that would have excluded those on low incomes from access to the courts.[175]

Further discussion of judicial review can be found in Chapters 12–15. For the time being, we simply note that the unusual nature of the separation of powers in the UK means, as we have already seen, that the executive is strongly placed to get Parliament to confer upon it such lawmaking powers as it desires; against that background, the courts' jurisdiction to determine whether delegated legislation has been made outwith the authority conferred by the parent Act is an important constitutional safeguard. Not only can the courts ensure that executive lawmakers act in accordance with whatever requirements Parliament stipulates, but they can also, as the cases considered above indicate, ensure that the executive does not (unless Parliament has unambiguously authorised such action) legislate contrary to fundamental notions of fairness, dignity, and human rights.[176]

4.3 **Prerogative powers**

So far, we have been concerned with general statutory powers and statutory powers to enact delegated legislation. However, certain important executive powers take the form of prerogative—or common law—rather than statutory powers. At one time, the prerogative was the principal legal means by which government was carried on. However, whenever Parliament enacts a statute conferring power on the executive, any prerogative power with which it overlaps is supplanted.[177] Gradually, the metaphorical ocean of prerogative power shrank as islands and later larger land masses of statutory power grew up;[178] today, the vast array of statutory powers that exist means that the prerogative remains only in the form of isolated pockets of power. But those remaining pockets are important. Among the things that Parliament has never authorised the executive to do—and which therefore remain the preserve of prerogative power—are the declaration of war, the disposition of the armed forces, the signing of treaties,[179] the granting of mercy and of honours, the issuing of passports, and the conduct of international relations. For public lawyers, the fact that such matters remain the subject of prerogative—rather than of statutory—power is of interest for two reasons.

First, the exercise of prerogative powers, unlike the exercise of statutory powers, was traditionally not subject to judicial review. This was regarded, at least by some writers, as strong grounds for objecting to the existence of the prerogative. However, as we explain

---

[175] *R v Lord Chancellor, ex p Witham* [1998] QB 575.

[176] The courts' hand is further strengthened in this regard by the Human Rights Act 1998, on which, see Chapter 19 below.   [177] See further Chapter 14, section 2.2.2, below.

[178] Nolan and Sedley, *The Making and Remaking of the British Constitution* (London 1997), p 15.

[179] Although still founded in the prerogative, this power is now subject to statutory regulation that gives Parliament the right to veto the UK's entering into treaty obligations: Constitutional Reform and Governance Act 2010, Pt 2.

in Chapter 14, the position has now changed, and the exercise of the prerogative can generally be examined by the courts in much the same way as the use of statutory powers.

Second, notwithstanding that their use is now amenable to judicial scrutiny, prerogative powers may be regarded as objectionable at a more fundamental level. In considering these matters further, it is helpful to distinguish between two rather different forms of prerogative power. We have already considered the *monarch's personal prerogatives* concerning such matters as the appointment of Prime Ministers and the conferral of royal assent upon Bills (without which they cannot become law). In these matters, the monarch is directly—personally—involved. Viewed in such baldly legal terms, the monarch appears to enjoy considerable powers and to occupy a role that is at odds with democratic principle. However, we saw earlier in this chapter that the exercise of these prerogatives is heavily regulated by convention. In this way, political practice supplements the legal constitution, producing a 'real' constitution that is markedly less anachronistic than the purely legal position implies.

Q Would it be better if the monarch were stripped of these powers, so as to remove any impression that she has a say in relation to such questions as who should lead the government? If so, how should the answers to such questions be determined instead?

Alongside the monarch's personal prerogatives, we find a wider set of *executive prerogative powers*. Into this category fall the powers mentioned at the beginning of this section, including the declaration of war and the signing of treaties. As noted above, the prerogative is effectively a residual power: to the extent that it exists today, it is what remains of the power that monarchs used in earlier times to govern the country. However, it is not only the width of the prerogative that has changed over the centuries as statute has gradually encroached. Save in relation to her personal prerogatives, the general position is that, as Markesinis has observed, what we used to call the *royal* prerogative is today 'to all intents and purposes [a] government or even prime ministerial prerogative'.[180] In other words, while prerogative power belongs, in constitutional theory, to the monarch, who has been said to have the rights 'to be consulted', 'to encourage', and 'to warn',[181] the exercise of executive prerogative powers is essentially a matter for the government of the day. This begs the question whether it is acceptable in a twenty-first-century liberal democracy for that branch of government to be endowed with common law powers that have not been conferred by, and which have therefore not been the subject of debate in or restriction by, Parliament. Such a situation might be thought to be profoundly undemocratic.[182] More specifically, it has

---

[180] Markesinis, 'The Royal Prerogative Revisited' (1973) 32 CLJ 287, 288.

[181] Bagehot, *The English Constitution* (London 1968), p 111.

[182] For critical views of the prerogative, see Institute of Public Policy Research, *The Constitution of the United Kingdom* (London 1991); Syrett, 'Prerogative Powers: New Labour's Forgotten Constitutional Reforms?' [1998] Denning Law Journal 111.

been suggested that it is unduly difficult for Parliament to hold Ministers to account for decisions taken under the prerogative—according to former Prime Minister John Major, it is 'for individual Ministers to decide on a particular occasion whether and how to report to Parliament on the exercise of prerogative powers'.[183] It is also felt by some to be objectionable that the scope of the prerogative is unclear: Ministers have said that it would be impossible to produce a precise list of prerogative powers.[184] We note (in passing for now, although we return to this point in Chapter 14) that this lack of transparency is also problematic in terms of judicial review of decisions taken under the prerogative: in a recent case, the House of Lords divided three–two on whether a power to expel an indigenous population from a British colony *existed*.[185]

An obvious response to criticism of the prerogative is that Parliament could, if it wished, abolish any prerogative powers it regarded as objectionable, replacing them, if it desired, with more limited statutory powers. The fact that certain prerogatives remain may, on this view, be taken to imply that Parliament is content with such a state of affairs. However, the view that at least some prerogatives should be replaced with statutory powers is now gaining ground—including within Parliament. In an influential report in 2004, the Public Administration Select Committee recommended that the government should compile a comprehensive list of prerogative powers and that legislation should then be enacted putting certain powers, where appropriate, on a statutory footing.[186] It appears that three policy considerations lay behind these recommendations. First, the Committee thought it objectionable that—as Brazier puts it—the government should possess 'imprecise powers'; instead, Ministers should be able to identify the 'nature and extent of their powers'.[187] Second, transparency was felt to be important not only as an end in itself, but also as a means by which to make possible the effective parliamentary supervision of executive action. The Committee pointed out that 'Because Parliament does not know what Ministers are empowered to do until they have done it, Parliament cannot properly hold government to account'.[188] Third, the Committee wished to see limitations placed on certain prerogative powers—for example, it felt strongly that decisions to engage in armed conflict should not be made without the consent of Parliament.[189]

Ministers were persuaded by at least the general thrust of some of these arguments. In 2007, the government said that 'in general the prerogative powers should be put onto a statutory basis and brought under stronger parliamentary scrutiny and control'.[190] As a result, legislation has recently been enacted placing the organisation of the Civil

---

[183]   HC Deb, vol 220, col 19W (1 March 1993).

[184]   House of Commons Public Administration Select Committee, *Taming the Prerogative: Strengthening Ministerial Accountability to Parliament* (HC 422 2003–04).

[185]   *R (Bancoult) v Secretary of State for Foreign and Commonwealth Affairs* [2008] UKHL 61, [2009] 1 AC 453.   [186]   *Taming the Prerogative*.

[187]   *Taming the Prerogative*, p 24.   [188]   *Taming the Prerogative*, p 17.

[189]   *Taming the Prerogative*, p 16.

[190]   Ministry of Justice, *The Governance of Britain* (Cm 7170 2007), pp 15–17.

Service on a statutory footing and introducing statutory regulation of the government's treaty-making powers.[191]

> **Q** Would abolishing or converting all prerogative powers into statutory powers be a good idea? What would be the advantages and disadvantages of doing so?

4.4 'Third source powers'[192]

Legal scholars disagree about the precise definition of the prerogative. Dicey argued that '[e]very act which the executive government can lawfully do without the authority of an Act of Parliament is done in virtue of... [the] prerogative',[193] whereas Blackstone thought the prerogative to be 'singular and eccentrical', comprising only 'those rights and capacities which the King enjoys alone, in contradistinction to others, and not... those which he enjoys in common with any of his subjects'.[194] The subject of this disagreement is therefore the sort of things that ordinary people can do (for example, enter into contacts). Do such acts—when committed by the executive—fall under the prerogative? And, if not, how do we account for the fact that the executive can do such things? The disagreement between Blackstone and Dicey relates principally to the first of these questions. For Dicey, anything done by the government not under statutory power—including things that individuals can do—must be done under the prerogative; Blackstone confined the prerogative to those things that only the executive can do, such as sign treaties. What, then, of situations in which the government wishes to commit acts that an individual could lawfully commit, but in which it does not have statutory power to do so?

It may be that if the government is unable to point to a specific statutory or prerogative power, it is simply not able lawfully to act. But this view is strongly counterintuitive. It is clearly impossible for the government to point to a specific power in relation to *everything* it does—ordering paper clips being the standard example—and yet it would be ridiculous to suggest that, in the absence of a specific power, the government may not lawfully do such things.

It might therefore be preferable to accept that Dicey was right all along: the prerogative should be construed widely, as including not only special governmental powers such as to declare war, but also as authorising the government to do that which everyone else can do. The courts have, on the whole, tended to prefer—or at least to assume the correctness of—Dicey's definition. For example, on more than one occasion, it has been judicially taken for granted that government schemes (not established under statute) to compensate victims of crime must have been set up under the prerogative,

---

[191] Constitutional Reform and Governance Act 2010, Pts 1 and 2.

[192] See generally Harris, 'The "Third Source" of Authority for Government Action' (1992) 108 LQR 626 and 'The "Third Source" of Authority for Government Action Revisited' (2007) 123 LQR 225.

[193] *An Introduction to the Study of the Law of the Constitution* (London 1964), p 425.

[194] *Commentaries on the Laws of England* (Oxford 1765), vol 1, p 239.

notwithstanding that any sufficiently wealthy individual could establish such a scheme.[195] Yet this view is problematic. As Wade has pointed out, there is nothing 'prerogative' about the government doing such things: it can do them 'because any one and every one can do them, and it has no need of "singular and eccentrial" power for the purpose'.[196] The better view, therefore, is that, as Lloyd LJ put it, 'the term "prerogative" should be confined to those powers which are unique to the Crown'.[197]

How, then, are we to account for the fact that the government does many things for which it has no specific statutory authorisation and no prerogative power (unless we are prepared to accept Dicey's overly broad definition of the prerogative)? Our response to this question must depend on whether we prefer one or other of two rival views of the government's legal and constitutional position.

The first view, set out by Laws J in the *Fewings* case, is that whereas individuals 'may do anything…which the law does not prohibit', the 'opposite' rule applies to public bodies: anything that they do 'must be justified by positive law'.[198] The principal argument in favour of this view is that considerations of transparency and legal certainty require that the government's powers should be enumerated, and that it should have no capacity to do anything not permitted by its enumerated powers. However, two difficulties arise. It would, in practice, be impossible to anticipate everything that the government might wish to do, and there would therefore need to be a conferral of a very general power upon the government that would hardly advance the interests of legal certainty and transparency. Moreover, Laws J's view that a special rule (requiring positive authorisation for everything) applies to 'public bodies' introduces practical difficulties: UK constitutional law is not predicated on a clear conception of the state, and it is therefore unclear to whom Laws J's special rule would apply.

The alternative view—and, it is submitted, the better one—is that that everyone (including the government) may do anything that is not unlawful. This position was endorsed by Carnwath LJ in *Shrewsbury and Atcham Borough Council v Secretary of State for Communities and Local Government*,[199] when he said that executive powers 'are not confined to those conferred by statute or prerogative, but extend, subject to any relevant statutory or public law constraints, and to the competing rights of other parties, to anything which could be done by a natural person'. The government's freedom to do anything that is not unlawful constitutes what Harris calls the 'third source' of government power, alongside statutory and prerogative powers.[200] The main

---

[195] *R v Criminal Injuries Compensation Board, ex p Lain* [1967] 2 QB 864; *R v Secretary of State for the Home Department, ex p Fire Brigades Union* [1995] 2 AC 513.

[196] 'Procedure and Prerogative in Public Law' (1985) 101 LQR 180, 191.

[197] *R v Panel on Takeovers and Mergers, ex p Datafin plc* [1987] QB 815, 848.

[198] *R v Somerset County Council, ex p Fewings* [1995] 1 All ER 513, 524. See also the comments of Sir Thomas Bingham MR in the same case in the Court of Appeal: [1995] 1 WLR 1037, 1042.

[199] [2008] EWCA Civ 148, [44].

[200] See Harris, 'The "Third Source" of Authority for Government Action' (1992) 108 LQR 626 and 'The "Third Source" of Authority for Government Action Revisited' (2007) 123 LQR 225. See also *Malone v Metropolitan Police Commissioner* [1979] Ch 344, 367.

objection to this view is that it appears to concede wide, almost infinite, powers to the government. For example, it was held in *Malone* that the government could lawfully listen into telephone conversations because no law prevented this.[201] However, properly understood, the difficulty highlighted by *Malone* is not with the view advocated by Harris, but simply that, when it was decided, English law did not make it unlawful to invade people's privacy. Had there been such a law, the government, lacking specific legal powers to tap telephones, would have been acting unlawfully in doing so. The position, therefore, is that the government may do anything that is not unlawful. What that means in effect is that anything that it does must either (i) not be prohibited by the general law applicable to individuals; or (ii) if it is contrary to the general law, be permitted by reference to specific statutory or prerogative powers. For example, agents of the state may only lawfully enter onto private property to carry out a search in relation to a criminal investigation provided that there is positive authority in law to justify such conduct (which would otherwise constitute trespass to land). Similarly, the government can only imprison certain convicted criminals and deport certain foreign nationals because statute law allows it to do these things (that would otherwise constitute, *inter alia*, trespass to the person).

4.5 **Contractual power**

Finally, we should mention the role that contractual power occupies in relation to the executive. It is important to begin by noting that such power is functionally different from statutory and prerogative powers. As Figure 4.4 shows, Acts of Parliament and the prerogative have the effect of *empowering* the executive to do certain things. This notion of empowerment may be resolved into two component elements.

First, Acts of Parliament and the prerogative constitute a *source of authority*, in that they make it possible for the government lawfully to do things that could not otherwise be lawfully done. For example, it is generally unlawful to erect buildings without planning permission. Such permission—the effect of which is to render lawful construction that would otherwise be unlawful—cannot be granted except by those governmental bodies that are statutorily authorised to do so. The relevant legislation therefore empowers such bodies to do that which they could not otherwise do—namely, to grant planning permission.

Second, statutory and prerogative powers constitute a *means by which the government may get things done, project influence, and implement policy*. This follows because its decision whether (and, if so, how) to exercise its statutory and prerogative powers will produce legal consequences—which may, in turn, produce practical consequences. For example, if the government decides that planning permission for a particular project should be granted subject to certain conditions (for example, as to

---

[201] *Malone* above; cf *Malone v United Kingdom* (1985) 7 EHRR 14, in which the European Court of Human Rights found that there had been a breach of Art 8 of the European Convention on Human Rights. See now Pt 1 of the Regulation of Investigatory Powers Act 2000.

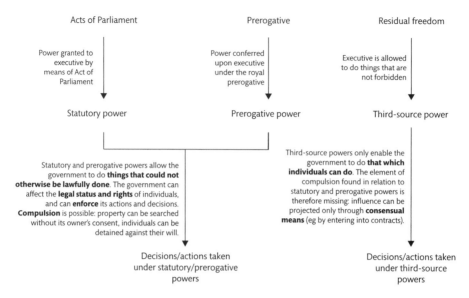

Figure 4.4 Three types of governmental power

the height of the building) that the developer goes on to flout, the latter will thereby act unlawfully; enforcement action may be taken that might culminate in the punishment (for example, the imposition of fines) upon those responsible for carrying on the unauthorised building work. The fact that such consequences may ensue incentivises compliance with the terms of the original decision, thus underlining the capacity of decisions taken under statutory (or prerogative) powers to project influence, further the government's policy objectives (for example, of not allowing tall buildings in architecturally sensitive areas), and so on.

Contractual power exists only in the latter, not the former, sense—that is, it does not constitute a source of authority; it is merely a means by which the government may seek to secure objectives and implement policies that it is already allowed to pursue. For example, in order to implement a statutorily authorised decision to deport a failed asylum seeker, the government may enter into a contract with an airline in order that the individual may be returned to his home country. It is the relevant statutory power, not the contract, that *empowers* the government to have the person deported; the contract with the airline merely *facilitates* the statutorily authorised deportation—it is a means of ensuring that the decision taken under statute produces the practical consequences desired by the government.

Nevertheless, the importance of contractual power should not be underestimated. It is frequently used by government bodies today, and is an important tool by which modern government is carried out.[202] Indeed, the use of contracts by government as

---

[202] See generally Harden, *The Contracting State* (Buckingham 1992).

a way of doing things that it is required or permitted to do is now commonplace. Of course, it has always been necessary—as in the example given above of the deportation of an asylum seeker—for public bodies to enter into contracts in order to fulfil certain aspects of their legal obligations and execute certain decisions. However, the contracting out of such matters has been far more common since the 1980s, when the Thatcher government procured the enactment of legislation *requiring* local authorities to put the provision of many services out to tender. As we note when we consider this matter in more detail in Chapter 7, this changed the role of local government quite radically, shifting its focus from the provision to the commissioning of services. Moreover, it is possible for statutory functions themselves to be contracted out.[203] This means that Ministers (and others[204]) may transfer the performance of statutory functions to contractors, such that the latter may (as Freedland puts it) 'exercise the powers and perform the duties which make up the statutory function in question'.[205] The use of contractual power by government bodies is of interest to public lawyers in relation both to the *act of contracting out* and the *results of contracting out*.

First, in entering into contracts for the provision of public services and the suchlike, the government exercises considerable power. Such contracts may be very valuable, and the government will often find itself in a strong bargaining position. Thus the government is able to wield considerable power in relation both to its choice of contractor and the terms on which it contracts. The entry by the government into such contracts is therefore tightly regulated by law in order to ensure that the process by which contracts are awarded is transparent, that potential contractors compete with one another on a level playing field, and that contractors are selected by government for legitimate (rather than corrupt) reasons.[206]

Second, contracting out—particularly where this involves authorising non-governmental bodies to exercise statutory powers—raises important and difficult questions that go to the heart of our key theme of executive accountability. A central concern is that public bodies that contract out the performance of their functions may thereby evade (or at least render themselves less amenable to) both political and legal scrutiny.[207] In turn, the interests of individuals may be prejudiced. As we will see, a particular difficulty in this sphere is that courts are generally reluctant to hold bodies providing public services under contract to the same legal standards as those to which public bodies would be held if they were providing the service directly.[208]

---

[203] Deregulation and Contracting Out Act 1999, Pt 2.

[204] The Act applies to local authorities, too: s 70.

[205] Freedland, 'Privatising *Carltona*: Part II of the Deregulation and Contracting Out Act 1994' [1995] PL 21, 24.

[206] See generally Arrowsmith, *The Law of Public and Utilities Procurement* (London 2005). Public procurement law in the UK also seeks to ensure that, as EU law requires, the tendering process is open, on equal terms, to companies from all EU member States.   [207] See, eg Freedland.

[208] See Chapter 14, section 2.2.3, and Chapter 19, section 3.5.2, below.

5. Conclusions

We have seen in this chapter that the executive occupies a pivotal role in the UK constitution. The absence of any absolute separation of powers between the legislative and executive branches places the latter in an unusually strong position. It has considerable powers at its disposal and is strongly situated to obtain, via the enactment of primary legislation, further legal powers on favourable terms. There are, in effect, three possible responses to this state of affairs. First, we might not regard it as problematic: we might think that the fact that the government has to submit to elections every five years provides an adequate safeguard against, or corrective in the event of, misuse of power. Second, we might advocate radical constitutional change, perhaps arguing that the UK should embrace a more full-blooded version of the separation of powers doctrine, such that the executive and the legislature are rendered more distinct. Under such arrangements, the executive might be less capable of getting Parliament to confer powers on it (or at least on the terms that it desires) and Parliament might be better able to hold the executive to account. Third, we might opt to steer a middle course, recognising that, in practice, such radical change is unlikely, instead seeking to rely upon—and where necessary improve—existing systems such that the executive is held to account in a more rigorous fashion. If such an approach is to be pursued, then Parliament must play a central role. It is to Parliament that we turn in the next chapter.

Further reading

DAINTITH AND PAGE, *The Executive in the Constitution* (Oxford 1999)

DREWRY, 'The Executive: Towards Accountable Government and Effective Governance?', in Jowell and Oliver (eds), *The Changing Constitution* (Oxford 2007)

FOSTER, 'Cabinet Government in the Twentieth Century' (2004) 67 MLR 753

McHARG, 'Reforming the United Kingdom Constitution: Law, Convention, Soft Law' (2008) 71 MLR 853

Useful websites

http://www.number10.gov.uk
The website of 10 Downing Street

http://www.cabinetoffice.gov.uk
The Cabinet Office website

http://www.civilservice.gov.uk
The Civil Service website

http://www.cabinetoffice.gov.uk/resource-library/ministerial-code
Online access to the Ministerial Code

Parliament

1. Introduction

The central concern of this chapter is Parliament—that is, the United Kingdom Parliament, which meets in the Palace of Westminster in London.[1] We focus on three principal issues. First, we address the *democratic credentials* of Parliament. It is trite to state that Parliament is a democratic institution, but what exactly does this mean? Who sits in Parliament? How do they get there? And is the form of democracy that the UK Parliament can lay claim to a satisfactory one? Second, we consider *Parliament's legislative role*. What is the contribution of Parliament to the making of legislation and what does this tell us about the relationship between Parliament and the executive government? Third, we examine *Parliament's powers*. We will see that, at least in constitutional theory, Parliament is 'sovereign', meaning that its authority to legislate is legally unlimited. We will consider why this is, whether it is acceptable, and whether the notion of parliamentary sovereignty remains accurate today.

In addressing these questions, we will encounter the three key themes that run throughout this book. First, we will need to consider *Parliament's role in holding the executive government to account*. Although we look at the accountability of the executive to Parliament in a later chapter—Chapter 10—we will see in this chapter that Parliament's lawmaking function itself raises questions about Parliament's capacity to hold the executive to account, bearing in mind that, as we explained in Chapter 4, Parliament is not really a lawmaker, but rather a scrutiniser of the executive's legislative agenda. Second, we will encounter questions concerning *the relationship between legal and political forms of constitutionalism*. In particular, in the section on Parliament's powers, we will see that, for all that the legal constitution allocates unlimited lawmaking power to Parliament, the political constitution imposes real limits upon Parliament's authority. We will need to ask whether it is right to leave that task to the political process, or whether the legal constitution should—or in fact already does—play a part in controlling Parliament's freedom to make law. Third, we will see that Parliament does not enjoy a monopoly on lawmaking power: in our contemporary *multilayered constitution*, the UK Parliament is an important—but is far from the only—legislative body.

---

[1] The Scottish Parliament and the Northern Ireland and Welsh Assemblies are considered in Chapter 7.

2. Parliament and democracy

2.1 **Why democracy?**

The word 'democracy' is used in many different ways and contexts.[2] At its most basic, it describes a system in which the people have a decisive say over how and by whom they are governed. This is most obviously so where the government is selected by the people via an election. It follows that countries that embrace democracy also, at least implicitly, embrace the notion that no individual or group has the right to govern, and that, instead, the people have the right to be governed as they wish. The opposite of democratic government is dictatorship: a system in which a particular individual or group obtains or retains power without in any formal way securing public assent. All government, whether democratic or undemocratic, is ultimately about the exercise of power, including doing inherently unpopular things such as collecting taxes. The key difference, however, is that whereas dictatorship involves the naked exercise of power by those with the means and audacity to seize it and who rule by force rather than consent, power in democracies is clothed in legitimacy through the existence of accepted systems for determining by whom, and on what terms, power should be wielded.

Q Is dictatorship 'wrong'? Can you identify principled arguments (as opposed to relying on an instinctive reaction) to justify your answer?

It is possible to divide the main attractions of—and hence reasons for embracing—democratic government into two broad categories.

The first consists in deductions drawn from *a particular normative view of the human condition*, which holds that every individual should be recognised as autonomous and that all people are equally valuable in moral terms. Various consequences flow from this, one of which is that everyone should, in general, be allowed to make their own decisions about how they live their lives. At an individual level, this philosophy is institutionalised in many countries in human rights laws that guarantee freedom of speech, religion, movement, and so on. But because it would be impossible for everyone to do what they wanted (since people's wishes would conflict), a system of government is required to provide a framework within which the autonomy of individuals can be reconciled with the existence of an ordered civil society in which people are able peacefully to coexist. However, recognition of the autonomy and dignity of individuals means that the system of government must be one in which they have a say. When questions arise about whether one person's freedom (for example, to protest by lying in the middle of a road) should be restricted for the benefit of another

---

2 See Morison, 'Models of Democracy: From Representation to Participation?', in Jowell and Oliver (eds), *The Changing Constitution* (Oxford 2007).

person (for example, who wishes to drive down the road), democracy requires that they are resolved in a manner recognised as legitimate by the people collectively. In this way, the autonomy of the individual is translated into the autonomy of the people: the people collectively are free to order society in the way in which they see fit; they are also treated as equals. Mill argued that a person's interests 'are only secure from being disregarded' when he is 'able and habitually disposed to stand up for them'. Since the interests of the 'excluded'—that is, those who play no role in or have no influence over government—are, at the very least, 'always in danger of being overlooked', giving everyone a voice is a way of preventing anyone's interests from being overlooked and of, in turn, recognising the equality of individuals.[3]

Second, there are *practical reasons for preferring democratic government*. Mill argued that giving people a 'voice in their own destiny' promotes the flourishing of individuals: it encourages intellectual endeavour and the development of 'moral capacities' by incentivising participation in the business of, and debate about, government.[4] Such participation in turn makes it likely that the society will be better governed: harnessing the wisdom, insight, and experience of many people is more likely to produce good results than reliance on the views of a few.

> **Q** Not everyone shares this view. The philosopher Plato wrote that 'when a man is ill, whether he be rich or poor, to the physician he must go, and he who wants to be governed, to him who is able to govern'.[5] Although his argument was complex, its essence was that governing is a complicated business, that few people are qualified to do it, and that the masses might well be ill-equipped to identify such people. Do these arguments constitute a convincing case against democratic government?

Even if it is accepted that democracy is, on balance, a good thing, it is a concept that can be implemented in different ways. Two should be noted. *Representative democracy* involves the public selecting, through elections, people who will represent them and make decisions on their behalf. In such a system, there is usually no requirement (at least, no *legal* requirement) for the representatives, once elected, to satisfy themselves that they are acting consistently with the wishes of those whom they represent—although in systems that allow representatives to stand for re-election, there is a strong practical incentive for them to act in a way that will please the majority of the represented. *Participative democracy*, meanwhile, entails forms of public participation in the governmental process that extend beyond voting for representatives. An extreme form of participative democracy is known as 'direct democracy', in which at least the more important changes in public policy and law must be approved by the public through referendums before they can take effect. More modest implementations of participative democracy seek to ensure an ongoing dialogue—rather than one that

---

[3] *Considerations on Representative Government* (New York 1862), ch 3.
[4] *Considerations on Representative Government*, ch 3.   [5] *Republic*, ch VI.

exists only when elections loom—between the people and the government; this might, for example, involve requiring government to supply extensive information to the public before decisions are made, and obliging the government to consult the public and take into account views thereby obtained.

In reality, many systems of government built on the representative notion of democracy also embrace aspects of participative democracy. For example, in the UK, although the election of representatives to Parliament is the most high-profile manifestation of democracy, the public is occasionally asked to vote on important constitutional changes in referendums, and is routinely informed about and consulted upon the development of public policy.[6] Indeed, once we recognise that democracy exists in a range of different forms, it becomes apparent that the distinction drawn above between democracies and dictatorships is an ultimately arid one: even a government that is unelected may exhibit vestiges of participative democracy by consulting people on certain matters or informally taking account of public sentiment. This is not to suggest that such a system of government could reasonably claim to be democratic in a conventional sense—but it is important to recognise that the more meaningful inquiry is not *whether* a country is democratic, but *how* democratic it is.

How democratic, then, is the UK?

2.2 Elections to the House of Commons

2.2.1 The point of general elections

The UK Parliament is bicameral—that is, it consists of two chambers. For the time being, we are concerned only with the House of Commons. The other chamber, the House of Lords, is considered below.

General elections in the UK serve two functions. First, they determine membership of the House of Commons. Members of the House of Commons—known simply as 'members of Parliament' (MPs)[7]—are thus selected by the electorate pursuant to the representative conception of democracy described above. Second, under the UK's system of 'parliamentary democracy', general elections determine which political party forms the executive government: as explained in Chapter 4, members of the government are drawn from the party (or from a coalition of parties) with more than half of the seats in the Commons. General elections are thus formally elections to the legislature, but they also, in effect, determine the political composition of the government.

2.2.2 Calling a general election

It has long been the case that no more than five years may elapse between general elections in the UK.[8] However, within that five-year period, Prime Ministers have had a discretion to call an election at a time of their choosing by asking the monarch to

---

[6] See further Ministry of Justice, *A National Framework for Greater Citizen Engagement* (London 2008).

[7] Members of the House of Lords, although members of Parliament, are known as peers rather than as MPs.　　　　　　　　　　　　　　　　　　　　　　　　　　[8] Septennial Act 1715.

dissolve Parliament, thus triggering an election.[9] The absence of fixed-term Parliaments has been a double-edged sword for governments. It has afforded them the opportunity to hold an election at a time of their choosing, but has also reflected the fact that government has required the ongoing confidence of the House of Commons, the convention being that (on a simple majority) a vote of 'no confidence' in the government triggered the dissolution of Parliament and so a general election.

Following the 2010 election, which produced no overall majority for any party, a coalition government was formed. Under this arrangement, it was agreed that five-year fixed-term Parliaments should be introduced so that the Prime Minister would lose his discretion to decide when to call an election. In principle, this is a good idea. There is no valid reason why the incumbent should have the advantage conferred by such discretion. But fixed-term Parliaments raise practical difficulties. On the one hand, a government may lose the confidence of the Commons (whether through the break-up of a coalition or internal dissension within a single governing party) part-way through a Parliament. This suggests the need for an escape clause whereby an early election can be triggered to avoid the prospect of a 'lame duck' government unable to get its Bills enacted. On the other hand, retaining the traditional rule—whereby a simple majority on a no-confidence vote leads to dissolution—undermines the notion of fixed-term Parliaments, since a governing party or coalition, provided that it controlled more than half the seats in the Commons, would be able to engineer a vote of no confidence in order to trigger an election.[10] Similarly, a coalition partner could withdraw at any time and join with opposition parties to vote against the government, again triggering an election.

The coalition government, when it was in the process of being formed, recognised the existence of these issues.[11] At the time of writing, the Fixed-term Parliaments Bill is being considered by Parliament. If enacted in its present form, it will make it possible to hold an early election—that is, prior to the expiry of the normal five-year term—in one of two circumstances: if two-thirds of MPs support such a proposal or if the government loses (on a simple majority) a confidence vote and a new government—for example, through the formation of a (new) coalition—cannot be formed within 14 days. Under these arrangements, a government (unless it had a substantial—that is, two-thirds—majority) could not directly trigger an early election; although there would be the option of engineering a vote of no confidence, an election would not automatically follow—other parties would first have the option of trying to work together to form a new government.

2.2.3 Voting and standing in elections

It follows from what was said in section 2.1 above that genuine democracy calls for the widest possible involvement of the public. This implies two requirements: that

---

[9] See Marshall, *Constitutional Conventions* (Oxford 1987), ch 3; Blackburn, 'The Prerogative Power of Dissolution of Parliament: Law, Practice and Reform' [2009] PL 766.

[10] This issue has arisen elsewhere. See, eg Apel et al, 'The Decision of the German Federal Constitutional Court of 25 August 2005 Regarding the Dissolution of the National Parliament' (2005) 6 German Law Journal 1243.   [11] HM Government, *The Coalition: Our Programme for Government* (London 2010), p 26.

the widest possible range of people should be entitled to *stand for election* and to *vote in elections*. As to the former, UK citizens, citizens of the Republic of Ireland, and certain Commonwealth citizens may stand for election to the House of Commons provided that they are over the age of 18 when they are nominated.[12] However, certain people are expressly disqualified from membership of the House of Commons. They include many judges, civil servants, members of the armed forces and the police, and many public office-holders.[13] Members of the House of Lords are also disqualified from membership of the Commons,[14] as are those detained for more than six months on grounds of mental illness,[15] bankrupts,[16] and those convicted of corrupt or illegal practices committed in relation to an election.[17] There is also a statutory limit of 95 on the number of government Ministers who may sit in the House of Commons.[18]

The entitlement to vote in parliamentary elections extends, subject to certain exceptions, to all UK and Irish and to certain Commonwealth citizens who are over the age of 18 and who have complied with the necessary formalities concerning registration.[19] The exceptions mentioned above concern convicted criminals serving custodial sentences,[20] certain people who are detained for mental health reasons,[21] and those convicted of corrupt or illegal practices as mentioned in the previous paragraph.[22]

In general, these eligibility rules are consistent with the view that democracy requires the widest possible range of people to be able to participate in elections (both in terms of voting and standing for election). To the extent that the rules disbar certain categories of person from standing or voting, it is generally possible to identify rational justifications based on age, mental capacity, and so on. Two points, however, should be highlighted. First, the breadth of participation provided for by the current rules is a relatively recent phenomenon. Historically, the right to vote in elections was tied to the ownership of land: the majority of people—bearing in mind that home ownership has only recently become commonplace—were therefore disenfranchised. It was not until the enactment of the Representation of the People Act 1918 that the modern system based on one vote per person was introduced; in particular, it was only in 1918 that women were allowed to vote. Second, the exception concerning convicted prisoners was considered by the Grand Chamber of the European Court of Human Rights (ECtHR) in 2006. The European Convention on Human Rights (ECHR) enshrines the right to vote in, and stand for, elections to national legislatures.[23] Although the

---

[12] Act of Settlement 1700, s 3; Electoral Administration Act 2006, ss 17–18.

[13] House of Commons Disqualification Act 1975, s 1.

[14] However, hereditary peers who are barred from membership of the House of Lords by s 1 of the House of Lords Act 1999 are not (by operation of s 3 of the 1999 Act) disqualified from membership of the Commons. On hereditary peers and the 1999 Act, see section 2.3.1 below.   [15] Mental Health Act 1983, s 141.

[16] Insolvency Act 1986, s 427.   [17] Representation of the People Act 1983, s 160.

[18] House of Commons Disqualification Act 1975, s 2.

[19] Representation of the People Act 1983, s 1.   [20] Representation of the People Act 1983, s 3.

[21] Representation of the People Act 1983, s 3A.

[22] Representation of the People Act 1983. The position concerning members of the House of Lords is the same as for eligibility to stand for election: they may not do so, subject to the proviso in s 1 of the House of Lords Act 1999.

[23] Protocol 1, Art 3, as interpreted in *Mathieu-Mohin v Belgium* (1988) 10 EHRR 1, [46]–[51].

Grand Chamber held that this is not an absolute right, it held that the UK's blanket ban on voting by convicted prisoners was incompatible with the Convention.[24] Firm proposals for remedying this situation are still awaited.

2.2.4 **The voting system**

To date, elections to the House of Commons have been based on the 'first-past-the-post' (FPTP) voting system. Under it, the UK is divided into a number of geographical areas known as 'constituencies'—there were 650 of these at the 2010 election—each of which is represented by one MP in the House of Commons.[25] In a general election, the votes in each constituency are counted up and the candidate with the most votes becomes the MP for that constituency. This means that it is possible—indeed, it is extremely likely—for the winning candidate to have fewer than 50 per cent of the votes cast in the constituency. Bearing in mind our general discussion of democracy above, there are three issues that should be considered in relation to the FPTP system.

First, as we saw above, democracy is partly underpinned by the concept of equality: everyone should be allowed to vote, and *everyone's vote should count equally*. Whether FPTP meets this requirement is doubtful. Everyone gets one vote—but, in practice, people's votes do not count equally. For example, in the 2010 general election in the constituency of East Ham, the Labour candidate got 70 per cent of the vote; the Conservative candidate got only 15 per cent. In such constituencies, the outcome is, in practice, a foregone conclusion, and it is unsurprising that voters in such areas feel that their vote is unlikely to make a real difference. As a result, the focus of campaigning is always in marginal constituencies in which two or more candidates have a real chance of winning. Consider, for example, the constituency of Bolton West: in 2010, the winning Labour candidate got 18,327 votes, while her Conservative rival got 18,235.

Second, *the only thing votes count for under FPTP is determining which candidate has the most votes in the constituency in question.* It makes no difference whether a candidate wins with a majority of 27,826, as in East Ham, or 92, as in Bolton West. Votes for losing candidates therefore have no effect on the national picture: a Conservative voter in East Ham cannot comfort himself by thinking that, although his vote did not succeed in getting a Conservative MP elected for that constituency, it might help the Conservatives to win power nationally. Once the winner in a given constituency has been decided, that is the end of the matter—which is why this system is sometimes dubbed 'winner takes all'. FPTP may therefore produce a House of Commons the political composition of which does not closely (or at all) reflect how people voted nationally in a general election. This is apparent from Figure 5.1, which shows the relationship between the percentage of votes cast for each party and the percentage of constituencies won by each party in 2010. This system tends to work to the particular disadvantage of smaller parties: in 2010, the Liberal Democrats secured 6.8 million votes against Labour's 8.6 million—but Labour got over four times more seats in the House of Commons than the Liberal Democrats.

---

[24] *Hirst v UK (No 2)* (2006) 42 EHRR 41.   [25] Parliamentary Constituencies Act 1986, s 1.

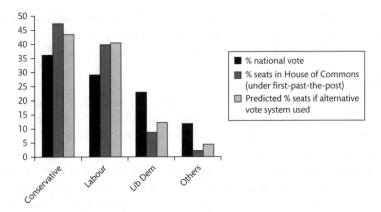

Figure 5.1 General election, May 2010

Third, it follows from what has been said so far that *the way in which constituency boundaries are drawn is very important*—at least in relation to marginal constituencies. Where, say, the Labour Party has a small majority in a mainly urban constituency, a small boundary change could make all the difference: if a Conservative-supporting suburban area were to be brought within the constituency, that might tip the balance at the next election. The practice of manipulating boundaries so as to influence election results is known as 'gerrymandering', after Elbridge Gerry, a US state governor, who caused the redrawing of electoral districts—the shape of one of which was said to resemble a salamander—to the benefit of his party. UK law attempts to ensure that this does not happen. The Parliamentary Constituencies Act 1986 provides for the independent determination of the boundaries of parliamentary constituencies. The bodies responsible are the Boundary Commissions for England, Northern Ireland, Scotland, and Wales. Each of the Boundary Commissions is chaired by an Electoral Commissioner. The latter are appointed by the Queen on the recommendation of the House of Commons, and each must be an independent person in the sense of not being a member of or a current or recent employee of a registered political party.[26] They are required to review, every eight to twelve years, the boundaries of parliamentary constituencies, applying the rules laid down in the Act. Those rules, *inter alia*, prescribe the total number of constituencies,[27] and that, in general, all constituencies should contain roughly equal numbers of voters[28]—although in practice there can be significant variations between constituencies, not least because the present approach aims to align parliamentary constituencies with local authority boundaries. The Parliamentary Voting System and Constituencies Bill, which is being considered by Parliament at the time of writing, will, if enacted in its present form, reduce by 50 the

---

[26] Political Parties, Elections and Referendums Act 2000, s 3.
[27] Parliamentary Constituencies Act 1986, Sch 2, para 1.
[28] Parliamentary Constituencies Act 1986, Sch 2, para 5.

total number of constituencies and will render them of more equal size. The Bill has proven controversial, not least because it would abolish the Boundary Commissions' powers to hold public inquiries into proposed changes to constituency boundaries.

2.2.5 Reform

Many people argue that democracy in the UK is not in the best of health. There is evidence, both statistical and anecdotal, of disaffection with politicians and the political process. A good example of the latter type of evidence is the extraordinary public backlash in 2009 when extensive information was made public concerning MPs' expenses claims. A strong sense emerged—whether fairly or not—that politicians were living the high life at public expense and were out of touch with ordinary people. Meanwhile, membership of the two main parties has plummeted dramatically over the last 50 years[29] and turnout at recent general elections shows a sharp decline.[30] As people lose faith in representative democracy, there is greater resort to other forms of participation, such as protest and direct action.[31]

The reasons for this apparent disaffection with conventional politics are contested and no doubt complex. They may be partly mundane—it may be, for example, that turnout would be improved by holding elections at weekends and allowing voting via the Internet rather than in person[32]—but it has been persuasively argued that the voting system is likely to be an important factor.[33] In particular, FPTP may act as a disincentive to voting if people feel that their vote will not really count if they wish to support a party that is unlikely to win in their particular constituency, or which stands no realistic chance of getting enough seats to secure a majority in the House of Commons.[34] This can lead to a sense of powerlessness and may require people to resort to tactical voting: for example, in a constituency in which the Conservatives stand no chance, a Conservative supporter might vote Liberal Democrat in an attempt to defeat the Labour candidate. FPTP's obvious problems notwithstanding, its great strength was always said to be that it tended to deliver a clear majority for one party, resulting in stable government. However, as the result of the 2010 election shows, this is not inevitable—particularly in a system increasingly characterised by three-party politics.

Against this background, reform of the voting system is now high up the political agenda. There are many different kinds of electoral system.[35] The one that most obviously contrasts with FPTP is the *party list* system, often referred to simply as *proportional representation*, under which people are asked to vote for a party rather than an

---

[29] Kavanagh et al, *British Politics* (Oxford 2006), p 445.

[30] From 1945 to 1997, turnout was always above 70 per cent and sometimes above 80 per cent, but turnout dropped to 60 per cent, 61 per cent, and 65 per cent in 2001, 2005, and 2010, respectively. See House of Commons Research Paper 01–37, *UK Election Statistics: 1945–2000* (London 2001) and online at **http://www.electoralcommission.org.uk**   [31] Kavanagh et al, ch 22.

[32] See, eg Ministry of Justice, *Election Day: Weekend Voting* (London 2008).

[33] See, eg *Power: An Independent Inquiry into Britain's Democracy* (London 2006).

[34] *Power: An Independent Inquiry into Britain's Democracy*, p 182.

[35] See generally **http://www.electoral-reform.org.uk**

individual candidate. Seats in the legislature are then shared out in direct proportion to the votes cast: if a given party were to obtain 32 per cent of the national vote, it would be given 32 per cent of the seats in the legislature. The individual party members who are allocated the seats are determined by reference to the party list: each party has a rank order of candidates; it works down that list until all of the seats that it has won have been allocated. All votes therefore count equally, and the legislature precisely reflects each party's share of the vote. There are, however, significant disadvantages with such a voting system. There is no link between MPs and constituencies (because there are no constituencies), and a profusion of small parties is encouraged, resulting in fragile coalition governments, which frequently collapse.[36] Although a version of the party list system is used for elections in the UK to the European Parliament, and although, as we discuss below, it may be appropriate in relation to the House of Lords, there is little prospect of its being adopted for elections to the House of Commons.

As a precursor to its unfulfilled 1997 manifesto commitment to a referendum on electoral reform, the Blair administration established the Jenkins Commission to review the voting system. In doing so, it made it plain that a party list system would be unacceptable, requiring the Commission to design a system that would maintain 'a link between MPs and geographical constituencies'.[37] In reaching its conclusions, the Commission was impressed by two voting systems.

The first is known as *alternative vote*. It can best be explained through an example. Assume that, as in Figure 5.2, there are three candidates—A, B, and C—standing for election in a given constituency. Voters can rank the candidates in order of preference. For example, if a voter were to want to see candidate A elected, the voter would put a '1' next to that candidate's name, and would put a '2' next to C's name if he were to prefer C to B. When the votes are initially counted, only the 'first preference votes'—that is, the '1's—are taken into account. If a candidate gets more than half of such votes, she wins outright. But if (as in our example) no such candidate emerges, then there is a second round of counting. In it, the candidate with the fewest first-preference votes—C in our example—is eliminated, and the second-preference votes of voters who put that candidate first are allocated to the remaining candidates. In the example, of the twenty people who put '1's next to C's name, twelve put '2's next to A's name, and eight put '2's next to B's name. In the second round of counting, therefore, A is given twelve and B is given eight additional votes. This gives A 57—more than half of the total 100 votes—and so A is the winner. If, after a given round, no one emerges with more than half the votes, the most unpopular remaining candidate is eliminated and his votes reallocated, the process being repeated until someone gets a majority.

The Jenkins Commission noted this system's 'very considerable advantage of ensuring that every constituency member gains majority acquiescence' and its capacity to free voters from their present dilemma of voting ideologically (for the candidate whom

---

[36] This problem can be alleviated by requiring a party to cross a minimum threshold before becoming eligible for legislative seats.

[37] *The Report of the Independent Commission on the Voting System* (Cm 4090 1998), [1].

Candidate	Count 1 (taking into account only first preference votes)	Count 2 (taking into account second-preference votes of voters who put 'C' first)
A	45	45 + 12 = 57 (wins with more than half of the votes)
B	35	35 + 8 = 43
C	20 (of whom 12 put 'A' as second preference and 8 put 'B' as second preference)	n/a

Figure 5.2 Alternative vote

they really like) or practically (for the candidate whom they like best out of the two or three with a realistic chance of winning).[38] However, Jenkins recognised that this is not a system of proportional representation. Like FPTP, it is based on constituencies and is unlikely to produce a legislature the political composition of which precisely mirrors the various parties' national shares of the vote. While it might increase the number of seats obtained by third parties such as the Liberal Democrats, it is also likely—particularly where the winning party is very popular, as with Labour in 1997—to give the main opposition party an even smaller—more disproportionate—number of seats than FPTP.[39]

The Jenkins Commission therefore looked at other systems—in particular, the *additional member* system. This applies, *inter alia*, in elections to the Scottish Parliament and Welsh Assembly, and is described in Chapter 7. For now, it suffices to say that it combines a constituency-based system (like FPTP or alternative vote) with the party list system: people cast two votes—for an individual to represent their constituency, and for a party. Some seats in the legislature are occupied by constituency representatives, with the remainder being filled by candidates on party lists, the idea being that the party list seats can be used to adjust the political make-up of the legislature to render it more proportionate than it would otherwise be. In the end, the Jenkins Commission recommended that 80–85 per cent of seats in the House of Commons should be filled by constituency MPs selected using the alternative vote system, and that the balance should be filled by candidates chosen through the party list system. This, the Commission felt, would harness the strength of the alternative vote system while offsetting the risk that it might otherwise lead to serious under-representation in the Commons of the main opposition party.[40]

At the time of writing, it is expected that a referendum on voting reform, proposing the adoption of the alternative vote system, will be held in 2011. Figure 5.1 shows the Electoral Reform Society's predictions of how many seats each party would have got in 2010 had this system been used.[41] It can be seen that use of the alternative vote system would have affected the outcome—in particular, the Conservatives would have

---

[38] Cm 4090, [46] and ch 9.

[39] Cm 4090, [82]; Baston, *A Better Alternative? What AV Would Mean for Westminster* (London 2008).

[40] Cm 4090, ch 9.   [41] See http://www.electoral-reform.org.uk

got fewer, and the Lib Dems more, seats—but it would not have yielded a House of Commons strictly representative of each party's share of the national vote.

> **Q** Which voting system do you prefer, and why? Which system do you think would best be capable of reinvigorating democracy in the UK and enhancing public trust in politicians and the political process?

A further proposed reform that should be noted concerns the creation of 'recall' powers. Following the 2009 MPs' expenses scandal, many MPs, anticipating the wrath of the electorate, chose not to stand for re-election in 2010. However, it was felt in some quarters that voters should be empowered, in effect, to sack MPs *between* elections. The government has therefore proposed that if an MP is guilty of serious wrongdoing and if 10 per cent of voters in the constituency sign a petition, a by-election should be triggered, giving the local electorate the opportunity to select a new MP between general elections.[42]

2.2.6 Political parties

There is nothing in principle that says that politics has to be dominated by political parties—and yet, all over the world, democracies *are* dominated by such parties. The UK is no exception. We have already seen in Chapter 4 that most politicians tend to behave tribally, expressing views and voting in ways that tow the party line. It follows that the House of Commons does not consist of 650 individuals each prepared to speak their own mind: in practice, it consists of two opposing sides—the government and the opposition parties. This is even reflected in the architecture of the House of Commons: government MPs sit on one side; opposition MPs on the other. Much of British political life is dominated by a seemingly continual election campaign between the main political parties. They will structure the policy choices presented to voters, select the candidates who become MPs and the leaders who become either Prime Ministers or leaders of the opposition, and also exert an enormous influence over how the government is both run and held to account. Within this system, people are unlikely to get anywhere in politics unless they ally themselves with a party. Although independent candidates occasionally succeed, the 2010 general election did not yield a single MP who was not a member of a political party.[43]

This is unsurprising. Political parties are both inevitable and desirable. They are inevitable because it is in the nature of like-minded people to gravitate together: such behaviour is both instinctive and purposeful, in that it enables such people to achieve more collectively than they could achieve acting wholly independently of one another. It is for precisely such reasons that political parties are formed. More than that, parties are desirable because, at least in parliamentary democracies, their absence would deprive voters of any meaningful way of influencing membership of the government.

---

[42] HM Government, *The Coalition: Our Programme for Government* (London 2010), p 27.

[43] As is conventional, the Speaker of the House of Commons stood, and was elected, as an independent candidate, but this is not a true exception: the Speaker had been a Conservative MP, and (again as is conventional) the main parties do not stand against the Speaker.

If people were simply to vote for independent MPs to represent their constituencies, who became Prime Minister and what policies his or her government followed would be wholly unpredictable, depending as it would upon which individual MP after an election had sufficient powers of persuasion to get others to rally around and support him or her as Prime Minister.[44] In a sense, then, the party system simply short-circuits, and makes rather more transparent, the sort of process that would have to precede the formation of a government: inevitably, each party is a reasonably 'broad church', encompassing people with a range of views, but before an election is held, each party, through its own internal processes, must decide on what its central policies and priorities will be. Of course, this system is not perfect. Political parties may not be straightforward with voters: they might, for example, try to conceal, or downplay, potentially unpalatable policies (for example, tax rises or public spending cuts)—and if, as in 2010, an election yields no overall majority for any party, a degree of horse-trading, with potentially unpredictable outcomes, must necessarily occur as potential coalition parties attempt to strike a bargain with one another.

However, while the party system is far from perfect, it is undoubtedly necessary. The existence of parties is therefore presupposed by the system of government that obtains in the UK (and in most democracies). Most political parties choose to register themselves under the relevant legislation.[45] This is not compulsory, but it does carry certain benefits: registered parties' logos may appear on ballot papers next to their candidates' names,[46] and only registered parties may make party-political broadcasts.[47]

2.2.7 Funding, spending, and fair play

It is in the nature of politics that politicians—and the parties into which they organise themselves—will attempt to persuade others of the correctness of their views. In this way, they seek to win power in order that they may put those views into practice. While this process of debate and persuasion is an ongoing one, it assumes particular prominence in the weeks immediately before a general election. Election campaigns are expensive: parties will inevitably want to spread their message as widely and as effectively as possible. This raises questions concerning the *funding of political parties* and the *rules on campaign spending*.[48]

The former has been the subject of considerable debate. Tony Blair was almost brought down six months into his first administration by allegations (which he denied) that a donation to the Labour Party of £1 million had influenced a subsequent government decision to exempt Formula One motor sport from a ban on tobacco advertising. More recently, a police investigation was held into allegations that certain individuals had been offered life peerages in return for making loans to the Labour

---

[44] For debate on this issue, see Tomkins, *Our Republican Constitution* (Oxford 2005), pp 136–9; Nicol, 'Professor Tomkins' House of Mavericks' [2006] PL 467.

[45] Political Parties, Elections and Referendums Act 2000.

[46] Political Parties, Elections and Referendums Act 2000, s 29.

[47] Political Parties, Elections and Referendums Act 2000, s 37. See further section 2.2.7 below.

[48] See generally Rowbottom, *Democracy Distorted* (Cambridge 2010).

Party.[49] And it was alleged that large accountancy firms gave hundreds of thousands of pounds' worth of resources to the Conservative Party before the 2010 election, hoping that they would retain and win new government contracts in the event of a Conservative government.[50] The suspicion—whether or not justified—to which such episodes give rise is that it is possible to purchase influence. Few people can be naive enough to think that politicians make decisions without thinking about what it is in it for them in terms of popularity, electoral success, and so on. But most people would also agree that the naked use of money to influence government policy is improper: it may be regarded as a form of corruption and certainly undercuts the principle of political equality by benefiting those who can afford to buy influence.[51] Debate has therefore focused on whether there should be changes to the way in which political parties are funded in order to remove or reduce the risk of such practices occurring. There are three main positions that one might adopt in this debate.

First, it might be argued that *people should be free to make whatever donations they wish* to political parties. Donating to political parties, it might be argued, is a form of participation in the political process that it would be improper to restrict. It is even said that any limitation on donations would restrict parties' capacity to communicate their messages and would thus represent a restriction upon freedom of expression.[52] It is not inconsistent with this position to accept that the identity of those making donations should be a matter of public record, the point of such transparency being that it allows people to judge whether money really is buying influence: although cause and effect might be hard to determine, the electorate is at least in a position to attempt to form a judgement if donations are public knowledge. For precisely that reason, UK law requires registered political parties regularly to report to the Electoral Commission on the size and source of any donation of more than £7,500.[53] Following the 'loans for peerages' allegations mentioned above, equivalent arrangements now apply to loans over £7,500.[54] The Electoral Commission maintains and publishes registers detailing all such donations and loans.

Second, there might instead be *a limit on the amount that any individual or organisation can donate* in a given year. Rowbottom explains that this form of regulation is motivated by concerns about equality—that is, that 'donation limits aim to restrict the activity of wealthy individuals to enhance the relative voice of others'.[55] A cap on donations thus has the potential to reduce the capacity of the rich to exert disproportionate influence—although that potential is unlikely to be fully realised unless the

---

[49] On life peerage, see section 2.3.1 below.

[50] 'Windfall for Tories as firms eye £4bn contracts', *The Independent*, 29 July 2009.

[51] See further Rowbottom, 'Political Donations and the Democratic Process: Rationales for Reform' [2002] PL 758.

[52] The closely related argument that limits on campaign spending may be an unlawful restriction on free speech have been accepted by the European Court of Human Rights and the US Supreme Court in *Bowman v UK* (1998) 26 EHRR 1 and *Buckley v Valeo* (1976) 424 US 1.

[53] Political Parties, Elections and Referendums Act 2000, s 62. There are also restrictions on who may make donations to registered political parties: eg individual donors must be registered to vote and resident for tax purposes in the UK (2000 Act, s 54).

[54] Political Parties, Elections and Referendums Act 2000, s 71M.   [55] Rowbottom, p 776.

cap is set low enough to be within the reach of everyone, which would be likely to drastically reduce the amount of funding available to political parties.[56] In the wake of the 'loans for peerages' allegations, an independent review of the funding of political parties was established under former senior civil servant Sir Hayden Phillips. It recommended new limits on election spending,[57] which would reduce the need for large donations, and a cap on donations of perhaps £50,000.[58] The review urged that any changes should be implemented on a consensual basis, but to date no consensus has emerged. A major sticking point has been the fact that the cap would drastically reduce the support available to major parties, which presently depend to a considerable degree on large donations from institutions and wealthy individuals.

Third, *state funding* might be made available to political parties in order to reduce reliance on donations. In fact, there is already limited state support in the UK: for example, election candidates get free postage so that they can send a mailing to voters in their constituency,[59] major parties get free airtime to make election broadcasts,[60] public money is given to the main opposition parties to support their parliamentary (but not campaigning) activities, and 'policy development grants' can be made to parties with more than one MP in the House of Commons.[61] The Electoral Commission has argued that state support should be increased modestly, partly through tax relief on individual donations,[62] and Phillips went much further, suggesting that public money should become a major source of income for political parties.[63] Phillips's main recommendations, on both state funding and a cap on donations, had not been implemented at the time of writing, although the coalition government said in 2010 that it would 'pursue a detailed agreement on limiting donations and reforming party funding in order to remove big money from politics'.[64]

Q Which of the three positions outlined above to you prefer? Why?

Like the way in which they raise their money, the way in which parties spend it—in terms of how much they are allowed to spend and on what—is subject to legal control. The purpose of such regulation is to attempt to create a level the playing field by preventing a very well-resourced party or candidate from being able to buy victory through sheer spending power (on advertising, for example). Four points arise.

First, there have, for a long time, been *constituency-level spending limits*. It is unlawful for any given candidate to spend more than approximately £10,500 on 'election

---

[56] Rowbottom, pp 776–7.   [57] Spending limits are addressed later in this section.

[58] Phillips, *Strengthening Democracy: Fair and Sustainable Funding of Political Parties* (London 2007).

[59] Representation of the People Act 1983, s 91.

[60] Election broadcasts are dealt with later in this section.

[61] Political Parties, Elections and Referendums Act 2000, s 12.

[62] *The Funding of Political Parties* (London 2004); for comment, see Rowbottom, 'The Electoral Commission's Proposals on the Funding of Political Parties' [2005] PL 468.   [63] Phillips, pp 17–20.

[64] HM Government, *The Coalition: Our Programme for Government* (London 2010), p 20.

expenses'[65]—which includes such things as advertising, transport, and administration.[66] It is also unlawful for others to spend more than £500 'with a view to promoting or procuring the election of a candidate'.[67] The sum used to be £5, but was raised after the ECtHR held—following the prosecution in the UK of an anti-abortion campaign group, which had exceeded the statutory spending limit—that such a severe restriction constituted an improper constraint upon freedom of speech.[68] This serves as a useful reminder of the tension between, on the one hand, permitting free and open debate, and, on the other hand, maintaining a playing field that is sufficiently level to enable a wide range of contributors to play an effective part in such debate.

Second, *national spending limits* were introduced in 2000. The amount that a party is allowed to spend (over and above the sums mentioned in the previous paragraph) depends on how many constituencies it is contesting.[69] If a party were to contest every seat in the UK, it would be allowed to spend £19.5 million. In the 2005 election, Labour and the Conservatives each spent £17.9 million and the Liberal Democrats spent £4.3 million.[70] This prompted Phillips to comment that 'the Conservative and Labour Parties spent on a scale which overwhelmed the resources which any other party was able to bring to bear'. His recommendation of stricter limits has not, to date, been implemented.[71]

Third, there are ways of levelling the playing field other than imposing quantitative caps on spending. For example, there may be *legal regulation of the way in which parties are allowed to campaign*. In the UK, strict impartiality requirements apply to television and radio programmes,[72] and there is an absolute ban on paid-for advertising by political parties on broadcast media.[73] However, certain broadcasters are required, free of charge, to make airtime available to major political parties for party-political broadcasts.[74] The relevant rules provide that the major parties will normally be offered a series of broadcasts before each election.[75] This system ensures that access to television and radio—which, notwithstanding the growth of the Internet, remain the most powerful advertising media—does not directly depend on the parties' resources.

Fourth, if elections are to be conducted in an even-handed and fair manner, it is clear that *the rules described above must be conscientiously enforced*, and that the fairness of elections must be ensured more generally in order to guard against fraud and other forms of improper behaviour that would pollute the democratic process. The

[65] Representation of the People Act 1983, s 76. The precise figure depends on the number of people on the electoral register in the relevant constituency.

[66] Representation of the People Act 1983, s 90ZA and Sch 4A.

[67] Representation of the People Act 1983, s 75.   [68] *Bowman v UK* (1998) 26 EHRR 1.

[69] Political Parties, Elections and Referendums Act 2000, s 79 and Sch 3.

[70] See http://registers.electoralcommission.org.uk/regulatory-issues/gbcampaignex.cfm

[71] Phillips, p 13.

[72] Communications Act 2003, ss 319–20, and Ofcom Broadcasting Code, ss 5 and 6. The BBC is subject to separate, but similar, rules under the terms of the agreement accompanying the BBC Charter.

[73] Communications Act 2003, s 321.

[74] Communications Act 2003, s 333, and Ofcom Rules on Party Political and Referendum Broadcasts. The BBC is subject to separate, but similar, rules under the terms of the agreement accompanying the BBC Charter.   [75] Ofcom Rules, r 10. See also http://www.broadcastersliaisongroup.org.uk

Electoral Commission is responsible for, *inter alia*: monitoring compliance with the rules concerning donations to, and spending by, political parties and candidates;[76] maintaining the register of political parties; monitoring and reporting on the conduct of elections;[77] keeping under review certain political and electoral matters, such as the regulation of income and expenditure by political parties, and political advertising;[78] reviewing constituency boundaries;[79] and promoting public understanding of the electoral systems in the UK.[80] The courts also play a significant role in two respects. First, there may be *criminal prosecutions* in respect of certain sorts of irregularity. Breach of many of the rules set out above concerning donations and election spending constitute criminal offences. The criminal law also deals with more direct attempts to subvert the democratic process: it is, for example, an offence for a candidate to bribe voters to vote for him.[81] Second, a constituency result can be questioned through an *election petition*.[82] Such petitions may be presented, *inter alia*, by candidates and by those entitled to vote[83] within 21 days of the result.[84] The courts have the power to determine that the election in the given constituency was void because of some relevant impropriety—for example, that spending limits were exceeded or that the candidate was not qualified to be a member of the House of Commons.[85]

2.3 The House of Lords

2.3.1 An anachronism?

Whatever the criticisms might be of the current system for electing MPs, the House of Commons is unquestionably a democratic institution. The same is manifestly not true of the House of Lords. There are four categories of 'peer'—members of the House of Lords—none of whom can claim any democratic mandate.

First, there are 26 Church of England *bishops and archbishops*. This has been criticised. The Royal Commission on House of Lords Reform—of which more later—concluded that while the inclusion of religious, as well as moral and philosophical, views in a second chamber may be valuable, such representation should not be restricted to a single denomination or faith given the religious diversity that characterises the UK today.[86]

Second, there are 23 *judicial members* of the House of Lords. This category (which will cease to exist when all of its present members die) is a leftover from the period before October 2009 when the UK's highest court was (for most purposes) the Appellate Committee of the House of Lords, the members of which were the 'Law Lords'. Now

---

[76] Political Parties, Elections and Referendums Act 2000, s 145.
[77] Political Parties, Elections and Referendums Act 2000, s 5.
[78] Political Parties, Elections and Referendums Act 2000, s 6.
[79] Political Parties, Elections and Referendums Act 2000, s 14.
[80] Political Parties, Elections and Referendums Act 2000, s 13.
[81] Representation of the People Act 1983, s 113.   [82] Representation of the People Act 1983, s 120.
[83] Representation of the People Act 1983, s 121.   [84] Representation of the People Act 1983, s 122.
[85] Representation of the People Act 1983, s 144.
[86] Commission on Reform of the House of Lords, *A House for the Future* (Cm 4534 2000), ch 15.

that the Appellate Committee has been superseded by the Supreme Court, no new Law Lords will be created. The original members of the Supreme Court were the 12 Law Lords then in post,[87] but they may not participate in the work of the House of Lords for as long as they are Supreme Court Justices.[88]

Third, there are approximately 90 *hereditary peers*. Such peerages are, as the name suggests, inherited: the death of a hereditary peer resulted in the peerage passing to his or her eldest son. Hereditary peers used to account for the majority of members of the House of Lords: there were over 700 such members by the end of the last century. Amid widespread recognition that if the legitimacy of an unelected second chamber was questionable, a second chamber dominated by hereditary members was undeniably improper in a supposedly meritocratic and democratic country, legislation was enacted in 1999 that provided that hereditary peers could no longer be members of the House of Lords.[89] However, as a token of its intention to undertake more thorough-going reform, the Labour government accepted that 92 hereditary peers should be allowed to remain pending such reform.[90]

Fourth, there are around 600 *life peers*. Such a person is appointed to the Lords for life, but when he or she dies, no hereditary principle applies: his or her child does not succeed to membership of the Lords. All life peerages are conferred by the Queen under the Life Peerages Act 1958, but the Queen does so only on the recommendation of the Prime Minister. There is no cap on the number of members of the House of Lords, and the number of life peers created each year varies: there were nearly 50 in 2004, but only ten in 2008. In effect, there are two types of life peer. About 70 per cent are *political peers*—that is, peers with a party affiliation whose names have been put forward to the Prime Minister by the leaders of each of the major parties. It is for the Prime Minister to decide how many new peers there should be from each party in any given year. The other 30 per cent of life peers are so-called *cross-benchers*. They have no party political affiliation and are now, in practice, appointed by the independent House of Lords Appointments Commission.[91]

> **Q** Is it acceptable for the Prime Minister to wield this sort of power? What difficulties might this pose in terms of the separation of powers doctrine?

2.3.2 Reform–framing the debate

Reform of the House of Lords has been on the political agenda for a very long time. Legislation enacted 100 years ago curtailing the Lords' legal powers was said, in its Preamble, to be a temporary measure pending the 'substitut[ion] for the House of Lords as it at present exists [with] a Second Chamber constituted on a popular instead

---

[87] Constitutional Reform Act 2005, s 24.   [88] Constitutional Reform Act 2005, s 137(3).
[89] House of Lords Act 1999, s 1.   [90] House of Lords Act 1999, s 2.
[91] See further **http://www.lordsappointments.independent.gov.uk**. The role of cross-benchers is considered in section 2.3.4 below.

of hereditary basis'.[92] Such a development is still awaited. The focus of the debate has always been on how people should get into the second chamber—in particular, whether they should be elected. That is clearly an important question, but it is not the only question; and it is not the question with which we should start. Rather, we must begin with two other (closely related) questions—what should the House of Lords do, and what powers should it have?

If the House of Lords were a co-equal partner with the House of Commons in the legislative process, with the power to veto Bills that the Commons had approved, then that would fundamentally influence the debate about the composition of the Lords. In such circumstances, it would be very difficult indeed for anyone committed to democratic principles to argue for anything other than a fully elected second chamber. However, that is not the current position, and nor is it how many of those who have contributed to the debate envisage a reformed House of Lords. The Royal Commission on House of Lords reform, which reported in 2000, took the view that the second chamber should complement, rather than replicate, the House of Commons—that it should be 'distinctively different'.[93] In many regards, the Royal Commission, like many others who have contributed to the debate, considered that a reformed second chamber should serve a broadly equivalent function to that which the present House of Lords fulfils: a revising chamber capable of providing thoughtful scrutiny of legislation and executive action in a manner that is, and from a range of perspectives that are, different from those found in the Commons. The job of the House of Lords, said that Royal Commission, was to make 'the House of Commons think again': 'The second chamber should engender second thoughts.'[94] If the role of the second chamber is conceived of thus, then this impacts on three particular matters.

2.3.3 Powers

First, it is relevant to the *powers* that the second chamber should have. At the moment, the House of Lords is less powerful than the House of Commons in two respects.

A *constitutional convention*, known as the Salisbury convention, provides that the House of Lords should not reject a government Bill that implements a manifesto pledge and for which the government therefore has an electoral mandate.[95] This convention recognises that it would be undemocratic for the Lords, lacking a democratic mandate, to block such legislation. The extent to which this convention is applicable to a coalition government remains to be seen; it should arguably apply only to commitments common to both coalition partners and for which there is therefore a clear mandate.

There is also a *legal restriction* on the Lords' powers in the form of the Parliament Acts 1911–49. In 1909, the Liberal government failed to secure the enactment of legislation imposing new taxes on landowners because the Conservative-dominated Lords

---

[92] See section 2.3.3 below on the Parliament Acts 1911–49.

[93] Commission on Reform of the House of Lords, *A House for the Future* (Cm 4534 2000), p 3; see also Chapter 3.   [94] Cm 4534, p 3.

[95] See further the report of the Joint Committee on Conventions (HL 265 HC 1212 2005–06).

refused to approve the Bill. Amid great controversy, which included the holding of two general elections in 1910, the government proposed legislation limiting the power of the Lords, and obtained the King's agreement that if the Lords were to refuse to approve such legislation, he would flood the second chamber with enough Liberal peers to out-vote the Conservatives on the matter. Faced with that prospect, the Lords agreed to the enactment of the Parliament Act 1911. That Act (as amended by the Parliament Act 1949) limits the Lords' powers in two ways. The first concerns *money Bills*—that is, Bills that the speaker of the House of Commons has certified as dealing with such matters as taxation and government spending. If such a Bill, having been passed by the Commons, is not passed without amendment by the Lords within a month of having been sent to the Lords, it can be enacted anyway.[96] The upshot is that, in respect of money Bills, the House of Lords has only a *one-month delaying power*. In relation to *non-money Bills* if, in two successive sessions (that is, parliamentary years), the Lords rejects a Bill approved by the Commons, the Bill may be enacted nevertheless.[97] Thus, in relation to legislation other than money Bills, the Lords has, in effect, a *one-year delaying power*.

There is one—and only one—exception to what may be done by the Commons, without the Lords' consent, under the Parliament Act. The Act explicitly states that it cannot be used in respect of 'a Bill containing any provision to extend the max-imum duration of Parliament beyond five years'.[98] It was suggested in *Jackson* that it would be open to the Commons—using the 1911 Act, without the Lords' consent—to enact two Bills. Act I would delete the exception regarding extending the life of Parliament.[99] Once that Bill were enacted, it would be possible for the Commons to use its 1911 Act powers to enact Act II—again without the Lords' consent—to extend the life of Parliament. This would make it possible for a government to extend its time in office by postponing a general election. All but one of the judges in *Jackson* rejected this analysis. The majority held that there was an implied prohibition in the 1911 Act on using it to pass anything resembling Act I: the Commons could not therefore unilaterally remove the exception regarding extending Parliament's life, and could not therefore pass Act II (an Act extending the life of Parliament) under the 1911 Act; such legislation would be possible only with the consent of the House of Lords.

Although welcome, this conclusion—that the Commons cannot unilaterally post-pone general elections—is a modest one. *Anything* else, said the court in *Jackson*, could be done by the Commons under the 1911 Act, including the enactment of major con-stitutional changes. Some of the judges acknowledged that, viewed thus, the effect of the Parliament Acts had been to 'erode the checks and balances inherent in the British constitution' by making it easier for the executive-dominated House of Commons to legislate without hindrance by the Lords.[100] This is an important point, but one that should not be overstated, bearing in mind that the Lords' power to delay legisla-tion for a year is not insignificant: such delays can wreck the government's legislative

---

[96] Parliament Act 1911, s 1.   [97] Parliament Act 1911, s 2.   [98] Parliament Act 1911, s 2(1).

[99] *R (Jackson) v Attorney General* [2005] UKHL 56, [2006] 1 AC 262.

[100] *Jackson* at [41], *per* Lord Bingham.

programme, and it will often prefer to reach a compromise with the Lords rather than wait a year to push the Bill through without the Lords' consent. This does, however, underscore the fact that control of the government-dominated Commons is ultimately political rather than legal—something that, in turn, reflects one of this book's key themes: the importance of political constitutionalism in the UK.

2.3.4 Complementarity

If, as suggested above, the role of a second chamber is to 'engender second thoughts', then it should *complement*, rather than *replicate*, the first chamber. Whatever its shortcomings, this is a criterion that the House of Lords presently fulfils, at least to some extent, in three ways—which, it is fairly broadly agreed, should be retained even if the Lords is subject to further reform.[101]

First, whereas the Commons is a highly political chamber, in the sense that it is *dominated by the political parties*, the House of Lords is not. No political party has an *overall majority*, making it impossible for a single-party government unilaterally to get legislation through the Lords. Nor does the Conservative–Liberal Democrat government formed in 2010 have an overall majority, although it has signalled that, pending full reform of the House of Lords, it will make appointments 'with the objective of creating a second chamber reflective of the share of the vote secured by the political parties in the last general election'[102]—which means more peers from the coalition parties. Moreover, a quarter of the Lords' members have *no party-political affiliation*. This dilutes the importance of party politics in the Lords and is said to encourage a more independent, objective, thoughtful way of conducting business. It is also important to bear in mind that even those members of the Lords who are affiliated to a political party are *more likely to be independent-minded*, in the sense of not slavishly following the party line, because most peers (in contrast to most MPs) are not career politicians: even those affiliated to a party are likely either to have a professional life outside of politics or to be towards the end of their political careers. This means that promises of promotion to the front benches are likely to be less appealing in the Lords, giving the parties less of a hold over the second chamber.

Second, the Lords is regarded as complementing the Commons in that it is able to bring *particular expertise* to the discharge of its functions. This reflects the fact that membership of the Lords is, at least in one sense, more diverse than that of the Commons. It is increasingly the case that the latter is dominated by career politicians who have spent most of their working lives in politics. Although there is no shortage of former MPs in the Lords—there are currently about 170—there is a substantial number of people who have been made members of the Lords because they have achieved distinction or prominence in some other field of activity, such as business, science, or the arts. In this sense, the House of Lords is able to scrutinise Bills and government activity with the benefit of a particular breadth of experience and depth of expertise.

---

[101] See, eg HM Government, *The House of Lords: Reform* (Cm 7027 2007), ch 6.

[102] HM Government, *The Coalition: Our Programme for Government* (London 2010), p 27.

Third, we noted above that the FPTP voting system means that large political parties dominate in the Commons; *small parties, and groups seeking to highlight a particular issue*, are unlikely to win enough votes in any given constituency to secure even a single seat in the Commons. The House of Lords is arguably capable of giving a voice to issues and groups unlikely to be well served by a first chamber the members of which are eager to appeal to the majority whose interests naturally dominate in the Commons. This is not, however, to suggest that, in its present incarnation, the Lords is a perfect representation of contemporary Britain: only 20 per cent of its members are women, and only 4 per cent are non-white.[103]

2.3.5 Composition

It is against the background of the foregoing discussion that questions about the composition of the Lords must be tackled. There are, broadly speaking, three options: a wholly appointed second chamber; a wholly elected one; or a hybrid system, with some members elected and some appointed.

Many of the factors considered above might be thought to point towards a wholly appointed second chamber. Such a system could ensure that political parties do not dominate, that a wide range of views and interests are represented, and that a wider range of people than those likely to stand for election is brought into the political process. But this overlooks one crucial point: that, in a democratic system, a legislature must be regarded as legitimate.[104] This is not an unanswerable argument against an appointed second chamber, particularly if, like the present House of Lords, it is less powerful than the first chamber. It was also argued by the then Lord Chancellor in 2003 that legitimacy may be conferred other than by the ballot box: judges, for example, are not elected, their legitimacy deriving instead from their independence and expertise. It is clear, however, that this argument has been considered largely unpersuasive. Phillipson, for example, retorts that, as part of the legislature itself, the second chamber 'exercises direct political power... the legitimacy for [which] can flow only from election'.[105]

> **Q** This argument begins with the fact that the House of Lords has legislative authority (albeit limited) and concludes that it must therefore have democratic legitimacy. Bingham[106] advances the opposite argument: that the second chamber should be stripped of its legislative power entirely and constituted as an advisory body consisting (like the current House of Lords) of a broad range of people who can bring experience and expertise to the scrutiny of legislation. Bingham argues that, thus constituted, the second chamber would not need democratic legitimacy. Do you agree?

---

[103] House of Commons Library Paper SN/SG/1156, *Ethnic Minorities in Politics, Government and Public Life* (London 2008).

[104] See, eg Public Administration Select Committee, *The Second Chamber: Continuing the Reform* (HC 494-I 2001–02), [68].

[105] Phillipson, ' "The Greatest Quango of Them All", "A Rival Chamber" or "A Hybrid Nonsense"? Solving the Second Chamber Paradox' [2004] PL 352, 366.   [106] 'The House of Lords: Its Future?' [2010] PL 261.

Recent debate has therefore focused on whether the Lords should become a wholly or only partly elected chamber. The Royal Commission recommended a mainly appointed House, but with a 'significant minority' of members elected to represent and 'provide a voice for the nations and regions of the United Kingdom'.[107] This position was endorsed by the government in 2002, which argued that a mainly elected second chamber would suffer from several 'practical disadvantages', including loss of independence and dominance of political parties.[108] Yet, in 2007, the government announced that it would attempt to build consensus around the view that the second chamber should be half appointed and half elected.[109] And by 2008, the government had decided that a reformed second chamber should be mainly elected, but that, in order to preserve an independent element, perhaps 20 per cent of members should be appointees independent of any political party.[110] Following the 2010 general election, the new government announced that it favoured a wholly or mainly elected second chamber, with elections on the basis of proportional representation.[111] At the time of writing, more detailed proposals are awaited.

Phillipson agrees that there should be an appointed element, but doubts whether 20 per cent would be sufficient.[112] Referring to the enactment of the Anti-terrorism, Crime and Security Act 2001—one of the case studies with which we opened this book—he argues that the architecture of the British constitution means that the 'composition of its second chamber must guarantee the presence of members who will instil a particularly strong culture of mature, objective, and long-termist scrutiny of the wisdom and necessity' of proposed legislation.[113] This is a persuasive argument that raises an important conundrum. In the absence of a written constitution limiting the power of Parliament and of a thoroughgoing separation of powers between the executive and the Commons, the existence of the Lords as an internal check upon the executive-dominated Commons is imperative—yet its effectiveness as a real counterweight to the power of the executive and the Commons is dependent upon its capacity for independent-minded scrutiny that is not stifled by the sort of party politics likely to be engendered by elections. The capacity of a small unelected element goes some way towards addressing this problem, but whether it goes far enough is debatable. For that reason, it has been suggested that elected members should serve for one long (for example, 15-year) term without any possibility of re-election in order to enable them to act as independently as possible.[114] This appears to be what the government now has in mind.[115]

---

[107] Commission on Reform of the House of Lords, *A House for the Future* (Cm 4534 2000), p 114.

[108] HM Government, *The House of Lords: Completing the Reform* (Cm 5291 2002), [36]–[40].

[109] HM Government, *The House of Lords: Reform* (Cm 7027 2007), p 5.

[110] Ministry of Justice, *An Elected Second Chamber: Further Reform of the House of Lords* (Cm 7438 2008).

[111] HM Government, *The Coalition: Our Programme for Government* (London 2010), p 27.

[112] Phillipson at 379.   [113] Phillipson at 371.

[114] Commission on Reform of the House of Lords, *A House for the Future* (Cm 4534 2000), ch 12; Ministry of Justice, *An Elected Second Chamber: Further Reform of the House of Lords* (Cm 7438 2008), ch 15.

[115] Conservative–Liberal Democrat Coalition Agreement, 11 May 2010.

Q Do you agree that a hybrid second chamber with a majority of elected members is the best way forward for the House of Lords? Why, or why not?

3. Parliament and the legislative process

In this section, we turn to consider the role of Parliament in the legislative process. The phrase 'the legislative process' refers to the process by which legislation—statute law or Acts of Parliament—is enacted. This often appears to be a long, complex, and tortuous procedure by which detailed legislative rules are produced, scrutinised, revised, amended, subjected to further scrutiny, and so on: 'A long, long road winds from initial idea to royal assent for the statute which embodies it.'[116] One view is that it is best to avoid examining this process altogether. As Bismarck once observed: 'Laws are like sausages: it is better not to see them being made.' But it is important that we examine the legislative process for a number of reasons.

First, there is the pre-eminent significance of legislation. Legislation affects us all: most of the rules that regulate our daily lives—whether by requiring or forbidding us to do certain things—originate either from legislation or from the numerous rules and regulations made under such legislation. Legislation is the single most important source of law in our society and is produced via the legislative process. The volume of legislation enacted today is enormous—but, as we shall see, quantity does not necessarily mean quality.

Second, legislation is used to achieve a variety of different and important public purposes. It can create new criminal offences, increase taxes, distribute welfare, enable government to make appropriations of public money, and authorise the use of such resources. Legislation is a vital resource of public policy.[117] Virtually all of the areas of public policy for which government is responsible depend partly or wholly upon legislation. While government retains certain prerogative powers—to go to war and issue passports, for example—such powers can be circumscribed by legislation and are relatively few in number when compared with the range of statutory powers and functions that government now has.[118]

Finally, the legislative process is closely intertwined with the broader political process. Acts of Parliament are the product of political debate. In a democracy, we would expect the legislative process to be as open as possible and for the legislature to scrutinise effectively all proposed legislation—'Bills'—before they became law. However, the degree to which Parliament does engage in effective scrutiny is, as we shall see, open to question. This relates to one of our principal themes—ensuring the responsible

---

[116] Hennessy, *Whitehall* (London 2001), p 280.

[117] Rose, 'Law as a Resource of Public policy' (1986) 39 Parliamentary Affairs 297.

[118] On the prerogative, see Chapter 4, sections 3.1 and 4.3, above.

exercise of executive power. Parliament's role in the legislative process is centred not upon making legislation itself, but upon scrutinising the legislation that the government would like to be enacted. The purpose of this section of the chapter is then to examine the effectiveness of Parliament as a scrutiniser of legislation.

3.1 The legislative process—Parliament and government

3.1.1 Types of legislation

Let us start by clarifying the different types of Bill that are put before Parliament. First, there are *public or government Bills*. These make up the government's annual legislative programme, which normally consists of about 30 such Bills that aim to give effect to the government's policy objectives. Second, there are *private members' Bills*, which are introduced by individual MPs and members of the House of Lords (peers), who are not members of the government. Most private members' Bills stand little, if any, chance of being enacted, unless they have government support, but they may raise the political profile of a particular topic.[119] Those private members' Bills that do become law are often minor or technical pieces of legislation when compared with government Bills. Third, there are *private Bills*, which are usually promoted by organisations, such as local authorities or private companies, to give themselves powers beyond, or in conflict with, the general law. Fourth, there are *hybrid Bills*, which mix the characteristics of public and private Bills, because they affect the general public, but also have a significant impact for specific individuals or groups.[120] Fifth, *members of the public* are to be given the power to put Bills forward. The coalition government announced in May 2010 that petitions that secure 100,000 signatures 'will be eligible for debate in Parliament' and that the 'petition with the most signatures will enable members of the public to table a bill eligible to be voted on in Parliament'.[121] We will concentrate largely upon the legislative process as regards public or government Bills, as these are the predominant type of legislation that is enacted.

3.1.2 Roles—Parliament, Ministers, and government departments

Before we examine that process in detail, it is necessary to make some preliminary points concerning the roles of different constitutional actors in the enactment of legislation.

The need to consider this matter may seem surprising: surely the position is straightforward—Parliament, as the legislature, enacts legislation? However, as we saw in Chapter 4, this is very far from the case. For the reasons set out in Chapter 4,

---

[119] Marsh and Marsh, 'Tories in the Killing Fields? The Fate of Private Members' Bills in the 1997–2001 Parliament' (2002) 8 Journal of Legislative Studies 91; House of Commons Information Office, *The Success of Private Members' Bills* (London 2009).

[120] The Channel Tunnel Act 1987, for example, was a hybrid Bill.

[121] HM Government, *The Coalition: Our Programme for Government* (London 2010), p 27.

the legislative process in the UK is dominated from beginning to end by the executive branch of government. Parliament's role is therefore a limited one, which focuses upon scrutinising and enacting legislation. This is why it is more accurate to describe Parliament not as a lawmaking, but as a *law-effecting*, institution.[122] Of course, this does not mean that Parliament is irrelevant: only Parliament has the constitutional authority to create Acts of Parliament. It is this constitutional authority that establishes Parliament's role in scrutinising legislation. Nonetheless, Parliament's constitutional authority is heavily conditioned by the degree of political control that the government of the day is able to exert over it.

The executive, then, is, in many senses, in the driving seat. But what, in this context, is meant by the 'executive'? Given the importance of legislation to policy, Ministers are certainly involved, but their involvement is largely at a managerial and strategic level. There is a Cabinet Committee on Parliamentary Business and Legislation, which manages the government's current legislative programme on behalf of the Cabinet, advises the Cabinet on strategic management of the forthcoming programme, and ensures that the government's legislative programme reflects the government's overall priorities and that the passage of each of those Bills through Parliament is as smooth as possible.[123] However, the detailed work of turning policy proposals into Bills is undertaken not by Ministers, but by civil servants, who are organised into Bill teams. Such teams operate under the general direction of Ministers, but work with a substantial degree of autonomy in developing legislative policy. In turn, Bill teams' instructions are turned into draft legislation by the Office of Parliamentary Counsel, a specialised team of 60 lawyers with expertise in legislative drafting, based in Whitehall. So, as Page has noted: 'The idea that the politician is the author of legislation confuses constitutional formality with empirical reality.'[124]

The influential policy role of civil servants throughout the legislative process may appear surprising. After all, our basic notions of how lawmaking ought to be conducted in a democracy would strongly suggest that the legislative process should be an exclusively democratic one in which elected politicians play the prominent role. However, in the context of the many large-scale administrative programmes that government now manages, it is natural that government departments will themselves play a substantial role in the legislative process. Government departments are, in most instances, responsible for administering and implementing that legislation after it has been enacted: they often see legislation as another means by which they can administer policy.[125] 'A Bill is first and foremost the legal expression of a policy developed

---

[122] Norton, 'Parliament and Legislative Scrutiny: An Overview of Issues in the Legislative Process', in Brazier (ed), *Parliament, Politics and Law Making: Issues and Developments in the Legislative Process* (London 2004), p 5.

[123] Cabinet Office, *Guide to Legislative Procedure* (London 2009).

[124] Page, 'The Civil Servant as Legislator: Law Making in British Administration' (2003) 81 Public Administration 651, 674.

[125] Walkland, *The Legislative Process in Great Britain* (London 1968), p 23.

within a particular Government department.'[126] Nor has this been a recent development. As Low noted in 1904, 'the Ministry is the real law-making organ and...it can
count on the support of its Parliamentary majority for any legislative project, so long
as the majority holds together'.[127]

3.2 Parliamentary scrutiny

3.2.1 Introduction

So far, we have seen that Parliament's role is to scrutinise the government's legislative
proposals, rather than to formulate its own proposals. This raises two fundamental
questions: what form does this scrutiny take; and how well does Parliament discharge
this function?

Scrutiny of legislation is a fundamental aspect of Parliament's work. Parliament
spends more of its time scrutinising legislation than on any other activity, and its
assent is required before a Bill can become law. Without robust and rigorous parliamentary scrutiny, the risk is that poor-quality legislation may be enacted. Such
legislation may not achieve its goals, may impose undue burdens upon individuals
or businesses, may have undesirable or unintended side effects, may violate human
rights standards, or may be counterproductive. Effective parliamentary scrutiny is
therefore essential and can perform a number of important functions. Parliament
can examine the policy justifications underpinning a Bill to ensure that the measure is desirable in principle. It can examine whether the means devised to accomplish policy goals are adequate and fit for purpose. Parliament can also scrutinise
the technical quality of legislation. On the whole, better scrutiny tends to produce
better legislation. Finally, Parliament provides the vital representative link between
the government and the people who will be governed by legislation, and the process
of parliamentary scrutiny has the advantage that it is structured, transparent, and
public. More generally, parliamentary scrutiny is one aspect of Parliament's broader
function of holding government to account.

Nevertheless, despite the significance of parliamentary scrutiny of legislation, it has
been widely recognised for many years that Parliament is often unable effectively to
scrutinise legislation.[128] The complaint has often been that governments have forced
important—and sometimes poorly thought through—laws through a complaisant
and submissive Parliament in which they receive little, if any, effective scrutiny. In
1953, Amery described Parliament as 'an overworked legislation factory'.[129] More
recently, Tony Wright, former chair of the House of Commons Public Administration

---

[126] Goldsmith, 'Parliament for Lawyers: An Overview of the Legislative Process' (2002) 4 European
Journal of Law Reform 511, 513.

[127] Low, *The Governance of England* (London 1904), p 65. According to Rose, *Politics in England: Change
and Persistence* (Basingstoke 1989), p 112: 'Laws are described as Acts of Parliament, but it would be more
accurate if they were stamped: Made in Whitehall.'

[128] Rippon, *Making the Law: The Report of the Hansard Society on the Legislative Process* (London 1992).

[129] Amery, *Thoughts on the Constitution* (Oxford 1953), p 41.

Committee, has noted that the ineffectiveness of parliamentary accountability is most apparent in its scrutiny of legislation:

> In outward form legislation is carefully scrutinized through an elaborate series of parliamentary stages, including detailed consideration in committee. The reality is that the whole process is firmly controlled by the government, serious scrutiny by government members is actively discouraged, any concession or amendment is viewed as a sign of weakness, and the opposition plays a game of delay. The result is that much legislation is defective, vast quantities of amendments have to be introduced by the government at the House of Lords stage, and the government's control of the parliamentary timetable means that many of these amendments are then simply voted through by the Commons without any scrutiny at all. It is all deeply unsatisfactory, and felt to be so by almost everyone involved in it.[130]

This portrayal may conjure up a rather jaundiced image of MPs acting as lobby fodder—that is, waiting to be told on their pagers and Blackberries how to vote by their 'party whips' (that is, those MPs or peers appointed by a political party to maintain parliamentary discipline among its members so as to ensure attendance and voting). This is perhaps an oversimplification—not all MPs and peers are willing to do precisely what they are told—but there is more than a grain of truth in this general depiction of parliamentary scrutiny. There are several reasons why the effectiveness of parliamentary scrutiny of legislation is limited.

3.2.2 Adversarial party politics and government dominance of the House of Commons

The first, and perhaps the principal, constraint upon the effectiveness of parliamentary scrutiny arises from two defining and interlocking features of the UK's parliamentary system: the dominance of the government of the day over the House of Commons, and the pervasive adversarial culture of Westminster party politics. We have already noted that virtually every aspect of Parliament's work is dominated by party politics; the same applies to the legislative process. The overriding assumption is that MPs support or oppose a Bill according to their party loyalties. And because the government (whether composed of a single party or a coalition of parties) will normally have more than half of the MPs, this means that the government can generally be confident of getting its Bills through the House of Commons.[131] The degree to which backbench government MPs refuse to support government Bills is normally seen as a test of the government's strength. Most MPs are loyal to their party or else placed under pressure by the government's whips to support the government's legislative programme; if the government whips declare that a particular vote will be subject to a 'three-line whip', then rebellious MPs risk being expelled from the governing party or parties. This

---

[130] Wright, *British Politics: A Very Short Introduction* (Oxford 2003), p 89.

[131] For reasons considered earlier in this chapter, the position in the House of Lords is different, but the likelihood of the government facing insuperable obstacles in the Lords is reduced by virtue of the Salisbury convention and the Parliament Acts.

does not mean that the whips are always successful in maintaining party discipline. The government may offer concessions in order to prevent a rebellion, but this is the exception rather than the norm, because the government will usually have a sufficient number of MPs to prevent a defeat.[132] For example, the Labour government elected in 1997 experienced its first defeat in the House of Commons only in 2005 when backbench Labour MPs refused to approve the government's proposal to allow the pre-charge detention of terrorist suspects for up to 90 days.[133] By contrast with government backbench MPs, opposition parties will often oppose government Bills, but will, by definition, lack the necessary support with which to defeat the government.

Parliament can, of course, offer criticism and advice, and can subject legislation to public scrutiny. However, it is important to recall that the legislative process is primarily a political process and one in which the governing party—the government—almost always holds the upper hand. Consequently, rather than being primarily focused upon the scrutiny of legislation, Parliament's role in the legislative process is often that of providing a forum in which the political parties engage in a continuous electoral campaign by seeking to score political points off one another.

An illustration of this adversarial culture is to be found in the role of Ministers within the legislative process. Ministers tend to view the size and importance of the Bills that they present to Parliament as a demonstration of their own strength. It has been noted that there has been a distinct culture prevalent throughout Whitehall that the standing and reputation of Ministers have been dependent on their Bills getting through largely unchanged, meaning that Ministers are resistant (for fear of appearing weak) to alterations to their Bills, not only on the main issues of substance, but also on matters of detail.[134] If Ministers see amendments as a threat to their personal reputations and seek to reinforce party discipline through the whips, then the possibilities for effective scrutiny are likely to be small.

3.2.3 Parliament's limited competence

A second constraint upon parliamentary scrutiny of legislation concerns the competence of Parliament. In the nineteenth century, John Stuart Mill noted that to determine 'what portions of the business of government the representative assembly should hold in its hands, it is necessary to consider what kinds of business a numerous body is competent to perform properly'. He concluded that 'a numerous assembly is...little fitted for the direct business of legislation': the 'detailed and skilled work of legislation' should be left to those 'with the requisite skill', with the legislature's role being limited to 'either approving or disapproving the results'.[135]

The complexity of public policy and legislation has increased exponentially since Mill made these comments. In the context of the contemporary legislative process, the

---

[132] See Cowley, *The Rebels: How Blair Mislaid His Majority* (London 2005).
[133] Terrorism Act 2006.
[134] House of Commons Modernisation Committee, *The Legislative Process* (HC 190 1997–98), [7].
[135] Mill, *Considerations on Representative Government* (New York 1862), pp 277–9.

competence of parliamentarians to perform even this scrutiny function has often been questioned. It has been noted that there is a 'contemporary shortage in the House of Commons itself of the kind of experience and skills demanded by the task' of scrutinising legislation.[136] So, what do MPs themselves think of their own ability to scrutinise the mass of complex legislation put before them? According to a recent empirical study of the legislative process (which drew upon interviews with MPs and peers):

> Parliamentarians were often open in admitting that coping with the reality of massive amounts of complicated legislation severely compromised their effectiveness, and that they often do not understand the subject matter of the Bills they are scrutinizing...a number of parliamentarians explained...that the content of anywhere from a quarter to a half of all legislation they voted on was effectively a mystery to them...MPs and Peers tend to focus on bits they understand but often do not understand the larger picture.[137]

The reason for the limited competence of Parliament is that MPs are generalists; at best, they can develop an expertise in only a handful of areas of public policy. After all, Parliament is a relatively small institution when compared with the scale and complexity of the largest organisation in the UK: the government. We saw above that one of the arguments against a fully elected House of Lords is that an appointed element makes room for people who, not being career politicians, may bring other forms of expertise and experience to the scrutiny process.

3.2.4 The government's dominance of the legislative procedure

A third constraint arises from parliamentary procedure and, in particular, the government's influence over the procedure by which legislation is scrutinised by Parliament. Most Bills are introduced by the government and the government has the ability to specify precisely how much time is to be allocated to parliamentary discussion of Bills. This is known as *programming*—that is, the government's imposition of a timetable for the passage of a Bill after its second reading (the first substantive and general debate that a Bill receives). Although there is a legitimate public interest in arranging matters such that the government is able to have Bills enacted in reasonable time, the risk (and often the reality) is that government programming prevents a Bill from being scrutinised in adequate depth; it is sometimes even the case that some parts of a Bill receive no scrutiny at all because time runs out.[138] As the House of Commons Reform Committee—established to suggest how confidence in politics might be restored following the MPs' expenses scandal—put it, 'the Government enjoys not

---

[136] Johnson, *Reshaping the British Constitution: Essays in Political Interpretation* (Basingstoke 2004), p 109.

[137] Brazier, Kalitowski, and Rosenblatt, with Korris, *Law in the Making: Influence and Change in the Legislative Process* (London 2008), p 194.

[138] House of Commons Modernisation Committee, *Programming of Bills* (HC 1222 2002–03); House of Commons Procedure Committee, *Programming of Legislation* (HC 325 2003–04); Brazier, 'Programming of Legislation: From Consensus to Controversy', in Brazier (ed), *Parliament, Politics and Law Making: Issues and Developments in the Legislative Process* (London 2004), p 130.

merely precedence but exclusive domination of much of the House's agenda, and can stop others seeking similar control'.[139] Following the 2010 general election, the new government indicated that, by 2012–13, it would introduce reforms that would reduce its control over the programming of business—including government business.[140]

3.2.5 Assessing the legislative process—different perspectives

It is apparent from the preceding discussion that the ability of Parliament effectively to scrutinise legislation is hindered in a number of respects largely because it is dominated by the government. And coalition government does not necessarily change this position fundamentally: provided that the coalition parties are able to impose sufficient discipline on their respective MPs, the government remains capable of pushing its legislation through. Whether this is an acceptable state of affairs very much depends on the perspective from which matters are approached.

From the governmental perspective, the legislative process is a tool by which the governing party can get its policies enacted into law. Governments are elected on a legislative platform and have an electoral mandate in order to implement their manifesto; this often requires legislation and there is a strong desire in the executive to ensure that its legislative programme can be implemented as easily and efficiently as possible. From this perspective, parliamentary scrutiny should not prevent the government from carrying out the work that it was elected to do. Indeed, from this perspective, the present system is generally seen to work quite well.

From an entirely different (antithetical) standpoint—that is, the non-executive parliamentarian perspective—the legislative process currently functions quite badly indeed. The whole process is almost entirely executive-driven: Parliament simply functions as a rubber-stamp mechanism approving laws that have been written elsewhere; and parliamentarians lack the necessary time and resources to subject legislation to robust scrutiny. From this perspective, urgent reform of the whole process is required so as to enable fuller debate of legislation. Parliamentary scrutiny of legislation needs to be strengthened considerably and executive domination needs to be ended. As we shall see, current debate over the legislative process in the UK tends to characterised by a constant tension between these two perspectives. The governmental perspective is generally predominant, although there have been some recent concessions to the non-executive parliamentarian perspective.

Given the dominance of the executive, what then are the purposes of parliamentary scrutiny in the legislative process? It has been suggested that parliamentary scrutiny of legislation serves three principal purposes.[141] First, Parliament can act as an *inhibitor* of the government. Even though a government will normally have a majority, the fact that it must justify its proposals will itself inhibit it from advancing proposals

---

[139] House of Commons Reform Committee, *Rebuilding the House* (HC 1117 2008–09), [126].

[140] On the backbench business committee, see Chapter 10, sections 5.3 and 6.2, below.

[141] Oliver, Evans, Lee, and Norton, 'Parliament's Role and the Modernisation Agenda', in Giddings (ed), *The Future of Parliament: Issues for a New Century* (London 2005), pp 118–19.

that would expose it to political embarrassment. Second, Parliament can act as a *collaborator* with government in the legislative process in order to make better law. Third, and more cynically, parliamentary scrutiny may serve a *theatrical* function in that it provides for a ritual public affirmation of policy decisions already taken by the government.

> **Q** What role do you think Parliament should play in the legislative process?

3.3 Parliamentary scrutiny and the legislative process

We can now turn to consider the different stages of the legislative process and, in this way, to examine in more detail the effectiveness of parliamentary scrutiny of legislation. We also consider in this section two related topics: the question of the standards by which legislation should be scrutinised, and the degree of scrutiny afforded to fast-track legislation—that is, emergency legislation that has departed from the normal legislative process because it has been expedited through Parliament.

3.3.1 The pre-legislative process

Until 2007, the government's legislative programme would not be known until a list of Bills was announced in the Queen's Speech at the start of the parliamentary year (typically in November). The Queen's Speech is a ritual symbolising the involvement of the sovereign as a constituent part of the legislature—but beneath the pomp and pageantry of the state opening of Parliament lies a barely concealed and efficient aspect of the constitution at work. As legislation is essential to a government's ability to get on with the job of running the country and its political fortunes, the Queen's Speech is actually prepared by government officials in the Legislation Secretariat of the Cabinet Office on behalf of the Legislation Committee.[142] In 2007, the Labour government introduced a new process, the Draft Legislative Programme, by which the government made a public commitment in the late spring preceding the start of the new parliamentary session in the autumn. The government's Draft Legislative Programme set out the Bills that the government proposed to bring forward, grouped by theme to illustrate the government's overarching priorities, and was followed by a period of formal public consultation. Its aim was to enhance transparency as regards what the government planned to achieve through legislation.[143] However, the Liberal Democrat–Conservative coalition has indicated that this process will not be maintained.[144]

---

[142] Cabinet Office, *Guide to Making Legislation* (London 2009), [2.21].

[143] House of Commons Modernisation Committee, *Scrutiny of the Draft Legislative Programme* (HC 81 2007–08).

[144] Sir George Young MP, 'Parliamentary reform: the Coalition Government's agenda after Wright', Speech by Leader of the House of Commons to the Hansard Society, 16 June 2010, available online at http://www.hansardsociety.org.uk/files/folders/2619/download.aspx

There are, however, other important aspects of the pre-legislative stage. First, proposed government Bills are subjected to internal legal scrutiny within government. This is to ensure that each Bill complies with European Union (EU) law and that legislation is expressed in the clearest possible language so as to reduce the risk of subsequent legal challenge; the courts are reluctant to interfere with an action that is clearly in accordance with the express wish of Parliament. Consideration is also given to whether proposed legislation complies with the Human Rights Act 1998 (HRA) and whether it affects matters devolved to Scotland, Wales, or Northern Ireland.[145]

Second, government Bills are nowadays accompanied by various ancillary documents, to which members of the public and parliamentarians may turn in order to make sense of them. One of the distinctive characteristics of UK legislation is that it is often written in precise and highly legalistic language; there is great emphasis upon exactness in statutory provisions. This is because the government will want its legislation interpreted by the courts in a manner that advances rather than defeats its policy objectives. Because legislation is therefore often virtually incomprehensible to most people, a number of other documents are now published alongside it, as Figure 5.3 shows.

3.3.2 Pre-legislative scrutiny

Most Bills are introduced directly into Parliament, but some may first be subject to pre-legislative scrutiny. This is a comparatively recent feature of the legislative process and involves the publication of a draft Bill by the government and its scrutiny by a parliamentary committee, usually in the parliamentary session preceding that in which the Bill is formally introduced to Parliament. The purpose of pre-legislative scrutiny is to produce better law by enabling Parliament and the public to have a real input into the making of legislation before the minds of Ministers are set. A number of Bills are dealt with in this way each year. Pre-legislative scrutiny may be carried out by a variety of types of Committee, including departmental select committees,[146] a joint committee of both Houses, or an ad hoc committee.[147]

Pre-legislative scrutiny has been generally welcomed for its ability to improve the quality of legislation, smooth the passage of legislation during the subsequent legislative process, and to achieve cross-party consensus.[148] Nonetheless, the role and effectiveness of pre-legislative scrutiny is limited in various ways. A major constraint is that the decision whether or not to subject a Bill to pre-legislative scrutiny

---

[145] The UK Parliament remains free to legislate contrary to the Human Rights Act 1998 and the schemes concerning devolution, but, as we explain in Chapters 7 and 19, it generally tries to avoid doing so.

[146] On which, see Chapter 10, section 5.4, below.

[147] For example, the Joint Committee on the draft Bribery Bill in 2009 was convened to subject the draft Bribery Bill to pre-legislative scrutiny; by contrast, the draft Heritage Protection Bill was subject to pre-legislative scrutiny by the House of Commons Select Committee on Culture, Media and Sport.

[148] See Kennon, 'Pre-Legislative Scrutiny of Draft Bills' [2004] PL 477; House of Commons Modernisation Committee, *The Legislative Process* (HC 1097 2005–06), [12]–[29]; Smookler, 'Making a Difference? The Effectiveness of Pre-Legislative Scrutiny' (2006) 3 Parliamentary Affairs 522.

Prior to introduction into Parliament	Parliament	Royal assent
Initial steps Bill may be foreshadowed in governing party's (or parties') *manifesto(s)* Issues to be addressed in Bill may be the subject of a *consultation exercise* **Draft Bill** Draft Bill will be *scrutinised within government* for *(inter alia)* compliance with human rights and devolution implications Draft Bill may be *published and examined by a parliamentary committee* **Preparation of accompanying documentation** *Explanatory notes* (to help the reader to understand what a Bill does, how it does it, and to provide helpful background) *Impact Assessment* (explains the costs and benefits of the Bill) *Equality Impact Assessment* (must, by law, be published; sets out race, gender, and disability implications of legislation) *Delegated Powers Memorandum* (for the House of Lords Delegated Powers and Regulatory Reform Committee: identifies every provision conferring powers to enact delegated legislation, explaining why the matter has been left to delegated legislation rather than included in the Bill, and the form of parliamentary scrutiny to which the enactment of delegated legislation will be subject)	**House of Commons** *First reading* (formal introduction of Bill without debate) *Second reading* (general debate on the policy of Bill) *Committee stage* (detailed examination, debate, and amendments; in the House of Commons, this stage takes place in a Public Bill Committee) *Report stage* (opportunity for further amendments) *Third reading* (final chance for debate; amendments are possible in the Lords) **House of Lords** Bill, in its amended state, goes to the House of Lords, where it is put through a similar process. **Ping pong** Unless the Lords approves the Bill in precisely the form in which it left the Commons, the Bill, as amended by the Lords, must go back to the Commons. The Bill bounces back and forth between the two Houses until they both agree on the text. NB A Bill can commence its passage in the Lords, in which case the process set out above is reversed.	The Bill becomes an Act, and thus a law, when it is granted *royal assent* by the monarch. This may not, however, result in the entirety of the Act entering into force: it may provide that certain parts of it are to enter into force only *when a Minister decides* that this should happen. This allows practical arrangements to be made for the entry into force of the new law.

Figure 5.3 The legislative process

is one for the government rather than Parliament. Parliamentarians have warned that if the government is serious about consulting the House, then there needs to be a more transparent and better-organised process for deciding upon arrangements for pre-legislative scrutiny than has been the case in the past.[149] Other constraints upon the effectiveness of pre-legislative scrutiny include the resources and time that committees need in order to perform such scrutiny seriously. There is also the issue of whether or not the government is willing to take on board the results of such scrutiny. A widely held view is that pre-legislative scrutiny is an innovative development and has the potential to enhance parliamentary scrutiny, but that its use needs to be more widespread for it to become a truly effective mechanism for scrutinising legislation.

3.3.3 Legislative scrutiny

While pre-legislative scrutiny only applies to a relatively small number of Bills, the main process of legislative scrutiny applies to all of them. However, a general word of warning is needed before proceeding further: parliamentary procedure is arcane and complex, and this section merely seeks to provide an overview. The key point is that underpinning the details of parliamentary procedure for scrutinising legislation is to be found a basic tension, reflecting the different perspectives on the legislative process. From the non-executive parliamentarian standpoint, the rules of parliamentary procedure ought to facilitate effective scrutiny of legislation by Parliament; from the governmental perspective, it has been argued that parliamentary procedure is best understood as a political instrument largely designed to enable the governing party to legislate.[150] At the same time, over recent years, there has been an initiative to modernise parliamentary procedures and to enhance parliamentary scrutiny of legislation.[151] The rules of parliamentary procedure are, then, in a sense, the product of the tension between two different and competing pressures: the government's desire to get its legislation through Parliament and the desire of Parliament to scrutinise that legislation.

What, then, is the procedure for passing Bills through Parliament? This procedure is broadly similar in both Houses of Parliament and consists of a number of stages, as Figure 5.3 shows. Bills can be introduced into either House. Whether a Bill is introduced into the Lords or the Commons will often depend upon the nature of the Bill itself and parliamentary timetabling. It has been customary for politically high-profile Bills to be introduced in the Commons; Ministers, most of whom are MPs not peers, tend to prefer to be personally associated with such Bills. By contrast, non-controversial Bills conventionally start off in the Lords. The advantage of this practice is that it spreads the legislative work of a parliamentary session more evenly than might otherwise be the case.

---

[149] House of Commons Liaison Committee, *The Work of Committees 2007–08* (HC 291 2008–09), [28].

[150] Walkland, *The Legislative Process in Great Britain* (London 1968), p 68.

[151] House of Commons Modernisation Committee, *The Legislative Process* (HC 190 1997–98).

The first reading of a Bill is a mere formality; the Bill will simply be presented before Parliament. At the second reading stage, there will be a debate on the general policy of the Bill. In most instances, this will involve the government Minister reading out a speech in support of the Bill that has been written by a civil servant. The opposition spokesperson will then make a speech criticising both the Bill and the government. Some backbench MPs or peers will contribute to the debate either in support of or opposition to the Bill (depending on their party membership), or to indicate their areas of concern, which will be raised at a later stage of the process. The Bill will then be voted upon and, if it is a government Bill, it will almost always survive this stage. While the ostensible purpose of second reading is to scrutinise a Bill by means of a general debate, its real purpose is to enable the political parties to state their respective positions.

The main parliamentary stage of the process is the committee stage in the Commons. At committee stage, a Bill will be discussed in detail—line by line—by a committee of MPs reflecting the political composition of the Commons. At this stage, amendments can be tabled, debated, and voted upon. Until 2007, these committees were known as standing committees. However, for a number of reasons, the operation of standing committees was one of the most criticised aspects of the legislative process—as Tony Wright, former chair of the Public Adminstration Select Committee, put it: 'We should thank our lucky stars that most of the public never get inside Standing Committees.'[152] Such committees failed to deliver genuine and analytical scrutiny of Bills, they were dominated almost exclusively by the government, they failed to engage with the public and the media, and they did not adequately utilise the evidence of experts or interested parties.[153] In the case of particularly important Bills, finance Bills, or those of constitutional importance, the committee stage in the Commons can take place in the Commons chamber—that is, it will be a committee of the whole House. In the committee stage in the Lords, most Bills are considered in this way.

In 2007, standing committees were replaced with Public Bill Committees. The difference is that Public Bill Committees have the ability to take oral and written evidence, as well as to question Ministers. It has been recognised that these committees have added slightly to Parliament's scrutiny of legislation. Nevertheless, the degree of scrutiny that committees offer is often constrained because the government is still able to influence their composition and to ensure that the committees are made up of backbench MPs who will vote for the government. For example, one backbench MP who served on a Public Bill Committee tabled various amendments to the Bill, but never voted against the government; he had agreed with the whips not to vote against the government in return for being selected as a member of the committee.[154] Following the 2010 general election, the coalition government announced the introduction of a new 'public

---

152 HC Deb, vol 442, cols 1073–4, 9 Feb 2006 (Tony Wright MP).
153 House of Commons Modernisation Committee, *The Legislative Process* (HC 1097 2005–06), [50].
154 Brazier, Kalitowski, and Rosenblatt, with Korris, *Law in the Making: Influence and Change in the Legislative Process* (London 2008), p 93.

reading stage' whereby the public would be given an opportunity to comment on Bills; such comments to be considered on a dedicated 'public reading day' in committee.[155]

In addition to the consideration of a Bill in a Public Bill Committee, the departmental select committees may also have a role in scrutinising legislation passing through the House by producing a report on a Bill.[156] Such committees are not obliged to scrutinise every piece of legislation being promoted by the government department that they oversee, but they may nevertheless decide to produce a report on a particular Bill. One advantage of select committees is that they are cross-party committees, which tend to operate in a relatively non-partisan manner. Another advantage is that departmental select committees have a degree of expertise in scrutinising the expenditure, administration, and policy of the relevant government department, and can therefore also exhibit similar expertise in the scrutiny of legislation. However, such committees are primarily reactive: they will scrutinise the government's legislative proposals, but rarely put forward their own. In response to their recommendations, the government may make concessions, but more often than not the government will simply respond to a select committee's report without actually changing the Bill. This is not to say that committees exert no influence upon the government. It is clear that critical reports from committees can force the government to think again. A good illustration is the episode in 2004 when the government sought to restrict access to the courts for asylum seekers. Three select committees were highly critical of the government's plans and although the Bill was passed by the Commons, the government retreated when the Bill was sent to the House of Lords.[157]

After the committee stage, the Bill (as amended) will then return to the main chamber for its report stage; at this point, there will be further debate, and more amendments may be tabled. In particular, the government may, at this stage, table various new amendments to a Bill. If this is done, then such amendments will not necessarily receive detailed scrutiny, as the Bill will not return to the committee stage; rather, it will be for the other House (typically the Lords) to undertake the detailed line-by-line scrutiny. Immediately following the report stage, a Bill will receive its third reading. The Bill will be considered again as a whole in a short debate and, if approved, sent to the other House. Again, the opportunity provided by third reading debates is normally limited. As the Commons Modernisation Committee has observed: 'Third reading debates are often no more than an opportunity to offer perfunctory congratulations to all those involved in the bill's passage; they are rarely if ever now an opportunity for substantial debate on the bill, as amended.'[158]

---

[155]   HM Government, *The Coalition: Our Programme for Government* (London 2010), p 27.

[156]   On select committees, see Chapter 10, section 5.4, below.

[157]   The Bill was what became the Asylum and Immigration (Treatment of Claimants, etc.) Act 2004. See House of Commons Constitutional Affairs Committee, *Asylum and Immigration Appeals* (HC 211 2003–04); House of Commons Home Affairs Committee, *Asylum and Immigration (Treatment of Claimants, etc.) Bill* (HC 109 2003–04); Joint Committee on Human Rights, *Asylum and Immigration (Treatment of Claimants, etc.) Bill* (HL 35 HC 304 2003–04).

[158]   House of Commons Modernisation Committee, *The Legislative Process* (HC 1097 2005–06), [94].

If a Bill is amended by one House, then these amendments will need to be considered by the other House. If there is a difference between the two Houses, then this will need to be reconciled. The process by which this happens is potentially the most complex part of the legislative process. For example, if a Bill has completed its passage through the Commons but is then amended by the Lords, it will have to return to the Commons to be considered again. If the amendments are accepted, then the Bill will then proceed to royal assent; if they are rejected, the Bill will be sent back to the Lords for further consideration. Both Houses must agree on the final text and there may be several rounds of exchanges between the two Houses until agreement is reached on every word of the Bill. This process is known both colloquially and formally as 'ping pong', because the Bill may bounce back and forth between the two Houses until agreement has been reached. If no agreement can be reached, then the House of Commons (or rather the government) may decide to use the procedure under the Parliament Acts.[159] Once agreement has been reached between the two Houses or the Parliament Acts have been invoked, the Bill will then proceed to the next stage—that of royal assent; the Queen will give formal approval to the Bill. As with the Queen's Speech at the start of the parliamentary session, royal assent is merely a ritualistic formality. Once a Bill has received royal assent, it will become an Act of Parliament and can be brought into force.

To what extent does Parliament's scrutiny of legislation exert influence upon the content of legislation? There is clearly a perception that the passage of legislation through Parliament is often a mere formality and Parliament does not normally make much, if any, impact upon the content of legislation. It is important to recognise that there has never been a 'golden age' in which Parliament subjected all legislation to detailed scrutiny. At the same time, it would be incorrect to assume that Parliament has no influence at all. From a study of the impact of parliamentary scrutiny upon government Bills in the 1970s, Griffith concluded that it was undeniable that Parliament makes an impact on legislation, but that governments, backed up by their majorities, almost always get the greater part of what they want.[160] More recently, the Hansard Society has concluded that Parliament does have an influence on government legislation, although it is hard to quantify that influence because it may be difficult or impossible to determine whether any given change was really the result of Parliament's actions.[161]

3.3.4 Scrutiny and standards

It is all very well to say that Parliament should scrutinise legislation—but what standards and criteria should it apply when doing so? The answer may seem obvious: because the legislative process is pre-eminently a political process, politics provides the criteria against which the value of legislation can be scrutinised. Parliament (specifically

---

[159] See section 2.3.3 above.
[160] Griffith, *Parliamentary Scrutiny of Government Bills* (London 1974), p 13.
[161] Brazier et al, p 12.

the House of Commons) is broadly representative of the electorate's political views and, reflecting those views, MPs bring their minds to bear upon the government's legislative proposals. Within this framework, the fact that the government normally gets its way is neither surprising nor troubling, given that its MPs are in the majority and, in approving government Bills, are presumably broadly reflecting the views of the majority of people in the country. There are, however, two fundamental problems with this analysis: it drastically overstates the representative capacity of MPs; and it assumes that the overriding criterion by which scrutiny should be conducted is merely an imprecise one of political acceptability. Each of these points needs to be unpacked.

First, the fact that a majority of MPs are willing to vote in favour of a government Bill does not necessarily mean that such legislation reflects the general will of the people. Of course, MPs may, at a very crude level, sometimes be able to represent their constituents' views. For example, an MP for a constituency blighted by very high levels of unemployment and social deprivation may well know that she is reflecting most of her voters' wishes by voting against large cuts in state benefits. But matters are rarely this straightforward: it is often the case that fewer than half of her constituents who voted at all will have voted for a given MP;[162] Bills may well raise issues that did not feature in the party's manifesto or otherwise in the election campaign; and, anyway, MPs may vote for things with which they and their constituents disagree because the party whips order them to do so. For all of these reasons, the notion that MPs can be trusted to subject legislation to adequate scrutiny by doing what their political antennae tell them to does not withstand analysis. It is self-evident that such an approach may—and does—result in legislation that may overlook or prejudice the interests, or go against the wishes, of small minorities, large minorities, or even a majority of people.

To the extent that this is precisely the sort of scrutiny supplied by the House of Commons, it is possible that the House of Lords may, to some extent, compensate. Legislative scrutiny in the Lords is typically less dominated by party-political considerations. As we noted above, although the House of Lords is organised along party lines, peers include retired politicians and others with experience and expertise in particular areas, which enables the House of Lords to bring a different perspective from that of the Commons. As members of the Lords currently have life tenure, they possess greater security and therefore independence of judgement than backbench MPs, who may fear that a reputation as a serial voter against the government may mean de-selection at the next general election. But it would be mistaken to think that the House of Lords represents some sort of panacea. Its powers are, as we have seen, limited, and for all that it may reflect views unrepresented in the Commons, the social and ethnic composition of the Lords, together with the fact that it remains unelected, tells against assuming that its involvement adequately overcomes the shortcomings of the lower chamber.

This leads on to our second point. Scrutiny, properly and conscientiously undertaken, must be about something more—and something more precise—than whether those

---

[162] The position would be different under the alternative vote system: see section 2.2.5 above.

conducting the scrutiny agree with the proposal in question. The elucidation of more specific standards can elevate Parliament's scrutiny function above adversarial exchanges and party-political considerations. Such standards include compatibility with the ECHR and EU law, value for money, risk assessment, clarity in legislative aims and objectives, equality assessments, and impact assessments, so that legislation does not impose disproportionate regulatory burdens upon businesses that hinder their competitiveness. To an extent, this form of scrutiny is evident in existing arrangements. For example, the Joint Committee on Human Rights scrutinises Bills against ECHR standards, the House of Lords Constitution Committee examines the constitutional implications of all public Bills, and the House of Lords Delegated Powers and Regulatory Reform Committee scrutinises proposals in Bills to delegate legislative power from Parliament to another body (usually Ministers). Such committees perform an important role in terms of scrutinising legislation against constitutional values.[163] However, Oliver has suggested that the legislative process could be enhanced by pulling together the various standards into a formal checklist of legislative scrutiny standards against which legislation could be assessed by Parliament.[164] There is little doubt that the use of such standards can improve the quality of legislation precisely because they are (or purport to be) unencumbered by the kind of partisan, adversarial-style politics that permeate Parliament. Such a checklist could promote careful, rational, consistent, and systematic scrutiny of legislation in order to raise its quality and effectiveness. It has also been suggested that particular types of legislation—for example, 'constitutional' Bills—should be subject to an enhanced procedure so that they can be subject to greater scrutiny.[165]

The desirability of scrutiny by reference to more precise standards is clear. However, it is also clear that such scrutiny cannot *replace* conventional political scrutiny. Any attempt to substitute a checklist-based approach for the scrutiny of legislation against the differing political stances taken both inside and outside Parliament would risk making the legislative process an unduly technocratic exercise. In the final analysis, and despite all of its flaws and imperfections, the Commons remains the best means of expressing the democratically expressed wishes of the nation. Its role is, and should remain, the scrutiny of legislation by reference to the differing political views that it broadly represents—but that is not to say that that primary function could not usefully be augmented by reference to the more objective criteria mentioned above.

Q What standards do you think should be used to scrutinise legislation? How might the concerns set out above concerning the adequacy of political scrutiny of legislation relate to the debate, considered earlier in the chapter, about the voting system used for elections to the House of Commons?

---

[163] Hazell, 'Who is the Guardian of Legal Values in the Legislative Process: Parliament or the Executive?' [2004] PL 495; Feldman, 'Parliamentary Scrutiny of Legislation and Human Rights' [2002] PL 323.

[164] Oliver, 'Improving the Scrutiny of Bills: The Case for Standards and Checklists' [2006] PL 219.

[165] Hazell, 'Time for a New Convention: Parliamentary Scrutiny of Constitutional Bills 1997–2005' [2006] PL 247.

3.3.5 **Post-legislative scrutiny**

After legislation has been enacted, it needs to be implemented. Precisely how legislation is implemented will depend upon the nature of the legislation. For example, legislation creating new criminal offences may be enforced by the police and the criminal courts. As most legislation is concerned with governmental policy, its implementation will depend upon how it is administered by the relevant government agencies. There is, though, no guarantee that legislation is always effective in securing its objectives. Legislation can have positive, negative or unintended consequences, or may be of no consequence at all. It might stand the test of time, or it might very quickly be subject to repeal or amendment. In many policy areas, such as criminal justice, immigration, and social security, government has repeatedly resorted to legislation in attempts to correct problems with previous legislation, but in many instances has only succeeded in increasing the complexity of the law without resolving the underlying policy and administrative issues. Such difficulties are not necessarily an indication of failure, but more a reflection of the deep policy challenges that any government faces. They do, though, raise the question as to whether or not Parliament should be involved not only with the scrutiny of Bills before they become law, but also the scrutiny of what happens after they become law. This is post-legislative scrutiny—the examination of how legislation is implemented in order to determine whether or not that legislation has been successful and, if not, what lessons can be learnt.

It is always open for Parliament or the government to subject legislation to post-legislative review, but in practice this has tended to happen rarely and unsystematically. Given the volume and complexity of legislation, the absence of effective post-legislative scrutiny has been widely acknowledged to be a major gap in Parliament's oversight of both legislation and of government. In 2004, the House of Lords Constitution Committee therefore recommended that there ought to be a systematic process of post-legislative scrutiny in order to determine if legislation has achieved its purpose.[166] This the government duly announced in 2008.[167] Three to five years after legislation has been enacted, the relevant government department will—for most Acts—publish and submit to the relevant parliamentary select committee a document summarising how the Act has been implemented. This will include a short preliminary assessment of how the Act has worked in practice. The relevant departmental select committee, or other parliamentary bodies, will then be able to assess whether a fuller review is necessary at that point. The purpose of this process is to identify those legislative contexts in which things need to be put right, as well as those in which things have gone well (and which might therefore serve as examples for the future).

---

[166] House of Lords Select Committee on the Constitution, *Parliament and the Legislative Process* (HL 173 2003–04), [165]–[193].

[167] Office of the Leader of the House of Commons, *Post-Legislative Scrutiny: The Government's Approach* (Cm 7320 2008). See also Law Commission, *Post-Legislative Scrutiny* (Cm 6945 2006).

It has been recognised that the introduction of a system of post-legislative scrutiny 'has the potential to make a valuable difference to the scrutiny of legislation'.[168] However, it remains to be seen how this process will operate in practice. It is apparent that any such system will face a number of challenges. One such challenge is the limited resources of departmental select committees; another challenge is simply the pace of legislative change. As it has been noted: 'In many of the areas where legislation is controversial—health, social security, taxation, criminal justice, and asylum and immigration, for example—the statute book rarely stays static long enough to be put under the microscope.'[169] The political demands that governments face to legislate in order to be seen to be doing something, and to be seen to have fresh ideas, mean that Bills are rarely coherent packages; they tend to amend other Acts of Parliament before it would be possible to undertake an examination of whether those original Acts were successful in resolving the problems that they were enacted to resolve. In some instances, the government has proposed new legislation even before previous legislation has been brought into force.

A further challenge is that most legislation merely provides a broad framework—that is, the legislation will not provide a comprehensive statement of the law, but in many instances merely confer upon government Ministers and other public agencies the ability to make rules and regulations (subordinate or delegated legislation) by which the primary legislation is to be implemented. There are different views upon this practice. One view is that secondary legislation is often necessary because parliamentary time is limited and the subject matter is often of a technical nature. Another view is that secondary legislation is often used by government to bypass full parliamentary scrutiny.[170] Yet another view is that the notion that secondary legislation is delegated legislation is a misnomer because it hardly involves any delegation at all; after all, both primary and secondary legislation is produced by government. What is apparent, though, is that the volume of secondary legislation, which is far greater that the volume of primary legislation, can pose a challenge to post-legislative scrutiny. As we noted in Chapter 4, parliamentary scrutiny of delegated legislation is itself often limited—principally because of the volume of such legislation and because few parliamentarians have much interest in scrutinising it closely.[171]

In summary, the development of formal arrangements between government and Parliament for post-legislative scrutiny has the potential to enhance the scrutiny of

---

[168] House of Commons Liaison Committee, *The Work of Committees 2007–08* (HC 291 2008–09), [69].

[169] Oliver, Evans, Lee, and Norton, 'Parliament's Role and the Modernisation Agenda', in Giddings (ed), *The Future of Parliament: Issues for a New Century* (London 2005), p 123.

[170] See, eg the comments of Chris Huhne MP during the second reading of what subsequently became the Borders, Citizenship and Immigration Act 2009:

There is an astonishing degree of reliance of statutory instruments. When in doubt, the Government want to give Ministers the power to make things up at a later date. This is yet another 'Trust me, I'm a Minister' Bill. Well, this House should not trust Ministers with clean-sheet powers. We do not even know who those Ministers will be this time next week, let alone in a year's time. (HC Deb, vol 493, col 192, 2 June 2009)

[171] See Chapter 4, section 4.2, above.

legislation, but its effectiveness will depend upon both government and Parliament playing a full part in the process. Departments must publish timely memoranda about the Acts concerned, and select committees will need to make a careful assessment of the value of a full follow-up exercise.

3.3.6 Fast-track legislation

A final topic to consider is the scrutiny provided by Parliament to fast-track legislation. Occasionally, legislation might have to be fast-tracked through Parliament—that is, the Bill will be scrutinised by Parliament through an accelerated procedure and the normal legislative timetable, which will ordinarily take several months, will be set aside; the Bill may be considered not in months, but weeks—or, in some instances, days.[172] One of our case studies in Chapter 1 concerned an example of fast-tracked legislation—the Anti-terrorism, Crime and Security Act 2001, which was enacted by Parliament in response to the terrorist attacks on the 11 September 2001 ('9/11') and gave the Home Secretary draconian powers to detain indefinitely foreign nationals suspected of involvement in terrorism. This is only one amongst many instances of legislation that has been fast-tracked through Parliament. A more recent illustration is provided by the Parliamentary Standards Act 2009, which was introduced following the MPs' expenses affair in 2009 and took one month to complete its passage through Parliament.

In such instances, government may come under enormous political pressure to do something—and to be *seen* to be doing something—about a particular issue. However, the difficulty is that legislating at speed inevitably leaves less time for scrutiny and weakens even further the degree of scrutiny that Parliament is able to provide. The accelerated nature of the legislative process in such instances will mean that the procedure will be characterised, even more so than normal, by dominance of the government. At the same time, when a Bill is fast-tracked, there are obvious risks that it may turn out to be bad legislation—especially when the Bill deals with a complex social and legal problem: 'Act in haste and repent at leisure.'

Should such legislation attract additional safeguards to ensure that, despite the accelerated nature of the scrutiny process, an attempt is made to ensure that it is good law? The House of Lords Constitution Committee certainly thinks so.[173] While recognising the need for fast-track legislation in exceptional circumstances, the Committee has made various recommendations as to how such legislation should to be handled. The government should make a proper case to Parliament as to why it is fast-tracking the legislation. There should be a presumption in favour of such legislation being subject to a sunset clause—that is, a provision by which the legislation will expire after a certain date, unless renewed by Parliament. Furthermore, said the Committee, there

---

[172] For example, the Criminal Justice (Terrorism and Conspiracy) Act 1998, introduced after the Omagh bombing in Northern Ireland in 1998, went through Parliament in two days.

[173] House of Lords Select Committee on the Constitution, *Fast-track Legislation: Constitutional Implications and Safeguards* (HL 116 2008–09).

should be a presumption in favour of early post-legislative scrutiny of fast-tracked legislation. While professing sympathy with some of the views advanced by the Committee, the Labour government's response in 2009 stopped short of a specific undertaking to implement the Committee's principal recommendations.[174]

3.4 Summary

Given the UK's basic constitutional set-up—the executive's political control of the legislature—the legislative process is an almost exclusively governmental process. Only in formal terms can Parliament be described as a lawmaking body. Government is the dominant force in this process: it formulates legislation, retains firm control of the process, and is extremely reluctant to cede any of this control. While Parliament plays a role in scrutinising legislation, it is a largely subsidiary one. The government's dominance of Parliament and the legislative process does not arise because the UK is subject to governmental dictatorship; rather, it is because the UK constitution places a high priority upon the ability of government to ensure that its policies can be enacted in law. There is much debate as to whether or not this set of arrangements is ideal. Some argue that governmental influence is advantageous because it enables the government to fulfil its electoral mandate; yet others bemoan excessive governmental influence over the legislative process.

Two remaining points need to be emphasised. First, parliamentary scrutiny of legislation has, in recent years, improved in certain respects.[175] And future changes to parliamentary procedure—such as giving Parliament more control over the program-ming of business[176]—may further enhance the degree of scrutiny that Parliament is able to afford to legislation. Second, absent some radical redesign of the UK constitu-tion by which the legislative and executive powers are entirely separated through the adoption of a written constitution, it is very unlikely that the government will cede its control over the legislative process. In a constitution in which the government has political control of Parliament, it is highly doubtful whether Parliament could become a lawmaking, as opposed to a law-effecting, body.

4. Parliament's powers

In this section, we turn away from Parliament's role in the legislative process and focus on the *powers* that Parliament enjoys. What, exactly, can Parliament (or, taking account of our discussion above, the *government* through Parliament) do? It

---

[174] House of Lords Select Committee on the Constitution, *Government Response to Fast-track Legislation: Constitutional Implications and Safeguards* (HL 11 2009–10).

[175] For example, see above on Public Bill Committees (section 3.3.3) and greater post-legislative scrutiny (section 3.3.5). [176] See section 3.2.4 above.

is generally, although not universally, accepted that the Westminster Parliament is legally 'sovereign'. We will see that what this means is open to debate; for now, it is enough to say that a legally sovereign legislature is capable of enacting, amending, and repealing any law—there is no legal restriction on the laws that it may enact.[177] In this section, we are concerned with three principal questions: should Parliament be sovereign? If it is sovereign, what exactly does that mean? And is the conventional wisdom holding that Parliament is sovereign really correct?

4.1 Should Parliament be sovereign?

4.1.1 Political and legal constitutionalism

To say that a legislature can enact *any* law—that there is *nothing* that it is legally incapable of doing—is, on the face of it, an extravagant claim. Stephen famously pointed out that '[i]f a [sovereign] legislature decided that all blue-eyed babies should be murdered, the preservation of blue-eyed babies would be illegal'.[178] This prompts several questions, the answers to most of which are—to anyone with a conventional moral compass—obvious. Should such a law be enacted? No. Should legislators be free to enact such a law if they so wish? No. What should stop them from doing so? Here, the answer is perhaps less obvious—and it is here that we encounter a fissure between the traditions of legal and political constitutionalism, the distinction between which is one of the key themes running throughout this book.

Political constitutionalism holds that non-legal factors will prevent the enactment of laws such as that described above. Legislators' own sense of morality means, it is to be hoped, that they would never be tempted to enact such a law. And even if they were, self-interest would ensure that they did not: public opinion would not stand for it. Any politician who voted in favour of such a law would be almost certain to lose his or her parliamentary seat at the following election, and it is highly likely that, in such an extreme case, there would be widespread civil and official disobedience, with individuals refusing to obey, and organisations such as the police refusing to enforce such a law. The essential point, then, is that political constitutionalism puts its faith in the political process—legislators will do the right thing because that is what public opinion will require of them—making legal restrictions upon their powers unnecessary.

It is hard to dispute this analysis in relation to truly extreme laws: it is impossible to imagine circumstances in which the political process would yield a law such as that referred to by Stephen. But what about a law that denied members of one gender the right to vote? Or which required racial segregation on public transport? Or which denied to suspected terrorists the right to liberty and to a fair trial in an attempt to enhance the safety of everyone else? These are not far-fetched examples: they are all things that have been done in the last hundred years in Western countries. Indeed,

---

[177] Dicey, *An Introduction to the Study of the Law of the Constitution* (London 1959), p 10.
[178] Stephen, *The Science of Ethics* (London 1882), p 137.

as we saw in Chapter 1, a law along the lines of the last example was enacted in the UK in 2001.[179] The political process may not—and indeed has not—been sufficient to prevent the enactment of laws such as these. (This might either be because a majority of people are happy to see such laws enacted or because politicians take it upon themselves to do things that are out of step with public opinion. The former point raises questions about democracy that we address in the next section; the latter point, meanwhile, underlines the fact that if political constitutionalism is to be embraced, the political process must be of a sufficient quality to justify the faith thereby placed in it.[180]) That is precisely why, legal constitutionalists argue, we should not put all of our faith in politics. Legislators, left to their own devices, may do the wrong thing—and while, in a democracy, they must generally be allowed to do as they think best, we must look to the law to remove unacceptable choices from them in the first place. Legal constitutionalism therefore has no truck with legislative sovereignty; instead, it holds that legislators should be given only limited powers and that courts should have the authority to strike down legislation enacted outwith such powers. The best-known example of such a system is the USA. The US Constitution confers only limited powers upon Congress—the American equivalent of Parliament—and authorises the courts to set aside unconstitutional legislation (that is, laws that transgress the constitutional limits on Congress's power).

4.1.2 Democracy

The foregoing discussion implicitly suggests that legal constitutionalism's central thesis is that *legislators* cannot be trusted to do the right thing. But the position is actually more subtle. Legislators' desire to be re-elected will generally ensure that they do only popular things, making it unlikely that they would enact a law that they anticipate would displease most people. Viewed thus, it seems that legal constitutionalism's thesis is really that *people generally*—or at least *the majority*—cannot be trusted to do the right thing. They might—indeed they may be quite likely—to act in a self-interested way that prioritises their own interests over those of others. The majority might therefore wish laws to be enacted that benefit themselves at the expense of the minority—wishes to which legislators, wanting to be re-elected, might accede. Legislation such as that which was enacted in the UK in the wake of the 9/11 attacks incarcerating suspected foreign terrorists—an unpopular minority if there ever were one—is a prime example of such behaviour.

If, then, legal constitutionalism's mission (or part of it) is to protect minorities against the tyranny of a self-interested majority, does this not make it profoundly undemocratic? On a so-called *majoritarian* view of democracy, it certainly does. That view holds that democracy simply means giving effect to the wishes of the majority of people: if they wish to organise society in a way that advantages them at the expense of smaller, weaker groups, then so be it. Of course, in enlightened societies, majorities

---

[179] Anti-terrorism, Crime and Security Act 2001.
[180] See generally Tomkins, *Our Republican Constitution* (Oxford 2005).

may not behave thus: they might, for example, recognise a moral code that embraces concern for the dignity and equality of individuals, and that precludes the exploitation of those who are insufficiently powerful to safeguard their own interests through the political process. The key point, however, is that, on a majoritarian view of democracy, whether the majority behaves self-interestedly or altruistically is a matter of choice— for the majority. Legislative sovereignty, on this view, is therefore wholly justified; indeed it is imperative—it would be undemocratic to constrain the legislature from doing whatever it is that the majority wants it to do.[181]

But this is not the only—and may not be the best—view of democracy. The opposing view, known as *countermajoritarianism*, holds that true democracy requires society to be governed in a way that takes due account of everyone's interests, not only those of 50.1 per cent of the people. James Madison, who played a leading role in the drafting of the US Constitution, warned against making laws 'not according to the rules of justice and the rights of the minor party, but by the superior force of an interested and overbearing majority'.[182] There are a number of ways in which this objective might be realised. Some are political: the voting system may be designed so as to make it unlikely that two big parties will dominate the legislature,[183] some or all votes in the legislature may be capable of being carried only with support in excess of a bare majority,[184] opposing parties might even be forced to work together in order to instil a consensual approach.[185] Instead, or as well, the power of the legislature might be legally limited in order to ensure that particular values, including minority interests, cannot be overridden.

This is generally how systems based on written constitutions work. Paradoxically, the adoption and maintenance of a constitution denying the legislature the legal capacity to subjugate minority interests requires, in the first place, that the majority is prepared to go along with such arrangements, assuming that the constitution is adopted pursuant to and/or can be amended by a popular vote. In this sense, the sort of legal constitutionalism engendered by such arrangements *is* democratically endorsed, even if, once such arrangements are in place, they result in specific instances of courts setting aside as unconstitutional legislation that the majority would like to see enacted. Since it is usually possible to amend a written constitution—typically through a process that includes asking the people to vote—it is normally possible in systems based on written constitutions for the people to remove some constitutional inhibition that would otherwise prevent the enactment of a law that they wished to see passed. However, most written constitutions require something more than a simple majority—and the greater the size of the majority required for constitutional amendment, the harder it is for the majority to shift the ground rules in their favour and to the disadvantage of smaller interest groups.

---

[181] See generally Bickel, *The Least Dangerous Branch* (New Haven 1986).
[182] *The Federalist Papers*, no 10.
[183] See discussion of proportional representation at section 2.2.5 above.
[184] For example, a two-thirds majority might be required.
[185] As in Northern Ireland: see Chapter 7 below.

4.1.3 Constitutional interpretation and judicial politics

In many systems based on written constitutions, the constitution is very hard indeed to amend. In such circumstances, the meaning of the existing text becomes all-important.[186] This, in turn, gives considerable power to the judiciary, the job of which it ultimately is in most countries to interpret the constitution. For example, in the famous case of *Roe v Wade*, the US Supreme Court was asked to determine whether the US Constitution meant that a Texan law prohibiting abortion except in very limited circumstances was unconstitutional.[187] Although the US Constitution did not explicitly address this question, the Supreme Court held that it contained an implied right to privacy that included a right to abort pregnancies in a much wider range of circumstances than those permitted by the Texan law. This is a good example of the way in which a system based on legal constitutionalism that incorporates legal restrictions on legislative power can result in certain matters being taken out of the hands of legislators and placed in the hands of judges. Once the Court determined that abortion was a matter that engaged the US Constitution, it was for the Court to determine whether and in what circumstances women should be permitted to terminate pregnancies. This is not an argument clearly in favour of or against legally limiting the powers of the legislature; rather, it is merely an implication of doing so.

4.1.4 Conclusion

The foregoing discussion does not lead to a definitive conclusion about whether it is right that the UK Parliament should be sovereign, for there is no objectively correct answer to that question. It is ultimately a matter of opinion. The division of opinion between those who support and oppose a legally untrammelled legislature is not, in reality, between those who do and do not think that a law should be enacted to the effect that all blue-eyed babies should be killed; rather, the disagreement is about what it is that should prevent the enactment of unacceptable laws—and about how the limits of acceptability should be determined in the first place.

Q Reflecting on the discussion so far, what is *your* view? Should courts in the UK have the power to strike down unacceptable laws? Or should we continue to rely on the self-restraint of legislators, and the controlling effect of public opinion and the electoral process?

4.2 What does 'parliamentary sovereignty' mean?

Orthodox constitutional doctrine says,[188] and the courts accept,[189] that the Westminster Parliament is sovereign. There is no legal limit to the laws that it may enact: any restraint that Parliament exercises therefore flows from the political, not the legal,

---

[186] See further Chapter 1, section 2.4, above.   [187] 410 US 113 (1973).
[188] See generally Goldsworthy, *The Sovereignty of Parliament* (Oxford 1999).
[189] See, eg *British Railways Board v Pickin* [1974] AC 765, 782, *per* Lord Reid.

system. The constitutional writer Dicey observed that the flip side of this coin is that no one can lawfully override, derogate from, or set aside an Act of Parliament.[190] On this view, then, UK courts cannot strike down or refuse to apply Acts of Parliament because there are no *external constraints* upon what Parliament can do: in the absence of constitutional restrictions on its authority, orthodox theory says that there are no benchmarks against which courts can test the constitutionality of legislation. The notion of an unconstitutional Act of Parliament is therefore a contradiction in terms: Parliament is incapable of acting unconstitutionally because it is constitutionally unrestrained.

We will see in section 4.3 below that this orthodox position is open to question on a number of grounds. But if the position described in the foregoing paragraph is, for now, accepted, a separate question arises. Even if the constitution imposes no *external constraints* upon Parliament, are *self-imposed constraints* a possibility? In other words, could Parliament limit its own powers? This question raises a paradox. If Parliament can do literally *anything*, then that must include the competence to limit its own powers—but if Parliament were so to exercise its powers, surely it would no longer be sovereign? We need to examine this matter more closely, but it is important to say at the outset that this question is not merely of philosophical interest; it is also of practical significance, and it raises fundamental questions about the nature and source of the principle of parliamentary sovereignty.

The question is, in essence, whether Parliament is capable of *entrenching* legislation. In other words, could it enact legislation and stipulate either that it could not be repealed or amended *at all*, or alternatively that it could not be repealed or amended *in the absence of compliance with some special condition* (such as securing a majority bigger than the bare majority that is normally needed)? For example, could Parliament enact a Bill of Rights stipulating that all future Parliaments were required to respect the Bill of Rights and that any Bills enacted in breach of it would be invalid?

4.3 Model I—parliamentary sovereignty as a constitutional fixture

4.3.1 No entrenchment

For some writers, the answer to that question is straightforwardly 'no'. The commentator most closely associated with that view was Wade. In an influential article published in 1955, Wade argued that it is impossible for Parliament to entrench legislation because the courts are constitutionally required to give effect to the most recent expression of parliamentary intention whenever two Acts conflict.[191] The implications of this are twofold.

First, it is always possible for Parliament to state in a later Act that some or all of an earlier Act is repealed. When Parliament lays down a new set of laws in a given Act, it

---

[190] Dicey, *An Introduction to the Study of the Law of the Constitution* (London 1959), p 38.
[191] 'The Basis of Legal Sovereignty' [1955] CLJ 172.

often adds to that Act a schedule listing the older Acts (or provisions in older Acts) that are repealed. This is known as *express repeal*.

But, second, if Parliament enacts new legislation that is at odds with an earlier statute and fails explicitly to address this matter, it is still the courts' constitutional duty to enforce the new law and, therefore, to disregard the older law to the extent of any inconsistency between the two. This is known as *implied repeal*: in the absence of express words of repeal in the later Act, the earlier Act is nevertheless treated as impliedly repealed to the extent that the two Acts are incompatible with one another. The doctrine of implied repeal was endorsed in *Ellen Street Estates Ltd v Minister of Health*.[192]

The doctrines of express and implied repeal are merely manifestations of the underlying principle that the courts are constitutionally obliged to give effect to the most recent expression of parliamentary intention, preferring more recent legislation over earlier legislation when the two conflict. Crucially for the purposes of our inquiry about entrenchment, Wade argued that this principle admits of no exceptions: there is no way in which the doctrines of express and implied repeal can be displaced. If this is true, two conclusions follow; they are best explained through examples.

First, assume that Parliament enacts legislation on a given matter, and that the Act contains a section that says: 'This Act may not be repealed.' On Wade's view, that section would be without legal effect. It would still be the courts' job to give effect to the most recent expression of Parliament's will in the event of a conflict between two Acts, meaning that any subsequent legislation that contained either express words of repeal or a provision impliedly incompatible with the earlier Act would result in the repeal of the latter. *Absolute entrenchment*—that is, placing an Act wholly beyond repeal—is, then, impossible.

Second, assume that the original Act says not that it cannot be repealed *at all*, but that it cannot be repealed unless some condition is first fulfilled—for example, a two-thirds (as opposed to a simple) majority in the House of Commons. What would then happen if Parliament were subsequently to legislate expressly to repeal, or impliedly legislate inconsistently with, the earlier Act without fulfilling the condition? On Wade's view, the latter Act would succeed in repealing the earlier Act whether or not the condition stipulated in the latter had been fulfilled. Again, this follows from the fundamental principle that the courts' duty is to implement the most recent expression of parliamentary intention. It follows that *contingent entrenchment*, like absolute entrenchment, is impossible. This, in turn, means that all Acts of Parliament are legally equal: none can be made harder or impossible to repeal.

Two questions arise.

4.3.2 Continuing and self-embracing sovereignty

First, how is it possible for Wade simultaneously to assert (i) that Parliament is sovereign, but (ii) that there is something—namely entrenching legislation—that it

---

[192] [1934] 1 KB 590.

cannot do? The apparent paradox raised by this question is resolved by recognising that when we say that Parliament is 'sovereign', we must mean one of two things. One possibility is that Parliament has a *self-embracing sovereignty*, meaning that its power extends to destroying its own sovereignty. It could, on this view, pass a law entrenching legislation, and the entrenchment would be effective: Parliament would subsequently be incapable of amending or repealing the law in question, and so would no longer be sovereign. The other possibility is that Parliament has a *continuing sovereignty*— one that cannot be destroyed, and which therefore means that the one thing that it cannot do is entrench legislation (because that would detract from the authority of future Parliaments to do whatever they like). Wade says that the UK Parliament has the second kind of sovereignty, which explains why he thinks that it cannot entrench legislation.

4.3.3 Why continuing sovereignty?

Yet this just begs a second question: *why* does Wade think that Parliament has a continuing, rather than a self-embracing, sovereignty? In order to answer this question, we need to consider what it is that gives Parliament the authority to make law in the first place. In most developed countries, the legislature is authorised to make law by a constitutional text. That text will prescribe the limits of the legislature's authority and will set out a process whereby the constitution can be amended so as to increase or reduce the legislature's powers. In such systems, legislative authority can be traced to a *legal source* in the form of the written constitution.

But of course the UK does not have a written constitution—so what is it that authorises Parliament to make the law? The answer (at least as far as Wade is concerned) lies in an event known as the Glorious Revolution. Seventeenth-century England witnessed considerable tumult that included a civil war and a period of republican government. An important factor underlying those events was a running tension between the monarchy and Parliament. The two were, in effect, vying for constitutional primacy; successive monarchs asserted powers to dispense with—that is, to disregard—Acts of Parliament. In 1688, when a new king took to the throne, it was agreed that the monarchy would no longer lay any claim to constitutional primacy in the sense of having any power to dispense with Acts of Parliament. And the courts, which at the beginning of the seventeenth century had suggested that *they* could dispense with Acts of Parliament by setting them aside if they offended basic principles of justice,[193] accepted, along with the monarch, that duly enacted parliamentary legislation had to be recognised as the law of the land. The basis of Parliament's authority to make law is therefore said to consist in this *political agreement* between the monarchy, Parliament, and the courts. That agreement gave rise to a constitutional rule to the effect that Parliament can enact any law and that the courts will recognise parliamentary enactments as valid laws. But Wade argues that this rule is not a *legal* rule in any

---

[193] See, eg *Dr Bonham's Case* (1610) Co Rep 113.

recognisable sense—Parliament did not legislate its own sovereignty into existence; how could it?—but is, rather, 'the ultimate *political* fact upon which the whole system of legislation hangs'.[194]

This rule, or political fact, is what Hart refers to as a 'rule of recognition'—that is, the rule that tells everyone, including courts, what to recognise as law.[195] Hart goes on to explain that '[i]n the day-to-day life of a legal system its rule of recognition is very seldom expressly formulated'; rather, 'its existence is *shown*'—and its content deduced— 'in the way in which particular rules are identified'.[196] Subject to that caveat, it seems likely that the rule of recognition in the UK provides that something will constitute a valid and enforceable Act of Parliament if it

   (i) has been approved by the House of Commons, and

  (ii) has been approved by the House of Lords (unless the Parliament Acts apply),[197] and

 (iii) has been granted royal assent by the Monarch, but

 (iv) only to the extent that it is not inconsistent with any provision in a subsequently enacted Act of Parliament.

Element (iv) of the rule of recognition can be deduced from the fact that courts give effect to later Acts of Parliament when they are inconsistent with earlier ones. If courts were to behave differently—that is, if they were to be required to give effect to certain legislation, such as a Bill of Rights, even if it were inconsistent with a later Act—it stands to reason that the rule of recognition would have to be altered. Specifically, element (iv) of the rule of recognition would need to be made subject to a proviso, so that it read:

 (iv) only to the extent that it is not inconsistent with any provision in a subsequently enacted Act of Parliament *except that the Bill of Rights shall take priority over all other inconsistent legislation, whether enacted before or after the Bill of Rights.*

Wade says that changing the rule of recognition—and hence entrenching legislation—is the one thing that Parliament cannot do. Why? Because whereas, in most countries, that rule is to be found in some shape or form in a written constitution—and can therefore be amended through whatever legal means the constitution prescribes—in the UK, it exists only in the form of Wade's 'political fact' that emerged because of the Glorious Revolution. It follows that although Parliament is sovereign in the sense of being able to make and change any *law*, this does not mean that it can change the rule of recognition, because the rule of recognition is *not* a law; it exists only in the political realm, and changing it is therefore beyond Parliament's legislative reach. Wade therefore argued that the rule of recognition could only alter—precipitating a

---

[194] Wade, 'The Basis of Legal Sovereignty' [1955] CLJ 172, 188.

[195] Hart, *The Concept of Law* (Oxford 1961), ch 6.   [196] Hart, p 98.

[197] The complications raised by the Parliament Acts are considered in detail below.

change in the powers enjoyed by Parliament—if the political agreement underpinning the rule of recognition were to collapse. The most obvious way in which this might happen would be if the courts were to refuse to recognise an Act of Parliament as a valid law. This, said Wade, would be a 'revolution', in that it would entail the courts acting unconstitutionally by disregarding the agreement reached at the end of the seventeenth century: if parliamentary sovereignty is ultimately sustained only by that political compact, it can only in practice exist for as long as the parties to it continue to agree to it.

4.3.4 Evaluation

Although highly influential, Wade's analysis is open to criticism on three principal grounds. The first is that it provides *an exclusively historical explanation* for the sovereignty of Parliament and takes no account of what principled justification might exist for ascribing lawmaking power to Parliament today. The most obvious such justification, as we noted above,[198] is that Parliament[199] is now (but was not 300 years ago) a democratic institution. We will see below that some writers argue that this raises questions about the contemporary appropriateness of Wade's analysis. Some, for example, argue that if democracy justifies Parliament's exercising lawmaking power today, that same principle must limit its authority, meaning that it would be unconstitutional and unlawful for Parliament to attempt to enact legislation at odds with basic principles of democracy.

Second, Wade's theory is *arguably incoherent judged even on its own terms*. Even if we accept Wade's premise that the rule ascribing lawmaking authority to Parliament was generated through non-legal means, it does not necessarily follow that that rule cannot be legislatively manipulated. The fact that the original source of the rule is political does not conclusively determine whether the rule permits Parliament to (for example) limit its own powers; that question can be determined only by reference to the *content* of the rule.[200]

Third, in the absence of any constitutional text setting out the extent and nature of parliamentary authority, the content of the rule has to be deduced from what actually happens—*which is arguably at odds with what Wade's theory says should happen*. The central tenet of that theory is that the sovereignty of Parliament is an absolute fixture that cannot be changed through any legal or constitutional means;[201] in particular, Parliament cannot, by enacting legislation, impose limits upon itself. Yet there are two situations in which Parliament appears to have succeeded in doing precisely that.

The first concerns the European Communities Act 1972, which gives effect in the UK to laws enacted by the EU. The nature of the EU and the way in which the 1972

---

[198] In section 4.1.2.   [199] Or at least the House of Commons.

[200] Bradley, 'The Sovereignty of Parliament: Form or Substance?', in Jowell and Oliver (eds), *The Changing Constitution* (Oxford 2007), p 38; Gordon, 'The Conceptual Foundations of Parliamentary Sovereignty: Reconsidering Jennings and Wade' [2009] PL 519, 531–4.

[201] Albeit that it would, in practice, collapse if the courts were to act unconstitutionally by refusing to recognise Acts of Parliament as valid laws.

Act works are considered in detail in Chapter 8. For the time being, we simply note that, in the 1972 Act, Parliament provided that EU law should take priority over UK law, including over Acts of Parliament, thereby effectively restricting its own powers. Although Wade suggested that this development could be reconciled with his theory by characterising it as a revolution,[202] we suggest in Chapter 8 that this is not a convincing explanation, bearing in mind that it was *Parliament*—which is supposed to be incapable of legislating away its sovereignty—that was responsible for bringing about this new state of affairs.

Second, there are the Parliament Acts 1911–49. The background to, and effect of, those Acts are considered above.[203] However, the way in which they work on a technical level calls into question Wade's theory. If the rule of recognition is as stated above, how is it possible for a Bill to 'become an Act of Parliament', as ss 1(1) and 2(1) of the 1911 Act put it, without the Lords' approval? Wade argued that legislation enacted under the Parliament Acts is not *really* an Act of Parliament; rather, he said, Parliament in 1911 in effect created a separate body—an inferior legislature—consisting of the monarch and the Commons. Measures enacted by it were therefore delegated legislation, not Acts of Parliament proper. While enabling Wade to reconcile the 1911 Act with his theory, this analysis compelled him to argue that the 1949 Act—and all legislation passed there under—is invalid, because it would have been impossible for the inferior legislature to extend its own powers: only Parliament proper could delegate further powers to the inferior body.[204] Precisely this argument was put to the Appellate Committee of the House of Lords in the *Jackson* case, in which it was contended that the Hunting Act 2004 was invalid, having been enacted by the monarch and the Commons under the 1911 Act, as amended by the 1949 Act.[205] It was argued that the 1949 Act was (for the reasons given by Wade) invalid and that the 2004 Act was therefore invalid too. The Appellate Committee rejected this argument and the analysis on which it was based. It held that, by enacting the 1911 Act, Parliament had created not a subordinate legislature capable only of enacting delegated legislation, but a parallel route whereby full Acts of Parliament could be enacted. In other words, it had amended the rule of recognition by inserting into it a proviso whereby the House of Lords' assent is needed *unless the Parliament Acts apply*.

This suggests that Parliament in 1911 did the very thing that Wade said was impossible in that it manipulated the rule of recognition. But this does not quite answer the question with which we started this section—namely, whether Parliament can *entrench* legislation. The Parliament Acts make it *easier* for legislation to be passed by creating a second mechanism for enactment alongside that which requires the assent of monarch, Lords, and Commons. Does this mean that, by the same logic, Parliament could make it *harder* to enact legislation by, for example, stipulating that a given Act cannot be repealed or amended unless special conditions are met?

---

[202] 'Sovereignty: Revolution or Evolution?' (1996) 112 LQR 568. [203] In section 2.3.3 above.
[204] Wade, 'The Basis of Legal Sovereignty' [1955] CLJ 172, 193–4.
[205] *R (Jackson) v Attorney-General* [2005] UKHL 56, [2006] 1 AC 262.

4.4 Model II—Parliament capable of controlling certain aspects of legislative process

4.4.1 The 'new view'

Proponents of the *new view* of parliamentary sovereignty—or the *manner and form theory* as it is sometimes called—have argued that the answer to that question is 'yes'.[206] Their central contention is that Parliament is, and should be, capable of laying down binding conditions concerning *how and in what form* legislation is to be enacted, but that it is not, and should not be, capable of tying future legislators' hands as to *what* legislation they may enact. This boils down to the propositions that (i) Parliament can and should be able to make it *harder than usual* for a given statute to be amended or repealed, but that (ii) it cannot and should not be able to make it *impossible* for any law to be amended or repealed. Let us unpack each of these propositions.

As to the former, adherents to the new view agree with Model I in that they too think that *absolute entrenchment*—that is, placing an Act wholly beyond repeal—is, and should be, impossible. This is entirely sensible. Allowing absolute entrenchment would enable a given Parliament—controlled by a given government—to enshrine its views in legislation that could never be altered. This would be both undemocratic (what if people in future were to decide that they do not like those policies?) and impractical (what if circumstances were to change such that those policies become inappropriate?). Even countries with written constitutions make provision for the constitution to be amended; constitution drafters might deliberately make amendment difficult, but it is widely recognised that no group of people can be so prescient as to be capable of laying down rules that will be appropriate for the rest of time.

But the new view does allow for *contingent entrenchment* of legislation. Assume that Parliament enacts legislation that stipulates that it can only be repealed by subsequent legislation that meets certain conditions—for example, that it is supported by a two-thirds (as opposed to a simple) majority in the House of Commons. If Parliament were subsequently to seek to repeal that Act by means of legislation not supported by the requisite majority, the earlier Act would (according to the new view) remain in force. Supporters of the new view argue that permitting Parliament to entrench legislation in this way is a good thing because it steers a desirable middle course between two undesirable extremes. The first such extreme—permitting absolute entrenchment—we have already encountered; the second extreme is permitting no entrenchment whatsoever. This, say proponents of the new view, is also undesirable. If Parliament cannot make it harder than usual to repeal or amend certain laws, this means that, in effect, all laws are equal: all can be repealed or amended with the same ease—it takes only a bare majority in Parliament. This, in turn, means that there can be no hierarchy of laws—no set of laws (such as laws dealing with important constitutional matters) that are marked out as especially significant, and with which interference is made commensurately difficult. For example, in 2010, the coalition government announced its

---

206 See Heuston, *Essays in Constitutional Law* (London 1964), ch 1; Jennings, *The Law and the Constitution* (London 1959), ch 4.

intention to create a 'referendum lock', whereby a treaty transferring additional powers to the EU could be entered into by the UK only if approved in a referendum.[207] This undertaking is legally worthless unless the new view obtains, since legislation providing for a referendum lock could be overridden simply by passing a further Act of Parliament and without holding the stipulated referendum.

Proponents of the new view argue that it is consistent with the notion of parliamentary sovereignty because, they contend, saying that Parliament is sovereign merely means that it is capable of enacting, amending, or repealing any law—and it continues to be capable of all of those things even if certain laws can only be enacted, amended, or repealed if certain conditions are first fulfilled.[208]

> **Q** Do you agree that the new view strikes the right balance between the two extreme positions mentioned above? Do you think that the distinction between (prohibited) substantive and (permissible) formal modes of entrenchment can be clearly drawn? For example, on which side of the line would you put a condition in an Act stipulating that it could be repealed or amended only by a unanimous vote in both Houses of Parliament?

4.4.2 Is the new view correct as a matter of UK law?

Those who support the new view do not merely argue that it is a good idea; they also contend that it accurately describes the position currently adopted by UK law. But certain cases suggest that this is not so. The most direct judicial consideration of this point is to be found in two 1930s cases concerning the relationship between the Acquisition of Land Act 1919 and the Housing Act 1925.[209] The former set out a scheme for assessing the compensation that should be awarded to landowners whose property was compulsorily purchased by the state—and s 7(1) said that other legislation 'shall, in relation to the matters dealt with in this Act, have effect subject to this Act, and so far as inconsistent with this Act those provisions shall cease to have or shall not have effect'. It was argued that the 1919 Act was contingently entrenched—that it could only be repealed or departed from by subsequent legislation that used express words of repeal or derogation. And, it was said, since the 1925 Act did not explicitly depart from the 1919 Act, the 1919 Act should take priority over the later legislation. This suggestion was roundly rejected by the courts. Maugham LJ said that Parliament 'cannot...bind itself as to the form of subsequent legislation';[210] similar views were expressed by other judges.[211] Much more recently, Laws LJ said in *Thoburn v Sunderland City Council*[212]

---

[207] HM Government, *The Coalition: Our Programme for Government* (London 2010), p 19.

[208] Heuston, p 9.

[209] *Vauxhall Estates Ltd v Liverpool Corporation* [1932] 1 KB 733, *Ellen Street Estates Ltd v Minister of Health* [1934] 1 KB 590. [210] *Ellen Street Estates* at 597.

[211] *Ellen Street Estates* at 595–6, *per* Scrutton LJ; *Vauxhall Estates* at 743, *per* Avory J, and at 746, *per* Humphrys J.

[212] [2002] EWHC 195 (Admin), [2003] QB 151, [59]. Of course, proponents of the new view would say that the imposition of formal restrictions on future Parliaments does not constitute the abandonment of sovereignty, because future Parliaments would remain free to pass any laws that they wished provided that they complied with the conditions laid down in the earlier Act.

that 'Parliament cannot bind its successors by stipulating against repeal' and 'cannot stipulate against implied repeal any more than it can stipulate against express repeal': 'Being sovereign, it cannot abandon its sovereignty.'

Until recently, the principal judicial authorities that were said to support the new view were cases concerning legislatures other than the UK Parliament, but which proponents of the new view said were analogically relevant.[213] For example, in *Ranasinghe*,[214] legislation enacted under the royal prerogative established a constitution for what was then the British colony of Ceylon[215] and provided, *inter alia*, that the Ceylon legislature could legislate contrary to the constitution only if such legislation were supported by a two-thirds (rather than the usual bare) majority of legislators. When the Ceylon legislature purported to enact a Bill that departed from the constitution, but which had not been passed with a two-thirds majority, it was judicially held that the Bill was invalid. Although supporters of the new view say this proves the correctness of their argument, it does nothing of the sort. It is entirely unsurprising that a legislature that derives its power from a constitutional text must abide by whatever *conditions the constitutional text lays down*. But this says nothing about whether a sovereign legislature that is not governed by any constitutional text can be subject to *binding conditions imposed by itself at an earlier point in time*.[216]

However, in *Jackson*, there was some *obiter* support for the new view. Some of the judges paid at least lip service to Wade's orthodoxy: Lord Hope, for example, reiterated that 'no Parliament can bind its successors'.[217] But others accepted that if (as in relation to the Parliament Acts) Parliament could legislate to make it easier to enact laws, it could also make it harder by imposing binding conditions on future Parliaments. As Baroness Hale put it, if Parliament—as in the Parliament Acts—can 'redefine itself downwards', by subtracting requirements (such as the Lords' consent) from the rule of recognition, then 'it may very well be that it can redefine itself upwards, [for example] to require a particular parliamentary majority'.[218] Lord Steyn was even more certain about this: he unequivocally said that 'Parliament could for specific purposes provide for a two-thirds majority in the House of Commons and the House of Lords', and went on to cite with approval the work of writers associated with the new view.[219] So while it remains the case that no UK judgment has unequivocally held that the Westminster Parliament can formally entrench legislation—all discussion of this in *Jackson* being *obiter*—some of the speeches in *Jackson* at least give succour to that view; the decision itself in *Jackson* is certainly at odds with Wade's view that the rule of recognition

---

[213] *Attorney-General for New South Wales v Trethowan* [1932] AC 526, *Harris v Minister of the Interior* 1952 (2) SA 428, *Bribery Commission v Ranasinghe* [1965] AC 172.   [214] [1965] AC 172.

[215] Now the independent state of Sri Lanka.

[216] This distinction was, without explanation, dismissed by Lord Steyn in *R (Jackson) v Attorney-General* [2005] UKHL 56, [2006] 1 AC 262, [85].   [217] *Jackson* at [113].

[218] *Jackson* at [163].   [219] *Jackson* at [81].

is immune from any attempt by Parliament to mould it through the enactment of legislation.

4.5 Is Parliament really sovereign?

4.5.1 The story so far—and a final question

So far, our inquiry has focused on whether Parliament is capable of imposing any sort of limits on itself. We have seen that Wade's continuing theory answers this question firmly in the negative, but that its veracity is open to question in the light of both the Parliament Acts and the European Communities Act. We have also seen that the new view holds that although Parliament cannot absolutely entrench legislation, it can impose conditions that must be fulfilled before legislation can be repealed or departed from. But while the continuing theory and the new view differ on whether a given Parliament can ever be subject to *intended constraints*—that is, constraints that exist because of the intention of earlier Parliaments—they agree on one thing: that Parliament is sovereign in the sense that it can make any law.[220] It is therefore said that Parliament is free from *unintended constraints*—that is, constraints that do not derive from conditions imposed by Parliament itself at an earlier point in time. Our final question is whether that supposition is correct.

4.5.2 Model III—unintended constraints on parliamentary authority

We already know from our discussion in section 4.1 above that not everyone thinks that Parliament *should* be free from unintended constraints: legal constitutionalists argue that legislative power should subject to legal restrictions that can, if necessary, be enforced by the courts. But our question now is a different one: is the UK Parliament *actually* subject to such constraints? In order to answer this question, we need to distinguish between two sorts of such constraint.

It is obvious that there are *practical constraints* upon what Parliament may accomplish. Even if it has the legal power to enact any law, a law directing that the sun should never set over the UK again would accomplish nothing in practice. This reduces to the issue of enforceability: Parliament, if it is sovereign, can make any legal provision that it wishes, but whether it can secure real-world compliance with stipulations set down in legislation is another matter entirely. For example, it has been observed that if Parliament enacts 'that smoking in the streets of Paris is an offence, then it *is* an offence' as a matter of *UK* law—but the *French* police and courts would take no notice of that law.[221] Similarly, if Parliament is sovereign, then it can undo anything that it has previously done. It has therefore been noted that, as a matter of law, Parliament could repeal legislation conferring independence on countries that used to form part of the British Empire such that, as a matter of UK law, Parliament's authority to legislate for such countries would resume. But Lord

---

[220] Even if, on the new view, Parliament might have to comply with certain conditions when doing so.

[221] Jennings, *The Law and the Constitution* (London 1959), pp 170–1 (original emphasis).

Denning pointed out that 'Freedom once given cannot be taken away. Legal theory must give way to practical politics'.[222]

The fact that there are things such as those mentioned above that Parliament cannot practically accomplish is not inconsistent with asserting that it is legally sovereign, since that concept simply means that Parliament can enact any laws that it wishes (whether or not they are sensible or practically enforceable). But are there also *legal constraints* on what Parliament can do? Are there some laws that it is not constitutionally competent to enact—and which, even if *practically* enforceable, would not be *legally* enforced by the courts? The answer to this question, in the absence of a written constitution in the UK, might seem obvious. How can there be legal constraints on Parliament's power if no written constitution prescribes any such constraints? But some writers—and now some judges—argue that the *unwritten* constitution may contain fundamental principles that are so important as to be immovable by Parliament.

There are a number of ways in which this argument has been expressed. Allan, one of its leading proponents, argues that Wade was wrong to suppose that parliamentary sovereignty simply has to be accepted as a matter of historical fact;[223] rather, he contends, the authority of a legislature to make law must derive from some recognised and accepted principle. And whatever the position might have been in 1688, the principle that today underpins Parliament's authority is democracy. He goes on to argue that because democracy constitutes the moral *foundation* of Parliament's lawmaking authority, it also traces the *extent* of that authority. It follows, says Allan, that if Parliament were to enact a law the 'effect [of which] would be the destruction of any recognizable form of democracy'—such as 'a measure purporting to deprive a substantial section of the electorate of the vote on the grounds of their hostility to government policies'—the courts should not enforce it.[224]

Other writers have expressed their arguments in different terms, but agree with Allan that Parliament is subject to constraints imposed by the unwritten constitution. Writing extrajudicially, the Court of Appeal judge Sir John Laws said that basic rights, such as freedom of expression, form part of a 'higher-order law'—that is, they constitute a set of principles that 'cannot be abrogated as other laws can'.[225] This analysis situates Parliament not (as traditional sovereignty theory would have it) *at the apex* of the constitutional order, unconstrained by anything or anyone, but *beneath* a set of fundamental constitutional principles that bind Parliament and with which it is therefore impotent to interfere. This point was captured by Lord Woolf, writing extrajudicially before he became Lord Chief Justice, when he asserted that 'both Parliament and the courts derive their authority from the rule of law' and that both are therefore bound by it. It follows, he said, that 'there are ... limits on the sovereignty of Parliament which

---

[222] *Blackburn v Attorney-General* [1971] 1 WLR 1037, 1040.
[223] *Law, Liberty, and Justice* (Oxford 1993), ch 11.   [224] Allan, p 282.
[225] 'Law and Democracy' [1995] PL 72, 84.

it is the courts' inalienable responsibility to identify and uphold'.[226] More recently, Lord Phillips, the President of the UK Supreme Court, said in a radio interview that 'if Parliament did the inconceivable [by legislating contrary to a fundamental constitutional principle], we [the judges] might do the inconceivable as well'.[227] These are radical assertions that depart markedly from orthodox thinking about parliamentary sovereignty. Would the courts really take such a drastic step?

4.5.3 Constitutional values and the interpretation of legislation

The short answer to that question is that we simply do not know for sure—but there are several clues in the case law and related developments that allow for informed speculation. Although, as noted above,[228] judicial dicta in the early seventeenth century appeared to assert a strike-down power in respect of legislation that was repugnant to fundamental principles of justice,[229] such assertions fell away following the Glorious Revolution during which the sovereignty of Parliament was firmly established. However, we should not be too quick to assume that the matter is therefore settled. It is absolutely clear that courts do not approach legislation from a position of constitutional neutrality—that is, when presented with legislation in a particular case, they do not interpret and apply it without regard to its constitutional implications; rather, courts normally attempt to find an interpretation of the law that is consistent with fundamental constitutional principles such as those falling under the rubric of the 'rule of law'.[230] This is often rationalised by the courts through reliance on a presumption about what Parliament intends when it enacts Bills. For example, in the *Pierson* case, Lord Steyn said: 'Parliament does not legislate in a vacuum. Parliament legislates for a European liberal democracy founded on the principles and traditions of the common law. And the courts may approach legislation on this initial presumption.'[231]

In many situations, this technique can readily be applied—for example, by reading a generally worded statutory provision as being subject to implied restrictions. *Ahmed v HM Treasury*[232] is a case in point. Following the 9/11 attacks in the USA in 2001, the United Nations Security Council required states to freeze the assets of 'persons who commit, or attempt to commit, terrorist acts or participate in or facilitate the commission of terrorist acts' and of specific individuals connected with Al-Qaeda and the Taliban.[233] In response, the UK enacted two pieces of secondary legislation under s 1(1) of the United Nations Act 1946, which authorises the enactment of Orders in Council (a form of delegated legislation) when this is 'necessary or expedient' for the purpose of giving effect to UN Security Council directions.[234] The claimants in *Ahmed* contended that the Orders in Council were unlawful on the ground that, properly

---

226 'Droit Public: English Style' [1995] PL 57, 68–9.
227 BBC Radio 4, *Today*, 2 August 2010.   228 *Dr Bonham's Case* (1610) Co Rep 113.
229 Compare Williams, 'Dr Bonham's Case and "Void" Statutes' (2007) 26 Journal of Legal History 111.
230 On the rule of law, see Chapter 2, section 4.4, above.
231 *R v Secretary of State for the Home Department, ex p Pierson* [1998] AC 539, 587.
232 [2010] UKSC 2, [2010] 2 WLR 378.   233 UN Security Council Resolution 1373, para 1(c).
234 On secondary legislation, see generally Chapter 4, section 4.2, above.

construed, s 1(1) of the 1946 Act did not authorise them. These arguments rested on two main premises: that one of the Orders, by permitting the government to freeze the assets of anyone *reasonably suspected* by it of terrorist involvement, went beyond what the UN direction required;[235] and that the other Order undermined the right of access to courts by permitting the UK government to freeze the assets of people designated as suspected terrorists by the UN without affording them any opportunity to mount a judicial challenge to the UN's decisions so to designate them.[236]

These arguments succeeded in the Supreme Court. Lord Hope noted that the effect of freezing someone's assets 'can be devastating', not least because 'their freedom of movement is severely restricted without access to funds or other economic resources', which 'strike[s] at the very heart of the individual's basic right to live his own life as he chooses'.[237] The Supreme Court concluded that, as Lord Hope put it, 'by introducing the reasonable suspicion test..., the Treasury exceeded [its] powers under section 1(1) of the 1946 Act'. This, he said, was 'a clear example of an attempt to adversely affect the basic rights of the citizen without the clear authority of Parliament'.[238] Similarly, the attempt to subject people to asset-freezing on the basis of their designation by the UN was unlawful: if Parliament were to have intended s 1(1) of the 1946 Act to authorise the enactment of Orders fundamentally at odds with the right of access to courts, it would have said so in clear language. As Lord Mance put it: 'The words of section 1(1) are general, but for that very reason susceptible to the presumption, in the absence of express language or necessary implication to the contrary, that they were intended to be subject to the basic rights of the individual.'[239] This approach to interpretation—whereby legislation is, where possible, interpreted consistently with basic constitutional principles and rights—is one that has a long pedigree in English law, but it is worth noting at this point that it is now bolstered by the HRA, s 3(1) of which requires courts to interpret legislation compatibly with certain fundamental rights when it is possible to do so.[240]

While cases like *Ahmed* demonstrate a willingness on the courts' part to do their best to give Acts of Parliament a meaning that is consistent with fundamental constitutional values, they do not provide evidence that—in line with the views of writers such as Allan, Laws, and Woolf considered above—the UK constitution contains 'higher order' principles contravention of which renders legislation unlawful and ineffective. (Indeed, the immediate response of the UK government to *Ahmed* was to procure the enactment of primary legislation conferring validity on the secondary legislation impugned by the Supreme Court.[241]) However, Allan argues that the distinction between *interpreting* a provision in an Act and *refusing to apply* it is an elusive and,

---

[235] Terrorism (United Nations Measures) Order 2006.
[236] Al-Qaida and Taliban (United Nations Measures) Order 2006.
[237] [2010] UKSC 2, [2010] 2 WLR 378, [60].   [238] *Ahmed* at [61].   [239] *Ahmed* at [249].
[240] See further Chapter 19, section 3.4, below.
[241] Terrorist Asset-freezing (Temporary Provisions) Act 2010. As its name implies, this Act was a stop-gap measure, pending more detailed legislative reform.

ultimately, unhelpful one.[242] In essence, his contention is that if a court were to adopt an interpretation of a statute that was so radical as to change its meaning entirely, that would be tantamount to a refusal to apply it whether or not the court openly admitted that it was doing so. It has been suggested by some commentators that that is precisely what happened in the *Anisminic* case.[243]

The case concerned a provision contained in an Act of Parliament that provided that decisions made by a particular public body known as the Foreign Compensation Commission 'shall not be called in question in any court of law'.[244] The meaning of such so-called *ouster* clauses seems perfectly clear: Parliament surely intends to displace (to oust) the power of judicial review—that is, the power to adjudicate on the legality of decisions—that courts would normally exercise in relation to public bodies.[245] The difficulty, of course, is that interpreting the Act in that way would wholly prevent the courts from upholding the law and would result in the existence of a public body entirely free from any form of legal control. Such a situation would fundamentally threaten the rule of law. It is hardly surprising, then, that in *Anisminic* the Appellate Committee of the House of Lords attempted to find an interpretation of the ouster clause that would preserve judicial review; what *is* surprising, given the clarity with which the clause was drafted, is that the majority succeeded—or at least claimed to have done so. It was held that when Parliament had said that the Commission's determinations could not be questioned in any court, it had *meant* that no *lawful* determination could be questioned.

This interpretation left intact the courts' normal powers to overrule public bodies' unlawful decisions, and the Law Lords claimed that this result had been achieved simply by construing the ouster clause in a proper way: Lord Wilberforce, for example, said that the Appellate Committee was merely 'carrying out the intention of the legislature'.[246] Some writers, however, have professed themselves unconvinced by this analysis: if a particular provision is interpreted in a way that runs wholly counter to its natural meaning, this inevitably begs the question whether the Court was really just engaging in interpretation or was, in effect, refusing to apply the provision at all. Wade argued that, in *Anisminic*, the Court was 'applying a presumption'—that courts must have the power to keep public bodies within the law—'which may override even their constitutional obedience [to Acts of Parliament]'. This, he went on, 'is tantamount to saying that judicial review [of government and public bodies' decisions] is a constitutional fundamental which even the sovereign Parliament cannot abolish'.[247]

4.5.4 Beyond interpretation?

But why is there no unequivocal evidence of courts refusing—and openly acknowledging that they are refusing—to apply Acts of Parliament? The first, and most

---

[242] 'Parliamentary Sovereignty: Law, Politics, and Revolution' (1997) 113 LQR 443, 447.
[243] *Anisminic Ltd v Foreign Compensation Commission* [1969] 2 AC 147.
[244] Foreign Compensation Act 1950, s 4(4).   [245] On judicial review, see Chapters 12–15 below.
[246] [1969] 2 AC 147, 208.   [247] Wade and Forsyth, *Administrative Law* (Oxford 2008), p 616.

obvious, possibility is that courts are simply *not prepared to* refuse to apply duly enacted primary legislation. On this view, writers such as Allan, Laws, and Woolf, who contend that Parliament's lawmaking authority is limited and subject to judicial control, are plainly wrong. The second possibility is that although courts *are prepared* to refuse to apply 'unconstitutional' legislation, they have never yet been faced with an Act of Parliament that is so repugnant to fundamental principles as to justify a refusal to apply it. This view is made more convincing by virtue of the fact that a dominant theme within this school of thought is that the limits on Parliament's lawmaking power that writers postulate relate to truly extreme legislation, the enactment of which is—for political reasons considered earlier in the chapter—unlikely.[248] It is also important to bear in mind that, as we explained in Chapter 1, for as long as the HRA is in force, the courts, because they are empowered by that Act to declare legislation to be incompatible with fundamental rights, are not presented with a stark choice between applying or refusing to apply legislation that offends such rights.[249] There is, however, a third possibility: that the courts wish to characterise—perhaps even *disguise*—their endeavours as the interpretation of, rather than as a refusal to apply, legislation. In relation to this third possibility, three points should be considered.

First, why might courts want to avoid explicitly refusing to apply legislation? Everyone accepts that it is the courts' job to interpret and apply laws enacted by Parliament. It follows that while a very bold interpretation may (by giving the legislation a meaning radically different from that which was intended by Parliament) have a similar effect to refusing to apply it at all, such an approach is less likely to attract the criticism that judges are overstepping the mark. Even in countries with written constitutions, judicial powers to strike down unconstitutional legislation are not uncontroversial. For example, the US Constitution does not explicitly confer such powers on the courts. When, in the seminal case of *Marbury v Madison*,[250] the US Supreme Court held that such powers were *implicit* in the Constitution—why would the framers have limited the powers of government if they had not intended the courts to be able to enforce such limits?—this conclusion was not universally welcomed: the Court was criticised in some quarters for assuming powers that had not clearly been allocated to it by the Constitution.

Second, UK courts would find themselves in a particularly exposed position if they were to assert such powers. In the USA, there was no doubt that the *Constitution imposed limits* on (*inter alia*) the legislative authority of Congress, albeit that there was some room for disagreement about *whether the Constitution assigned to the courts the task of policing those limits*. In the UK, in contrast, there is no written constitution to which judges can point in the first place to establish that Parliament's authority *is limited*—and even if we are prepared to accept that it is, there is no written constitution telling us (or the judges) *what those limits are*. It follows that if UK courts were to assert US-style powers to strike down Acts of Parliament, they would not only be

[248] Lord Woolf, '*Droit Public*: English Style' [1995] PL 57.   [249] See further Chapter 19 below.
[250] 5 US 137 (1803).

assuming an enforcement function not explicitly assigned to them by the constitution, but would also be determining, without any evidence in the form of a written constitution, that *there are constitutional limits to Parliament's lawmaking authority* and *what those limits are*. As Griffith—a prominent critic of extensive judicial power—remarks, the 'trouble' with the argument that there are 'higher-order' laws restricting Parliament's authority and enforceable by courts is that they 'must be given substance, be interpreted, and be applied'. This, he says, leads to judges claiming 'superiority over democratically elected institutions' and prefers 'philosopher-kings to human politicians'.[251] It is perhaps for precisely these reasons that those who argue in favour of UK judges possessing a power to disregard unconstitutional legislation suggest that it arises only in extreme circumstances: Woolf, for example, said that he envisaged limits upon Parliament's lawmaking authority only 'of the most modest dimensions which I believe any democrat would accept'.[252]

> **Q** In section 4.1.2 above, we considered the 'majoritarian' objection to courts having powers to strike down legislation enacted by democratically elected legislatures. In the absence of a written constitution imposing limits on the legislature, do you regard those objections as unanswerable?

Third, however, it seems that it is not only the courts that are, for the reasons explored above, keen to avoid the sort of confrontation that would bring out into the open the question of whether there are legally enforceable constitutional limits upon Parliament's lawmaking power. In 2003, the government published a Bill that later became the Ayslum and Immigration (Treatment of Claimants, etc.) Act 2004. The Act created a new body—the Asylum and Immigration Tribunal—responsible for hearing appeals against government decisions on matters such as whether someone claiming asylum meets the requirement of having a well-founded fear of persecution in his or her home country.[253] As originally drafted, the Bill contained a clause providing that there should be no oversight whatever of the tribunal by the ordinary courts. This would have displaced what we have seen is regarded as the fundamental constitutional right of access to courts; indeed, the clause had been specifically drafted with a view to precluding the sort of interpretation accorded to the ouster clause in *Anisminic*. A furore ensued: as we have already noted, parliamentary select committees opposed the clause. The Bar Council said that to oust the jurisdiction of the courts completely 'would be startling if done in a dictatorship' and that it was 'incredible that it is proposed in the UK'.[254] And the then Lord Chief Justice, Lord Woolf, said that if the clause were enacted, 'it would be so inconsistent with the spirit

---

[251] 'The Brave New World of Sir John Laws' (2000) 63 MLR 159, 165.   [252] Lord Woolf at 69.

[253] See Thomas, 'After the Ouster: Review and Reconsideration in a Single-Tier Tribunal' [2006] PL 674.

[254] Quoted in Le Sueur, 'Three Strikes and it's Out? The UK Government's Strategy to Oust Judicial Review from Immigration and Asylum Decision-Making' [2004] PL 225.

of mutual respect between the different arms of government that it could be the catalyst for a campaign for a written constitution'.[255] In the face of such opposition, the clause was withdrawn.

There is, therefore, something of a stand-off. The courts, for the reasons discussed above, are reluctant to assert a power to strike down Acts of Parliament that offend fundamental constitutional principles; but Parliament and the executive are also reluctant to put the courts in a situation in which they are forced to nail their colours to the mast by choosing between, on the one hand, the application of an Act that is incontrovertibly contrary to fundamental principles and, on the other hand, enforcing such principles notwithstanding the existence of such legislation. Although this means that we still cannot clearly say what would happen if such a situation were to arise, it is fair to say that judicial rhetoric has become notably bolder in recent years. In particular, judges' scepticism about Parliament having untrammelled powers has now found expression not only in extra-curial speeches, but also in remarks (albeit *obiter* ones) in decided cases. For example, following the controversy over the ouster clause in 2004, in the *Jackson* case, Lord Steyn said that as a matter of 'logic' and '[s]trict legalism', Parliament could enact 'oppressive and wholly undemocratic legislation', for example 'abolish[ing] judicial review of flagrant abuse of [executive] power'.[256] But, he said, this analysis was based on a 'pure and absolute' conception of parliamentary sovereignty that was 'out of place' in modern Britain. He went on to argue that the supremacy of Parliament depends on judicial recognition of it, and that, if Parliament were to assert an extravagant power by, for example, seeking to remove judicial review, the courts 'may have to consider whether this is a constitutional fundamental which even a sovereign Parliament...cannot abolish'.[257] Lord Hope expressed similarly striking views, opining that 'parliamentary sovereignty is no longer, if it ever was, absolute',[258] and Baroness Hale thought it possible that the courts may reject an attempt by Parliament to 'subvert the rule of law by removing governmental action affecting the rights of the individual from all judicial scrutiny'.[259]

These comments are consistent with dicta of Laws LJ, who we already know to be a critic of parliamentary sovereignty in his extrajudicial capacity. He argued in *International Transport* that the constitution stands 'at an intermediate stage between parliamentary supremacy and constitutional supremacy', that the courts are in the process of exposing the fundamental principles of the constitution, and that they will ultimately (even though they have not yet) hold those principles to be constraints upon the legislative authority of Parliament.[260] He employed similar reasoning in *Thoburn*, in which he argued that Parliament is constrained by whatever limits the contemporary

---

[255] 'The Rule of Law and a Change in the Constitution' [2004] CLJ 317, 329.

[256] *R (Jackson) v Attorney-General* [2005] UKHL 56, [2006] 1 AC 262, [102].

[257] *Jackson* at [102].   [258] *Jackson* at [104].   [259] *Jackson* at [159].

[260] *International Transport Roth GmbH v Secretary of State for the Home Department* [2002] EWCA Civ 158, [2003] QB 728, [71].

constitution imposes upon it.[261] He said that, in its present state of development, the constitution imposes only formal limits upon Parliament, such that 'constitutional statutes'—that is, legislation of fundamental constitutional importance—can only be repealed or amended through the use of specific language, and not impliedly.[262] Importantly, however, he conceptualised the authority of Parliament not as something that is outside the realm of, or superior to, constitutional law, but rather as a function of constitutional law, the implication being that as the constitution develops—or rather, as judges' thinking about what the constitution means develops—it is possible that substantive limits upon Parliament's authority may emerge. In this analysis, therefore, lie the seeds of a vision of the constitution in which it would be perfectly proper for judges to strike down legislation enacted outwith the limited powers accorded by the unwritten constitution to Parliament—provided that we are prepared to take the judges' word for it that they know what those limits are.

Whether or not the courts will one day decide to strike down legislation as unconstitutional remains to be seen. The episode of the ouster clause was perhaps the nearest we have come in recent years to the courts being placed in a position in which they would have been forced to decide whether to maintain traditional orthodox theory and apply legislation that ousted their own jurisdiction, or to depart from orthodox theory and strike down legislation on constitutional grounds. In any event, the ouster clause was never enacted and the whole episode will serve as a glaring warning to any future government contemplating a similar proposal. Nevertheless, it is not inconceivable that circumstances might, in the future, arise in which the courts decide to take UK constitutional law into hitherto unchartered territory by acknowledging substantive limits upon parliamentary sovereignty.

However, it is important to recognise two broader points. First, even if the courts were one day to decide that they had the constitutional ability to enforce such constraints, those limits would be likely to be at the very extremes. Absent some large-scale public and political debate as to whether or not the courts should be able to have such a power and also an agreed constitutional statement of the values against which the courts would assess the constitutionality of legislation, it is unlikely that legislation would be struck down except if it were to offend absolutely fundamental principles.

Second, if the courts were ever to take such a step, it would be highly likely to raise the hackles of politicians who resent unelected judges interfering with the powers of the elected Parliament. For example, David Blunkett MP, a former Home Secretary, has argued that it is necessary to have clarity about the relationship between Parliament

---

[261] *Thoburn v Sunderland City Council* [2002] EWHC 195 (Admin), [2003] QB 151. This case, and its implications vis-à-vis parliamentary sovereignty, are considered in more detail in Chapter 8, section 4.6, below in relation to EU law.

[262] *Thoburn* at [62]–[63]. Laws LJ defined a 'constitutional statute' as 'one which (a) conditions the legal relationship between citizen and state in some general, overarching manner, or (b) enlarges or diminishes the scope of what we would now regard as fundamental constitutional rights'. Into this category, he suggested, would fall legislation such as the European Communities Act 1972, the Human Rights Act 1998, and the various statutes enacted in 1998 instituting devolution in Scotland, Wales, and Northern Ireland.

and the courts to ensure that judges can strike down decisions by the *government* that exceed the powers given to it by Parliament, but that they do not have the power to decide that *Parliament* is wrong.[263] The difficulty for the courts is that entering into constitutional review of legislation may risk an unprecedented constitutional struggle with the government and/or calls for greater accountability of judges through, for example, pre-appointment hearings before Parliament in order to investigate the moral and political views of individual judges. The best solution all round would perhaps be for all three branches—Parliament, government, and the courts—to continue to respect each others' legitimate fields of action.

4.6 **Summary**

We have been concerned in this section with three models of parliamentary authority. Model I holds that Parliament is fully sovereign and that sovereignty is fixed (or 'continuing'); it is therefore (paradoxically) impossible for Parliament to do anything that would limit its own powers. Model II agrees that Parliament is sovereign, in that it is always possible for it to make, amend, or repeal any law, but says that it is possible for Parliament to lay down binding conditions as to the process that must be followed if (for example) a given Act were to be repealed or amended. Model III says that Parliament is not sovereign: it lacks the power to make laws that violate fundamental constitutional principles. The debate that underlies these three competing views ultimately turns on two questions: (i) can Parliament subject itself to any sort of limitations ('intended limitations'), and (ii) is Parliament subject to limitations that derive otherwise than from earlier Acts of Parliament ('unintended limitations')? We have seen that while there are no clear answers to either of these questions, there is at least circumstantial evidence that provides a basis for informed speculation.

The answer to question (i) is that while there is no unequivocal example of courts accepting that the UK Parliament can impose restrictions upon its successors, the reasoning, together with certain dicta, in the *Jackson* case provides some support for the view that Parliament *can* adapt the ground rules governing the enactment of legislation, thus allowing, for example, for legislation to be accorded limited entrenchment by precluding its amendment or repeal in the absence of express language or a super-majority.[264]

As far as question (ii) is concerned, we have seen that the courts—and indeed politicians—prefer, if possible, to avoid it. In particular, the courts seek to secure basic constitutional values by interpreting legislation consistently with them rather than by asserting a power to disregard Acts of Parliament that violate such values. And we know that the political process itself is likely to guard against the enactment of such legislation. However, we have also seen that some judges have asserted that if the unthinkable were to happen, they would be willing to consider refusing to apply such legislation.

---

[263] 'Sorry, m'lud, supremacy is not yours alone', *The Sunday Times*, 23 August 2009.

[264] For example, a two-thirds majority—something greater than the bare majority that is normally required.

Some of the heat has been removed from this debate by the fact that, as we saw in Chapter 1, courts are able under the HRA to declare that legislation is incompatible with fundamental rights.[265] But that Act, at least in its present form, may not remain on the statute book forever; in any event, the underlying question—whether there are any enforceable limits on Parliament's lawmaking authority—remains an important one that goes to the heart of the nature of the British constitution. We know that there are many things that Parliament is, in reality, extremely unlikely to do. What we do not know is whether, if the political process were to fail to prevent such legislative conduct, the courts would step in and provide legal redress by striking down the relevant Act. Ultimately, therefore, this question is about the extent to which the British tradition of political constitutionalism is supplemented—or has been replaced—by a legal form of constitutionalism that supplies clear lines that may not lawfully be crossed by legislators. And it is, as we have seen, a question that both judges and politicians seem anxious should never be allowed to arise.

5. Concluding remarks

In this chapter, we have explored three principal issues relating to Parliament's role within the UK constitution: its democratic credentials, its efficacy as a lawmaker (or, more accurately, as a scrutiniser of government Bills), and the extent of its legal powers. In addressing these matters, we have encountered all three of the key themes that run throughout this book. First, we have noted that the Westminster Parliament is not the only lawmaking body in the UK: in our contemporary *multilayered constitution*, legislative authority is shared between institutions at several different levels. Second, we have seen that because of the UK constitution's idiosyncratic implementation of the separation of powers doctrine, Parliament is, in practice, dominated by the executive branch. As a result, its capacity effectively to scrutinise government Bills is limited, and Parliament as a lawmaker can, without exaggeration, be regarded as, in some senses, an offshoot of the executive. This engages our theme concerning the *importance of holding the government to account*. If Parliament is, in effect, part of the government rather than an independent scrutiniser of it and of its Bills, then this raises questions about the need for effective scrutiny *of Parliament*—whether internally (through the relationship between the two chambers) or externally (for example, via judicial review of legislation). Third, we have seen that the debate concerning the extent of Parliament's powers goes to the heart of the wider debate about *the balance in the UK between political and legal forms of constitutionalism*. Although we were unable definitively to determine whether Parliament *is* truly sovereign, we *do* know for sure that whether we think that Parliament *should* be sovereign will depend on the faith that we are willing to put in politicians and in judges respectively.

---

[265] See further Chapter 19 below.

Further reading

General

GIDDINGS, *The Future of Parliament: Issues for a New Century* (Basingstoke 2005)

NORTON, *Parliament in British Politics* (Basingstoke 2005)

Parliament and democracy

The Report of the Independent Commission on the Voting System (Cm 4090 1998), available online at **http://www.archive.official-documents.co.uk/document/cm40/4090/4090.htm**

COMMISSION ON REFORM OF THE HOUSE OF LORDS, *A House for the Future* (Cm 4534 2000), available online at **http://www.archive.official-documents.co.uk/document/cm45/4534/4534.htm**

PHILLIPS, *Strengthening Democracy: Fair and Sustainable Funding of Political Parties* (London 2007), available online at **http://www.partyfundingreview.gov.uk/files/strengthening_democracy.pdf**

MORISON, 'Models of Democracy: From Representation to Participation?', in Jowell and Oliver (eds), *The Changing Constitution* (Oxford 2007)

PHILLIPSON, '"The Greatest Quango of Them All", "A Rival Chamber" or "A Hybrid Nonsense"? Solving the Second Chamber Paradox' [2004] PL 352

Parliament and the legislative process

BRAZIER (ed), *Parliament, Politics and Law Making: Issues and Developments in the Legislative Process* (London 2004)

BRAZIER, KALITOWSKI, AND ROSENBLATT, WITH KORRIS, *Law in the Making: Influence and Change in the Legislative Process* (London 2008)

HOUSE OF COMMONS MODERNISATION COMMITTEE, *The Legislative Process* (HC 1097 2005–06)

HOUSE OF LORDS SELECT COMMITTEE ON THE CONSTITUTION, *Parliament and the Legislative Process* (HL 173 2003–04)

Parliament's powers

ALLAN, 'Parliamentary Sovereignty: Law, Politics, and Revolution' (1997) 113 LQR 443

GOLDSWORTHY, *The Sovereignty of Parliament* (Oxford 1999)

GORDON, 'The Conceptual Foundations of Parliamentary Sovereignty: Reconsidering Jennings and Wade' [2009] PL 519

LAWS, 'Law and Democracy' [1995] PL 72

WADE, 'The Basis of Legal Sovereignty' [1955] CLJ 172

Useful websites

General

http://www.parliament.uk
The website of the UK Parliament

Parliament and democracy

http://www.electoral-reform.org.uk
The website of the Electoral Reform Society

http://www.lordsappointments.gov.uk
The website of the House of Lords Appointments Commission

Parliament and the legislative process

http://www.cabinetoffice.gov.uk/resource-library/guide-making-legislation
The Cabinet Office's Guide to Making Legislation

http://www.legislation.gov.uk
An online UK legislation service

6

The Judiciary

1. Introduction

We have, inevitably, already mentioned the role of the courts on several occasions. In this chapter, however, we focus specifically on the judiciary—and on two issues in particular.

First, *what are courts and judges for?* The answer to this question may seem so obvious as to make it unnecessary to pose it in the first place. However, we will see that it is worth reflecting upon the proper role of the judiciary, both in general terms and with specific reference to the constitutional role played by the courts. This will enable us to appreciate both the function that the courts fulfil in upholding key constitutional principles such as the separation of powers and the rule of law, and the way in which such principles, in turn, inform the proper conception of the judicial role.

Second, having identified the functions that courts do and should serve, we will consider what *characteristics* they have (and should have) in order that they may effectively discharge these functions. In this context, we will pay particular attention to the notion of judicial independence: the idea that judges should be free to interpret and apply the law in an objective way, free from political interference, and free from any need to worry about public opinion. But while judicial independence is undoubtedly important, we will also ask whether this orthodoxy should be accepted unquestioningly. In particular, as judges acquire greater powers to pronounce on controversial matters—as a result of, among other things, the growth of judicial review of government action and the increasing prominence of human rights law—we will consider whether it is realistic to suppose that the business of judging is an activity wholly distinct and separate from the broader political process. We will also, in this regard, consider what characteristics, other than judicial independence, the judiciary should possess. How important, for example, is it that judges are representative—in gender, ethnic, social, and other terms—of the population at large?

2. The structure of the judicial system

Before addressing these matters, it is necessary first to outline the structure of the judicial system in the United Kingdom. It is beyond the scope of this book to examine in

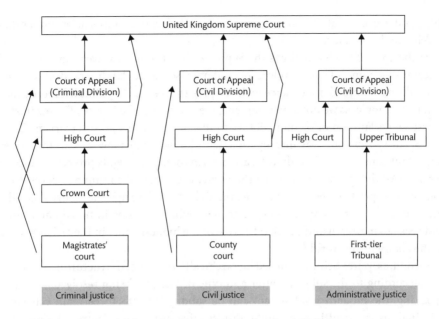

Figure 6.1 The structure of the judicial system in England and Wales

any detail the way in which the system of courts is organised and the exact scope of the respective jurisdictions of the courts that form that system.[1] It is, however, necessary to consider the general shape of the system. Figure 6.1 shows the basic architecture of the system, and should be read subject to the following points.

First, the judicial structure is a hierarchical one. Different courts undertaking different tasks are located at different levels of the hierarchy. Broadly speaking, there are three main levels of this hierarchy. The bottom tier is made up of lower courts and tribunals, such as magistrates' courts, the county court, and the First-tier Tribunal. These are first-instance courts. This means that they will always be involved in hearing cases for the first time. Normally, the role of such courts and tribunals involves fact-finding. They will hear witnesses and consider the evidence to make findings of fact.

Above this level are courts of higher standing, such as the High Court and the Court of Appeal. Such courts may have either a first-instance or appellate jurisdiction. For example, the High Court is a first-instance court in some types of litigation, such as judicial review. By contrast, the Court of Appeal is an appellate court—that is, it only ever deals with cases that are appeals against decisions of a lower court or tribunal. Likewise, the Upper Tribunal, which has an equivalent status to the High Court, determines appeals on a point of law from the First-tier Tribunal. Courts at

---

[1] On such matters, see Bailey, Ching, and Taylor, *The Modern English Legal System* (London 2007), chs 2 and 18.

this middle level are almost always concerned with deciding points of law rather than making findings of fact.

At the apex of the hierarchy is the Supreme Court. It is only ever concerned with determining points of law. Its role is focused upon so-called 'landmark' decisions that generally have a broad importance in developing the law and to public life more generally. For example, as we noted in Chapter 1, the decision of the House of Lords in 2004 to issue a declaration of incompatibility to the effect that the Anti-terrorism, Crime and Security Act 2001 was incompatible with human rights law was an immensely important constitutional landmark case in terms of human rights protection and terrorism.[2] All the indications are that the Supreme Court will continue to develop this role in appropriate cases. For example, the website of the Supreme Court states that the Court concentrates on cases of the greatest public and constitutional importance, and seeks to maintain and develop the role of the highest court in the UK as a leader in the common law world.[3]

Second, as well as being organised hierarchically, the judicial structure is also organised according to the subject matter and type of disputes being resolved. Generally speaking, the modern legal system can be subdivided into three main categories: criminal justice, civil justice, and administrative justice. As Figure 6.1 shows, the structure of the judicial system is arranged accordingly. We need to say something about each of the three main elements of the system.

The *criminal justice* process is concerned with the criminal prosecution of alleged offenders. Nearly all criminal cases begin in the magistrates' court. Cases concerning less serious offences are heard in that court, while more serious cases (for example, murder) can—and in some cases must—be transferred to the Crown Court. A key difference is that while cases in the magistrates' court are heard by a panel of lay justices or a single judge, Crown Court cases involve trial by jury. Appeals from decisions of the magistrates' court can be made to the Crown Court[4] (and thereafter, on a point of law only, to the High Court,[5] and subsequently to the Supreme Court[6]) or (on points of law only) directly to the High Court[7] (and thereafter the Supreme Court[8]). Appeals in cases heard by the Crown Court lie to the Court of Appeal (Criminal Division)[9] and thereafter to the Supreme Court.[10]

Meanwhile, the *civil justice* process is concerned with civil liability (for example, actions for personal injury or breach of contract). Some lower-value claims must be brought in the county court, but many civil claims can be brought either in that court or in the High Court.[11] In such circumstances, cases can be transferred between the

---

    [2] *A v Secretary of State for the Home Department* [2004] UKHL 56, [2005] 2 AC 68; see Chapter 1, section 3.1.2, above.   [3] **http://www.supremecourt.gov.uk/about/role-of-the-supreme-court.html**

    [4] Magistrates' Courts Act 1980, s 108.   [5] Senior Courts Act 1981, s 28.

    [6] Administration of Justice Act 1960, s 1.   [7] Magistrates' Courts Act 1980, s 111.

    [8] Administration of Justice Act 1960, s 1.

    [9] Criminal Appeal Act 1968, Pt I. In relation to certain other matters with which the Crown Court deals, appeals can be made to the High Court.   [10] Criminal Appeal Act 1968, s 33.

    [11] High Court and County Courts Jurisdiction Order 1991, SI 1991/724.

High Court and the county court on a discretionary basis.[12] In exercising that discretion, factors such as the financial value of the claim, the availability of judges specialising in the matter concerned, and the complexity of the legal and factual issues are to be taken into account.[13] Appeals against county court decisions can be made to the High Court[14]—and thereafter to the Court of Appeal (Civil Division)[15] and the Supreme Court[16]—or, in limited circumstances, directly to the Court of Appeal (Civil Division)[17] and thereafter to the Supreme Court.[18] Appeals against High Court decisions can be made to the Court of Appeal (Civil Division)[19] and thereafter to the Supreme Court;[20] in limited circumstances, an appeal can be made directly to the Supreme Court.[21]

By contrast with the criminal and civil justice processes, the *administrative justice* process, or the public law system, is concerned with legal challenges against public or governmental decisions. Such challenges fall into two general categories. First, there are judicial review challenges against the legality of public decisions, which are determined by the Administrative Court (part of the High Court). We deal with judicial review in more detail in Chapters 12–15. Second, there are appeals against administrative decisions made by public bodies (such as welfare and immigration decisions). These appeals are determined by the First-tier and Upper Tribunals. Tribunals handle an enormous volume of cases each year and are now considered to be part of the broader judicial system.[22] We consider tribunals further in section 3.3.1 below and, in more detail, in Chapter 17.

Some additional points need to be made here. First, the *legal jurisdictions* of the different courts and tribunals vary. Many courts have a statutory jurisdiction. By contrast, other courts have an inherent, non-statutory jurisdiction. For example, the jurisdiction of the High Court is inherent: it is not conferred by legislation—and, at least on one view, cannot be excluded by legislation.[23] There are three 'divisions' of the High Court: the Family Division, the Chancery Division, and the Queen's Bench Division.[24] The last, as well as dealing with many commercial and other private law matters, also encompasses the Administrative Court, which handles judicial review cases.

Second, the structure is more complicated than so far indicated. Figure 6.1 is concerned only with the structure of the judicial system in England and Wales. The system in *Northern Ireland* is distinct, but very similar, with appeals lying ultimately (as in England and Wales) to the Supreme Court. The structure of the *Scottish* system is

---

[12] County Courts Act 1984, ss 40–42.   [13] Civil Procedure Rules, Pt 30, r 3.

[14] Access to Justice Act 1999 (Destination of Appeals) Order 2000, SI 2000/1071, art 3(1).

[15] Senior Courts Act 1981, s 16(1).   [16] Constitutional Reform Act 2005, s 40.

[17] Access to Justice Act 1999 (Destination of Appeals) Order 2000, art 4.

[18] Constitutional Reform Act 2005, s 40.   [19] Senior Courts Act 1981, s 16(1).

[20] Constitutional Reform Act 2005, s 40.   [21] Administration of Justice Act 1969, Pt II.

[22] Figure 6.1 shows only the tribunals that comprise the new tribunals system introduced in 2008. We explain in Chapter 17 that other tribunals exist outside that system.

[23] See Chapter 5, section 4.5.3, above.   [24] Senior Courts Act 1981, s 5.

different, although the Supreme Court is the final court of appeal in respect of all non-criminal matters.[25]

Third, brief mention should be made of the *Judicial Committee of the Privy Council*. It acts as the court of final appeal for Jersey, Guernsey, and the Isle of Man, UK overseas territories, and certain Commonwealth countries. The Judicial Committee also used to have jurisdiction over devolution issues within the UK, but that function is now undertaken by the Supreme Court.[26] When it hears cases, the Committee normally comprises five judges drawn from the Supreme Court.[27]

Finally, an overview of the UK's judicial systems would not be complete without mention of two international courts. First, there is the *Court of Justice of the European Union* (CJEU), which deals with matters concerning European Union (EU) law and sits in Luxembourg. Second, there is the *European Court of Human Rights* (ECtHR), which is concerned with the interpretation and application of the European Convention on Human Rights (ECHR) and sits in Strasbourg. Neither court can straightforwardly be said to form an integral part of the UK's judicial systems, but both nevertheless play a crucial role. As we explain in Chapter 8, UK courts can, and sometimes must, refer to the CJEU contested questions of EU law, the CJEU's role being to render an authoritative interpretation of the provision in question. Meanwhile, the ECtHR's influence is felt in two particular respects. First, UK courts, when deciding cases under the Human Rights Act 1998 (HRA), are statutorily required to take into account the ECtHR's case law[28] and have indicated that they will 'follow any clear and constant jurisprudence' of that Court unless special circumstances apply.[29] Second, the ECtHR's judgments are binding upon the UK as a matter of international law.[30]

If this brief summary of the judicial structure seems complex and intricate, then that is simply because the structure itself is complicated. In a modern legal system, courts and tribunals are required to handle a wide variety of types of case—criminal, civil, administrative. Furthermore, the total volume of cases determined by the courts is enormous. In 2008, there were approximately 30,000 magistrates, 140 district judges, and 170 deputy district judges operating in the roughly 330 magistrates' courts throughout England and Wales; an estimated 1.92 million defendants were proceeded against for criminal offences (excluding breaches) in magistrates' courts.[31] By contrast, higher courts deal with a far lower caseload—the Supreme Court heard approximately 60 cases in its first year of operation—but such cases typically have a wider public importance. The complexity of the judicial structure partly reflects the complexity of modern law and modern society. A further point to note—and one

---

[25] For an overview of the Scottish system, see **http://www.scotcourts.gov.uk**

[26] Constitutional Reform Act 2005, s 40(4)(b) and Sch 9.

[27] For more detailed information, see **http://www.jcpc.gov.uk**

[28] Human Rights Act 1998, s 2(1).

[29] *R (Alconbury Developments Ltd) v Secretary of State for the Environment, Transport and the Regions* [2001] UKHL 23, [2003] 2 AC 295, [26], *per* Lord Slynn. This dictum has been endorsed in several subsequent cases.   [30] ECHR, Art 46.

[31] Ministry of Justice, *Judicial Statistics 2008* (Cm 7697 2008), p 135.

that should already be apparent—is that the judicial structure is often the subject of reforms and reorganisations to ensure that it can provide effective and independent access to justice.

3. **The role of the judiciary**

3.1 **General matters**

At root, the function of the judicial system is straightforward. It exists to resolve disputes in accordance with the law; put simply, courts decide cases. Whatever the context—whether it is a criminal trial, a civil matter, or a judicial review case—first-instance courts undertake three principal tasks: (i) they find the relevant facts, (ii) they determine the relevant law, and (iii) they apply the law to the facts as found.

First, then, the court must *ascertain what the relevant facts are.* Depending on the circumstances, this may require the court to resolve disputes of fact. For example, in a criminal case, the prosecution may contend that the defendant was present when the alleged offence was committed, whereas the defendant may claim that he has an alibi that establishes that he was elsewhere. As we noted above, courts and tribunals at the lower level of the judicial hierarchy—magistrates' courts and the First-tier Tribunal, for example—are primarily fact-finding bodies. By contrast, in some other types of litigation, there will be no dispute over the facts between the parties. For example, in judicial review proceedings, the parties normally agree on the facts; their dispute will centre upon whether or not a public decision is lawful.

Second, the court must *determine what the relevant legal rules or principles are.* In some instances, this may be quite straightforward; in others, the court might have to wrestle with points of law that are unclear or complex. The court might even end up making law, by clarifying, developing, or supplementing existing principles or articulating new ones. While lower courts and tribunals are largely concerned with fact-finding, the role of higher appellate courts, such as the Court of Appeal, is to resolve points of law. Cases that raise difficult points of law of broader importance might proceed to the Supreme Court for an authoritative resolution by the top judges, the Supreme Court Justices, which, because of the status of that court, will be binding on all lower courts.

Third, the court must *apply the law to the facts*: it must decide whether the facts satisfy the relevant legal test. In a murder trial, for example, the court has to determine whether the evidence establishes that the defendant unlawfully caused the death of the victim and, in doing so, intended that the victim should either die or should suffer really serious harm. In a negligence action, the court may have to determine whether, for example, the driver of a car acted negligently when he drove his car into a pedestrian. By contrast, in a judicial review case, the High Court may have to decide whether a decision or policy announced by a government department constitutes a disproportionate interference with an individual's human rights.

Courts and tribunals are not, of course, uniquely capable of carrying out functions such as these. Other bodies can and do resolve disputes. For example, a contract might stipulate that disputes arising under it are to be resolved by an arbitrator rather than by a court, and that the parties are to accept the arbitrator's ruling. People may also resolve disputes in much more informal ways such as negotiation or early neutral evaluation. These processes are collectively known as alternative dispute resolution (ADR) in that they provide a method of resolving disputes without going to court. However, the fact that courts are not the only bodies capable of resolving disputes does not mean that they are unnecessary. They are, in fact, essential in any civilised society. This is so for three main reasons.

First, *courts operate as a longstop*. It is, as we have already indicated, possible in some situations for people to arrange to resolve disputes otherwise than by recourse to the courts. But in many instances, no such provision will or could have been made. This is most obviously the case when there is no pre-existing relationship between the parties. If X is injured by the carelessness of Y, a stranger, no arrangement will exist between X and Y as to how it should be decided whether, and if so to what extent, Y should compensate X. It would, of course, be possible for X and Y to reach a negotiated settlement—but, in contrast to a situation in which a contract provides for binding arbitration, neither party is locked into any extrajudicial process for the resolution of the dispute. This means that one of the parties might simply refuse to participate in an informal dispute resolution process, or that the parties might reach an impasse that cannot be resolved except by involving an independent third party capable of authoritatively determining the disputed point. It is unsurprising, therefore, that in many situations such as this the parties end up in court. Although unnecessary recourse to litigation is not to be encouraged—indeed there is a growing emphasis on the desirability of resolving disputes in other, cheaper ways—it is essential that courts exist as a longstop. In the absence of such an arrangement, some people would inevitably resort to less civilised means by which to resolve disputes. The risk would arise that the stronger party—whether in physical, social, or financial terms—would be likely to prevail. Such a system would be antithetical to justice and equality. In short, an effective and independent judicial system is necessary to the preservation of social order.

Second, *courts can exercise the coercive powers of the state*. Often, one party will not wish to participate in a dispute resolution process (particularly if she thinks that she will lose). And even if the parties do participate in such a process, the 'losing' party may, on reflection, be unwilling to do whatever was undertaken (for example, to pay compensation). One of the main differences between courts and other dispute resolution mechanisms, then, is that the courts have coercive powers. If one party validly issues legal proceedings against another, the latter cannot choose whether to allow the court to rule on the matter: submission to the court's jurisdiction will be compulsory, not a matter of election. Similarly, if the court issues a remedy—for example, if it requires the wrongdoer to pay compensation to the injured party or, in a criminal case, to pay a fine—it has a range of coercive powers that can be used to secure compliance. Ultimately, if someone refuses to do as a court lawfully instructs, they can be imprisoned for contempt of court. Furthermore, while courts exercise the coercive powers of the state, they are also able to exercise those powers against government itself. For example, if a court, through judicial review proceedings, determines that a government decision is unlawful, then the court can issue a remedy striking down that decision and the government must comply with the court's ruling in order to uphold the rule of law.

Third, that point leads on to a broader one: the courts' role is not confined to deciding disputes between individuals; rather, they are also *a necessary part of a balanced machinery of government under the separation of powers doctrine*. In this sense, they form a crucial part of the network of checks and balances that are needed if the powers of the other branches of government are to be adequately controlled. This aspect of the courts' role is of particular importance to the subject matter of this book. In the next section, therefore, we explore three particular issues that concern the courts' place within, and responsibility for upholding the principles of, the constitution.

3.2 **The courts and the constitution**

3.2.1 **Courts are referees in public law cases**

Just as courts act as referees in private disputes between individuals in civil litigation, they also adjudicate upon disputes with a public dimension to them. Some such cases involve disputes between two public bodies, but most concern situations in which a governmental body has made a decision that adversely affects the rights or interests of an individual who wishes to challenge the legality of that decision before the courts. In such 'judicial review' cases, the function of the court is not radically different from that which it performs in other contexts: its ultimate responsibility is to determine the dispute by reference to the relevant facts, and in accordance with the relevant legal rules and principles. However, in cases involving government bodies, a further layer of issues is in play.

When the court is adjudicating upon a dispute between an individual and a public body, it will be concerned to see that the latter has respected the special legal standards to which government is required to adhere. As we explain elsewhere, those standards include the principles of good decision-making enforceable through judicial review proceedings,[32] relevant aspects of the rule of law,[33] and the rights protected by the HRA.[34] The fact that public bodies are bound by these special standards implicitly acknowledges that the relationship between the individual and the state is an unequal one, with the state having the upper hand, and that this calls for particular safeguards to be enforced. It also recognises that public bodies are fundamentally different from private bodies (such as companies) and individuals. This is because public bodies exist

---

[32] See Chapter 13. [33] See Chapter 2, section 4.4, above. [34] See Chapter 19.

in order to advance the broader public interest: for example, the Environment Agency exists in order to protect the environment while the UK Border Agency is responsible for controlling migration into the UK. However, in order to promote the broader public interest, a public body may often need to make decisions that adversely affect the rights and interests of an individual or business: for example, the Environment Agency will seek to protect the environment by fining a polluting business, while the UK Border Agency will seek to enforce immigration control by deporting a foreign national who has unlawfully entered the UK. It is inevitable that tensions will arise between individuals' rights and interests, and public bodies' pursuit of the public interest. For precisely that reason, the state, in its various emanations, is subject to a set of distinctive public law principles that seek to maintain an appropriate balance between providing adequate protection for the rights and interests of individuals, on the one hand, and enabling public bodies to make decisions in pursuit of their policy goals, on the other. This aspect of the courts' role has grown substantially in recent decades, partly but not exclusively as a result of the HRA. This reflects one of the key themes of this book and constitutes part of another: the growing prominence of the courts' role as a constitutional watchdog is born, at least in part, of concern about the peculiarly powerful position of the executive branch in the UK[35]—and the way in which the courts' role has expanded in this area is a key driver of the shift from a more political to a more legal form of constitutionalism.

In addition, disputes between one public body and another—as well as some disputes between individuals and public bodies—will raise demarcation-of-powers issues. For example, questions may arise about whether it is lawful for a given action to be undertaken by a particular body, or whether the matter concerned properly falls within the constitutional province of another government institution. A good example is the *Fire Brigades Union* case,[36] considered in Chapter 3, in which the court was, in effect, called upon to draw a dividing line between the respective powers of the UK executive and the UK Parliament. When it ruled that the government—by attempting, in effect, to repeal legislation—had asserted a power that belonged rightfully to Parliament, the court attempted to uphold the separation of powers.[37] The multilayered nature of the modern constitution—the third of our three key themes—increases the scope for disputes of this nature: questions may, for example, arise about whether a devolved legislature, such as the Scottish Parliament, possesses constitutional authority to legislate on a given matter, or whether responsibility for the issue in question remains exclusively with the UK Parliament at Westminster.[38]

One final point should be noted in this regard. It is that the courts' role as a constitutional 'policeman' in the senses set out above is ultimately constrained by the principle of parliamentary sovereignty, under which the courts have to apply primary legislation

---

[35] On which, see generally Chapter 4.

[36] *R v Secretary of State for the Home Department, ex p Fire Brigades Union* [1995] 2 AC 513.

[37] However, as we saw in Chapter 3, the minority judges were concerned that, by intervening, the court itself would be asserting undue power.   [38] See further Chapter 7.

and possess no jurisdiction to strike down such legislation as unconstitutional. If the full force of that principle is accepted, it follows that the courts' ability to uphold (and hence resolve disputes in accordance with) constitutional principles such as the rule of law and the separation of powers can be limited by clear contrary provision in an Act of Parliament. The doctrine of parliamentary sovereignty has traditionally been viewed as the foundation of the UK constitution. However, as we saw in Chapter 5, over recent years it has increasingly been doubted whether Parliament enjoys legal powers that are wholly unlimited: on one view, the unwritten constitution conceals certain fundamental principles that even Parliament is unable to transgress and which are capable of judicial enforcement. If UK courts were to begin to assert such powers, this would represent a considerable extension of the judicial role.

3.2.2 Beyond dispute resolution

It is clear from what has been said so far that the courts' dispute resolution function is a vitally important component of a democratic society. But is it—and should it be—their only function? Resolving disputes is a retrospective, backward-looking business: at root, it involves examining what has already happened and determining whether the defendant was, as the claimant[39] asserts, in the wrong. However, the law—and the courts—can also operate in a more prospective, forward-looking manner. At a basic level, this is obvious. For example, under the doctrine of precedent, higher courts, such as the Supreme Court, make decisions that bind the lower courts in future cases and which also guide the future conduct of people. If, for example, a court interprets a piece of legislation so as to establish (contrary to previous understandings) that a given form of conduct is unlawful, then people may, in the future, choose to modify their behaviour in order to take account of the new interpretation of the statute. Similarly, the principles of public law articulated by the courts have the potential to influence the future behaviour of public bodies anxious to ensure that they behave in a lawful manner. This is illustrated by a government publication, entitled *The Judge Over Your Shoulder*, which aims to convey to public servants the legal principles with which their actions must comply if they are to survive scrutiny by the courts.[40] In this sense, the body of public law created and applied by the courts through decisions in individual cases has come to constitute a template of best practice that can, and often does, inform the way in which public administration is undertaken.

However, the sense in which the courts' function transcends one of dispute resolution is not confined to the fact that they (inevitably) set out legal principles that shape responsible parties' subsequent conduct. In some (albeit limited) circumstances, courts are prepared to involve themselves in situations that do not disclose any live dispute. The form that such involvement is most likely to take is the issuing of an 'advisory declaration', which states whether a given action (or omission) would, if it

---

[39] Or, in a criminal case, the prosecution.

[40] The most recent edition was published by the Treasury Solicitor's Office and the Government Legal Service in 2006.

were to arise, be lawful. When courts do this, the relevant parties are not left (as in the situation described in the previous paragraph) to deduce from already-articulated principles whether a given course of conduct would be lawful; rather, the court indicates in specific terms how those principles apply to the situation in question, notwithstanding that the situation has not arisen (or at least is not in issue in the proceedings). For example, in the case of *Airedale NHS Trust v Bland*,[41] the House of Lords issued a declaration to the effect that if a hospital were to end the life support of a patient in a persistent vegetative state, then this would not amount to unlawful homicide. In this way, claimants are able to establish in advance whether or not a particular course of action would be lawful. And courts, meanwhile, expand their role from one that is concerned only with resolving disputes to one that encompasses expository justice— that is, the provision of guidance outside the confines of live disputes.[42]

The extent to which courts are prepared to provide such guidance is considered in more detail below.[43] For the time being, we simply note that this sort of anticipatory intervention by courts is arguably especially appropriate in relation to matters of public law. Laws observes (as we did above) that there is a crucial difference between public bodies and private actors (such as individuals and companies). Whereas the latter can, and often do, act in a purely self-interested manner, public bodies cannot lawfully do so: having no interests of their own, the public official must act 'in the perceived interests of…his constituency, whether the public as a whole or a defined section of it'.[44] There is, says Laws, 'a clear distinction between a case where the claimant seeks in effect the court's advice only so that he can further his own private interests, and one where he seeks judicial guidance for the fulfilment of [public] duties which he owes or…are actually or putatively owed to him'.[45] On this view, courts should not be wedded, in the public law realm, to their traditional dispute resolution function; rather, there is a strong public interest in courts readily issuing advisory declarations in order to articulate or clarify the legal framework within which those who owe duties to the public are required to operate. In this way, the judicial role becomes a more forward-looking one that aims to ensure that public administration is conducted in a lawful manner in the first place.

Q Do you agree with Laws' argument? He goes on to suggest that if the government were contemplating the enactment of secondary legislation,[46] it should be possible for an advisory declaration to be obtained as to the legality of the draft legislation. This is not something that courts are currently willing to do—but should they be?

---

[41] [1993] AC 789.

[42] See further Miles, 'Standing under the Human Rights Act 1998: Theories of Rights Enforcement and the Nature of Public Law Adjudication' [2000] CLJ 133.   [43] See Chapter 14, section 4.5, below.

[44] 'Judicial Remedies and the Constitution' (1994) 57 MLR 213, 215–16.

[45] 'Judicial Remedies and the Constitution' (1994) 57 MLR 213, 217.

[46] On which, see generally Chapter 4 above.

3.2.3 **Judicial lawmaking and the separation of powers**

The adage that 'Parliament makes the laws, the judiciary interpret them'[47] is technically correct, but is misleading to the extent that it implies that *only* Parliament makes law. For example, we have already seen that administrative bodies have wide lawmaking powers—and that even though Acts of Parliament are formally enacted by Parliament, the reality is that it merely considers (and usually approves) the government's legislative proposals. Furthermore, it is undeniable that the courts, as well as applying the laws enacted by the other branches of government, themselves contribute to the lawmaking enterprise. This is so in two senses.

When courts *interpret legislation*, they can be said to be making law. It might be retorted that this is not the case, and that there is a difference between interpreting and making law. However, a debate conducted on that basis would be an ultimately arid one, for the distinction that it postulates, if it exists at all, is one of degree. There are, of course, situations in which a legislative rule is crystal clear, and in which the task of applying it to the established facts is a relatively mechanical one. However, surprisingly often, the precise meaning of legislation may be unclear and may be disputed between two parties. As the legal philosopher HLA Hart explained, legal rules are inherently 'open textured': a legislative rule might possess a core of settled meaning, but it will also contain a penumbra of uncertainty in which the meaning of the rule may be unclear and indeterminate.[48] The meaning of the rule in such instances will depend upon how it is interpreted. The classic example is the meaning of a rule to the effect that 'no vehicles may be taken into the park': this would clearly prohibit the driving of a car or a bus through the park, but what of a child's toy car, a pram, or a wheelchair? The general point is that it is very often the case that a legislative text will be unclear or that it does not precisely answer the question raised by the factual matrix before the court. In such circumstances, the judge will be forced to choose between competing interpretations of the statute, and in doing so, will refine its meaning.

In other situations of statutory interpretation, the scale of the courts' role may be greater still. For example, we saw above that courts will often strain to interpret legislation compatibly with fundamental constitutional principles;[49] we explain below that similar considerations may arise when a court is faced with legislation that, if accorded its natural meaning, would be incompatible with EU law[50] or with the rights protected by the HRA.[51] In such situations, the courts' role goes well beyond ascertaining the dictionary definition of the statutory text and applying it to the facts of the case; rather, the courts are called upon to find an interpretation of the legislation that can most comfortably be accommodated within the pre-existing legal and constitutional framework. Whether we call this 'interpretation' or 'lawmaking' is an ultimately semantic question; the reality is that, in interpreting legislation, judges are

---

[47] *Duport Steels Ltd v Sirs* [1980] 1 WLR 142, 157, *per* Lord Diplock.
[48] *The Concept of Law* (Oxford 1994), p 128.
[49] See Chapter 2, section 4.4, and Chapter 4, section 4.5.3, above.
[50] See Chapter 8, section 3.2.6, below.   [51] See Chapter 19, section 3.4, below.

themselves, in a sense, often acting as judicial legislators. This point is reinforced by three basic facts about the operation of law in a modern legal system. First, legislation is inevitably the largest and most dominant source of law, and most legislation is the legal expression of government policy. Second, the major part of the work of the higher courts—'perhaps as high as 90 per cent'—is concerned with the interpretation and application of legislative rules.[52] Third, the courts have the final say on the meaning of legislation. So, when they interpret legislation, courts are not merely technical interpreters of legislation (although they may sometimes present themselves as such); rather, they form part of the lawmaking enterprise.

More obviously still, judges make law when they *develop the common law*. Although (as a consequence of the doctrine of parliamentary sovereignty) legislation displaces common law when the two overlap, certain areas of the law are either devoid of legislation or are only peripherally affected by it. For example, large swathes of private law—such as contract, tort, and restitution—are centrally based upon common law, albeit that certain aspects of those areas have been supplemented or modified by statute. By contrast, the overwhelming proportion of public law is governed by primary and secondary legislation that lays down the powers, duties, and policies of public governmental agencies and the administrative rules that such agencies apply. Such matters are regulated by an enormous amount of legislation. But, of course, the exercise of those powers and duties by such public bodies will only be lawful if compliant with the principles of judicial review that, as common law principles, have been developed by the courts. For example, the well-known principle of judicial review that a public body cannot make a decision that is irrational because it outrageously defies logic or accepted moral standards does not derive from any Act of Parliament; rather, it has been created and developed by the courts through the common law. There is no room for even semantic debate here: the common law is judge-made law.

Is judicial lawmaking, in either of the above senses, inconsistent with the separation-of-powers doctrine? This largely depends on what we mean by the separation of powers. We saw in Chapter 3 that the concept is a malleable one: it can bear a variety of meanings, although a broad distinction between two schools of thought may be drawn. If we adopt what was referred to in Chapter 3 as a 'pure' conception of the separation of powers, then it follows that any form of judicial lawmaking is improper. On that view, the three principal functions of government would have to be performed by wholly separate institutions; it would therefore be unacceptable for the judicial branch to be involved in lawmaking as well as adjudication. However, we saw in Chapter 3 that this model of the separation of powers is both impossible to implement in practice and arguably unnecessary in principle. The fundamental purpose of the separation-of-powers doctrine is to guard against the abuse of power. It seeks to realise this objective by prescribing an institutional architecture that prevents any branch of government both from possessing too much power, and from wielding its power in a way that

---

[52] Steyn, 'Dynamic Interpretation Amidst an Orgy of Statutes' (2003–04) 35 Ottawa Law Review 163, 164.

cannot adequately be checked and controlled by the other branches. On this—the better—view, the exercise by one branch of functions lying within the core responsibility of another is not objectionable per se; rather, the question is whether, by allowing such a situation to obtain, the fundamental objective—of guarding against abuse of power—is compromised.

In addressing that question vis-à-vis the courts' lawmaking powers, it is significant, therefore, that those powers are limited. Although it was argued above that courts make law by interpreting legislation, the extent of such lawmaking is evidently constrained by the text concerned. Even in circumstances in which the courts have been given explicit licence by Parliament to adopt a very bold interpretative approach, they have been sensitive not to usurp the function of the legislature. For example, s 3(1) of the HRA instructs courts to interpret all legislation compatibly with the rights protected by that Act '[s]o far as it is possible to do so'.[53] While, pursuant to this obligation, the courts have been willing to adopt interpretations that depart dramatically from the natural meaning of the legislation concerned, they have, nevertheless, remained mindful of the fact that the courts' role is distinct from that of the legislature. They are therefore unwilling to adopt an interpretation of an Act of Parliament that goes against 'the grain of the legislation',[54] or which is 'inconsistent with a fundamental feature' of it.[55] And, of course, if it is felt that the courts have overstepped the mark by adopting an inappropriate interpretation, it is always open to the relevant legislature to amend the provision in question.[56]

Similar considerations apply to the lawmaking function performed by courts when they develop the common law. Here, the courts' role is inherently limited by a number of factors. First, common law can exist only to the extent that the relevant matter has not been dealt with by means of legislation. Second, when developing common law rules, courts typically act in an incremental fashion—moving slowly, one step at a time; courts are generally limited by precedent and they follow previous case law. Third, should the courts develop the common law in a way that is considered to be unacceptable, then their decisions may be replaced by legislation, because it is always open to Parliament to reverse a judicial decision through legislation. To illustrate this point, consider the law on whether witnesses in criminal trials may give evidence anonymously. In 2008, the Appellate Committee of the House of Lords (since replaced by the Supreme Court) handed down its ruling in *R v Davis*[57] that restricted the courts' ability at common law to allow witnesses to give evidence anonymously in criminal trials. However, shortly after the ruling, Parliament enacted the Criminal Evidence (Witness Anonymity) Act 2008, which reversed the ruling by conferring upon the

---

[53] For detailed discussion of this point, see Chapter 19 below.

[54] *Ghaidan v Godin-Mendoza* [2004] UKHL 30, [2004] 2 AC 557, [121], *per* Lord Rodger.

[55] *Ghaidan* at [33], *per* Lord Nicholls.

[56] This is necessarily so in relation to the UK Parliament (because it is sovereign), and is so in relation to other legislative bodies (such as administrators exercising subordinate lawmaking power and devolved legislatures) to the extent that they have the legal authority to amend the provision in such a way as to override the court's interpretation.   [57] [2008] UKHL 36, [2008] 1 AC 1128.

criminal courts a statutory power to grant witness anonymity where this would be consistent with the right of a defendant to a fair trial.[58] It is clear therefore that legislation can be enacted in order to replace or modify common law rules—although, in practice, this occurs relatively infrequently.

3.2.4 Reasons for judicial restraint–democratic and institutional considerations

From all of this, it follows that the courts' lawmaking function is subject to real and significant limits, the existence of which mean that judicial lawmaking is not usually problematic in separation of powers terms. Such limits partly arise from the nature of judicial decision-making itself. For example, unlike legislatures, courts are unelected and not politically accountable. Unlike government, courts are unable to consult more broadly about possible changes to the law. Furthermore, courts are generalists in the sense that they are expected to deal with a dispute from any area of law; by contrast, government can draw upon the views of expert and specialist administrators and professionals when designing possible changes to the law. For these reasons, courts generally recognise that while they possess some lawmaking capacity, it must be exercised cautiously so as to ensure that courts do not overreach themselves. As Lord Phillips, a former Lord Chief Justice, put it when speaking for the judiciary as a whole: 'We recognise the boundaries of our role and the need to accord proper respect to the respective roles of the other two branches of the state . . . and we hope and expect that they will do the same in respect of our role.'[59]

The existence of such self-imposed limits that the courts apply to their lawmaking role is abundantly apparent both in relation to the interpretation of legislation and the development of the common law. For example, when interpreting legislation in circumstances in which s 3(1) of the HRA is in play, the courts recognise that it would be inappropriate for them to adopt an interpretation that would involve the making of a major policy choice.[60] In doing so, the courts acknowledge that such choices properly fall to be made by the democratic branches. Similarly, the courts have declined to develop the common law in ways that would involve the making of such choices. For example, English law has long been criticised for not providing adequate protection of individuals' privacy. While legislation protects certain aspects of privacy, and the common law in this area has been developed in some respects, the courts have nonetheless signalled that it would be inappropriate for them to engage in thoroughgoing law reform in this sphere. In *Wainwright v Home Office*,[61] Lord Hoffmann said that this is 'an area which requires a detailed approach which can be achieved only by legislation rather than the broad brush of common law principle'. In doing so, Lord

---

[58] The 2008 Act has now been largely superseded by ss 86–97 of the Coroners and Justice Act 2009.

[59] *The Lord Chief Justice's Review of the Administration of Justice in the Courts* (HC 448 2007–08), [1.4]. (Lord Phillips is now the President of the Supreme Court.)

[60] See, eg, *R (Anderson) v Secretary of State for the Home Department* [2002] UKHL 46, [2003] 1 AC 83; *In Re S (Minors) (Care Order: Implementation of Care Plan)* [2002] UKHL 10, [2002] 2 AC 291. These cases are discussed in Chapter 19 below.   [61] [2003] UKHL 53, [2004] 2 AC 406, [33].

Hoffmann recognised that the courts' lawmaking role is properly constrained not only by concerns about democratic legitimacy, but also by considerations of institutional competence: very often, the lawmaking process, if conscientiously executed, requires extensive research, consultation, and discussion—tasks that the courts, operating within the limits of the adversarial process, are simply incapable of undertaking. In other words, by recognising their own institutional limitations, the courts are defining the limits of their own lawmaking role.

> **Q** It might be argued that the considerations highlighted in the previous paragraph point towards the conclusion that judges should not have any involvement in lawmaking. Would you agree with such an argument?

4. The characteristics of the judiciary

Given that the judiciary is required to perform functions of the nature set out so far in this chapter, what characteristics should it possess? And what steps are taken to ensure that the judiciary actually possesses those characteristics? These questions need to be asked both in relation to individual judges and the system as a whole—although it is meaningless to attempt to draw a clear distinction between those two matters, since the nature of the system is, at least to some extent, determined by the nature of the individuals who comprise it.

4.1 Judicial appointments

For two reasons, the process by which judges are appointed is of fundamental importance in this area. First, that process is a key way in which steps can be taken to ensure that members of the judiciary possess the qualities necessary to be a good judge. According to the body responsible for appointing judges in England and Wales, those qualities include a high level of expertise in the relevant area of the law, integrity, independence of mind, objectivity, an ability to deal with people fairly and courteously, efficiency, authority, and good communication skills.[62] Second, it is imperative not only that the appointments process actually results in the appointment of appropriate individuals, but also that the process is of such a nature as to lead people to trust that the system is staffed by people who have the necessary integrity and skills. If trust in the judicial system breaks down, the risk arises that people will seek to resolve their differences in other, less civilised, ways. It follows that the appointments process must be one that is not only rigorous and fair, but is also perceived as such.

---

[62] See **http://www.judicialappointments.gov.uk**

The way in which judges are appointed has changed dramatically in recent years. Until recently, most judges were appointed by the Queen on the advice of the Lord Chancellor or the Prime Minister (who, in practice, relied on the Lord Chancellor's advice).[63] Although there have long been (and remain) concerns about the diversity of the judiciary,[64] there was a general consensus that, in practice, this system delivered a high-quality judiciary. But there were two major difficulties with it. First, although, in recent times, Lord Chancellors appeared to act in an even-handed fashion by appointing candidates on merit,[65] the system was not, and could not be perceived to be, independent of the government. Given that courts—through judicial review and the HRA—are increasingly concerned with scrutiny of the government, it became highly anomalous for a Minister to be centrally involved in the appointments process. Second, the process was anything but transparent: vacancies at senior levels were not even advertised; rather, people were invited to apply on the basis of informal, confidential soundings.

In 2003, the government published proposals for radical reform of the appointments process.[66] This culminated in the Constitutional Reform Act 2005. Reflecting reforms that had already taken place in Scotland and Northern Ireland, that Act established a new body, the Judicial Appointments Commission (JAC), which is responsible for making judicial appointments in England and Wales. Four points should be noted in this regard.

First, the JAC is *independent of the government*.[67] It consists of a chairman and 14 other commissioners, and must include lay, judicial, and professional members; the chairman must be a lay member. Although commissioners are appointed on the recommendation of the Lord Chancellor, he does not have a free hand in making such recommendations; rather, he is only permitted to recommend the appointment of individuals who are nominated by the Judges' Council or by a panel that includes the Lord Chief Justice. Second, when deciding which candidate it should recommend in respect of a given vacancy, the JAC is *required by law to apply certain criteria*. There is, for example, an experience requirement, as Figure 6.2 shows.[68] The JAC is also required to make appointments solely on merit and to select someone only if satisfied that she is of good character.[69] Third, the process is much more transparent than it used to be. Vacancies are advertised, and the JAC publishes extensive information about the criteria and processes used in selection.[70]

---

[63] See further Department for Constitutional Affairs, *Constitutional Reform: A New Way of Appointing Judges* (London 2003), ch 1.   [64] On which, see section 4.6 below.

[65] Not that this has always been the case: see Stevens, 'Reform in Haste and Repent in Leisure' (2004) 24 LS 1, 10–13.   [66] *Constitutional Reform: A New Way of Appointing Judges.*

[67] The composition etc, of the Commission is prescribed in the Constitutional Reform Act 2005, Sch 8.

[68] Although Figure 6.2 mentions Justices of the Supreme Court (JSCs), the JAC has no involvement in their selection; the arrangements for appointing JSCs are set out below. For the position regarding eligibility for senior judicial offices in Scotland, see Law Reform (Miscellaneous Provisions) (Scotland) Act 1990, s 35 and Sch 4.   [69] Constitutional Reform Act 2005, s 63.

[70] See http://www.judicialappointments.gov.uk

Judicial office	Requirement	Source
Justice of the Supreme Court	High judicial office (ie High Court or above) for two years, or qualified lawyer or holder of other relevant qualification for 15 years	Constitutional Reform Act 2005, s 25
Lord Chief Justice, Master of the Rolls, President of the Queen's Bench Division, President of the Family Division, Chancellor of the High Court	Already a Court of Appeal judge or eligible for appointment to the Court of Appeal	Senior Courts Act 1981, s 10(3)(a)
Court of Appeal judge	Qualified lawyer or holder of other relevant qualification for seven years, or already a High Court judge	Senior Courts Act 1981, s 10(3)(b)
High Court judge	Qualified lawyer or holder of other relevant qualification for seven years, or two years' experience as a circuit judge	Senior Courts Act 1981, s 10(3)(a)

Figure 6.2 Eligibility for appointment to senior judicial offices

Fourth, *the role of the government* in the selection of judges is now very limited. It was noted above that, in effect, judges used to be appointed by a government Minister in the form of the Lord Chancellor. While the Lord Chancellor retains a role under the new system, it is much more modest than his former role. When a vacancy arises, the Lord Chancellor may (and in some circumstances must) seek to fill it.[71] He does this by asking the JAC to select a candidate. When such a request is made, this triggers a process that culminates in a JAC selection panel (the composition of which varies depending on the nature of the office that has fallen vacant) selecting one person. That name is then put to the Lord Chancellor. He does not have to accept it: he can either reject it outright or can ask the JAC to reconsider the matter.[72] If the Lord Chancellor rejects a given candidate, the JAC cannot select that person again, meaning that the Lord Chancellor has a right of veto. But this is very different from the sort of power of selection that the Lord Chancellor used to enjoy. Moreover, the Lord Chancellor cannot keep rejecting candidates until the JAC comes up with a name that he likes. In any given selection process, he may exercise his power to reject only once, and his power to require reconsideration only once. At most, then, the process will have three stages; at the final stage, the Lord Chancellor is statutorily required to accept either the name put to him at that stage or a name not rejected by him earlier in the process.

[71] Constitutional Reform Act 2005, ss 68 and 69.
[72] Constitutional Reform Act 2005, ss 73, 75E, 82, and 90.

> **Q** Is it a good thing that the government now has only a marginal role in judicial appointments? Can you think of any arguments in favour of the government having a greater role than that which it currently has?

One final point should be noted. The JAC has no involvement in appointments to the Supreme Court. The initial Justices of the Supreme Court were the judges in post as Law Lords immediately before the Supreme Court began to operate.[73] Vacancies are filled by the Queen on the recommendation of the Prime Minister. But the Prime Minister has no discretion in this matter. The name that he passes to the Queen must be the one notified to him by the Lord Chancellor.[74] And, in turn, the Lord Chancellor has only very limited discretion. When a vacancy arises, the Lord Chancellor must convene a selection commission[75] normally consisting of the President and Deputy President of the Court, a member of the JAC, and one member from each of the equivalent bodies in Scotland and Northern Ireland.[76] The process is then very much as described above: a name is recommended to the Lord Chancellor, who must either accept it, notifying the Prime Minister accordingly, reject it, or require the matter to be reconsidered.[77]

4.2 Independence–an introduction

It is an article of faith that the judiciary should be 'independent'; indeed, courts should not only *be* independent, but should be *perceived* to be so. This relates back to the point made above: that people should have confidence in both the integrity and fairness of the system, the risk being that, in the absence of such confidence, resort may be made to less desirable forms of dispute resolution. The requirement of judicial independence arises both in relation to individual judges and the system more generally.[78] Indeed, the right to have legal proceedings dealt with in a manner that is both actually and apparently unbiased is a fundamental right, and as such is enshrined in ECHR, Art 6, to which the HRA gives effect in UK law.

As far as individual judges are concerned, it stands to reason that if they have, or are perceived to have, an interest in the outcome of the case, this will constitute grounds for doubting the integrity of the process and the fairness of the outcome. In the light of that, judges are disqualified from sitting in cases in which they are (or are in a position equivalent to that of) a party, in that they have a financial interest, or in which they have some other interest that would lead a fair-minded and informed observer to entertain a reasonable suspicion of bias. These matters are considered in detail in Chapter 13, and therefore need not be expanded upon for the time being. Instead,

---

[73] Constitutional Reform Act 2005, s 24.   [74] Constitutional Reform Act 2005, s 26(3).
[75] Constitutional Reform Act 2005, s 26(5).   [76] Constitutional Reform Act 2005, Sch 8, para 1.
[77] Constitutional Reform Act 2005, s 29.
[78] When applied to individual judges, the term 'impartiality', rather than 'independence', is normally used.

our present focus is on the importance of, and the steps that are taken to secure, the independence of the judicial system itself.

4.3 **Independence—the institutional situation of the courts**

If the judiciary is to be—and is to be seen to be—independent, then this must mean that it is separate from, and immune from undue influence that might otherwise be exerted by, the other branches of government. Although, as we saw in Chapter 3, the doctrine of the separation of powers in the UK does not apply in a rigorous fashion in the context of the relationship between the executive and legislature, the doctrine has long been taken with greater seriousness in relation to the judiciary. Even here, of course, segregation is not complete: for example, as we have already seen in this chapter, judges exercise lawmaking functions. But the key question is whether the judiciary, in discharging its core adjudicatory function, is (and is perceived to be) able to get on with this task independently—in particular, without meddling or undue influence by politicians, legislators, or administrators.

There are two ways of approaching this question. The first is to consider the matter on an institutional level:[79] are the courts sufficiently separate, in institutional terms, from the other branches of government? Such separation is important both because its absence may increase the practical scope for political interference in judicial matters, and because, even if such interference does not actually occur, the absence of clear dividing lines may lead people to perceive that the judiciary is not truly independent. Approaching the matter on this institutional level, it is noteworthy that significant steps have been taken in recent years in order to enhance the level of separation between the judiciary and the other branches of government. In many respects, these steps were taken not so much to put an end to interference that was occurring—because, largely speaking, such interference was, as far as it is possible to tell, not taking place—but rather make it clear to the world at large that there is a real institutional separation between the courts and the other parts of the government. Three examples should be noted.

4.3.1 **The UK Supreme Court**

First, the most visible manifestation of the trend referred to above is the creation of the UK Supreme Court. Until October 2009, the UK's highest court was, for most purposes, the Appellate Committee of the House of Lords. It acted as the court of final appeal in all civil and criminal matters in the UK, with the exceptions of Scottish criminal matters and 'devolution issues'.[80] On the face of it, this situation constituted a bizarre and flagrant breach of the separation of powers doctrine: the

---

[79] The second way, explored in section 4.4 below, involves examining the position of individual judges.

[80] That is, questions whether given matters lie within the competence of devolved bodies. See further Chapter 7, section 2.4.2, below.

inappropriateness of allowing a committee of one of the legislative chambers to act as a court—let alone as the highest court in the land—is so obvious that it need not be spelled out. Yet in this context, as in many other matters of UK public law, not all was as it appeared to be. The Appellate Committee's members were the Lords of Appeal in Ordinary, or the 'Law Lords'—senior judges who were typically promoted from the Court of Appeal in England and Wales (or the equivalent courts in Scotland and Northern Ireland). The Law Lords decided cases in the same way as other judges—by reference to relevant facts and legal principles—and, although members of the House of Lords in its legislative capacity, by convention did not participate in debates or votes concerning politically contentious matters. It follows that, in most practical senses, the Appellate Committee, although technically a parliamentary committee, functioned as an independent court of law.

To those who understood how the system worked, there was little scope for doubting this. But that is not the point (or at least, is not the whole point). As noted above, public trust, and so perception, is crucial in this area. The physical location of the UK's highest court in the Palace of Westminster (hearings were held in a House of Lords committee room; judgments were delivered in the chamber) gave the strong impression that the apex of the constitutional system was characterised not by a separation, but by a fusion, of power. This difficulty was exacerbated by the facts that people (for good reason, as we saw in Chapters 4 and 5) often do not distinguish between the executive and the legislature, and that the Appellate Committee was increasingly concerned with judicial review and human rights cases involving the political branches. As Steyn has noted:

> When judgments were delivered in *Pinochet No. 1*[81] [in which the Appellate Committee decided that Augusto Pinochet, the former Chilean head of state, could be extradited to stand trial for crimes against humanity] the crowded benches of the chamber apparently led foreign television viewers to believe that Lady Thatcher [who was present in the chamber whilst judgment was being delivered] was part of the dissenting minority who opposed the extradition of General Pinochet![82]

Because Thatcher was a former UK Prime Minister who had opposed the extradition of Pinochet, the perception that could reasonably arise was that the Appellate Committee of the House of Lords was not sufficiently independent. In such circumstances, the case in favour of abolishing the Appellate Committee and replacing it with a *transparently* independent body was a strong one—although it did not convince everyone. Most of the Law Lords who were in post in 2003, when the proposal for a Supreme Court was consulted upon,[83] argued that the established arrangements worked well and that there was no need for change.[84] However, the

---

[81] [2000] 1 AC 61.   [82] 'The Case for a Supreme Court' (2002) 118 LQR 382, 382.

[83] We noted in Chapter 1 that the process by which these reforms were introduced was regarded by many people as a shambles: the Law Lords, for example, were only consulted *after* the proposal was made public.

[84] *The Law Lords' Response to the Government's Consultation Paper on Constitutional Reform: A Supreme Court for the United Kingdom* (London 2003), p 1.

contrary view, advanced by a minority of the Law Lords in 2003, prevailed. They said that 'the functional separation of the judiciary at all levels from the legislature and the executive [is] a cardinal feature of a modern, liberal, democratic state governed by the rule of law',[85] and that this should be reflected by creating an institutionally separate court of final appeal.

Although provision for the UK Supreme Court was made in the Constitutional Reform Act 2005, the Court did not start work until 2009.[86] The Supreme Court is, in many respects, identical to the Appellate Committee. The *jurisdiction* of the former is the same as the latter, save that the Supreme Court also decides devolution issues;[87] the Supreme Court, like the Appellate Committee before it, does not, however, deal with Scottish criminal appeals.[88] Meanwhile, the Supreme Court has the same *powers* as those that the Appellate Committee had: the new nomenclature does not imply that the Court is able, for example, to strike down Acts of Parliament. And the *role* of the Supreme Court is the same as that which the Appellate Committee formerly fulfilled. Although the role of 'top courts' can be conceived of in many different ways—for example, rather than acting as courts of final appeal, they may simply receive references on points of law from lower courts, to which the matter is then sent back once the legal problem has been resolved[89]—the Supreme Court decides cases in the same way as the Appellate Committee.

It is apparent, then, that the changes wrought by the creation of the new Court were largely cosmetic. This might be perceived as a damning criticism—as evidence that the whole project was nothing more than an expensive rebranding exercise—but this would be to miss the crucial point that, in this sphere, appearance matters. The old system worked: a mixture of law, tradition, and convention ensured that the Appellate Committee functioned, in practice, as an independent court. The new system is different in two ways. First, the independence of the Court is provided for not by unwritten convention, but by law, in the sense that the Supreme Court is constituted by legislation as an institution that is separate from the other branches of government. In this way, the creation of the new Court reflects one of this book's key themes—namely, the growing emphasis on more legal, formal notions of constitutionalism. Second, the Supreme Court is visibly independent of both Parliament and the government. This is most obviously apparent in physical terms: whereas the Appellate Committee conducted its business within the precincts of the Palace of Westminster, the new Court occupies separate premises.[90] Perhaps more subtly, but no less importantly, the

---

[85] *The Law Lords' Response to the Government's Consultation Paper on Constitutional Reform*, p 1.

[86] It was a given that the new court should have its own premises, rather than operate from the Palace of Westminster. The delay between the enactment of the 2005 Act and the entry into force of the relevant provisions was largely due to the need to identify and obtain a suitable building. The building that was eventually chosen was Middlesex Guildhall on Parliament Square in London.

[87] Previously, such matters were dealt with by the Judicial Committee of the Privy Council.

[88] The High Court of Justiciary is the final court of appeal in relation to such matters.

[89] This model applies to the Court of Justice of the European Union, on which, see Chapter 8, sections 2.3.4 and 3.2.1, below.   [90] See n 86 above.

Justices of the Supreme Court, unlike the Law Lords, do not have a legislative, as well as a judicial, role. As noted above, the latter were full members of the House of Lords in its legislative capacity.[91] Although the initial Justices of the Supreme Court, as former Law Lords, remain members of the legislative House of Lords, they are prohibited, whilst serving in the former capacity, from participating in the work of the upper chamber.[92] Meanwhile, Justices appointed directly to the Supreme Court (as distinct from those who transferred to it from the Appellate Committee) do not, by virtue of such appointment, become members of the House of Lords.

> **Q** It follows from what has just been said that the link between active membership of the House of Lords and the UK's highest court has been broken. Is this to be welcomed? Might it, for example, be convincingly argued that the legislative process will be poorer because senior serving judges are now unable to participate in the business of the House of Lords?

4.3.2 **The Lord Chancellor**

The developments considered above cannot be fully understood without mention of the Lord Chancellor. We explained in Chapter 4 that, until recently, the Lord Chancellor held senior positions in all three branches of government, and, in that sense, was a powerful symbol of the UK constitution's failure to embrace a full-blooded notion of the separation of powers. Of particular concern to the present discussion is the fact that the Lord Chancellor was both a Cabinet Minister—and so a senior member of the executive government—and the head of the judiciary. Not only did this mean that a senior Minister was (as we saw above) responsible for appointing judges, but the Lord Chancellor was also entitled to—and did—sit as a member of the Appellate Committee of the House of Lords.

Whereas the general difficulties considered above concerning the Appellate Committee were principally ones of appearance, allowing a member of the government to sit as a senior judge raised concerns of an altogether different order. Such concerns were, to some extent, assuaged by practice: Lord Chancellors did not sit in cases directly involving the government, and generally delegated their functions in terms of the management of the Appellate Committee's judicial business to the senior Law Lord. But the position nevertheless remained that, in the person of the Lord Chancellor, there existed a fundamental breach of the separation of powers doctrine right at the apex of the judicial system. The defence, such as it was, of the Lord Chancellor's judicial role was (in the words of a Minister in 2001) that 'through it the judiciary has a representative in the Cabinet and the Cabinet has a representative in the judiciary. As such,…the Lord Chancellor is well placed mutually to represent the views of each branch of our constitution to the other'.[93] However, in a devastating critique of the office of Lord

---

[91] Albeit that, by convention, they did not involve themselves in politically contentious matters.
[92] Constitutional Reform Act 2005, s 137(3).
[93] Michael Wills MP, HC Deb, 4 December 2001, col 155.

Chancellor as it then existed, Lord Steyn—then a sitting Law Lord—said in 2002 that this argument was specious. He argued that the judiciary could speak for itself, and did not require a spokesperson in Cabinet. Meanwhile, the notion of a government representative in the judiciary was fundamentally misconceived, because it 'openly asserts that it is proper for the Lord Chancellor in his political function to inform the judiciary of the wishes of the Government of the day'.[94] Under the separation of powers, informing the judiciary of such matters is, of course, as unnecessary as it is improper.

Reform of the office of Lord Chancellor and the creation of a Supreme Court necessarily went hand in hand: accepting the case for the creation of the latter inevitably meant acknowledging the inappropriateness of the former's judicial role.[95] After initially announcing that the office of Lord Chancellor was to be abolished, the government eventually accepted that the office should remain, but that it should be substantially reformed. Of particular interest for present purposes are the facts that the Lord Chancellor ceased to be head of the judiciary, this function being taken over by the Lord Chief Justice;[96] lost (as we saw above) much of his involvement in judicial appointments; and ceased to be a judge.[97]

In practice, then, the Lord Chancellor is now simply a government Minister with responsibility for, as opposed to direct involvement in, the judicial system. This is reflected in the fact that the Lord Chancellor is also styled Secretary of State for Justice, in which capacity he is in charge of the Ministry of Justice—the government department responsible for, among other things, courts, tribunals, prisons, and probation. These reforms constituted a major change in the relationship between the executive and judicial branches. The new division of responsibility between the Ministry of Justice and the judiciary was laid down in an agreement, or 'concordat',[98] made by the then Lord Chancellor and the then Lord Chief Justice in 2004, key elements of which were then incorporated in the Constitutional Reform Act 2005. Since the Lord Chancellor no longer sits as a judge, there is no expectation that he be legally qualified.[99] However, like all other Ministers, the Lord Chancellor is under a statutory obligation to uphold the independence of the judiciary.[100] Meanwhile, in the absence of the Lord Chancellor as a direct means of communication between the executive and the judiciary, the Constitutional Reform Act 2005 makes provision for the Lord Chief Justice of England and Wales[101] to make written representations to Parliament 'on matters that appear to him to be matters of importance relating to the judiciary'.[102]

---

[94] 'The Case for a Supreme Court' (2002) 118 LQR 382, 392.

[95] Although it is unclear whether the real reason for proceeding with either reform was driven by constitutional principle or base politics. We noted in Chapter 1 that the proposals appeared to be rushed out in the context of a botched Cabinet reshuffle.   [96] Constitutional Reform Act 2005, s 7(1).

[97] The other main reform involved stripping the Lord Chancellor of his role as speaker of the House of Lords.   [98] See **http://www.dca.gov.uk/consult/lcoffice/judiciary.htm**

[99] The Prime Minister must be satisfied that a person is 'qualified by experience' before appointing him or her to the office of Lord Chancellor, but experience other than as a lawyer can be taken into account: Constitutional Reform Act 2005, s 2.   [100] Constitutional Reform Act 2005, s 3(1).

[101] And, in the respective cases of Scotland and Northern Ireland, the Lord President of the Court of Session and the Lord Chief Justice of Northern Ireland.   [102] Section 5(1).

4.3.3 **The new tribunals system**

An enormous number of cases are adjudicated upon not by courts, but by tribunals. With some notable exceptions, such as the employment tribunals, such bodies are concerned with disputes between individuals and public bodies. They deal with matters as diverse as immigration and asylum, provision of welfare benefits, tax disputes, and the detention of individuals on mental health grounds. We examine the role of tribunals in detail in Chapter 17. For the time being, we merely note that, in 2008, the tribunals system was the subject of a major reform programme, an important strand of which involved recasting the relationship between tribunals and the executive government.[103] Previously, tribunals were often 'sponsored' (which, among other things, meant funded) by the very government departments involved in the disputes upon which tribunals were required to adjudicate. It was noted that such arrangements resulted 'in tribunals and their departments being, or appearing to be, common enterprises', and might even have made tribunal members feel 'that their prospects of more interesting work, of progression in the tribunal, and of appointments elsewhere depend on the departments against which the cases that they hear are brought'.[104] As such, the old structure was inimical to the independence of tribunals, both actual and perceived. That structure has been replaced by one within which administrative responsibility for tribunals rests not with individual government departments, but with the Tribunals Service, an executive agency under the auspices of the Ministry of Justice.[105] Since that department does not itself make the type of decisions that are subject to appeals in tribunals, its having responsibility for the tribunals system better reflects—and demonstrates—the independence of that system. However, the changes to the tribunals system have not been purely administrative; rather, they have also mirrored developments to enhance the judicial independence of the courts. For example, the statutory obligation of the Lord Chancellor under the Constitutional Reform Act 2005 to uphold the continued independence of the judiciary has been extended so as to include the tribunals' judiciary.[106] Furthermore, the appointment of tribunal judiciary is now, as with the courts, the responsibility of the JAC.[107] Put together, this reform of tribunals has been described as 'a profound constitutional change, completing the process of embedding the tribunals judiciary in the judicial system'.[108]

4.4 **Independence—judicial seclusion**

In the previous section, we saw that judicial independence must be confronted at an institutional level—and that several recent developments in the UK have enhanced

---

[103] Tribunals, Courts and Enforcement Act 2007.

[104] Leggatt, *Tribunals for Users: One Service, One System* (London 2001), [2.20].

[105] The Tribunals Service is to be merged with HM Courts Service: see Chapter 17, section 3.3, below.

[106] Tribunals, Courts and Enforcement Act 2007, s 1.

[107] Tribunals, Courts and Enforcement Act 2007, Pt 2.

[108] Sir Robert Carnwath, Senior President of Tribunals, *Second Implementation Review* (London 2008), [11].

that sense of independence. However, institutional independence is merely a necessary, not a sufficient, condition for an adequately independent judicial system. The ultimate goal is that the judges responsible for making decisions in particular cases are, and are perceived to be, capable of doing so free from the influence of improper extrinsic factors. While considerations of institutional architecture such as those addressed above are important in this regard, it is also necessary to examine the position of individual judges. What steps need to be taken in order to ensure that they are equipped to decide cases on their legal merits, rather than with reference to, say, public opinion or political pressure? In other words, how can a situation of judicial seclusion—in the sense of freedom from undue incentives to take account of legally irrelevant matters—be brought about? In this section, we consider three potential forms of pressure that might lead judges to decide cases otherwise than on their legal merits.

4.4.1 Litigation

Lord Denning MR once remarked that each judge 'should be able to do his work in complete independence and free from fear. He should not have to turn the pages of his books with trembling fingers, asking himself: "If I do this, shall I be liable in damages?"'[109] It follows that, 'So long as he does his work in the honest belief that it is within his jurisdiction, then he is not liable to [legal] action'—even if he is 'mistaken in fact' or 'ignorant in law'.[110]

Q Is this acceptable? Circumstances might, for example, arise in which, during the time taken to correct on appeal an erroneous judgment rendered at first instance, real losses (financial or otherwise) are suffered by one of the parties. What are the public policy reasons that would justify the application of the principles set out by Lord Denning in such a situation?

4.4.2 Security of tenure

It stands to reason that judges may not act in a fearless and independent way if, by doing so, they risk personal disadvantage such as dismissal.[111] It is unsurprising, therefore, that one of the central planks of judicial independence is security of tenure. This point is of particular (but far from unique) importance in relation to adjudication on public law matters. Just as a self-serving government with influence over judicial appointments might seek to fill the courts with judges likely to allow Ministers to do as they please, so such a government might attempt to use dismissal, or the threat thereof, as a means of ensuring judicial complaisance.

---

[109] *Sirros v Moore* [1975] QB 118, 136.   [110] *Sirros* at 136, *per* Lord Denning MR.

[111] This is not to suggest that all judges would compromise their personal and professional integrity by yielding to the threat of dismissal. But that possibility cannot be discounted—and, in any event, people would *perceive* that, in such circumstances, judges might be inclined to decide cases otherwise than on their legal merits.

The terms on which senior judges in the UK hold office make this sort of interference by the government impossible in practice. Judges of the senior courts in England and Wales—that is, the High Court and the Court of Appeal—normally hold office until retirement. They can only be dismissed in one of two circumstances. The Lord Chancellor can dismiss on medical grounds, but only with the concurrence of a relevant senior judge.[112] Otherwise, judges of the senior courts hold office 'during good behaviour, subject to a power of removal by Her Majesty on an address presented to Her by both Houses of Parliament'.[113] Equivalent provisions apply in relation to the Justices of the Supreme Court.[114] Finally, in this regard, it is worth noting that pressure can be brought to bear on judges in ways more subtle than (threatened) dismissal—for example, by slashing the pay of judges who make life difficult for the government. For this reason, legislation provides that the salaries of senior judges are protected and cannot be reduced.[115]

> **Q** The protections afforded to less senior judges are less extensive. For example, circuit, district, and tribunal judges can be dismissed by the Lord Chancellor (with the Lord Chief Justice's agreement) on the ground of incapacity or misbehaviour.[116] How, if at all, can the different levels of protection offered to judges of differing seniority be justified?

4.4.3 Judges, politics, and public debate

Conventional wisdom holds that judges and politics do not, and should not, mix.[117] This follows, it is said, because if judges are to be, and are to be seen as, independent, they should be separate from—even above—the political maelstrom. In fact, the point is rather broader than this. If judges are to be (and perceived as) independent, objective appliers of the law, then they should arguably play no part in public debate generally, not just in relation to matters that have a party-political dimension to them. These points, if accepted, cut two ways. On the one hand, judges should not involve themselves either in party politics or, more generally, in matters of public or political controversy. On the other hand, judges should be protected from others' attempts to draw them into such matters. We consider each of these issues in turn.

On the first issue, it is relatively obvious that judges should not be directly involved in party politics. So, although they are allowed to vote in elections, they are required,

---

[112] Senior Courts Act 1981, s 11(8). The judge or judges whose concurrence is required depends on the nature of the office held by the person being dismissed.

[113] Senior Courts Act 1981, s 11(3). Similar arrangements exist in relation to judges of the Court of Session: Scotland Act 1998, s 95(6)–(10).   [114] Constitutional Reform Act 2005, ss 33 and 36.

[115] Senior Courts Act 1981, s 12(3) (judges of the Senior Courts); Constitutional Reform Act 2005, s 34(4) (Justices of the Supreme Court).

[116] Courts Act 1971, s 17(4) (circuit and district judges); Tribunals, Courts and Enforcement Act 2007, Sch 2, paras 3 and 4 (judges of the First-tier Tribunal), and Sch 3, paras 3 and 4 (judges of the Upper Tribunal). (The 2007 Act uses the word 'inability' rather than 'incapacity'. The roles of the First-tier and Upper Tribunals are explained in Chapter 17.)

[117] Whether we should accept that conventional wisdom is a matter to which we turn in the next section.

upon appointment, to 'forego any kind of political activity'.[118] This means that judges must 'sever all ties with political parties' and avoid attendance at events (such as political gatherings or fundraising events) and conduct (such as financially supporting political parties) that would give an appearance of continuing ties.[119] Outside the specifically party-political sphere, the rules concerning judicial participation in public debate are less restrictive than they once were. Under the 'Kilmuir rules',[120] the general position was that judges should not give radio or television interviews, the thinking being that '[s]o long as a judge keeps silent his reputation for wisdom and impartiality remains unassailable'.[121] Things have moved on somewhat since that view was articulated in 1955. The current guidance issued to judges says that they are free to contribute to public debate (including via the broadcast media) 'provided the issue directly affects the operation of the courts, the independence of the judiciary or aspects of the administration of justice'.[122] However, this is subject to the caveats that a judge should not speak out in circumstances that would 'cause the public to associate the judge with a particular organisation, group or cause', and that the risk should be borne in mind of 'expressing views that will give rise to issues of bias or pre-judgment in cases that later come before the judge'.[123]

One further point should be noted in this regard. It is increasingly common for judges to be appointed by the government to chair inquiries into matters of public controversy. While this has obvious attractions—not least the perception that a judge will get to the heart of the matter by adopting an independent and objective approach—serious concerns have been voiced about this practice. In particular, the risk arises that involvement in inquiries into very controversial matters may taint the judge in a way that subsequently compromises her (perceived) independence. For example, Lord Hutton, a Law Lord who chaired an inquiry that raised highly charged issues concerning the Blair government's claims about the case for war against Iraq, was strongly criticised when he produced a report that was perceived in some quarters as unduly pro-government. This matter is considered in more detail in Chapter 18.

The other side of the coin concerns judges being involuntarily drawn into matters of public or political controversy in ways that may damage the dignity and independence of the judicial system. The most obvious way in which this might happen is through public criticism of judges' decisions. The rule here is that such criticism is lawful provided that it keeps 'within the limits of reasonable courtesy and good faith'.[124] Criticism falling on the wrong side of this line, such as allegations that a judge is corrupt, is a criminal offence.[125] (There are, however, official channels for complain-

---

[118] Judges' Council, *Guide to Judicial Conduct* (London 2008), [3.3].

[119] *Guide to Judicial Conduct*, [3.3].

[120] So-called after the Lord Chancellor who articulated them in a letter to the then Director-General of the BBC. The letter was printed at [1986] PL 383, 384–6.   [121] [1986] PL 383, 385.

[122] *Guide to Judicial Conduct*, [8.2.1].   [123] *Guide to Judicial Conduct*, [8.2.4].

[124] *R v Commissioner of Police of the Metropolis, ex p Blackburn (No 2)* [1968] 2 QB 150, 155, *per* Salmon LJ.   [125] See Chapter 20, section 3.3.2, below.

ing about judges).[126] Although lesser forms of criticism will not be *unlawful*, it does not follow that they will be *legitimate*. A particular issue here concerns the appropriateness of politicians criticising judges. Under the separation of powers, each branch of government ought to respect the others' decisions made within their respective constitutional provinces. On this view, it is unseemly (at best) and wholly inappropriate (at worst) for politicians publicly to berate judges who make decisions with which they disagree.

The growth of judicial review and the implementation of the HRA have enhanced the scope for discord between courts and politicians, given that the former are increasingly called upon to pronounce upon the lawfulness of the conduct of the latter. Of course, a degree of tension between the courts and the other branches may be healthy. As Lord Woolf remarked, it may demonstrate 'that the courts are performing their role of ensuring that the actions of the Government of the day are being taken in accordance with the law'. Such tension may therefore be 'a necessary consequence of maintaining the balance of power between the legislature, the executive and the judiciary upon which our constitution depends'.[127] On occasions, however, a line has arguably been crossed between legitimate disagreement and inappropriate confrontation; some examples were given in Chapter 1 and need not be repeated here.[128] The difficulty is that such episodes present the courts with an uncomfortable dilemma: either judges adhere to the normal convention whereby they do not speak publicly about individual cases, or they allow themselves to be dragged into a public row. The choice is thus between, on the one hand, allowing allegations of incompetence or wrongheadedness to stand and, on the other hand, compromising the independence and dignity of the judiciary by publicly locking horns with Ministers. In an attempt to find a way through these difficulties, the England and Wales judiciary now undertakes greater central coordination of media issues through the Judicial Communications Office (JCO). This affords an opportunity, where appropriate, for misconceptions and criticisms to be dealt with in a way that avoids the individual judge concerned being drawn into the fray. For example, in December 2009, in a very high-profile case, Cox J issued an injunction against a union, preventing a strike that would have grounded British Airways (BA) flights over the holiday period.[129] Thereafter, there were allegations that the judge had flown with BA during the period that would have been affected by the strike, and had therefore had a personal interest

---

[126] Complaints can be made to the Office for Judicial Complaints. Its role is to arrange for a judge to advise the Lord Chancellor and the Lord Chief Justice as to whether a formal investigation is appropriate. In such cases, the Lord Chancellor and the Lord Chief Justice appoint an investigating judge to advise them on whether disciplinary action should be taken. This may involve removal from office (or, in respect of judges of the Senior Courts or Justices of the Supreme Court, invoking the procedure set out in section 4.4.2 above), a formal warning, or a reprimand (Constitutional Reform Act 2005, s 108). See further Judicial Discipline (Prescribed Procedures) Regulations 2006, SI 2006/676.

[127] 'Judicial Review: The Tensions between the Executive and the Judiciary' (1998) 114 LQR 579, 580.

[128] See Chapter 1, section 3.3.3, above.

[129] *British Airways plc v Unite the Union* [2009] EWHC 3541 (QB).

in preventing the strike. In response, the JCO issued a media statement refuting the allegations.[130]

4.5 **Independence—concluding remarks**

The appropriateness of the notion of judicial independence elaborated above rests on an important set of assumptions concerning the judicial role. That judges should be independent in the senses just considered is unarguable if their function is an essentially mechanical one of applying established rules to fact situations. In such circumstances, the technically most able people should be appointed as judges and their independence should be jealously guarded so that they can get on with the business of applying the law to the facts.

However, the greater the extent to which the role of judges extends into the making of law and policy choices, the less obvious it becomes that they need to—or even should—be independent in the traditional sense. Imagine, for example, if UK judges were given the task of interpreting and enforcing a constitutional Bill of Rights that prevailed over all other law: even Acts of Parliament that were inconsistent with the Bill of Rights would be vulnerable to being struck down by the courts. Imagine, too, if the Bill of Rights were drafted in general, lofty terms, conferring such entitlements as 'the right to life'. And imagine if the courts were then asked to strike down legislation legalising abortion on the ground that it interfered with foetuses' rights to life. The judicial task in such a scenario would patently transcend the mechanical application of established law to the facts: in the absence of clear textual guidance from the Bill of Rights, judges would have to decide by reference to other factors the stage of pregnancy, if any, at which a foetus acquired a constitutional right to life. It is unlikely that judges would be able to carry out such a task without (even if only subconsciously) being influenced by their own attitudes and experience. In such circumstances, a judge's outlook and background would be highly pertinent to the way in which he would be likely to approach his task. It is unsurprising, therefore, that in legal systems in which judges are called upon to perform functions such as the one sketched above, a great deal of interest is taken, before candidates are appointed to judicial office, in their views on the sort of matters upon which they might subsequently be asked to adjudicate. In the USA, for example, appointments to the Supreme Court are one of the most *politically* significant functions performed by the President: if a given President can achieve a situation in which the balance of opinion on the Court is sympathetic to his general philosophy, this will reduce the likelihood that his agenda will be thwarted by adverse judgments. As such, judicial appointments are regarded as a legitimate subject of political inquiry, debate, and influence.

Within such a framework, conventional notions of judicial independence are arguably inapposite for a combination of two reasons. On the one hand, in our example,

---

[130] JCO statement, 20 January 2010.

the loose wording of the Bill of Rights—it does not say *who* has a right to life—leaves considerable scope for judicial choice. On the other hand, the consequences of that choice are substantial, bearing in mind the existence of a strike-down power that means that courts ultimately have the last word in the event of a disagreement with the other branches. There are two possible responses to this state of affairs. One is to say that the courts are still engaged in a classically judicial endeavour involving the construction of a legal text; the other is to acknowledge that, in such circumstances, judges are executing an essentially political task. The latter view, if adopted, begs the questions why extensive steps should be taken to render judges immune from public and political pressure, and why they should be appointed solely on the grounds of technical legal ability. If the distinction between the legal and political processes is less watertight than we thought, then arguably the justification for judicial independence—which is, to a large extent, concerned with separating judges from the world within which politicians operate—is substantially weakened.

Q Do you agree with the argument outlined above?

Of course, the scenario sketched at the beginning of this section does not reflect the situation currently obtaining in the UK, in which judges do not have the power to strike down Acts of Parliament. But that does not make the foregoing discussion irrelevant to the UK. Judges have very considerable powers in both of the senses described above. First, they are increasingly called upon to interpret legal texts—most obviously the ECHR—the vague language of which leaves considerable scope for the making of judicial policy choices. And, second, while (for as long as the UK Parliament is sovereign) the courts are ultimately unable to insist that their view should prevail, the practical effect of such choices is nevertheless considerable, particularly where the legislation at stake has been enacted by a body, such as one of the devolved legislatures, which is not sovereign. This is not to say that the existing concept of judicial independence should be torn up. It is, however, important to take account of the fact that that concept is, or ought to be, a function of the judiciary's role. As that role evolves, this needs to be reflected in the operative principles of judicial independence and the practical arrangements that flow from them. Two examples will be given by way of conclusion.

First, if the courts' task is just mechanically applying rules, then the identity of the judge(s) assigned to a particular case is irrelevant, save to the extent that some may be more technically proficient at ascertaining and applying the law, and so more likely to get it 'right'. If, however, the courts' role is more open-ended—for example, if it involves choosing between competing possible meanings of the law, or developing legal rules against a largely blank canvas—then the position is very different. Here, the judges who are assigned to the case may crucially affect the outcome.[131] Against this

---

[131] In the example given above, judges with strong religious views might be more willing than, say, judges with a liberal secular outlook to be persuaded that the right to life extends to foetuses.

background, it has been argued that it is unacceptable that the Supreme Court (like the Appellate Committee of the House of Lords before it) sits in panels (five of the twelve Justices typically sit on each case) and that judges are not assigned to cases in a transparent manner.[132]

Second, in many jurisdictions, the problem mentioned above is avoided by the practice of top courts sitting *en banc*, meaning that all members of the court sit in all cases. Of course, this has resource implications: the UK Supreme Court would have to reduce substantially the number of appeals that it hears each year if it were to adopt such a practice. More fundamentally, however, such an approach shifts the difficult question to a different stage. If all of the judges sit in all of the cases, then the crucial question concerns the balance of opinion within the Court as a whole. Without the element of randomness that might arise as a result of panel selection, outcomes might well be influenced through appointments to the Court. For precisely this reason, appointments to the US Supreme Court (which sits *en banc*) are, as foreshadowed above, the subject of intense political interest, and the political (if not *party*-political) views of candidates on such matters as abortion and freedom of speech are probed in great depth as part of the process whereby the legislature can confirm or reject candidates put forward by the President. Whatever the other arguments for and against this system, it at least has the virtue of acknowledging that the work of the US Supreme Court has a strongly political dimension to it.

> **Q** As we saw above, politicians have almost no involvement in the reformed judicial appointments process in the UK. It might be argued that this reform was wholly misconceived, bearing in mind that the role of UK judges is broader than it has ever been in the light of the growth of judicial review and the implementation of the HRA. Would you agree with such an argument?

4.6 Judicial diversity

In recent years, increasing emphasis has been placed on the need for a judiciary that is more diverse, particularly in terms of gender and ethnicity. The perception that the judiciary is mainly comprised of white males is an accurate one. At present, only one of the twelve Justices of the Supreme Court is a woman, and women make up less than 10 per cent of the Court of Appeal judiciary; meanwhile, fewer than 2 per cent of High Court judges are from ethnic minorities.[133] Against this background, two questions arise.

First, *why does diversity matter*? Naturally, it matters if its absence (in this sphere as in any other) implies unlawful or otherwise unfair discrimination. But, irrespective of such concerns, is diversity a particularly desirable quality in the judicial context? According to an advisory panel on judicial diversity established by the Lord Chancellor, it is—for two reasons. It is argued that a 'judiciary which is visibly more

---

[132] Buxton, 'Sitting *En Banc* in the New Supreme Court' (2009) 125 LQR 288.
[133] *The Report of the Advisory Panel on Judicial Diversity 2010* (London 2010), [19].

reflective of society will enhance public confidence'.[134] Furthermore, it is said that a more diverse judiciary would allow a greater range of perspectives to be reflected in judicial decision-making—a quality that is 'particularly important where there is scope for the exercise of judicial discretion or where public interest considerations are a factor'.[135]

Second, *what steps can and should be taken to increase the diversity of the judiciary?* At present, the JAC is under a statutory duty to 'have regard to the need to encourage diversity in the range of persons available for selection for appointments'.[136] However, this is subject to the overriding requirement that '[s]election must be solely on merit'.[137] It follows that while the JAC is required to take steps to encourage a broad range of people to apply, it may not engage in 'positive discrimination' when it comes to deciding between candidates—that is, the positive promotion of an individual for a particular judicial office because of his or her gender or ethnicity. This is summed up in the JAC's 'guiding principle'—'diversity in the field, merit in the selection'.[138]

The advisory panel established by the Lord Chancellor made a large number of recommendations as to how diversity might be enhanced. For present purposes, those recommendations can be divided into two broad categories.

First, in terms of the selection process itself, the panel agreed that selection should remain merit-based, but that the JAC's definition of 'merit' should be extended such that it takes account of candidates' 'awareness and understanding, acquired by relevant experience, of diversity of the communities which the courts serve'.[139] While rejecting quotas or targets, the panel argued that the JAC should favour candidates from under-represented groups when choosing between two otherwise indistinguishable applicants.[140] It was also suggested that the procedures for appointing to the Court of Appeal and the Supreme Court should be changed so as to reduce the involvement of members of those courts in order to diminish the likelihood of appointments panels recruiting 'in their own image' and thereby perpetuating homogeneity.[141]

Second, the panel argued that in order to stimulate applications from under-represented groups, it was necessary to address systemic issues that transcend the appointments process.[142] Thus it was necessary to encourage a greater diversity of entrants into the legal profession, and to encourage a greater diversity of members of

---

[134] *The Report of the Advisory Panel on Judicial Diversity 2010*, [25].

[135] *The Report of the Advisory Panel on Judicial Diversity 2010*, [26].

[136] Constitutional Reform Act 2005, s 64(1).   [137] Constitutional Reform Act 2005, s 63(2).

[138] See **http://www.judicialappointments.gov.uk**

[139] *The Report of the Advisory Panel on Judicial Diversity 2010*, [31].

[140] *The Report of the Advisory Panel on Judicial Diversity 2010*, [33]. The Equality Act 2010, s 159, provides that it is lawful, in certain circumstances, for candidate A to be offered employment in preference to candidate B on the ground that A (unlike B) possesses a 'protected characteristic'. However, candidate A must be as qualified as candidate B, and it must be the case that people with the characteristic in question are under-represented. This means that it would be lawful for the JAC to (for example) favour female or minority ethnic candidates. At the time of writing, the Equality Act 2010 had not entered into force.

[141] *The Report of the Advisory Panel on Judicial Diversity 2010*, [41]–[42].

[142] *The Report of the Advisory Panel on Judicial Diversity 2010*, [4].

the profession to apply for judicial posts. Achieving the latter objective, it was argued, would be aided by, among other things, dispelling myths about the nature of the judiciary (for example, that, in order to be appointed. it is necessary to be 'part of the "club"').[143]

4.7 Other necessary judicial characteristics

A final point needs to be made here. Courts make decisions that, more often than not, intimately affect the lives of the people involved and can have drastic repercussions. In order to discharge this function responsibly, judges need to possess certain attributes, such as knowledge of the law, the ability to conduct a fair trial or hearing, and judicial independence. At the same time, acting as a judge requires the possession of other qualities in order to make sometimes difficult decisions as to how the law applies in any given instance. As the current Lord Chief Justice, Lord Judge, has explained:

> The men and women who serve the Crown in judicial office engage daily with their fellow citizens, often when they are at their most vulnerable. They are asked to make extremely difficult and sensitive decisions affecting their lives and to do so calmly and with fair and measured patience. The work is unremitting and at times very stressful and the moral courage required properly to exercise judicial authority can be considerable.[144]

5. Concluding remarks

An independent judiciary is a prerequisite in any civilised society subject to the rule of law. Only through the existence of such an institution is it ultimately possible to ensure that disputes are generally settled in a way that is just and which does not simply result in the victory of the stronger party.[145] But we have also seen in this chapter that the courts play a special role in constitutional terms. Under the separation of powers, the judiciary forms an essential element of the checks and balances system that is needed if the other branches of government are to be confined to their appropriate constitutional provinces and if fundamental constitutional principles are to be upheld. It follows that an independent judiciary is needed if the separation of powers is to be meaningfully enforced—but also that the separation of powers is necessary if there is, in the first place, to be a truly independent judiciary. It is noteworthy, then, that although the separation of powers is generally implemented in the UK in a rather half-hearted way, it rightly finds its fullest and clearest expression in the doctrine of judicial independence.

---

[143] *The Report of the Advisory Panel on Judicial Diversity 2010*, [49].

[144] *The Lord Chief Justice's Review of the Administration of Justice in the Courts* (London 2010), p 5.

[145] An independent judiciary is, of course, a necessary, but not a sufficient, condition in this respect: the law that falls to be applied by the courts must be consonant with outcomes that are just and fair.

Further reading

BAILEY, CHING, AND TAYLOR, *The Modern English Legal System* (London 2007), ch 4

BELOFF, ' "Better that a Horse Should Have a Voice in That House [of Lords] than that a Judge Should" (Jeremy Bentham): Replacing the Law Lords by a Supreme Court' [2009] PL 723

LE SUEUR (ed), *Building the UK's New Supreme Court* (Oxford 2004)

The Lord Chief Justice's Review of the Administration of Justice in the Courts (London 2010)

STEYN, 'The Case for a Supreme Court' (2002) 118 LQR 382

Useful websites

http://www.bailii.org
The website of the British and Irish Legal Information Institute

http://www.hmcourts-service.gov.uk
The website of the Courts Service of England and Wales

http://www.judicialappointments.gov.uk
The website of the Judicial Appointments Commission

http://www.judiciary.gov.uk
The website of the Judiciary of England and Wales

http://www.justice.gov.uk
The website of the Ministry of Justice

http://www.courtsni.gov.uk
The website of the Northern Ireland Courts Service

http://www.scotcourts.gov.uk
The website of the Scottish Courts

http://www.supremecourt.gov.uk
The website of the Supreme Court

7 Devolution and Local Government

1. Introduction

So far in this book, we have been mainly concerned with the United Kingdom's institutions of government. Our focus now shifts to the other tiers of government that give rise to the UK's multilayered governance arrangements mentioned in Chapter 1 and illustrated in Figure 7.1. In the next chapter, we consider the European Union (EU); here, our concern is with local government and, first, devolution.

2. Devolution

2.1 Where should governmental power lie?

Devolution has involved creating new governments in Scotland, Northern Ireland, and Wales, and investing them with powers that were previously exercised at a UK level. Devolution in the UK is therefore intended to be part of the answer to questions that must be confronted in all political systems: where should governmental power lie? And at what level should laws be enacted and the business of government transacted?

There are no objectively correct answers to these questions: ultimately, everything turns (in democracies, at least) on what sort of arrangements will be considered legitimate by the people. This helps to explain why there is great diversity of practice internationally. In states in which there is a strong sense of shared identity and destiny, it may be acceptable—even desirable—for there to be a highly centralised system of government; this is most likely to be the case where the population of a country is homogeneous in cultural, linguistic, ethnic, and economic terms. But it is not uncommon for a state to consist of a looser association of peoples lacking that sort of homogeneity; they may be content to live under the umbrella of a single state—allowing it to deal with such high-level issues as defence, national security, and so on—while demanding regional governments to represent and serve their diverse interests and outlooks. Meanwhile, the peoples within in a state may occasionally conclude that their interests are so distinct (or even conflicting) and affinities so lacking that they should go their

Policy area

Tier of government	Foreign affairs	Defence	Competition and single European market	Planning	Education	Taxation	Social services	Immigration and nationality	Health and health services	Agriculture	Crime and justice
EU	European coordination of some aspects of foreign policy	European Defence Agency, common foreign and security policy	Main responsibility	Environment and planning powers	Student exchange schemes, exchange of ideas	Some harmonisation, EU fundamental principles constrain national policy		Increasing harmonisation in area of asylum	Powers to protect and improve public health	Common Agricultural Policy, rural development	Common policies on some aspects of justice and home affairs
UK	Main responsibility for conduct of foreign relations	Main responsibility for defence	Duty to implement relevant EU laws	Policy and legislative framework for England	Policy and legislative framework for England	Main responsibility	Policy and legislative framework for England	Main responsibility	Policy and legislative framework for England	Policy and legislative framework for England	Criminal law and judicial system in England and Wales
Devolved			Duty to implement relevant EU laws	Policy and legislative framework for devolved nations	Policy and legislative framework for devolved nations	Scottish Parliament's limited power to vary income tax	Policy and legislative framework for devolved nations		Policy and legislative framework for devolved nations	Policy and legislative framework for devolved nations	Criminal law and judicial system in Scotland and Northern Ireland
Local				Planning decisions	Implementation	Council Tax (but subject to control by central government)	Implementation		Delivery by local NHS trusts		Power to enact by-laws, some enforcement powers

Figure 7.1 The UK's multilayered governance arrangements

separate ways entirely, leading to the break-up of the state—something that may either occur peacefully, through mutual consent, or as a result of civil war.

Systems, like devolution, that allow for the diffusion of power within a state are relevant to the second of these situations—and may help to avoid the third. Affording a degree of autonomy to regions within a state enables them to pursue their own interests in ways of their own choosing. This can ultimately enhance the integrity of the state by allowing regional differences—which might otherwise create tensions, and even found arguments in favour of the break-up of the country—to be accommodated.

Against this background, we can begin to consider why devolution was introduced in the UK, which, as the name suggests, is a sovereign state formed through the union of several nations. The history by which England and Wales were joined is complex, but a key milestone was reached in 1535 when, among other things, Welsh constituencies came to be represented in the English Parliament.[1] The United Kingdom of Great Britain was formed by the joining of England and Wales with Scotland in 1707,[2] and later became the United Kingdom of Great Britain and Ireland in 1800.[3] Thereafter, all four of the so-called home nations were governed at a UK level; the laws applicable in them were enacted by the Westminster Parliament, and they were administered by the UK executive. That does not mean that the home nations were treated identically to one another—the UK Parliament frequently enacted legislation that applied only to Scotland, or only to England and Wales, while the UK executive established separate departments to deal with certain administrative matters in Northern Ireland, Scotland, and Wales. But there was no escaping the fact that the UK had one executive government and one legislature controlled by whichever political party secured a majority in the House of Commons.[4] It followed that even if a particular part of the UK voted overwhelmingly for a given political party in a general election, it was possible for a different party to win control of the UK legislature and form the executive government.

For example, in 1992, the Labour Party won 68 per cent of Scottish seats in the UK Parliament, but the Conservatives gained an overall majority of seats across the UK, and Scotland was therefore governed by a Conservative-controlled Parliament and executive. Of course, it is hardly unusual for the majority of voters in one part of the country to favour a given party that nevertheless fails to gain an overall majority in a general election—but the position was complicated by the fact that Scotland identified itself as a distinctive political unit within the UK, given its former status as an independent country and the fact that it has subsequently retained a sense of separateness in cultural and political terms. It was this alignment of factors—namely, Scotland's propensity to regard itself as a discrete unit and the capacity of the electoral system to frustrate the clear wishes of its electorate, leading to a sense of disenfranchisement—that

---

[1] Law in Wales Act 1535.   [2] When the Acts of Union 1706 entered into force.

[3] Union with Ireland Act 1800.

[4] This statement needs to be qualified in that, for part of the twentieth century, devolved government existed in Northern Ireland. See section 2.2 below.

fuelled enthusiasm for the devolution of power to new Scottish institutions of government. This reflects the more general point that the case for devolution is most keenly felt where the members of a community consider themselves to be part of a cohesive political unit that itself is perceived, to some degree, as separate from the rest of the political system.

2.2 Demand and supply

How, then, did devolution come about in practice in the UK? In contrast to countries such as the USA, the UK's constitution was not designed as such: no one sat down with a blank sheet of paper and sketched the powers of, and relationships between, the different institutions and tiers of government. Rather, the constitution is the product of centuries of gradual change—of pragmatic responses to issues that have arisen from time to time. Devolution is of a piece with this tradition: it occurred *because* it was desired and *to the extent* that it was desired. In this sense, it has been governed by the laws of demand and supply.

This helps to explain why devolution in the UK is *asymmetrical*, meaning that different amounts and types of power have been devolved to different parts of the country. For example, as noted above, there was real dissatisfaction, and so a real appetite for change, in Scotland. Short of independence—a step that the Scottish people have not, to date, clearly shown themselves willing to take[5]—self-rule *within* the UK was the obvious answer. Aware of the strength of feeling in Scotland, one of the first acts of Tony Blair's new administration in 1997 was to publish proposals for an extensive devolution of power to new Scottish institutions[6]—proposals that won the strong support of the Scottish people in a referendum.[7] Scots wanted their own system of government with substantial powers, and, as we will see shortly, got precisely that.

The law of demand and supply also operated—but with different results—in Wales, where the desire for devolution was not as strong.[8] A form of devolution less radical than that proposed for Scotland was therefore put to the Welsh people, who made their ambivalence about devolution manifest: only 50.3 per cent of those who voted were in favour.[9]

---

[5] The Scottish National Party, which favours independence, won more seats than any other party in the 2007 elections to the Scottish Parliament, but failed to gain an overall majority.

[6] Scottish Office, *Scotland's Parliament* (Cm 3658 1997).

[7] Of those who voted in the referendum, 74.3 per cent favoured devolution.

[8] Indeed, in a referendum in Wales in 1979, 79.9 per cent of those who voted were *against* devolution.

[9] Cause and effect is difficult to establish here; arguably, the modest nature of the proposals may have led to the perception that devolution in Wales would have little impact, thereby reducing support. On the other hand, as Williams, 'Devolution: The Welsh Perspective', in Cambridge Centre for Public Law, *Constitutional Reform in the UK: Practice and Principles* (Oxford 1998), pp 43–4, notes, Wales 'offers a very different historical, constitutional and cultural pattern' from Scotland, which may help to explain divergent attitudes to devolution.

Q What might be the practical limitations of this demand-and-supply model of constitutional reform? Why, for example, may be it be difficult to establish precisely what the people of a particular nation or region want?

Northern Ireland is different again. There, the position was complicated by clear divisions—expressed through decades of terrorist atrocities that claimed over 3,000 lives—between Nationalists (who favoured Northern Ireland's cession from the UK) and Unionists (who did not). Devolution—which had existed in Northern Ireland for much of the twentieth century, but which ended in the early 1970s as violence escalated— was an obvious compromise, but one that risked pleasing no one. In this context, the law of demand and supply eventually delivered an unusual and highly bespoke form of devolution, including provision for Northern Ireland to leave the UK if such a step is supported in a referendum.[10] This scheme would have been no one's first choice, yet represented a compromise acceptable to both sides.[11] Despite this, devolution had a very difficult start in Northern Ireland: it was suspended, and direct rule by the UK government reinstated, on a number of occasions, most notably from 2002 to 2007, the main sticking point being whether terrorist weapons had been put beyond use.

England, meanwhile, has no system of devolved government. This apparent anomaly is explored below; for the time being, we simply note that England's exclusion from the devolution programme is but one aspect of the latter's highly unusual character. It has certainly not produced neat results; indeed, to the casual observer ignorant of the under- lying history and politics, the structure of the UK post-devolution must seem bizarre. The situation obtaining today is undoubtedly not one that would have eventuated had the constitution been designed from scratch; in this sense the story of devolution is part of a much wider narrative. The UK's constitutional arrangements are informed by a raw pragmatism that accepts a certain roughness around the edges as the acceptable cost of accommodating diversity, history, and tradition.[12] Nevertheless, there comes a point at which such a relentlessly pragmatic approach—the absence of any 'strategic vision', as the Justice Select Committee put it[13]—begins to create problems of its own. We will argue later that this is the case with devolution, in relation to which there are so many loose ends, particularly with regard to England, that the fabric of the system starts to look worryingly fragile. First, however, we need to consider how devolution works where it presently *does* exist—in Northern Ireland, Scotland, and Wales.

---

[10] Northern Ireland Act 1998, s 1. At present, the majority in Northern Ireland favours the union with Great Britain, but demographic trends suggest that this position may change over time.

[11] Of the 81.1 per cent who voted, 71.1 per cent were in favour of the devolution proposals.

[12] This is not to deny that devolution is underpinned by ideological concerns such as democracy and sub- sidiarity (that is, the taking of decisions at an appropriate level), but it is plain that the response to such con- cerns has been heavily influenced by factual, historical, and cultural differences between the home nations. See further McCrudden, 'Northern Ireland and the British Constitution Since the Belfast Agreement', in Jowell and Oliver, *The Changing Constitution* (Oxford 2007), ch 10.

[13] House of Commons Justice Committee, *Devolution: A Decade On* (HC 529 2008–09), [6].

2.3 **Devolution in action**

2.3.1 **Legislative power**

The extent to which devolved governments possess legislative power is a key index of their ability to act independently; the differences on this front between the UK's devolution schemes are therefore telling.

The Scottish Parliament and the Northern Ireland Assembly possess *general legislative competence*: they are authorised to enact legislation on *any* issue, subject to certain exceptions.[14] Those exceptions relate both to specific legislation that the devolved legislatures are unable to alter, such as the Human Rights Act 1998 (HRA),[15] and particular subject areas, such as international relations and defence of the realm.[16] In addition, neither legislature can validly enact legislation that conflicts with EU law or certain provisions of the European Convention on Human Rights (ECHR).[17] Although broad, these legislative powers cannot be equated with the sovereign power that the Westminster Parliament enjoys (at least in orthodox theory).[18] It follows that if the Scottish Parliament or the Northern Ireland Assembly exceeds its legislative authority, the courts can intervene.

The National Assembly for Wales (more commonly known as the Welsh Assembly), rather than having general legislative competence, is empowered only to enact legislation in certain specified fields[19]—and even then only if it has first secured permission, in effect from the UK government, to legislate on a particular matter within one of those fields.[20] These are much more modest powers than those wielded by the other devolved legislatures; they result in a complicated division of power and a cumbersome legislative process that straddles both Cardiff and London.[21] Ron Davies, who, as Secretary of State for Wales, was instrumental in introducing Welsh devolution, said that devolution was a 'process not an event'. History has proved him right. The Welsh Assembly lacked even the powers described above until reforms contained in Pt 3 of the Government of Wales Act 2006 entered into force. And even those reforms were envisaged only as a stop-gap measure. Part 4 of the Act provides that the need to seek permission before legislating can be removed—but only if such reform is approved by the people of Wales in a referendum. At the time of writing, it is expected that a referendum will be held in 2011.

The nature of devolution as an ongoing process is evident in Scotland and Northern Ireland, too. Justice and policing powers—originally excluded from the devolution

---

[14] Northern Ireland Act 1998, ss 5–8; Scotland Act 1998, ss 28–30.

[15] Northern Ireland Act 1998, s 7; Scotland Act 1998, s 29(2)(c) and Sch 4.

[16] Northern Ireland Act 1998, s 6(2)(b) and Sch 2; Scotland Act 1998, s 29(2)(b) and Sch 5.

[17] Northern Ireland Act 1998, s 6(2)(c) and (d); Scotland Act 1998, s 29(2)(d).

[18] *Re Axa General Insurance Ltd* [2010] CSOH 2.

[19] The specified fields include agriculture, economic development, the environment, health services, housing, and local government. For a complete list, see Government of Wales Act 2006, Sch 5.

[20] Government of Wales Act 2006, ss 94–95.

[21] See *Report of the All Wales Convention* (Cardiff 2009).

settlement as part of a compromise—were transferred to Belfast in 2010. Meanwhile, the extent of the Scottish institutions' powers has been the subject of considerable attention in recent years. The Calman Commission, established by the Scottish Parliament and the UK government, recommended a modest extension of Edinburgh's powers, most notably in relation to taxation.[22] Following the 2010 general election, the UK government announced its intention to implement the Calman Commission's proposals.[23]

As well as considering the *extent* of the power wielded by the devolved legislatures, it is necessary to consider the *type* of legislative power that they each exercise. Since the inception of devolution in 1999, the Scottish Parliament and (whilst it has sat) the Northern Ireland Assembly have wielded primary lawmaking power: they are capable, within their legislative competence, of amending, repealing, and replacing Acts of the UK Parliament in so far as they apply to Scotland and Northern Ireland respectively. This allows them, should they so wish, to set out in fundamentally different policy directions from other parts of the UK.

In contrast, the system originally obtaining in Wales was merely one of *administrative* or *executive*—as opposed to *legislative*—devolution. The Welsh Assembly was only empowered to exercise in relation to Wales certain administrative powers that would otherwise have been exercised by UK Ministers. This meant, for example, that where an Act of the UK Parliament gave Ministers discretionary power to make certain choices, they could be made, as far as they affected Wales, by the Welsh Assembly.[24] Equally, if UK legislation authorised Ministers to make secondary legislation,[25] this power could be exercised for Wales by the Assembly.[26] None of this, however, really enabled Wales to pursue a truly distinctive legislative agenda: at best, it allowed the Assembly to finesse the details of how legislation applied to Wales. This was a source of dissatisfaction: it was felt in some quarters that the Assembly lacked the power to be truly useful.[27] In a further example of the operation of the law of demand and supply in this sphere, the UK Parliament responded with fresh legislation in 2006 that wrought major changes to the Welsh system.[28] So today, subject to the limitations mentioned above,[29] the Assembly is able to enact legislation that replaces, amends, or repeals UK legislation in so far as it applies to Wales.

---

[22] Commission on Scottish Devolution, *Serving Scotland Better: Scotland and the United Kingdom in the 21st Century—Final Report* (Edinburgh 2009). The Scottish Parliament has always had limited powers to vary income tax in Scotland: Scotland Act 1998, Pt IV.

[23] HM Government, *The Coalition: Our Programme for Government* (London 2010), p 28.

[24] Provided that the function in question had, in the first place, been transferred to the Welsh Assembly.

[25] See Chapter 4, section 4.2, above on secondary legislation.   [26] Subject to the above proviso.

[27] *Report of the Richard Commission* (Cardiff 2004), ch 3.

[28] Government of Wales Act 2006, which replaces (and in many respects replicates) the Government of Wales Act 1998. For background, see Wales Office, *Better Governance for Wales* (Cm 6582 2005).

[29] See the text above. In addition, the Assembly, like its counterparts in Scotland and Northern Ireland, cannot validly legislate contrary to European Union (EU) law or the European Convention on Human Rights (ECHR): Government of Wales Act 2006, s 94(6)(c).

2.3.2 **Executive power**

All three of the UK's devolution schemes include the transfer of executive power to new devolved executive bodies—but, as with legislative authority, there are important differences between the schemes.

The position in Scotland is perhaps the most straightforward because it is the most familiar. Following elections, members of the Scottish Parliament (MSPs) must nominate one of their number to be appointed First Minister by the Queen.[30] If one party secures an overall majority, its leader is highly likely to become First Minister; otherwise, a coalition is likely to be formed, with the leader of the biggest coalition party becoming First Minister.[31] He then appoints the other Ministers drawn from MSPs who are members of his own party and any others with which it has formed a coalition.[32] This largely follows the UK model of a 'parliamentary government'—that is, an executive drawn from, and held to account by, the legislature. Like its Westminster counterpart, the Scottish Parliament can confer discretionary and delegated lawmaking powers on the Scottish Ministers,[33] who also exercise in relation to Scotland all powers relating to devolved matters that had been conferred on UK Ministers prior to devolution.[34] The upshot is that the Scottish Executive now acts as Scotland's government save in relation to those matters that remain the responsibility of the UK authorities. As a result, the role of UK Ministers in relation to Scotland is now relatively slight, given that the major domestic areas of governance—including the most politically high-profile issues of health and education—are largely devolved to Scotland.

Originally, the position in Wales was very different: *only* executive power was transferred, and this vested in the Assembly itself, albeit that it could delegate such power.[35] Today the position is different again: legislative powers, as explained above, have now been conferred upon the Assembly, and a formal legal distinction is made between the Assembly, as a legislative body, and the executive branch, known as the Welsh Assembly Government.[36] The Assembly's role is to enact primary legislation and hold the executive branch to account, while the latter now exercises the administrative powers that formerly vested in the Assembly. A First Minister and other Welsh Ministers are appointed in broadly the same way as their Scottish counterparts; all must be Assembly Members, thus conforming to the familiar model of parliamentary government.[37]

Arrangements in Belfast also follow that pattern, with a separate Northern Ireland Executive drawn from the membership of the Assembly. However, the Northern Ireland Executive differs in important respects from its Scottish, Welsh, and UK counterparts. The way in which the Northern Ireland Executive is appointed and composed represents a highly bespoke solution to the specific problems faced by Northern

---

[30] Scotland Act 1998, ss 45–46.

[31] The Scottish elections in 2007 produced no overall majority for any party. The leader of the largest party in the Parliament, the Scottish National Party, became First Minister, but was able to do so only with the support (direct and, through abstentions, indirect) of other parties' MSPs.

[32] Scotland Act 1998, s 47.   [33] Scotland Act 1998, s 52.   [34] Scotland Act 1998, s 53.

[35] See Rawlings, *Delineating Wales* (Cardiff 2003), ch 3.

[36] Government of Wales Act 2006, ss 1 and 45.   [37] Government of Wales Act 2006, ss 46–48.

Ireland. In particular, it was clear that, in a sharply divided community, devolved government would only be perceived as legitimate—and have any prospect of contributing to the ending of terrorist violence—if it enjoyed the support of both Nationalists and Unionists. This meant that it would be unacceptable to follow the normal model to the extent that it allows the majority party in the legislature, or a coalition of like-thinking parties, to form the executive government. Instead, it was felt necessary to *require* parties representing *both* sections of the community to share executive power. So, following elections to the Assembly, the nomination for First Minister is made by the nominating officer of the largest political party of the largest political designation (currently the Unionists), while the nomination for Deputy First Minister is made by the nominating officer of the largest political party of the *second largest* political designation (currently the Nationalists). In practice, this means that the two senior ministerial offices are held by one Nationalist and one Unionist politician.[38] Moreover, detailed rules ensure that no political party[39] can monopolise the other ministerial portfolios.[40] Northern Ireland is thus administered by a power-sharing executive, coalition government being the legally stipulated norm—a highly unusual approach that seeks to solve a set of very particular and hitherto intractable problems. There is no clearer illustration than this of the British approach to devolution, in which pragmatism is paramount: a 'differential approach to the arrangements for each country', reflecting their individual 'histories and contemporary circumstances'.[41]

> **Q** Conducted in this way, constitutional reform produces undeniably messy results. Is this acceptable? What problems might follow from embracing this 'asymmetric' model of devolution?

2.3.3 Democracy

As we saw earlier, one of the objectives underlying devolution is the enhancement of democracy by enabling people to be governed by institutions over which they feel they have real influence, and to which they therefore consider themselves genuinely connected. Devolution mainly pursues this goal by providing institutions that are more proximate—geographically, politically, and culturally—to the people. But it is, of course, also important that the *process* whereby representatives are elected to serve in the new devolved legislatures is a democratic one.

The system used for elections to the Scottish Parliament and Welsh Assembly differs from that used for elections to the House of Commons. Known as the *additional member system*, it involves dividing Scotland and Wales into both *constituencies* and larger *regions*. Voters cast ballots to select both constituency members and regional (so-called additional) members. The former are elected under the first-past-the-post

---

[38] Northern Ireland Act 1998, s 16A.   [39] And, in practice, neither Nationalists nor Unionists.

[40] Northern Ireland Act 1998, s 18.

[41] Irvine, *Human Rights, Constitutional Law and the Development of the English Legal System* (Oxford 2003), p 90.

(FPTP) system: the candidate with the greatest number of votes in each constituency becomes its representative in the legislature. This ensures the valuable link between constituents and their representatives. Meanwhile, additional members—of whom there are several for each region—are chosen by voters casting ballots for political parties rather than individuals. The regional seats are then allocated by applying a mathematical formula that seeks to ensure that a party's total number of seats in the legislature broadly reflects its overall share of the vote. As Figure 7.2 shows, this can have the effect of both disadvantaging parties that have done disproportionately well in constituency elections and advantaging (for example) smaller parties that are not strong enough to win in any particular constituency, but which may nevertheless garner sufficient support across a larger region to secure at least one seat.

A system known as the *single transferable vote* is used for elections to the Northern Ireland Assembly; this is different from the model that applies in Scotland and Wales, but is also designed to ensure that the political make-up of the legislature closely reflects each party's share of the popular vote.[42]

One important consequence of the additional member system and the single transferable vote is that they make it unlikely that any one party will gain an overall majority, thus necessitating minority or coalition government.[43]

Party	Constituency seats (%)	Total seats (%) once additional members taken into account
Scottish National	28.8	36.4
Labour	50.7	35.7
Conservative	5.5	13.2
Liberal Democrat	15.1	12.4
Green	0	1.6
Other	0	0.8

Figure 7.2 Scottish elections 2007

2.4 **Devolution in context**

So far, we have observed a number of distinctive features of the UK system of devolution. It is now time to take stock of these by placing them in a broader context. One way in which the sometimes idiosyncratic nature of devolution may be appreciated is by contrasting it with other systems, such as federal ones, in which power is divided or shared between different layers of government.

---

[42] The single transferable vote is the system favoured by the Electoral Reform Society. For detailed information on how it works, see **http://www.electoral-reform.org.uk**

[43] Coalition is in any event a legal requirement in Northern Ireland: see section 2.3.3 above.

2.4.1 Federalism and devolution contrasted

Federalism exists in some form in many constitutions, but here we focus in particular on the version of it found in the USA. The USA consists of 50 states, each with its own legislature and administration. Certain matters, however, are dealt with on a national level by the federal legislature—Congress—and the US administration. On the basis of this brief description, federalism in the USA may seem similar to devolution in the UK. However, any similarity is only skin deep: there are three crucial differences.

First, the UK's system is, as we already know, *asymmetrical*: different parts of the UK have different amounts and types of devolved power. In the USA, however, all states possess the same legal powers as one another. It follows that, in the UK, the central institutions of government exercise different degrees of power over different parts of the country: for example, the UK Parliament makes relatively little law pertaining to Scotland and Northern Ireland (because they have their own legislatures with extensive powers), while it enacts all primary legislation relating to England (which lacks its own legislature). Again, this contrasts with the US federal system, in which the federal government exercises the same degree of power in relation to all 50 states.

The reasons underlying our first distinction partly consist in a second distinction. The USA was formed by a number of individual states deciding to join together in order that certain matters could be dealt with collectively by a federal government. An agreed position was therefore worked out among the original states as to what should be done at state level and what should be conceded to the new federal government. This *bottom-up* approach—in which power originated at state level and was transmitted to the federal level only to a limited degree and along uniformly agreed lines—produced a symmetrical distribution of powers in both of the above senses.[44] In contrast, devolution in the UK is a *top-down* system: the UK Parliament is legally sovereign, but has chosen to confer limited powers on the new devolved governments. And those conferrals of power were effected not on the basis of a single set of negotiated principles as to how the line should be drawn between central and devolved government, but in light of the differing histories, attitudes, and politics of the UK's constituent nations.

A third difference between UK devolution and US federalism concerns the *constitutional security* of those systems of government. In the USA, the balance of power between federal and state levels is set by the Constitution—and the Constitution can be changed only by going through a lengthy procedure requiring, *inter alia*, approval by 75 per cent of the states.[45] The balance of power between state and federal levels therefore enjoys a high degree of security: changes are difficult to effect because they require a very wide consensus. The situation in the UK is very different. Devolution was simply effected by passing Acts of Parliament—and, as we saw in Chapter 4, it is always open to Parliament to amend its own enactments. This has three implications in the present context. First, it is theoretically possible for the UK Parliament simply to repeal the devolution legislation, abolishing at a stroke the devolution system. Second, short of such drastic action, the Westminster Parliament could amend

---

[44] An analogy may be drawn with the relationship between the EU and its member States: see Chapter 8.
[45] US Constitution, art 5.

the devolution legislation: for example, it may add to or subtract from the powers of the devolved legislatures. Third, being sovereign, the UK Parliament may override the devolved legislatures: if, for example, one of them were to enact legislation to which the Westminster Parliament took exception, it would be open to the latter Parliament to pass an Act overriding the offending devolved legislation.[46] In legal terms, therefore, the UK's devolved system of government is far less secure than the federal system obtaining in the USA, since the former can be undone or changed without the need to go through any elaborate—and hard-to-comply-with—constitutional amendment procedure.

> **Q** Would it have been better if the UK had adopted federal arrangements? Why, or why not?

2.4.2 Legal and political constitutionalism—law and convention

This difference between the UK and US systems illuminates a deeper point of distinction that speaks volumes about the British constitution itself and returns us to one of the key themes of this book. The US model is one of legal constitutionalism, which emphasises law as a means of controlling government. Hence key restrictions on the powers of government in the USA—from the human rights of individual citizens to the limitations inherent in the division of power between state and federal levels—are laid down in a written Constitution and enforced by the courts. In contrast, the UK constitution often lacks these legal bright lines; instead, it remains, in important respects, a political constitution. Among other things, this means that we place a good deal of emphasis on the political process—including the restraint that is induced by requiring politicians to submit regularly to re-election—as the force that constrains government.

This is clearly illustrated in relation to devolution. We observed above that, *in theory*, the UK Parliament may unilaterally abolish or radically change the devolution settlement. Yet in the absence of exceptional circumstances, it would be nigh on impossible for it to do any of these things. Here, then, we encounter a familiar characteristic of the British constitution as a political constitution—namely, a disjunction between the positions prescribed by legal theory, on the one hand, and real-world politics, on the other. It is often the case that the gap between these two positions is bridged by constitutional convention, and devolution is no exception to this norm. It was recognised in the early days of devolution that it would be wholly contrary to the spirit of the new constitutional arrangements if the UK Parliament were to interfere unilaterally in devolved matters. However, it was also recognised that circumstances can arise in which it makes sense for legislation impinging on devolved issues to be enacted on a UK basis at Westminster.[47] For example, to legislate satisfactorily on a given matter, it may be necessary to enact a scheme that covers both devolved and reserved matters, or legal obligations flowing

---

[46] See Scotland Act 1998, s 28(7).

[47] See, eg HL Deb, 21 July 1998, col 791 (Lord Sewell, speaking during the committee stage of the Scotland Bill).

from international or EU law may require all parts of the UK to implement uniform legal changes. In such situations, it is most efficient for UK-wide legislation to be enacted.[48] Crucially, however, it has been accepted that the UK Parliament should not normally legislate on devolved matters *unless the relevant devolved legislature consents*. Thus a *political* agreement—now regarded as a constitutional convention, known as the Sewel convention[49]—has emerged, regulating the exercise of the Westminster Parliament's *legal* sovereignty and rendering its practice consistent with the spirit of devolution.

Indeed, convention is important not only as regards the relationship between Westminster and the devolved legislatures, but also in relation to how the various administrations relate to one another. Devolution has radically changed the British system of government by creating new seats of political and administrative authority in Edinburgh, Cardiff, and Belfast, all of which must relate to the UK government and, to some extent, one another. It might therefore seem surprising that, as Rawlings has noted, 'almost nothing is said in the [devolution] legislation about the structures and processes of intergovernmental relations', thus creating a 'vast constitutional space'.[50] In the absence of law, that vacuum has been filled by 'concordats', which are best thought of as instant conventions: whereas conventions traditionally emerge implicitly through long practice, concordats are explicit, but legally non-binding, agreements entered into between political institutions.[51] A multilateral concordat known as the Memorandum of Understanding[52] sets out in general terms how the UK and devolved governments should relate to one another, while myriad bilateral concordats lay down the ground rules for relationships between particular central and devolved government departments. This heavy reliance on extra-legal agreements further illustrates the importance of the political nature of the British constitution generally, and its devolution settlement in particular.

That said, there are, of course, legal dimensions to the devolution scheme—most notably in terms of the statutorily prescribed limitations on the powers of the devolved bodies—and the courts have a role in enforcing these. The devolution legislation makes special provision for judicial resolution of 'devolution issues'—that is, issues as to whether devolved bodies are acting or proposing to act beyond their legal competence—with final appeals on such matters ultimately lying to the Supreme Court.[53]

---

[48] See further Burrows, 'This is Scotland's Parliament: Let Scotland's Parliament Legislate' (2002) 5 Juridical Review 213, 222–6; Page and Batey, 'Scotland's Other Parliament: Westminster Legislation about Devolved Matters in Scotland Since Devolution' [2002] PL 501, 508–19.

[49] So-called because it was first proposed by Lord Sewel: see above. He made this suggestion during the committee stage of the Scotland Bill, but the UK government accepts that the same principle applies when Westminster contemplates legislating on matters over which *any* devolved legislature has competence: Office of the Deputy Prime Minister, *Devolution Memorandum of Understanding and Supplementary Agreements* (Cm 5240 2001), p 8.

[50] Rawlings, 'Concordats of the Constitution' (2000) 116 LQR 257, 258–9.

[51] Purists might argue that conventions, by definition, cannot be instantly created. For discussion, see Jaconelli, 'The Nature of Constitutional Convention' (1999) 19 LS 24.

[52] Office of the Deputy Prime Minister, Cm 5240.

[53] See Scotland Act 1998, Sch 6; Government of Wales Act 2006, Sch 9; Northern Ireland Act 1998, Sch 10 (as amended by Constitutional Reform Act 2005, Sch 9, Pt 2).

2.5 England—'the spectre at the feast'?[54]

In relation to Northern Ireland, Scotland, and Wales, the UK government's role is residual: it does those things that the devolved institutions are not authorised to do. In England, however, there are no devolved institutions. The UK Parliament and the UK executive are therefore the *de facto* government of England.

2.5.1 Implications

England's exclusion from the devolution settlement, according to one commentator, means that the 'new constitutional architecture of the United Kingdom is rightly seen as lop-sided'.[55] This has important implications, two of which we address here.

First, as Oliver notes, no governmental institution exists that can provide a 'voice for England' by legitimately arguing its case 'as against Scotland, Wales, and Northern Ireland'.[56] Although the UK government acts *de facto* as England's government, she argues that it cannot properly act as England's advocate—this 'would be seen as partisan, given that it is supposed to be promoting the interests of the UK as a whole'—thus giving rise to 'inequalities' within the UK that are not 'consistent with principles of good governance, transparency, and equality'.[57] Logically, this point is difficult to refute; instead, those who seek to defend the current situation question the underlying premise that England *needs* such an advocate. For example, Lord Falconer, when he was Lord Chancellor, argued that the 'essence of devolution is to protect the legitimate interests of Scotland and Wales'[58]—a requirement based on the fact that 'England and English MPs represent over 80% of the population and over 80% of MPs'.[59] England, on this view, is big enough to look after itself; only the smaller nations require the special voice afforded by devolution.

> **Q** Do you find Falconer's approach on this point convincing? Can you think of any counter-arguments?

The second implication of the absence of devolution in England presents a more profound difficulty, commonly known as the *West Lothian question*.[60] Although first posed specifically in relation to proposals for Scottish devolution, the essence of the question is simply whether it is legitimate for MPs representing non-English constituencies to vote on matters that will affect *only* England. If the instinctive response

---

[54] England was so described by Rawlings at 266.   [55] Rawlings at 266.

[56] Oliver, *Constitutional Reform in the UK* (Oxford 2003), p 290.   [57] Oliver, p 290.

[58] Northern Ireland was not mentioned, presumably because, when this speech was made, devolution there was suspended.

[59] Speech to ESRC Devolution and Constitutional Change Programme Final Conference, March 2006.

[60] So-called because, when devolution was considered in the late 1970s, this problem was most notably raised by the then MP for West Lothian in Scotland, Tam Dalyell, a staunch opponent of devolution.

to this question is 'no', two factors may help to explain this.[61] First, there is a lack of reciprocity in these arrangements: it is not immediately obvious why, for example, Scottish MPs should vote in Westminster on education law, given that—education being a devolved matter in Scotland—English MPs have no influence over Scottish education law. Second, the fact that English law can be made by MPs unaccountable to the English electorate arguably raises problems of democratic legitimacy.[62]

These are difficult issues that go to the heart of the nature of the Union following devolution. The only potentially viable defence of England's post-devolution situation is a pragmatic one—that although the position looks odd, it is acceptable because it does not, in practice, matter. On this view, lop-sidedness is acceptable, even desirable, since it 'balance[s] out England's overwhelming size':[63] England will get its own way on English matters *because of its size*, while devolution ensures that the smaller nations are heard *in spite of their size*. However, experience indicates that this is not necessarily so. For example, in 2003, a health Bill was put before Parliament concerning, *inter alia*, National Health Services (NHS) reforms entailing the creation of so-called foundation hospitals. That part of the Bill pertained *only* to England—and as Figure 7.3 shows, although a majority of *all* MPs supported the proposals, a majority of *English* MPs did not.

Q Do you think that these voting figures imply some sort of unfairness? If so, can you pinpoint exactly what it is that gives rise to such unfairness?

2.5.2 Possible ways forward

Lord Irvine—who, as Lord Chancellor from 1997 until 2003, was instrumental in many of the Blair government's constitutional reforms, including devolution—once remarked that 'the best thing to do about the West Lothian question is to stop

Nation	For foundation hospitals	Against foundation hospitals
England	234	251
Scotland	44	17
Wales	24	11
Northern Ireland	0	6
All	302	285

Figure 7.3 MPs' votes on amendment to Health Bill, November 2003*

* See Constitution Unit, *Devolution and the Centre* (November 2003), 8.

[61] See Hadfield, 'Devolution, Westminster and the English Question' [2005] PL 286, 286–7.
[62] Hadfield at 286–7.
[63] Straw, 'The future for Parliament' (speech to Hansard Society, July 2006).

asking it'.[64] This flippant remark conceals an important insight: the problems thrown up by the West Lothian question are very difficult to solve, and there may be little point in attempting to do so unless the general public is clamouring for this to be done. For the first decade or so of devolution, there was no such clamour, because the Labour governments of 1997–2010 enjoyed comfortable—and usually very large—majorities. The implementation of their legislative programmes therefore rarely depended on non-English votes, the example of the health Bill given above being exceptional. But the position is now different. As Figure 7.4 shows, the outcome of the 2010 general election threw the West Lothian question into sharp relief: while the Conservative Party did not secure a majority of *all* seats in the UK Parliament, it secured a clear majority of *English* seats. England now therefore finds itself in the very position that triggered calls for Scottish devolution: a clear majority (at least expressed through the current voting system) expressed a preference for one party, yet voting patterns elsewhere meant that that party could not (on its own) form a government.

Following the 2010 election, the coalition government announced that it would create a commission to consider the West Lothian problem.[65] There are at least three possible solutions to it.

The first would involve devolution to *English regions*. In fact, this was proposed by the Labour government in 2003: England was to be divided into eight regions,[66] each with its own elected regional assembly.[67] However, the powers with which such

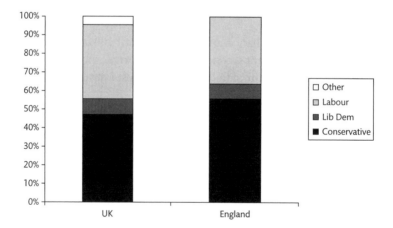

Figure 7.4 2010 general election results

[64] HL Deb, 25 June 1999, col 1201.

[65] HM Government, *The Coalition: Our Programme for Government* (London 2010), p 27.

[66] In addition to London, where a form of regional government—in the shape of the Greater London Authority—already exists.

[67] See Department for Transport, Local Government and the Regions, *Your Region, Your Choice: Revitalising the English Regions* (Cm 5511 2002); Regional Assemblies (Preparations) Act 2003.

assemblies were to be invested were modest, and the proposal disintegrated when it was resoundingly rejected in a referendum in north-east England in 2004.

The second, and most drastic, option would be to create a separate English parliament (and administration) along the lines of the Scottish Parliament (and Executive), in effect moving the UK towards a federal structure, with the Westminster Parliament and UK executive dealing only with matters not devolved to the four nations. There is little political appetite for change on such a massive scale, in part because it is feared by some that it would presage the break-up of the Union by fatally loosening the ties that bind England and the other home nations together.

Critics of the current position have therefore tended to concentrate on a third option—that is, 'English votes for English laws'. The idea is simple—measures pertaining to England should be voted on only by English MPs—but implementing it would be fraught with difficulty.[68] For example, it is said that it would be practically hard to delineate England-only measures, given that many Bills contain some clauses that apply only to England, others to England and Wales, and yet others to the UK as a whole. Although this would be procedurally unwieldy—the Speaker would have to determine which MPs were eligible to vote on each part of a Bill—it is not an insuperable obstacle.

Adopting such an approach would, however, raise other, more far-reaching—and more intractable—problems. In particular, precluding non-English MPs from voting on England-only matters might mean that the governing party had a majority for some purposes, but not others. For example, a government with a small majority *in Parliament as a whole* might not have a majority *amongst English MPs*, potentially preventing it from getting its England-only legislation through the House of Commons. This would represent a fundamental departure from the way in which government has traditionally worked: Bogdanor has argued that it would 'destroy the principle of collective responsibility, according to which government must stand or fall as a whole, commanding a majority on all the issues that come before Parliament, not just a selection'.[69] On the other hand, as Hadfield notes, there is a fairly obvious response to this—one that goes against the grain of our 'executive-dominated constitution but actually has democratic principle...behind it':

> if there is, say, a UK Labour government, in power because of the number of Scottish Labour MPs but controlling only a minority of English MPs, and it cannot secure the passage into law of its proposals for England then so be it...If the result is a hiatus on any given topic, then let the Labour government seek a wider consensus on the matter.[70]

Q If the idea of 'English votes for English laws' were embraced, how could these problems be resolved? Would it, for example, be feasible to distinguish between a UK executive (formed by the party with an overall majority in the House of Commons) and an English executive (formed by the party with an overall majority of English seats)?

---

[68] See Hadfield.   [69] *Financial Times*, 10 February 2006.   [70] Hadfield at 301.

This discussion shows us that if we were to begin unpicking the fabric of the constitution by, for example, embracing the idea of 'English votes for English laws', then it would begin to unravel in other respects: changing the way in which Parliament legislates would have consequences for the executive branch, and so on. This is not necessarily an argument against change—simply a recognition that it is likely to have wider implications, potentially necessitating further reform. But, as we have seen, such an approach to constitutional change—involving stepping back and looking at the bigger picture—is not typical of the British way in these matters.

3. Local government

3.1 Why *local* government?

Local government is important.[71] It employs hundreds of thousands of people, spends tens of billions of pounds annually, and plays a key role in the making of decisions, the formulation of policy, and the delivery of public services across a very wide range of areas, including education, housing, personal social services, transport, and planning control. That certain decisions should be made and tasks performed at a local level seems obvious on an instinctive level, but it is nevertheless worth reflecting on why we have local government—and why we have it in its current form.

A good starting point is the conclusions of the Widdicombe Committee, a body set up in the 1980s by central government to inquire into the conduct of local authority business.[72] It argued that the value of local government consists in three principal factors. First, it was said, local government is important for reasons of *pluralism*. Rather than having a single (central) seat of government, the existence of local authorities ensures that governmental power is, to some extent, diffused, thus avoiding the hegemony of central government. Second, local government facilitates *participation* in the business of governance—both by equipping citizens to shape local policy through regular elections to councils and by virtue of the fact that individuals can more easily become directly involved in local, than in national, governance. The liberal writer John Stuart Mill considered these participative virtues of local government to be of great importance, arguing that they help to provide citizens with an education in democracy.[73] Third, the Widdicombe Committee emphasised the *responsiveness* of local government—that is, its capacity to make decisions and deliver services in ways that are appropriate to the particular needs of localities. Such responsiveness is facilitated by the proximity of local government to the electorate and the area concerned,

---

[71] Lyons, *Place-Shaping: A Shared Ambition for the Future of Local Government* (London 2007), contains detailed discussion of the role of local government, past, present, and future.

[72] Committee of Inquiry into the Conduct of Local Authority Business, *The Conduct of Local Authority Business* (Cmnd 9797 1986).

[73] Mill, *Considerations on Representative Democracy* (New York 1862), pp 288–9.

equipping it with local knowledge and sensitivity to local mores. A more recent inquiry concluded that local government's key role is 'place-shaping', meaning 'the creative use of powers and influence to promote the general well-being of a community and its citizens'—an endeavour in which responsiveness, as we have defined that notion, is obviously imperative.[74]

In what follows, we consider whether local government in the UK today corresponds to these ideals.

3.2 **What should local government do?**

Whether local government enjoys sufficient authority and autonomy to realise the potential that the Widdicombe Committee perceived depends on a broad range of factors, the most important of which is perhaps the way in which the respective roles of central and local government are formulated. It stands to reason that if local government can do little more than implement central government policy, then it will not exist in the form described above.

Although there is no magic formula for determining precisely how responsibility should be divided between localities and the centre, there is certainly scope for drawing the line—or assessing how the line has been drawn—by reference to normative criteria. For example, the European Charter of Local Self-Government states that 'Public responsibilities shall generally be exercised, in preference, by those authorities which are closest to the citizen'.[75] This reveals a general preference for power being exercised at the lowest practicable level, but it does not provide tangible criteria for drawing the line between local and central government business. Mill's writings are more helpful in this regard. He argued that while 'all business purely local—all which concerns only a single locality—should devolve upon the local authorities', some duties, although capable of being performed by local officials, 'might with equal propriety be termed national, being the share belonging to the locality of some branch of the public administration in the efficiency of which the whole nation is alike interested'.[76] Mill developed this idea, going on to argue that 'localities may be allowed to mismanage their own interests, but not to prejudice those of others, nor violate those principles of justice between one person and another of which it is the duty of the state to maintain the rigid observance'.[77]

> **Q** Can you think of examples of matters that would fall into each of Mill's two categories? More broadly, consider whether the distinction postulated by Mill is capable of being drawn as a bright line: is anything *purely* local?

[74] Lyons, p 60.

[75] Article 4(3). The Charter is an international treaty, to which the UK is a party. It does not, however, form part of domestic law.   [76] Mill, p 299.

[77] Mill, p 305.

While the division of functions between central and local government is important, it is beyond the scope of this book to provide a detailed account of how that line is drawn in the UK. Instead, our focus is on more general aspects of the relationship between central and local government that affect the capacity of the latter to play the role ascribed to it by the Widdicombe Committee. Is local government a secure part of a pluralist constitution, able to act independently and responsively by using local knowledge and sensitivity to fashion policies that are appropriate to particular localities? Or is local government essentially an agent of the centre, the role of which is merely to implement the policies of the latter?

3.3 Local and devolved government compared

One way of tackling these questions is to compare the constitutional position of local government with that of devolved government. As we saw earlier in this chapter, the devolved governments in Edinburgh, Cardiff, and Belfast were created by the UK Parliament. It is therefore possible, at least as a matter of constitutional theory, for the latter to interfere in the devolution settlements—for example, by curtailing the devolved governments' powers, making changes to how devolution works, or overriding laws passed by devolved legislatures. Local government is also a creation of the UK Parliament. Local authorities therefore possess only the powers given to them via Acts of the Westminster Parliament. And, just as that Parliament could, if it wished, fundamentally rewrite the devolution legislation, so it may interfere with local government, effecting major changes to its powers, structure, and so on.

It follows that, in *legal* terms, the UK level of government, via Acts of Parliament, has the capacity to intervene in the affairs of both devolved and local government. But does central government possess the *political* capacity to exploit such legal powers? We have already seen that it would be politically very difficult for central government to interfere in the devolution settlements without the consent of the devolved governments concerned. Now that devolution has allowed the genie of self-government out of the bottle, it would be nigh on politically impossible to put it back in. The same is not, however, true of local government. Although local, like devolved, government exists (*inter alia*) to allow communities to order their own affairs in ways that best meet their peculiar needs and priorities, the institutions of local government—city councils, county councils, and so on—do not, in general, enjoy the same status or security as their devolved counterparts.

Why is this so? The political capacity of central government to intervene in other tiers of government within the UK is principally dependent upon citizens' perceptions of, and attitudes towards, the latter. People are most likely to entertain a sense of connection with—even the possession of a stake in—institutions with which they identify closely. National institutions, such as the devolved legislatures and administrations, enjoy a particular status deriving from the sense of shared identity and common destiny that nationhood inspires. This does not, of course, mean that people support everything that their devolved governments do—but the ties that bind the citizens of the devolved nations together are likely to lend a degree of popular legitimacy to, and support for the existence of, their national institutions. In contrast, senses of identification with institutions of local government may be less strong, bearing in mind that we live in an increasingly mobile society in which the membership of many communities is transient to a significant degree,[78] and that such institutions may not, in the first place, necessarily be aligned with such senses of local identity as exist.[79] A further, related point is simply that local government generally has rather a low profile: people's awareness of the role that it plays is often rudimentary at best; this, too, inhibits the development of the sort of strong sense of connection with local authorities that might guard against central government interference. Thus the Conservative governments of 1979–97 'were able to remove functions and finance because local government was not greatly loved or respected by its electorates'.[80]

> **Q** Does this lower level of identification with localities, as distinct from nations, *necessarily* follow? What factors might mean that in some areas—towns, cities, counties, regions—there is a stronger sense of local identity?

Central government, then, has both the legal and political capacity to intervene in local government matters. Does such intervention actually occur, and, if so, why?

3.4 **The role of the centre**

3.4.1 **Intervention by the centre**

The first half of that question can be answered quite easily. The UK government frequently intervenes—on both the administrative and legislative planes—in matters pertaining to local government. Three points should be considered in this regard.

First, Parliament may intervene directly so as to alter the fundamental nature and structure of local government. The UK government, through its control of the House of Commons, is thus able to assert considerable influence over local government. The most dramatic example is perhaps the Thatcher administration's procurement of legislation to abolish the Greater London Council, which, under the control of the Labour Party, was highly and very publicly critical of central government policies in the 1980s.[81] The Thatcher government, informed by its ideological predilection for

---

[78] According to Young et al, *In Search of Community Identity* (Joseph Rowntree Foundation 1996), who surveyed community identity in the shire counties of England in the mid-1990s: '[T]he largest group [of people] have no sense of attachment to any of their neighbourhood/village, their district or their county. Nearly one in three fall into this category.'

[79] For example, in England in the 1970s, some new county-level authorities (such as Avon and Humberside) were created with boundaries dictated by considerations of administrative convenience rather than respect for local mores. These authorities have since been abolished.

[80] John, 'Strengthening Political Leadership? More than Mayors', in Stoker and Wilson (eds), *Local Government into the 21st Century* (Basingstoke 2004), p 47.   [81] Local Government Act 1985.

market economics, also made radical changes to how local authorities operated by requiring many services that had traditionally been provided by councils themselves to be put out to tender (albeit that the local authority could itself bid for the work). This led to the contracting out of many of the councils' core functions (for example, housing management and refuse collection) and transformed councils in some spheres from service-providing to service-commissioning bodies.[82]

Second, the governing UK party may choose to impose its own policy preferences on local government by requiring it to undertake or desist from undertaking certain actions. An example of the former is furnished by the attempts of Labour governments in the 1960s and 1970s to introduce a new system of secondary education. Legally, it was for local authorities to decide on the organisation of schools within their areas, but the government wished to institute the 'comprehensive' system on a national basis.[83] It attempted to do this by issuing administrative directions requiring local authorities to formulate plans for shifting to comprehensive education. When this met with opposition from some councils, legislation was introduced requiring local authorities to submit plans for the reorganisation of schools along the lines of the comprehensive model.[84] Meanwhile, the Thatcher administration secured the enactment of s 28 of the Local Government Act 1988, which banned local authorities from 'promot[ing] the teaching in any maintained school of the acceptability of homosexuality as a pretended family relationship'. This is a very clear example of the ability and willingness of central government to use primary legislation as a means of imposing its policy (including moral) preferences on local authorities, rather than allowing such issues to be debated and decided at a local level.[85]

Third, as well as using primary legislation directly to intervene in local affairs, the UK executive possesses numerous administrative powers[86] to intervene in, scrutinise, regulate, and even override the conduct of local government. An important element of this relates to financial affairs, in which local authorities lack any substantial measure of real autonomy. Although local authorities raise funds directly by levying the Council Tax, this accounts for less than a fifth of their total budget,[87] and this revenue-raising capacity is itself constrained by the Secretary of State's power to 'cap' Council Tax if he considers a local authority's budget to be 'excessive'.[88] Councils depend for the remainder—that is, the vast majority—of their income on various types of grant from central government. This clearly gives the latter considerable influence, which is wielded, *inter alia*, by attaching conditions to such grants.

---

[82] The Blair government abolished compulsory competitive tendering, replacing it with a regime known as 'best value', under which councils are expected to contract out the provision of services where this represents the best option judged by a range of criteria (including non-financial ones). See Local Government Act 1999, s 3(1).

[83] This system was intended to replace that under which pupils were sent to grammar or secondary modern schools depending on an assessment of their academic ability at age 11.   [84] Education Act 1976.

[85] Section 28 of the 1988 Act was repealed in 2003.

[86] Themselves conferred by primary legislation.

[87] Lyons, *Place-Shaping: A Shared Ambition for the Future of Local Government* (London 2007), p 223.

[88] Local Government Finance Act 1992, ss 52A–52Z.

Although local authorities enjoy significant discretionary powers, these discretions are bounded by the terms of the relevant legislation and some local government decisions may need to be approved by central government before taking effect. For example, local councils are able to make local laws, known as by-laws, on certain matters, but some of these cannot take effect without the say-so of the 'confirming authority'—who, unless the relevant legislation says otherwise, is the Secretary of State.[89] Leigh observes that where this task falls to the Home Office, it has shown itself reluctant to confirm by-laws that depart from the terms of its model by-laws—that is, the standard, centrally approved template—'even on topics as mundane as dog-fouling or control of ice-cream van chimes'.[90]

Meanwhile, legislation conferring powers on local government may allow Ministers to make regulations prescribing in great detail how local authorities may exercise such powers, or enable Ministers to issue legally enforceable directions to a local authority that is failing to discharge its statutory duties to the satisfaction of central government. For example, local government is legally required to 'make arrangements to secure continuous improvement in the way in which its functions are exercised, having regard to a combination of economy, efficiency and effectiveness'.[91] If satisfied that a local authority is failing to do this, the Secretary of State may direct 'that a specified function of the authority shall be exercised by the Secretary of State or a person nominated by him for a period specified in the direction or for so long as the Secretary of State considers appropriate'.[92]

A further strand within the central–local dynamic must also be appreciated. During the period of Conservative government from 1979, the courts became an important—and novel—theatre in which the outworking of tensions between central and local government occurred. Writing in 1986, Lord Woolf remarked that while it was 'rare' before 1979 'to have one public body challenging before the courts a decision of another, it is now commonplace to have central government attacking local government decisions, local government attacking central government decisions and one local authority challenging the decisions of another'.[93]

Where does this leave us? Is local government essentially a delivery mechanism—an 'executory agency for national policies', as one commentator has put it?[94] Or is local government truly autonomous, able to develop and implement its own policies in a

---

[89] Local Government Act 1972, s 236. The Local Government and Public Involvement in Health Act 2007 amended the 1972 Act, inserting a new s 236A under which the Secretary of State can permit certain classes of by-laws to be enacted without his confirmation.

[90] Leigh, *Law, Politics, and Local Democracy* (Oxford 2000), p 52. But see now s 236A of the 1972 Act, discussed above.   [91] Local Government Act 1999, s 3(1).

[92] Local Government Act 1999, s 15(6)(a).

[93] 'Public Law—Private Law: Why the Divide?' [1986] PL 220, 220. For prominent examples of such litigation, see *Bromley London Borough Council v Greater London Council* [1983] 1 AC 768; *Hammersmith and Fulham London Borough Council v Secretary of State for the Environment* [1991] 1 AC 521. For discussion of this trend and its implications, see Loughlin, *Legality and Locality* (Oxford 1996), especially pp 399–416.

[94] Loughlin, *Local Government in the Modern State* (London 1986), p 186, suggesting that some aspects of the work of local government could be described thus.

way that is appropriate to the needs of individual communities—thus realising the potential that the Widdecombe Committee saw? Inevitably, these questions are not as simple as might be implied by the stark terms in which we have posed them: the real concern is the *degree* to which local government enjoys genuine autonomy and the *degree* to which it is merely an implementer of central government policy.

Nothing that has been said so far should be taken to imply that local government is unimportant or lacking in power. It plays a fundamental role and exercises real power; local authorities are free, in many respects, to adopt their own policies and to develop distinctive solutions to local problems. It is also important to appreciate that the degree of central control of local government tends to ebb and flow; having reached a high-water mark in the 1990s and early 2000s, it is now beginning to recede somewhat. The Labour government stated in 2006 that 'we must have the courage at the centre to let go', in order to 'give local people and local communities more influence and power to improve their lives'.[95] To this end, it gave councils greater flexibility over (*inter alia*) the enactment of by-laws[96] and the assessment of allegations of misconduct against individual councilors, reduced the number of targets and eased the system of inspection to which councils are subject, and gave local authorities new powers to promote or improve the economic, social, and environmental well-being of their areas.[97] In 2010, the new coalition government signaled an intensification of this approach. It undertook (*inter alia*) to 'promote radical devolution of power and greater financial autonomy to local government', to give councils extended powers, including a 'general power of competence', and to reduce inspection and audit.[98] It remains to be seen (at the time of writing) precisely what those undertakings amount to in practice.[99] While the coalition's proposals countenance greater autonomy for local authorities, centralising tendencies are not wholly absent, especially in the financial sphere: it has proposed that any local authority that wishes to increase Council Tax beyond a centrally prescribed level should be forced to hold a referendum.[100] This implies that local representative politics is judged an inadequate mechanism of control in relation to fiscal matters.

For the time being, at least, it remains the case that local government is subject to a good deal of oversight and intervention by central government. This is important; it goes to the heart of one of the main themes with which we are concerned in this book—namely, the extent to which governance in modern Britain is genuinely

---

[95] Department for Communities and Local Government, *Strong and Prosperous Communities* (Cm 6939 2006), p 4. Ironically, however, the empowerment of *local people* involved the imposition of new policies on *local authorities* so as to guarantee individuals choice over such matters as childcare and housing. See Cm 6939, p 27.   [96] See above.

[97] Local Government Act 2000, s 2.

[98] HM Government, *The Coalition: Our Programme for Government* (London 2010), p 12.

[99] Although, at the time of writing, one concrete measure—the abolition of the Audit Commission—had been announced. On this, see further Chapter 11, section 4.2, below.

[100] Department for Communities and Local Government, *Local Referendums to Veto Excessive Council Tax Increases* (London 2010).

multilayered. Clearly, the greater the extent to which central government intervenes in local government, the lower the degree of autonomy enjoyed by the latter, and the less it can lay claim to being a real counterweight to the power of the central bodies. If the diffusion of power—by means of constitutional arrangements under which authority and influence are shared rather than within the grasp of all-powerful central institutions—is the essence of multilayered governance, then local government clearly makes a contribution to this. But that contribution is constrained by the capacity and preparedness of central government to intervene in local government matters. Indeed, the Lyons Inquiry—a major inquiry into the role and funding of local government, which reported in 2007—found that the 'high degree of central control' over local authorities has 'inhibited' the ability of the latter to 'respond to local needs and preferences and manage pressures on their budgets'. The inquiry concluded that the 'breadth and detail of central prescription . . . effectively prevents [local] authorities from shaping services and taking action on local, rather than national priorities'.[101] In similar vein, it has been suggested that the post-1997 Labour government's approach to local government was 'hierarchist'—'or, in the more common parlance of some newspapers, "control freakery gone mad"'.[102]

3.4.2 Why intervene?

Although intervention and control by central government is now beginning to decline somewhat, it is arguable that local government's capacity to fulfil the role envisaged by the Widdicombe Committee remains compromised. This begs an obvious question: why does central government not simply leave local authorities to do as they wish, relying on the local electorate to step in if things go awry by electing new councillors? After all, the national democratic process is ultimately what checks the power of central government: why not rely on local democracy to do the same in respect of local government? This is not to suggest that other mechanisms should not be relied upon as well: local (like central) government is subject to judicial review;[103] councillors are bound by a code of conduct, breaches of which may result in suspension or even temporary disqualification[104] (as Ministers are expected to abide by the ethical standards of the Ministerial Code);[105] and allegations of maladministration against central and local government alike can be investigated by ombudsmen.[106] Nevertheless, it is clear that local government is subject to a degree of regulation and intervention that simply does not apply to central government. Why is this so? Three factors help to explain the particular dynamics that are at work in the relationship between central and local

---

[101] Lyons, *Place-Shaping: A Shared Ambition for the Future of Local Government* (London 2007), pp 80–1.

[102] Stoker, 'Life is a Lottery: New Labour's Strategy for the Reform of Devolved Governance' (2002) 80 Public Administration 417, 430.   [103] See Chapters 12–15 below.

[104] See Local Government Act 2000, Pt 3 (as amended by Local Government and Public Involvement in Health Act 2007, Pt 10). However, it was announced by central government in 2010 that the Standards Board for England (which is responsible in certain cases for enforcing the code) would be abolished.

[105] See Chapter 4, section 3.4, above.   [106] See Chapter 16 below.

government, all of which tend to induce intervention by the former in relation to the latter.

First, local authorities, having been stripped over time of many of their responsibilities, are now principally concerned with redistributive welfare functions such as education, housing, and personal social services. As Loughlin notes: 'It is a basic principle of public finance that there are severe limitations on a local authority's ability successfully to undertake independent policies of income redistribution.' This follows because '[i]f a local authority sought to do so a more equal distribution of income might be achieved but "through the emigration of the rich and possibly also the immigration of the poor"'.[107] This suggests that some central involvement in the redistributive activities of local government is necessary, or at least sensible.

Second, it may well be tempting for those involved in central government to seek to advance their general programme[108] or impose specific policy preferences[109] even if this involves restricting local authorities' autonomy. This has led to what one commentator has called '[c]ommand-and-control delivery of public services from Whitehall'.[110]

A third set of factors explains the tendency of central government not merely to constrain local government through the imposition of specific policies, but also to institute the sort of detailed arrangements for the oversight and regulation of local authorities that we sketched above. The existence, on the part of central government, of an obvious instinct to put in place such arrangements implies that central government sees it as its job to ensure that local government does not go off the rails. Fearful that if local authorities are allowed to fail in their provision of important public services, it will be central government that takes the rap, the latter seeks to put in place systems that guard against such eventualities, to demonstrate vigilance and concern on the part of central government, and ultimately to empower central government to intervene and take corrective action in the event of failure. This has a standardising effect that, rather than permitting local diversity (or a 'postcode lottery', depending on one's perspective), leads central government to use its powers so as to ensure a degree of consistency in the provision of services. Lyons noted that such thinking 'can lead us to value uniformity far above the need to find the right solution for each area'.[111]

This takes us to the heart of the issue. The high degree of control exercised by central over local government can be traced, in large measure, to the fact that it is principally to the former that the electorate looks when there are failures in important public services. This incentivises interventionism on the part of central government, rather than a laissez-faire attitude that puts its faith in the self-correcting capacity of local democracy. As Jones and Stewart have argued: 'At the heart of central–local relations

---

[107] Loughlin, *Local Government in the Modern State* (London 1986), p 6, quoting Foster et al, *Local Government Finance in a Unitary State* (London 1980), p 44.

[108] As in the case of comprehensive education, discussed above.

[109] As in the case of banning the promotion of homosexuality, discussed above.

[110] White, 'From Herbert Morrison to Command and Control: The Decline of Local Democracy', available online at **http://www.historyandpolicy.org**

[111] Lyons, *Place-Shaping: A Shared Ambition for the Future of Local Government* (London 2007), p 79.

lies a dilemma between a commitment to local government and decentralisation, and distrust of local government.'[112] This tension is illustrated nowhere better than in difficulties encountered in the course of attempts to reform local government finance in the late 1980s and early 1990s. Local taxes, known as 'rates', based on property values were replaced by the 'Community Charge', a flat-rate local tax introduced with the intention of producing a transparent system that would enable people to judge whether their council provided good value for money. Margaret Thatcher—who, as Prime Minister, was instrumental in the introduction of the Community Charge—later explained in her memoirs that the principle underlying the new tax was that 'everyone should contribute something, and therefore have something to lose from electing a spendthrift council'.[113] Ironically, however, when local authorities levied high levels of Community Charge, it was not they who were principally blamed for overspending, but central government for introducing the new regime in the first place.[114] The reason for this is not hard to discern. The Thatcher government had spent the previous ten years intervening to an unprecedented degree in local government finance—breaking with past political practice by taking powers to cap high-spending councils' local tax levels while imposing compulsory competitive tendering—and it is therefore hardly surprising that when difficulties arose, it was to central government that the electorate looked.

This leads us to a final important question: is central government right to suppose that local democracy and accountability is so weak that it must itself intervene to curb the excesses of profligate councils and remedy the failures of incompetent ones? And if this is indeed so, is further centralisation and control the only solution, or might local authorities be made more accountable to their electorates, thus facilitating democratic control in the place of regulation by the centre?

3.5 **Local democracy and accountability**

As elected bodies, local authorities are subject to democratic control. If the electorate dislikes a council's policies, or regards it as inept, discontent can be expressed at the next election, and new councillors chosen. That, at least, is the theory. However, democratic control does not generally work well in the local government context. For example, far fewer people (typically only around 35 per cent) bother to vote in local than in general elections. A number of factors have conspired to create a situation in which there is a sense of disconnection from local government—although, as we will see, change is afoot. Here, we focus on three sets of key issues: the organisation of local government, its internal structure, and local government elections.

---

112 'Central–Local Relations since the Layfield Report', in Carmichael and Midwinter (eds), *Regulating Local Authorities: Emerging Patterns of Central Control* (London 2003), p 26.

113 *The Downing Street Years* (London 1993), p 648.

114 Indeed, criticism of the community charge played an important role in Margaret Thatcher's resignation as Prime Minister and Leader of the Conservative Party in 1990. Her successor, John Major, abolished the Community Charge, replacing it with Council Tax, another property-based tax.

3.5.1 **Organisation**

Our first concern is with the *organisation* of local government. People are often less conscious of local than of central government in relation to its role and its decisions—even its existence. Part of the explanation for this may be the rather complex way in which local government has (until quite recently) been organised. The Local Government Act 1972 provided for a two-tier system. Broadly speaking, England was divided into counties, and each county into districts. County councils were responsible for some matters; district councils for others. Similar arrangements applied in Wales. This scheme was complex—there is obvious scope for confusion, at least in the minds of voters, over which authority is responsible for any given matter—and serves to obscure lines of accountability. Research conducted for the Electoral Commission in relation to the May 2003 local elections revealed that many people had 'little understanding of which authority the elections were actually for', with nearly one in five respondents uncertain whether the elections were for county or district councils.[115] The position is complicated even further by the fact that one local authority may delegate powers to another. Such conditions are not ideal for the effective functioning of democratic control: if voters find it difficult to ascertain which authority is responsible for particular policies or failures in implementation, this is likely to engender apathy born of a sense of powerlessness. And if local democracy is thus compromised, this may, in turn, encourage central government intervention as an alternative means of exercising control over local authorities.

The replacement of two-tier arrangements with 'unitary authorities' goes some way towards addressing these issues. All metropolitan, and many other, areas in England, along with all parts of Wales, have now been brought within this system.[116] The decision whether to retain the two-tier structure in non-metropolitan English areas is taken by central government in light of advice tendered by the Local Government Boundary Commission for England.[117]

The position in London is rather different. Most local government functions in the capital are performed by the borough councils, but a need was felt for an overarching authority capable of making some decisions on a wider, coordinated basis.[118] As a result, the Greater London Authority (GLA) was created, comprising an elected mayor and an assembly that holds him to account, with strategic responsibility for matters such as transport, planning, and the environment.[119]

The very fact that two-tier arrangements have been reintroduced in London shows that unitary local government is not a panacea. Nevertheless, an obvious virtue is its capacity to enhance local democracy by creating clearer lines of authority,

---

[115] Electoral Commission, *The Cycle of Local Government Elections in England* (London 2004), p 13.
[116] Unitary councils are also the norm in Northern Ireland and Scotland.
[117] Local Government and Public Involvement in Health Act 2007, Pt 1.
[118] No such authority existed following the abolition of the Greater London Council in 1986, on which, see section 3.4.1 above.   [119] See Greater London Authority Act 1999, as amended.

responsibility, and accountability. Voters in areas covered by unitary authorities are more likely to know who to blame (or praise) when things go wrong (or well).

> **Q** What might be the implications of shifting to a system of unitary local authorities in a given area? Should they cover large areas or small areas? What factors would decision-makers have to grapple with in deciding whether to abolish certain district councils and establish a unitary county council, or to abolish the county council and create a number of unitary district councils?

3.5.2 Structure

These organisational reforms are a necessary, but not a sufficient, condition for reinvigorating local democracy so as to empower voters to exercise real control over local government. A second key issue concerns the internal structure of local authorities. Whatever its faults, the UK's system of central government is, in certain important respects, straightforward: the electorate votes at a general election, one party normally secures an overall majority of seats in the House of Commons, that party forms the executive government, and the government is scrutinised by the legislature. These arrangements are comfortably familiar, and have the merit of making it clear who is in charge and whose job it is to hold them to account.

To the vast majority of people, whose awareness (such as it is) of the functioning of government is based on the way in which the UK system operates, arrangements at local level are somewhat mysterious. Historically, the distinction between an executive and a body the role of which is to oversee and hold to account the executive has not formally existed in local government. As corporations, local authorities comprise a single legal entity: statutory powers have traditionally vested in the local authority itself, not in an executive body or a leader (albeit that authorities have long been able to delegate their powers to committees, subcommittees, and officers[120]). Of course, in such a system, the political party with the most councillors will exercise the greatest power and, if a party has an overall majority, it will be in a position (provided that there is adequate party discipline) to push through its programme—but three difficulties remain.

First, in the absence of the traditional distinction between an executive body and a scrutiny body, local authorities have tended to seem amorphous: it may be hard to work out who is in charge and whose job it is to hold them to account. Second, the electoral system often delivers 'hung' councils—that is, councils in which no single party holds more than half the seats.[121] Such circumstances may exacerbate the difficulties just mentioned. Third, the absence of a formal executive body within local authorities caused a distinction to open up between appearance and reality: while

---

[120] Local Government Act 1972, s 101.

[121] At any one time, typically around one-third of councils are 'hung'. See Gains, *The Implementation of New Council Constitutions in Hung Authorities* (London 2005), p 6.

powers were formally exercised by the council as a whole (or by the committees and officers to which powers had been delegated), the real decisions were often made outside formal meetings by the majority group of councillors. Such arrangements, it has been observed, can give rise to a 'lack of clarity about where decisions are taken and by whom. The role of the council's officers to provide professional advice to the decision takers is clouded. People do not know who to praise, who to blame, or who to contact with their problems'.[122]

Against this background, major reforms were made via the Local Government Act 2000 that, for the first time, created legally distinct executives within local authorities. Under the Act (as amended by the Local Government and Public Involvement in Health Act 2007), councils can choose one of three options.[123] The first possibility—and the most radical break with traditional arrangements—is a *directly elected mayor*. Under this arrangement, individuals vote not only for their ward councillor, but also for the mayor, who then selects from the other councillors the members of his cabinet. Cabinet members have responsibility for particular areas of policy, and the mayor can delegate executive powers to such members, individually or collectively. Few councils have opted for elected mayors. Most have instead taken the second option—an *indirectly elected leader*. This is similar to the first model except that no mayor is elected; rather, following elections to the council, the councillors choose a leader, whose role is then essentially the same as that of a directly elected mayor. Third, there may be a *directly elected executive*: groups of candidates (united no doubt by party affiliation) may put themselves forward in local elections as the prospective council leader and cabinet, and the group that gains the most votes goes on to form the executive. Against this background, three points should be noted.

First, whereas traditionally council committees and subcommittees were legally required to be politically balanced,[124] the new executives (under all three models) can consist of members of just one party.[125] Council executives can thus formally be captured by a single political party (or a coalition of parties), just like the UK and devolved executives. This allows council executives to function in an explicitly political fashion. Although to some extent this merely formalises a situation that already existed *de facto*—as noted above, the majority group of councillors in effect took the major decisions outside formal council meetings—it is nevertheless important. The new arrangements increase transparency and accountability by making it clear to all concerned, including the general public, where power lies. This enables individuals to perceive clearly who is running the council and who they should vote for if they want change (or, for that matter, more of the same), thereby helping to counter the notion that local authorities are amorphous and remote. The new arrangements thus aim to enhance the visibility of leadership within local councils and therefore public

---

[122] Office of the Deputy Prime Minister, *Local Leadership, Local Choice* (Cm 4298 1999), [1.13].

[123] A small number of local authorities, on account of their small size, are permitted not to use any type of executive model.   [124] Local Government and Housing Act 1989, s 15.

[125] Local Government Act 2000, s 24.

awareness of, and interest in, local government and politics—although an early review of the reforms introduced by the 2000 Act did not find that it was succeeding in these respects.[126] In 2010, the coalition government said that councils should not be forced to adhere to an executive model, and that those that wished to should be allowed to 'return to the committee system'.[127]

Second, to the extent that the purpose of the reforms has been to increase the visibility and public awareness of council leaderships, they are most likely to succeed where there is a high-profile figurehead in the form of a directly elected mayor. For that reason, the 2007 Act made it easier for councils to shift to a directly elected mayor by removing the requirement (originally imposed by the 2000 legislation) that a referendum be held before introducing such arrangements.[128] Moreover, in 2010, the coalition government indicated that it would take the initiative by holding referendums on directly elected mayors in England's 12 largest cities.[129]

Third, for the reasons discussed above, all three models entail a distinction between the executive and the council generally. What, then, is the role of councillors who are not members of the executive? Under the old system, all councillors were involved in decision-making by virtue of sitting on the council and its committees. In contrast, backbench councillors today appear to have a much more peripheral role (although this perhaps overstates the extent to which councillors outwith the inner circle would have directly influenced decision-making under the committee system).[130] Perhaps unsurprisingly, then, a parliamentary inquiry in 2002 expressed concern that so-called backbench councillors 'feel "excluded" from the decision-making process' and 'less well informed'.[131] The 2000 reforms justified these changes to the role of backbench councillors on two grounds. They would enable such councillors to focus on 'their vital representative work in the community' by freeing them from participation in 'largely unproductive committee meetings'.[132] But councillors also have a new role under the new system: they sit on 'overview and scrutiny' committees,[133] of which there must be at least one in each council operating executive arrangements. These are modelled on parliamentary select committees:[134] their membership cannot include executive members of the council[135] (just as Ministers may not sit on select committees) and they must be politically balanced.[136] The role of such committees is (*inter alia*) to

---

[126] Transport, Local Government and the Regions Select Committee, *How the Local Government Act 2000 is Working* (HC 602-I 2002), vol 1, p 13.

[127] HM Government, *The Coalition: Our Programme for Government* (London 2010), p 12.

[128] Local Government Act 2000, ss 33A and 33M, as inserted by the 2007 Act.

[129] *The Coalition: Our Programme for Government*, p 12.

[130] See Snape, 'Liberated or Lost Souls: Is there a Role for Non-Executive Councillors?', in Stoker and Wilson (eds), *Local Government into the 21st Century* (Basingstoke 2004), p 68.

[131] Transport, Local Government and the Regions Select Committee, *How the Local Government Act 2000 is Working* (HC 602-I 2002), p 7.

[132] Office of the Deputy Prime Minister, *Local Leadership, Local Choice* (Cm 4298 1999), [1.16].

[133] See Local Government Act 2000, s 21.   [134] On which, see Chapter 10, section 5.4, below.

[135] Local Government Act 2000, s 21(9).

[136] Local Government Act 2000, s 21(11)(b).

review, scrutinise, make reports on, and issue recommendations in respect of matters pertaining to the council's executive functions.[137] Overview and scrutiny committees may also recommend that decisions that have been taken (but not yet implemented) be reconsidered by the relevant executive member or even arrange for such matters to be dealt with by the whole council instead.[138]

The 2007 reforms sought to enhance the role of overview and scrutiny committees by, *inter alia*, legally requiring councils to respond publicly to such committees' recommendations within two months of their having been made.[139] It is also worth noting at this point that other aspects of the 2007 reforms seek to strengthen councils' capacity to put their own houses in order. Most notably, the 2007 Act enhanced the role of local authorities in investigating complaints of unethical conduct against individual councillors,[140] placing less reliance on external regulation of such matters.[141]

3.5.3 Elections

If local democracy is to thrive, and democratic control of local authorities is to be a reality, then as well as organising and structuring councils such that electorates can identify with them, understand what they do, and appreciate where power and responsibility lie, the electoral system must itself enable people to feel engaged with, and empowered to influence, local government.

These objectives have not always been realised in the recent past—something that is evidenced by far lower turnout in local than national elections, and in UK compared to many other European local elections[142]—and the situation has not been helped by inconsistent central government policy. In 1998, the government took the view that the interests of accountability and responsiveness to, and participation by, the electorate could best be served by frequent local elections. As a result, government announced its intention to extend the practice (already followed by some councils) of electing 'by thirds'.[143] Under this system, councillors serve a four-year term of office, and in years one, two, and three of the four-year cycle, one-third of councillors stand down and elections are held to fill the vacant seats.[144] In effect, therefore, one-third of the council is up for election almost every year, but the whole council is never elected at the same time.

There are obvious problems with such a system. Frequent elections can cause fatigue and confusion, with voters uncertain what exactly it is they are voting for—a prob-

---

[137] Local Government Act 2000, s 21(2).

[138] Local Government Act 2000, s 21(3).   [139] Local Government Act 2000, s 21B(3).

[140] See Local Government and Public Involvement in Health Act 2007, Pt 10, amending the Local Government Act 2000, Pt 3.

[141] In 2010, the coalition government announced that it would abolish the external regulator: see further section 3.4.2 above.

[142] For relevant statistics, see Office of the Deputy Prime Minister, *Local Leadership, Local Choice* (Cm 4298 1999), [1.18].

[143] Department for Environment, Transport and the Regions, *Modern Local Government: In Touch with the People* (Cm 4014 1998), ch 4.

[144] Of course, the councillors who were required to stand down can put themselves forward for re-election.

lem that is exacerbated where two-tier arrangements (county and district councils) remain in place.[145] Just as importantly, as the government recognised in a 2006 White Paper, the system of election by thirds creates a perception 'that the elector cannot affect the overall control of the council', thus discouraging voters from participating in local elections.[146] It is hardly surprising, therefore, that turnout in 'whole council' elections, in which all council seats are voted upon, is 'systematically higher compared to other authorities'.[147] In light of such concerns, the Electoral Commission, in 2004, recommended that all English local authorities should be elected via whole-council elections.[148] The government accepted the arguments in favour of such a change of policy,[149] and therefore made it easier for local authorities to shift to whole-council elections, although it did not go as far as to impose this model across the board.[150]

Finally, we should note that there are ways other than via the electoral system in which people can be made to feel involved, and to have a stake, in local government. For example, members of the public have recently been given the right to submit petitions to local authorities. Councils are required to act upon such petitions by, for example, discussing the matter at a council meeting or holding the relevant council officer to account via an overview and scrutiny committee.[151]

Q Think back over the three issues—the organisation of, structure of, and elections to local authorities—that we have discussed in this section. How would you sum up the various changes that have been made (and that we have outlined above) in each of these three areas? Do they imply a particular view of local government? In particular, do these changes strengthen or weaken local government as an autonomous tier of government within a pluralist, multilayered system?

4. Conclusions

In this chapter, we have seen that governance in the UK is, at least to some extent, multilayered. Although media coverage of matters pertaining to government and politics often focuses on the UK government, it does not enjoy a monopoly of power. In reality, the work of governing the UK is a shared endeavour—one that involves

[145] See section 3.5.1 above.

[146] Department for Communities and Local Government, *Strong and Prosperous Communities* (Cm 6939 2006), p 60. This perception has some foundation in reality: if no more than a third of seats are voted on at any one time, this reduces the likelihood that overall control of the council will change, although such change is of course possible if the largest party's majority is sufficiently small.

[147] Department for Communities and Local Government, Cm 6939.

[148] Electoral Commission, *The Cycle of Local Government Elections in England* (London 2004), p 21.

[149] Department for Communities and Local Government, Cm 6939, p 60.

[150] Local Government and Public Involvement in Health Act 2007, Pt 2.

[151] Local Democracy, Economic Development and Construction Act 2009, ss 10–22.

local authorities, the devolved institutions in Belfast, Cardiff, and Edinburgh, and (as we will see in the next chapter) the EU. This makes for a picture that is complicated (a term that we do not, at least here, intend pejoratively) and, to an extent, unfamiliar. The idea of the UK as a unitary state governed from the centre—always incorrect given the long tradition of local, alongside national, government—is an increasingly inaccurate one in light of developments such as devolution and EU membership. Although, as a matter of orthodox constitutional theory, most governmental power continues to emanate from, and can be recovered by, the UK Parliament, this sort of one-dimensional account of the constitution, founded on the doctrine of legislative supremacy, is becoming less and less sustainable. Our new constitutional reality is one in which the UK-tier authorities are part of a network of institutions of government, operating at local, devolved, state, and supranational levels. And the assumption that the UK tier holds the trump card by virtue of the sovereignty of the Westminster Parliament is increasingly misplaced as other seats of government become politically embedded aspects of our constitutional architecture. As the idea that governmental power is genuinely diffused among different institutions grows to be the new orthodoxy, so the notion of multilayered governance—of power shared by bodies with different roles and operating at different levels—takes root.

However, while it is important to recognise the changing dynamics within our constitution, it is also crucial not to exaggerate them. The essence of truly multilayered governance (as we use that term in this book) is a situation in which all power does not reside at, or emanate from, the centre because other institutions exist that enjoy a legitimacy and a status that lend them a degree of permanence, thus giving rise to a genuinely pluralist constitution. The extent to which the different layers of governance in the UK have achieved such standing is debatable—and variable. For example, the strength of feeling in favour of devolution and public attachment to, and identification with, the new institutions of government in Scotland confers upon them the sort of status that makes them secure features of the UK constitution—and a true example of its multilayered nature. However, local government, for reasons that we have explored, generally finds itself in a more fragile position.

The story of our multilayered constitution is therefore an uneven one. But it is also a story that is far from complete. The devolution settlement is deepening as the Welsh Assembly acquires more powers and Scotland explores the possibility of enhancing its legislative competence.[152] Meanwhile, change is afoot in local government. For decades, local government in the UK has been locked into a vicious circle: electors feel disconnected from it, perceiving it as amorphous, unaccountable, and unresponsive. Central government therefore seizes the initiative, placing local government in an ever-tighter straitjacket of regulation, control, and assessment. True autonomy thus seeps away from local government, electors feel increasingly disconnected, and so a self-sustaining cycle develops. As one commentator has put

---

[152] See section 2.3 above.

it: 'Small wonder...that national politicians bemoan participation rates or turnout figures at local elections. They are indeed risible. But why should people vote for organisations that have so little power to change things on the ground?'[153] There are, however, now signs that national policymakers—national, because it is, of course, they who are in overall control of the framework in which local government operates—are attempting to break this cycle by simultaneously extending the freedom of local authorities and enhancing voters' capacity to hold them to account. Should these endeavours prove successful, local government will have a stronger claim to be regarded as a real seat of power—and a pluralist counterweight to the centre—within our multilayered constitution.

Further reading

BOGDANOR, *Devolution in the United Kingdom* (Oxford 2001)

Report of the Calman Commission on Scottish Devolution, available online at **http://www .commissiononscottishdevolution.org.uk**

HAZELL (ed), *The English Question* (Manchester 2006)

HIMSWORTH AND O'NEILL, *Scotland's Constitution: Law and Practice* (Edinburgh 2003)

JENKINS, *Big Bang Localism* (London 2004)

JOWELL AND OLIVER (eds), *The Changing Constitution* (Oxford 2007), chs 9 (Winetrobe), 10 (McCrudden), 11 (Hadfield), and 12 (Leigh)

LEIGH, *Law, Politics, and Local Democracy* (London 2000)

LYONS, *Place-Shaping: A Shared Ambition for the Future of Local Government* (London 2007), available online at **http://www.lyonsinquiry.org.uk**

RAWLINGS, *Delineating Wales: Constitutional, Legal and Administrative Aspects of National Devolution* (Cardiff 2002)

Useful websites

http://www.scottish.parliament.uk
http://www.scotland.gov.uk
Websites of the Scottish Parliament and the Scottish Executive

http://www.niassembly.gov.uk
http://www.northernireland.gov.uk
Websites of the Northern Ireland Assembly and the Northern Ireland Executive

---

[153] White, 'From Herbert Morrison to Command and Control: The Decline of Local Democracy', available online at **http://www.historyandpolicy.org**

http://www.assemblywales.org
http://www.wales.gov.uk
Websites of the Welsh Assembly and the Welsh Assembly Government

http://www.lga.gov.uk
Website of the Local Government Association

8 The European Union

1. Introduction

The European Union (EU) is an unusual—in many ways unique—organisation. The member States of the EU have each entered into agreements that bind them in international law to work together so as to pursue a number of objectives, including the promotion of peace and well-being; sustainable development; economic growth; full employment; social progress; environmental protection; social justice; equality; the safeguarding of Europe's cultural heritage; economic and monetary union, including a single currency; and, in its relations with the rest of the world, free and fair trade, eradication of poverty, and protection of human rights.[1] But the international agreements, or treaties, establishing the EU do not merely state objectives; they also establish institutions—including a court, a legislature, and an executive branch—that in some respects make the EU look more like a state than an international organisation, and which ensure that the lofty aims spelt out in the treaties can be pursued in meaningful, concrete ways.

The law relating to the EU is a vast subject, and the purpose of this chapter is not by any means to summarise that body of law; rather, it has two, more specific objectives, both of which relate to the study of the EU as an aspect of United Kingdom constitutional law. First, we seek to convey a sense of what the EU is for, how and why it was formed, what it does, and how it does it. Second, we address the way in which the EU legal system interacts with those of members States—in particular, the UK.

The UK's membership of the EU illuminates and impacts upon the key themes of this book. EU membership is an important factor contributing to *the multilayered nature of the UK constitution*. In the EU, we encounter a striking example of how the notion of the UK as a unitary state, with power concentrated at the centre, is wholly inapposite. By joining the EU, the UK has transferred a significant amount of power, including considerable lawmaking power, to external institutions—a shift of authority that may be, for all practical purposes, irreversible. EU membership has therefore radically changed the landscape within which UK constitutional law falls to be understood. Most significantly, perhaps, the idea encountered in earlier chapters that

---

[1] Treaty on European Union, Art 3.

the British constitution lacks rigid dividing lines that place absolute limits on the powers of government—a notion that derives from the absence of a written constitution and which is most completely expressed in the orthodox notion of parliamentary sovereignty—finds itself under considerable pressure once account is taken of the legal consequences of Britain's membership of the EU. This, in turn, feeds into our second key theme—*the shift from political to legal constitutionalism*—to the extent that EU membership entails the imposition of absolute, legally enforceable limits on the powers of the UK's institutions of government. It will also be necessary to assess the implications of EU membership through the lens of our third theme—namely *the importance of effective systems of accountability*. The perceived absence of such systems is a running sore within discourse concerning the EU. It is epitomised in the charge levelled by its critics that the EU's legitimacy is fatally undermined by a so-called 'democratic deficit': that the EU is remote from, and ultimately unaccountable to, the peoples of the member States.

2. The EU in context

2.1 The development of the EU—four milestones

The roots of what we know today as the EU can be traced to the Treaty of Paris, which was signed by Belgium, West Germany, France, Italy, Luxembourg, and the Netherlands in 1951. It created the European Coal and Steel Community (ECSC)—a common market in coal and steel. This may seem a rather mundane matter, but, in the immediate aftermath of the Second World War, it was a radical and highly political step. As the French Foreign Minister Robert Schuman explained in 1950, introducing solidarity in relation to the extraction and production of coal and steel—two ingredients crucial to the economy of the industrialised Europe of the mid-twentieth century—was intended to 'make it plain that any war between France and Germany becomes not merely unthinkable, but materially impossible'.[2] This was, and was always meant to be, a precursor to embarking upon a more thoroughgoing project of European cooperation and integration—'the first concrete foundation of a European federation indispensable to the preservation of peace'.[3]

The second, and still the most significant, such foundation was laid in 1957 when the six ECSC members signed the Treaty establishing the European Economic Community (EEC Treaty)[4]—later known as the Treaty establishing the European Community (TEC)—as well as the Treaty establishing the European Atomic Energy Community ('Euratom'). The Preamble to the EEC Treaty records the member States' intentions to 'lay the foundations of an ever closer union among the peoples of Europe' and to

---

[2] Schuman Declaration, 9 May 1950.   [3] Schuman Declaration.
[4] Often referred to as the Treaty of Rome, after the city in which it was signed.

'ensure the economic and social progress of their countries by common action to eliminate the barriers which divide Europe'. The central idea underlying the EEC was, and remains, the creation of a common market based on 'four freedoms': the freedom of goods, persons, services, and capital to move between member States.[5] This explains why citizens of one member State have the right to live and work in any member State, and why manufacturers and producers have the right to export their goods from one such state to another without, *inter alia*, any requirement to pay customs duties.

The third milestone in the development of the EU was the Treaty on European Union (TEU, or the 'Maastrict Treaty'), which was signed in Maastricht in 1992 and introduced a number of important structural changes. Until the entry into force of the TEU, there had been no entity known as the 'European Union'; rather, there were the three separate Communities: the ECSC, Euratom, and the EEC. The Maastricht Treaty changed the name of the EEC to the European Community (EC), and placed the ECSC, Euratom, and the EC Treaties beneath a new overaching structure: the EU. It also introduced a framework for member States to work together in new policy areas such as policing, justice, foreign affairs, and security. But perhaps the most tangible consequence of the TEU was that it laid the legal basis for the introduction of a single European currency—the euro—now used in 17 member States, although not in the UK.

An important aspect of the EU's development not so far mentioned is its enlargement. Four main waves of growth saw additional western European countries—the UK, Denmark, and Ireland—join in 1973, followed by the southern countries of Greece, Spain, and Portugal in the 1980s, the northern states of Austria, Finland, and Sweden in 1995, and ten eastern European countries,[6] as well as Malta and Cyprus, in 2004–07. With a membership of 27 states (and thus a population of around 500 million), and a likelihood that it will expand further, the EU spent much of the last ten years thinking about how it should redesign itself to meet the challenges posed by its dramatic enlargement, as well as by dissatisfaction with certain aspects of how things are presently done.

This began with the creation in 2001 of the Convention on the Future of Europe, which was charged by the EU with the task of proposing constitutional changes in order to make the Union more democratic, transparent, and effective. This resulted in a Treaty establishing a Constitution for Europe.[7] However, in order to be implemented, the Constitutional Treaty had to be ratified—that is, approved—by all member States. In some states, this involved the holding of referendums, and in 2005, the electorates of France and the Netherlands voted against ratification. But many of the

---

[5] EC Treaty, Art 3(1). See generally Barnard, *The Substantive Law of the EU: The Four Freedoms* (Oxford 2007).

[6] Namely, Bulgaria, the Czech Republic, Estonia, Hungary, Latvia, Lithuania, Poland, Romania, Slovakia, and Slovenia.

[7] The final version of the Treaty can be found online at **http://eur-lex.europa.eu/JOHtml.do?uri=OJ:C :2004:310:SOM:en:HTML**. For discussion, see Kokott and Rüth, 'The European Convention and Its Draft Treaty Establishing a Constitution for Europe: Appropriate Answers to the Laeken Questions?' (2003) 40 CML Rev 1315; Tomkins, 'The Draft Constitution of the European Union' [2003] PL 571.

reforms that the Constitutional Treaty would have introduced re-emerged in the form of the Lisbon Treaty, which finally entered into force in December 2009, having initially been rejected in an Irish referendum, but approved at a second referendum in Ireland.[8] The Lisbon Treaty is, then, our fourth, and most recent, milestone. Two preliminary points about it should be noted.

First, the Lisbon Treaty amended the TEU, which sets out the EU's basic constitutional architecture. The Lisbon Treaty also renamed and substantially amended the TEC. That treaty is now known as the Treaty on the Functioning of the European Union (TFEU); it deals with more detailed matters such as the EU's specific legal powers. The most visible consequences of the Lisbon reforms are the creation of the new offices of President of the European Council, and High Representative of the Union for Foreign Affairs and Security Policy—popularly referred to as the EU President and EU Foreign Minister, respectively—but its implications are much more far-reaching than this. They will be addressed throughout this chapter.

Second—unhelpfully, but inevitably—the Lisbon amendments resulted in the renumbering of the provisions in the Treaties. Where key provisions in the post-Lisbon versions of those treaties have direct analogues in the pre-Lisbon versions, we give the numbers for both versions.

2.2 **The EU's areas of activity**

As noted above, the notion of the single market lies at the heart of the EU, and many, but by no means all, of the policies adopted and laws implemented by the EU relate directly to the single market. However, the EU's involvement is not limited to areas directly connected to the single market: for example, it is authorised to undertake such activities as research, technological development, space exploration,[9] and the provision of humanitarian aid.[10] In practical terms, the impact of the EU is felt in three main ways.

First, it *makes law*. Indeed, a great deal of the law now applicable in the UK, as in other member States, is either law enacted by the EU or domestic law enacted at its behest. Prominent and recent examples of laws authored by the EU and applicable in the UK (and in all other member States) include those that limit working time and require employees to be given paid annual leave,[11] require equal pay for men and women,[12] introduce a greenhouse gas emissions trading scheme within the EU,[13] make provision for the safety of consumer products,[14] enable the EU to take action to investigate and terminate anti-competitive practices,[15] set minimum levels of value

---

[8] See generally Dougan, 'The Treaty of Lisbon 2007: Winning Minds, Not Hearts' (2008) 45 CML Rev 617.   [9] TFEU, Art 4(3).
[10] TFEU, Art 4(4).   [11] Directive 2003/88/EC.   [12] Directive 2006/54/EC.
[13] Directive 2003/87/EC.   [14] Directive 2001/95/EC.
[15] Council Regulation (EC) No 1/2003.

added tax (VAT);[16] and require compensation to be paid to air passengers in the event of certain delays and cancellations.[17] This highly selective list merely gives an indication of the range of areas into which EU law reaches.

Second, the EU *redistributes wealth*. The money that is redistributed is acquired principally from national governments (and hence taxpayers), which generally pay into the EU in proportion to the size of their respective economies: at present, the EU's total income each year is approximately €140bn—just over 1 per cent of the combined gross national income of the member States.[18] Two main areas—'cohesion' and agriculture—account for the lion's share of the EU's expenditure. The former concerns measures to assist economically poorer regions of the EU by, for example, providing funds for the improvement of infrastructure. Meanwhile, the large proportion of the EU's budget devoted to agriculture is accounted for by the Common Agricultural Policy (CAP). Its objectives include increasing agricultural productivity, ensuring a fair standard of living for farmers, and assuring the availability of supply[19]—aims that reflect concerns that were particularly acute when the EEC, as it then was, was founded in the aftermath of the Second World War. The practice under the CAP of subsidising food production and buying up surpluses so as to ensure the security of the supply chain—thus literally creating EU wine lakes and grain mountains—was heavily criticised. The CAP has, however, been substantially reformed in recent years, and as a result its claim on the EU budget has fallen from (at its peak) roughly two-thirds to one-third.[20]

Third, the EU *facilitates cooperation between member States and the coordination of policy*. Of course, much of this is achieved by making EU laws laying down common standards throughout the Union; but much else is done in other ways. For example, it is increasingly the case that the member States adopt a coordinated approach to their relations with other (that is, non-EU) countries. Under its common foreign and security policy, the EU is an important player on the world stage, and its members increasingly project global influence by acting in concert rather than alone. The most tangible examples of this are the involvement of the EU member States' military and police forces—under the auspices of the EU, not of the individual states—in (among other places) the Balkans, the Democratic Republic of the Congo, Afghanistan, and the Middle East. The Lisbon Treaty has sought to lend greater coherence to the EU's external relations by creating, as noted above, the post of High Representative (or 'Foreign Minister'),[21] supported by a new EU diplomatic corps known as the External Action Service.

Q Are there particular issues for which you think the EU should or should not be responsible? What principles would you wish to see employed in determining those matters for which member States remain responsible and those in relation to which the EU has authority to adopt a coordinated, pan-European approach?

[16] Council Directive 2006/112/EC.   [17] Regulation (EC) No 261/2004.
[18] See further **http://ec.europa.eu/budget/index_en.htm**   [19] TFEU, Art 39.
[20] See further European Commission, *The Common Agricultural Policy Explained*, available online at **http://ec.europa.eu/agriculture/publi/capexplained/cap_en.pdf**   [21] TFEU, Art 18.

Legislative/scrutiny functions	Executive functions	Judicial functions
Parliament		
Commission	Commission	Court of Justice
Council		
Court of Auditors		

Figure 8.1 Institutional architecture

2.3 The institutional architecture of the EU

So much for what the EU does. *How* does it do it? In this section, we explain and evaluate the role of the EU's principal institutions.

2.3.1 Separation of powers–the Commission, the Council, and the Parliament

As Figure 8.1 shows, the EU fails, in two senses, to adhere to an orthodox conception of the separation of powers.[22] First, *the Commission straddles the distinction between executive and legislative functions.* The Commission is made up of one Commissioner from each of the member States, each of whom has responsibility for a particular portfolio (for example, trade, external relations, competition, and so on) and who must act independently rather than as a representative of the government responsible for his or her appointment.[23] However, unless the European Council unanimously decides otherwise, the number of Commissioners will be reduced by a third from November 2014.[24] This is one of the streamlining measures introduced by Lisbon in recognition of the growing membership of the EU.

In its *executive* guise, the Commission is responsible for seeing that EU law is applied: for example, it can take legal action against member States[25] or other EU institutions[26] that it believes to be in breach of EU law. But the Commission also has a pivotal *legislative* role: in general, a proposal from the Commission is required before the legislative process can get under way.[27] In this respect, a loose analogy may be drawn between the Commission and the executive branch in the UK: each is, within its respective system, the primary initiative-taker within the legislative process.

This leads on to the distinct, but related, point that the EU possesses *no single body that is identifiably the legislature*; rather, three institutions—the Commission, the Council, and the Parliament—are involved in the enactment of legislation. Once the Commission has initiated the process, its proposal is considered by the Parliament (considered below) and the Council.[28] The Council is, in a sense, the hardest of the EU institutions to place within a traditional tripartite separation-of-powers model.

---

22 On the separation of powers generally, see Chapter 3.   23 TEU, Art 17(4).
24 TEU, Art 17(5); TFEU, Art 244.   25 TFEU, Art 258 (formerly TEC, Art 226).
26 TFEU, Art 263 (formerly TEC, Art 230).   27 TFEU, Arts 289–294; Arts 251–252 EC.
28 TFEU, Art 294 (formerly TEC, Art 251).

It carries out 'policy-making and coordinating functions'[29] and plays a central role in the enactment of legislation. It is therefore best thought of primarily as a legislative institution—but one which has a somewhat unusual membership. It consists of 'a representative of each Member State at ministerial level, who may commit the government of the Member State in question and cast its vote'.[30] In practice, the membership of the Council is fluid: the Minister nominated by a member State to attend a particular Council meeting depends on the subject matter of the meeting.[31] For example, if the Council is to discuss economic matters, it will be the Finance Ministers who attend; if it is to discuss agricultural policy, the Agriculture Ministers will attend; and so on. Countries take it in turn to hold the presidency of the Council[32] (except when it meets to discuss foreign policy, when the EU 'Foreign Minister' presides[33]). Although, in theory, holding the presidency affords each member State an opportunity to shape the direction, including in terms of legislation, of EU policy, the fact that the presidency rotates every six months limits the practical capacity of the country holding it to engage in agenda-setting activity.

Moreover, the agenda-setting role of the Council is necessarily reduced by the existence, post-Lisbon, of a separate institution, known as the *European* Council. This used to be the informal name given to (usually biannual) meetings of heads of EU governments. However, as a result of the Lisbon Treaty, the European Council now constitutes a separate entity under the leadership of a President who will serve for a period of up to five years. Its role is to provide the 'necessary impetus for [the] development' of the EU and to 'define the general political directions and priorities thereof'.[34]

2.3.2 Democracy—the European Parliament

The third institution involved in the enactment of legislation is the European Parliament. Elections are held simultaneously every five years in all member States, with each member State sending to the Parliament a number of members of the European Parliament (MEPs) that relates to the size of its population.[35] The Parliament provides a form of interest representation that is more familiar than that supplied by the Council. Whereas the latter permits the advancement of specifically national interests, the Parliament functions, to an extent, as a more conventional legislature in which the dividing lines are political or philosophical rather than national. Although MEPs tend to be members of national political parties, many of those parties are, in turn, affiliated to larger groupings within the Parliament. As a result, the sort of dividing lines that are familiar within national political discourse—left-wing versus right-wing, socialism versus conservatism—are also evident in the European Parliament.

Representing a citizenry approximately 500 million-strong, the European Parliament is one of the world's largest democratic legislatures. It is therefore (at least *prima facie*) perverse that one of the most persistent criticisms levelled at the EU is that it suffers

---

[29] TEU, Art 16(1).   [30] TEU, Art 16(2).   [31] TEU, Art 16(6).   [32] TEU, Art 16(9).
[33] TEU, Art 18(3).   [34] TEU, Art 15.
[35] For example, Luxembourg has only 6 MEPs; Germany has 99.

from a 'democratic deficit'. The reasons for this are several, but one important factor is that, until recently, a substantial amount of EU legislation could be enacted without the consent of the Parliament—meaning that the EU's most obviously democratic institution was effectively sidelined. The Lisbon Treaty sought to address this problem by substantially expanding the range of legislation that can be enacted only with the consent of the Parliament. It did so by increasing the number of subject areas in which the 'ordinary legislative procedure' has to be used.[36] As Figure 8.2 shows, under this procedure, a proposal cannot become law without the Parliament's approval.

2.3.3 National interests and the legislative process—the Council

Although the EU undoubtedly represents an unparalleled example of nation states pooling resources and authority in order to further their common interests, it is impossible to escape the fact that individual states' interests do not always coincide. Until recently, this was reflected by the fact that states could generally veto legislative proposals—a situation attributable to the fact that Council decisions generally had to be made unanimously. However, as the EU has grown, unanimity has become harder to secure, and member States have—as a price that has to be paid if things are ever to be done—agreed, in many subject areas, to give up their veto powers.

Although there are still some areas in which unanimity is needed,[37] they are much fewer now that the Lisbon Treaty has entered into force. Today, in many areas, a system known as *qualified majority voting* (QMV) allows measures to be enacted—and thereafter to be applicable to *all* member States—even if some object; in other words, no single member State may veto a proposed measure. Under QMV, each member State has a number of votes relating to the size of its population: for example, Malta has three votes, while the UK has twenty-nine. In order for a proposal to be adopted, there must be at least 255 votes in favour (74 per cent of the total) *and* the countries casting those votes must account for at least 62 per cent of the EU population.[38] As a result of the Lisbon Treaty, the rules will change in November 2014. From then, each member State will have one vote, and a measure will be passed if it is supported by at least 55 per cent of member States, representing at least 65 per cent of the EU population.[39]

The debate about the acceptability of QMV (in place of a unanimity requirement) reflects a much deeper discourse about the nature of the EU itself. We noted in Chapter 7, when discussing devolution, that the extent to which the populations of different geographical areas within a country are willing to submit to common sets of laws, notwithstanding that some such laws might benefit some areas more than others, turns on whether those areas identify themselves as separate political units or as parts of a single political unit. If a given geographical area identifies itself as a distinct

---

[36] TFEU, Art 294.

[37] For example, decisions under the common security and defence policy can only be made on this basis: TEU, Art 42(4).   [38] TEU, Art 16(5); Protocol on Transitional Provisions, Art 3.

[39] TEU, Art 16(4). Moreover, a blocking minority must consist of at least four states: this means that a very small number of large states will be unable to block proposals. The old QMV arrangements may, at the request of a member State, be applied in a given case until 2017.

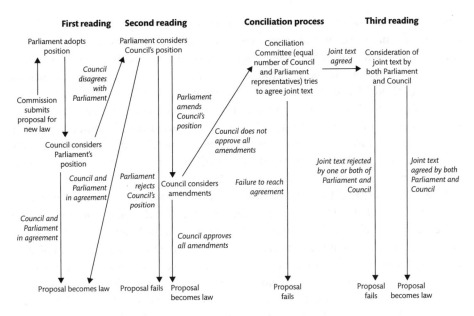

Figure 8.2 The ordinary legislative procedure

political unit (as is the case, to an extent, in relation to Scotland within the UK), its population is less likely to be prepared to tolerate what might be perceived as the imposition of laws by a central legislature that may favour the interests of other areas (for example, England). These issues also arise—in a more acute form—in relation to the EU. It is for precisely that reason that national interests are explicitly represented in the legislative process through the medium of the Council—but the extent to which the Council facilitates the prosecution of such interests is clearly limited if QMV, rather than unanimity, applies. Following the 2010 general election, the UK's coalition government signaled its resistance to the extension of QMV.[40]

> **Q** Why do you think the issues referred to above may arise 'in a more acute form' in relation to the EU than in relation to a single state such as the UK? What do you think might be the principal obstacles to member States' willingness to give up their national veto in particular policy areas?

2.3.4 Accountability—Parliament and the courts

In most constitutional systems, the Parliament is responsible not only for legislating, but also for holding the executive branch to account. The view that the EU suffers

[40] It said that it would amend the European Communities Act 1972 so as to require primary legislation before Ministers would be permitted to agree to any such extension: HM Government, *The Coalition: Our Programme for Government* (London 2010), p 19.

from a democratic deficit reflects the perception held in some quarters that the EU is a distant and remote organisation over which individual citizens have little influence or control, and which is not sufficiently accountable for its use of public power and money. The Lisbon Treaty attempts to introduce some innovations in this regard, such as requiring national Parliaments to be consulted as part of the EU lawmaking process[41] and requiring the Commission to consider proposing legislation when requested to do so by at least 1 million EU citizens.[42] The general requirement of 'subsidiarity'—that the EU should act only if action at member State level would not be appropriate[43]—is also given some teeth by allowing national Parliaments to object (but not to veto) legislative proposals on subsidiarity grounds.[44]

However, a deeper difficulty is that the levers of democratic control do not work in relation to the EU in the same way as they function in relation to, for example, the UK government. If the British public is dissatisfied with the latter, it can precipitate a change of government at the next election. No equivalent democratic mechanism is open to EU citizens who disapprove of how the EU is run. Although they can vote in elections to the European Parliament, membership of that Parliament has no effect upon the identity or political outlook of the Commissioners and Council Members who, as we have seen, find themselves in the driving seat when it comes to initiating and pushing through legislative changes. And although citizens in a given state can, in theory, exert pressure on their national government with respect to who it nominates as its Commissioner and how its Ministers bargain at Council meetings, voters in one state have no way of influencing the behaviour of the other 26 Commissioners and the other 26 Council Members.

As in most systems, the EU has legal, as well as political, accountability mechanisms. The Court of Justice of the European Union (CJEU) consists of judges drawn from across the EU who must be relevantly legally qualified persons 'whose independence is beyond doubt'.[45] Many of the Court's functions are connected with ensuring that EU law is correctly interpreted and applied by and within the member States—functions that we consider below.[46] But the Court also plays an important role in ensuring that institutions of the EU act lawfully. Thus it is possible, under TFEU, Art 263,[47] for proceedings to be initiated before the Court by individuals, member States, and certain EU institutions for judicial review of the legality of action taken by the Parliament, the Council, the Commission, and the European Central Bank (ECB). The Court can intervene if the relevant institution has acted beyond its legal powers—the EU has only those powers conferred upon it by the Treaty[48]—or has infringed an 'essential procedural requirement', acted contrary to the EU Treaty or any relevant rule of law, or has otherwise misused its powers.

---

[41] Protocol on the Role of National Parliaments in the EU.   [42] TEU, Art 11(4).
[43] TEU, Art 5(3).   [44] Protocol on the Principles of Subsidiarity and Proportionality, Arts 6 and 7.
[45] TFEU, Art 254.   [46] See section 3 below.   [47] Formerly TEC, Art 230.
[48] TEU, Art 5 (formerly TEC, Art 5).

Many of the misgivings that contribute to the perception that the EU is not properly accountable relate to concerns about financial probity. In this context, the Court of Auditors plays a central role. Its name notwithstanding, this body is not a court in the normal sense of that word, but the EU's auditing agency. It is then more closely analogous to the UK's National Audit Office,[49] in that it is an independent (but not judicial) body responsible for scrutinising the way in which money is spent. Its tasks are, *inter alia*, to 'examine the accounts of all revenue and expenditure of the Union' and to 'examine whether all revenue has been received and all expenditure incurred in a lawful and regular manner and whether the financial management has been sound'.[50] The Court is also required each year to provide the Council and the Parliament with a 'statement of assurance as to the reliability of the accounts and the legality and regularity of the underlying transactions'[51]—something that it frequently finds itself unable to do.[52] The Commission, however, points out that the Court's inability to give the accounts an entirely clean bill of health is not necessarily indicative of fraud, and may be attributable to less sinister causes such as 'inadequate documentation'.[53] In a report published in 2009, the Court acknowledged that the Commission had made progress in relation to its systems for supervising and controlling expenditure, albeit that these had been more successful in some areas of activity than in others.[54]

3. **EU law and national law**

Having looked at what the EU does, and at the various institutions that comprise it, it is now necessary to turn our attention to a more specific matter. If the EU is to achieve its objectives, it is often necessary for it to make law that applies throughout the 27 member States. For example, in order to facilitate the free movement of workers, it was necessary to enact legislation concerning the recognition of professional qualifications.[55] Requiring member States to adopt common legal rules on this matter—under which, *inter alia*, certain qualifications obtained in one member State must be automatically recognised by others—makes it easier for professionals who are qualified in one member State to work in another; this, in turn, helps to make the single market a reality.

It is self-evident, however, that the EU will only be able to use law as an instrument of policy in this way—that is, as a way of advancing its purposes—if two conditions are met. First, EU law must be enforceable in member States' courts. Second, member

---

[49] See Chapter 11, section 4.1.2, below.   [50] TFEU, Art 287(1)–(2).   [51] TFEU, Art 287(1).
[52] See, eg its 2008 Annual Report, pp 12–13, available online at **http://eca.europa.eu/portal/pls/ portal/docs/1/3258349.PDF**
[53] *EU Spending: A Myth-Buster*, p 3, available online at **http://ec.europa.eu/budget/library/ publications/financial_pub/pub_eu_spending_en.pdf**
[54] Court of Auditors, *Annual Report for Financial Year 2008*, at pp 60–1, available online at **http://eca .europa.eu/portal/pls/portal/docs/1/3258349.PDF**   [55] Directive 2005/36/EC.

States must not be allowed to pick and choose the EU laws that are permitted to operate within their national legal systems, since it is central to the purpose and ethos of the EU that common legal standards must (in relevant fields) apply throughout the Union. In other words, EU law must take priority over any conflicting domestic law.

3.1 **Types of EU law**

The two requirements set out above are, as we will see, met through the principles, developed by the CJEU, of *direct effect* and *supremacy*. Before addressing those principles, however, it is necessary to say something about the different types of EU law that exist. A good deal of such law is contained in the treaties themselves. For example, TFEU, Art 30 prohibits (*inter alia*) customs duties on imports and exports between member States, thus helping to facilitate free movement of goods. This part of the TFEU can properly be thought of as a law, in that it sets out a specific, prescriptive rule that is directly enforceable in courts.[56] However, the treaties often serve not as a source of *law*, but as a source of *lawmaking authority*, laying down general principles with a view to the EU enacting more specific measures that will give effect to them. For example, TFEU, Arts 191–192 authorise the enactment of legislation for the purpose of 'preserving, protecting and improving the quality of the environment'. So, as Figure 8.3 indicates, the relationship between the treaties and (other forms of) Union legislation is analogous to that which exists between a national constitution and legislation enacted thereunder, or between Acts of Parliament and secondary legislation. This analysis requires elaboration of two further points.

The first is that the EU is allowed to do only those things that the treaties authorise it to do: it has no 'inherent' or 'original' power.[57] Hence there is no question of the EU enjoying 'sovereign' lawmaking power in the way that the UK Parliament (at least on a traditional analysis) does; rather, the EU finds itself in a position much more closely analogous to that of a legislature operating in a state that possesses a written constitution which defines the respective powers of the branches of government. In this sense, the treaties can quite sensibly be thought of as the EU's constitution. Its legislative acts are therefore vulnerable to judicial review if, for example, they are enacted in a constitutionally unauthorised manner[58] or if they deal with subject areas with which the EU has not been authorised to deal.

Second, there are two principal types of legislation the enactment of which is authorised by the treaties: *regulations* and *directives*.[59] TFEU, Art 288[60] states: 'A regulation shall have general application. It shall be binding in its entirety and directly

---

[56] Case 26/62 *Van Gend En Loos* [1963] ECR 1.   [57] TEU, Art 5 (formerly TEC, Art 5).

[58] Case C/84-94 *United Kingdom v Council* [1996] ECR I-5755, [1996] 3 CMLR 671.

[59] We do not here address a third form of legislation, known as 'decisions', in any detail. It is sufficient for present purposes to say that decisions are equivalent to regulations, save that the former are binding only upon those individuals to whom they are addressed, whereas the latter are of general application.

[60] Formerly TEC, Art 249.

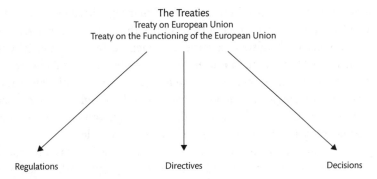

Figure 8.3 Types of EU law

applicable in all Member States.' Regulations are thus, in one sense, the most easily understood form of Union legislation, since they possess the characteristics that we usually associate with laws in that they are binding upon the whole world and are legally enforceable. In contrast, TFEU, Art 288 provides that 'A directive shall be binding, as to the result to be achieved, upon each Member State to which it is addressed, but shall leave to the national authorities the choice of form and methods'. This suggests that directives merely constitute an instruction to member States to take whatever steps are necessary in terms of enacting domestic law to see that the requirements laid down in the directive are fulfilled.

3.2 **Direct effect**

3.2.1 **The reasons for, and nature of, the principle**

We have already seen that there exists, in the form of the CJEU, a mechanism for enforcing EU law. For example, it is possible for the Commission and member States to issue proceedings in the CJEU if they believe that a member State is acting contrary to EU law; if so, and if the state in question fails to comply with the judgment of the Court, then the Court can impose financial penalties.[61] And it is possible for national courts, under TFEU, Art 267,[62] to refer to the CJEU questions concerning the interpretation of Union law.

However, it is both necessary and desirable that responsibility for enforcing EU law should not rest exclusively with the CJEU. As the CJEU has explained, the EU is intended to constitute a 'new legal order..., the subjects of which comprise not only the Member States but also their nationals'.[63] It follows that Union law does not merely create legal obligations and rights for the *states*; the Court famously said in the *Van Gend en Loos* case that it also imposes 'obligations on individuals' and is 'intended to

---

[61] TFEU, Arts 258–260 (formerly TEC, Arts 226–228).   [62] Formerly TEC, Art 234.
[63] *Van Gend En Loos* at 12.

confer upon them rights which become part of their legal heritage'.[64] The legal system created by the EU treaties therefore straddles the distinction between international and national law: the system exists because member States created it by entering into agreements that bind them in *international* law—but, having done so, they have opened the doors of their respective *national* legal systems to EU law. Individuals within the member States are intended to acquire new legal rights and responsibilities by virtue of the operation of EU law, and if those new rights and responsibilities are to exist in any meaningful sense, they must be legally enforceable.

This points towards two conclusions. First, because the EU exists in this sense—that is, as a legal system affecting the 500 million or so people, rather than only its 27 constituent states—it would be impossible for the CJEU to deal with all cases concerning alleged breaches of EU law. In practice, it is necessary for the many thousands of member States' courts to be involved in the enterprise of adjudicating upon disputes concerning, and thus enforcing, Union law. Second, the involvement of national courts is appropriate in philosophical, as well as pragmatic, terms: EU law is not meant to be something exotic, which stands apart from national law; it is supposed to become part of the 'legal heritage', as the Court put it, of individuals and member States, and as such should be enforceable in just the same way as other applicable (national) legal norms.

For these reasons, the CJEU, in the very early days of what we now call the EU, developed the principle of direct effect. At root, this can be explained very simply: the EU laws to which the principle applies are enforceable in ordinary legal proceedings before national courts without further ado. It follows that national courts must now resolve legal disputes by applying both relevant domestic law and directly effective EU law: the latter is just as much a part of the applicable body of law as the former.[65] It is therefore commonplace for individuals to take action in national courts against the government, companies, and other individuals in order to enforce rights derived from EU law just as they do in relation to rights granted by national law.

3.2.2 **Regulations and treaty provisions**

How do we know whether a given EU law is directly effective? The answer, as Figure 8.4 indicates, is that it depends on the *type* of EU law concerned.

The position in relation to *regulations* is the most straightforward: all regulations have direct effect.[66] There is a clear basis for this in the Treaty—TFEU, Art 288 says that a regulation is 'binding in its entirety and directly applicable in all Member States'— and the CJEU therefore had little difficulty in arriving at the view that regulations are directly effective.[67]

In contrast, the treaties do not explicitly say that *treaty provisions* themselves are directly effective. Nevertheless, the Court held in *Van Gend En Loos* that the doctrine

---

[64] *Van Gend En Loos* at 12.

[65] Indeed, the primacy doctrine, the meaning of which we set out below, means that EU law is ultimately *more important* than domestic law.

[66] The same is true of decisions: see TFEU, Art 288; *Franz Grad v Finanzamt Traustein* [1970] ECR 825, [5].   [67] Case 39/72 *Commission v Italy* [1973] ECR 101, [17].

Type of EU law	Directly effective?
Regulations	Yes
Treaty provisions	Only if unconditional and sufficiently precise
Directives	Only against the state, and even then only if
	(a) the implementation date has passed, and
	(b) the provisions are unconditional and sufficiently precise

Figure 8.4 Direct effect

of direct effect was, for the reasons considered in the last section, in principle applicable to treaty provisions. However, whereas regulations are inevitably drafted with the intention of being enforceable—and therefore are, or at least should be, worded with the sort of precision that makes it possible for courts to make sense of them—that is not true of every part of the treaties. Thus the CJEU has held that treaty provisions will only be enforceable in national courts if they meet certain conditions for direct effect. Those conditions, which have been relaxed over the years, are that the provision in question must be 'unconditional' (meaning that it must set out 'an obligation which is not qualified by any condition, or subject, in its implementation or effects, to the taking of any measure either by the Community institutions or by the Member States') and 'sufficiently precise' (in the sense of being 'unequivocal').[68] Ultimately, these conditions reduce to a test of justiciability: is the provision clear and complete enough to be capable of being applied as a legal rule? It follows that while certain treaty provisions, such as TFEU, Art 30—which, as noted above, lays down a clear rule banning customs duties on goods moving between member States—are directly effective,[69] many, such as TFEU, Art 145—which requires member States and the EU to 'work towards developing a coordinated strategy for employment'—are not.

3.2.3 Directives

In a perfect world, it would be unnecessary to consider whether *directives* are or should be capable of direct effect. As explained above, member States are required to take all necessary steps to ensure that, by whatever deadline is stated in it, national law complies with the terms of the directive. If all member States always were to do so, it would never be necessary to attempt to invoke directives before national courts because national law would make substantively identical provision. This, as we have seen, and as Figure 8.5 illustrates, represents the principal distinction between directives, on the one hand, and regulations,[70] on the other: the latter puncture the distinction between European and national law by automatically becoming enforceable in domestic courts, whereas the former are only intended to stimulate the amendment by national legislative authorities of domestic law.

---

[68] Joined Cases C 246–249/94 *Cooperativa Agricola Zootecnica S Antonio v Amministrazione delle Finanze dello Stato* [1997] 1 CMLR 1112.   [69] *Van Gend En Loos.*

[70] And, as discussed above, certain Treaty provisions.

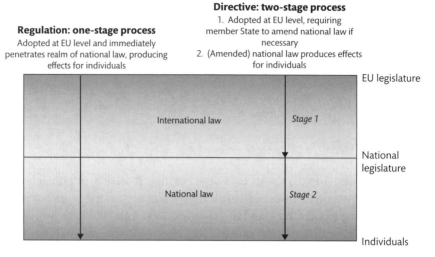

Figure 8.5 Direct effect—regulations and directives compared

But what if a member State fails to implement (either at all or correctly) a directive? Is the directive itself enforceable—can it have directive effect? Faced with this question, the CJEU has found itself walking something of tightrope. On the one hand, it has, as we have seen, taken the general view that EU law should be enforceable (in order that the EU may take effect as a real legal order): this suggests that directives should be directly effective, so as to ensure that, whether by accident or design, they cannot be rendered unenforceable by the failure of member States correctly to implement them. On the other hand, TFEU, Art 288 seems to indicate with reasonable clarity that directives are not directly effective.

In an attempt to resolve the tension between these competing forces, the Court has held that directives may have direct effect—but only in limited circumstances. First, and unsurprisingly, the conditions for direct effect must be met, so only those parts of directives that are *clear and unconditional* (in the senses set out above) can have direct effect.[71] Second, as mentioned above, directives specify a date by which they must be accommodated within national law, and it has been held that directives can only acquire direct effect once that *implementation period has expired*.[72] Third, directives are capable only of *vertical, not horizontal, direct effect*.[73] This means that (if the first two conditions are met) they can be enforced by citizens in legal proceedings against the state (so they have *vertical* effect—that is, they are effective as against state bodies), but not against other parties such as individuals

---

[71] Case 41/74 *Van Duyn v Home Office (No 2)* [1974] ECR 1337.

[72] Case 148/78 *Pubblico Ministero v Ratti* [1979] ECR 1629.

[73] Case 152/84 *Marshall v Southampton and South West Hampshire Area Health Authority* [1986] ECR 723, Case C-91/92 *Faccini Dori v Recreb Srl* [1995] 1 CMLR 665.

and companies (so they have no *horizontal* effect—that is, they are ineffective as against non-state bodies).

3.2.4 Why vertically, but not horizontally, effective?

On the face of it, it seems arbitrary that directives can be enforced only against state bodies. However, the Court has identified a justification for permitting directives to have vertical, but not horizontal, effect. The *default position* must, because of what is said in TFEU, Art 288, be that directives do not have any direct effect—but it is legitimate to carve out an *exception* to that rule to the extent that it would, if applied, produce unconscionable results. This can best be explained by reference to an example.

> Assume: that the EU adopts a directive requiring member States to ensure that all employees have the right to work in a smoke-free environment, that a given state fails to implement the directive by the relevant date, and that two people wish to sue their respective employers—a government department and a private company—for failing to provide such an environment. Ideally, they would each like a court order requiring the provision of such an environment: in other words, they want to enjoy the substance of the benefit referred to in the directive.

The government employee would be seeking to enforce the directive vertically. If the general principle that directives do not have direct effect were applied in such a case, the defendant (the state) would be able to evade liability by arguing that the directive, lacking direct effect, cannot be enforced. This would, in effect, reduce the state to pleading its own unlawful inaction—that is, its failure to implement the directive—as a defence, and would offend against the general principle of fairness, known as the *estoppel principle*, which holds that no one should be allowed to profit (for example, by escaping legal liability) from their own unlawful conduct. The doctrine of vertical effect prevents states from profiting in that way.[74]

But the same point does not apply when the case is a horizontal one. If an employee sues a company complaining that a smoke-free environment has not been provided, there is nothing unconscionable in the company relying on the state's failure to implement the directive. In doing so, it would not be profiting from any unlawful conduct on its own part, because it was never its responsibility to enact a national law entitling employees to a smoke-free working environment. In horizontal cases, then, there is no justification for departing from the general rule, as set down in TFEU, Art 288, that directives do not have direct effect. Indeed, as the Court has recognised, if directives were capable of horizontal as well as vertical effect, this would largely assimilate them with regulations. This, the Court maintains, would be unacceptable, because it would disregard the clear distinction drawn in the Treaty between regulations and directives.[75]

---

[74] *Faccini Dori* at [23].   [75] *Faccini Dori* at [24].

3.2.5 **The scope of the vertical direct effect doctrine**

If directives are capable only of vertical, and not horizontal, direct effect, it is important to know where and how to draw the line between those two categories. If directives, to the extent that they are not (correctly) implemented in national law, can be enforced only against state bodies, exactly what is a 'state body'? The discussion in the last section points towards an obvious answer to this question. If the justification for vertical effect is to preclude state bodies benefitting (by escaping legal liability) from their wrongful failure to take steps to implement directives, then surely the vertical effect doctrine should apply only to those state bodies responsible for taking such steps. This suggests that a very narrow range of public bodies—for example, central government departments responsible for seeing that EU law is implemented—should be subject to vertical effect. However, in this sphere, as in many others, the Court has felt the strong pull of its desire to see that EU law is as effective as possible.[76] It has therefore defined the state in much broader terms—thereby ensuring that unimplemented (or incorrectly implemented) directives are enforceable against a wide range of defendants—by reference to such factors as whether the defendant is responsible for providing a public service, has special powers, and is under government control.[77] These tests are applied in a relaxed fashion: they are merely 'indicia which point to the appropriateness of treating the body in question as an emanation of the state', and courts should therefore refer to them simply as guidelines rather than as absolute preconditions all of which must be met before the defendant can be characterised as a state body.[78] As well as central government departments, it has been held that unimplemented directives can be enforced against the police,[79] publicly run hospitals,[80] nationalised utility companies,[81] privatised utility companies,[82] and even a Church of England primary school.[83]

> **Q** Is it acceptable for the CJEU to have characterised public authorities so broadly? Has it managed satisfactorily to balance fidelity to the treaties with its policy of ensuring the effectiveness of EU law?

The CJEU's case law notwithstanding, many defendants remain immune from claims arising from unimplemented directives because they cannot be characterised as state bodies. Individuals who want to rely on unimplemented directives against such bodies cannot do so. This is problematic for two reasons: it compromises the effectiveness

---

[76] See further Spink, 'Direct Effect: The Boundaries of the State' (1997) 113 LQR 524.

[77] Case C-188/89 *Foster v British Gas plc* [1991] 1 QB 405.

[78] *National Union of Teachers v Governing Body of St Mary's Church of England (Aided) Junior School* [1997] 3 CMLR 630.

[79] Case 222/84 *Johnston v Chief Constable of the Royal Ulster Constabulary* [1987] QB 129.

[80] *Marshall v Southampton and South West Hampshire Area Health Authority (No 2)* [1994] 1 AC 530.

[81] *Foster v British Gas plc* [1991] 2 AC 306.

[82] *Griffin v South West Water Services Ltd* [1995] IRLR 15.   [83] *St Mary's School.*

of EU law; and it creates arbitrary distinctions. In the example given above, the government employee is able to enforce the right to a smoke-free environment, yet the company employee is not. For both of these reasons, the CJEU, as Figure 8.6 shows, has developed four ways of filling the gap left by the fact that directives are incapable of horizontal effect.

3.2.6 Indirect effect

The doctrine of indirect effect goes some distance towards doing so. TEU, Art 4(3) requires member States to 'take any appropriate measure' to fulfil their obligations under EU law. This means, *inter alia*, that each state authority is expected to play its own part in ensuring that the obligations placed on member States by directives are fulfilled. Most obviously, legislative authorities are required to take the necessary steps to make sure that national law is drafted in a way that gives effect to the directive. However, the Court has held that (the predecessor to) TEU, Art 4(3) also applies to national courts.[84] If, therefore, a given member State's legislature fails to take steps to implement a directive, its courts are nevertheless required to do 'whatever lies within [their] jurisdiction, having regard to the whole body of rules of national law, to ensure that [the directive is] fully effective'.[85]

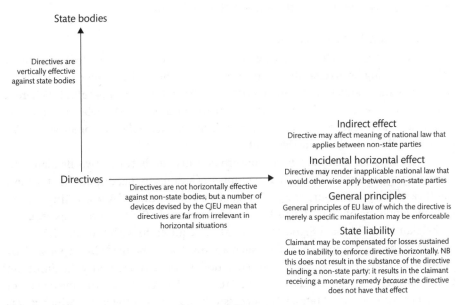

Figure 8.6 The legal effects of unimplemented directives

---

[84] Case 14/83 *Von Colson v Land Nordrhein-Westfalen* [1984] ECR 1891, [26].

[85] Case C-397/01 *Pfeiffer v Deutsches Rotes Kreuz, Kreisverband Waldshut Ev* [2005] 1 CMLR 44, [118]. This obligation of consistent interpretation is not restricted to directives: all legislation must, whenever possible, be interpreted compatibly with all relevant forms of EU law.

Reverting to the example given above, assume that a particular member State has taken no steps to enact specific legislation entitling workers to a smoke-free environment, but that national law already requires employers to provide a 'safe and healthy working environment'. The principle of indirect effect would enable an employee to sue his private sector employer for failing to provide a smoke-free environment by arguing that it is possible—and therefore compulsory—for national courts to interpret the domestic requirement of a 'safe and healthy' environment as including a working environment free from smoke. Crucially, such an argument would be open to someone taking legal action against a non-state body—but, for two reasons, it does not equate to the conferral of direct (horizontal) effect on the directive. Indirect effect is *conceptually distinct* from direct effect: whereas the latter enables the claimant to enforce the directive itself against the defendant, the former involves the enforcement of national law—albeit national law the meaning of which has been determined in the light of the unimplemented directive. Moreover, indirect effect is *not a panacea*: it can only work if national laws already exist that are amenable to being interpreted in a way that gives effect to the directive. If, in our example, no national law were to exist concerning the working environment—or if national law specifically were to say that employers were *not* required to provide a smoke-free environment—it simply would not be possible for national courts to interpret domestic law in line with the directive, and an argument based on indirect effect would therefore be doomed to failure.

3.2.7 Incidental horizontal effect

A second way in which unimplemented (or incorrectly implemented) directives, although lacking horizontal direct effect, may nevertheless have some impact other than upon state bodies is via the doctrine of *incidental horizontal effect*. Whereas indirect effect results in the modification of the *meaning* of the relevant domestic law, incidental direct effect is concerned with the *enforceability* of domestic law. An example will help to illustrate the point.

CIA Security SA v Signalson SA concerned a dispute between two Belgian suppliers of burglar alarms.[86] There were a number of strands to that dispute, but the most significant, for present purposes, was Signalson's claim that CIA was acting unlawfully by supplying burglar alarms that had not received official approval as required by Belgian law. CIA, said Signalson, should be required to withdraw its alarm system from the market until or unless such approval was obtained. In response, CIA pointed out that an EU directive required national authorities to notify the European Commission if they proposed to enact certain laws that restrict the free movement of goods between member States. CIA successfully argued that the law of which it was allegedly in breach fell into that category, and that the requisite notification had not been given. The CJEU held that the Belgian law in question was therefore unenforceable, that CIA was therefore not acting unlawfully, and that, as a result, it was free to continue to market its product notwithstanding the absence of official approval.

---

[86] Case C-194/94 *CIA Security SA v Signalson SA* [1996] ECR I-2201.

This illustrates the operation of the principle of incidental horizontal effect, and the ways in which it differs from related principles. CIA did not *enforce* the directive against Signalson as such, and therefore the directive cannot be said to have been accorded *full horizontal effect*. Nor was the directive used to assist with the *interpretation* of national law, meaning that the principle of *indirect effect* was not in play. Rather, the principle of incidental horizontal effect, as applied in this case, means that when a directive is sufficiently clear and precise, it will render any conflicting domestic law unenforceable, including in legal proceedings between private parties. As a result, directives that have not been implemented (in the sense that national law does not fully comply with them) may nevertheless affect the legal position as between private parties: thus, in the case considered above, the directive precluded Signalson from invoking Belgian law so as to stop CIA from marketing its product.[87]

3.2.8 State liability

All of the devices so far considered for ameliorating the impact of the absence of horizontal direct effect have one thing in common: they make it possible for cases to be decided in ways that are consistent with directives that have not been properly implemented in national law. The state liability principle, in contrast, may assist when cases *cannot* be decided in a way that is consistent with the directive.[88] The state liability principle facilitates the payment of money to compensate an individual who, because the state has failed to implement a directive fully or at all, is denied some right or benefit that would otherwise have been enjoyed.

This point can be illustrated by referring back to our example. Imagine that a member State fails by the due date to implement the directive concerning the provision of smoke-free working environments, that national law cannot be interpreted as requiring such provision, that the claimant works for a company that cannot be regarded as a state body, and that the claimant is allergic to cigarette smoke. In such circumstances, there is no prospect of the claimant being able to enforce the directive against his employer,[89] meaning that there are no legal means at his disposal for securing the substantive benefit—that is, a smoke-free working environment—envisaged by the directive. The question then becomes whether the claimant can obtain damages to compensate him for the fact that he is being denied that benefit. Faced with a question

---

[87] While this may appear to be a substantial exception to the rule that directives do not have horizontal effect, it seems that its compass may be restricted to 'public' directives that are addressed principally to the exercise of member States' powers, as distinct from directives that predominantly concern legal relationships between individuals. See further Dashwood, 'From *Van Duyn* to *Mangold* via *Marshall*: Reducing Direct Effect to Absurdity?', in Barnard (ed), *Cambridge Yearbook of European Law*, vol 9 (Oxford 2007).

[88] This is not to imply that state liability is simply a substitute for direct effect. In appropriate fact situations, claimants may seek to enforce a right contained in a directive *and* obtain compensation, under the state liability principle, for past denials of the right.

[89] Because this is clearly a horizontal, not a vertical, situation, and none of the principles considered above would provide any assistance: in particular, the doctrine of indirect effect would not be of any help in light of the fact that national law is clearly inconsistent with the directive.

of this type in *Francovich*, the CJEU developed the principle of state liability.[90] The Court concluded that its policy of attempting to ensure the 'full effectiveness' of EU law would be thwarted 'if individuals were unable to obtain compensation when their rights are infringed by a breach of [Union] law for which a member-State can be held responsible'.[91] Put bluntly, the Court was saying that if an individual is denied EU law rights through the unlawful action (or inaction) of a member State, that state should be responsible for compensating the individual. Over time, the conditions for state liability have been refined, and the current position is that the individual will be able to recover damages if

(i)   the directive 'intended to confer rights on individuals',

(ii)   the state's breach of EU law is 'sufficiently serious', and

(iii)   there is a 'direct causal link between the breach...and the damage sustained by the injured [party]'.[92]

It is unnecessary to say much about the first and third conditions: the former will depend on the wording of the directive, while the latter has to be determined by domestic courts applying national rules on causation.[93] The second condition requires more detailed explanation. Its purpose is to draw a line between those breaches of EU law for which member States can and cannot be held liable in damages. The Court has indicated that, in deciding whether any given breach is sufficiently serious, it will consider such matters as the clarity and precision of the EU law that has been breached, whether the breach and the damage thereby caused was intentional, and whether any legal error committed by the member State is excusable or inexcusable.[94] In practice, where a member State is under a specific obligation to enact national law implementing a directive that is clear, it will almost inevitably be guilty of a sufficiently serious breach.[95] On the other hand, a member State may be able to escape liability where it has taken some steps to implement a directive, but, in doing so, turns out to have misunderstood what the directive requires such that national law is imperfectly aligned with the directive. When such circumstances arose in *Denkavit*, the CJEU held that the member State concerned should not be held liable to pay compensation because it, like several other states, had adopted a reasonable—albeit incorrect—interpretation of an ambiguous directive.[96]

---

[90] Cases C-6/90 and 9/90 *Francovich v Italy* [1991] ECR I-5357.   [91] *Francovich* at [33].

[92] Joined Cases C-46/93 and C-48/93 *Brasserie du Pecheur SA v Federal Republic of Germany; R v Secretary of State for Transport, ex p Factortame (No 4)* [1996] QB 404, [51].

[93] *Factortame (No 4)* at [65]. Other relevant national rules, eg as to procedure, can be applied to state liability claims, provided that they are not less favourable than those rules applicable to equivalent claims under domestic law: Case C-118/08 *Transportes Urbanos v Administracion del Estado* [2010] 2 CMLR 39.

[94] *Factortame (No 4)* at [56].

[95] Case C-5/94 *R v Ministry of Agriculture, Fisheries and Food, ex p Hedley Lomas (Ireland) Ltd* [1997] QB 139, [28].

[96] Case C-283/94 *Denkavit International BV v Bundesamt fur Finanzen* [1996] ECR I-5063.

As we have seen, state liability was originally developed to compensate claimants unable to secure rights due to them under unimplemented (or incorrectly implemented) directives. But the principle is now acknowledged to be much more widely applicable.[97] It is therefore possible, for example, to claim damages where the state has breached directly effective treaty provisions.[98] The Court has also made clear that the conduct of any branch of the state, including the legislature,[99] the executive,[100] and the judiciary,[101] can give rise to liability in damages. However, outside the context of straightforward obligations to implement directives, the CJEU recognises that liability must not be imposed so readily as to paralyse the exercise of legislative and judicial discretion by member States. As a result, the bar for establishing a sufficiently serious breach of EU law is higher in such circumstances, the test being 'whether the member state...manifestly and gravely disregarded the limits on its discretion'.[102]

3.2.9 Directives that reflect general principles of EU law

There is one further way in which an unimplemented (or incorrectly implemented) directive may be relevant in situations in which enforcement is desired against non-state bodies. In *Mangold*,[103] the claimant sued his employer. He alleged that a term in his contract—which, if enforced, would be disadvantageous to him—was incompatible with a directive concerning equal treatment (specifically age discrimination) in employment. Although facing apparently insuperable difficulties—domestic law permitted the inclusion of the disadvantageous term; the directive was not horizontally enforceable against the employer, which was a non-state body; and the implementation date had not expired—the claimant was successful. The CJEU held that the directive was merely a specific manifestation of a general principle of EU law requiring equal treatment and therefore prohibiting age discrimination, that the principle (unlike the directive) was horizontally effective,[104] and that the claimant could therefore sue the employer for breaching the general principle notwithstanding that the directive could not be horizontally enforced.

This decision has been heavily criticised on a number of counts, including that it risks entirely consuming the rule that says directives are not horizontally effective. A sufficiently bold Court would be capable of relating many, if not all, directives to some general principle of law. As one commentator has noted, if pressed to its logical conclusion, the *Mangold* doctrine means that there is no 'real sense in which the no

---

[97] *Factortame (No 4)* at [17]–[22].   [98] *Factortame (No 4)*.   [99] *Factortame (No 4)*.

[100] *Hedley Lomas*.

[101] Case C-173/03 *Traghetti del Mediterraneo SpA v Italy* [2006] ECR I-5177. See also *Cooper v Attorney General* [2010] EWCA Civ 464.

[102] *Factortame (No 4)* at [55]. The test in relation to the judicial branch is whether 'the court has manifestly infringed the applicable law': Case C-224/01 *Köbler v Austria* [2003] ECR I-10239.

[103] Case C-144/04 *Mangold v Helm* [2005] ECR I-9981.

[104] This in itself is controversial, as it had not previously been established that general principles of EU law were horizontally effective.

horizontal direct effect rule for directives can be said to survive'.[105] The alarm bell was sounded by Advocate-General Mazák,[106] who argued that the *Mangold* doctrine 'call[ed] into question the distribution of competence between the [Union] and the Member States' by enabling the imposition of EU law obligations upon individuals in a way that runs directly contrary to the way in which TFEU, Art 288 limits the effect of directives.[107] The CJEU, however, appears unmoved by such concerns. The facts of *Kücükdeveci* were similar to those of *Mangold*, but the implementation period for the directive had expired, and, although Germany had taken steps to implement it, it had failed to do so correctly.[108] While reiterating that directives are not horizontally effective, the Court nevertheless held that German law should be disapplied to the extent of any inconsistency with the general principle (non-discrimination on grounds of age) underlying the directive, even though the case involved two private parties. It therefore seems that, as Albors-Llorens puts it, the *Mangold* approach 'is very much alive'.[109]

4. The supremacy of EU law and UK parliamentary sovereignty

4.1 **Introduction**

If the EU is to be a functioning legal order capable of securing the Union's objectives, it is imperative that, in relevant fields, common legal rules apply throughout the member States. We have seen that direct effect plays a major part in ensuring that this is so, by rendering many forms of EU law domestically enforceable without the need for further legislation on the part of the states. However, direct effect is merely a necessary, not a sufficient, condition precedent to the EU's working in the way in which it is intended to. It is self-apparent that the Union could not work in that way if a given member State were free to opt out of EU law—by enacting or preserving contrary national measures—whenever the Union adopted rules that it disliked.[110]

---

[105] Dashwood, 'From *Van Duyn* to *Mangold* via *Marshall*: Reducing Direct Effect to Absurdity?', in Barnard (ed), *Cambridge Yearbook of European Law*, vol 9 (Oxford 2007), p 8. Other commentators have presented *Mangold* as a less radical decision, suggesting that it is simply an application of the incidental horizontal effect principle: Jans, 'The Effect in National Legal Systems of the Prohibition of Discrimination on Grounds of Age as a General Principle of Community Law' (2007) 34 Legal Issues of Economic Integration 53.

[106] The role of advocates-general is advisory: they present reasoned opinions to the Court prior to judgment.

[107] Case C-411/05 *Palacios de la Villa v Cortefiel Servicios SA* [2007] ECR I-8531, [AG138].

[108] Case C-555/07 *Kücükdeveci v Swedex GmbH* [2010] 2 CMLR 33.

[109] 'Keeping Up Appearances: The Court of Justice and the Effects of EU Directives' [2010] CLJ 455, 457.

[110] However, special provision is made for the UK and Ireland whereby they may be excluded from measures concerning 'freedom, security and justice' under TFEU, Arts 67–89.

This point was recognised by the CJEU in the early days of what is now the EU. The *Costa* case concerned a law, enacted by Italy to nationalise its electricity industry, which was allegedly incompatible with certain provisions of what is now the TFEU. Asked whether a national law enacted after Italy's accession to the Union could prevail over EU law, the Court remarked that the 'strength of [EU] laws cannot vary from one State to the other in favour of later internal laws without endangering the realisation of the aims envisaged by the Treaty'.[111] The CJEU concluded that it was not legally possible for member States to derogate from EU law by enacting conflicting domestic provisions because 'the member-States, albeit within limited spheres, have restricted their sovereign rights and created a body of law applicable both to their nationals and to themselves'.[112]

> **Q** Why must EU law take priority over conflicting domestic law? In what senses would the purposes of the EU be thwarted if such domestic law could prevail over Union law?

4.2 The scope and implications of the supremacy principle

Although *Costa* clearly established the principle of supremacy of EU law, questions remained about its precise scope and implications. Subsequent case law clarified two important points.

First, in *Simmenthal*, the CJEU addressed *the implications of the supremacy principle for national courts*.[113] The case arose from an Italian law requiring meat importers to pay for veterinarian checks at the national border. Although it was established that this was contrary to directly effective EU law concerning the free movement of goods, the Italian government argued that domestic courts could not order it to repay the fees until and unless the Italian Constitutional Court annulled the law in question. This view did not find favour with the CJEU, which took the opportunity to spell out the practical consequences of the supremacy doctrine for domestic courts faced with incompatible national laws. It was, said the CJEU, the task of national courts to protect the rights conferred upon individuals by EU law.[114] Domestic courts therefore had to 'apply [Union] law in its entirety', disregarding 'any provision of national law'—whenever enacted—'which may conflict with it', and ignoring any national rules that, if applied, would compromise domestic courts' capacity to do the foregoing things.[115]

Second, in *Internationale Handelsgesellschaft*, the CJEU held that the principles laid down in *Simmenthal* applied to *all* types of national law, including provisions of member States' constitutions, and including provisions in such constitutions

---

[111] Case 6/64 *Costa v Enel* [1964] CMLR 425, 455.   [112] *Costa* at 455.

[113] Case 106/77 *Amministrazione delle Finanze dello Stato v Simmenthal SpA* [1978] ECR 629.

[114] *Simmenthal* at [16].

[115] *Simmenthal* at [17]–[22].

concerning the protection of human rights.[116] It was therefore the duty of national courts to disapply national constitutional human rights guarantees to the extent that EU law was inconsistent with them. Unsurprisingly, this conclusion provoked a good deal of disquiet, but the Court was careful to say that such situations should arise rarely if at all. This was because EU law itself recognised the fundamental rights common to the constitutional traditions of member States. As a result, the Union was bound by those rights and powerless to legislate or otherwise act in breach of them.[117] It would therefore rarely, if ever, be the case that a national court was forced to choose between a national human rights law and a *valid* EU provision. An obvious difficulty with this approach is that it fails to identify with any precision the body of human rights recognised by EU law (particularly now that the membership is so large and diverse).[118] For that reason (among others), the member States adopted a Charter of Fundamental Rights in 2000 that was made legally effective by the Lisbon Treaty.[119]

4.3 **Parliamentary sovereignty**

The principle of supremacy of EU law poses an obvious difficulty as far as the UK constitutional system is concerned. If the UK Parliament is sovereign in the traditional sense considered in Chapter 5, how can EU law be supreme? The orthodox doctrine of parliamentary sovereignty holds that Acts of Parliament are the highest form of law known in the UK, and that it is the first duty of UK courts to give effect to them. It is unclear whether—and, if so, how—that view can be reconciled with the EU supremacy principle. As we will see, various attempts have been made to square this circle; whether any of them are convincing is a different matter. However, before assessing judges' and commentators' attempts to explain *how* UK constitutional law may accommodate the supremacy principle, it is necessary to set out *what* the current position is.

In doing so, it is difficult to know what to choose as a starting point, because two quite different possibilities arise. From *the perspective of EU law*, the starting (and, for that matter, finishing) point is simply the supremacy principle itself. The CJEU's view is that EU law enjoys priority over national law *as a matter of EU law*.[120] The Court has said that the Treaty of Rome—the forerunner of today's treaties—created 'its own legal system which, on the entry into force of the Treaty, became an integral part of

---

[116] Case 11/70 *Internationale Handelsgesellschaft mbH v Einfuhr- und Vorratsstelle fur Getreide und Futtermittel* [1970] ECR 1125.

[117] Case 4/73 *J Nold Kohlen- und Baustoffgrosshandlung v Commission of the European Communities* [1975] ECR 985. See further Tridimas, *General Principles of EU Law* (Oxford 2005), ch 7.

[118] Carruthers, 'Beware of Lawyers Bearing Gifts: A Critical Evaluation of the Proposals on Fundamental Rights in the EU Constitutional Treaty' [2004] EHRLR 424.

[119] TEU, Art 6(1). The UK and Poland have a so-called opt-out from the Charter (see Protocol on the Application of the Charter of Fundamental Rights of the European Union to Poland and to the United Kingdom). However, Dougan, 'The Treaty of Lisbon 2007: Winning Minds, Not Hearts' (2008) 45 CML Rev 617, 665–71, persuasively argues that the legal effect of the so-called opt-out may be extremely limited.

[120] An argument of this nature was canvassed, but ultimately rejected, in *Thoburn v Sunderland City Council* [2002] EWHC 195 (Admin), [2003] QB 151, [53]–[57].

the legal systems of the Member States and which their courts are bound to apply'.[121] On this view, national law cannot detract from the supremacy of EU law: such law is, and will be, supreme within all member States for as long as they remain members of the Union.

However, from *the perspective of British constitutional law*, this analysis is problematic. As a matter of domestic law, treaties to which the UK is a party only produce effects in national law—for example, only give rise to rights and obligations enforceable in British courts—to the extent that they are incorporated by means of an Act of Parliament. On this approach, it is the Act of Parliament that incorporates the European treaties that must form our starting point if we wish to understand the status of EU law in the UK. The legislation in question is the European Communities Act 1972 (ECA).

Section 2(1) of this Act provides that

> All such rights, powers, liabilities, obligations and restrictions from time to time created or arising by or under the Treaties, and all such remedies and procedures from time to time provided for by or under the Treaties, as in accordance with the Treaties are without further enactment to be given legal effect or used in the United Kingdom shall be recognised and available in law, and be enforced, allowed and followed accordingly.

Although drafted in somewhat archaic language, the effect of s 2(1) is simple: it is the domestic counterpart to the doctrine of direct effect, in that it provides that all EU provisions that have direct effect as a matter of Union law should be regarded as legally effective as a matter of UK law. In this way, s 2(1) can be thought of as the gateway through which EU law enters the domestic system.

Meanwhile, s 2(4) says that 'any enactment passed or to be passed...shall be construed and have effect subject to the foregoing provisions of this section'. What does this mean? One of the 'foregoing provisions of this section' is s 2(1)—which, as we have just seen, makes directly effective EU law domestically effective. Section 2(4) is, then, saying that any Act of Parliament, whether enacted before or after the entry into force of the ECA, 'shall be construed and have effect subject to' directly effective EU law. But what does 'shall be construed and have effect subject to' mean? The former part of that phrase—*shall be construed* subject to—suggests that UK courts are merely being instructed, where possible, to interpret domestic legislation consistently with EU law. On this view, s 2(4) merely amounts to a *rule of interpretation*. But saying that UK legislation shall *have effect* subject to EU law hints at something else altogether: it suggests that Acts of Parliament are only effective to the extent that they are consistent with EU law, and that they are ineffective, or unenforceable, to the extent that they are not. This implies that s 2(4) constitutes not only a rule of interpretation, but also a *rule of priority*—one that determines which of two conflicting laws should apply, and which stipulates that, in the event of such conflict, it is ultimately EU law that takes precedence.

---

[121] Case C-6/64 *Costa v Enel* [1964] ECR 585, 593–4.

As the House of Lords' historic decision in *Factortame* demonstrates, it is the latter view that has prevailed in the UK.[122] The dispute centred upon (what is now) TFEU, Art 49, which (*inter alia*) entitles EU nationals to establish businesses in any EU state. Contrary to that right, the UK Parliament enacted the Merchant Shipping Act 1998, the aim of which was to protect the British fishing industry by preventing foreign (specifically Spanish) nationals from exploiting British fish stocks. The CJEU eventually held that the nationality restrictions imposed by the Act were incompatible with Art 49.[123] However, it took several years to obtain this ruling, and in the meantime the claimants asked the British courts to suspend the operation of the Act. As the House of Lords noted,[124] the traditional doctrine of parliamentary sovereignty would clearly prevent the setting aside—whether permanently or merely temporarily—of primary legislation.[125] The CJEU, however, reminded the Law Lords that the supremacy principle requires national courts to apply EU law in preference to national law, and to ignore any national rule or principle—including the doctrine of parliamentary sovereignty—that would impede domestic courts in that endeavour.[126] The House of Lords therefore took the unprecedented step of issuing an injunction disapplying the relevant parts of the Merchant Shipping Act 1988 in order that the claimants could exercise their conflicting rights under the Treaty.[127] Although, as explained above, *Factortame* was concerned with *temporary* disapplication of a statute, pending a final decision about its compatibility with EU law, it is clear from the later *EOC* case[128] that UK courts can—indeed, must—*permanently* disapply Acts of Parliament that conflict with EU law.

How can this novel judicial power to set aside primary legislation be accounted for in terms of constitutional law and theory? *Factortame* itself is far from illuminating in this respect. Only one of the judges, Lord Bridge, considered the matter directly, and even his analysis was sparse. He observed that the supremacy of EU law was 'well established in the jurisprudence of the [CJEU] long before the United Kingdom joined the [Union]', such that 'whatever limitation of its sovereignty Parliament accepted when it enacted the European Communities Act 1972 was entirely voluntary'.[129] In the following sections, we evaluate the position arrived at in *Factortame* against the backdrop of the three interpretations of parliamentary sovereignty advanced in Chapter 5.

---

[122] *R v Secretary of State for Transport, ex p Factortame Ltd (No 2)* [1991] 1 AC 603. See further Barnard, *The Substantive Law of the EU: The Four Freedoms* (Oxford 2007), pp 334–40.

[123] Case C-221/89 *R v Secretary of State for Transport, ex p Factortame Ltd* [1992] QB 680.

[124] *R v Secretary of State for Transport, ex p Factortame Ltd (No 1)* [1990] 2 AC 85.

[125] As explained in Chapter 7 above, no such complications arise in relation to the devolved legislatures, since they are in no sense sovereign; the devolution legislation provides a clear and straightforward legal basis for courts to set aside devolved legislation that contradicts EU law.

[126] Case C-213/89 *R v Secretary of State for Transport, ex p Factortame Ltd* [1990] ECR I-2433.

[127] *Factortame (No 2)*.

[128] *R v Secretary of State for Employment, ex p Equal Opportunities Commission* [1995] 1 AC 1.

[129] *Factortame (No 2)* at 658–9.

Q Before reading on, review the three models of parliamentary sovereignty discussed in Chapter 5 above. How do you think proponents of each of the three models might attempt to explain the outcome of *Factortame*?

4.4 **Model I—parliamentary sovereignty as a constitutional fixture**

Lord Bridge's assertion that Parliament had 'voluntarily' accepted limitations upon its sovereignty presupposes that it is *capable* of doing so. The difficulty with this analysis— and one that remained unconfronted by the Law Lords in *Factortame*—is that it is wholly at odds with the premise underlying what is, or at least was, generally regarded as the dominant account of parliamentary sovereignty. As we saw in Chapter 5, the so-called *continuing theory* propounded by Wade holds that the constitutional rule that establishes the sovereignty of Parliament—by requiring courts to recognise all Acts of Parliament as valid laws and to prefer the most recent expression of parliamentary intention over any earlier conflicting intentions—is ultimately a political, not a legal, one. This, said Wade, means that it is 'a rule which is unique in being unchangeable by Parliament'. On this view, while Parliament, being sovereign, is capable of changing any *law*, it is incapable of changing the rule that ascribes sovereignty to it because that rule is not a law in any conventional sense; rather, it is the peg 'upon which the whole system of legislation hangs'.[130]

For Wade, therefore, there are two central truths about parliamentary sovereignty. First, as a matter of constitutional law, the sovereignty of Parliament is fixed: it is a given that cannot be changed by legislation or by any other legal means. It is therefore simply not open to Parliament to accept, voluntarily or otherwise, limitations upon its sovereignty. But, second, the sovereignty of Parliament may be diminished (that is, destroyed)[131] through non-legal means. This would involve courts acting unconstitutionally in refusing to recognise an Act of Parliament as an enforceable law. They would thereby bring the old constitutional order (in which Parliament was sovereign) crashing down and, as a matter of practical politics, establish a new order (in which Parliament is not sovereign). Thus Wade says that the sovereignty of Parliament can be 'changed [only] by revolution not by legislation'.[132] This analysis forces Wade to characterise *Factortame* as a judicial revolution: the judges refused to do what the old constitutional order required of them (namely, applying the Merchant Shipping Act 1988) and instead shifted their allegiance to EU law as the highest form of law applicable in the UK.[133] For this reason, Wade sees this change as a permanent one, in the sense that it does not follow that Parliament can simply repeal the ECA and thus restore its 'ultimate' sovereignty;[134] rather, the pre-1973 position could be restored

---

[130] Wade, 'The Basis of Legal Sovereignty' [1955] CLJ 172, 188–9.

[131] The diminution of sovereignty necessarily constitutes its destruction: Parliament is either all-powerful (sovereign) or it is not.   [132] Wade, 'The Basis of Legal Sovereignty' at 189.

[133] Wade, 'Sovereignty: Revolution or Evolution?' (1996) 112 LQR 568.

[134] Wade, 'Sovereignty: Revolution or Evolution?'.

only if a further revolution were to occur in which judges shifted their allegiance back to the Westminster Parliament as supreme lawmaker for the UK—something that is, self-evidently, not within *Parliament's* gift.

Rationalising *Factortame* in this way is consistent with Wade's general theory of parliamentary sovereignty, but is problematic on two levels. First, it does not accord with Lord Bridge's (admittedly sparse) analysis in *Factortame* itself, in which he implied that legislation, not a judge-led 'revolution', constituted the death warrant of parliamentary sovereignty. Second, Wade's attempt to accommodate *Factortame* within his theory of sovereignty highlights substantial problems with that theory. If Wade is to be believed, the authority to make laws applicable in the UK—whether by Parliament, the EU, or some other body—is a house of cards propped up by judicial acquiescence alone. Any institution possesses lawmaking authority only to the extent to which, and for as long as, the judges are prepared to tolerate it; it can be removed by judicial whim. As Goldsworthy points out, this highlights what might be considered a fallacy at the heart of Wade's theory—that just because Parliament could not logically have conferred sovereignty upon itself, the judges must have done so. Goldsworthy argues that, in reality, the authority of the legislature must depend upon and be sustained by something both broader and deeper than merely the courts' recognition of it. At the very least, there must be a consensus across the various branches of government—and, it might be added, in wider society—about where lawmaking power resides.[135] All branches of government were involved in the UK's becoming a member of the EU and in EU law becoming effective in the UK, and that membership of the EU was supported by the public in a referendum. To suggest that the supremacy of EU law supplanted the sovereignty of Parliament merely because the judges said so fails to chime with that historical reality, and paints a one-dimensional picture of a constitution propped up by a judicial elite.

4.5 **Model II—Parliament capable of controlling certain aspects of legislative process**

How else, then, might the contemporary status of EU law in the UK be explained? Wade's model sees sovereignty as absolutely fixed in a legal sense (albeit that judges, acting unconstitutionally, might bring it crashing down). As we saw in Chapter 5, other writers take a more nuanced view by distinguishing between the substance of parliamentary sovereignty and the formal conditions according to which it may be exercised. Proponents of the so-called *new view* contend that while Parliament cannot do anything that would cut down its sovereignty in the substantive sense, it may require future Parliaments to comply with certain formal conditions when making law.

Can this analysis provide a convincing rationalisation of the status of EU law in the UK? It has been suggested that it can.[136] The ECA, the argument runs, can be read as

---

[135] *The Sovereignty of Parliament* (Oxford 1999), pp 238–46.
[136] See, eg Laws, 'Law and Democracy' [1995] PL 72, 88–9.

laying down a formal requirement such that any Parliament wishing to legislate contrary to EU law would have to use express language indicating such an intention.[137]
So when it enacted the Merchant Shipping Act 1988, Parliament, being substantively
sovereign, could have succeeded in its attempt to deprive the Spanish fishermen of
their EU law rights, but only if it exercised its sovereignty in the correct way—that
is, by complying with the procedural requirement of express language supposedly
laid down in the ECA. The absence of such language in the 1988 Act explains why
Parliament failed to revoke the claimants' EU law rights.

There are, however, two difficulties with this analysis. First, it sits uncomfortably with
the language of s 2(4) of the ECA, which says that UK law takes effect 'subject to' EU law.
This suggests that Parliament was attempting to create a rule of priority, rather than
simply to lay down a formal requirement about how Parliament should go about enacting legislation that is inconsistent with EU law. Second, it is based on an approach that is
somewhat parochial. Lord Denning said that if Parliament were deliberately to attempt
to act inconsistently with EU law and '[say] so in express terms then…it would be the
duty of our courts to follow the statute of our Parliament'.[138] But this presupposes that
the matter can and should be analysed purely in terms of domestic law. It also overlooks,
or at least attaches no weight in domestic legal terms to, the fact that the use of express
language would cut no ice whatever at the EU level. At that level, Union law is regarded
as supreme. Member States are incapable of opting out of EU law in any way,[139] including by enacting inconsistent national legislation—however explicitly the intention to
derogate might be stated. Characterising the EU-related limitations on Parliament's
legislative freedom as purely formal ones may, in conjunction with the new view, provide a workable explanation of why the Merchant Shipping Act 1988 was disapplied in
Factortame—but by proceeding on the implicit premise that Parliament remains truly
sovereign in the substantive sense, and could have overridden EU law if only it had used
express language, this analysis is ultimately weakened by an air of unreality. For as long
as the UK remains a member of the EU, it is forbidden, as a matter of Union law, from
legislating contrary to it. If the purpose of theory is to help us to make sense of reality,
then a theory that fails to accord with reality can hardly be regarded as a good one.[140]

4.6 Model III—EU law as a substantive limit on Parliament's lawmaking authority

The two models so far considered have arguably failed to supply a convincing account
of how EU law has acquired its present status in the UK. A third possibility lies in
rejecting the premise of the first model by characterising the sovereignty of Parliament

---

[137] For example, by stating that the relevant provisions of the Act were to take effect notwithstanding any
inconsistency with EU law.   [138] *Macarthys v Smith* [1979] 3 All ER 325, 329.

[139] Except by negotiating an amendment to the Treaty.

[140] The same criticism can be made of the analysis advanced by Laws LJ in *Thoburn v Sunderland City
Council* [2002] EWHC 195 (Admin), [2003] QB 151, in which he presupposed that Parliament can derogate
from EU law if it makes its intention to do so sufficiently clear. See further Chapter 5, section 4.4.2, above.

as a *legal phenomenon* rather than a purely political one, such that it can be manipulated like other legal norms, and by saying that it has been so manipulated such that EU law now truly is supreme and Parliament is *no longer sovereign* (as opposed to being subject, as the second model would have it, only to formal constraints).

This view, which shares some common ground with the third model of sovereignty considered in Chapter 5, is perhaps the most radical one. It is certainly the approach that most directly forces constitutional lawyers to face up to hard facts. It rules out hiding behind the fiction that Parliament is still sovereign in the sense that it can override EU law if only it has the courage to use express language. And by characterising the authority of Parliament as a legal phenomenon it requires lawyers to engage with these difficult, but important, questions, rather than to seek refuge in the notion that they belong exclusively to the realm of politics. We saw in Chapter 5 that the courts are increasingly—but tentatively at this stage—developing the idea that the authority of Parliament to make law is something that is subject to, and therefore controllable by, constitutional law—that there is a line that Parliament is not allowed to cross, albeit that the location of the line remains, for now, uncertain. This view presents the authority of Parliament as a dynamic, legal phenomenon: its scope is a function of the contemporary constitution as interpreted by the judges. On that view, EU law may well be regarded as forming part of the line delimiting the authority of Parliament to make law. For example, in *Jackson*, Lord Hope went as far as to say that 'the supremacy of [Union] law restricts the absolute authority of Parliament to legislate as it wants in this area'.[141]

Yet this view is not without difficulty. It is one thing to say that the width of Parliament's authority to make law is itself a function of law and may therefore be changed by legal means. But precisely what are those legal means? In *Jackson*, Lord Hope said that the restriction on parliamentary sovereignty inherent in EU membership was a 'product of measures enacted by Parliament' itself—that, by enacting the ECA, Parliament had limited its future lawmaking power.[142] In contrast, Laws LJ in *Thoburn* suggested that the width of Parliament's lawmaking power is set not by Parliament, but by the constitution.[143] This presupposes that, as in a system with a written constitution, Parliament has only so much power as the constitution concedes to it; as the constitution evolves over time, the amount of power wielded by Parliament may alter. On this analysis, if Parliament is today incapable of enacting enforceable legislation that is contrary to EU law, that is because the UK constitution, as presently interpreted, prevents it from doing so. The problem, of course, is that, in the absence of a written constitution, we have only the word of the judges that such is the position.

The truth probably lies somewhere between the positions adopted by Lord Hope in *Jackson* and Laws LJ in *Thoburn*. The emerging modern orthodoxy is that the capacity of Parliament to legislate is a legal, not a purely political, phenomenon. In other words, the width of Parliament's power is determined by constitutional law and can be changed if, and only if, the relevant constitutional law changes. The key questions

---

[141] *Jackson v Attorney-General* [2005] UKHL 56, [2006] 1 AC 262, [105].   [142] *Jackson* at [105].
[143] *Thoburn v Sunderland City Council* [2002] EWHC 195 (Admin), [2003] QB 151.

are: how can the constitutional law that determines the extent of Parliament's authority be changed? And who decides whether such change has occurred? For the reasons considered in Chapter 5, to suggest that this is a matter entirely within the hands of Parliament is unsatisfactory—not least because it would be dangerous to concede entirely to the legislature control over this matter. That Parliament is not master of its own destiny in this respect is reflected in the suggestions in *Jackson* that there might be some limits on Parliament's authority—for example, it might be impotent to abolish judicial review of executive action—that are wholly unattributable to any intention evidenced in Acts of Parliament.

> **Q** Why would it be dangerous to recognise in Parliament an unqualified power to impose substantive limits on its own and its successors' legislative authority?

But it is equally unsatisfactory to suggest that this is a matter wholly in the hands of the judges such that neither Parliament's nor anyone else's view is relevant, since that way lies the risk of uncontrolled judicial supremacism. In any event, it does not chime with reality: it is self-evident that the judges did not simply take it on themselves to decide that EU law should take priority over domestic law, just as they did not unilaterally decide that it should be possible for legislation to be enacted without the involvement of the House of Lords;[144] rather, they were clearly influenced by legislation in arriving at those conclusions.

Laws LJ's view that it is the unwritten constitution, as interpreted by the judges, that ultimately sets the terms on which Parliament wields power must therefore be supplemented by recognising that the judges' interpretation of the constitution will and should be influenced by Acts of Parliament. It follows that the constitutional terms on which Parliament holds legislative power are within the exclusive control of neither Parliament nor the courts; rather, they are set by the constitution, the content of which necessarily falls to be determined by judges, but which can be influenced by Acts of Parliament. It is hard to resist the conclusion that, at its present stage of development, the UK constitution has reached the point at which, for as long as the UK remains a member of the EU, Parliament is denied the power to enact enforceable laws that are contrary to Union law. As Lord Bridge pointed out in *Factortame*, that is precisely what Parliament wanted when it enacted the ECA, and the outcome of *Factortame*, like the dictum of Lord Hope quoted above, indicates that the courts have accepted that the constitution has evolved (under the influence of that legislation) to deny Parliament the authority to contravene EU law for the time being.

It follows, on this view, that the question of whether Parliament can restore its 'ultimate' sovereignty—for example, by repealing the ECA—does not have a straightforward answer. Rather, it depends on the answer to a more fundamental question: whether the constitution has evolved to a point at which EU law, and membership of the EU,

---

[144] See discussion in Chapter 5, section 2.3.3, above of the Parliament Acts.

have become fully entrenched features of it. Most judges and commentators[145] accept that it is currently possible for Parliament to restore its ultimate sovereignty by revoking the ECA. But even if this is true now, it may not always be true. 'If', writes Allan, 'the [Union] ever came to replace the United Kingdom as the fundamental political entity to which the average or representative citizen owed his first and natural allegiance', the courts could be expected to reflect this by denying Parliament the opportunity to derogate in *any* way from EU law—including, presumably, by attempting to revoke the ECA.[146] It is at that point that EU law would truly become one of the lines—like, arguably, the abolition of judicial review or of any recognisable form of democracy—that Parliament is impotent to cross in any way. But, of course, the remote possibility of Parliament attempting to cross any of these lines means that the courts are unlikely to be called upon authoritatively to determine that they exist.

5. Conclusions

So much for the various ways of theorising the status of EU law in the UK—but does any of this really matter? For two reasons, it does.

First, theory should aid our understanding of reality—and this, in turn, should provide a framework within which to decide hard cases. The fact that it is far from clear which, if any, of the various theoretical accounts considered above—and summarised in Figure 8.7—is the right one is problematic. This uncertainty deprives the courts of a clear conceptual framework within which to decide hard cases. Although unlikely, it is far from inconceivable that a Eurosceptic government might secure the enactment of legislation explicitly derogating from EU law. Indeed, in its 2010 election manifesto, the Conservative Party undertook to pass legislation making 'it clear that ultimate authority stays in this country, in our Parliament'.[147] At the time of writing, the European Union Bill is before Parliament. As presently drafted, it provides, *inter alia*, that: 'It is only by virtue of an Act of Parliament that directly applicable or directly effective EU law…falls to be recognised and available in law in the United Kingdom.' The implication of this seems to be that the door opened to EU law by s 2 of the ECA could be closed, either fully or in respect of particular pieces of Union law. If this legislation is enacted, and if Parliament seeks to rely on it in order to derogate from EU law, the courts will have to decide whether Parliament has succeeded in putting back into the bottle the genie that it arguably let out by enacting the ECA. That, too, is a question that can only be tackled by reference to a clear theoretical framework. For example, if Wade's view were to be adopted, Parliament cannot return the genie to the bottle— whereas, if the ECA is regarded merely as having implanted a rule of construction, the scope for rowing back (at least as a matter of *UK law*) is considerably greater.

---

[145] With the exception of Wade, for the reason given above at section 4.4.
[146] Allan, 'The Limits of Parliamentary Sovereignty' [1985] PL 614, 618.
[147] Conservative Party, *An Invitation to Join the Government of Britain* (London 2010), p 114.

Theory	Summary	Possible to derogate from EU law?	Possible to restore 'ultimate' sovereignty?
Model I: Continuing theory	A 'revolution' has occurred: EU law now recognized as supreme law in UK, parliamentary sovereignty no longer exists	Not in any circumstances: judicial loyalty has switched to the EU as supreme lawmaker	Only if there is another 'revolution' in which judicial loyalty switches back to UK Parliament as supreme lawmaker
Model II: EU law as a formal limit on Parliament's freedom to make law	Parliament is subject to the formal requirement that express language must be used if it wishes to derogate from EU law	Yes, as a matter of UK law, provided that express language is used—but derogation would be unlawful as a matter of EU law	'Ultimate' sovereignty has not been lost: Parliament can derogate in particular situations through use of express language, and can cast EU law aside wholesale by repealing the ECA
Model III: EU law as a substantive limit on Parliament's freedom to make law	The constitution, interpreted by courts in the light of the ECA, ascribes priority to EU law over Acts of Parliament	An Act of Parliament attempting to derogate from or revoke in its entirety EU law would need to be interpreted by courts in the light of the constitution and other relevant norms. A time may come when membership of the EU is such an entrenched feature of the British polity that it will be constitutionally impossible for the UK Parliament to restore its ultimate sovereignty or derogate in particular situations.	

Figure 8.7 Explaining the status of EU law in the UK

Second, the theoretical debate sketched above is relevant to—and is informed, although not necessarily explicitly, by—the competing notions of political and legal constitutionalism, the relationship between which forms one of this book's key themes. To the extent that EU membership entails legal, judicially enforceable limits on Parliament's freedom to make law, such as that revealed in *Factortame*, it contributes towards the shift, which we have already noted in several contexts, to a more legal form of constitutionalism. Indeed, it is only in relation to EU law that UK courts have to date asserted jurisdiction to disapply Acts of Parliament, judicial review of primary legislation being one of the clearest and most distinctive hallmarks of legal constitutionalism. However, the extent to which there has been a shift towards a hard form of legal constitutionalism in this sphere—whereby there are judicially enforceable boundaries that Parliament is legally incompetent to cross—depends upon which of the various above theoretical accounts is preferred. Reliance on the new view, for example, implies the emergence in this area of a softer form of legal constitutionalism, in the sense that any legal limits on Parliament's authority are formal only. In contrast, the third model, which envisages substantive—and, on Allan's argument, potentially immovable—limits, reflects a harder form of legal constitutionalism. But, more fundamentally, whatever form of legal constitutionalism is hinted at by these developments, it is hard to deny that British membership of the EU (and the resulting questions about the status of EU law that arise) demonstrates the poverty of any theory of parliamentary sovereignty that attempts to present it as a wholly political phenomenon. Questions about the relationship between UK and EU law have to be confronted by courts and lawyers, and it is desirable, if not necessary, that such confrontation should take place within a well-understood framework of legal and constitutional principle. Seeking refuge from such facts of life in the argument that the British constitution is a political one no longer cuts any ice.

This new reality also impacts on another of our key themes—that of the increasingly multilayered nature of the British constitution. Although attempts have been made to play down the consequences of EU membership by presenting it as a delegation of authority by the UK to EU, or as a merely temporary state of affairs that can be undone by the stroke of a legislative pen in Westminster, the reality, as we have seen, is different. The EU as a tier of government is—and will, for the foreseeable future, remain—a reality. If the essence of multilayered constitutionalism is the existence of multiple loci of power the ongoing existence of which is not contingent upon the UK government's acquiescence, there can hardly be clearer evidence of such multilayeredness than the existence of the EU and the fact that it is now deeply, if not irreversibly, ingrained with the UK's constitutional arrangements.

Further reading

CRAIG, 'Sovereignty of the United Kingdom Parliament after *Factortame*' (1991) 11 *Yearbook of European Law* 221

DASHWOOD, 'From *Van Duyn* to *Mangold* via *Marshall*: Reducing Direct Effect to Absurdity?', in Barnard (ed), *Cambridge Yearbook of European Law*, vol 9 (Oxford 2007)

DOUGAN, 'The Treaty of Lisbon 2007: Winning Minds, Not Hearts' (2008) 45 CML Rev 617

WADE, 'Sovereignty: Revolution or Evolution?' (1996) 112 LQR 568

Useful websites

http://europa.eu/index_en.htm
Website of the European Union

http://eur-lex.europa.eu/en/treaties/index.htm
Online access to the Treaty on European Union and Treaty on the Functioning of the European Union

PART III

Good Governance— Scrutiny, Accountability, and Transparency

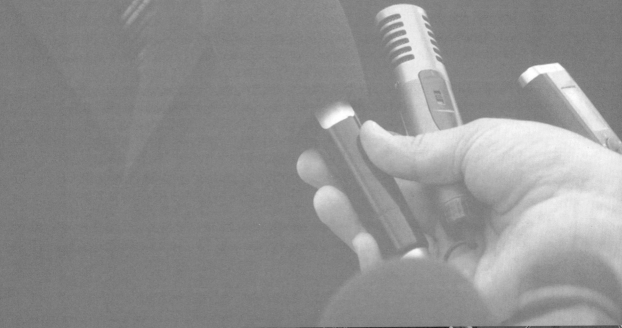

9 Good Governance—An Introduction

1. Introduction

So far, this book has considered the structures and institutions of government in the multilayered constitution of the UK. It has also examined the key principles—such as the separation of powers, the sovereignty of Parliament, and the rule of law—that help to explain and inform the powers exercised by those institutions and the relationships between them. The focus now shifts to a different, but related, set of issues that are ultimately concerned with one overarching question: what are the practical arrangements for ensuring that the institutions of government adhere to principles of good governance? In tackling this question, we must start by considering two logically prior questions. What, in the first place, is meant by good governance? And why is it important that the standards of good governance are upheld? In practice, these two questions represent two sides of the same coin.

The *importance of good governance* lies in the fact that it is a prerequisite if people are to accept, cooperate with, and recognise the legitimacy of the institutions of government—all of which are imperative to the existence of a peaceful, well-functioning, civilised, and productive society. Mechanisms must therefore exist that require, or at least encourage, those in power to adhere to the standards of good governance. And while the electoral process is clearly important in this regard—the prospect of having to submit to re-election incentivises responsible behaviour by politicians—it is not, by itself, adequate. Not all institutions of government are under the direct control of elected politicians. And even in relation to those that are, infrequent elections constitute a crude, insufficiently granular form of scrutiny: the electorate can do no more than pass broad judgement on the performance of the government as a whole.

Good governance, then, is integral to the legitimacy of government. But while the desirability of good governance is beyond dispute, it is more difficult to define *what it actually means and how to achieve it.* There is no definitive set of standards of good governance upon which everyone agrees. Nonetheless, it could be said that there is a set of core principles that, together, are widely regarded as comprising good governance, although their precise details may vary and change over time. But before we articulate those core principles, it is worth saying something about their source. The notion of good governance is inseparable from that of democracy. Good governance ultimately reduces to the idea of government being conducted in ways that are *acceptable to* the (majority of) people—hence our point above that good governance is necessary for the *acceptance of* government by the people.

From this, it follows that the principles of good governance derive from—indeed, are constituted by—values that are widely held within society. Some such values are reflected in the sort of constitutional principles that we encountered in earlier chapters. This is unsurprising: as we explained in Chapter 1, one of the purposes of a constitution is to capture and institutionalise values that are deep-seated and enduring within the relevant society. So, while the average person may not readily adopt the language of 'separation of powers' or 'rule of law', he or she would most likely subscribe to propositions inherent in those constitutional principles—for example, that politicians should not interfere in judicial proceedings, that retrospective criminal liability should not be imposed, and so on. A government that sought to do things such as these could fairly be said to have failed to adhere to standards of good governance. However, those standards are not confined to ones reflected in fundamental constitutional principles. The concept of good governance encompasses a broader range of norms—expectations widely held by those subject to government—concerning how institutions of government should behave. People expect the government, and the politicians running it, to behave in ways—honestly, openly, straightforwardly, competently, with integrity, selflessly—that are not necessarily, or not comprehensively, mandated by law.

From this, it follows that lawful governance is a necessary, but not sufficient, condition for good governance—and that the standards of good governance therefore fall to be upheld not only through legal, but also through political, means. This raises a fundamental question that is central to one of this book's key themes: are the political mechanisms responsible for upholding standards of good governance adequate? And, if not, should legal control of government be expanded? In other words, what is the right balance in this context between legal and political modes of constitutionalism? These are questions for later chapters. We return now to the question that is most pertinent to this stage of our inquiry—namely, what is good governance?

2. **What is good governance?**

As foreshadowed, no definitive or universally accepted list of standards of good governance exists. This means that we have to look at a variety of sources in order to locate what can be regarded as the prevailing standards of good governance—including the standards upheld by those bodies responsible for upholding good governance. For example, in 2009, the House of Commons Public Administration Select Committee identified five requirements as prerequisites for good government: good people, good process, good accountability, good performance, and good standards.[1] In the following discussion, we have attempted to divide the standards of good governance into different categories in order to aid explanation. However, in practice, many of the standards are interrelated.

2.1 Governing in the public interest

First of all, good governance requires that government acts in the public interest. Governments have no legitimate interests of their own, and nor, when acting in their official capacities, do the individuals who lead and work in governments. In a democracy, citizens elect a government in order to protect, advance, and serve their interests. In normative terms, we could say that democratic governance presupposes that government acts as the servant—rather than the master—of the people. There are two dimensions to this notion that good governance means (among other things) governing in the public interest.

The positive dimension is that *government should make decisions that advance the public good*. Of course, what constitutes the public good is a highly contestable notion. Concepts such as good governance and the public good do not supply objective yardsticks against which the legitimacy of governmental action can be determined. But the notion of good governance does require the existence of mechanisms whereby the wisdom of government policy and decisions can be measured and judgement pronounced. In a democracy, the ultimate question is not whether the government is acting in an objectively correct way (whatever that might mean); rather, it is whether it is governing in a manner that is regarded as broadly acceptable.[2] As noted above, elections are an important, but—taken on their own—inadequate, means of doing this. Good governance requires government to be kept on a shorter leash than that supplied by the electoral process. There are a number of different ways that enable or require government to take account of the views and wishes of the people: the need to obtain parliamentary approval of legislative proposals; submission to scrutiny by Parliament, the media, courts, tribunals, and ombudsmen; and public participation in government decision-making (for example, by consulting with the public).

To take one specific example, it is a relatively uncontentious proposition that, when using public resources—especially public money—government should, so far as possible, seek to attain value for money. That is, because government is largely funded by the public through taxation, the public can, in turn, rightfully expect that government should not waste its money; rather, government should endeavour to use public money

---

[1] House of Commons Public Administration Select Committee, *Good Government* (HC 97 2008–09).

[2] This does not necessarily reduce to a notion of majoritarianism under which anything goes provided that it is supported by a bare majority. Some constitutional systems deliberately put in place arrangements to ensure that government is carried on in a more consensual manner. Such mechanisms may be political (eg an electoral system unlikely to deliver a majority for a single party) or legal (eg judicial powers to strike down as unconstitutional legislation that conflicts with minority interests).

wisely so that the public receives value for its money. As we shall see in Chapter 11, detailed arrangements exist for overseeing—and thereby helping the public to form a view about—whether the government is acting responsibly in this regard.

Governing in the public interest has a second, negative dimension. It demands that *government must not act in a self-interested manner*. It follows from what was said above—namely, that governments do not have any *legitimate* interests of their own— that self-interested behaviour by governmental institutions is necessarily improper, and a breach of the standards of good governance. The notion operates on at least two levels. On a general level, it would be improper for an elected public body—whether the UK central government or a local authority—to elevate *political gain* above the public good. Assume, for example, that a government Minister is choosing between two potential locations for a new airport: all other things are equal, save that site X is near several economically depressed marginal constituencies to which a new airport would bring much-needed jobs (and probably electoral popularity for the governing party), whereas choosing site Y would bring equal economic benefits, but would cause far less environmental damage. It would be improper—indeed, unlawful—for the Minister, motivated by electoral calculations, to choose site X over site Y.

The proscription on self-interested governance also means that those involved in government must not act for improper *personal gain*. If, in our example, the Minister were choosing between two potential sites for a new airport and the arguments were otherwise evenly balanced, it would be improper (and, again, unlawful) for her to choose one site over the other if she would stand to gain financially by that decision.[3] The impropriety of such behaviour is widely recognised. For example, a wide-ranging and broadly applicable list of principles has been devised by the Committee on Standards in Public Life, the independent public body that advises the UK government on ethical standards across the whole of public life in the UK. Among those principles are the requirements that those involved in public life act with selfless-ness (acting in public, not private, interest), integrity (freedom from influence from outside interests), objectivity (making decisions on merit), and honesty.[4] These principles are not legally binding. They have, though, come to inform public life and other codes of conduct, such as the Ministerial Code and the Civil Service Code, which are respectively applicable to government Ministers and civil servants. Public oppro-brium is highly likely to be attracted by politicians and officials who fall short of these standards. A prime example of this was the public revulsion exhibited in relation to the 2009 MPs' expenses scandal—discussed in more detail in the next chapter—when it transpired that some MPs had made expenses claims that were widely regarded as highly improper.

---

[3] For example, if she owned land consisting of part of one of the potential sites, such that choosing that site would increase the value of that land.

[4] See **http://www.public-standards.gov.uk**. The other principles are accountability and transparency (which we address below) and leadership (meaning that '[h]olders of public office should promote and support [the other] principles by leadership and example').

2.2 **Governing transparently**

It is implicit in what has already been said that it can be hard to distinguish the content of the principles of good governance from the mechanisms necessary to secure (or at least to incentivise) it.[5] So it is with the requirement of transparency or openness—another of the principles articulated by the Committee on Standards in Public Life and upheld in a number of different ways, including, now, via the Freedom of Information Act 2000. According to the Committee, openness requires that '[h]olders of public office should be as open as possible about all the decisions and actions that they take', 'should give reasons for their decisions', and should 'restrict information only when the wider public interest clearly demands'. Transparency is arguably desirable in and of itself—it recognises that people are 'grown-ups' who deserve to be told what is being decided and why—but it is also a means to another, important, end. As Brandeis observed: 'Sunlight is said to be the best form of disinfectant.'[6] A government that is both open and transparent is likely to avoid acting in a way that is otherwise improper, and which may undermine the trust that people place in it. It is unsurprising, for example, that the new regulatory body set up in response to the MPs' expenses scandal now publishes MPs' expenses claims as a matter of course.[7] Good governance therefore implies not merely that government pursues the public interest (and only the public interest), but also that it does so openly and transparently.

2.3 **Respecting the dignity, rights, and interests of individuals**

Transparency, as indicated above, is one way of respecting the dignity of people—that is, of recognising that they are individuals whose views and interests deserve to be taken into account, as opposed to mere pawns who must unquestioningly accept the government's dictates. But good governance requires much more than this. This is reflected in many of the legal standards by which government is required to abide. These standards are anchored in the rule of law. As we saw in Chapter 2, this concept requires that government act in accordance with the law and the principles of legality that have been developed by the courts. It is, for example, a long-established legal principle that government is obliged to adopt a fair decision-making process when it goes about the task of making decisions that affect individuals. This means, among other things, that government must afford affected individuals an opportunity to be heard—to put their side of the story—rather than simply make decisions without knowledge of, or regard to, such individuals' circumstances and interests. The courts enforce this principle—known as *procedural fairness*—and other legal principles through the process known

---

[5] For example, because what constitutes the public interest is highly contestable, the requirement of governing in the public interest practically reduces to the requirement that mechanisms should exist for testing and challenging the wisdom of government policy and decisions.

[6] 'Other people's money', *Harper's Weekly*, 20 December 1913.

[7] Independent Parliamentary Standards Authority, *The MPs' Expenses Scheme* (London 2010).

as judicial review, which we will examine in detail in Chapters 12–15. A related point is that, under the Human Rights Act 1998 (HRA), government must respect individuals' human rights.

2.4 **Governing competently**

Many of the foregoing requirements of good governance are underpinned by or related to a further, and very basic, requirement—that of competence. As we have already seen, modern government is not merely a collection of government Ministers, but a very much larger enterprise. In addition to Ministers, government consists of the many departments and agencies that exist in order to make and administer public policy. When members of the public interact with government, they rarely, if ever, do so by way of direct contact with the Prime Minister or government Ministers; rather, they are far more likely to come into contact with the many officials and public servants located within the multitude of governmental bodies. Unlike government Ministers, these officials are neither directly elected nor accountable to Parliament; instead, they are appointed as full-time public employees on the basis of their knowledge and expertise. The public rightfully expects that these officials and public agencies operate in accordance with the above standards—that is, they seek to further the public interest, are open and transparent, obey the law, and do not infringe human rights. However, the public also expects these officials and public servants to adhere to basic principles of good administration. These principles require *inter alia* that governmental agencies advise individuals correctly and precisely on the detailed rules governing, for example, their tax liability or entitlement to welfare benefits, that they are customer-focused, and that, when mistakes are made, these are acknowledged and corrected quickly and effectively.[8]

Furthermore, good governance often requires the potential for incompetence to be recognised and anticipated. This means that when an individual receives a negative decision from a government agency (for example, when an individual's application for a welfare benefit has been refused), it is often appropriate that some form of redress is available via, for example, a complaints scheme, a tribunal, or an ombudsman. It also means that when a major issue of public concern has arisen because of some failing within government, the issue is properly investigated by an independent inquiry. Institutions such as these—ombudsmen, tribunals, and inquiries—form the 'administrative justice' system, and their operation is examined in Chapters 16–18. Finally, competent government requires that those in power are able and willing to learn lessons when things go wrong so as to prevent the recurrence of similar errors in the future.

---

[8] See, eg Parliamentary and Health Service Ombudsman, *Principles of Good Administration* (London 2009).

2.5 **Some preliminary conclusions**

The foregoing discussion is necessarily tentative: much of the rest of this book is devoted to detailed examination of the principles of good governance and the mechanisms for their enforcement. Nevertheless, it is appropriate, at this stage, to make two points by way of preliminary conclusion.

First, it is apparent that there is no comprehensive and definitive list of standards that together comprise good governance; nor, perhaps, could there be. The standards that define good governance are likely to vary and change in response to changes within public life itself. For example, the Committee on Standards in Public Life was itself established, in 1994, in the context of much concern about propriety in public life following the 'cash for questions' affair in which it was disclosed that some MPs had been asking parliamentary questions in return for financial payments. While basic lapses of probity were not, before that episode, regarded as acceptable, it placed such concerns centre-stage, resulting in a renewed emphasis upon them. We will also see that the need to ensure that proper control over public expenditure and that government secures value for taxpayers' money has evolved over time. Likewise, the precise nature of the legal controls over governmental action imposed by the courts have, over recent decades, intensified often as a result of changes in the courts' own perceptions as to the necessary demands of legality and of the (in)adequacy of alternative methods of scrutinising government. Furthermore, the recognition that openness and transparency within government are important standards that need to be secured was, after many years of persuasion, finally formally recognised by Parliament when it enacted the Freedom of Information Act 2000. The broader picture is, then, that the notion of good governance is dynamic, because it reflects contemporary and changing social, moral, and democratic mores.

Our second preliminary conclusion follows from the first: it is that the nature of *modern* government makes good governance a more acute concern than ever before. While there are various different ideas as to what government should and should not do, it could be said that there are four basic responsibilities that any legitimate government owes to its own citizens.[9] The first, and perhaps most fundamental, responsibility of government is to protect its own citizens by preserving their freedom so that they can live safe and secure lives. Governments seek to protect their own citizens in various ways. For example, through its relations with other states, a government will seek to protect its own territory from invasion; by organising a police service and criminal justice process, government will seek to maintain law and order. The second responsibility of government is to promote the welfare of its citizens. This is undertaken by, for example, managing the economy and providing a level of social protection for those individuals who are unable to provide for themselves. The third responsibility of government is to enforce justice by punishing crimes and resolving disputes, while the fourth responsibility is to promote truth and knowledge.

---

[9] Mulgan, *Good and Bad Power: The Ideals and Betrayals of Government* (London 2006), pp 44–58.

Exactly how government seeks to discharge these responsibilities will vary over time and between different countries. Perhaps the most noticeable development over the last two hundred years or so in most Western countries has been the growth in the scale and complexity of governmental action deemed necessary to fulfil these basic responsibilities. Modern government is a large and complex organisation comprising many different public agencies pursuing a multitude of important public goals. If the public desires some change or other in society—for example, a better transport system, better provision of public services such as education and health, more effective regulation of banks and financial institutions, or protection from worldwide flu pandemics—then it is usually government that is called upon to act. This is because government is often the only means by which the necessary resources can be collected, organised, and mobilised. Moreover, it is certainly plausible to assume that the scope and role of government is unlikely to diminish significantly in the future. If, for example, countries are to attempt to confront some of the world's major challenges—global terrorism, climate change, maintaining the supply of energy, and managing the global economy—then it is governmental action that will be required.

One important consequence of all of this is that people cannot seek to lead their lives without some element of governmental influence. If citizens wish to pursue collective goals, then they must generally agree to confer power on government to achieve these goals for them. Of course, this means that government itself becomes very powerful. Governmental power may be used for either good or ill—and the notion of good governance provides a blueprint, a template, that seeks to ensure that such powers are used only for good, and that there are adequate systems in place to provide correction and redress if they are used for ill. In this way, the idea of good governance is a necessary corollary to the very powerful systems of government found in many countries, including the UK, today. However, it is not enough that good governance exists as an idea: if the risk exists, as it surely does, that powerful governments may misuse their authority, then there need to be adequate systems in place to identify whether such abuse is happening—and, if so, to deal with such conduct. This leads us to the concept of accountability.

3. Accountability

3.1 The concept of accountability

In an ideal world, all governments and public office-holders could be expected to uphold the standards of good governance. Alternatively, if those standards were considered to be either ambiguous or insufficiently precise, then government could be expected to determine what those standards required in any particular set of circumstances and then respect them. There would consequently be little, if any, need to have other bodies to oversee government in order to check for compliance with these standards. But of course we do not live in an ideal world. It would be hopelessly naive simply to have blind faith in government, trusting it to adhere to the standards of good governance. The constant risk is that government may simply fail to live up to these standards or that it may seek to misuse its powers. While the public expects certain standards from government, no particular government—or even system of government—is either perfect or infallible. On the contrary, ordinary experience often demonstrates that those who hold public office sometimes fall short of the standards expected of them.

To ensure that government does act in accordance with the standards of good governance, it is therefore necessary that it be overseen by various accountability mechanisms. The purpose of such mechanisms is to ensure that government is held to account, that it properly observes the standards of good governance, and that its activities are properly scrutinised. In other words, for the standards of good governance to have real, practical effect, government needs to be subject to extensive mechanisms of accountability and oversight. An absence of effective mechanisms for holding government to account—and therefore a lack of accountability—diminishes good governance.

Over recent decades, the concept of accountability has increasingly come to prominence and is widely viewed as a key concept within modern, democratic constitutions. For that reason, the importance of holding government to account is one of the key themes of this book. Yet, while accountability has become ubiquitous, it is also an elusive concept that can mean different things to different people. We therefore need to take some care when considering this concept.

In essence, the concept of accountability represents the response of democracies to the need to oversee government. As Mulgan has noted, accountability—the obligation to be called to account—is

> a method of keeping the public informed and the powerful in check. It implies a world which is at once complex, where experts are needed to perform specialised tasks, but still fundamentally democratic in aspiration, in which members of the public assert their right to question the experts and exercise ultimate control over them.[10]

The concept reflects the recognition that no government is perfect. Given that government may get things wrong—whether by deciding upon a bad policy, by using an inadequate means of implementing a good policy, by wasting public money, or by acting unlawfully—it is essential that a constitution possesses adequate and effective safeguards. The purpose of these safeguards is to uncover bad government, to lay blame and criticism where it is required on those in power, and in that way to seek to prevent bad governance while at the same time promoting good governance.

What then does the concept of accountability mean? At its most basic level, accountability can be understood as a relationship between an actor and an accountability forum.[11] To be held to account, an actor (for example, the government or a government Minister) is obliged to explain and to justify his or her conduct. The relevant

---

[10] Mulgan, *Holding Power to Account: Accountability in Modern Democracies* (London 2003), p 1.

[11] Bovens, 'Public Accountability', in Ferlie, Lynn, and Pollitt (eds), *The Oxford Handbook of Public Management* (Oxford 2005), pp 184–5.

accountability forum (for example, Parliament or the courts) can ask questions and pass judgement. The actor may then face consequences: the accountability forum can either reward or punish the actor on the basis of the conduct or explanation given. The precise identity of both the actor and the accountability forum can, of course, vary. The actor will normally be someone or something that has the ability to exercise public power and so will often be a government Minister, a civil servant, a government department or agency, or the government as a whole. Likewise, the accountability forum will assume different guises. It may be the public, Parliament (whether an individual member of Parliament, a parliamentary select committee, or Parliament as a whole), a court of law, an audit agency, an ombudsman, a public inquiry, or a tribunal. Depending on who or what the actor is and what the accountability forum is, the relationship between the two will differ. For example, the process by which Parliament holds a government Minister to account is very different from that adopted by a court of law. In the former instance, politically aligned parliamentarians will ask questions of the Minister either in Parliament or in a committee hearing; in the latter, an individual will challenge the legality of the Minister's decision before an independent court. The nature of the actor and the forum will then influence both the operative procedure and the applicable standards of good governance.

One important upshot of this is that there is no single mechanism by which government is held to account. Another is that the idea of accountability does not possess a single meaning. Broadly speaking, in relation to holding government to account, there are three different types of accountability that recur over and over again.[12] First, there is the *political accountability* which seeks to ensure that government is subject to democratic and popular control. This form of accountability is exercised by the public through elections and on their behalf by Parliament. Second, there is the *legal accountability* of government, the purpose of which is to ensure that government acts according to law. This form of accountability is undertaken normally, although not exclusively, by the courts. The purpose is to guard against the abuse of public power and to protect the rights and interests of individuals adversely affected by governmental action in order to maintain the rule of law. In addition to courts that review the legality of public decisions, tribunals also determine appeals against negative administrative decisions. Third, there is *administrative accountability*. This type of accountability operates both within government itself and is also undertaken by independent audit agencies. This type of accountability is concerned with ensuring that government is both effective and efficient in administering and implementing public policy. Administrative accountability is concerned with neither the political desirability of government action, nor with its legality; rather, it is concerned with managing the

---

[12] See Day and Klein, *Accountabilities: Five Public Services* (London 1987), pp 4–29; Flinders, *The Politics of Accountability in the Modern State* (Aldershot 2001); Mashaw, 'Accountability and Institutional Design: Some Thoughts on the Grammar of Governance', in Dowdle (ed), *Public Accountability: Designs, Dilemmas and Experiences* (Cambridge 2006), pp 120–2; Bovens, 'Analysing and Assessing Accountability: A Conceptual Framework' (2007) 13 European Law Journal 447, 462–4.

machinery of government effectively so that the desired policy goals can be successfully and efficiently secured.

Each of these types or models of accountability are loosely connected with each other in that they all share the overriding purpose of holding government to account, but there are also, as we will see, important differences between them. It is necessary to elaborate on these different types of accountability.

3.2 Political accountability

In democracies, the most important type of accountability is political accountability. Government is politically accountable to both the public and Parliament, which represents the views of the public, for its policies. The rationale for political accountability reflects the nature of public power in a democracy. In a democracy, power is presumed to reside with the people. It is the people who decide to delegate power to government to achieve common goals. Government is legitimate only if it acts in the name of the people via the power they have conferred upon it. The corollary of this is that the people have the right to call government to account for how it has or has not exercised that power. The people are thereby equipped to exercise a form of control over those in public office by expressing their own views as to what the public interest requires. Since, as we noted earlier, there is no objectively correct definition of what the public good requires, political accountability forms an imperative connection between the views of the public at any given time and those in power who are charged with pursuing the public good.

The most conspicuous form of political accountability is the election. Elected officials are accountable to the electorate; by voting for elected representatives, the public delegates power to them. In the UK, the electorate votes, *inter alia*, for MPs to be returned to the House of Commons and members to the devolved legislatures. This, in turn, determines who forms the government. Of course, if the people elect a government of which they subsequently disapprove, then the next election will give them the opportunity to pass judgement.

Virtually all Western democracies owe a huge intellectual debt to ancient Greece, which is where the concept of democracy originates.[13] According to Aristotle, democracy meant direct democracy in which all citizens were to rule and to be ruled in turn.[14] However, while elections remain the basic foundation of any country's claim to be a democracy, they are, for a variety of reasons, by themselves usually less than fully effective mechanisms for holding government to account. Elections are not normally held that frequently. In the UK, general elections to Parliament are usually held every four to five years.[15] Consequently, the involvement of voters in the governmental process is not continuous, but intermittent: there are many decisions that government

---

[13] Dunn, *Setting the People Free: The Story of Democracy* (London 2005).

[14] Aristotle, *The Politics* (Harmondsworth 1962).

[15] On proposals to introduce fixed-term parliaments, see Chapter 5, section 2.2.2, above.

must take that are neither discussed during elections nor upon which the public has a direct say. Elections are then inherently constrained in the extent to which they enable government to be held to account. The function of elections is usually just to determine the composition of the political executive—which political party should form the government—and therefore the broad direction of government policy. A more granular form of control must therefore be exercised by holding government to account for its specific policies and decisions, as well as passing a global judgement upon it at elections.

In the UK, this is achieved, in part, by making government Ministers accountable to Parliament through the doctrine of ministerial responsibility. This requires them to provide an account of their actions and conduct in a variety of different ways.[16] For example, MPs are able to table parliamentary questions in order to elicit information from the government. Debates on the floor of both Houses of Parliament enable government policy and action to be queried and discussed. Furthermore, Parliament has specialist select committees that scrutinise the work of government. Each government department is overseen by a departmental select committee—a cross-party committee of MPs. These committees examine the expenditure, administration, and policy of government departments. Such committees regularly produce reports on aspects of government policy and administration, some of which can, on occasion, prove to be highly critical. Meanwhile, public inquiries into matters of grave public concern[17]—such as extreme incompetence or highly questionable judgement on the part of government—provide an alternative, or supplement, to parliamentary mechanisms of accountability.[18]

The effectiveness of the sanctions that may flow from such forms of political accountability are, though, far from certain. Parliament may, of course, criticise a particular government policy. However, whether such criticism will prompt the government to think again will often depend not only upon the cogency of that criticism, but also upon whether sufficient MPs are prepared to vote against the government. In a parliamentary system such as that of the UK, there have long been concerns that the process of political accountability is not as effective as it should be. Parliament is rarely successful in overturning government decisions because it is dominated by the government of the day that exerts control over its own MPs. Equally, if a public inquiry contains excoriating criticism of government, there is no guarantee that anything in particular will happen as a result. This is not to say, however, that the absence of coercive power robs inquiries and parliamentary forms of accountability of any teeth. Given the right political circumstances,[19] government may, in effect, have no choice but to take whatever corrective action Parliament or an inquiry demands. Nonetheless, concerns as to

---

[16] For more detail, see Chapter 10.

[17] The decision to go to war in Iraq—which has been the subject of several public inquiries—being an obvious example.   [18] On inquiries, see Chapter 18 below.

[19] For example, if the report of an inquiry or parliamentary committee captures public attention and harnesses public anger, the government may find itself backed into a corner.

the ineffectiveness of political and parliamentary accountability of the government have been one of the defining features of the contemporary British constitution, and it remains to be seen whether and, if so, how, Parliament can become more effective in scrutinising government.

3.3 Legal accountability

Legal accountability is a central aspect of the rule of law. Like everyone else, government is obliged to follow the law. However, the nature of the legal relationship between government and individuals is of a completely different nature from that between one individual and another. Whereas private law regulates those forms of activity that anyone can undertake (such as entering into contracts), public law embodies distinctive rules and principles that regulate the activity of governing. The most fundamental principle is that of legality. Whereas individuals can do anything that is unlawful, the general principle[20] is that government can do only that which it is legally authorised to do: if it undertakes unauthorised tasks, or undertakes authorised tasks in an improper way, it acts unlawfully. Unlawful governmental acts are invalid (of no legal effect) and, as such, can be struck down by the courts via judicial review.[21]

The rationale behind legal accountability is that anyone whose rights or interests have been adversely affected by the actions of someone else has the right to hold that person to account. In particular, because government has extensive and coercive powers that can be used to the detriment of people, it is necessary that there are special arrangements to protect individuals against excessive or abusive use of those powers. As a method of control over governmental activity, legal accountability is largely concerned with protecting individuals against the infringement of their interests and rights by government. The courts do this by examining whether public decisions— that is, decisions taken by government—comply with the following public law principles: *legality* (public decisions should be made within the scope of the legal powers of government), *procedural fairness* (government must adopt a fair decision-making process), and *rationality* (public decisions must not outrageously defy logic or accepted moral standards). Furthermore, under the HRA, the courts can strike down public decisions that constitute a disproportionate infringement of an individual's rights, as laid down in the European Convention on Human Rights (ECHR), and may also declare primary legislation to be incompatible with such rights.

There are, though, some inherent limitations as to how legal accountability by courts operates. First, the courts do not have a free-roaming mandate to rule upon the legality of any government decision; their jurisdiction is only engaged if they have been called to adjudicate upon a legal dispute in which an individual or other body wishes to challenge a government decision. Second, the courts can only review

---

[20] But cf Harris, 'The "Third Source" of Authority for Government Action Revisited' (2007) 123 LQR 225.

[21] Judicial review is considered in detail in Chapters 12–15 below.

whether a government decision is unlawful; they have no jurisdiction to consider whether a public decision is either right or wrong, or to substitute it with a decision of their own. The courts therefore need to be careful when reviewing the legality of a public decision to ensure that they do not themselves lapse into error by telling the government whether or not a particular policy or decision is a good one. If the courts were to do this, then they would be intruding into the realm of political accountability. While legal accountability is subject to these constraints, it does possess a particular strength: the effectiveness of its sanctions or remedies. Legal remedies against a government that has acted unlawfully are legally binding; government has no choice whether or not to comply with a court judgment and can be compelled by the courts to do so.

Finally, it is important to bear in mind that the courts are not the only mechanism for ensuring that government acts according to law. In many instances, an individual who has received a negative decision from a government agency (for example, refusal of a welfare benefit) can appeal against that decision to an independent, judicial tribunal. Tribunals handle vastly more cases each year than the courts. Tribunals are less formal than courts; they are staffed by tribunal judges who specialise in the particular area of law, and, unlike courts, tribunals can substitute their own decision for that produced by the government.[22]

3.4 **Administrative accountability and audit**

Administrative accountability and audit are concerned with ensuring that government 'gets the job done'—that it implements policy effectively and efficiently. It also provides government and public office-holders with feedback on their conduct that may induce them to improve their future performance. From this perspective, responsible and accountable government is likely to be better government and therefore more likely to achieve desired policy goals. Administrative accountability focuses upon the organisation and management of government agencies. It is concerned with issues such as whether, for example, government agencies are well organised, staffed by competent and honest people, and able to perform and deliver public services effectively and efficiently.

On one level, administrative accountability and audit operates internally within government—that is, as a means whereby government can exercise control over itself. Given the scale of modern government, the Prime Minister cannot hope to exert much effective control over the operations of the governmental machine. He therefore appoints Ministers who, in turn, are able to instruct their civil servants and officials as to how they ought to operate. The Civil Service itself is made up of different grades, and civil servants work within different government departments and agencies. To ensure coordination and control, higher-level officers are able to issue instructions

---

[22] On tribunals, see Chapter 17 below.

to lower-level officers. Such instructions can take a number of different forms, such as rules, policies, and guidance that lower-level officials need to follow and apply. These factors—hierarchy of authority, specialisation, and a system of rules—are the basic characteristics of public administration.[23] Given the essentially administrative nature of modern government, it is necessary to design mechanisms of administrative accountability to ensure that administrative agencies work effectively and efficiently.

A particularly noticeable form of administrative accountability over the last decade or so has been the system of public service agreements (PSAs) introduced by the 1997–2010 Labour administration. Under this system, targets and performance indicators were established by government itself. Government departments and agencies were then expected to meet these targets and performance indicators. As we noted above, officials and civil servants are not usually subject to political accountability, whereas government Ministers are. However, such officials are accountable to Ministers, and PSAs were a means of establishing objective yardsticks by which the performance of departments and agencies, and the individuals within them, could be monitored.[24]

Administrative accountability does not, though, operate solely within the governmental machine itself. There are various other bodies that have been established in order to oversee government and to hold it to account. Consider, for example, the audit agencies, such as the National Audit Office and the Audit Commission, which oversee public spending by central and local government, respectively.[25] These bodies—colloquially known as the 'spending watchdogs'—were created to ensure that government spends public money wisely and that it secures value for money in the delivery of public services.[26] These bodies are neither judicial nor legislative, but are themselves administrative agencies established by Parliament. Their purpose is to inspect the government's accounts and to examine the economy, efficiency, and effectiveness with which government agencies use their resources when discharging their functions. The benefit of such bodies is that they are non-political institutions, and possess the requisite independence and expertise with which to examine whether public money is being spent effectively and prudently.

There are other public bodies that oversee government. For example, ombudsmen investigate complaints lodged by individuals complaining of maladministration—bad administrative practice—by government agencies.[27] The purpose of such ombudsmen is to investigate those instances of maladministration that are productive of injustice for the individual concerned, to ensure that government learns the necessary lessons, and also to promote the principles of good administration, so that government can improve the quality of public services. To these ends, ombudsmen have the

---

[23] Blau and Meyer, *Bureaucracy in Modern Society* (New York 1987).

[24] The system of PSAs was abolished in 2010 by the Conservative–Liberal Democrat coalition government, but was replaced by another internal system of administrative accountability known as structural reform plans, on which, see Chapter 11, section 3.2, below.

[25] However, see Chapter 11, section 4.2, below on proposals announced in 2010 to abolish the Audit Commission.   [26] See further Chapter 11 below.

[27] See further Chapter 16 below.

ability to make recommendations to government, for example, that it reorganise its processes and administrative systems in order to prevent similar injustices reoccurring. Ombudsmen can also recommend that government pays out compensation to individuals who have suffered some loss as a result of its maladministration. Unlike the audit agencies, ombudsmen are not concerned with either auditing government accounts or promoting value for money; rather, they are concerned with promoting adherence to the principles of good administration by government in order to ensure a better quality of government.

A distinctive feature of such agencies—the audit agencies and ombudsmen—is that they provide expert and non-political oversight of government. They are generally accepted to be credible and trustworthy mechanisms for holding government to account, and their reports often become topics of political and public comment. At the same time, this type of accountability has its limitations. Unlike the courts, neither the audit agencies nor ombudsmen can impose legally binding sanctions or remedies upon government. However, their recommendations are usually accepted and acted upon by government. It is also important to recognise that accountability systems do not exist in complete isolation from one another. Audit and administrative accountability often feeds into political accountability. For example, reports by the National Audit Office are often followed up by parliamentary select committees—in particular, the House of Commons Public Accounts Committee. Likewise, when the government refuses to comply with a recommendation of the Parliamentary Ombudsman, the House of Commons Public Administration Select Committee often conducts an inquiry to assess whether or not the government's refusal is justified—and, if it thinks not, this may put the government under additional pressure to comply. In this way, different accountability mechanisms—and, indeed, different forms of accountability—overlap with and complement one another.

4. Conclusion

We have seen in this chapter that the public has a variety of different expectations as to how government should conduct itself. The standards of good governance should not therefore be understood as being either fixed or static; rather, since these standards develop over time, they are both fluid and dynamic. They reflect some of the most basic standards of a polity and, as a polity changes, so will the standards of good governance. At the most basic level, however, the standards of good governance require that government acts for the public good, that it acts lawfully, and that it is both effective and efficient in performing its assigned tasks. In order to ensure that government adheres to these broad standards, it is necessary that it is held to account by different bodies in different ways.

From one perspective, the imposition of extensive and complex webs of accountability upon government may present its own risks. Government may spend so much of its time being held to account that its capacity to govern effectively is undermined; too much accountability may be just as problematic as insufficient or deficient accountability. Furthermore, there may often be tensions between different accountability processes. As Bovens has noted, public institutions are not infrequently faced with the '*problem of many eyes*: they are accountable to a plethora of different forums, all of which apply a different set of criteria'.[28] At the same time, it is important to recall that accountability is necessary in order to fulfil the ideals of good governance. The crucial issue that arises is then the operation and effectiveness of particular types of accountability. Examining the operation of the different accountability mechanisms that function in the context of the UK is the task of the chapters that follow.

Further reading

BOVENS, 'Analysing and Assessing Accountability: A Conceptual Framework' (2007) 13 European Law Journal 447

DOWDLE (ed), *Public Accountability: Designs, Dilemmas and Experiences* (Cambridge 2006)

HOUSE OF COMMONS PUBLIC ADMINISTRATION SELECT COMMITTEE, *Good Government* (HC 97 2008–09).

MULGAN, *Holding Power to Account: Accountability in Modern Democracies* (London 2003)

---

[28] Bovens, 'Analysing and Assessing Accountability: A Conceptual Framework' (2007) 13 European Law Journal 447, 455. See also Bovens, Schillemans, and Hart, 'Does Public Accountability Work? An Assessment Tool' (2008) 86 Public Administration 225, 227–30.

10 Parliamentary Scrutiny of Central Government

1. Introduction

The central concern of this chapter is the accountability of government—in particular, the accountability of the United Kingdom's central government to the UK Parliament. It is a fundamental principle of the British constitution that government Ministers, who together comprise the government, are responsible—both collectively and individually—to Parliament. The UK government derives its authority, legitimacy, and ability to govern from Parliament by virtue of its majority in the House of Commons. In turn, government is responsible to Parliament and it is for Parliament to hold the government to account by scrutinising its policies, decisions, and actions. As we noted in the previous chapter, political accountability of government takes two principal forms: electoral and non-electoral accountability. General elections determine the political composition of the government and provide the democratic basis of the constitution, but they occur relatively infrequently.[1] In the meantime, political accountability is dependent upon Parliament's ability to scrutinise government actions. Parliament is, then, amongst the most important institutions for holding government to account. In this chapter, we examine the constitutional relationship between government and Parliament, the mechanisms used by Parliament to scrutinise governmental action, the effectiveness of such mechanisms, and their possible reform.

To state the obvious, the focus of this chapter directly relates to one of our major themes—namely, the accountability of government to Parliament, and, in particular, the ability of Parliament effectively to scrutinise government and to hold it to account for its actions or inactions. Central to any consideration of the accountability of government to Parliament is the convention of ministerial responsibility—namely, the obligation of Ministers to account to Parliament and to be held to account for governmental policies and decisions. At the same time, Parliament's role in scrutinising government is directly related to, and in some senses dependent upon, another major aspect of any constitution—the ability and power of the executive to govern. It is therefore necessary that we consider the broader relationship between Parliament and government in the UK and the constitutional doctrine of ministerial responsibility in

---

[1] See further Chapter 5, section 2.2, above.

some detail. As we have emphasised throughout this book, that relationship is characterised by the government's dominance over Parliament—particularly the House of Commons. We will explore the following questions: what is Parliament's proper role in scrutinising government? What does the constitutional convention of ministerial responsibility mean? And how does it operate in practice?

Another initial point needs to be made. In other chapters of this book, we have identified a tension between political and legal forms of constitutionalism, and the possible move toward a more legal constitution. There is, of course, no prospect of this transition occurring in relation to parliamentary scrutiny of government, because that is an inherently political process—although, as we explain in Chapter 12, concern about the effectiveness of parliamentary scrutiny is arguably one reason why greater emphasis is increasingly being placed on legal forms of accountability.

Having examined parliamentary scrutiny of government, the chapter examines two topics of particular importance to the accountability of government. The first is freedom of information law—that is, the law governing the extent to which individuals are able to access information held by government agencies. The second topic is the accountability of the security and intelligence services.

2. Parliamentary control and government

2.1 Political accountability

All democratic constitutions possess an inevitable and built-in tension between two major forces: governing and scrutinising. The first force reflects the essential need for a polity to be governed—that is, for a collection of people (the government) to decide how they are going to govern the country, which policies they will adopt, and how those policies are to be implemented. The basic responsibilities of government are to protect its own people and to promote their welfare. No successful country has ever existed without an effective government.

The second force in a democratic constitution is the need to call to account those who do the governing, to scrutinise their actions, to ask questions of them to determine whether their policies are, in fact, beneficial and well considered, and whether such policies are being implemented effectively, fairly, and efficiently. In a democracy, government can only rule by consent and only if it is open to scrutiny. The need for government is logically prior to the need for scrutiny—but scrutiny is a prerequisite of *legitimate* government.

Political accountability of government is of fundamental importance for a number of reasons. First, it enables *democratic control* over government. Much of the scrutinising has to be done by people—elected representatives, such as MPs—who are themselves representative of, and accountable to, the people. Second, political accountability requires government to *explain and justify* its actions and policies. In turn, this encourages better-thought-out policymaking and implementation by government. It also requires government to listen to, take account of, and respond to views different from its own. Finally, political accountability will often involve the *making of judgements* as to the success or otherwise of governmental action. These judgements often inform citizens' votes and so the formation of future governments.

However, while political accountability is of fundamental importance, it can often be difficult to secure in practice. This is because the two forces—governing and scrutinising—very often compete with one another. If too much emphasis is placed upon governing, that may unduly restrict the scope for effective scrutiny of government. Conversely, if too much emphasis is placed upon effective scrutiny, then the task of governing will be impeded. The solution, then, is to find some appropriate balance between governing and scrutiny, but, as we will see, this is no easy task.

2.2 Political accountability in the UK

In the UK, political scrutiny of government is undertaken primarily by Parliament. There are various different aspects to Parliament's scrutiny of government. One of these—its scrutiny of government Bills—has already been considered in Chapter 4. Our conclusion there was that while Parliament enacts legislation and possesses some influence over the content of legislation, its role is limited, because it is the government that dominates the legislative process. In Chapter 11, we will examine another aspect of Parliament's scrutiny function—namely, its scrutiny of public expenditure—that is, its oversight of government decisions both to raise and to spend public money. Meanwhile, in this chapter, we are principally concerned with Parliament's role as regards political and administrative oversight of government. Political oversight concerns the policy choices and decisions that government makes, while administrative oversight involves scrutinising, on a more technical level, the way in which government programmes are implemented and delivered.

The general issue of the accountability of one branch of the state—the executive—to another—the legislature—raises a number of questions. How does the legislature seek to scrutinise the executive? What are the particular tools or mechanisms at Parliament's disposal? How effective are such mechanisms in holding the executive to account? What are their limitations? To the extent that such scrutiny mechanisms are deficient, then how, if at all, could they be improved? Because accountability is (for the reasons set out above) important, questions such as these are of considerable constitutional significance in any democratic country. However, over recent years, these questions have assumed particular importance in the UK for a number of reasons.

First, there have long been *concerns about whether the UK Parliament can and does subject the government to effective scrutiny*. Public confidence in Parliament is perhaps the lowest it has been for decades, due in part to the fact that Parliament's agenda and composition are largely dominated by the government of the day. At the time of writing, there is, unusually, a coalition government: a government comprised of two political parties. Although the two parties that form the coalition had to (and continue to have to) compromise with one another in deciding which policies to implement, the coalition, as a block, nevertheless numerically dominates the House of Commons, with well over half of the MPs. Coalitions may be peculiarly fragile, because they bring together MPs with explicitly different views, but similar problems can beset single-party governments too: John Major's administration in the 1990s was riven by internal dissent, resulting in a relatively weak government. These phenomena are, however, without prejudice to the fact that the UK system often delivers strong governments able to dominate Parliament.

Second, Parliament—in particular, the House of Commons—has come to be seen as *increasingly remote from the concerns of the public.* All too often, the public's perception of the House of Commons is that it is either the scene of 'Punch and Judy politics', in that the apparent role of MPs is to cheer for their own side and jeer at the other side, or else that the Commons chamber is almost entirely empty, with only a handful of MPs discussing a particular issue. These images contrast sharply with the ideal of a modern, professional legislature—one that closely scrutinises executive policies and decisions, and is able to extract information from the executive, point out wrongdoing, and prevent its reoccurrence.

Third, these specific institutional concerns over the scrutiny role of Parliament are connected to a broader political problem: *widespread public cynicism and even contempt for politicians.* In the UK, public confidence in Parliament received a considerable battering when, in 2009, the MPs' expenses scandal erupted. It was disclosed that many, although not all, MPs had made expenses claims from which they were able to profit personally. While one upshot of this episode was changes to the law governing parliamentary standards, another was the establishment of the House of Commons Reform Committee to consider how to improve parliamentary scrutiny of the government, which is considered below.

More generally, the wider problem is *public disengagement from politics.* Despite the fact that politics affects virtually every aspect of our lives, paradoxically many people have little, if any, interest in it. Of course, this problem has various causes and is by no means confined to the UK. It is, though, credible to suppose that responsibility can partly be ascribed to the sort of concerns about Parliament and politicians considered above. This suggests that the issues considered in this chapter concerning parliamentary scrutiny of government possess a wider political and constitutional relevance in relation to the political process and the democratic system.

In practical terms, scrutiny is carried out via three main mechanisms: oral and written questions to Ministers, parliamentary debates, and inquiries by 'select committees'. To assess the effectiveness of these mechanisms as devices by which Parliament can hold government to account, we will need to consider each in turn. First, however, it is necessary to consider the general institutional setting within which they are deployed by considering the political relationship between government and Parliament and the constitutional doctrine of ministerial responsibility. It is important to consider both of these topics because, as we noted earlier, parliamentary scrutiny of government takes place within a context characterised by the tension between governing and scrutinising. To appreciate that context fully, it is necessary to consider the nature of the power relationship between government and Parliament.

3. Parliament and government

3.1 Roles and responsibilities

The relationship between the UK government and Parliament is both complex and dynamic. As we have seen, there are two defining aspects of that relationship: first, it is wholly governed by political considerations; and, second, governments are normally able to dominate Parliament through their majority in the House of Commons. From one perspective, this domination gives rise to an undesirable 'elective dictatorship' by which the government is able to force through any measure.[2] However, from a different perspective, to describe this situation as an 'elective dictatorship' is merely to adopt a simplistic cliché because the UK constitution actually requires that the government dominate Parliament; if government were not to do so, then it would forfeit its right to govern. The government only acquires its authority from its majority in the House of Commons and the first obligation of government is to govern—that is, to make and implement public policy.

To understand Parliament's scrutiny function, it is necessary to understand the respective roles of Parliament and government. The Victorian Prime Minister Gladstone once said to the House of Commons: 'Your business is not to govern the country, but it is, if you see fit, to call to account those who govern it.'[3] In a similar vein is the following statement by JS Mill:

> Instead of the function of governing, for which it is radically unfit, the proper office of a representative assembly is to watch and control the government: to throw the light of publicity on its acts: to compel a full exposition and justification of all of them which any one considers questionable; to censure them if found condemnable, and, if the men who compose the government abuse their trust, or fulfil it in a manner which contradicts with the deliberate sense of the nation, to expel them from office, and either expressly or virtually appoint their successors.[4]

Parliament does not govern because it is neither intended nor equipped to do so. Indeed, the British people have never had government *by* Parliament simply because it has always been accepted that this would not work. What the British people do have, though, is government *through* Parliament. Parliament provides the government of

---

[2] Hailsham, *The Dilemma of Democracy: Diagnosis and Prescription* (Glasgow 1978).
[3] HC Debs Series 3, vol 136, col 1202 (29 January 1855).
[4] 'Considerations on Representative Government' [1861], in Mill, *On Liberty and Other Essays* (Oxford 1991), p 282.

the day with the authority to govern: the government can then get on with the job of governing, subject to the fact that Parliament also seeks to hold the government of the day to account.

To understand further the role of the UK Parliament, it is profitable to draw upon the distinction between 'transformative' and 'arena' legislatures. A 'transformative' legislature is one that possesses its own 'independent capacity, frequently exercised, to mold and transform proposals from whatever source into laws'.[5] Such legislatures have an existence separate from that of the executive branch; the classic example is the US Congress. By contrast, 'arena' legislatures 'serve as formalized settings for the interplay of significant political forces in the life of a political system'.[6] Whereas transformative legislatures are able to exert significant influence over how a country is governed and hold government robustly to account, arena legislatures tend merely to provide a forum in which the theatre of politics is conducted, and exercise little real power. The focus for arena legislatures is not upon governing, but upon debating what the government does.

The UK Parliament has long been held up as the archetypal arena legislature. As King explains, Parliament 'is simply not equipped to function as a transformative legislature, and of course governments of all political parties are anxious to ensure that it never, ever becomes so equipped'.[7] Parliament provides the forum in which competing political parties confront each other through the roles of government and opposition. Parliament is also a reactive legislature in the sense that much of its time is spent not in developing its own laws or policy proposals, but in responding to and scrutinising the government's proposals for new laws or policies. As we noted in Chapter 4, in the UK, the initiative rests with the government of the day. Finally, Parliament is also a reactive legislature in the sense that all of the work of government—the delivery and administration of government policy—is undertaken outside of Parliament by government departments and other public bodies. As Flinders has explained, the UK's constitutional framework is such that Parliament adopts 'a passive rather than active role in relation to the administration' by 'hold[ing] ministers responsible for the way in which they steer the ship of state'.[8] In other words, the role of Parliament is to provide a forum in which political debate occurs, to enable different views within society to be represented, but real power remains with the government and its heavy, complex administrative machinery.

Q What are the roles of Parliament in relation to the government? Why would changing the role of Parliament require a wider redesign of the UK's system of government?

---

[5] Polsby, 'Legislatures', in Greenstein and Polsby (eds), *Handbook of Political Science Vol 5: Governmental Institutions and Processes* (Reading, MA 1975), p 277.   [6] Polsby, p 277.

[7] *The British Constitution* (Oxford 2007), p 332.

[8] 'MPs and Icebergs: Parliament and Delegated Governance' (2004) 57 Parliamentary Affairs 767, 778.

3.2 **The nature of parliamentary control of government**

The nature of the political relationship between the government and Parliament has important consequences as regards the nature of Parliament's control of government. Whatever form that control takes, it does not—because it cannot—consist in outright parliamentary *direction* of government. The government's inevitable majority in the House of Commons means that the Commons cannot readily defeat the government or tell the government what to do. Governments rarely lose votes in the Commons because they enjoy both numerical dominance and, usually, a high degree of discipline over their backbench MPs. The political reality, then, is that Parliament does not control the government; rather, it is the government that controls Parliament. And there is no reason why this should not be so when, as at present, the government consists of a coalition of two (or more) parties, provided that those parties have a sufficiently strong relationship with one another.

At the same time, the relationship between Parliament and government is a complex and subtle one. Parliament may be dominated by the government, but government must take seriously the views of Parliament. Backbench MPs may raise concerns about a particular policy and threaten to rebel against the government. Parliamentary select committees often produce reports on governmental activities that are highly critical. MPs can ask questions of Ministers and debate policy issues. Government cannot afford to ignore such questions and debates or the views articulated within Parliament. So, while Parliament cannot realistically command the government and tell it what it ought to do, it is, nonetheless, able to exert influence. It follows that, as Crick has explained, parliamentary control of government in the UK context 'means *influence*, not direct power; *advice*, not command; *criticism*, not obstruction; *scrutiny*, not initiation; and *publicity*, not secrecy'.[9]

What this means in practice is that the relationship between government and Parliament tends to operate along the following lines. The government will make a policy decision to do something; the right of initiative always rests with the government. Parliament may then seek to scrutinise the decision taken. MPs and peers may debate the matter and/or put questions to Ministers. A parliamentary select committee may even undertake an inquiry into the issue, and produce a report that is critical of the government's policy and/or its administration by a particular public body. By raising criticisms of the policy, Parliament will perform its role in throwing light upon the issue and reflecting public opinion on the particular matter. Parliament might even seek to influence the content of government policy. It is, of course, possible that, as a result of such scrutiny, the government might completely change its policy. But no one really expects this to happen and the vast majority of the time it will not happen. Typically, the government will respond by providing Parliament with an explanation and a defence of its decision. Parliament might, of course, be able to win some concessions—even to prompt the government to rethink how it might seek to achieve

---

[9] *The Reform of Parliament* (London 1969), p 80.

a particular outcome. Nevertheless, Parliament will rarely be able to command the government to take, or to refrain from taking, a particular course of action.

The extent of Parliament's influence over government is dependent on the political context—that is, the strength of the government's majority in the House of Commons, whether there are fault lines within the government (be it a single-party or coalition government), the nature of the particular policy or administrative issue, the attitudes of the opposition parties, the feelings amongst the government's backbench MPs, and media and public opinion. Occasionally, such factors conspire to force a government to change its policy—for example, if there is widespread public opposition to a policy proposed by a weak government—but that is the exception, the norm being that Parliament has very limited capacity directly to determine the course that the government adopts.

A further exception, albeit a minor one, should also be noted. It is that Parliament (or, more accurately, the House of Commons) can exercise genuine control, as opposed to mere influence, over the government through the medium of a confidence motion. By convention, the government must resign if it loses a vote of confidence. This can certainly happen. For example, the 1979 Labour government fell because it lost a confidence vote (by a single vote) in the House of Commons. However, votes of no confidence are exceedingly rare and highly unusual. They represent the breakdown of the relationship between Parliament and government rather than the assertion of ordinary parliamentary control. The position has always been that the loss of a confidence vote by the government triggers the dissolution of Parliament and a general election. However, the Fixed-term Parliaments Bill, which is before Parliament at the time of writing, would (if enacted in its current form) simply require the government to resign upon losing a confidence vote. An election would only be triggered if a new government—for example, via the formation of a (new) coalition—could not be formed within 14 days. These issues were considered in Chapter 4. For now, the important point is that governments, in practice, rarely face the threat of being overthrown by Parliament.

The role of sustaining the government in power is undertaken by the government's backbench MPs—its majority. The opposition parties will criticise the government, oppose its policies, and present their own policies. However, opposition parties do such things not in the hope or expectation that the government will actually change its policy, but rather in an attempt to convince the public of their own fitness for government. In this sense, parliamentary scrutiny is as much concerned with the political 'game', in that the parties vie for public attention and approval, as it is with genuine oversight of government.

It might be asked: why does the relationship between Parliament and government operate in this way? The answer is simple: the British governmental tradition has a particularly pronounced disposition toward strong and stable government; government must get on with governing. Irrespective of which political party or parties form the government of the day, the deeply embedded cultural and political attitude within the UK constitution is that, first and foremost, government must have the ability to act and to take the initiative; this is not only an essential attribute of government, but also of the constitutional system of which it forms the central part. It is for this reason that the UK constitution has often been described as a 'power-hoarding' constitution because power is largely concentrated within the government of the day. So long as the government retains its Commons majority, it is given considerable freedom to make and implement its policies. This essential aspect of the constitution is reflected in many aspects of British political culture, such as the adversarial nature of politics, the party system in which political parties engage in an almost continual general election campaign with each other, and also the convention of ministerial responsibility.

> **Q** What does it actually mean to say that Parliament 'controls' the executive in the UK? What does the meaning of parliamentary control tell us about the relationship between government and Parliament?

4. Ministerial responsibility

4.1 Introduction

Now that we have considered the broader political relationship between government and Parliament, and the nature of parliamentary control over government, we can turn to consider the constitutional doctrine concerning the responsibility of government to Parliament. This is the doctrine of ministerial responsibility, which means that Ministers are responsible to Parliament for their decisions and policies and those of their departments.

It is generally said that there are two aspects to the concept of ministerial responsibility. The notion of *collective responsibility* was considered in Chapter 4.[10] Our concern here is with *individual ministerial responsibility*. It is important to note at the outset that while the doctrine of ministerial responsibility lies at the heart of the constitution, its *place and status* have often been contested. Sometimes ministerial responsibility is described as a fundamental part of the UK constitution; sometimes it is dismissed as a myth because of its ineffectiveness in practice. Meanwhile, the *meaning* of ministerial responsibility is itself contested and it can possess different meanings depending on the context. The purpose of the discussion that follows is to elucidate both the constitutional meaning of the doctrine and its operation in practice.

It is important to recall that governmental power is held and exercised largely, although far from exclusively, by government Ministers. Ministers comprise the leading politicians of their day who belong to the governing political party (or coalition) with a Commons majority; collectively, they form the government. As we emphasised

---

[10] See Chapter 4, section 3.5, above.

in Chapter 4, Ministers are an essential, although very small, part of the much larger governmental machine. Ministers are the political heads of government departments, but these departments and their agencies are staffed by half a million civil servants. By convention and political practice, Ministers must also be members of either House of Parliament. As such, Ministers provide the vital link between the governmental machine and Parliament, and the convention of ministerial responsibility seeks to condition the nature of that relationship.

The official definition of ministerial responsibility is set out in the government's Ministerial Code. It says, 'Ministers have a duty to Parliament to account, and be held to account, for the policies, decisions, and actions of their departments and agencies.'[11] This may sound straightforward, but we will see that the official definition conceals several complexities. As we examine them, it will be useful (as it is when considering any particular accountability mechanism) to pose the following questions. First, who is accountable? Second, to whom are they accountable? Third, for what are they accountable? Fourth, how are they accountable? And, fifth, with what consequences?

In terms of governmental accountability to Parliament, the answers to these questions are provided by the convention of ministerial responsibility. The answers to the first and second questions—who can be called to account and by whom—are that government Ministers are accountable and answerable to Parliament. With regard to the third question—the matters on which Ministers can be called upon to explain or defend—the answer is that Ministers are responsible for the policies adopted by the government, in addition to the decisions and actions undertaken by their departments and agencies. Ministers are also responsible for their own personal conduct.

In addressing the fourth question, which concerns *how* Ministers are held to account, it is important to recognise that the duty under the Ministerial Code is twofold: Ministers are obliged both *to provide an account to Parliament* of the policies, decisions, and actions of the relevant government department; and to be *held to account by Parliament* for those policies, decisions, and actions. The first aspect of ministerial responsibility simply requires that Ministers render an account to Parliament by making statements and answering questions. By contrast, being held to account involves something more than only the provision of information; it also implies taking responsibility when things have gone wrong, and putting them right. There is no single mechanism by which accountability in either of these senses is enforced; rather, there are, as we have already noted, several such processes: questions to Ministers, debates in Parliament, and the work of parliamentary select committees.

The final question concerns the potential consequences or sanctions when wrongdoing or failure is uncovered. The question of the sanctions attendant upon being held to account is a problematic one because it will often depend upon numerous political

---

[11] Cabinet Office, *Ministerial Code* (London 2010), [1.2b]. This definition was approved by a parliamentary resolution in 1997.

factors such as the strength of criticism against the government Minister, what went wrong, who was actually responsible for it, the strength of the Minister's response to the criticism, the habitual desire of Ministers to seek to avoid political embarrassment, the strength of the government's majority in Parliament, the attitude of the Prime Minister, how the story can be 'spun' by the government to the media, the media's own reaction, and the views of the public toward the government. The vast majority of the time when government Ministers are called upon to answer for a government policy or decision, the Minister will simply explain and defend that policy or decision. This explanation and defence may sometimes be accompanied by an attack upon the policies of the opposition parties. By explaining and defending the policy or decision, the government will, with the support of its Commons majority, in most instances be able to continue with its policy. Having seen off the attack, the business of government can continue unhindered.

4.2 **Ministerial resignations**

One issue frequently discussed in relation to the consequences of ministerial responsibility concerns the most extreme sanction available—namely, whether or not a Minister should resign from his or her post because some wrongdoing has been uncovered. The convention of ministerial responsibility has sometimes been taken to mean that not only do Ministers have to assume responsibility for mistakes, but also that they have to accept whatever Parliament considers the appropriate penalty to be. However, ministerial resignations as a result of parliamentary pressure are extremely rare indeed. As Johnson has noted:

> Far more common has been the determination of ministers to fight off criticism, to deny or qualify their own responsibility, or simply to hang on to office for as long as the prime minister and their colleagues seem ready to stand behind them ... [I]n its penal application ministerial responsibility is rather like a paper tiger: it is often waved in front of ministers, but only rarely does it really frighten them.[12]

Whether or not a Minister resigns will depend upon a number of factors. First, there is the seriousness of the wrongdoing that has been uncovered. For example, no one would expect a Minister to resign because a civil servant within the Minister's department has made an erroneous decision with which the Minister had never been personally involved. On the other hand, the Ministerial Code states that a Minister who 'knowingly misleads' (that is, lies to) Parliament will be expected to resign.[13] In the former case, a ministerial resignation would not be warranted because the government is nowadays so large that no Minister could ever possibly know of, let alone oversee, all of the decision-making within his or her department. Indeed, if a Minister really were to resign every time that the relevant government department made a mistake, however minor, then it would be virtually impossible for government

---

[12] *Reshaping the British Constitution* (London 2004), pp 87–8.   [13] *Ministerial Code*, [1.2c].

to carry on: some ministerial offices would be subject to regular, if not daily, personnel changes. By contrast, lying to Parliament is at the other end of the scale. This still remains the biggest political sin that any politician can commit because it undermines the whole system of parliamentary control of government, which depends upon the government providing Parliament with accurate and truthful information.

Other crucial determinants of whether a Minister resigns include the Minister's own personal feelings, whether the Minister has the support of the Prime Minister, and the feelings within the political party.[14] All of those factors can be affected, often decisively, by the attitude of the media.[15] Once the media scents ministerial blood, intense pressure is today commonplace; beleaguered Ministers often go from having the 'full support' of the Prime Minister to resigning within a matter of hours or days.

Note that there is one important omission from this list of factors—namely, Parliament: ministerial resignations rarely, if ever, occur as a result of parliamentary pressure. Of course, there may be calls within Parliament from the opposition for a Minister to resign; this is all part of the political contest between the political parties that occurs in Parliament. Pressure brought to bear within Parliament (for example, via embarrassing questions put to Ministers or the Prime Minister) may help to increase the pressure on an embattled Minister, but the government's majority in the House of Commons will help to insulate it, to some extent, from such attacks. There are, inevitably, a number of reasons that may lead to ministerial resignations, but three types of situation may usefully be distinguished.

First, many resignations occur not because the Minister accepts responsibility for some political or administrative failing within his department, but because his own personal conduct has become a source of embarrassment to the government. The most obvious example of a purely personal issue likely to result in resignation is the disclosure that a Minister has behaved reprehensibly in his private life—for example, by having an affair. While not necessarily grounds for resignation, such conduct may result in pressure to resign if the Minister is thereby exposed as a hypocrite (for example, because he has previously championed 'family values').[16] Meanwhile, in 2010, David Laws, after less than three weeks in office, resigned as Chief Secretary to the Treasury when it was alleged that he had breached (at least the letter of) the rules on MPs' expenses: as the Minister responsible for implementing huge public spending cuts, it was felt in some quarters that questions over his personal financial propriety made his position untenable.

Second, a Minister's private life may more directly collide with his public duties. For example, when a Minister acts in a way that fails to recognise that a conflict of interests exists, this raises questions about his integrity and fitness for office.[17] In 2004, David

---

14 Finer, 'The Individual Responsibility of Ministers' (1956) 34 Public Administration 377.

15 Woodhouse, 'UK Ministerial Resignations in 2002: The Tale of Two Resignations' (2004) 82 Public Administration 1.   16 See, eg the resignation of Tim Yeo from John Major's administration in 1994.

17 The Ministerial Code (at [7.1]) requires Ministers to ensure that 'no conflict arises, or could reasonably be perceived to arise, between their public duties and their private interests, financial or otherwise'.

Blunkett was forced to resign as Home Secretary when an inquiry found that there had been a 'chain of events' linking him to a request to the Immigration and Nationality Directorate (IND) to fast-track a visa for his lover's nanny.[18] As the IND was a directorate within the Home Office, which is headed by the Home Secretary, Blunkett was forced to resign because of concern that his public role as Home Secretary may have been used for his private benefit.

Third, it is sometimes, but rarely, the case that a Minister resigns straightforwardly because he is responsible for, or has presided over, administrative chaos. Consider the dismissal of Blunkett's successor as Home Secretary, Charles Clarke. In 2006, it was disclosed that the IND had failed to deport over 1,000 foreign national prisoners who had completed their prison sentences. This was a major administrative failure. While the Home Secretary could not have been expected to have known about every aspect of the work of the IND, he took responsibility for it. In the event, the public and media pressure on the Prime Minister was so great that Clarke was, in effect, forced out from the government. But even when, as here, resignation is linked with departmental failure, it might be asked: what was the purpose of this resignation? It is apparent that Clarke's removal from the office of Home Secretary did nothing whatsoever to rectify the administrative problems within the Home Office (which would require major administrative reorganisation). Furthermore, Clarke was generally recognised to be an able and competent Minister. Rather, Clarke's resignation may have served a 'sacrificial' purpose: the failings within the Home Office were so serious, and public and media pressure was so immense, that the Prime Minister felt compelled to act in order to abate the media storm.

It might be thought that the infrequency of ministerial resignations means that the doctrine of ministerial responsibility is hollow and without substance. This would be wrong. The notion of government being responsible and accountable usually has a much wider meaning than the narrow question as to whether or not a Minister should resign. As we have noted above, more often than not, in order to discharge the obligation of ministerial responsibility, Ministers will answer questions put to them in Parliament and elsewhere, and then face up to whatever response their answer provokes in those to whom it is provided. Ministers have to devote a considerable amount of time and effort to their parliamentary work. This principally involves answering questions within Parliament, explaining governmental decisions and policies, appearing before select committees, and responding to criticisms of those decisions and policies. This is what lies at the heart of ministerial responsibility. While it would be going too far to say that whether a Minister should resign is inevitably a distraction, it is rarely the most important issue: resignation may, by itself, do little, if anything, to remedy the situation, and whether resignation occurs is likely to be determined by nothing more significant than chance political factors.

---

[18] Budd, *An Inquiry into an Application for Indefinite Leave to Remain* (HC 175 2004–05), [3.35].

4.3 **The different meanings of ministerial responsibility**

It was noted above that the doctrine of ministerial responsibility is a fundamental part of the UK constitution. Nonetheless, the doctrine presents both constitutional scholars and students with something of a paradox. On the one hand, Ministers are, *in theory*, responsible to Parliament; on the other hand, it is widely believed that Ministers are not *in practice* held to account by Parliament. It has, for example, been noted that the doctrine has a 'largely fictional character' and that it 'has every advantage except that it is not true. It is contrary to both the administrative and political realities'.[19] If this is so, then is it correct to describe ministerial responsibility as a fundamental part of the constitution? And how are Ministers in practice responsible to Parliament?

The key to understanding this paradox is to start by recognising that the convention of ministerial responsibility has different meanings and can operate in different ways with different implications.[20] Indeed, ministerial responsibility is a good illustration of what is sometimes described as an 'essentially contested concept'—that is, a concept that does not possess a single definitive meaning, but which instead possesses various different, even contradictory, meanings; in other words, an idea that means different things to different people.[21] It is, therefore, necessary to clarify the contrasting meanings sometimes ascribed to the notion of ministerial responsibility.

A second reason for examining ministerial responsibility in detail is that it is important not to take constitutional doctrines, such as ministerial responsibility, at face value. Constitutional conventions are not legal rules; treating them as if they were always poses the risk that they will conceal or confuse as much as they reveal.[22] Conventions such as ministerial responsibility always operate within a broader political context, with all of the messy and imperfect compromises that characterise politics. The ever-present risk is that political actors may give lip service to grand constitutional ideals that are, in practice, subordinated to political realities.

In terms of seeking to understand the different meanings often ascribed to the convention of ministerial responsibility, the critically important factor to bear in mind is the broader political relationship between government and Parliament. From this starting point, the following questions arise. Do the decisions and actions of government Ministers reflect the wishes of Parliament? Should they? Or, alternatively, do Ministers decide upon their own decisions and actions irrespective of the wishes of Parliament? There are different answers to these questions that, in turn, reflect different meanings attributed to ministerial responsibility.[23] Consider the following views of ministerial responsibility.

---

[19] Drewry, 'The Executive: Towards Accountable and Effective Governance?', in Jowell and Oliver (eds), *The Changing Constitution* (Oxford 2007), p 205; Gilmour, *The Body Politic* (London 1969), p 163.

[20] Marshall and Moodie, *Some Problems of the Constitution* (London 1971), p 52.

[21] Gaillie, 'Essentially Contested Concepts' (1955–56) 56 Proceedings of the Aristotelian Society 167.

[22] On constitutional conventions generally, see Chapter 2, section 3.5, above.

[23] Beattie, 'Ministerial Responsibility and the Theory of the British State', in Rhodes and Dunleavy (eds), *Prime Minister, Cabinet, and Core Executive* (London 1995), p 158. See also Birch, *Representative*

First, there is the 'Whig' view.[24] On this view, ministerial responsibility means that Ministers should be responsive to the views expressed in the House of Commons. This is because the House of Commons is a democratic and representative institution. Parliament should, therefore, exercise strong political control over the government and the doctrine of ministerial responsibility should be used to ensure that governmental decisions reflect the wishes of the House of Commons. Ministers, on this view, should also be held culpable when government fails in some way and should bear the consequences (that is, resign). Ministers should also listen and respond to views expressed in Parliament. Looked at in this way, ministerial responsibility is designed to promote representative government that is responsive to views expressed in Parliament—in particular, the House of Commons. This view of ministerial responsibility is often advanced by those who emphasise the importance of Parliament, who are sceptical of governmental power, and who would like government to pay more attention to views expressed in Parliament. But while this is the meaning often attached to the doctrine of ministerial responsibility, it is not the only one, and it is certainly not always reflected in reality.

The 'Whig' view should be compared with what has been termed the 'Peelite' view of ministerial responsibility.[25] On this view, ministerial responsibility means that the government—rather than Parliament—is responsible for governing. Ministerial responsibility ensures that Ministers are able to make government policy and decisions because they are able to command a majority in the House of Commons. Government decisions need not therefore reflect the wishes of the House of Commons; if they were to have to do so, then government would be weak and indecisive. Instead, ministerial responsibility means that Ministers make their own decisions, albeit that they have to explain and defend them before Parliament. The Minister is thus the government's spokesperson in Parliament who informs it of government decisions and answers questions. This view, then, reflects a conception of the relationship between the government and Parliament that is very different from that on which the Whig view is premised. The Peelite view presupposes the government's role as initiative-taker: backbench and opposition MPs do not tell Ministers how to act; rather, it is the government that is able to exercise control over its backbenchers through the whips. In this sense, ministerial responsibility is a means of limiting parliamentary involvement in order to ensure strong, stable, and effective government. While this view of

---

and Responsible Government: An Essay on the British Constitution (London 1964), pp 139–49; Flinders, 'The Enduring Centrality of Individual Ministerial Responsibility within the British Constitution' (2000) 6 Journal of Legislative Studies 73.

[24] The Whig Party was the reforming and constitutional party that sought the supremacy of Parliament and was succeeded by the Liberal Party during the nineteenth century.

[25] This view is named after Robert Peel, who was Prime Minister 1841–46. According to Hurd, *Robert Peel: A Biography* (London 2007), p 226, when Peel became Prime Minister in 1841, he considered that it was the duty of his backbench MPs to follow him: 'The country needed strong government. Peel…could never accept that it would be the duty of his government to consult, let alone follow, the views of backbenchers who by definition knew less than he and his colleagues on any subject under discussion.'

ministerial responsibility is rarely articulated, it has long found favour with those within government, such as Ministers and senior civil servants.

The notion of ministerial responsibility is often used in both of the senses set out above, but with different implications. Those who adhere to the Whig view are likely to be disappointed with the operation of ministerial responsibility in practice. For example, Barendt has lamented that it is now 'rare for the House of Commons to hold an individual minister to account'.[26] Furthermore, Jowell and Oliver have noted that 'the domination of party, especially the party of government serves to suppress any sense of a *corporate* House of Commons function or identity in holding government to account as opposed to sustaining it in power'.[27] These views clearly reflect the Whig view of ministerial responsibility: government should be made fully accountable to the House of Commons and should listen to the views expressed in the Commons. The fact that government rarely does this today strongly suggests that ministerial responsibility has been weakened so much that it can no longer be said to be a fundamental doctrine of the constitution.

But, from the Peelite standpoint, these views seem naive. From this perspective, ministerial responsibility is not Parliament's sword, but a Minister's shield: it was never intended to ensure that ministerial actions reflected the wishes of the House of Commons; rather, it was intended to preserve executive power and Ministers', rather than Parliament's, responsibility for governing. Furthermore, the assumption that the House of Commons possesses a corporate identity—that it comprises a single, unified entity devoted to scrutinising government—is at odds with reality. Instead, the UK Parliament is, as we noted above, an arena legislature that serves as the formalised setting for the interplay of political forces. In other words, Parliament does not function as a corporate, collective body, but as a setting in which different political parties are present; so long as the government has a majority in Parliament and is able to exert authority over its backbenchers, it need not genuinely consult with Parliament or be responsive to the views expressed therein.

Which view of ministerial responsibility now has the upper hand and which best reflects the practice of parliamentary control? It has been noted that 'the Whig tradition has always been paraded as the public face of ministerial responsibility, but the Peelite view has formed a strong undercurrent in governing attitudes'.[28] The Peelite view has considerable attractions for government: it offers Ministers flexibility and a strong platform from which to implement their policies. As Flinders has noted: 'The ascendancy of the Peelite strand is now complete. Ministerial responsibility has endured because it allows ministers to govern with a minimal level of Parliamentary interference while also, in the main, delivering stability.'[29] The basic point, then, is

---

26 Barendt, *An Introduction to Constitutional Law* (Oxford 1998), p 116.

27 Jowell and Oliver (eds), *The Changing Constitution* (Oxford 2007), p x.

28 Weir and Beetham, *Political Power and Democratic Control in Britain* (London 1998), p 338.

29 Flinders, 'The Enduring Centrality of Individual Ministerial Responsibility within the British Constitution' (2000) 6 Journal of Legislative Studies 73, 79.

that the notion of ministerial responsibility is viewed differently by different people and different actors within the political system. When opposition MPs complain (as they often do) that the government is not being properly held to account, they are subscribing to the Whig view of ministerial responsibility. By contrast, government Ministers and senior civil servants tend to adopt the Peelite view. Which view is adopted depends almost entirely upon whether or not it suits the immediate purposes of the actor involved.

Q Which view of ministerial responsibility—the Whig or the Peelite view—do you think best describes the practice and reality of parliamentary control of government? Which view do you think ought to inform parliamentary control of government?

4.4 Ministerial responsibility and administrative government today

4.4.1 Introduction

The doctrine of ministerial responsibility developed in the nineteenth century when government was much smaller and more limited than it is today. Furthermore, during this period, it became accepted that the general structure of government was to be organised through ministerial departments—that is, government departments staffed by civil servants and headed up by a government Minister.[30] Ministerial responsibility was designed to suit the needs of the relatively small structure of government and to ensure that Ministers were responsible to Parliament. Today, however, the situation is much more complex, and the purpose of this section is to examine the particular challenges to ministerial responsibility posed by modern government.

As we noted in Chapter 4, government is now a very large organisation composed of various central government departments, executive agencies, and non-departmental bodies. Today, no one seriously supposes that a government Minister actually performs much—if, indeed, any—of the administrative work that goes on within a government department. The volume of such work is enormous and of necessity must be undertaken by departmental officials. Ministers are not trained administrators, but mere politicians: it is not for them to manage government departments or undertake administrative tasks; rather, their role is to provide effective political leadership to the administrative apparatus of government. It would be simply impossible for a small collection of politicians, Ministers, to run the vast complex of the modern state without the assistance of a large bureaucracy comprised of civil servants and other administrators. Furthermore, Ministers are, by definition, temporary holders of public office, whereas officials form the permanent bulk of the administrative machinery.

---

[30] Parris, *Constitutional Bureaucracy: The Development of British Central Administration Since the Eighteenth Century* (London 1969), pp 80–105; Chester, *The English Administrative System 1780–1870* (Oxford 1981).

There is, however, a paradox: while much of the work of government is undertaken by civil servants, they are not themselves elected or accountable directly to Parliament. The traditional constitutional response to this position is that civil servants—as servants of the Crown, which, for all practical purposes, simply means the government of the day[31]—operate as part of a clear line of accountability. Civil servants take decisions under the authority of the Minister, the Minister is constitutionally responsible to Parliament, and Parliament is democratically elected and therefore able to hold the Minister to account for the decisions of his or her civil servants.

However, while this theory may have been tenable in the past, it now finds itself under considerable strain. The basic reason for this is that the traditional theory becomes unworkable when 'administrative life parts company from [the] constitutional doctrine [on which it is based], and government departments become too large and too complex for ministers to accept personal responsibility for what is done in their name by their civil servants'.[32] There are several reasons why the traditional constitutional theory of ministerial responsibility for the decisions and actions of government departments and agencies has become problematic.

4.4.2 **Three issues**

First, there are severe constraints as to the amount of *time and resources* that Parliament can devote to the scrutiny of government departments and agencies. In terms of its size and scale, government is a vastly larger enterprise than Parliament. Parliament simply possesses neither the resources nor the ability to subject each and every unit within the governmental machine to detailed and searching scrutiny. In practice, Parliament is really only ever able to examine a tiny proportion of the actual work of government, while the vast majority goes unscrutinised.

These difficulties are exacerbated by a second set of phenomena—namely, the *expansion of government activity* and *changes to the structure of government*. The notion of ministerial responsibility implies that governmental action is undertaken by government departments that are headed up by Ministers. However, there have always been other bodies that have exercised public power, but which have not been part of ministerial departments. This obviously raises particular problems for the effective accountability of government: if there is no Minister to answer for such bodies, then who can Parliament call to account in order to scrutinise the exercise of public power? Today, the number of public bodies that operate at 'arm's length' from Ministers—sometimes collectively called the 'quango state'—is extensive.[33] The nature and range of such bodies was considered in Chapter 4. But, for present purposes, the important point is that public power is exercised by a range of public bodies that are often sometimes

---

[31] House of Commons Treasury and Civil Service Committee, *Civil Servants and Ministers: Duties and Responsibilities* (HC 92 1985–86), vol II, pp 7–8, memorandum from the Cabinet Secretary entitled, 'The Duties and Responsibilities of Civil Servants in Relation to Ministers' (the Armstrong memorandum).

[32] Day and Klein, *Accountabilities: Five Public Services* (London 1987), pp 33–4.

[33] Albeit that the number of such bodies is presently being reduced in an effort to cut public spending.

only tenuously connected with government Ministers. While many of these public bodies are overseen by their parent government department, which is headed up by a Minister, in practice, many such bodies have significant room for manoeuvre and are rarely subject to detailed scrutiny by either Ministers or Parliament. As Flinders puts it: '[M]inisterial departments are bureaucratic icebergs, under which the greater part of the state structure operates in delegated organisational forms largely beyond public view or parliamentary oversight.'[34] In other words, as the scale of government has grown, the ability of Ministers to oversee their departments and associated public bodies has diminished—and so too has the ability of Parliament. The reality is that much of the work of government carries on with little effective parliamentary oversight.

Third, even when Parliament does scrutinise the work of government, the convention of ministerial responsibility will often be used by Ministers as a means of *shielding government from parliamentary interference* rather than as a means of enabling Parliament to secure proper accountability. If government is to get on with the business of governing, there needs to be some balance drawn between democratic control through Parliament, on the one hand, and governmental independence and organisational effectiveness, on the other. Ministerial responsibility provides the buffer that shields government departments from parliamentary interference. To illustrate the point, consider, for example, the following comment from the nineteenth-century constitutional writer Bagehot: 'The incessant tyranny of Parliament over the public offices…can only be prevented by the appointment of a Parliamentary head, connected by close ties with the present Ministry and the ruling party in Parliament.' According to Bagehot, this 'parliamentary head'—a Minister—acts as a 'protecting machine' that 'stands between the department and the busybodies and crotchetmakers of the House and the country'.[35] In other words, ministerial responsibility can be used by Ministers to prevent MPs from interfering with the business of government so that the government department is able to get on with the task of governing. This is the classic Peelite view of ministerial responsibility: the convention is being used as a tool to limit parliamentary scrutiny so that strong and effective government can be delivered, uninhibited by 'meddlesome' MPs. The role of the Minister is to defend his or her department and to limit the involvement of Parliament in the task of governing. From this perspective, the *real* purpose of the doctrine of ministerial responsibility has nothing to do with facilitating parliamentary accountability of government, but with protecting the workings of government from parliamentary 'interference'.

This view of ministerial responsibility is, at least in part, informed by certain value assumptions—namely, that Parliament is simply not competent itself to govern or administer, that public administration is a skilled business, and that parliamentary 'scrutiny' is likely to hinder and interfere with the skilled work of government. But a further point that has to be kept in mind is that both Ministers and civil servants have

---

[34] Flinders at 772.   [35] *The English Constitution* [1867] (London 1993), p 193.

an interest in avoiding blame. It is not too cynical to suggest that much energy goes into avoiding scrutiny and 'passing the buck'—that is, seeking to pass the blame on to someone else. Ministers are normally extremely reluctant to take the blame if they do not perceive themselves to have been at fault. The Minister remains constitutionally responsible to Parliament, but in practice this simply means that the Minister is the man or woman who tells Parliament that he or she was not responsible for the mistake.[36]

For their part, civil servants are not directly accountable to Parliament, but act in the name of the Minister, and the tradition and ethos of the Civil Service is that it is independent and politically neutral. While civil servants are theoretically accountable to Ministers, the doctrine of Civil Service independence makes it difficult for this accountability to be exercised effectively, and may prevent a Minister from dismissing or disciplining individual civil servants. It has been suggested that it serves the interests of civil servants to portray themselves as merely obedient executors of the will of elected politicians who are responsible to Parliament.[37] This is because civil servants themselves have an interest in avoiding accountability and the best way for them to do this is to emphasise that it is Ministers, not civil servants, who are accountable to Parliament. Of course, the reality is that civil servants do not merely execute the will of Ministers, but themselves possess significant power in terms of making and implementing policy. As we noted above, Ministers are there to provide political leadership, whereas civil servants do the vast majority of the work involved in governing. The upshot is that the traditional theory of ministerial responsibility may often have the effect of shielding civil servants from effective accountability.

It should also be noted that the attitudes of civil servants may not be conducive to effective parliamentary scrutiny of government. Consider, for example, the following comments by Chris Mullin MP, a junior Minister at the Foreign Office between 2003 and 2005. In his diaries, Mullin noted that Foreign Office civil servants often 'regard ministers as a temporary inconvenience and barely conceal their contempt. Especially, they don't like ministers who overrule them'. Furthermore, according to Mullin, 'accounting to Parliament is a low priority' for many Foreign Office civil servants.[38] It is unsurprising, therefore, that it can be extremely difficult for Parliament to hold civil servants effectively to account through Ministers.

It is apparent that there is considerable ambiguity in the doctrine of ministerial responsibility. Indeed, both Ministers and civil servants sometimes disagree upon how ministerial responsibility both does and should operate. For example, according to David Blunkett MP, a former Home Secretary, it sometimes appears that Ministers have to cover for civil servants who are 'utterly useless, incompetent, and ineffective'.[39] By contrast, civil servants might sometimes think that Ministers are able to shift the

---

[36] Gilmour, *The Body Politic* (London 1969), p 166.
[37] Riddell, *Parliament Under Pressure* (London 1998), p 77.
[38] Mullin, *A View from the Foothills: The Diaries of Chris Mullin* (London 2009), pp 166 and 508.
[39] Blunkett, *The Blunkett Tapes* (London 2006), p 607.

blame onto civil servants rather than assume responsibility themselves. The upshot in practice is that there is an 'accountability gap' in which Ministers and civil servants can hide behind each other, so that no one is really held to account.[40] As the House of Commons Public Administration Select Committee has noted: 'It is clear that there is no consensus, either among politicians or officials, about the way in which ministerial and civil service responsibilities are divided. This means there can be no consensus about where accountability should lie.'[41]

4.4.3 An example

As an illustration of how both Ministers and civil servants can, in practice, evade accountability, consider the sorry episode of the Rural Payments Agency (RPA) and its failure adequately to implement the 'single farm payment system'. The RPA is an executive agency of the Department for Environment, Food and Rural Affairs (DEFRA). Since 2006, it has had the task of implementing a system of payments to farmers. This required the processing of thousands of applications from farmers. However, the RPA was unable to process all of the applications by the deadline that had been set. Consequently, many farmers did not receive their payments and suffered significant financial losses. The RPA itself had failed largely because DEFRA had asked it to do too much in too short a period of time and did not pay enough heed to the Agency's warnings about the risks of what was being proposed. According to the parliamentary select committee overseeing DEFRA, the failure in administering the payments was a catastrophe for many farmers, as well as a serious and embarrassing failure for both DEFRA and the RPA: it represented a fundamental failure by DEFRA to carry out one of its principal tasks—namely, to pay farmers their financial entitlements on time.[42]

Who, then, was held to account? Accountability for the failure was limited to the removal and eventual dismissal of the RPA's chief executive. By contrast, those responsible within DEFRA—the Minister and other senior officials—escaped accountability by either moving on to other posts unscathed or staying in post. The select committee was highly critical of DEFRA, its Minister, and senior civil servants:

> A culture where ministers and senior officials can preside over failure of this magnitude and not be held personally accountable creates a serious risk of further failures in public service delivery. Accountability should mean that good results are rewarded, but a failure as serious as this of a Department to deliver one of its fundamental functions should result in the removal from post of those to whom the faulty policy design and implementation can be attributed. We recommend new guidance to make clear to ministers what they should do to take responsibility in the event of serious departmental failure.[43]

---

[40] House of Commons Public Administration Select Committee, *Politics and Administration: Ministers and Civil Servants* (HC 122 2006–07), [22].

[41] *Politics and Administration: Ministers and Civil Servants*, [39].

[42] House of Commons Environment, Food, and Rural Affairs Select Committee, *The Rural Payments Agency and the Implementation of the Single Payment Scheme* (HC 107 2006–07).

[43] *The Rural Payments Agency and the Implementation of the Single Payment Scheme*, [7].

Given such strong criticism, one might have expected that DEFRA would have recognised the need to own up to its failure and to display some degree of contrition (even if only a tokenistic display). But instead DEFRA—in what the select committee considered a 'shoddy' and 'superficial' response—strongly regretted that the select committee had made criticisms of named civil servants and rejected the need for any new guidance concerning the responsibility of Ministers for serious departmental failures.[44] In short, those who (according to the select committee) were responsible for a serious government failure were, in effect, easily able to evade responsibility.

4.4.4 Conclusions

So, what are we to make of ministerial responsibility for governmental decision-making and action? The overall view is that parliamentary control over, and ministerial responsibility for, the vast majority of the decisions and actions taken by the governmental machine is very weak indeed. Most of the decisions and actions produced by government are not made by Ministers, but by civil servants, administrators, and other public officials. These officials work within a plethora of public bodies, many of which are not headed up by a Minister or otherwise directly accountable to Parliament. The traditional theory of ministerial responsibility for official decision-making is based on the fiction that Ministers are inevitably involved in policymaking; the reality is that civil servants, even middle-ranking ones, are often intimately involved in both policymaking and implementation tasks over which there may be little, if any, ministerial supervision. Parliament, for its part, has failed to develop new mechanisms of accountability in order to scrutinise the detailed work and operations of public bodies that operate at arm's length from Ministers.

One possible solution to the problem of effective accountability of civil servants would be to institute direct accountability of civil servants to Parliament. However, this has always been resisted on the grounds that it would produce a division of loyalties for civil servants and thereby politicise the Civil Service. So, when civil servants do become involved in, for example, select committee hearings, the position is that they are not themselves being held to account, but that they are assisting Parliament in holding Ministers to account. This is made clear in the relevant Cabinet Office rules, which state that '[c]ivil servants who give evidence to Select Committees do so on behalf of their Ministers and under their directions', reflecting the fact that 'it is Ministers who are accountable to Parliament' and that civil servants 'are not directly accountable to Parliament in the same way'.[45] Furthermore, the constitutional position of civil servants is that they work for the government of the day; direct accountability to Parliament, in which both the government and opposition parties are present, would blur lines of control. Another suggestion has been to establish a new 'public

---

[44] House of Commons Environment, Food, and Rural Affairs Select Committee, *The Rural Payments Agency and the implementation of the Single Payment Scheme: Government Response to the Committee's Third Report of Session 2006–07* (HC 956 2006–07).

[45] Cabinet Office, *Departmental Evidence and Response to Select Committees* (London 2009), [40]–[41].

service bargain' between Ministers and civil servants underpinned by a governance code that would clarify formally their respective roles and responsibilities.[46]

> **Q** What is the traditional theory of ministerial responsibility for civil servants? Why does the theory sometimes seem at odds with the practice?

4.5 Ministerial responsibility as prudential government

Finally, we might note that there is another sense in which ministerial responsibility is sometimes used: government Ministers are responsible for adopting a wise, prudential policy irrespective of whether or not it meets with public approval. Recall that the task of governing belongs not to Parliament, but to the government. It has been noted that the UK government is an independent body that, upon taking office, assumes responsibility for leading and directing both Parliament and the nation in accordance with its own judgement and convictions.[47] Government is expected to act responsibly not only in the sense of providing explanations for its decisions, but also in the sense of pursuing a responsible policy in the public interest regardless of its popularity. Responsibility in this sense means acting wisely and prudently, rather than being responsive to Parliament and the public.

The bailout of the banks by the UK government in 2008 provides a good illustration of responsible government in this sense. The government used hundreds of billions of pounds of taxpayers' money to bail out the banking system in 2008—but why? It is abundantly apparent that the government did not take this action to fulfil any manifesto pledge, or because Parliament had commanded it to do so, or because of a desire to enhance its political standing; rather, the government itself decided that this would be the responsible thing to do—an effective banking system is essential to the functioning of a capitalist economy, and the government took the action that it considered necessary to maintain the banking system. Had such action not been taken, the banking system—and, with it, the UK economy—could have collapsed. The government was aware that its actions would increase public borrowing and thereby produce a large fiscal deficit that would need to be paid off at some future stage. It was also aware that the action would be politically unpopular in some quarters, but the government considered it to be the prudential, responsible thing to do. Of course, after the government had taken the action, Parliament debated and scrutinised it; Parliament provided the public arena in which the merits or demerits of the action were discussed—but Parliament did not in any way tell the government what to do. Government acted, then Parliament debated.

---

[46] House of Commons Public Administration Select Committee, *Politics and Administration: Ministers and Civil Servants*.

[47] Amery, *Thoughts on the Constitution* (Oxford 1953), p 31; Birch, *Representative and Responsible Government: An Essay on the British Constitution* (London 1964), pp 18–19.

'Responsibility' in this sense is used by government to justify unwelcome decisions and policies, and to explain to the public that the broader notion of responsible government sometimes requires tough decisions to be taken in order to advance the wider public interest. Of course, 'responsible' decisions in this sense are sometimes highly contested ones. The government's contention that its action to save the banks was necessary in order to avoid imminent financial meltdown was not universally accepted, but Ministers decided that it was the best action to take in the broader public interest. Similarly, the decision to invade Iraq—which the government claimed to have taken in order to safeguard vital national interests—proved highly unpopular, and hindsight has shown it to have been an arguably unwise one. To some people, decisions such as these are the epitome of *irresponsible* government—of decisions being taken that have serious, even disastrous, long-term consequences, in the face of strong public opposition. But to say that such action is at odds with the notion of responsible government rather misses the point if we recognise that the concept of ministerial responsibility is itself a highly contested one that is arguably as much about facilitating strong government as it is about aligning governmental decision-making with public or parliamentary opinion.

4.6 **Summary**

The above discussion of ministerial responsibility is complex. No apology is made for that: the convention of ministerial responsibility is itself a complex and ambiguous notion. It is central to the British constitution and to parliamentary accountability of the government. The above discussion has sought to highlight two main points: first, there are different meanings attributed to the convention of ministerial responsibility; second, the operation of that doctrine in practice is heavily influenced by the government's dominance of Parliament. We can now turn to consider the mechanisms by which Parliament seeks to scrutinise government and their effectiveness.

Q What are the main meanings of ministerial responsibility? What are the reasons for its essentially contested nature?

5. **Parliamentary scrutiny of government**

Parliament has three principal mechanisms by which it seeks to scrutinise government—namely, parliamentary questions, parliamentary debates, and inquiries by select committees. These mechanisms are used, respectively, to extract information and explanations from government, to debate government policy and administration, and to undertake detailed inquiries into government operations. However, before examining these mechanisms in detail, it is appropriate to consider a broader issue: the constraints on parliamentary scrutiny.

5.1 **Constraints on parliamentary scrutiny**

Parliamentary control of government is an inherently political activity and politics is not an exact science. We have already examined some of the broader structural aspects of the political relationship between government and Parliament. It is also important to recognise the party-political dimension to parliamentary accountability. For good or ill, modern British politics is dominated by political parties that are engaged in a continuous electoral campaign with each other. MPs in the House of Commons, whose role it is to scrutinise government, are themselves politically aligned to either the governing political party (or parties) or to an opposition party. The House of Commons is itself divided into three main groups: members of the government; backbench MPs who are members of the governing party (or parties), but not themselves members of the government; and the opposition parties.

Political factors, therefore, influence the effectiveness of parliamentary scrutiny of government in numerous ways. For example, opposition MPs commonly oppose the government, but this may be because they are motivated by a desire to engage in political point-scoring rather than by an inclination to subject governmental activity to meaningful scrutiny. Meanwhile, the purpose of government whips is to exert control over the government's backbench MPs in order to sustain it in power. While the role of the whips may seem inimical to the ideal of representative democracy, it is long established and without it government would be unable to get its business through Parliament.[48] The personal views of individual MPs are then often subject to an 'iron cage of party discipline'.[49] The government does not, therefore, normally have to respond to individuals MPs; rather, it will generally be confident of the outcome of votes in the Commons because of its majority. This necessarily limits the capacity of the Commons to hold the government to account. This is true whether or not the government is composed of a single party or a coalition of parties, provided that, in the latter event, the relationship between the coalition partners is sufficiently strong.

Indeed, an experienced parliamentarian and former chair of the House of Commons Public Administration Select Committee, Tony Wright, has noted that 'all the textbook talk about Parliament's role in scrutiny and accountability' is misleading as it 'frequently fails to get inside the skin of an institution whose members have a quite different agenda'.[50] In the real world of politics, the agenda of most MPs is either to get promoted into government or to the opposition frontbench or, at the worst, to get re-elected back into Parliament. Most people become MPs not in order to scrutinise the government or even necessarily to represent the views of their constituents, but

---

[48] Renton, *Chief Whip: People, Power and Patronage in Westminster* (London 2004).
[49] Rose, *Politics in England: Change and Persistence* (London 1989), p 121.
[50] Wright, *British Politics: A Very Short Introduction* (Oxford 2003), p 85.

because they wish to have a successful political career—and the principal, if not exclusive, way of achieving this is by becoming a government Minister. As Wright puts it: 'Every parliamentary foot-soldier dreams of one day holding a ministerial baton.'[51]

The consequence of this is that it cannot be assumed that the activity of seeking to subject government to scrutiny is always uppermost in the minds of most MPs. As Rush has explained, the partisan role of MPs—that of supporting their party and attacking opposition parties—has become dominant and their scrutiny role has declined.[52] This, of course, is not to say that MPs never vigorously subject governments to scrutiny; some individual backbench MPs have made their reputations out of criticising their own party when it has been in office. And the awareness that backbenchers might rebel over a particular issue will make government Ministers pay attention to the opinions expressed by backbenchers. The key point, however, is that there is an inherent tension between the partisan and scrutiny roles of the backbench MP—and that, for the reasons set out above, the partisan role is often the dominant one.

Despite its pervasive influence (at least in the Commons), party politics is not the only constraint upon Parliament as a scrutiniser of government. Parliamentary time and resources are also limited. Furthermore, over recent years, MPs have increasingly come to spend a greater proportion of their time dealing with complaints and issues of concern raised by their constituents. It is often doubted whether this increasing constituency workload is compatible with MPs also being able to scrutinise government. For example, in the opinion of one MP:

> Too many Members of Parliament see themselves as super-councillors, who take up issues that should be handled by citizens' advice bureaux and local law centres, rather than as representatives who hold the government to account, which is a particularly important role for backbenchers in government.[53]

Moreover, some MPs have second jobs. Obviously, given that MPs have limited time, one role or other will have to give way.

Another inherent constraint on parliamentary accountability is that individual MPs, and so Parliament collectively, may simply not be equipped to subject government to detailed scrutiny. Most MPs are generalists. They may, of course, bring experience of outside interests with them when they enter Parliament, but there has been a discernible trend for more MPs to be professional politicians and not to have much experience from outside politics. In any event, modern government is complex and this can make it difficult for MPs to offer informed criticism, except in those areas (if any) in which they possess real experience or on which they have been briefed (in an inevitably skewed way) by lobbyists.

Much of what has been said so far relates mainly or wholly to the House of Commons. We saw in Chapter 5 that the House of Lords is a radically different chamber from the

---

[51] Wright, p 85.

[52] Rush, *The Role of the Member of Parliament Since 1868: From Gentlemen to Players* (Oxford 2001).

[53] HC Deb, 15 Dec 2009, col 201WH (Mark Field MP).

Commons.[54] For as long as it remains an unelected chamber, the Lords is less affected by the tribalism of party politics and, as a result, is arguably capable of subjecting the government to more serious, thoroughgoing scrutiny. This is not necessarily a knock-out argument against an elected House of Lords—but it does underline the tension just described between partisanship and scrutiny.

> **Q** What are the practical constraints upon parliamentary scrutiny? How, if at all, could such limitations be ameliorated?

5.2 **Parliamentary questions**

With the foregoing general points in mind, we turn to consider the particular mechanisms at Parliament's disposal for scrutinising the government. One simple and sometimes effective way by which parliamentarians can seek to hold government to account is to ask questions of the government. Such questions can be asked to extract information, or to require the government to explain and defend its policies, actions, and decisions.

5.2.1 **Oral questions**

Oral questions to Ministers are perhaps amongst Parliament's most publicly recognisable activities. Prime Ministers' questions (PMQs) takes place for half an hour each week and is televised. This regular and frequent questioning of the Prime Minister is a relatively recent innovation, having been introduced in 1961. PMQs usually shows the House of Commons at its most directly adversarial, especially in terms of the confrontation between the Prime Minister and the leader of the opposition. The latter often seeks to highlight some defect in the government or its policy, and then the Prime Minister seeks to defend the government and highlight the failings of the opposition party. MPs from opposition parties put questions to the Prime Minister not in the expectation or hope that this will actually prompt any change of government policy, but to highlight to the general public their perception both that the government is deficient and that their own party would be able to form a better government. In this sense, PMQs is simply part of the theatre of politics in which the main parties assail each other in order to score political points. This perception is reinforced by the frequent practice of government backbench MPs asking sycophantic questions congratulating the Prime Minister upon the government's ostensible successes ('Does the Prime Minister agree that what the government is doing is wonderful?'). This is not to say that backbench MPs do not ask searching questions at PMQs, but scrutiny is very often subordinated to partisanship. That said, PMQs does serve an important public function: that of highlighting for the public the ideological and policy differences between the government and the opposition.

---

[54] See Chapter 5, section 2.3, above.

Question time for other Ministers operates on a departmental rota; each Minister appears once in a five-week cycle in order to answer questions that fall within his or her particular area of responsibility. So, for example, an MP's question about terrorism would be put to the Home Secretary or another Home Office Minister. Question times for Ministers are still 'often adversarial but usually less gladiatorial than PMQs'.[55] Nevertheless, ministerial question time has been likened to a 'daily opportunity for the rival parliamentary armies to lob custard pies at each other'.[56] It follows that while the asking of oral questions serves a political purpose, it achieves relatively little—except perhaps at a symbolic level—in terms of real scrutiny.

5.2.2 Written questions

MPs can put questions in writing as well as orally. This is an important tool that MPs have at their disposal in terms of extracting information, especially detailed information, from the government. The daily record of parliamentary proceedings—Hansard—contains the reports of debates and statements in the Chamber, and also a long list of answers to written questions. The total number of questions tabled by MPs is substantial: in 2009, the daily number of questions tabled was over 500. It is clear that the continuing increase in the number of questions tabled has placed some strain on the systems both within Parliament and government that handle written parliamentary questions. Written questions are highly valued by MPs as a means of scrutinising government and obtaining information; the advantage of this tool is its transparency, and the fact that, because the answer is placed clearly on record, it can be followed up by any MP who takes an interest.

There are, though, some constraints upon the effectiveness of this method of extracting information from the government. First, there is an advisory cost limit, known as the *disproportionate cost threshold*, of £750. This is the cost level above which a government department can refuse to answer a parliamentary question—although, in practice, this is rarely exceeded.

Second, there is widespread concern amongst MPs that many answers to written parliamentary questions are unsatisfactory. For example, rather than giving detailed answers, some government departments have a practice of giving evasive or anodyne 'non-answers' to questions, which in turn prompt further questions or even resort to the Freedom of Information Act 2000.[57] This is notwithstanding the fact that the Ministerial Code states:

> [I]t is of paramount importance that Ministers give accurate and truthful information to Parliament, correcting any inadvertent error at the earliest opportunity…Ministers should be as open as possible with Parliament and the public, refusing to provide information only when disclosure would not be in the public interest.[58]

---

[55] Rush, *Parliament Today* (Manchester 2005), p 211.   [56] Wright, p 83.
[57] On the Act, see section 7.2 below.   [58] *Ministerial Code*, [1.2c]–[1.2d].

For their part, government departments have expressed frustration when dealing with questions that seem frivolous. Meanwhile, Parliament has expressed concern that, in some areas, the government does not seem to be meeting its responsibilities for answering questions and has sought to remind government of those responsibilities.[59]

It is also important to note another parliamentary mechanism—the written ministerial statement—which is commonly used by government to make formal announcements to Parliament. For example, written ministerial statements are often used to provide or announce detailed information and statistics from the government, the publication of reports by government agencies, findings of reviews and inquiries, and the government's responses to such inquiries. Such statements are not, then, a tool by which government can be held to account by Parliament, but a means by which the government can make important announcements to Parliament. If anything, the use of such statements reflects a broader set of understandings between Parliament and government—namely, that the government generally accepts the discipline of informing Parliament as to important changes in governmental policy as an aspect of the principle of responsible government.[60] At the same time, this conception of responsibility—as a duty to inform—reflects the view, dominant within government, that Parliament's role is an essentially passive one.

5.3 **Parliamentary debates**

Debates are the oldest method by which Parliament can critically scrutinise government decisions and actions. Debates are held in Parliament on particular issues, and they allow for the expression and representation of different political views. Such debates are held in both the chamber of the House of Commons and now the satellite debating chamber, Westminster Hall. Two questions arise.

First, *who has the power to decide what does and does not get debated in Parliament?* A long-standing concern has been that business in the House of Commons is too closely controlled by the government, enabling it to determine what does and does not get discussed. This is reflected in Standing Order No 14 of the House of Commons, which states that the general principle is that 'government business shall have precedence at every sitting'. The main exceptions, until recently, were that 20 days are set aside for debates initiated by the opposition parties—'opposition day debates'—while 13 Fridays are used for discussion of private members' Bills.[61] However, in 2010, an important new exception was added: that backbench MPs, via a newly created Backbench Business Committee, should control at least 27 days' worth of business in the Commons, enabling them to hold debates on matters of their choosing.[62] This

---

[59] House of Commons Procedure Committee, *Written Parliamentary Questions* (HC 859 2008–09).

[60] However, successive governments have been criticised by MPs for often *first* announcing new initiatives via the media, only informing Parliament thereafter.

[61] On private members' Bills, see Chapter 5, section 3.1.1, above.

[62] HC Deb, 15 June 2010, cols 842–5, approving new standing orders relating to the Backbench Business Committee and amending Standing Order 14.

reform—part of a package of changes intended to reinvigorate the House of Commons in the wake of the 2009 MPs' expenses scandal[63]—is intended to reduce the government's hegemony and to strengthen the Commons' capacity to hold it to account.

Second, *are debates an effective instrument of accountability?* For Wright, it is a mistake to use the word 'debate' to describe events that often involve prepared speeches served up to a largely empty chamber in which neither votes nor minds are likely to be changed by what is said.[64] The partisan nature of the House of Commons means that debates often have a ritualistic character in which party considerations are so dominant that they serve little real purpose. According to Norton, 'there is little evidence that opposition day debates have affected government actions: they are simply part of the partisan conflict in the chamber and rarely reported by the media'.[65] Even when backbench MPs are able to raise their own issues for debate, debates often have a very low profile. For example, it is not at all uncommon for 'adjournment debates' tabled by backbenchers to take place late at night in an almost deserted Commons chamber with only a handful of MPs present. The situation may improve now that backbenchers have greater influence over the parliamentary timetable, although it is too early to assess the impact of that change.

5.4 Select committees

On the whole, the effectiveness of parliamentary questions and debates as a means of holding government to account seems to be limited. What, then, of select committees?

5.4.1 House of Commons departmental select committees

The current structure of departmental select committees is relatively new and dates from 1979. This system was introduced in order to extend parliamentary scrutiny of government policy and administration. Under it, the policy and administration of each government department is overseen by a dedicated House of Commons select committee. So, the House of Commons Home Affairs Committee scrutinises the work of the Home Office and its associated public bodies, while the House of Commons Health Committee scrutinises the work of the Department of Health and its public bodies, and so on.

There are currently 18 departmental select committees. If the remit of a government department changes, or if a new government department is established, then the remit of the relevant select committee will change to reflect it. For example, following the 2010 election, the Deputy Prime Minster was given particular responsibility for political and constitutional reform; in response, a new select committee was created in order to scrutinise his work in that area. Each select committee comprises between 11 and 16 MPs, all of whom are backbench MPs. Each select committee is

---

[63] See section 6.2 below for more on the Wright Committee.
[64] Wright, *British Politics: A Very Short Introduction* (Oxford 2003), p 85.
[65] Norton, *Parliament in British Politics* (Basingstoke 2005), p 131.

cross-party—that is, no single party will have a majority of MPs in any particular committee, so as to reduce partisanship. Until recently, party whips determined who became chairs of select committees—and the temptation for the government whips to exert partisan influence sometimes proved irresistible. For example, in 2001, the Labour government whips sought, unsuccessfully as it happened, to deselect two MPs as select committee chairs because of their willingness to subject government to independent scrutiny; one of those MPs, Gwyneth Dunwoody, was subsequently described as one of Parliament's 'most fearless inquisitors', who set 'a gold-standard for independent and robust parliamentary scrutiny'.[66] The more general concern is obvious: 'Those being scrutinised should not have a say in the selection of the scrutineers . . . the present system does not, and should not, have the confidence of the House and the public.'[67] Against this background, it is significant that, after the 2010 election—in a bid to reinvigorate Parliament following the MPs' expenses scandal of 2009—the system was changed: select committee chairs are now chosen by MPs through a secret ballot, thereby drastically reducing the power of the whips in this area.

The formal remit of select committees—that of examining the administration, expenditure, and policy of the government departments to which they are attached—may sound a little dry, but according to King, select committees function as 'goaders, gadflies, and critics' of government departments.[68] The committees operate by conducting inquiries into areas of policy and administration within the responsibility of the government department that the committee oversees. Each committee selects its own subjects of inquiry and seeks written and oral evidence from a wide range of relevant groups and individuals. Hearings take place in committee rooms in Parliament in which witnesses are questioned by committee members. While select committees do not have the power to compel Ministers and civil servants to attend before them, in practice, Ministers and civil servants tend to appear for fear that political embarrassment will otherwise result. At the end of an inquiry, the relevant committee produces a report setting out its findings and making recommendations to the government. The government aims to produce a considered response to a select committee report within two months of its publication.[69] In 2002, the House of Commons produced (and subsequently amended) a formal list of the core tasks of departmental select committees in order to provide a framework for committees as they hold Ministers and their departments to account. The current core tasks of select committees are set out in Figure 10.1.[70]

---

[66] House of Commons Transport Committee, *Work of the Committee in 2007–08* (HC 211 2008–09), [5].

[67] House of Commons Liaison Committee, *Independence or Control? The Government's Reply to the Committee's First Report of Session 1999–2000* (HC 748 1999–2000), [28].

[68] King, *The British Constitution* (Oxford 2007), p 333.

[69] Cabinet Office, *Departmental Evidence and Response to Select Committees* (London 2005), [108].

[70] Figure 10.1 is based on a report of the House of Commons Liaison Committee entitled *The Work of Committees in 2008–09* (HC 426 2009–10), [12]. The relevant part of the report refers to public service agreements (PSAs). However, PSAs have now been discontinued (see Chapter 11, section 3.2, below), and the text of Figure 10.1 has been adapted accordingly.

| | OBJECTIVES | | | |
TASKS TO BE UNDERTAKEN IN PURSUIT OF OBJECTIVES	Policy	Expenditure	Administration	Assisting House
	Examine and consider appropriateness of policy proposals		Assess department's performance against relevant targets and performance indicators	
	Identify and examine areas of emerging policy, or in which existing policy is deficient, and make proposals	Examine expenditure plans and out turn of the department and associated bodies	Monitor work of department's executive agencies and other associated public bodies	Produce reports that are suitable for debate in the House, including Westminster Hall, or debating committees
	Scrutinise relevant draft Bills		Scrutinise major appointments made by department	
	Examine departmental 'output' (eg decisions)		Examine implementation of legislation and major policy initiatives	

Figure 10.1 Objectives and tasks of departmental select committees

5.4.2 Other committees

There are other House of Commons committees that cut across departmental boundaries. These include the Public Accounts Committee, the Environmental Audit Committee, the European Scrutiny Committee, the Public Administration Select Committee, and the Liaison Committee.

- The Public Accounts Committee, which investigates whether public expenditure by government offers value for money, is considered in more detail in Chapter 11.

- The Environmental Audit Committee was established in 1997 to consider whether government policies and programmes contribute to environmental protection and sustainable development, and to audit the performance of government against specified targets.

- The European Scrutiny Committee assesses the legal and/or political importance of each document produced by the European Union (EU), decides which EU documents are debated, monitors the activities of UK Ministers in the Council of Ministers, and keeps legal, procedural, and institutional developments in the EU under review.

- The Public Administration Select Committee oversees the work of the Parliamentary Ombudsman,[71] and considers matters relating to the quality and standards of administration provided by government departments, and other matters relating to the Civil Service.

- Finally, the Liaison Committee comprises the chairmen of all of the House of Commons select committees and oversees the work of all select committees. The Prime Minister appears before the Liaison Committee twice a year.

Like the House of Commons, the House of Lords has a number of select committees, but they are not organised on a departmental basis. The following House of Lords select committees are worth highlighting.

- The House of Lords Constitution Committee examines the constitutional implications of all public bills coming before the House and keeps under review the operation of the constitution.

- The Delegated Powers and Regulatory Reform Committee scrutinises proposals in Bills to delegate legislative power from Parliament to another body (usually Ministers).[72]

- The EU Select Committee considers EU documents and other matters relating to the EU and works through some seven sub-committees.

- The House of Lords Merits of Statutory Instruments Committee reports to the House those statutory instruments that are of political or legal significance.

- Other committees—for example, the Science and Technology Committee and the Economic Affairs Committee—play to the strengths of members of the House of Lords who possess expertise in those particular subject areas.

Finally, there are some joint committees of both Houses, of which the Joint Committee on Human Rights is perhaps the most high profile.[73]

5.4.3 Assessment

How effective are select committees in scrutinising government? This is a complex question because the current system of select committees has a number of advantages and disadvantages. We begin with the former.

First, select committees provide a forum in which the work of government departments can be subject to *more detailed scrutiny* than would be possible in the chamber of the House of Commons. Committees can undertake detailed inquiries, amass evidence from experts and those affected by the administration of government policy, and then question the relevant Minister. According to the House of Commons Modernisation Committee:

> Select committees have served Parliament and the public well. They have enabled Members of Parliament to hold the Executive to account through more rigorous scrutiny than is

---

[71] On which, see Chapter 16 below.   [72] See further Chapter 4, section 4.2, above.
[73] See further Chapter 19, section 3.3.2, below.

possible on the floor of the House and they have brought before the public matters which otherwise might have remained concealed.[74]

Select committees also offer the least partisan of the mechanisms available in that they offer a more considered form of scrutiny when compared with politically-charged, debates in the Commons chamber.

Second, the ability of select committees to scrutinise government departments has *strengthened over time*. The work of select committees is more focused, more extensive, better resourced, more visible, and reveals greater engagement with the public than ever before. In the 2008–09 parliamentary session, select committees held 664 public hearings and produced some 371 reports.[75] In the opinion of Natzler and Hutton, select committees have come a long way since 1979—over recent years, two significant trends in the work of select committees have been their more systematic approach in terms of both breadth and depth of coverage, and the growth in public awareness and media coverage of committees' activities: 'The conditions are arguably now in place to allow a significant and mutually reinforcing acceleration of those two trends in the years ahead and for that acceleration to be accompanied by a steady growth in the committees' influence.'[76]

Third, select committees have enabled individual MPs to *develop their own expertise* in particular areas of government, thereby tending to enhance the quality of scrutiny.

On the other hand, virtually all commentators would agree that the current system of select committees operates under various constraints that restrict the degree of scrutiny that they are able to offer. First, the *powers* of select committees are weak in comparison with those in other legislatures. The committees cannot amend, veto, or propose legislation. They have no right to have their reports debated in the House of Commons, let alone voted upon; whether a committee's report gets debated depends on whether or not the government is minded to allow time for debate and, as we noted above, the government dominates the scheduling of business in the House of Commons.

Second, the *resources* of select committees to scrutinise the workings of government are limited. As one select committee chairman once noted:

[T]here simply isn't time for Select Committees to look at each and every one of the quangos[77] within their remit...The problem is that Select Committees just don't have the

---

[74] House of Commons Modernisation Committee, *Select Committees* (HC 224 2001–02), [59]. See also Rush, *Parliament Today* (Manchester 2005), p 239.

[75] House of Commons Liaison Committee, *The Work of Committees in 2008–09* (HC 426 2009–10), [52]–[53].

[76] 'Select Committees: Scrutiny à la Carte?', in Giddings (ed), *The Future of Parliament: Issues for a New Century* (London 2005), p 97.

[77] This is the informal name for public bodies associated with, but outside of, the main structure of government departments.

time and resources to do what they already do, never mind having their burdens added to. I regard this as disappointing, but an acceptance of reality.[78]

One of the most significant pressures on select committees is the availability of MPs' time; if MPs are unable to commit sufficient time to working on a committee, then the quality of scrutiny is likely to suffer.

Third, there is the paradox that *more committees with larger remits* might diminish the quality of scrutiny that they are able to provide. Over recent years, the remits of select committees have been expanded to include pre- and post-legislative scrutiny, and pre- and post-appointment hearings of appointments to public bodies. However, such tasks inevitably make further demands on MPs' time and concerns have been frequently been expressed that many MPs do not attend committee hearings.

Finally, *whether or not government accepts the recommendations* in a select committee report ultimately depends simply upon whether or not the relevant department is inclined to accept them. Often, government departments take little notice of select committee reports. For example, some select committees have noted the occasionally poor quality of government replies and of long delays by departments in producing responses to committees' reports.[79]

The general conclusion is, then, that while select committees are an important mechanism for holding government to account, their effectiveness is limited. As King has noted, 'no one denies the committees' utility, but at the same time no one claims that they have had a more than marginal effect on the relations between governments and parliament'.[80] This is because government departments can, and frequently do, simply disregard recommendations from select committees and are able to do so without creating much political controversy. Of course, there are instances in which select committees have made recommendations and the government has then taken the action recommended. It is, however, very difficult to quantify the extent to which select committees cause Ministers to take action that they would not have otherwise have taken. Indeed, it is plausible that, from the perspective of government Ministers, select committees provide a forum in which Ministers can seek to *overcome* opposition within their own political party to a particular policy idea, in that appearances before select committees enable Ministers to communicate directly and in depth with their own backbenchers.[81]

Even when government has sought to increase the powers of select committees, this has usually been accompanied by concerns that any such enhancement of committees' powers has been largely cosmetic. Consider, for example, the role of select committees as regards pre-appointment hearings. Government Ministers are responsible

---

[78] Evidence of Peter Luff MP, Chairman of the Agriculture Select Committee, to House of Commons Public Administration Select Committee, *Quangos* (HC 209 1998–99).

[79] *The Work of Committees in 2008–09*, [86].

[80] King, *The British Constitution* (Oxford 2007), p 334.

[81] Hindmoor, Larkin, and Kennon, 'Assessing the Influence of Select Committees in the UK: The Education and Skills Committee 1997–2005' (2009) 15 Journal of Legislative Studies 71.

for making some 21,000 appointments to public bodies. Ultimately, Ministers are accountable to Parliament for such appointments. In 2007, the government decided that its nominees for key positions should be subject to pre-appointment hearings in which select committees address issues such as the candidate's suitability for the role, his or her key priorities, and the process used in selection. While such hearings were never meant to be binding, Ministers undertook that they would consider the committee's report when deciding whether to proceed with the appointment.[82]

The real test over this function was only ever going to come once a select committee had disapproved of the government's nominee for a public appointment. This happened in 2009 when the House of Commons Children, Schools and Families Select Committee concluded that the government's nominee for the post of Children's Commissioner (a post with responsibility for promoting awareness of the views and interests of children in England) was not sufficiently independent of the government.[83] The government Minister rejected the Committee's report; while the Minister was obliged to take into account the Select Committee's view, he was not bound by it.[84] This episode, like so many others related in this chapter, is indicative of a conception of governmental responsibility that is more facilitative of government action than of parliamentary control. However, the coalition government appears to recognise that it may sometimes be appropriate to give select committees real powers over appointments to public bodies. For example, the Treasury Select Committee is to be given the power to veto the appointment of the Chair of the Office of Budget Responsibility, a body established by the coalition to provide independent assessments of the public finances.[85]

> **Q** What is your assessment of the degree of scrutiny offered by parliamentary select committees? How do you think that their effectiveness might be enhanced?

6. Current and future parliamentary scrutiny

6.1 Assessing parliamentary scrutiny

Is parliamentary scrutiny of government adequate—and, if not, what should be done to improve it? According to Norton, Parliament cannot claim to subject the conduct of government to continuous and comprehensive scrutiny. Government is frequently

---

[82] HM Government, *Governance of Britain* (Cm 7170 2007), [76]. See further *The Work of Committees in 2008–09*, Annex 3.

[83] House of Commons Children, Schools and Families Select Committee, *Appointment of the Children's Commissioner for England* (HC 998 2008–09).   [84] HC Deb, vol 497, cols 639–48 (19 October 2009).

[85] Written evidence submitted by the Chancellor of the Exchequer to the Treasury Select Committee, 23 July 2010.

able to avoid parliamentary oversight of much—if not most—of what it does. When governmental action is the subject of parliamentary scrutiny, the attention that it receives is often sporadic and fleeting, affected by party-political considerations, time pressures, and a lack of knowledge amongst MPs. Ministers are often able to deflect probing by parliamentarians and can always, in any event, simply ignore recommendations for a change in government policy or administration.[86] All of this reinforces the sense that the role of Parliament is, and always has been, a passive rather than an active one.

At the same time, while Parliament's capacity to review government actions and administration is clearly limited, it is not so limited as to be irrelevant. It may be common to assume that Parliament merely acts as a rubber stamp and that its scrutiny role has diminished to the point of non-existence. But Parliament still matters. Governments must listen to, and respond to, concerns raised in Parliament. Governments profess a commitment to engaging with Parliament. The answers that Ministers give to parliamentary questions may at times seem evasive, but Ministers must give them nonetheless. Furthermore, the general principle is still that when Parliament is in session, the most important announcements of government policy should be made in the first instance to Parliament[87]—a principle that is often, but not (given the temptation to make announcements to the media in a bid to grab headlines) uniformly, followed. Ministers are also aware that they have no alternative but to interact with select committees, to explain and defend government policy, and to answer questions. So, while Parliament is unable to direct the government to undertake or refrain from specific action, it is able to influence government in at least two ways.

First, there is the *negative influence* of Parliament: parliamentary scrutiny can exert a deterrent effect upon government. If the government is aware that a particular issue might be raised in Parliament and prompt adverse public reaction, this may induce government to be more circumspect as to what it does. In other words, the threat of parliamentary scrutiny may prompt government to abandon some of its proposals or to water them down so that they survive parliamentary scrutiny without undue embarrassment

Second, parliamentary scrutiny can also exercise a *positive, agenda-setting function*. By asking questions of Ministers and contributing to debates, parliamentarians can cause certain issues to be brought on to the government's agenda. MPs can alert Ministers to a particular issue—the significance or existence of which they might not have appreciated—and then induce a response from the Minister and/or prompt some further attention or action. Parliament may not be able to dictate to government what it should do—but it can occasionally place particular issues on the broader political agenda and arouse interest in the matter.

These forms of influence notwithstanding, it is generally recognised that the effectiveness of parliamentary scrutiny of government is less than adequate and could be

---

[86] Norton, *Parliament in British Politics* (Basingstoke 2005), p 131.   [87] *Ministerial Code*, [9.1].

enhanced. It has become quite common to lament the decline—indeed, the irrelevance—of Parliament. And while the reasons for this decline and the potential solutions to the problem (if it is perceived as such) consist partly in the technical minutiae of how Parliament works, there is one, overwhelming issue at the root of all of this—namely, the executive's dominance of Parliament. For example, according to the Power Inquiry, the executive in Britain is now more powerful in relation to Parliament than it has been probably since the time of Walpole, who was Prime Minster from 1721 to 1742.[88]

There is then a compelling case for increasing the role of Parliament and its ability to scrutinise government effectively. The principal argument is that this would enhance democratic control over, and the accountability of, government. Additionally, government decisions are more likely to be accepted if they are subject to thorough parliamentary scrutiny. Strong and stable government needs to be complemented by robust parliamentary control; enhanced parliamentary scrutiny does not necessarily imply a reduction in the ability of government to govern. As Crick has noted: 'Parliamentary control of the executive—rightly conceived—is not the enemy of effective and strong government, but its primary condition.'[89]

> **Q** Should parliamentary scrutiny of government be enhanced?

6.2 Improving parliamentary scrutiny—Rebuilding the House

There have, for many years, been suggestions that Parliament ought to subject government to more thorough scrutiny by, for example, reducing the influence of the whips, increasing the powers, role, and status of select committees, and reducing the ability of the government to set Parliament's agenda. However, such proposals have met with resistance from successive governments. This is unsurprising, since it is generally not in the interests of the government of the day to strengthen Parliament's capacity to hold it to account.

However, recent discussion of improving the scrutiny role of Parliament has taken place in unusual circumstances—most obviously the fallout from the MPs' expenses scandal and, subsequently, the formation of a coalition government. The expenses scandal damaged public confidence not only in some individual MPs, but also in the House of Commons as an institution. The crisis prompted a number of responses, such as immediate reforms of the system of MPs expenses.[90] But it was also accepted that further changes were needed to the functioning of Parliament in order to instil new

---

[88] The Power Inquiry, *Power to the People: An Independent Inquiry into Britain's Democracy* (London 2006), p 128.   [89] Crick, *The Reform of Parliament* (London 1969), p 259.

[90] Parliamentary Standards Act 2009. See Parpworth, 'The Parliamentary Standards Act 2009: A Constitutional Dangerous Dogs Measure?' (2010) 73 MLR 262.

public confidence in it. As the then Prime Minister, Gordon Brown, told the House of Commons, 'the battered reputation of this institution cannot be repaired without fundamental change'.[91] A special House of Commons Committee was established—the Reform Committee, chaired by Tony Wright MP—to consider reforms to parliamentary procedures. Its report, entitled *Rebuilding the House*, was published in late 2009.[92]

According to the Committee, public confidence in the House of Commons was too low, and fundamental structural and cultural change was required: 'We believe that the House of Commons has to become a more vital institution, less sterile in how it operates, better able to reflect public concerns, more transparent, and more vigorous in its task of scrutiny and accountability.'[93] As the Committee noted, the great majority of MPs work extremely hard, but 'at present many Members do not see the point in attending debates or making the House the primary focus of their activities'.[94] To address this, the Committee considered that it was necessary to give MPs back a sense of ownership of Parliament by enabling them to set its agenda and take meaningful decisions, and to ensure that the business of the House is responsive to public concerns.

The Committee's work was informed by its view that while the government should get its business through the Commons, the House, in turn, should get its scrutiny and the public should get listened to. We have already noted two of the Committee's major proposals, both of which have already been implemented—giving backbench MPs more influence over debates in the House of Commons via a Backbench Business Committee, and the election by secret ballot of select committee chairs. The Committee also recommended that the House of Commons should engage more with the public by actively assisting a greater degree of public participation through giving a higher profile to public petitions, opening up the process of legislation, and giving the public an opportunity to influence the content of draft laws. The coalition government that took office in 2010 agreed to implement these proposals in full. The need to further strengthen Parliament's role has also been recognised by Sir George Young MP, the Leader of the House of Commons. In a speech to the Hansard Society, he advocated launching important select committee reports in the chamber of the House of Commons with a vote on their conclusions.[95]

It is too early to assess the impact of these reforms. However, it can be said with confidence that, cumulatively, they represent a significant strengthening of Parliament's position vis-à-vis the executive. Whether they will succeed in substantially bolstering parliamentary scrutiny of government remains to be seen.

---

[91] HC Deb, vol 493, col 795, 10 June 2009.

[92] House of Commons Reform Committee, *Rebuilding the House* (HC 1117 2009–10).

[93] *Rebuilding the House*, [3].   [94] *Rebuilding the House*, [3].

[95] See **http://www.hansardsociety.org.uk/files/folders/2619/download.aspx**

7. Freedom of information

In this section, we turn to consider freedom of information. If government is to be held to account, then it is necessary to have access to information from government. Transparency and openness in government are essential to effective public and political scrutiny.

This area is governed by the Freedom of Information Act 2000 (FOIA), which came into force in 2005. This Act enshrines in UK law the principle that citizens have a (qualified) right of access to government information.[96] As we have already seen, two of the branches of the state—the courts and Parliament—have a long tradition of acting in an open manner; courts are bound by the principle of open justice; likewise, parliamentary proceedings are public and open. However, government—and especially British government—has long been characterised by a culture of—some would say almost an obsession with—official secrecy.[97] In this culture, access to information has more often than not been tightly controlled by Ministers and civil servants.

It is difficult to overemphasise how deeply embedded this attitude is within British government. Calls for freedom-of-information legislation long met with resistance, with only limited statutory rights of access to official information being conceded prior to the enactment of the FOIA.[98] In a notable development in 1993, the then Conservative government adopted a code of practice under which individuals could request access to information held by central government departments.[99] While this code was non-statutory, its administration was overseen by the Parliamentary Ombudsman. Despite these developments, there were still calls for specific legislation on freedom of information. Following the election of the Labour government in 1997, the FOIA was enacted. The purpose of this section is to analyse critically the regime established by that Act—but first we need to consider the reasons for having freedom-of-information legislation.

7.1 The rationale for freedom of information

There are various reasons why such legislation might be thought desirable. First, freedom of information advances transparency and openness in government. This is likely to enhance the accountability of government by revealing abuses of power, and is also likely to make government act more responsibly given the enhanced likelihood of poor administration (or worse) coming to light. Second, freedom of information can also advance the cause of democratic government by enabling citizens to participate

---

[96] In Scotland, see the Freedom of Information (Scotland) Act 2002.

[97] See Vincent, *The Culture of Secrecy: Britain 1832–1998* (Oxford 1998).

[98] See, eg Public Records Act 1958; Local Government (Access to Information) Act 1985; Access to Personal Files Act 1987; Access to Medical Records Act 1988; Environmental Information Regulations 1992, SI 1992/3240; Data Protection Act 1998 (replacing Data Protection Act 1984).

[99] *Code of Practice on Government Information* (Cm 2290 1993).

in government decision-making on a fully informed basis rather than in light only of such information as the government chooses to release. This, in turn, recognises individuals as democratic citizens rather than as subjects of government.

However, while there is an important public interest in freedom of information, there can often be a countervailing public interest in the non-disclosure of information. For example, there may be little point in requiring government to disclose sensitive information about the operations of the security services if the very disclosure of such information may enable suspected terrorists to evade the state's surveillance of their activities and thereby jeopardise public safety. Likewise, there may be little value in government disclosing the details of a future military campaign if such disclosure undermines the potential effectiveness of that campaign.

The general point is that, while important, the principle of freedom of information is not absolute. Exceptions and limitations are inevitably necessary in order to ensure an appropriate balance between the public interest in freedom of information and competing public interests served by non-disclosure. Saying that there should be some balance is, though, the easy part; the more difficult matter is deciding precisely where that balance should lie in any particular instance and, just as importantly, who should have the power to decide where the balance should lie. A further important point to bear in mind at the outset is that legitimate *public* interests in non-disclosure should not be confused with considerations of *governmental* convenience. Withholding information because its release would, for example, jeopardise the safety of UK soliders is one thing; suppressing it in order to spare ministerial blushes is quite another.

7.2 The Freedom of Information Act 2000

As noted above, the FOIA creates a general right of access to information held by public authorities.[100] Any person making a Freedom of information request is entitled to be informed by the public authority whether it holds the information requested, and, if so, to have that information communicated to him.[101] The Act applies to over 100,000 public authorities, including central government departments, local authorities, schools, colleges and universities, the health service, the police, and a range of other public bodies.[102] All public authorities must adopt and maintain a publication scheme—that is, a scheme relating to the publication of its information, which is subject to the approval of the Information Commissioner.[103]

While the principle of the Act is that individuals have a general right of access to government information, this principle is subject to severe limitations. First, there are *absolute (or class-based) exemptions.* Information that falls within an absolute exemption is excluded from the general duty of disclosure and not subject to any public interest test. This means that once it is established that information falls within a relevant

---

[100] Freedom of Information Act 2000, s 1.   [101] Freedom of Information Act 2000, s 1(1).
[102] Freedom of Information Act 2000, s 3 and Sch 1.
[103] Freedom of Information Act 2000, s 19.

class, the Act does not require it to be disclosed even if, in relation to the *particular* information in question, the public interest would favour its disclosure. Absolute exemptions cover information available through other means; information supplied by, or relating to, the government intelligence services; information in court records; information the disclosure of which would infringe parliamentary privilege; information held by either House of Parliament the disclosure of which might 'prejudice the effective conduct of public affairs'; information provided in confidence; and information the disclosure of which is positively prohibited by statute, court order, or EU law.[104] The appropriateness of having classes of information subject to absolute exemptions is questionable, bearing in mind that the effect of this regime is to deny access to information falling within such classes even if disclosure would have positive and no (or less compelling) negative consequences in public interest terms.

Second, the Act sets out a further category of *non-absolute public-interest-based exemptions*. Here, a two-stage analysis applies. The first question is whether the information falls into one of the relevant categories. Information concerning such matters as national security, defence, international relations, the economy, and formulation of government policy falls into such categories.[105] The second question is whether the public interest in maintaining the exemption outweighs the public interest in disclosing the information.[106] It is clearly easier to justify a system of non-absolute exemptions, although this aspect of the Act is also open to criticism—not least given the breadth of the categories of information qualifying for exemption on this basis.

There are other limitations on the general right of access to information. For example, a public authority need not release information—and, if it chooses to do so, may charge a fee—when the cost of supplying the information would exceed a prescribed limit (currently £600).[107] Another limitation is that public authorities need not comply with vexatious or repeated requests for information.[108]

The FOIA is administered in the following way. Individuals may make requests to the relevant public authority to disclose requested information. The public authority must then, within 20 days, either confirm or deny whether it holds the information requested.[109] If the authority holds the information, then the authority should disclose the information, unless it considers the information to be exempt from disclosure. If the authority refuses to disclose, then the individual may request an internal review of that refusal by the public authority.[110] If the public authority still refuses to

---

[104] Freedom of Information Act 2000, ss 23, 32, 34, 36, 41, and 44, read with s 2(3).

[105] Freedom of Information Act 2000, ss 24, 26, 27, 29, and 35, read with s 2(3).

[106] Freedom of Information Act 2000, s 2(2)(b).

[107] Freedom of Information Act 2000, ss 12 and 13; the Freedom of Information and Data Protection (Appropriate Limit and Fees) Regulations 2004, SI 2004/3244. A lower limit of £450 applies in relation to certain public bodies.   [108] Freedom of Information Act 2000, s 14.

[109] Freedom of Information Act 2000, s 10.

[110] *Secretary of State for Constitutional Affairs' Code of Practice on the Discharge of Public Authorities' Functions under Part I of the Freedom of Information Act 2000 Issued under Section 45 of the Act* (November 2004).

disclose, then the individual may complain to the Information Commissioner, which will decide whether the public authority's decision was correct.[111] The Information Commissioner is an independent body separate from government. If necessary, the Information Commissioner can issue an enforcement notice requiring the authority to disclose.[112] Either party (that is, the complainant or public authority) affected by a decision of the Information Commissioner may appeal to the First-tier Tribunal (Information Rights), and, from there, to the Upper Tribunal.[113] However, all of this is subject to a ministerial power of veto on the disclosure of information even though its disclosure has been ordered by the Information Commissioner or the Tribunal. This power of ministerial veto, or executive override, means that Ministers are able to refuse to disclose information even though such information would otherwise need to be disclosed under the Act.[114]

7.3 **The operation of the Act**

How, then, has the FOIA operated in practice? In 2009, central government bodies received over 40,000 requests for information. Of these requests, only 3 per cent were subject to a fee. In 2009, 86 per cent of requests were answered 'in time', in that they either received an answer within the standard 20-day deadline or were subject to a permitted deadline extension. As regards the use of the exemptions under the Act, these were applied in relation to just over 8,500 requests in 2009. The most commonly applied exemptions or exceptions were those relating to personal information, and investigations and proceedings conducted by public authorities.[115]

To date, the FOIA has been used to extract information from a number of different public authorities, and a great variety of information has been released—from Ministry of Defence records concerning supposed UFO sightings in the UK, to Ministry of Justice information concerning the highest paid legal aid lawyers. Two particularly high-profile cases deserve special mention here: the controversy of MPs' expenses and the use of the ministerial veto to prevent the disclosure of Cabinet discussions concerning the decision to go to war in Iraq in 2003.

7.3.1 **MPs' expenses**

In the first case, a request to disclose the expenses payable to MPs was initially refused under the Act by the House of Commons.[116] Following protracted legal proceedings, the High Court eventually held that this information should be disclosed under the

---

[111] Freedom of Information Act 2000, s 50.
[112] Freedom of Information Act 2000, s 52.   [113] Freedom of Information Act 2000, ss 57–59.
[114] Freedom of Information Act 2000, s 53.
[115] All of the statistical information in this paragraph is taken from Ministry of Justice, *Freedom of Information Act 2000: 2009 Annual Statistics on Implementation in Central Government* (London 2010), p 5.
[116] See Leyland, 'Freedom of Information and the 2009 Parliamentary Expenses Scandal' [2009] PL 675.

Act.[117] However, before the deadline for disclosing the information had passed, a national newspaper in 2009 published the complete information that it had obtained from a leak within Parliament. This information revealed that some MPs had made quite spurious expenses claims—for example, for mortgage interest payments when the mortgage had already been paid off, and for gardening costs such as the clearing of a moat and for the construction of a duck island. As noted earlier in this chapter, the whole saga of MPs' expenses aroused considerable public concern and anger. In the then Prime Minister's words, Parliament could no longer regulate itself like a gentleman's club and legislation was quickly enacted to establish the Independent Parliamentary Standards Authority in an attempt to restore public confidence.[118] Even then, when the information was finally disclosed under the FOIA, it transpired that various parts of it had been heavily redacted—that is, so edited for publication that it was incomplete when compared with the full information leaked to the newspaper. In other words, while the FOIA eventually lead to the disclosure of the information, the public was only made fully aware of the extent of the misuse of the MPs' expenses system because the full information had been published by the newspaper concerned.

7.3.2 Iraq Cabinet minutes

The second case—relating to the minutes of Cabinet meetings concerning the decision to go to war in Iraq—raised the question of how to balance two important public interests: the public interest in disclosing information concerning the hugely important and politically controversial decision to go to war in Iraq, and the public interest in maintaining the confidentiality of information relating to the formulation of government policy—in particular, the long-standing convention of collective Cabinet responsibility.[119] While the government considered that collective Cabinet responsibility precluded disclosure, the Information Tribunal[120] held that, given the exceptional circumstances, there were very powerful reasons why disclosure of the minutes would be in the public interest. According to the Tribunal, the disclosure of the Cabinet minutes was of 'crucial significance to an understanding of a hugely important step in the nation's recent history and the accountability of those who caused it to be taken'.[121]

However, the government then decided to exercise its power of ministerial veto under the FOIA to override the tribunal ruling. When using the veto, the government has to lay a statement before Parliament giving its reasons for the use of its override power.[122] In this instance, the government's argument was that Cabinet discussions needed to remain private because of the need for full and frank discussion of government policy, which could be inhibited by disclosure; consequently, the government

---

[117] *Corporate Officer of the House of Commons v Information Commissioner* [2008] EWHC 1084 (Admin), [2009] 3 All ER 403.   [118] Parliamentary Standards Act 2009.

[119] An aspect of this convention, as noted above, is that the details of cabinet meetings are confidential.

[120] Since superseded by the First-tier Tribunal (Information Rights).

[121] *Cabinet Office v Information Commissioner and Dr Lamb* (EA/2008/0024 and 29), [79].

[122] Freedom of Information Act 2000, s 53(3)(a).

exercised its ultimate right to make the final decision that the public interest justified the non-disclosure of information.[123] While the use of executive override was permissible under the FOIA, this merely serves to illustrate that the FOIA regime—designed, like all legislation, by government—is structured so as to give government the last word, thereby enabling it to decide that other interests are, in the circumstances, more valuable than those, such as transparency and accountability, that would be served by disclosure.

Q A government that chooses to exercise its veto in order to suppress information concerning matters of great controversy may, of course, have to suffer political consequences, such as sharp criticism and even electoral unpopularity. Is this a sufficient safeguard against the misuse of the veto power, or is it objectionable in the first place that such a power should exist?

7.4 Assessing the Freedom of Information Act 2000

It is undoubtedly the case that the FOIA has provided unprecedented access to information held by government and that a diverse array of information has entered the public domain that would otherwise not have been disclosed. The introduction of freedom of information legislation therefore represents a positive step forward in terms of promoting greater transparency, accountability, and understanding of the way in which public authorities work and how they make decisions. Freedom of information is now embedded within the UK constitution and presents a welcome challenge to the culture of secrecy that has long characterised UK government.

However, it is necessary to guard against being excessively sanguine over the effectiveness of the FOIA. The Act has certainly been criticised on a number of grounds for casting in unduly narrow terms the right of access to information. The Act was less rigorous in allowing access to information than freedom of information campaigners had wanted, and the Bill was substantially watered down within government before being presented to Parliament. The exemptions in the FOIA to the general duty of disclosure are wider and more extensive than those found in comparable legislation elsewhere. The risk is that the exemptions may be used to prevent disclosure of information necessary to hold public authorities to account. Moreover, the existence of the ministerial veto to overturn decisions of two politically independent bodies—the Information Commissioner and the Tribunal—enables the executive always to have the last word as to whether information is released. There will therefore always be the suspicion—as in the case of the Iraq Cabinet minutes—that governments will give in to their natural impulse towards secrecy in order to evade political accountability for

---

[123] Ministry of Justice, *Exercise of the Executive Override under Section 53 of the Freedom of Information Act 2000: Statement of Reasons* (23 February 2009).

their actions, especially when the information concerns events or actions that may threaten the political reputation of a government.

Indeed, some have argued that the limitations and restrictions built into the FOIA are so extensive that they effectively undermine the purported purpose of the Act to allow greater access to government information. According to Austin, the FOIA is a 'brilliant piece of *trompe l'oeil*, a sheep in wolf's clothing'.[124] On this view, the Act really only gives the *illusion* of a robust right of access to information: it is so hedged around with restrictions and qualifications that it represents a far more modest advance than at first appears. We conclude by noting that the coalition government that took office in 2010 publicly committed itself to a policy of greater transparency, including a commitment to 'extend the scope' of the FOIA.[125] At the time of writing, it is unclear precisely what this commitment involves.

8. Accountability and oversight of the security and intelligence services

We can now turn to consider the accountability and oversight of the security and intelligence services. We do so for the following reasons. First, the security and intelligence agencies undertake some of the most sensitive and important activities of government; indeed, such agencies are essential to the survival of government and society. Second, because of the nature of their task, there are special considerations concerning how to hold these agencies to account, and they have their own special accountability and oversight arrangements. Indeed, in this context, the basic tension seen throughout this chapter between effective government and effective scrutiny arises in a particularly acute form, given that the very nature of the security and intelligence services' activities precludes the use of many of the normal tools of accountability.

8.1 The security and intelligence services

It is a basic fact that, in the modern world, democratic states and the lives of their peoples are under threat from a number of different sources, including rogue states, global terrorism, the proliferation of weapons of mass destruction, and illegal narcotics. The scale of the danger posed by such threats and how they should be dealt with are both very difficult and complex questions over which different people can

---

[124] Austin, 'The Freedom of Information Act 2000: A Sheep in Wolf's Clothing?', in Jowell and Oliver (eds), *The Changing Constitution* (Oxford 2007), p 397. Translated literally, *trompe l'oeil* means 'deceives the eye' and is used to refer to a visual illusion, in this case, to highlight that legislation enacted to provide freedom of legislation, in fact does little to enable access to government information.

[125] HM Government, *The Coalition: Our Programme for Government* (London 2010), p 11.

reasonably disagree. However, one does not have to subscribe to the notion of a 'global war on terrorism' to accept that there is a real terrorist threat and that the development of nuclear weapons by a rogue state or a non-state group may pose something of a danger to the lives of ordinary people in Western countries such as the UK. In 2010, the UK government's Joint Terrorism Analysis Centre raised the threat to the UK from international terrorism from 'substantial' to 'severe': this means that a terrorist attack is regarded as highly likely.

National security, or, in older language, 'defence of the realm', is perhaps the most essential function of government. Government is the principal institution that is able to protect people against a threat to national security. Indeed, the most basic responsibility of any government is to protect the security of its own people, which means protecting them against terrorism and attack from other states and groups. To this end, the UK government has its intelligence and security machinery. There are three intelligence and security services, collectively known as 'the agencies'. First, there is the Security Service, also known as MI5. It is responsible for protecting the UK against covertly organised threats to national security, such as terrorism, espionage, and the proliferation of weapons of mass destruction. Second, there is the Secret Intelligence Service (SIS), also known as MI6. Its principal function is the collection of foreign intelligence on issues concerning Britain's vital interests in the fields of security, defence, serious crime, and foreign and economic policies. Third, there is Government Communications Headquarters (GCHQ), which gathers intelligence through the interception of communications and provides intelligence in support of government decision-making in the fields of national security, military operations, and law enforcement.

Both the Security Service and the SIS were established in 1909, and GCHQ was established in 1929. For much of their history, the security services were, in effect, a 'secret state'.[126] For many decades, the agencies had no formal existence and no legal basis or framework whatsoever; indeed, the government officially denied their existence, and there were no arrangements whereby Parliament could hold them to account for their actions. This state of affairs could exist because politicians across the political spectrum subscribed to two basic principles in this area: that it was not possible even to discuss the work of the agencies in public or in Parliament; and that Parliament must entirely abdicate its powers in this field to the executive.[127] As Andrew has observed, the assumption was 'that the mysteries of intelligence must be left entirely to the grown-ups (the agencies and the government) and that the children (parliament and the public) must not meddle in them'.[128] However, over recent decades, the context in which the agencies operate has changed considerably, and there have been persistent calls for more transparency and scrutiny of the work of the agencies. There are two main reasons for this.

---

[126] See Hennessy, *The Secret State: Whitehall and the Cold War* (London 2003).

[127] Andrew, *The Defence of the Realm: The Authorised History of MI5* (London 2009), p 753.

[128] Andrew, p 753.

First, concerns that arise in relation to other government bodies apply equally to the agencies. Like the rest of government, the agencies are not immune from the most ludicrous incompetence. For example, in 2008, it was discovered that a digital camera used by a Security Service agent containing sensitive data had been put up for sale on eBay—'a clear breach of data security procedures'.[129]

Second, however, there is also the potential for the agencies, given the nature of their work and the secrecy with which it is necessarily conducted, to engage in particularly dubious practices. Consider the case of Binyam Mohamed. Before being charged with terrorist offences by the US government, he was held in various locations around the world by and on behalf of the US authorities, during which time, he alleged, confessions were extracted from him under torture. He further claimed that members of the UK's Security Service were involved in facilitating his questioning while the alleged programme of torture was being undertaken. The claimant sought judicial review of the UK government's refusal to disclose to him evidence that, he asserted, would support his argument that he had been tortured and which would therefore assist in his defence against the charges brought by the US government. The Administrative Court concluded that the 'relationship of the UK government to the US authorities in connection with [the claimant] was far beyond that of a bystander or witness to the alleged wrongdoing',[130] and that the treatment to which the claimant had allegedly been subject 'could easily be contended to be at the very least cruel, inhuman and degrading treatment'.[131] In an extraordinary passage, publication of which the government sought unsuccessfully to suppress, Lord Neuberger MR, in the Court of Appeal, said that 'some Security Services officials appear to have a dubious record relating to actual involvement, and frankness about any such involvement, with the mistreatment of Mr Mohamed when he was held at the behest of US officials'.[132]

Against this background, it is unsurprising that the traditional position, whereby the agencies existed in a legal black hole and were essentially immune from scrutiny, came to be regarded as unsustainable. The position today is different in two senses.

8.2 **The legal framework and powers of the agencies**

First, the agencies now have a legal, statutory basis and certain legal powers. The Interception of Communications Act 1985 allowed communications (telephone, fax, telex, and post) to be intercepted when authorised by a warrant signed by a Secretary of

---

[129] Intelligence and Security Committee, *Annual Report 2008–09* (Cm 7807 2010), p 21.

[130] *R (Mohamed) v Secretary of State for Foreign and Commonwealth Affairs (No 1)* [2008] EWHC 2048 (Admin), [2009] 1 WLR 2579, [88].

[131] This part of the Administrative Court's judgment was published, following further litigation, as an appendix to the judgment of the Court of Appeal in *R (Mohamed) v Secretary of State for Foreign and Commonwealth Affairs* [2010] EWCA Civ 65.

[132] This passage formed [168] of Lord Neuberger's judgment in *Mohamed*, but was only published, following further litigation, in *R (Mohamed) v Secretary of State for Foreign and Commonwealth Affairs* [2010] EWCA Civ 158, [28].

State for the highlighted reasons.[133] This was followed by the Security Service Act 1989, which established a legal framework for the Security Service. The legal framework for both the SIS and GCHQ was subsequently established by the Intelligence Services Act 1994.

There is now, therefore, a legal framework that sets out the powers and functions of the agencies. For example, the Security Service is responsible for protecting the UK against threats to national security from espionage, terrorism, and sabotage, from the activities of agents of foreign powers, and from actions intended to overthrow or undermine parliamentary democracy by political, industrial, or violent means.[134] The operations of the Security Service are principally directed toward counter-terrorism activities. The SIS, meanwhile, is directed by statute to obtain and provide information relating to the actions or intentions of persons outside the British Islands, and to perform other tasks relating to the actions or intentions of such persons.[135] This enables the SIS to conduct covert operations and to act clandestinely overseas in support of UK government objectives. The statutory function of GCHQ is to monitor and decipher communications.[136]

Under statute, the agencies have the ability to apply to the relevant Secretary of State for a warrant in order to authorise certain actions, such as entry into or interference with property or the interception of communications (for example, phone-tapping).[137] Such actions would normally be unlawful, but the simple grant of a warrant by the Secretary of State renders such action by the agencies lawful.[138] It was considered necessary to establish a legal framework for the agencies in order to comply with the European Convention on Human Rights (ECHR).[139] Under ECHR, Art 8, everyone has the right to respect for their privacy, home, and correspondence, but this right may be interfered with when it is necessary in the interests of national security, public safety, or the economic well-being of the country, for the prevention of disorder or crime. Under the Security Service and Intelligence Services legislation, the agencies are empowered to act only in the interests of the national security of the UK, in the interests of its economic well-being, or in support of the prevention or detection of serious crime.[140]

8.3 **Accountability framework**

The second major development has been the establishment of a formal accountability framework for the security and intelligence agencies. Such accountability and oversight is provided in three different ways.

---

[133] The 1985 Act was superseded by the Regulation of Investigatory Powers Act 2000.

[134] Security Service Act 1989, s 1(2).   [135] Intelligence Services Act 1994, s 1.

[136] Intelligence Services Act 1994, s 3(1).

[137] Security Service Act 1989, s 3; Intelligence Services Act 1994, s 5; Regulation of Investigatory Powers Act 2000.

[138] It is also possible, under the Regulation of Investigatory Powers Act 2000, for warrants for certain forms of interception of communication to be issued to other bodies, such as police forces.

[139] See *Malone v UK* (1985) 7 EHRR 14.

[140] Security Service Act 1989, s 1; Intelligence and Security Act 1994, ss 1(2) and 3(2).

First, the agencies are accountable to government Ministers, who, in turn, are accountable to Parliament. Overall responsibility for intelligence and security matters rests with the Prime Minister, who is answerable to Parliament on matters affecting the agencies collectively. The Home Secretary is responsible for the Security Service, and the Foreign Secretary for the SIS and GCHQ.

Second, the agencies are subject to a degree of political accountability to Parliament. This is provided by the Intelligence and Security Committee (ISC). The role of the ISC is to provide politically independent oversight of the agencies' activities and is considered in more detail below.

Third, the agencies are subject to a degree of judicial oversight. This is provided by the Commissioners and a tribunal. There are two Commissioners—the Intelligence Services Commissioner and the Interception of Communications Commissioner—who oversee the agencies' performance of their statutory duties and review the lawfulness of their actions.[141] Both Commissioners must be judges of high standing. Judicial accountability is also provided by the Investigatory Powers Tribunal, which investigates complaints by individuals about the agencies' conduct towards them or about interception of their communications.[142] Together, the Commissioners and the Tribunal provide independent judicial oversight of the activities of the agencies.

However, we should not blithely accept that the existence of these arrangements means that adequate provision is now made for holding the agencies to account. What type of accountability can there really be, given the hidden and secret world of the intelligence and security services? How effective is such accountability? And how, if at all, can such accountability mechanisms be improved? Given the focus of this chapter on political and parliamentary accountability of government, we shall address these questions by focusing specifically upon the role and effectiveness of the ISC, because it is the principal method by which parliamentary scrutiny of the agencies is supposed to be facilitated.

8.4 The Intelligence and Security Committee

There is a basic and unavoidable dilemma in seeking to scrutinise the activities of the security and intelligence services, and to hold them to account. To maintain their effectiveness, the agencies must of necessity operate in secret. If information concerning their activities were to become public knowledge, then this could endanger lives and undermine the effectiveness of the agencies in seeking to protect national security. On the other hand, it is important in a democratic society that there are effective safeguards and means of overseeing the work of the agencies, and that they are, as far as possible, held to account for their activities. As with political accountability in general, the requirement to explain and justify actions encourages

---

141 Regulation of Investigatory Powers Act 2000, ss 57 and 59.
142 Regulation of Investigatory Powers Act 2000, s 65.

better-thought-out policy, better control of expenditure, and adherence to accepted principles and practices. Oversight of the intelligence and security agencies is no different—and, if anything, is even more essential given that most of their work is kept secret from the general public. What kind of political oversight and accountability does the ISC then provide?

The ISC is an independent committee, established by the Intelligence Services Act 1994. Its purpose is to examine the policy, administration, and expenditure of the three agencies.[143] ISC members are appointed by the Prime Minister after consulting with the leader of the main opposition party.[144] The ISC has a cross-party membership of nine non-ministerial parliamentarians, drawn from both Houses of Parliament. The ISC reports directly to the Prime Minister, and through him to Parliament. Sometimes, the ISC is asked to look into a particular matter, but most of the time it is able to set its own agenda. The ISC determines how and when it is to conduct and conclude its programme of work; this gives it the freedom to pursue avenues of inquiry to its satisfaction. The ISC publishes an annual report and also produces ad hoc reports. These reports are published (although with deletions of sensitive material), laid before Parliament together with the government's response, and then debated in Parliament.

While the ISC is a committee of parliamentarians, it is important to recognise that it is not itself a parliamentary select committee. Indeed, when compared with select committees, the ISC is unique in a number of respects.

First, ISC members are appointed by, and report to, *the Prime Minister* rather than Parliament itself. The separation between the ISC and Parliament is not only physical—the ISC does not sit in Parliament itself, but in a government building—but also administrative—the ISC is hosted and supported by a government department: the Cabinet Office.

Second, while the ISC holds evidence sessions and considers written evidence like other select committees, its evidence sessions are held *in secret* and written evidence is not publicly disclosed.

Third, the Prime Minister has a *statutory power to exclude material* from a report of the ISC, if it appears to him that its publication would prejudice the continued discharge of the functions of any of the agencies.[145] While ISC reports are published, sensitive material that would damage national security is deleted (or 'redacted'). It is therefore never possible to know for certain whether an ISC report has been censored and, if it has, for what reason.

Fourth, the ISC operates within a *'ring of secrecy'* by operation of the Official Secrets Act 1989. ISC members have access to a great deal of classified information and the agencies' future plans, but in return, they are 'notified' under the 1989 Act. This means that a criminal offence is committed, under the 1989 Act, by any ISC

---

[143] Intelligence Services Act 1994, s 10(1).   [144] Intelligence Services Act 1994, s 10(3).
[145] Intelligence Services Act 1994, s 10(7).

member who discloses information relating to the security agencies without lawful authority.[146]

All of these features place the ISC in a highly unusual position—one that, in the minds of some, drastically restricts its ability to exercise effective oversight of the agencies. The cynical criticism of the ISC is that it merely serves a 'window-dressing' function—that is, that it holds out the promise of political accountability, but without actually providing it. Those who advance this criticism often highlight how the above features of the ISC can be used to suit the needs of government and the agencies rather than those of Parliament. For example, because ISC members are appointed by the Prime Minister, the risk is that they are the Prime Minister's placemen—that is, parliamentarians carefully selected so as to give the agencies an easy ride rather than to subject them to robust scrutiny.

This line of criticism is fortified with respect to other features of the ISC. For example, the fact that ISC evidence sessions are conducted in private may give rise to suspicion (whether or not well founded) over the robustness of ISC scrutiny. Another suspicion is that the Prime Minister's power to insist upon deletions from ISC reports can provide a useful means of excising valid criticisms of the agencies. A more general criticism of the ISC is that it is a creature of the executive rather than Parliament: an arrangement that is at odds with the purpose of the ISC—namely, to provide political, parliamentary scrutiny of the agencies.

It is important, though, not to dismiss the ISC out of hand, but to recognise the difficult challenge posed by the basic dilemma involved in exercising political oversight of the security and intelligence agencies. For example, there is really no alternative to the ISC holding its evidence sessions in private. If the process were to occur in public, certain information would simply never be disclosed to the ISC *at all* (because *public* disclosure would be gravely damaging to the national interest and could put individuals at risk), meaning that the ISC itself would be deprived of an accurate picture of the agencies' activities and plans. The government has, in fact, suggested that the ISC hold *some* evidence sessions in public, but the ISC itself has, so far, been reluctant to take this step. It has argued that, in public sessions, it would only be able to ask 'patsy' questions—that is, questions that can only evoke bland and uninformative answers. In March 2010, Kim Howells, the ISC's then chair, said: '[W]e do not expect our agencies to spill secrets all over the place because they are in the business of trying to keep this country safe from terrorists and other murderous lunatics.'[147] Meanwhile, although the Prime Minister is able to insist upon redactions to ISC reports, he is obliged to consult with the ISC on any proposed redaction and, to date, no material has been excluded without the ISC's consent.[148] Furthermore, the ISC includes parliamentarians from opposition parties (as well as

---

[146] Official Secrets Act 1989, s 1. On the Official Secrets Acts, see Chapter 20, section 7.2, below.

[147] HC Deb, vol 507, col 994, 18 March 2010 (Kim Howells MP).

[148] Open letter from the then Chair of the ISC to the Director of Human Rights Watch, 19 February 2010.

the governing party (or parties)) who have a recognised knowledge and expertise in the work of the security agencies.

What, then, is to be made of the ISC? When he was chair, Howells strongly defended the robustness of the scrutiny supplied by the Committee, asserting that 'giving evidence before us is not a comfortable experience for anyone. The questioning is robust, often combative, issues are returned to, further explanations demanded, documents examined and the end results are often critical, albeit not sensationalist'.[149] The Committee has also asserted that, as the agencies have learnt to trust the ISC, the agencies have become increasingly willing to be open with the Committee.[150] Howells said that the ISC's experience has been that the harder it investigates and questions the agencies, the better they understand the need to be fully accountable.[151]

There is, however, one persistent issue with the ISC: who should have ownership of the committee—the government or Parliament? In 1999, the House of Commons Home Affairs Committee noted that the ISC's establishment constituted a significant step forward over previous arrangements for providing democratic accountability. However, it was concluded that the ISC should be replaced by a parliamentary select committee or committees. Such a system would draw heavily on the ISC, and would be grafted onto the select committee system with appropriate adaptations. But the key point for the Home Affairs Committee was that scrutiny of the agencies should be more independent of the executive.[152] This recommendation was not accepted by the government, and indeed, when he was ISC chair, Howells said that making the ISC a parliamentary select committee would be counterproductive because it would not get access to the same information as the ISC—meaning that oversight would not be strengthened, but weakened.[153]

But this is not to imply that the current arrangements are adequate; on the contrary. In 2010, the ISC itself expressed some concerns with respect to its relationship with government. The Committee recognised that certain of its administrative arrangements were no longer appropriate and required not only updating, but also changing if there was to be confidence in the Committee's independence.[154] More explicitly, the then ISC chair told Parliament that

> there are some within the Whitehall bureaucracy who...have not understood or have refused to accept that the independence of the ISC is sacrosanct. Some of them have given the impression that they regard the ISC as an irritation—a problem that they could well do without.[155]

---

[149] Open letter from the then Chair of the ISC to the Director of Human Rights Watch.

[150] Intelligence and Security Committee, *Intelligence Oversight* (London 2002), p 12.

[151] HC Deb, vol 507, cols 996–7, 18 March 2010 (Kim Howells MP).

[152] House of Commons Home Affairs Committee, *Accountability of the Security Service* (HC 291 1998–99).   [153] HC Deb, vol 507, col 993, 18 March 2010 (Kim Howells MP).

[154] Intelligence and Security Committee, *Annual Report 2009–10* (Cm 7844 2010), pp 4–5.

[155] HC Deb, vol 507, col 996, 18 March 2010 (Kim Howells MP).

The Committee therefore made two recommendations.[156] First, the ISC stated that its independence must be strengthened and made more transparent. To this end, it said that it was absolutely fundamental that it could not continue to sit within, and depend upon, a government department—the Cabinet Office—which itself has a central role concerning the very agencies that the ISC oversees.

Second, the ISC also recommended that it should have its own separate budget rather than have its budget drawn from that of the agencies and therefore, in effect, be determined by the organisations that it oversees.

In response, the government, in what may be perceived as a classic delaying tactic, noted that the ISC's recommendations required further consideration.[157]

Q Why does oversight of the security and intelligence services pose a problem for accountability? How, if at all, could oversight of the security and intelligence agencies be enhanced? Should the ISC become a parliamentary select committee?

9. Conclusion

This chapter has examined a central, although complex, aspect of the UK constitution: the political accountability of government to Parliament. It has been seen that the degree to which Parliament is able effectively to scrutinise government policy and actions is largely dependent upon the political relationship between the two institutions—in particular, the dominance of Parliament by the government of the day. This basic feature of the constitution exerts considerable influence over how institutions, such as Parliament, and constitutional conventions, such as ministerial responsibility, operate in practice. It also influences the nature and type of control that Parliament is able to exercise over government. As we noted above, Parliament's role is not that of directing, commanding, or obstructing the government; rather, it is there to influence, advise, criticise, and scrutinise the government.

There is, however, a strong and justified perception amongst many politicians and commentators that Parliament is unable to discharge even these relatively modest functions adequately. We have seen that there are several interlocking reasons for this, including the executive's pervasive influence on Parliament, political party discipline, the career aspirations of MPs, ambiguities in the relationship between Ministers and civil servants, and the temptation for them to play the blame game when things go wrong. These difficulties are not (either individually or collectively) easily resolvable. However, the reforms being undertaken in response to the House of Commons Reform

---

[156] Intelligence and Security Committee, Cm 7844.

[157] HM Government, *Government Response to the Intelligence and Security Committee's Annual Report 2009–10* (Cm 7845 2010).

Committee's report, *Rebuilding the House*, represent a starting point for enhancing the ability of Parliament to scrutinise government more effectively.

Finally, it is important to note that while this chapter has emphasised that parliamentary scrutiny of government is a matter of politics not law, political and legal forms of accountability are closely connected with each other. Indeed, the concerns identified in this chapter as regards the relative ineffectiveness of political accountability have prompted the courts to subject government to a more intensive and searching form of legal accountability through the process of judicial review. In this sense, the weakness of political forms of control has been a driving force behind the development of the forms of legal control that we examine in Part IV of the book.

Further reading

Parliamentary scrutiny of government

NORTON, *Parliament in British Politics* (Basingstoke 2005), ch 6

OLIVER, 'The "Modernisation" of the United Kingdom Parliament?', in Jowell and Oliver (eds), *The Changing Constitution* (Oxford 2007)

WOODHOUSE, 'Ministerial Responsibility', in Bogdanor (ed), *The British Constitution in the Twentieth Century* (Oxford 2003)

Freedom of information

AUSTIN, 'The Freedom of Information Act 2000: A Sheep in Wolf's Clothing?', in Jowell and Oliver (eds), *The Changing Constitution* (Oxford 2007)

BIRKINSHAW, *Freedom of Information: The Law, Practice, and the Ideal* (London 2010)

Useful websites

Parliamentary scrutiny of government

http://www.parliament.uk
Website of the UK Parliament, with links to select committees and daily reports of parliamentary proceedings, known as Hansard

Freedom of information

http://www.informationtribunal.gov.uk
Website of the First-tier Tribunal (Information Rights)

http://www.ico.gov.uk
Website of the Information Commissioner's Office

http://www.itspublicknowledge.info
Website of the Scottish Information Commissioner

Accountability and oversight of the security and intelligence services

http://www.gchq.gov.uk
Website of the Government Communications Headquarters

http://www.ipt-uk.com
Website of the Investigatory Powers Tribunal (also includes the Intelligence Services Commissioner and Interception of Communications Commissioner)

http://www.mi5.gov.uk
Website of the Security Service (MI5)

http://www.sis.gov.uk
Website of the Secret and Intelligence Service (MI6)

The Control of Public Expenditure

11

1. Introduction

We saw in Chapter 4 that, in a modern administrative state such as the United Kingdom, the executive is necessarily a large and highly complex network of numerous agencies and organisations—departments of state, executive agencies, and non-departmental public bodies. That the executive now has such an intricate and highly differentiated structure is largely a product of the range and complexity of public functions that it is expected to perform. However, none of this governmental activity comes for free. It must all be paid for and the vast majority of the funding for government expenditure comes from public money—that is, from taxpayers. Given the scale and breadth of public activity, government spends public money in a variety of different ways. Much of the expenditure is accounted for by a handful of big spending departments such as the Department of Work and Pensions in dispensing social security benefits, the Department of Health, which funds the National Health Service (NHS), and the Department for Education, which pays for schools. Public spending takes less remarkable forms, too: the purchase of paperclips by a governmental agency or the cost of a Minister's chauffeur, for example. What is abundantly clear, though, is that, irrespective of precisely how government spends public money, the total amount of public spending is substantial. At the time of writing, annual UK public expenditure (that is, the money spent by government) exceeds £700 billion—48 per cent of gross domestic product (the total value of the goods produced and services provided by the UK in a single year).[1]

This chapter examines the control of public expenditure in the UK, and, in particular, how government acquires the resources needed to administer public policy and how it is held to account for the raising and spending of public money. Such 'financial scrutiny' is imperative in any political system and generally assumes considerable constitutional significance. As it has been noted, '[m]oney is central to the constitution, whether the focus be effective power, legitimate authority, or both'.[2]

It is important that we examine financial scrutiny for two principal reasons. First, financial scrutiny is itself a *significant mechanism for holding government to account*.

---

[1] HM Treasury, *Budget 2010: Securing the Recovery* (HC 451 2009–10), p 11.
[2] Harden, 'Money and the Constitution: Financial Control, Reporting and Audit' (1993) 13 LS 16.

This topic therefore bears directly upon one of the central themes of this book—namely, how the executive is held to account. Government spends vast sums of public money and it is essential that it is properly held to account. It is therefore necessary to analyse the processes by which the raising and spending of public money is subject to scrutiny and oversight, and to consider the effectiveness of such accountability processes. A second reason for examining this topic arises from the fact that financial scrutiny is not only an important topic of public law in its own right, but can also offer us some insight into *broader issues of constitutional design*—in particular, the relationship between the executive and the legislature. It is, after all, the executive that typically raises and spends public money, and the legislature that holds it to account. By examining financial scrutiny, we can therefore better appreciate basic aspects of the UK's constitutional structure.

We begin our analysis of these matters by looking at the role and importance of financial scrutiny, and its constitutional significance in the context of the relationship between Parliament and the executive. The next section examines the planning and scrutiny of public expenditure by considering the process by which government raises public money—that is, the *supply procedure*. The focus then turns to the accountability processes for scrutinising planned governmental expenditure; these controls are both internal—that is, within government itself—and external—that is, by Parliament. Finally, we examine the accountability processes concerning the actual expenditure of public money: in other words, once government has spent public money, how do we know that it has been well spent and what are the processes for scrutinising such expenditure?

The central theme of this chapter is the role of financial scrutiny as an important aspect of accountability and the effectiveness of the processes of financial scrutiny over governmental expenditure. At the same time, we will also see another of our general themes materialise in this context—the increasingly multilayered nature of the UK's constitutional arrangements—when we turn to consider how financial scrutiny and audit operates at different levels of government—national, devolved, and local—in the UK.

2. Financial scrutiny of government

2.1 The importance of financial scrutiny

So, what actually is financial scrutiny of public expenditure? And why do we need it? One way of seeking to understand the role and importance of financial scrutiny is to compare it with other accountability mechanisms—political and legal—that oversee governmental activities. We saw in Chapter 10 that government is subject to political control by elected representatives in Parliament via the doctrine of ministerial responsibility, and we explain in Chapters 12–15 that government is also subject to legal control by the courts via judicial review proceedings. Financial scrutiny sits alongside political and legal control as another important form of public accountability. It is fundamentally concerned with holding government to account for its financial decisions by requiring it to justify its revenue-raising and spending plans, and then, subsequently, to explain whether the expenditure achieved its objective and, if not, why not. Indeed, it might be said that this form of scrutiny is central to the concept of accountability—that those in power produce *an account* of their actions—because that concept itself derives in large part from the need to provide a statement of financial expenditure relating to a particular purpose.[3]

However, when compared with other accountability mechanisms and processes, financial scrutiny serves slightly different ends. If political and legal forms of accountability are respectively concerned with the merits and legality of the government's policies and decisions, then the focus of financial scrutiny is upon efficiency, effectiveness, and economy in the use of public money to deliver public services (often referred to as the 'three Es'). While these related values are each distinct, they are usually captured together by one catch-all phrase: 'achieving value for money' (often referred to by its acronym VFM)—that is, making sure that public money is used appropriately and that it is not wasted. This is a legitimate concern. Almost everyone pays tax in one form or another or benefits from public services. How valuable public assets and services are funded, safeguarded, and paid for is a key issue in any democratic society. In short, the proper and productive use of public money is an indispensable component of the democratic process. Furthermore, given the pressure on public spending in the UK and the need to reduce the deficit, it can only be expected that the need for accountability and transparency in public spending will increase.[4]

An equally important rationale behind effective financial scrutiny is that it goes to the heart of the broader political process and the wider set of constitutional relationships between the executive and the legislature. Consider, first, the importance of public expenditure and financial scrutiny to the political process. The task of undertaking financial scrutiny of public money might, at first glance, appear to involve merely a narrow exercise of poring over figures on a balance sheet—although the most mundane practices often perform an unacknowledged, but pivotal, role in social life. In any event, financial scrutiny is nowhere near as lacklustre or peripheral as this image suggests. This is because financial scrutiny is really about ensuring the effective management of limited public resources so that important public purposes—protecting people from crime, funding hospitals and schools, promoting international development, and so on—can be successfully achieved. The crux of the issue is that all government activity needs to be funded, but public resources are always finite. Indeed, one of the principal reasons why we have the political process is to determine society's collective priorities when it comes to raising and spending public money, to decide who gets

---

[3] Day and Klein, *Accountabilities: Five Public Services* (London 1987), p 8.
[4] See HM Treasury, *The Spending Review Framework* (Cm 7872 2010).

what, when, and how.[5] Every government needs public money in order to make and implement policy, but how much money should government raise and how should it be spent? These questions raise some of the most highly politicised, contentious, and problematic issues that any political system has to address.

During the course of general elections, political parties make commitments and pledges on public spending and taxation in their manifestos, and the electorate can vote on this basis in such elections. Elections certainly have a role to play with regard to the financial scrutiny of government by determining which political party forms the government. However, elections are, in general terms, inadequate mechanisms for subjecting public expenditure to detailed scrutiny. For example, the 2010 general election campaign was fought on the understanding that sweeping austerity measures would be necessary, but the main political parties were reluctant (for fear of courting unpopularity) to spell out in detail how they would cut public spending and/or raise taxes if returned to government. In practice, Parliament has a unique constitutional function in authorising and scrutinising governmental expenditure, and has a responsibility to hold government to account between general elections for the money that it raises and then spends. Parliament provides the important link between government and the public. Financial scrutiny of government therefore goes to the centre of the constitutional relationship between government, Parliament, and the public.

Another set of reasons for having financial scrutiny concerns the unique nature of the many tasks for which government has assumed responsibility. Many public tasks—delivering public services, regulating businesses, protecting the environment, and promoting social equality amongst many others—could not realistically be achieved unless government, as opposed to private sector businesses, assumed responsibility for them. One particular concern is that governmental agencies may often be inherently prone to inefficiency and waste because, unlike commercial businesses, they do not compete in the marketplace, but instead rely on the taxpayer for their funding. Whereas companies and businesses are accountable to their shareholders, government is accountable to the public. Particular processes of financial scrutiny and accountability are therefore required with respect to governmental expenditure.

A final rationale for having effective financial scrutiny relates to the effectiveness of government itself. How government spends public money and the value for money achieved strongly influence the effectiveness of governmental policies and their administration. Public money raised and spent by government directly determines important aspects of the decisions made by government about public services, whether those decisions concern the number of police officers and nurses, the provision of local bus services, or the grant of international development aid to developing countries. Financial scrutiny of governmental expenditure—in particular, effective accountability and transparency—tends to promote better government. The quality of governmental decisions concerning the raising of public money and its expenditure

---

5 Lasswell, *Politics: Who Gets What, When, How* (New York 1950).

are likely to be better if those responsible are aware that their decisions are likely to be subject to robust and thorough scrutiny, and that mismanagement is likely to be revealed. Financial scrutiny and enhanced governmental performance—making government work better—are, then, inseparable.

Given the importance of financial scrutiny, we now need to consider what it actually involves. Broadly speaking, it is concerned with two distinct tasks. First, there is scrutiny of planned governmental expenditure and taxation; this we might term *forward-looking scrutiny* because it looks at the amount of public money that the government plans to raise in the future and at how it proposes to finance such spending. Second, there is scrutiny of past government expenditure, which we might term *backward-looking scrutiny*. This focuses upon how effectively public money has been used by government once it has been spent. In this chapter, we consider how both types of financial scrutiny operate in the UK.

The processes of financial scrutiny of government and public expenditure take various forms, and are undertaken by a variety of different institutions. Financial scrutiny can be undertaken internally within government itself; it can also be undertaken externally (in both its forward- and backward-looking guises) by Parliament and independent audit agencies. While Parliament can act as a whole to hold the government to account, more often than not it acts through its select committees—in particular, the Public Accounts Committee—so as to provide a degree of specialist scrutiny. A further point to note is that Parliament is often dependent upon the support provided by independent non-political audit agencies, in particular the National Audit Office (NAO). The importance of financial scrutiny therefore implicates the relationship between the government and Parliament, and it is to this that we now turn.

> **Q** Why is financial scrutiny of government so important? How does financial scrutiny differ from other forms of accountability?

2.2 **Parliament, government, and public expenditure**

The control of public expenditure is central to contemporary British constitutional arrangements and the relationships between government, Parliament, and the public. The basic constitutional principle is that government expenditure must be authorised by legislation, and therefore by Parliament. This principle underpins Parliament's constitutional right and duty to subject the executive to financial scrutiny and accountability of governmental financial decisions. It is important to appreciate that this principle is not merely a recent invention; rather, it is intimately intertwined with the development both of Parliament as an institution and of its constitutional relationship with the executive.

The origins of Parliament owe more to its financial rather than legislative functions. As Erskine May, the leading authority on parliamentary powers and procedures, explains, the obligation upon the sovereign to obtain the consent of Parliament to the levying of taxes to meet the expenditure of the state 'was a central factor in the historical development of parliamentary influence and power'.[6] The basis of Parliament was founded largely upon the practice of medieval monarchs summoning members of Parliament principally in order to receive their assent to taxes.[7] The notion that taxation was only lawful if the common consent of the realm was obtained in Parliament was almost universally accepted from at least the fifteenth century onwards.[8] However, during the seventeenth century, the English civil war between the monarch and Parliament was fought directly over whether or not the monarch had the inherent power to raise revenue without the approval of Parliament. Stuart monarchs, such as Charles I, wanted to raise money, but, as Parliament opposed this, they resorted to indirect taxation, which was imposed without parliamentary assent.[9] Parliament opposed this on the basis that it was nothing other than royal absolutism or despotism. The eventual winner was Parliament. In 1689, the Bill of Rights declared that 'levying money for or to use of the Crown by pretence of prerogative without grant of Parliament for longer time or in other manner than the same is or shall be granted is illegal'.[10]

This provision reflects a fundamental principle of British constitutional arrangements: government cannot raise or allocate public money without parliamentary consent. As no government can exist without raising and spending public money, the importance of Parliament is thereby ensured by this principle. Furthermore, Parliament's supremacy, and with it the constitutional principle of parliamentary sovereignty, is built upon its control of taxation. As Dicey explained, it is Parliament's financial muscle—the 'power of the purse', as White and Hollingsworth put it—that provides the legal basis for the constitutional supremacy of Parliament over the executive.[11]

More specifically, precedence in financial matters belongs to one particular part of Parliament—namely, the House of Commons rather than the House of Lords. Nowadays, it is solely the House of Commons that has precedence in financial matters. The House of Lords has no power to block or amend the Commons' approval of public expenditure: it merely endorses what the Commons has approved. The restricted powers of the House of Lords arise from the ancient rights and privileges of the House

---

[6] McKay (ed), *Erskine May's Treatise on The Law, Privileges, Proceedings and Usage of Parliament* (London 2004), p 848.

[7] Gneist, *The English Parliament* (London 1886), pp 131–8, 199–200; Einzig, *The Control of the Purse: Progress and Decline of the Parliament's Financial Control* (London 1959).

[8] Goldsworthy, *The Sovereignty of Parliament: History and Philosophy* (Oxford 1999), p 69.

[9] For example, the ship money tax introduced by Charles I. See Hill, *The Century of Revolution 1603–1714* (London 1980), pp 43–6.

[10] Bill of Rights 1688, art 4. See Maitland, *The Constitutional History of England* (Cambridge 1908), pp 306–11.

[11] Dicey, *An Introduction to the Study of the Law of the Constitution* (London 1959), ch 10; White and Hollingsworth, *Audit, Accountability, and Government* (Oxford 1999), p 3.

of Commons established in the seventeenth century and the restrictions on the House of Lords under the Parliament Acts.[12]

However, the financial precedence of the Commons is not absolute in terms of constitutional theory, let alone practical operation. By a long-standing constitutional convention, the right of financial initiative lies not with Parliament, but with the Crown—or rather, the government. This right of financial initiative means that only the government can make decisions to propose increases in taxation or public expenditure. In other words, decisions to raise public money can only be put before Parliament if they have first been made by the government. While Parliament—or rather, the House of Commons—may have *precedence* in financial matters, it is only the government that has the right of *initiative*. Perhaps surprisingly, this principle is enshrined not in any piece of legislation, but within Parliament's own internal laws: its Standing Orders and long-standing constitutional practice. Under Standing Order 48 of the House of Commons (first introduced in 1713), Parliament is unable to impose taxes or permit public expenditure unless first requested to do so by the government.[13] As we noted in Chapter 4, the executive is the only branch of government that can fairly be described as an *initiative-taker*, and the right of financial initiative is a crucial dimension of this. This right originated from the idea that what the monarch did with his or her money was his or her own business. According to Erskine May, the Crown's financial initiative is a 'long-established and strictly observed rule of procedure, which expresses a principle of the highest constitutional importance'.[14] Since the emergence of large-scale and responsible government, this right is now exercised by the political executive of the day in the name of the Crown.

This right of financial initiative needs to be understood in the context of the broader relationship between the government and Parliament—in particular, the capacity of a government with a working majority to dominate Parliament. It is the executive that is both (indirectly) elected on the basis of its policy commitments in its party-political manifesto, which need to be funded, and which (normally) has a majority in the House of Commons. The government's right of financial initiative is a major constraint upon legislative power. It also 'represents the recognition by Parliament of its own innate incapacity to act as the manager of public funds'.[15] At best, Parliament's role is limited to that of criticising governmental proposals for the raising and spending of public expenditure rather than constructively formulating its own view as to how public money should be spent. However, as we will see below, there are serious concerns as to whether or not Parliament possesses the ability even to engage in effective scrutiny of planned governmental expenditure.

---

[12] See Chapter 5, section 2.3.3, above.

[13] *Standing Orders of the House of Commons: Public Business* (2007), Standing Order 48.

[14] McKay (ed), *Erskine May's Treatise on The Law, Privileges, Proceedings and Usage of Parliament* (London 2004), p 852.   [15] Daintith and Page, *The Executive in the Constitution* (Oxford 1999), p 108.

Q If it is the government and not Parliament that has the right of initiative in financial matters, then how, if at all, can Parliament be described as sovereign? For all practical purposes, is it not the case that the government's financial initiative operates as a constitutional, albeit non-legal, constraint upon the exercise of legislative power?

3. Planning and scrutinising public expenditure

In order to examine the effectiveness of financial scrutiny of planned governmental *expenditure*, we first need to consider the procedure by which government *raises* public money. This is called the *supply procedure*—the process by which public funds are placed into the government's hands by Parliament.

3.1 The supply procedure

The constitutional arrangements by which public money is raised and allocated can be summed up in a simple maxim: 'The Crown requests money, the Commons grant it, and the Lords assent to the grant.'[16] The development of modern democratic government and the assumption by the government of the day of the traditional role and powers of the Crown in relation to public finance has not altered this basic constitutional principle. In today's constitutional system, we would say that the government presents to the House of Commons its detailed requirements for public expenditure, the Commons then authorises the relevant expenditure, or 'supply', and then provides through taxes and other sources of public revenue the necessary 'ways and means' to meet the supply so granted. The broader public expenditure process has four successive stages:

(i) expenditure planning by the government,
(ii) parliamentary debate and approval,
(iii) spending of the money involved, and
(iv) accounting for the money spent.[17]

It is in the first stage that the government will determine the total amount of public expenditure and how that is to be divided between different priorities. Such decisions are made internally within government. The government will then request funds from Parliament by presenting to it *supply estimates* of public expenditure.

Estimates are simply the vehicle by which government departments request supply—that is, public money—to fund their spending programmes. The supply procedure is the main formal avenue for parliamentary scrutiny of government

---

[16] *Erskine May*, p 848.
[17] White and Hollingsworth, *Audit, Accountability, and Government* (Oxford 1999), p 1.

spending plans. The process commences when the main estimates are presented to Parliament by the Treasury at the start of the financial year to which they relate. Estimates are prepared by government departments and examined by the Treasury, and then presented to Parliament. The bulk of such requests are typically laid before Parliament in April or May each year shortly after the Budget, which is typically delivered in April. The Treasury presents alongside the main estimates a set of supplementary budgetary information tables reconciling the estimates to departmental report tables. At various points in the year, the Treasury presents new, revised, and/or supplementary estimates, as appropriate, asking Parliament for approval for any necessary additional resources and/or cash or for authority to incur expenditure on new services. After the end of the financial year (around July), the Treasury publishes the public expenditure outturn White Paper to Parliament, providing provisional outturn figures for public expenditure by departments—that is, how much money government has spent.

Mere presentation of the main estimates to Parliament is not, by itself, sufficient to provide government with authority for expenditure. Statutory authority is required. Government acquires this legal authority to spend the funds set out in estimates through the passage of at least two Appropriation Acts and one Consolidated Fund Act during each parliamentary session. These statutes are amongst the most important that Parliament passes because they give statutory authority for both the consumption of resources and for cash to be drawn from the *consolidated fund* (the government's general bank account at the Bank of England). These statutes are also amongst the most distinctive types of legislation. The Appropriation Act, for example, sets out in detail the resources allocated to different government departments and agencies. By contrast, the Consolidated Fund Act consists of only a few sections detailing the total amounts of resources to be issued out of the consolidated fund. Furthermore, these statutes are distinctive in that they are addressed primarily to the executive itself rather than the public. Finally, unlike other statutes, they are not normally the subject of detailed debate in Parliament.

While the supply procedure provides the legal basis for constitutional subordination of the executive to Parliament, there are two further constitutional purposes served by parliamentary involvement in the public expenditure process.[18] The first is to require government to make promises about how the money provided by Parliament will actually be spent. The second constitutional purpose of parliamentary involvement in the public expenditure process is to provide a legal framework that comprises the basis for financial control, reporting, and accountability within government. These two purposes can only be achieved if there are appropriate mechanisms for checking whether or not public money has been spent in accordance with the purposes for which it was granted.

---

[18] White and Hollingsworth, p 3.

3.2 **Internal governmental financial controls**

While parliamentary approval for public expenditure is of constitutional importance, in practice, the external control exercised by Parliament is highly dependent upon internal control of public expenditure within government itself. In this respect, HM Treasury, as the UK's economics and finance ministry, plays a fundamental role. It is responsible for formulating and implementing the government's financial and economic policy. In terms of internal financial control, it is principally HM Treasury—the most powerful government department and also one of the smallest—that both oversees and controls public expenditure within government. As the Treasury's handbook *Managing Public Money* puts it, government seeks to deliver public services, but is only able to do so when Parliament grants the right to raise, commit, and spend resources; it therefore falls to the Treasury to respect and secure the rights of both government and Parliament in this process.[19] Parliament therefore looks to the Treasury to ensure that government departments use their powers only as Parliament has intended and that revenue is raised, and resources spent, only within agreed limits and that it is used properly. The Treasury must then set the ground rules for administering public money and account to Parliament for doing so. There is then an 'alliance' or 'mutual dependence' between Parliament and the Treasury in pursuit of a common interest—namely, the control of public expenditure.[20]

From the Treasury's perspective, its duty to safeguard public funds is a constant one, but precisely how this control is carried out changes over time. The Treasury's system of internal financial control includes many different mechanisms or disciplines. For example, all legislation with expenditure implications must have Treasury support. Government departments must also secure Treasury approval for public expenditure; this is one aspect of the long-standing convention that Parliament expects the Treasury to control all other departments in expenditure matters. In practice, the Treasury delegates to departments the authority to enter into spending commitments within agreed limits.

Given the scale of government, it is important that internal financial control within government extends beyond the Treasury itself and into each department and agency, which together make up the broader governmental machine. Here, a key role is played by *accounting officers*. Each organisation in central government—departments and agencies, for example—must have an accounting officer who is responsible for departmental expenditure. This position is normally held by the Permanent Secretary, the most senior official in a government department. This is a personal responsibility for the propriety and regularity of the public finances, for keeping proper accounts, for prudent and economical administration, for the avoidance of waste and extravagance, and for the efficient and effective use of all available resources.[21] The Treasury also sets out certain standards expected of accounting officers—in particular, responsibility for

---

[19] HM Treasury, *Managing Public Money* (London 2007), p 7.   [20] Daintith and Page, p 105.
[21] *Managing Public Money*, ch 3.

the regularity and propriety of public resources. Regularity means that resource consumption should accord with the relevant legislation, the relevant delegated authority, and the Treasury's own guidance as to how public money should be managed. Propriety requires that patterns of resource consumption should respect Parliament's intentions, conventions, and control procedures.[22]

Given these responsibilities, and also the need to secure efficiency, economy, effectiveness, and prudence in the administration of public resources, accounting officers have particular obligations. For example, accounting officers advise Ministers as to whether or not a proposed action would provide value for money. If a Minister decides to proceed with a course of action against her accounting officer's advice, then the accounting officer must seek written instruction to proceed so that she does not bear personal responsibility.[23] While the accounting officer will be obliged to comply with the Minister's instructions, she must also send relevant papers to the Comptroller and Auditor General, the independent auditor. Furthermore, accounting officers also answer personally to the House of Commons Public Accounts Committee (which is considered in more detail below) on the efficient and effective use of resources. Although accounting officers thus play a central role, effective financial control in large organisations such as government departments and agencies cannot be secured by one person alone. However, it has been found that the lack of financial skills and awareness amongst non-finance staff is one of the most significant barriers to improving and embedding financial resource management capability in departments.[24]

Some other important developments in the control and management of public money also need to be highlighted: first, changes to the accounting system used by government. In 2000, the basis on which government bodies account for public money, set out in legislation dating from 1866, was brought into line with commercial practice and placed on an 'accruals basis' under the Government Resources and Accounts Act 2000.[25] Producing resource accounts on an accruals basis involves departments matching expenditure to the period in which the costs were incurred (rather than paid) and fully recognising the cost of owning assets (such as buildings). This was introduced in order to enable government departments to determine relative value for money of different activities, identify areas of waste or low productivity, improve the management of assets and liabilities, and increase the quality of services delivered.

Another major development has been how government manages its public expenditure. From the late 1960s until 1998, government spending was subject to annual limits arising from the annual public expenditure survey. In 1998, the Labour government introduced the first comprehensive spending review—a complete 'root and branch' examination of public spending: whether it was being used to meet governmental objectives, and whether it was being properly and efficiently

---

[22] *Managing Public Money*, p 13.   [23] Cabinet Office, *Ministerial Code* (London 2010), [5.4]–[5.5].

[24] House of Commons Public Accounts Committee, *Managing Financial Resources to Deliver Better Public Services* (HC 519 2007–08), [16].   [25] Government Resources and Accounts Act 2000.

used. Spending reviews have set out the expenditure allocations between different government departments over a three-year period and the government's objectives against which such spending is measured. The reviews have also placed great importance on effective management of financial resources. In 2004, the government's Gershon Review set out how the government could achieve over £20 billion worth of efficiency gains.[26]

The comprehensive spending reviews also established public service agreements (PSAs) as a key instrument of allocating funding. These agreements laid down performance targets for government departments and were akin to a contract between different parts of the executive, specifying the objectives of governmental activity and detailing how delivery of each objective is to be achieved and monitored. The responsibility for delivering each PSA lay with a number of government departments. For example, Public Service Delivery Agreement 1 from the 2007 comprehensive spending review was for government to raise the productivity of the UK economy—a wide-ranging objective that required substantial cooperation between different government departments. The system of PSAs was completely overhauled in the 2007 spending review. Of course, because PSAs specified the performance targets of government departments, their effect was to increase substantially the Treasury's power over the activities of spending departments in order to ensure internal governmental control of public expenditure. More broadly, it is apparent that the Treasury's influence over the strategic direction of the government has grown through the Treasury taking a lead in significant areas of social policy, such as welfare reform, social security, pensions, and health care.

In 2010, the coalition Conservative–Liberal Democrat government announced that it was abandoning the complex system of PSAs because they relied upon 'top-down management and too many politically motivated targets'.[27] PSAs have been replaced by a new system, structural reform plans, for setting clear priorities and measureable milestones for government departments.[28] These plans are described by the government as a key tool for making government departments accountable for the implementation of government policy. Under this new system, each government department will have its own structural reform plan, which will identify the resources, structural reforms, and efficiency measures that the department is to put in place to deliver public services. Furthermore, the coalition government has committed itself to greater transparency by publishing details on public spending and the performance of public services.[29] In short, while the precise mechanisms may change, the centre of government has to have some mechanism for holding spending departments to account and for overseeing what they do.

---

[26] Gershon, *Releasing Resources to the Front Line: Independent Review of Public Sector Efficiency* (London 2004); National Audit Office, *Progress in Improving Government Efficiency* (HC 802 2005–06).

[27] HM Treasury, *The Spending Review Framework* (Cm 7872 2010), [2.7].

[28] Speech by David Cameron on Structural Reform Plans, 8 July 2010.

[29] See **http://transparency.number10.gov.uk**

3.3 **Parliamentary scrutiny of planned governmental expenditure**

As we have already noted, financial scrutiny of government expenditure is a constitutional imperative. More specifically, financial scrutiny of government by the House of Commons has various and related purposes: to make the government's financial decisions transparent, including the relationship between its stated priorities and its funding decisions; to engage bodies and individuals outside Parliament and give them the opportunity to comment; and to enable the Commons to have the opportunity to influence the government's financial decisions. Furthermore, financial scrutiny aims to hold the government, individual departments, and other public bodies to account for their financial decisions and financial management, and thereby to contribute to an improvement in the quality of government departments' financial decisions and management, and improve value for money in public services.[30] In constitutional theory, the government must obtain Parliament's approval before raising taxation, but how effective is parliamentary scrutiny of planned governmental expenditure in practice? There are two principal ways in which Parliament can scrutinise planned governmental expenditure: debates on the floor of the House on 'estimates days'; and through select committees.

Let us consider first scrutiny on the floor of the House. On at least three occasions each year, the House of Commons is required to authorise public spending on the basis of estimates and supplementary estimates that are debated on the floor of the House. Such debates focus upon select committee reports linked to the estimates that have been selected by the House of Commons Liaison Committee (which is comprised of the chairs of all House of Commons select committees).[31] The Commons therefore has the opportunity to scrutinise and debate estimates on the floor of the House.

However, such debates tend to involve little, if any, thorough scrutiny of government expenditure plans. The debates themselves tend to focus on policy rather than expenditure. Furthermore, the debate is linked to an estimate and therefore the Commons' intervention is placed too late in the expenditure planning cycle to be effective. But, most of all, the problem is that the only real sanction Parliament has is to reject or reduce the government's estimates because the right of financial initiative is with the government rather than Parliament. Parliament cannot, for example, decide for itself how much public money should be raised; it can only consider the government's proposals. Even then, the scrutiny provided by the Commons through such debates is highly restricted because of the government's influence over Parliament. In principle, the Commons could reject the government's taxation and spending proposals. However, bearing in mind that the government normally has a working majority, meaning that members of the governing party (or parties) usually make up more than half of the membership of the

---

[30] House of Commons Liaison Committee, *Parliament and Government Finance: Recreating Financial Scrutiny* (HC 426 2007–08), [9].   [31] Standing Order No 54.

Commons, estimates are rarely rejected. The last occasion such an event occurred was in 1919.[32]

The widely held view is, then, that the scrutiny offered by the House of Commons on such Estimates debates amounts to very little scrutiny in practice. Of course, Parliament does have control in the sense that the government cannot obtain funding from the public purse without Parliament's consent. The government must also present financial information to the House. But this is the limit of the power of the Commons. As one select committee has commented, if parliamentary control of governmental expenditure is 'not a constitutional myth, it is close to one'.[33] In 2002, one backbench MP denounced estimates debates as a 'charade' in which the 'House of Commons rubber stamps tablets of stone handed down by the executive of the day', while another noted that the Commons has 'no record of scrutinising expenditure measures as many other legislatures throughout the world do'.[34] As McEldowney has noted: 'In modern times the Commons has not rejected an estimate and the scrutiny function appears a limited one.'[35] Moreover, the government has been resistant to proposals that would give Parliament a more influential role in the supply procedure. For example, in 1999, the Procedure Committee proposed that rather than accepting the government's own allocation of resources between different government departments, Parliament should be able to adjust such allocations. This proposal was, though, rejected by the government on the ground that it would undermine the financial initiative of the Crown.[36]

What then of the financial scrutiny of planned expenditure by government departments, and their agencies, undertaken by the House of Commons select committees that oversee such departments? One of the most important roles played by departmental select committees is to scrutinise expenditure by the government departments that they monitor. (The House of Commons Public Accounts Committee takes a broader view by examining expenditure across government and its role is examined in more detail below.) Departmental select committees have three main roles in relation to financial scrutiny: to examine the relevant department's main reporting documents; to examine how a department allocates its spending totals across its programmes; and to take account of finance and performance in the context of inquiries mainly concerned with policy and administration.

Scrutiny of government departments' expenditure and resources is undertaken mainly, although not exclusively, by departmental select committees in the context

---

[32] In 1919, the House of Commons rejected an estimate produced by the Royal Palace to make provision for an additional bathroom for the Lord Chancellor in the Houses of Parliament.

[33] House of Commons Procedure Committee, *Resource Accounting and Budgeting* (HC 438 1997–98), [10].

[34] HC Deb, vol 395, cols 871 and 873 (3 December 2002).

[35] McEldowney, 'The Control of Public Expenditure', in Jowell and Oliver (eds), *The Changing Constitution* (Oxford 2007), p 366.

[36] House of Commons Procedure Committee, *Procedure for Debate on the Government's Expenditure Plans* (HC 295 1998–99), [27]; House of Commons Procedure Committee, *Government Response to the Sixth Report of Session 1998–99: Procedure for Debate on the Government's Expenditure Plans* (HC 388 1999–2000).

of their annual inquiries into departmental annual reports. Since 1991, every government department has published its own departmental annual report each spring, setting out the department's aims and objectives, principal activities, expenditure plans, and achievements. The standard procedure is for each committee to receive an analysis of their department's annual report from the Committee Office Scrutiny Unit, and then to follow this up with an evidence session with Ministers and senior officials. In 2002, the Scrutiny Unit was established in order to maintain and improve the ability of the House of Commons—in particular, through its select committees—to perform its scrutiny function. It has been noted that the ability of select committees to undertake effective financial scrutiny has been greatly increased by the assistance provided by the Scrutiny Unit.[37]

Concerns have, though, been raised as to the quality of financial information provided by government departments in their annual reports. Particular problems can arise if several government departments are involved in a particular project. As one select committee noted, it may be difficult in such circumstances, in the absence of detailed information, to determine the extent of the financial commitments into which any given department has entered—which, in turn, increases the difficulty of the select committee's task of holding that department, and thus the government, to account.[38]

Select committees can also scrutinise estimates themselves. This is normally conducted by way of correspondence with the relevant Minister, the exception being the House of Commons Defence Committee, which reports to the House on all of the Ministry of Defence's estimates. (The cost of military operations has not traditionally been covered in the main estimates, but, following the Defence Committee's insistence, this cost is now included in some detail in the main estimate.[39]) In 2004, estimates memoranda were introduced, at the behest of the Liaison Committee, to accompany the actual estimates, but have themselves been described by that Committee as 'the least comprehensible reporting documents'.[40] While such memoranda are a potentially valuable tool for select committees scrutinising both the estimates and the financial management of departments more generally, some concern has been expressed that some memoranda have been judged to be inadequate.[41] Nevertheless, the improved quality of such memoranda has assisted select committees in scrutinising estimates.[42]

---

[37] House of Commons Liaison Committee, *Parliament and Government Finance: Recreating Financial Scrutiny* (HC 426 2007–08), [85].

[38] House of Commons Children, Schools and Families Committee, *Public Expenditure* (HC 46 2008–09), [25].

[39] House of Commons Defence Committee, *The Work of the Committee in 2007–08* (HC 106 2008–09), [28].

[40] *Parliament and Government Finance: Recreating Financial Scrutiny*, [3].

[41] For example, the House of Commons Business and Enterprise Committee, *Funding the Nuclear Decommissioning Authority* (HC 394 2007–08), [21], concluded that a Spring supplementary estimate memorandum 'did not give an entirely accurate picture of the situation'.

[42] House of Commons Liaison Committee, *Estimates Memoranda* (HC 1685 2005–06).

So, what of parliamentary scrutiny of planned governmental expenditure? There is near-universal general agreement within the House of Commons that its scrutiny of the government's finances is in need of improvement.[43] Outside Parliament, the Hansard Society, an independent and non-partisan body that exists to promote parliamentary democracy, has concluded that 'Parliament's influence over government spending proposals is virtually non-existent...all too often it simply acquiesces to requests from government, without sufficient scrutiny or debate'.[44] From a different perspective, the passivity of Parliament is not itself necessarily a problem; what really matters is that Parliament's assent to the government's planned expenditure is needed. The mere fact that Parliament's approval is required may be of considerable importance, irrespective of the actual degree of scrutiny in which Parliament engages. The principal reason for this is that democratic control of planned government expenditure by Parliament often operates to sustain and legitimise internal governmental control of expenditure, and it is these internal controls—especially the extensive influence of the Treasury—that are typically most effective. Parliament acts as the 'ever-present outsider, a political counterweight sustaining trustful behaviour within the executive'.[45] However, merely assuming the role of an outsider or spectator means that Parliament is excluded from much of the action and that, consequently, the degree of financial scrutiny that it provides is far from adequate in order properly to hold government to account for its planned expenditure.

> **Q** According to Harden, '[t]he great myth of the British constitution is the Sovereignty of Parliament. The idea that Supply procedure gives Parliament control of public money is one of its facets'.[46] Do you agree?

So what type of financial scrutiny can Parliament reasonably be expected to undertake? This question directly concerns broader issues of constitutional design—especially the relationship between the legislature and the executive. In normal circumstances in the UK, the governing party possesses a majority in the legislature; it is therefore unlikely that a majority of MPs would ever vote down spending plans put forward by the government. By contrast, in political-constitutional systems in which there is a strict separation of powers between the legislature and the executive such that the two are entirely separate institutions, different considerations apply. For example, in the USA, the legislature—Congress—has the ability to amend or reject the executive's spending proposals and to formulate its own proposals.[47] The form and intensity

---

[43] *Parliament and Government Finance: Recreating Financial Scrutiny*, [1].

[44] Brazier and Ram, *The Fiscal Maze: Parliament, Government and Public Money* (London 2006), p 75.

[45] Heclo and Wildavsky, *The Private Government of Public Money: Community and Policy inside British Politics* (London 1974), p 244.

[46] Harden, 'Money and the Constitution: Financial Control, Reporting and Audit' (1993) 13 LS 16, 33.

[47] Tushnet, *The Constitution of the United States of America: A Contextual Analysis* (Oxford 2009), pp 107–8.

of financial scrutiny exercised by legislatures over the planning of governmental expenditure is largely determined by its broader constitutional relationship with the executive.

At the same time, the fact that the UK Parliament is normally comprised of a majority of MPs from the party that forms the government of the day does not imply that the only choice is between a legislature that is wholly obsequious or servile and one that is always able to defeat the government. Financial scrutiny—and, as we saw in Chapter 10, accountability more generally—is often a more nuanced endeavour, one concerned with probing decisions, requiring an adequate justification, and, if necessary, requesting the decision-taker to think again: in short, with exercising influence rather than dominance. So, how could Parliament's influence with regard to government expenditure be enhanced?

3.4 Strengthening financial scrutiny of planned expenditure

For the House of Commons Liaison Committee, the problem is not so much the lack of the House's powers in financial matters as it is the lack of ability and willingness amongst its members to scrutinise government spending in the degree of detail necessary to hold the government to account. The Committee has highlighted three factors that make financial scrutiny difficult and unattractive for Parliament: the unnecessary complexity of government finances; the fact that the financial information presented by government to Parliament is often hard to understand and does not, in any event, provide all of the information needed for scrutiny; and the difficulty of pursuing financial matters, and attracting wider media and public interest.

As regards the complexity of the financial reporting methods used by government to present its expenditure to Parliament, it is apparent that such complexity can inhibit transparency and accountability of government expenditure. There are a number of different systems used by the government to present public expenditure: the Budget is used to plan what the government will spend; estimates are then presented to Parliament for approval; and then finally after the end of the year, government publishes its resource accounts. The basic problem is that there is significant misalignment between the different bases on which financial information is reported to Parliament, making it difficult for MPs to read across different sources of information. Further, the government's financial documents are published in different formats and on different occasions during the year, making it difficult to understand the relationship between them. Complexity therefore arises because there are three different financial frameworks within the financial reporting system, each of which were created at different times for different purposes; such complexity can undermine transparency.

As we have seen, the House of Commons is required to authorise public spending on the basis of estimates on at least three occasions each year. However, the figures presented in estimates are not always easy to reconcile with the totals established in spending reviews, in part because spending reviews cover three-year periods whereas estimates are yearly. As the Treasury Committee has explained, the disjunction between the amounts that the Commons is formally expected to authorise and the totals contained in the comprehensive spending review that will form the centrepiece of the political process of resource allocation does little to enhance understanding of the role of the House of Commons in financial scrutiny and authorisation. Consequently, it has been argued that the government should replace the current system based on estimates with one linked more clearly with the public expenditure planning and control system, so that the Commons could consider and evaluate individual expenditure limits for government departments and an annual total for annually managed public expenditure.[48] To put the same point in a different way, most major decisions on public expenditure are made not in estimates, but in the comprehensive spending review; however, this is primarily a governmental process in which there is little scope for the House of Commons to engage. As the Liaison Committee has noted, '[i]t is absurd that the outcome of the Comprehensive Spending Review was discussed for only an hour and a half in the Chamber, and makes a mockery of the House's right to scrutinise government expenditure'.[49]

Calls for the reform of the government's financial reporting have therefore been made by parliamentary select committees. According to the Liaison Committee, the government's financial reporting should be characterised by comprehensiveness, clarity, and transparency, but its financial arrangements and reporting are exceptionally complex. Such complexity can have damaging consequences for financial scrutiny by Parliament. According to the Liaison Committee, 'even MPs with financial or business experience struggle to understand the financial information provided', and it is extremely difficult to follow through from planned spending to actual spending and subsequent examination of what the spending has achieved.[50] Furthermore, even 'government Departments themselves struggle to compile and understand the figures'.[51] As the Liaison Committee has noted, '[h]ad such a system been deliberately designed, it could fairly be assumed that it had been set up with the specific purpose of making it impossible to hold the government and Departments to account'.[52]

In response, the government has accepted the need to make it easier for Parliament to hold the government to account for its expenditure by improving the transparency and accountability of government expenditure.[53] It has stated that it will simplify its financial reporting to Parliament to ensure that it reports in a more consistent fashion at all three stages in the process: on plans, estimates and actual expenditure outturns. To this end, it has established the 'alignment', or 'clear line of sight', project in order to 'make it easier for Parliament to understand how the

---

[48] House of Commons Treasury Committee, *The 2007 Comprehensive Spending Review: Prospects and Processes* (HC 279 2006–07), [110].

[49] House of Commons Liaison Committee, *Parliament and Government Finance: Recreating Financial Scrutiny* (HC 426 2007–08), [66].

[50] *Parliament and Government Finance: Recreating Financial Scrutiny*, [30].

[51] *Parliament and Government Finance: Recreating Financial Scrutiny*, [31].

[52] *Parliament and Government Finance: Recreating Financial Scrutiny*, [30].

[53] Ministry of Justice, *The Governance of Britain* (Cm 7170 2007), [109]–[111].

government has used the resources voted to it, and thus to hold the government to account'.[54]

Another important factor that constrains the potential of the Commons to engage in thorough financial scrutiny concerns both the willingness and ability of MPs to engage in this activity. After all, it is not reasonable to expect most MPs to possess considerable understanding of the technical details of government finance: they are not technicians, but politicians. In 2002, the Commons Scrutiny Unit was established in order to maintain and improve the ability of the Commons—especially its select committees—to perform its scrutiny functions principally with regard to government expenditure. There is little doubt that the Scrutiny Unit has enhanced the degree of scrutiny provided by the House of Commons.[55] At the same time, the Scrutiny Unit operates on a relatively small scale. If the ability of MPs and, in particular, select committees in undertaking financial scrutiny is to be strengthened, then the Scrutiny Unit will need more resources. There have, for example, been calls for the Scrutiny Unit to develop into something akin to the US government's Accountability Office, which provides both an information and support system for members of Congress to study government figures and a check on the assumptions on which government makes its decisions. An enhanced Scrutiny Unit would clearly have the potential to augment Parliament's ability to hold government to account in relation to expenditure.[56] Another way of increasing the capacity of MPs to undertake financial scrutiny may be to make more training available to them.

The view of the Liaison Committee is clear: financial scrutiny is a fundamental responsibility of the House of Commons, but for far too long the House has 'shirked the task of providing itself with the means to carry out financial scrutiny effectively, and it is time that the House was more assertive in this area'.[57] In the view of the Committee, three practical steps must be taken so that the Commons can scrutinise properly the government's financial decisions: simplification of the government's over-complex financial system, improvement of the quality of the financial information provided to Parliament, and the creation of opportunities for MPs to challenge the government in financial matters and hold it to account.

Q Do you think that the recommendations made by the House of Commons Liaison Committee would enable Parliament to undertake effective financial scrutiny of planned governmental expenditure? If not, then what other reforms might you propose?

---

[54] Ministry of Justice, Cm 7170, [111]. See further HM Treasury, *Alignment ('Clear Line of Sight') Project (Memorandum submitted to the House of Commons Liaison Committee)* (London 2008); HM Treasury, *Alignment (Clear Line of Sight) Project* (Cm 7567 2009).

[55] See House of Commons Commission, *Supporting the House and its Committee* (HC 791 2003–04), [66]; House of Commons Liaison Committee, *The Work of Committees in 2007–08* (HC 291 2008–09), app 2.

[56] Brazier and Ram, *The Fiscal Maze: Parliament, Government and Public Money* (London 2006), pp 69–71.

[57] House of Commons Liaison Committee, *Parliament and Government Finance: Recreating Financial Scrutiny* (HC 426 2007–08), [88]–[89].

4. Scrutinising past government expenditure

So far, we have been concerned with forward-looking scrutiny—that is, scrutiny of planned government expenditure. But once public money has been spent, it is imperative that backward-looking scrutiny takes place. This section is concerned with the latter.

Backward-looking scrutiny is important in order to hold government to account with respect to how it has actually spent public money. This type of scrutiny is usually concerned with investigating whether, having spent public money, government has used that money effectively—whether it has delivered value for money. As noted at the beginning of the chapter, this concept is often reduced to the 'three Es':

- *economy*—the minimising of costs of resources used for an activity, having regard to appropriate quality;
- *efficiency*—the relationship between the output in terms of goods, services, or other results and the resources used to produce them; and
- *effectiveness*—the relationship between the intended impact and the actual impact of an activity or product.

More generally, this type of scrutiny is typically described as that of *audit*—the official inspection of an organisation's accounts, typically by an independent body. Audit has become an increasingly common technique because of increased demand for public accountability. Indeed, it has been argued that we now live in what has been called an 'audit society', in which there has been an explosion in the number and intensity of audits of virtually all organisations.[58]

At the UK level, financial scrutiny of past government expenditure is undertaken by the House of Commons Public Accounts Committee (PAC) on the basis of investigations undertaken by the National Audit Office (NAO). While the composition of these bodies differ drastically—the PAC comprises some 15 elected MPs, while the NAO comprises some 850 accountants—both act in order to investigate whether or not government has delivered value for money. The PAC and NAO work together in order to scrutinise public spending by UK central government. Separate arrangements apply for scrutinising the use of public money by local government and the devolved administrations in Scotland, Wales, and Northern Ireland. Furthermore, there is also the issue as to what, if any, role the courts have in relation to financial scrutiny. In this section, we examine the effectiveness of backward-looking financial scrutiny, beginning with the role of Parliament in this area.

4.1 Parliamentary scrutiny and audit of government expenditure

4.1.1 The Public Accounts Committee

While parliamentary control of taxation was established in the seventeenth century, parliamentary control and scrutiny of expenditure was only gradually established

---

[58] Power, *The Audit Society: Rituals of Verification* (Oxford 1997).

between the 1780s and 1860s. Since 1861, the PAC has acted on behalf of Parliament to examine and report on accounts, and the regularity and propriety of expenditure. The advantage of focusing parliamentary scrutiny of public expenditure in a select committee rather than through debates in the Commons chamber is that a dedicated committee can investigate public expenditure in more depth and thereby build up its own expertise. The Committee is, and also sees itself as, a key part of the accountability arrangements to safeguard public money.[59] The PAC does not consider either the formulation or merits of policy—this falls within the scope of other, departmental select committees; instead, it focuses on value for money criteria—the three Es. The Committee is chaired by a senior opposition MP and adopts a non-party-political approach to its task. The PAC is certainly one of the most high-profile and productive of the Commons select committees. In a single year, the PAC generally holds more evidence sessions and produces more reports than most other select committees. Between 1995 and 2005, the PAC issued over 400 reports.[60] A debate is also held biannually in the Commons Chamber to 'take note' of the PAC's reports.

4.1.2 The National Audit Office

The NAO provides a critical support to the work of the PAC. It is headed by the Comptroller and Auditor General, whose function, since 1866, has been to examine accounts on behalf of the House of Commons.[61] In recognition of the importance of audit of government, the Comptroller and Auditor General in 1983 became an officer of the House of Commons.[62] Furthermore, the NAO was established. In broad terms, the NAO performs a number of roles: holding government to account for the way in which it uses public money, helping public service managers to improve performance, safeguarding the interests of taxpayers who pay for public services, and championing the interests of citizens as users of public services. According to the NAO, its work in 2009 resulted in savings of £768 million, a return of over £10 for every £1 spent running the office.[63]

More specifically, the NAO has two principal functions: to audit the accounts of all government departments and agencies, as well as a wide range of other public bodies (known as *certification audit*); and to report to Parliament on the economy, efficiency, and effectiveness with which these bodies have used public money (known as *value for money audit*).[64] The NAO has a professional staff, largely comprising accountants who are not civil servants and are independent of government. It has comprehensive

---

[59] See House of Commons Public Accounts Committee, *Holding Government to Account: 150 Years of the Committee on Public Accounts* (London 2007).

[60] House of Commons Public Accounts Committee, *Achieving Value for Money in the Delivery of Public Services* (HC 742 2005–06), p 5. [61] Exchequer and Audit Departments Act 1866.

[62] National Audit Act 1983, s 1(2). [63] National Audit Office, *Annual Report 2009* (London 2009).

[64] National Audit Act 1983, 6(1). Under the Finance Act 1998, ss 156 and 157, the NAO also has the power to examine and report on conventions and assumptions underlying the Treasury's fiscal projections in the Budget that are submitted to it by the Treasury for examination.

statutory rights of access to the bodies it audits.[65] It is, though, specifically prohibited from examining the merits of governmental policy objectives.[66]

Over recent years, the PAC's main work has become the examination of the NAO reports as to the 'value for money' of public services delivered by government. About 60 of these reports are adopted each year by the PAC as the basis for a follow-up inquiry. The PAC will proceed by means of an oral evidence session in which it will hear oral evidence from and question the appropriate accounting officer. As we noted earlier, it is the accounting officer who is personally responsible for both regularity and propriety in the use of public money. This therefore distinguishes the role of the accounting officer from that of the appropriate Minister. While the Minister is accountable to Parliament for the policies, actions, and conduct of her department, the accounting officer is responsible for value for money issues. The PAC's principal objective is to draw lessons from past successes and failures that can be applied to future activity by the department examined or more generally. PAC inquiries result in a published report that highlights any inefficient use of public resources and, if appropriate, makes recommendations to government. By convention, the government must reply to the Committee's recommendations within two months, indicating whether or not it accepts them.

> **Q** Why is it significant that, at PAC hearings, it is the accounting officer rather than the Minister who appears before the Committee? Does this practice contravene the doctrine of ministerial responsibility to Parliament? Or does it mean that the doctrine of ministerial responsibility is necessarily subject to an exception in relation to matters of financial scrutiny?

4.1.3 Some examples

To give a flavour of the combined work of the PAC and the NAO, and also some indication of how government occasionally spends public money, we can consider the following instances (selected from numerous examples).

- In 2002, Parliament established the Assets Recovery Agency in order to recover assets from criminals by using its special powers of civil recovery. By 2006, the Agency had recovered assets amounting to £23 million, but the Agency had itself cost £65 million. The Agency was subsequently merged with the Serious Organised Crime Agency.[67]

- In 2004, the Home Office commenced a major information technology (IT) project under which prison and probation officers in the National Offender Management Service would have electronic access to offenders' records. The

[65] National Audit Act 1983, s 8.   [66] National Audit Act 1983, s 6(2).

[67] Proceeds of Crime Act 2002; House of Commons Public Accounts Committee, *Assets Recovery Agency* (HC 391 2006–07); Serious Crime Act 2007.

IT system was intended to support a new 'end-to-end' offender management process in order to reduce the risk of reoffending by improving information-sharing about offenders. The IT system was originally estimated to cost £234 million. However, by 2008, the IT project was three years overdue and its cost had more than doubled to £513 million. The NAO undertook a 'value for money' investigation of the project and found various problems including inadequate oversight, poor programme management, and underestimation of its technical complexity. The NAO concluded that the project had been 'handled badly and the value for money achieved was poor'. The PAC's chairman castigated the project as a 'spectacular failure' and a 'masterclass in sloppy project management'.[68]

- In order to deliver efficiency savings, government has increasingly sought to introduce greater sharing of corporate services (for example, human resources, payroll, and finance support services). In 2005, the Department for Transport sought to introduce such a system for its various agencies and estimated that this would yield a net benefit (the long-term benefit minus the initial start-up costs) of £57 million. However, a demanding timetable for implementation and poor project management meant that, by 2008, the Department had forecast that, rather than produce savings, the programme would impose a net cost of £81 million. The PAC trenchantly criticised the Department, noting that its project management had been 'extremely poor' and 'one of the worst that this Committee has seen'.[69]

- In 1995, the Ministry of Defence ordered fourteen Chinook Mk3 helicopters, eight of which were to be modified for use by special armed forces. However, delays and problems arose with modifying the helicopters. The PAC considered it to be one of the worst examples of equipment procurement that it had ever seen. The absence of these helicopters had increased the risks for British troops in Afghanistan, because they had been compelled to make more dangerous journeys by road. Following their modification, costs had increased to over £422 million, making the helicopters more expensive than alternative types available at the time that the original order had been placed by the Ministry.[70]

- In 2003, the government introduced the system of tax credits in order to help families with children and working people on low incomes. Some £85 billion was paid out under this scheme in its first five years. Tax credits are administered on an annual basis; a provisional award is made by HM Revenue and Customs (HMRC) based on a claimant's income, and adjustments are

[68] National Audit Office, *The National Offender Management Information System* (HC 292 2008–09); Ford, '"Spectacular IT failure" costs taxpayer millions', *The Times*, 12 March 2009.

[69] House of Commons Public Accounts Committee, *Shared Services in the Department for Transport and its Agencies* (HC 684 2007–08).

[70] House of Commons Public Accounts Committee, *Ministry of Defence: Chinook Mk3* (HC 247 2008–09).

then made if income changes. During the first four years, HMRC had made overpayments of £7.3 billion. While the government had changed the system to reduce overpayments, many vulnerable people were overpaid, thereby generating distress that they would have to pay back the money that they had received. The government recognised that it was unlikely to recover all of the money that had been overpaid. Furthermore, the system also suffered from high rates of error and fraud. Both the PAC and the NAO suggested a range of remedial action to prevent overpayments and to reduce errors and fraud in the system.[71]

What these illustrations reveal is that independent audit, backed up by the authority of the PAC, can provide an effective means of laying bare instances of inefficient and wasteful use of public resources by government. The NAO provides the PAC with independent investigations into value for money that the Committee could not itself be expected to undertake; indeed, it is no exaggeration to say that the PAC simply could not function without the NAO's support.

4.1.4 The effectiveness of the PAC and the NAO

How effective, though, is this accountability mechanism for holding government to account for public expenditure? At a simple level, the PAC can be seen as effective in terms of publicly highlighting the inefficient use of public money by government; the Committee's reports often command media attention and, despite its party membership, the Committee is generally accepted to be non-party-political. However, merely highlighting poor value for money is, by itself, insufficient if government repeats its mistakes. Another test of the effectiveness of this accountability process concerns the frequency with which the government accepts the PAC's recommendations. The majority of the PAC's specific recommendations are positively received and acted upon by government. As the government has itself stated, it takes the PAC's recommendations 'seriously as the fruit of the accountability process... The Committee has thus helped the government to secure financial savings, raise the standards of public services and improve the quality of delivery'.[72]

However, as well as identifying (and suggesting remedial action in respect of) particular areas of difficulty, the PAC has increasingly sought to draw broader lessons as to how government should plan and deliver value for money more generally. Here, the PAC has identified several causes for concern, including policies not being properly planned or thought through; improvements not materialising or taking place slowly, despite promises; failure to apply more widely the lessons learned in one part of the public sector; the repetition of mistakes, even after the causes have been

---

[71] National Audit Office, *HM Revenue and Customs 2007–08 Accounts: Tax Credits Part Two and Part Three—Follow-up on the Collection of Income Tax* (HC 674 2007–08); House of Commons Public Accounts Committee, *HM Revenue and Customs: Tax Credit and Income Tax* (HC 311 2008–09).

[72] HM Treasury, *Treasury Minutes on the Thirteenth to Seventeenth Reports from the Committee of Public Accounts 2005–06* (Cm 6743 2006), p 33.

identified; failure to exploit commercial opportunities; and slow progress in making the most of opportunities offered by new developments in technology.[73] The fact that such difficulties persist, scrutiny by the PAC and NAO notwithstanding, does not detract from the importance of such scrutiny. It is generally accepted that financial scrutiny undertaken by Parliament is much more effective when it comes to examining past expenditure (backward-looking scrutiny) than as regards planned expenditure (forward-looking scrutiny).[74]

There are, however, various factors that constrain the effectiveness of the PAC's scrutiny. An inherent constraint arises from the limited amount of resources devoted to accountability processes. The PAC's remit covers a vast area—the whole of central governmental activity. Given its limited resources, and even with assistance from the NAO, the PAC's scrutiny inevitably has to focus upon particular areas of government. The risk is that, despite the PAC's successes in uncovering and exposing governmental inefficiency, there are always likely to be many areas that elude detailed scrutiny. A second issue concerns the extent to which government does actively seek to take account of the PAC's recommendations. Those recommendations are often accepted by the government, in the sense that they are not explicitly rejected. However, what is often less certain is the extent to which government actively seeks to act upon the PAC's recommendations in order to ensure future efficiency in the use of public money by learning appropriate lessons and thereby preventing future mistakes. In practice, the action taken by government in response to PAC reports may be quite limited. It has, then, been suggested that there should be a more coordinated follow-up system after the PAC has published a report. More generally, the Hansard Society has recommended that there should be a move towards a deeper notion of accountability to ensure that individual lessons are translated into general reforms of public institutions that are found to be flawed.[75]

> **Q** To what extent do the PAC and NAO together provide an effective means of financial scrutiny? How do you think that their effectiveness can be enhanced?

4.1.5 Departmental select committees

We explained above that select committees have a role in relation to the scrutiny of planned expenditure. Here, our concern is with their role in scrutinising public expenditure after the money has been spent. There is an argument that financial scrutiny is more effective when it is conducted in conjunction with an analysis of the governmental policies to which such expenditure is allocated and of the outcomes of that expenditure. Knowledge of a government department's finance should underlie

---

[73] House of Commons Public Accounts Committee, *Achieving Value for Money in the Delivery of Public Services* (HC 742 2005–06), pp 6–7.

[74] House of Commons Liaison Committee, *Parliament and Government Finance: Recreating Financial Scrutiny* (HC 426 2007–08), [6].

[75] Brazier and Ram, *The Fiscal Maze: Parliament, Government and Public Money* (London 2006), p 39.

and inform much of a departmental select committee's activity, including the scrutiny of policy and administration.[76]

As we saw in Chapter 10, one of the core tasks of departmental select committees is to examine the effectiveness of governmental activity. Because those committees are composed of MPs who oversee the activities of a particular governmental department, the committees should be able to combine a knowledge and awareness of a particular area of governmental activity with financial scrutiny. This potential is limited by the fact that, as noted above, MPs do not, on the whole, possess sufficient capacity and willingness to undertake thorough financial scrutiny, although some assistance is available from the Commons Scrutiny Unit. Furthermore, the NAO provides select committees with a wide range of support in addition to its core work for the PAC—for example, by producing performance briefings to assist select committees' annual oversight of departments' performance.

It has also been suggested that select committees could occupy a more fundamental role in financial scrutiny by undertaking the more detailed follow-up of the implementation or otherwise of the PAC's recommendations.[77] As the PAC's resources are limited, it seems apposite that the responsibility for more detailed follow-up should rest primarily with departmental select committees. After all, departmental select committees that oversee individual government departments are especially well placed to monitor the progress of such departments and their agencies in acting upon the recommendations of the PAC and the NAO. Some committees have occasionally performed this function—for example, in 2006, the Foreign Affairs Committee examined the progress of the Foreign and Commonwealth Office in implementing a range of recommendations from the NAO[78]—but this is not the norm. Select committees choose their own subjects of inquiry and there is no normal expectation that they will routinely monitor whether or not departments have, in fact, acted upon the PAC's recommendations.

4.2 **Local government and the Audit Commission**

So far, we have focused exclusively upon the work of the NAO, the PAC, and the Commons' departmental select committees; as we have seen, the work of these bodies illustrates one of our general themes—namely, the importance of holding UK central government to account (in this context, for its spending of public money). However, another general theme of this book is that the nature of the UK's constitution has increasingly come to be characterised by its 'multilayered' nature. As public power has increasingly come to be exercised at various different levels—EU, national, regional, and local—so too has the constitution itself come to formulate rules and structures that operate at these different levels. This is reflected in contemporary arrangements

---

[76] *Parliament and Government Finance: Recreating Financial Scrutiny,* [11].

[77] Brazier and Ram, p 41.

[78] House of Commons Foreign Affairs Committee, *Annual Report* (HC 903 2005–06).

for financial scrutiny. As White and Hollingsworth have explained, 'the constitutional role of audit implies that its institutional arrangements should reflect constitutional differences between layers of government, as well as the relationship between the layers'.[79] If so, then it also needs to be accepted that the nature and activity of public sector auditing needs to be designed and operated in a manner appropriate to the characteristics of the layer of government that is subject to financial scrutiny. In this section and the next, we therefore consider briefly the role of the audit agencies that oversee public spending by local government and the devolved administrations in Scotland, Wales, and Northern Ireland.[80]

Like UK central government, local government is also a big spender of public money. However, due in large part to constraints imposed by central government, local authorities have far less freedom to decide for themselves how they use or spend their resources. As we noted in Chapter 7, the UK government frequently intervenes in matters pertaining to local government. One principal mechanism of such intervention is through the control by central government of the amount of resources spent by local government. For example, charge-capping—by which central government can constrain the amount of Council Tax raised by local authorities—is the principal means by which central government exerts control over local government finance.

Another means of overseeing public expenditure by local government is provided by the Audit Commission. This body was established in 1982 and comprises 15–20 members appointed by the Secretary of State for Communities and Local Government.[81] Before that time, scrutiny of local government spending had been overseen through a number of haphazard systems. The establishment of the Audit Commission 'marked a decisive watershed in the nature and function of public sector auditing' by establishing a single body tasked with responsibility for ensuring efficiency, economy, and effectiveness in the use of public money by local authorities.[82] Its work spans the range of local government activity including health, housing, community safety, and fire and rescue services.

More specifically, the Audit Commission has been assigned various statutory functions. First, it audits the accounts of local public bodies. Second, the Commission has been involved in carrying out 'comprehensive area assessments' drawing together the findings of a range of audit bodies, including those with a specific focus on education and health, in order to provide a global indication of the performance of public bodies in each area. Comprehensive area assessments also involved scoring local authorities' performance against a set of national performance criteria. Third, the Audit Commission undertakes a 'national studies programme' that aims, among other things, to identify, disseminate, and encourage best practice. Fourth, an auditor may

---

[79] White and Hollingsworth, *Audit, Accountability, and Government* (Oxford 1999), p 198.

[80] Financial scrutiny in the EU is the responsibility of the Court of Auditors. See Chapter 8, section 2.3.4, above.   [81] Local Government Finance Act 1982, Audit Commission Act 1998.

[82] Leigh, *Law, Politics, and Local Democracy* (Oxford 2000), p 129.

institute legal proceedings against a local public body if it appears to him or her that unlawful spending has taken place.[83]

In general terms, it is broadly accepted that the Audit Commission provides an effective means of financial scrutiny over local government. It has, for example, been noted that 'the Audit Commission has established itself as a key player, alongside the NAO, in ensuring proper accountability for the use of public money'.[84] As with the NAO, the utility of the Audit Commission is that it provides independent audit findings that represent a valuable source of expert information that can then be used in order to hold those responsible for spending decisions to account.

At the same time, various concerns have been raised with regard to both the work and the constitutional position of the Audit Commission. First, with regard to its audit role, perhaps the principal concern has been that the Commission has increasingly placed local authorities under pressure to act in accordance with its own views as to how public money should be spent best. As Leigh has noted, the most significant feature of the Audit Commission's work 'has been its proactive role in disseminating management practice, ostensibly under the authority of its statutory functions of promoting value for money'.[85] In other words, the concern is that underlying the Audit Commission's use of technocratic language—'best value', 'comprehensive area assessments', and 'value for money'—lie value judgements as to how public money should be allocated. Local government is democratically elected and therefore one might expect that political judgements by local councillors should generally be accepted, subject to the controlling influence of local elections. However, as we noted in Chapter 7, central government is remarkably reluctant to entrust such matters to the local democratic process. Another concern has been that the volume of inspection and audit imposed upon local government has progressively diverted its attention from its primary role of delivering local public services. Whether or not this is correct has been a contested question, but it is a salutary reminder that while it is important to ensure that government is held to account, it also needs freedom to perform the tasks that it exists to do.

Another set of concerns relates to the constitutional position of the Audit Commission. First, there is the independence of the Commission: while the Audit Commission is independent of those local public bodies that it audits, its members are appointed by the Secretary of State—that is, by central government—thereby augmenting the control of central government over local government. It has been noted that the 'unfettered ministerial patronage in appointments and unconfined ministerial powers of direction under the Audit Commission Act 1998' are both strikingly unsatisfactory features of the Audit Commission's current constitutional arrangements.[86] A further concern relates to the absence of a direct link between the Audit Commission and Parliament. Unlike the NAO, which reports to the PAC, there is no equivalent select committee to which the Audit Commission reports. In 2000, a Commons select

---

[83] Audit Commission Act 1998, s 17.   [84] White and Hollingsworth, p 161.   [85] Leigh, p 130.
[86] White and Hollingsworth, p 165.

committee rejected a proposal that a new select committee be established to consider and report upon the work of the Audit Commission; the committee explained that services provided by local authorities should be accountable to local electorates and that Parliament should not attempt, even indirectly, to hold them to account.[87] At the same time, there is a strong case for Parliament having a greater role in considering both the areas audited and scrutinised by the Audit Commission and the work of the Audit Commission itself. As McEldowney has commented, the absence of a select committee equivalent to the PAC to oversee local government expenditure and the Audit Commission is a 'weakness' in existing arrangements.[88]

Like so many other parts of the constitution, things rarely stand still. In 2010, the coalition government announced its intention to reduce local government inspection and abolish the comprehensive area assessment by the Audit Commission.[89] Furthermore, the coalition announced that it would implement the Sustainable Communities Act 2007 to enable citizens to know how taxpayers' money is spent in their local area and to have greater involvement over how it is spent. Under this Act, the Secretary of State for Communities and Local Government is obliged to produce local spending reports—that is, reports on expenditure by local authorities.[90] However, in an abrupt change of policy, the Secretary of State, Eric Pickles MP, subsequently announced that the coalition government intended to abolish the Audit Commission. According to the Secretary of State, the Audit Commission had 'lost its way. Rather than being a watchdog that champions taxpayers' interests, it has become a creature of the Whitehall state'.[91] It is currently uncertain what arrangements will replace the Audit Commission. It is possible that some of the Audit Commission's functions, such as the auditing of local government accounts, could be undertaken by private sector audit companies.

4.3 Devolution and audit

While the devolution of power to Scotland, Wales, and Northern Ireland has resulted in the creation of new government institutions, it has also affected the system of financial control within the UK government. Before explaining these changes, it is necessary to consider some of the basic financial implications of the UK's system of asymmetrical devolution. The general principles governing the funding of the devolved administrations are set out by the Treasury in its Statement of Funding Policy.[92] In most

---

[87] House of Commons Environment, Transport and Rural Affairs Select Committee, *Audit Commission* (HC 174 1999–2000).

[88] McEldowney, 'The Control of Public Expenditure', in Jowell and Oliver (eds), *The Changing Constitution* (Oxford 2007), p 383.

[89] HM Government, *The Coalition: Our Programme for Government* (London 2010), pp 11–12.

[90] Sustainable Communities Act 2007, s 6.

[91] 'Eric Pickles announces plans to scrap Audit Commission', BBC News website, 13 August 2010.

[92] HM Treasury, *Funding the Scottish Parliament, National Assembly for Wales and Northern Ireland Assembly: Statement of Funding Policy* (London 2007).

cases, these arrangements represent the continuation of long-standing conventions concerning the funding of public spending outside England prior to devolution. Overall responsibility for fiscal policy remains with the Treasury—that is, central UK government. As a result, the budgets of the devolved administrations—the Scottish Executive, the Northern Ireland Executive, and the Welsh Assembly Government— continue to be determined by reference to the UK's public expenditure regime. The amounts allocated to the devolved administrations are determined by reference to the 'Barnett Formula', which takes account of the population sizes of Scotland, Wales, and Northern Ireland compared with that of England. However, once funding has been allocated to the devolved governments, it is for them to decide how to allocate it between the services for which they are responsible.[93]

So, with the devolution of power comes the ability of the devolved administrations to decide how to spend and allocate their resources; so, also, must come scrutiny mechanisms to oversee such expenditure. This is essentially undertaken in the following way. Forward-looking scrutiny of the devolved administrations' proposed expenditure—in particular, annual budgets—is undertaken by the finance committees of the National Assembly for Wales, the Northern Ireland Assembly, and the Scottish Parliament. As regards backward-looking scrutiny of actual expenditure, arrangements broadly replicate those at Westminster. The spending of each devolved administration is audited by an independent auditor: the Wales Audit Office, the Northern Ireland Audit Office, and Audit Scotland. Like the NAO, these audit agencies undertake financial audit by certifying accounts and examine value for money issues by reporting on the economy, efficiency, and effectiveness of government services. They also oversee the auditing of local government. These audit bodies are independent of the devolved administrations and report to the appropriate assembly or Parliament. Furthermore, as with the relationship between the NAO and the PAC, reports by these independent audit bodies can be taken up in inquiries undertaken by the audit committee of the appropriate assembly or Parliament, or, in the case of the Northern Ireland Assembly, its Public Accounts Committee.

4.4 **The courts**

We can now turn to consider the role of the courts: what role, if any, do they have with regard to financial scrutiny? Typically, the attitude of the courts is that they are unwilling to involve themselves in scrutinising either the raising of revenue or how public money has been spent by government. From the judicial perspective, the raising and spending of public money raise difficult resource allocation issues that the courts are generally reluctant to subject to thorough scrutiny. They implicitly accept that

---

[93] Not all of the devolved governments' money comes via the UK Treasury. Devolved governments receive some money from locally collected taxes, and the Scottish Parliament also has a tax-varying power, meaning that it can increase (or indeed reduce) income tax payable in Scotland by up to 3 per cent as compared with the basic rate applicable elsewhere in the UK. See Scotland Act 1998, ss 73–74.

because there are competing claims upon the public purse, it is generally preferable that any disputes that arise are best resolved through the political process. This, of course, is not to imply that the courts have no role whatsoever with regard to financial scrutiny.

Since the sixteenth century, the courts have accepted the primacy of Parliament's role in financial control and have indicated that they will, if necessary, intervene in order to protect individuals against attempts by the executive to raise money without parliamentary authority (and in that way bolster Parliament's constitutional authority). So, for example, in *Congreve v Home Office*, a challenge was made to the legality of an attempt by government to revoke a television licence purchased by the claimant (and countless others) before his old one had expired, so as to avoid an imminent price rise. By holding that the Home Office's decision to revoke such licences, thereby forcing affected individuals to buy new, more expensive ones, was an unlawful 'means of extracting money which Parliament has given the executive no mandate to demand', the Court of Appeal was essentially sustaining the primacy of Parliament's role in assenting to increases in revenue.[94]

What, then, of the role of the courts in assessing the legality of governmental expenditure? According to Esrkine May, the constitutional position—that legislation is necessary to sanction governmental expenditure—is based on 'ancient constitutional usage'.[95] In practice, few questions as to the technical legality of governmental expenditure are raised before the courts, but it is clear that the courts have a jurisdiction to determine legality in this context, as the *Pergau Dam* case illustrates.[96]

At stake here was UK government funding of £200 million for an international development scheme to fund the construction of a dam in Malaysia. The PAC, basing itself on an NAO report, was highly critical, and official advice tendered to the government indicated that the scheme represented poor value for money. The suspicion was that the international development funding had been granted by the UK government as a 'sweetener' to induce the Malaysian government to agree an arms contract. However, importantly, for present purposes, when the decision to fund the scheme was challenged by way of judicial review, the High Court concluded that it was unlawful: the legislation, which permitted the government to promote international development, was to be read as implicitly limited to the promotion of economically sound development.[97] The Court noted that where the contemplated development is so economically unsound that there is no economic argument in its favour, it is not possible to draw any material distinction between questions of propriety and regularity,

---

[94] *Congreve v Home Office* [1976] 1 QB 629, 662, *per* Geoffrey Lane LJ. See also *Attorney-General v Wilts United Dairies* (1922) 91 LJKB 897.

[95] McKay (ed), *Erskine May's Treatise on The Law, Privileges, Proceedings and Usage of Parliament* (London 2004), p 850.

[96] *R v Secretary of State for Foreign and Commonwealth Affairs, ex p World Development Movement Ltd* [1995] 1 WLR 386.   [97] Overseas and Development Co-operation Act 1980, s 1(1).

on the one hand, and those of economy and efficiency, on the other.[98] The decision to make the grant was, therefore, unlawful.

Both the government and the NAO's reaction to this ruling was that it did not possess any wider ramifications other than in relation to the specific statutory context from which it arose. It has, though, been argued that the judgment represents a general principle of public law applicable across the whole range of public spending: proposed expenditure by the government of money voted by Parliament will be unlawful if, in relation to the object for which the money has been provided, no reasonable Minister could think that it represented value for money.[99] More generally, it has been noted that this decision 'makes clear that legality and value for money cannot be treated as entirely separate matters'.[100] In other words, while public law principles will not require every spending decision to represent the best possible value for money, not least because this would be unrealistic and unachievable, the courts may intervene to strike down spending decisions that represent extremely poor value for money and at which no reasonable decision-maker could ever have arrived. Furthermore, it is worth noting that Parliament subsequently amended the relevant legislation so that international development funding could, in future, only be provided by the government if it were satisfied that it was likely to contribute to a reduction in poverty.[101]

> **Q** Should the courts have a jurisdiction in relation to scrutinising the legality of spending decisions?

5. Conclusion

The essential theme of this chapter has been that financial scrutiny is an important mechanism of accountability over government: because government spends public money, it is essential that it should be held to account for its spending proposals and actual expenditure. We already know from our discussion of accountability in Chapters 9 and 10 that it is a broad concept. Government is constrained, overseen, and scrutinised in a number of ways. Some of those processes, such as judicial review of the legality of administrative action, will involve legally enforceable outcomes, whereas others, such as political accountability, will not. The precise nature of the accountability method will depend largely upon which particular end or objective it is seeking to achieve. In the case of financial scrutiny, the end or objective is the proper use of public money—that is, value for money, and its economic, efficient, and effective use by government. The mechanisms used to advance financial scrutiny are a mixture

---

[98] *Pergau Dam* case at 402, *per* Rose LJ.   [99] White and Hollingsworth, above n 17 at 70.
[100] Harden, White, and Hollingsworth, 'Value for Money and Administrative Law' [1996] PL 661 at 680.
[101] International Development Act 2002, s 1.

of political, parliamentary processes and independent audit by specialist audit agencies. The courts' involvement, meanwhile, is relatively modest in this sphere. Furthermore, it is important to note that the focus of accountability is not always on preventing or curbing the excesses of governmental action; it is just as, if not more, often concerned with promoting effective governmental action or, as in the case of financial scrutiny, making sure that government seeks to achieve its objectives without wasting public money.

Financial scrutiny is of obvious practical importance—but it is also constitutionally important: 'External audit in the public sector is an essential part of a constitution which is premised on the accountability of government to Parliament and to citizens.'[102] The value for money principles—efficiency, effectiveness, and economy—do not enjoy the same constitutional status as, for example, manifestations of the separation of powers or the rule of law, such as judicial independence and the right of access to courts. But this does not render them constitutionally insignificant. The responsible use of power is one of the fundamental expectations that individuals rightly hold in relation to government and the responsible use of public money is central in this regard. It follows that it is imperative that the constitution supplies adequate machinery for holding government to account in financial terms.

This, in turn, takes us back to the central issue of the relationship between the executive and Parliament. We have seen that the development of Parliament as an institution came about in large measure because it was summoned in order to approve the Crown's demands for supply. In the contemporary context, the government enjoys considerable influence in establishing the amount of public expenditure and the purposes to which it is committed. This influence merely reflects the broader dominance that a government with a majority in the House of Commons is able to exert over Parliament. It would be mistaken to conclude that Parliament is impotent in this regard, but there is clearly room for improvement. Scrutiny of past government expenditure is generally considered to be more effective than forward-looking financial scrutiny of proposed government expenditure, although there is no doubt that the influence of both the PAC and the NAO could be enhanced. If the proposals of the Liaison Committee[103] are successful in reinvigorating financial scrutiny by Parliament, then perhaps the balance may be restored so that financial scrutiny regains its proper position as one of Parliament's core activities.

Further reading

Brazier and Ram, *The Fiscal Maze: Parliament, Government and Public Money* (London 2006)

Daintith and Page, *The Executive in the Constitution* (Oxford 1999), chs 4–6

---

[102] White and Hollingsworth, *Audit, Accountability, and Government* (Oxford 1999), p 197.
[103] On which, see section 3.4 above.

McEldowney, 'The Control of Public Expenditure', in Jowell and Oliver (eds), *The Changing Constitution* (Oxford 2007)

White and Hollingsworth, *Audit, Accountability, and Government* (Oxford 1999)

Useful websites

http://www.audit-commission.gov.uk
The website of the Audit Commission

http://www.audit-scotland.gov.uk
The website of Audit Scotland

http://www.parliament.uk/business/committees/committees-a-z/commons-select/public-accounts-committee/
The website of the House of Commons Public Accounts Committee

http://www.nao.org.uk
The website of the National Audit Office

http://www.niauditoffice.gov.uk
The website of the Northern Ireland Audit Office

http://www.wao.gov.uk
The website of the Wales Audit Office

PART IV

Judicial Review

12 Judicial Review—An Introduction

1. An example

Thousands of decisions are made by the government and public bodies every day, affecting individuals in myriad ways. We begin with just one example.

> Imagine that a government Minister is in the process of deciding whether to grant permission for the construction and operation of a new airport. This decision will impact upon huge numbers of people in many different ways. Some might welcome it for the ready access to air travel that it would provide, for the employment it would create, and for the prosperity that it might bring to the surrounding area. Others will oppose it vehemently in light of the noise pollution that it would bring, the likely reduction in the value of nearby properties, the despoilment of the countryside, and the contribution that the new airport would make to the environmental damage caused by air travel. The decision is, therefore, an obviously difficult one for the Minister. He will have to weigh up all of these different—and conflicting—considerations, and ultimately make a judgement about whether giving the go-ahead to the new airport is in the public interest.

We saw in Chapter 10 that the actions of government Ministers are open to political control by Parliament via the doctrine of ministerial accountability. However, the actions of Ministers, and of other public bodies, are open to scrutiny in a number of other ways—including judicial review. The law of judicial review sets the legal framework within which decisions such as this, affecting the rights, interests, or legitimate expectations of individuals, are taken. A Minister deciding whether our hypothetical new airport should be built would therefore find himself subject not just to political scrutiny—for example, by being asked questions by MPs in the House of Commons—but also to a wide range of legal requirements that, if breached, would enable a court to strike down the decision on judicial review. For example, the Minister would be required to give all interested parties—such as those living near the proposed airport—a fair opportunity to express their views, and then to take those views into account when making a decision. He would be required to disregard any legally irrelevant considerations (for example, it would be unlawful for him to take into account the fact that it would be personally convenient to him to have a new airport in the location under consideration) and prohibited from acting for an improper purpose (for example, to boost the government's popularity by creating jobs in a marginal constituency). He might also be legally required to honour any promises made in the course of considering the issue (for example, the courts may hold him to an undertaking to compensate householders whose homes would be rendered less valuable owing to their proximity to the new airport) and he might well be required to give reasons for his decision.

2. What judicial review is and is not about

Traditionally, the principal focus of judicial review has been on *the way in which the decision is taken*, rather than on *the decision itself*. So, if the government, having complied with all of the legal requirements mentioned above, were to conclude that the airport should be built in the locale under consideration because, on balance, it felt that the transport, economic, and environmental arguments justified such a decision, a court, on judicial review, could not second-guess this—that is, a judge, in a judicial review case, cannot overturn a government decision simply because she disagrees with it. This is not to say that the court cannot examine *any* aspect of the decision itself (as distinct from the way in which it was made). For example, as we will see, if the government were to make a wholly unreasonable decision,[1] or a decision that unacceptably compromised individuals' human rights,[2] a court could intervene—but this is very different from courts being able to overturn decisions simply because they disagree with them. As Laws LJ has explained, the court 'does not ask itself the question, "Is this decision right or wrong?"', and judicial review has 'nothing to do with the question, "Which view is the better one?"'.[3]

This limitation on the power of the court reflects the so-called distinction between 'appeal' and 'review'. If Parliament has created a statutory right of appeal, authorising some appellate tribunal to substitute its view for that of the original decision-maker, there can be little scope for disagreement about the legitimacy of such arrangements. But where Parliament has not put such measures in place, meaning that the decision can be challenged only via judicial review, it is generally held that the courts have no mandate to interfere with the decision itself. There are several reasons that explain

---

[1] For example, if the case against locating the airport in a particular place were overwhelmingly strong on all relevant bases—environmental, economic, and so on—but the Minister, for no demonstrable reason, nevertheless were to approve its construction, this decision could be overturned by the court.

[2] For example, if the Minister were to refuse to compensate people whose houses had to be demolished to make way for the airport (thereby violating their right to property) or to impose restrictions on night flights so as to ensure that noise pollution did not lead to an unacceptable level of sleep deprivation (thereby violating the right to private and family life).

[3] *R v Somerset County Council, ex p Fewings* [1995] 1 All ER 513, 515.

why courts are, in general, prepared to accept that their powers of judicial review are limited in this way.[4] Two merit particular attention.

The first concerns the *institutional capacity* of the court to determine whether a decision is flawed. Where the ground of challenge relates, for example, to an alleged procedural error—perhaps the Minister in our example fails to give local residents an opportunity to voice their objections—the court can assess such a situation by reference to general principles of procedural fairness, the application of which calls for no expertise that is particular to the decision under consideration. The reviewing court is therefore perfectly capable of forming a judgment about whether the procedure used by the Minister was fair. In contrast, if the content of the decision is challenged—for example, if a pressure group argues that the airport should not be built because the environmental damage that it would cause outweighs any economic advantages that it might bring—the court is not really qualified to assess the merits of these competing arguments. Indeed, the Minister, together with his departmental officials and advisers, is likely to be in a much stronger position to evaluate the relative environmental and economic implications of giving the go-ahead to the new airport. Recognising that they lack expertise on these sorts of questions, courts have therefore traditionally accepted that they should not second-guess the decision-maker on matters of substance.

The second reason for judicial reticence in relation to such matters relates to concerns about *democratic legitimacy*. To understand this point, we need to appreciate the consequences of a court striking down a government decision as unlawful. If a reviewing court concludes that a Minister has acted in a procedurally unfair manner, and quashes the decision on that basis, it is open to the Minister to retake the decision in a procedurally fair manner, perhaps eventually reaching the same conclusion— that the new airport should be built. Judicial review, in such circumstances, does not therefore curtail the ultimate discretion of the decision-maker; rather, it ensures that the decision-maker exercises his discretion in a fair and lawful way. In contrast, if the court were to strike down the decision on the basis of the pressure group's argument that the environmental damage would be unacceptably great, this makes it legally impossible for the Minister to sanction the new airport: the court has, in effect, prohibited him from giving it the go-ahead. This may be regarded as objectionable, since it involves the court taking out of the democratically accountable Minister's hands a matter that, in the first place, Parliament had given him the authority to decide.

Q Do you find these arguments persuasive? What counter-arguments might be marshalled against them?

We will see in the next chapter that these arguments do not mean that courts never look at the content of government decisions (as distinct from the process by which

---

[4] See generally Irvine, 'Judges and Decision-Makers: The Theory and Practice of *Wednesbury* Review' [1996] PL 59.

they are made)—but they do continue to exert considerable influence in this area, and it remains the case that courts exercise far greater restraint when called upon to scrutinise the substance of executive decisions.

3. Judicial review and administrative law

The phrase 'administrative law' is often ascribed two different meanings. First, it is often used to describe the collective legal remedies that individuals may pursue in order to challenge public decisions. Judicial review is an important aspect of administrative law, but it is by no means the only available mechanism for challenging government decisions. In later chapters, we will examine other ways—including complaints to ombudsmen and appeals to tribunals—whereby such challenges can be made.[5] These three mechanisms—judicial review, ombudsmen, and tribunals—have their own distinct processes, but all are largely concerned with enabling individuals to hold government to account by going to an independent third party. That party assesses whether or not the individual's case is made out and then, if so, provides some sort of remedy. It is primarily in this sense that we shall be examining administrative law in this section of the book dealing with judicial review, and in subsequent chapters on ombudsmen and tribunals.

However, it is important to note that there is a second and alternative meaning of 'administrative law'.[6] The phrase is also used to refer to the law governing the organisation and activities of administrative agencies. In this sense, administrative law concerns the powers of public authorities, their duties, the rules that they must apply in order to administer and implement policy, and the decision-making processes that they adopt. Rather than just detailing the legal mechanisms of challenging government decisions, administrative law also concerns the rules governing the powers, duties, and organisation of public agencies, and how such agencies are to undertake their functions (for example, their decision-making processes).

Administrative law in this sense is not to be found primarily in courts' judgments, tribunals' decisions, or ombudsmen's reports—although they are important; rather, it is to be found in the legislation establishing public agencies. Furthermore, because many statutes governing public administration delegate the power to make further rules or delegated legislation to the relevant government Minister or public agency, it is also necessary to consider the enormous volume of detailed rules and regulations that govern the performance of public functions and which are continuously generated by public agencies themselves in order to implement their policy objectives. Administrative law in the broader sense is also to be found in the reality of

---

[5] See Chapters 16 and 17.

[6] See Gellhorn and Robinson, 'Perspectives on Administrative Law' (1975) 75 Columbia LR 771; Arthurs, 'Rethinking Administrative law: A Slightly Dicey Business' (1979) 17 Osgoode Hall Law Journal 1.

governmental practices—how the rules are applied and how decisions are reached by public authorities. In this sense, administrative law is often broken down into the law governing discrete areas of administration spanning the entire range of functions that the modern administrative state performs. This is because the law governing public administration is often specific to governmental activities that attempt to achieve particular public goals. For example, rather than the general principles of judicial review, there is social security law, prison law, police law, food law, education law, immigration law, agricultural law, and so on. Administrative law, in this sense, is also subject to constant change as policy goals alter and as government seeks to enhance the effectiveness of public agencies.

This book does not focus on administrative law in this second, broader sense—indeed, no single book could do so; rather, we will be considering the mechanisms through which individuals may challenge governmental decisions, and the general principles applied by courts, tribunals, and ombudsmen. But it is important to recognise that administrative law also has the second meaning identified above, and that there therefore exist detailed bodies of law that regulate the several and contrasting spheres within which public administration is conducted.

4. Judicial review and our three key themes

At the beginning of this book, we highlighted three key themes that are crucial to an understanding of the modern British constitution. It is fitting, therefore, that we begin our consideration of judicial review by considering how it relates to those themes.

4.1 **Accountability**

We noted in Chapter 2, and examined in more detail in Chapter 4, the dominant role of the executive in the United Kingdom's constitution today. This is doubtless one of the defining features of our contemporary constitution. In 1888, the legal historian Maitland noted that 'we are becoming a much governed nation, governed by all manner of councils and boards and officers, central and local, high and low, exercising the powers which have been committed to them by modern statutes'.[7] In the intervening years since Maitland wrote these words, this trend—the growing scale and complexity of public action—has accelerated. Today, we might say that we live in an administrative state. Government has taken responsibility for large areas of social regulation and public services, which means that it possesses an enormous ability to affect people's lives.

---

[7] Maitland, *Constitutional History of England* [1888] (New Jersey 2001), p 501.

The unusually powerful position in which the UK executive finds itself is, as we have seen, a composite function of several interlocking features of the British constitution, including a highly incomplete separation of powers that enables the executive government to arrogate power to itself through its effective control of the sovereign legislature. The dominant position of the executive raises obvious challenges in terms of accountability—and an associated paradox. The more powerful the executive, the greater the need for effective systems of accountability to guard against and deal with abuses of power—and, yet, as we saw in Chapters 5 and 10, the very dominance of the executive is an obstacle to such accountability. Against the background of a powerful government that exerts enormous influence over nearly every aspect of life, and a Parliament that is limited in its capacity to hold that government to account, people have unsurprisingly looked increasingly to other institutions, including courts, to fill the accountability deficit that has arguably arisen. As the former Lord Chancellor, Lord Irvine, has explained, it has been 'the massive expansion of the administrative state, which more than any other factor' has prompted the judges to develop the principles of judicial review.[8]

However, it is important to bear two further points in mind. First, judicial review lies in relation to all governmental (and some other public) powers, not only those of the executive branch of the central government. While difficulties at the centre—including Parliament's difficulties in holding the executive to account—have formed part of the impetus for the development of the courts' powers of judicial review, it is necessary to recognise that judicial review is a mechanism for holding a much broader range of bodies, including local authorities, legally to account. Second, notwithstanding that it has developed, in part, because of concerns about the effectiveness of other (especially parliamentary) accountability mechanisms, judicial review nevertheless remains (as noted above) just one way of holding the government to account: it exists, as Figure 13.1 shows,[9] as part of a network of overlapping mechanisms for securing executive accountability.

4.2 **Political and legal constitutionalism**

It is clear from what we have said so far that judicial review is an important accountability tool—and one upon which reliance has grown because of the weakness of parliamentary accountability. But no one would seriously suggest that government's legal accountability to the courts should or could entirely replace its political accountability to Parliament. What, then, is the right balance between these two forms of accountability? This question squarely raises the second of our key themes—that is, the notions of political and legal constitutionalism; whereas the former emphasises

---

[8] *Human Rights, Constitutional Law and the Development of the English Legal System* (Oxford 2003), p 52.
[9] See Chapter 13, section 2.1, below.

political means of controlling the executive, the latter puts its faith in legal regulation of government.

The respective weight that should be placed upon these two approaches is highly controversial. Harlow and Rawlings have pointed out a fissure in public law scholarship, separating schools of thought that are respectively enthusiastic and distinctly sceptical about judicial review.[10] The former school embraces a minimalist conception of the state in which administrative law's main role is to limit government power and subject it to judicial control. Here, then, emphasis is placed on the role of the courts in securing good administration, and the administrative law enforced by courts is viewed as a valuable and necessary external limitation upon government. Whether it is right to put courts centre-stage in this way depends on the position that one adopts in relation to a range of other issues.

First, enthusiasm about judicial review may reflect a particular *ideological* bent. Those who emphasise the law's role in safeguarding the basic rights of individuals tend to favour extensive powers of judicial review. This prompts us to think back to the contrasting conceptions of democracy considered in Chapter 5. Sedley, for example, considers that democracy is best served by a system in which 'individuals and minorities have an assurance of certain basic protections from the majoritarian interest'—and that this requires 'independent courts of law' to be given responsibility for upholding 'the interests of every individual, not merely the represented majority'.[11] On this view, the courts' role is pivotal: their unique position as neutral, independent arbiters allows them to ensure that the rights and interests of the former are not unacceptably sacrificed for the sake of the majority. In similar vein, some judges have sought in recent years to articulate a more principled justification for judicial intervention: for example, Laws LJ has argued that the principles of judicial review constitute ethical principles as to the virtuous conduct of the state's affairs.[12] To put these rather abstract-sounding ideas in context, it would, within this tradition, be acceptable for a court to strike down a ministerial decision allowing extensive night flights to take off from and land at the new airport referred in our example above. While this might be convenient for the vast majority of people, and for the airport operator and its client airlines, this would be at the expense of the interests—indeed, the human rights[13]—of those whose lives would be blighted by the inevitable nocturnal noise pollution. An important role of the court, on this view, is to provide an independent assessment of whether an acceptable balance has been struck between the interests of the minority and the majority.

Second, acceptance of extensive judicial powers to review executive action may arise for *pragmatic* reasons. For example, Farwell LJ remarked (around 100 years ago) that because (as he saw it) ministerial responsibility was no more than 'the mere

---

[10] *Law and Administration* (Cambridge 2009), ch 1.

[11] Sedley, 'The Common Law and the Constitution', in Nolan and Sedley (eds), *The Making and Remaking of the British Constitution* (London 1997), p 25.   [12] Laws, 'Law and Democracy' [1995] PL 72.

[13] See *Hatton v United Kingdom* (2003) 37 EHRR 28.

shadow of a name', the role of the courts was crucial: they were, he said, 'the only defence of the liberty of the subject against departmental aggression'.[14] Viewed thus, judicial review is a practical response to the weakness of ministerial accountability—hence the shift of emphasis from *parliamentary* to *judicial* means of controlling government, which forms an important part of the trend towards *legal* (and away from *political*) constitutionalism.

The ideological argument in favour of giving courts extensive powers of judicial review postulates that individuals' interests can, on the whole, *best* be safeguarded by independent judges against state interference, while the pragmatic argument rests on the more modest claim that judicial review is at least an *acceptable substitute* for political modes of accountability. We need to assess each of these claims.

The latter was made by Lord Mustill in the *Fire Brigades Union* case[15] (the facts of which are set out in Chapter 3.[16]) Having noted that parliamentary methods for holding the executive to account had 'been perceived as falling short, and sometimes well short, of what [is] needed to bring the performance of the executive into line with the law', he went on to explain (and generally to approve of the fact) that

> To avoid a vacuum in which the citizen would be left without protection against a misuse of executive powers the courts have had no option but to occupy the dead ground [left by Parliament] in a manner, and in areas of public life, which could not have been foreseen 30 years ago.[17]

Lord Mustill's account is doubtless historically accurate: one of the main driving forces behind the growth of judicial review has been the perceived shortcomings of parliamentary modes of accountability. However, this trend—and Lord Mustill's account of it—takes for granted the capacity of judicial review to make up for these shortcomings. Yet we should not accept this idea unquestioningly. To a large extent, it is arguable that judicial review and ministerial accountability constitute *complementary*—not *alternative*—mechanisms for holding the executive to account. The latter is concerned principally with the wider picture—with questions about policy and the management of government departments—while the former enables individuals to litigate specific grievances against administrative bodies. The view that judicial and political systems for securing accountable government are complementary is further underlined by the orthodox view, outlined above, under which it is considered improper for courts to enquire into the sort of substantive policy questions that are the traditional focus of parliamentary processes for holding the executive to account. For these (and other) reasons, writers such as Griffith and Tomkins counsel against viewing judicial review as some sort of panacea, capable of filling the 'dead ground' referred to by Lord Mustill, and argue instead that Parliament should be reformed

---

[14] *Dyson v Attorney-General* [1911] 1 KB 410, 423.

[15] *R v Secretary of State for the Home Department, ex p Fire Brigades Union* [1995] 2 AC 513.

[16] See Chapter 3, section 4, above.

[17] *Fire Brigades Union* at 567.

and reinvigorated, enabling it to play a fuller role in calling the executive branch to account—and thereby reducing the need to rely on the courts.[18]

This, however, would be unlikely to satisfy those writers whose enthusiasm for judicial review springs not from the practical consideration that it is an *acceptable substitute* for political accountability, but from the ideological view that courts are the *best-placed* institutions to scrutinise government decisions when they impact on the rights and interests of individuals. Paradoxically, while, for such writers, the independence and supposed neutrality of the courts is what uniquely equips them to stand as an honest broker between individual and public interests, those characteristics of the judicial branch are also grist to the mill of judicial review *sceptics*. How can this be? The answer lies in the fact that those who are sceptical about affording courts wide powers of judicial review contend that the enthusiasts' position is built on the false premise that questions about individuals' rights are legal (rather than political) and should therefore be answered by independent courts. In truth, say the sceptics, even if judges are given power to adjudicate on such questions—rendering them, in that sense, legal questions—this cannot deprive them of their fundamentally political character, thereby placing judges in positions where they are forced to make political choices.[19]

For example, if night flights at our hypothetical airport are regarded as interfering with the rights of nearby residents,[20] the resulting question—whether those rights or the convenience of the wider public, which would be served by allowing night flights, should prevail—involves the making of a policy choice. In other words, it is not a question with a single, objectively correct answer. It has been argued that accepting judges' authority to determine such questions amounts to dangerous judicial supremacism by which unelected judges are able to arrogate to themselves too much power at the expense of the democratic process.[21] Sceptics argue that there is no positive reason why judges should be responsible for making such 'political' choices, and that there are good reasons—including the narrow social, educational, and ethnic backgrounds from which the judiciary is presently drawn, together with its lack of democratic credentials—why it should not.[22] They therefore argue that scrutiny of such (as they see them) policy questions is best left to Parliament. Of course, all judicial decision-making involves an element of discretion that may be exercised by reference to policy considerations:[23] even questions such as whether a duty of care in negligence should be imposed may well involve policy choices about the extent to which people should be required to assume responsibility for their own actions. Judicial review sceptics,

[18] Griffith, 'The Common Law and the Political Constitution' (2001) 117 LQR 42; Tomkins, *Our Republican Constitution* (Oxford 2005).

[19] See generally Griffith, *The Politics of the Judiciary* (London 1997).

[20] Such interference was held to exist in *Hatton v United Kingdom* (2003) 37 EHRR 28.

[21] Griffith, 'The Brave New World of Sir John Laws' (2000) 63 MLR 159; Griffith, 'The Common Law and the Political Constitution' (2001) 117 LQR 42.

[22] See further Griffith, above; Campbell, Ewing, and Tomkins (eds), *Sceptical Essays on Human Rights* (Oxford 2001).   [23] Robertson, *Judicial Discretion in the House of Lords* (Oxford 1998).

though, contend that in this area, the scope for judicial policymaking is unusually great.

> **Q** Are you persuaded by the sceptics' view?

It is important not to overstate the disagreement between judicial review enthusiasts and sceptics. Few, if any, commentators advocate that there should be no judicial review at all. Disagreement centres on the *extent* to which courts should be permitted to examine the substance of executive decisions (as opposed to the propriety of the process by which they are made). We return to this issue when we consider the law of substantive judicial review in Chapter 13.

4.3 Demarcation disputes in the multilayered constitution

Much of what we have said thus far has been concerned with the role of judicial review in relation to protecting the interests and rights of individuals against unlawful executive action. There is, however, a further—and, in many respects, relatively new—dimension to judicial review. As well as providing a forum in which the proper boundaries of the *relationship between the individual and the state* can be determined, judicial review also—and increasingly—operates as a mechanism for resolving disputes about the *relationship between different parts of the multilayered constitution*.

It stands to reason that the more multilayered the constitution becomes—that is, the more that responsibility and authority are divided between different institutions—the greater the scope for disagreement about the respective competences of different bodies. Of course, in one sense, this is not a new phenomenon: as we know from Chapter 7, power has long been shared between central and local government, and courts have therefore been called upon from time to time to resolve demarcation disputes between the two. For example, the courts have been called upon to determine the extent to which central government can impose its policy preferences on local authorities,[24] and the extent of ministerial powers to curb increases in local taxes.[25] Demarcation disputes can also occur as between the UK and the European Union (EU). As we saw in Chapter 8, circumstances have arisen—most famously in the *Factortame* case[26]—in which courts have had to determine whether an Act of Parliament should be disapplied on account of the fact that it conflicts with directly effective EU law. And we saw in Chapter 7 that courts now also have a role in determining 'devolution issues'— that is, issues as to whether devolved bodies are acting or proposing to act beyond their legal competence (and thereby interfering in matters reserved to the UK tier of government).

---

[24] *Secretary of State for Education and Science v Tameside Metropolitan Borough Council* [1977] AC 1014.   [25] *Nottinghamshire County Council v Secretary of State for the Environment* [1986] AC 240.
[26] *R v Secretary of State for Transport, ex p Factortame Ltd (No 2)* [1991] 1 AC 603.

This role—which, in effect, involves acting as a referee between different foci of power within the constitutional order—is one that is familiar to courts in many countries, particularly those with federal systems in which power is clearly divided between different levels of government.[27] It is a role that is less familiar to UK courts, but one in which they are, of necessity, growing in experience. That said, it is important to remember that while judicial review serves an important function in terms of facilitating legal regulation of intra-governmental relations, non-judicial mechanisms—such as negotiation and constitutional convention—also play a very significant part in shaping the relationship between the various seats of government that exist today within our multilayered constitution.

Indeed, the question considered in the last section—concerning the appropriate balance between legal and political regulation—arises here too. The *Fire Brigades Union* case[28] illustrates the point (albeit that it involved a demarcation dispute between different arms of the national government rather than between different tiers of the multilayered government). As we saw in Chapter 3,[29] the Home Secretary, by refusing to bring into force a statutory scheme for compensating victims of violent crime, effectively sought to repeal the relevant provisions of the legislation. The question of whether it was appropriate for a court to resolve this demarcation dispute between the executive and legislative branches divided the Appellate Committee of the House of Lords: there was a three–two division of opinion in favour of judicial intervention. This demonstrates just how difficult it is for courts to determine when it is appropriate for them to act, and when it is better to recognise that the essentially political character of a question makes it better suited to non-judicial resolution. As we will see through our study, in Chapter 13, of the content of the law of judicial review, this is a pervasive problem that courts have to face up to very frequently indeed.

5. The constitutional basis of judicial review

Before we begin that study, however, one further, and obvious, preliminary question arises: what is it, in the absence of a written constitution making clear provision for judicial review, that authorises courts to intervene in (and, where appropriate, strike down) decisions made by government bodies?

5.1 The *ultra vires* doctrine

An obvious answer is that courts enforce whatever limits the relevant legislation imposes upon ministerial powers. For example, if legislation were to authorise the

---

[27] For discussion of federalism, see Chapter 7, section 2.4.1, above.

[28] *R v Secretary of State for the Home Department, ex p Fire Brigades Union* [1995] 2 AC 513.

[29] See Chapter 3, section 4, above.

Minister in our example to 'give permission for the construction and operation of new *airports*', a court, on judicial review, would be perfectly justified in striking down a decision, purportedly taken under this power, to give permission for the construction and operation of a new *prison*. In such a situation, the Minister would self-evidently be acting outside his powers, and it seems natural that courts, as enforcers of the law, should be entitled to take appropriate steps to deal with such action.

Administrative lawyers refer to this line of thinking as the *ultra vires* doctrine, *ultra vires* literally meaning 'beyond the powers'. It provides a simple and—superficially— attractive justification for judicial review, because it says, on judicial review, that courts are simply policing the boundaries upon government power stipulated by Parliament. This can be seen from Figure 12.1. The shaded area represents the Minister's power: he is authorised by the statute to do things lying inside that area, but not to do anything else. In our example, the statute allows him to approve new airports: a decision to do so (represented by point 1 in the diagram) would therefore lie within his statutory power and would be lawful. In contrast, a decision to approve a new prison (point 2) would be outside the power and unlawful. The justification for courts striking down such decisions is clear, since it 'consists of nothing other than *an application of the law itself, and the law of Parliament to boot*'.[30]

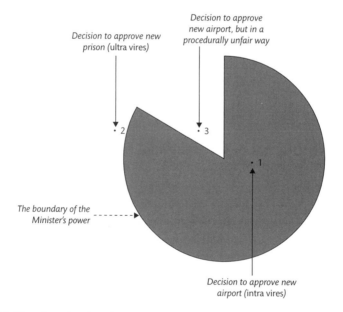

Figure 12.1 The *ultra vires* doctrine

[30] Baxter, *Administrative Law* (Cape Town 1984), p 303.

This proposition is easy to make out where courts enforce limits that are explicit in the statute: in our example, it is tolerably clear that Parliament intended the power to be used *only* to approve the construction and operation of new airports; if it were to have intended the power to extend to prisons, it would surely have said as much. The reality, however, is that judicial review goes far beyond the enforcement of limits on power that are explicit in the statute. This much is obvious from the overview we gave above[31]—and from that which is given in Figure 13.1[32]—of the many and various grounds on which courts can intervene in executive decisions. The Minister exercising the power to grant permission for a new airport would be required by the courts to exercise it fairly, reasonably, on the basis of all relevant (but no irrelevant) information, and subject to a host of other requirements (all of which we will consider in detail in the next chapter) that are neither mentioned explicitly nor even hinted at by the text of the statute. *Ultra vires* theorists respond to this difficulty by saying that Parliament intends to limit decision-makers' powers in all of these ways, even if it fails to *say* so explicitly. For example, if a Minister were to decide to grant permission for a new airport, but make his decision in a procedurally unfair way, *ultra vires* theorists would say that the decision would lie outside his powers, because Parliament never intended to give him the power to act unfairly. Figure 12.1 illustrates this idea. The missing part of the circle represents the never-granted power to act unfairly (or in breach of any of the other principles of judicial review): hence a decision (represented by point 3) marred by unfairness lies outside the Minister's power and can justifiably be struck down by the courts.

There is, however, an obvious difficulty with this argument: it is implausible.[33] If Parliament has not *said* that it is withholding from decision-makers the power to act contrary to the principles of judicial review, how do we *know* that it meant to withhold such powers? From this criticism flow several others.[34] First, as we will see in Chapter 14, the range of bodies and powers that are subject to judicial review has expanded significantly in recent decades. Importantly, courts are now willing to review the exercise of *non-statutory powers*, such as decisions taken under the royal prerogative. This presents an apparently insurmountable obstacle to the *ultra vires* principle: how can that principle—which says that judicial review is constitutionally acceptable because courts are simply enforcing those limits on power that Parliament intended when it created the power—explain judicial review of powers that were not, in the first place, created by Parliament? Second, we will see in Chapter 13 that the principles of judicial review—that is, the limits on power that courts are prepared to enforce—have evolved considerably in recent years. Entirely new limits have developed, and other principles have changed. Adherents of the *ultra vires* doctrine would

---

[31] See section 1 above.   [32] See Chatper 13, section 2.1, below.

[33] See Laws, 'Law and Democracy' [1995] PL 72, 78–9; Forsyth, 'Of Fig Leaves and Fairy Tales: The *Ultra Vires* Doctrine, the Sovereignty of Parliament and Judicial Review' [1996] CLJ 122, 136.

[34] See Craig, '*Ultra Vires* and the Foundations of Judicial Review' [1998] CLJ 63.

be forced to argue that any such developments were directly related to changes in Parliament's intention concerning the limits that courts should impose on executive power via judicial review—yet there is no evidence that this is so. Third, we explain in Chapter 14 that courts have fiercely resisted parliamentary attempts to prevent judicial review of certain matters. When Parliament has inserted an 'ouster clause' into legislation, providing in clear terms that (in effect) there should be no judicial review of certain decisions, the courts have generally struggled (successfully) to interpret such clauses in a highly artificial and restrictive way, in order to preserve the possibility of judicial review. This is hard for *ultra vires* theorists to explain: how can the courts, in exercising powers of judicial review, be doing Parliament's bidding if they insist upon exercising those powers even when Parliament appears to have told them not to?

5.2 **The common law theory**

In light of these difficulties, an alternative view—the common law theory—has been put forward in an attempt to provide a sounder justification for judicial review.[35] Whereas the *ultra vires* doctrine characterises the restrictions enforced via judicial review as limitations that are contained (explicitly or implicitly) in the statute conferring the relevant power, the common law theory postulates that they are common law rules, just like those that make it unlawful to cause foreseeable harm to one's neighbour or to breach a contract without lawful justification. Viewed in this way, if a court were to strike down our hypothetical Minister's decision to grant permission for a new airport, on the ground that the decision had been taken in a procedurally unfair way, this would have nothing to do with the intention of Parliament: the court would simply be enforcing a common law rule to the effect that decision-makers must act fairly.

This view avoids many of the difficulties encountered by the *ultra vires* doctrine. It avoids the artificiality of arguing that the detailed principles of judicial review are intended (yet never actually articulated) by Parliament. Instead, it is possible to acknowledge that the law of judicial review has been developed by judges in much the same way as the law of tort and the law contract—by incrementally fashioning legal principles through the development of case law. The common law theory also allows the principles of judicial review to be applied to decision-making powers whether or not the powers have been created by Parliament (because, according to the common law theory, the principles enforced by courts in judicial review proceedings have nothing to do with the intention of Parliament). And the common law theory can account for changes to the law of judicial review over time. Such developments need not (as under the *ultra vires* theory) be justified by reference to supposed (but unexpressed) changes in parliamentary intention; instead, they can be accounted for in the same way as any other change in the common law—by reference to the fact that it is the

---

[35] See Oliver, 'Is the *Ultra Vires* Rule the Basis of Judicial Review?' [1987] PL 543; Craig, above; Laws, above.

courts' role to develop the common law as new situations emerge and as social, moral, and legal mores change.

However, these substantial benefits notwithstanding, some commentators argue that the common law theory does not adequately fit with the basic architecture of the constitution.[36] As we have seen, in order to escape the difficulties that beset the *ultra vires* doctrine, the common law theory holds that the grounds of judicial review—that require decision-makers to act fairly, reasonably, and so on—have nothing to do with the intention of Parliament; they are instead common law rules. It has been said that this line of argument gives rise to the following problem. If, when it grants a ministerial power to approve the construction of new airports, Parliament is taken not to have *prohibited* the making of (for example) procedurally unfair decisions, then it must have *authorised* the making of such decisions. Forsyth puts the point in the following terms: '[I]f Parliament grants a power to a minister, that minister either acts within those powers or outside those powers. There is no grey area between authorisation and the denial of power.'[37]

Assume that our hypothetical Minister makes a procedurally unfair decision to approve a new airport. On Forsyth's view, the Minister either *is* or *is not* authorised by Parliament to make procedurally unfair decisions. If he is not so authorised, then the position is as shown in Figure 12.1. It will be unlawful—*ultra vires*—for the Minister to act unfairly, and a common law requirement to act fairly will be redundant (because its effect would merely require the Minister to desist from conduct that Parliament has, in the first place, omitted to authorise). In the alternative scenario, the Minister *is* authorised by Parliament to make unfair decisions: as in Figure 12.2, no chunk (representing the power to act unfairly etc) is missing from the power granted in the statute. Here, the common law is not (as in the first scenario) redundant: a common law rule requiring Ministers to act fairly *would* make a difference, because, without such a rule, it would be lawful for them to act unfairly. But there is an obvious problem. If Parliament has authorised the making of unfair decisions, it is constitutionally impossible—if Parliament is sovereign—for the common law to prohibit the making of such decisions. In effect, the common law is removing from the Minister authority that was given to him by Parliament. Critics of the common law theory therefore contend that it is unconstitutional to the extent that it purports to enable courts to prevent decision-makers from doing things that the sovereign Parliament has authorised.

If this argument is accepted (and we will see below that it is certainly not universally accepted), then something of an impasse seems to have been reached. On the one hand, the *ultra vires* doctrine fits with the principle of parliamentary sovereignty, but is otherwise highly implausible; on the other hand, the common law theory is said to conflict with parliamentary sovereignty, but is otherwise plausible. We end this chapter by considering three potential ways out of this impasse—concluding with a radical

---

[36] Forsyth, above; Elliott, 'The *Ultra Vires* Doctrine in a Constitutional Setting: Still the Central Principle of Administrative Law' [1999] CLJ 129.   [37] Forsyth at 133.

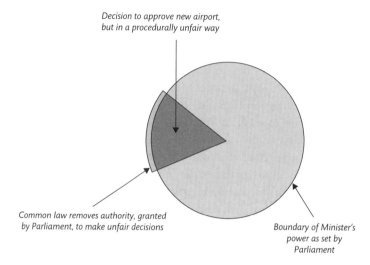

Figure 12.2 The common law theory

solution that calls into question the doctrine of parliamentary sovereignty itself and the very nature of our constitutional order.

5.3 **Defence of the common law theory**

Some writers have sought to demonstrate that the common law theory is *not* incompatible with the principle of parliamentary sovereignty. In particular, Laws argues that Forsyth is wrong to suppose that a Minister is either authorised or not authorised to act: Parliament may be agnostic—it may have no opinion one way or the other—about how the powers that it confers should be exercised. This, says Laws, gives rise to a 'vacuum'—created through the absence of any relevant parliamentary intention—that can legitimately be filled by common law principles of judicial review.[38] Applying this argument to our example, when Parliament granted the power to our hypothetical Minister to approve the construction of new airports, it would be taken to have no view as to whether or not the Minister should be allowed to exercise the power unfairly—and it would therefore be legitimate for the courts to determine whether or not the Minister should be free so to act. However, there are two difficulties with this argument.

First, just as the argument underpinning the *ultra vires* doctrine that *all* of the grounds of judicial review relate *directly* to parliamentary intention is implausible, so is the common law theory's contention that *none* of the grounds of judicial review relate *at all* to the will of Parliament. It is, for example, obvious that when a court

---

[38] 'Illegality: The Problem of Jurisdiction', in Supperstone et al (eds), *Judicial Review* (London 2005).

strikes down a ministerial decision that violates the express terms of the relevant statute, the court is enforcing parliamentary intention; even where courts are enforcing more general principles, such as those of procedural fairness, they may well be influenced by the statute when determining what fairness requires in the context.[39] It may therefore be thought that the common law position—that legislative intention is wholly irrelevant to the grounds of judicial review—is an overreaction to the *ultra vires* doctrine's admitted shortcomings.

Second, the common law theory's ascription of agnosticism to Parliament sits uncomfortably with broader ideas—explored in Chapter 5—about the relationship between legislation and the rule of law. As we have seen, while it is generally accepted that Parliament is sovereign—meaning that it can, in theory, do as it pleases—substantial protection is conferred upon the rule of law by means of statutory interpretation.[40] Courts habitually and consistently justify this approach by recourse to the simple, but important, presumption that Parliament legislates not in a vacuum, but 'for a European liberal democracy founded on the principles and traditions of the common law'.[41] The difficulty, therefore, with Laws' defence of the common law theory of judicial review is that it requires us to suppose that Parliament is agnostic about the rule-of-law values that judicial review protects. That supposition is diametrically opposed to the usual (and arguably more natural) presumption that Parliament intends to respect the rule of law—a presumption that is widely invoked by the courts as an aid to statutory construction.

5.4 Development of the *ultra vires* theory

Those commentators who do not find the defence of the common law theory convincing have instead focused on developing the *ultra vires* theory, with the intention of equipping it to provide a more convincing account of the constitutional justification for judicial review.[42] It will be recalled that the principal difficulty with the *ultra vires* theory relates to the *direct* relationship that it postulates between the intention of Parliament and the various, detailed grounds of judicial review that courts enforce today. This, as we have seen, is fundamentally implausible: as Forsyth acknowledges, '[n]o-one is so innocent as to suppose that judicial creativity does not form [in the sense of having contributed to the development of] the grounds of judicial review'.[43] It follows that the question for *ultra vires* theorists is whether it is possible to identify a more plausible relationship between the will of Parliament and the grounds of judicial review. In this regard, it has been argued that such a relationship may be articulated—based not on the discredited assumption that every last detail of the grounds of judicial

---

[39] See, eg *Lloyd v McMahon* [1987] AC 625, *per* Lord Keith.

[40] See, eg *Anisminic Ltd v Foreign Compensation Commission* [1969] 2 AC 147; *R v Lord Chancellor, ex p Witham* [1998] QB 575.

[41] *R v Secretary of State for the Home Department, ex p Pierson* [1998] AC 539, 587, *per* Lord Steyn.

[42] See Forsyth, above; Elliott, above.   [43] Forsyth at 136.

review can be traced to (largely unexpressed) parliamentary intention, but on the more modest presumption that Parliament intends the powers that it creates to be exercised in conformity with the rule of law, while leaving it to the courts to work out what this means in individual cases.

On this view, there is a connection—but merely an indirect connection—between what courts do in judicial review proceedings and the intention of Parliament. The courts' role is to take Parliament's (presumed) intention that decision-makers should respect the rule of law, and to work out what limitations or grounds of review should be developed to give effect to that constitutional principle. On this view, our hypothetical Minister, when exercising his power to decide whether to grant permission for a new airport, would find himself obliged to exercise the power subject to (*inter alia*) the various principles of procedural fairness that we consider in Chapter 13—not because Parliament intended the detailed content of those principles, but because the courts have developed them against the background of Parliament's general intention that ministerial discretion should be exercised compatibly with the rule of law.

5.5 **A more radical view**

The differences between the *ultra vires* and common law schools of thought represent a disagreement about the *implications* of parliamentary sovereignty—in particular, whether (as the *ultra vires* theorists would have us believe) it requires judicial review to be justified by reference to the will of Parliament, if only indirectly, or (as the common law theory holds) mandates no such relationship between parliamentary intention and the grounds of judicial review. Yet the *ultra vires* and common law schools are united in one important respect: both assume Parliament to be sovereign, and then attempt to justify judicial review taking parliamentary sovereignty as a given.

It is this aspect of the debate with which Allan takes issue.[44] He accepts that the common law theory is, as the *ultra vires* theorists contend, incompatible with full respect for the sovereignty of Parliament—but goes on to argue that since, in his view, Parliament is *not* sovereign, it is unnecessary to justify judicial review by reference to the intention of Parliament. In particular, Allan says that the principles that courts uphold on judicial review are constitutional fundamentals, hardwired into the constitution as restraints on the authority of Parliament itself. So while, to the question 'why are decision-makers required to act fairly?', *ultra vires* theorists would respond, 'because Parliament, directly or indirectly, so intends', Allan would say, 'because Parliament can only create decision-making powers which can be exercised in line with fundamental constitutional principles such as procedural fairness'. In this sense, Allan's view can be thought of as a form of *constitutional* theory of *ultra vires*. The end result (that the power to breach important rule of law-based principles is withheld

---

[44] 'The Constitutional Foundations of Judicial Review: Conceptual Conundrum or Interpretative Inquiry?' [2002] CLJ 87.

from decision-makers) is the same whether we subscribe to the standard *ultra vires* theory or Allan's constitutional version thereof. The reasoning, however, is significantly different: in Allan's argument, the intention of Parliament is beside the point, because higher-order constitutional principles prevent it, in the first place, from creating decision-making powers that are free from obligations to respect the fundamental norms enforced via judicial review.

Q Would Allan's argument, if accepted, support or undermine the common law theory of judicial review?

Approached on this basis, the debate over the constitutional foundations of judicial review is part of the much broader debate that we encountered in Chapter 5 concerning the constitutional status of Parliament—and, in particular, the question of whether its lawmaking power is legally unbounded. Allan's position is logically unassailable. If, as he contends, Parliament is not sovereign, and if, as he contends, the principles of judicial review are constitutional fundamentals from which Parliament is impotent to deviate, then it is the constitution itself—not the intention of Parliament—that justifies courts in striking down administrative decisions that contravene those principles. But this merely begs the bigger questions: is Parliament sovereign? And do the principles of judicial review have the fundamental status that Allan ascribes to them?

As we saw in Chapter 5, these questions are difficult to answer, at least by reference to positive law, because courts are rarely required to face squarely up to them—and even when they are, they generally prefer to avoid directly answering them. For example, we saw in Chapter 5 that, in the *Anisminic* case,[45] when faced with an 'ouster clause' that seemed to prevent judicial review of certain decisions—a situation that would have been inconsistent with the requirements of the rule of law—the House of Lords chose to neutralise it by engaging in what it characterised as statutory interpretation (so as to preserve a veneer of fidelity to parliamentary intention) rather than asserting a power to strike down, or refusing to apply, the offending clause. Yet some commentators, reading between the lines, argue that the Lords' policy in that case was actually 'one of total disobedience to Parliament', the implication being that judicial review was actually regarded as a constitutional fundamental that Parliament was powerless to displace.[46]

Succour has recently been given to this point of view by the *Jackson* case,[47] in which Lord Steyn remarked that if Parliament were to attempt to abolish judicial review, the courts would have to determine 'whether this is a constitutional fundamental which

---

[45] *Anisminic Ltd v Foreign Compensation Commission* [1969] 2 AC 147.

[46] Wade and Forsyth, *Administrative Law* (Oxford 2009), p 616.

[47] *R (Jackson) v Attorney General* [2005] UKHL 56, [2006] 1 AC 262; see Chapter 5, section 4.5.4, above for fuller discussion.

even a sovereign Parliament…cannot abolish'.[48] Similarly, Baroness Hale said: 'The courts will treat with particular suspicion (and might even reject) any attempt to subvert the rule of law by removing governmental action affecting the rights of the individual from all judicial scrutiny.'[49] Of course, these were merely *obiter dicta* and, in any event, their Lordships were guarded in how they expressed their views. Yet the very fact that the Law Lords were prepared to make such statements from the bench demonstrates that the supremacy of Parliament is not the sacred beast that it once was—and that if the judges ever decide that our unwritten constitution has evolved to a point at which the doctrine of parliamentary sovereignty can be discarded, the principles of judicial review are prime candidates for recognition as constitutional fundamentals limiting the legislature's freedom of action. If that day ever comes, it will have important consequences for the debate about the constitutional foundations of judicial review, and it will be difficult to resist the logic of Allan's position.

6. Concluding remarks

In the next chapter, we will focus on the law of judicial review as a subject in its own right by examining the content of the principles to which courts require decision-makers to adhere when exercising statutory and other powers. But, in this chapter, we have seen that judicial review is not something that can, or should, be studied in isolation. We have, for example, seen that the debate about the constitutional foundations of judicial review is, in truth, part of a much broader discussion concerning *the relationship between Parliament and the courts*—and even about *the veracity of the doctrine of parliamentary sovereignty* itself. We have also seen that judicial review impacts upon—and can only properly be understood in relation to—the three key themes with which we are concerned in this book. Thus, judicial review is an important mechanism for *holding the executive branch of government to account*, and the reliance that we place on judicial—as opposed to, say, parliamentary—systems of accountability is an important facet of the broader debate about *political and legal constitutionalism*. Meanwhile, the *multilayered nature* of the modern British constitution means that courts have acquired new responsibilities for settling demarcation disputes between different governing institutions. For all of these reasons, studying the law of judicial review—which is the task to which we now turn—is important not only for its own sake, but also for what it tells us about these broader and deeper issues with which we must grapple as we come to terms with the contemporary UK constitution.

---

[48] *Jackson* at [102]. See also Lord Hope's remarks at [104].   [49] *Jackson* at [159].

Further reading

ARTHURS, 'Rethinking Administrative Law: A Slightly Dicey Business' (1979) 17 Osgoode Hall
    Law Journal 1

FORSYTH (ed), *Judicial Review and the Constitution* (Oxford 2000)

GRIFFITH, 'The Common Law and the Political Constitution' (2001) 117 LQR 42

HARLOW AND RAWLINGS, *Law and Administration* (Cambridge 2009)

SEDLEY, 'Governments, Constitutions and Judges', in Richardson and Genn (eds), *Administrative Law and Government Action* (Oxford 1994)

13 The Grounds of Judicial Review

1. An example

In this chapter, we explore the content of the law of judicial review—that is, the legal standards to which the courts require government decision-makers to adhere.[1] In order to provide a practical context in which to explore these matters, we will make use, throughout this chapter, of an example. It will be developed as the chapter progresses, but for the time being, it takes the following form:

> The (imaginary) Planning and Infrastructure Act 2010 provides that, whereas requests for planning permission are normally dealt with by local authorities, 'the Secretary of State may decide whether—and, if so, subject to what conditions, if any—permission should be granted for major infrastructure projects'.
>
> A major airport operating company wishes to build a new airport. However, it anticipates that the local authority, which has a track record of refusing to allow developments unless they are environmentally friendly, will decline to grant permission. It therefore asks the Secretary of State to intervene by exercising the power set out above.

2. Interpreting and applying the statute

2.1 Introduction

Most power exercised by public bodies is granted by statute. Parliament enacts legislation authorising Ministers (and others) to make certain decisions. Our example, above, is a case in point. We noted in Chapter 12 that the law imposes numerous conditions on the exercise of such powers. Many such conditions are not immediately obvious from the

---

[1] This chapter is concerned principally with English law, but virtually all of what is said here is equally applicable in Scotland, given that, according to the Court of Session, there is 'no substantial difference between English law and Scots law as to the grounds on which the process of decision-making may be open to review': *West v Secretary of State for Scotland* 1992 SC 385, 413. This statement notwithstanding, there is at least one area in which a different approach appears to prevail in Scotland: see section 2.2 below.

text of the legislation;[2] but we begin with those that are. When legislation authorises a Minister or another public body to do something, it is implicit in the wording that the power is limited. For example, the above statute only authorises the Secretary of State to deal with 'major infrastructure projects'. What if the Minister, purporting to exercise this power, grants permission for the construction of a small airport? Is this within his power? Who should decide what counts as a 'major infrastructure project'? And who should decide whether a small airport falls into this category?

These may appear to be very lawyerly questions, which concern fine distinctions—but they raise important practical issues. Suppose, for example, that a government committed to economic growth, but unconcerned about the environmental consequences of air transport, attempted to use this power to override the views of an eco-conscious local authority that was opposed to the construction of the new airport. The questions here under consideration—that is, those that are set out in the bottom left-hand portion of Figure 13.1—may be of crucial importance. If it is for the court to decide whether the airport constitutes a 'major infrastructure project', and if it decides that it is not, this will prevent the Minister from intervening, because his power only applies to 'major infrastructure projects'. And these questions about the demarcation of powers—here, the demarcation of Ministers' and local authorities' powers—reflect

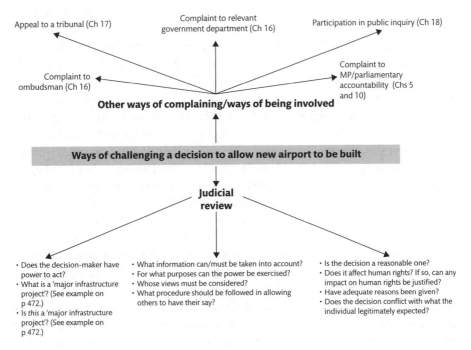

Figure 13.1 Judicial review and the wider administrative justice system

---

2 For example, the above imaginary statute does not say that the Minister must act fairly.

important underlying policy concerns. In our imaginary statute, Parliament has evidently made a policy decision about the respective roles of local councils and central government in relation to the planning process—the thinking being that the former should generally have responsibility (given the obvious local sensitivities involved in planning decisions), but that the latter should become involved where the scale of a project is such as to make it of more than merely local significance.

Whenever a Minister or other decision-maker is contemplating exercising a statutory power, he must, before addressing the *merits question* over which he would have discretion ('should I allow this project to go ahead?'), address a prior issue, known as the *jurisdictional question* ('do I have power to decide this matter?'). Jurisdictional questions can conveniently be broken down, at least for the purposes of explanation, into two stages.

2.2 **The meaning of the statute**

The first question concerns the meaning of the statute. If the Minister is to try to work out whether he has the power to deal with the matter, and if he only has power if the matter concerns a 'major infrastructure project', then he must first address the meaning of that term. Such questions, since they involve the interpretation of a statute, are generally regarded as *questions of law*. The general principle is that, while Ministers and other decision-makers must inevitably try to answer such questions (in order to work out whether they have power to deal with the matter at hand), the courts (if the matter reaches them by virtue of being litigated) have the final say. This is the principal hallmark of judicial review of jurisdictional questions: whereas courts will not second-guess decision-makers on the merits of the decision ('should the airport be built?'), courts can and do override decision-makers on jurisdictional questions ('what does "major infrastructure project" mean?'). What this means, in other words, is that judges can *substitute* their view of the meaning of the statute for that of the Minister.

This matter was addressed by the House of Lords in the celebrated case of *Anisminic*.[3] Property belonging to the claimant company, Anisminic, had been confiscated by the Egyptian authorities in 1956; the Egyptian government later paid a lump sum to the United Kingdom government to be distributed by the latter to those whose assets had been affected in this way. This task fell to the Foreign Compensation Commission,[4] to which Anisminic applied without success. The Commission ruled that Anisminic was ineligible for compensation because, in its view, the relevant legislation precluded claims in which the successor-in-title to the property concerned—that is, the subsequent owner—was a non-British national. Anisminic, on the other hand, contended that the Commission had misunderstood the legislation, and that, properly construed, it imposed no requirement with respect to the nationality of the subsequent owner. The question for the Court, therefore, was whether the Commission's interpretation of the legislation should stand. Their Lordships held that it should not. Lord Wilberforce pointed out that

---

[3] *Anisminic Ltd v Foreign Compensation Commission* [1969] 2 AC 147.
[4] Established by the Foreign Compensation Act 1950.

the Commission had 'a derived authority, derived, that is, from statute: at some point, and to be found from a consideration of the legislation, the field within which it operates is marked out and limited'.[5] In similar vein, Lord Reid observed that '[i]t cannot be for the commission to determine the limits of its powers.... [I]f they reach a wrong conclusion as to the width of their powers, the court must be able to correct that'.[6] By a majority, their Lordships concluded that just such a conclusion had been reached, ruling that, on the correct interpretation—that is, the *judges'* interpretation—the legislation did not require consideration of the nationality of Anisminic's successor-in-title.

After this decision was handed down, there was some confusion as to its precise effect.[7] Clearly, their Lordships had treated the *particular question of law* that arose in *Anisminic* as one on which they, as a court, had the final say. But did this mean that *all questions of statutory interpretation* should be treated in this way, such that the decision-maker's conclusion would always be capable of being overturned if a reviewing court were to take a different view? There was little clarity on this point until the later decision of the House of Lords in *Page*, in which Lord Browne-Wilkinson articulated the general principle that decisions affected by errors of law can be quashed on judicial review.[8] This prompts us to ask two questions: *why should courts exercise such power* and *what are the exceptions to this general principle*? It is convenient to deal with these questions in tandem because, as we will see, the limits of the justifications for the general principle help to shape the exceptions to it.

The first (of three) potential justifications concerns the notion of *relative institutional competence*—which essentially holds that courts, being better qualified than decision-makers in relation to legal matters, should have the final say on them. Although this argument is superficially attractive, the assumption upon which it rests is, at best, a half-truth, for it does not follow that courts are *inevitably* better placed than decision-makers to interpret the statute.

> **Q** Arden LJ has noted that courts often approach questions of statutory interpretation 'by peeling away the layers of meaning and by analysing the policy choices that have been made to arrive at the form of words that has been used. In other words, statutory interpretation is an intensive exercise that involves *drilling down* into the substratum of meaning of the statutory provision'.[9] In the example set out at the beginning of the chapter, the Minister is only authorised to take planning decisions in relation to 'major infrastructure projects'. What sort of policy and other factors might influence the court in attaching meaning to the term 'major infrastructure project'?

---

[5] *Anisminic* at 207.   [6] *Anisminic* at 184.

[7] See, eg *Pearlman v Keepers and Governors of Harrow School* [1979] QB 56; *South East Asia Fire Bricks Sdn Bhd v Non-Metallic Mineral Products Manufacturing Employees Union* [1981] AC 363.

[8] *R v Lord President of the Privy Council, ex p Page* [1993] AC 682. No such general principle is recognised in Scotland, where the concept of non-jurisdictional errors of law continues to be recognised: *Watt v Lord Advocate* 1979 SC 120, 131. However, in *Eba v Adovate General for Scotland* [2010] CSIH 78, [46], the Inner House of the Court of Session (in *obiter* comments) cast some doubt on this view.

[9] Arden, 'The Changing Judicial Role: Human Rights, Community Law and the Intention of Parliament' [2008] CLJ 487, 490.

Arden LJ's comments indicate that judges may not have a monopoly of wisdom in this area: answering 'legal' questions of statutory interpretation may require policy choices to be made. English courts have therefore recognised (with varying degrees of clarity) a number of exceptions to the general principle that they should have the last word on questions of law. For example, when, in *Page*, the reviewing Court was confronted with a system of law (the statutes of a university) unfamiliar to it, it did not substitute its interpretation for that of the decision-maker. And even if the law in question is the regular law of the land, the reviewing court may still be willing to allow the decision-maker's interpretation of it to stand if the decision-maker is a legally competent one, such as another court.[10] More generally, it has been said that when the statutory provision under consideration is extremely vague, the reviewing court will not simply impose its own view—because it cannot be confident that it is the correct one. Instead, it will interfere only if the decision-maker has adopted an unreasonable definition of the term.[11]

The second factor that arguably justifies giving courts ultimate power over questions of law is the *independence of the judiciary*. Farina argues that where 'the consequence of adopting one interpretation of the statute over another is to subject an individual to civil or criminal penalties for her past behavior', fairness demands that the decision is taken by one 'whose life tenure and salary protection promote impartiality, objectivity and insulation from political pressure'—in other words, a judge.[12] However, this argument will not always be compelling. Not all questions of interpretation are like the ones Farina describes. If a statute confers discretion in broad terms that raise controversial policy questions, the reverse argument may apply: it may be more appropriate to leave the decision to (for example) an elected decision-maker. For example, in *Puhlhofer*, the claimant was eligible for assistance from his local authority if he was homeless—which he would be if he had no 'accommodation' within the meaning of the relevant legislation.[13] Rather than treating the meaning of the word 'accommodation' as a question of law, the House of Lords instead said that it was a question of fact for the local authority to determine. This carried significant consequences for the power of local authorities in this area. Allowing councils to reach their own definition of 'accommodation' meant that they could control the breadth of the category of persons eligible for homelessness support.

The final factor said to justify giving the last word to courts is *consistency*. In *Pearlman*, Lord Denning argued that it would be 'intolerable' if different decision-makers were allowed to reach conflicting interpretations of legislation.[14] He therefore

---

[10] *Re Racal Communications Ltd* [1981] AC 374, 383, *per* Lord Diplock. See also *R (Cart) v Upper Tribunal* [2010] EWCA Civ 859, discussed in Chapter 17, section 5.6, below.

[11] *R v Monopolies and Mergers Commission, ex p South Yorkshire Transport* [1993] 1 WLR 23.

[12] Farina, 'Statutory Interpretation and the Balance of Power in the Administrative State' (1989) 89 Columbia Law Review 452, 453. See also Hare, 'The Separation of Powers and Judicial Review for Error of Law', in Forsyth and Hare (eds), *The Golden Metwand and the Crooked Cord* (Oxford 1998).

[13] *R v Hillingdon London Borough Council, ex p Puhlhofer* [1986] AC 484.

[14] *Pearlman v Keepers and Governors of Harrow School* [1979] QB 56.

thought that reviewing courts should always have the ultimate power to determine the meaning of the law in the interests of consistency. However, while consistency may often be desirable, it is not necessarily a knock-out argument. There may, for example, only be one decision-maker, in which case the need for consistency as between decision-makers is irrelevant. And even if there are many different decision-makers (for example, if the power is given to all local authorities), it does not automatically follow that consistency is more important than, say, allowing each body to reach its own interpretation in the light of its own expertise and experience of local circumstances.

Q Think back to the example, given above, of a ministerial power to approve 'major infrastructure projects'. Should the definition of this statutory term be regarded as a question of law such that the reviewing court, if it were to disagree with the Minister's definition, could substitute it with its own?

The position, then, is that (subject to the exceptions considered above) questions of law are jurisdictional ones. The upshot is that decision-makers have very little latitude in this area: the court's view will generally prevail in the event of disagreement. Whether this state of affairs is acceptable depends on how convincing the justifications set out above are considered to be. Williams, for one, thinks that the present position emphasises judicial control at the expense of administrative autonomy. She argues that courts should only substitute their view for that of the decision-maker where the question at issue has only one, objectively correct answer, otherwise limiting themselves to intervening where the decision-maker has adopted an unreasonable interpretation of the statute.[15] So, in our hypothetical case, the Minister would be free to adopt any reasonable definition of 'major infrastructure project', since this term does not have one inherently and objectively correct meaning. The position would only be different if the legislation were to provide an objective definition. For example, if the statute were to say that a 'major infrastructure project' was one that would, when built, cover an area of at least 10 km^2, there would be no room for argument, and the court could intervene if the Minister were to adopt a different definition. Williams adopts this approach because, she says, 'where there is no objectively right answer the court must accept that it is not detecting errors at all, rather it is reviewing the exercise of the initial decision-maker's discretion'—and it must therefore limit itself to interfering only if the decision-maker has acted unreasonably.[16]

Q Do you agree? How does Williams's approach relate to the arguments about institutional competence, independence, and consistency, considered above, in favour of stricter judicial control?

---

[15] Williams, 'When is an Error Not an Error? Reform of Jurisdictional Review of Error of Law and Fact' [2007] PL 793.   [16] Williams at 798.

Williams's approach would, if adopted, have important implications, enhancing the autonomy of government decision-makers, while restricting the power of courts to intervene in their decisions. The fact that, at present, the courts exert a relatively high degree of control in this context relates back to our key themes, since it implies an emphasis on legal, rather than political, mechanisms for securing the responsible use of governmental power.

2.3 **Applying the statute to the facts**

Even if our hypothetical Minister adopts a lawful *definition* of 'major infrastructure project', this is not an end of the matter, for he must, within our example, then decide whether the proposed airport is, *in fact*, such a project. As indicated in Figure 13.2, this is analogous to working out whether two pieces of a jigsaw fit together. In strict logic, a distinction should be drawn between what we call in Figure 13.2 'questions of fact' and 'questions of fit'—that is, it must logically be necessary to determine *both* what the relevant factual characteristics are *and* whether those factual characteristics fit the statutory definition. In relation to our example, depending on the correct definition of 'major infrastructure project', the relevant questions of fact may involve looking at the physical size and location of the proposed airport, its likely economic impact, and its overall significance. Having determined these matters, it would then be necessary to move on to the question of fit: given the proposed airport's size, impact, and on so, does it constitute a 'major infrastructure project', thus triggering the Minister's legal capacity to wrest from the local authority the power to decide whether the scheme should go ahead?

In reality, neither decision-makers nor reviewing courts necessarily draw a clear distinction between questions of fact and fit, often treating them as linked or even inseparable matters. This notwithstanding, the key question for our purposes is: who has the final say as to whether the facts satisfy the statutory test? For example, is it ultimately for the Minister to decide whether the characteristics of the proposed

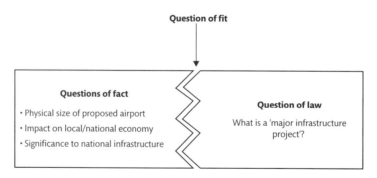

Do the two pieces of the jigsaw fit together?
Who decides whether they fit together?

Figure 13.2 Applying the facts to the law

airport satisfy the statutory definition of 'major infrastructure project', or can the court overturn the Minister's view on this point if it disagrees with him?

There is no 'one-size-fits-all' answer to this question. The case law reveals varying judicial attitudes, principally informed, it seems, by the objectivity of the criterion laid down by the statute. This is illustrated by the Supreme Court's decision in *R (A) v Croydon London Borough Council*.[17] The case centred upon s 20(1) of the Children Act 1989. The section states that local authorities must provide accommodation for any 'child in need' within their area who appears to require accommodation on one of several grounds.[18] There was no dispute as to the meaning of the statute—the Act says that 'child' means 'person under the age of 18'[19]—but the defendant councils asserted that the claimants were not under the age of 18 and that no duty to provide accommodation therefore arose. Were the councils' views final (unless unreasonable) or could the court overturn them if it disagreed? The Supreme Court held that the clarity and objectivity of the term 'child' pointed to the latter conclusion: as Baroness Hale put it, 'the question whether a person is a "child"...is a [question with a] right or wrong answer'.[20] The position is different in relation to the question whether an individual is a 'child *in need*', however. As Baroness Hale observed, answering this question involves making value judgements that 'it is entirely reasonable to assume that Parliament intended...to be [made] by the public authority'.[21] This case shows, then, that the more objective a statutory term, the more likely the court is to insist on the final word on questions of fit. It also shows that where a composite term, such as 'child in need', is used, different approaches may apply to each component if one is more objective than the other.

> **Q** In our example, the question is whether the proposed airport is a 'major infrastructure project'. In light of the discussion above, do you think that a reviewing court would interfere with the Minister's conclusion on that point if it were to disagree with it, or only if the Minister were to have come to a perverse or unreasonable conclusion?

3. Acting fairly

3.1 Introduction

Up to now in this chapter, we have been concerned with how to determine *whether a decision-maker's power (or duty) to act is triggered*. In our example, therefore, the question has been whether the Minister has power to decide (in place of the local authority) whether a new airport should be built. This, as we know, depends on

---

[17] [2009] UKSC 8, [2009] 1 WLR 2557. See also *Khawaja v Secretary of State for the Home Department* [1984] AC 74.   [18] For example, that there is no one who has parental responsibility for him.
[19] Children Act 1989, s 105(1).   [20] *Croydon* at [27].   [21] *Croydon* at [26].

whether the airport constitutes a 'major infrastructure project'. If it is, the Minister has the power to decide, but this does not mean that he has free reign to do as he wishes. The role of the law in this sphere is not limited to determining whether there has been compliance with the statute so as to trigger the legitimate exercise of power: the law is also concerned to ensure that administrative power, when it is exercisable, is used only in legally acceptable ways. To this end, the courts have developed a range of principles with which decision-makers must comply when exercising power.[22] We begin with the principles of natural justice.

3.2 **Different senses of 'fairness'**

Most people have an instinctive sense of what it means to act 'fairly'. Administrative law imposes upon decision-makers a *duty to act fairly*, the content of which is perhaps more precise and limited than—but still related to—colloquial notions of fairness. In particular, administrative lawyers make a distinction between two sorts of fairness that are not, in popular consciousness, necessarily differentiated. The distinction relates to *procedural* and *substantive* notions of fairness. The former is concerned with *process* (was the decision made in a fair way?), the latter with *outcomes* (was the decision, at the end of the day, a fair one, or did it, for example, benefit one person or group at the expense of unjustly penalising some other person or group?).

Administrative law is not unconcerned with fairness in the substantive, outcomes-oriented sense. This sense of fairness is protected, *inter alia*, by the requirements—which we will examine later—that decision-makers should, in certain circumstances, act consistently with their own policies or with what the individual in question reasonably expected, and that they must not unjustifiably sacrifice the individual's human rights for the benefit of others.

However, when we speak of the duty to act fairly—or of the doctrine of 'natural justice'—in administrative law, we are almost invariably referring to fairness in its procedural sense. It is with that type of fairness that we are concerned in this section. In particular, we are concerned with three elements of procedural fairness: the absence of bias, the existence of institutional independence, and the right to participate in the decision-making process (commonly, but inaccurately, called 'the right to a fair hearing'). We will unpack each of these three notions in what follows, but it may be helpful to say something briefly about each of them—by reference to our example—at the outset.

Let us assume that our imaginary Minister does have the power to decide whether or not permission should be given for the new airport to be built. In exercising that power, he is obliged to act fairly. This means, first of all, that he must not be (or appear to be) biased—that is, he must not be subject, actually or apparently, to being influenced by extraneous factors such as financial benefit or personal connections with the

---

[22] See the bottom-centre and bottom-right portions of Figure 13.1 above.

parties. Second, the law requires certain decisions to be taken with some degree of independence from the executive branch of government: we shall explore later whether this requirement applies in circumstances such as those of our example. Third, our hypothetical Minister is required to allow certain parties—for example, those living near the site of the proposed airport—to participate appropriately in the decision-making process. There are many different ways in which such participation may be facilitated and, depending on the circumstances, something as modest as allowing people to make written representations may suffice, whereas sometimes nothing short of a full oral hearing will do.

3.3 **Why act fairly?**

In the following sections, we will consider the three aspects of procedural fairness outlined above. First, however, we address a more general issue. The desirability of acting fairly is perhaps obvious—why would anyone *not* want an unbiased decision-maker who allows them to have their say by participating in the process?—but is nevertheless worth addressing. When we stop to think about this matter, it becomes apparent that there are two distinct reasons for requiring public bodies to adopt fair procedures.

The first reason is a predominantly practical one. Good government, in the sense of making sensible, evidence-based decisions that best promote the public interest and strike an appropriate balance between competing sets of interests, is possible only if those who are responsible for taking decisions are in the first place in receipt of as much relevant information as they reasonably can be. For example, it is obviously desirable that our hypothetical Minister, before deciding whether to authorise construction of the new airport, should be aware of relevant information about the proposal. Is a new airport needed in this location? Could the existing road network cope with the extra traffic that an airport would generate? What would be the environmental impact of the scheme? Would the scheme bring sufficient economic gains? Only if the Minister is in a position to answer these questions can he sensibly exercise his discretion. It therefore follows that a procedure must be adopted that will harvest the raw data on which the decision will be based. As we will see, this may, for example, involve taking expert evidence about the probable impact of the airport, allowing environmentalists and business lobbyists to present—and challenge one another's—contrasting views, and listening to local people's opinions about whether their area should be transformed by such a major project. Viewed in this way, the notion of procedural fairness is a means to an end: it ensures that an information-gathering process is conducted in order that good decisions might be made.

For some, this *instrumental* view of fairness is predominant: it supplies the main justification for requiring decision-makers to act fairly.[23] Others, however, emphasise

---

[23] See, eg Galligan, *Due Process and Fair Procedures: A Study of Administrative Procedures* (Oxford 1996); *Secretary of State for the Home Department v AF (No 3)* [2009] UKHL 28, [2009] 3 WLR 74, [60], *per* Lord Phillips.

what we might call a *non-instrumental* conception of fairness that presents proced-ural fairness as an end in itself, not merely a means to some other end.[24] This view is premised on what Tribe has called 'the elementary idea that to be a *person*, rather than a *thing*, is at least to be *consulted* about what is done with one'.[25] In other words, if the dignity and status of individuals is to be properly respected, they must at least be given the opportunity to have their views listened to before the taking of decisions that are liable to affect them.

Of course, these two views are not necessarily in tension: it might reasonably be argued that fair treatment should be accorded to individuals *both* because this is necessary if due respect is to be accorded to their status as a human being *and* because it is likely to enable better decisions to be taken.[26] However, there may be circumstances in which the two views conflict. For example, where the evidence in favour of a par-ticular decision is very strong, going through some form of fair procedure may seem to serve little practical purpose: it seems obvious from the outset what the decision should be, and it is arguably a waste of time and money to delay the inevitable by first holding (for example) a hearing. Courts have certainly found this argument persua-sive on occasion. Consider, for example, the case of *R (National Association of Health Stores) v Department of Health*,[27] which concerned the legality of the defendant's deci-sion to ban on health grounds a herbal remedy known as kava-kava from being sold for medicinal purposes and used in foodstuffs. Having (as statutorily required) consulted certain parties, on both the possibility of banning kava-kava outright and making it available only on prescription, the Minister imposed an outright ban. The claimant challenged the decision, arguing that the consultation was flawed because there had been no consultation on the option of compulsory labelling of products containing kava-kava. The Department, however, argued that this would have made no differ-ence: since it had concluded that making the substance available only on prescription would not have constituted an adequate safeguard, it was inevitable that the less dras-tic option of compulsory labelling would have been judged inadequate, whether or not it had been consulted upon. The court agreed with this analysis.

The broad conclusions that we can draw from this case—and indeed from the gen-eral tenor of the case law—are as follows. First, the court's willingness, in the *Health Stores* case, to accept the claimant's argument—that a particular procedural step did not have to be taken because it would have made no difference to the outcome of the decision-making process—implies that the court took a predominantly instrumental view of fairness: dispensing with a particular form of procedure was acceptable pro-vided that the court was satisfied that this had not undermined the quality of the deci-sion itself. Second, however, this does not imply that courts will readily sacrifice due

---

[24] The other end being the making of good decisions.

[25] *American Constitutional Law* (New York 1988), p 666.

[26] See further Allan, 'Procedural Fairness and the Duty of Respect' (1998) 18 OJLS 497.

[27] [2005] EWCA Civ 154; The Times, 9 March 2005. See also *Cinnamond v British Airports Authority* [1980] 1 WLR 582; *Malloch v Aberdeen Corporation* [1971] 1 WLR 1578.

process on the altar of efficiency. The danger of doing so was highlighted by Megarry J in *John v Rees*,[28] who cautioned that 'the path of the law is strewn with examples of open and shut cases which, somehow, were not; of unanswerable charges which, in the event, were completely answered; of inexplicable conduct which was fully explained; of fixed and unalterable determinations that, by discussion, suffered a change'. Thus it is plain that courts should view with extreme caution the argument that adopting a given procedure would make no difference to the outcome, since it cannot generally be predicted what information would turn up if a given procedure were adopted. Against this background, we can appreciate why the *Health Stores* case was decided the way that it was. Sedley LJ said that it was a 'laboratory example' of a case in which it *was* safe to assume that the more extensive consultation contended for by the claimant would have made no difference: given that 'it was concluded that placing usage and dosage in the hands of qualified medical practitioners was not a sufficient safeguard, the rule-maker could not rationally have concluded, whatever the input from consultation, that a warning on the label would suffice'.[29]

Q Do you agree that decision-makers should be relieved of the obligation to act fairly to the extent that it would make no difference to the outcome? Is the emphasis, which is apparent in the case law, on the instrumental value of fairness always appropriate? For example, should Ministers and other public bodies ever be excused from adopting a fair procedure because it would make no difference in circumstances in which the personal liberty of an individual is at stake?

3.4 **Impartiality**

Against this background, we begin our examination of the principles of natural justice with the requirement that decision-makers be impartial. As we do so, it is worth pointing out that although many of the cases considered in this section concern judges, the same principles, subject to what is said below in section 3.4.3, apply to administrative decision-makers.

It stands to reason that if a decision-maker is actually biased, the process cannot be said to be fair. It is therefore unlawful for a decision-maker to decide a case in order (for example) to secure some financial benefit for himself or in order to do a favour for a friend. However, actual bias is hard to establish. Showing that a decision-maker *stood to gain* financially from his decision is one thing; proving that he was *actually influenced* by such selfish considerations is a different, and more difficult, matter. It follows that if the law were to go no further than a rule against actual bias, many situations would arise in which there was a suspicion that the decision-maker may have been improperly influenced, but the decision would nevertheless stand in the absence

---

[28] [1970] Ch 345, 402.   [29] *National Association of Health Stores* at [21]–[22].

of clear evidence. This, in turn, would be likely to undermine public confidence in the integrity of the decision-making system.

The law in this area therefore embraces not only a rule against actual bias, but also a rule against apparent bias. The principle was famously set out in *R v Sussex Justices, ex p McCarthy*,[30] in which a justices' clerk who retired with the magistrates in a dangerous driving case also happened to be a partner in the law firm that was acting against the defendant in a related civil action. When this fact came to the notice of the defendant, he sought to have his dangerous driving conviction quashed. Lord Hewart CJ, giving judgment in the Divisional Court, accepted that the clerk had, in fact, played no part in the justices' decision: he had been in the room when the decision was made, but the justices had not found it necessary to consult him. Nevertheless, said Lord Hewart, 'it is not merely of some importance but is of fundamental importance that justice should not only be done, but should manifestly and undoubtedly be seen to be done'.[31] Applying this principle, the conviction was quashed because the clerk's conflict of interest gave rise to a sufficient appearance of bias; proof of actual bias was unnecessary.

3.4.1 Interests that automatically disqualify the decision-maker

Ideally, situations such as those that arose in *McCarthy* should not arise. Decision-makers should decline to act if their participation would give rise to an appearance of bias (unless the parties are willing to overlook the apparent conflict of interests[32]). The advantages of this approach are considerable: situations are avoided in which decisions are made pursuant to long, complex, and costly processes, only to be overturned in light of a conflict of interest that should have been apparent all along. However, if the law is to work in this efficient manner, it must be sufficiently clear and straightforward: decision-makers must be able to determine with some certainty whether, in the first place, they have a sufficient interest in the outcome of the process as to require them to disclose it to the parties. In order to obviate the need for decision-makers to agonise or weigh finely balanced arguments, the law has come to recognise three types of interest that automatically disqualify the decision-maker: interests arising from being a party, from having a financial interest in the outcome of the decision, and from particularly close alignment with a party and its interests. Applying a rule of automatic disqualification to such interests promotes legal certainty, which is advantageous for the reasons just mentioned.

First, then, and most straightforwardly, there are those cases in which the decision-maker is a party. This reflects what Lord Browne-Wilkinson referred to as the 'fundamental principle...that a man may not be a judge in his own cause'.[33] The reason for

---

30 [1924] 1 KB 256.   31 *McCarthy* at 259.

32 Provided that the parties are in full receipt of the relevant facts and unequivocally signal that they are content to allow the decision-maker to participate, they may not subsequently raise an objection on the grounds of apparent bias: *Locabail (UK) Ltd v Bayfield Properties Ltd* [2000] QB 451, 475.

33 *R v Bow Street Metropolitan Stipendiary Magistrate, ex p Pinochet Ugarte (No 2)* [2000] 1 AC 119, 132.

treating such a situation as automatically disqualifying the decision-maker needs no explanation.

It is also widely held that where the decision-maker has a financial or proprietary interest in the outcome of the decision, this is tantamount to his acting as a judge in his own cause; such interests are therefore held to disqualify the decision-maker automatically. The classic application of this principle occurred in *Dimes v The Proprietors of the Grand Junction Canal*,[34] in which the decision of no less a figure than the then Lord Chancellor, Lord Cottenham—who had, in legal proceedings, granted relief to a company in which he was a shareholder—was quashed. Giving judgment in the House of Lords, Lord Campbell said that 'the maxim that no man is to be a judge in his own cause... is not to be confined to a cause in which he is a party, but [also] applies to a cause in which he has an interest'.[35] Two points should be noted in connection with the *Dimes* principle.

First, its usefulness has been called into question. Lord Campbell argued that it was necessary to disqualify Lord Cottenham notwithstanding that '[n]o one [could] suppose that [he] could be, in the remotest degree, influenced by the interests that he had in [the company]'.[36] This prompts Olowofoyeku to point out that if this is so, then it is unclear what purpose was served by disqualifying Lord Cottenham in the absence of both real and apparent bias. He therefore contends that 'automatic disqualification is draconian, disproportionate and unnecessary'—in other words, it may be said to be over-inclusive.[37]

This leads on to our second point. The problem of over-inclusiveness may be avoided if the category of disqualifying financial interests is constructed in a sufficiently subtle manner. Olowofoyeku's point clearly has purchase if any financial interest, however small and remote, triggers the automatic disqualification rule. But if we restrict the rule to significant financial interests that give rise to plausible concerns about impartiality, then the problem of over-inclusiveness evaporates. This, to some extent, is what the courts have done. In *Locabail*,[38] a judge was alleged to have a financial interest in the outcome of the case, and it was said that he was disqualified from acting on that basis. However, this argument failed because the possibility of the judge benefiting from deciding the case in a particular way was so small: it was contingent upon a long and uncertain chain of events unfolding. In ruling that the judge was not disqualified in these circumstances, the Court of Appeal in *Locabail* recognised that a highly speculative financial interest will be insufficient to trigger the automatic disqualification rule, so going some way towards meeting Olowofoyeku's point about its over-inclusiveness.[39]

---

[34] (1852) 3 HLC 759. At this time, the Lord Chancellor sat as a judge, although he no longer does so: see Chapter 6, section 4.3.2, above.   [35] *Dimes* at 793.

[36] *Dimes* at 793.

[37] 'The *Nemo Judex* Rule: The Case against Automatic Disqualification' [2000] PL 456, 475.

[38] *Locabail (UK) Ltd v Bayfield Properties Ltd* [2000] QB 451.

[39] See also *R v Bristol Betting and Gaming Licensing Committee, ex p O'Callaghan* [2000] QB 451, decided with *Locabail*.

Q Do you agree that the sort of financial interest said to exist in *Locabail* should fall outside the scope of the automatic disqualification rule? Where exactly should the line be drawn between interests that are and are not sufficient to trigger its operation? To what extent may excluding insubstantial or tenuous financial interests be incompatible with the existence of a simple rule that provides clear guidance to decision-makers?

For some time, it was thought that automatic disqualification could occur only on the basis of being a party or having a financial or proprietary interest. However, in *Pinochet (No 2)*,[40] Lord Browne-Wilkinson said that just as financial interests were automatically disqualifying because of their similarity with to actually being a party, so other analogous interests may arise. This point is best explained by reference to the facts of the case.

The claimant, Pinochet, following his role in a successful military coup, was head of state in Chile from 1973 to 1990. Reports published in 1991 and 2004–05 alleged that Pinochet's regime killed over 2,000 people for political reasons and tortured many times that number.[41] While he was in the UK in 1998, Spain issued arrest warrants against Pinochet, alleging crimes against humanity, and sought his extradition.[42] The claimant argued that, as a former head of state, he was immune from arrest and extradition in respect of events alleged to have occurred whilst in office. This point was ultimately argued before the House of Lords in *Pinochet (No 1)*.[43] It found, by a majority of three–two, in favour of extradition. When hearing the case, their Lordships allowed Amnesty International (AI), a well-known group that campaigns against human rights abuses, to intervene.[44] It later became apparent that Lord Hoffmann, one of the majority judges, was a director of Amnesty International Charity Ltd (AICL), a charity that was intimately related to, and undertook work on behalf of, AI in the UK. Pinochet therefore asked the House of Lords to set aside its decision.

The House of Lords did precisely that in *Pinochet (No 2)*.[45] In itself, that result is unsurprising. Whether or not Lord Hoffmann was actually influenced by his association with AICL, it was certainly arguable that there was reasonable cause to suspect that he may have been influenced. As we explain in the next section, this is, in itself, a sufficient ground for setting a decision aside. However, their Lordships chose instead to decide the case by extending—or, according to Lord Browne-Wilkinson, clarifying—the automatic disqualification principle. While Lord Hoffmann was not actually party to the case—because 'Lord Hoffmann, AICL and the executive committee of AI are in law

---

[40] *R v Bow Street Metropolitan Stipendiary Magistrate, ex p Pinochet Ugarte (No 2)* [2000] 1 AC 119.

[41] *The National Commission for Truth and Reconciliation Report* (Santiago 1991); *The National Commission on Political Imprisonment and Torture Report* (Santiago 2004–05).

[42] That is, his removal to Spain to stand trial.

[43] *R v Bow Street Metropolitan Stipendiary Magistrate, ex p Pinochet Ugarte* [2000] 1 AC 61.

[44] This means that it was allowed, through counsel, to put certain arguments to the court.

[45] *R v Bow Street Metropolitan Stipendiary Magistrate, ex p Pinochet Ugarte (No 2)* [2000] 1 AC 119.

separate people[46]—he was nevertheless held to have an interest that automatically disqualified him. This did not arise straightforwardly on the ground that his affiliation with AICL evidenced an interest in promoting respect for human rights; rather, AI and AICL were 'parts of an entity or movement working in different fields towards the same goals' of procuring the abolition of (*inter alia*) torture and extrajudicial detention, and Lord Hoffmann's association with AI—a party—through AICL meant that he was involved 'in promoting the same causes in the same organisation as is a party to the suit'.[47]

The upshot of this decision is that automatic disqualification now extends beyond cases in which the decision-maker is actually a party or has a financial interest in the outcome. It has been criticised on a number of grounds—most notably because it creates uncertainty, the precise circumstances that trigger application of the *Pinochet* rule being far from clear. It has also been argued that an unintended consequence of the decision may be that judges will decide to withdraw to some extent from public life—for example, as directors or trustees of charitable organisations—in order to ensure that they do not find themselves disqualified from deciding cases.[48] These concerns should not, however, be overstated. In *Pinochet* itself, Lord Browne-Wilkinson emphasised the 'very unusual circumstances' of the case,[49] while the Court of Appeal in *Locabail* subsequently implied that the *Pinochet* rule should be read narrowly.[50] As a result, the cases in which *Pinochet* applies are likely to be few and far between.

Q Look back to our hypothetical case set out at the very beginning of this chapter. If the Minister were to make a decision on the construction of the new airport, would he be automatically disqualified on the basis of:

(i) owning land in a nearby town that, some property experts claim, is likely to appreciate in value if the airport is built?

(ii) the fact that his son is employed by a construction firm that would likely be awarded a contract to build part of the airport?

(iii) his membership of an environmental pressure group that is vehemently opposed to any expansion of air travel?

3.4.2 Situations giving rise to the appearance of a real possibility of bias

The circumstances thus far considered, in which decision-makers are automatically disqualified, are far from exhaustive of the situations in which a perceived lack of impartiality may render their involvement unlawful. Beyond cases involving financial interests and the suchlike, a broader test falls to be applied, the purpose of which is to ensure the disqualification of decision-makers whose participation would undermine public confidence in the fairness of the system.

---

[46] *Pinochet (No 2)* at 134, *per* Lord Browne-Wilkinson.

[47] *Pinochet (No 2)* at 134, *per* Lord Browne-Wilkinson.

[48] Malleson, 'Judicial Bias and Disqualification after *Pinochet (No 2)*' (2000) 63 MLR 119.

[49] *Pinochet (No 2)* at 135.   [50] *Locabail (UK) Ltd v Bayfield Properties Ltd* [2000] QB 451.

Following a good deal of instability in the case law,[51] the House of Lords, in *Porter v Magill*,[52] settled on a test for identifying when there will be a disqualifying level of apparent bias. The question that courts must now ask themselves is *whether the circumstances would lead a fair-minded and informed observer to conclude that there was a real possibility of bias*.[53] Three key issues arise in relation to the meaning and application of this test.

The first matter relates to the *level of concern* that must exist before the propriety of the decision becomes open to question. Part of the uncertainty that afflicted the case law prior to *Porter v Magill* related to precisely this question—in particular, whether a *probability* of bias was required, or whether a mere *possibility* would suffice. The position is now clear: the question is whether there is a 'real possibility' of bias; it is not necessary to establish a probability (in the sense of bias being more likely than not).[54] This approach is consistent with the *McCarthy* principle's emphasis on the importance of public perception, bearing in mind that confidence is liable to be damaged by the perception that it is possible—whether or not probable—that a decision was tainted by bias.

Second, *through whose eyes* does this assessment fall to be made? In particular, is it for the court to make this decision in its own right, or should the court be attempting to ascertain what the ordinary, reasonable person is likely to think? In *R v Gough*, Lord Goff created great confusion by eliding these two possibilities, arguing that it was unnecessary 'to require that the court should look at the matter through the eyes of a reasonable man, because the court in cases such as these personifies the reasonable man'.[55] However, this formulation was taken in some subsequent cases to imply wholesale departure from the *McCarthy* principle, such that it was for reviewing courts to determine the likelihood of actual bias, whether or not reasonable people might have perceived a risk of bias.[56] Orthodoxy was restored in *Porter v Magill*, which emphasises that the court must ask whether *a fair-minded and informed observer* would perceive a real possibility of bias. As Lord Philips MR acknowledged in the *Medicaments* case, such an approach caters for the possibility that even if the court is 'inclined to accept a statement about what the judge under review knew at any material time', there may still be 'public scepticism'.[57] This recognises that judicial and public perceptions may diverge—because judges are 'adept, by training and experience, at reaching decisions by objective appraisal of the facts'[58]—and that since this branch of the law is intended

---

[51] See, for conflicting judicial views, *Metropolitan Properties Co (FGC) Ltd v Lannon* [1969] 1 QB 577; *R v Rand* (1866) LR 1 QB 230; *Frome United Breweries Co Ltd v Bath Justices* [1926] AC 586; *R v Gough* [1993] AC 646; *R v Inner West London Coroner, ex p Dallaglio* [1994] 4 All ER 139.

[52] [2001] UKHL 67, [2002] 2 AC 357.

[53] *Porter v Magill* at [102]–[103], adapting a test laid down by the Court of Appeal in *Re Medicaments and Related Classes of Goods (No 2)* [2001] 1 WLR 700.

[54] *R v Gough* [1993] AC 646; *Porter v Magill* at [103].   [55] *Gough* at 670.

[56] See, eg *R v Inner West London Coroner, ex p Dallaglio* [1994] 4 All ER 139.

[57] *Re Medicaments and Related Classes of Goods (No 2)* [2001] 1 WLR 700, [67].

[58] *Medicaments* at [68].

to uphold public confidence in decision-making systems, it is public, rather than judicial, perceptions that must ultimately hold sway.

Thus it has been held that the fair-minded observer would consider a real possibility of bias to exist where, for example, a barrister appeared before a tribunal comprising lay members with whom he had previously sat on the tribunal in his judicial capacity,[59] and where someone involved in making or publicly advising upon the meaning of rules was subsequently called upon to interpret them[60] or to pronounce upon their legality.[61] In some cases, however, courts have arguably been too quick to imbue the notional fair-minded observer with the sort of ability to distinguish the relevant from the irrelevant that is more accurately the province of the professional judge. For example, in *Gillies*, a tribunal's decision to terminate the payment of Disability Living Allowance to the claimant was challenged on the ground that a member of the tribunal was a doctor who also worked for a company that provided reports on benefit claimants to the government agency the decision of which the claimant was challenging before the tribunal.[62] The claimant's argument before the House of Lords—that the doctor's two roles risked a perception of bias sufficient to impugn the tribunal's decision—failed. Lord Hope thought that it should be assumed that the fair-minded observer is 'able to distinguish between what is relevant and what is irrelevant, and that he is able when exercising his judgment to decide what weight should be given to the facts that are relevant'.[63] The observer would therefore appreciate that the doctor was capable of exhibiting sufficient 'professional detachment' to enable her to 'exercise her own independent judgment' when sitting on the tribunal, uninfluenced by the fact that she also performed work on behalf of the government agency that was a party to the dispute that fell for determination before the tribunal.[64]

The risk, of course, is that the more judge-like the fair-minded observer is deemed to be, the less likely is the fair-minded observer test to yield results that sufficiently reflect public perceptions—and that therefore uphold public confidence. This leads on to our third point, which concerns the *amount of knowledge* to be imputed to the observer. The test laid down in *Porter v Magill* refers to a 'fair-minded *and informed* observer'— but just *how* informed is he? In principle, the observer should know only that that is within 'the ken of ordinary, reasonably well informed members of the public', since it is their perceptions of the integrity of the decision-making system around which this branch of the law is designed.[65] On occasion, however, the courts have perhaps shown undue enthusiasm for imputing knowledge to the observer—with the result, intended or otherwise, that his viewpoint becomes indistinguishable from that of the court itself. For example, in *Taylor v Lawrence*,[66] it transpired that a judge had received free legal

---

[59] *Lawal v Northern Spirit Ltd* [2003] UKHL 35, [2004] 1 All ER 187.
[60] *Davidson v Scottish Ministers (No2)* [2004] UKHL 34, 2005 1 SC (HL) 7.
[61] *R (Carroll) v Secretary of State for the Home Department* [2005] UKHL 13, [2005] 1 WLR 688.
[62] *Gillies v Secretary of State for Work and Pensions* [2006] UKHL 2, [2006] 1 WLR 781.
[63] *Gillies* at [17].   [64] *Gillies* at [18].   [65] See *Medicaments* at [65].
[66] [2002] EWCA Civ 90, [2003] QB 528.

services from the claimants' solicitors the day before he gave judgment in favour of the claimant. To the average layperson, this may well give rise to a suspicion of bias, but the Court of Appeal held that the fair-minded and informed observer would not share this perspective. However, the Court could only reach this conclusion by imputing to the notional observer extensive knowledge of the legal community and of the way in which judges and lawyers interact with one another—knowledge that the average person almost certainly lacks. The difficulty with this approach is that the fair-minded observer is taken to know so much about the legal professions and the judiciary that his perceptions are likely to be substantially at odds with those of ordinary members of the public—whose perceptions are supposed to be paramount in this context.

> **Q** Look back at the example given at the very beginning of this chapter. What would be the legal implications (if any) if our hypothetical Minister were to refuse permission to build the new airport, and it later come to light that he was having an affair with the chief executive of a company backing a rival site for a new airport?

The sort of difficulties highlighted above prompt Olowofoyeku to argue that the fair-minded observer test is incapable of being sensibly applied. He contends that it would be better if the courts were to dispense with the observer—'a fictional and theoretical "middle-man"'—and simply assess matters from their own perspective.[67] This would have the benefit of simplicity, since it would no longer be necessary for courts to second-guess how the observer would perceive the situation. However, it is arguable that such an approach, by removing the focus from ordinary people's perceptions, might inadequately uphold public confidence.

3.4.3 Politics and administration

So far, we have been mainly concerned with cases in which the impartiality of *judges* has been in doubt. Are other sorts of decision-makers—Ministers, local authorities, government agencies, and so on—held to the same standards? Although other views prevailed in the past,[68] the answer to this question is now, in essence, 'yes'.[69] As Sedley J held in the *Kirkstall* case, the normal test for impartiality 'is of general application in public law and is not limited to judicial or quasi-judicial bodies or proceedings'.[70] This means that the automatic disqualification principle and the fair-minded observer test apply to political and administrative, as well as to judicial, decision-makers.

However, this notwithstanding, politicians cannot—indeed, should not—be expected to behave in the same way as judges. In particular, as Sedley J went on to observe in *Kirkstall*, the law must accommodate the fact that such decision-makers—particularly

---

[67] Olowofoyeku, 'Bias and the Informed Observer: A Call for a Return to *Gough*' [2009] CLJ 388, 406–7.

[68] See, eg *Franklin v Minister of Town and Country Planning* [1948] AC 87.

[69] *R v Secretary of State for the Environment, ex p Kirkstall Valley Campaign Ltd* [1996] 3 All ER 304; *R (Island Farm Development Ltd) v Brigend County Borough Council* [2006] EWHC 2189 (Admin), [2007] BLGR 60.   [70] *Kirkstall* at 325.

if they are elected—'will take up office with publicly stated views on a variety of policy issues'.[71] This issue arises when politicians are alleged not to have acted impartially on account of having decided a matter in line with a previously articulated policy position, rather than by approaching it with an entirely open mind. Consider, for example, the *Island Farm* case.[72] The claimant company had been negotiating with the respondent council over the purchase of a piece of land. A local election interrupted the negotiation process, and the new council then refused to sell. That refusal was challenged by the company on the ground that certain councillors were tainted by a lack of impartiality given that they had spoken out, during the election campaign, against the sale of the land. Collins J held that, 'whatever their views, [councillors] must approach their decision-making with an open mind in the sense that they must have regard to all material considerations and be prepared to change their views if persuaded that they should'.[73] However, that did not make it improper for them to approach the issues with a particular view as their starting point. It followed that while it would be wrong for councillors—and, by extension, other decision-makers—to lapse into *predetermination* (in the sense of refusing to engage with the issues or listen to the arguments), it was entirely acceptable for them to have a *predisposition* in favour of a given policy. Concluding that 'the fair-minded and informed observer must be taken to appreciate that predisposition is not predetermination and that Councillors can be assumed to be aware of their obligations', Collins J refused to uphold the claimant's complaint.[74]

> **Q** Do you agree that, in the respect outlined above, political decision-makers should be regarded differently from judges? Might it be possible to go further and argue that democracy *requires* such differential treatment?

3.5 Independence

3.5.1 The issue—and an example

So far, we have been concerned with the importance of decision-makers acting impartially—a requirement that is centrally concerned with their *personal circumstances and characteristics*.[75] The need for impartiality therefore impacts upon whether a *given individual* can properly make a particular decision. We now turn to the distinct question of *independence*—and we begin with an example.

---

[71] *Kirkstall* at 325.

[72] *R (Island Farm Development Ltd) v Brigend County Borough Council* [2006] EWHC 2189 (Admin) [2007] BLGR 60. See, to similar effect, *R (Condron) v National Assembly for Wales* [2006] EWCA Civ 1573, [2007] 2 P & CR 4.   [73] *Island Farm* at [31].

[74] *Island Farm* at [32].

[75] For example, questions about whether someone stands to gain financially or is motivated by self-interest or ill will turn on his personal situation.

Although those convicted of murder by the courts of England and Wales are automatically subject to a life sentence, few, in practice, spend the rest of their lives in prison. Until comparatively recently, the procedure was that, following conviction, the judiciary would make recommendations to the Home Secretary as to the 'tariff' (the minimum period for which the prisoner should be held before being considered for release on parole[76]), but the Home Secretary had the final say over the length of the tariff. The legality of this system was challenged in *Anderson*.[77] The claimant, a convicted murderer, argued that deciding on the tariff was, in effect, part of the process of sentencing—and that this should be carried out by an independent judge, not by a government Minister susceptible to political pressure. We will see later that the House of Lords agreed with this argument. For now, however, two points fall to be made.

First, the type of argument canvassed in *Anderson* raises quite different issues from those that we encountered in the previous section. The claimant in *Anderson* based his case not on the personal characteristics of the *particular* Home Secretary who had set his tariff, but on the argument that *no* Home Secretary could legitimately make sentencing decisions. It is in this way that the requirement of independence, with which we are concerned here, differs from that of impartiality.

Second, it is only recently that English courts have had to concern themselves with the former requirement. This is because, in most instances, the choice of decision-maker is ordained by Parliament itself through primary legislation. Indeed, this was so in *Anderson*: s 29 of the Crime (Sentences) Act 1997 unambiguously assigned the ultimate power of tariff-setting to the Home Secretary. And, of course, there has traditionally been nothing that courts can do in such situations: where Parliament makes its wishes sufficiently clear, orthodox theory teaches that it is for judges to implement it. However, a requirement of institutional independence is included in the European Convention on Human Rights (ECHR), to which the Human Rights Act 1998 (HRA) gives effect in UK law. Although courts cannot override or disapply legislation that conflicts with the ECHR, they can—as did the House of Lords in *Anderson*—issue a 'declaration of incompatibility' when an Act of Parliament is at odds with rights protected by the HRA.[78] This means that courts can now rule on whether decision-making arrangements are sufficiently independent, even if laid down in primary legislation.

3.5.2 When is an independent decision-maker required?

The part of the ECHR that is of present concern is Art 6(1): 'In the determination of his civil rights and obligations or of any criminal charge against him, everyone is entitled to a fair and public hearing within a reasonable time by an independent and impartial tribunal established by law.' It is well-established that 'independent'

---

[76] Parole is release subject to the possibility of recall to prison in the event of improper behaviour.

[77] *R (Anderson) v Secretary of State for the Home Department* [2002] UKHL 46, [2003] 1 AC 837.

[78] See further Chapter 19, section 3.4.5, below.

here means independent of (*inter alia*) the executive branch of government.[79] It is easy to see why such a requirement should apply to the conduct of civil and criminal proceedings: it is axiomatic, under the separation of powers, that the criminal liability and legal rights of individuals should be determined in a forum that is above the political fray.[80]

However, Art 6(1) has also been held to apply to the making of some administrative decisions.[81] This raises significant questions about *accountability*—one of the key themes with which we are concerned in this book. It is important to recall that one of the hallmarks of independence (in the sense in which we are presently using that term) is freedom from external pressures, such as public opinion, parliamentary scrutiny, and the electoral process. It is precisely because judges are free from such pressures that we entrust to them decisions about criminal and civil liability—decisions that are best made in an objective, detached, evidence-based way. But, for precisely the same reasons, where decisions fall to be made about controversial issues of policy, there is a strong argument for saying that they should *not* be made by independent bodies such as courts, but by a politically accountable government decision-maker. As Lord Nolan has pointed out, to entrust such decisions to 'an independent and impartial body with no central electoral accountability would not only be a recipe for chaos: it would be profoundly undemocratic'.[82] This is not to imply that judges are unaccountable; they are required to provide reasoned justification for their decisions, and most are subject to a form of oversight in that superior courts can overturn their decisions on appeal. But accountability can take many forms—and most would agree that political accountability is most apt in relation to the taking of policy decisions. What, then, is the effect of Art 6(1)? Where does it draw the line between decisions that have to be taken by independent judges and those that can be taken by accountable politicians? And does it draw that line in an acceptable place?

Article 6(1) stipulates that matters must be entrusted to independent decision-makers when they entail determining either criminal liability or civil rights and obligations. Few administrative decisions involve determining criminal liability,[83] and so our focus here is on 'civil rights and obligations'. It has been held that such rights and obligations are at stake in, for example, disciplinary proceedings impacting upon a person's right to pursue his profession,[84] compulsory purchase by the state of an individual's land,[85] and decisions about parents' rights of access to their children.[86] In contrast, it has been held that civil rights and obligations are not in play in decisions

---

[79] *V v United Kingdom* (2000) 30 EHRR 121, [114].   [80] See further Chapter 6, section 4, above.

[81] *Ringeisen v Austria (No 1)* (1979–80) 1 EHRR 455.

[82] *R (Alconbury Developments Ltd) v Secretary of State for the Environment, Transport and the Regions* [2001] UKHL 23, [2003] 2 AC 295, [60]. See also *Runa Begum v Tower Hamlets London Borough Council* [2003] UKHL 5, [2003] 2 AC 430.

[83] But some do—eg prison authorities' rulings on whether a prisoner has breached disciplinary rules and should therefore have his sentence extended: *Ezeh v United Kingdom* (2004) 39 EHRR 1.

[84] *König v Federal Republic of Germany* (1979–80) 2 EHRR 170.

[85] *Sporrong v Sweden* (1983) 5 EHRR 35.   [86] *W v United Kingdom* (1988) 10 EHRR 29.

about taxation[87] and immigration.[88] Giving examples is one thing—but what is the principle?

This question was tackled by the Supreme Court in *Ali v Birmingham City Council*.[89] Section 193 of the Housing Act 1996 obliges local authorities to provide accommodation to certain homeless persons—but it relieves councils of that obligation if an applicant declines, without good reason, an offer of suitable accommodation having been warned that, if he does so, the authority will regard itself as having discharged its duty. In *Ali*, a dispute arose over whether the council had, in the way just described, been relieved of its duty—and the claimants alleged that because the statutory machinery for resolving such disputes involved a local authority housing officer, it lacked independence in the Art 6(1) sense. Whether this argument could be sustained turned on whether, in the first place, Art 6(1) applied: did the claimants have a 'civil right' to be given accommodation? The Supreme Court held that they did not. Whether there was a duty to house them (and so whether they had a corresponding right to be housed) depended on the making of judgements about compliance with statutory criteria that were not clear-cut. The council had to ask itself whether the claimants were homeless (which involves asking whether it would be reasonable for them to continue to occupy given accommodation) and, if so, whether they had become homeless intentionally. This meant, said Lord Hope, that no civil right arose: all that the claimants sought was a benefit that might or might not be conferred in the light of 'a series of evaluative judgments...as to whether the statutory criteria are satisfied'.[90] A civil right, he said, only arises when there is 'an individual right of which the applicant can consider himself the holder'.[91] Or, as the European Court of Human Rights (ECtHR) has put it, Art 6(1) is only likely to apply when a public body is making a determination concerning an 'assertable right'.[92] Such a right is only likely to exist when the relevant legislation sets out clear criteria as to when the entitlement arises. From all of this, it follows that the acid test concerns the extent to which the benefit or entitlement in question depends on the exercise of evaluative or discretionary judgement on the public body's part. The less objective and clear-cut the statutory criteria, the less likely it is that a civil right within the meaning of Art 6(1) will exist.

Q Look back at our example at the beginning of the chapter. Is this the sort of decision to which the requirement of independent decision-making ought to apply? What if the decision to give the go-ahead to the new airport were to entail forcing people to sell to the government land comprising part of the site of the new airport? Would this be a matter to which Art 6(1) would apply?

---

[87] *Ferrazzini v Italy* (2002) 34 EHRR 45.
[88] *Uppal v United Kingdom* (1981) 3 EHRR 391; *Maaouia v France* (2001) 33 EHRR 42.
[89] [2010] UKSC 8, [2010] 2 WLR 471. The conclusion reached in *Ali* was foreshadowed in *R (A) v Croydon London Borough Council* [2009] UKSC 8, [2009] 1 WLR 2557.   [90] *Ali* at [49].
[91] *Ali* at [49].   [92] *Stec v United Kingdom* (2005) 41 EHRR SE295, [50].

3.5.3 **What does Art 6(1) require?**

When it applies, Art 6(1) demands an 'independent' decision-maker—a requirement that means different things in different circumstances. As Figure 13.3 shows, we can broadly distinguish between two types of case.

At one end of the spectrum are cases concerning the exercise of *policymaking functions*. The *Alconbury* case concerned a challenge to the involvement of the Environment Secretary in deciding whether a company should be given permission to develop a disused airfield owned by the Ministry of Defence.[93] Lord Hoffmann emphasised that the decision did 'not involve deciding between the rights or interests of particular persons'; rather, it entailed 'the exercise of a power delegated by the people as a whole to decide what the public interest requires'—a 'policy decision', in other words.[94] In such circumstances, the House of Lords, applying ECtHR case law,[95] concluded that the requirement for an independent decision-maker would be satisfied provided that the decision of the Minister, who was himself clearly *not* independent of the executive, was open to review by a 'court of full jurisdiction'—a requirement that was met by the possibility of seeking judicial review of the Minister's decision. We therefore refer

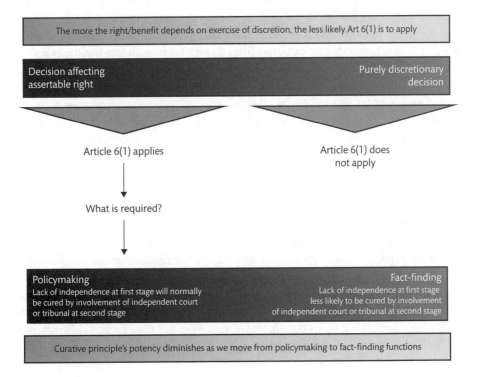

Figure 13.3 Article 6 ECHR

[93] *R (Alconbury Developments Ltd) v Secretary of State for the Environment, Transport and the Regions* [2001] UKHL 23, [2003] 2 AC 295.   [94] *Alconbury* at [74].
[95] Including *Albert and Le Compte v Belgium* (1983) 5 EHRR 533; *Zumtobel v Austria* (1993) 17 EHRR 116.

in this context to the *curative principle*—the idea that the possibility of subsequent judicial review by an independent court can make up for any lack of independence in the making of the original decision.

At the other end of the spectrum, we find cases involving *fact-finding functions*. The applicant in *Bryan v United Kingdom*[96] was ordered to demolish buildings that, said the local authority, he had erected without planning permission. The applicant, contending, *inter alia*, that the buildings were for agricultural use and that no such permission was therefore needed, appealed, without success, to the Secretary of State—who appointed a planning inspector to determine the appeal—and thereafter, again unsuccessfully, on a point of law to the High Court. Subsequently, the applicant contended that the Secretary of State's involvement was improper because he lacked the independence required by Art 6(1). This argument failed, and the curative principle was held to apply: the possibility of appeal to the High Court meant that, taken as a whole, the system was sufficiently independent. However, in reaching this conclusion, emphasis was placed on the fact that while the planning inspector who decided the appeal on behalf of the Minister was not independent in the way that a judge is,[97] there was nothing to suggest that such an inspector 'acts anything other than independently, in the sense that he is in no sense connected with the parties to the dispute or subject to their influence or control; his findings and conclusions are based exclusively on the evidence and submissions before him'.[98] The conclusion that we can draw from this is that, in such fact-finding cases, the curative principle is less potent: while the possibility of review by or appeal to a court may inject sufficient independence into the decision-making process to render it compatible with Art 6(1), this cannot be taken for granted. Where fact-finding is required, the curative principle can only do so much: in effect, it is limited to rescuing regimes in which (as in *Bryan*) the fact-finder already enjoys substantial independence in practice.

This may seem very technical, but can be summed up quite briefly. The underlying issue is whether the function in question is one that should be performed by an independent, court-like body, or by a politically accountable decision-maker. Since matters involving broad questions of policy fall into the latter category, the requirement of independence is, in effect, diluted: politicians and administrators can take the decisions provided that there is adequate oversight by a court. Meanwhile, since fact-finding functions fall into the former category, the requirement of independence applies more rigidly here: such functions must be performed by persons or bodies with substantial independence, albeit that if they lack the very high degree of independence enjoyed by judges, the possibility of oversight by a court may be enough to bridge the shortfall.[99] It turns out, therefore, that what is, *prima facie*, a very technical

---

[96] (1996) 21 EHRR 342.

[97] The independence of judges is attributable in large part to the substantial security of tenure (see Chapter 6, section 4.4.2, above) that they, unlike planning inspectors, enjoy.

[98] (1996) 21 EHRR 342 (concurring opinion of Mr N Bratza).

[99] If, however, a fact-finding function is ancillary to a decision involving the exercise of discretion, this may enhance the potency of the curative principle. This point was acknowledged by the Supreme Court in *Ali*.

issue concerning the meaning of 'civil rights and obligations' and of 'independence' in fact turns on a much more substantive debate about the appropriateness, under the separation of powers, of allocating particular types of function to particular types of institution. This requires us to confront fundamental questions about accountability, and to recognise that different forms of accountability and oversight will be called for in relation to different types of decision.

3.6 **The right to be heard**

3.6.1 **Introduction**

Most people would regard it as fundamentally unfair if a decision affecting them in some important way were to be taken without first giving them an opportunity to address the decision-maker. For example, a person who stands accused of a crime will want to address the court—probably through his legal representative—in order to challenge the prosecution's version of events. Equally, an asylum seeker will want an opportunity of explaining—before any decision is taken—why she fears for her life if returned to her home country. As we noted above,[100] that people should be afforded such a 'right to be heard'[101] is important both for practical reasons, because a process that harvests information from all relevant parties will likely yield better, more informed decisions, and for normative reasons, in that making decisions without affording those likely to be impacted a chance to advance their point of view fails to acknowledge the status and dignity of such individuals.

At one time, it was held that the right to be heard applied only if the decision-maker was discharging a judicial function. This concept came to be applied in a way that meant that administrative decision-makers were often not subject to any legal duty to act fairly. Even decisions that affected people's livelihoods—for example, whether a trading licence or taxi licence should be revoked—did not necessarily have to be accompanied by any sort of hearing, or indeed any other opportunity to allow the individual to advance his side of the story.[102] Happily, courts now take a different approach in this area. That approach is informed by two central considerations: that *fairness is required* whenever an administrative decision affects someone's rights, interests, or legitimate expectations; but that *what fairness requires* is heavily dependent upon the circumstances.

The first of those two points can be traced to the seminal decision of the House of Lords in *Ridge v Baldwin*.[103] The case arose from a decision to dismiss the Chief Constable of Brighton, who had been acquitted of conspiracy to obstruct the course of justice and corruption—but had also been the subject of adverse judicial comments—in

---

[100] See section 3.3 above.

[101] This right is sometimes expressed in terms of a correlative duty to 'hear the other side'—which sometimes appears as a Latin maxim: *audi alteram partem*.

[102] *Nakkuda Ali v Jayaratne* [1951] AC 66; *R v Metropolitan Police Commissioner, ex p Parker* [1953] 1 WLR 1150.   [103] [1964] AC 40.

two criminal trials. The decision was taken by a 'watch committee'—a body that had responsibility for overseeing the work of the local police force, but which could not in any sense be regarded as a 'judicial' body—without first giving the Chief Constable any opportunity of being heard.[104] The House of Lords held that this failure rendered unlawful the watch committee's decision, which was therefore quashed,[105] notwithstanding that it was not a judicial body. This laid the foundation for a much more expansive approach whereby administrative decision-makers are almost inevitably required to act fairly.

The second point, though, is that the expansive effect of *Ridge* was (quite properly) balanced by growing judicial recognition that the right to be heard should mean different things in different contexts.[106] There is, as Figure 13.4 shows, a spectrum of possibilities, ranging from a rudimentary right to make written representations at one extreme, to something resembling a full-blown criminal trial at the other. The key issue becomes how to decide where a given case should be placed on that spectrum. Here, two central factors come into play: the *implications of the decision for the individual* and *the practical need for particular forms of procedure*.

> **Q** Why do you think procedural fairness is rationed in this way? Why not say that anyone who is affected by a decision—however important or trivial—is entitled to a full-blown hearing along the lines of a criminal trial?

3.6.2 Setting the level of fairness—normative considerations

The first of those considerations reflects the normative value of fair procedures, since it effectively amounts to asking the question: 'What degree of fairness is appropriate, given what is at stake for the individual?' Two factors are important here. The first concerns the impact of the decision on the *status quo*. If the individual stands to lose something important—something that he currently has—this would seem, on an instinctive level, to demand a higher level of fairness than a situation in which someone applies for a benefit over and above that which they already have. On this basis, a person whose house is at risk of demolition to make way for a new airport would be entitled to a higher degree of procedural fairness than someone seeking permission to build a new house.[107] Second, the normative case for procedural fairness will be stronger—and so, other things being equal, the level of procedural justice due to the individual will be higher—where the rights or interests at stake are especially important. So, for example,

---

[104] He was later allowed to make representations through his solicitor, but the dismissal was not overturned in light of these.

[105] It was also held that the watch committee's subsequent willingness to receive representations did not, on the facts, cancel out the unfairness involved in denying the Chief Constable an opportunity to participate *before* the decision to dismiss was taken.

[106] For early recognition of this point, see *Re HK (An Infant)* [1967] QB 617, 630, *per* Lord Parker CJ.

[107] See further *McInnes v Onslow-Fane* [1978] 1 WLR 1520; *R (Khatun) v Newham London Borough Council* [2004] EWCA Civ 55, [2005] QB 37.

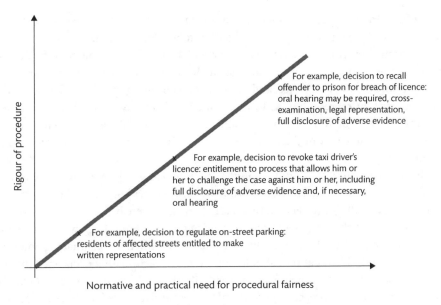

Figure 13.4 Procedural fairness—a sliding scale

if the decision may result in loss of liberty, this would point towards a particularly rigorous procedure.[108] It follows that where the task being undertaken by the public body is general in nature—for example, developing policy—this is likely to call for far less by way of procedural fairness than tasks involving adjudication on individual cases.[109]

3.6.3 Setting the level of fairness—practical considerations

Practical considerations must also be taken into account when deciding how rigorous the procedure should be and what features it should include—a point that we illustrate through the following examples.

First, assuming that the relevant statute is silent on the point, *how do we decide whether an oral hearing is required, or whether it will suffice to allow individuals to make written representations?* The House of Lords had to address this question in *Lloyd v McMahon*.[110] Certain Liverpool councillors were found guilty by the relevant regulatory agency—the district auditor—of wilful misconduct occasioning substantial financial losses to the city council. As a result, the councillors were made personally liable—meaning that they could be required to reimburse the council—and banned from holding public office for five years. The councillors mounted a legal challenge to the auditor's decision, arguing that, by denying them an oral hearing, he had acted

---

[108] See, eg *R v Secretary of State for the Home Department, ex p Tarrant* [1985] QB 251; *R (Smith) v Parole Board* [2005] UKHL 1, [2005] 1 WLR 350.

[109] In situations not involving individual adjudication, it may well be sufficient for the public body to consult in broad terms, eg on proposed changes to policy. [110] [1987] AC 625.

unlawfully. In an oft-repeated dictum, Lord Bridge observed that 'the so-called rules of natural justice are not engraved on tablets of stone';[111] instead, their content depends on the circumstances of the case. In this particular case, there was no need for an oral hearing. The liability of the councillors fell to be determined by reference to large volumes of documentary evidence, and in this context limiting the councillors to a right to make written representations to the auditor was entirely appropriate. Moreover, an oral hearing would have added nothing: it might have allowed the councillors to emphasise the sincerity of their motives, but, as Lord Keith observed, this was irrelevant to their liability.[112]

This can be contrasted with the *Smith* case,[113] which was brought by two individuals who had been released on licence from prison after serving part of their sentences. However, it was alleged (*inter alia*) that one of them had thereafter assaulted his former partner and that the other had used illegal drugs. As a result, both were recalled to prison. It then fell to the Parole Board to decide whether the claimants should be re-released. It decided that they should not—and, in reaching that decision, it did not afford either claimant an oral hearing. That failure, the claimants argued on judicial review, amounted to a breach of procedural fairness and rendered the Board's decision unlawful. The House of Lords agreed. Lord Bingham emphasised a key feature of oral hearings that distinguishes them from written proceedings—namely, that the former are more flexible than the latter: they facilitate dynamic and immediate interchange between the individual and the decision-maker, allowing the former to develop and adapt his arguments in light of the latter's responses.[114] This means that oral hearings will be particularly appropriate where, for example, the case turns on disputed questions of fact or upon the credibility or truthfulness of a witness.

> **Q** Look back at our discussion of normative and instrumental views of fairness (in section 3.3 above). Does the courts' preparedness, as evidenced by *Lloyd*, to limit procedural rights where a practical case for more rigorous procedures cannot be made out imply support for one or other of those views?

The case law shows that practical considerations also help to determine *whether the decision-maker is obliged to allow the individual to be legally represented*. Consider *Tarrant*,[115] for example, in which serving prisoners were alleged to have committed offences of assault and mutiny. The disciplinary body that heard their cases—and which had the power, *inter alia*, to order that they should spend longer in prison than they otherwise would—rejected the prisoners' requests that they be allowed legal

---

[111] *Lloyd v McMahon* at 702.   [112] *Lloyd v McMahon* at 708.

[113] *R (Smith) v Parole Board* [2005] UKHL 1, [2005] 1 WLR 350.

[114] In making this point (at [32]), Lord Bingham relied on comments made by Brennan J in the US Supreme Court in *Goldberg v Kelly* (1970) 397 US 254, 269.

[115] *R v Secretary of State for the Home Department, ex p Tarrant* [1985] QB 251. See also *R v Board of Visitors of HM Prison, The Maze, ex p Hone* [1988] AC 379.

representation. They therefore sought judicial review, arguing that this amounted to a denial of procedural fairness. Webster J considered that a number of practical considerations—in addition to the seriousness of the allegations—should be taken into account in deciding whether legal representation was necessary as a matter of fairness. In particular, he thought it important to consider the capacity of the individual to present his own case (something that would be affected by the legal and factual complexity of the case, as well as by personal factors such as articulacy and literacy) and whether denial of representation would pose procedural difficulties (for example, the judge noted that prisoners awaiting adjudication are normally segregated, and that this might inhibit preparation of their defence). The court concluded that legal representation was necessary in the mutiny cases—because they raised complex questions, for example, about whether prisoners had acted together in order to challenge the prison authorities—but that it would not normally be unfair to deny representation in more straightforward cases such as those involving allegations of assault.

> **Q** Consider the position of the Minister—set out in our example at the very beginning of this chapter—who has to decide whether to allow a new airport to be built. To what extent would the following have to be heard by the Minister before he takes the decision?
>
> (i)   The owner of a house that will be compulsorily purchased and demolished if the airport is built.
> (ii) Local residents concerned about likely increases in traffic congestion.
> (iii) Environmental campaigners anxious about the contribution that the new airport would make to carbon emissions.

3.6.4 Trading fairness off against other considerations

We have seen so far that the right to be heard is not fixed and absolute; rather, it is conceded in particular cases to the extent that is necessary, judged by reference to both normative and practical considerations. Nevertheless, the principles set out above should, if applied correctly, ensure that each individual is accorded whatever procedural rights are necessary and appropriate to his case. The question to which we now turn is whether the law ever allows decision-makers to accord a *lower* degree of procedural fairness than this. In other words, can (and should) the right to a fair hearing be traded off against other considerations?

This question arises in particularly stark form in relation to the 'right to notice', which is generally regarded as an essential component of procedural fairness.[116] As Lord Denning MR put it: 'If the right to be heard is to be a real right which is worth anything, it must carry with it a right in the accused man to know the case which is

---

[116] See, eg *R v Secretary of State for the Home Department, ex p Doody* [1994] 1 AC 531; *Chief Constable of North Wales Police v Evans* [1982] 1 WLR 1155; *R v Secretary of State for the Home Department, ex p Fayed* [1998] 1 WLR 763.

made against him.'[117] The precise implications of the right obviously depend on the circumstances—for example, if the government is obliged, for the sake of fairness, to consult before making a decision about something, the right to notice would require the government to publish sufficient information about its proposals to enable people to respond sensibly—but the gist is clear: the right to be heard is only valuable if one knows what it is one is arguing against (or about).

Against this background, we turn to *R (Roberts) v Parole Board*.[118] The claimant was a life-sentence prisoner who had served enough of his sentence to be considered by the Parole Board for release on licence. When the Board came to make a decision, it was alleged that Roberts had engaged in drug-dealing whilst in prison—which, if true, would weigh strongly against release. However, the Board was caught on the horns of a dilemma: ignoring the allegations may have resulted in Roberts being released inappropriately, but admitting them into evidence, it was said, would have endangered the informant. The Board attempted to steer a middle course by deciding to appoint a 'special advocate'—a barrister to whom the drug-dealing allegations would be disclosed, but who would not be allowed to discuss them with Roberts. The intention was that the special advocate would challenge the allegations in a special session of the hearing from which Roberts would be excluded: Roberts would therefore remain ignorant of key evidence against him—but it would at least be tested on his behalf. This approach would clearly represent a major departure from the normal principles of fairness, by denying the individual any notice of (one aspect of) the case against him and in that way—and by physically excluding him from part of the proceedings—substantially eroding his right to be heard.

The question for the House of Lords was whether, in principle, such arrangements would ever be lawful. Lords Bingham and Steyn, dissenting, thought not. The latter considered that what the Board proposed 'undermines the very essence of elementary justice' and would entail 'a phantom hearing only'.[119] The majority, however, were willing to countenance the possibility that, in some circumstances, the sort of arrangements proposed by the Board may be lawful. However, Lord Woolf CJ, with whom Lord Carswell agreed, stressed that this possibility would only arise where departure from the normal principles could be justified (for example, by a serious threat to life or limb), and where alternative arrangements ensured that the individual was treated in accordance with a minimum acceptable level of fairness.

The majority's approach in *Roberts* was considered by the House of Lords in the subsequent case of *Secretary of State for the Home Department v AF (No 3)*.[120] In the latter case, particular emphasis was placed on the fact that restricting the amount of information given to the individual might well undermine the usefulness of procedural devices such as special advocates, thereby unacceptably compromising the overall fairness of the proceedings. (For example, if the individual is wholly in the dark as

---

[117] *Kanda v Government of Malaysia* [1962] AC 322, 337.
[118] [2005] UKHL 45, [2005] 2 AC 738.   [119] *Roberts* at [88].
[120] [2009] UKHL 28, [2009] 3 WLR 74.

to the content of the allegations, she is unlikely to be able to give adequate instructions to those representing her interests.) It was therefore held in *AF (No 3)* that the individual must always be given enough information to enable her to instruct her special advocate so as to facilitate an effective challenge to the case against her. The broader point that can be drawn from this case is that it may be lawful to water down the right to notice, but it must not be diluted to such an extent as to deprive the individual of a fair hearing.

Finally, a caveat should be entered. *AF (No 3)* concerned circumstances to which Art 6(1) of the ECHR was applicable, and some of the Law Lords indicated that they would or may not have reached the same conclusion had that not been so. The significance of this point is underlined by *W (Algeria) v Secretary of State for the Home Department*,[121] in which the Court of Appeal held that, in deportation proceedings to which Art 6(1) did *not* apply, the appellants (who were represented by special advocates) could be denied knowledge of even the gist of the case against them. This was not because the common law was unconcerned with the provision of procedural fairness; rather, the Court held that the Act of Parliament concerned was so clear as to displace the common law principles of fairness.[122]

3.7 Giving reasons for decisions

The requirement of notice, considered above, relates to the giving of information to relevant parties *before* a decision is made, so that they can effectively exercise their right to be heard. A distinct, but related, question is whether there is any right to be told the reasons for a decision *once it has been taken*. Whereas administrative law has long regarded the duty to give *notice* as essential to procedural fairness, a more ambivalent attitude exists in relation to the giving of *reasons*. This reflects the view that it is entirely possible to conduct a process that is fair—in the sense of according an appropriate form of hearing and equipping the individual with sufficient information to engage with the process—without giving reasons for the eventual decision. It is, however, strongly arguable that decision-makers ought, in most cases, to be required to give reasons for their decisions. The arguments in favour of such a requirement reflect the two general arguments in favour of procedural fairness considered above.[123] On an *instrumental* level, it has been observed that if '[c]onsciously duty-bound to articulate their reasons, decision-makers' minds are [likely to be] more focused and their substantive decision-making…better'.[124] And, in *non-instrumental* terms, the giving of reasons is necessary if the status and dignity of the individual as a human

---

[121] [2010] EWCA Civ 898.

[122] If Art 6(1) were to have been applied, the court would have been obliged, if at all possible, to read the legislation compatibly with it (HRA, s 3); if that had not been possible, a declaration of incompatibility could have been issued (s 4).

[123] See section 3.3 above. For general discussion, see Le Sueur, 'Legal Duties to Give Reasons' (1999) 52 CLP 150. [124] Fordham, 'Reasons: The Third Dimension' [1998] JR 158.

being are to be properly acknowledged: as Collins J put it, 'individuals directly affected [by a decision] should not suffer without...at least knowing why they [are] suffering'.[125] For example, in *Doody*, Lord Mustill regarded the giving of reasons as essential when the executive branch exercised its (now defunct) power to decide the minimum term for which convicted murderers should be imprisoned: this, he noted, was 'the most important thing in the prisoner's life', and it was fundamentally unfair if the decision was (as far as the prisoner could see) conjured 'out of thin air' without any accompanying reasons.[126]

Although concluding that, in such a case, the Home Secretary should be—and was—legally required to give reasons, Lord Mustill said that the law did not recognise 'a general duty to give reasons for an administrative decision'.[127] This remains the case today.[128] However, there are a number of exceptions to the general rule that reasons need not be given, four of which we address in what follows.[129]

First, there may be a *statutory obligation* to give reasons; many statutes specifically require public agencies to provide reasons for their decisions.[130] For example, s 10 of the Tribunals and Inquiries Act 1992 directs that reasons must accompany the decisions of certain tribunals and certain ministerial decisions made after a statutory inquiry has been held (or in circumstances in which such an inquiry could have been required). An individual may also be able to use the Freedom of Information Act 2000 to extract reasons from a decision-maker.[131] Although the Act does not impose a reason-giving duty per se, it requires—subject to certain exceptions—that public authorities supply individuals with requested 'information'.[132] Reasons for a decision will fall under the statutory definition of 'information'—and so be liable to disclosure—if, but only if, they are 'recorded in any form'.[133] The Act will not, therefore, help individuals in circumstances in which, at the time of their freedom of information request, reasons have not been recorded (for example, by writing them down or storing them electronically).

Second, *fairness as understood at common law* may require the giving of reasons. In order to decide whether this is so, the reviewing court examines the circumstances of the case, balancing any arguments for and against the giving of reasons in order to come to a rounded view about what fairness requires.[134] Prominent among the factors that weigh in favour of the imposition of a reason-giving duty is the importance of the right or interest that is at stake. So if, as in *Doody*, the decision affects the claimant's liberty, this will be a strong indication that reasons should be given, as will the fact

---

[125] *R (Hasan) v Secretary of State for Trade and Industry* [2007] EWHC 2630 (Admin), [21].

[126] *R v Secretary of State for the Home Department, ex p Doody* [1994] 1 AC 531, 564.

[127] *Doody* at 564.   [128] *Hasan* at [20].

[129] For comment on the relative merits of this approach and one based on a general duty subject to exceptions, see Neill, 'The Duty to Give Reasons: The Openness of Decision-Making', in Forsyth and Hare (eds), *The Golden Metwand and the Crooked Cord* (Oxford 1998).

[130] See Le Sueur, 'Legal Duties to Give Reasons' (1999) 52 CLP 150.

[131] See further Chapter 10, section 7, above.   [132] Freedom of Information Act 2000, s 1.

[133] Freedom of Information Act 2000, s 84.

[134] *R v Higher Education Funding Council, ex p Institute of Dental Surgery* [1994] 1 WLR 242.

that the decision impacts on other important interests such as professional standing, reputation,[135] or bodily integrity.[136] A duty to give reasons is also likely to be imposed in respect of decisions that are aberrant—that is, decisions that, on the face of it, seem inexplicable, perhaps because they appear to fly in the face of the great weight of evidence.[137] On the other hand, the court also has to weigh factors that point away from a duty to give reasons: this may be so where, for example, giving reasons would place 'an undue burden on the decision-maker' or 'call for the articulation of sometimes inexpressible value judgments'.[138]

Q Where reasoning-giving would be especially burdensome for the decision-maker, should this wholly relieve it of the obligation to give reasons, or might it be more appropriate to impose a lighter duty—for example, to outline its thinking without going into detail?

Third, where a public authority has an established administrative practice of giving reasons or has made an express promise that it will do so, this may create a *legitimate expectation* that reasons will be given. The courts will generally insist that such an expectation be honoured by the decision-maker. We consider legitimate expectations below.[139]

Fourth, Art 6 of the ECHR requires that decisions to which it is applicable be accompanied by an indication of the grounds on which they are based.[140] So, where Art 6 applies, a duty to give reasons can be said to exist without more: there is no need to engage in the common law analysis discussed above. In this sense, Art 6 imposes a clearer and more certain duty to give reasons. However, the important caveat must be entered that—as we saw above—Art 6 does not apply to all administrative decisions.[141]

It only remains to consider what the duty to give reasons requires when it applies. Courts—both domestic and European—have said that the content of the duty depends on the circumstances.[142] Some general principles, however, were set out by Lord Brown in *South Buckinghamshire District Council v Porter*.[143] He said that while reasons must enable people to understand why the decision was reached and what the conclusions were on the main points of controversy, they need refer only to the 'main issues' and not to 'every material consideration'. It also seems that the court will take into account the burden that a requirement to give reasons imposes on the decision-maker: where, for example, decisions are taken by groups of people, it has been held that it would be unduly burdensome to require each individual decision-maker's thinking to be set out, such that very broad-brush reasons may suffice in such situations.[144]

---

[135] *R v Ministry of Defence, ex p Murray* [1998] COD 134; *R v City of London Corporation, ex p Matson* [1997] 1 WLR 765.   [136] *R (Wooder) v Feggetter* [2002] EWCA Civ 554, [2003] QB 219.

[137] *Institute of Dental Surgery* at 263.   [138] *Institute of Dental Surgery* at 257.

[139] See section 4.3 below.   [140] *Hadjianastassiou v Greece* (1993) 16 EHRR 219, 237.

[141] See section 3.5.2 above.

[142] *Helle v Finland* (1997) 26 EHRR 159, 183; *Stefan v General Medical Council* [1999] 1 WLR 1293, 1301 and 1304.   [143] [2004] UKHL 33, [2004] 1 WLR 1953, [36].

[144] *R (Asha Foundation) v Millenium Commission* [2003] EWCA Civ 88.

4. Exercising discretion

4.1 Introduction

We began this chapter with the example of a Minister empowered to 'decide whether—and, if so, subject to what conditions, if any—permission should be granted for major infrastructure projects'.[145] This enables—indeed requires—the Minister to exercise *discretion*: to choose whether or not to grant permission for a given 'major infrastructure project' and, if so, what conditions, if any, should be attached. Naturally, the principles of fairness, considered above, apply to the exercise of discretionary power where this impacts on the rights, interests, or legitimate expectations of individuals. In this section, we are concerned with a further set of principles of judicial review that apply specifically to the exercise of discretion.

4.2 The need to retain discretionary power

An obvious—and logical—starting point is with the general principle that those to whom discretionary power has been granted must retain it. This means that they must exercise *genuine discretion* (rather than, for example, making decisions according to a fixed rule) and must exercise it *themselves* (instead of getting others to do so).

4.2.1 The non-delegation principle—exercise of discretion by the chosen decision-maker

Unless the legislation conferring the power in question provides otherwise, the presumption is that discretionary power may only lawfully be exercised by the person or body upon whom it is conferred by statute.[146] Three reasons underlie this presumption. First, and most obviously, it reflects *parliamentary intention*: if Parliament has specified that a particular agency should take the decision, then Parliament's will ought to prevail. Second, Parliament is likely to have chosen a particular decision-maker because it is *institutionally qualified* to act: it may, for example, possess expertise on the issue to which the power relates. And, third, if the power may only be used by the person or body named in the statute, this ensures that—in the event of an improper or unlawful decision—the responsible party can readily be identified and held *accountable*. Courts have therefore held that it is unlawful not only for the statutorily ordained decision-maker straightforwardly to delegate power to another person or body,[147] but also for it to enter into arrangements in which the *real* power is exercised by someone other than the person identified in the statute. So, for example, it is unlawful for the statutory decision-maker automatically to adopt someone else's view[148] or to make their decision conditional on another's approval.[149]

---

[145] See section 1 above.
[146] *Barnard v National Dock Labour Board* [1953] 2 QB 18.   [147] *Barnard.*
[148] *High v Billings* (1903) 89 LT 550.
[149] *Lavender and Sons Ltd v Minister of Housing and Local Government* [1970] 1 WLR 1231.

However, problems would arise if these principles were applied too strictly. First, this may actually inhibit good government. Consider our example of a Minister called upon to decide whether to allow the construction of a new airport. While it is, for the reasons set out above, important that he[150] takes the ultimate decision, it is also acceptable—indeed, desirable—that he should do so having taken full account of the views of others, such as those with expertise on the likely environmental and economic implications of the proposed airport. For this reason, courts must—and do—distinguish between taking account of others' views (which is legitimate) and ascribing so much weight to them that the statutory decision-maker can no longer be said to be bringing his own judgement to bear on the issues.

> **Q** Assume that, in our example, the Minister, having decided that the new airport should be built, consults an expert environmental campaign group about what conditions he should attach to the grant of planning permission. The group replies to the Minister, recommending restrictions on the number of runways, the size of the terminal buildings, and the amount of car-parking. The next day, the Minister formally imposes exactly those conditions. Would the Minister have acted lawfully in such circumstances?

Second, in some circumstances, it is simply impractical to insist that discretionary power must always be exercised by the person named in the statute. For example, in *Re Golden Chemical Products Ltd*,[151] the Secretary of State was authorised by statute to take steps to arrange for the winding up[152] of a company where this appeared to be in the public interest. In fact, the power had actually been exercised by a civil servant in the Secretary of State's department, in apparent breach of the requirement that discretionary power is exercised only by the person named in the statute. However, the court noted that, in the earlier case of *Carltona*, Lord Greene MR had treated Ministers as a special case, on account of the fact that their functions are 'so multifarious that no Minister could ever personally attend to them': public business, he said, 'could not be carried on' if Ministers were to have to exercise all of their powers personally.[153] Thus, applying the so-called *Carltona* doctrine, the court in *Golden Chemical* held that the civil servant could lawfully exercise the ministerial power. Some judges have attempted to rationalise this position by holding that, in such circumstances, the 'civil servant acts not as the delegate, but as the *alter ego*, of the Secretary of State'.[154] The better view, however, is that when Parliament confers discretion on a *Minister*, its intention is to entrust the discretion not only to him, but also to his *departmental officials* for whose actions he is legally responsible to the courts and politically responsible to Parliament.[155]

---

[150] Or at least his department: see below for discussion of this point.   [151] [1976] Ch 300.
[152] That is, putting its affairs in order (for example, by paying creditors where possible) and closing it down.   [153] *Carltona Ltd v Commissioners of Works* [1943] 2 All ER 560, 563.
[154] *R v Secretary of State for the Home Department, ex p Oladehinde* [1991] 1 AC 254, 284, *per* Lord Donaldson MR.
[155] *Bushell v Secretary of State for the Environment* [1981] AC 75, 95, *per* Lord Diplock.

This raises difficult questions in light of recent changes to the structure of government in the UK. In particular, it is increasingly common for certain functions to be performed not by traditional government departments, but by executive agencies.[156] For example, the Ministry of Justice is not itself involved in the day-to-day running of prisons: this is the role of the Prison Service. While the Secretary of State for Justice determines the policy framework within which the Service works (for example, setting targets and budgets), the relationship is an arm's-length one, and Ministers are not in the traditional sense responsible for the day-to-day decisions made by such agencies. In light of this, it has been argued that applying the *Carltona* doctrine in such contexts is objectionable because the very assumption underpinning it—of ministerial responsibility for departmental officials' actions—does not meaningfully apply in relation to agencies.[157] Nevertheless, the courts have held that powers conferred on Ministers can lawfully be exercised by executive agencies.[158]

4.2.2 The non-fettering principle—discretion, policy, and rules

As Figure 13.5 shows, the holder of a discretionary power—such as the Secretary of State in our example—might exercise it in one of a number of ways. First, he may choose to adopt an absolutely rigid rule that he will only grant permission for new airports in the northern half of the country. Second, at the other extreme, he might approach each new case with a completely open mind, without any prior view about whether (and, if so, in what circumstances) new airports should be built. Or, third, he might adopt an interim position: a general policy that no new airports should be built in the south, coupled with a willingness to make exceptions to that policy if it can be shown (for example) that there is a compelling economic case.

Traditionally, administrative law has held that while holders of discretionary power may adopt policies to guide the exercise of discretion, they may not lawfully adopt

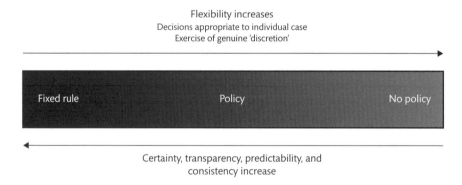

Figure 13.5 Rules, policy, and discretion

---

[156] On executive agencies, see further Chapter 4, section 3.10, above.

[157] Freedland, 'The Rule against Delegation and the *Carltona* Doctrine in an Agency Context' [1996] PL 19.

[158] *R v Secretary of State for Social Services, ex p Sherwin* (1996) 32 BMLR 1.

rigid rules that fetter the exercise of such discretion. The difficult question concerns how to draw the line between a lawful policy and an unlawful rule. The general principle is that a position from which the decision-maker is prepared to resile in exceptional circumstances will be acceptable, and treated as falling on the 'policy' side of the line, whereas an unwillingness to make exceptions is suggestive of a 'rule'.[159] On this basis, the third position set out above would be lawful. For example, in *British Oxygen Co Ltd v Minister of Technology*,[160] the Minister, having been given a discretionary power to provide businesses with grants to assist with the purchase of industrial machinery and having resolved to make no grants in respect of machinery costing less than £25, refused assistance to the claimant company, which had spent some £4 million on numerous items of equipment costing £20 each. Holding that the Minister had acted lawfully, Lord Reid thought it almost inevitable that large departments called upon to decide many cases would evolve 'a policy so precise that it could well be called a rule'—an approach that he regarded as acceptable provided that 'the authority is always willing to listen to anyone with something new to say' (and to make exceptions to the policy, or rule, if that is appropriate in the circumstances).[161]

However, in some circumstances, the courts are less willing to tolerate the sort of approach that was permitted in *British Oxygen*. For example, in a case concerning the exercise of a discretionary power to provide assistance (including accommodation) to homeless families with young children, it was considered imperative that each case be looked at on its own merits, and Templeman LJ was not 'persuaded that even a policy resolution hedged around with exceptions would be entirely free from attack'.[162]

> **Q** Is it possible to account for these different approaches? Do the underlying policy factors considered above—certainty, flexibility, consistency, transparency, and so on—help to explain why the courts' willingness to accept the legitimacy of structuring discretion by reference to policies may vary?

4.3 Legitimate expectations

The legal principle addressed in the previous section concerns situations in which decision-makers adopt policies or rules to the disadvantage of the claimant—raising the question of whether the claimant may challenge the decision on the ground that the executive unlawfully fettered its discretion. What of the obverse situation, in which the individual wishes to hold the government to a policy that it has announced or an undertaking that it has given, but the government wishes to act otherwise? Consider,

---

[159] *R v Port of London Authority, ex p Kynoch Ltd* [1919] 1 KB 176. If exceptions are never, in fact, made, this will be strong evidence that a rigid rule is being applied, even if the defendant professes a preparedness to make exceptions: *R v Warwickshire County Council, ex p Collymore* [1995] ELR 217.

[160] [1971] AC 610.   [161] *British Oxygen* at 625.

[162] *Attorney-General ex rel Tilley v Wandsworth London Borough Council* [1981] 1 WLR 854, 858.

for example, the facts of *Coughlan*.[163] The claimant, having been seriously injured in 1971, became a long-term hospital patient. In 1993, the health authority, in order to secure the claimant's agreement to be moved to a new care facility, told her and a small number of others that they could remain 'for as long as they wished to stay there': it would be their 'home for life'. Yet, just five years later, the health authority resolved to close the new facility, arguing that it had become 'prohibitively expensive' to run. Cases such as this raise very difficult questions.[164] Clearly, if the health authority were to be allowed to resile from its promise, the claimant, having relied upon it, would suffer profound unfairness; moreover, there is a strong argument—based on the idea of legal certainty[165]—that individuals should be able to trust and rely safely on what public authorities have told them.[166] Yet it is also arguable that public bodies should be free to act in the *public* interest—for example, by using scarce financial resources efficiently—even if this occasions unfairness to some individuals.[167]

These are the sort of arguments with which courts have had to grapple as they have developed the *doctrine of legitimate expectation*, the essence of which is that judicial review will lie where a public authority's conduct is inconsistent with that which the claimant is legitimately entitled to expect. Two key questions arise: how do we work out what the claimant can legitimately expect; and what can courts do when public bodies refuse to give them it?

4.3.1 What can the claimant legitimately expect?

Unsurprisingly, the law does not straightforwardly protect people's actual expectations. So if a person reads a government statement and unreasonably misinterprets it, such that they expect to receive something that was not, on a reasonable interpretation, promised, no *legitimate* expectation will arise. For this reason, the courts require that, in order to give rise to such an expectation, the undertaking must be 'clear, unambiguous and devoid of relevant qualification',[168] like the representation made to the claimant in *Coughlan*. It appears that a conditional statement (at least when the condition is not met) will not suffice.[169] The requirement of a clear undertaking does not, however, mean that it must be explicit: an undertaking may be inferred from previous conduct.[170]

---

[163] *R v North and East Devon Health Authority, ex p Coughlan* [2001] QB 213.

[164] We will see what answers the court came to in *Coughlan* in section 4.3.2 below.

[165] See Chapter 2, section 4.4.3, above.

[166] See further Schønberg, *Legitimate Expectations in Administrative Law* (Oxford 2000), ch 1.

[167] Indeed, as we saw in section 4.2.2 above, the importance of *preserving* discretion underlies the unlawfulness of exercising discretion pursuant to a strict rule (as opposed to a policy). For comment, see Hilson, 'Policies, the Non-Fetter Principle and the Principle of Substantive Legitimate Expectation: Between a Rock and a Hard Place?' [2006] JR 289.

[168] *R v Inland Revenue Commissioners, ex p MFK Underwriting Agencies Ltd* [1990] 1 WLR 1545, 1569, *per* Bingham LJ.

[169] *R (Bancoult) v Secretary of State for Foreign and Commonwealth Affairs (No 2)* [2008] UKHL 61, [2009] 1 AC 453.

[170] For example, in *Council of Civil Services Unions v Minister for the Civil Service* [1985] AC 374, a legitimate expectation that civil servants would be consulted before their terms of employment were changed

Additional restrictions on the circumstances in which a legitimate expectation can arise were highlighted by *Begbie*.[171] The case arose out of the Blair administration's decision—implemented, shortly after its election, via the Education (Schools) Act 1997—to wind up a scheme that had offered state funding to enable children of insufficient financial means to attend independent schools. The 9-year-old claimant was a pupil at an 'all-through school'—that is, a school that educated children from the age of 5 through to the age of 18—and sought to enforce undertakings that such children would receive state funding throughout, rather than having it stopped at the age of 11 upon completion of primary education. Rejecting the claimant's case, the court held that undertakings given by Labour politicians, including Tony Blair, *before* the 1997 general election could not give rise to legitimate expectations. Peter Gibson LJ stated that an 'opposition spokesman, even the Leader of the Opposition, does not speak on behalf of a public authority', such that 'when a party elected into office fails to keep its election promises, the consequences should be political and not legal'.[172] It was also held in *Begbie* that the claimant could not establish a legitimate expectation because this would run directly contrary to the scheme Parliament had laid down. The statute envisaged that funding would continue beyond primary education only where, on the particular facts of the case, the Secretary of State was satisfied that that should happen—yet the claimant's legitimate expectation, if accepted by the court, would have required funding to be continued in a broad category of cases without reference to the circumstances of individual children.

Finally, it seems intuitively right that individuals should only be able to claim a legitimate expectation where, in the first place, they have *knowledge* of the representation giving rise to the expectation. After all, it is not possible to expect something of which one is ignorant. However, the courts have not taken this view. For example, the High Court of Australia held that an individual could establish a legitimate expectation on the basis that the Australian government, by ratifying a treaty, had held itself out as willing to comply with certain standards of behaviour—notwithstanding that he was aware of neither the existence nor the content of the treaty when the decision about which he complained was taken.[173] The majority judges considered this irrelevant: it was reasonable to expect the Australian government to act in conformity with the standards in the treaty, and that was sufficient, in the circumstances, to give rise to a legitimate expectation. English courts have now adopted the same view. So, for example, in *R (Rashid) v Secretary of State for the Home Department*,[174] an asylum seeker—who, it had been decided, should be returned to Iraq contrary to a Home Office policy—established a legitimate expectation that he would *not* be returned in breach of the policy,

---

could be inferred from the fact that previous such changes had always been preceded by consultation. (The legitimate expectation was not, however, enforced, due to national security considerations.)

[171] *R v Department of Education and Employment, ex p Begbie* [2000] 1 WLR 1115.
[172] *Begbie* at [55]–[56].
[173] *Minister of State for Immigration and Ethnic Affairs v Teoh* (1995) 183 CLR 273.
[174] [2005] EWCA Civ 744, [2005] Imm AR 608.

notwithstanding that, when the decision was taken, neither he nor the officials concerned knew of the policy. Dyson LJ thought the claimant's ignorance 'immaterial'.[175] There is a strong policy argument in favour of this approach, in that it ensures that the law does not discriminate between well-informed and less well-informed individuals. However, it is difficult to overlook the fact that cases such as *Rashid*, in which the claimant knows nothing about the policy, are different from cases such as *Coughlan*, in which there is a breach of a clear undertaking on which the claimant relied.[176] It may therefore be desirable if the law were to distinguish between these types of case more clearly, regarding the latter as raising legitimate expectations proper, while dealing with the former by reference to a separate principle requiring public bodies—in the absence of reasonable justification—to act consistently with their own policies.[177]

4.3.2 What can courts do if legitimate expectations are dashed?

If a claimant establishes that he had a legitimate expectation that has been frustrated by a public body, the options open to a reviewing court, as Figure 13.6 shows, depend, in the first place, on the *content* of the expectation.

One possibility is that the claimant may be entitled to expect that his case will be considered in a particular way—for example, that he will be consulted or be given a fair hearing. Here, the claimant has a *procedural legitimate expectation*, and the most that the court can do is to require the public body to accord to the claimant whatever procedural niceties it led him to expect. Of course, as we have already seen, decision-makers are very often required to treat individuals in a procedurally fair manner whether or not they have created an expectation of such treatment.[178] But legitimate expectation may be relevant in one of two ways. First, if there would not otherwise be a duty to act fairly, a procedural legitimate expectation will enable the individual to insist upon fair treatment to which she would not otherwise be entitled.[179] Second, if, as a general matter of procedural fairness, an individual would be entitled in the circumstances only to a modest degree of fairness (for example, a right to make written representations), but is promised something more than this (for example, an oral hearing), this is likely to give rise to a procedural legitimate expectation entitling him to the more elaborate style of fair treatment.

The other possibility is that the claimant may have a *substantive legitimate expectation*—that is, he may legitimately expect a particular outcome to the decision-making process: for example, that he will receive the licence for which he applied or, as in *Coughlan*, a 'home for life'. Here, as Figure 13.6 indicates, a number of options are open to reviewing courts.

---

[175] *Rashid* at [47].

[176] If knowledge of the representation is not required in order to *establish* a legitimate expectation then, logically, there can be no absolute requirement of reliance. However, absence of reliance makes it less likely that the court will judge it unfair (and hence unlawful) to *breach* a legitimate expectation: *R v Secretary of State for Education and Employment, ex p Begbie* [2000] 1 WLR 1115, 1124, *per* Peter Gibson LJ.

[177] See further Dotan, 'Why Administrators Should be Bound by Their Policies' (1997) 17 OJLS 23.

[178] See section 3.6 above.   [179] *Attorney-General of Hong Kong v Ng Yuen Shiu* [1983] 2 AC 629.

First, the court may decide whether or not frustration of the expectation is lawful by asking whether this would be 'so unfair as to be a misuse of the authority's power'.[180] This involves balancing the unfairness that would be occasioned to the individual if the expectation were dashed against the damage that would be caused to the public interest if the decision-maker were held to its promise. In *Coughlan*, for example, the court felt that it would be grossly unfair to the claimant if her expectation of a home for life were dashed, bearing in mind that the promise had been directed to her (rather than to a large group of people of which she was a member). This made it more likely that she would (and more reasonable for her to) rely on the promise, which she had duly done (by moving to the new care facility in the first place). Moreover, the court did not consider that the defendant had established an adequate justification for overriding the claimant's legitimate expectation: the health authority cited scarcity of resources, arguing that it could make more efficient use of its budget by rehousing the claimant, but it was held that these obstacles to fulfilling the claimant's expectation were 'financial only', and insufficient to justify not doing what had been promised.[181]

The approach adopted in *Coughlan* was highly interventionist: it has been argued that the court was 'dismissive' of the health authority's arguments and failed to adhere to the orthodox view—about which we say more in the next section—that 'discretionary decisions as to the allocation of finite resources subject to many competing individual demands [should] generally [be] left to bodies subject to democratic accountability and with a complete view of all the claims upon those resources, not the courts'.[182] However, it is important to bear in mind that the court indicated that such an approach would be adopted only in very specific circumstances—such as those of *Coughlan* itself—'where the expectation is confined to one person or a few people, giving the promise or representation the character of a contract'.[183]

Outwith such circumstances, reviewing courts are likely to be less interventionist. For example, in *R (Bibi) v Newham London Borough Council*,[184] it was held that a local authority's promise to provide the claimant with permanent accommodation gave rise to a substantive legitimate expectation that such accommodation would indeed be provided, but the court did not apply the *Coughlan* test. Instead, it required the local authority—which, in deciding that the claimant should *not* be offered permanent accommodation, had ignored its earlier promise—to reconsider the matter, taking due account of the legitimate expectation that it had engendered. This (unlike the approach in *Coughlan*) leaves the decision-maker with ultimate discretion over whether to prioritise the interests of the claimant or the public.

A further possibility, as Figure 13.6 shows, lies in '*Wednesbury* protection' of substantive legitimate expectations. For example, in *R v Secretary of State for the Home*

---

[180] *R v North and East Devon Health Authority, ex p Coughlan* [2001] QB 213, [83].
[181] *Coughlan* at [60].
[182] Sales and Steyn, 'Legitimate Expectations in English Public Law: An Analysis' [2004] PL 564, 591.
[183] *Coughlan* at [59].   [184] [2001] EWCA Civ 607, [2002] 1 WLR 237.

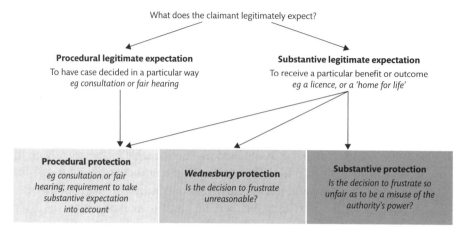

Figure 13.6 Legitimate expectations

Department, ex p Hargreaves,[185] a legitimate expectation arose when prisoners were promised (in return for good behaviour) temporary home release upon serving one-third of their sentence. When the claimant prisoner later challenged the Home Secretary's decision to defer home release until completion of *half* of the sentence, it was held that the decision would be lawful provided that it was not manifestly unreasonable (which it was not). Like the approach in *Bibi* (and in contrast to that which was adopted in *Coughlan*), the test applied in *Hargreaves* ensured that the decision-maker retained a degree of discretion to decide for himself whether to prioritise the interests of individual promisees or those of the general public.

So how do courts—when faced with a substantive legitimate expectation—decide which of the three approaches shown in Figure 13.6 to adopt? The key to understanding this point is to recognise that when an individual seeks to enforce a substantive legitimate expectation, he is effectively asking the court to hold the public authority to an 'advance decision' from which it now wishes to resile because it judges that some other decision would better serve the public interest. Sales argues that the more opportunity the public body has had, at the advance stage, to appreciate the likely consequences of its representations or policy, the more legitimate it is for the court to hold it to the 'advance decision'.[186] *Coughlan*-style substantive protection is therefore most likely where a promise is made to an individual,[187] or to a group of individuals with similar interests. Where, however, legitimate expectations are founded on general statements of policy capable of impacting unpredictably on large numbers of people, there is a strong argument for the public authority to be permitted to retain discretion, so as to enable it later to make an informed decision.[188]

---

[185] [1997] 1 WLR 906.   [186] Sales, 'Legitimate Expectations' [2006] JR 186, 189.
[187] As in *Coughlan*.   [188] Sales at 189.

Finally, we should note that the courts' capacity to protect legitimate expectations is severely limited where the expectation relates to *unlawful conduct*.[189] For example, in *Rowland v Environment Agency*,[190] the owners of a house were led by the respondent to believe that an adjoining stretch of the River Thames was not subject to public rights of access. It later transpired that such rights did exist, but the Environment Agency had no legal power to extinguish them. The Court of Appeal therefore concluded that although the claimant had a legitimate expectation concerning the status of the relevant stretch of river,[191] the Agency could not be ordered to fulfil the expectation because it lacked legal capacity to do so. Instead, the Court held that the Agency was required to act towards the claimant as favourably as its limited legal powers permitted—by not drawing attention to the existence of the rights of access.

4.4 Inputs to the decision-making process

It stands to reason that if the quality of the material that is put into a process is high, this increases the chances of a high-quality outcome—and vice versa. This is true of manufacturing processes (high-quality raw materials will help to produce a high-quality product) and it is equally true of decision-making processes. In light of this, it is unsurprising that administrative law seeks to exert some control over the inputs into such processes. It does so through the *relevancy doctrine*, which requires decision-makers to *take into account all legally relevant matters* and to *ignore legally irrelevant matters*.[192]

Before looking at how this works in practice, we should note two connections between these requirements and those of procedural fairness, considered above. First, as we have seen, one of the purposes of according fair hearings to individuals liable to be affected by government actions is to ensure that, before anything is done, decision-makers are in receipt of relevant information. In this way, the concept of natural justice helps to ensure on a practical level—by obliging decision-makers to listen to individuals—that the former will be well-placed to exercise their power sensibly. The relevancy doctrine goes further by insisting that such matters are *actually taken account of* when decisions are made. Second, the requirement to ignore irrelevant matters overlaps with the rule against bias: for example, if a Minister or official were to take a particular decision because he stood to benefit financially from it, this would be unlawful according to both the rule against bias and the relevancy doctrine (personal financial gain being a legally irrelevant consideration). That said, the rule against bias and the relevancy doctrine do not cover identical ground: the latter requires proof that

---

[189] See further Hannett and Busch, '*Ultra Vires* Representations and Illegitimate Expectations' [2005] PL 729.   [190] [2002] EWCA Civ 1885, [2005] Ch 1.

[191] This conclusion was based in part on the fact that the claimant's right to property under the ECHR was at stake.

[192] *Hanks v Minister of Housing and Local Government* [1963] 1 QB 999; *Padfield v Minister of Agriculture, Fisheries and Food* [1968] AC 997. Some matters may fall into neither category—it may be permissible, but not obligatory, to consider them. For discussion, see *Ashby v Minister of Immigration* [1981] 1 NZLR 222, 224.

irrelevant matters have been considered; the former requires only a perception that this may have happened.[193] Meanwhile, as we will see, the range of matters liable to be considered legally irrelevant is broader than the category interests likely to give rise to a perception of bias.[194]

An obvious question arises. How do we decide whether a particular matter is legally relevant or irrelevant? For example, how does our hypothetical Minister, when required to decide whether to allow a new airport to be built, know what he must and must not take into account? The difficulty is that the language of our imaginary statute[195]—like that of most actual statutes—gives no real steer. Courts, when called upon to apply the relevancy doctrine, must therefore often rely on relatively general, including practical, considerations. As Cooke J explained in a New Zealand case, 'the more general and the more obviously important the consideration, the readier the court must be to hold that Parliament must have meant it to be taken into account'.[196] So, for example, when faced with the question of whether the financial implications of a decision are legally irrelevant, the courts have indicated a willingness to allow such matters to be considered where to do otherwise would expose a public authority to potentially unlimited expense.[197] In contrast, when the Home Secretary—in deciding on the minimum period that two children who had murdered another child should spend in prison[198]—took into account public opinion, including a petition organised by a national tabloid newspaper, it was held that he had acted unlawfully.[199] The Minister was, in effect, exercising a judicial function, and had therefore to adopt the sort of objective, independent approach expected of judges; as a result, public opinion was legally irrelevant. Similarly, it was said by Lord Reid in *Padfield* that it was unlawful for a Minister, in refusing to order an investigation into arrangements for the sale of milk, to take into account the fact that such an investigation may arrive at politically embarrassing conclusions.[200]

Finally, we should note the implications of the relevancy doctrine for the decision-maker's ultimate discretion. The *Padfield* case is a famous example of the fact that it is possible to win the battle at judicial review while losing the war: the Minister's decision was quashed, but he took the same decision again (without apparent reliance on irrelevant considerations). That judicial review of the *inputs* to the decision-making process does not necessarily circumscribe the *conclusions* the decision-maker may reach is underlined by the fact that the courts have held that while relevant factors must be *taken into account*, the *amount of weight* to be ascribed to them is, in general, a matter

---

[193] Judged by reference to the fair-minded and informed observer test. See section 3.4.2 above.

[194] The *Venables* case, considered in the next paragraph, illustrates this point.

[195] See section 1 above.

[196] *CREEDNZ v Governor-General of New Zealand* [1981] 1 NZLR 172, 183.

[197] *R v Gloucestershire County Council, ex p Barry* [1997] AC 584.

[198] The Home Secretary no longer exercises this power: such decisions are now taken exclusively by the judiciary. See discussion in section 3.5.1 above.

[199] *R v Secretary of State for the Home Department, ex p Venables* [1998] AC 407.

[200] *Padfield v Minister of Agriculture, Fisheries and Food* [1968] AC 997.

purely for the relevant public authority.[201] That said, we should not underestimate the relevancy doctrine or its capacity to enable judges to give vent to their own policy preferences: in the early twentieth-century case of *Roberts v Hopwood*, it was held that a local authority, in deciding to pay male and female employees equally, had acted improperly by taking into account what Lord Atkinson called 'eccentric principles of socialistic philanthropy' and 'a feminist ambition to secure the equality of the sexes'.[202]

> **Q** In our example, would it be lawful for the Minister, in deciding whether to grant permission for the new airport, to take into account the environmental impact of and public demand for air travel? Would it be unlawful for him not to take into account local opposition to the proposed airport and likely increases in congestion on roads in the vicinity of the airport?

4.5 **Motives and purposes**

It has been said that 'no statute can be purposeless': every grant of discretionary power to a public authority must be for some purpose (or purposes), and the power can lawfully be used *only* for that purpose (or those purposes).[203] This principle is an essential safeguard against the misuse of power—for example, it prevents powers conferred on public authorities from being lawfully used for self-serving political reasons—and its application is relatively straightforward where the statute contains an explicit statement of purpose. For example, in *Municipal Council of Sydney v Campbell*,[204] a local authority had been given power to purchase land compulsorily for the purposes of 'carrying out improvements in or remodelling any portion of the city' and widening or constructing new highways. Purporting to exercise these powers, the defendant council resolved to improve a major thoroughfare and, in this context, to purchase land covering a considerable area, including neighbouring streets. However, the purchase of much of the land was not necessary for the purpose of carrying out the improvements to the highway, and it transpired that the purpose underlying the purchase of the excess land was to realise a profit by selling it after completion of the highway scheme. This was not one of the purposes for which the power had been conferred—and so the council's resolution was unlawful.

Where the statute makes no explicit provision about the purpose underlying a discretionary power, the court must nevertheless determine the uses to which it may legitimately be put. In *Congreve v Home Office*,[205] the Home Secretary revoked a television licence that the claimant—in order to avoid a scheduled 50 per cent rise in the price of licences—had purchased before his old one expired. This revocation, said the Court of Appeal, was unlawful: the Minister was seeking to use his power 'as a

---

[201] *Tesco Stores Ltd v Secretary of State for the Environment* [1995] 1 WLR 759.
[202] [1925] AC 578, 594.
[203] *R v Somerset County Council, ex p Fewings* [1995] 1 All ER 513, 525, *per* Laws J.
[204] [1925] AC 339.   [205] *Congreve v Home Office* [1976] QB 629.

means of extracting money which Parliament ha[d] given the executive no mandate to demand'; he had thus acted for an improper purpose.[206]

The court's role in determining the purposes for which a discretion may and may not be used places it in a powerful position, since its decision on this point may have serious consequences for the scope of the government's discretion. This point is clearly illustrated by the *Pergau Dam* case.[207] We saw in Chapter 11 that, in this case, the Foreign Secretary—in purported exercise of a statutory power to grant aid 'for the purpose of promoting the development or maintaining the economy of a country or territory outside the United Kingdom, or the welfare of its people'—approved financial support of over £200 million for the construction of a hydroelectric power station on the Pergau river in Malaysia. When he proposed to proceed notwithstanding a report that concluded that the project was economically unviable and a 'very bad buy', judicial review was sought. Holding that the Minister had acted unlawfully, the court concluded that, properly interpreted, the power could only be used for the purpose of promoting *economically sound* development. The effect of this interpretation was to curtail the Minister's discretion significantly: unless the court were satisfied of the economic viability of the scheme—and, in this case, the court was *not* satisfied—it would be unlawful to offer financial assistance.[208] It is clear, therefore, that by implying particular purposes into a discretionary power, the courts are able to exert considerable influence over the uses to which it may be lawfully put.

4.6 Review of the outcome of the decision-making process

So far, our focus has principally been on aspects of the decision-making *process*, such as the procedure to be adopted, and the matters that can and cannot lawfully be taken into account. We now turn to the *decision itself*—and therefore enter more controversial territory.

4.6.1 *Wednesbury* unreasonableness

As we saw in the previous chapter, a distinction has traditionally been drawn between 'appeal' and 'review'. So, returning to our example,[209] while it is uncontroversial that a court could strike down the Minister's decision to allow the new airport to be built if he were to appear to be biased, or to have failed to act fairly, or to have taken into account improper considerations, it would not be open to a judge to quash the decision simply because he disagreed with it. It might well be the case that, if the judge were asked to

---

[206] *Congreve* at 662, *per* Geoffrey Lane LJ.

[207] *R v Secretary of State for Foreign and Commonwealth Affairs, ex p World Development Movement Ltd* [1995] 1 WLR 386.

[208] For criticism, see Irvine, *Human Rights, Constitutional Law and the Development of the English Legal System* (Oxford 2003), pp 164–5. If economic soundness had been characterised simply as a relevant matter that had to be considered, rather than part of the statutory purpose, the outcome would have been different, since it would have been sufficient for the Minister to have taken the issue into account.

[209] See section 1 above.

make the decision himself, he would consider that (for example) the environmental damage likely to be caused by the new airport outweighed the economic gains that it would bring. But such disagreement about the merits of the decision would not, in itself, be grounds for striking it down.

Instead, courts have traditionally confined themselves to asking whether—as Lord Greene MR put it in the *Wednesbury* case— the decision is 'so unreasonable that no reasonable authority could ever have come to it',[210] citing the example[211] of dismissing a red-haired teacher simply because of the colour of her hair.[212] Meanwhile, in the so-called *GCHQ* case, Lord Diplock preferred to speak of a decision 'which is so outrageous in its defiance of logic or of accepted moral standards that no sensible person who had applied his mind to the question to be decided could have arrived at it'.[213] The most significant characteristic of such dicta is that they characterise unreasonableness (in the present sense) as something quite exceptional, bordering on the absurd. The clear intention behind this approach is to ensure that courts do not transgress the hallowed line between legality and merits by second-guessing public bodies, interfering simply because they disagree with decision-makers' conclusions.

In reality, however, the position is more complex, and the willingness of the courts to examine the outcomes of decision-making processes varies depending on the circumstances. The reasons for judicial restraint in this sphere, as we saw in Chapter 12, lie in *democratic* and *institutional* considerations—and it stands to reason that such concerns play out differently in different contexts. For example, the courts have identified some categories in which they will be even *less* willing than usual to examine, on reasonableness grounds, the outcome of a decision-making process. Where, for example, certain councils challenged a Minister's decision (which had been approved by Parliament) to limit the levels at which they could set local taxes, Lord Scarman (whose speech commanded the assent of the other Law Lords) said that judicial intervention was improper in the absence of evidence that the Minister had acted in bad faith or that his decision was 'so absurd that he must have taken leave of his senses'.[214] His Lordship sought to justify this 'hands-off' approach to substantive review on both democratic grounds (the Minister's policy had been approved by Parliament) and institutional grounds (the decision raised complex issues of national economic policy, the appropriateness of which the court lacked the expertise to judge). Indeed, there are several reasons why courts may consider themselves institutionally ill-equipped to form a judgment about the content of a policy or decision. The difficulty may be one straightforwardly of expertise if the matter is highly technical or esoteric. Alternatively, where a decision is 'polycentric'—that is, where it is likely to have many,

---

[210] *Associated Provincial Picture Houses Ltd v Wednesbury Corporation* [1948] 1 KB 223, 230.

[211] Given by Warrington LJ in *Short v Poole Corporation* [1926] Ch 66, 90–1.

[212] Of course, such a decision would also be unlawful on the grounds of having taken account of a legally irrelevant consideration.

[213] *Council of Civil Service Unions v Minister for the Civil Service* [1985] AC 374, 410.

[214] *Nottinghamshire County Council v Secretary of State for the Environment* [1986] AC 240, 247.

perhaps unpredictable, consequences—the court, by virtue of the fact that it hears only the limited amount of evidence put to it by the two parties to the dispute, will probably not be in a position to form a view about the appropriateness of whatever decision has been made.[215] For example, the decision in *Coughlan*[216] can be characterised as polycentric: the health authority was seeking to close the home in which the claimant was accommodated because it felt that scarce resources could be better used. In order to evaluate such an argument fully, it would be necessary to identify and ascribe value to all of the different uses to which the health authority could put its available funds—a task that the reviewing court was self-evidently not well situated to undertake.

> **Q** Do you agree that the decision under review in *Coughlan* was a polycentric one? If so, was the court right to review the decision in the way that it did?

Just as courts are sometimes *less* willing to review the outcomes of decision-making processes, situations also arise in which they are *more* willing than usual to do so. For example, well before the entry into force of the HRA, English courts indicated a preparedness to adopt a more searching form of judicial review when decisions were said to infringe fundamental rights. As Sir Thomas Bingham MR put it in *R v Ministry of Defence, ex p Smith*:[217] 'The more substantial the interference with human rights, the more the court will require by way of justification before it is satisfied that the decision is reasonable.' The thinking, essentially, was that reasonable people do not infringe human rights without good reason—and reasonable people do not gravely infringe such rights without very good reason.

However, while this approach enabled courts to look rather more critically at decisions that impacted upon human rights, the courts' role remained very modest, as the *Smith* case itself illustrates.[218] The claimants, all of whom had been dismissed from the British armed forces solely on the grounds of their sexual orientation, challenged the legality of those dismissals and the government's then policy, on which the dismissals were based, under which gays and lesbians were banned from serving in the military. Notwithstanding that the case predated the HRA, Sir Thomas Bingham MR, in the Court of Appeal, said that the claimants' 'rights as human beings' were 'very much in issue'.[219] In the Divisional Court (the judgment of which was upheld by the Court of Appeal) Simon Brown LJ concluded that the government's justification for the ban—that military effectiveness and morale would be undermined by the presence of gays and lesbians—was unconvincing, and reflected a 'wrong view…that rests too firmly upon the supposition of prejudice in others and which insufficiently recognises the damage to human rights inflicted'.[220] Nevertheless, he went on to conclude that the policy was not unlawful, because the court's role was limited to applying

---

[215] The concept of polycentricity is discussed in more detail in Chapter 15, section 3.2, below.
[216] *R v North and East Devon Health Authority, ex p Coughlan* [2001] QB 213.
[217] [1996] QB 517, 554.   [218] *Smith* at 554.   [219] *Smith* at 556.   [220] *Smith* at 540.

the unreasonableness doctrine—and, quoting Lord Diplock's formulation, which we set out above, he did not think the policy could be characterised as 'outrageous in its defiance of logic'. That Simon Brown LJ could simultaneously regard the ban on gays and lesbians as *wrong*, but *lawful*, graphically demonstrates that the *Wednesbury* unreasonableness test reserves considerable discretion to decision-makers, thereby preventing judicial interference except in extreme circumstances.

This characteristic of the test is, depending on one's perspective, either its greatest strength or its greatest weakness. For some commentators, the wide discretion with which *Wednesbury* furnishes decision-makers strikes the right balance between judicial control and government freedom.[221] For others, however, the latitude that decision-makers enjoy under the unreasonableness doctrine is unacceptably broad. Lord Cooke, for example, castigated *Wednesbury* as 'an unfortunately retrogressive decision', doubting that the law should ever 'be satisfied... merely by a finding that the decision under review is not capricious or absurd'.[222] The very low level of review supplied by *Wednesbury* was considered especially problematic in human rights cases in which, many commentators felt, it would be appropriate for courts to scrutinise government decisions more rigorously. *Wednesbury* has also been subjected to criticism on other grounds. It has been observed that it is somewhat circular (defining unreasonableness as a lack of reasonableness) and unstructured; as a result, a finding of unreasonableness may not pinpoint exactly what was wrong with the decision.[223]

4.6.2 Proportionality–introduction

Those who are dissatisfied with *Wednesbury* have tended to look to the proportionality test as a more satisfactory principle by which to evaluate the outcomes of decision-making processes. It differs from *Wednesbury* in two main respects.

First, the *intensity of review* under proportionality may well be greater than that under *Wednesbury*, and the amount of discretion enjoyed by the decision-maker will be correspondingly smaller.[224] As Figure 13.7 shows, a decision that is reasonable might nevertheless be disproportionate, because the decision-maker's discretion is confined more tightly by the proportionality doctrine than by the reasonableness test. Second, the proportionality test is more *structured* than *Wednesbury*. There are a number of different formulations of the former, but it may conveniently be thought of as involving four questions, as follows:[225]

---

[221] See, eg Irvine, 'Judges and Decision-Makers: The Theory and Practice of *Wednesbury* Review' [1996] PL 59.

[222] *R (Daly) v Secretary of State for the Home Department* [2001] UKHL 26, [2001] 2 AC 532, [32].

[223] See further Jowell and Lester, 'Beyond *Wednesbury*: Substantive Principles of Administrative Law' [1987] PL 368.

[224] See, eg the speeches of Lords Steyn and Cooke in *R (Daly) v Secretary of State for the Home Department* [2001] UKHL 26, [2001] 2 AC 532.

[225] These are the questions that a reviewing *court* is likely to ask. Although *decision-makers* must comply with the requirements inherent in these questions—by not restricting protected interests except where this is necessary and proportionate—there is no need for the decision-maker specifically to address the four

(i)   Has a *protected interest* (for example, a human right) been compromised by the decision in question?

(ii) Was the interest compromised in the pursuit of some *legitimate aim*?

(iii) Was it *necessary* to compromise the protected interest (to whatever extent it has been compromised) in order to achieve the legitimate aim?

(iv) Is there an *adequate relationship of proportionality*[226] between the damage caused to the protected interest and the positive consequences that flow from achieving the legitimate aim?[227]

This may seem rather abstract, but an example will help to clarify what these questions mean in practice. Indeed, an example is provided by the *Smith* case, considered above. The claimants, having lost in the English courts, took their case to the ECtHR, which used the proportionality test to assess the legality of the UK's policy banning gays and lesbians from the armed forces.[228]

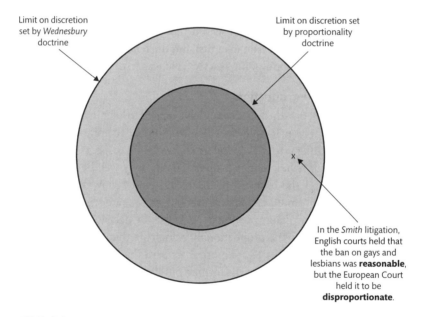

Figure 13.7 Substantive review

questions: *Belfast City Council v Miss Behavin' Ltd* [2007] UKHL 19, [2007] 1 WLR 1420; *R (SB) v Governors of Denbigh High School* [2006] UKHL 15, [2007] 1 AC 100.

[226] Somewhat confusingly, the term 'proportionality' appears only in the fourth question—but all four stages of the test are generally referred to as the 'proportionality test'.

[227] This final question was recognised in *Huang v Secretary of State for the Home Department* [2007] UKHL 11, [2007] 2 AC 167, [19], although courts do not always clearly distinguish the third and fourth questions.   [228] *Smith v United Kingdom* (2000) 29 EHRR 493.

First, the Court held that a *protected interest*—the right to respect for private and family life, guaranteed by Art 8 of the ECHR—had been compromised by the policy. This followed, in part, because it is recognised that respect for the 'sexual life' of the individual is an intrinsic element of respect for private life.[229]

Second, it was held that the UK's policy pursued a *legitimate aim*. Art 8(2) permits respect for private life to be compromised to the extent that this is necessary in 'the interests of national security' and 'for the prevention of disorder'. The Court accepted that the policy was designed to pursue these objectives, bearing in mind the UK's contention that it promoted 'the maintenance of the morale of service personnel and, consequently, of the fighting power and the operational effectiveness of the armed forces'.[230]

These conclusions required the Court, third, to consider whether it was *necessary* to ban gays and lesbians from the armed forces in order to achieve the legitimate aim. The British government argued that this was so, contending that the presence of gays and lesbians in the armed forces would have had a destabilising effect, given the close quarters in which service personnel must live, and the trust and confidence that they have to repose in one another. The UK's argument was based, in part, on research that indicated that existing service personnel did not welcome the prospect of serving alongside gay and lesbian colleagues. Although the government resisted such a characterisation, its argument essentially reduced to the proposition that it was necessary to ban gays and lesbians because institutional homophobia would otherwise have compromised the forces' effectiveness. The Court rejected this submission. In doing so, it noted that it is only possible to establish that a given course of action is necessary for the achievement of some aim if the aim could not be realised by other—less drastic—means. The crucial question, therefore, was whether it was possible to preserve the effectiveness of the armed forces by taking steps that would inflict less (or no) damage on the claimants' right to respect for private life. The Court answered this question in the affirmative, noting that the UK's arguments 'were founded solely upon the negative attitudes of heterosexual personnel towards those of homosexual orientation'.[231] It was held that the government had not demonstrated that less drastic measures—such as the adoption of appropriate codes of conduct, disciplinary rules, and education programmes—would be inadequate to address issues arising from the admission of homosexuals to the armed forces. The UK policy was therefore held to be in breach of the ECHR.[232]

In light of that conclusion, it was not necessary for the Court to address the fourth question—that is, whether the restriction of the applicants' rights was proportionate to the aim being pursued. However, it did note that 'when the relevant restrictions concern "a most intimate part of an individual's private life"'—in other words, where there is a serious limitation of a core aspect of the right—'there must exist "particularly

---

[229] *Dudgeon v United Kingdom* (1982) 4 EHRR 149, 160.

[230] *Smith v United Kingdom* at 522.

[231] *Smith v United Kingdom* at 532.　　　[232] The policy was later abandoned.

serious reasons" before such interferences can satisfy the requirements of Article 8(2) of the Convention'.[233] Conversely, when the House of Lords was called upon, in the *Miss Behavin'* case, to decide whether a council's decision to refuse to license a sex shop unlawfully breached the owner's right to freedom of expression, Lord Hoffmann regarded this as representing (at most) a minor qualification of the right. Noting that the 'right to vend pornography is not the most important right of free expression in a democratic society', his Lordship concluded that denying a licence to a sex shop 'would require very unusual facts for it to amount to a disproportionate restriction on Convention rights'.[234] The general principle, therefore, is that the more serious the interference with the right, the weightier the justification must be.

> **Q** How, exactly, does the ECtHR's analysis of the *Smith* case differ from that of the English courts? Which analysis do you prefer, and why?

4.6.3 Proportionality, and the distinction between appeal and review

The proportionality test is a long-standing feature of the case law of the ECtHR. It is the means by which the Court tests the legality of measures that interfere with so-called qualified rights—that is, rights that can lawfully be restricted if this is necessary in order to pursue some conflicting legitimate interest. (The right to respect for private life, mentioned above, is an example of a qualified right.[235]) Following the entry into force of the HRA,[236] English courts have also adopted the proportionality test in cases concerning qualified rights. Indeed, the House of Lords indicated in *Daly* that—although the HRA's incorporation of the ECHR was the obvious catalyst for the use of proportionality by national courts—the test should be regarded not as some sort of foreign import, but as something that has been embraced by, and absorbed into, the common law.[237] This indicates that the proportionality test may be applicable not only in relation to cases brought under the 1998 Act: for example, in *R (Nadarajah) v Secretary of State for the Home Department*,[238] Laws LJ said that when courts assess the legality of decisions to frustrate substantive legitimate expectations (as in the *Coughlan* case, considered above[239]), they apply a form of proportionality test.

However, some domestic judges were very reluctant to welcome proportionality into domestic law. For example, in 1991, Lord Ackner argued that '[t]he European [proportionality] test...must ultimately result in the question "Is the particular decision acceptable?" and this must involve a review of the merits of the decision'.[240] His fear was

---

[233] *Smith v United Kingdom* at 529, quoting from *Dudgeon* at [52].

[234] *Belfast City Council v Miss Behavin' Ltd* [2007] UKHL 19, [2007] 1 WLR 1420, [16].

[235] In contrast, 'absolute rights'—such as the right, under Art 3, not to be subjected to torture or to inhuman or degrading treatment—may not lawfully be restricted.

[236] See Chapter 19 below for detailed discussion of the HRA.

[237] *R (Daly) v Secretary of State for the Home Department* [2001] UKHL 26, [2001] 2 AC 532.

[238] [2005] EWCA Civ 1363, [68].   [239] See section 4.3.2 above.

[240] *R v Secretary of State for the Home Department, ex p Brind* [1991] 1 AC 696, 762–3.

that the distinction between appeal and review[241] could not survive adoption by English courts of the proportionality doctrine. The challenge, then, is to apply the proportionality test in a way that recognises that the roles of judges and decision-makers are distinct: as Laws LJ put it in *R (Mahmood) v Secretary of State for the Home Department*,[242] there must continue to be 'a principled distance between the court's adjudication...and the Secretary of State's decision, based on his perception of the case's merits'.

Experience teaches that it *is* possible to embrace proportionality while keeping the roles of the court and the decision-maker separate, thereby ensuring that the decision-maker maintains a measure of discretion, and that the distinction between appeal and review is preserved. This is so because the role of the court, when applying the proportionality doctrine, is not to identify the one and only *proportionate* decision that is open to the decision-maker; rather, its function is to determine whether the decision that has been taken is *disproportionate*, and therefore unlawful. Unless the court applies the proportionality test in an extremely rigorous manner, it is perfectly possible for certain decisions to be ruled out as disproportionate, while leaving several proportionate options open to the decision-maker. In this way, the proportionality test and administrative discretion are capable of coexisting. For example, in *Smith*, the ECtHR ruled that a complete ban on gays and lesbians was disproportionate, but this left the UK government with discretion as to what steps should be taken so as to ensure that the presence of homosexual service personnel did not compromise the effectiveness of the armed forces.

4.6.4 Deference

The amount of discretion with which the proportionality test leaves a decision-maker depends on the rigour with which the test is applied. In this context, English courts have embraced the idea that they should exhibit *deference* towards the decision-maker in certain circumstances. The meaning and appropriateness of this concept have been the subject of heated academic debate. Two principal schools of thought may be distinguished. Allan argues that when courts 'defer', they effectively refuse to determine whether the decision in question is lawful.[243] Allan is rightly critical of this extreme sort of deference, arguing that judges who engage in it are guilty of dereliction of duty. However, while there is some judicial support[244] for the sort of deference that Allan criticises, the dominant view favours a more subtle, and more defensible, idea of deference.[245] On this second, more moderate view, deference simply

---

[241] On which, see Chapter 12 above.   [242] [2001] 1 WLR 840, [33].

[243] 'Human Rights and Judicial Review: A Critique of "Due Deference"' [2006] CLJ 671.

[244] See, eg *R v Director of Public Prosecutions, ex p Kebilene* [2000] 2 AC 326, 380, *per* Lord Hope; *International Transport Roth GmbH v Secretary of State for the Home Department* [2002] EWCA Civ 158, [2003] QB 728, [77], *per* Laws LJ.

[245] Advocates of this view include Hunt, 'Sovereignty's Blight: Why Contemporary Public Law Needs the Concept of "Due Deference"', in Bamforth and Leyland (eds), *Public Law in a Multi-Layered Constitution* (Oxford 2003); Young, 'In Defence of Due Deference' (2009) 72 MLR 554; Kavanagh, 'Defending Deference in Public Law and Constitutional Theory' (2010) 126 LQR 222.

involves the court, where appropriate, attaching more weight, or respect, to the view of the decision-maker—thus making it less likely that that view will be overturned on judicial review. There is clear authority, at the highest judicial levels, supporting this approach, albeit that some judges have been reluctant to adopt the 'deference' label.[246] In practice, deference (understood in the latter sense) can operate in relation to two matters.

First, deference may be appropriate in relation to the question of whether it is *necessary* to compromise (say) a human right in order to achieve some legitimate (but conflicting) aim. Whether the court is in a position to form its own view on this point, or whether it is appropriate for the court to take the government's word at face value (or at least to attach considerable respect to the government's view), depends principally on the *relative institutional competence* of the judge and the decision-maker. In other words, does the court have the necessary expertise to form a judgment? For example, in the *Belmarsh* case, the House of Lords had to determine whether detaining suspected foreign terrorists without charge or trial was necessary in order to uphold public safety.[247] The Court had no difficulty in holding that such measures were *not* necessary, since the government had not detained UK nationals posing an equivalent threat. As Baroness Hale put it: '[I]f it is not necessary to lock up the nationals it cannot be necessary to lock up the foreigners.'[248]

In other circumstances, however, working out whether it is necessary to take certain steps so as to realise a given objective may be a far more difficult matter—because, as Rivers has observed, 'we often do not know how much any particular act will achieve its end'.[249] This point was taken by the Court of Appeal in *R (Farrakhan) v Secretary of State for the Home Department*,[250] which concerned the Home Secretary's decision to ban the claimant—the spiritual leader of a religious, political, and social movement known as the 'Nation of Islam'—from entering the UK. Since the ban would frustrate the claimant in his objective of meeting and addressing his followers in the UK, it clearly impacted upon his right of freedom of speech, and the Court therefore had to determine whether the ban was necessary in order to achieve a legitimate end.[251] The Home Secretary argued that the ban was necessary because he considered that, if allowed to enter the country, the claimant would make inflammatory speeches that would threaten community relations and provoke public disorder. The Court, in upholding the Secretary of State's decision, attached considerable respect to

---

[246] See, eg *Huang v Secretary of State for the Home Department* [2007] UKHL 11, [2007] 2 AC 167, [16], *per* Lord Bingham.

[247] *A v Secretary of State for the Home Department* [2004] UKHL 56, [2005] 2 AC 68. See further Chapter 1, section 3.1.2, above.

[248] *A* at [231]. It is noteworthy that the House of Lords took such a robust approach in this case, bearing in mind that English courts have traditionally been extremely deferential in cases concerning national security: cf *Secretary of State for the Home Department v Rehman* [2001] UKHL 47, [2003] 1 AC 153, *per* Lord Hoffmann.   [249] Rivers, 'Proportionality and Variable Intensity Review' [2006] CLJ 174, 199.

[250] [2002] EWCA Civ 606, [2002] QB 1391.

[251] ECHR, Art 10 (on which, see further Chapter 20 below) protects freedom of speech—but it is a qualified right, and may be curtailed if this is necessary to uphold (*inter alia*) public safety or public order.

his assessment of the situation, noting that he 'is far better placed to reach an informed decision as to the likely consequences of admitting Mr Farrakhan to this country than is the court'.[252]

Second, it may—for different reasons—be appropriate for the court to defer to the decision-maker's view in the context of determining whether there is an *adequate relationship of proportionality* between the restriction on the right and the positive consequences flowing from the restriction. Imagine that the Court, in the *Belmarsh* case, had been faced with the rather different scenario of a policy that, in order to realise a governmental objective of ensuring a very high level of national security, all suspected terrorists (foreign *and* British) should be detained indefinitely without charge or trial. If—as might well be the case—such draconian measures were deemed necessary in order to attain the desired (very high) level of national security, the court would then have had to turn to the question of proportionality per se. This question—is the national security 'gain' flowing from detention of suspects worth the human rights 'loss' flowing from such detention?—is one of *policy*. Whereas it may be appropriate for courts to defer to decision-makers on the necessity question—is there a more efficient way of achieving the desired outcome?—on grounds of *lack of competence*, deference on the proportionality question may be appropriate on grounds of *democracy*. Whether the human rights sacrifice is worth the national security gain depends on the relative importance that one attaches to those two interests. It might be perfectly straightforward for courts to intervene and hold disproportionate decisions that involve a massive loss in human rights terms in return for little or no clear gain in terms of public policy—but where the scales are more finely balanced, it may well be appropriate for courts to defer to the view of democratically accountable decision-makers. This is a further example of the point considered in Chapter 12 concerning the appropriate balance between legal and political accountability, and relates directly to the debate, outlined in that chapter, between those who are sceptical and those who are enthusiastic about the role of judicial review.

In conclusion, therefore, we can say that applying the proportionality test does not necessarily threaten the distinction between appeal and review, and it does not result in courts entirely removing discretion from decision-makers. The court's role is to identify—and rule out of contention—measures that would disproportionately impact on protected interests (most obviously human rights). In doing so, however, courts may attach weight to—and leave undisturbed—the views of decision-makers where this is appropriate on grounds of either institutional competence or democracy. It follows that the reviewing court does not simply substitute its view for that of the decision-maker: the court's role is still to identify the limits of the decision-maker's discretion, albeit that the proportionality test—as Figure 13.7 shows—generally draws those limits more tightly than the *Wednesbury* principle. It is, all things being equal, easier to establish that a decision is disproportionate than it is to establish that it is

[252] *Farrakhan* at [73].

unreasonable—but establishing disproportionality is emphatically not simply a matter of finding a judge who disagrees with the decision.

4.6.5 **Proportionality and *Wednesbury***

The adoption of the proportionality test in human rights cases raises the question of whether it should be adopted in all cases: should it replace *Wednesbury* entirely, or should the tests coexist? Many leading commentators on administrative law argue that *Wednesbury*'s days are numbered, and that proportionality will—and should— replace it.[253] Proportionality, it is said, is a superior principle: it provides a structured form of review that forces the courts to articulate the different values being balanced against one another, in contrast with the more opaque *Wednesbury* doctrine. Indeed, in 2003, the Court of Appeal said that it had 'difficulty in seeing what justification there now is for retaining the *Wednesbury* test', although it held that (for reasons of precedent) only the House of Lords could 'perform its burial rites'.[254]

So far, those rites have not been performed—and it is at least arguable that they should not be. While the structured proportionality test is obviously well suited to situations in which one interest has to be balanced against another—for example, where a human right or a substantive legitimate expectation is in tension with the public interest—proportionality principles, as Fordham has pointed out, 'will not always be helpful' and are not 'universally applicable'.[255] Outside the context of cases in which some protected interest falls to be balanced against a competing legitimate aim, it is difficult to see how the four-stage proportionality test can be meaningfully applied. So, for the time being at least, the proportionality and *Wednesbury* tests exist side by side, with the former limited to cases concerning fundamental rights and, arguably, substantive legitimate expectations.

5. **Concluding remarks**

In this chapter, we have seen that there exist many and varied grounds on which courts may review decisions taken by public bodies. A notable theme in this area concerns the *deepening*, in recent years, of judicial scrutiny of the executive. This is apparent from a number of the developments traced in this chapter. New grounds of review—such as legitimate expectation and proportionality—have emerged, often involving a greater degree of judicial oversight of executive decisions than has traditionally existed. This prompts, by way of conclusion, two sets of comments.

---

[253] Wade and Forsyth, *Administrative Law* (Oxford 2004), p 371 (although a more nuanced view is expressed in the 2009 edition at p 314); Craig, *Administrative Law* (London 2008), pp 635–40.

[254] *R (Association of British Civilian Internees (Far East Region)) v Secretary of State for Defence* [2003] EWCA Civ 473, [2003] QB 1397, [34]–[35].

[255] Fordham, '*Wednesbury*' [2007] JR 266, 267. See further Taggart, 'Proportionality, Deference, *Wednesbury*' [2008] NZLR 423.

First, these developments reflect the way in which two of the key themes of this book—the importance of ensuring adequate oversight of executive power, and the shift from a more political to a more legal constitution—intersect in this context. The emergence of more stringent judicial control of executive power—through the development of principles such as substantive legitimate expectation and proportionality, aided by the enactment of the HRA—underlies increasing reliance on the courts as a mechanism for ensuring the responsible use of executive power. And this, in turn, reflects a growing emphasis on legal, as distinct from political, arrangements for the control of governmental power. In this way, questions of substantive policy—should public authorities be allowed to renege on their promises? Should gays and lesbians be allowed to serve in the armed forces?—have acquired new legal dimensions, opening them up to legal, as well as political, challenge. Whether this is a good or a bad thing depends on one's perspective. For many, it is entirely appropriate that courts should act as guardians of individuals' fundamental rights and interests, standing as independent arbiters of whether, and if so on what conditions, such rights and interests may be sacrificed by governments for the greater good (as it sees it). But for writers, such as those we met in Chapter 12, who are deeply suspicious of judicial interference (as they would see it) in the business of government, the growing depth of modern judicial review is doubtless a source of concern. In all of this, it is important to recognise that no simple choice, between judicial *or* political control of the executive, falls to be made. It is inevitable and desirable that both forms of control should coexist, but it is important to take stock of whether the modern British constitution strikes the right balance between these two methods by which responsible government can be promoted. In particular, it is crucial to recognise that greater reliance on judicial review is not the only—and is certainly not necessarily the right—response to the weaknesses of the political system.[256]

Second, the deepening of judicial review, through adoption of concepts such as proportionality, requires us to re-evaluate received wisdom in this area. As we noted in Chapter 12—and as we have mentioned in this chapter—orthodox theory ascribes a highly limited role to the courts in exercise of their powers of judicial review. A bright line is envisaged between questions of legality (which are for courts) and questions of merits or policy (with which it is improper for courts to engage). This distinction has always been difficult to maintain, but it makes less and less sense as we begin to embrace substantive principles of justice as legal constraints on governmental power. Once it is acknowledged that rights to respect for private life, freedom of speech, freedom of religion, and so on constitute legal restrictions on administrative discretion, it is impossible to avoid some degree of judicial engagement with the substance of executive decisions, thus blurring the appeal/review distinction as traditionally conceived. While this may be a source of regret for purists, orthodox teaching concerning the proper role of the courts is not *inherently* right: it merely reflects a particular conception

---

[256] On which, see further Chapters 5 and 10.

of the separation of powers doctrine generally, and of the relationship between judges and decision-makers in particular. The challenge that now faces administrative lawyers and judges is to establish a new vision of how the courts and the executive should relate to one another, and of where the boundaries between their respective provinces should lie. That is the challenge that underlies (for example) attempts to articulate a doctrine of deference so as to enable courts applying the proportionality doctrine to pay appropriate (but only appropriate) respect to executive decisions. We therefore end this chapter by reiterating the point that we developed in the last one, by observing that administrative law, for all of its technicality and detail, is part of our wider constitutional fabric, and represents the working out, in a particular legal context, of much broader debates about the proper relationship between the different branches of the constitution.

Further reading

CRAIG, 'The Human Rights Act, Article 6 and Procedural Rights' [2003] PL 753

FORSYTH AND HARE (eds), *The Golden Metwand and the Crooked Cord* (Oxford 1998)

GALLIGAN, *Due Process and Fair Procedures: A Study of Administrative Procedures* (Oxford 1996)

JOWELL AND LESTER, 'Beyond *Wednesbury*: Substantive Principles of Administrative Law' [1987] PL 368

LE SUEUR, 'Legal Duties to Give Reasons' (1999) 52 CLP 150

RIVERS, 'Proportionality and Variable Intensity Review' [2006] CLJ 174

SALES AND STEYN, 'Legitimate Expectations in English Public Law: An Analysis' [2004] PL 564

TAGGART, 'Proportionality, Deference, *Wednesbury*' [2008] NZLR 423

WILLIAMS, 'When is an Error Not an Error? Reform of Jurisdictional Review of Error of Law and Fact' [2007] PL 793

14 Judicial Review—Scope, Procedures, and Remedies

1. Introduction

In the previous chapter, we examined the various grounds upon which it is possible to challenge administrative decisions by way of judicial review. We now turn to address a number of practical matters that must be confronted by litigants who propose to launch judicial review proceedings, and by courts dealing with such claims.

First, we consider the *sort of decisions* that can be reviewed. It is clear from the examples and cases encountered in Chapter 13 that (at least some) decisions taken by public authorities under statutory powers are open to review—but what about other decision-makers and other types of power? And what if the subject matter of the decision is something that courts feel unqualified to consider, or if Parliament has stipulated that judicial review of a particular decision should not occur? These questions are important both for their own sake and for their relevance to our key themes. For example, if courts are prepared to assert authority to review the making of a broad range of decisions, this implies that they consider themselves to have a key role in ensuring the accountable use of power.

Second, we examine the *procedure* under which courts subject decisions to judicial review. Although questions about procedure may seem—and to an extent are—technical, they also invite answers that are of wider significance to the book's key themes. For example, should courts allow government decisions to be challenged by anyone at all, or only by those who are directly affected? Favouring a broad approach (which, as we will see, the courts do) implies a general preference for judicial control of government, and chimes with our theme of the shift from a more political to a more legal constitution.

Third, we look at the *remedies* that courts may issue in judicial review proceedings. This, too, will cast light on matters of general importance. For example, to what extent should courts intervene pre-emptively by ruling that it would be unlawful for public authorities to engage in certain kinds of conduct? A narrow view of the courts' function would imply that they should limit themselves to resolving disputes, pronouncing only upon the legality of actions already undertaken. But if the courts' role is conceived of more broadly, it might be appropriate for courts to enter the fray at an earlier stage—for example, by pronouncing on the legality of *proposed* government action.

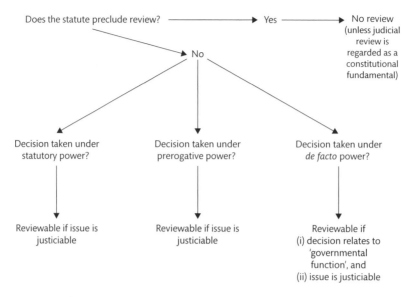

Figure 14.1 Can the decision be judicially reviewed?

2. What decisions can be judicially reviewed?

As Figure 14.1 illustrates, whether a decision is judicially reviewable turns on three factors: whether the statute contains an *ouster clause* prohibiting judicial review; the *type of power* under which the decision was taken; and whether the claimant's case raises *justiciable issues*.

2.1 Ouster clauses

If Parliament is sovereign, it stands to reason that it can, if it so chooses, prohibit judicial review of decisions taken under certain (or even all) powers.[1] The Foreign Compensation Act 1950 appears to be a rare example of Parliament seeking to do precisely this. The Act provided: 'The determination by the [Foreign Compensation Commission] of any application made to them under this Act shall not be called in question in any court of law.'[2] When a company, Anisminic, sought to challenge the Commission's decision to refuse compensation, the House of Lords had to rule on whether the Act precluded judicial review.[3] The House of Lords therefore found itself in a delicate position. Two fundamental constitutional principles appeared to be pulling in different directions: fidelity to the sovereign will of Parliament seemed, at least *prima*

---

[1] See Chapter 5, section 4, above.   [2] Section 4(4) as originally enacted.
[3] *Anisminic Ltd v Foreign Compensation Commission* [1969] 2 AC 147.

facie, to require the Court to rule that judicial review was unavailable; the rule of law—which requires, *inter alia*, that people should be able to have legal disputes resolved by independent courts[4]—demanded the opposite outcome. Presented with this dilemma, their Lordships deftly—or disingenuously, depending on one's perspective—ruled that the Act did not really mean what it seemed to mean. Lord Pearce observed that Parliament had only precluded judicial review of 'determinations'. By this, he said, Parliament 'meant a real determination, not a purported determination': review of the former was precluded by the statute; review of the latter was not.[5] The question, therefore, was whether the Commission's determination was 'real' or 'purported'. This, said their Lordships, turned on whether the Commission had exceeded its powers by misinterpreting the rules governing the eligibility for compensation. In other words, the ouster clause did not preclude judicial scrutiny.

The *Anisminic* decision can be viewed on two levels. Superficially, the Court appeared to act in an entirely orthodox way. The word 'determination'—the meaning of which was, as we have seen, pivotal—was said to be ambiguous, and the Court, forced to choose between rival interpretations, felt that it should favour the one that preserved judicial review.[6] So, said Lord Wilberforce, the Court was merely 'carrying out the intention of the legislature', and it would be wrong to suggest that the decision was evidence of 'a struggle between the courts and the executive'.[7] However, there is an important subtext to the case. Since, on the majority's view, *any* unlawful determination by the Commission would merely have constituted a 'purported' determination, and would thus be reviewable notwithstanding the ouster clause, the clause was essentially deprived of any effect.[8] It has therefore been argued that the Court in *Anisminic* adopted a 'policy...of total disobedience to Parliament'.[9] On this view, the House of Lords, without admitting as much, gave priority to the rule of law (by preserving the availability of judicial review) over the intention of Parliament as stated in the ouster clause.

This discussion leads on to three more general points. First, *Anisminic* is ultimately an ambiguous case that can be read in either of the two ways sketched above. It therefore does not provide definitive guidance as to *what a court would do if it were faced with an indisputably clear statutory provision ousting judicial review.* We saw in Chapter 12 that senior judges have recently indicated, albeit in *obiter dicta*, that they may refuse to enforce ouster clauses—although whether Parliament would enact a wholly unambiguous ouster,

---

[4] See Chapter 2, section 4.4, above.   [5] *Anisminic* at 199.   [6] *Anisminic* at 170, *per* Lord Reid.
[7] *Anisminic* at 208, *per* Lord Wilberforce.

[8] The only exception is that, at the time that *Anisminic* was decided, an anomalous category of unlawful decisions, known as 'non-jurisdictional errors of law on the face of the record', was recognised. However, that category is now largely irrelevant given that, as we saw in Chapter 13, section 2.2, above, the general principle is that all errors of law (whether or not 'on the face of the record') are jurisdictional. The position in Scotland, however, is different, where the courts have 'never had power to correct an *intra vires* error of law made by a statutory tribunal or authority exercising statutory jurisdiction': *West v Lord Advocate* 1979 SC 120, 131.   [9] Wade and Forsyth, *Administrative Law* (Oxford 2009), p 616.

thereby forcing the courts to choose between fidelity to the rule law and adherence to legislative intention, is another matter.[10]

Second, leaving aside the 'parliamentary sovereignty *versus* rule of law' point, the general approach in *Anisminic* is indicative, in broader terms, of *how courts perceive judicial review*. Particularly noteworthy is the justification offered by Lord Wilberforce for a robust reading of the ouster clause. 'What', he asked, 'would be the purpose of defining by statute the limit of a tribunal's powers if, by means of a clause inserted in the instrument of definition, those limits could safely be passed?'[11] The obvious answer to this question is that even if *courts* could not (because of the ouster clause) enforce limits on the decision-maker's power laid down in the statute, there might be other, political, means by which such limits could be enforced. Lord Wilberforce's premise therefore presents a notably court-centric view: it implies an emphasis on the judiciary as the primary means by which to hold the executive to account, and thus buys into a more legal form of constitutionalism.

Third, attempts to exclude judicial review entirely should be distinguished from *two other statutory devices, the effect of which may be to limit judicial review*. One option that Parliament sometimes takes is to, in effect, rule out the exercise of the courts' normal judicial review powers while giving them statutory powers of judicial review. The only real practical impact of this is that such statutory powers are normally exercisable within a narrower time frame (typically six weeks) than the courts' normal powers.[12] A further possibility is that Parliament might create a statutory body that has court-like characteristics. Here, the perceived constitutional need for judicial review may be weaker (because the body in question is an independent judicial, as opposed to executive, body), and the High Court may be willing to concede that judicial review should lie only in exceptional circumstances.[13]

2.2 **Type of power**

2.2.1 **Statutory powers**

The majority of governmental decisions are taken under statutory powers. As a general rule, such decisions are judicially reviewable to the extent that they raise justiciable issues. It is convenient to defer discussion of the concept of justiciability until we have addressed prerogative powers.

---

[10] The closest that Parliament has recently come to doing so was in the Asylum and Immigration (Treatment of Claimants, etc.) Bill in 2003, which, as originally drafted, contained a stronger ouster clause than that which was at stake in *Anisminic*. However, Parliament ultimately withdrew the clause in the face of intense criticism from judges and others. [11] *Anisminic* at 208.

[12] See, eg Acquisition of Land Act 1981, ss 23 and 25.

[13] This view was adopted in relation to the Upper Tribunal in *R (Cart) v Upper Tribunal* [2010] EWCA Civ 859. See Chapter 17, section 5.6, below.

2.2.2 **Prerogative powers**

As we saw in Chapter 4, the Crown—which, in practice, means the executive branch of government—possesses a number of non-statutory powers, known as *prerogative powers*, covering matters as diverse as the granting of honours, the declaration of war, and the making of treaties. Is the exercise of such powers susceptible to judicial review? It was established as long ago as the early seventeenth century that courts could determine whether a prerogative claimed by the Crown actually existed[14]—a jurisdiction famously exercised in the *De Keyser* case,[15] in which it was held that prerogative powers are placed in abeyance, or suspended, when statutory powers cover the same ground.

However, deciding whether a particular power exists constitutes a very modest form of judicial review: it is analogous to deciding whether a statutory power under which a Minister claims to be acting really exists or applies to the sort of conduct that he is undertaking. Yet we know that the exercise of statutory powers can be reviewed in myriad other, more sophisticated, ways by applying the various grounds of judicial review that we encountered in Chapter 13. For many years, however, the courts refused to hold that those grounds of review were applicable to exercises of prerogative power. Such reticence was attributable to two factors.

First, it was felt that it would have been *constitutionally improper*, or at least unseemly, to interfere with the exercise of the royal prerogative. Such an attitude reflected the fact that, historically, prerogative power was actually wielded by the sovereign himself or herself. However, this is not, generally speaking, the case today, as the House of Lords recognised in the seminal *GCHQ* case, which concerned a challenge to a ministerial decision, taken under prerogative power, banning workers at the government's communications headquarters from belonging to trade unions.[16] It was argued that previous important changes to employment conditions had been preceded by consultation, and that failure to consult on the occasion in question caused a breach of legitimate expectations.[17] The most significant aspect of the case is that all five Law Lords were willing to countenance judicial review of the manner of exercise of the prerogative by requiring it to be used in line with the usual requirements—respect for legitimate expectations and natural justice, reasonableness, and so on—that are enforced via judicial review. Lord Scarman, for example, could see 'no reason why simply because a decision-making power is derived from a common law and not a statutory source, it should *for that reason only* be immune from judicial review'.[18] In doing so, their Lordships recognised that prerogative power today is, as Markesinis puts it, 'to all intents and purposes [a] government or even prime ministerial prerogative'.[19] To overlook this, said Lord Roskill,

---

[14] *Case of Proclamations* (1611) 2 Co Rep 74.

[15] *Attorney-General v De Keyser's Royal Hotel Ltd* [1920] AC 508.

[16] *Council of Civil Service Unions v Minister for the Civil Service* [1985] AC 374. See also *R v Criminal Injuries Compensation Board, ex p Lain* [1967] 2 QB 864, in which the developments in *GCHQ* were, to an extent, prefigured.   [17] See section 4.3 above on legitimate expectations.

[18] *GCHQ* at 410.   [19] Markesinis, 'The Royal Prerogative Revisited' (1973) 32 CLJ 287, 288.

would be to hark back to 'the clanking of mediaeval chains of the ghosts of the past'.[20] *GCHQ* was concerned with the exercise of a power conferred upon a Minister under the prerogative. In this sense, it concerned the use of 'delegated' prerogative power. It is now clear, following the *Bancoult* case, that exercises of the prerogative itself—not only of powers conferred under it—are also, in principle, reviewable.[21]

The second factor that explains judges' traditional reticence in the face of the prerogative concerns the *subject matter* of many such powers. For example, in *Chandler v Director of Public Prosecutions*,[22] it was said that courts could not rule on matters concerning 'the methods of arming the defence forces' or their 'disposition'; this was a matter 'at the decision of Her Majesty's Ministers', and it was 'not within the competence of a court of law to try the issue whether it would be better for the country that that armament or those dispositions should be different'. However, the force of this argument—that decisions about the deployment of the armed forces are likely to raise nonjusticiable questions of policy on which courts are not qualified to rule—can be accepted without going so far as to assume that no exercise of prerogative power will ever give rise to justiciable matters. This was recognised in *GCHQ*, Lord Scarman opining that 'if the subject matter in respect of which prerogative power is exercised is justiciable, that is to say if it is a matter upon which the court can adjudicate, the exercise of the power is subject to review in accordance with the principles developed in respect of the review of the exercise of statutory power'.[23] It followed, said Lord Roskill, that the exercise of powers concerning the making of treaties, the defence of the realm, the granting of mercy, the conferral of honours, the dissolution of Parliament, and the appointment of Ministers would not be reviewable because '[t]he courts are not the place wherein to determine whether a treaty should be concluded or the armed forces disposed in a particular manner or Parliament dissolved on one date rather than another'.[24]

The difficulty with Lord Roskill's view is that it presupposes that there are certain prerogative powers that will *never* raise justiciable issues. Of course, there are certain powers the exercise of which is highly unlikely to generate justiciable questions. For example, it was recently held that a government promise to hold a referendum before ratifying a treaty could not be said to have given rise to an enforceable legitimate expectation because 'a promise to hold a referendum lies so deep in the macro-political field that the court should not enter the relevant area at all'.[25] This does not, however, mean that everything to do with treaty-making is necessarily non-justiciable.[26] The better view, therefore, is that there is no such thing as a non-justiciable *prerogative*;

---

[21] *GCHQ* at 417.

[22] *R (Bancoult) v Secretary of State for Foreign and Commonwealth Affairs (No 2)* [2008] UKHL 61, [2009] 1 AC 453.   22 [1964] AC 763, 798, *per* Viscount Radcliffe.

[23] *GCHQ*, at 407. However, the decision in *GCHQ* was ultimately not quashed because the Court was satisfied that national security reasons justified the government's failure to consult.

[24] *GCHQ* at 418.   25 *R (Wheeler) v Prime Minister* [2008] EWHC 1409 (Admin).

[26] Note that the prerogative power to conclude treaties on behalf of the UK is now qualified in the sense that most treaties can only be ratified (that is, made legally binding upon the UK) if Parliament has not exercised its new statutory right to object: Constitutional Reform and Governance Act 2010, Pt 2.

rather, there are merely *issues* arising from the exercise of a prerogative—or any other kind of power, including statutory power—upon which the courts may consider themselves unable to adjudicate.[27]

This idea has clearly taken root in relation to the prerogative of mercy, under which pardons can be granted to individuals convicted of criminal offences.[28] Clearly, whether such a pardon should be granted in any particular case is ultimately a moral value judgement, and it is difficult to see how a court could sensibly or appropriately review the substance of such a decision. Yet this does not mean that justiciable issues cannot arise in the course of exercising the power. For example, it was held in *R v Secretary of State for the Home Department, ex p Bentley*[29] that, when the Home Secretary refused to grant a posthumous pardon to the claimant's brother, who had been hanged for inciting murder, he had failed to appreciate the full width of his legal powers. In particular, he had overlooked the possibility of a partial pardon (the effect of which would have been to acknowledge that the person concerned should not have been hanged without going so far as to imply that no punishment should have been imposed). Similarly, in *Lewis v Attorney General of Jamaica*,[30] the Privy Council concluded that decisions not to grant mercy to prisoners sentenced to death could be challenged on account of the fact that a fair decision-making process had not been adopted.

Nevertheless, it is clear that there are certain prerogatives—such as the power to make representations to foreign governments in support of British nationals and those with permission to reside in the United Kingdom—in relation to which the scope for judicial review is distinctly limited. In *R (Abbasi) v Secretary of State for Foreign and Commonwealth Affairs*,[31] concerning the extrajudicial detention of a British citizen by the USA at Guantanamo Bay in Cuba, the Court of Appeal refused to hold that the UK government had acted unlawfully by declining to make such representations. Although the prerogative in question was not considered to be non-justiciable per se, it was felt that the Court could not 'enter...forbidden areas, including decisions affecting foreign policy', and that it was 'highly likely that any decision of the Foreign and Commonwealth Office, as to whether to make representations on a diplomatic level, will be intimately connected with decisions relating to this country's foreign policy'. It followed that while the prerogative in question was not off-limits to the courts, it would be rare for a judge to be able to go further than to require the Foreign Secretary to 'give due consideration to a request for assistance'.[32]

Q Do you think that there might be some prerogative powers the exercise of which will never raise justiciable issues? For example, what, if any, justiciable issues might be raised by the exercise of powers to (i) grant honours, and (ii) declare war?

---

[27] See further Daly, 'Justiciability and the "Political Question" Doctrine' [2010] PL 160.
[28] See generally Harris, 'Judicial Review, Justiciability and the Prerogative of Mercy' [2003] CLJ 631.
[29] [1994] QB 349.   [30] [2001] 2 AC 50.   [31] [2002] EWCA Civ 1598, [2003] UKHRR 76.
[32] *Abbasi* at [106].

Finally, in this regard, we should note that the idea of justiciability is closely related to the notion of deference that we encountered in Chapter 13. Justiciability and deference may be thought of as different points on a continuum. To characterise an issue as 'non-justiciable' is to regard it as something upon which courts *cannot adjudicate at all*. Meanwhile, even if a court does not regard a question as wholly non-justiciable, it may, as we saw in Chapter 13, choose to *exhibit considerable deference* when considering the legality of the decision-maker's conduct. So, for example, in *R (Al Rawi) v Secretary of State for Foreign and Commonwealth Affairs*,[33] which arose on similar facts to *Abassi*, the argument that the Foreign Secretary had not taken into account relevant considerations when declining to make representations on the claimants' behalf failed because, as the Court of Appeal put it, it was 'the government's responsibility to make decisions touching the conduct of foreign relations' such that 'the class of factors which … it is open to the decision-maker to treat as relevant or not … must be particularly wide'. It follows that, from the claimant's perspective, persuading a court that a question is justiciable does not guarantee victory: the court may still, because of the sensitive nature of the subject matter of the decision, refuse to subject it to rigorous scrutiny.

> **Q** How do you think courts should decide whether to treat an issue as non-justiciable, or simply to exercise deference when reviewing the legality of the decision? Is the distinction between non-justiciability and deference a helpful one?

2.2.3 *De facto* powers

So far, we have seen that the position regarding decisions taken under statutory and prerogative powers is that they can be judicially reviewed provided that the issues raised are justiciable. The willingness of courts to bring the use of the prerogative within the ambit of judicial review reflects two of our key themes—namely, judicial recognition of the importance of ensuring that the *executive is held to account* for its use of power, whatever the source of that power, and judicial willingness to play a key role in securing such accountability rather than to rely on parliamentary processes. This provides further evidence of the growing emphasis in the UK on *legal constitutionalism* as distinct from *political constitutionalism*.

However, as we saw in Chapter 4, many decisions are taken—by government bodies and others—under neither statutory nor prerogative powers.[34] Are such decisions also open to judicial review?[35] Figure 14.2 shows a number of different types of decision, based on real cases that we consider below, which might be taken under '*de facto* powers'—so-called because they are powers that, as a matter of *fact*, the

---

[33] [2006] EWCA Civ 1279, [2008] QB 289, [140].   [34] See Chapter 4, section 4.4, above.

[35] If they are, then, of course, judicial review will lie only in relation to justiciable matters—but here we are concerned with the prior question whether the exercise of such powers is open to review *at all*.

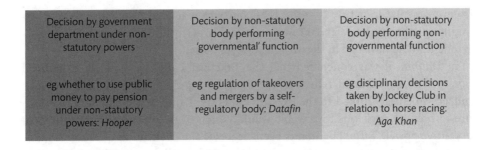

Figure 14.2 Decisions taken under *de facto* powers

decision-maker possesses, even though there is nothing in *law* that specifically gives them such powers.

The *Datafin* case is a good starting point.[36] The claimant, which was attempting to take over company X, complained to the Panel on Takeovers and Mergers that company Y, which was also trying to take over company X, had acted in breach of the Panel's code of conduct, which stipulated how companies should behave in such situations. When the Panel dismissed the complaint against company Y, the claimant sought judicial review of that decision, arguing that the Panel was not enforcing the code correctly. Ultimately, the Court of Appeal ruled that the Panel had not acted unlawfully. However, the most significant point is that the Court was willing to subject the Panel's decision to review at all, bearing in mind that the Panel was not exercising any legal powers.[37] Its code had no legal force—breach of it was not per se unlawful— but, in practice, companies were obliged to play by the Panel's rules; if they did not, they would find it impossible to do business in the City of London. Organisations such as the Panel are often called 'self-regulatory bodies' consisting of a 'group of people, acting in concert, [and using] their collective power to force themselves and others to comply with a code of conduct of their own devising'; as such, it was noted in *Datafin* that the Panel 'exercise[d] immense power *de facto*'.[38] Yet judicial review does not lie in relation to the decisions of any and every body with 'immense power'; if it were to do so, then even large corporations would be susceptible to judicial review. In reality, the purpose, and so the scope, of judicial review are conceived of more narrowly: courts have settled on the view that judicial review is for controlling the use of *governmental* power. The acid test for whether decisions taken under *de facto* powers can be reviewed is therefore whether the relevant decision-maker is performing a public function that

[36] *R v Panel on Takeovers and Mergers, ex p Datafin plc* [1987] QB 815.
[37] The position is now different: see Companies Act 2006, ss 942–965.
[38] *Datafin* at 826, *per* Sir John Donaldson MR.

is governmental in nature[39]—a test that courts have tended in practice to apply by asking whether, if the defendant were not already performing the function, the government would have had to step in and perform it itself.

In *Datafin*, it was concluded that the Takeover Panel was subject to judicial review. The government relied on the Panel to regulate takeovers and mergers; indeed, so closely linked to the executive was the Panel that it was said that failure to hold its decisions reviewable would be to fail to 'recognise the realities of executive power'.[40] The position is even clearer if the decision in question is made (albeit under *de facto* powers) by a body that is *formally* part of the government. For example, in *R (Hooper) v Secretary of State for Work and Pensions*,[41] the Court of Appeal held that the Minister had acted unlawfully by failing to pay pensions to certain categories of widower despite the lack of any specific statutory power to do so. This may be taken as evidence of the courts' willingness to review all justiciable decisions pertaining to governmental functions, whether or not they are taken under identifiable legal powers. In contrast, it was held in the *Aga Khan* case that the Jockey Club's decision to disqualify the claimant's horse after it failed a drugs test could not be reviewed because, as Hoffmann LJ put it, '[t]here is nothing to suggest that, if the Jockey Club had not voluntarily assumed the regulation of racing, the government would feel obliged or inclined to set up a statutory body for the purpose'.[42] Similarly, in *Wachmann*, it was held that there could be no judicial review of the Chief Rabbi's decision that the claimant—who had been accused of adultery with members of his congregation—was no longer religiously and morally fit to occupy his position as rabbi.[43]

Q Some governments might be more inclined than others to regulate particular areas of life. For example, although a laissez-faire government might take the view that it would not (in the absence of the Jockey Club) be necessary for the state to regulate horse racing, a more interventionist government might take the opposite view. What difficulties does this imply as regards the test that courts use in this area, and how might courts seek to resolve such problems?

Experience shows that the courts find it especially difficult to work out whether judicial review should lie in areas in which contracts are involved. Here, we should distinguish two situations, beginning with those in which there is a *contract between the claimant and the defendant*. This was the case in *Aga Khan*, and it is clear that, for two of the judges, this was a major factor against the possibility of judicial review.[44] Indeed, the

•

---

[39] *R v Disciplinary Committee of the Jockey Club, ex p Aga Khan* [1993] 1 WLR 909; *R v Chief Rabbi of the United Hebrew Congregations of Great Britain and the Commonwealth, ex p Wachmann* [1992] 1 WLR 1036.   [40] *Datafin* at 838, *per* Sir John Donaldson MR.

[41] [2003] EWCA Civ 813, [2003] 1 WLR 2623. The Court of Appeal's decision was overturned by the House of Lords ([2005] UKHL 29, [2005] 1 WLR 1681) on presently irrelevant grounds.

[42] *Aga Khan* at 932.   [43] *Wachmann*.

[44] Namely, Sir Thomas Bingham MR and Farquharson LJ.

idea that there should be no judicial review of decisions taken under contract is a long-standing one.[45] It reflects the idea that contractual arrangements are a private matter—to be dealt with by private law—between the parties, and that there is no need for public law remedies such as judicial review to intrude. The difficulty, of course, is that individuals may have little choice but to enter into contracts with powerful bodies on terms of the latter's choosing; it is therefore arguable that, where such bodies are performing governmental functions, individuals should enjoy the additional protections that judicial review brings.

Second, there are situations in which there is a *contract between a government body and a service provider*. The practice of 'contracting out', whereby public bodies pay companies or charities to deliver public services, is increasingly common,[46] but the courts have generally ruled against the possibility of judicially reviewing the service provider. For example, in *R v Servite Houses, ex p Goldsmith*,[47] a local authority engaged the defendant to provide accommodation that it was legally obliged to arrange for certain categories of person. When the defendant reneged on a promise given to the claimants that they could remain in their accommodation for life, they sought judicial review, alleging breach of legitimate expectation.[48] However, the court held that judicial review could not occur in such circumstances—a conclusion that has been strongly criticised on the ground that there is 'nothing in the logic of contracting out' that means that the service provider, if it is performing a governmental function, should not be amenable to judicial review.[49] The courts' present approach enables the government, in effect, to place matters beyond the reach of judicial review by contracting them out to private sector bodies in relation to which only private law remedies will apply.[50]

When we consider the Human Rights Act 1998 in Chapter 19, we will see that similar issues have arisen in that context. Just as courts have struggled to demarcate the range of bodies that should be required to adhere to the principles enforced via judicial review, so they have found it difficult—especially when contracting out has occurred—to decide which bodies should be required to respect human rights.

Finally, the above position, adopted by English law, does not reflect the position in Scotland, where the availability of judicial review is governed by a different, more inclusive, test that, in particular, is not limited by reference to any public/private distinction. In Scots law, judicial review lies in respect of decisions 'taken by any person or body to whom a jurisdiction, power or authority has been delegated or

---

[45] See, eg *R v Criminal Injuries Compensation Board, ex p Lain* [1967] 2 QB 864, 882, *per* Lord Parker CLJ, and 884, *per* Diplock LJ.   [46] See Chapter 4, section 4.5, above.

[47] (2001) 33 HLR 369.   [48] On legitimate expectations, see Chapter 13, section 4.3, above.

[49] Craig, 'Contracting Out, the Human Rights Act and the Scope of Judicial Review' (2002) 118 LQR 551, 564–7.

[50] See Hunt, 'Constitutionalism and the Contractualisation of Government in the United Kingdom', in Taggart (ed), *The Province of Administrative Law* (Oxford 1997); Freedland, 'Government by Contract and Public Law' [1994] PL 86.

entrusted by statute, agreement or any other instrument'.[51] This requires a 'tripartite' relationship—between the body that *conferred* the jurisdiction, the body *exercising* it, and the person *affected* by the exercise of jurisdiction. While this means that judicial review does not lie in straightforward, two-party contractual situations (for example, employer–employee), its reach is greater in Scots than in English law. For example, when members of a golf club, purporting to exercise jurisdiction conferred upon them by the rules of the club, decided to expel an individual member, this decision was held amenable to judicial review.[52]

> **Q** Is the test adopted in Scots law preferable to that which is used by English law?

3. Procedure

3.1 The judicial review procedure

There is a special procedure that those wishing to issue judicial review claims are generally expected to use.[53] The procedure that applies today is laid down in Pt 54 of the Civil Procedure Rules,[54] and has its origin in, and much in common with, major reforms to judicial review proceedings introduced in the period 1977–81.[55] Judicial review procedure is different from that relating to ordinary civil proceedings,[56] in that it contains several protections for respondents—which will usually be public authorities. This, it is said, is justified by the need for public bodies to be protected against vexatious and unreasonable legal challenges so as to avoid unacceptable distraction from their core task of serving the public interest.[57] Against that background, we briefly consider in this section four limitations that apply to judicial review proceedings to the advantage of public bodies—but, arguably, to the disadvantage of members of the

---

[51] *West v Secretary of State for Scotland* 1992 SC 385, 412–13. See further Wolffe, 'The Scope of Judicial Review in Scots Law' [1992] PL 625.

[52] *Crocket v Tantallon Golf Club* 2005 SLT 663. See further Munro, 'Sport in the Courts' [2005] PL 681.

[53] In this chapter, we are concerned with judicial review proceedings in the High Court of England and Wales. The same (or similar) procedural and remedial regimes apply to the Upper Tribunal when it exercises its powers of judicial review. The Upper Tribunal's judicial review powers are considered in Chapter 17, section 5.5, below. Footnotes indicate the principal respects in which the position described in the text differs from that obtaining in Scotland.

[54] See also Senior Courts Act 1981, s 31. For background to the changes introduced by Pt 54, see Bowman, *Review of the Crown Office List* (London 2000); Law Commission, *Administrative Law: Judicial Review and Statutory Appeals* (Law Com No 226 1994). For the position in Scotland, see ch 58 of the Rules of the Court of Session.

[55] For background and discussion, see Law Commission, *Remedies in Administrative Law* (Law Com No 73 1976); *O'Reilly v Mackman* [1983] 2 AC 237, 280–5, *per* Lord Diplock.

[56] For example, for claims in tort or contract.

[57] For a more critical view, see Oliver, 'Public Law Procedures and Remedies: Do We Need Them?' [2002] PL 91.

public seeking to bring claims. In doing so, we make reference to the following version of the example that we used in the previous chapter:

> The (imaginary) Planning and Infrastructure Act 2010 provides that 'the Secretary of State may decide whether—and, if so, subject to what conditions, if any—permission should be granted for major infrastructure projects'. A major airport operating company that wishes to build a new airport asks the Secretary of State to exercise this power by granting it permission to do so.

First, in contrast to claims in private law, litigants must secure the *permission of the court* to launch a judicial review challenge.[58] Judicial review is therefore a two-stage process: first, the court's permission must be sought, and then, if permission is granted, there can be a substantive hearing of the issues. It has been argued that this system is advantageous to *public bodies*, because it allows unmeritorious cases to be filtered out with relatively little fuss,[59] to *the courts*, since it provides a means by which they can dispose of such cases quickly and efficiently,[60] and to *claimants*, because it allows them to obtain the opinion of the court speedily and cheaply.[61] The test that courts apply to determine whether permission should be granted is whether there appears to be 'an arguable ground for judicial review having a realistic prospect of success',[62] although researchers have found that there is considerable diversity of practice in this area, with some judges apparently much more willing to grant permission than others.[63]

Second, claimants are generally required to *take various steps before seeking judicial review*, including utilising alternative methods of dispute resolution (such as mediation) and exhausting alternative remedies (such as rights of appeal).[64] So, for example, if in our example the company were denied permission to build the new airport in question, but had a statutory right of appeal to a planning tribunal, it would normally be expected to exercise that right before seeking judicial review. Viewed thus, judicial review is a remedy of last resort.[65] There are several reasons that explain why courts have adopted this position: for example, it reduces the number of cases that go forward for judicial review, thus helping to stop the system from becoming clogged up; and appellate tribunals, because they focus on a narrow range of cases, may well be better equipped than the High Court to bring relevant expertise to

---

[58] Civil Procedure Rules, Pt 54, r 4. There is no such requirement in Scotland.

[59] Law Com No 226, [3.5]–[3.6].   [60] Law Com No 226, [5.6].

[61] Le Sueur and Sunkin, 'Applications for Judicial Review: The Requirement of Leave' [1992] PL 102, 107.

[62] *Sharma v Brown-Antoine* [2006] UKPC 57, [2007] 1 WLR 780, [14], *per* Lords Bingham and Walker.

[63] Le Sueur and Sunkin; Bondy and Sunkin, 'Accessing Judicial Review' [2008] PL 674.

[64] See, eg *R v Inland Revenue Commissioners, ex p Preston* [1985] AC 835, 852, *per* Lord Scarman. The same is true in Scotland: Rules of the Court of Session, r 58(3).

[65] *R (Cowl) v Plymouth City Council* [2001] EWCA Civ 1935, [2002] 1 WLR 803.

bear on the issues.[66] Nevertheless, the requirement to exhaust other remedies is not applied unswervingly: courts have shown themselves willing to waive it where, for example, the alternative remedy would be inadequate[67] or would require the claimant to wait an unreasonable length of time for justice.[68] However, the mere fact that it would be more convenient for the individual to use judicial review as opposed to lodging an appeal may not, on its own, be sufficient.[69]

Third, anyone wishing to bring a judicial review claim *must act very quickly*. Whereas claims based on contract or tort can be brought within six years of the accrual of the cause of action,[70] judicial review claims must generally be brought within three months of the date on which the relevant decision was made.[71] They must *also* be brought 'promptly', meaning that courts can rule a claim to be out of time even it if is initiated within three months (although, in practice, courts rarely do this).[72] Where claimants have failed to comply with the time limit, courts have discretion to allow the case to continue in spite of this provided that there is a 'good reason' for doing so[73]— for example, a claimant who tries to exhaust other remedies before seeking judicial review would generally be regarded as having a good reason for failing to comply with the time limit.[74] However, even if there is a good reason for extending time, the court may refuse to do so if this 'would be detrimental to good administration' (for example, if a successful late challenge to a particular decision would require the government to unpick many other decisions taken in reliance upon it).[75] An extension of time may also be refused if it would 'be likely to cause substantial hardship to, or substantially prejudice the rights of, any person'.[76] So if, in our example, the company were to be granted permission to build the new airport and local residents were to wish to object, it is very unlikely that they would be granted permission to seek judicial review outside the usual three-month time limit if building work had started, since this might well cause 'substantial hardship' to the company, which would, by that point, have begun to invest considerable amounts of money in the project.[77] The short time limit for judicial review is obviously problematic for prospective claimants, who must act swiftly, but is said to be justified by the need for certainty: government bodies need to know where

---

[66]   See further Lewis, 'The Exhaustion of Alternative Remedies in Administrative Law' [1992] CLJ 138.

[67]   *Leech v Deputy Governor of Parkhurst Prison* [1988] AC 533.

[68]   *R v Chief Constable of the Merseyside Police, ex p Calveley* [1986] QB 424.

[69]   *R (Lim) v Secretary of State for the Home Department* [2007] EWCA Civ 773, [2008] INLR 60.

[70]   Limitation Act 1980, ss 2 and 5.

[71]   Civil Procedure Rules, Pt 54, r 5(1)(b). No specific time limit applies in Scotland, but the courts have a discretion to dismiss applications where there has been unwarranted delay. This discretion is exercised particularly readily in judicial review cases: *Watt v Secretary of State for Scotland* [1991] 3 CMLR 429, [21].

[72]   Civil Procedure Rules, Pt 54, r 5(1)(a).

[73]   Civil Procedure Rules, Pt 3, r 1(2), as interpreted in *R (M) v The School Organisation Committee, Oxfordshire County Council* [2001] EWHC Admin 245.

[74]   As in *R v Rochdale Metropolitan Borough Council, ex p Cromer Ring Mill Ltd* [1982] 3 All ER 761.

[75]   Senior Courts Act 1981, s 31(6). See further *R v Dairy Produce Quota Tribunal for England and Wales, ex p Caswell* [1990] 2 AC 738.   [76]   Senior Courts Act 1981, s 31(6).

[77]   See *R v North West Leicestershire District Council, ex p Moses* [2000] Env LR 443.

they stand, it is argued, and it would be detrimental to the public interest if decisions could be challenged years after being taken.[78]

> **Q** Oliver has argued that while it is right that certain decisions should be open to challenge for only a very short period, there is no good reason why the three-month rule should apply to all government decisions.[79] Do you agree? What sort of decisions might be most deserving of protection by means of very short time limits?

Fourth, and finally, courts in judicial review cases are generally *reluctant to resolve disputes of fact*.[80] For example, although the Civil Procedure Rules make provision for courts to allow cross-examination in judicial review proceedings,[81] the power is rarely used: Lord Diplock said that 'it will only be upon rare occasions that the interests of justice will require that leave be given for cross-examination'.[82] Similarly, courts are generally reluctant to require disclosure of documentary evidence in judicial review cases. This reluctance was reaffirmed by the House of Lords in *Tweed v Parades Commission for Northern Ireland*:[83] Lord Brown said that 'disclosure orders are likely to remain exceptional in judicial review proceedings', although he went on to acknowledge that when—as, for example, in cases arising under the Human Rights Act 1998—the court's scrutiny of the decision is to be unusually rigorous, a more generous approach to disclosure may be warranted. The general reluctance of courts to grapple with and resolve disputes of fact in judicial review proceedings may therefore provide an additional incentive for the use of other avenues of challenge. For example, if, in our example, the company were to be denied permission on the ground that the Minister considered that the new airport would have a serious negative environmental impact, appeal to a planning tribunal (should the Act grant such a right of appeal) might be an attractive way forward for the company, because the tribunal would be more likely to be able and willing to examine and resolve differences between conflicting evidence as to the environmental implications of the project.

3.2 **Procedural exclusivity**

It is apparent from the previous section that the judicial review procedure is, in some respects, not especially attractive to prospective claimants. They therefore sometimes seek to avoid these procedural obstacles by issuing ordinary proceedings to challenge government decisions rather than making a claim for judicial review. The main differences between the two forms of proceeding are set out in Figure 14.3. Given a free

---

[78] See, eg *O'Reilly v Mackman* [1983] 2 AC 237, 280–1, *per* Lord Diplock.

[79] Oliver, 'Public Law Procedures and Remedies: Do We Need Them?' [2002] PL 91, 98–9.

[80] Scottish courts seem to be less reluctant to resolve factual disputes via cross-examination: *Walker v Strathclyde Regional Council (No 2)* 1987 SLT 81.   [81] Civil Procedure Rules, Pt 54, r 16(1).

[82] *O'Reilly* at 282.   [83] [2006] UKHL 53, [2007] 1 AC 650.

	Judicial review proceedings	Ordinary proceedings
Time limit	Three months	Six years
Permission needed?	Yes	No
Cross-examination?	Rarely available	More liberal approach
Disclosure?	Rarely available	More liberal approach

Figure 14.3 Ordinary and judicial review proceedings compared

choice, then, people might prefer to use ordinary proceedings. The difficulty, however, is that some features of the judicial review procedure that constitute *restrictions* from the perspective of claimants are, as discussed above, *safeguards* as far as public authorities are concerned. If those safeguards are to have any practical impact, then it would seem to be necessary to force litigants to use judicial review proceedings if they wish to challenge public bodies' decisions.

Precisely that point was taken by the House of Lords in *O'Reilly v Mackman*,[84] in which the claimant prisoners sued the prison authorities, alleging that certain disciplinary decisions had been taken in a procedurally unfair way, and were therefore unlawful. The House of Lords ruled that, by using ordinary—rather than judicial review—proceedings, the claimants had committed an 'abuse of process', and therefore struck out their claims. Lord Diplock said that, as a general principle, courts should not

> permit a person seeking to establish that a decision of a public authority infringed rights to which he was entitled to protection under public law to proceed by way of an ordinary action and by this means to evade the protection of such authorities [which inheres in the judicial review procedure].[85]

There is also a practical argument that judicial review claims should be channelled into the Administrative Court, which is staffed by judges with special expertise in public law.

The effect of *O'Reilly* was that ordinary proceedings could be used to vindicate private law rights, but that public law matters had to be litigated by means of the special judicial review procedure. We can use our example to illustrate the point. Imagine that two householders whose land adjoins the proposed site of the new airport wish to mount legal challenges to the Secretary of State's decision to allow it to be built. The first householder wishes to argue that the Minister failed to take into account local opposition to the scheme. In other words, he contends that the Secretary of State did not take into account certain relevant considerations as he is duty-bound to do as a matter of public law. This is a straightforward public law argument and would have to be made in judicial review proceedings. In contrast, assume that the airport is to be

---

[84] [1983] 2 AC 237.   [85] *O'Reilly* at 285.

built partly on a field next to the second householder's home, and that the land was sold several years ago by the second householder (and subsequently acquired by the airport operator) subject to a condition (known as a 'restrictive covenant') that it was not to be used for commercial purposes. The second householder would be free to enforce the restrictive covenant in ordinary proceedings, because he would be seeking to protect a private law property right.

We can see, therefore, that the *O'Reilly* case established the principle of *procedural exclusivity*, such that the judicial review procedure was the only way in which claimants could raise public law issues in the courts. This caused numerous problems, not least because it required English courts to distinguish between public and private law in a way that they had never previously done. This resulted in considerable uncertainty and consumed a great deal of the courts' time.[86] As a result, the courts softened their stance on procedural exclusivity in a series of cases that followed *O'Reilly*. Two main sets of developments should be noted.

First, the courts have recognised a *number of exceptions* to the requirement that judicial review proceedings must be used to litigate public law issues. For example, it appears that courts may be prepared to allow the use of ordinary proceedings in cases that turn on disputed points of fact;[87] this is obviously sensible given the inability, or at least unwillingness, noted above, of judicial review courts to resolve such disputes. It has also been recognised that the principle of procedural exclusivity should not prevent people from attacking the legality of government decisions and measures in order to defend themselves in criminal[88] or civil[89] proceedings. For example, in *Boddington*,[90] it was held that a defendant charged with breaching a by-law could argue in his defence that the by-law was being unlawfully applied; it was not necessary for him to launch separate judicial review proceedings in order to litigate that point. Meanwhile, it was established in *Roy v Kensington and Chelsea and Westminster Family Practitioner Committee*[91] that, where a case raises a mixture of public and private law points, they can all be dealt with in ordinary proceedings.[92]

Second, even if a case does not fall within one of the above exceptions, there is now a *more sophisticated approach* to enforcing the policy that underpinned the House of Lords' decision in *O'Reilly*.[93] If a court concludes that judicial review proceedings should have been, but were not, used, it no longer automatically follows that there has been an abuse of process; rather, the court asks itself whether, if judicial review were

---

[86] As Lord Woolf MR noted in *Trustees of the Dennis Rye Pension Fund v Sheffield City Council* [1998] 1 WLR 840, 842.   [87] *Dennis Rye*.

[88] *Boddington v British Transport Police* [1999] 2 AC 143.

[89] *Wandsworth London Borough Council v Winder* [1985] AC 461.

[90] *Boddington v British Transport Police* [1999] 2 AC 143.   [91] [1992] 1 AC 624.

[92] The position in Scotland is broadly comparable. Those wishing to raise public law challenges must generally make an application for judicial review under ch 58 of the Rules of the Court of Session, but exceptions (eg permitting collateral challenge) are recognised. See further Clyde and Edwards, *Judicial Review* (Edinburgh 2000), ch 8.

[93] *Clark v University of Lincolnshire and Humberside* [2000] 1 WLR 1988.

to have been used, the case would have passed muster—would permission have been granted? Had the claimant complied with the time limit? If not, would there have been a good reason for allowing the claim to proceed anyway? If the answers to these questions are 'yes', then the claim will be allowed to continue because the claimant will not have gained an unfair advantage by failing to use judicial review proceedings, since the case would, in such circumstances, have been permitted to go ahead even if such proceedings were to have been issued.[94] This approach is to be welcomed, since it upholds the policy underlying *O'Reilly*, but in a less dogmatic, more subtle, way.

Q Why did the courts establish and then modify the principle of procedural exclusivity?

3.3 **Standing**

3.3.1 **Introduction**

We now turn to the question of who may issue a claim for judicial review.[95] Generally speaking, if one party to a contract fails to do what she has promised, only the other party—or, in limited circumstances, third parties who are affected—can initiate a claim for breach of contract. Similarly, if one person's negligent driving causes harm to another, it is generally only the latter who can issue a claim in tort.[96] These matters are regarded as essentially private: it is therefore for the victims to decide whether they wish to make a claim; it is they who have suffered as a result of the unlawful conduct of the other parties; and if the victims do not wish to seek legal redress, then that is no one else's business.

So much for private law—but what about public law? Do (and should) a wider range of people have standing to issue claims for judicial review?[97] Returning to our example, it is clear that, even if a narrow, private-law-style approach were adopted, people directly affected by a decision to allow the new airport to be built—for example, those whose lives would be blighted by noise pollution by virtue of living close to the proposed site of the airport—would have standing to issue judicial review proceedings. What, however, about people with a less direct interest? Could, for example, people who live several miles from the new airport seek judicial review on account of the fact that, if built, it would cause traffic congestion that would reduce their quality of life or damage their businesses? And what of people with even less direct interests? Could a

---

[94] Indeed the court may, under the Civil Procedure Rules, Pt 54, r 20, transfer such a case into the judicial review procedure.

[95] A related question—who may issue a claim under the Human Rights Act 1998—is considered separately. See Chapter 19, section 3.5.4, below.

[96] There are, however, certain limited circumstances in which it may be possible for someone else to sue on behalf of the victim of the breach of contract or tort—eg where the victim is a child or a person who lacks mental capacity within the meaning of the Mental Capacity Act 2005. See Civil Procedure Rules, Pt 21.

[97] In this context, to have standing—or *locus standi*, as it is sometimes called—is to have legal capacity to proceed with judicial review in respect of a particular matter.

member of an environmental pressure group—or even just an environmentally concerned member of the public—issue a claim in order to argue that the Minister had failed adequately to consider the ecological implications of the new airport?

The standing rules for judicial review are set out in the Senior Courts Act 1981, which provides that a court may not grant permission for judicial review 'unless it considers that the [claimant] has a *sufficient interest* in the matter to which the application relates'.[98] However, this provision, by itself, offers little guidance: it could be read narrowly, so as to allow standing only to those who have been directly adversely affected by a public decision (for example, to an asylum seeker who wishes to argue that his asylum application has been unlawfully rejected), or more widely, so as to allow anyone to challenge such a decision (because we all have an interest in making sure that the government respects the law).

3.3.2 Possible approaches to standing

In terms of policy, there may be good reasons for adopting a narrow approach to standing.[99] A broad approach might, for example, risk opening up public authorities to large volumes of vexatious litigation brought by busybodies. However, this is not, in itself, a convincing argument in favour of a narrow approach to standing, bearing in mind that other control devices, unrelated to the identity of the prospective claimant, are, in any event, at the courts' disposal.[100]

At the same time, there are strong arguments in favour of the courts adopting a generous approach towards standing. This is because we think differently about the public law that is enforced via judicial review than we do about the private law that is enforced in claims brought in contract, tort, and so on. When claimants seek judicial review, they are not seeking to vindicate *rights* that have allegedly been infringed by, for example, a procedurally unfair government decision; rather, they are seeking to enforce the *duties*—for example, the duty to act fairly—under which public law places government bodies.[101] This is a subtle, yet important, distinction. It reflects the fact that whereas the prevailing view is that a breach of contract is an essentially private matter, such that only a person who suffers because of the breach should be able to sue,[102] breach of public law duties is *not* a purely private issue. Instead, it is regarded

---

[98] Section 31(3) (emphasis added). No equivalent provision applies in Scotland, where the approach to standing is set at common law. See further below.

[99] See further Schiemann, 'Locus Standi' [1990] PL 342, 348–9.

[100] For example, permission to initiate judicial review can be withheld if the claimant appears to have no realistic prospect of success: see section 3.1 above.

[101] See, eg *R v Somerset County Council, ex p Dixon* [1998] Env LR 111, 121, *per* Sedley J.

[102] There is, of course, a clear public interest in having an effective legal system for providing remedies to victims of breach of contract. If such a system did not exist, then people would feel free to breach contracts with impunity (thus deterring entry into contracts in the first place, with obvious social and commercial consequences) and/or there would be attempts to enforce contractual obligations other than through recourse to the courts (for example, by the use or threat of violence). However, the fact that there is a strong public interest in having a *system* for dealing with breaches of contract does not change the fact that any *particular* breach of contract is a private matter between the parties.

as something in which the public generally has a legitimate interest: even if a specific individual suffers particular harm as a result of an unlawful decision by a public body, the public as a whole has an interest in ensuring that government authorities respect the principles of good administration that the courts have developed.

Miles notes that this perspective embraces a *communitarian* view of public law that 'focuses not on the specific interest of the individual victim in seeing government illegality against him or her checked, but on a broader public interest in lawful government'.[103] She goes on to argue that, on this view, it is inappropriate to allow those affected by unlawful decisions to 'veto' litigation that would aim to determine whether the government action in question were unlawful.[104] Whether a narrow or a broad approach to standing is to be preferred ultimately depends on the role that courts ought to serve in this context. A broad approach to standing may allow the judicial process to become a surrogate political process, by enabling individuals and interest groups who are not themselves directly affected by particular decisions to raise their objections to them by means of judicial review. Whether this is a good or a bad thing turns on the extent to which it is felt legitimate for courts to assume such a pseudo-political role—a question that goes to the heart of our key themes about how executive power should be controlled, and about the balance between legal and political notions of constitutionalism.

3.3.3 The current position

As Figure 14.4 shows, there are several possibilities regarding standing to seek judicial review, ranging from a very restrictive, private-law-like approach (shown at the left-hand side of the diagram) to an extremely liberal approach (shown at the right-hand side). As we explain in the remainder of this section, English law generally adopts a liberal approach to standing, although it does not go as far as to allow anyone at all to challenge any decision.[105]

The basis of the modern law of standing is the *Fleet Street Casuals* case, so-called because it involved a dispute about the taxation of casual print workers on national newspapers, many of which used to be based on Fleet Street in London.[106] It was well known that some such workers avoided paying income tax by falsifying information provided to the tax authorities. In an attempt to regularise the situation, a deal was offered: if the workers would register for tax purposes and pay tax in future, no inves-

---

[103] Miles, 'Standing under the Human Rights Act 1998: Theories of Rights Enforcement and the Nature of Public Law Adjudication' [2000] CLJ 133, 150.   [104] Miles at 152.

[105] Scottish courts adopt a narrower approach than their English counterparts. This is, in part, because, under Scots law, there must be both 'title' and 'interest' to sue. The former requirement means that the applicant must be 'a party (using the word in its widest sense) to some legal relation which gives him some right which the person against whom he raises the action either infringes or denies': *D & J Nicol v Dundee Harbour Trustees* [1915] AC 550, 562, *per* Lord Dunedin. See further Hope, 'Mike Tyson Comes to Glasgow: A Question of Standing' [2001] PL 294.

[106] *R v Inland Revenue Commissioners, ex p National Federation of Self-employed and Small Businesses Ltd* [1982] AC 617.

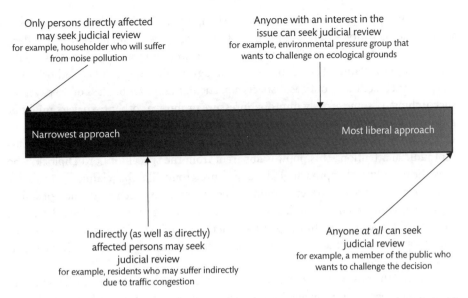

Figure 14.4 Standing: a range of possible approaches (with reference to example on p 543 above)

tigations would be undertaken into previous infractions. The claimant, a body representing the interests of self-employed people and small businesses, sought to challenge the tax authorities' offer of an amnesty in respect of past tax avoidance, arguing that this was unfair to law-abiding taxpayers such as its members.

The great irony of the *Fleet Street Casuals* case is that while it is invariably cited as the bedrock of the modern, liberal law of standing, the House of Lords held, on the facts, that the claimant did *not* have standing to pursue its claim. Their Lordships noted that the claimant had no particular interest, over and above that of any taxpayer, in the tax affairs of the print workers, and a majority was unwilling to accept—at least on these facts—that the requirement of 'sufficient interest' under the Senior Courts Act 1981 was so wide as to enable a legal challenge in such circumstances. However, in reaching this conclusion, their Lordships laid down a fundamental principle that has profoundly influenced the subsequent development of the law in this area— that is, that standing is not to be assessed as a purely preliminary matter separate from the substance of the case itself; rather, whether a claimant has standing is to be judged within 'the legal and factual context' of the case.[107] The question of standing must therefore be addressed with reference to the strength and seriousness of the claimant's case.

This, in turn, helps to explain why the claimant in *Fleet Street Casuals* did not secure standing. Lord Fraser was willing to countenance the possibility that even an individual taxpayer may be granted standing to challenge a decision by the tax authorities

---

[107] *Fleet Street Casuals* at 630, *per* Lord Wilberforce.

about another person's affairs 'if he was relying upon some exceptionally grave or widespread illegality'—but, said his Lordship, 'such cases would be very rare indeed and this is not one of them'.[108] Similarly, Lord Roskill said that if—in contrast to the present case—a claimant were to seek to impugn a failure by the tax authorities to 'perform their statutory duty as respects a particular taxpayer or class of taxpayer' by succumbing to 'some grossly improper pressure or motive', other taxpayers might be granted standing to mount a judicial review challenge.[109] This suggests that no one will be denied standing if the court is persuaded that the case is serious enough to warrant judicial attention. This point is apparent from the speech of Lord Diplock, who took the most liberal approach of all: 'a pressure group, like the [claimant], or even a single public-spirited taxpayer' should not be prevented by 'technical rules' of standing from getting a court 'to vindicate the rule of law and [getting] ... unlawful conduct stopped'.[110] Cane has therefore suggested that the *Fleet Street Casuals* case marked the end of standing as an independent requirement, so bound up is it now with the merits of the claim itself.[111]

However, the position is arguably more complex than this. It is clear that where an individual is personally affected by a decision, she will undoubtedly have standing to sue. (Whether she has a strong case is another matter.) As we move away from that paradigm, standing may still be a possibility, but prospective claimants will, in effect, have to compensate for their lack of personal involvement with the issue by persuading the court that the matter is so important that it should nevertheless be litigated—by them. Subsequent case law confirms that courts may entertain challenges by claimants who are not themselves affected by the relevant decision, but that such claimants—and their cases—will be subjected to greater and stricter scrutiny than victims. It is helpful to distinguish between two types of case in considering this further.

First, the courts now clearly recognise the possibility of *associational standing*, which, as Cane puts it, generally involves a group or corporation 'claiming on behalf of (the interests of) identifiable individuals who are its members or whom it claims to represent'.[112] For example, in *R v HM Inspectorate of Pollution, ex p Greenpeace (No 2)*,[113] the court allowed an environmental pressure group to seek judicial review, on behalf of local residents among its membership, of a decision to allow a nuclear reprocessing plant to open in spite of safety concerns. The court was clearly influenced by Greenpeace's 'particular experience in environmental matters' and 'its access to experts in the relevant realms of science and technology (not to mention the law)', which meant that it was 'able to mount a carefully selected, focused, relevant and well-argued challenge'.[114] This suggests that where a case is brought not by a victim, but by a campaigning organisation seeking to represent others' interests, the court will scrutinise that organisation's credentials to ensure that it is capable of arguing the case

---

[108] *Fleet Street Casuals* at 646.   [109] *Fleet Street Casuals* at 662.

[110] *Fleet Street Casuals* at 644.   [111] 'Standing, Legality and the Limits of Public Law' [1981] PL 322.

[112] Cane, 'Standing Up for the Public' [1995] PL 276 at 276.   [113] [1994] 4 All ER 329.

[114] *Greenpeace (No 2)* at 350, *per* Otton J.

sensibly, and is not simply an interfering and ill-informed busybody liable to waste the court's time.

Second, the courts are also willing to recognise *public interest standing*,[115] as the decision in the *Pergau Dam* case illustrates.[116] When we examined that case in Chapter 13, we saw that the claimant persuaded the court that the Foreign Secretary had acted unlawfully by funding a development project in Malaysia despite concerns that it was economically suspect.[117] Our present interest in the case relates to the claimant itself—a highly respected pressure group that, as Rose LJ put it, 'actively campaign[ed] through letter-writing, lobbying and other democratic means to improve the quantity and quality of British aid to other countries'.[118] Neither the group itself nor any of its members were directly affected—at least, no more than any other taxpayer. Furthermore, the pressure group was not acting, in a representative capacity, on behalf of people who were peculiarly affected. The court therefore had to decide whether standing could ever be generated on purely public interest grounds: could a claimant be permitted to litigate not because it purported to be (or to speak for those) affected by a decision, but simply because it would be in the public interest for a court to rule on its legality? This question was answered in the affirmative, although the court made it clear that it would not be easy to secure standing on such grounds. But, it said, standing was appropriate on the facts of this case due to the intersection of a number of factors: the seriousness of the allegations (£200 million of public money was at stake); the strength of the claimant's case; the absence of an alternative challenger (because no one was peculiarly affected—all taxpayers were affected equally and imperceptibly); and the expert and informed character of the claimant, which enabled it to present a well-informed challenge to the court.

Finally, it should be noted that a party that may lack standing to initiate judicial review proceedings may nevertheless be granted permission to intervene in proceedings brought by someone else.[119] Today, the courts exercise their discretion to permit such intervention fairly liberally—a development that has been welcomed, bearing in mind that, in judicial review cases, courts are frequently asked to examine multifaceted questions that engage interests beyond those of the actual parties.[120]

English law's liberal approach to standing, important in itself, also tells us something more profound about the role of judicial review. It implies that English law embraces what, as we saw above, has been referred to as a 'communitarian' view of public law, in which value is attached not just to righting wrongs suffered by individual victims of illegal decisions, but also to the wider project of 'vindicating the rule of law'.[121] Importantly, that wider project may require courts to hear cases in which

---

[115] See further Cane 'Standing Up for the Public'.

[116] *R v Secretary of State for Foreign and Commonwealth Affairs, ex p World Development Movement Ltd* [1995] 1 WLR 386.   [117] See Chapter 13, section 4.5, above.

[118] *Pergau Dam* at 393.   [119] Civil Procedure Rules, Pt 54, r 17.

[120] For contrasting views on the value of permitting intervention, see Harlow, 'Public Law and Popular Justice' (2002) 65 MLR 1; Fordham, '"Public Interest" Intervention: A Practitioner's Perspective' [2007] PL 410.

[121] *Pergau Dam* at 395.

victims do not wish or are unable to come forward, or in which the illegality is victim-less in the sense that no particular individual or group of individuals is specifically or identifiably disadvantaged by it. The fact that judges are, in appropriate circum-stances, willing to hear such cases is significant to our key themes. In particular, it implies that courts attach importance to ensuring the *accountable use of executive power* and that they perceive, pursuant to the notion of *legal constitutionalism*, a sig-nificant role for the judiciary in this enterprise. Viewed in this way, the law relating to standing provides an insight into the significance of judicial review in the modern British constitution.

> **Q** What range of factors do the courts consider when deciding whether or not a claimant has standing to challenge an administrative decision by way of judicial review?

4. Remedies

4.1 The discretionary nature of remedies in public law

If a claimant succeeds in establishing that a defendant is acting or proposing to act unlawfully, the court must then decide what remedy, if any, to issue. In judicial review proceedings, remedies are not available as of right, but are *discretionary*. This means that even if a public authority has acted unlawfully, the court may still refuse to issue a remedy if it would be in the public interest to do so. Assume, for example, that a Minister uses statutory powers to enact secondary legislation establishing a state-funded compensation scheme for victims of violent crime and then, under that scheme, grants compensation to thousands of such victims over the following three months.[122] If a claimant were later to persuade a court that the Minister had acted unlawfully by enacting the secondary legislation, the court might nevertheless refuse to set aside that legislation if doing so would cause chaos and hardship by making all of the subsequent grants of compensation unlawful too. In such circumstances, the court may instead exercise its discretion to withhold relief in order to safeguard a broader public interest.[123]

The discretionary nature of remedies in public law is an important factor that dis-tinguishes it from private law, in which remedies issue as of right—that is, the claim-ant is *entitled* to relief if she establishes (for example) that the defendant committed a breach of contract or a tortious act. In turn, this distinction reflects a deeper differ-ence between public and private law: the former, unlike the latter, is not solely about regulating the relationship between the (individual) claimant and the (government)

---

[122] After three months, judicial review would most likely be time-barred: see section 3.1 above.
[123] See, eg *Glynn v Keele University* [1971] 1 WLR 487.

defendant; rather, public law also allows for the holding of the government to account in the public interest, and it is therefore entirely appropriate that courts, in deciding whether to issue a remedy when unlawful conduct is established, should take into account whether this would be in the public interest. Having said all of this, it is not common for courts to refuse relief in public law litigation.

4.2 **Quashing orders**

The three main remedies that are available in judicial review proceedings are quashing, mandatory, and prohibiting orders.[124] These remedies, unlike those that we consider at sections 4.4 and 4.5 below, can *only* be secured through judicial review, as opposed to ordinary, proceedings.[125] Quashing orders are the most commonly sought of the remedies: they quash, or reject as invalid, unlawful administrative decisions. Two issues in relation to quashing orders require discussion.

First, what is the impact of such orders? This depends fundamentally on the kind of illegality that induced the court to issue it. If the court finds that a decision was *made in an unacceptable way* (for example, that irrelevant considerations were taken into account, or that an unfair procedure was adopted), the decision can be quashed and the decision-maker required to reconsider the matter and reach a decision in accordance with the findings of the reviewing court.[126] However, there may be nothing to stop the decision-maker from making the same decision again, given that the original decision was struck down because of *how* it was made, not *what* the decision itself was. On the other hand, it is open to courts in appropriate circumstances to rule that *the decision itself* is unlawful. It might, for example, be regarded as *Wednesbury* unreasonable, disproportionate, or incompatible with the claimant's substantive legitimate expectation, or it might be a decision that, in the first place, the decision-maker had no jurisdiction to take. Here, the impact of the quashing order will be greater, since it will no longer be open to the decision-maker to reach whatever conclusion the court found unlawful. Where, therefore, a decision is quashed on substantive, as opposed to procedural, grounds, it is not open to the public body concerned to make the same decision again in that case.[127] Indeed, in some circumstances, a quashing order may not simply prevent a decision-maker from making a particular decision; it might also *compel the making of a particular decision*. For example, if a decision-maker has only two options open to it—such as granting or not granting a licence to do something—and the court rules that one of those options is unlawful, then this effectively forces the decision-maker to choose the other option.[128]

---

[124] Formerly known as *certiorari, mandamus,* and *prohibition*. Different remedies are available in Scotland. They are (and correspond to the English remedies of), reduction (quashing order), suspension/interdict (prohibiting order/injunction), specific performance/statutory order for performance (mandatory injunction/mandatory order), and declarator (declaration).   [125] Senior Courts Act 1981, s 31(1).

[126] Senior Courts Act 1981, s 31(5)(a).

[127] Unless circumstances change such that it is, for example, no longer unreasonable to adopt a particular decision.

[128] It is sometimes possible, in such circumstances, for the reviewing court to make the required decision itself, rather than to remit the matter to the decision-maker: Senior Courts Act 1981, s 31(5)(b) and (5A).

Second, when is it necessary or desirable for an individual to obtain a quashing order? When such an order is granted, the quashing occurs with retrospective effect, meaning that its net result is to create a situation as if the decision in question had never been taken. This reflects the fact that, in theory, an unlawful act is void *ab initio*, or invalid from the very beginning: if a Minister never had legal authority to make a particular decision, it can never have legally existed. Quashing orders do not therefore *render* unlawful acts invalid; rather, they simply 'make it quite plain that this is the case'.[129] It follows that, in some circumstances, an individual may simply choose to ignore an unlawful decision rather than go to the trouble of having it quashed—but whether such a strategy is advisable depends on a number of factors. Two are particularly important.

First, if someone simply elects to ignore something that they consider to be unlawful, this will generally involve *the taking of a risk*. For example, in *Boddington v British Transport Police*,[130] an individual smoked on a train in breach of a by-law making it unlawful to do so. He did not seek to have the by-law in question quashed in judicial review proceedings, but when prosecuted, he argued that the way in which the by-law had been implemented was unlawful. It is perfectly acceptable to make such arguments—known as *collateral challenges to administrative measures*—by way of a defence to criminal or civil proceedings.[131] If successful, such an argument provides a good defence. It allows the individual to argue that he has done nothing unlawful because the measure that he is accused of contravening does not actually exist: it was unlawfully adopted and is therefore void *ab initio*. The risk, however, is that the individual may be wrong—as, indeed, Mr Boddington was. In that case, the House of Lords ruled that the by-law had been lawfully implemented; the defence therefore failed and the individual was convicted. People may therefore choose to launch judicial review proceedings, with a view to obtaining a quashing order, in order to avoid this sort of risk by having a court authoritatively determine the legality of the measure in question.

Second, *practical reasons* may sometimes mean that an individual has no option but to seek a quashing order if she wishes to avoid being affected by an unlawful administrative act. The strategy adopted (ultimately without success) in *Boddington* is only potentially useful if an individual wishes to behave *as if the measure in question did not exist*. So if, for example, an invalid by-law criminalises certain conduct, an individual who is confident as to the by-law's invalidity can simply choose to ignore it, behaving as if it did not exist and collaterally challenging it should prosecution occur subsequently. However, such an approach is of no use if the person requires the taking of a positive administrative act, such as the conferral of a licence. Here, the fact that a licence has been unlawfully denied (for example, because an

---

[129] *Ahmed v HM Treasury (No 2)* [2010] UKSC 5, [2010] 2 WLR 378, [4], *per* Lord Phillips.

[130] [1999] 2 AC 143.

[131] There are some exceptions to this principle. For example, the relevant legislation may, explicitly or impliedly, exclude the possibility of collateral challenge in particular cases: see, eg *R v Wicks* [1998] AC 92.

unfair procedure was adopted) does not change the fact that the individual lacks a licence. A quashing order followed by a fresh decision will be needed if the individual is to have any prospect of obtaining the licence. Equally, a quashing order may be practically imperative if the individual wishes to *convince others* of the unlawfulness of an administrative measure. For example, if a bank has frozen someone's assets pursuant to an unlawful administrative order, it is unlikely that the bank will release the assets without judicial confirmation (by way of quashing) of the invalidity of the order.[132]

4.3 Mandatory and prohibiting orders

Mandatory and prohibiting orders can be considered more briefly. Whereas quashing orders deal after the event with unlawful action already committed, prohibiting orders are anticipatory in their effect: they are issued to prevent unlawful action being taken where it seems that such action is being planned. For example, in *R v Liverpool Corporation, ex p Liverpool Taxi Fleet Operators' Association*,[133] a local authority decided that it would issue a number of new taxi licences. This was in breach of an assurance that, for the time being, the number of licences would be capped. Existing licence-holders objected to this proposed course of action because, by increasing the number of taxis allowed to operate in the city, it would compromise the viability of their own businesses. In these circumstances, the court issued a prohibiting order preventing the council from implementing its decision pending consultation with existing licence-holders.

Mandatory orders, meanwhile, compel public authorities to do things that they are legally required to do. Such relief is most obviously pertinent where a statute places a public body under an explicit duty to do something; if the duty is not discharged, a mandatory order may be sought in order to make the public body discharge it. However, mandatory orders are also relevant in relation to discretionary powers. As we saw in Chapter 13, no discretion is unlimited, and courts often find that duties—to act fairly, to take into account relevant factors, and so on—are implicit within discretionary powers. A mandatory order may therefore be issued to require a decision-maker to exercise discretion in line with such implied duties.[134]

4.4 Injunctions

The effect of an injunction is equivalent to that of a prohibiting order—it prevents a public body from undertaking unlawful conduct—but there are two reasons why an injunction may be preferable to a prohibiting order. First, injunctions can be obtained in ordinary, as well as in judicial review, proceedings, whereas prohibiting

---

[132] *Ahmed (No 2)*.
[133] [1972] 2 QB 299.
[134] See, eg, *Padfield v Minister of Agriculture, Fisheries and Food* [1968] AC 997.

orders can only be obtained in the latter—and, as we saw above, the use of ordinary proceedings has certain attractions for prospective claimants.[135] Second, injunctions can be obtained in interim, as well as final, form. This means that it is possible to get a temporary injunction—for example, preventing a decision from being implemented—pending the court's final ruling on whether or not the decision is lawful. This is especially useful if there is a risk of the issue becoming moot by the time the court is likely to reach a final decision. For example, a court may grant an interim injunction preventing the deportation of an asylum seeker pending judicial review of whether the decision to deport him was lawful.[136] Granting such relief may be necessary to ensure that the person concerned is still in the country by the time the court actually rules on the legality of the decision.

In deciding whether to grant interim relief, the courts apply a three-stage test. First, has the claimant shown *prima facie* that there is a 'serious issue to be tried'?[137] If so, then, second, would the claimant have an adequate remedy in damages if the act in question were to be carried out and later be found to be unlawful? For example, damages would clearly not be an adequate remedy for an asylum seeker whose life would be at risk if (unlawfully) deported to his home country.[138] Third, the court has to apply what is known as the *balance of convenience test* by considering the implications for the parties of granting and not granting temporary relief: in effect, the court has to work out how damaging it would be to the claimant's interests if an interim injunction were not granted and balance this against the likely damage to the defendant's interests if such an injunction were granted.[139]

Finally, we should note that, after a period of considerable uncertainty, it was eventually established in *Re M* that injunctions, including interim injunctions, can be issued against Ministers acting in their official capacity.[140] This means that failure to comply with the terms of an injunction can lead to a finding of contempt of court, which is a criminal offence, although in *M* the House of Lords emphasised that any such finding would be against the Minister in his official, not his personal, capacity. Lord Woolf explained: 'By making the finding against the minister in his official capacity the court will be indicating that it is the department for which the minister is responsible which has been guilty of contempt.'[141] It follows that there is no prospect of Ministers being imprisoned or personally fined in such circumstances, and that a finding of contempt is therefore largely symbolic. It has been argued by one commentator that this represents 'a very dangerous concession' because it means that there is ultimately no

---

[135] See section 3.2 above.   [136] As in *Re M* [1994] 1 AC 377.

[137] *R v Secretary of State for Transport, ex p Factortame Ltd (No 2)* [1991] 1 AC 603, 671, *per* Lord Goff.

[138] Claimants, if granted an interim injunction, are usually required to give an undertaking that they will pay damages to the defendant if it later turns out that the act in question is lawful. The court must consider whether, in such circumstances, payment of money would adequately compensate the defendant for having been prevented from carrying out a lawful act.

[139] *American Cyanamid Co v Ethicon Ltd* [1975] AC 396, 406.   [140] *Re M* [1994] 1 AC 377.

[141] *M* at 426.

coercive means of enforcing the court's orders.[142] We should not, however, lose sight of the likely political impact of a finding of contempt against a government Minister. In this sphere, therefore, notions of legal and political constitutionalism potentially coalesce: it is for the court to determine whether the Minister has breached the terms of the injunction and hence the legal rules of the constitution, while the outworking of this *legal* infraction will principally be by means of the *political* ramifications of the court's judgment.

4.5 **Declarations**

Declarations do exactly what their name implies: they are, in effect, an authoritative statement by the court about the legal issue that has been brought to its attention. So, for example, a court might declare that it would be unlawful for a public body to refuse to consult the claimant before making a decision, or that it would be unlawful to make a particular decision because the decision-maker in question does not have jurisdiction to do so. Although declarations share two characteristics with injunctions—they are available in both ordinary and judicial review proceedings, and in both final and interim form—they differ in an important respect. Unlike injunctions, declarations are *non-coercive remedies*, meaning that they can be disregarded without legal consequence. Clearly, if a court declares that a given course of action would be unlawful and a public body adopts it anyway, the body will have acted unlawfully—but the existence of the declaration does not itself generate any liability (for example, for contempt).

Why, then, would a claimant bother seeking, or a court bother issuing, a declaration? In some circumstances, a declaration might be regarded as the most appropriate form of relief. For example, courts might sometimes consider it more seemly to issue a declaration: in *M*, Lord Woolf thought that it would rarely be necessary to issue an injunction against Ministers because it could, in general, be reasonably assumed that they would fully respect a declaration.[143]

In addition, declarations are more appropriate when courts are asked to rule on questions that have not yet fully crystallised into crisp legal disputes. For example, where an act has already been committed, the most obvious remedy, assuming that the court can be persuaded that the act is unlawful, is a quashing order; if the act is imminent, then a prohibiting order is most apt. But in other circumstances, a declaration might be more suitable. For example, a claimant might want to the court to rule not on the legality of a decision that has been taken or is imminent, but on whether something the government has said—by way of advice, guidance, or recommendation—might lead, for example, to the commission of unlawful acts by others. In such

---

[142] Harlow, 'Accidental Loss of an Asylum seeker' (1994) 57 MLR 620, 623. For further discussion, see Sedley, 'The Crown in Its Own Courts', in Forsyth and Hare (eds), *The Golden Metwand and the Crooked Cord* (Oxford 1998).

[143] *Re M* [1994] 1 AC 377, 423. An interim injunction was granted in *M*, but at that time there was no such thing as an interim declaration.

circumstances, there is no actual act or decision that can sensibly be quashed, nor is it appropriate to seek a prohibiting order unless there is clear evidence that some other body is about to act on what was said.

Precisely such a situation arose in *Royal College of Nursing v Department of Health and Social Security*[144] concerning a government circular that said that nurses could lawfully undertake part of a procedure for termination of pregnancy without a doctor's supervision. The claimant, which had already issued its own guidance saying that nurses risked criminal liability if they took part in the procedure in the way advocated by the government, sought a declaration to the effect that the government circular was wrong in law; the government, for its part, counterclaimed for a declaration that it was not. A declaration in the latter terms was granted and the courts did not consider there to be any difficulty in the parties litigating what was, in the absence of any actual prosecutions of nurses, an abstract point of law. In a later case, however, the House of Lords signalled that the courts' willingness to rule on such a point in *Royal College of Nursing* could be traced to the facts that an authoritative ruling was obviously desirable 'in the interests both of the nursing profession and of the public' and that the case raised 'a pure question of law'.[145]

These comments indicate that the courts are not prepared to declare open season, such that litigants can require them, by means of what are often called *advisory declarations*, to answer any legal question, however abstract.[146] While judges are clearly unwilling to rule on academic questions—that is, questions 'which [do] not need to be answered for any visible practical purpose', concerning such matters as the interpretation of long-ago repealed statutes—they are prepared to entertain at least the possibility of answering hypothetical questions.[147] In other words, adjudication on matters that have not yet, but which have the potential to, become concrete legal disputes is at least a possibility—and the more likely it is that the matter will become relevant to a real dispute, the more likely the court is, all things being equal, to be prepared to intervene with an advisory declaration. For example, in the *Royal College of Nursing* case, Lord Edmund-Davies observed that 'several thousand' of the procedures in question were carried out each year, making clarification of the legal position obviously desirable.[148] In contrast, the House of Lords refused to grant a declaration, sought by the editor of *The Guardian* newspaper, to the effect that, on a proper interpretation of the Treason Felony Act 1848, it would be lawful to publish articles advocating abolition of the monarchy by peaceful means. Lord Steyn concluded that it was obvious that, properly construed in line with the European Convention on Human Rights (ECHR),[149] such

---

[144] [1981] AC 800.

[145] *Gillick v West Norfolk and Wisbech Area Health Authority* [1986] AC 112, 193, *per* Lord Bridge.

[146] See further Beatson, 'Prematurity and Ripeness for Review', in Forsyth and Hare (eds), *The Golden Metwand and the Crooked Cord* (Oxford 1998).

[147] Laws, 'Judicial Remedies and the Constitution' (1994) 57 MLR 213, 214. See also *R (McKenzie) v Waltham Forest London Borough Council* [2009] EWHC 1097 (Admin).

[148] *Royal College of Nursing* at 833.

[149] As is required by s 3 of the Human Rights Act 1998. See Chapter 19 below.

conduct was not unlawful, and that 'the courts ought not to be troubled further with this unnecessary litigation'.[150] The courts' preparedness to rule on hypothetical matters is also tempered by judicial caution about giving a legal opinion that is divorced from a factual context.[151] So while they are, in principle, willing to rule on 'a discrete point of statutory construction...which does not involve detailed consideration of facts',[152] judges are not, in general, prepared to issue advisory declarations about how the law applies to complex fact situations that have not yet eventuated. Thus, in *Pretty*, the House of Lords made it clear that it would not be prepared to rule in advance on the legality of the terminally ill claimant's husband helping her to commit suicide.[153]

The courts very sensibly accept that they should be cautious in their use of advisory declarations. However, the fact that such relief is available in some circumstances is in itself important. It implies that the courts perceive their role in expositive, not merely dispositive, terms: in other words, that they consider that their function extends beyond the resolution of disputes to the elaboration of the legal framework—by, for example, clarifying the law in advance of real disputes arising. This contributes to the planning function of law—it enables people and government bodies to plan their conduct on the basis of a due appreciation of the legal position—and thus buttresses the rule of law concept of certainty. In turn, the fact that courts perceive their function in these relatively expansive terms contributes, in so far as it impacts upon the executive's legal position, to the role of legal constitutionalism, by enabling individuals to seek the courts' assistance not only when government bodies have acted unlawfully, but also by obtaining advance judicial opinions as to the legal constraints subject to which governance must occur.

5. Conclusions

Our focus in this chapter has been on a number of practical issues concerning procedures and remedies. In one respect, these are matters of technical, black-letter law. However, we have seen that questions of procedure and relief can also offer an insight into quite fundamental aspects of the subject—and that a consistent narrative can be deduced from what might superficially seem to be a disjointed set of rules. Many of the issues that we have studied in this chapter tell a story of a judiciary that has a very particular vision of the role of judicial review within the modern British constitution. The great reluctance of the courts to allow their supervisory jurisdiction to be ousted by legislation, their preparedness to hear claims from parties unaffected

---

[150] *R (Rusbridger) v Attorney General* [2003] UKHL 38, [2004] 1 AC 357, [28].

[151] *R (Burke) v General Medical Council* [2005] EWCA Civ 1003, [2006] QB 273, [21], *per* Lord Phillips MR.

[152] *R v Secretary of State for the Home Department, ex p Salem* [1999] 1 AC 450, 457, *per* Lord Slynn.

[153] *R (Pretty) v Director of Public Prosecutions* [2001] UKHL 61, [2002] 1 AC 800.

by the impugned decision when this is necessary for the maintenance of the rule of law, and their willingness to rule in advance on important legal questions all paint a picture in which judicial review—and therefore law—play a fundamental role in ensuring good governance. So, as we noted at the beginning of this chapter, the technical issues considered within it are closely related to two of our key themes, since they serve to underline the important role that courts play in securing the accountability of the executive branch and therefore the contemporary significance of legal constitutionalism.

Further reading

BEATSON, 'Prematurity and Ripeness for Review', in Forsyth and Hare (eds), *The Golden Metwand and the Crooked Cord* (Oxford 1998)

FELDMAN, 'Public Interest Litigation and Constitutional Theory in Comparative Perspective' (1992) 55 MLR 44

HARRIS, 'Judicial Review, Justiciability and the Prerogative of Mercy' (2003) 62 CLJ 631

LEWIS, 'The Exhaustion of Alternative Remedies in Administrative Law' [1992] CLJ 138

MILES, 'Standing under the Human Rights Act 1998: Theories of Rights Enforcement and the Nature of Public Law Adjudication' [2000] CLJ 133

SCHWARTZ, '*Anisminic* and Activism: Preclusion Provisions in English Administrative Law' (1986) 38 Administrative Law Review 33

TAGGART (ed), *The Province of Administrative Law* (Oxford 1997)

15 The Effectiveness and Impact of Judicial Review

The preceding three chapters have considered the procedure and legal principles of judicial review. This chapter is also concerned with judicial review, but it seeks to offer a different perspective upon the operation of judicial review. The purpose of this chapter is to examine the effectiveness of judicial review as a mechanism of legal accountability and its impact upon public administration. We are therefore concerned with how law works in practice. This requires a shift of approach: rather than examining legal doctrines, we shall focus upon the broader political and administrative context in which judicial review operates.

1. Judicial review and government

1.1 Judicial review—effectiveness and impact

It might be asked why it is necessary to consider the effectiveness and impact of judicial review. Under the traditional constitutional principles of parliamentary sovereignty and the rule of law, Parliament makes the law and the courts enforce it; the role of government is to administer the law and to comply with judicial interpretations of it. From this perspective, the relationship between the courts and public administration is, or should be, relatively non-problematic: court judgments expounding the law should be directly reflected in governmental practices. But, as this chapter will seek to demonstrate, the reality is rarely so simple. So far, we have considered the detailed and complex legal principles governing judicial review; however, a solely legal analysis does not, by itself, exhaust consideration of all of the issues raised by judicial review. It is necessary also to examine how judicial review works in practice and its impact upon government. After all, judicial review is concerned not only with the development of legal principles, but also with how public administrators are to perform their functions; every judicial review case, however routine, has some implication for policy development and administration, and for how these tasks are to be performed. While traditional separation of powers theory tends to rely upon clear distinctions between politics, law, and administration, in practice, these distinctions can become blurred. Court judgments—and, indeed, even the possibility of applying for judicial review—can have major consequences for governmental administration; alternatively, the government may seek to undermine court rulings.

This chapter therefore examines a number of issues concerning the effectiveness and impact of judicial review. However, the concepts of 'effectiveness'—the propensity of something such as judicial review to produce a desired outcome—and 'impact'—its influence or effect on public administration—are both complex. In the context of this chapter, the effectiveness of judicial review is taken to have three aspects. First, there is effectiveness in relation to the *accessibility* of the judicial review procedure—that is, the extent to which potential claimants are able to access judicial review. Second, there is effectiveness in terms of the *competence and capacity* of the courts to review administrative action. Third, there is the effectiveness of the *output* of judicial review and its impact upon government—in particular, the ability of judicial review to affect the behaviour and operations of government agencies.

Attention will focus on three sets of questions. First, in relation to the accessibility of judicial review, what are the dynamics of judicial review litigation? How many judicial review applications do the courts receive and in which particular administrative contexts? What obstacles are there to using judicial review? Second, to what extent does and should the likely impact of judicial review (if undertaken) influence the courts' decisions whether to undertake such review in the first place? In particular, where—in relation to so-called 'polycentric' issues—courts are faced with situations in which it is difficult to predict the likely impact of intervention, does (and should) this deter courts from engaging in judicial review? Third, what actually is the impact of judicial review on government? This question is 'probably the least studied but most important issue surrounding administrative law'.[1] The court's decision in a judicial review case is not usually the end of the story of a legal challenge to government action, but rather a chapter in the ongoing and evolving relationship between the courts and public authorities. How do public authorities react to judicial review? What factors tend to increase or diminish the impact of judicial review?

These questions require consideration because they are of direct relevance to one of our principal themes: the processes by which government is held accountable. Because holding public decision-makers to account is a central concern for public lawyers, it is important to examine the effectiveness of judicial review as a mechanism of legal accountability. If judicial review is able to exert influence on government, then its effectiveness for securing legal accountability can be said to be strengthened; if judicial review exerts little influence, then it may only provide a minimal form of legal accountability. Whether or not administrative law is able to achieve its primary goal—ensuring that government acts according to law—depends largely on the effectiveness of judicial review.

---

[1] Schuck and Eliot, 'To the *Chevron* Station: An Empirical Study of Federal Administrative Law' [1990] Duke Law Journal 984, 1044.

As we have already emphasised, judicial review provides only one means of controlling governmental decision-making; the legal norms articulated by the courts may often be only a subordinate part of the broader political–administrative context in which public authorities operate.[2] There is often a complex and dynamic interrelationship between law, politics, and public administration. It cannot be assumed that public authorities always enthusiastically welcome judicial scrutiny or comply with court judgments. Government reaction to judicial review may be positive or negative, formal or informal. Furthermore, there is always a risk that a court judgment, especially in the public law context, may have broader consequences and ramifications on governmental procedure and policy beyond its particular circumstances. It is therefore dangerous to assume that the relationship between court judgments and administrative practice is a straightforward one in which the latter automatically mirrors—by falling into line with—the former. The reality, as we will see, is far murkier—particularly in relation to the impact of judicial review decisions outwith the narrow confines of the actual case.

In considering the effectiveness and impact of judicial review, it is important to bear in mind the general expectation that all public authorities will comply with and implement court decisions holding their actions (or inactions) unlawful without delay or objection. This assumption is a central consequence of the rule of law. All public authorities take very seriously the obligation to act in accordance with the law and court judgments.[3] While, in formal constitutional terms, this obligation derives from the rule of law, it also reflects a deeply ingrained mental attitude having roots in British constitutional history—in particular, the victories of Parliament and the judiciary over the Stuart kings in the seventeenth century, as reflected in Dicey's formulation of the rule of law.[4] Outright refusal by public authorities to comply with court rulings may be a feature in other jurisdictions, but it is extremely unusual in the United Kingdom.[5] From the court's perspective, the proper constitutional relationship between the executive and the courts is that the courts will respect all acts of the executive within its lawful province, while the executive will respect all decisions of the courts as to what its lawful province is.[6] The rule of law enforced by the courts is the ultimate controlling factor on which the constitution is based. According to the courts, the task of judicial review—the protection of individual legal rights and clarification of the legal framework within which government operates—requires a partnership between the

---

[2] Prosser, 'Politics and Judicial Review: The *Atkinson* Case and Its Aftermath' [1979] PL 59.

[3] For example, the *Ministerial Code* (London 2010), [1.2] states that it 'should be read against the background of the overarching duty on Ministers to comply with the law'.

[4] See Chapter 2, section 4.4, above on the rule of law, and Chapter 4, section 4, above on parliamentary sovereignty.

[5] In the USA, 'non-acquiescence' by administrative agencies with court rulings is a recognised phenomenon. See Maranville, 'Non-Acquiescence: Outlaw Agencies, Imperial Courts, and the Perils of Pluralism' (1986) 39 Vanderbilt Law Review 471; Estreicher and Revesz, 'Non acquiescence by Federal Administrative Agencies' (1989) 98 Yale Law Journal 679.   [6] *Re M* [1992] 4 All ER 97, 146, *per* Nolan LJ.

courts and public authorities 'based on a common aim, namely the maintenance of the highest standards of public administration'.[7]

1.2 The development of judicial review

To place the discussion within a historical perspective, it is important to acknowledge the development of the judicial review jurisdiction.[8] Taking the 1950s as a starting point, the courts are generally considered to have exerted little, if any, influence on government. The prevalent judicial attitude, exemplified by the *Wednesbury* case decided in 1947 and considered in Chapter 13,[9] was that the courts should generally defer to administrative decisions and only intervene on the extreme basis that the impugned decision was so unreasonable that no reasonable authority could ever have arrived at it.[10] The very high level of deference shown by the courts toward the executive during the Second World War carried over into peacetime, even though this was a period during which the scale of administrative action was expanding significantly. In 1956, a senior judge expressed concern that the common law no longer possessed 'the strength to provide any satisfactory solution to the problem of keeping the executive…under proper control'.[11] As a leading commentator, de Smith, noted, judicial review was 'inevitably sporadic and peripheral'.[12]

However, as we saw in Chapter 13, during the 1960s and 1970s, the courts assumed a more active supervisory role by removing some of the most debilitating anachronisms, such as the distinction between errors of law inside and outside jurisdiction, and breathed new life into old concepts, such as the rules of natural justice and the doctrine of improper purpose.[13] New legal principles—notably the doctrines of legitimate expectations and proportionality—also developed.[14] Meanwhile, as noted in Chapter 14, the court's jurisdiction was expanded to include review of the prerogative and decisions produced by non-statutory bodies,[15] and the courts began to adopt a more generous approach toward standing and challenges brought by public interest groups.[16] Alongside doctrinal changes, procedural reforms were also occurring. In the

---

[7] *R v Lancashire County Council, ex p Huddleston* [1986] 2 All ER 941, 945, *per* Lord Donaldson MR.

[8] See generally Jowell, 'Administrative Law', in Bogdanor (ed), *The British Constitution in the Twentieth Century* (Oxford 2003), p 373; Rawlings, 'Modelling Judicial Review' (2008) 61 CLP 95.

[9] See Chapter 13, section 4.6.1, above.

[10] *Associated Provincial Picture Houses Ltd v Wednesbury Corporation* [1948] 1 KB 223.

[11] Devlin, 'The Common Law, Public Policy and the Executive' (1956) CLP 1, 14–15. See also Davis, 'The Future of Judge-Made Public Law in England: A Problem of Practical Jurisprudence' (1961) 61 Columbia Law Review 201.   [12] De Smith, *Judicial Review of Administrative Action* (London 1959), p 1.

[13] The landmark cases in this period are: *Ridge v Baldwin* [1964] AC 40; *Padfield v Minister for Agriculture, Fisheries and Food* [1968] AC 997; *Anisminic v Foreign Compensation Commission* [1969] 2 AC 147.

[14] *R v North and East Devon Health Authority, ex p Coughlan* [2001] QB 213; *R (Daly) v Secretary of State for the Home Department* [2001] 2 AC 532.

[15] See *Council of Civil Service Unions v Minister for the Civil Service* [1985] AC 374 (the *GCHQ* case); *R v Panel on Takeovers and Mergers, ex p Datafin plc* [1987] QB 815.

[16] *R v Inland Revenue Commission, ex p National Federation of Self-employed and Small Businesses* [1982] AC 617; *R v Secretary of State for Foreign Affairs, ex p World Development Movement Ltd* [1995] 1 WLR 386.

late 1970s and early 1980s, the procedures of judicial review were reformed to provide a coherent process for challenging administrative decisions before specialist judges sitting in the Crown Office List of the High Court.[17] The number of judicial review applications increased dramatically from some 500 in 1981 to over 4,000 in 1996. By this time, de Smith's comment required reformulation: '[T]he effect of judicial review on the practical exercise of power has...become constant and central.'[18] The next major developments occurred in 2000: a further set of procedural reforms[19] the renaming of the Crown Office List as the Administrative Court and the coming into force of the Human Rights Act 1998.

With these developments, it can now be said that judicial review possesses a distinctive role as a means for challenging public decisions. It exists alongside other accountability mechanisms such as parliamentary select committee inquiries,[20] ombudsmen investigations,[21] National Audit Office reports,[22] and media and political pressure. Often, these mechanisms may be used in combination, the distinctive aspect of judicial review being that it is a mechanism of *legal* accountability of government. This raises the questions of effectiveness and impact, to which we now turn.

2. Judicial review litigation

2.1 The dynamics of the judicial review jurisdiction

Let us start, then, by considering the nature of the Administrative Court's judicial review jurisdiction—not in terms of the legal principles of judicial review, but in terms of the number of judicial review claims lodged with the Court. Who lodged these claims, and against which public authorities? Figure 15.1 provides the statistics on the number of judicial review claims lodged with the Administrative Court.[23]

As can be seen from the diagram, the number of applications for judicial review varies from year to year. What is apparent is that the number of applications for permission to proceed to apply for judicial review is generally on an upward trend, apart from a decline in 2003–04. However, a significant proportion of these applications are refused permission to proceed by a High Court judge.[24] In 2008, 54 per cent of applications for permission to proceed were refused—that is, the judge decided that they did not raise an arguable legal challenge. The number of applications for judicial review granted permission to proceed—that is, allowed to proceed to a full hearing—has hovered around 1,000 for the last ten years. In 2008, 914 judicial review applications

---

[17] Senior Courts Act 1981, s 31; Rules of the Supreme Court (1977), Order 53.

[18] De Smith, Woolf, and Jowell, *Judicial Review of Administrative Action* (London 1995), p vii.

[19] Civil Procedure Rules (2000), Pt 54.   [20] See Chapter 10 above.   [21] See Chapter 16 below.

[22] See Chapter 11 above.

[23] These statistics are taken from the 1999–2008 editions of *Judicial and Court Statistics* published by the Ministry of Justice.   [24] On permission, see Chapter 14, section 3.1, above.

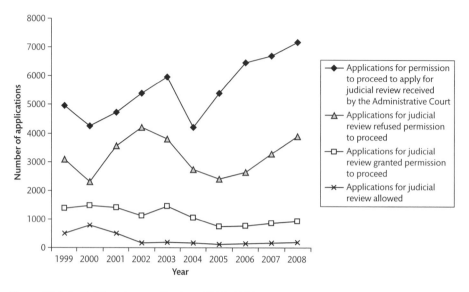

Figure 15.1 Judicial review applications 1999–2008

were granted permission to proceed. The bottom line of the table shows the actual number of judicial review applications that were allowed—that is, the number of cases in which the Court held that the challenged decision was unlawful. In 2008, the Administrative Court allowed 199 applications for judicial review.

A number of comments can be made on the basis of these statistics. First, there has certainly been an increase in the volume of judicial review challenges over recent years. However, considering the vast scale of governmental decision-making, the total number of such decisions challenged by way of judicial review is very small indeed. We noted in Chapter 12 that, according to some judges at least, judicial review has been developed in order to fill a gap that arises due to perceived problems with other remedies (most notably parliamentary accountability).[25] However, if we put this in the context of the statistics, then we find that the role of the courts has, in the grand scheme of things, increased only in a relatively modest way. Despite numerous factors that have expanded the role, scope, and intensity of judicial review in recent years—developments in the grounds of review, the expansion of standing, and the coming into force of the Human Rights Act 1998 in 2000—the number of successful applications for judicial review actually fell from 504 in 1999 to 199 in 2008.

It is, though, important to bear in mind that statistics cannot tell us everything. One application for judicial review may function as an important 'test case', with considerable repercussions for many other cases. An illustration is the House of Lords' decision in *Limbuela* concerning support for asylum seekers, the outcome of which influenced

---

[25] See Chapter 12, section 4, above.

several hundred other judicial reviews that were also pending.[26] Other judicial review challenges may be brought by a public interest body and may have wider ramifications for many thousands of individuals or on government policy. There is an important distinction, explored further below, between those judicial reviews that merely concern the individual redress of grievance and those that have a broader influence on governmental policy and procedure. Furthermore, the superior status of the Administrative Court within the legal system, staffed as it is by holders of high judicial office, means that its rulings possess a broader influence beyond individual cases.

Another point to note is that while judicial review can be used to challenge public decisions in any area of government, in practice, the use of judicial review tends to be concentrated in certain areas. In particular, immigration and asylum decision-making has, for several years, provided the principal source of judicial review. In 2008, this area accounted for 64 per cent of all judicial review claims received by the Administrative Court. As Rawlings has noted, 'it is today hard to avoid the impression of the Administrative Court as a specialist asylum and immigration court with knobs on'.[27] The second major area of judicial review pertains to the criminal justice system, and concerns decisions about sentencing, parole, and prison discipline and management.

The position, then, is that the experience of public authorities of judicial review varies enormously. Some public authorities have considerable experience of dealing with judicial review challenges. As the government department with responsibility for immigration and asylum decision-making, the Home Office is the archetypal 'repeat player' in the judicial review jurisdiction. By contrast, the exposure of other public authorities to judicial review may be more intermittent. Indeed, some may hardly ever, if at all, have their decisions legally challenged, which may, in turn, affect how they respond if and when they are subjected to an application for judicial review. For example, it is not unknown for the mere threat of judicial review proceedings to be sufficient inducement to prompt some public authorities to reconsider a decision—perhaps especially so if the public authority is not accustomed to having its decisions challenged by way of judicial review, or if it is unwilling to incur the expense, delay, and potentially adverse publicity of defending such proceedings.

Even the use of judicial review against a particular category of public authority may vary considerably *within the category*. For example, empirical research into the use of judicial review to challenge decisions of local authorities has indicated that while a few local authorities regularly experience judicial review challenges, for most, it remains a rarity; even within a single local authority, the focus of litigation on specific areas—for example, community care and housing—may mean that the influence of

---

[26] *R (Limbuela) v Secretary of State for the Home Department* [2006] 1 AC 396. As the Court of Appeal recognised, 666 other judicial review applications were affected by this decision: see [2004] EWCA Civ 540, [2].   [27] Rawlings, 'Modelling Judicial Review' (2008) 61 CLP 95, 111.

judicial review across areas of service provision varies.[28] Factors influencing the use of judicial review may include uneven geographical access to legal services, the link between deprivation and the presence of legal services in bringing challenges, and the dissatisfaction associated with poor-quality public services. In 'ground-level' contexts, such as community care and housing, judicial review is often used by the most marginalised groups of people—for example, homeless individuals seeking temporary accommodation—against hard-pressed local authorities in relation to some of the most intractable resource allocation issues.

Another point to note from the statistics is that the variation in the volume of judicial review challenges is, in practice, dependent upon a large number of different variables, such as the number of negative decisions made by government, the propensity of individuals and businesses to challenge such decisions, the availability of legal aid, the willingness of the court to grant permission to proceed for judicial review, the availability of judicial resources to deal with such challenges, and the availability of alternative methods of challenge.

To expand upon the last factor, it is apparent that the caseload of the Administrative Court is dependent upon the availability of tribunal appeal rights. The establishment of appeal rights can reduce the Court's caseload by diverting challenges away from judicial review into an appeal process. At the same time, restrictions on appeal rights to tribunals may mean that there is only one method of challenging decision-making—by way of judicial review. For example, during the 1980s, challenges lodged by individuals refused homelessness support by local authorities provided one of the principal areas of judicial review, but this aspect of the judicial review caseload fell away when a statutory right of appeal against homelessness decisions was created.[29]

Consider also the experience of immigration and asylum appeals and judicial review over the last decade. As noted above, immigration and asylum judicial review provide the bulk of the cases received by the Administrative Court. This has posed problems for the Court because there are a limited number of judges to deal with judicial review cases and an increase in the Court's caseload in one area is likely to mean delays in other areas. Add to this the government's concern that failed asylum seekers use legal challenges to prevent their removal from the country, and it is unsurprising that this area has been politically contentious and so subject to frequent change. Before 2003, a considerable number of immigration and asylum judicial review claims were lodged by individuals who, having had their immigration and asylum appeals dismissed by an immigration adjudicator and refused permission to appeal to the Immigration Appeal Tribunal, then sought judicial review of that refusal. In order to streamline this process, Parliament, in 2002, introduced a quick, paper-based statutory review procedure—a form of 'judicial review-lite'—under which individuals could challenge

---

[28] Sunkin, Calvo, Platt, and Landman, 'Mapping the Use of Judicial Review to Challenge Local Authorities in England and Wales' [2007] PL 545.

[29] Sunkin, 'What is Happening to Applications for Judicial Review?' (1987) 50 MLR 432; Housing Act 1996.

such decisions.[30] This diverted such cases away from the judicial review process, but it meant that the Administrative Court still had to deal with such challenges. The reduction in the overall number of applications for permission to proceed received in the years 2003 to 2005 may, in large part, be attributed to the introduction of this statutory review procedure.

In the face of a desire on the government's part to crack down on 'abuse' of judicial procedures, Parliament introduced a further change in 2005: the replacement of the two-tier appeal process with a single tier tribunal, the Asylum and Immigration Tribunal. This new system retained the ability of individuals to apply to the Administrative Court for a quick, paper-based review of the tribunal's decision.[31] In 2006, the Administrative Court received 3,306 such applications in addition to the already substantial volume of ordinary immigration and asylum judicial reviews.[32] The pressure posed by such applications created difficulties for both the Administrative Court itself and for the government department, the Home Office, the decisions of which were being challenged. As the Lord Chief Justice stated in 2008: '[T]he pressure of the asylum and immigration cases has meant that there are unacceptable delays. Claimants may wait 12 months or more. Understandably, concerns are being expressed at the delays.'[33]

In 2009–10, further restructuring was undertaken in order to relieve the Administrative Court of this caseload. First, the asylum and immigration appeals process was transferred into the new First-tier and Upper Tribunals established under the Tribunals, Courts and Enforcement Act 2007. Under this new framework, there is, in general, no ability to challenge Upper Tribunal decisions before the Administrative Court. Second, the 2007 Act allows for certain classes of judicial review challenge to be transferred to the Upper Tribunal, which is able to exercise its own 'judicial review' jurisdiction.[34] In 2009, Parliament legislated to transfer certain immigration and asylum judicial review challenges from the Administrative Court to the Upper Tribunal in order to relieve further the pressure on the Administrative Court.[35]

What this indicates is that the volume of judicial review applications can itself put pressure on the courts, and prompt government and Parliament to introduce changes, such as creating rights of appeal to a tribunal or transferring judicial review cases to the Upper Tribunal, to reduce that pressure. There is then a close interaction between the work of the Administrative Court and that of tribunals.

---

[30] Nationality, Immigration and Asylum Act 2002, s 101(2).

[31] Asylum and Immigration (Treatment of Claimants, etc.) Act 2004, s 26, inserting new s 103A into the Nationality, Immigration and Asylum Act 2002.

[32] Ministry of Justice, *Judicial and Court Statistics 2006* (Cm 7273 2007), table 1.14.

[33] Lord Phillips, Lord Chief Justice, *The Lord Chief Justice's Review of the Administration of Justice in the Courts* (HC 448 2008–09), p 36.

[34] Tribunals, Courts and Enforcement Act 2007, ss 15–19. For discussion of the Upper Tribunal's judicial review powers, see Chapter 17, section 5.5, below.

[35] Borders, Citizenship and Immigration Act 2009, s 53.

The overall picture is that the use of judicial review remains sporadic, with the bulk of it focused in particular areas. This, in turn, may affect its effectiveness in ensuring accountability; to be effective, controls over public authorities usually need to be systematic and continuous, whereas judicial review, as de Smith noted, tends to be more episodic. Consequently, its effectiveness in ensuring legal accountability may be constrained.

2.2 **The accessibility of judicial review**

How accessible, then, is the judicial review procedure? Judicial review is claimant-driven: the Administrative Court, like all courts, is essentially reactive in the sense that it can only consider the legality of a public decision if requested to do so by an individual. A claimant seeking judicial review must overcome a number of obstacles: he or she must comply with the three-month time limit, possess standing, and have exhausted alternative remedies. Claimants must also be granted permission to proceed for judicial review by demonstrating that they have an arguable case.[36] While this requirement acts as a filter mechanism, providing the Court with a useful tool of case management, it tends to operate on a highly discretionary basis, with substantial variations in the grants of permission between individual judges: the definition of what comprises an 'arguable' case leaves scope for judicial discretion.[37]

Other important practical difficulties may arise from the variable geographical availability of legal advice and services—for example, while some law firms may be very familiar with judicial review proceedings, others may not. Then there are the financial costs of securing such services. Many claimants may be unable to afford the substantial sums of money required to pursue judicial review proceedings and are compelled to rely on legal aid—but this may not be available where the prospects of success are either unclear or borderline.[38] Furthermore, as legal costs must normally be borne by the losing party, this may dissuade potential claimants from seeking judicial review. Of course, a claimant must also have good legal reasons for arguing that the challenged decision was unlawful. Even then, if a claimant overcomes all of these hurdles, there is no remedy as of right because public law remedies are discretionary. The paradox is that, while the courts often state that access to justice is a fundamental right, this right is, in practice, hedged around with numerous restrictions.

Another factor of some importance is that the Administrative Court, like virtually all courts, operates under constraints that limit the number of cases that it can handle at any one time. Courts are prone to overload because, typically, 'there are far more claims than there are institutional resources for full dress adjudication of

---

[36] For detailed discussion of these procedural matters, see Chapter 14.

[37] Le Sueur and Sunkin, 'Applications for Judicial Review: The Requirement for Leave' [1992] PL 102; Bridges, Mezaros, and Sunkin, *Judicial Review in Perspective* (London 1995), pp 164–70.

[38] Bridges, Meszaros, and Sunkin, 'Regulating the Judicial Review Case Load' [2000] PL 651, 658–64.

each'.[39] Such institutional limits may manifest themselves in stringent scrutiny of applications for permission to proceed and a search for ways to divert cases out of the ordinary judicial process, such as settlement and alternative dispute resolution (ADR), which are considered below. Furthermore, overload can lead to delays in the processing of cases.

In terms of the Administrative Court, judicial resources are comparatively constrained. One practical difficulty is that the number of High Court judges nominated to decide judicial review cases and who are therefore able to be deployed in the Administrative Court is limited.[40] As noted above, in light of the increasing caseload of judicial review claims and asylum-related review applications, the Court has experienced practical difficulties in coping with its workload; the average length of a judicial review case from initial application to a substantive hearing is approximately 18 months. Considerable delays in the judicial review process can create substantial adverse consequences for both claimants and public authorities, reducing the effectiveness of the process for reviewing the legality of public action. Justice delayed is justice denied.[41]

A final feature of judicial review litigation has been the uneven geographical spread of judicial review applications: a substantial number are lodged by individuals located in London and south-east England.[42] The precise causes of this are unknown and are likely to include many variables such as the willingness or otherwise of individuals to challenge public authorities, and access to legal advice and services. One suggestion has been that the location of the Administrative Court itself in London might inhibit people living elsewhere from seeking judicial review. In 2008, a judicial working group recommended that the Administrative Court establish regional hearing centres outside of London on the ground that proper access to justice cannot be achieved if those in the regions can only bring judicial review and other claims in the Administrative Court in London.[43] Following this, the Administrative Court has been regionalised, with hearing centres now operating in Cardiff, Manchester, Birmingham, and Leeds. The purpose of regionalisation is to facilitate access to

---

[39] Galanter, 'Why the "Haves" Come Out Ahead: Speculations on the Limits of Legal Change' (1974) Law and Society 95, 121.   [40] Report of Judicial Working Group, *Justice Outside London* (London 2007), [131].

[41] According to Cragg, 'Legislation update', *The Times*, 16 October 2007: 'There is a crisis in the Administrative Court...the court is now overloaded with cases and waiting times for even initial consideration of applications, even in urgent cases, has extended to months.' In *R (Casey) v Restormel Borough Council* [2007] EWHC Admin 2554, [29] and [33], Munby J noted:

> It is no secret that the Administrative Court is having great difficulty coping with its present workload...Hard pressed local and other public authorities should not be prejudiced,...tax payers and ratepayers should not be financially disadvantaged, other more deserving claimants seeking recourse to over-stretched public resources should not be prejudiced, because of delays in the Royal Courts of Justice.

The phrase 'justice delayed is justice denied' is often attributed to Magna Carta (1297), ch 29, which reads: 'To no one will we sell, to no one will we deny or delay, right or justice.'

[42] Bridges, Mezaros, and Sunkin, *Judicial Review in Perspective* (London 1995).

[43] Report of Judicial Working Group, [50]–[52].

justice by enabling judicial review cases to be administered and determined in the most appropriate location.[44]

2.3 **Settlement**

Looking at Figure 15.1 above, it is clear that many applications for judicial review do not proceed to a full hearing even if granted permission to proceed. This may be because a claimant withdraws the claim because it is without merit. Another explanation has been the increasing use of out-of-court settlements. Settlement refers to the ability of the litigants to resolve their differences before the case gets to court. For example, a public authority facing a judicial review challenge may concede the case. There may often be a temptation on the part of public authorities to settle or concede a judicial review challenge, especially where the claimant has been granted permission to proceed. The Home Office has often adopted this approach in relation to immigration and asylum judicial reviews.[45] For example, in 2008, there were 4,643 claims for judicial review lodged in respect of immigration and asylum decisions; 2,677 were refused permission to proceed and 353 were granted permission, yet only 134 claims were actually decided by the Administrative Court (46 were allowed, 88 were dismissed, and 10 withdrawn). What, then, happened to those applications that were neither granted nor refused permission to proceed, and those that were granted permission, but never actually got as far as a substantive hearing? The answer is likely to be that a fair number of such claims were settled by the Home Office out of court.

A public authority may settle cases out of court for a variety of reasons. The authority might recognise that its initial decision was unlawful; if so, then it makes little sense to defend that decision before the Court, as this will take up time and money. By contrast, conceding the case out of court saves time and the expense of defending a flawed decision. Indeed, recent research suggests that parties are increasingly prepared to settle. Bondy and Sunkin found that 62 per cent of judicial review 'threats' are resolved by dialogue between the parties, and that, of those cases that get as far as the issue of proceedings, 34 per cent are resolved before permission is granted, while 56 per cent of cases in which permission is granted are settled prior to the substantive hearing.[46]

Settlement of judicial review challenges may have both positive and negative aspects. The advantage for the individual claimant is that his or her grievance will be remedied, because the public authority will have recognised that its initial decision was in error and will have to replace it with a new one. From the public authority's perspective, settlement of challenges can avoid further delays and costs in the decision-making

---

[44] CPR Practice Direction 54d, 'Administrative Court (Venue)'. See also Nason, 'Regionalisation of the Administrative Court and the Tribunalisation of Judicial Review' [2009] PL 440.

[45] Bowman, *Review of the Crown Office List: A Report to the Lord Chancellor* (London 2000), p 33.

[46] Bondy and Sunkin, 'Settlement in Judicial Review Proceedings' [2009] PL 237.

process; if the initial decision was flawed, then it is more efficient and quicker simply to concede the challenge and produce a new decision.

At the same time, settlement can also be used by public authorities for less respectable reasons. By conceding, the public authority may be able to neutralise a legal challenge in order to avoid unfavourable publicity and attention, and/or to reduce the risk of the court issuing a judgment adverse to its policy interests. For example, an individual challenging the interpretation of a statutory provision may have considerable impact on hundreds, even thousands, of other cases. If the public authority wishes to avoid a potentially adverse interpretation from the courts, then settling the challenge out of court may give the public authority the upper hand in being able to maintain its favoured interpretation of the law. Paradoxically, while the courts are there to ensure government according to law, a public authority will, in practice, be able to influence to some degree which cases go forward for potential creation of precedent by conceding challenges before they get to court.

2.4 **Alternative dispute resolution**

In recent years, the practical pressures on the Administrative Court have prompted a search for ways to divert challenges out of the Court into other routes, such as ADR techniques—that is, the resolution of disputes through informal processes, such as mediation, rather than via formal judicial procedures.

Traditionally, public lawyers have been resistant to the use of ADR because public law litigation concerns both the rights and interests of individuals, and the duties and obligations of public authorities; the concern is that use of ADR should not be used as a substitute for judicial review when the legality of a public decision is being challenged or where an important precedent might be established.[47] However, ADR can have some advantages and its use has been encouraged by the courts as an alternative to judicial review even though it may not amount to an alternative remedy in the strict sense, such as an appeal to a tribunal.[48] For example, in *Cowl*, Lord Woolf noted that 'insufficient attention' had been paid to the 'paramount importance of avoiding litigation whenever this is possible'.[49] ADR can make a contribution to resolving disputes in a manner that meets the needs of the parties and saves time, money, and stress; the courts should not, without good reason, permit judicial review proceedings to proceed if a significant part of the issues could be resolved outside the litigation process. As Lord Woolf noted, due to the 'unfortunate culture in litigation' of over-judicialising the processes involved, parties to litigation can insist on arguing about

---

[47] In 2001, the government made a commitment that government departments and their agencies should use ADR in the resolution of disputes, but recognised that there may be some cases in which ADR would not be suitable. See Ministry of Justice, *Annual Pledge Report: Monitoring the Effectiveness of the Government's Commitment to Using Alternative Dispute Resolution 2006–07* (London 2008).

[48] Supperstone, Stilitz, and Sheldon, 'ADR and Public Law' [2006] PL 299; Boyron, 'The Rise of Mediation in Administrative Law Disputes: Experiences from England, France and Germany' [2006] PL 320.

[49] *R (Cowl) v Plymouth City Council* [2002] 1 WLR 803.

what has occurred in the past rather than focus on the future. The emphasis on ADR is now reflected in the Pre-action Protocol for Judicial Review, which states that the parties should consider whether some form of ADR procedure would be more suitable than litigation.[50]

> **Q** Should access to judicial review be limited in the ways that it is? How, if at all, might the accessibility of judicial review be improved? Is the use of settlement or ADR desirable in the context of judicial review challenges?

3. Judicial competence and capacity

The discussion so far has considered the dynamics of judicial review litigation. However, it is important to appreciate that questions concerning the impact of judicial review also fall to be addressed in relation to more substantive issues. In particular, we must recognise that considerations about the impact of judicial review have influenced—and ought to influence—the courts' development of the grounds of judicial review. This raises questions, first encountered in Chapter 13, about the institutional competence of the courts. We saw there that, in some situations, judges recognise that they ought not to engage in judicial review—or ought at least not to engage in intensive review—where they lack adequate competence. For the purposes of our present discussion, an important respect in which courts may lack competence is that they may be ill placed to understand the likely *impact* of their decisions. As we explain in the following sections, there are two (related) reasons why this might be so.

3.1 Judicial expertise and procedure

First, the ability of the courts to review administrative decisions may, in some areas, be constrained because of the limits of judicial expertise. It is important to emphasise here the different perspectives of administrators and judges.[51] Public authorities have responsibility for making and implementing policy with regard to whatever public function they have been assigned. They are therefore often concerned with the delivery of public services, administrative efficiency, and the public interest. Public authorities tend to develop an expertise in the particular area of administration for which they are responsible. By contrast, the principal function of the courts is to adjudicate on disputes. Judges decide cases; they are not responsible for administering

---

[50] Ministry of Justice, *Pre-action Protocol for Judicial Review* (London 2007), [3.1]. While the Protocol notes that it is not practicable to address in detail ADR procedures, it mentions some of the options: discussion and negotiation, ombudsmen, early neutral evaluation, and mediation.

[51] See Blom-Cooper, 'Lawyers and Public Administrators: Separate and Unequal' [1984] PL 215; Drewry, 'Public Law' (1995) Public Administration 41, 48–51.

or managing whole areas of policy. Even though the courts have developed a degree of specialisation in public law litigation, through channelling judicial review cases to nominated judges in the Administrative Court, such judges do not normally have the benefit of administrative experience. This has prompted Lord Woolf to suggest that Administrative Court judges should have exposure to government departments as part of their training so that they can appreciate the pressures and forces faced by those making the decisions upon which judges adjudicate.[52]

The general point is that while the courts are specialists in administrative law principles, they are not necessarily specialists in all areas of public administration. As judicial review can have significant repercussions on complex areas of public administration, the courts need to be aware of the potential effect of their rulings. Furthermore, while public authorities must have regard to the broader public interest, the judicial perspective tends to concentrate on individual interests and rights. There is an inherent tension in *judicial* review of *administrative* action.

In some contexts, the courts have recognised that public decision-making can be sufficiently removed from their own area of expertise as to be non-justiciable and therefore not susceptible to review. For example, decisions taken under the prerogative about foreign policy, such as whether or not to declare war or to authorise the use of the armed forces, are considered 'no go' or 'forbidden areas' by reason of self-denying judicial ordinance.[53] As Lord Diplock noted, such decisions normally involve questions to which the judicial process is ill adapted to provide the right answer; furthermore, the policy considerations involved require 'a balancing exercise which judges by their upbringing and experience are ill-qualified to perform'.[54] As the courts have themselves recognised, in a society based on the rule of law, it is necessary to decide which branch of government has, in any particular instance, the decision-making power and what the legal limits of that power are; this is a question of law to be decided by the courts. However, this means that the court will itself often have to decide the limits of its own decision-making power. In doing so, the courts will have regard to democratic accountability, efficient administration, and parliamentary sovereignty.[55]

In other administrative contexts, however, the courts have intervened in administrative decision-making and opened themselves up to criticism on the basis that they have simply not possessed sufficient knowledge or expertise in order effectively to review the legality of public action. A related concern is that the bipolar and adversary nature of the judicial process, in which the claimant seeks to challenge the respondent public authority's decision before the court, has not always been an appropriate procedure given the complex and multidimensional nature of much public administration.

---

[52] Woolf, *Protection of the Public: A New Challenge* (London 1990), pp 115–20; Woolf, 'Has the Human Rights Act made judicial review redundant?', ALBA annual lecture, November 2005.

[53] *Campaign for Nuclear Disarmament v Prime Minister of the United Kingdom* [2002] EWHC 2777.

[54] *Council of Civil Service Unions v Minister for the Civil Service* [1985] AC 374, 411, *per* Lord Diplock.

[55] *R v British Broadcasting Corporation, ex p ProLife Alliance* [2003] UKHL 23, [2004] 1 AC 185, [75]–[76]; *R (Runa Begum) v Tower Hamlets Borough Council* [2003] UKHL 5, [2003] 2 AC 430, [35].

Often, a public authority will have to consider not only the position of the individual claimant, but all individuals affected by its decision and the broader public interest. As courts typically decide by hearing a case between two parties, other parties liable to be affected by the outcome are not normally represented before the court.

Consider, for example, the House of Lords' decision in *Bromley*, in which the (now defunct) Greater London Council (GLC) implemented a manifesto commitment to reduce public transport fares by 25 per cent, which was to be funded by increases in local taxation.[56] The House of Lords held that the policy was unlawful because the GLC had failed to have proper regard to its statutory duty to promote the provision of integrated, efficient, and economic transport facilities under s 1(1) of the Transport (London) Act 1969. By placing a financial burden on local taxpayers, the GLC had not acted economically in the sense that it was not making the most cost-effective use of its resources. However, the Law Lords did not recognise the social purposes of the GLC's policy: reducing traffic congestion and pollution by subsidising public transport. The Law Lords' decision has therefore been criticised on a number of grounds. First, the Lords failed to take into account the policy background to the 1969 Act, which envisaged the subsidy of public transport.[57] Second, there was, one commentator noted, a paucity of reference by the Law Lords 'to the social impact of the GLC's policy and the consequences of holding it unlawful'—for example, reduced passenger flows leading to higher fares, an increase in road traffic causing more accidents and pollution, and a less frequent public transport service. It was therefore said that 'it is objectionable that the judiciary should purport to construe admittedly ambiguous legislation without regard to the consequences' of its decision.[58] Furthermore, as the judgments 'were not only extremely convoluted, but also bordered on the incoherent', they provided little legal certainty for local authorities.[59]

Other illustrations could be given. It has been argued that many of the judicial review cases concerning relations between central and local government highlighted the limitations of judicial understanding of complex areas such as local authority finance—for example, the House of Lords' decision concerning the legality of local authority involvement with the swaps market, which provided local authorities with an innovative way around the complex rules limiting their ability to borrow money, was

---

[56] *Bromley London Borough Council v Greater London Council* [1983] AC 768.

[57] Griffith, 'Judicial Decision-Making in Public Law' [1985] PL 564, 575–9.

[58] Pannick, 'The Law Lords and the Needs of Contemporary Society' (1982) 53 Political Quarterly 318, 322.

[59] Loughlin, *Legality and Locality: The Role of Law in Central–Local Government Relations* (Oxford 1996), p 34. Commenting on the judgments, one MP stated that he could not

> believe that the House of Lords judgment will go down as illustrating a clear distillation of principles from the words of a statute and the circumstances of the case. Each of the five judgments rambles over the territory in what can only be called a head-scratching way, making it impossible for the consumer of the judgment to know at the end just what the law is held to be, except negatively, and then only negatively on a few points. When one puts the five judgments together, the effect is chaos. (HC Deb, vol 15, col 905, 22 December 1981, George Cunningham MP)

based on a misunderstanding of how that market operated.[60] As a consequence of such decisions, it has been argued that judicial review has the worst of both worlds: an interventionist judiciary that is limited by procedures, and practices that exclude sources of information relevant to administrative and political decision-making.[61] Complex judicial review challenges can therefore pose a difficult dilemma for the courts: '[J]udicial restraint is unsatisfactory while judicial activism is ill-informed.'[62]

It is, though, important to bear in mind that the courts do often accept the limits of their own competence—they have, for example, been generally reluctant to intervene in contexts such as macro-economic policy[63]—while recognising that they have particular competence in other areas. For example, in the context of the prison discipline system, by which prisoners accused of a disciplinary offence are subject to an adjudication process that may result in punishment, courts have imposed norms of procedural fairness to ensure that prisoners are treated fairly.[64] The courts ensured that, when exercising sentencing powers, the Home Secretary had to give reasons for his decisions and subsequently ruled that the allocation of such judicial powers to a member of the executive did not comply with the right to a fair trial under Art 6 of the European Convention on Human Rights (ECHR).[65] The courts also held that the executive's influence and control over the Parole Board meant that it was not sufficiently independent and impartial to exercise its judicial functions.[66] The degree of judicial intervention may, then, often depend on the context in which a judicial review challenge is brought. As Lord Steyn once put it: 'In law context is everything.'[67]

Another aspect of judicial review procedure that might, on occasion, limit its effectiveness concerns the procedural dependence of the court on public authorities to present factual material concerning an impugned decision. Public authorities are expected to assist the court with full and accurate explanations of all of the facts relevant to a challenge, but the court has no power to investigate factual issues; furthermore, there is no general duty of disclosure in judicial review proceedings.[68] In

---

[60] *Hazell v Hammersmith London Borough Council* [1992] 2 AC 1; Loughlin, 'Innovative Financing in Local Government: The Limits of Legal Instrumentalism' [1991] PL 568, 590–5.   [61] Griffith at 580.

[62] Allison, 'The Procedural Reason for Judicial Restraint' [1994] PL 452, 466.

[63] See, eg *Nottinghamshire County Council v Secretary of State for the Environment* [1986] AC 240; *R v Secretary of State for the Environment, ex p Hammersmith and Fulham London Borough Council* [1991] 1 AC 521; *Donoghue v Poplar Housing and Regeneration Community Association Ltd* [2001] EWCA Civ 595, [2002] QB 48.

[64] See Loughlin and Quinn, 'Prisons, Rules and Courts: A Study of Administrative Law' (1993) 56 MLR 497; Loughlin, 'The Underside of the Law: Judicial Review and the Prison Disciplinary System' (1993) 46 CLP 23; Livingstone, 'The Impact of Judicial Review on Prisons', in Hadfield (ed), *Judicial Review: A Thematic Approach* (Dublin 1995).

[65] *R v Secretary of State for the Home Department, ex p Doody* [1994] 1 AC 531; *R v Secretary of State for the Home Department, ex p Anderson* [2002] UKHL 46, [2003] 1 AC 837.

[66] *R (Brooke) v Parole Board* [2008] EWCA Civ 29, [2008] 1 WLR 1950.

[67] *R (Daly) v Secretary of State for the Home Department* [2001] 2 AC 532, 548.

[68] *R v Lancashire County Council, ex p Huddleston* [1986] 2 All ER 941, 945, *per* Lord Donaldson MR; *Marshall v Deputy Governor of Bermuda* [2010] UKPC 9; Woolf, 'Public Law–Private Law: Why the Divide?' [1986] PL 220, 225. See further Chapter 14, section 3, above.

other words, the ability of a claimant to challenge a decision may be contingent on what information the public authority is prepared to release; if the court is unable to probe behind the formal account of the decision-making process, then this may limit its ability to correct abuses of power. However, the courts have mounted something of a fight-back in this respect. In cases in which a claimant has been met with a deliberate wall of silence from the government or prevarication in full disclosure, the courts have made it clear that they may either draw adverse inferences against the public authority or impose indemnity costs against the public authority as a mark of the court's disapproval.[69]

> **Q** To what extent should judicial experience and knowledge of public administration (or lack of it) affect how the courts review public decision-making? In light of the importance of context to judicial review, is it still meaningful to identify general principles of judicial review?

3.2 The concept of polycentricity

We first encountered the concept of polycentricity in Chapter 13.[70] We saw that a polycentric issue is one that affects a number of different interacting and interlocking interests; a polycentric task is one that is 'many centred' or involves the balancing of a number of elements that may be interdependent.[71] According to Fuller, a distinguishing feature of adjudication is that the parties affected by a decision may participate in judicial proceedings. However, what of those cases in which the outcome of a judicial decision may have implications for many other individuals who have not been party to the proceedings? The basic concern is that judicial review may be unsuited to the resolution of disputes that arise from a polycentric situation, because the judicial process is primarily bipolar and adversary; it only tends to allow the individual claimant and the respondent public authority to appear before the court, yet many

---

[69] *R (Quark Fishing Ltd) v Secretary of State for Foreign and Commonwealth Affairs* [2002] EWCA Civ 1409, [50], *per* Laws LJ; *R (Karas and Miladinovic) v Secretary of State for the Home Department* [2006] EWHC 747 (Admin), [53]–[57], *per* Munby J; *R (S) v Secretary of State for the Home Department* [2006] EWHC 1111 (Admin), [115]–[119], *per* Sullivan J; *Marshall* at [29], *per* Lord Phillips.

[70] See Chapter 13, section 4.6.1, above.

[71] As Fuller, 'The Forms and Limits of Adjudication' (1978) 92 Harvard Law Review 353, 395, explained:

We may visualise this kind of situation by thinking of a spider web. A pull on one strand will distribute tensions after a complicated pattern throughout the web as a whole. Doubling the original pull will, in all, likelihood, not simply double each of the resulting tensions but will rather create a different complicated pattern of tensions. This would certainly occur, for example, if the doubled pull caused one or more of the weaker strands to snap. This is a 'polycentric' situation because it is 'many centered'—each crossing of strands is a distinct center for distributing tensions.

According to Jowell, 'The Legal Control of Administrative Discretion' [1973] PL 178, 213: 'Polycentric problems involve a complex network of relationships, with interacting points of influence. Each decision made communicates itself to other centres of decision, changing the conditions, so that a new basis must be found for the next decision.'

other individuals may, in practice, be affected by the court's decision.[72] In other words, the polycentric nature of the issue before the court may induce judicial restraint on account of the court's inability adequately to appreciate the likely impact if it were to intervene by way of judicial review.

Polycentric situations often arise in the context of resource allocation decisions. If an administrative decision-maker has to make decisions as regards the distribution of limited resources (for example, whether through the award of compensation or issue of licences), then a decision to make an award in favour of one party will inevitably impact upon the decisions to be made with respect to other parties because the resources being allocated are limited. If one of those parties seeks to challenge a decision not to make an award in their case, then the limits of adjudication are highlighted because the outcome of the challenge will, if successful affect other parties who have received positive decisions. In any event, litigation may delay any fulfilment of those awards to such parties. Either way, the limitations of the judicial process are highlighted.

A good illustration is provided by the well-known case of *Anisminic*.[73] As we saw above,[74] the case concerned a challenge to a decision of the Foreign Compensation Commission, which had the task of assessing applications for compensation by companies that had suffered losses overseas—in other words, it had to decide how to distribute limited resources. The House of Lords held that the Commission's decisions were susceptible to judicial review in spite of an 'ouster clause' that appeared to preclude intervention by the courts. From the doctrinal legal perspective, *Anisminic* is viewed as a landmark decision that liberated English public law from esoteric distinctions between errors of law inside and outside jurisdiction, and signalled the court's unwillingness to acquiesce in the exclusion of judicial scrutiny of public decisions.[75]

However, from the government's perspective, the ruling was far from welcome. This was because it had adverse consequences for the administration of the whole compensation scheme. The Commission's task was to allocate a finite amount of resources. Opening up decisions refusing compensation to judicial review was problematic because the length of time taken to resolve such challenges would mean delays for those who had received positive decisions. This was because the amount of compensation to be allocated to each could not be determined until the total number of successful applicants was known.[76] Parliament responded by establishing a right of appeal against decisions of the Commission direct to the Court of Appeal.[77]

---

[72] For judicial recognition of this concept, see *R v Secretary of State for the Home Department, ex p P* [1995] 1 All ER 870, [38]–[39].

[73] *Anisminic v Foreign Compensation Commission* [1969] 2 AC 147. See also our discussion of *Coughlan* in Chapter 13, section 4.3, above.

[74] In Chapter 13, section 2.2, above and Chapter 14, section 2.1, above.

[75] See, eg Wade, 'Constitutional and Administrative Aspects of the *Anisminic* case' (1969) 85 LQR 198.

[76] HL Deb, vol 299, col 17, 4 February 1969 (Minister of State at the Foreign and Commonwealth Office).

[77] Foreign Compensation Act 1969, s 3.

The polycentric nature of certain issues has therefore been used as an argument for judicial restraint. To avoid exceeding the limits of its own competence, the court must refrain from two kinds of activism: it must not change the law where an appreciation of repercussions is required for sensible legal development; and in so far as the court has a choice under existing law, it must avoid choosing a legal solution that necessitates an appreciation of complex repercussions.[78] The concept assists in bringing home to the court the wide-ranging implications that may flow from any unsettling of a finely balanced policy decision and is of particular relevance in challenges against the allocation of scarce resources, which courts are ill-equipped to decide.

In more recent decisions, the courts have differed over whether or not they should review administrative decisions that raise polycentric questions. Consider, for example, the case of a child diagnosed with leukaemia who had been refused treatment by her health authority. This is a clear illustration of a very difficult polycentric situation: health authorities frequently have to decide how best to prioritise the uses to which limited resources may be put; funding treatment of one patient may mean refusing it to others. In this case, the child challenged the refusal of funding on the basis that it infringed her right to life without good reason. In the High Court, Laws J held that because the decision affected the right to life, it should be closely scrutinised by the courts—and that, because the health authority had failed to provide sufficient justification for its refusal of funding, it should reconsider its decision.[79] However, the Court of Appeal reversed this ruling. Sir Thomas Bingham MR said that 'difficult and agonising judgments have to made as to how a limited budget is best allocated to the maximum advantage of the maximum number of patients. That is not a judgment which the court can make'.[80] While expressing sympathy with the claimant, the Court was emphatic that it did not wish to review decisions in a field of activity in which it was not itself fit to make any decision favourable to the patient.

It is, though, important to bear in mind that the polycentric nature of a particular issue does not necessarily preclude judicial scrutiny. Courts have long reviewed administrative decisions concerning tax liability, a heavily polycentric area of administration, in order to protect individuals and companies against the abuse of power.[81] Furthermore, the polycentric nature of a particular issue is often a matter of degree: are the polycentric elements of the situation so significant and predominant that the proper limits of the adjudicative process have been reached? This question clearly involves some assessment of the degree of polycentricity involved, but provides only an uncertain guide. While a polycentric element may not preclude judicial review, it may affect the degree of scrutiny that the courts are willing to give. For example, the courts have indicated that anyone wishing to challenge the legality of the criteria governing a compensation scheme will face an uphill struggle.[82]

---

[78] Allison, 'The Procedural Reason for Judicial Restraint' [1994] PL 452, 455.
[79] *R v Cambridge Health Authority, ex p B* (1995) 25 BMLR 5.   [80] [1995] 2 All ER 129, 137.
[81] King, 'The Pervasiveness of Polycentricity' [2008] PL 101, 111–24.
[82] See, eg *R v Ministry of Defence, ex p Walker* [2000] 1 WLR 806; *R v Secretary of State for Defence, ex p Association of British Civilian Internees* [2003] EWCA Civ 473, [2003] QB 1397.

Q To what extent, if at all, should the polycentric nature of a particular issue affect how a court examines the legality of a public decision?

4. Judicial impact and administrative reaction

What then happens after the court decides a judicial review case? Does judicial review exert an important influence on government? Is it irrelevant? Or is the law merely one influence amongst many others that conditions public administration?

In general terms, comparatively little is known about the impact of judicial review on government.[83] What is apparent is that governmental reaction to judicial review can take different forms: positive or negative; formal or informal. A positive reaction to judicial review implies that the public authority is willing to abide by the court's decision, whereas a negative reaction implies disapproval by the public authority of the court's decision and a willingness either to reverse or limit its impact. Meanwhile, a formal reaction to judicial review is one that has been formalised in a rule or a particular decision; an informal reaction is one that is represented in other ways such as in the attitudes and feelings of officials.[84]

4.1 Understanding the impact of judicial review

4.1.1 Individual judicial review

To get a feel for the issues raised by the impact of judicial review on public administration, let us consider a mundane, though typical, example of judicial review litigation.

Suppose that a foreign national lawfully present in the UK, Shabina, applies to the immigration authorities to extend her period of leave in the UK. Shabina lodges her application, which is accompanied by various supporting documents. The application is considered by the UK Border Agency. One of the agency's hundreds of caseworkers (acting on behalf of the Home Secretary) refuses Shabina's application, but the reasons for refusal do not demonstrate that the supporting documentation has been considered. Shabina then seeks judicial review, which is granted on the basis that the Secretary of State erred in law by failing to take into account a relevant consideration—namely, the supporting documentation. Shabina's case is then sent back to the agency to be reconsidered in a lawful manner.

Does this mean that Shabina will ultimately receive a decision in her favour? While the legal challenge was successful, this does not, of course, imply that Shabina will ultimately receive a positive decision. As the courts have often acknowledged, 'dependent upon reconsideration on sufficient and proper evidence, the Secretary of

---

[83] Richardson, 'Impact Studies in the United Kingdom', in Hertogh and Halliday (eds), *Judicial Review and Bureaucratic Impact: International and Interdisciplinary Perspectives* (Cambridge 2004), p 107.

[84] Sunkin, 'Issues in Researching the Impact of Judicial Review', in Hertogh and Halliday (eds), p 62.

State may reach exactly the same decision'.[85] Of course, it may be the case that Shabina receives a positive decision because her supporting documents demonstrate that she fulfils the relevant criteria. The chance of a fresh reconsideration is, therefore, worth fighting for, but it does not guarantee a positive decision.

This is an example of 'bureaucratic', or 'individualised', judicial review.[86] Such challenges are typically against a low-level administrative decision and its outcome; while of considerable importance to the individuals concerned, they may have little, if any, broader impact on administrative procedure or policy. Much, although not all, judicial review litigation falls into this category. In such cases, it can be seen that the judicial review process functions as part of the machinery for the redress of grievances and adheres to the important merits/legality distinction. The reviewing court is operating in a similar way to a tribunal, the principal difference being that because tribunals have an appeal, rather than a review, jurisdiction, they can replace the initial decision with one of their own, whereas a reviewing court may not.[87] Indeed, in some of the best-known public law cases, following the court's judgment, the public authority arrived at exactly the same decision while taking care not to repeat the earlier legal error; the *Padfield* case is a good illustration.[88]

Our example may seem very simple, although it actually raises broader and more complex questions concerning the 'impact' and purpose of judicial review. From Shabina's perspective, judicial review provided for the redress of a grievance. At the same time, judicial review could also be seen here as fulfilling another purpose: that of ensuring compliance with standards of good administration, taking into account relevant considerations when making a decision being an elementary standard of good administration.

But what is the ability of judicial review to ensure compliance with such standards by administrative decision-makers? For example, will the caseworker who refused the application make the same mistake when considering subsequent applications? Will other caseworkers learn of the court's decision? Will, for example, the agency incorporate the decision into its training programme and/or internal guidance issued to all caseworkers? How does the judicial review case compete for influence with other forces? For example, what if the volume of such applications increases or if the agency has to cut its workforce: is there a risk that administrative imperatives of efficiency may override adherence to administrative law norms? To what extent, if at all, will other public agencies learn from the court's decision?

It is impossible to answer these questions without having some further information about how the particular government agency operates and whether—and, if so,

---

[85] *R (Ali) v Secretary of State for the Home Department* [2003] EWHC 899 (Admin), [31].

[86] Cane, 'Understanding Judicial Review and Its Impact', in Hertogh and Halliday (eds), p 17.

[87] See Chapter 17, section 2.1, below.

[88] In *Padfield v Minister for Agriculture, Fisheries and Food* [1968] AC 997, the House of Lords held that a ministerial decision not to refer a complaint concerning milk prices to a committee of investigation was vitiated by improper purpose; after the case, the Minister did refer the complaint to the committee, which recommended change, which the Minister refused to accept.

how—it incorporates a judicial review case into its procedures. It might be the case that a court ruling does have a broader impact; it might not. The point here is merely to highlight the type of questions with which we must engage if we are to understand the impact of judicial review—something that requires empirical study of administrative reaction to judicial review.

4.1.2 Policy judicial review

Now let us consider a different form of judicial review that might be termed 'policy', or 'high-profile', judicial review. These types of challenge typically have far-reaching consequences for governmental procedure and/or policy, and can impact on a much wider range of people than the particular claimants involved. Such challenges may be brought in the wider public interest and the courts sometimes allow interventions by third parties.[89] Such challenges may settle important constitutional issues— for example, that European Union (EU) law prevails over incompatible primary legislation.[90] Such cases might also raise matters of acute political sensitivity and involve decisions taken by politically accountable government Ministers. Such cases also include those in which there is a challenge, under the Human Rights Act 1998, to the compatibility of primary legislation with the European Convention on Human Rights (ECHR).

By way of illustration, let us consider the decision of the House of Lords in *Smith*—which we encountered in Chapter 13—on whether or not the Parole Board should hold oral hearings. One function of the Parole Board is to decide whether or not the Secretary of State is justified in recalling to prison an individual who has been released from prison on licence, but who goes on to breach licence conditions (the rules that must be observed upon release). For many years, the Parole Board had been reluctant to hold oral hearings in such cases and instead determined them solely 'on the papers'. However, as we saw in Chapter 13, the House of Lords held that the Board had acted in breach of its duty of procedural fairness by not offering the claimant prisoners the opportunity to make representations at an oral hearing against their recall to prison, given the importance of a recall decision in terms of a prisoner's personal liberty.[91] Lord Bingham set out a number of general principles concerning when oral hearings would be necessary, and the House ruled that the Parole Board should be prepared to reconsider its approach and hold more oral hearings.

In such a case, judicial review may be said to be serving a number of different purposes. In *Smith*, judicial review clearly provided means for redress of grievances of the two prisoners concerned. But the Lords were also seeking to impose standards of good administration on the Parole Board, through the elaboration of normative common

---

89 See Chapter 14, section 3.3.3, above.

90 *R v Secretary of State for Transport, ex p Factortame Ltd (No 2)* [1991] 1 AC 603. See Chapter 8, section 4.3, above.

91 *R (Smith) v Parole Board* [2005] UKHL 1, [2005] 1 WLR 350. See Chapter 13, section 3.6.3, above.

law principles of fairness. And, in turn, the House was clearly, although not explicitly, performing a policy function: the House of Lords was not merely ruling that the two prisoners had been treated unfairly; its judgment also had implications for the general policy of the Parole Board concerning oral hearings.

What was the impact of the decision? Following *Smith*, the Parole Board adopted a new policy to the effect that it would grant an oral hearing for recalled prisoners whenever asked to do so. This policy change had a number of consequences. The number of oral hearings increased substantially.[92] Because a number of hearings had to be held in prisons, the number of cases that the Parole Board could hear in a single day reduced. There were also significant resource implications: the additional cost of oral hearings, as compared with paper-only decisions, was about £1,200 per case. Furthermore, because of the strain placed on the Parole Board to convene panels, it proved impossible in a number of cases to find sufficient members to make decisions, which resulted in delay—which, in one case, itself resulted in a successful judicial review action taken by prisoners against the Parole Board.[93] To some extent, the problems could be ascribed to an overreaction by the Parole Board: its policy of granting an oral hearing whenever a recalled prisoner asked for one meant that, in many instances, an oral hearing was held even though it added nothing to the information already before the Board on paper. The Parole Board then adopted a stricter policy to the effect that it would no longer automatically grant an oral hearing when requested to do so, but would instead require reasons from the prisoner when applying for an oral hearing, which would be considered on a case-by-case basis.[94] Oral hearings would normally be granted where there were realistic prospects of success or if the risk assessment required live evidence.[95]

The Law Lords' decision therefore raised complex issues concerning the basis of judicial intervention, the competence of the court, and judicial impact. Let us consider the following questions: was the House conscious of the likely impact of its judgment? Was the House's judgment desirable? Do oral hearings actually improve the quality of Parole Board decision-making?

With respect to whether or not the House of Lords was aware of the likely impact of its judgment, it is apparent that oral hearings impose a cost both in terms of financial resources and time. In their speeches, the Law Lords did not consider the cost of oral hearings or the possible effect of an increase in the number of hearings upon the Parole Board's budget and operational procedures—a factor that might indicate that their judgment was ill informed. However, matters are not so simple. It is important

---

[92] The number of oral hearings increased by 400 per cent, from 500 in 2002–03 to just over 2,500 in 2006–07: Parole Board for England and Wales, *Annual Report and Accounts 2006–07* (HC 1022 2007–08), p 30.

[93] Parole Board for England and Wales, HC 1022; *R (Cooper) v Parole Board* [2007] EWHC 1292 (Admin). See also National Audit Office, *Protecting the Public: The Work of the Parole Board* (HC 239 2007–08).

[94] Parole Board, *Change of Policy on Granting Oral Hearings in Smith and West Cases* (London 2007).

[95] Parole Board, *Criteria for Refusing an Oral Hearing* (London 2009).

not to underestimate the intrinsic difficulty for the court of weighing up whether the additional cost and delays imposed by oral hearings would be justified. This is because the other interests at stake—the importance of the decision to the prisoner (and the potential deprivation of liberty) and the public interest (the possible risk of future reoffending)—are not susceptible to being assigned a monetary value. The House of Lords' decision therefore reflected a value judgement that a particular interest—the liberty of recalled prisoners—should receive priority.

Assessing whether the judgment had a beneficial influence is similarly problematic because there is scope for different views here. From one perspective, it might be argued that the decision was beneficial in terms of extending procedural fairness into an administrative decision-making system affecting the personal liberty of a group of people—prisoners—who rarely attract public sympathy. Realistically, it is unlikely that the Parole Board would have changed its policy on oral hearings had it not been for the court ruling. However, from a different perspective, it might be contended that the imposition of procedural requirements was counterproductive by disrupting the work of the Parole Board, reducing administrative efficiency, causing delays, and increasing costs.

As to whether or not the decision improved the quality of Parole Board decisions, it is difficult to provide an answer simply because such decisions often involve an attempt to predict the future risk to the public posed by a recalled prisoner; there may be no single correct answer. It is possible that making such decisions on the basis of a prisoner's evidence presented at an oral hearing is likely to be better than considering it solely on the papers. If so, then the quality of such decisions is likely to be higher, but it is impossible to assess whether or not this is actually the case.

We have already seen that the allocation of resources is a polycentric issue often unsuited to judicial decision-making—but even cases that are, on the surface, about other matters (such as the fairness of procedures) may well have hard-to-predict resource implications. It can be seen, then, that assessing the impact of judicial review often raises complex questions as to how public authorities respond to court judgments, and the relationship between judicial supervision and bureaucratic behaviour.

4.2 Forms and effects of judicial control

How, then, do the principles of judicial review—legality, fairness, rationality, and proportionality—contribute to the control of administrative action? Feldman has suggested that the courts adopt three different techniques for controlling administrative action: directing, limiting, and structuring.[96] Judicial *directing* of administrative behaviour refers to the ability of the courts to require government to adhere to its stated powers and obligations. Here, the control is undertaken by reference to the legislative power that the public authority possesses and reflects the traditional *ultra vires* principle that a public authority cannot lawfully act outside the four corners of its

---

[96] Feldman, 'Judicial Review: A Way of Controlling Government?' (1986) 66 Public Administration 21.

statutory powers.[97] Judicial *limiting* of administrative action refers to the way in which courts establish the scope of, or set, limits applicable to the exercise of administrative discretion. For example, if a court holds that a public authority has either fettered its discretion or unlawfully delegated its powers to another,[98] then the court is placing limits on the exercise of the public authority's power. The third technique—*structuring* administrative decision-making processes—involves making explicit some of the values and goals that either should or should not guide decision-makers. For example, when a court decides that the decision-maker adopted an unfair procedure, took account of an irrelevant consideration, or reached an irrational decision, then the court is structuring how the decision-maker ought to make its decisions. Judicial structuring of administrative action may exert far more influence on the day-to-day activities of public authorities than directing or limiting.

The implications of judicial review for public authorities may then depend on which particular legal principle is being applied by the court. However, much may depend on the particular administrative context. For example, a judicial decision that concerns a narrow technical point—how a particular statutory provision is to be interpreted—might assist a public authority by providing greater clarity in respect of its legal obligations, but have little broader impact. At the same time, it is equally possible that narrow technical questions of statutory interpretation may have substantial resource implications if, for example, a court has held that a public authority owes a duty to provide services to a broader class of person than was previously thought to be the case. For example, when the Administrative Court held, interpreting the Children Act 1989, that local authorities owe a duty to provide after-care for unaccompanied asylum-seeking children when they reached the age of 18, the judgment had considerable economic significance for local authorities, because their legal obligations were extended to a broader group of people for whom the resources had to be found.[99]

Similarly, a judicial decision that a public authority has to afford an individual a right to a fair hearing might have little broader impact if it only affects a very small number of individuals—for example, taxi drivers whose licences have been revoked. By contrast, if the court holds that a public authority must apply the principles of procedural fairness to a wider range of persons, then this may have substantial resource implications, as the case of *Smith* illustrates. The application of other legal principles, such as legitimate expectation and proportionality, might also have a broader influence on administrative culture and practices by requiring public authorities to consider more carefully how their policies are to be applied in the circumstances of particular individuals who either hold certain expectations or whose rights might otherwise be adversely affected. More generally, it has been suggested that public authorities may be more able to accommodate some legal principles, such as procedural fairness, within their

---

[97] See Chapter 12, section 5.1, above.   [98] See Chapter 13, section 4.2, above.

[99] *R (Behre) v London Borough of Hillingdon* [2003] EWHC 2075 (Admin), [2004] 1 FLR 439; *R (London Borough of Hillingdon) v Secretary of State for Education and Skills* [2007] EWHC 514 (Admin).

decision-making process than substantive principles: '[a]lthough the ability of juridical norms to infiltrate administrative cultures is likely to be limited, it may be that certain values, those associated with process for example, are more readily internalised than others.'[100]

4.3 Judicial review from the administrator's perspective

What, then, is the administrator's perspective on judicial review? In considering this, it is important to recall that public administration in the UK does not comprise a single, undifferentiated public authority called 'the government'; rather, it is made up of a vast array of highly complex organisations operating at different levels of our multilayered constitution: central government departments and their executive agencies and non-departmental public bodies, local authorities and independent regulatory bodies, in addition to the devolved executives and non-statutory bodies.[101] Furthermore, each public agency is typically a complex organisation comprising different hierarchies, such as higher-level policy officials, legal advisers, and front-line or 'street-level' operational staff, within which judicial decisions will need to be both interpreted and communicated if they are to exert influence.

The impact of judicial review on different officials may, then, vary. The task of interpreting a judicial decision is often one for government lawyers, while senior policy officials will often consider how, if at all, policy needs to be reformulated in light of the decision. By contrast, a court judgment may, by itself, have little, if any, effect on front-line decision-makers. For example, officials responsible for making decisions in large areas of administration—social security, tax, immigration, and so on—make literally millions of decisions each year without consulting either a statute or a court decision; they do, though, on the whole, consider themselves obliged to follow the internal guidance and policy instructions—often collectively referred to as 'soft law'—issued by senior officials. From a legal perspective, soft law may be viewed as relatively low down in the hierarchy of legal rules, certainly beneath both primary and secondary legislation. However, for officials within government agencies, soft law is often the first source of guidance that they consult. If judicial review decisions are to influence routine administrative decision-making within large bureaucratic organisations, then they often need to be internalised within such organisations and communicated to front-line staff through such guidance. To be effective, such guidance must correctly interpret the court's decision and then also be applied in practice by front-line officials.

When viewed from the perspective of public administrators, judicial review may have both advantages and disadvantages. On the positive side, judicial review performs an important function of clarifying the law and rules that must be administered. As public authorities must operate lawfully, judicial review may assist by providing greater

---

[100] Richardson and Sunkin, 'Judicial Review: Questions of Impact' [1996] PL 79, 103.

[101] See Chapters 4 and 7 above.

clarity on what the law means in any particular instance. Judicial review may also perform an educative role by indicating the legal principles that should inform and guide administrative decision-making. The addition of procedural requirements—reason-giving, opportunities to make representations, oral hearings—into administrative decision-making may promote higher-quality decisions and also greater transparency in public administration.[102] Furthermore, judicial review may focus the mind of a public authority on a particular area of its responsibility and prompt reconsideration of how the discharge of its duties could be improved.

But judicial review may also have disadvantages from the administrator's perspective. For example, the very generality of the principles of judicial review can create uncertainty for administrators because they 'offer comparatively little guidance in dealing with complex situations' and, consequently, it can be difficult to determine how such principles will be applied in any particular case.[103] This uncertainty can leave administrators with the dilemma of choosing between a cautious, risk-averse approach, which may compromise the achievement of policy objectives, or a more adventurous approach, which risks legal challenge.[104] Judicial review may discourage long-term planning by public authorities if they need to respond to court judgments. Judicial review may also increase the use and influence of lawyers in public authorities (with obvious resource implications). Further, while the task of dealing with judicial review challenges is necessary for a public authority to defend its decisions, this can inevitably take up time and resources that could be expended elsewhere: 'The very business of going to court is fraught with danger and inconvenience for officials.'[105] While the availability of judicial challenge does not inevitably induce administrative and political timidity, public authorities would perhaps avoid going to court if possible. The mere fact that a public authority is being subject to legal challenge may have adverse reputational consequences that the authority might seek to avoid. Then there is always the risk that exposure to judicial review may lead public authorities to adopt a defensive style of administration designed to reduce the risk that their decisions will be challenged rather than to seek to improve their quality. Another concern is that there is a risk that the delay and uncertainty created by judicial review litigation may itself be deliberately exploited by those wishing to disrupt the policy process.

One indication of growing governmental awareness of judicial review has been the publication by central government of a pamphlet entitled *The Judge Over Your Shoulder*—sometimes affectionately known within government as 'JOYS'—which provides guidance to junior officials in the practical application of legal principles.[106]

---

[102] Hammond, 'Judicial Review: The Continuing Interplay between Law and Policy' [1998] PL 34, 42.

[103] Kerry, 'Administrative Law and Judicial Review: The Practical Effects of Developments over the Last 25 Years on Administration in Central Government' (1986) 64 Public Administration 163, 171.

[104] James, 'The Political and Administrative Consequences of Judicial Review' (1996) 74 Public Administration 613, 625.   [105] James at 619.

[106] Treasury Solicitor, *The Judge Over Your Shoulder* (London 2006).

While the first edition received criticism for its negative tone and for treating law as distinct from good administration, subsequent editions have stressed that their purpose is not to teach public administrators how to survive judicial review, but to inform and improve the quality of administrative decision-making.[107] Of course, if the guide does improve the quality of decision-making, then an incidental effect of this would be to make decisions less vulnerable to judicial review.

Q Why do you think administrators have mixed feelings about judicial review? Is it unrealistic to expect administrators to be anything other than ambivalent about having their decisions challenged by way of judicial review?

4.4 **Positive reaction**

For the most part, public authorities react positively to judicial review. Positive reactions may take different forms: for example, a change of policy or decision-making procedure, or the laying of a new statutory instrument to modify the effect of a previous instrument that has been declared unlawful.

By way of illustration, consider the case of *FP (Iran)*, in which the Court of Appeal declared unlawful a rule governing the procedure for appeal hearings conducted by the Asylum and Immigration Tribunal.[108] The relevant rule stated that the tribunal had to hear an appeal in the absence of a party or his representative if satisfied that the party or his representative had been given notice of the hearing, but had not given any satisfactory explanation for his absence. The Court held that this rule was productive of irremediable procedural unfairness because it could deny a party the opportunity to be heard due to the error of their representative: the rule prioritised speed over fairness. Following the judgment, the rules were amended so that the tribunal would have the discretion to proceed in a party's absence, rather than a duty to do so.[109] This, the government contended, would remove the rigidity in the previous rule and enable the tribunal to assess in each individual case whether there was no good reason for the party's absence. This, then, might be instanced as a positive reaction by the government to a court ruling: the Court held the rule invalid and the government duly sought to comply with the ruling.

The reaction by government to a court ruling may depend on the particular legal principle applied by the court. For example, if a blanket policy adopted by a public authority has been held to be disproportionate, then the public authority will need to revise the blanket or 'catch-all' nature of the policy either by creating appropriate exceptions or by reformulating the policy altogether. To illustrate this point, consider *Smith and Grady v United Kingdom*, which concerned a legal challenge to the Ministry

---

107 Bradley, 'The Judge over Your Shoulder' [1987] PL 485.
108 *FP (Iran) v Secretary of State for the Home Department* [2007] EWCA Civ 13.
109 The Asylum and Immigration Tribunal (Procedure) (Amendment) Rules 2007, SI 2007/835, r 2.

of Defence's policy that homosexuality was incompatible with membership of the armed forces. This was a blanket policy in the sense that all gay or lesbian members of the armed forces were to be discharged irrespective of their personal service record and whether or not their sexual orientation had, in fact, adversely affected the operational effectiveness of the armed forces. It was precisely because of its blanket nature that the policy was found to be disproportionate by the European Court of Human Rights: it went further than was necessary in order to achieve its objective of maintaining the operational effectiveness of the armed forces. Following the judgment, the Defence Secretary informed Parliament that a new policy had been devised to comply with the Court's ruling.[110] At the centre of the new code of conduct was a new service test: have the actions or behaviour of an individual adversely affected the efficiency or operational effectiveness of the armed services? So, as the previous blanket policy had been held to be a disproportionate interference with individuals' right to private life, policy had been reformulated. Rather than a blanket policy that homosexuality per se was incompatible with membership of the armed forces, the new policy sought a more individuated approach: were the actions of a particular individual likely adversely to affect operational effectiveness? The new policy was specifically designed in order to produce a more appropriate balance between the legitimate desire for the armed forces to be effective and the rights of individuals.

A similar point can be made in relation to *Daly*.[111] Here, a prison policy concerning cell searches was challenged on the ground that such searches would be conducted in the absence of the prisoner and would include an examination of the prisoner's correspondence with his legal advisers. The policy was introduced following a number of serious breaches of prison security, its justification being that it was necessary to search such correspondence to ensure that the prisoner had not written or secreted within it anything that might endanger security. However, the House of Lords concluded that the blanket policy was an unjustifiable and disproportionate infringement of a prisoner's right to the protection of his legal correspondence. Following the decision, the Prison Service devised a new policy under which a prisoner normally had to be present when legal correspondence was being searched, although a prisoner could be excluded if he were to attempt to disrupt the search or because of sudden operational emergencies or urgent intelligence.[112]

There may be other forms of positive reaction. For example, public authorities may particularly welcome judgments that provide guidance on the approach to be taken to cases in the future or which clarify an important point of law. Broadly speaking, public authorities tend to welcome clarity in their legal powers and obligations, because

---

[110]   *Smith and Grady v United Kingdom* (2000) 29 EHRR 493; Hansard HC Deb, vol 342, col 287, 12 January 2000 (Secretary of State for Defence). See further Chapter 13, section 4.6.1, above.

[111]   *R (Daly) v Secretary of State for the Home Department* [2001] 2 AC 532.

[112]   HM Prison Service, *Revision to the Security Manual after the* Daly *Judgment* (2001). In *Daly*, at 545, Lord Bingham, while noting that it would be inappropriate for the court to attempt to formulate or approve the terms of the new policy, in effect suggested a new rule that was, for all practical purposes, exactly the same as that which was subsequently adopted.

it enables them to put in place systems and decision-making processes in order to administer policy effectively and to prevent other legal challenges.

The methodological difficulties of assessing the impact of judicial review should not, though, be overlooked. It is important to recall that court rulings are only one influence on government; there are many other influences, such as political pressures, limited resources, demands for efficiency, and the administrative imperative to implement policy. If the courts comprise only one of many different pressures, how then is it possible to isolate their influence?

A good illustration of such difficulties is presented by the issue of whether the Home Secretary should give reasons when refusing applications for British nationality. Traditionally, the Home Secretary had an absolute discretion whether to grant or refuse an application for British nationality: under statute, no reason needed to be assigned when refusing an application.[113] In *Fayed*, the Court of Appeal ruled that although statute did not require that refusal reasons be given by the Home Secretary, the decision-making process adopted must nevertheless be fair.[114] In particular, the Home Secretary should have, before reaching a final decision, informed the applicants of any adverse concerns so as to afford them a reasonable opportunity to respond to such concerns. Following the judgment, the Home Secretary decided that, in light of the importance of transparency in public administration, reasons would in future be given—a policy change subsequently confirmed by Parliament.[115]

Did the Court's ruling influence the change in policy? On the one hand, the Court recognised that, in light of the express prohibition on requiring the Home Secretary to give reasons, there was no such duty. On the other hand, the Court ruled that the Home Secretary was, in the interests of fairness and natural justice, under a duty of disclosure to the applicants; in practice, there may be little practical difference between raising adverse concerns *prior* to a decision and giving reasons *after* a negative decision has been reached. Even though the case was decided on procedural grounds, it had important policy implications. At the same time, there were also broader political factors present here. The change in policy was announced once the Labour government—which had a commitment to greater openness in government (for example, it secured the enactment of the Freedom of Information Act 2000)—had come to power in 1997. So, while the Court's judgment may not be said to have been the sole cause behind the policy change, it did highlight a particular area of decision-making in which reasons had not hitherto been provided. In light of a change in the political environment toward greater transparency, the gap in administrative reason-giving was closed.

Putting to one side the issue of whether it is possible to isolate the influence of judicial review from other influences on government, questions of 'impact' are not, in any

---

[113] Maitland, *The Constitutional History of England* (Cambridge 1908), p 428; British Nationality Act 1981, s 44(2).   [114] *R v Secretary of State for the Home Department, ex p Fayed* [1997] 1 All ER 228.
[115] HC Deb, vol 303, col 564W, 22 December 1997 (Secretary of State for the Home Department); Nationality, Immigration and Asylum Act 2002, s 7(1).

event, so easily settled. For example, what has been the impact of a duty to give reasons on the Home Office? While reason-giving might promote transparency in public administration, it might equally impede efficient administration and increase costs because providing reasons might lengthen the decision-making process. Alternatively, there is always the risk that decision-makers may seek to fulfil this duty by merely issuing pro forma or 'standard paragraph' reasons.

4.5 **Negative reaction**

Administrative reaction to judicial review can also be negative. Why? Negative reaction may be prompted by several considerations, such as the disruption caused to administrative procedures and policy implementation, governmental antipathy toward judicial interference, and the financial and other costs imposed by judgments. Ministers accustomed to being held to account in Parliament may take personal umbrage at having their decisions struck down by judges, especially in politically sensitive areas of administration. Indeed, it has been argued that an inevitable consequence of stronger judicial review may be a corresponding governmental disinclination to accept court decisions.[116] Negative reactions may take many forms. Public authorities may seek to neutralise or limit the effect of judicial review through delaying tactics. They may reach the same substantive decision again, but in accordance with the court's judgment. Alternatively, they may seek direct legislative reversal of the judgment.

One example of negative reaction to judicial review has been the insertion of 'ouster clauses' in primary legislation. Such clauses seek to protect the policy from judicial challenge by stating that a decision 'shall not be called into question in any court'. By virtue of parliamentary sovereignty, such clauses should be given effect. However, the courts have considered such clauses to be constitutionally suspect on the ground that they restrict a fundamental constitutional principle—the right of access to justice— and thereby undermine respect for the rule of law. The *Anisminic* case,[117] considered in Chapter 14,[118] is the paradigm example of this. More recently, the Home Office in 2003 sought to oust judicial review of certain immigration and asylum decisions on the basis that there were so many such cases—many of which were unmeritorious and abusive—as to impose an undue burden on the courts. This provoked a wide-ranging legal and political conflict of considerable constitutional significance; in the face of strong opposition from Parliament, the legal profession, and the judiciary, the government backed down.[119]

Earlier, it was noted that outright failure by a public agency to comply with a court ruling is extremely unusual; it is not, though, unknown. One area in which this issue

---

[116] Harlow, 'Administrative Reaction to Judicial Review' [1976] PL 116, 117.

[117] *Anisminic v Foreign Compensation Commission* [1969] 2 AC 147.

[118] See Chapter 14, section 2.1, above.

[119] Woolf, 'The Rule of Law and a Change in the Constitution' [2004] CLJ 317, 327–9; Rawlings, 'Review, Revenge and Retreat' (2005) 68 MLR 378.

has arisen has been in relation to the removal of failed asylum seekers by the Home Office in the face of a court injunction prohibiting removal. Over recent years, this area has been a source of much judicial review litigation. The basic tension here is between the Home Office's policy interest in maintaining effective immigration control and the ability of individuals to challenge the legality of removal decisions. The Home Office has been under enormous political pressure to increase the rate of removals, and has tended to view judicial review applications by individuals subject to removal action simply as a means of disrupting and frustrating the removals process.[120] At the same time, if an Administrative Court judge issues an injunction requiring the Home Office not to remove the claimant, it is axiomatic that it should be complied with—yet this has not always happened.[121] For example, in the case of *Re M*,[122] considered in Chapter 14 above,[123] the House of Lords held that, where the Home Office had failed to comply with an interim injunction not to remove a claimant, the court not only possessed the power to issue such an injunction, but could also hold the Secretary of State in contempt of court.

Nevertheless, despite this decision, the Home Office failed to learn the lessons. For example, in both 2004 and 2006, the Home Office removed asylum seekers despite injunctions issued by the High Court prohibiting removal.[124] In both instances, the Home Office subsequently explained to the Court that there had been a 'breakdown in communications' and 'regrettable failings' on its behalf, while the Administrative Court found that 'substantial blame' attached to the Home Office over its failure to comply with the injunctions.[125] The Home Office responded by issuing new guidance to ensure that officials complied with injunctions against removal.[126] This episode might then be taken as an example of the temporary impact of judicial review. Even a 'high-profile' and constitutionally important decision such as *M* may only exert a temporary impact on governmental practice. In light of increased political pressure to enforce removals and systemic failures within its large administrative organisation, the Home Office was again found to be acting in breach of court injunctions, prompting it to issue stronger guidance to its operational staff.

---

[120] Indeed, in the battle over the inclusion of an ouster clause in what subsequently became the Asylum and Immigration (Treatment of Claimants, etc.) Act 2004, the Home Office had sought to prevent individuals subject to removal action from applying for judicial review.

[121] Such cases usually come before the 'duty judge' at the Administrative Court, who may issue an emergency injunction against the Home Office; this often occurs late at night and over the telephone.

[122] [1994] 1 AC 377.   [123] In Chapter 14, section 4.4, above.

[124] 'Asylum error judge demands answer', BBC News website, 27 August 2004; 'Home Office ignored judge over deportation', *The Times*, 27 August 2004; 'Mother of three was deported after court ruled she could stay', *The Times*, 16 August 2006; 'Home Office ignored court injunction on deportation', *The Guardian*, 16 August 2006; 'Judge raps Home Office over deportation blunder', *The Times*, 18 August 2006.

[125] Thereby illustrating the adage that failures within government are perhaps more often the product of cock-up than conspiracy.

[126] Home Office, *Process Communication: Revised Instructions for Handling Injunctions against Removal* (16 August 2006).

However, the story did not end there. The Home Office was still concerned that its efforts to remove asylum seekers were being thwarted by a high number of last-minute judicial review applications (160 per month), a number of which were found to be without merit.[127] In 2007, the Home Office changed its policy as regards the handling of such judicial review applications in order to ensure the swift disposal of weak claims.[128] Under the new policy, reflected in amended Civil Procedure Rules, the Home Office will not defer removal simply if an individual has lodged a judicial review claim, but only if the claim is accompanied by a detailed statement of the claimant's grounds for bringing the claim.[129] The general point is that in areas of mass use, such as immigration, public agencies may view the use of judicial review—even the submission of judicial review claims—as an impediment to effective policy implementation and seek to tighten up procedures for lodging such claims.

Immigration is perhaps atypical in that the tensions between administrative implementation of policy and judicial review are extremely acute. By contrast, in other contexts, administrative failure to comply with a court ruling may prompt follow-up oversight by other administrative law bodies such as the ombudsman, which investigates individuals' complaints of maladministration against government.[130] Consider the *Coughlan* case, for example.[131] One aspect of that case, concerning legitimate expectations, was considered in Chapter 13. Another aspect concerned who should pay for the long-term care of older and disabled people: could such care be provided by a local authority as a social service (in which case, the patient paid according to their means), or was it to be provided free of charge by the National Health Service (NHS)? The court decided, from its interpretation of the relevant legislation, that such long-term care was generally to be provided by the NHS. Following the decision, the Department of Health drew the court's judgment to the attention of local health authorities so that they could revise their criteria for funding long-term care in line with the judgment. However, many individuals complained to the ombudsman on the basis that they were being denied NHS-funded long-term care because health authorities had been acting unlawfully by not applying the relevant criteria in light of the *Coughlan* judgment. Four years after the judgment, the Health Service Ombudsman, finding such complaints to be justified, recommended that health authorities comply with the judgment and provide financial redress for affected individuals.[132] What this episode illustrates is that it

---

[127] For example, in 2006, the Home Secretary issued a 'warning' to the Administrative Court that, because of the practical difficulties of removing failed asylum seekers, the Home Office would not defer removal in the face of last-minute applications for judicial review or threats to issue such applications. See 'Reid warns judges not to block Iraqis' deportation', *The Guardian*, 5 September 2006. See also 'Judges told: do not delay Iraq deportations', *The Guardian*, 9 June 2010.

[128] Home Office, *Immigration and Nationality Directorate Statement of Policy: Judicial Review Challenges Following Notification of Removal Directions* (2 March 2007).

[129] Civil Procedures Rules, Pt 54, Practice Direction, para 18.2(c). See also *Madan and Kapoor v Secretary of State for the Home Department* [2008] 1 All ER 973.   [130] See Chapter 16.

[131] *R v North and East Devon Health Authority, ex p Coughlan* [2001] QB 213.

[132] Health Service Ombudsman, *NHS Funding for Long Term Care* (HC 399 2002–03). See also Health Service Ombudsman, *NHS Funding for Long Term Care: Follow Up Report* (HC 144 2004–05).

cannot be assumed that public authorities will automatically comply with important court rulings; in the event of non-compliance, the intervention of another administrative justice institution, such as on ombudsman, may be necessary.

Direct legislative reversal of a court judgment is another strong form of negative reaction: if the government is particularly concerned about the impact of a judicial decision, then it may seek to reverse it by causing an Act of Parliament to be enacted. A classic example is provided by the *Burmah Oil* case.[133] The House of Lords had held that a company, the property of which had been destroyed by British armed forces during the Second World War, and had therefore suffered substantial losses, was able to sue for compensation. However, immediately following the case, the government introduced legislation into Parliament that retrospectively nullified the effect of the decision.[134] Concerned at the amount of compensation payable and the need for equal treatment of all of those who suffered losses during the war, the government, in effect, reversed the House of Lords' decision.

More recently, in the context of asylum and immigration judicial reviews, the government has been particularly ready to reverse the effect of court rulings through legislation.[135] Consider, for example, the ruling of the Court of Appeal in 1999 to the effect that the Home Office could not remove certain asylum seekers to other European countries through which they had passed en route to the UK for determination of their asylum claims there, because those countries adopted a less favourable interpretation of the Refugee Convention.[136] This is an illustration of a 'test case' that would impact on hundreds of other individuals in a similar position seeking to challenge, by way of judicial review, their removal to European countries. Uppermost in the government's mind was the broader influence of the ruling: in light of the number of other judicial review challenges, the risk was that the delays caused by legal challenges could, in themselves, impede the policy objective of maintaining immigration control. The government therefore introduced legislation that created an irrebuttable presumption that other European countries are safe, which the courts subsequently accepted.[137]

From one perspective, legislative reversal illustrates the continuing supremacy of Parliament and an expression of democracy: if elected politicians dislike the effect of a court ruling, then it should be open to them to reverse it. At the same time, it illustrates the very limited effect of judicial review and the ability of government to shape the law

---

[133] *Burmah Oil Ltd v Lord Advocate* [1965] AC 75.   [134] War Damage Act 1965.

[135] For example, the Court of Appeal's decision in *R v Secretary of State for Social Security, ex p Joint Council for the Welfare of Immigrants* [1996] 4 All ER 385, in which secondary legislation restricting support for asylum applicants was declared unlawful and was subsequently reversed by the Asylum and Immigration Act 1996.

[136] *R v Secretary of State for the Home Department, ex p Adan, Subraskran and Aitsegeur* [1999] 4 All ER 774; aff'd [2001] 2 AC 477, HL.

[137] Immigration and Asylum Act 1999, s 11(1); *R (Yogathas and Thangarasa) v Secretary of State for the Home Department* [2003] 1 AC 920. For other examples of legislative reversal, see Zellick, 'Government beyond law' [1985] PL 283.

to its own needs.[138] However, direct legislative reversal does not imply that judicial review is without any impact. By seeking to reverse a court judgment through legislation, the government must seek publicly to justify its action; the very task of legislating opens up policy issues to debate and campaigning by affected interests. This, in turn, may mean that the government has to offer concessions to secure the passage of legislation. Moreover, legislative reversal will not be lightly undertaken by a government given that the need to enact legislation may disrupt its legislative programme: legislation is itself a scarce resource. In any event, legislative reversal is very much the exception rather than the norm. Furthermore, it is really only an option for central government (and, even then, not in the context of EU law[139]), whereas many judicial review claims are brought against local authorities and other public bodies.

Another form of negative reaction to judicial review that has been more common in recent years has been direct criticism of the courts by politicians. Ministerial familiarity with judicial review may both breed contempt and prompt criticism. For example, in response to a High Court decision declaring Home Office asylum procedures unlawful, the then Home Secretary, David Blunkett MP, expressed his frustration: 'Frankly, I am personally fed up with having to deal with a situation where Parliament debates issues and the judges overturn them.'[140]

Such criticism of judges by politicians has been viewed as part of a government strategy to cope with legal challenge.[141] At the same time, it is unsurprising that such comments have also been viewed as undermining the convention that, irrespective of what government Ministers might think of a judicial decision, they should not publicly criticise it because of the constitutional importance of the executive respecting the independence of the judiciary. Indeed, this may illustrate a more general development in our constitution: the passing away of old unwritten conventions and their replacement with more formal (and sometimes legally binding) duties—a trend that relates to one of our key themes concerning the transition from a more political to a more legal constitution. So, following repeated criticism of the judiciary by government Ministers, Parliament decided, in the Constitutional Reform Act 2005, to impose a statutory duty on the Lord Chancellor to uphold the continued independence of the judiciary.[142] This duty, though, does not prevent politicians from criticising judges. At the same time, the rhetoric of political criticism may simply act as a pressure

---

[138] As Cranston, 'Reviewing Judicial Review', in Richardson and Genn (eds), *Administrative Law and Government Action: The Courts and Alternative Mechanisms of Review* (Oxford 1994), p 70, has noted: 'Legislative reversal of the effects of particular decisions on judicial review is at once a tribute to its potency but also a reminder that at the end of the day parliamentary power trumps judicial power.'

[139] See Chapter 8, section 4, above on the supremacy of EU law.

[140] Quoted by Bradley, 'Judicial Independence under Attack' [2003] PL 397, 400. These comments were made in response to the Administrative Court's decision in *R (Q) v Secretary of State for the Home Department* [2003] EWHC 195 (Admin), which was upheld on appeal ([2003] EWCA Civ 364, [2004] QB 36).

[141] See Le Sueur, 'The Judicial Review Debate: From Partnership to Friction' (1996) 31 Government and Opposition 8. See also Rozenburg, *Trial of Strength: The Battle between Ministers and Judges over Who Makes the Laws* (London 1997).   [142] Constitutional Reform Act 2005, s 3.

valve through which politicians express their displeasure at court rulings, but which, in the absence of legislative reversal, they are compelled to follow.[143]

On occasion, political criticism of the courts may combine with legislative changes. Consider, for example, the episode of the 'Afghan hijackers', in which a number of Afghan nationals, having arrived in the UK on a hijacked plane, succeeded in their appeals that their removal to Afghanistan would be contrary to ECHR, Art 3. Following this, the Home Office delayed in applying its own policies by refusing immigration status to a number of the individuals concerned; the Administrative Court concluded that this delay resulted in 'conspicuous unfairness amounting to an abuse of power'.[144] The immediate reaction of the then Prime Minister was that the Court's decision amounted to 'an abuse of common sense'.[145] While dismissing the government's appeal, the Court of Appeal indicated that it would be open to Parliament to create a new immigration category for people whose conduct the government considered had disentitled them from the ordinary immigration status.[146] Subsequently, the government introduced legislation to introduce a special immigration status for such people.[147]

There are other, lesser forms of negative reaction apart from legislative reversal and political criticism. Public agencies may give 'lip service' to a court ruling, but fail to comply with its spirit. Consider, by way of example, the Home Office's response to the Court of Appeal's ruling in *Dirshe*, in which it was held that, in the interests of procedural fairness, audio recordings should be made of interviews with asylum seekers.[148] Following the case, the Home Office did change its policy to the effect that it would record interviews if so requested; however, it was not Home Office policy to inform applicants that they could make such a request.[149]

Q To what extent, if at all, is it permissible for public authorities to react negatively toward judicial review?

4.6 **Informal reaction**

So far, the reactions to judicial review that we have considered, whether positive or negative, have been formal, such as a change in policy or procedure. However, the

---

[143] It should also be noted that the judges have themselves not been immune from such rhetoric. Consider the case of *R (SK) v Secretary of State for the Home Department* [2008] EWHC 98 (Admin), in which the Home Office had unlawfully detained foreign nationals subject to removal. Munby J, at [2], described the actions of the Home Office as 'both shocking and scandalous ... for what they expose as the seeming inability of that Department to comply not merely with the law but with the very rule of law itself'.

[144] *R (S) v Secretary of State for the Home Department* [2006] EWHC 1111 (Admin).

[145] 'Blair dismay over hijack Afghans', BBC News website, 10 May 2006.

[146] *S v Secretary of State for the Home Department* [2006] EWCA Civ 1157, [47].

[147] Criminal Justice and Immigration Act 2008, ss 130–137.

[148] *R (Dirshe) v Secretary of State for the Home Department* [2005] EWCA Civ 421, [2005] 1 WLR 2685.

[149] Home Office, *Asylum Process Guidance: Conducting the Asylum Interview* (London 2007).

limitation of studying formal reactions is that they provide little information on the extent of indirect impact outside the particular public agency, nor do they illuminate the more diffuse and informal impact on decision-makers further away from the formulation of policy.[150] While it may be easier to identify a formal reaction to judicial review—whether positive or negative—than an informal reaction, this does not imply that informal responses are any less important. Indeed, it has been argued that the most profound and enduring influences of judicial review are not to be found by examining the statute book or by seeking formalised and public shifts of policy in response to litigation; rather, they are to be found in the effects of litigation on the less accessible aspects of government—the internal and informal working practices of public agencies, their management systems, and their decision-making regimes.[151] However, it is often harder to trace the impact of judicial review on patterns of bureaucratic behaviour than on the outcome of individual cases, because administrative action is usually influenced by so many factors.[152]

In this context, empirical studies of the impact of judicial review are particularly important.[153] A common theme of such studies is that the ability of judicial review to influence routine administrative decision-making may be constrained. Why might this be so? Administrative decision-makers may be unaware of elementary principles of judicial review. There may be are other pressures—political, administrative, and financial—with which judicial review must compete in order to have any impact. Public authorities typically operate in a highly complex political–administrative context and are subject to all sorts of pressures, such as centrally imposed targets and performance indicators. In the organisational context in which public authorities operate, compliance with judicial review may often be a low priority. Furthermore, judicial review has an effect of isolating a single administrative decision—possibly out of very many other decisions—for scrutiny; this might be beneficial for the recipient of that particular decision, but it does not necessarily mean that other decisions will receive similar scrutiny.

For example, homelessness decision-making by local authorities is a high-pressure, 'street-level' environment far removed from legal norms and the courts. Studies of the impact of judicial review in this context have revealed that decision-making is informed by a number of different concerns, such as the allocation of limited resources, administrative and managerial pressures, and decision-makers' own perceptions of the moral worthiness of homeless applicants. In this context, judicial review is unlikely to exert much influence and may prompt negative reaction. For example, increased compliance with legal requirements might stem from a defensive concern by decision-makers to safeguard their decisions from challenge rather

---

[150] Richardson, 'Impact Studies in the United Kingdom', in Hertogh and Halliday (eds), *Judicial Review and Bureaucratic Impact: International and Interdisciplinary Perspectives* (Cambridge 2004), p 109.

[151] Sunkin and Le Sueur, 'Can Government Control Judicial Review?' (1991) 44 CLP 161, 162.

[152] Mullen, Prosser, and Pick, *Judicial Review in Scotland* (Chichester 1996), p 115.

[153] For an overview of such studies, see Richardson, pp 107–15.

than a concern with improving their quality.[154] Halliday concluded, from empirical research into homelessness decision-making by three English local authorities, that, despite prolonged exposure to judicial scrutiny, unlawful homelessness decision-making was rife; paradoxically, exposure to judicial scrutiny might operate so as to reduce self-scrutiny by public authorities.[155]

By contrast, it might be thought that judicial review may exert more influence on adjudicative bodies, such as tribunals, that are made up of legally qualified decision-makers. However, this assumption may not be borne out in practice. For example, a study of the impact of judicial review on Mental Health Review Tribunals[156] concluded that, despite the legal and adjudicatory nature of the tribunals, the presence of lawyers, and the fact that fundamental rights were often at stake, the influence of judicial review was 'patchy at best, even with regard to procedural requirements'.[157]

Another theme from the literature is that the relationship between judicial review and public administration is not a static, but a complex and dynamic, one that varies over time and between different contexts. We have seen enough to demonstrate that, in some contexts, such as immigration and asylum, the government may view judicial review from a highly sceptical perspective; in other administrative contexts, judicial review may be of central importance to a new public agency. For example, when the Social Fund was established in 1986 to make discretionary 'crisis' payments to those in need, controversially, there was no right of appeal to a social security appeal tribunal.[158] The system did, though, include an Independent Review Service through which dissatisfied claimants could challenge the lawfulness of initial refusal decisions. During its first decade, judicial review was extremely important to the Independent Review Service in establishing its legitimacy. However, as the new agency came under pressure to ensure efficient service delivery, the influence of judicial review declined.[159] The broader lesson is that judicial review may exert an influence on public agencies if this coincides with the agency's goals; by contrast, the influence of judicial review may diminish if those goals change.

Which factors, then, condition the influence of judicial review on public administration? A number of different hypotheses have been advanced.[160] Judicial review is likely to exert a greater influence if public administrators possess legal knowledge of the principles of administrative law, if they are legally conscientious (they care about making lawful decisions), and if they are legally competent (they are able to apply their legal knowledge to produce lawful decisions). Additional factors conditioning the

---

[154] Loveland, *Housing Homeless Persons* (Oxford 1995).

[155] Halliday, 'The Influence of Judicial Review on Bureaucratic Decision-Making' [2000] PL 110.

[156] Now part of the Health, Education and Social Care Chamber of the First-tier Tribunal: see further Chapter 17 below.

[157] Richardson and Machin, 'Judicial Review and Tribunal Decision-Making: A Study of the Mental Health Review Tribunal' [2000] PL 494, 514.   [158] See generally Buck, *The Social Fund* (London 2000).

[159] Sunkin and Pick, 'The Changing Impact of Judicial Review: The Independent Review Service of the Social Fund' [2001] PL 736.

[160] Halliday, *Judicial Review and Compliance with Administrative Law* (Oxford 2003).

influence of judicial review concern the decision-making environment (is it conducive to producing lawful decisions or are there competing pressures?) and the law itself (are court rulings themselves clear and unambiguous?).[161]

5. Conclusions

In this chapter, we have examined the effectiveness and impact of judicial review in terms of the accessibility of judicial review, the competence and capacity of the courts to review administrative action, and the impact of judicial review on government. The purpose has not been to provide a comprehensive overview of these issues, but to illustrate their complexity in order to consider the effectiveness of judicial review as a means for securing legal accountability of governmental action.

In terms of accessibility of judicial review, the courts possess certain distinct advantages. They are, of course, independent of government and adjudicate on cases through fair procedures. Judicial review may be relatively rare, but it can be a potent remedy for aggrieved individuals seeking redress. Furthermore, the Administrative Court possesses a prominent position within the judicial hierarchy for determining administrative legality. However, as we have seen, access to judicial review is constrained in various ways. Legal costs, restrictions on legal aid, uneven access to legal advice and services, the variable operation by the court of the permission to proceed requirement, and delays within the court can limit the accessibility and effectiveness of the judicial review procedure. Overload has prompted greater use of ADR and settlement of cases in order to divert appropriate cases out of the court's caseload. While these alternatives might possess some advantages in terms of efficiency, it cannot be guaranteed that they will always be an effective substitute for full judicial scrutiny. At the same time, the establishment of regional hearing centres of the Administrative Court may improve its accessibility.

The effectiveness of the courts may also be affected by their institutional capacity. The ability of the courts to subject public administration to thorough legal scrutiny has been questioned. While the courts may be expert in some areas of administration, they may possess less experience and awareness of other areas; the courts need to be aware of the potential impact of their rulings on government and of the political context in which administration is undertaken. And, as we have seen, such awareness may, in turn, prompt judicial restraint in terms of the types of matter that courts are

---

[161] On this last point, the House of Lords' decision in *Bromley London Borough Council v Greater London Council* [1983] AC 768 is an instructive example of how it can be difficult for public authorities to derive clear guidance from multiple and complex judgments. A noticeable trend over recent years has been for the higher courts to deliver single, rather than multiple, judgments, other than in cases including dissenting judgments, which promotes clarity in working out their meaning.

prepared to review and the intensity with which they are prepared to conduct such review.

Despite renewed focus, the impact of judicial review on government remains, overall, a comparatively unexamined issue. One view has been that court judgments have little or no effect on government, although it has been argued that judicial review can be important not only on account of what it achieves in practice, but also because of its symbolic importance in terms of the values that it embodies and protects.[162] Another view is that there is always a risk that the courts may usurp the policymaking function and override the expertise of officials. What evidence there is suggests that neither of these views is accurate. Administrative reaction to judicial review can be both positive and negative. While judicial review has an important role to play in ensuring administrative legality, whether or not it can be successful in doing so often depends on the degree of receptiveness exhibited by public authorities. For judicial review to be effective, public authorities must be willing to internalise administrative law principles in their decision-making processes. However, judicial review is rarely the sole factor determining administrative behaviour.

Finally, while judicial review is undoubtedly of great importance, it is not the sole mechanism of legal accountability, let alone the only method of accountability in the modern state. The constitution possesses other mechanisms for holding government to account. While the significance of judicial review within our constitution has grown, it is unlikely ever to replace the traditional mechanisms of political accountability—scrutiny of governmental action by Parliament, the media, and general public opinion—as a means of holding government to account. We can therefore end this part of the book where we began in Chapter 12, by observing that judicial review is simply one part—albeit an important part—of a much wider framework within which the relationship between the individual and the state is played out, and within which the executive branch of government is held to account for its actions. It is fitting, therefore, that we now turn, in the next part of the book, to examine other aspects of that framework, such as ombudsmen, inquiries, and tribunals.

Further reading

HALLIDAY, *Judicial Review and Compliance with Administrative Law* (Oxford 2003)

HERTOGH AND HALLIDAY (eds), *Judicial Review and Bureaucratic Impact: International and Interdisciplinary Perspectives* (Cambridge 2004)

JAMES, 'The political and Administrative Consequences of Judicial Review' (1996) 74 Public Administration 613

---

[162] Cane, 'Understanding Judicial Review and Its Impact', in Hertogh and Halliday (eds), *Judicial Review and Bureaucratic Impact: International and Interdisciplinary Perspectives* (Cambridge 2004), p 41.

RAWLINGS, 'Modelling Judicial Review' (2008) 61 CLP 95

RICHARDSON AND SUNKIN, 'Judicial Review: Questions of Impact' [1996] PL 79

Useful websites

http://www.hmcourts-service.gov.uk/cms/admin.htm
Website of the Administrative Court

PART V

Administrative Justice

16 Ombudsmen and Complaints

1. Introduction

In the preceding chapters, we saw that one of the principal purposes of judicial review is to enable individuals to challenge the legality of governmental decisions and, in this way, to ensure that government and other public bodies uphold legal standards of good administration. Judicial review is therefore one way of securing administrative justice, but it is far from being the only technique through which administrative justice may be secured, and its counterpart, good government, promoted. In this part of the book, our focus shifts to a range of *non-court-based* mechanisms that, in different ways, seek to secure administrative justice for individuals (by providing redress when things go wrong) and/or to promote good government (by enabling lessons to be learned from past mistakes). In this chapter, we begin our examination of such mechanisms by looking at public sector ombudsmen. The word 'ombudsman' means literally a 'complaints man'; public sector ombudsmen are those independent bodies that investigate complaints of maladministration against public bodies.[1] In the next chapter, we will examine the operation of tribunals, which determine appeals against administrative decisions.

In the course of examining ombudsmen, we will encounter all three of the key themes of this book: ombudsmen constitute an important mechanism by which the executive (and other public bodies) can be *held to account*; the relationship between ombudsmen and other accountability mechanisms, together with questions concerning the legal enforceability of ombudsmen's findings, raise important issues about *legal and political forms of constitutionalism*; and the *multilayered nature of the United Kingdom's constitution* post-devolution has resulted in a diversity of ombudsman schemes and poses particular challenges in relation to the rationalisation of ombudsmen in England. We will unpack each of these points in the appropriate parts of the chapter.

---

[1] Throughout this chapter, we refer to 'ombudsmen', albeit that some of the offices considered are formally known as 'commissioners'. Notwithstanding its retention in some of the relevant legislation, the latter term has largely fallen into disuse.

2. An example—the 'debt of honour' case

One of the purposes of this chapter is to explain what ombudsmen do, and why and how they do it. But a good starting point (albeit one that will need to be refined) is to say that ombudsmen exist to: *investigate* complaints of maladministration; *secure redress* for injustice occasioned thereby; *identify the underlying reasons* for maladministration in order that appropriate lessons may be learned; and do all of these things in a way that *avoids the formality, cost, and legalism* associated with court proceedings. These points can be illustrated by means of an example: the 'debt of honour' case.

In 2000, the UK government announced the establishment of a compensation scheme for 'British' civilians interned by the Japanese during the Second World War. The terms in which the scheme was announced led to an expectation in some quarters that it would apply to a relatively broad range of people. However, subsequently, the government issued a clarification indicating that it would be limited to those who had been born in the UK or with at least one parent or grandparent who had been born in the UK. Judicial review proceedings were initiated by a group representing disappointed individuals who had anticipated benefiting from the scheme, but who fell outside the scope of its clarified terms.[2] Their claim was based in part on the legitimate expectation doctrine,[3] but the Court of Appeal held that the original announcement had been insufficiently clear to generate such an expectation, no definite indication having been given of who would count as 'British' for those purposes.

Following this, a complaint was made to the Parliamentary Ombudsman—that is, the ombudsman who investigates complaints of maladministration (bad administrative practice) made against UK central government departments. She conducted an investigation, examining the government's initial and subsequent statements, and concluded that the way in which the matter had been handled—in particular, the confusion created by the unclear and imprecise nature of the original announcement—constituted maladministration that had occasioned injustice to the complainant and similarly situated individuals.[4] The Ombudsman therefore recommended, among other things, that the government review the scheme that it had implemented, and fully reconsider the position of the complainant and those in a similar position to him.[5] However, the government refused to do so, prompting the Ombudsman to lay a special report before Parliament drawing its attention to what she regarded as unremedied injustice. This, in turn, was followed up by a report by the House of Commons Public Administration Select Committee—the select committee that, amongst other things, oversees the work of the Ombudsman. The report was highly critical of the

---

[2] *R (Association of British Civilian Internees: Far East Region) v Secretary of State for Defence* [2003] EWCA Civ 473, [2003] QB 1397.   [3] See Chapter 13, section 4.3, above.

[4] Parliamentary Ombudsman, 'A *Debt of Honour': The Ex Gratia Scheme for British Groups Interned by the Japanese During the Second World War* (HC 324 2005–06), [199].

[5] Parliamentary Ombudsman, HC 324, [212]–[216].

government's stance. Following this, the government backed down and accepted the need to review the compensation scheme.[6]

This episode points to several distinctive features of the ombudsman system. All of them will be considered in more detail later in the chapter, but we need to highlight them here. First, the Ombudsman considered maladministration to have occurred notwithstanding that the Court had found the government's conduct to be lawful. This shows that *the concept of good administration employed by ombudsmen is a broader one than that which is enforced by the courts via judicial review*—that is, a government decision may be lawful, but may nonetheless still result in maladministration. Second, the Ombudsman's recommendations were concerned not only with the case of the complainant, and not only with the circumstances of similarly situated individuals, but also with the general way in which government should implement compensation schemes: the Ombudsman said that, in future, due regard should be given to all relevant issues (for example, eligibility criteria) *before* any announcements are made, and that, once announced, any subsequent changes should be publicised and explained.[7] This demonstrates that ombudsmen are concerned not only with remedying injustice in individual cases, but also with *identifying general administrative deficiencies and disseminating good practice to guard against their recurrence*. Third, the fact that the government refused to implement the Ombudsman's key recommendations, and that the Ombudsman's only recourse was by way of drawing Parliament's attention to that fact, highlights the *legally non-binding nature of ombudsmen's recommendations* and the general principle that *ombudsmen form part of the political, not legal, system for securing good government*.

> **Q** These distinctive aspects of ombudsmanry that differentiate it from other modes of redress are generally seen as good things. Do you share that view? Why, or why not? How would you respond to someone who argued that ombudsmen are unnecessary and that it would be better to rely on judicial review?

3. Public sector ombudsmen in the UK

Before we unpack those points—and others concerned with the nature of the ombudsmen's role—it is necessary to deal with some of the 'nuts and bolts' issues about the ombudsman 'system'. Two initial matters should be noted.

First, a broad distinction must be drawn between *public* and *private sector ombudsmen*. The latter are typically established by particular industries and professions to act as complaints-handlers. Thus there is an Energy Ombudsman, a Legal Services

---

[6] See further Kirkham, 'Challenging the Authority of the Ombudsman: The Parliamentary Ombudsman's Special Report on Wartime Detainees' (2006) 69 MLR 792.

[7] Parliamentary Ombudsman, HC 324, [224]–[225].

	Part of the country to which alleged maladministration relates			
	England	Scotland	Wales	Northern Ireland
UK public bodies (general)	UK Parliamentary Ombudsman			
'National' (ie English, Scottish, etc) public bodies	UK Parliamentary Ombudsman	Scottish Public Services Ombudsman	Welsh Public Services Ombudsman	Assembly Ombudsman for Northern Ireland
Health service providers	Health Service Ombudsman	Scottish Public Services Ombudsman	Welsh Public Services Ombudsman	Northern Ireland Commissioner for Complaints
Local authorities	Local Government Ombudsmen	Scottish Public Services Ombudsman	Welsh Public Services Ombudsman	Northern Ireland Commissioner for Complaints
Social landlords	Housing Ombudsman			n/a

Figure 16.1 Public sector ombudsmen

Ombudsman, and even a Furniture Ombudsman.[8] Our concern, however, is with public sector ombudsmen—that is, with ombudsmen that are independent of government and investigate complaints against public bodies.

Second, within the category of public sector ombudsmen, there are two broad models. The distinction between them is evident from Figure 16.1. The first model adopts an integrated approach, with a single ombudsman service responsible for oversight of all relevant public bodies. So, after devolution to Scotland and Wales, the Scottish and Welsh Public Services Ombudsmen were established to handle complaints relating to all public bodies within those countries except for those complaints relating to UK-wide public bodies (such as central government departments).[9] In contrast, the system in England is fragmented, with different ombudsmen dealing with complaints pertaining to general public bodies (the Parliamentary Ombudsman),[10] health service providers (the Health Service Ombudsman),[11] local authorities (the Local Government Ombudsmen),[12] and social landlords (the Independent Housing Ombudsman Service).[13] The existence of such diversity is unsurprising in a multi-layered constitution:[14] the essential point of devolution is to enable each country within the UK to arrange its own affairs in the most appropriate way, and it is inevitable that

[8] For a list of ombudsman schemes, see **http://www.bioa.org.uk**

[9] Scottish Public Services Ombudsman Act (SPSOA) 2002, Public Services Ombudsman (Wales) Act (PSO(W)A) 2005.   [10] Parliamentary Commissioner Act (PCA) 1967.

[11] Health Service Commissioners Act (HSCA) 1993.   [12] Local Government Act (LGA) 1974.

[13] Housing Act 1996.

[14] In this regard, it should be noted that ombudsmen also exist at the EU level. The EU Ombudsman is responsible for investigating complaints of maladministration against certain EU institutions. See further Heede, *European Ombudsman: Redress and Control at Union Level* (The Hague 2000).

different views will prevail in different regions.[15] However, it is not clear that any-one actually regards the English system as superior to the integrated models adopted in Scotland and Wales. The public sector ombudsmen themselves have argued that people find it 'difficult to know to which Ombudsman to complain', and that par-ticular problems arise when complaints raise issues that fall within the jurisdiction of more than one ombudsman.[16] For example, the Scottish Ombudsman sees the breadth of his jurisdiction as a great strength—citing by way of example investigations into 'long-term care for the elderly [that] can involve a number of agencies in delivering the service including health providers, local government and housing associations'.[17] In contrast, such an investigation would engage the jurisdictions of a number of separate ombudsmen in England.

In light of such problems, a review by the Cabinet Office in 2000 concluded that the integrated model should be adopted in England by merging the Parliamentary, Health Service, and Local Government Ombudsmen.[18] However, as the Parliamentary Ombudsman has pointed out, this would raise fresh difficulties: she (unlike the Health and Local Government Ombudsmen) is not an *English*, but a *UK*, ombudsman, with jurisdiction over *both* English *and* UK-wide public bodies.[19] If the UK Parliamentary Ombudsman were to be merged with the English Health and Local Government Ombudsmen, would the resulting institution be an English or a UK one? If the former, why should it have jurisdiction over non-devolved matters pertaining to other parts of the country? And, if the latter, why should its jurisdiction be limited in some regards to England?

These complications are an artefact of the peculiarly British conception of multi-layered constitutionalism. The absence of England from the devolution settlement means that the line between English and UK matters and institutions is inevitably blurred, with English affairs often handled, in the absence of England-specific bodies, by UK institutions. Against that background, the line-drawing exercise that would have to be undertaken in order to create an integrated English ombudsman service separate from the UK Parliamentary Ombudsman would be a complicated, albeit not an impossible, one. It seems likely, therefore, that the fragmented system will remain in place in England, although the position has been improved to some extent by modest reforms introduced in 2007 permitting the Parliamentary, Health Service, and Local Government Ombudsmen to conduct joint investigations and issue joint reports on matters that cut across their respective jurisdictions.[20]

---

[15] As Figure 16.1 shows, the position in Northern Ireland is different again. See further Ombudsman (Northern Ireland) Order (O(NI)O) 1996, SI 1996/1298; Commissioner for Complaints (Northern Ireland) Order (CC(NI)O) 1996, SI 1996/1297.

[16] Collcutt and Hourihan, *Review of the Public Sector Ombudsmen in England: A Report by the Cabinet Office* (London 2000) (hereinafter the 'Cabinet Office Review'), annex A.

[17] Scottish Public Services Ombudsman, *Annual Report 2003–04* (Edinburgh 2004), p 24.

[18] The Cabinet Office Review, [4.3]–[4.4].

[19] Public Administration Select Committee, *Minutes of Evidence* (HC 506–i 2002–03) (annex). See further Elliott, 'Asymmetric Devolution and Ombudsman Reform in England' [2006] PL 84.

[20] See PCA 1967, s 11ZAA; HSCA 1993, s 18ZA; LGA 1974, s 33ZA.

It is beyond the scope of this chapter to provide a detailed account of the workings of each of the public sector ombudsmen that operate in the UK. Instead, our approach is to examine a number of general matters concerning the role and functions of public sector ombudsman, using the UK Parliamentary Ombudsman as our focus and referring to other ombudsman schemes by way of comparison.[21] References in the remainder of the chapter to the 'Ombudsman' are to the Parliamentary Ombudsman unless otherwise indicated.

4. The role of public sector ombudsmen

4.1 What are ombudsmen for?

Broadly speaking, there are two views about the role that ombudsmen should fulfil.[22] On the first view, the principal role of ombudsmen is to secure *redress* for individuals who suffer because of maladministration. Here, then, the focus is on dealing with individual grievances, getting public bodies to apologise and to put things right. The second view, in contrast, holds that ombudsmen should concentrate on broader *systemic* issues, trying to understand why things have gone wrong and identifying how things should be done differently to avoid a repetition of past mistakes. This is sometimes referred to as the *quality control* model of ombudsmanry—it is a forward-looking approach the focus of which is on improving the future quality of administration. Viewed in this way, ombudsmanry also becomes an important mechanism for holding government to account, capable of laying bare the nature and causes of systemic failure, and enabling others—the public, MPs, the media—to make informed judgements about the quality of public administration and the competence of those ultimately responsible for it.

Although these two models are helpful in that they assist in understanding the range of things that ombudsmen might do, it would be a mistake to think that an ombudsman system must adhere to either one model or the other. In reality, many ombudsmen seek to combine the two approaches. Indeed, this is not difficult, because they are, to a large extent, complementary.[23] By investigating large numbers of individual complaints, ombudsmen are able to build up a wealth of experience that helps them to understand why things go wrong, and to make constructive suggestions about how administrative systems and policies can be improved. For example, in 2003–05, the Parliamentary Ombudsman received large numbers of complaints about tax credits, a means-tested state benefits system, the principal concern being that some recipients

---

[21] For more detailed discussion of different ombudsman systems, see Seneviratne, *Ombudsmen: Public Services and Administrative Justice* (London 2002).

[22] Heede, *European Ombudsman: Redress and Control at Union Level* (The Hague 2000), pp 79–112; Seneviratne, pp 16–21.

[23] This is certainly the view of the Parliamentary Ombudsman: *Improving Public Service: A Matter of Principle* (HC 9 2008).

were being overpaid for relatively long periods and then subjected to unexpected demands for repayment, causing serious hardship to those on low incomes. As well as dealing—pursuant to her redress function—with the individual complaints received, the Ombudsman looked at the tax credits system as a whole, using experience gleaned in relation to individual complaints to identify systemic failures concerning the design and implementation of the scheme, and to suggest what corrective action might be taken.[24] Similarly, the Health and Local Government Ombudsmen conducted a joint investigation in 2008–09 concerning the treatment of six people with learning disabilities who had died in National Health Service (NHS) or local authority care between 2003 and 2005.[25] This revealed 'significant and distressing failures' leading to people with learning disabilities experiencing 'prolonged suffering and inappropriate care',[26] and led the Ombudsmen to recommend that all NHS and social care organisations in England should urgently review their arrangements for understanding and meeting the needs of people with learning disabilities. Some ombudsmen, such as the Welsh Public Services Ombudsman, have specific statutory powers to issue guidance about good administrative practice;[27] and although the Parliamentary Commissioner Act (PCA) 1967 makes no mention of such powers, the Parliamentary Ombudsman has nevertheless—in addition to seeking to disseminate good practice through her reports on investigations—issued a general code of good administration, setting out the standards to which public bodies are expected to adhere.[28]

While the redress and control functions of ombudsmen complement one another, there remains nonetheless a tension between the two models. The former encourages a high volume of investigations in order to provide as much redress to aggrieved individuals as possible; the latter, meanwhile, suggests that ombudsmen should be highly selective, investigating only those complaints that are likely to shine a light on systemic failures, thereby enabling them to make a contribution at the macro level. One way in which ombudsmen can seek to resolve that tension is by dealing differently with different sorts of complaints. For example, the Parliamentary and Health Ombudsmen[29] received (excluding those not validly made or outside the Ombudsmen's remit) 11,066 enquiries in 2009–10, but accepted only 356 cases for full investigation.[30] Other complaints were either rejected (for example, because they were premature[31] or because there was no reasonable prospect of securing a worthwhile outcome) or dealt with by raising the matter informally with the public body concerned. This reflects the Ombudsman's philosophy that there should be 'a diverse product range, and that the

---

[24] Parliamentary Ombudsman, *Tax Credits: Putting Things Right* (HC 124 2004–05).

[25] Parliamentary Ombudsman, *Six Lives: The Provision of Public Services to People with Learning Disabilities* (HC 203 2008–09).   [26] Parliamentary Ombudsman, HC 203, p 31.

[27] PSO(W)A 2005, s 31.   [28] See further section 5.3 below.

[29] Although legally distinct, the posts of Parliamentary and Health Ombudsmen are held by the same person, and statistical information regarding their workload is sometimes published in an aggregated form.

[30] Parliamentary Ombudsman, *Making an Impact* (HC 274 2009–10), p 18.

[31] Complaints are rejected as premature if complainants have not made recourse to the relevant public body's own complaints procedure.

serious, heavyweight, statutory investigation should not be the core product'[32]—an approach that allows a balance to be struck between redressing substantial numbers of grievances, while undertaking detailed investigations into matters of broader significance.

4.2 Ombudsmen and the political process

One way of attempting to understand the role of ombudsmen is to consider where they sit in relation to other parts of the constitutional system. We address their relationship with other aspects of the administrative justice system, including courts, in the next section, but first we address their position vis-à-vis the political process.

Part of the impetus for the creation of the Parliamentary Ombudsman—the first ombudsman in the UK—was concerns as to the inability of Parliament to deal with instances of apparent administrative failure. Former Ombudsman Sir Cecil Clothier wrote of a perception that Parliament's increasing focus on 'massive and detailed legislation' meant that it could not devote its time to 'those problems of individuals which lack a national or international dimension'.[33] The Parliamentary Ombudsman was therefore conceived, according to Drewry and Harlow, as 'an adjunct to the MP's traditional and cherished role as grievance-chaser on behalf of constituents'.[34] It was envisaged that the Ombudsman would augment the capacity of Parliament to deal with such matters: Richard Crossman MP, the government Minister responsible for piloting the Parliamentary Commissioner Bill through the House of Commons, said that the Ombudsman would be a 'servant of the House'.[35] The relationship between the Ombudsman and Parliament is cemented in a number of ways.

First, the Ombudsman is required to *report to Parliament* annually on the performance of her functions under the PCA 1967 and is permitted to report to Parliament on such other matters as she thinks fit.[36] The reports referred to above concerning the 'debt of honour' case, the overpayment of tax credits, and the treatment of people with learning disabilities were thus reports made *to Parliament*. Similarly, the Scottish, Welsh, and Northern Irish ombudsmen report to their respective legislatures.[37]

Second, when the Ombudsman concludes that maladministration occasioning injustice has taken place, but that it appears that the public body concerned is not going to remedy it, she can *lay a special report before Parliament* drawing the matter to its attention.[38] Again, equivalent provision is made in relation to most of the other ombudsmen.[39] This feature of the ombudsman systems arguably underscores the view that they are best thought of as part of the political process, in the sense that

---

[32] House of Commons Public Administration Select Committee, *Minutes of Evidence* (HC 506–i 2002–03), [70].   [33] 'The Value of an Ombudsman' [1986] PL 204, 205.
[34] 'A "Cutting Edge"? The Parliamentary Commissioner and MPs' (1990) 53 MLR 745, 753.
[35] HC Deb, vol 734, col 49.   [36] PCA 1967, s 10(4).
[37] SPSOA 2002, s 15; PSO(W)A 2005, Sch 1, para 14; O(NI)O 1996, art 17; CC(NI)O 1996, art 19.
[38] PCA 1967, s 10(3).   [39] SPSOA 2002, s 16; PSO(W)A 2005, s 24; O(NI)O 1996, art 17.

the enforceability (such as it is) of ombudsmen's recommendations derives from the pressure that representative legislatures are able to bring to bear upon governments. This leads onto the question of whether ombudsmen's findings and recommendations should ever be regarded as *legally* binding—a question that we address below.

Third, the Parliamentary Ombudsman has a *special relationship with the Public Administration Select Committee of the House of Commons*. The role of that committee in respect of the Ombudsman is twofold: it both scrutinises her work and, when it considers it appropriate, acts as her champion by orchestrating political pressure when the government proves reluctant to accept the Ombudsman's findings and recommendations.

Fourth, and most controversially, the Parliamentary Ombudsman's relationship with Parliament is evident in the so-called *MP filter*: the Ombudsman may investigate complaints, but *only* when they are referred to her by the complainant's MP.[40] This means that the Ombudsman cannot undertake investigations on her own initiative, and cannot undertake investigations in response to complaints received directly from members of the public. The latter phenomenon distinguishes the Parliamentary Ombudsman from most other UK public sector ombudsmen, to whom members of the public are able to complain directly,[41] and from most other public sector ombudsmen around the world. The MP filter, which was envisaged by the Justice Report that recommended the creation of an Ombudsman as a temporary measure,[42] may constitute an obstacle to access by making complaining to the Ombudsman relatively cumbersome and contingent upon finding an MP willing to refer the complaint. So why does it still exist? Two principal arguments are made (with less and less enthusiasm) in favour of the filter.

The first is a *pragmatic* one, which holds that the filter is needed in order to shield the Ombudsman from what would otherwise be an unsustainable workload. However, the theory that the filter 'allows the MP to settle the trivial administrative muddles', sending only the 'hard nuts' on to the Ombudsman,[43] does not seem to correspond to reality. Far from sending on only the hard cases that require the Ombudsman's specialised investigative skills, many MPs—over half, according to one study—*automatically* refer complaints to the Ombudsman when asked to do so.[44]

The pragmatic argument, then, cuts little ice. The second argument is a *constitutional* one. It is that the MP filter is a fitting reflection of the fact that the Ombudsman system forms part of the parliamentary process: that it is Parliament, and the MPs who partly comprise it, that bears primary responsibility for resolving constituents' grievances against public bodies and holding the executive to account, and that the Ombudsman

---

[40] PCA 1967, s 5(1), (1A).

[41] SPSOA 2002, s 9; PSO(W)A 2005, s 4; CC(NI)O 1996, art 8. The exception is the Northern Ireland Assembly Ombudsman, who may only investigate complaints referred to him by an Assembly Member: O(NI)O 1996, art 9(2). [42] *The Citizen and the Administration* (London 1961), [157].

[43] Harlow, 'Ombudsmen in Search of a Role' (1978) 41 MLR 446, 451.

[44] The Cabinet Office Review, [3.45].

is a functionary who better equips them to do those things. But this argument, too, is open to question.[45] The Cabinet Office Review of public sector ombudsmen in 2000 therefore recommended the abolition of the filter—a step supported by the Public Administration Select Committee[46]—arguing that the constitutional concerns just outlined could adequately be met by *permitting*, rather than *requiring all*, complaints to be routed via MPs, and by obliging the Ombudsman to keep MPs informed of her work and her findings.[47]

Persistent criticism notwithstanding,[48] the filter remains. It is worth noting, though, that the Ombudsman herself is ambivalent about it. On the one hand, she regards it as 'an anachronistic barrier to citizen access'; on the other hand, she sees some merit in it to the extent that, 'deployed properly', it might 'ensure the "buy in" of MPs to the effective operation of the Ombudsman system'.[49] It is important to note that these remarks were made against a background of government refusals to accept her findings and recommendations in a number of high-profile cases, which in turn raised questions about whether Parliament has sufficient political will and clout to hold the government to account in such circumstances. The essence of her argument is that cutting MPs out of the loop by removing the filter might hinder fulfilment of what she regards as the 'urgent need to re-engage the interest of MPs in the work of the Ombudsman and to reignite the feeling that the Ombudsman makes available to MPs an important resource at a time when discussion about the accountability of the executive has become especially acute'.[50] Similar thinking appears to underlie the Public Administration Select Committee's suggestion that parliamentary rules should be altered in order to facilitate a debate whenever the Ombudsman issues a report under s 10(3) of the PCA 1967 drawing Parliament's attention to the government's failure adequately to remedy injustice identified by the Ombudsman.[51] This recommendation was rejected by the then government,[52] although there is, as we saw in Chapter 10,[53] now greater scope for backbench MPs to trigger debates—a power that could be used to force discussion of government intransigence in the face of the Ombudsman's recommendations.

Q Should the MP filter be dropped? If it were, what practical steps, if any, should be taken in order to meet the Ombudsman's concerns set out above?

---

[45] See, eg Justice, *Our Fettered Ombudsman* (London 1977), pp 16–19; Justice-All Souls Committee, *Administrative Justice: Some Necessary Reforms* (London 1988), pp 88–9.

[46] House of Commons Public Administration Select Committee, *Ombudsman Issues* (HC 448 2002–03).

[47] The Cabinet Office Review, [3.43]–[3.51].

[48] The House of Commons Public Administration Select Committee reiterated its opposition to the filter and called for its removal in 2009: *Parliament and the Ombudsman* (HC 107 2009–10), [2]–[6].

[49] Abraham, 'The Ombudsman and the Executive: The Road to Accountability' (2008) 61 Parliamentary Affairs 535, 543.   [50] Abraham at 542–3.

[51] House of Commons Public Administration Select Committee, HC 107, [12].

[52] House of Commons Public Administration Select Committee, *Parliament and the Ombudsman: Further Report* (HC 471 2009–10).   [53] See Chapter 10, section 5.3, above.

4.3 **Ombudsmen within the administrative justice system**

As well as considering where in the constitutional landscape ombudsmen sit relative to legislatures and the political process, it is also necessary to address their relationship with other parts of the administrative justice system, such as courts and tribunals. Two sets of questions arise: in formal terms, how do the jurisdictions of ombudsmen relate to those of courts and tribunals? And, more broadly, how does the role of ombudsmen compare with that of courts and tribunals?

The answer to the latter question is that although the Ombudsman was created partly in response to concerns in the 1960s as to the unwillingness of courts to undertake rigorous judicial review[54]—a concern that is hardly felt today—the role of ombudsmen is largely complementary to that of other administrative justice institutions. In other words, ombudsmen bring something distinctive to the table, and do not simply replicate the work of courts and tribunals. There is certainly an overlap between the types of complaint that may be investigated by the Ombudsman and those that can be subjected to judicial review, but the two mechanisms differ markedly in several respects.[55]

First, as we have already seen in relation to the 'debt of honour' case, the Ombudsman applies a *broader concept of good administration* than the courts, such that she is able to deal with allegations—of rudeness, delay, general incompetence—that may not rob an administrative act of legality. Second, in contrast to making a claim for judicial review, complaining to the Ombudsman *costs nothing*. Third, the Ombudsman's *approach* is very different from that of the Administrative Court: she adopts an inquisitorial style that differs radically from the adversarialism of court proceedings; and whereas the Administrative Court is rarely willing or able to resolve disputes of fact, the Ombudsman readily and expertly does so. Fourth, as noted above, the Ombudsman is able to take a *broader view*: whereas courts (and tribunals) are principally concerned with resolving the dispute before them, the Ombudsman can step back with a view to identifying systemic failures and identifying how administrative practice should be improved in light of them.

The largely complementary role of ombudsmen, on the one hand, and courts and tribunals, on the other, means that the answer to our other question—about their respective jurisdictions—reveals something of a puzzle. Section 5(2) of the PCA 1967 says that the Parliamentary Ombudsman 'shall not conduct an investigation' when the person concerned has either a right of appeal to a tribunal or a remedy by way of court proceedings; equivalent provision is made in respect of the other public services ombudsmen.[56] But if the Ombudsman's role is largely complementary to that of other institutions, why make such provision? One reason may be to shield ombudsmen from an unmanageable workload by treating them as a remedy of final resort—although

---

[54] See Bradley, 'The Role of Ombudsmen in Relation to the Protection of Citizens' Rights' [1980] CLJ 304, 309.   [55] Bradley at 324–9.

[56] HSCA 1993, s 4(1); LGA 1974, s 26(6); SPSOA 2002, s 7(8); PSO(W)A 2005, s 9(1); O(NI)O 1996, art 10(3); CC(NI)O 1996, art 9(3).

workload-related problems are hardly an unknown phenomenon in other parts of the administrative justice system. The position can better be understood once it is recognised that the prohibition on ombudsmen taking on cases that could be pursued in other ways is not an absolute one. Section 5(2) of the 1967 Act—like equivalent provisions in the legislation concerning other ombudsmen[57]—contains the proviso that the Ombudsman may nevertheless investigate 'if satisfied that in the particular circumstances it is not reasonable to expect' the person concerned to pursue his or her complaint via tribunal or court proceedings. The question that ombudsmen must ask themselves when exercising this discretion is not whether legal proceedings would succeed, but whether 'the court of law is an appropriate forum for investigating the subject matter of the complaint'.[58] It might, for example, be unreasonable to expect someone to resort to judicial review if the cost of doing so would, in the circumstances, be prohibitively high, or if the case raises complex disputes of fact that the Ombudsman is more likely than the Administrative Court to be able to resolve. In practice, the Ombudsman tends to exercise her discretion generously, taking on investigations into complaints that could have been pursued via judicial review.[59]

What the legislation provides is a crude system of triage, whereby the ombudsmen, by exercising their discretion whether to investigate notwithstanding the availability of other remedies, are able in effect to direct cases to the most appropriate administrative justice institution. The system, though, is crude in the sense that it is not always apparent before an investigation is under way which institution that is. For that reason, the Law Commission has suggested that it should be possible for ombudsmen to refer cases to courts—and vice versa—when, in the course of an investigation or hearing, it becomes clear that the other institution would be better able to deal with the matter concerned.[60]

5. Investigations

The flowchart in Figure 16.2 indicates the range of questions that need to be considered in relation to whether the Ombudsman may investigate a given matter; if so, whether she will, in her discretion, undertake an investigation; and, if so, what that investigation, and its aftermath, is liable to entail.[61]

---

[57] HSCA 1993, s 4(1); LGA 1974, s 26(6); SPSOA 2002, s 7(8); PSO(W)A 2005, s 9(2); O(NI)O 1996, art 10(4); CC(NI)O 1996, art 9(4).

[58] *R v Commissioner for Local Administration, ex p Croydon London Borough Council* [1989] 1 All ER 1033, 1044, *per* Woolf J.

[59] The exercise of the Ombudsman's discretion in this regard is, however, subject to judicial review: *R v Commissioner for Local Administration, ex p Croydon London Borough Council* [1989] 1 All ER 1033.

[60] Law Commission, *Administrative Redress: Public Bodies and the Citizen* (CP 187 2008), ch 5; Law Commission, *Administrative Redress: Public Bodies and the Citizen* (Law Com No 322 2010), [5.89]–[5.91]. See also Kirkham, *The Parliamentary Ombudsman: Withstanding the Test of Time* (HC 421 2006–07), p 11.

[61] Figure 16.2 is concerned specifically with the Parliamentary Ombudsman, although most aspects of it (the obvious exception being the MP filter) apply to the other public sector ombudsmen.

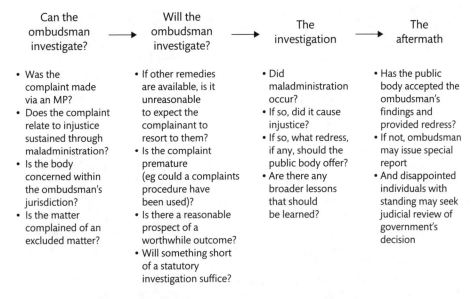

Figure 16.2 Ombudsman flowchart

5.1 **Bodies subject to investigation**

We have seen elsewhere in this book that, in several contexts, it has proven very difficult indeed for legislatures and courts to fashion coherent tests for what should count as a 'public' body or authority.[62] But no such difficulties arise in relation to the legislation conferring jurisdiction upon public sector ombudsmen in the UK. Rather than attempting to lay down a general definition of the type of bodies falling within that jurisdiction, the legislation simply lists each institution that is subject to investigation by the relevant ombudsman. So, for example, the Parliamentary Ombudsman is authorised to investigate complaints against only those bodies listed in Sch 2 of the 1967 Act.[63] This makes for a cumbersome system—every time a public body is created, abolished, or subject to a change of name, the list must be amended—but it at least results in clarity. Names can be added, removed, or altered via secondary legislation.[64] The lists of bodies subject to each ombudsman's jurisdiction can be found in the relevant legislation.[65] The length of many of those lists precludes their reproduction in this book; however, Figure 16.3 provides a broad indication, together with some illustrative examples, of the types of body subject to the various ombudsmen's jurisdictions.

---

[62] See Chapter 8, section 3.2.5, and Chapter 14, section 2.2.3, above, and Chapter 19, section 3.5, below.
[63] PCA 1967, s 4(1).　　[64] PCA 1967, s 4(2).
[65] PCA 1967, Sch 2; HSCA 1993, ss 2–2B; LGA 1974, s 25; SPSOA 2002, Sch 2; PSO(W)A 2005, Sch 3; O(NI)O 1996, Sch 2; CC(NI)O 1996, Sch 2.

Ombudsman	Types of body	Illustrative examples	Devolution
Parliamentary Ombudsman	UK public bodies	UK government departments, Civil Aviation Authority, National Lottery Commission	Devolved ombudsmen do not have jurisdiction over UK public bodies*
Parliamentary Ombudsman	English public bodies	English Tourist Board, Director of Fair Access to Higher Education, Natural England	The Scottish, Welsh, and Northern Ireland ombudsmen deal with Scottish, Welsh and Northern Irish bodies
Health Service Ombudsman	NHS bodies and health service providers	NHS Trusts, people providing medical or dental services pursuant to a contract with an NHS body	The Scottish, Welsh, and Northern Ireland ombudsmen deal with health matters in their respective parts of the country
Local Government Ombudsmen	Local authorities and certain other local bodies	Local authorities, National Park authorities, fire and police authorities	The Scottish, Welsh, and Northern Ireland ombudsmen deal with local government matters in their respective parts of the country

Figure 16.3 Ombudsmen's jurisdictions

* An exception concerns 'cross-border public authorities'—a special category over which devolved ombudsmen have jurisdiction to the extent that their actions pertain to a devolved part of the country.

5.2 **Excluded matters**

Even if the *body* to which the complaint relates is one falling within the relevant ombudsman's jurisdiction, he or she will be unable to investigate if it relates to an excluded *matter*.[66] The matters excluded from each ombudsman's jurisdiction vary. Those excluded from the Parliamentary Ombudsman's jurisdiction are set out in Sch 3 to the 1967 Act. They include matters certified by a Minister to affect international relations, the commencement or conduct of civil or criminal proceedings, and the grant of honours.

One exclusion—matters concerning 'contractual or commercial transactions' by public bodies—is particularly controversial for two reasons.[67] First, the effects of such transactions may be considerable. For example, they may involve very large amounts of public money, or they may have a particularly severe impact on given individuals.[68] Second, not only are the consequences of commercial and contractual decisions potentially *serious*, but the use of such arrangements, such as the contracting out of service

---

[66] PCA 1967, s 5(3); LGA 1974, s 26(8); SPSOA 2002, s 8; PSO(W)A 2005, s 10; O(NI)O 1996, art 10(1); CC(NI)O 1996, art 9(1).

[67] PCA 1967, Sch 3, para 9. The Welsh Public Services Ombudsman is not subject to this exclusion.

[68] Clothier, 'The Value of an Ombudsman' [1986] PL 204, 205, 210–11.

provision, has also become increasingly *common*,[69] meaning that their exclusion from the Ombudsman's purview represents a more far-reaching exclusion than was once the case. Although s 5(1) of the 1967 Act allows the Ombudsman to investigate action taken 'on behalf of', as well as 'by', the public bodies listed in Sch 2, thus raising the possibility of an investigation into the conduct of a commercial body providing government services to the public under contract, the point remains that the exclusion of contractual or commercial transactions by public bodies makes it impossible for the Ombudsman to investigate the propriety of decisions to make such arrangements in the first place. Thus, for example, if the government were to award a multimillion-pound contract to a given company that turns out to be incompetent, the Ombudsman would be able to investigate the company's conduct, but not the prior decision to engage it.

> **Q** Is this position acceptable? What justifications might be advanced for retaining the exclusion relating to contractual and commercial matters?

5.3 **Maladministration**

The concept of maladministration is central to the role of the Parliamentary Ombudsman for two reasons. First, it determines the scope of the Ombudsman's jurisdiction: subject to one limited exception,[70] the Ombudsman is only able to investigate complaints originating from members of the public who claim to have sustained 'injustice in consequence of maladministration'.[71] Second, the question of whether maladministration has occurred is (along with the question of whether, in the event of maladministration, injustice has been sustained as a result) therefore the key matter with which the Ombudsman's investigations are concerned. The notion of maladministration is central to other public sector ombudsmen schemes, although many of them also permit investigation into allegations of 'failure in a service' or 'failure to provide a service'.[72] What, then, is meant by 'maladministration'?

Given the pivotal role of the concept of maladministration in the UK's public sector ombudsmen schemes, it is perhaps curious that no positive attempt is made to define it in any of the relevant legislation. However, the legislation does indicate, in negative terms, what is *not* meant by maladministration: the 1967 Act says that nothing in it authorises or requires the Ombudsman to 'question the *merits* of a decision taken without maladministration',[73] while the other ombudsmen schemes make similar provision.[74] The implication, then, is that maladministration is concerned with the

---

[69] See Chapter 4, section 4.5, above.

[70] The Ombudsman may investigate, without reference to whether maladministration has occurred, an allegation of non-performance of certain duties owed to victims of sexual or violent offences: PCA 1967, s 5(1A)–(1C).   [71] PCA 1967, s 5(1)(a).

[72] HSCA 1993, s 3(1); LGA 1974, s 26(1); PSO(W)A 2005, s 7(1).

[73] PCA 1967, s 12(3) (emphasis added).

[74] HSCA 1993, s 3(4)–(6) (subject to a proviso concerning the merits of decisions taken in the exercise of clinical judgement: s 3(7)); LGA 1974, s 34(3); SPSOA 2002, s 7(1) (subject to an exception concerning

decision-making *process*, not with the substantive *merits* of administrative acts and decisions. This distinction is, as we saw in Chapters 12 and 13, a familiar one in administrative law, but one that is hard, if not impossible, to draw cleanly.

The legislation establishing the Ombudsman intentionally did not define the concept of maladministration. However, during the parliamentary debates, the government Minister responsible for the passage of the legislation through the House of Commons did provide an indicative list—the 'Crossman catalogue'—of the sort of things covered by the concept: 'bias, neglect, inattention, delay, incompetence, inaptitude, perversity, turpitude, arbitrariness and so on.'[75] By 1993, things had moved on and the Ombudsman's view was that the Crossman catalogue needed updating. Maladministration could include administrative failures such as rudeness, unwillingness to treat a complainant as a person with rights, knowingly giving misleading or inadequate advice, offering no redress or manifestly disproportionate redress, faulty procedures, failure to monitor compliance with adequate procedures, cavalier disregard of guidance designed to ensure equitable treatment, and failure to mitigate the effects of rigid adherence to the letter of the law that produces unequal treatment.[76] The flexibility inherent in the concept of maladministration allows room for manoeuvre by the Ombudsman to update its jurisdiction in accordance with developing ideas of the standards to be expected of government. However, it is not an unbounded concept: as we explain below, ombudsmen are amenable to judicial review, including in relation to the way in which they define maladministration.

More recently, the Parliamentary Ombudsman has made a conscious move away from defining maladministration and towards defining the principles of *good* administration.[77] As Figure 16.4 shows, the Ombudsman applies six key principles of good administration. Maladministration is defined by reference to those principles—in other words, maladministration is likely to be discerned when public bodies fall short of the Ombudsman's principles of good administration.

Q How do the Ombudsman's principles of good administration differ from those that courts uphold via judicial review? Why do you think the two sets of principles differ from one another?

5.4 **Injustice**

Ombudsmen are not concerned with maladministration per se, but maladministration productive of injustice to the complainant.[78] If, therefore, maladministration is found

---

the merits of decisions involving clinical judgement: s 7(2)); PSO(W)A 2005, s 11(1) (subject to a similar exception: s 11(2)); O(NI)O 1996, art 10(5); CC(NI)O 1996, art 9(5).

[75] Hansard HC Deb, vol 734, col 51 (Richard Crossman MP). See also Marshall, 'Maladministration' [1973] PL 32.   [76] Parliamentary Ombudsman, *Annual Report 1993* (HC 290 1993–94).

[77] Parliamentary and Health Service Ombudsman, *Principles of Good Administration* (London 2009).

[78] This underlines the fact that, as noted earlier in the chapter, the UK ombudsmen are concerned with 'redress', not exclusively with 'control'.

Principle	Examples
Getting it right	Acting in accordance with the law and with regard for the rights of those concerned; acting in accordance with the public body's policy and guidance (published or internal); taking proper account of established good practice; providing effective services, using appropriately trained and competent staff; taking reasonable decisions, based on all relevant considerations
Being customer-focused	Ensuring that people can access services easily; informing customers what they can expect and what the public body expects of them; keeping to its commitments, including any published service standards; dealing with people helpfully, promptly, and sensitively, bearing in mind their individual circumstances; responding to customers' needs flexibly, including, where appropriate, coordinating a response with other service providers
Being open and accountable	Being open and clear about policies and procedures, and ensuring that information and any advice provided is clear, accurate, and complete; stating its criteria for decision-making and giving reasons for decisions; handling information properly and appropriately; keeping proper and appropriate records; taking responsibility for its actions
Acting fairly and proportionately	Treating people impartially, with respect and courtesy; treating people without unlawful discrimination or prejudice and ensuring no conflict of interests; dealing with people and issues objectively and consistently; ensuring that decisions and actions are proportionate, appropriate, and fair
Putting things right	Acknowledging mistakes and apologising where appropriate; putting mistakes right quickly and effectively; providing clear and timely information on how and when to appeal or complain; operating an effective complaints procedure, which includes offering a fair and appropriate remedy when a complaint is upheld
Seeking continuous improvement	Reviewing policies and procedures regularly to ensure that they are effective; asking for feedback, and using it to improve services and performance; ensuring that the public body learns lessons from complaints, and uses these to improve services and performance

Figure 16.4 Ombudsman's principles of good administration

to have occurred, it is then necessary to consider whether injustice was sustained in consequence of it.[79] Like the concept of maladministration applied by ombudsmen, the notion of injustice is a broader one than that applicable in legal proceedings. It has been said judicially that, in the ombudsman context, 'injustice' covers 'not merely injury redressible in a court of law, but also "the sense of outrage aroused by unfair or incompetent administration, even where the complainant has suffered no actual

---

[79] PCA 1967, s 5(1)(a); HSCA 1993, s 3(1) ('injustice or hardship'); LGA 1974, s 26A(1); SPSOA 2002, s 5(3) ('injustice or hardship'); PSO(W)A 2005, s 4(1) ('injustice or hardship'); O(NI)O 1996, art 9(2); CC(NI)O 1996, art 8(3).

loss".[80] This means that 'the defence familiar in legal proceedings, that because the outcome would have been the same in any event there has been no redressible wrong, does not run in an investigation by the [Ombudsman]'.[81] For example, in the 'debt of honour' case, the Ombudsman concluded that 'the principal form of injustice [the complainant] has suffered is not financial';[82] rather, it consisted in the sense of outrage and distress engendered by the implication that he was 'not sufficiently British to receive a payment', having believed, on the basis of the Ministry of Defence's original, unclear statement, that he would receive such a payment.[83]

Finally, on this point, it should be noted that it is not sufficient that injustice has occurred: it must have occurred 'in consequence of' maladministration[84]—that is, the injustice must have been caused by maladministration. In the *Bradley* case, which we examine in detail below, Bean J said that this requires there to be 'at least a material increase in risk, or the loss of a chance of a better outcome, caused by maladministration in the individual case'.[85]

5.5 Judicial review

Ombudsmen, being public bodies themselves, are amenable to judicial review. So, while the legislation tends to be broadly drafted—'maladministration' is, as we have seen, largely undefined; Ombudsmen 'may', not 'must', investigate matters within their jurisdiction,[86] and so on—the discretionary powers of ombudsmen are not unlimited; rather, the courts are capable of stepping in if ombudsmen exceed the scope of their discretion or otherwise act contrary to the principles of judicial review. This has been established in several contexts, of which the following are illustrative.

First, the Ombudsman's discretion *whether to undertake an investigation* is open to judicial review. (In contrast, it seems that an MP's decision whether to *refer* a complaint to the Ombudsman is not[87].) For example, in *Dyer*, the claimant sought judicial review of the Ombudsman's decision to investigate only certain aspects of her complaint.[88] However, it was argued on behalf of the Ombudsman that judicial review was inappropriate in light of the drafting of the 1967 Act and the fact that the Ombudsman is accountable to Parliament via (what is now) the Public Administration

---

[80] *R v Parliamentary Commissioner for Administration, ex p Balchin (No 1)* [1997] JPL 917, 926, *per* Sedley J, endorsing the view of De Smith, Woolf, and Jowell, *Judicial Review of Administrative Action* (London 1999), [1.102], quoting Richard Crossman MP.   [81] *Balchin (No 1)* at 926, *per* Sedley J.

[82] Parliamentary Ombudsman, 'A Debt of Honour': *The Ex Gratia Scheme for British Groups Interned by the Japanese During the Second World War* (HC 324 2005–06), [203].

[83] Parliamentary Ombudsman, HC 324, [204].

[84] PCA 1967, s 5(1)(a); HSCA 1993, s 3(1) ('injustice or hardship'); LGA 1974, s 26A(1); SPSOA 2002, s 5(3) ('injustice or hardship'); PSO(W)A 2005, s 4(1) ('injustice or hardship'); O(NI)O 1996, art 9(2); CC(NI)O 1996, art 8(3).

[85] *R (Bradley) v Secretary of State for Work and Pensions* [2007] EWHC 242 (Admin), [2009] QB 114, [68].

[86] See, eg PCA 1967, s 5(1).

[87] *R (Murray) v Parliamentary Commissioner for Administration* [2002] EWCA Civ 1472, [17].

[88] *R v Parliamentary Commissioner for Administration, ex p Dyer* [1994] 1 WLR 621.

Select Committee. Simon Brown LJ, with whom Buckley J agreed, 'unhesitatingly' rejected that argument: '[m]any in government' were accountable to Parliament, but also subject to supervision by the courts, and there was nothing 'so singular [about the Ombudsman] as to take him wholly outside the purview of judicial review'.[89] However, his Lordship did accept that the 1967 Act was drafted so as to emphasise the width of the Ombudsman's discretion; taking that point into account, together with the fact that the exercise of such discretion 'inevitably involves a high degree of subjective judgment', intensive judicial review would be inappropriate.[90]

Second, the exercise of the discretion *whether to investigate notwithstanding the possibility of a judicial review or tribunal claim* is also amenable to review. In the *Croydon* case, following an adverse report by the Local Government Ombudsman about its arrangements for allocating secondary school places, a local authority sought judicial review alleging, among other things, that the Ombudsman had lacked jurisdiction to investigate given that the parents of the child concerned could have sought judicial review of its decision.[91] That argument did not persuade Woolf J to set aside the Ombudsman's report,[92] but the case established two presently relevant points: that when judicial review or appeal to a tribunal is possible, ombudsmen will generally act unlawfully if they fail to exercise their discretion by *considering* whether to refuse to investigate (or discontinue an investigation) on that ground; and that while such an exercise of discretion, if it takes place, is, in principle, amenable to judicial review, such review is unlikely to be intensive. This discretion is therefore a broad one.

Third, the courts have shown themselves willing to *limit the scope of ombudsmen's investigations*. In *Cavanagh*, the complainant's daughter was referred by one consultant to a second at the same hospital for specialist diagnosis and treatment, which the second consultant provided.[93] Some months later, the second consultant's department was closed by the hospital, and the girl's treatment ended. The complainant alleged to the Health Service Ombudsman that the hospital authorities were guilty of maladministration by failing to ensure continuing care following the closure of the relevant department. To the surprise of the complainant and the consultants—all three of whom sought judicial review—the Ombudsman concluded that the hospital authorities were not at fault, but that the doctors were by having misdiagnosed the girl's condition. Sedley LJ said that the Ombudsman 'has no power of investigation at large': her powers 'do not enable her to expand the ambit of a complaint beyond what it contains, nor to expand her investigation of it beyond what the complaint warrants'.[94] By investigating the quality of the clinical judgements in the case—matters that had not been complained about—the Ombudsman had therefore exceeded her powers.

---

[89] *Dyer* at 625.

[90] *Dyer* at 626. As a result, the Ombudsman's refusal to investigate certain aspects of the complaint withstood judicial scrutiny.

[91] *R v Commissioner for Local Administration, ex p Croydon London Borough Council* [1989] 1 All ER 1033.   [92] Although other arguments did lead to a declaration that the report was void.

[93] *R (Cavanagh) v Health Service Commissioner for England* [2005] EWCA Civ 1578, [2006] 1 WLR 1229.

[94] *Cavanagh* at [16].

Fourth, the courts are willing to scrutinise, applying the normal principles of judicial review, *whether an ombudsman's decision-making and conclusions are lawful.* These points emerge from the *Balchin* saga, which involved no fewer than three—successful—challenges to the Parliamentary Ombudsman's handling of a particular case.[95] The complainants were aggrieved by events surrounding a local authority's decision to build a new road near their house, the result of which was to reduce its value, and by the Department of Transport's refusal to insist, before granting permission for the road to be built, on the local authority's buying the house from the complainants at its original (higher) value. In the first case, Sedley J struck down the Ombudsman's report, which concluded that no maladministration had occurred, because he had failed to take account of a *relevant consideration*—namely, whether the Department ought to have drawn the local authority's attention to new statutory powers that it could have exercised to acquire the complainants' property. The Ombudsman (who by now was a different person) looked at the case again, and again concluded that there had been no maladministration; again, the court struck the report down, this time holding that the Ombudsman's *reasoning* was insufficient to demonstrate that he had a sound basis for concluding that the Department had not itself overlooked the existence of the new statutory powers. Finally, in the third case, the Ombudsman's third report was struck down again because of *inadequate reasons*: this time, the court found internal inconsistencies in the report that meant that there had been a 'failure to give adequate reasons for his decision that there was no maladministration' during a particular phase of the process.[96]

In the second of the *Balchin* cases, Dyson J defended the willingness of the courts—revealed by this series of judgments—to review the Ombudsman's decisions, arguing that the courts were engaging in scrutiny only of the Ombudsman's decision-making process, not of the substance of the decisions. However, it has been argued that the judicial attitude evidenced by the *Balchin* litigation is problematic for three reasons. First, it is not obviously appropriate or necessary: the rationale for judicial control of government Ministers and other public bodies is to ensure that they are not permitted to govern unlawfully. But the Ombudsman does not govern; as Endicott puts it, her role is simply 'to decide whether to make a public criticism of the government'.[97] Second, the risk arises of courts usurping the Ombudsman's role—something that would be justified only 'if judges were generally better at an ombudsman's work than ombudsmen are'.[98] Third, undue judicial control of ombudsmen risks the loss of their distinctiveness. Giddings argues that the prospect of judicial review may cause ombudsmen to act defensively by adopting a more formal method of working—which could 'put at risk the essential informality and accessibility' of ombudsmen.[99]

---

[95] *R v Parliamentary Commissioner for Administration, ex p Balchin (No 1)* [1997] JPL 917; *(No2)* (2000) 79 P & CR 157; *(No 3)* [2002] EWHC 1876 (Admin).   [96] *Balchin (No 3)* at [51].

[97] *Administrative Law* (Oxford 2009), p 490.   [98] Endicott, p 491.

[99] *'Ex p Balchin:* Findings of Maladministration and Injustice' [2000] PL 201, 203.

Q Do you share these concerns? Do they suggest that ombudsmen should never be subject to judicial review? Or should they be subject only to limited review—and, if so, in what circumstances do you think it would be appropriate for courts to intervene?

Finally, we merely note at present—because we address this point in detail below—that ombudsmen's decisions are subject to indirect judicial scrutiny when people (typically those whose complaints to an ombudsman have been upheld by him or her) seek judicial review of *government* decisions to reject the ombudsman's findings or to refuse to implement the ombudsman's recommendations.

6. Compliance

Can ombudsmen really make a difference? If they are to be effective, two essential requirements must be met. First, ombudsmen must be able to conduct their investigations in an effective manner—meaning, among other things, that they must be able to get answers to questions, access to relevant documentation, and so on. Second, when they find injustice occasioned by maladministration and accordingly make recommendations, the responsible public bodies must be, or must consider themselves to be, in some sense required to accept and act on such findings. If ombudsmen's reports were merely to gather dust on shelves, there would be little point in producing them in the first place: they would neither provide an effective means for the redress of grievances, nor an effective means of enhancing the quality of administration. The extent to which these two criteria are met by the UK's public sector ombudsmen schemes—and in particular by that pertaining to the Parliamentary Ombudsman—is the focus of concern in this part of the chapter.

6.1 Cooperation with the ombudsmen

Getting to the heart of matters complained of often requires careful evaluation of a range of evidence—indeed, one of the strengths of the system is that ombudsmen are more willing and better equipped than the Administrative Court to undertake such work—but such evaluation is possible only if, in the first place, ombudsmen can get at the raw factual material.

In the interests of natural justice, ombudsmen are required to afford the relevant public body a chance of putting its own side of the story: for example, the Parliamentary Ombudsman must give the principal officer of the public body concerned, along with anyone named in the complaint, an opportunity to comment on any allegations made in it.[100] However, ombudsmen will usually wish—indeed, need—to go further, by talking to, or otherwise communicating with, a range of officials and employees of the public

---

[100] PCA 1967, s 7(1).

body that is the subject of the complaint, and perhaps of other public bodies, and by gaining access to official papers, correspondence, minutes of meetings, emails, and so on. In many instances, public bodies will cooperate willingly with ombudsmen, granting interviews with staff and facilitating access to material. But ombudsmen may sometimes be faced with more obstructive attitudes, and it is therefore important that they have at their disposal a range of coercive powers that can be deployed if the evidence that they request is not forthcoming. Here, we focus on the Parliamentary Ombudsman, although similar powers are possessed by other public sector ombudsmen. Three points should be noted.

First, the Ombudsman is able to 'require any Minister, officer or member' of the department or body concerned, along with 'any other person who in his opinion is able to furnish information or produce documents relevant to the investigation', to provide such material.[101] Moreover, the Ombudsman, like a court, can require witnesses to attend for examination and to produce documents.[102]

Second, being authorised to require something is all very well—but what happens if those upon whom such requirements are placed refuse to fulfil them? Section 9 of the 1967 Act gives the Ombudsman real teeth in this regard. If, without lawful excuse, someone 'obstructs' an investigation, the Ombudsman can refer the matter to the High Court. The Court may then inquire into the matter, hearing witnesses, and may deal with the person concerned as 'if he had committed the like offence in relation to the Court'. What this boils down to is that failing to cooperate with the Ombudsman is equivalent to committing the criminal offence of contempt of court—an offence that is punishable by imprisonment.[103]

Third, it is worth emphasising the significance and breadth of the Ombudsman's powers to require the provision of information. It is not a power of unlimited breadth: the Ombudsman is explicitly *unable* to require information relating to Cabinet (including Cabinet committee) proceedings.[104] Importantly, however, the Act provides that obligations 'to maintain secrecy' and other restrictions concerning the disclosure of information imposed on 'persons in Her Majesty's service' do *not* apply for the purposes of the Ombudsman's investigations.[105] This means, among other things, that information the disclosure of which would normally be a criminal offence under the Official Secrets Act 1989 can (without criminal liability)—indeed, must—be disclosed to the Ombudsman when requested.[106] It should also be noted that the Ombudsman's ability to require the provision of information far exceeds that of members of the public under the Freedom of Information Act 2000: while, as we have seen,[107] that legislation is hedged around with exceptions and qualifications, those restrictions do not apply to the Ombudsman. It is important to note in this regard that the Ombudsman's investigations take place in private,[108] and it is therefore not the case that all information

---

[101] PCA 1967, s 8(1).   [102] PCA 1967, s 8(2).

[103] On contempt, see Chapter 20, section 3.3, below.

[104] PCA 1967, s 8(4).   [105] PCA 1967, s 8(3).

[106] On the Official Secrets Act, see Chapter 20, section 7.2, below.

[107] See Chapter 10, section 7.2, above.   [108] PCA 1967, s 7(2).

obtained by the Ombudsman finds its way into the public domain. Indeed, if the Ombudsman *publishes* information covered by the Official Secrets Act, that may constitute a criminal offence.[109] Getting the Ombudsman to conduct an investigation is therefore not a way of circumventing the limitations imposed by the official secrecy and freedom of information legislation: disclosure is only to the Ombudsman, although, of course, the information, once disclosed, will form part of the factual basis on which the Ombudsman makes her assessment of whether maladministration occasioning injustice has occurred. To the extent, then, that legal restrictions upon access to official information constitute an obstacle to holding government to account, the powers of the Ombudsman to obtain otherwise non-disclosable information represent an important qualification.

6.2 **Securing redress–politics**

Once an investigation has been completed by the Ombudsman, a report is produced and sent to (among others) the MP who originally referred the complaint to the Ombudsman and to the principal officer of the department or body against which the complaint was made.[110] In addition to such complaint-specific reports, the Ombudsman is required to lay an annual report before Parliament 'on the performance of his functions under [the 1967] Act' and is permitted to lay such other reports as is thought fit.[111] It is in reports laid before Parliament that the Ombudsman raises systemic problems uncovered as a result of investigations, whereas case-specific reports are concerned with determining whether maladministration occasioning injustice has occurred and, if so, what steps should be taken to remedy such injustice.

It is up to the Ombudsman—subject to the fact that her discretion is bounded by the normal principles of judicial review, such as rationality—to decide what, if any, redress she should recommend in a given case. The Ombudsman has publicly indicated the principles she applies when making such decisions.[112] Her aims are to secure 'suitable and proportionate remedies' for complainants and similarly situated individuals, and to require public bodies 'to be fair and to take responsibility, to acknowledge failures and apologise for them, to make amends, and to use the opportunity to improve their services'.[113] Applying these principles, the Ombudsman will recommend remedies that she considers appropriate to the circumstances of the case. These can include a simple apology, conferring upon the complainant a benefit or status denied to him, changes to an administrative scheme that has been found to be faulty,[114] and the payment of financial compensation. On the latter point, the Ombudsman recognises that public

---

109 This is explicitly contemplated by PCA 1967, s 11(2)(b).   110 PCA 1967, s 10(1)–(2).

111 PCA 1967, s 10(4).

112 Parliamentary and Health Service Ombudsman, *Principles for Remedy* (London 2009).

113 *Principles for Remedy*, p 1.

114 For example, in the 'debt of honour' case, considered above, the Ombudsman recommended that the Ministry of Defence should review the compensation scheme the terms and operation of which lay at the heart of the complaint.

bodies need to strike a 'balance between responding appropriately to people's complaints and acting proportionately within available resources', but has said that 'finite resources should not be used as an excuse for failing to provide a fair remedy'.[115]

The vast majority—typically over 99 per cent—of the Ombudsman's recommendations are followed.[116] But what if they are not? Should it be possible to *require* public bodies to implement the Ombudsman's recommendations? If so, what form should such a requirement take? Who should enforce it, and how? These questions ultimately resolve into a single dilemma: should the decision whether or not to implement the Ombudsman's recommendations be a political one, or, alternatively, should the Ombudsman's recommendations be legally enforceable, if necessary, by the courts? Thus we encounter one of our three key themes: the relationship between political and legal modes of constitutionalism. Who should we trust to see that the Ombudsman's reports are respected and her recommendations followed: politicians or judges? We address that question below; before doing so, it is necessary to consider what the current position actually is.

The position in relation to the Parliamentary Ombudsman, like nearly all other UK public sector ombudsmen,[117] is that her reports are not legally binding in the sense that a public body is not under any legal obligation to accept and follow them; rather, the system is premised on the twin notions that public bodies will generally do the right thing by implementing the Ombudsman's recommendations—and that when this does not happen, the political system, when appropriate, will facilitate a resolution of the matter. As to the last point, s 10(3) of the 1967 Act is pivotal. It empowers the Ombudsman, if it appears to her that injustice occasioned by maladministration 'has not been, or will not be remedied', to lay a special report before Parliament drawing its attention to the case. It is then for Parliament to take whatever steps, if any, it thinks appropriate to see that the public body concerned puts things right. Only very rarely has the Ombudsman considered it necessary to invoke her s 10(3) power: just six special reports have ever been laid before Parliament. But it is noteworthy that four of them have been issued since 2005,[118] raising concerns that, over recent years, government has become too willing to dismiss the Ombudsman's findings and recommendations.

6.3 The Equitable Life affair

A recent example concerns the affair of the Equitable Life Assurance Society, a pension provider. It made certain guarantees to policyholders about the level of

---

[115] *Principles for Remedy*, p 1.

[116] Parliamentary Ombudsman, *Every Complaint Matters: Annual Report 2008–09* (HC 786 2008–09), p 36.   [117] The exceptions are considered below.

[118] The four in question are the 'debt of honour' case, considered above, the Equitable Life and 'pensions promise' cases, considered in this and the following section, and the Cold Comfort case concerning maladministration by the Rural Payments Agency (*Cold Comfort: The Administration of the 2005 Single Payment Scheme by the Rural Payments Agency* (HC 81 2009–10)).

pensions that they would receive upon retirement, but subsequently found itself unable to pay out at the levels that had been indicated. Of course, the Parliamentary Ombudsman has no power to investigate complaints about *private* bodies such as insurance companies and societies, but complaints were made against the *public* bodies responsible for regulating insurers. It was alleged that the regulators were guilty of maladministration that had caused injustice to policyholders in the form of loss of anticipated income. After a four-year investigation, the Ombudsman concluded that there had been 'serial regulatory failure', that there had been a 'series of missed opportunities' for the responsible public bodies to identify and seek to deal with the difficulties that Equitable was getting into, and that the regulators had been 'passive, reactive and complacent' in their approach.[119] Against that background, she recommended, among other things, that the government should establish a compensation scheme with the aim of 'put[ting] those people who have suffered a relative loss[120] back into the position that they would have been in had maladministration not occurred'.[121]

The House of Commons Public Administration Select Committee, the job of which it is to scrutinise the Ombudsman's reports, responded by supporting the Ombudsman. It regarded her report as a 'compelling' one that painted a 'damning picture' of the regulation of Equitable Life, and supported her call for compensation.[122] While recognising the need to strike a balance between taxpayers' and policyholders' interests,[123] the Committee concluded that the compensation scheme should aim to 'restore individuals to the position they would have been in had maladministration not occurred',[124] and that it should apply to all of those who had suffered loss as a result of that maladministration. In particular, the Committee said that it would 'not be appropriate to compensate only those policyholders...who are experiencing financial hardship; the payment of compensation is not a matter of charity but a requirement of justice to redress a wrong'.[125] The Committee also warned that the government should not use a separate report, which had highlighted serious mismanagement at Equitable Life itself, to justify a refusal properly to compensate those who had suffered because of regulators' failure to identify and deal with that mismanagement.[126] It said that it would be 'deeply concerned if the Government chose to act as judge on its own behalf by refusing to accept that maladministration took place'.[127]

---

[119] Parliamentary Ombudsman, *Equitable Life: A Decade of Regulatory Failure* (HC 815 2007–08), pp 372–5.

[120] That is, a loss compared to the position in which they would have been had they invested elsewhere.

[121] Parliamentary Ombudsman, HC 815, p 395.

[122] House of Commons Public Administration Select Committee, *Second Report* (HC 41 2008–09), [17] and [47]–[50].

[123] House of Commons Public Administration Select Committee, HC 41, [47].

[124] House of Commons Public Administration Select Committee, HC 41, [65].

[125] House of Commons Public Administration Select Committee, HC 41, [84].

[126] House of Commons Public Administration Select Committee, HC 41, [49].

[127] House of Commons Public Administration Select Committee, HC 41, [117].

In fact, the government behaved precisely as the Committee had feared. It refused to accept several of the Ombudsman's specific findings of maladministration (and of injustice resulting therefrom),[128] it invoked the separate report mentioned above in exactly the way in which the Committee had said that it should not,[129] and it refused to implement a full compensation scheme, undertaking instead to compensate only those who had suffered a 'disproportionate impact'.[130] The Committee responded by saying that the government's proposal constituted an 'inadequate' remedy;[131] argued that the government, in responding to the Committee's earlier report, had misrepresented its views;[132] and said that the government's refusal to put right wrongs caused by maladministration was 'morally unacceptable'.[133] The Ombudsman responded by laying a special report before Parliament under s 10(3) of the 1967 Act[134]—but the then government stuck to its guns. One of the opposition parties insisted on a debate about the Equitable Life affair in October 2009 during which concerns were raised on all sides of the House of Commons about both the substance of the government's handling of the affair and its treatment of the Ombudsman. However, the Chief Secretary to the Treasury emphasised that the Ombudsman's report gave rise to no *legal* obligation to provide compensation and the government adhered to its view that the Ombudsman's recommendations should not be implemented in full.[135] The Chairman of the Public Administration Select Committee lamented the fact that the House of Commons had no formal machinery for resolving disputes between the government and the Ombudsman, and endorsed the view that whenever the government wishes to reject her findings or recommendations, it should be required to subject the matter to a debate and a free vote.[136] However, that not being the case, the government defeated, on a whipped vote, the opposition motion calling upon it to accept the Ombudsman's recommendations.

Following the 2010 general election, the new government said that it would implement the Ombudsman's recommendations,[137] although, at the time of writing, uncertainty remains about the level of compensation that will be offered. In any event, this episode remains instructive. Reflecting on it, the Ombudsman has drawn a distinction between the government's rejection of some of her findings of maladministration and its refusal to implement the compensation scheme that she considered necessary. As to the latter, she accepts that there are 'legitimate considerations of public policy and public purse'—that it is ultimately the government's responsibility to decide whether the

---

[128] HM Treasury, *The Prudential Regulation of the Equitable Life Assurance Society: the Government's Response to the Report of the Parliamentary Ombudsman's Investigation* (Cm 7538 2009), [4.4].

[129] HM Treasury, Cm 7538, [5.15].   [130] HM Treasury, Cm 7538, [5.22].

[131] House of Commons Public Administration Select Committee, *Sixth Report* (HC 219 2008–09), [2].

[132] House of Commons Public Administration Select Committee, HC 219, [33].

[133] House of Commons Public Administration Select Committee, HC 219, [60].

[134] Parliamentary and Health Service Ombudsman, *Injustice Unremedied: The Government's Response on Equitable Life* (HC 435 2008–09).   [135] HC Deb, vol 497, col 931.

[136] HC Deb, vol 497, cols 942–4.

[137] HM Government, *The Coalition: Our Programme for Government* (London 2010), p 26.

general good is served by doing what the Ombudsman recommends. But she takes strong issue with the government's refusal to accept her findings of maladministration, arguing that the government failed to show adequate 'constitutional respect' for her office.[138] This mirrors concerns expressed by the Public Administration Select Committee (in relation to another case[139]) that government rejection of the Ombudsman's findings of maladministration raises 'fundamental constitutional issues about the position of the Ombudsman and the relationship between Parliament and the Executive'.[140] It concluded that '[t]he Parliamentary Commissioner[141] is Parliament's Ombudsman: Government must respect her'.[142]

> **Q** Why do you think the Ombudsman's special report, laid before Parliament under s 10(3) of the 1967 Act, did not cause Parliament to put the government under sufficient pressure to accede to the Ombudsman's recommendations? Does this episode suggest that the Ombudsman's findings and/or her recommendations should be legally binding upon the government?

6.4 **Securing redress—law?**

It might be thought that the answer to the question above is 'yes'—that the intransigence of the government (before the 2010 election) in the face of the Ombudsman's report (and the Public Administration Select Committee's support for her position) demonstrates a need to render her findings and recommendations legally enforceable. Indeed, the possibility of legal redress on the basis of ombudsmen's findings is not an unknown phenomenon. When the Northern Ireland Complaints Commissioner makes a finding of maladministration occasioning injustice, the person aggrieved may ask the county court to require the public body concerned to pay damages.[143] And in certain circumstances, the High Court can issue an order, such as an injunction, requiring the public body concerned to desist from any further conduct of the type that the Northern Ireland Commissioner has found to have occurred as a result of maladministration occasioning injustice.[144]

However, the 1967 Act makes no equivalent provision in respect of the Parliamentary Ombudsman. Whether—and, if so, to what extent—her reports are legally binding was the question before the court in the *Bradley* case, which arose from another investigation by the Ombudsman that resulted in the government rejecting some of her findings and refusing fully to implement her recommendations. The so-called 'pensions promise' case concerned allegations that tens of thousands of people had ended up with

---

[138] House of Commons Public Administration Select Committee, *Sixth Report* (HC 219 2008–09), Ev 1.

[139] The 'pensions promise' case, considered below.

[140] House of Commons Public Administration Select Committee, *Sixth Report 2005–06* (HC 1081 2005–06), [78].

[141] This is the term used to describe the Ombudsman in the PCA 1967, although the term 'ombudsman' is now commonly used.   [142] House of Commons Public Administration Select Committee, HC 1081, [79].

[143] CC(NI)O 1996, art 16.   [144] CC(NI)O 1996, art 17.

occupational pensions worth less than they anticipated, and that this situation had come about because of (among other things) regulatory failure by public bodies. The Ombudsman concluded that maladministration had occurred: the public bodies concerned had given assurances to policyholders that had led them reasonably to believe that their pensions were safer than they turned out to be. Furthermore, those bodies had decided on the basis of an inadequate consideration of relevant evidence to cut the minimum amount of assets that pension providers were required to hold, meaning that some providers had found themselves with insufficient assets to pay pensions at levels that would meet policyholders' expectations.[145] The Ombudsman recommended that the government should consider making arrangements for the restoration of policyholders' benefits 'by whichever means is most appropriate, including if necessary by payment from public funds, to replace the full amount lost by those individuals'.[146] As in the Equitable Life case, the government rejected the Ombudsman's findings of maladministration and refused to implement the principal recommendation set out above.[147]

Against that background, four policyholders sought judicial review of the government's decision to reject the Ombudsman's findings and to refuse to implement her recommendations.[148] It is important at this stage to note the distinction between rejection of the Ombudsman's *findings* (of maladministration or of injustice) and rejection of her *recommendations*. Rejection of recommendations is of more obvious practical importance: it means that victims will not get the redress that the Ombudsman thinks they should; the government may end up rejecting recommendations because it thinks that taxpayers' money should not be used in the way or to the extent that the Ombudsman said that it should. In contrast, the government may reject findings because it does not wish to accept the blame laid upon it by the Ombudsman; the consequence of this type of rejection is less obvious: nothing directly turns upon it, although, as we will see, the more free the government is to reject findings of fault, the more likely it is to be able lawfully to refuse to offer redress.

The argument in *Bradley* centred upon the government's rejection of the Ombudsman's findings. The Ombudsman[149] argued that the government was legally obliged to 'proceed on the basis that the ombudsman's findings of injustice caused by maladministration are correct unless they are quashed in judicial review proceedings'.[150] This would make it possible for Ministers lawfully to reject the Ombudsman's findings only in very rare circumstances. For that reason, the Court of Appeal rejected this submission: Sir John Chadwick, giving the leading judgment, quoted with approval the view of the Royal Institute of Public Administration that 'if he is prepared to take

---

[145] Parliamentary Ombudsman, *Trusting in the Pensions Promise* (HC 984 2005–06), ch 5.

[146] Parliamentary Ombudsman, HC 984, [6.15].

[147] Although subsequent improvements to an existing financial assistance scheme went some way towards providing recompense.

[148] *R (Bradley) v Secretary of State for Work and Pensions* [2007] EWHC 242 (Admin); [2008] EWCA Civ 36, [2009] QB 114.

[149] Making submissions to the court as an interested party.   [150] *Bradley* at [135].

the consequences, and defend his position in Parliament, in the last resort a minister who genuinely believes that he and his department have been unfairly criticised by the commissioner, clearly has the right to say so'.[151] Sir John therefore concluded that Ministers and public bodies are free to reject the Ombudsman's findings provided that doing so is *rational*. On the face of it, this seems to give a broad discretion to reject such findings: as we have seen, the standard test for whether something is irrational is whether it outrageously defies logic or accepted moral standards.[152]

However, Sir John actually appeared to apply a more exacting concept of rationality, saying that the Minister had to have 'cogent reasons' for rejecting the Ombudsman's findings[153]—a test said in a later case to require the court to engage in a 'careful examination of the facts of the individual case'.[154] Applying that relatively strict version of the rationality test, the Court concluded that the Minister *had* acted irrationally in rejecting the Ombudsman's findings that the government's information had been potentially misleading and that the maladministration had caused some injustice. Varuhas argues that it was inappropriate for the Court to engage in such rigorous review of the government's decision to reject the Ombudsman's findings: he suggests that this risks displacing Parliament 'as the central institution for ensuring accountability', that this runs 'against the grain of the system of *political* accountability created by the [1967] Act', and that 'any challenge to the substance of the Minister's response [to the Ombudsman's report] is more appropriately made through political channels.'[155]

Q Do you agree? Are those 'political channels' sufficiently robust to permit meaningful challenges to ministerial rejections of ombudsmen's findings?

Notwithstanding that the outcome of *Bradley* was a victory for the policyholders, its practical consequences were limited. The judges, in effect, prevented the government from disclaiming its share of the responsibility for what had happened—the importance of which should not be underestimated in terms of government accountability—but their court victory did not get the policyholders any money. Instead, the government simply had to reconsider its rejection of the Ombudsman's *recommendation* concerning the provision of compensation in the light of the Ombudsman's *findings* of maladministration, which had effectively been reinstated by the Court. The reinstatement of those findings might make it more difficult for a Minister to conclude rationally that no compensation should be provided, but that is not inevitably the case.

This raises the question of whether it is possible to challenge government refusals to accept not only *findings*, but also *recommendations*. Precisely this point arose in

---

[151] *Bradley* at [135], quoting from Royal Institute of Public Administration, *The Parliamentary Ombudsman: A Study in the Control of Administrative Action* (London 1975), p 503.

[152] See Chapter 13, section 4.6.1, above.   [153] *Bradley* at [72].

[154] *R (Equitable Members Action Group) v HM Treasury* [2009] EWHC 2495 (Admin), [66].

[155] 'Governmental Rejections of Ombudsman Findings: What Role for the Courts?' (2009) 72 MLR 91, 111–12 (emphasis added).

the litigation arising out of the Equitable Life saga. A group representing Equitable policyholders sought judicial review of the government's refusal to accept the Ombudsman's *recommendation* concerning compensation.[156] They lost that part of the case. As in *Bradley*, the Court applied the rationality principle: the Minister could reject the Ombudsman's recommendation provided that to do so was not irrational. But, as we know, rationality can mean many different things[157] and, this time, the Court applied a much more relaxed standard: whether to establish a compensation scheme was 'a matter for the government, reporting to Parliament' and was 'not reviewable in the courts save on *conventional* rationality grounds'.[158] So it seems that getting courts to force the government to accept the Ombudsman's *recommendations* is harder than getting them to require the government to accept her *findings*.

> **Q** It might be argued that this is a perfectly sensible position, given that the decision whether to accept recommendations, unlike findings, is likely to have wide policy and/or financial implications. Would you agree with such an argument?

7. The wider complaints-handling system

We conclude this chapter with some necessary background about the wider complaints-handling system. It would be wrong to give the impression that ombudsmen exist in isolation; rather, they exist as part of, and in a sense at the apex of, a network of (non-judicial) public sector complaints-handlers. The importance of individuals having an effective opportunity to complain, and to have things put right when they have gone wrong, is especially important in the public sector, where there is often no possibility of 'exit'. This lack of 'exit' arises because people are often forced to deal with public bodies whether they like it or not: if someone wants a passport, their only option is to apply to the Home Office's Identity and Passport Service; there is not a range of providers competing on price and service levels.

Contemporary thinking about complaint-handling is based on a number of propositions. First, public bodies should operate systems for handling complaints that are both *effective and accessible*. Second, the design of any system of complaint-handling should acknowledge the importance of the notion of *proportionate dispute resolution*—that is, complaint-handling systems should be organised so that they only take up the time and resources that are necessary, bearing in mind the nature of the complaints and that complaints should be resolved as close to their source as is practicable. This means that complaints should, at the initial stage, be dealt with

---

[156] *R (Equitable Members Action Group) v HM Treasury* [2009] EWHC 2495 (Admin).
[157] See Chapter 13, section 4.6.1, above.
[158] *Equitable Members Action Group* at [132] (emphasis added).

in-house, if possible—that is, by the public body against which the complaint has been lodged. There is therefore a strong expectation that public bodies will have their own complaints procedures: indeed, as we have seen, the existence of effective complaints-handling systems forms part of one of the Parliamentary Ombudsman's principles of good administration.

There is no doubt that public bodies have responded to the expectation that complaints systems should exist: according to the National Audit Office, such systems are found in 'all government organisations'.[159] In most instances, public bodies operate their own complaint-handling systems, but Parliament has established independent bodies to investigate certain types of complaint. For example, the Independent Police Complaints Commission was established to provide an independent body to investigate complaints against the police because of the perceived lack of public confidence in, and independence of, the previous complaint-handling system.[160] Likewise, Parliament created the Office of the Independent Adjudicator to resolve students' complaints against higher education institutions.[161]

However, despite the proliferation of complaint-handling systems to be found throughout government, it has been recognised that the quality of those systems is not uniformly high. Indeed, it has been noted that '[c]omplainants often need time, persistence and stamina to pursue their complaint to a satisfactory conclusion and complaints processes can be difficult to access, understand and use'.[162] And complaints-handling is a time-consuming and costly business for government (and hence the taxpayer) too: the National Audit Office found that, in 2003–04, nearly 1.4 million complaints were made across central government, costing over £500 million.[163]

It is perhaps inevitable that the quality and nature of complaints systems across the breadth of the public sector will vary. Attempts are made, however, to disseminate and promote best practice. The Parliamentary and Health Service Ombudsman service has taken a lead in this area in recent years, seeing as an important part of its role the development and promotion of good practice. This culminated with the publication, in 2009, of its *Principles of Good Complaint Handling*, in which the Ombudsman implores public bodies (among other things) to provide clear information about complaints procedures, to make sure that staff are properly trained to handle complaints, to observe basic principles of fair and rational decision-making, to provide prompt and appropriate remedies, and to learn lessons from complaints.[164] The Ombudsman has also published a report specifically concerning the quality of complaints-handling in the Department for Work and Pensions—which, because of

---

[159] National Audit Office, *Citizen Redress: What Citizens Can Do if Things Go Wrong with Public Services* (HC 21 2004–05), p 19.　　　　　　　　　　　　　　　　[160] Police Reform Act 2002.

[161] Higher Education Act 2004.

[162] House of Commons Public Administration Select Committee, *Fifth Report* (HC 409 2007–08), [6].

[163] National Audit Office, HC 21, p 44.

[164] Parliamentary and Health Service Ombudsman, *Principles of Good Complaint Handling* (London 2009), pp 2–3.

the volume of decisions that it takes, receives a higher number of complaints than other public bodies.[165]

As well as acting as champions of best practice, ombudsman schemes exist as remedies of further resort in the event that complainants are unhappy with the outcome of local procedures. We saw earlier in this chapter that the Parliamentary and Health Service Ombudsman rejects large numbers of complaints each year because they are 'premature' in that complainants have failed to use local complaints procedures. It is in this sense that ombudsmen provide remedies of further, not first, resort: local mechanisms must be tried first. Indeed, in some areas of government that generate particularly high volumes of complaints—those in which the number of complaints are measured in the tens of thousands—intermediate complaints-handling systems have been interposed between in-house complaint procedures and the external investigation of complaints by the ombudsmen. For example, the Adjudicator's Office investigates complaints about HM Revenue and Customs (HMRC), while the Independent Case Examiner reviews complaints arising from the Department for Work and Pensions. These bodies are known as 'second-tier complaints handlers', with the Ombudsman standing as the 'ultimate independent arbiter of complaints about government administration and public services'.[166] The advantage of such second-tier complaint handlers is that they enable individuals who do not consider their complaints to have been satisfactorily dealt with by the public body then to pursue their complaints before an independent and external body. Such second-tier complaint handlers can also resolve many complaints informally through techniques such as mediation. This also has the advantages of avoiding the costs and lengthy delays associated with the more formal investigation of complaints and of ensuring that ombudsmen are not overwhelmed with a high volume of complaints. But, of course, the risk is that, in seeking to resolve complaints in this way, the overall system becomes more complex and hence more difficult for people to navigate. Indeed, the NHS complaints system was recently simplified: the second-tier adjudicator, the Healthcare Commission, was abolished, with complaints that cannot satisfactorily be resolved locally going directly (if complainants wish) to the Health Service Ombudsman.

A further means of complaint-handling that should be mentioned here is perhaps the most obvious of all: complaints taken up by MPs themselves. Anyone with a grievance can always simply write to his or her MP, who may then take the matter up with the relevant government Minister. After all, MPs are there not only to serve in the government or opposition, or to contribute to debates in Parliament, but also to act as constituency members—that is, taking up the interests and complaints of their constituents. Occasionally, an MP might take the matter further by raising a constituent's particular complaint through an adjournment debate in the House of Commons. It is not always apparent that government agencies respond to complaints made via MPs

---

[165] Parliamentary Ombudsman, *Putting Things Right: Complaints and Learning from the DWP* (HC 367 2008–09).   [166] Parliamentary Ombudsman, HC 409, [59].

satisfactorily. Consider, for example, the handling of MPs' letters by the UK Border Agency. As part of their constituency postbag, many MPs receive complaints concerning individuals' immigration difficulties and their interactions with the Border Agency, a body not always known for displaying high customer service standards. The MP may then take up the matter with the Agency. In 2008, the Agency received some 49,000 complaint letters from MPs, each of which cost £300 to process.[167] Even then, many MPs consider that the Agency's processing of such complaints is often poor, with both delays and inadequate replies being the commonest complaints.[168] The overall impression is that some government agencies have some way to go to improve both the quality of their basic administration and how they handle complaints.

From this broader discussion of complaint-handling, we can make a more general observation: ombudsmen are not the only formal administrative justice institutions to inhabit the world of complaints-handling. The type of things that may attract complaints are myriad, from delay and insensitivity at one end of the spectrum, through to fundamental mistakes of fact and law at the other. So the part of the administrative justice system to which a complaint progresses when it cannot satisfactorily be resolved through an informal, local procedure will depend largely upon its nature. If the grievance is one that goes to the substance of the public body's decision—if, for example, the individual considers that he has been wrongly denied a benefit to which he is entitled—then, in the absence of successful local resolution, its natural destination will be an appellate tribunal should one exist (and otherwise the Administrative Court). It is the tribunals system to which we turn our attention in the next chapter.

8. Concluding remarks

In this chapter, we have seen that ombudsmen play two key, and complementary, roles. They provide a mechanism by which individuals can obtain *redress* against public bodies that have caused injustice through maladministration, in circumstances in which the grievance has not been resolved by a local complaints procedure. And they also serve a *control* function by being able to identify, publicise, and recommend corrective action in the face of systemic administrative failure.

We have also seen that the role of ombudsmen raises important issues with respect to the key themes of this book—two of them in particular.[169] First, ombudsmen play an important role in relation to *the holding to account of the executive branch of*

---

[167] United Kingdom Border Agency, *Customer Strategy 2009–12* (London 2009), p 9.

[168] House of Commons Home Affairs Committee, *Managing Migration: The Points Based System* (HC 217 2008–09), [269]–[290].

[169] We also saw that our other key theme, that of the increasingly multilayered nature of the UK constitution, is engaged by the material covered in this chapter: ombudsman arrangements are increasingly diverse as a result of devolution, and the asymmetric nature of devolution poses particular challenges in respect of the reform of public sector ombudsmen in England, given its absence from the devolution settlement.

government (as well as of other public bodies). We know from earlier chapters that the capacity of Parliament effectively to call Ministers to account is limited in several respects and by several factors, not least the constitutional architecture of the UK, which entails only a limited separation of powers resulting in executive domination of the House of Commons. Against that background, the Parliamentary Ombudsman augments the capacity of MPs, and of Parliament as a whole, to hold the executive to account.[170] Investigations and reports by the Ombudsman are able to identify and expose administrative failures that might not otherwise come to light; the constitutional independence of the Ombudsman, together with her capacity to undertake detailed inquiries, means that her conclusions generally command respect. As such, investigations by ombudsmen represent a significant weapon in the armoury of politicians who wish to press the government for redress in particular cases and reform in the face of widespread maladministration.

However, we have also seen that the Ombudsman, even with the backing of the Public Administration Select Committee, does not always get her way. In recent years, the government has shown itself willing to reject her findings and recommendations, leaving identified injustice unremedied. Whether this is problematic—and, if it is, how the problem should be solved—is a matter of opinion. One response to the fact that the government sometimes disregards what the Ombudsman thinks is to say that such is the government's prerogative: it is (indirectly) elected; it enjoys the (indirect) imprimatur of the people; it should be free to conclude that the public good is best served by doing something other than that which the Ombudsman recommends, subject to the fact that such judgements may influence how people vote at the following general election. A second response is to say that the failure of politicians to secure implementation of the Ombudsman's recommendations in a number of recent high-profile cases is testimony to the fact that Parliament is a weak, ineffectual institution that is incapable of adequately holding the government to account. If that view is adopted, what should be done to improve things?

Here, we come up against—as we have throughout this book—the distinction between political and legal modes of constitutionalism. Whether the Ombudsman's findings and recommendations should carry the force of law to any extent—and, if so, to what extent: through mild or strong judicial review, or through legislative provision requiring public bodies to do what the Ombudsman tells them?—depends on whether we are more inclined to put our faith in the judges than in the political process. The former is tempting, but it is a temptation that should not be given into in this context. Rendering the Ombudsman's reports legally binding would make her, in effect, an adjunct of the judicial process, and would rob the ombudsman system of a great deal of its distinctiveness and utility. It is therefore strongly arguable that, in this area, at least, the drift towards greater reliance on legal control of government should be resisted.

---

[170] An equivalent point applies to other ombudsmen, such as the Scottish, Welsh, and Northern Irish Ombudsmen, who have reporting relationships with their respective legislatures.

Further reading

Abraham, 'The Ombudsman and Individual Rights' (2008) 61 Parliamentary Affairs 370

Abraham, 'The Ombudsman and the Executive: The Road to Accountability' (2008) 61 Parliamentary Affairs 535

Abraham, 'The Ombudsman as Part of the UK Constitution: A Contested Role?' (2008) 61 Parliamentary Affairs 206

Kirkham, *The Parliamentary Ombudsman: Withstanding the Test of Time* (HC421 2006–07)

Kirkham et al, 'Putting the Ombudsman into Constitutional Context' (2009) 62 Parliamentary Affairs 600

Seneviratne, *Ombudsmen: Public Services and Administrative Justice* (London 2002)

Useful websites

http://www.bioa.org.uk
Website of the British and Irish Ombudsman Association (with links to the various ombudsmen's websites)

17   Tribunals

One of the principal themes of this book is the effectiveness of the processes through which government is held to account. In Chapters 12–15, we examined one of the forms of legal accountability—judicial review. However, judicial review is not the sole, or even the most widely used, legal process through which government may be held to account. In most cases, when individuals wish to challenge an administrative decision, they appeal against that decision to an administrative tribunal. Tribunals are the primary mechanism provided by Parliament for the resolution of disputes between individuals and the state, and, in some instances, disputes between individuals. As a mechanism for providing judicial, legal accountability of governmental decision-making, tribunals determine vastly more cases than the higher courts. This chapter considers the constitutional importance of the many and various tribunals that determine appeals against initial decisions taken by governmental agencies. It also examines the place of tribunals within the United Kingdom's public law system and the recent reorganisation of the tribunals into a new, integrated and unified, tribunals system brought about by the Tribunals, Courts and Enforcement Act 2007 (TCEA). An overview of principal tribunal systems, tribunal procedures, and judicial oversight of tribunal decision-making is also provided.

1. Tribunals

1.1 What are tribunals?

Tribunals are statutory bodies that hear and determine appeals by individuals against initial decisions made by governmental decision-makers; in some instances, tribunals resolve disputes between individuals. Consider the following situations. A foreign national who has been refused political asylum by the Home Office may appeal against that decision to the Immigration and Asylum Chamber of the First-tier Tribunal (FTT).[1] An individual whose application for a welfare benefit has been refused by

---

[1] We explain what is meant by 'First-tier Tribunal' and its constituent chambers when we consider the structure of the new tribunals system in section 3 below.

the Department for Work and Pensions may appeal to the FTT's Social Entitlement Chamber. A child who has been refused admission to the school of his or her choice by a local authority may appeal to a school admissions appeal panel. In each of these instances, an individual dissatisfied with an initial decision taken by a governmental agency can appeal to an independent judicial tribunal. The individual concerned can either appear before the tribunal at an appeal hearing or submit written arguments in support of the appeal being allowed. The tribunal will then determine the appeal and can substitute its own decision for that of the initial decision-maker by either allowing or dismissing the appeal. The tribunal's decision will be binding upon the parties.

Tribunals are a vitally important part of the legal system, providing access to justice for a large community of users across a wide range of issues. As the courts have noted: 'In this day and age a right of access to a Tribunal or other adjudicative mechanism established by the state is just as important and fundamental as a right of access to the courts.'[2] As far as individual appellants are concerned, they are far more likely to have contact with a formal adjudication process by appealing to a tribunal rather than by applying for judicial review or, indeed, going to any other part of the legal system.

In many areas, tribunals are the primary avenue for challenging governmental decisions, and they specialise in determining appeals and administering the law in their own jurisdictions. Indeed, it is no exaggeration to say that some tribunal systems comprise legal systems in their own right, with their own procedural rules, judiciary, law reports, and legal cultures. When viewed collectively, tribunals comprise the most important component of the legal system for ensuring legality in respect of the mass of front-line decision-making that characterises modern government.

Like ombudsmen and complaint procedures, examined in the previous chapter, tribunals comprise a central part of the administrative justice system. In the modern state, all levels of government—central, devolved, and local—are responsible for administering complex public policy programmes across the range of political and social life. To administer such programmes, officials take decisions that can affect individuals' lives. However, no decision-making process is perfect: mistakes and errors may occur frequently and generate a sense of grievance on the part of those affected. Furthermore, the sheer scale of decision-making required by the administration of policies—for example, in the areas of social security, immigration, and education— creates the potential for an enormous volume of disputes.

The role of tribunals within the administrative justice system is to enable individuals dissatisfied with initial governmental decisions to appeal against them to an independent judicial decision-making body. Simply appealing to the government agency's sense of fairness is not, and never has been, sufficient; there has to be some further form of redress if the state is to discharge its responsibility for ensuring that its decisions are correct. Furthermore, the mechanism for securing such redress needs to be demonstrably independent of the governmental agency responsible for making the

---

2 *Saleem v Home Secretary* [2000] Imm AR 529, 544, *per* Hale LJ.

initial decision. Because tribunals enable individuals dissatisfied with an initial decision to challenge that decision by way of an appeal, they comprise an essential aspect of the administrative justice system.

Tribunals were created on an ad hoc basis in specialist areas of government with little consideration of the coherence of the 'tribunal system' as a whole. However, over recent years, government policy has shifted to ensure greater coherence. The TCEA has established a new simplified statutory framework for tribunals. The principal issues that we will be addressing will therefore be the extent to which tribunals now comprise a distinct system and the degree to which tribunals provide individuals with an effective remedy for challenging administrative decisions. However, it is necessary first to consider the historical development of tribunals and the nature of the 'tribunals world' today, before going on to examine the nature of tribunal appeals and the reasons for their creation.

1.2 **Historical background**

While the number of tribunals increased dramatically over the last century, tribunals have been with us for some time and are a well-established aspect of our legal system. The General Commissioners of Income Tax—the oldest form of tribunal—were established in 1799. During the nineteenth century, tribunals became a popular choice of government to resolve disputes speedily.[3] Tribunals such as the Board of Railway Commissioners were established. However, it was during the twentieth century, with the development of the welfare state, that tribunals proliferated. As government established schemes such as National Insurance and old-age pensions, it also established processes for determining appeals against administrative decisions. The development of tribunals therefore reflects changes in the scope of government. As government took on responsibility for the administration of new public functions, tribunals were established in order to resolve disputes.

With the growth in tribunals, the Franks Report in 1957 investigated the procedure and operation of tribunals. This report stated that tribunals should promote three values—openness, fairness, and impartiality—and recommended improvements in tribunals.[4] Following the Franks Report, Parliament provided that tribunals should be overseen by the Council on Tribunals, that they should give reasons for their decisions, and that there should be an appeal from the decisions of certain tribunals on a point of law to the High Court.[5] Following the report, the 'tribunals maze' continued to expand and concerns were expressed over the unsystematic nature of tribunals.[6]

---

[3] See generally Stebbings, *Legal Foundations of Tribunals in Nineteenth Century England* (Cambridge 2006).

[4] *Report of the Committee on Administrative Tribunals and Enquiries* (Cmnd 218 1959) (the Franks Report), [23].   [5] Tribunals and Inquiries Act 1958.

[6] Bradley, 'The Tribunals Maze' [2002] PL 200; Robson, *Justice and Administrative Law: A Study of the British Constitution* (London 1951), ch 3; Allen, 'Administrative Jurisdiction' [1956] PL 13.

New tribunals were established in the fields of immigration, mental health, and education, amongst others.

Over recent years, the government has introduced major reforms to the tribunal system. This reform agenda commenced with the Leggatt Report on tribunals published in 2001, which was followed by a White Paper published in 2004 entitled *Transforming Public Services.*[7] Parliament subsequently passed the TCEA. The changes introduced by this reform agenda, and their significance, are considered throughout this chapter.

1.3 **The tribunals world**

There is a bewildering diversity in the range of tribunals and the types of issue upon which they adjudicate. There are currently some 70 different tribunal systems that operate in a wide variety of areas that span our political and social life. The principal areas in which tribunals operate include social security; health; education and employment; tax, finance, and pensions; criminal injuries compensation; immigration and asylum; and traffic and transport. The broader picture is of an array of different tribunals that have been established across a range of governmental functions and resolve a number of different types of dispute.

1.3.1 **'State v party' and 'party v party' tribunals**

Most tribunals are required to resolve disputes between a government agency and an individual or business. Tribunals that determine such 'state v party' disputes might involve appeals against decisions of central or local government or an independent regulatory body. For example, the War Pensions and Armed Forces Compensation Chamber of the FTT hears appeals from ex-servicemen or women who have had their claims for a war pension rejected by the Ministry of Defence, a central government department. By contrast, valuation tribunals determine appeals against decisions taken by local authorities,[8] whereas the Tax and Chancery Chamber of the Upper Tribunal hears appeals against, *inter alia*, decisions made by the Financial Services Authority, an independent regulator.

Other tribunals determine 'party v party' disputes. For example, employment tribunals hear appeals concerning disputes between employers and employees over employment rights, concerning such matters as unfair dismissal, redundancy payments, and discrimination.[9] The Employment Appeal Tribunal hears appeals from decisions made by employment tribunals.

---

[7] Leggatt, *Tribunals for Users: One System, One Service—Report of the Review of Tribunals by Sir Andrew Leggatt* (London 2001) (the Leggatt Report); Department for Constitutional Affairs, *Transforming Public Services: Complaints, Redress and Tribunals* (Cm 6243 2004).

[8] Local Government Finance Act 1988, Sch 11.   [9] Employment Tribunals Act 1996, s 1.

Some tribunals determine both 'state v party' and 'party v party' disputes. For example, the Lands Tribunal resolves disputed claims for compensation for compulsory purchase of land, appeals from valuation tribunals in rating valuation cases, and discharge or modification of restrictive covenants affecting freehold land. The Residential Property Tribunal Service decides appeals against fair rent determinations, adjudicates in disputes about the enfranchisement of holding renewals and service charges/insurance, etc, and decides if an authority can prevent a home being bought on grounds of suitability for occupation by elderly people.[10]

1.3.2 Tribunals and government policy

Because tribunals are statutory creations, it is ultimately for Parliament, at the behest of the government of the day, to decide whether tribunals exist and, if so, how they are organised. This means that the shape of the tribunals system is highly sensitive to government policies and priorities—particularly in politically delicate or controversial areas.

For example, over recent years, pressures on the UK immigration system have presented unprecedented challenges for both government, and consequently, the tribunal system that determines appeals from initial decisions concerning the administration of immigration policy. It is therefore unsurprising that the administrative and political pressures have prompted government to undertake many different legal changes to the tribunal system. As the volume of initial decisions has increased, so has the caseload of the principal tribunal, known in its latest incarnation as the Immigration and Asylum Chamber of the FTT. In response, government has been keen to ensure that the tribunal can process quickly the high volume of appeals and, to this end, has frequently reformed the tribunal. Since the early 1990s, the immigration and asylum appeals system has then been subject to more statutory changes than any other tribunal system.[11] The most radical reform occurred in 2004, when the tribunal was reformed from an established two-tier structure, with appeals determined initially by the Immigration Appellate Authority and then by the Immigration Appeal Tribunal, to a single-tier structure in order to speed up the processing of appeals and to reduce the proportion of onward appeals.[12] But when immigration and asylum matters were absorbed into the new tribunals system in 2010, a two-tier structure was reintroduced. The Immigration and Asylum Chamber of the FTT now hears initial appeals against decisions concerning political asylum; entry, or leave to remain in, the UK for permanent settlement; deportation; and family visits. There is then the possibility of further appeal to the Immigration and Asylum Chamber of the Upper Tribunal.

---

[10] Rent Act 1977, Sch 10.

[11] Asylum and Immigration Appeals Act 1993; Asylum and Immigration Act 1996; Immigration and Asylum Act 1999; Nationality, Immigration and Asylum Act 2002; Asylum and Immigration (Treatment of Claimants, etc.) Act 2004; Immigration, Asylum and Nationality Act 2006; Transfer of Functions of the Asylum and Immigration Tribunal Order 2010, SI 2010/21.

[12] Asylum and Immigration (Treatment of Claimants, etc.) Act 2004, s 26. See Thomas, 'Evaluating Tribunal Aadjudication: Administrative Justice and Asylum Appeals' (2005) 25 LS 462.

1.3.3 What is at stake in tribunal proceedings?

Tribunals have been established in order to deal with a wide range of problems; they decide a vast number of cases in a large number of subject areas, and it is therefore unsurprising that a great diversity of rights and interests may be at stake in tribunal proceedings.[13]

For example, tribunals operating in areas such as asylum, immigration, and mental health determine cases in which fundamental human rights are often in issue.[14] In such areas, tribunals are not merely examining whether or not primary decisions affecting fundamental rights are lawful; they are also determining the boundaries of such rights. Indeed, some tribunals operate in acutely sensitive areas that concern both human rights and national security; their procedures reflect this. For example, the Special Immigration Appeals Commission (SIAC) hears appeals in cases in which the Home Office decides to deport foreign nationals on national security grounds or for other public interest reasons, and also hears appeals against decisions to deprive persons of British citizenship if this would be conducive to the public good. Given the sensitive nature of the evidence involved in such appeals, SIAC may sometimes hear evidence in closed session. An appellant will not be able to have their own legal representative, but a special advocate—a security-cleared barrister—will be appointed to represent the interests of the appellant.[15]

Other tribunals determine cases that do not directly raise human rights issues, but rather what might be termed 'political rights'. For example, the FTT General Regulatory Chamber hears appeals against, *inter alia*, data protection enforcement notices issued by the Information Commissioner, while the Administrative Appeals Chamber of the Upper Tribunal hears appeals concerning national security exemptions and freedom of information.[16] By contrast, the Proscribed Organisations Appeal Commission deals with appeals in cases in which the Home Office declines to de-proscribe organisations believed to be involved in terrorism.[17]

Meanwhile, some tribunals deal with appeals concerning an individual's entitlements to material benefits. For example, the Social Entitlement Chamber of the FTT—the largest component of the tribunals service judged in terms of caseload—hears appeals regarding social security, child support, vaccine damage, tax credit and compensation recovery, Housing Benefit, and Council Tax Benefit.[18] There is an onward

---

[13] Richardson and Genn, 'Tribunals in Transition: Resolution or Adjudication?' [2007] PL 116, 135–40.

[14] For example, asylum and immigration appeals often concern the application of ECHR, Arts 3 and 8, while appeals concerning the detention of the mentally ill raise questions concerning ECHR, Art 5.

[15] Special Immigration Appeals Commission Act 1997, s 6. See also House of Commons Constitutional Affairs Committee, *The Operation of the Special Immigration Appeals Commission (SIAC) and the Use of Special Advocates* (HC 323 2004–05).   [16] Data Protection Act 1988, s 6.

[17] Terrorism Act 2000, Sch 3.

[18] Social Security Act 1998, Pt 1. See Baldwin, Wikeley, and Young, *Judging Social Security: The Adjudication of Claims for Benefit in Britain* (Oxford 1992); Wikeley, 'Burying Bell: Managing the Judicialisation of Social Security Tribunals' (2000) 63 MLR 475. On child support appeals, see Davis, Wikeley, and Young, *Child Support in Action* (Oxford 1998).

right of appeal to the Administrative Appeals Chamber of the Upper Tribunal. The FTT Social Entitlement Chamber also hears appeals against decisions taken by the Criminal Injuries Compensation Authority on applications for compensation received from victims of criminal violence,[19] and appeals against the refusal of support to asylum applicants by the Home Office.[20] Whereas the foregoing tribunals deal with cases concerning an individual's entitlement to a material benefit, other tribunals determine appeals that concern an individual's financial liability. For example, the Tax Chamber of the FTT hears and determines appeals from taxpayers against tax decisions made by HM Revenue and Customs.

Other tribunals deal with cases that concern social rights that can be highly conditional on limited resources. For example, school admission appeal panels hear appeals by parents whose children have been refused admission to their preferred school by their local authority.[21] Schools adjudicators decide on objections to published admission arrangements for admitting children to schools, and decide on statutory proposals for school organisation.[22] Furthermore, the Health, Education and Social Care Chamber of the FTT determines appeals by parents against decisions of local education authorities (LEAs) concerning their children's special educational needs if parents cannot reach agreement with the LEA; the Chamber also hears appeals concerning disability discrimination.[23] Because such decisions involve the allocation of limited resources—for example, places at reputable schools—tribunal decision-making does not merely involve the determination of individual appeals, but can also involve decisions as to how the policy of school admissions should be administered.[24]

However, it would be mistaken to assume that all tribunals operating in the education context decide cases concerning social rights. For example, school exclusion appeal panels are constituted by LEAs or the governing bodies of schools to hear appeals against decisions related to school exclusion; this tribunal reviews disciplinary decisions.[25] Therefore, different tribunals operating within the same broad policy area may be allocated very different tasks.

To illustrate the point further, tribunals that operate in the health context similarly determine a diverse range of disputes. The Health, Education and Social Care Chamber of the FTT includes appeals against decisions of various government bodies in respect of independent residential care, nursing homes, voluntary homes, and registered children's homes,[26] and appeals against decisions of National Health Service

---

[19] Criminal Injuries Compensation Act 1995, s 5.   [20] Immigration and Asylum Act 1999, s 103.

[21] School Standards and Framework Act 1998, s 94. See Council on Tribunals, *School Admission and Exclusion Appeal Panels: Special Report* (Cm 5788 2003).

[22] School Standards and Framework Act 1998, s 25.

[23] First-tier Tribunal and Upper Tribunal (Chambers) Order 2008, SI 2008/2684, art 5; Equality Act 2010, Sch 17. See Harris, *Special Educational Needs and Access to Justice* (London 1997).

[24] Tweedie, 'Rights in Social Programmes: The Case of Parental Choice of School' [1986] PL 407.

[25] Education Act 2002, s 52. See Council on Tribunals, *School Admission and Exclusion Appeal Panels: Special Report* (Cm 5788 2003); Harris and Eden with Blair, *Challenges to School Exclusion: Exclusion, Appeals and the Law* (London 2000).   [26] Protection of Children Act 1999, s 9.

(NHS) primary care trusts (PCTs) to suspend or remove an individual from the list of practitioners.[27] It also reviews the cases of patients detained under the Mental Health Act 2007 and directs the discharge of any 'unrestricted' patients where the statutory criteria have been satisfied.[28]

Meanwhile, other tribunals determine appeals that concern an individual's reputation. For example, one of the roles of the FTT's General Regulatory Chamber is to hear and adjudicate on matters concerning the conduct of local authority members.[29] By contrast, other tribunals handle issues that intimately concern an individual's personal life and self-identity: the Gender Recognition Panel assesses applications from transsexual people for legal recognition in their acquired gender.[30]

The types of appeal determined by some tribunals might appear relatively trivial, but can nevertheless provoke a real sense of grievance amongst those affected. For example, agricultural land tribunals settle disputes and other issues that cannot be resolved by agricultural landlords and tenants, and drainage disputes between neighbours.[31] Meanwhile, parking adjudicators hear appeals concerning unauthorised vehicle parking.[32]

The volume of appeals determined by individual tribunals tends to fluctuate over time depending on the social and economic context in which such tribunals operate. For example, the number of appeals concerning asylum and immigration varies in line with the number of immigrants seeking to enter the country and the number of refusal decisions. The number of social security appeals will vary in line with the health of the economy, which affects the number of applicants for social security benefits; furthermore, the Department for Work and Pensions has been actively seeking to reduce the number of such appeals.[33] Nevertheless, the overall volume of appeals determined by tribunals is considerable. In 2009–10, the FTT and Upper Tribunal disposed of 639,600 cases.[34]

Q Why is there such diversity between different tribunals? Why do tribunals deal with very different types of appeals?

---

[27] National Health Act 2006, s 158.

[28] Mental Health Act 1983, Pt 5. See Peay, *Tribunals on Trial: A Study of Decision-Making under the Mental Health Act 1983* (Oxford 1989).   [29] Local Government Act 2000, s 77.

[30] Gender Recognition Act 2004, Sch 1.   [31] Agriculture Act 1947, s 73.

[32] Road Traffic Act 1991, s 73; Civil Enforcement of Parking Contraventions (England) General Regulations 2007, SI 2007/3483. See Sheppard and Raine, 'Parking Adjudicators: The Impact of New Technology', in Harris and Partington (eds), *Administrative Justice in the 21st Century* (Oxford 1999); Raine and Dunstan, *Mindsets, Myths and Misunderstandings at the Administrative–Judicial Divide: The Case of the Parking Appeals Tribunal* (Birmingham2005).

[33] Council on Tribunals, *Annual Report 2006–07* (HC 733 2006–07), p 32.

[34] Tribunals Service, *Annual Statistics for the Tribunals Service, 2009–10* (London 2010), p 4.

2. Tribunals—their place in the UK's public law system

2.1 **Tribunals and judicial review compared**

To understand the operation and function of tribunal appeal rights, it is useful to compare tribunals with the other form of legal accountability that we have already examined—namely, judicial review. Both tribunals and judicial review provide a mechanism of legal accountability and are similar in that they resolve disputes through an adjudication process. Adjudication involves the parties to a dispute having an opportunity to participate by presenting arguments to an independent third party— the judge or judges of the court or tribunal—who will impose a decision on the parties by applying pre-existing rules and principles.[35]

However, there are some fundamental differences between judicial review and tribunal appeals. First, *tribunals are directly responsible for reconsidering the merits of the initial decision.* While the jurisdiction of the reviewing court is limited to examining whether or not a decision is lawful, tribunals are specifically authorised to substitute their own decision for that of the governmental agency. Rather than sending the decision back to the initial decision-maker to be retaken, tribunals themselves retake the initial decision. In short, tribunals exercise a 'merits appeal' jurisdiction, whereas the reviewing court has a more limited, supervisory jurisdiction.

A second difference concerns *the basis on which the initial decision may be overturned*: whereas judicial review focuses on the legality of administrative decisions and is not normally involved in resolving factual disputes, the majority of tribunal appeals involve disputed factual issues. That tribunal appeals largely concern factual disputes does not mean that they are less important than other judicial proceedings; rather, it means that they serve a different purpose. For example, the Supreme Court determines the most important legal questions, but only hears approximately 90 appeals per year.[36] In 2008, the Administrative Court received over 7,000 judicial review claims.[37] By contrast, as we have already noted, tribunals determine a vastly higher number of cases: their role is the delivery of mass administrative justice.

A third, related point concerns the *different jurisdictional bases underpinning judicial review and tribunal appeals*. In exercising their judicial review jurisdiction, the courts apply general legal principles, such as legality, reasonableness, and procedural fairness, the basis of which is to be found in the courts' inherent common law jurisdiction. By contrast, tribunals are statutory creations: their jurisdiction depends solely on the legislation creating them; and the legislation concerning tribunals is located in many different statutes.

A fourth difference is that judicial review claims in England and Wales are channelled through the Administrative Court. Until recently, it sat only in London,

---

[35] See Fuller, 'The Forms and Limits of Adjudication' (1978) 92 Harvard Law Review 353.

[36] Based on typical workload of the Supreme Court's predecessor, the Appellate Committee of the House of Lords.   [37] Ministry of Justice, *Judicial and Court Statistics 2008* (Cm 7697 2009), p 16.

although some cases are now heard in Birmingham, Cardiff, Leeds, and Manchester. In contrast, tribunals have hearing centres located throughout the UK. A related point is that while the Administrative Court has a single set of procedural rules,[38] each tribunal (or, in the case of those tribunals within the new, unified tribunals system, each chamber) has its own procedural rules. Further, where Parliament has established a right of appeal against an initial decision to a tribunal, then the existence of that appeal right normally precludes any judicial review challenge.

Tribunals tend to occupy an ambiguous position between the judicial and executive branches of government. From one perspective, tribunals are part of the judicial system, but they are not, strictly speaking, courts of law; from another perspective, because tribunals can substitute their own decision for that of a government agency, they appear to be part of the administration.[39] The Franks Report concluded that tribunals should properly be regarded as machinery provided by Parliament for adjudication, rather than as part of the machinery of administration.[40] We explain later in the chapter that this view, endorsed in the Leggatt Report, has been embraced in the reforms introduced by the TCEA. The table in Figure 17.1 compares tribunals, judicial review, and ombudsmen.

Q How do tribunals differ from judicial review? Why do these differences exist?

2.2 **Justifications for tribunals**

Why do we have tribunals? The traditional rationale, as espoused by the Franks Report, was that tribunals have advantages over the ordinary courts in resolving disputes: their 'cheapness, accessibility, freedom from technicality, expedition and expert knowledge of their particular subject matter'.[41] Tribunals tend to deal with many more cases than the courts could deal with. Because tribunals are designed to be less adversarial and formal than the courts, the need for the parties to be legally represented, and so the need for legal aid funding, is reduced. Tribunals therefore cost less than the ordinary courts. As they are not bound by the formal procedures and rules of evidence that the higher courts must follow, tribunals can deal with appeals in a more informal, user-friendly way.

The relevant concept here is that of 'proportionate dispute resolution'—that is, ensuring that there is a proportionate relationship between the issues at stake in a dispute and the costs of the procedures used to resolve it.[42] For example, it would be out of proportion for disputes over entitlement to welfare benefits that, although of immense significance to individuals, might involve only comparatively small sums of money to

---

[38] On which, see Chapter 14 above.   [39] Farmer, *Tribunals and Government* (London 1974), p 4.
[40] Franks Report, [40].   [41] Franks Report, [38].
[42] Department for Constitutional Affairs, *Transforming Public Services: Complaints, Redress and Tribunals* (Cm 6243 2004), ch 2.

Administrative law mechanism	Source of power	Function	Procedure	Technique	Remedy
Tribunals	Statute	To determine merits appeals on issues of both fact and law	Appeal directly to tribunal or via public authority	Adversarial/ inquisitorial/ enabling	Allow/dismiss appeal
Ombudsmen	Statute	To investigate complaints of maladministration by a public authority	MP filter/ complain directly (See further above at p 615)	Investigative	Recommendations and compensation
Judicial review	Inherent common law jurisdiction	To review the legality of administrative decisions and the human rights compatibility of legislation	Judicial Review procedure in the Civil Procedure Rules, Pt 54	Adversarial	Discretionary public law remedy

Figure 17.1 Administrative law mechanisms

be resolved through a judicial process akin to that used by the higher courts, which might cost more than the amount of money at stake—especially when the volume of such disputes is substantial.

Tribunals can also provide a more effective means of redress than other forms of legal and political accountability. Government Ministers may be formally responsible for a decision made by civil servants. However, in practice, the ability of Parliament to hold Ministers to account for the mass of front-line administrative decisions is severely constrained simply because of the sheer volume of such decisions and the length of the decision-making chain between the initial official and the Minister. Furthermore, the avenue of seeking legal accountability of public decisions by way of judicial review cannot always be regarded as satisfactory or accessible because of the expense and difficulties involved—especially for individuals without legal assistance. The alternative of a tribunal can remedy these gaps in accountability by providing an accessible means of appealing against bureaucratic decisions.

Tribunals also provide a buffer for the courts by dealing with large volumes of individual appeals: this prevents the courts from becoming overloaded with a mass of cases, and allows them to focus on constitutional challenges on grounds such as the legality of public policy and compliance with human rights. If an individual wishing to challenge a decision can appeal to a tribunal, then he or she should pursue this avenue of challenge rather than make a judicial review claim. Appeal rights to a tribunal might therefore be established to reduce the pressure on the higher courts. For example, the introduction of a right of appeal to the county court for homeless individuals refused temporary accommodation by local authorities was motivated in part by the perceived need to reduce the number of homelessness judicial reviews received by the High Court.[43] Furthermore, judicial review procedures are not necessarily appropriate for determining some types of issue. Judicial review focuses on the lawfulness of administrative decisions and is not suited to resolving contested factual issues. By contrast, appeals involve a full, factual appeal on the merits.

It has, though, been questioned whether the traditional rationales for tribunals— their speed, convenience, accessibility, efficiency, and procedural simplicity—are, in reality, convincing. Empirical research on tribunals has indicated that, despite the supposed accessibility and informality of tribunals, most individuals who are entitled to appeal decline to do so; appeal hearings before tribunals can also be legally complex and unrepresented appellants can be at a disadvantage.[44] While the intention is that tribunals provide quick justice, in practice, delays may be common in some tribunal jurisdictions.

It may also be the case that governments are tempted to create tribunals for political reasons. For example, it has been argued that the reasons for establishing tribunals created during the early welfare state lay more with concerns that the ordinary courts were unsympathetic to new redistributive social policies and that channelling legal challenges into a specialist tribunal would therefore be more appropriate.[45] Governments might also establish appeal rights not in order to provide individuals with a mechanism for securing redress, but to enable government Ministers to avoid responsibility for individual decision-making and to defuse political opposition to controversial policies. Tribunals may thus only provide 'a symbolic appearance of legality'.[46] As Wraith and Hutchesson have noted: 'The British constitution tries to keep law and politics apart...but administrative tribunals inhabit a twilight world where the two intermingle.'[47]

The very existence of certain tribunals can prove to be a contentious matter raising complex legal, policy, and administrative issues. Consider the case of school exclusion appeal panels, which determine appeals against decisions to exclude children from schools. The panels have, on occasion, received criticism from some quarters for undermining the authority of school headteachers by overturning decisions to exclude disruptive pupils and it has been suggested that they be abolished. Yet the decision to exclude a child from school can have a significant impact on his or her future life, and it is important that there is an accessible means of

---

[43] Housing Act 1996, s 204.

[44] Genn, 'Tribunal Review of Administrative Decision-Making', in Richardson and Genn (eds), *Administrative Law and Government Action: The Courts and Alternative Mechanisms of Review* (Oxford 1994), p 249.   [45] Wraith and Hutchesson, *Administrative Tribunals* (London 1973), p 33.

[46] Prosser, 'Poverty, Ideology and legality: Supplementary Benefit Appeal Tribunals and Their Predecessors' (1977) 4 BJLS 39, 44. See also Bridges, 'Legality and Immigration Control' (1975) 2 BJLS 221.

[47] Wraith and Hutchesson, p 17.

challenging exclusion decisions. If the appeal right were to be abolished, the only available remedy would be the more expensive and time-consuming process of judicial review.

The Leggatt Report suggested three tests to determine whether tribunals rather than the courts should decide cases in any particular area:

(i)   direct participation by tribunal users,

(ii) the need for special expertise, and

(iii) expertise in administrative law.[48]

The first point refers to the fact that there is much greater scope for people to represent themselves in tribunal, as opposed to court, proceedings. Where such direct participation is possible—for example, because the legal and factual issues are unlikely to be particularly complex—the use of a tribunal is likely to be appropriate. Second, the membership of tribunals may include those with special expertise in the particular subject matter: for example, some tribunals consist of legally qualified members plus experts in relevant fields (such as doctors or accountants). When such breadth of experience is called for, again the case for a tribunal may be stronger. Third, because tribunals specialise in specific areas of administration, they are able to develop an expertise in their particular area of administrative law. In appropriate contexts, this, too, may point in favour of reliance on tribunals rather than on the necessarily generalist High Court.

Like all policy decisions, the establishment of a tribunal system involves balancing competing interests. On the one hand, because tribunals are more accessible than the higher courts, they can provide individuals with an informal and independent mechanism of redress that also combines fairness and expertise. On the other hand, there may be drawbacks from the government's perspective. Tribunal systems need to be funded; government must take responsibility for the costs of administering an appeals process, and for devoting resources to the preparation and representation of appeals. The introduction of appeal rights will also inevitably mean some delay in the implementation of decisions and government must be content to allow decisions to be taken by an independent decision-maker. Such considerations may lead government to restrict appeal rights in certain areas. For example, government has restricted appeal rights in relation to discretionary Social Fund decisions for welfare applicants and to decisions taken under the points-based immigration system for overseas applications.[49] Such developments simply illustrate the point that appeal rights are not entrenched; rather, they are granted, and can be withdrawn or restricted, by statute.

---

[48] Leggatt Report, [1.11]–[1.13].

[49] See Council on Tribunals, *Social Security—Abolition of Independent Tribunals under the Proposed Social Fund* (Cmnd 9722 1986); Immigration, Asylum and Nationality 2006 Act, s 4; Home Office, *A Points-Based System: Making Migration Work for Britain* (Cm 6741 2006).

3. The reorganisation of tribunals

3.1 The Leggatt Report and *Transforming Public Services*

Until the TCEA, tribunals had been created by individual pieces of primary legislation, without any overarching statutory framework. It was common to find that a tribunal was administered by the very government department responsible for making the decisions that fell to be challenged before the tribunal. A major problem with this arrangement was the impression that tribunals were not sufficiently independent. Tribunals had developed on an ad hoc basis, with new tribunals being established whenever government decided that a new tribunal was necessary. Furthermore, each government department was used to managing 'its' tribunal by having responsibility for providing administrative support to the tribunal, drafting its procedural rules, and sometimes even making judicial appointments to the tribunal. The consequence of this was that, while it was possible to identify tribunals as a discrete topic of administrative law, tribunals themselves did not comprise a coherent system in their own right.

In 2001, the Leggatt Report concluded that tribunals had developed in an almost entirely haphazard way with wide variations of practice and approach, almost no coherence, and little focus on the needs of tribunal users.[50] The lack of a coordinated approach to the establishment and operation of tribunals had contributed to a fragmented and complex administrative and judicial landscape without common standards for performance or accountability. Leggatt therefore recommended extensive reform to the tribunal system. The report stated that tribunals should be brought together in a single system and that they should become separate from their current sponsoring departments, to be administered instead by a single Tribunals Service—an executive agency under the auspices of the Ministry of Justice.

In 2004, the government published its White Paper, *Transforming Public Services: Complaints, Redress and Tribunals*, which accepted the Leggatt Report's recommendations.[51] This White Paper is significant in that it marked a distinct change of government policy and has been described as 'a radical advance in administrative justice'.[52] It represented a new focus on tribunals, and a recognition of their crucial role in dealing with the real-world legal problems faced by very large numbers of people. The government concluded that, overall, the tribunal system lacked systematic design and was poorly organised. The White Paper suggested a number of reforms. These included the bringing together of tribunals administered by central government departments in a unified Tribunals Service to provide a more coherent and independent

---

[50] Leggatt Report, [1.3]. See Adler, 'Who is Afraid of Sir Andrew Leggatt?' (2002) 9 JSSL 177.

[51] Department for Constitutional Affairs, *Transforming Public Services: Complaints, Redress and Tribunals* (Cm 6243 2004).

[52] Kirkham, 'Reforming the Tribunal Sector' (2005) 27 JSWFL 185, 196. See also Adler, 'Tribunal Reform: Proportionate Dispute Resolution and the Pursuit of Administrative Justice' (2006) 69 MLR 958, 961–4.

tribunals system, the introduction of proportionate dispute resolution mechanisms, the improvement of initial and tribunal decision-making standards, and the reform of the Council on Tribunals into an Administrative Justice and Tribunals Council. Many of these changes were implemented by the TCEA. We examine them in more detail in the following sections.

3.2 Judicial independence and tribunals

As tribunals are part of the judicial branch of government, they should be both impartial and independent. While the concepts of impartiality and independence are closely linked, they are not exactly the same.[53] Impartiality concerns the tribunal's approach toward the case before it in the sense of a lack of personal interest or bias, on the part of tribunal judges, in the outcome of a case. By contrast, independence requires that tribunals be structurally and institutionally separate from the executive branch of government.

Because tribunals were traditionally overseen and managed by the government departments the decisions of which tribunals had to scrutinise, there was an absence of structural independence and at least the risk of people perceiving an absence of impartiality. For example, until 1987, immigration adjudicators (now immigration judges) were appointed and paid by the Home Office—yet because they were determining appeals against decisions made by the Home Office, they could have no real claim to independence. Following political pressure, responsibility for appointments was transferred to a predecessor department of the Ministry of Justice to ensure judicial independence.[54] Similarly, it has been argued that school admission panels cannot appear to be entirely independent if they are appointed, trained, financed, and serviced by local education authorities.[55]

A broad consensus developed that tribunals should be, and be seen to be, more independent of the government. For example, the Council on Tribunals said that 'the principal hallmark of any tribunal is that it must be independent. Equally importantly, it must be perceived as such'.[56] Similarly, the Leggatt Report recommended that tribunals should be demonstrably independent of the governmental agencies that produce the primary decisions subject to appeal. Ensuring that tribunals are as independent as the courts is necessary if the public is to have full confidence in the

---

[53] *Gilles v Secretary of State for Work and Pensions* [2006] UKHL 2, [2006] 1 WLR 781, [38], *per* Baroness Hale.

[54] The Transfer of Functions (Immigration Appeals) Order 1987, SI 1987/465. Responsibility for the appointment of members of the Social Security Commissioners was transferred to the Ministry of Justice's predecessor in 1984.

[55] Council on Tribunals, *School Admission and Exclusion Appeal Panels: Special Report* (Cm 5788 2003), [2.7]. Similarly, the House of Commons Select Committee on Transport, *Parking Policy and Enforcement* (HC 748 2005–06), [139], has stated that the funding of parking adjudicators by participating local authorities projects an unfortunate appearance and does not convey the impression of independence.

[56] Council on Tribunals, *Tribunals: Their Organisation and Independence* (Cm 3744 1997), [2.2].

former. The TCEA recognised this point by placing the Lord Chancellor and other Ministers of the Crown under a duty to uphold the independence of the tribunals judiciary, just as they are under a duty to uphold the independence of the courts judiciary.[57]

3.3 The Tribunals Service

While important (at least symbolically), the imposition of such a duty was not sufficient on its own to meet the concerns, noted above, about the independence, actual and perceived, of tribunals. A major plank of the reform programme was therefore to shift administrative responsibility for tribunals from individual government departments to a new Tribunals Service. The Tribunals Service is an executive agency of the Ministry of Justice and was launched in April 2006.[58] The purposes of the Tribunals Service are to provide a responsive and efficient administration for tribunals, to contribute to the improvement of decision-making quality across government, to reform the tribunals system for the benefit of its users and the wider public, and to promote and protect judicial independence.[59] It is the task of the Tribunals Service to meet the vision of the Leggatt Report to achieve 'one system, one service' and to implement the 2007 Act. Many formerly separate tribunals have now migrated into the new tribunals system, meaning that they are part of the new structure described in the next section, and that they are administered by the Tribunals Service.

Some of the reasons for a unified tribunals administration—such as providing greater coherence and reducing costs—are managerial. But there is also an important constitutional issue here. Locating the Tribunals Service within the Ministry of Justice is important because that department does not take the kinds of decision that can be subject to appeals before tribunals; as the department responsible for the administration of justice, it has a special mission to protect judicial independence. The purpose of the unification of the tribunals system under the Ministry of Justice is to ensure that tribunals are seen to be manifestly independent from those the decisions of which they are reviewing. As Minister for Justice, the Lord Chancellor is under a general duty to ensure that there is an efficient and effective system to support the carrying on of the business of the new tribunals system and that appropriate services are provided for tribunals.[60] The Lord Chancellor must also report annually to Parliament on the discharge of this general duty in relation to tribunals.[61] In March 2010, the government announced proposals to merge the administration of courts and tribunals, with both functions discharged by a new, combined executive agency.[62]

---

[57] Both duties are imposed by the Constitutional Reform Act 2005, s 3, as amended by the TCEA, s 1.

[58] On executive agencies, see Chapter 4, section 3.10, above.

[59] Tribunals Service, *Annual Report and Accounts 2006–07* (HC 905 2006–07).   [60] TCEA, s 39(1).

[61] TCEA, s 39(3).   [62] Ministry of Justice media statement, 24 March 2010.

3.4 **The First-tier Tribunal and the Upper Tribunal**

Prior to the reforms introduced by the 2007 Act, there was great variety in the structure of tribunals. Some had a two-tier structure, with the first-instance tribunal hearing appeals from governmental decisions, and a second-tier body that determined appeals from the first-tier tribunal. Other tribunals were organised on a single-tier basis, albeit with the possibility of further challenges in the higher courts, by way of appeal or judicial review. Structural differences aside, the overall pattern was to have initial merits appeals determined by a fact-finding tribunal, with any further challenges, whether decided by a specialist tribunal or a higher court, focusing on whether any error of law afflicted the first-tier tribunal decision.

The 2007 Act establishes a new unified structure by creating two new generic tribunals: the First-tier Tribunal (FTT) and the Upper Tribunal.[63] Although some tribunals remain outside of the new structure, a large number of previously separate tribunals have been abolished, and their functions transferred to the FTT and the Upper Tribunal. As Figure 17.2 shows, the two new generic tribunals are themselves divided into 'chambers'. For example, the Health, Education and Social Care Chamber of the FTT deals with appeals previously heard by four separate tribunals—the Care Standards Tribunal, the Mental Health Review Tribunal, the Special Educational Needs and Disability Tribunal, and the Family Health Services Appeals Authority. This structure is more malleable than its predecessor: judges within a given chamber can work across different areas, enabling judicial resources to be deployed more flexibly and efficiently. Each chamber is headed by a chamber president and the tribunals judiciary is headed by the Senior President of Tribunals.

The primary role of the Upper Tribunal is to hear appeals on points of law against the FTT's decisions.[64] However, the Upper Tribunal also has first-instance jurisdiction in relation to a small number of matters.[65] It also has powers of judicial review in limited circumstances, as we explain below.[66]

Both the FTT and the Upper Tribunal are intended to be adaptable institutions, able to take on any existing or new tribunal jurisdictions. So, in the future, when Parliament decides to create a new appeal right or jurisdiction, it will not have to create a new tribunal to administer it. The Lord Chancellor also has the power to transfer the jurisdiction of existing tribunals to the two new tribunals.[67]

The Upper Tribunal is a superior court of record, like the High Court and the Employment Appeal Tribunal.[68] This underlines its status, and also raises questions about whether the Upper Tribunal's decisions may themselves be subject to judicial review—a point that we consider below.

---

[63] TCEA, s 3.   [64] TCEA, s 11.

[65] For example, individuals can apply to the Lands Chamber of the Upper Tribunal to ask it to modify or discharge restrictive covenants affecting land: Law of Property Act 1925, s 84.   [66] At section 5.5.

[67] TCEA, s 37.   [68] TCEA, s 3(5).

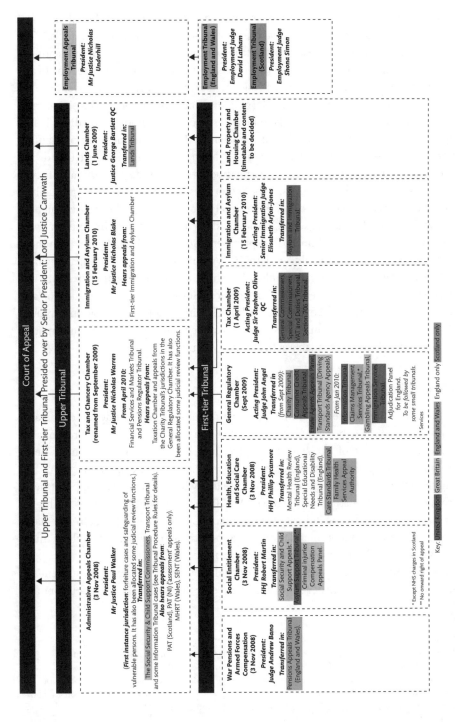

Figure 17.2 The new tribunals system

Source: Senior President of Tribunals, *The Senior President of Tribunals Annual Report: Tribunals Transformed*, February 2010, p 10, available online at <http://www.tribunals.gov.uk>

3.5 **The Senior President of Tribunals**

To provide senior judicial leadership of tribunals and to oversee the tribunal judiciary, the 2007 Act provides for a new judicial office—the Senior President of Tribunals.[69] The Senior President is the judicial leader of the tribunals system and holds a distinct statutory office. In carrying out the functions of that office, he is not subject to the direction of any other judicial office holder. The Senior President of Tribunals also presides over both the FTT and the Upper Tribunal.[70] In discharging his functions, the Senior President must have regard to the need for tribunals to be accessible; the need for proceedings before tribunals to be handled fairly, quickly, and efficiently; the need for members of tribunals to be experts in the subject matter of, or the law to be applied in, cases in which they decide matters; and the need to develop innovative methods of resolving disputes that are of a type that may be brought before tribunals.[71] The Senior President must also report annually to the Lord Chancellor.[72] The purpose of this annual report is to support improvement both in the workings of the tribunals, and in the standard of decision-making and review in cases that come before the tribunals. In September 2010, the Lord Chancellor announced that the Ministry of Justice would 'work towards a unified judiciary encompassing both courts and tribunals', which may involve abolishing the office of Senior President and transferring his powers to the Lord Chief Justice. However, the Lord Chancellor also proposed creating a new post of Head of Tribunals 'with a statutory obligation to protect and develop the distinct and innovative features of the tribunals'.[73] Detailed information on these proposals was unavailable at the time of writing.

3.6 **The tribunal judiciary**

The 2007 Act introduced measures to ensure judicial independence as regards appointments to the tribunal judiciary. In 2004, the Lord Chancellor was responsible for the appointment of 60 per cent of tribunal members, the remainder being appointed by the government department responsible for the original decision.[74] To bring the appointment of tribunal members in line with the changes to appointments introduced by the Constitutional Reform Act 2005, under which judges of the higher courts are appointed by the Judicial Appointments Commission,[75] the 2007 Act places the responsibility for recommendations for appointment of tribunal members under the remit of the Judicial Appointments Commission (JAC).[76]

The 2007 Act also introduces a new basis of eligibility for judicial appointment as a tribunal member.[77] The purpose of this is to increase the pool of those eligible for office

---

[69] TCEA, s 2.

[70] TCEA, s 3(4). The first Senior President of Tribunals is Carnwath LJ, a Court of Appeal judge.

[71] TCEA, s 2(3).   [72] TCEA, s 43.   [73] HL Deb, 16 Sept 2010, col 63WS.

[74] Department for Constitutional Affairs, *Transforming Public Services: Complaints, Redress and Tribunals* (Cm 6243 2004), [6.47].   [75] See Chapter 6, section 4.1, above.

[76] Constitutional Reform Act 2005, ss 85–93 and Sch 14 (as amended by TCEA).

[77] TCEA, s 50.

and to promote greater diversity in appointments, while maintaining appointments on merit. Furthermore, under the new unified system, tribunal members will also be able to sit in more than one jurisdiction if there is an operational need. The reforms will therefore make it easier for judiciary and staff to work more flexibly across different tribunals.

A distinctive feature of tribunals has been the participation of lay members—that is members without legal qualifications. At one time, many tribunals were composed of two lay members and a legally qualified chair. This allowed the tribunal to benefit from the experience of lay members with specialist knowledge relevant to the issues of the dispute. However, the role of lay membership has reduced dramatically in some tribunals. For example, lay membership of social security tribunals was abolished in 1998.[78] And when the government reformed the immigration and asylum appeals system in 2004, it defeated proposals made by the House of Lords that lay membership of the tribunal created by those reforms should be greater than that of its predecessor, so that all appeals would be heard with a lay member. Lay members do, though, still sit in some tribunals such as school admission appeal panels.

As regards training for tribunal members, the Judicial Studies Board (JSB) has established a competence framework for tribunal judiciary that provides that tribunal chairs and members should acquire the full range of competences required for their roles.[79] Complaints against tribunal members are dealt with under the Judicial Complaints (Tribunals) Rules 2006. The chairman or president of the tribunal will investigate the complaint, and if he or she believes that there may be a case for formal disciplinary action, then he or she will refer the case to the Office for Judicial Complaints. The Lord Chancellor and the Lord Chief Justice will then consider the evidence and decide what action, if any, should be taken.

3.7 The Administrative Justice and Tribunals Council

From 1958 until 2007, the Council on Tribunals had responsibility for the oversight of tribunals.[80] The statutory purpose of the Council was to keep under review, and report on, the constitution and working of tribunals under its supervision. The Council had to consider and report on particular matters referred to it under the Tribunals and Inquiries Act 1992 with respect to tribunals, and, where necessary, to consider and report on the administrative procedures of statutory inquiries. This was achieved by way of an annual report laid before Parliament. The primary concern of the Council was to ensure that tribunals met the needs of users through the provision of an open, fair, impartial, efficient, timely, and accessible service. The Council on Tribunals also had a right to be consulted by government departments in relation to draft tribunal

---

[78] See Adler, 'Lay Tribunal Members and Administrative Justice' [1999] PL 618; Wikeley, 'Burying Bell: Managing the Judicialisation of Social Security Tribunals' (2000) 63 MLR 475, 484–6.

[79] Judicial Studies Board, *Competence Framework for Chairmen and Members of Tribunals* (2002).

[80] Tribunals and Inquiries Act 1992, s 1.

procedure rules.[81] The Council on Tribunals produced a guide to drafting tribunal procedure rules[82] and also established a framework of standards for tribunals.[83] This framework stated that tribunals should be independent, and should provide open, fair, and impartial hearings. It also said that they should also be accessible to their users and focus on the needs of users, and that tribunals should offer cost-effective procedures, and be properly resourced and organised.

However, the Council on Tribunals was criticised for being an ineffectual body with limited powers.[84] It had no parliamentary select committee to which to report, meaning that its reports rarely attracted much political (or public) attention. While government departments were under an obligation to consult the Council on Tribunals in relation to draft rules concerning tribunal procedure, they were under no obligation to consult in relation to draft Bills concerning tribunals. In any event, government departments were under no obligation to respond to criticisms made by the Council on Tribunals and therefore the work of the Council could, on occasion, be ignored by government departments. However, with the reform of the tribunal system, the name, role, and status of the Council on Tribunals has changed. The Leggatt Report recommended that the Council on Tribunals should play a central role in the new tribunals system, acting as the hub of the wheel of the administrative justice system.[85] Its primary duty, said Leggatt, should be the championing of users' causes, and it should include members with the experience and perspective of users. Furthermore, the Council should go beyond its merely advisory role and become more proactive by making recommendations to government about how improvements might be made to the tribunal system. The government subsequently recommended that, in the wider context of its reform of the administrative justice system, the Council should take on a broader remit to become an Administrative Justice and Tribunals Council, with a particular remit to focus on the needs of the public and users.[86]

The 2007 Act therefore established the Administrative Justice and Tribunals Council (AJTC).[87] The AJTC is of a comparable size to the Council on Tribunals, with between ten and fifteen members appointed by the Lord Chancellor, and by Ministers from the devolved administrations, under an independent chair. Whereas the Council on Tribunals had only a Scottish Committee, the AJTC has both Scottish and Welsh Committees.

The AJTC has a similar role in relation to the supervision of tribunals as that of its predecessor. However, in addition to taking on the Council on Tribunals' previous

---

[81] Tribunals and Inquiries Act 1992, s 8.

[82] Council on Tribunals, *Guide to Drafting Tribunal Rules* (London 2003).

[83] Council on Tribunals, *Framework of Standards for Tribunals* (London 2002).

[84] See, eg Lomas, 'The 25th Annual Report of the Council on Tribunals: An Opportunity Sadly Missed' (1985) 48 MLR 694.   [85] Leggatt Report, [7.46]–[7.55].

[86] Department for Constitutional Affairs, *Transforming Public Services: Complaints, Redress and Tribunals* (Cm 6243 2004), ch 11.   [87] TCEA, s 44 and Sch 7.

remit, the AJTC also has responsibility for keeping the administrative justice system as a whole under review.[88] That wider remit is concerned with ensuring that the relationships between the courts, tribunals, ombudsmen, and alternative dispute resolution (ADR) routes satisfactorily reflect the needs of users. With respect to the administrative justice system, the responsibilities of the AJTC are to keep the administrative justice system under review; consider ways in which to make the system accessible, fair, and efficient; advise the Lord Chancellor, devolved administrations, and the Senior President of Tribunals on the development of the system; refer proposals for changes in the system to those persons; and make proposals for research into the system.[89] The 'administrative justice system' is defined as being the overall system by which decisions of an administrative or executive nature are made in relation to particular persons, including the procedures for making such decisions, the law under which such decisions are made, and the systems for resolving disputes and airing grievances in relation to such decisions.[90] This enlarged remit has much to commend it. One of the criticisms of the Franks Report was that, by focusing on tribunals, which are predominantly open, fair, and impartial, the Council on Tribunals had been precluded from considering the 'closed, dark and windowless' procedures of governmental decision-making.[91] With its broader remit, the AJTC has the ability to examine initial decision-making procedures.

As regards tribunals, the responsibility of the AJTC is to keep under review, and report on, the constitution and working of tribunals; to consider, and report on, any other matter that relates to listed tribunals[92] in general or to a particular listed tribunal, and that the AJTC determines to be of special importance; and to consider, and report on, any particular matter referred to the AJTC that relates to tribunals in general or to any particular tribunal that has been referred to the AJTC by the government and devolved administrations.[93] The AJTC may also scrutinise and comment on legislation, existing or proposed, relating to tribunals or to any particular tribunal.[94] Lord Newton, the former (and inaugural) chairman of the AJTC, indicated that the new body would focus, amongst other things, on how the tribunals system can be made more user-friendly.[95] However, in October 2010, the coalition government announced that the AJTC, along with many other public bodies, would be abolished (in order to save money). It appears that the 'key functions' of the AJTC will now be performed in-house by the Ministry of Justice, although the details of these arrangements were unavailable at the time of writing.[96]

---

[88] TCEA, Sch 7, para 13(1).   [89] TCEA, Sch 7, para 13(1).   [90] TCEA, Sch 7, para 13(4).
[91] Griffith, 'Tribunals and Inquiries' (1959) 22 MLR 125, 127.
[92] That is, those tribunals the oversight of which falls within the AJTC's remit. Those tribunals include the First-tier Tribunal and the Upper Tribunal: TCEA, Sch 7, para 25.   [93] TCEA, Sch 7, para 14(2).
[94] TCEA, Sch 7, para 14(2).
[95] Newton, 'The Role of the Administrative Justice Council' (2006) 13 JSSL 98, 101.
[96] Ministry of Justice media statement, 14 October 2010.

> **Q** Think back over the issues examined in this section. What prompted the reform of tribunals? Will the reforms achieve their purposes? Do you think that the tribunals system is more independent and coherent as a result of them?

4. Tribunal procedures

How do tribunals operate in practice? Are there obstacles that prevent potential appellants from pursuing appeals? What procedures do tribunals adopt? Should they mimic the courts by adopting an adversarial style or should they be more interventionist? What is the role of legal representation? Do tribunals fulfil the promise of being less informal than the courts, or are they adversarial and legalistic? To what extent should they give reasons for their decisions? Examining tribunal procedures is complex because of the range of questions raised and also because practice varies so considerably between different tribunals. With this caveat in mind, the overview presented here seeks to illuminate some of the issues raised by tribunal procedures in order to consider how effective tribunals are in controlling governmental decision-making.

4.1 Preliminary reviews of initial decision-making

In many decision-making systems, an individual dissatisfied with a decision must first ask for a review of the decision before pursuing any appeal to a tribunal. This review can be conducted internally by the same governmental agency that made the primary decision. For example, an individual may ask the decision-maker responsible for the initial decision to undertake a 'fresh look' at his or her case by conducting an internal review.[97] Alternatively, the review can be external in the sense that it is undertaken by a different agency altogether.[98] Some review processes are established by statute; others are not.[99] Where there is a procedure for the review of initial decisions, dissatisfied individuals must normally first apply for such a review before appealing against the

---

[97] See, eg Housing Act 1996, s 202 (an applicant for homelessness assistance has the right to request a review by the local authority); the Social Security and Child Support (Decisions and Appeals) Regulations 1999, SI 1999/991 (an applicant for social security benefit has the right to request the Secretary of State to revise his decision); Education Act 2002, s 52 (a child excluded from school has the right to request a review of the decision by a responsible body). Immigration decisions made by entry clearance officers at UK visa sections based overseas are subject to an internal review by an entry clearance manager.

[98] See, eg, Social Security Act 1998, s 38 (Social Fund decisions can be reviewed by a Social Fund inspector); School Standards and Framework Act 1998, s 25 (objections to school admission arrangements devised by a school can be referred to the schools adjudicator).

[99] For example, the system of administrative review of points-based immigration decisions for overseas applicants is laid down not in legislation, but in administrative guidance issued by the Home Office. See also House of Commons Home Affairs Select Committee, *Immigration Control* (HC 775 2005–06), [137]–[140]. The Committee recommended that there should be clear rules and procedures as to how entry clearance managers carry out their reviews.

decision to a tribunal. The advantage of such review mechanisms is that they can filter out clearly wrong initial decisions; at the same, the drawback is that, because they do not offer an independent mechanism for reviewing the primary decision, individuals may have little confidence in such reviews.[100] Initial decision-makers undertaking internal reviews may not be inclined to undertake a thorough review of the decision and such reviews may, in practice, become little more than 'rubber-stamping' exercises.[101]

4.2 **Access to tribunals**

While tribunals hear more appeals than the courts, it is apparent that most individuals who can pursue an appeal to a tribunal decide not to do so. For example, the administration of social security policy requires civil servants to make millions of decisions concerning applicants' eligibility for welfare benefits. However, fewer than 1 per cent of unsuccessful applicants decide to appeal even though the success rate of appeals is 40 per cent. Why do so many people decide not to appeal—even with an apparently high chance of success?

Despite the claims that tribunals are accessible to their users, empirical research has identified several practical barriers that may prevent potential appellants from appealing.[102] First, potential appellants might be ignorant of tribunal appeal rights and procedures. For example, it has been suggested that the low number of appeals to parking adjudicators can be explained by the relative obscurity of the service and that there should be greater public awareness of it.[103] Second, there is the cost of pursuing an appeal. While tribunals generally do not charge fees in order to appeal, potential appellants may not appeal because of the costs of legal advice and/or representation. There may, though, be additional costs in preparing an appeal, such as the commissioning of expert evidence in relation to an appeal concerning an assessment of special educational needs.[104] Third, the complexity of the appeal process and the absence of appropriate help may mean that many potential appellants find appealing a confusing

---

[100] See further Sainsbury, 'Internal Reviews and the Weakening of Social Security Claimants' Rights of Appeal', in Genn and Richardson (eds), *Administrative Law and Government Action: The Courts and Alternative Mechanisms of Review* (Oxford 1994); Harris, 'The Place of Formal and Informal Review in the Administrative Justice System', in Harris and Partington (eds), *Administrative Justice in the 21st Century* (Oxford 1999).

[101] This was the view of the House of Commons Constitutional Affairs Committee, *Asylum and Immigration Appeals* (HC 211 2003–04), [107] as regards internal reviews conducted by entry clearance managers.

[102] See Genn, 'Tribunal Review of Administrative Decision-Making', in Richardson and Genn (eds), *Administrative Law and Government Action: The Courts and Alternative Mechanisms of Review* (Oxford 1994), pp 265–8; Adler and Gulland, *Tribunal Users' Experiences, Perceptions and Expectations: A Literature Review* (London 2003); Cowan and Halliday, *The Appeal of Internal Review: Law, Administrative Justice and the (Non-) Emergence of Disputes* (Oxford 2003).

[103] House of Commons Select Committee on Transport, *Parking Policy and Enforcement* (HC 748 2005–06), [127].

[104] House of Commons Education and Skills Select Committee, *Special Educational Needs* (HC 478 2005–06), [211]–[215].

and therefore off-putting prospect. Fourth, physical barriers to accessing tribunals might pose difficulties to disabled appellants and those with health problems, while some individuals—for example, potential immigration appellants—might experience language and literacy difficulties.

Another concern has been that individuals from deprived socio-economic back-grounds tend not to pursue appeals.[105] Potential appellants might also be deterred from appealing in light of the perceived lack of independence of tribunals from initial governmental decision-makers, and the perception that pursuing an appeal may be difficult and time-consuming. It is therefore likely that some individuals with legit-imate grievances may not pursue an appeal. Ison has noted that 'the total volume of injustice is likely to be much greater among those who accept initial decisions than among those who complain or appeal', whereas Genn has argued that the prevalent failure of potential appellants to exercise their right of appeal demonstrates the very limited contribution that tribunals can make as a corrective to inaccurate initial decision-making.[106]

While there may be obstacles that discourage individuals from pursuing appeals, higher appeal rates can cause practical difficulties for tribunal systems, including delays in processing appeals and extra costs; after all, if everyone who could appeal were to do so, then the tribunal system would, like other parts of the legal system, become unmanageable. This is why government departments occasionally introduce plans to reduce the volume of appeals or recovery plans to deal with a backlog of appeals.[107]

Some cases may proceed to the appeal stage because the governmental agency has failed either to allow individuals to explain their circumstances clearly or to explain properly its decisions to their recipients. Many cases that proceed to an appeal concern issues of fact that, had they been known or considered at the initial stage, might have resulted in a different outcome. The consequence of this is that the appeal process can become burdened with appeals that could have been resolved satisfactorily at an earlier stage.

Appeal rates against initial decisions are generally low, but there is one exception to this: the immigration and asylum appeals jurisdiction is marked out by an exception-ally high rate, which has been characterised as a 'culture of pervasive challenge'.[108] On the one hand, the high rate of challenge by asylum applicants might be seen as a necessary feature of a decision-making process in which matters of personal liberty, and even life and death, are at stake, and in which the quality of decision-making at both initial and appeal stages has regularly been criticised. On the other hand, this

---

[105] House of Commons Education and Skills Select Committee, HC 478, [216]–[220].

[106] Ison, ' "Administrative Justice": Is it Such a Good Idea?', in Harris and Partington (eds), *Administrative Justice in the 21st Century* (Oxford 1999), p 23; Genn, p 266.

[107] See, eg the Department of Work and Pensions' plan to reduce the volume of social security appeals and the recovery plan introduced by the Asylum and Immigration Tribunal in 2005 to deal with a backlog of appeals. See Council on Tribunals, *Annual Report 2006–07* (HC 733 2006–07); Tribunals Service, *The AIT Review Report* (London 2006).   [108] Leggatt Report, Pt 2.

high rate of challenge has been seen by the government as evidence that many asylum appellants are inclined to use the appeals process to prolong the final determination of their claims, and therefore their stay within the country.

4.3 Tribunal procedure rules

Prior to the implementation of the TCEA, each tribunal had its own rules. Such rules were typically made by the Lord Chancellor or the Secretary of State in the department with the decisions of which the tribunal was concerned. This gave rise to problems both of coherence and (in the case of rules made by the relevant Secretary of State) independence. In light of this, the 2007 Act provides that Tribunal Procedure Rules governing the practice and procedure of the FTT and the Upper Tribunal are to be made by the Tribunal Procedure Committee,[109] which consists of the Senior President (or his nominee), four people appointed by the Lord Chancellor (one of whom must be an AJTC member), three people (who must include tribunal judges) appointed by the Lord Chief Justice, and one person appointed by the Lord President of the Court of Session in Scotland. Further appointments may be made at the Senior President's request subject to the consent of a senior judge, such as the Lord Chief Justice.[110]

The Tribunal Procedure Rules must be made with a view to ensuring that the tribunals provide justice, that the tribunal system is fair and accessible, that proceedings are handled quickly and efficiently, that the rules are simple, and that, where appropriate, responsibility is conferred on tribunal members for ensuring that proceedings are handled quickly and efficiently.[111] The Senior President of Tribunals also has a power to make practice directions concerning the practice and procedure of the FTT and the Upper Tribunal.[112]

4.4 The conduct of tribunal hearings

There are three principal ways in which tribunal hearings may be conducted: through adversarial or inquisitorial hearing styles, or through an enabling approach.[113] Each of these three approaches involves a different role for the tribunal judge or panel.

Adversarial hearings have traditionally been adopted in common law jurisdictions. In an adversarial hearing, the judge is enabled to get at the truth by holding the ring between the parties, while each side presents its own case and assails that of its opponent. In order to maintain judicial independence, the judge does not descend into the arena between the two parties to the proceedings by asking his or her own questions or by any interventions; instead, the two parties are expected to engage in gladiatorial conflict. The advantage of this approach is that the tribunal can maintain its independence because it does not intervene directly in the proceedings and cannot

---

109 TCEA, s 22(1).   110 TCEA, Sch 5, para 2.   111 TCEA, s 22(4).

112 TCEA, s 23.   113 Leggatt Report, [7.2]–[7.5].

therefore be seen as taking the side of one party or the other. However, difficulties with the adversarial approach can arise when the parties are not on a level playing field because, for example, the appellant is unrepresented.

In an *inquisitorial* process, the judge or adjudicator takes full control of the proceedings, governs the participation of the parties, and intentionally descends into the arena to elicit the necessary facts to make a decision. The advantage is that the tribunal controls the proceeding, but at the risk of appearing to favour one party. Few tribunals in the UK adopt an inquisitorial approach.

Third, there is the *enabling* approach in which the tribunal supports the parties in ways that give them confidence in their own abilities to participate in the process, and in the tribunal's capacity to compensate for the appellant's lack of skills or knowledge. An enabling approach is designed to avoid some of the problems for unrepresented appellants posed by the adversarial approach, but without requiring the tribunal to take full control of the proceedings.

Because different tribunal systems operate in different contexts, it is unsurprising that each have developed their own culture and approach. For example, some tribunals have an adversarial culture, whereas others adopt the enabling approach.[114]

The Leggatt Report was convinced that tribunals should adopt an enabling approach in order to assist appellants.[115] An enabling approach is particularly important when appellants are unrepresented, the context concerns a dispute between the individual and the state, and the respondent authority or government department is represented by an official or advocate who is familiar with the law, the tribunal, and its procedures. In these circumstances, the Leggatt Report noted that tribunal chairmen may find it necessary to intervene in the proceedings more than might be thought proper in the courts in order to hold the balance between the parties, and to enable citizens to present their cases. Tribunal members should do all that they can to understand the point of view, as well as the case, of the appellant.

A further point should be noted. There is an important difference between tribunals determining 'state v party' disputes, in which there is an underlying public interest in ensuring that the law is being correctly applied, and ordinary civil litigation, which typically has no broader impact beyond the two parties involved. To ensure that individuals' appeals are properly investigated in 'state v party' disputes, the tribunal may have to intervene more proactively than would normally be considered appropriate in other litigation to ensure that cases are properly investigated—even if this means raising issues that can be, but are not always, potentially favourable to an appellant's case.[116]

---

[114] For example, asylum and immigration appeals are more adversarial. In contrast, an enabling approach tends to be adopted in appeals concerning decisions about social security, child support, criminal injuries compensation, and special educational needs.   [115] Leggatt Report, [7.5].

[116] See Criminal Injuries Compensation Appeals Panel, *Annual Report and Accounts 2005–06* (HC 1428 2005–06), p 14; *M (Chad) v Secretary of State for the Home Department* [2004] UKIAT00044, [16].

4.5 **Legal representation**

The question of legal representation before tribunals raises a number of issues. As tribunals have been designed to be accessible by individuals, legal representation has traditionally not been considered to be necessary or even desirable, because it might add to the cost, length, and formality of tribunal proceedings. Representation might also make tribunal hearings more legalistic. However, appellants may be unaware of tribunal procedures, the applicable rules, and how best to prepare their cases, and may lack advocacy skills. Representation may therefore significantly enhance an individual's chances of success. At the same time, as many appellants are unable to afford legal representation, the costs of representation would have to be borne by the government's legal aid budget—something that successive governments have refused to countenance. Debate has therefore focused on how, if at all, tribunals can ensure that tribunal users are not disadvantaged by the general unavailability of legal representation—for example, through the adoption of an 'enabling' approach by the tribunal.

While legal aid funding is not generally available for tribunal proceedings, it is available in relation to proceedings before the Employment Appeal Tribunal; the Health; Education and Social Care Chamber of the FTT (in mental health cases); the Special Immigration Appeals Commission; and the Proscribed Organisations Appeal Commission. Legal aid is also available for asylum and immigration appeals, although representatives can only provide publicly funded representation if the case has merit. The Lord Chancellor also has the power, on receipt of a recommendation from the Legal Services Commission, to authorise 'exceptional funding' for representation in those few cases in which representation may be essential for a fair hearing, and in which no other sources of help can be found, but this power is rarely used.[117]

Despite the general absence of publicly funded legal aid, there are some forms of assistance. Funding for general legal advice (falling short of representation at appeal hearings) is available to those who qualify financially, under the Legal Help scheme, which allows legal aid solicitors to advise clients on tribunal procedures, and can include the provision of written or oral advice, obtaining counsel's opinion if appropriate, and the preparation of a case to present at a tribunal. Furthermore, representation does not necessarily have to mean representation by a qualified lawyer, although representation by non-lawyers has caused concern in some jurisdictions.[118] Assistance is sometimes available via advice agencies such as the National Association of Citizens' Advice Bureaux, the Free Representation Unit, and other advice agencies and pro bono services.[119]

[117] Access to Justice Act 1999, s 6(8)(b).

[118] For example, in 1999, Parliament established the Office of the Immigration Services Commissioners to regulate non-professional immigration representatives in response to concerns over the variable quality of representation provided. See Immigration and Asylum Act 1999, s 83.

[119] For example, in 2005–06, 39.5 per cent of oral hearings before the Criminal Injuries Compensation Appeals Panel (the functions of which have now been transferred to the First-tier Tribunal) were repre-

As regards the impact of representation for appellants, empirical research has demonstrated that having specialist representation at tribunals significantly increases the likelihood that appellants will have their appeals allowed.[120] Representation is valuable to appellants in several ways: it can help them to prepare their appeals and navigate unfamiliar law and precedents, it can help them through the tribunal process, and it can help to defend them against inappropriate cross-examination. By performing these functions, good-quality representation can also assist the tribunal itself by furnishing all of the available information needed to reach a decision and promote the efficiency of the process by narrowing down the issues in contention. Representation can ensure that cases are investigated thoroughly by the tribunal, and also increase the likelihood that appellants and the broader public will perceive the proceedings to be fair. Furthermore, as the initial decision-maker may also be represented before the tribunal, the presence of a representative on behalf of the appellant promotes an equality of arms. Representatives can advise appellants aggrieved with a tribunal decision of onward rights of challenge.

Finally, much of the law administered by tribunals is highly complex and not easily accessible to the average individual. The complexity, for example, of social security and immigration law—the two largest tribunal jurisdictions—is generally recognised.[121] This complexity can have adverse consequences, such as reducing the efficiency of decision-making and increasing the likelihood of incorrect and inconsistent decisions, which may then be appealed against. The level of complexity can also make it extremely difficult for individuals to navigate the plethora of rules, regulations, and case law that govern entitlement either to welfare benefits or immigration status, making it very difficult for individuals to represent themselves effectively before tribunals.

In response to concerns that many unrepresented appellants are disadvantaged, the Leggatt Report noted that it was convinced that representation not only often added unnecessarily to cost, formality, and delay, but that it also worked against the objective of making tribunals directly and easily accessible to the full range of potential users. The report noted that this objective of providing accessible and fair justice for unrepresented appellants is challenging and will not always be achievable. However, it suggested measures that, it argued, would achieve these objectives for most appellants and, therefore, should radically reduce the need for representation. A combination of good-quality information and advice, effective procedures, and well-conducted hearings, along with competent and well-trained tribunal members, could go a very

---

sented. See Criminal Injuries Compensation Appeals Panel, *Annual Report and Accounts 2005–06* (HC 1428 2005–06), p 14.

[120] Genn and Genn, *The Effectiveness of Representation at Tribunals: Report to the Lord Chancellor* (London 1989).

[121] See, eg National Audit Office, *Department for Work and Pensions: Dealing with the Complexity of the Benefits System* (HC 592 2005–06); House of Commons Work and Pensions Select Committee, *Benefits Simplification* (HC 463 2006–07); Home Office, *Simplifying Immigration Law: An Initial Consultation* (London 2007).

long way to helping the vast majority of appellants to understand and put their cases properly themselves. The report noted that it was of fundamental importance that the tribunals system be viewed as participatory, and for every effort to be made to achieve and maintain such a state of affairs.[122] There is, however, little research-based support for the view that the sort of measures advocated by Leggatt actually enhance the ability of most appellants to put their cases properly themselves—that is, without representation.[123]

For obvious, cost-related reasons, the government is also anxious to implement measures that facilitate the effective participation of unrepresented appellants.[124] In particular, the government has proposed greater use of 'early neutral evaluation', which involves an independent person assessing an appellant's claim and giving an opinion on its likely outcome in a tribunal and on any technical or legal points. While this evaluation is non-binding and does not prevent an appellant from subsequently pursuing an appeal, it might provide assistance for appellants by preventing unrealistic appeals from proceeding.[125] However, the concern is that early neutral evaluation might interfere with users' rights to conventional appeal hearings.

How do tribunals, in practice, handle hearings at which the appellant is unrepresented? While tribunals should provide assistance to unrepresented appellants by adopting the 'enabling' approach advocated by Leggatt, in practice, much will depend on the personal preference of the tribunal judge or panel. On the one hand, the fact that an appellant is unrepresented may require the tribunal judge to play a much more active role in the proceedings than would normally be expected of a judge. Some judges may therefore spend some time in hearings questioning appellants, checking documentation, and ensuring that appellants understand the submissions being made by the governmental agency. On the other hand, some tribunal judges may be concerned that to provide such assistance might undermine their perceived independence and consequently provide little assistance to unrepresented appellants beyond asking them whether there is anything they would like to say.[126] Such concerns notwithstanding, there is much to commend the adoption of the 'enabling' approach as regards unrepresented appellants.

---

[122] Leggatt Report, [4.21].

[123] Adler and Gulland, *Tribunal Users' Experiences, Perceptions and Expectations: A Literature Review* (London 2003), p 27.

[124] Department for Constitutional Affairs, *Transforming Public Services: Complaints, Redress and Tribunals* (Cm 6243 2004), [10.14]. For example, in response to concerns raised by parliamentary select committees concerning the absence of legal aid funding, the government has argued that it is not necessary that legal representation be available for tribunal hearings if the tribunal adopts an inquisitorial or 'enabling' approach. See, eg Joint Committee on Human Rights, *The Treatment of Asylum Seekers* (HL 81 HC 60 2006–07), [99].

[125] In 2006, the President of Social Security and Child Support Appeal Tribunals commenced a pilot project to test the viability of early neutral evaluation and employment tribunals have introduced a mediation pilot to resolve discrimination claims. See Tribunals Service, *Strategic and Business Plan for 2007–08: Delivering the Future. One System, One Service* (London 2007), pp 16–17.

[126] Genn, 'Tribunals and Informal Justice' (1993) 56 MLR 393, 407.

In addition to representation of appellants, it is also important to consider representation of the governmental agency the decision of which is being appealed against. The agency will normally be represented at tribunal hearings by one of its officials—a presenting officer, whose function it is to defend the initial decision and to assist the tribunal in coming to a legally correct decision. The presenting officer may cross-examine the appellant to establish the facts of the case and may make submissions to the tribunal as to why the appeal should be dismissed. The risk here is that unrepresented appellants may be disadvantaged by an inequality of arms. After all, government agencies are 'repeat players', in that they frequently appear before tribunals, and are fully aware of tribunal procedure and case law.[127] By comparison, most appellants are 'one-shotters' who are appealing for the first time; unfamiliarity with the system may place them at a disadvantage. For example, the Council on Tribunals expressed concern about the legal representation of headteachers and schools before school exclusion appeal panels, because this raises inequality-of-arms issues given that the parents of an excluded child are often unrepresented.[128]

In the two largest tribunal systems—social security, and immigration and asylum—the declining attendance of presenting officers at appeal hearings has become a feature of such appeals and has been subject to criticism.[129] While this may reduce any inequality in relation to an unrepresented appellant, it may, at the same time, pose some difficulties for the tribunal judge, because the tribunal will still want to have the appellant's evidence tested properly. Without a presenting officer to conduct cross-examination, the tribunal will have to ask its own questions, but will need to be careful not to be seen to be undertaking cross-examination, as this might imply that the judge has descended into the arena and compromised his or her independence and impartiality. Equally, in other jurisdictions, the approach of the relevant government agency has been criticised. For example, the Chief Parking Adjudicator has repeatedly criticised local authorities for the late disclosure of evidence at appeal stage and the high proportion of appeals that are uncontested.[130]

4.6 **Informality of tribunal hearings**

Should appeal hearings be informal? To what extent do tribunals achieve informality? The degree of formality or informality in tribunal hearings depends on several

---

[127] Galanter, 'Why the "Haves" Come Out Ahead: Speculations on the Limits of Legal Change' (1974) Law and Society 95.

[128] Council on Tribunals, *School Admission and Exclusion Appeal Panels: Special Report* (Cm 5788 2003), pp 17–18.

[129] For example, in 2006–07, presenting officers attended 81 per cent of social security appeal hearings. For criticism of the decline in presenting officers, see Harris, *President's Report: Report by the President of Appeal Tribunals on the Standards of Decision-Making by the Secretary of State 2006–07* (London 2007), [1.13]; House of Commons Home Affairs Select Committee, *Immigration Control* (HC 775 2005–06), [364].

[130] House of Commons Select Committee on Transport, *Parking Policy and Enforcement* (HC 748 2005–06), [120]–[123].

factors. First, tribunals are tending to move away from traditional, adversarial court procedures and toward the more 'enabling' approach advocated by Leggatt. Tribunals are not bound by strict court procedure. Second, there is the process through which evidence is given by the appellant and any witnesses. Tribunals are not bound by the ordinary rules of evidence used in courts. Third, there is the physical nature of the hearing room itself. Is the hearing room set out like a court or are hearings more like case conferences? Does the tribunal judge or panel sit on a raised platform or do all of the parties sit around the same table (more suggestive of an informal discussion of an individual's case)? Fourth, there is the general atmosphere of the appeal hearing. Fifth, the formality of tribunal hearings can be affected by the presence of a representative.

Tribunals were designed to have less formal procedures than the ordinary courts, and to be more user-friendly and accessible than the courts. However, there may be substantial differences in the (in)formality of tribunal appeal hearings not only between different tribunal systems, but also between different hearings of the same tribunal conducted by different tribunal judges. For example, social security appeals are amongst the more inquisitorial and informal hearings, with the tribunal acting more as a panel of experts than as a court substitute. This is reflected in the stipulations in procedure rules that require such appeals to be conducted without 'unnecessary formality' and that, as far as possible, 'the parties are able to participate fully in the proceedings'.[131] However, in other jurisdictions, such as asylum and immigrations, the tribunal operates as a court in all but name.[132] In this jurisdiction, there is a well-entrenched adversarial culture in which both sides—the appellant and the Home Office—strongly contest the immigration status to which the appellant is entitled.

Further, it might be questioned whether informality is really a desirable attribute of tribunals. Genn, for example, has argued that it has been assumed that tribunals ought to be informal because they are largely concerned with resolving simple disputes in which relatively small sums of money might be at stake. The reality is that much of the law involved is complex and the issues at stake in tribunal proceedings can be of great significance to individuals' lives.[133]

While tribunals may profess to adopt informal procedures, the extent to which they actually do so in practice may vary. From the perspective of the tribunal judge, it might be beneficial to have some degree of informality in order to put appellants at their ease; at the same time, too much informality may mean that the proceedings are not treated with the degree of seriousness that they deserve. Research has suggested that many appellants find tribunals more formal than they had expected.[134] Many

---

[131] These requirements apply to the Upper Tribunal and to most chambers of the FTT.

[132] The Asylum and Immigration Tribunal (Procedure) Rules 2005, SI 2005/230, which govern proceedings in the Immigration and Asylum Chamber of the FTT, do not contain the stipulations as to flexibility and participation mentioned above.

[133] Genn, 'Tribunals and Informal Justice' (1993) 56 MLR 393.

[134] Adler and Gulland, *Tribunal Users' Experiences, Perceptions and Expectations: A Literature Review* (London 2003).

tribunals operate on an adversarial and legalistic basis. For example, special educational needs appeals should not be adversarial, but they can become so if parents seek to protect their children's best interests.[135]

In any event, informality of procedure does not absolve the need for tribunals to perform their central function: the application of legal tests to the factual circumstances of an individual's case. It has therefore been argued that the informality of tribunals may present a trap for unwary appellants.[136] Having formed the impression that tribunals are informal, appellants might gain a false impression in thinking that their cases are to be heard and decided with informality as regards both the procedure at appeal hearings and as regards the application of the relevant legal rules. In other words, appellants might think that they simply need to tell the tribunal about their case and that the tribunal will, irrespective of the law, dispense justice. The difficulty, of course, is that tribunals can only allow or dismiss appeals according to the relevant legal rules: appellants must fit their factual circumstances, as supported by evidence, within the applicable rules; tribunal hearings are necessarily legalistic. The upshot is that unrepresented appellants who are misled by the impression of informality may be at a serious disadvantage. Some cases that possess merit may therefore nevertheless be lost by default.

4.7 **Oral and paper appeals**

To what extent do tribunals determine appeals through an oral hearing and what are the implications for this as regards the effectiveness of tribunals? In most, although not all, tribunals, oral hearings are the norm. In some jurisdictions, such as social security and criminal injuries compensation appeals, there is no automatic right to an oral hearing; rather, appellants have to 'opt in'—although they are advised that those who do attend their hearing usually do better than those who do not. By comparison, other tribunals, such as the parking adjudicators, determine the majority of their appeals solely on the basis of written documents.

There are a number of advantages to having appeals heard through an oral hearing.[137] Oral hearings may be more user-friendly than written procedures. They might be particularly suitable in cases that turn on many disputed facts or complex issues, making it necessary to have the evidence tested rigorously. For example, if the credibility of a witness has been questioned, then the tribunal might be assisted by an oral hearing at which the tribunal can assess the witness in person. Oral hearings might also give the tribunal a better opportunity to uncover information not available in the documentary evidence. Appellants attending oral hearings may present additional

---

[135] House of Commons Education and Skills Select Committee, *Special Educational Needs* (HC 478 2005–06), [222].   [136] Genn at 401–2.

[137] See Council on Tribunals, *The Use and Value of Oral Hearings in the Administrative Justice System: Consultation Paper* (London 2005); Council on Tribunals, *Consultation on the Use and Value of Oral Hearings in the Administrative Justice System: Summary of Responses* (London 2006).

evidence or shed new light on existing evidence; tribunal members have the opportunity to check information and elicit evidence that may have appeared irrelevant to the appellant.

Oral hearings may also perform a symbolic role in enabling appellants to have their 'day in court' and might allow justice to be seen to be done in a more transparent way than written procedures. Attendance by appellants at oral hearings might have a positive impact on their comprehension of, and confidence in, the tribunal process. Furthermore, there is always the risk that, without an oral hearing, the tribunal may simply confirm the initial refusal decision by rubber-stamping it. For example, the Asylum and Immigration Tribunal[138] noted that if tribunal judges, when considering an appeal without an oral hearing, fail to make a proper assessment of the evidence, then this is inconsistent with judicial independence.[139]

The importance of oral hearings by tribunals has been recognised by the higher courts. For example, in *FP (Iran)*, the Court of Appeal struck down a procedural rule regarding immigration and asylum appeals that stated that the tribunal *must* hear an appeal in the absence of an appellant if satisfied that the appellant had been notified of the hearing, but had not satisfactorily explained his or her absence.[140] The Court of Appeal concluded that the procedural rule was productive of irremediable unfairness, because it penalised appellants who had lost the opportunity to an oral hearing (for example, through the fault of their representative) and unnecessarily sacrificed fairness to speed.

Empirical research has demonstrated that there is a strong correlation between an appellant's attendance at an oral hearing and the successful outcome of appeals.[141] For example, in the social security context, 63 per cent of appellants who attended their hearing with a representative were successful, while 45 per cent for those who attended without a representative were successful; by comparison, only 17 per cent of those appellants who did not attend were successful.[142]

However, this is not to deny that there may be problems associated with oral hearings. They can be costly, time-consuming, and inefficient. As some tribunals deal with mass adjudication, an expectation that all appeals be dealt with through oral hearings can substantially increase costs and delays. Determining appeals solely on the basis of papers can reduce operating costs and enable large volumes of appeals to be dealt with more speedily. Appellants may also find oral hearings daunting and legalistic, and

---

[138] The functions of which have now been taken over by the Immigration and Asylum Chamber of the FTT.   [139] *Oyeleye v Entry Clearance Officer, Lagos* (01TH02325), [6].

[140] *FP (Iran) v Secretary of State for the Home Department* [2007] EWCA Civ 13. See also *R (Smith) v Parole Board* [2005] UKHL 1, [2005] 1 WLR 350.

[141] Genn, 'Tribunal Review of Administrative Decision-Making', in Richardson and Genn (eds), *Administrative Law and Government Action: The Courts and Alternative Mechanisms of Review* (Oxford 1994), pp 270–2; Thomas, 'Immigration Appeals for Family Visitors Refused Entry Clearance' [2004] PL 612, 631–9.

[142] House of Commons Social Security Committee, *The Modernisation of Social Security Appeals* (HC 581 1998–99), [42].

prefer not to attend if their appeal could otherwise be adequately determined. The government has expressed the view that its aim is to reduce the need for hearings before tribunals through better decisions and innovative proportionate dispute resolution methods, such as early neutral evaluation.[143]

4.8 **Tribunal reason-giving**

We saw in Chapter 13 that there is increasing recognition of the importance of giving reasons for public decisions.[144] The provision of reasons ensures that the decision-maker has addressed his or her mind to the basis of the decision. Reason-giving may then promote the aim of reaching accurate decisions by demonstrating that the decision-maker has collected and analysed the relevant facts, and applied the applicable legal rules. It also performs a key role in legitimising decisions and ensuring their acceptability. By detailing adequate reasons, the tribunal is able to tell the losing party why he or she has lost, demonstrate that it has adequately addressed the factual and legal issues that have arisen in the case, and enable the losing party to appreciate whether or not there has been any appealable error.

Although, as explained in Chapter 13, there is still no overarching common law duty to give reasons for administrative decisions, tribunals are statutorily required to give reasons.[145] However, the way in which tribunals discharge this duty varies. Some tribunals have conventionally given reasons only in summary form, with greater detail being provided only upon request, while in some areas—most notably, asylum and immigration—judges usually produce a lengthy, written determination in each appeal containing the reasons for the decision.

As regards the standard of reasons, it is a well-established principle of administrative law that reasons should be proper, adequate, and intelligible, and should deal with the substantial points that have been raised.[146] A failure to give such reasons may amount to an error of law. Indeed, most challenges to tribunal decisions are made on the ground that the reasons given were inadequate. How detailed, then, must the reasons be? There is an obvious tension here between the pressure on a tribunal to process a large number of appeals quickly, and the need to reach demonstrably robust and adequate decisions. Tribunal reasons should deal with the principal issues in disputes, but do not need cover every single issue. As the Court of Appeal has noted, it is 'a long established principle of administrative law that it is not to be assumed that a decision-maker has left a piece of evidence out of account merely because he does not refer to it

---

[143] Department for Constitutional Affairs, *Transforming Public Services: Complaints, Redress and Tribunals* (Cm 6243 2004), [10.11].   [144] See Chapter 13, section 3.7, above.

[145] Tribunals and Inquiries Act 1992, s 10; Procedure Rules for the Chambers of the First-tier Tribunals and the Upper Tribunal.

[146] *Re Poyser and Mills' Arbitration* [1964] 2 QB 467, 478, *per* Megaw J. See also *Save Britain's Heritage v Secretary of State for the Environment* [1991] 1 WLR 153; *South Bucks District Council v Porter* [2004] UKHL 33, [2004] 1 WLR 1953.

in his decision'.[147] A tribunal decision should not therefore be set aside for inadequacy of reasons unless the tribunal had failed to identify and record the matters that were critical to the decision in such a way that a reviewing court is unable to understand why the decision was reached.

4.9 **Improving initial decision-making—feedback from tribunals**

To what extent are tribunal decisions used as feedback to initial decision-makers in order to improve the quality of initial decision-making? While the purpose of tribunals is to determine appeals in individual cases, it is apparent that initial governmental decision-makers could learn broader lessons from tribunal decisions in order to improve the quality of initial decisions and thereby prevent some cases from proceeding to the appeal stage. The broader concern here is that the quality of initial decision-making across many areas of administration is not of a sufficiently high and robust standard. Concerns have been frequently raised that initial decisions are not always made on the basis of a full appreciation of the relevant facts, that initial decision-makers do not thoroughly investigate initial claims, or that they misapply the relevant rules. It has also been argued that initial decision-makers are not sufficiently well trained and prepared, and that organisational pressures to process a mass of decisions quickly might dilute their quality. Tribunals have themselves often raised concerns as to the quality of initial decision-making.[148]

At the same time, it should be recognised that taking decisions is often a complex activity requiring the sensitive exercise of judgement.[149] For example, social security decision-making can require careful judgement and assessment of the effect of an applicant's illness or disability on his or her life, while asylum adjudication is perhaps the most problematic form of decision-making in the legal system.[150] It is rarely possible to know whether or not decisions are objectively correct. It is therefore possible for different decision-makers to reach quite different conclusions about the same case. That an initial decision is overturned at the appeal stage by a tribunal may simply reflect the fact that the tribunal judge made a different judgement from that of the initial decision-maker. Furthermore, appellants may often present new information

---

[147] *RG (Ethiopia) v Secretary of State for the Home Department* [2006] EWCA Civ 339, [37].

[148] For example, see the report produced by the President of Social Security and Child Support Appeal Tribunals: Harris, *President's Report: Report by the President of Appeal Tribunals on the Standards of Decision-Making by the Secretary of State 2006–07* (London 2007). In *IO v Entry Clearance Officer, Lagos ('Points in Issue') Nigeria* [2004] UKIAT 00179, [3], the Asylum and Immigration Tribunal noted that the reasons provided in the initial decision were 'quite inadequate' and that it was 'disappointing to see that decisions of this quality' were still being prepared.

[149] See Baldwin and Hawkins, 'Discretionary Justice: *Davis* Reconsidered' [1984] PL 570, 580–6.

[150] National Audit Office, *Getting it Right, Putting it Right: Improving Decision-Making and Appeals in Social Security Benefits* (HC 1142 2002–03), pp 21–8; Thomas, 'Risk, Legitimacy and Asylum Adjudication' (2007) 58 NILQ 49.

or evidence concerning their case to the tribunal that was not available to the initial decision-maker.

It is generally recognised that the quality of primary decision-making—getting it 'right first time'—is central to providing a high-quality public service to individuals and that it is fundamental to how administrative justice operates. Tribunals are well placed to pick up systemic problems in decision-making within governmental agencies, from decision letters that are confusing, through administrative systems that muddle key facts, to flawed decision-making processes that lead to misconceptions of the law. If the feedback provided by tribunals is used to improve the quality of initial decisions, then this can have several advantages. Higher-quality decision-making at the initial stage may reduce the need to appeal, and so the need for lengthy and costly appeal proceedings. On this basis, the National Audit Office—unsurprisingly, given its focus on achieving better value for money—has emphasised the financial case for raising the quality of initial decision-making.[151] Better initial decisions benefit both the wider public and individuals.

On a practical level, tribunals provide feedback to governmental agencies responsible for initial decision-making on the standard of decisions many times every day—by making their decisions and passing them back to the agency to put into effect. The issue, though, is the extent to which such agencies take account of such feedback in order to improve decision-making systemically. Research into social security appeals has indicated that the impact of appellate decisions may be greater if the official responsible for making the initial decision appears before the tribunal as the presenting officer charged with defending the decision.[152] For example, the official may become more aware of the need to substantiate decisions more carefully to ensure that they withstand scrutiny before the tribunal. However, it is apparent that, in many cases, the same official will not be responsible both for making the initial decision and for defending it before the tribunal. Furthermore, levels of attendance by presenting officers in some jurisdictions can be low. Even if feedback is received, initial decision-makers may have neither the time nor the inclination to learn from the tribunal's decision. In some areas, the legal consciousness of initial decision-makers—their awareness of the importance of legal norms—and their understanding of, or even their willingness to understand, tribunal decision-making may be limited. Further, the low rate of appeals inevitably limits the amount of feedback that tribunals can provide.

In any event, as the Leggatt Report noted, the provision of formal, systematic feedback from tribunals to initial decision-makers is an underdeveloped practice in many jurisdictions.[153] Yet there are examples of good practice: for example, the

---

[151] See National Audit Office, p 42; National Audit Office, *Visa Entry to the United Kingdom: The Entry Clearance Operation* (HC 367 2003–04), p 28.

[152] Wikeley and Young, 'The Administration of Benefits in Britain: Adjudication Officers and the Influence of Social Security Appeal Tribunals' [1992] PL 238.

[153] Leggatt Report, [9.12].

President of Social Security and Child Support Appeal Tribunals used to report annually on primary decision-making standards.[154] However, tribunals have not generally developed robust mechanisms through which initial decision-makers may learn lessons; they are simply at the end of the decision-making process with no mechanism to feed back their views on decision-making or any expectation that such views would be acted upon if they were to do so. Furthermore, some tribunals may be disinclined to engage in such a dialogue because of concerns that it might undermine their independence. Such concerns, though, may be misplaced: providing feedback to initial decision-makers seeks to improve the quality of decisions and does not necessarily jeopardise the perception of judicial independence. A broader difficulty is that legal accountability of governmental decision-making, as provided by tribunals, is only one of the pressures on governmental agencies; they are also subject to political and administrative accountability. For example, there is an obvious tension between political and administrative pressures on a governmental agency to determine a large number of decisions quickly, and legal pressures from the tribunal to raise decision-making quality.

In order to provide a formal mechanism of feedback from tribunals to initial decision-makers in the reformed tribunal system, the Senior President of Tribunals must report annually to the Lord Chancellor bringing matters to his attention.[155] The purpose of this annual report is to support improvement both in the workings of the tribunals and the standards of primary decision-making in cases that come before the tribunals. The report must cover appeals coming before the FTT, the Upper Tribunal, the Employment Appeal Tribunal, and the employment tribunals.[156] In its White Paper announcing the new tribunals system, the government indicated that the Senior President's formal reports should be underpinned by a cooperative approach between the Tribunals Service and initial decision-makers. The White Paper noted that this approach was to be facilitated by 'partnership agreements' between the Tribunals Service and decision-makers, which set out the way in which the two bodies are intended to relate to one another, including in relation to the provision of feedback by tribunals.[157] However, because no such agreements have yet been published, it remains to be seen whether government departments are receptive to the whole notion of learning from tribunal feedback.

Finally, it should be observed that while feedback from tribunals may improve initial decision-making, there are a host of other devices that governmental agencies may use to raise initial decisional quality. These include: the redesign of administrative processes and applicable legal rules to minimise the risk of error and uncertainty; better training and support for decision-makers; and quality assurance techniques that

---

[154] Such reports were made pursuant to a statutory obligation. This arrangement has now been superseded by the one described in the following paragraph.   [155] TCEA, s 43.

[156] TCEA, s 43(3).

[157] Department for Constitutional Affairs, *Transforming Public Services: Complaints, Redress and Tribunals* (Cm 6243 2004), [6.33].

monitor decision-making quality irrespective of whether individuals appeal against negative decisions.[158]

4.10 **Tribunals and legal precedent**

Given their status within the legal hierarchy, tribunals are, of course, bound by legal precedents created by the higher courts—but to what extent do tribunal decisions themselves create legal precedents? This question is often wide of the mark because the vast majority of the work of tribunals involves merits appeals—making decisions in individual cases—in which precedents concerning points of law are unlikely to be set in the first place. However, this is not to deny that tribunals are sometimes presented with cases that can be determined only by confronting contested points of law. Against this background, some of the larger, high-volume tribunal jurisdictions have developed their own ways of creating legal precedent.[159]

Strictly speaking, as creatures of statutes, tribunals are not able to establish their own legal precedents: that ability is reserved for the higher courts. However, it has long been recognised that some system is needed whereby tribunals can make authoritative decisions rather than make individual adjudications. Most tribunal systems are relatively self-enclosed: because of the low rate of onward challenge against tribunal decisions, the opportunities for the higher courts to establish precedents on the many and various legal issues that arise in tribunal adjudication are, in practice, limited. At the same time, because such tribunals specialise in large and legally complex areas, some form of precedent has been necessary in order to ensure consistency. Most tribunals undertake precisely the same type of work as the higher courts in clarifying important points of law, and interpreting primary and secondary legislation. If tribunals in practice perform a role in clarifying important legal points, it is therefore desirable that such decisions form legal precedents in order to promote consistency and to prevent subsequent tribunals from rehearing the same issues. These arguments are widely recognised: the higher courts have approved of tribunals establishing their own legal precedents,[160] and the Leggatt Report saw advantages in tribunals having the ability to designate some cases as binding.[161]

Tribunals can designate as binding important precedents to ensure consistency amongst their tribunal judiciary. This also provides a degree of certainty for tribunal users. The establishment of the Upper Tribunal presents an obvious opportunity for the development of a principled and consistent approach towards the role of tribunals in creating legal precedents. To enable the Upper Tribunal properly to fulfil

---

[158] For discussion, see Adler, 'Tribunal Reform: Proportionate Dispute Resolution and the Pursuit of Administrative Justice' (2006) 69 MLR 958, 971–85.

[159] See generally Buck, 'Precedent in Tribunals and the Development of Principles' (2006) 25 CJQ 458; Carnwath, 'Tribunal Justice: A New Start' [2009] PL 48, 58–60.

[160] See, eg *Sepet and Bulbul v Secretary of State for the Home Department* [2001] Imm AR 452, 488, *per* Laws LJ.   [161] Leggatt Report, [6.26].

its role in achieving consistency in the application of the law and so as to encourage the development of precedent across tribunals, a series of common principles with regard to precedent is to be developed in partnership with the jurisdictional presidents. This will promote a common view of how these issues should be tackled across jurisdictions, but leave scope for a flexible approach in particular jurisdictions.[162] Meanwhile, some established protocols predating the new tribunals system have been accommodated within it. For example, the Upper Tribunal (Immigration and Asylum Chamber) issues both 'starred' decisions, which are generally binding on points of law, and 'country guidance' decisions, which are generally binding as to the factual conditions in countries from which political asylum has been sought.[163]

4.11 Enforcement of tribunal decisions

To what extent can tribunal decisions be enforced? Such decisions are just as binding on the parties as court decisions, but, unlike the courts, tribunals have no direct powers of enforcement. In most cases, both parties will accept the tribunal's decision unless they wish to challenge it through the appropriate legal procedures. In the rare cases in which a government agency refuses to give effect to a tribunal's decision, then direct enforcement of the tribunal's decision can be sought in the courts. For example, in *R (S) v Secretary of State for the Home Department*,[164] the Home Secretary had deliberately delayed giving effect to the Asylum and Immigration Tribunal's decision that the removal of nine Afghan nationals from the UK, who had arrived on a hijacked plane, would contravene the prohibition on torture and inhuman and degrading treatment under Art 3 of the European Convention on Human Rights (ECHR). The Administrative Court concluded that this delay amounted to conspicuous unfairness and an abuse of power. While the case had raised sensitive political issues, there was an important public interest in ensuring that the executive acted lawfully in implementing tribunal decisions. The Home Secretary could not seek deliberately to circumvent a decision of an independent tribunal simply because he disagreed with the outcome, unless the decision could be set aside through the appropriate legal procedures, because this would undermine the rule of law.

Q Think back through the topics raised in this section concerning tribunal procedures. To what extent do tribunals provide individuals with an effective mechanism of redress against initial governmental decisions? How could tribunal procedures be improved?

---

[162] Department for Constitutional Affairs, *Transforming Public Services: Complaints, Redress and Tribunals* (Cm 6243 2004), [7.20].

[163] Practice Direction concerning the Immigration and Asylum Chambers of the First-tier Tribunal and the Upper Tribunal (2010), [12]. See also Thomas, 'Consistency in Asylum Adjudication: Country Guidance and the Asylum Process in the United Kingdom' (2008) 20 International Journal of Refugee Law 489.

[164] [2006] EWHC 1111 (Admin); [2006] EWCA Civ 1157.

5. Judicial oversight of tribunal decision-making

5.1 Judicial control of tribunals

Lord Denning MR once said that 'if tribunals were to be at liberty to exceed their jurisdiction without any check by the courts, the rule of law would be at an end'.[165] This reflects the fact that tribunals are creatures of statute: they have limited powers, and the rule of law requires that they, like other holders of statutory power, be kept within the confines of their jurisdiction. Until recently, this task necessarily fell to the higher courts, but was accomplished through what was fairly described as a 'hotchpotch' of arrangements:[166] some tribunals' decisions could be appealed to the High Court on points of law;[167] others could be judicially reviewed; and, in some cases, there were rights of appeal against tribunals' decisions to second-level appellate tribunals such as the Social Security and Child Support Commissioners. The unstructured and incoherent nature of these arrangements was unsurprising, given the unstructured growth of tribunals themselves.

5.2 Appeals from the First-tier Tribunal to the Upper Tribunal

To remedy this rather confusing situation, the TCEA introduced new uniform arrangements for judicial oversight of tribunal decisions. In general, appeals against decisions taken in an FTT chamber lie to the Upper Tribunal, which can identify any error of law in the initial tribunal decision (see Figure 17.2[168]). The policy behind the new arrangements is that onward appeal rights should be based on a simple and coherent appellate system; tribunal cases should proceed to the higher courts only when issues of sufficient weight and importance need to be resolved.

There is a general right of appeal from decisions of the FTT to the Upper Tribunal by any party to an appeal.[169] However, certain tribunal decisions are excluded.[170] Permission to appeal may be given by either the FTT or the Upper Tribunal. An appellant may only appeal to the Upper Tribunal on the ground that the FTT made an error of law.[171] If the Upper Tribunal finds that the FTT has made an error of law, then it may set aside the decision and either remit the case back to the FTT with directions for its reconsideration or make the decision that it considers should have been made. If it takes the latter option, it can make findings of fact. If the Upper Tribunal sends

---

[165] *R v Medical Appeal Tribunal, ex p Gilmore* [1957] 1 QB 574.
[166] Woolf, 'A Hotchpotch of Appeals: The Need for a Blender' (1988) 7 CJQ 44.
[167] Tribunals and Inquiries Act 1992, s 11.   [168] At section 3.4 above.
[169] TCEA, s 11.
[170] TCEA, s 11(5). For example, criminal injury compensation appeals against decisions on reviews, data protection and freedom of information appeals against national security certificates, and decisions of the FTT to review, or not to review, an earlier decision are excluded from appeal to the Upper Tribunal.
[171] TCEA, s 12.

the case back to the FTT, it may direct that a different panel reconsiders the case. The Upper Tribunal may also give procedural directions in relation to the case. If the Upper Tribunal decides that the error of law does not invalidate the decision of the FTT, it must let that decision stand.

Both the FTT and the Upper Tribunal can review their own decisions without the need for a full onward appeal, and, where the tribunal concludes that an error was made, it can re-decide the matter.[172] The purpose of this review is to capture decisions that are clearly wrong, so avoiding the need for an onward appeal. The power of review of both tribunals is provided in the form of a discretionary power, so that only appropriate decisions are reviewed. Both tribunals may review a decision made within the tribunal either of its own initiative or on application by any party who has a right of appeal in respect of the decision. Both tribunals have the power to correct accidental errors in the decision or in a record of the decision, amend the reasons given for the decision, or set aside the decision. If the decision is set aside, then the tribunal concerned must re-decide the matter.

5.3 **Error of law**

Appeals to the Upper Tribunal are confined to examining whether there is an error of law in the initial tribunal's merits appeal decision. What is an error of law? The higher courts have identified a number of grounds that illustrate the range of errors that count as errors of law:

(i) Making perverse or irrational findings on a matter or matters that were material to the outcome ('material matters').

(ii) Failing to give reasons or any adequate reasons for findings on material matters.

(iii) Failing to take into account and/or resolve conflicts of fact or opinion on material matters.

(iv) Giving weight to immaterial matters.

(v) Making a material misdirection of law on any material matter.

(vi) Committing or permitting a procedural or other irregularity capable of making a material difference to the outcome or the fairness of the proceedings.[173]

A poor factual decision by a tribunal will not normally, by itself, qualify as an error of law unless the reasons given are clearly inadequate or the findings are irrational. However, it is possible that a mistake concerning a factual issue can be an error of law if the mistake can be established by objective and uncontentious evidence, the

---

[172] TCEA, ss 9–10.

[173] *R (Iran) v Secretary of State for the Home Department* [2005] EWCA Civ 982, [2005] INLR 633, 640, *per* Brooke LJ.

appellant and/or his advisers were not responsible for the mistake, and unfairness resulted from the fact that a mistake was made.[174]

This list is indicative. It is not possible to provide an exhaustive list of all errors of law. This is because the concept of 'error of law'—and thus the distinction between errors of law and errors of fact—is not entirely clear. In other words, because 'error of law' has never been precisely and conclusively defined by the higher courts, there remains some latitude for a second-tier tribunal such as the Upper Tribunal to define the scope of that principle through its application in individual cases. The scope of the concept may depend on a number of factors, such as the relationship between the second-tier tribunal and the first-tier tribunal, and the willingness or otherwise of the former to intervene. For example, if the second-tier tribunal considers that the decision of the first-tier tribunal was clearly wrong, then it may be more inclined to adopt a broad conception of 'error of law' (that is, manufacture an error of law), so that it has some basis on which to interfere with the first-tier tribunal's decision. On the other hand, if a second-tier tribunal regularly upsets tribunal decisions on error of law grounds, then it may find itself, in effect, overturning such decisions merely because it does not like them—in other words, substituting its own judgment for that of the first-tier tribunal on the merits of individual cases even though its jurisdiction is limited to identifying errors of law. The consequence of this might be to undermine the role of the first-tier tribunal in determining merits appeals, and to increase the length and cost of the process. Other factors—in addition to just outcomes, and the timeliness and cost of appeal processes—might also inform the scope of the concept of 'error of law' as applied by a second-tier tribunal. For example, the need for consistency in tribunal decision-making, the perceived expertise of the first-tier tribunal, the particular demands of the context in which such challenges arise (for example, social security, immigration), the volume of the second-tier tribunal's own caseload, and the personal assessments of judges in the second-tier tribunal concerning the desirability of intervention might all influence how widely or narrowly the concept of 'error of law' is drawn.

5.4 **Further appeals to the Court of Appeal**

Appeals against substantive decisions of the Upper Tribunal lie to the Court of Appeal.[175] The link between tribunal appeals structures and the higher courts is important both to maintain the independence of tribunals and to ensure fidelity to general principles of law. Where the Court of Appeal determines that the Upper Tribunal has made an error of law, it has power to set aside the decision and either send the case back to the Upper Tribunal to be re-decided (or, where the decision of the Upper Tribunal was on an appeal or reference from another tribunal or some

---

[174] *E v Secretary of State for the Home Department* [2004] EWCA Civ 49, [2004] QB 1044.
[175] TCEA, s 13.

other person, to that other tribunal or person, with direction for its reconsideration), or to make the decision that it considers the Upper Tribunal (or the other tribunal or person) should have made.[176]

However, there are two features that will tend, in practice, to limit the scope for onward appeals from the Upper Tribunal to the Court of Appeal. First, under the 2007 Act, the Court of Appeal can only grant permission to appeal against a decision of the Upper Tribunal if the case raises 'some important point of principle or practice' or if there is 'some other compelling reason' for the appeal to be heard.[177] This means that, to obtain the Court of Appeal's permission to appeal, it is insufficient that there is merely some error in the individual case concerned; there must also be some wider point of legal principle or practice that justifies the case proceeding to the Court. Second, the higher courts have been developing an approach under which, while they retain jurisdiction over tribunal decisions, they will normally adopt an appropriate degree of caution because of the special knowledge, expertise, and competence of such tribunals.[178] In practice, this means that higher courts, such as the Court of Appeal, will recognise that tribunals specialise in their particular areas of law and that

> [t]heir decisions should be respected unless it is quite clear that they have misdirected themselves in law. Appellate courts should not rush to find such misdirections simply because they might have reached a different conclusion on the facts or expressed themselves differently.[179]

5.5 The Upper Tribunal's 'judicial review' jurisdiction

As noted above, tribunals determine appeals; they do not possess powers of judicial review. However, the 2007 Act provides that the Upper Tribunal has a 'judicial review' jurisdiction and can exercise judicial review powers in appropriate cases.[180] This allows the parties to have the benefit of the specialist expertise of the Upper Tribunal in cases similar to those with which the Upper Tribunal routinely deals in the exercise of its statutory appellate jurisdiction.

Certain conditions must be met for the Upper Tribunal to exercise its judicial review jurisdiction.[181] The first is that the applicant in question is only seeking a remedy that the Upper Tribunal is able to grant. In this regard, it should be noted that the Upper

---

176 TCEA, s 14.

177 TCEA, s 13(6); Appeals from the Upper Tribunal to the Court of Appeal Order 2008, SI 2008/2834, para 2.

178 See, eg *R v Preston Supplementary Benefits Appeal Tribunal* [1975] 1 WLR 625; *Cooke v Secretary of State for Social Security* [2002] 3 All ER 279; *Napp Pharmaceutical Holdings Ltd v Director-General of Fair Trading* [2002] EWCA Civ 796, [2002] 4 All ER 376; *Hinchy v Secretary of State for Work and Pensions* [2005] UKHL 16, [2005] 1 WLR 967; *Akaeke v Secretary of State for the Home Department* [2005] EWCA Civ 947, [2005] Imm AR 701; *AH (Sudan) v Secretary of State for the Home Department* [2007] UKHL 49; [2008] 1 AC 678, HL, [30].

179 *AH (Sudan) v Secretary of State for the Home Department* [2007] UKHL 49; [2008] 1 AC 678, HL, [30], *per* Baroness Hale.   180 TCEA, s 15.

181 TCEA, s 18.

Tribunal cannot grant declarations of incompatibility under s 4 of the Human Rights Act 1998. The second condition is that the application does not call into question anything done by the Crown Court. This is because it would be anomalous to give the Upper Tribunal, a superior court of record, supervisory powers over another superior court of record. The third condition is that the application falls within a class of case designated by a direction made by, or on behalf of, the Lord Chief Justice, with the concurrence of the Lord Chancellor. The fourth condition is that the judge presiding at the hearing of the application is either a High Court judge or a judge who has the authority of the senior judiciary to do so.

If all four of the above conditions are met, judicial review proceedings must be commenced in the Upper Tribunal; if they are improperly commenced in the High Court, the High Court must transfer them to the Upper Tribunal.[182] Cases satisfying the first two conditions, but which do not fall within one of the categories prescribed for the purposes of the third condition, cannot be commenced in the Upper Tribunal, although the High Court has a discretion to transfer such cases to the Upper Tribunal.[183] Such transfers are likely to occur in cases raising issues closely related to the Upper Tribunal's areas of expertise.

To date, some limited categories of case have been specified for the purpose of the third condition (meaning that they can, and must, be commenced in the Upper Tribunal). These categories concern FTT decisions against which, unusually, there is no right of appeal to the Upper Tribunal, such as FTT decisions concerning criminal injuries compensation. Under the 2007 Act, as originally enacted, it was not possible for cases to be transferred to the Upper Tribunal if they involved immigration or nationality matters.[184] However, this has been amended to allow a particular category of immigration judicial review case—fresh asylum claim judicial reviews—to be transferred from the High Court to the Upper Tribunal.[185] Over recent years, the number of such judicial reviews in the High Court has been very numerous and the Court itself has recognised that such cases could be dealt with appropriately in the Upper Tribunal by senior tribunal judges with immigration law expertise. An incidental benefit of such a transfer is that it relieves the pressure of caseload on the High Court and helps it to speed up its work.

In exercising its judicial review jurisdiction, the Upper Tribunal may grant certain forms of relief in the same way as the High Court on an application for judicial review. For example, it may grant a mandatory order, a prohibiting order, a quashing order, a declaration, or an injunction.[186] Awards made by the Upper Tribunal in exercising

---

[182] Senior Courts Act 1981, s 31A(2).

[183] Senior Courts Act 1981, s 31A(3).   [184] Senior Courts Act 1981, s 31A(7).

[185] Borders, Citizenship and Immigration Act 2009, s 53. This type of case involves a judicial review challenge against a decision by the UK Border Agency not to consider an asylum claim as a fresh claim on the ground that the substance of the claim is not significantly different from material previously considered. Over recent years, the Administrative Court has been receiving approximately 1,000 such judicial review claims per year.   [186] TCEA, s 15(1).

its 'judicial review' jurisdiction may be enforced as if they were awards of the High Court.[187]

5.6 Judicial review of tribunals' decisions

One final question concerning the relationship between the tribunal and court systems needs to be considered: can tribunals' decisions be judicially reviewed? There is no statutory bar against judicial review of the FTT's decisions. However, there is no need to seek judicial review of the FTT because, in general, there is a right of appeal to the Upper Tribunal on error of law grounds; the principle of the exhaustion of alternative remedies precludes the use of judicial review in such circumstances.

What, then, of the Upper Tribunal—can its decisions be judicially reviewed? To consider this question, it is important to recognise the distinction between two types of decision that the Upper Tribunal makes. First, it determines substantive appeals against decisions of the FTT. As we have noted, there is a right of further appeal from the Upper Tribunal to the Court of Appeal in such cases. Second, even before an appeal gets to the Upper Tribunal for substantive consideration, it must first be granted permission to appeal by the Upper Tribunal. If permission to appeal is refused by the Upper Tribunal, then the case cannot proceed to substantive consideration. As there is no right of appeal against the decision to refuse permission, the question of whether such a decision is susceptible to challenge by way of judicial review is a practically important one.

This question arose in *R (Cart) v Upper Tribunal*.[188] The Court of Appeal[189]— upholding conclusions at which the Administrative Court[190] had arrived, but not the entirety of its reasoning—reached two fundamental conclusions. First, in the absence of the 'plainest possible statutory language' in the TCEA, the Upper Tribunal, like any statutory body, was subject to judicial review by the High Court.[191] Second, however, it did not follow that the Upper Tribunal was vulnerable to review on all of the standard grounds; rather, its decisions would be subject to review only if vitiated by a fundamental denial of justice or an assertion of jurisdiction over something plainly beyond the Upper Tribunal's statutory authority.[192]

Q Why is it important for there to be control over tribunal decisions? Does the 2007 Act succeed in establishing a simple and coherent system of judicial control of tribunal decisions?

---

[187] TCEA, s 16(6).   [188] [2009] EWHC 3052 (QB).

[189] [2010] EWCA Civ 859.   [190] [2009] EWHC 3052 (QB).   [191] [2010] EWCA Civ 859, [20].

[192] [2010] EWCA Civ 859, [36] and [42].

6. Conclusions

In this chapter, we have seen that tribunals perform a major role in ensuring the legal accountability of governmental decision-making. While such decision-making is often portrayed as involving high-level decisions by government Ministers, the reality is that the vast majority of the millions of decisions concerning the administration of public policy are of necessity taken by officials within central and local government. In many cases, neither parliamentary accountability, in the form of ministerial responsibility, nor judicial review will provide an adequate and easily accessible mechanism by which people can seek to challenge such decisions. Tribunals have been designed to fill this gap by providing people with an accessible mechanism by which they can challenge initial governmental decisions that they consider to be incorrect.

There are, though, aspects of tribunals that constrain their effectiveness as mechanisms for ensuring legal accountability of governmental decisions. For example, tribunals, like courts, cannot subject the activities of government to systematic scrutiny; they can deal only with the cases that come before them, and the low rate of appeals to tribunals strongly suggests that many incorrect governmental decisions are allowed to stand. The general absence of publicly funded legal representation at appeal hearings disadvantages those appellants who do appeal, while it appears that appellants whose appeals are determined on paper (a practice that is increasingly common) experience a lower rate of success than those who attend oral hearings. The effectiveness of tribunals is also limited by broader policy and organisational factors—not least the pressure on tribunals to process a high volume of cases within prescribed time limits and limited public funding. Furthermore, the tribunals system has, until recently, suffered through the lack of any sort of coherent structure.

These limitations notwithstanding, the tribunals system has recently experienced a period of unprecedented reform initiated by the Leggatt Report, developed by the *Transforming Public Services* White Paper, and implemented by the 2007 Act. Looked at as a whole, this reform package comprises the most radical overhaul of the tribunal system ever undertaken. The establishment of the First-tier Tribunal and the Upper Tribunal introduces a simple structure for tribunals. The Lord Chancellor is under statutory obligations to protect the independence of tribunals, and to ensure that there is an efficient and effective tribunal system administered by the Tribunals Service. The Senior President of Tribunals provides (previously lacking) senior judicial leadership for tribunals.[193] Further, tribunals themselves are undertaking significant reforms: wider use of the 'enabling' approach, better mechanisms for providing feedback to primary decision-makers, and greater use of early neutral evaluation to prevent unnecessary appeals. Of course, the inherent tensions in the concept of administrative justice between the competing imperatives of (on the one hand) public administration and

---

[193] However, as noted in section 3.5 above, the government proposes to abolish the post of Senior President of Tribunals, albeit that a new post of Head of Tribunals would be created.

policy implementation and (on the other hand) the fair and just resolution of disputes are unlikely ever to be fully resolved. However, the changes taking place within tribunals and broader organisational reforms have the potential to secure a more structured and coherent tribunals system that better achieves justice for individuals and legal accountability of government.

Further reading

ADLER, 'Tribunal Reform: Proportionate Dispute Resolution and the Pursuit of Administrative Justice' (2006) 69 MLR 958

CARNWATH, 'Tribunal Justice: A New Start' [2009] PL 48

DEPARTMENT FOR CONSTITUTIONAL AFFAIRS, *Transforming Public Services: Complaints, Redress and Tribunals* (Cm 6243 2004)

GENN, 'Tribunal Review of Administrative Decision-Making', in Richardson and Genn (eds), *Administrative Law and Government Action: The Courts and Alternative Mechanisms of Review* (Oxford 1994)

LEGGATT, *Tribunals for Users: One System, One Service: Report of the Review of Tribunals by Sir Andrew Leggatt* (Lord Chancellor's Department 2001), available online at **http://www .tribunals-review.org.uk**

RICHARDSON AND GENN, 'Tribunals in Transition: Resolution or Adjudication?' [2007] PL 116

Useful websites

http://www.ajtc.gov.uk
Website of the Administrative Justice and Tribunals Council

http://www.justice.gov.uk
Website of the Ministry of Justice

http://www.tribunals.gov.uk
Website of the Tribunals Service (with links to the websites of individual tribunals)

Inquiries

18

1. Introduction

When it appears that something has gone wrong either within government or society—for example, a disaster has happened or a major public scandal or alleged political misconduct has been uncovered—there are invariably calls for a full and independent public inquiry to investigate precisely what happened and what, if anything, can be done to ensure that it is not repeated. Government Ministers may come under pressure to establish an inquiry—that is, an official investigation into the particular source of public concern with a view to making recommendations. Such inquiries are relatively common in the United Kingdom and are both 'a pivotal part of public life in Britain, and a major instrument of accountability'.[1] In this chapter, we consider the role, function, and operation of public inquiries established by government in order to undertake an official investigation into a matter of public concern. This topic is of significance to one of our central themes—the constitutional processes that ensure accountability of government. Attention will therefore be focused on the way in which inquiries are established, their effectiveness, and proposals for their reform.

2. Inquiries—nature, function, and legal framework

2.1 What are inquiries?

The phrase 'independent public inquiry' is often used loosely to refer to a range of different official investigations, such as inquiries into transport or industrial accidents, as well as planning inquiries as to whether, for example, an airport ought to have an additional runway or a new motorway ought to be built. Such routine inquiries—routine in the sense that they are customarily, or legally, required to be held in particular circumstances—serve an important function. However, our concern in this chapter is with inquiries of a different type—namely, those established by

---

[1] House of Commons Public Administration Select Committee (PASC), *Government by Inquiry* (HC 51 2004–05), [2].

government Ministers in order to undertake an official investigation into a particular matter of public concern. These types of inquiry are established on an ad hoc basis in response to a particular event. While such inquiries are not numerous, they often address particularly important, controversial, and difficult issues. Let us start with some examples of recent inquiries.

- The Stephen Lawrence inquiry, which reported in 1999, investigated the circumstances surrounding the racially motivated killing of a black teenager and, in particular, sought to identify the lessons to be learned for the police as regards the investigation and prosecution of racially motivated crimes.[2] The report concluded that the police's handling of the investigation had been marked by institutional racism, a wider problem within the police that needed to be addressed.

- Various inquiries have been conducted into organisational failures within the National Health Service (NHS). For example, the Bristol Royal Infirmary (BRI) inquiry investigated the deaths of children receiving complex cardiac surgical services and found serious clinical and organisational failings.[3] The Royal Liverpool Children's Hospital (Alder Hey) inquiry investigated the removal and retention of organs from children after death without their parents' knowledge or consent, and found serious failings in clinical practice and managerial arrangements.[4] The Shipman inquiry investigated the conduct of a general practitioner (GP) who had been responsible for killing many of his patients.[5] All of these inquiries investigated matters of acute sensitivity to those concerned and uncovered systemic failings within the NHS.

- In 2004, the Hutton inquiry reported into the suicide of a government scientist, Dr David Kelly, who had been the source of a story by a BBC radio reporter claiming that the government had embellished, or 'sexed up', its intelligence material concerning the existence of weapons of mass destruction in Iraq in order to justify the allied invasion of that country.[6] The inquiry took place in the context of great controversy over whether the government's intelligence had been correct. The inquiry was chaired by Lord Hutton—then a serving Law Lord—and concluded that the allegation of the BBC reporter was unfounded and that the BBC had not exercised sufficient editorial controls over its reporter. Following the report's publication, the BBC's Director-General resigned. The

---

[2] *The Stephen Lawrence Inquiry: Report of an Inquiry by Sir William MacPherson of Cluny* (Cm 4262 1999).

[3] *Learning from Bristol: Report of the Public Inquiry into Children's Heart Surgery at the BRI 1984–95* (Cm 5207 2001). [4] *The Royal Liverpool Children's Hospital (Alder Hey) Inquiry* (HC 12 1998–99).

[5] *The Shipman Inquiry* (six reports published 2002–05), available online at **http://www.the-shipman -inquiry.org.uk**

[6] *Report of the Inquiry into the Circumstances Surrounding the Death of Dr David Kelly* (HC 247 2003–04). See also **http://www.the-hutton-inquiry.org.uk**

report was itself the subject of much public discussion over its correctness and was criticised by some as being little other than a 'whitewash'.[7]

- Following the Hutton inquiry, the government established the Butler inquiry following widespread public concern about the reliability of pre-war intelligence that claimed that Iraq had weapons of mass destruction. The inquiry was composed of five Privy Counsellors and chaired by a former Cabinet Secretary (the most senior position in the Civil Service), Lord Butler. The inquiry found serious weaknesses in the preparation of intelligence dossiers concerning the supposed existence of weapons of mass destruction in Iraq.[8] At the time of writing, a further, broader inquiry concerning the Iraq war is ongoing.[9]

- The Bloody Sunday inquiry was established in 1998 to inquire into the events concerning a disturbance in Londonderry (Derry) in 1972 following a civil rights march during which shots were fired by the British Army and 13 people were killed. This incident was the subject of an initial inquiry by the then Lord Chief Justice, Lord Widgery, which took only a matter of weeks to report, and the outcome of which was badly received; the inquiry had reported quickly and had been perceived by some to have produced a report that was unduly favourable to the government. For some years, there was a campaign for a new inquiry, to which the Labour government agreed in 1998. The new inquiry was chaired by a Law Lord (and subsequently Supreme Court Justice), Lord Saville.[10] It was the most protracted and the costliest inquiry ever held in the UK. It lasted for over a decade and considered the statements of 2,500 witnesses, of whom 922 were called to give direct evidence. It resulted in a ten-volume report that condemned the actions of the British Army as unjustified. The inquiry cost approximately £200 million, a significant proportion of which was spent on legal services.

Each of these inquiries was unique. Each was established as a result of a particular set of circumstances that gave rise to public concern, and each generated a degree of controversy and public debate in its own particular way. But what are the functions served by such inquiries and why are they established?

2.2 **The role and functions of inquiries**

As the examples just considered illustrate, each public inquiry is a creature of the particular circumstances that led to its establishment. This might be a particular

---

[7] See Blom-Cooper and Munro, 'The Hutton Inquiry' [2004] PL 472, 474, reporting the findings of an opinion poll. See further Hutton, 'The Media Reaction to the Hutton Report' [2006] PL 807.

[8] The Butler Committee, *Review of Intelligence on Weapons of Mass Destruction* (HC 898 2003–04).

[9] The Iraq Inquiry, chaired by Sir John Chilcot: see **http://www.iraqinquiry.org.uk**

[10] *Principal Conclusions and Overall Assessment of the Bloody Sunday Inquiry* (HC 30 2010–11), available online at **http://www.bloody-sunday-inquiry.org**. For critical comment, see Blom-Cooper, 'What Went Wrong on Bloody Sunday: A Critique of the Saville Inquiry' [2010] PL 61.

event, such as a death in custody, or a series of events, such as the development of BSE in cattle—a disease that can be passed to humans who consume meat from infected cows.[11] It is, though, possible to enumerate some more generic reasons for the establishment of inquiries, and their role and functions. It is apparent that there are a number of different rationales.[12]

First, inquiries enable an official investigation into a matter of public concern in order to provide a *full and fair account of the relevant facts*. This can be especially important when the facts are disputed or unclear. In this way, inquiries provide a mechanism for investigating and determining the facts in a way different from either formal court litigation or the more knockabout style of politics found in the House of Commons.

Second, inquiries enable government to *learn from events in order to prevent their recurrence*. Inquiries are frequently tasked with fact-finding and also framing recommendations that will prevent repetition of the particular problem that gave rise to the inquiry in the first place. For example, the Stephen Lawrence inquiry made some 70 recommendations concerning, *inter alia*, the investigation and prosecution of racist crimes by the police. Inquiries may then perform a powerful role in holding public bodies to account by ensuring that the facts are properly investigated so that lessons may be distilled and practice changed accordingly. While an inquiry may have been prompted by a particular event, this will often provide the basis for the inquiry to range more broadly into a certain aspect of government and to frame appropriate recommendations. In this sense, inquiries may be viewed as case studies in organisational or governmental failure. In another sense, inquiries can be viewed, alongside royal commissions and parliamentary select committees, as a 'decision advice process' as to how that organisational failure can be corrected and, in future, prevented.[13] Compared with these other methods, the distinctive feature of inquiries is that they are typically established as a result of a specific event, or set of events, the investigation of which may prevent similar events from recurring.

Third, inquiries may help to *restore public confidence* after a major failure by demonstrating that a particular issue is being fully investigated. Inquiries can also provide a forum for accountability of government: by finding the facts, inquiries can hold people and organisations to account and apportion blame.

Fourth, inquiries may provide an opportunity for the *reconciliation or resolution of difficult issues* by bringing all of the protagonists together; in other words, they might provide opportunities for a form of communal catharsis. Inquiries often concern difficult and sensitive issues. By holding an inquiry to investigate painful matters—for example, failings in the healthcare system—it may then be possible to put those issues

---

[11] *The BSE Inquiry Report* (London 2000).

[12] For discussion, see Howe, 'The Management of Public Inquiries' (1999) 70 Political Quarterly 294; PASC, *Government by Inquiry* (HC 51 2004–05), [10]–[12].

[13] Barker, 'Public Policy Inquiry and Advice as an Aspect of Constitutional Reform' (1998) 4 Journal of Legislative Studies 107.

to rest or to ensure that there is a degree of 'closure' in respect of them. Inquiries can also improve both the understanding and resolution of complex issues.

Finally, it cannot be overlooked that governments may be motivated to establish inquiries by more *self-interested and political considerations*. For example, if government is faced with a difficult issue that has aroused public concern, it may be tempted to give in to demands for a public inquiry that will satisfy immediate public pressure by ensuring that the particular issue is being seen to be investigated, while simultaneously deflecting short-term scrutiny and criticism of the government—in other words, to 'kick the issue into the long grass'. It has been noted that a government is likely to view the decision to establish an inquiry as presenting 'a difficult choice between the short-term attractions of removing a contentious issue from public controversy and the more remote dangers of prolonging the embarrassment through an extended investigation and an ultimate report over which it has little control'.[14] Establishing an inquiry may also justify governmental inaction while satisfying public demands that 'something must be done' about an issue of public concern.

A related point is that government may attempt to dispose of a difficult political issue by establishing an inquiry, but then seek to constrain the scope of that inquiry by limiting its terms of reference. To illustrate the point, in the aftermath of the Iraq war, there were calls for a full public inquiry into the invasion. The government established two inquiries: the Hutton and Butler inquiries. However, as noted above, those inquiries were limited to examining specific issues arising from the war, such as the events surrounding the death of Dr David Kelly and the use of intelligence concerning the existence of weapons of mass destruction in Iraq. Meanwhile, the government steadfastly refused to establish a more wide-ranging inquiry into the whole war and its planning, and whether or not the decision to invade Iraq was the right one. Although a broader inquiry into the Iraq war is now under way,[15] it was not convened until some years after the invasion, by which time some of the political heat surrounding the issue had dissipated. Most notably, the inquiry was established towards the end of the Blair–Brown government's period of office; by the time the report is published, all of the major political players involved in the invasion of Iraq will have been out of office for some time.

It has therefore been suggested that inquiries are often instituted in order to serve a symbolic function by reassuring the public that a particular event, or series of events, has been fully investigated. Most cynically, a former Deputy Prime Minister, Michael Heseltine, has noted that if a government feels that it has to hold an inquiry, the saying 'Reach your conclusion and then choose your chairman and set up the inquiry' may apply.[16] However, governments can never wholly dictate how an inquiry will actually proceed, or what findings and recommendations it may make. Furthermore,

---

[14] Leigh and Lustgarten, 'Five Volumes in Search of Accountability: The Scott Report' (1996) 59 MLR 695.

[15] The Iraq Inquiry, chaired by Sir John Chilcot: see **http://www.iraqinquiry.org.uk**

[16] PASC, *Minutes of Evidence*, 11 November 2004, Q615.

governments both cooperate with and fund inquiries; there are also examples of governments responding constructively to inquiries' recommendations.[17]

How, then, are we to classify inquiries? Are they administrative or judicial? This issue is not altogether easy because inquiries possess some features of both the administrative and the judicial processes. Like courts and tribunals, inquiries usually have to make findings of fact. However, unlike courts, inquiries cannot determine criminal or civil liability or make legally binding decisions; rather, their role is to investigate a particular issue of public concern. The final decisions contained in an inquiry's report will not have been reached by the application of pre-established rules; they will be the result of the exercise of wide discretion in the balancing of private and public interests. Unlike the courts, inquiries often make recommendations that have broader implications for public policy and administration. At the same time, unlike administrative decision-makers, inquiries often sit in public and hear evidence through an orderly procedure, sometimes approximating that of the courts. As we shall see, many, but not all, inquiries have been chaired by judges. Furthermore, while the decision to establish an inquiry is one for a government Minister, inquiries themselves are—or should be—independent of the government. Inquiries cannot then be classified as being purely administrative or judicial, but are best viewed as a hybrid of the two.

Q Why do we have inquiries? Do you think that it is realistic to assume that inquiries can fulfil all of the expectations placed on them?

2.3 **The legal framework of inquiries**

While inquiries have been used as a tool of government for many years, the legal framework underpinning them was, until recently, quite confused. Inquiries could be established in one of three possible ways. First, an inquiry might be established under the Tribunals of Inquiry (Evidence) Act 1921, which was enacted by Parliament in order to create a mechanism for the investigation of allegations of improper behaviour by certain government officials in the then Ministry of Munitions in relation to armament contracts. Inquiries under the 1921 Act had to be held in public, and had the power to compel witnesses to attend and give evidence. Another distinctive feature of such inquiries was that they had a direct connection with Parliament. Such inquiries could only be established through a resolution of both Houses of Parliament 'for inquiring into a matter... of great public importance'.[18] Furthermore, there was a practice of Parliament debating the inquiry report on a substantive motion following its publication. In other words, the 1921 Act introduced a direct link between an inquiry and Parliament. Some recent inquiries have been held under the 1921 Act, including the Bloody Sunday and Shipman inquiries. However, use of this Act declined as government established inquiries through the following alternative means.

---

[17] See section 4.1 below for examples. [18] Tribunals of Inquiry (Evidence) Act 1921, s 1(1).

Second, then, inquiries could be established under a *specific statutory provision* governing the general area of activity. For example, the Stephen Lawrence inquiry was established under the Police Act 1996, under which the Home Secretary could direct an inquiry to be held into any matter connected with the policing of any area; such inquiries could be conducted either in public or in private, as the Home Secretary directed.[19] Other inquiries—for example, the Royal Liverpool Children's Hospital (Alder Hey) and Bristol Royal Infirmary inquiries—were held under specific statutory powers concerning inquiries into the NHS.[20]

Third, an inquiry could be established *on a non-statutory basis under a general ministerial prerogative power*. Both the Hutton and Butler inquires were established on this basis. Lacking formal legal powers, such non-statutory inquiries were dependent upon the active cooperation of government and other public bodies. Compared with inquiries established under the 1921 Act, the second and third types of inquiry, once they reported, typically received less thoroughgoing attention in Parliament.

In 2004, the government decided to reform the law in this area, and Parliament subsequently passed the Inquiries Act 2005.[21] The Act creates a comprehensive statutory power to establish inquiries and consolidates other legislation concerning inquiries. The Act also seeks to make inquiry procedures faster and more effective, and to contain the escalation of their costs.

In respect of these goals, the Act has been welcomed. At the same time, other aspects of the Act have nevertheless raised some concerns. One concern is that because the 2005 Act repealed the 1921 Act, it has removed the opportunity for formal parliamentary involvement in inquiries. In other words, there has been a long-term diminution in Parliament's role in the process of inquiries, which the 2005 Act has finally extinguished. As one function of inquiries is to secure accountability of government, it might appear odd that there should now be no formal role for Parliament in relation to them. A second concern is that, while reducing the role of Parliament, the 2005 Act has simultaneously strengthened the executive's position by enabling Ministers to decide not only the form, personnel, and terms of reference of an inquiry, but also to influence its operation. Under the 2005 Act, Ministers now have the power to end or suspend inquiries.[22] However, to evaluate the Act properly, we need to examine the processes by which inquiries are established and undertaken.

3. The inquiry process

3.1 Establishing an inquiry

There is no obligation on government to establish an inquiry; rather, the decision whether to do so is a discretionary one, and is therefore often informed by various

---

[19] Police Act 1996, s 49.   [20] National Health Service Act 1977, ss 2 and 84.

[21] Department for Constitutional Affairs, *Effective Inquiries*, DCA Consultation Paper 12-04 (London 2004).   [22] Inquiries Act 2005, ss 13 and 14.

policy considerations. Given the diversity of situations that might generate calls for an inquiry, the 2005 Act places only the very loosest limits on the exercise of this power. Under the Act, a government Minister may cause an inquiry to be held where it appears that particular events have caused, or are capable of causing, public concern, or there is public concern that particular events may have occurred.[23] Clearly, in considering whether or not to establish an inquiry, a Minister may have regard to a range of competing considerations: the gravity of the event(s) generating calls for an inquiry; the need to maintain public confidence; public and media opinion; the probable costs and length of an inquiry; and, cynically, the perceived need to establish an inquiry in order to relieve pressure upon the government. The decision regarding whether an inquiry should be established is itself often a contentious matter that is the subject of public and political debate.

Indeed, a Minister's refusal to establish an inquiry may attract not only political debate, but also legal challenge by way of judicial review. Consider, for example, the case of Zahid Mubarek, a young prisoner in a young offender institution, who had been placed in a cell with another offender who was known to be both violent and racist, and who subsequently murdered Mubarek. Mubarek's family were concerned to know why he had been placed in the cell in such circumstances. However, the Home Secretary refused to hold a public inquiry into the circumstances surrounding the death. The family therefore challenged this decision on the ground that it breached Art 2 of the European Convention on Human Rights, which provides that everyone's right to life shall be protected by law. The House of Lords concluded that Art 2 was to be interpreted as including not only a duty on the state not to take life, but, in some circumstances, a duty to take steps to prevent life from being taken and, as part of that duty, an obligation to investigate the circumstances surrounding a death.[24] The Home Secretary's refusal to establish an inquiry was, the House of Lords concluded, unlawful because it resulted in a violation of a Convention right. The Home Secretary subsequently established an inquiry that was chaired by a High Court judge, who was ultimately highly critical of systemic shortcomings within the Prison Service that had exposed a vulnerable prisoner to attack by his cell mate.[25]

The Mubarek case is, of course, fact-specific. It does not follow that all governmental refusals to hold an inquiry will be quashed by way of judicial review. It does, though, illustrate a developing role for the courts in reviewing the legality of such decisions—especially when Convention rights are involved. As regards the character of such an inquiry into a death, the European Court of Human Rights has itself held that the nature and degree of public and independent scrutiny required by Art 2 will depend on the circumstances of the particular case, and the European Court has

---

[23] Inquiries Act 2005, s 1(1).

[24] *R (Amin) v Secretary of State for the Home Department* [2003] UKHL 51, [2004] 1 AC 653. See also *R (JL) v Secretary of State for the Home Department* [2007] EWCA Civ 767, [2008] 1 WLR 158.

[25] *Report of the Zahid Mubarek Inquiry* (HC 1082 2005–06).

recognised that, in the light of such factors, the form of investigation required may also vary.[26]

As well as having the discretionary power to decide whether to establish an inquiry at all, the government also has considerable discretion when it comes to the setting of an inquiry's terms of reference. These will often be crucial to determining its scope, length, complexity, cost, and success. For example, whether an inquiry is to establish particular facts and make recommendations will normally be explicitly detailed in its terms of reference. The relationship between an inquiry and the government will also be determined by its terms of reference. Under the Inquiries Act, it is for the Minister to set out an inquiry's terms of reference and there is a duty on the Minister to inform Parliament (or, if the matter concerns devolved issues, the relevant devolved legislature) as to those terms.[27] In practice, the terms of reference may often be a matter for negotiation between the chair of the inquiry and the Minister. Other interested parties might also make representations as to an inquiry's terms of reference. It is clearly important to the success of an inquiry that its terms of reference are precise, command broad consensus, and enable the inquiry to undertake its task without undue constraint. However, while Parliament must be informed as to the terms of reference, it has little input in determining what those terms should be. An important limit on the government's discretion over terms of reference is that no inquiry panel may rule on, or have the power to determine, any person's civil or criminal liability.[28] Such tasks are for the ordinary criminal and civil justice processes.

Finally, we should note that, although the Inquiries Act 2005 sets out a framework for inquiries that is comprehensive in the sense that it creates a general, rather than subject-specific, ministerial power to establish inquiries, the holding of inquiries other than under the Act is not ruled out by it. In particular, while the 2005 Act extinguished many discrete statutory powers to hold inquiries, the option still remains of using prerogative powers to establish an inquiry on a non-statutory basis. Indeed, the Iraq Inquiry was established in that way. It appears that this decision may have been taken on the basis that an inquiry under the Act was considered unsuitable given that there is a (qualified) duty to hold such inquiries in public.[29] Announcing the inquiry, the then Prime Minister, Gordon Brown, said that 'evidence will be heard in private' because the inquiry would be concerned with matters entailing 'a degree of confidentiality that would not suit a public inquiry, where all witnesses give evidence in public'.[30] However, this prompted a good deal of controversy—the suspicion being that Ministers were seeking to avoid the potential embarrassment of giving public evidence—and the chairman of the inquiry, Sir John Chilcot, later announced that hearings would be held

---

[26] *McCann v United Kingdom* (1995) 21 EHRR 97, [193]; *Jordan v United Kingdom* (2001) 37 EHRR 52, [105].   [27] Inquiries Act 2005, ss 5 and 6.

[28] Inquiries Act 2005, s 2(1).   [29] Inquiries Act 2005, ss 18 and 19.

[30] HC Deb, 15 June 2009, cols 23–4.

in public wherever possible. As a result, leading politicians—including Tony Blair, the Prime Minister at the time of the invasion of Iraq—gave evidence in public.

3.2 The membership of inquiries

A crucial aspect of inquiries concerns their membership: who precisely is to chair an inquiry? Because inquiries are established on an ad hoc basis, they have no set membership; rather, this will vary from inquiry to inquiry. Some inquiries may have a sole chair; others will be composed of a panel or committee of inquiry members; other inquiries may have a chair with assessors. Some inquiries may be chaired by a judge, with two or more panel members who possess particular expertise of assistance to the inquiry. Other inquiries may be chaired by a former and experienced civil servant with panel members. As inquiries are established by the government, it is primarily for the Minister to decide upon questions of membership.

A particular issue is whether or not it is appropriate for a judge to chair an inquiry. Not all inquiries have been chaired by judges. However, there has been an increasing trend for government to appoint judges to chair inquiries. Many recent inquiries—the Stephen Lawrence, Bloody Sunday, and the Hutton inquiries, for example—have all been chaired by senior judges. There are various arguments in favour of using judges in this respect. In addition to their legal expertise, judges have experience in assessing evidence—a particularly important skill, because inquiries are often established in order to clarify disputed factual issues. Judges are also impartial and independent from the government—a factor that will enhance public confidence in the inquiry because they are free from party-political bias. From a practical point of view, judges are often more readily available than other individuals to chair inquiries. In the context of inquiries into areas of extreme controversy, a judge may offer a seal of credibility because he or she will be independent, non-party-political, and impartial. Indeed, when Sir John Chilcot—a former senior civil servant—was appointed to chair the Iraq Inquiry, there were suggestions in some quarters that the government was seeking to avoid the sort of forensic scrutiny and consideration of the legality of the Iraq war that a judicially led inquiry might have facilitated.[31]

At the same time, there are countervailing arguments against the employment of judges in this respect. One argument concerns the range of skills that judges possess. While judges are skilled in fact-finding, they may not necessarily be equipped to frame appropriate recommendations, particularly when an inquiry is essentially concerned with a widespread and systemic governmental failure. Many recent inquiries have concerned the operation of public sector bodies of which judges normally have little or no experience; if inquiries are to lead to effective improvement of such bodies, then it is arguably best that their membership includes those

---

[31] See, eg 'Iraq inquiry: Civil servant Sir John Chilcot "incapable of addressing legal issues"', *The Daily Telegraph*, 24 November 2009.

individuals with experience of the policy and administrative contexts within which such bodies operate.

Perhaps the strongest argument against the use of judges to chair inquiries concerns the political nature of the subject matter to be investigated. As Beatson has noted, the involvement of a judge will not depoliticise an inherently controversial political matter, which cannot itself be resolved through the application of judicial standards and court-like procedures.[32] From the government's perspective, however, using a judge may well be attractive: it may enable the government to claim that the issue has been taken out of the political domain merely because an independent judge is chairing the inquiry, thereby providing public reassurance.[33] If there are obvious advantages to government Ministers in appointing judges to chair inquiries, the gains to the judiciary are perhaps less easily discernible. Judges may chair inquiries out of a sense of public duty. Yet, by chairing inquiries, judges may run the risk of being drawn into areas of acute political controversy, opening themselves up to criticism. As a former Attorney-General has put it: 'When a judge enters the market place of public affairs outside his court and throws coconuts he is likely to have the coconuts thrown back at him. If one values the standing of the judiciary…the less they are used [in relation to inquiries] the better it will be.'[34] In other words, there is a risk that the judiciary's own reputation and authority could itself be damaged in the aftermath of an inquiry—especially if there is public dissension over the correctness of the findings, and criticism of the judge's impartiality and objectivity. It has therefore been argued that it is wrong in principle for judges to chair inquiries of a political nature because this may exert a more general corrosive effect on public trust in the judiciary; the judiciary's political independence may be threatened by its entanglement in controversial political affairs.[35]

The Hutton inquiry is a recent illustration of the difficulties that a judge chairing a public inquiry can face and has been instanced as a case in which it is questionable whether a judge should have chaired an inquiry that took place in a highly controversial political context. While Lord Hutton—then a Law Lord—viewed his role solely as one of fact-finding, he was criticised for interpreting his terms of reference too narrowly, for being too establishment-minded, and for showing a lack of understanding of the broader political context of the inquiry. For Jowell, the difficulty is that while judges possess special expertise in analysing evidence, assessing the credibility of witnesses, and resolving complex factual issues, they are reluctant to engage in the broader political context in which an inquiry operates.[36] According to Blom-Cooper and Munro, there was room to doubt whether a Law Lord's 'borrowed authority' ought to have been lent to the Hutton inquiry, which 'may represent the classic instance of

[32] Beatson, 'Should Judges Chair Public Inquiries?' (2005) 121 LQR 221, 236.
[33] Drewry, 'Judicial Inquiries and Public Reassurance' [1996] PL 368.
[34] HL Deb, vol 648, col 883, 21 May 2003 (Lord Morris of Aberavon QC).
[35] Steele, 'Judging Judicial Inquiries' [2004] PL 738, 745.
[36] Jowell, The Guardian, 3 February 2004.

why we should question the public's ready acceptance of asking a judge to hold a public inquiry'.[37]

Some have therefore argued that the involvement of senior judges in inquiries in general should be avoided as it gives rise to serious constitutional concerns.[38] This view is fortified if we consider experience elsewhere. For example, there is a well-established consensus in the USA that it is constitutionally and politically inappropriate for judges to undertake inquiries because of the doctrine of the separation of powers. As we have previously considered, that doctrine is not as firmly embedded in the UK constitution as it is elsewhere.[39] Nevertheless, it has been argued that it is inappropriate for judges to chair inquiries because of the constitutional demands of the separation of powers. However, in this respect, the 2005 Act makes little change as to the use of judges, because it does not remove the possibility of appointing a judge to chair an inquiry. The Act does, though, add an important safeguard by requiring a Minister proposing to appoint a judge to an inquiry to consult first with a senior member of the judiciary, such as the senior Law Lord or the Lord Chief Justice.[40] This allows scope for the senior judiciary to consider whether it would be appropriate for a judge to chair an inquiry before agreeing to such a request from the government. However, this duty to consult does not go as far as some would have liked: during the passage of the Inquiries Act, some senior judges argued that judges should be appointed to inquiries only with the *approval* of the Lord Chief Justice.[41]

If a judge is not appointed to chair an inquiry, then another suitable person will be. Such categories of person have included former senior civil servants (for example, the Butler and Iraq inquiries) or those with particular experience in the subject matter of the inquiry (for example, the Bristol Royal Infirmary inquiry was chaired by an academic lawyer specialising in medical law and ethics). Under the 2005 Act, the Minister must ensure that the inquiry panel possesses the necessary expertise to undertake the inquiry.[42] This can be particularly important if the inquiry is to consider a complex or sensitive social issue or area of governmental activity and if the inquiry is to frame effective recommendations. For example, the Butler inquiry panel, which was concerned with the handling of intelligence concerning weapons of mass destruction in Iraq, was comprised of Privy Councillors. As members of both Houses of Parliament and experts who possessed independence and prior experience of handling intelligence information, they were well placed to inquire into sensitive matters. The inquiry was able to investigate effectively issues that were highly controversial and which involved matters of national security, and which needed to be discussed in private, although a report was subsequently published.

In any event, whoever is appointed—a judge or a specialist with or without other panel members—it is imperative that they both are and are seen to be wholly impartial.

---

[37] Blom-Cooper and Munro, 'The Hutton Inquiry' [2004] PL 472, 476.   [38] Steele, above.

[39] See Chapter 3 above.   [40] Inquiries Act 2005, s 10.

[41] See, eg Beatson, 'Should Judges Chair Public Inquiries?' (2005) 121 LQR 221, 251; Lord Woolf, memorandum to Public Administration Select Committee, November 2004.   [42] Inquiries Act 2005, s 8.

The Minister must not appoint a person as a member of an inquiry panel if it appears that the person either has a direct interest in the matters to which the inquiry relates or a close association with an interested party.[43] The requirement of impartiality is essential if the inquiry itself is to command public confidence.

In addition to inquiry panel members, the Minister may also appoint assessors who can assist the inquiry panel with their expert knowledge and advice.[44] Again, the particular individuals chosen for this task will depend on the nature of the inquiry. It is apparent that the chair of an inquiry may be able to exert some influence with regard to the areas of expertise that any assessors or advisers appointed to assist the inquiry should possess. For example, Keith J, the High Court judge who chaired the Zahid Mubarek inquiry, told senior Home Office officials before the inquiry was announced that he wished to have the assistance of independent advisers on a number of areas—race and diversity, the management and operation of prisons and young offender institutions, and prison life—on which he himself lacked both special experience and expertise. The advisers assisted the inquiry by informing its analysis and recommendations, thereby augmenting the credibility and authority of the final report.

Q What are the arguments for and against judges undertaking public inquiries? Why, if at all, is it constitutionally inappropriate for judges to chair inquiries? Are there particular types of inquiry that may be either particularly suited or unsuited to judicial involvement?

3.3 Inquiries—public or private?

Should an inquiry be held in public or in private? The principal argument in favour of holding inquiries in public is that this is often the only way in which to maintain public confidence that the particular events of concern—for example, the alleged misconduct of office-holders or failure of governmental systems—are being both fully and properly investigated. Private inquiries give rise to a suspicion that they are not being conducted sufficiently vigorously and thoroughly or that something is being hushed up. Publicity enables the public to see for itself how the investigation is being carried out and accordingly dispels suspicion. Holding inquiries in public also ensures that information surrounding the matter in question is brought to light. This means that, whatever the conclusions of the inquiry panel, members of the public, the media, and parliamentarians gain access to facts that will enable them to form their own judgements about (for example) who should be blamed.

On the other hand, it may be easier to elicit the truth from witnesses if their questioning is not conducted in the full glare of publicity; individuals who can assist as to the failings of others, errors by public bodies, and administrative flaws are likely to be far more forthcoming and candid in private. However, a counter-argument is that allowing witnesses to testify out of the glare of public scrutiny may allow them to

---

[43] Inquiries Act 2005, s 9.   [44] Inquiries Act 2005, s 11.

embellish their testimony rather than require them to adhere to the truth; it may also enable them to cast blame on others. There may be other justifiable reasons for holding an inquiry in private: national security, legal barriers to the disclosure of documents, personal privacy, and avoiding unnecessary intrusion or distress to witnesses. It is also important to consider concerns as to the costs and time involved: private inquiries tend to be both quicker and less costly than public inquiries.

The importance placed on this issue is illustrated by the fact that legal challenges have been made as to whether inquiries should be held either in public or private. Consider, for example, the Shipman inquiry into the activities of a doctor who had killed many of his own patients. The Health Secretary had decided that the inquiry should sit in private. However, this was successfully challenged through judicial review proceedings by the victims' families, who wanted the inquiry to be held in public. The court reasoned that if the inquiry were conducted in public, then its report and recommendations would command greater public confidence. Furthermore, the court noted that because all members of the public are accustomed to placing trust in the medical profession, the restoration of public confidence was a matter of high importance.[45] It is apparent that this legal challenge had a broader significance on the role of this particular inquiry. The Health Secretary had initially wanted a limited inquiry into the safeguards over doctors, while the victims' families wanted a much more wide-ranging inquiry. Following the court's decision, not only was the inquiry held in public, but it also became much more broad-ranging than the government had initially envisaged. It was also held under the 1921 Act and chaired by a High Court judge.

By contrast, in other cases, the courts have rejected legal challenges against a government's refusal to hold an inquiry in public. Following the outbreak of foot-and-mouth disease in 2001, which had a considerable adverse impact on the farming community and the rural economy more generally, the government refused to hold a public inquiry, preferring instead to have three separate independent inquiries that received evidence for the most part in private. A legal challenge against the decision not to hold a public inquiry was unsuccessful. The court held that the circumstances were strikingly different from those appertaining to the Shipman inquiry, and concluded that there was no legal presumption of an open, public inquiry. The court pointed out that there were arguments both for and against full-scale inquiries sitting in public, and that a range of considerations could be taken into account, such as cost, speed, and the desirability of candour on the part of witnesses. The decision as to the nature of an inquiry was therefore an essentially political one to be taken by Ministers and not one that the court could take.[46]

The 2005 Act clarifies the position by requiring that an inquiry chairman must take reasonable steps to secure public access both to inquiry proceedings, and the evidence and information provided to the inquiry panel.[47] However, public access may be

---

[45] *R v Secretary of State for Health, ex p Wagstaff* [2001] 1 WLR 292.

[46] *Persey v Secretary of State for Environment, Food and Rural Affairs* [2002] EWHC 371 (Admin), [2003] QB 794.   [47] Inquiries Act 2005, s 18.

restricted if either the Minister or the inquiry chairman considers it to be conducive to the inquiry fulfilling its terms of reference or to be necessary in the public interest having regard to specified matters. Those matters are the extent to which any restriction on access might inhibit the allaying of public concern; any risk of harm or damage that could be avoided or reduced by any such restriction; any conditions as to confidentiality; and the extent to which not imposing any restriction would be likely to cause delay, or impair the efficiency or effectiveness of the inquiry, or otherwise to result in additional cost.[48] In summary, then, the general principle is that an inquiry should be held in public, but this is subject to specified restrictions.

Q To what extent, if at all, is it acceptable for inquiries to be held in private?

3.4 **Inquiry proceedings**

Inquiry proceedings need to be highly flexible and adaptable to the particular circumstances: the 2005 Act therefore provides that the procedure and conduct of an inquiry are to be such as the chairman may direct.[49] It is axiomatic that the proceedings should be fair, and that the decisions and procedures of inquiries are susceptible to challenge by way of judicial review on the basis that they are either unlawful, irrational, or procedurally unfair. For example, the Bloody Sunday inquiry prompted a judicial review challenge concerning the anonymity of witnesses, which is considered below.

Inquiries often adopt an inquisitorial approach in which the inquiry chair or panel will frame the issues to be addressed, lead the investigation, and both call and question witnesses. The advantage of this approach is that it may assist the inquiry in drawing out the facts, while at the same time preventing the inquiry from becoming a confrontational, adversarial process. For example, the procedures of the Bristol Royal Infirmary inquiry were designed to be wholly inquisitorial and sensitive to witnesses' needs.[50] An inquiry will normally have its own counsel, who will undertake the questioning of witnesses. A witness or core participant of an inquiry is entitled to have legal representation. However, the role of that representation is limited to making opening and closing statements. Questions of a witness will primarily be asked by the inquiry's own counsel unless the inquiry itself directs that a witness may be asked questions by his or her own legal representative.[51]

The cost and length of inquiries can, of course, vary. The Hutton inquiry reported eight months after it was established. By contrast, the Bloody Sunday inquiry took over a decade. As that particular example demonstrates, lengthy inquiries are likely to be more costly. As inquiries are funded by the sponsoring government

---

[48] Inquiries Act 2005, s 19(4).   [49] Inquiries Act 2005, s 17(1).

[50] Maclean, 'How Does an Inquiry Inquire? A Brief Note on the Working Methods of the Bristol Royal Infirmary Inquiry' (2001) 28 JLS 590.   [51] Inquiry Rules 2006, SI 2006/1838, rr 10 and 11.

departments, the government will always have a concern as to their cost, because this inevitably draws resources away from other areas of governmental work. Therefore, while there is a need to ensure that an inquiry is able to undertake a thorough investigation and produce workable recommendations, there is also a need to ensure that it is conducted with reasonable expedition and does not cost too much. In this respect, changes introduced under the 2005 Act have been designed to contain the length of inquiries and their costs. For example, legal challenges (by way of judicial review) to the way in which inquiries are being conducted can cause substantial delay (resulting in significant additional costs). The 2005 Act therefore requires that any application for judicial review must normally be brought no more than 14 days after the applicant became aware of the matter concerned.[52] Furthermore, the Act also provides that, in making any decision as to the procedure or conduct of an inquiry, the chairman must not only act with fairness, but must also consider the need to avoid any unnecessary cost (whether to public funds, or to witnesses or others).[53]

3.5 **Witnesses**

One contentious aspect of inquiry proceedings concerns how to resolve the tension between achieving the inquiry's purpose of eliciting the truth while also protecting those individuals against whom findings of culpability may have to be made. If an inquiry operates under an inquisitorial process, then some witnesses might feel that they have not been treated fairly because the basic safeguards of the more usual adversarial court process have not been followed. On the other hand, inquiries undertake a primarily investigative function and do not, as with court litigation, necessarily need to operate on an adversarial basis.

If this issue seems somewhat abstruse, imagine that you are to appear as a witness before an inquiry. There is a chance that the inquiry may be critical of your conduct. While you will be found neither guilty of a criminal office nor liable for any civil wrongdoing, there is a chance that your personal reputation or career may be harmed—yet you may neither be legally represented nor cross-examined by your own representative. In this situation, you may feel at risk of being subjected to an unfair process. At the same time, the inquiry will want to establish the truth as to what has occurred.

It was because of concerns over the fairness of inquiry processes that the Salmon Commission was established to examine the operation of inquisitorial procedure by inquires.[54] Noting that the inquisitorial approach is alien to the concept of justice generally accepted in the UK, the Commission proposed that inquiries should adhere to

---

[52] Inquiries Act 2005, s 38.   [53] Inquiries Act 2005, s 17(3).
[54] *The Report of the Royal Commission on Tribunals of Inquiry* (Cmnd 3121 1966).

six principles that roughly equate with more traditional adversarial process. The six 'Salmon principles' are as follows:

(i)   Before any person becomes involved in an inquiry, the inquiry must be satisfied that there are circumstances that affect her and that the Tribunal proposes to investigate.

(ii)   Before any person involved in an inquiry is called as a witness, she should be informed of any allegations that are made against her and the substance of the evidence in support of them.

(iii) That person should be given an adequate opportunity of preparing her case and of being assisted by her legal advisers, and legal expenses should normally be met out of public funds.

(iv)   That person should have the opportunity of being examined by her own lawyer and of stating her case in public at the inquiry.

(v)   Any material witness whom she wishes called at the inquiry should, if reasonably practicable, be heard.

(vi)   Finally, she should have the opportunity of testing, by cross-examination conducted by her own lawyer, any evidence that may affect her.

The degree to which an inquiry adheres to these principles reflects a choice for an inquiry chairman as to their appropriateness in the context of the specific nature of the investigation to be undertaken. If an inquiry follows the Salmon principles, then there is a risk of making the inquiry too confrontational and adversarial—in other words, the inquiry process could resemble that of the courts. Furthermore, there is always the risk that greater involvement of lawyers throughout the process will add to the length and cost of an inquiry. Some inquiry chairs have noted that, while an inquiry needs to be fair to witnesses, this does not necessarily require strict adherence to the Salmon principles. The principles are, then, not to be applied inflexibly or rigidly, but adapted to the circumstances of the particular inquiry.[55]

In some inquiries, the principles have been discarded altogether. For example, for the purposes of his inquiry into the export of defence equipment to Iraq ('arms to Iraq'), Lord Scott decided not to adhere to the Salmon principles because he was of the view that they would have been inoperable, ineffective, and inefficient. As Lord Scott has argued, an inquiry has an investigative purpose to determine the truth, and therefore an inquisitorial mode of procedure, is more appropriate. It is not a process designed to adjudicate on a dispute between two parties because, in an inquiry, there are no litigants; the adversarial style of procedure adopted in court litigation in which each side seeks to promote its own 'case' is therefore not appropriate in the context of an investigative inquiry.[56] It was not therefore necessary to adhere strictly to the

---

[55] PASC, *Government by Inquiry* (HC 51 2004–05), [100]–[104].
[56] Scott, 'Procedures at Inquiries: The Duty to be Fair' (1995) 111 LQR 596. See also Winetrobe, 'Inquiries after Scott: The Return of the Tribunal of Inquiry' [1997] PL 18.

Salmon principles; instead, the Scott inquiry adopted an inquisitorial procedure, with questions being posed by the chairman and his assisting counsel. This was, however, a controversial way of proceeding. Lord Howe—a former government Minister who, as a lawyer, had been involved in two earlier inquiries and who appeared as a witness at the Scott inquiry—condemned Scott's refusal to permit legal representation of witnesses and their cross-examination on the basis that this was contrary to established inquiry procedure, was unfair, and undermined the inquiry's ability to operate effectively and to reach valid conclusions.[57]

What, then, is the current status of the Salmon principles? It has been noted that the 'issue has yet to be satisfactorily resolved'.[58] However, in order to reconcile the competing demands of fairness and efficiency, the Inquiry Rules 2006 introduced a system of 'warning letters' in order to notify inquiry witnesses of potential criticism.[59] Under this system, the inquiry chairman may send a warning letter to any person who may be subject to criticism in the inquiry proceedings or report, outlining the potential criticism and the evidence in support of it. The inquiry panel may only include any criticism of a person in the inquiry report if that person has both been sent a warning letter and also given a reasonable opportunity to respond to it. Furthermore, before the publication of a final report, the chair is to provide a copy to each core participant in the inquiry.[60] In this way, the rules ensure that those potentially subject to criticism are treated fairly, while at the same time enabling the inquiry chairman to control its proceedings, and to prevent extensive and costly cross-examination of witnesses.

In some inquiries, the particular issue of witness confidentiality has arisen. For example, early in the Bloody Sunday inquiry, the inquiry panel decided that witnesses should, in the interests of open justice, give evidence in public and be named. However, former British soldiers, who had fired live rounds after the civil rights march and who were to give evidence, sought judicial review of this decision. While recognising that the inquiry was the master of its own procedure and that it had considerable discretion as to the procedure it adopted, the court nevertheless held that the decision to release the names of the witnesses was unlawful because the inquiry had not accorded requisite weight to the fundamental rights of the witnesses, including their right to life.[61] While the courts therefore provide oversight of the fairness of the inquiry process, inquiries themselves must first decide how they are to proceed. In a complex and protracted inquiry such as the Bloody Sunday inquiry, this task may itself lead to the production of numerous formal procedural rulings. For example, the Bloody Sunday inquiry issued rulings deprecating repetitive or hostile questioning of witnesses by counsel and as regards the standard of proof that the inquiry should apply before making findings in its report.[62]

---

[57] Howe, 'Procedure at the Scott Inquiry' [1996] PL 445.   [58] PASC, HC 51, [100].

[59] The Inquiry Rules 2006, SI 2006/1838, r 13.   [60] The Inquiry Rules 2006, SI 2006/1838, r 17.

[61] *R v Lord Saville of Newdigate, ex p A* [2000] 1 WLR 1855. See also Hadfield, '*R v Lord Saville of Newdigate, ex p Anonymous Soldiers*: What is the Purpose of a Tribunal of Inquiry?' [1999] PL 663.

[62] See http://www.bloody-sunday-inquiry.org/rulings-and-judgments/index.html

3.6 **Publication of inquiry reports**

After the inquiry has taken evidence and written its report, that report must then be delivered to the Minister.[63] Before doing so, the inquiry chairman may submit an interim report.[64] It is normally the duty of the Minister to arrange for inquiry reports to be published, although the inquiry chairman can have responsibility for this.[65] The general principle is that an inquiry report must be published in full. However, there is scope for the withholding of material in the report from publication to the extent that this is required by law or is considered necessary in the public interest. Such public interest matters can include, for example, the extent that the withholding of such material might inhibit the allaying of public concern, any risk of harm or damage that could be avoided or reduced by withholding any material, and any conditions as to confidentiality subject to which a person acquired information that he has given to the inquiry.[66] Furthermore, as we have seen, an inquiry may have to disclose its report to each core participant before its publication. The final report must be laid by the Minister before the UK Parliament or the relevant devolved legislature.[67] Few inquiry reports are brief; most inquiries typically produce a lengthy report, with various recommendations. Consequently, few people will read inquiry reports in full, but the majority will instead rely on executive summaries and press reports.

4. The effectiveness of inquiries

4.1 **Implementing and monitoring inquiry recommendations**

Once an inquiry has reported, it is for government to decide whether or not to accept the recommendations and, if so, whether and how to implement them. Implementing recommendations is crucial: identifying the lessons is one thing, but recurrence will be prevented only if appropriate practical steps are then taken. In some instances, an inquiry may lead to changes in the law. For example, the Bristol Royal Infirmary and Royal Liverpool Children's Hospital (Alder Hey) inquiries established that organs and tissue from children who had died had often been removed, stored, and used without proper consent. Parliament subsequently passed the Human Tissue Act 2004, which established a consistent legislative framework for this issue, and made consent the fundamental principle underpinning the lawful storage and use of human bodies. In other instances, following an inquiry report, changes in the law may be made albeit belatedly. For example, the Scott inquiry into the export of defence equipment, which reported in 1996, concluded that the then legislative structure concerning export controls was inadequate and lacked proper parliamentary scrutiny, and should be

---

[63] Inquiries Act 2005, s 24(1).   [64] Inquiries Act 2005, s 24(3).
[65] Inquiries Act 2005, s 25(1) and (2).   [66] Inquiries Act 2005, s 25(4) and (5).
[67] Inquiries Act 2005, s 26.

replaced as soon as possible. However, it was not until 2002, when it enacted the Export Controls Act 2002, that Parliament sought to remedy the situation.

These examples notwithstanding, inquiries are not always regarded as a success in terms of producing practical changes that secure real improvements. Failure in this regard may be attributable to shortcomings in the inquiry itself, or in governmental and legislative responses to it. For example, with regard to other inquiries held into aspects of the provision of health care by the NHS, it has been concluded that the consistency with which successive inquiries have highlighted 'similar causes suggests that their recommendations are either misdirected or not properly implemented'.[68]

Part of the problem here is that there are few formal mechanisms that allow for any follow-up in relation to the findings and recommendations of inquiries. An inquiry will report and it is then for the relevant government department to decide how it will act on the recommendations. However, in the absence of a formal mechanism for checking whether or not the government department has taken adequate steps to change the relevant law, policy, or procedure, there is always the risk that the impetus behind an inquiry report might dissipate as time passes, the political scenario changes, and competing priorities come to the fore. This, in turn, raises the concern that the cost and resources devoted to inquiries may have been wasted if their reports and recommendations are merely 'shelved' rather than effectively implemented by government. In other words, the fear is that government may give 'lip service' to inquiry recommendations—but without ongoing monitoring, it is difficult to ensure that the recommendations are actually implemented.

Occasionally, inquiries themselves decide to reconvene in order to assess the extent to which their recommendations have been implemented by government. For example, the Bichard inquiry into the murder of two schoolgirls by a man who worked as their school's caretaker reconvened six months after the publication of its report. The inquiry chairman considered it essential to reconvene the inquiry to ensure that its recommendations had been properly taken on board by the government.[69] Furthermore, parliamentary select committees occasionally decide to hold a follow-up investigation into the work of an inquiry. For example, ten years after the Stephen Lawrence inquiry reported, the House of Commons Home Affairs Committee found that the police service had made progress towards tackling racial prejudice and discrimination since 1999.[70]

However, these examples of subsequent follow-ups on inquiry reports are very much the exception rather than the norm. To remedy the problem, the House of Commons Public Administration Select Committee (PASC) has suggested that gov-

---

[68] Walshe and Higgins, 'The Use and Impact of Inquiries in the NHS' (2002) 325 British Medical Journal 895, 899.

[69] *An Independent Inquiry Arising from the Soham Murders* (HC 653 2003–04) (the Bichard Inquiry); PASC, *Government by Inquiry* (HC 51 2004–05), [140].

[70] House of Commons Home Affairs Committee, *The Macpherson Report: Ten Years On* (HC 427 2008–09).

ernment departments should report on the implementation of inquiry recommendations at regular intervals, and, in any event, within the first two years of the end of an inquiry. Such reports should cover the extent to which recommendations have been implemented and describe the wider cultural changes that have been brought about as a result. PASC argued that institutional responsibility for scrutinising such reports should lie with parliamentary select committees, which should be well placed to undertake such work.[71] In response, the government accepted that it is important for government departments to maintain a focus on the implementation of inquiry recommendations and that they should publicise how they have dealt with such recommendations.[72] There is, however, no formal statutory process in this area; the 2005 Act is silent on the issue of follow-up.

Q Should there be a more formal process for following up the implementation of inquiry recommendations? If so, then who should have this responsibility: Parliament or the government?

4.2 **Parliamentary commissions of inquiry**

Should Parliament have a more prominent role with regard to inquiries? As we saw in Chapter 10, under the doctrine of ministerial responsibility, Ministers are accountable to Parliament for their own actions and those of their departments. Inquiries can play an important role in this process by bringing to light information that may better equip Parliament to hold Ministers to account. However, there has been a 'long-term diminution of Parliament's role in the process of public inquiries'.[73] This process began with fewer inquiries being held under the 1921 Act, which required a resolution of both Houses of Parliament. Formal parliamentary involvement with inquiries has now been finally terminated by the 2005 Act, which itself makes no provision for such involvement and which abolished the 1921 Act. To what extent should Parliament itself be able to establish its own inquiries and investigations into matters of concern? And why is it important for there to be a close connection between Parliament and inquiries?

As the PASC has emphasised, the importance of parliamentary involvement in the inquiry process derives from the basic constitutional tenet that Parliament should be able to scrutinise the actions of the executive and to hold it to account. For example, the government may be reluctant to establish an inquiry into a particular matter because it may result in politically embarrassing or awkward findings for it. At the same time, Parliament and the public may consider it imperative to hold an inquiry into the particular area of concern in order to hold the government accountable for its actions. It

---

[71] PASC, HC 51, [147].

[72] Department for Constitutional Affairs, *Government Response to the Public Administration Select Committee's First Report of the 2004–05 Session: "Government by Inquiry"* (Cm 6481 2005), pp 18–19.

[73] PASC, HC 51, [13].

has therefore been argued that it would be more constitutionally appropriate and legitimate for Parliament, rather than the executive, to have 'ownership' of inquiries.[74] As the House of Commons is democratically elected, it would strengthen Parliament's role in both scrutinising government and representing the public if it were to have the power to establish its own inquiries. If we look at current arrangements from a realistic perspective, the temptation for the government to be influenced by political considerations when deciding whether or not to hold an inquiry (and, if so, on what terms) may simply be too great. Rather than relying on the government to establish inquiries, Parliament could itself both institute and oversee the operation of inquiries. However, while the PASC has recommended that there should be a mechanism by which Parliament can decide to establish inquiries where the events causing concern may involve the conduct of Ministers, this has not been accepted by the government.[75]

What other options are there, then, for greater parliamentary involvement with inquiries? One option is for Parliament, if it so chooses, to legislate for a specific inquiry—but because Parliament is dominated by the government of the day, this is, in reality, unlikely. Another option is for parliamentary select committees to conduct their own inquiries. However, this option also has its limitations. Select committees have limited capacity (in terms of time and resources); their main focus is upon wider scrutiny of government departments, rather than specialised investigations of particular events, and they may not be adequately equipped effectively to carry out such investigations. Moreover, there are limits on the degree of governmental cooperation with select committees. For example, when investigating the decision to go to war in Iraq, the Foreign Affairs Select Committee met with continued refusal by Ministers to allow access to intelligence papers and personnel, which hampered the Committee's inquiry.[76] Because such committees are comprised of party politicians, there will always be concerns arising from perceptions of partisanship. Furthermore, select committees shadow individual government departments, whereas some matters of concern that prompt calls for public inquiries cover issues that cut across several government departments in addition to other agencies.

A third option, suggested by the PASC, is for Parliament to be able to commission and initiate its own inquiries through a special process known as 'parliamentary commissions of inquiry'.[77] Such commissions would, like other inquiries, be established on an ad hoc basis. Their membership would include parliamentarians and others with appropriate expertise. However, the fundamental difference between such commissions and inquiries under the 2005 Act is that the former would be established not by government, but by Parliament. Consequently, such commissions would possess a

---

[74] Barker, 'Public Policy Inquiry and Advice as an Aspect of Constitutional Reform' (1998) 4 Journal of Legislative Studies 107, 124.

[75] PASC, HC 51, chs 6 and 7; Department for Constitutional Affairs, Cm 6481, p 22; PASC, *Parliamentary Commissions of Inquiry* (HC 473 2007–08).

[76] House of Commons Foreign Affairs Committee, *The Decision to go to War in Iraq* (HC 813 2002–03).

[77] PASC, HC 51, [208]–[215]; PASC, HC 473.

superior legitimacy because they would be initiated by Parliament in order to investigate the conduct and actions of the government rather than by the government itself. The justification for Parliament being able to create such commissions is then central to Parliament's function in holding the government to account. As the Committee explained, it is crucial, in a constitutional sense, that Parliament has the necessary powers and abilities to scrutinise the executive and to hold it to account. As we saw earlier, the ability of Parliament to undertake effective scrutiny of governmental action is limited in various ways.[78] If Parliament's capacity in this area is to be enhanced, then as the Committee has explained, proper parliamentary scrutiny should include the ability to establish and undertake inquiries into significant matters of public concern.[79]

To illustrate the Committee's argument, consider the controversy surrounding inquiries into the government's actions in relation to the Iraq war. Following the invasion and the failure to locate weapons of mass destruction in Iraq, considerable public controversy arose over the purpose and planning of the war, and there were calls for a full public inquiry to investigate all aspects of the war. Furthermore, there was a precedent, because previous governments had held inquiries into other military campaigns: following the Falklands war in 1982, the then government had established an inquiry.[80] However, in relation to the Iraq war, the government steadfastly refused, for several years, to establish a general, wide-ranging inquiry (as opposed to the more focused Butler and Hutton inquiries), while Parliament was unable to establish its own inquiry even though this has been the most significant issue of public concern in recent years. As explained above, a wider-ranging inquiry—the Iraq inquiry, chaired by Sir John Chilcot—was eventually established in 2009, but at a time, and with an inquiry panel, of the government's choosing.

According to the PASC, Parliament's inability to establish an inquiry in such circumstances reflects a fundamental problem in the UK's current constitutional arrangements. It is for Parliament to hold the executive accountable for its actions, and, on occasion, this involves Parliament investigating and inquiring into important matters of public concern. However, the inability of Parliament to initiate its own inquiries highlights a significant gap in its power to hold the government to account. The Committee's proposal that Parliament should have the power to establish of its own volition parliamentary commissions of inquiry was, then, in the interests of promoting effective parliamentary accountability of government.

Q Is it desirable for Parliament to have greater involvement with inquiries? Do you think that parliamentary commissions of inquiry would enhance Parliament's ability to secure accountability of government? What, in practical terms, might prevent Parliament from implementing the PASC's recommendations by establishing a new system of parliamentary commissions?

---

[78] See Chapters 5 and 10 above.   [79] PASC, HC 473, p 3.

[80] *Falkland Islands Review* (Cm 8787 1983) (the Franks review).

5. **Conclusion**

So what, then, are we to make of inquiries? Are they an effective mechanism for holding government to account? From one perspective, inquiries have been the subject of much criticism because of their chequered history—one that has been characterised by lengthy proceedings, high costs, and reports that have often been met with public dissension over the correctness of the conclusions reached or indifference from the government. Inquiries are also often the object of criticism on the ground that they are susceptible to being manipulated by the government for its own political interests. Nevertheless, it is apparent that inquiries are an important mechanism for undertaking a detailed investigation into an issue of public concern and for holding government accountable. There remains a need for some form of inquiry process—albeit one that sits uneasily at times between court litigation and the ordinary political process—the purpose of which is to undertake such investigations and make recommendations. At the same time, aspects of the inquiry process could be enhanced in order to strengthen its effectiveness. Parliamentary select committees could take a more active role in scrutinising whether government departments fully implement inquiry recommendations. Furthermore, the long-term uncoupling of Parliament from inquiries needs to be addressed. If Parliament is to undertake an effective scrutiny of government and hold it to account over major matters of public concern, such as the invasion of Iraq, then it should have the ability to initiate its own inquiries independent of the government.

The role and effectiveness of inquiries is a matter that is central to one of our key themes—namely, the dominance, within the UK's constitutional arrangements, of the executive branch, and the consequent importance of having effective mechanisms for holding it to account. For the reasons considered in this chapter, inquiries have a crucial role to play in this regard: a fact that raises a second of our key themes—namely, the relationship between legal and political forms of constitutionalism. There is widespread recognition of the weaknesses, within the UK system, of political—in particular, parliamentary—control of the executive.[81] As a result, there has been a tendency to place increasing emphasis on legal forms of control—most obviously, judicial review. Indeed, this sort of thinking, born of despair at the inadequacies of the political system, has been one of the main drivers behind the shift to a more legal form of constitutionalism. But the PASC's proposals for strengthening Parliament's capacity to hold the government to account serve as an important reminder that political control of government need not be written off as irremediably weak. Properly understood, legal and political forms of control are complementary; one cannot wholly substitute for the other. The trend, identified in this book, towards legal and away from political modes of constitutionalism, should not therefore be viewed as one that will or should

---

[81] See Chapters 5 and 10 above.

inevitably consign political control of government to the sidelines. The reinvigoration of political mechanisms for securing executive accountability is essential to the health of the UK's constitutional arrangements. Against that background, the PASC's proposals are to be welcomed.

Further reading

BEATSON, 'Should Judges Chair Public Inquiries?' (2005) 121 LQR 221

HOUSE OF COMMONS PUBLIC ADMINISTRATION SELECT COMMITTEE, *Government by Inquiry* (HC 51 2004–05)

HOUSE OF COMMONS PUBLIC ADMINISTRATION SELECT COMMITTEE, *Parliamentary Commissions of Inquiry* (HC 473 2007–08)

STEELE, 'Judging Judicial Inquiries' [2004] PL 738

WRAITH AND LAMB, *Public Inquiries as an Instrument of Government* (London 1971)

PART VI

Human Rights

19 Human Rights and the UK Constitution

1. Introduction

A good deal has already been said in this book about human rights. This is inevitable. The language of human rights is increasingly prevalent in public law in the United Kingdom (as elsewhere). Thus far, discussion of matters pertaining to human rights has been incidental to the analysis of other issues. In this part of the book, however, our focus shifts much more specifically to human rights law and its place within the UK constitution.

In this chapter, we examine a number of general issues. We begin by considering the notion of human rights itself: it is, as we will see, a flexible concept that people use in different ways, and there is plenty of debate and disagreement about exactly what it should (and does) mean. There is disagreement, too, about whether human rights—at least as they are normally conceived—are good things. This might seem surprising, not least because the very term 'human rights' seems to immunise the concept against rational objection. But, as we will see, the position is more complex. The way in which we view such rights depends upon a range of other factors, such as exactly which rights are placed within that category in the first place, how they are balanced against other interests, such as those of society generally, and who is ultimately responsible for protecting them.

This chapter is concerned not only with human rights at a general or conceptual level; it also examines, in more practical terms, the extent to, and the way in, which human rights are recognised and protected within the UK's constitutional arrangements. This analysis engages all three of the book's key themes. First, it is in this context that we see one of the clearest examples of the *shift in emphasis from a more political to a more legal notion of constitutionalism*. The Human Rights Act 1998 (HRA), which has already been mentioned on several occasions in the book, has dramatically extended the legal protection afforded to human rights. However, we will see that the Act stopped short of conferring upon the courts powers to strike down Acts of Parliament inconsistent with human rights law, such that, in this ultimate sense, the ongoing existence of human rights is dependent upon the restraint of the political branches of the state—namely, the government and Parliament. Second, one of the principal effects of the HRA (as we have already seen in Chapter 13) has been to enhance the courts' powers to review the legality of administrative action. In this sense, the HRA can be seen, at least in part, as recognition of *the unusually powerful position occupied by the executive branch* within the UK constitution, and the resulting importance of ensuring *adequate oversight* of it. Third, we will see that, while the HRA does not ultimately restrict the UK Parliament's legislative authority, the law-making powers of the devolved legislatures are limited by it. Understanding the role of human rights in the constitution thus requires us to engage with our third theme, by appreciating *the multilayered nature of the UK's constitutional arrangements.*

This chapter is the first of three in this, the final section of the book. The remaining two chapters are concerned with two specific human rights—the right of freedom of expression and the right to protest. It would be impossible in a book like this, as opposed to a specialist work on human rights, to consider all such rights in detail— that is the task of more focused textbooks and works on human rights law. A principal rationale for specific examination of the rights of expression and protest is that they are especially relevant to the effective functioning of the democratic process, and are therefore of particular interest from the standpoint of constitutional law.

2. Human rights

2.1 What are human rights?

'Human rights' are much talked about these days. To some extent, this has devalued the term: there is a tendency, in popular discourse, to invoke the language of human rights in a much wider range of situations than those in which it is really appropriate. The reality is that while people have many legal rights, only a small subset of such rights falls into the category of 'human rights'. Generally speaking, when the law imposes a duty on one person, someone else will acquire a corresponding right. For example, if A enters into a contract under which he is to clean B's house in return for payment, A's contractual duty vests in B a corresponding contractual right to have her house cleaned—but B does not thereby acquire a *human* right. What is it, then, that distinguishes human rights from other legal rights?

There are two main ways in which this question may be approached. On a practical level, human rights are normally accorded special treatment within any given legal system. Of course, all legal rights are protected in the sense that legal consequences will flow from their breach: in the example above, B's contractual right enables her (among other things) to bring a claim for damages against A if the latter fails to do what he promised. One of the hallmarks of human rights, however, is that they are accorded a form of protection that goes beyond that which is normally afforded to legal rights. The paradigm form of protection given to human rights involves not simply rendering unlawful *conduct* (for example, by an individual or public body) that is inconsistent with such rights, but, at a constitutional level, making it impossible or difficult for *legislation* to be enacted that is incompatible with such rights. Viewed thus, a key difference between human rights and other legal rights is that the existence of (and hence the unlawfulness of conduct that is incompatible with) the latter is precarious in the sense that regular legal rights can be modified or removed by legislation. In many legal systems, the position as regards human rights is different, because the constitution prevents (or makes difficult) the enactment of legislation modifying or removing such rights; as such, human rights acquire a degree of permanence that other rights do not necessarily enjoy.[1]

But this practical answer to the question 'what are human rights?' is ultimately unsatisfying because it simply begs a further question: *why* are some rights, through their characterisation as human rights, singled out for this special treatment?

Naturally, people will disagree about what factors should be relevant for this purpose—and hence about the range of rights that should count as human rights. However, the sort of rights to which legal systems around the world generally provide special protection suggests that an important idea in this sphere is the concept of human autonomy. On this view, the political notion of liberalism—that is, the idea that people should, as far as possible, be allowed to do as they please—lies at the root of human rights.[2] Such rights, then, should restrict the capacity of the state to interfere in individuals' lives, thereby enabling them to pursue particularly important forms of human activity (for example, to express themselves freely and to protest—which is imperative if the democratic process is to function properly), and to be free from certain forms of unwanted interference (for example, from being subject to deprivation of physical liberty or torture).

However, few people would argue that all such freedoms should be unlimited. For example, an exercise of a right by one person may result in interference with someone else's right. If A has a right to say what he likes, and exercises it by spreading false rumours that cast doubt upon B's honesty, this involves interference with B's right to be free from unwarranted interference with his reputation. It follows that even within a human rights framework that is exclusively concerned with the freedom of the individual, restrictions upon such freedoms will have to be contemplated in order that an appropriate balance may be struck when they are in tension with one another.

In truth, however, few legal systems adopt a view of human rights that is oriented exclusively towards the freedom of the individual. Although it is obvious (as in the example above) that an exercise of liberty by one person may interfere with *the rights of other individuals*, it is equally clear that such an exercise of liberty may interfere

---

[1] Where human rights are guaranteed by a constitution, it follows that the extent of the degree of permanence enjoyed by such rights depends upon how easy or difficult it is to amend the constitution.

[2] This, too, begs a question—albeit not one that can be addressed here in any detail: why might it be regarded as a good thing that people should be able to live their lives in this way? While some responses to this question focus on arguments related to the individual (for example, that respect for human dignity, and the nature of the human condition, demands individual liberty), others focus on broader social interests (for example, that society as a whole will flourish if people are largely able to live their lives as they wish). For detailed discussion, see Feldman, *Civil Liberties and Human Rights in England and Wales* (Oxford 2002), ch 1.

with *the interests of the community*. Consider, for example, a former intelligence agent who exercises her right of free speech by publishing information that is highly damaging to national security, or a group of protestors who blockade oil refineries, choking off petrol supplies and bringing the country to a standstill. In these cases, the exercise of individuals' rights arguably interferes with the general interests of the community as a whole: what level of inconvenience or disruption should the community have to bear in order that particular people may exercise their individual rights? In most legal systems, the rights of the individual are qualified, to some extent, by the interests of the community—thus recognising that while the principle of autonomy that animates the concept of human rights is an important one, it is not the only value that is in play.

2.2 **Other views**

The foregoing is a (necessarily) brief sketch of the way in which human rights are conceptualised in many legal systems—including, as we will see shortly, the UK legal system. However, in four main senses, the view outlined should not be unquestioningly accepted as the right one.[3]

First, even if we accept that human rights should be used to safeguard individual autonomy, questions remain about *the range of rights necessary to secure that objective*. It is unsurprising that, if autonomy is the principal driver, emphasis is placed upon negative rights—that is, rights to be free from certain forms of interference in order that individuals may live their lives however they see fit.[4] Yet it is self-evident that interference by others is not the only potential reason why a given individual may be unable to live her life as she wishes: other factors may mean that a particular freedom, although guaranteed by law, is practically worthless. For example, the law may guarantee the right to freedom of expression—but it is clear that some people will be better equipped than others to exercise this right. Compare, for example, a university-educated columnist who writes for an influential newspaper with someone struggling to survive on the minimum wage who is ill-educated, illiterate, and inarticulate. The practical scope for the latter person to exercise his freedom of speech by, for example, contributing to public discourse on matters of political controversy is clearly more restricted than that of the former person. This involves a form of inequality: in pragmatic, if not legal, terms, there is unequal access to the right of free speech. One response to this problem—if it is perceived as such—is that negative, autonomy-based rights should be supplemented by such positive rights as are necessary for the effective exercise of the former. On this view, people should, for example, have a positive right to a good education in order that they may be equipped in practice to exercise their right to freedom of speech. It follows that, on this approach, the range of rights

---

[3] See generally Campbell et al, *Sceptical Essays on Human Rights* (Oxford 2001).
[4] See, eg Laws, 'The Constitution: Morals and Rights' [1996] PL 622.

that will qualify as human rights will be broader: in particular, it will encompass those rights of a social and economic nature that are necessary for the effective exercise of those rights that safeguard individual autonomy.

Second, the approach described in the former paragraph does not fundamentally challenge the proposition that the core purpose of human rights is to safeguard human autonomy; rather, it adopts a relatively sophisticated view of the form that human rights may need to take if that objective is to be realised. In that sense, it views positive rights as ancillary to negative rights: people should have the right to a good education not because that is intrinsically important, but because the provision of such a right will better equip people to exercise their right of free speech. That view is therefore still fundamentally premised upon the liberal philosophy that prizes individual autonomy. Those who disagree with that view emphasise *other values that are important in themselves*, not merely because they are capable of better equipping people to exercise their liberties. Prominent within this strand of criticism is the argument that considerations of *liberty* should not be emphasised at the expense of *equality*—and that while equality requires equal access to negative rights, it also requires the provision of positive entitlements because they are worthwhile in themselves, not simply because they may enhance people's capacity to exercise negative rights. This view supports a much wider set of human rights than that which emphasises autonomy and hence liberty. In particular, it supports recognition of a broad range of social and economic rights, such as the right to a decent standard of living, the right to adequate housing, and the right to health care, thereby guaranteeing to everyone at least a minimum standard of provision in these areas.

Q Should the law guarantee rights such as those mentioned in the previous sentence? What difficulties might arise if courts were required to interpret and enforce such rights?

Third, although different in some respects, both of the foregoing approaches assume that rights are an appropriate vehicle for upholding important values—but this view is not universally held. Some writers argue that *human rights are inappropriately individualistic in nature*. On this view, it is paradoxical to try to base an understanding of society and the political order upon individual rights precisely because individual rights emphasise the primacy of the individual, whereas one of the most basic facts of life is that people are bound together with each other in a community or society. From this perspective, to rely upon the notion of individual rights as the basis for society is to rely upon an asocial principle. Instead, it should be recognised that individuals are first and foremost members of a community, and that the interests of the individual should have a secondary role. Broadly speaking, this point of view is often labelled as *communitarian*—that is, a world view that places particular weight upon the responsibility of the individual to the community and society, as opposed to emphasising individual freedom and rights.

One response to this criticism is, as noted above, to acknowledge that individuals' rights should be capable of being overridden by sufficiently important community interests. For many people, this response is sufficient: it strikes an appropriate balance between the interests of the individual and society. For others, however, it does not go far enough because it retains the presumption that individuals' rights must be upheld unless it can be shown that there is some community interest that, in the particular circumstances of the case, should be allowed to prevail over the right and thus restrict the extent to which it may be lawfully exercised. Those who question the appropriateness of human rights from a communitarian perspective do not agree that the rights of the individual should, in this way, enjoy presumptive priority. This does not mean that communitarians reject the norms that underpin rights—but they do reject the notion that such norms should operate as trumps that generally override other interests.

Fourth, the communitarian perspective is distinct from, but connected to, a further issue concerning human rights: *who should decide on how far human rights should go and what they mean in any particular situation?* Once human rights are enshrined in law, it inevitably follows that the courts will play a key role in adjudicating upon disputes concerning whether or not such rights have been violated. For supporters of this approach, one of its greatest strengths is that the courts are independent and free from political interference from the legislature and the executive. The independence of the judges enables disputes to be decided in an objectively rational way—by reference to reason and principle, rather than by reference to the political maelstrom. In turn, this should lead to better protection of fundamental rights. In the UK constitution, there are important considerations arising from the constitutional relationship between the government and Parliament that are relevant here. As the legislature is dominated by the government, the risk is always that Parliament may not provide proper scrutiny and accountability of government decisions that adversely affect the human rights of the individual. By contrast, because the courts are independent, they are able to provide a useful check on the exercise of governmental power, and human rights norms provide a benchmark by reference to which such scrutiny may be carried out.

However, there are also arguments against such judicial involvement. From a very different perspective, the independence of the courts is one of their greatest weaknesses. This is because there are few, if any, objectively correct answers to the questions that arise in this arena. Consider the following questions, for example: does burning a flag constitute a form of expression falling within the protection of the right to freedom of expression? When, if at all, will national security concerns justify the restriction the rights of suspected terrorists? Should the right to freedom of religion mean that schools should be prevented from banning certain forms of religious dress? Questions such as these raise exceedingly problematic issues, because they involve the balancing up of different rights; people will legitimately disagree as to where the balance should lie. Such disagreements, it can be argued, can only legitimately be resolved through the political process. From this perspective, the meaning of human rights (and the extent to which they can legitimately be qualified by competing interests) are ultimately political, not legal, questions: answering them involves making hard choices on policy matters. As Loughlin has noted: 'Rights adjudication is intrinsically political; it requires judges to reach a determination on the relative importance of conflicting social, political, and cultural interests in circumstances where there is no objective—or even consensual answer.'[5] On this view, the very notion of legally enforceable human rights is, at best, questionable and, at worst, misconceived. Embracing such rights simply dresses up inherently political issues as legal questions. And that, it is said, is undemocratic, because it removes such issues from the sphere of representative politics, placing them in the hands of judges who are unelected and politically unaccountable.[6]

It should be apparent that there is no 'right' answer to the question of whether political or legal institutions should decide on human rights. Ultimately, the debate comes down to the underlying values that one prefers. Those who would leave it to Parliament and the government, and who are sceptical of allocating the task of deciding on human rights to courts, tend to emphasise the inherently political nature of human rights and tend to prefer political accountability. By contrast, those who are inclined toward the courts having the principal responsibility for such matters tend to stress that they are, on the whole, better placed to decide on human rights because they cannot be subject to political influence. In this way, this debate illustrates one of our key themes: the contrasting notions of political and legal constitutionalism, and the fact that the appropriate balance between those two forms of constitutionalism is a contentious matter.

The disagreement alluded to above is not one that can readily be resolved. Nevertheless, it is possible to make the following points. First, the question as to whether or not judges should be entrusted with the protection of human rights is distinct from the question as to whether the whole notion of human rights is itself a good thing. Those sceptical of allocating to the courts the task of adjudicating upon human rights disputes do not reject the notion of human rights altogether; rather, they simply think that these disputes are, on the whole, best resolved through the political rather than the judicial process.

Second, the extent to which judicial protection of human rights is disquieting will, to some extent, turn upon which rights are recognised as human rights. For example, the right to freedom of expression is a traditional civil and political right, because it is central to the functioning of a democracy. Contrast this with social rights, such as the right to adequate health care, which, some argue, should also be recognised as human rights. But if such rights were to be protected by courts, then it is highly likely that judges would be drawn into enormously difficult and controversial questions concerning spending priorities, the allocation of scarce public money, and the like.

Third, the extent of the courts' powers in relation to human rights is an obviously relevant consideration in this regard: the more extensive those powers, the greater the

---

5 Loughlin, *The Idea of Public Law* (Oxford 2003), p 129.

6 Griffith, 'The Brave New World of Sir John Laws' (2000) 63 MLR 159; Tomkins, *Our Republican Constitution* (Oxford 2005); Waldron, 'The Core of the Case against Judicial Review' (2006) 115 Yale LJ 1346.

scope for objecting to them.[7] At the same time, account must be taken of the source of such powers. When Parliament enacted the HRA, it was making a conscious political choice that, in most—although not all—instances, the courts were best placed to decide upon human rights. In other words, Parliament was making a clear political choice to recognise that human rights should be legally enforceable. Parliament did not have to do this and it is entirely feasible to suppose that Parliament might one day reverse or alter its decision. But the point is that, by enacting the HRA, Parliament granted the courts a clear and unequivocal jurisdiction to adjudicate on human rights disputes. Importantly, for the purposes of the present discussion, this jurisdiction cannot be criticised as undemocratic precisely because it was conferred upon the courts by a democratic lawmaking institution— namely, Parliament. Against this background, we turn to consider the way in which human rights are protected in UK law.

Q Who do you think should decide on human rights disputes: government and Parliament, or the courts? Why?

3. Human rights in the UK

3.1 Two models—'liberties' and 'rights'

In this sphere, UK law has traditionally recognised the notion of 'liberties' rather than 'rights'. So far in this chapter, we have used those terms largely interchangeably, but we need to distinguish between them now. The difference was clearly expressed by Browne-Wilkinson LJ in *Wheeler v Leicester City Council*[8] when he said (long before the enactment of the HRA) that

> Basic constitutional rights in this country such as freedom of the person and freedom of speech are based not on any express provision conferring such a right but on freedom of an individual to do what he will save to the extent that he is prevented from so doing by the law.

The difference, then, is that having the liberty to do something means that it is lawful to do it because *the law does not prohibit it*. By contrast, to say that someone has a right to do something means that *the law specifically says that it can be lawfully done*. The notion of liberties is residual, whereas the notion of rights is both positive and declaratory. The difference between these two positions may seem subtle, even unimportant. However, there are three reasons why the difference is practically significant. (These differences between the 'rights' and 'liberties' models are summarised in Figure 19.1.)

---

[7] We develop this point below when we consider the current extent of the powers that UK courts have to uphold human rights.   [8] [1985] AC 1054, 1065.

Liberties	Rights
Absence of state power to interfere, but no positive action required by state	Rights may require state not to interfere and/or positively to do certain things
Conduct is lawful because no law makes it unlawful—hence scope of lawful conduct is a function of prohibitions: whatever is not unlawful is lawful	Conduct is lawful because law grants a specific right to engage in it: scope of lawful conduct is determined by the right
Scope of lawful conduct not fixed: may expand or contract depending on operative legal prohibitions	Scope of lawful conduct is fixed: changes only if the right itself is amended

Figure 19.1 Liberties and rights

First, an approach based exclusively upon liberties rather than rights necessarily *restricts the type of protection thereby afforded to the individual*. If people possess a liberty to do something, then (unless the law is changed) doing it will not be unlawful. In this sense, the correlative of a liberty is a requirement of passivity on the part of the state: the state may not, for example, punish someone for doing that which he is at liberty to do. The same applies in relation to some rights. For example, if someone has the right to freedom of expression, the state may not punish him for expressing himself (unless, in doing so, he exceeds the boundaries of his right). But it follows from what was said in the previous section that rights may require not only passivity, but also positive action on the part of the state. This is true most obviously—but not exclusively[9]—in relation to social rights, such as the right to adequate housing or the right to adequate health care. Such rights transparently impose a positive obligation on the state to provide and deliver appropriate public services. They cannot meaningfully be conceptualised as liberties: being free (at liberty) to receive health care is not the same thing as having a right to be provided with health care.

Second, individuals are likely to be in a better position in that they can *ascertain their position more readily and more straightforwardly within a framework based on rights* as opposed to one based on residual liberties. Within the former approach, an individual trying to answer the question, 'Am I allowed to do X?' would seek to establish whether the law furnished him with a right to engage in the conduct concerned. In contrast, in a framework based on liberties, it would be necessary to identify all laws potentially impinging upon the activity in question in order to determine what, if any, scope there were for lawfully engaging in it. However, while this analysis suggests that the rights-based model is clearer, this point should not be overstated: rights may be stated in broad terms that leave people uncertain as to whether particular forms of conduct are protected.

---

[9] Even rights that, on their face, simply require the state *not* to do things might implicitly require it also to *do* certain things. For example, a right to be free from inhuman or degrading treatment may implicitly require the state to provide people on the verge of destitution with basic food and shelter.

Third, *liberties are at constant risk of erosion*. Liberties are freedoms that are left over once all relevant legal prohibitions have been taken into account. For example, in a system based on liberties rather than rights, freedom of speech exists only to the extent that people can lawfully say those things that they are not legally prohibited from saying. The extent of the liberty is therefore a function of the relevant legal prohibitions (the law of libel, the law of official secrecy, the law of privacy, and so on). If, over time, legislators (or, for that matter, judges in their development of the common law) impose more and more restrictions upon what may lawfully be said, the liberty to speak freely will correspondingly shrink. The position may be different, however, in a rights-based system. If (as is the case in many legal systems) no public body, including the legislature, is permitted to act contrary to constitutionally protected rights, the erosion of the legal freedoms created by such rights cannot be eroded (whether intentionally or accidentally). This is because any conduct by public bodies (including legislation) that conflicts with such rights can be challenged before a constitutional court on the ground that its interference with human rights renders it unlawful and ineffective.

> **Q** Lord Irvine—who, as Lord Chancellor, was a principal architect of the HRA—said: 'The view that because we have liberty we have no need of human rights must be rejected.'[10] What do you think he meant by this—and do you agree with him?

3.2 Before the Human Rights Act 1998

In the previous section, we sketched two models—two ways in which legal freedom may exist within a given legal system. The HRA was enacted because it was felt (at least by those responsible for its enactment) that the rights-based model is superior. It might therefore be thought that the effect of the HRA was to flick a switch, such that a liberties-based approach was replaced by a rights-based approach. However, the position is actually more complex, both because the HRA does not fully implement a rights-based model (in the sense set out above) and because the pre-HRA position did not fully conform to the liberties-based framework. In reality, the two models set out above are not binary alternatives; rather, they describe points on a continuum. Thus the UK has not swapped an approach based on liberties for one based on rights; rather, it has shifted from an approach lying towards the liberties end of the spectrum to one lying nearer the rights end. In order to substantiate this proposition, we need to examine how the HRA works and why it does not fully implement a rights-based model—a task that we undertake in the next section. First, however, it is necessary to say something about the position that obtained before the HRA entered into force.[11]

---

[10] Irvine, *Human Rights, Constitutional Law and the Development of the English Legal System* (Oxford 2003), p 24.

[11] See generally Hunt, *Using Human Rights in English Courts* (Oxford 1997).

A pure liberties-based approach to legal freedom—that is, one lying at the far left of the continuum shown in Figure 19.1—would be wholly agnostic about such freedom. Within such a framework, a court seeking to ascertain whether an individual could lawfully undertake a given form of conduct—publishing an article calling for the abolition of the monarchy, for example—would undertake a morally neutral, factual inquiry. Normative considerations, such as the desirability of free political debate, would not enter into the inquiry. The court would simply examine, interpret, and apply any relevant laws without reference to the fact that an important liberty was at stake.

The key point for present purposes is that the approach described in the previous paragraph does not accurately reflect that which obtained in the UK prior to the HRA's entry into force—nor does it accurately reflect the approach that would be applied if the HRA were to be repealed. This is partly because *other legislation* confers specific rights on individuals. For example, long before the HRA was enacted, legislation existed that protected the right (in certain contexts) not to be discriminated against on grounds such as gender and race.[12] More generally, there are countless examples of decisions by the UK courts, long before the HRA began to operate, recognising individuals' rights and seeking (often with success) to protect them in the face of administrative and legislative measures arguably at odds with such rights.[13] We have already met a clear example of this in Chapter 13. We saw there that, when public bodies exercise discretionary powers, the courts are prepared to uphold (what amounts in practice to) a right to good administration, by requiring agencies to act in accordance with a series of principles of good decision-making. We also saw in Chapter 14 that, in cases such as *Anisminic*,[14] the courts have gone to considerable lengths in order to interpret Acts of Parliament in such a way as to leave the right of access to the courts intact. In such cases, the courts are far from agnostic about the right that is at stake, and it is in this sense that the pre-HRA position did not wholly conform to the pure liberties-based model.

In order to understand the pre-HRA position more fully—thereby allowing us to appreciate the impact of the HRA—it is necessary to consider two questions. First, *at common law, which rights are courts prepared to recognise and attempt to uphold* in the face of conflicting administrative or legislative action? Unsurprisingly, no definitive list of such rights exists, but the courts' focus has generally been on matters concerning due process and access to the courts. *Anisminic* itself involved an 'ouster clause', which, on the face of it, seemed to preclude judicial review of a government agency's decisions; other cases were concerned with such matters as the right to launch legal proceedings irrespective of financial means[15] and the right of

---

[12] See now the Equality Act 2010, which addresses discrimination on various grounds, including gender, race, age, disability, gender reassignment, religion, belief, and sexual orientation.

[13] See, eg *Anisminic Ltd v Foreign Compensation Commission* [1969] 2 AC 147; *R v Lord Chancellor, ex p Witham* [1998] QB 575; *R v Secretary of State for the Home Department, ex p Pierson* [1998] AC 539; *R v Secretary of State for the Home Department, ex p Simms* [2000] 2 AC 115.

[14] *Anisminic Ltd v Foreign Compensation Commission* [1969] 2 AC 147.

[15] *R v Lord Chancellor, ex p Witham* [1998] QB 575.

legal professional privilege (that is, the right to communicate confidentially with one's legal representative, which is necessary if the right of access to court is to be fully enjoyed).[16] Even in cases concerned with different rights, such as the right to freedom of expression, the courts, prior to the HRA's entry into force, tended to be at their boldest when the exercise of such a right could be related to the core of rights, concerning access to courts and due process, which the judiciary was evidently most willing to uphold.[17] This may have had something to do with what Sir John Laws, a Court of Appeal judge, has described as the 'settled, overarching quality' of rights of due process.[18] His point is that such rights are relatively uncontroversial, such that the courts, in recognising and trying to protect such rights, considered themselves to be on relatively firm ground, even though they had no explicit mandate, such as a Bill of Rights, for doing so. It is clear, then, that, by the time the HRA was enacted, the protection of rights at common law, although a reality, operated within a relatively narrow field.

Second, if willing to recognise a given right at common law, *what exactly can courts do in order to protect it?* The answer to this question depends in large part upon who has acted (or is proposing to act) contrary to the right. If the actor in question is a body other than the UK Parliament, the courts (subject to an important proviso explained below) can and do strike down its acts and decisions if they contravene what are often called 'common law constitutional rights'. In contrast, if the actor is Parliament—if, in other words, an Act of Parliament unambiguously conflicts with a common law constitutional right—the courts cannot strike down or refuse to apply the relevant provision.[19] If, then, an Act of Parliament is inconsistent with a right, the legislation must be applied and the right must yield. From this, it follows that if a public body other than Parliament is authorised by an Act of Parliament to act inconsistently with common law constitutional rights, the courts are powerless to intervene.[20]

The key question is, therefore, this: what can courts do if an Act of Parliament appears to be inconsistent with a common law constitutional right such that it apparently provides for some eventuality that would deny an individual the full enjoyment of that right? Given that *disapplication* of Acts of Parliament is not a tool at the courts' disposal (unless Parliament is no longer regarded as sovereign[21]), the primary technique by which they seek to uphold common law rights is the *interpretation* of legislation. The idea is a very simple one. If the legislative provision in question can be made to mean something that is, in fact, consistent with the right in question, the fact that

[16] *R (Daly) v Secretary of State for the Home Department* [2001] UKHL 26, [2001] 2 AC 532. This case was decided after the HRA had entered into force, but, in his leading judgment, Lord Bingham relied principally upon a common law right to legal professional privilege.

[17] *R v Secretary of State for the Home Department, ex p Simms* [2000] 2 AC 115.

[18] Laws, 'The Limitations of Human Rights' [1998] PL 254, 260.

[19] The only established exception is in relation to Acts of Parliament that conflict with directly effective European Union law. See Chapter 8, section 4, above.

[20] This is the proviso referred to earlier in the paragraph.

[21] For criticism of parliamentary sovereignty, see Chapter 5, sections 4.1 and 4.5, above.

the courts are (because Parliament is sovereign) duty-bound to apply the provision presents no problem from a rights perspective. We saw in Chapter 5 that the courts are prepared to uphold a range of important constitutional values in this way, including common law constitutional rights, and that, in doing so, they have, on some occasions, been prepared to adopt extremely strained interpretations of the legislation in question. Indeed, we noted in Chapter 5 that it has even been suggested that in certain cases—most obviously *Anisminic*[22]—the courts' interpretation of legislation has been so radical as to amount, in effect, to a refusal to apply that legislation. Whether or not this view is accurate, it is certainly the case that courts were prepared to uphold common law constitutional rights unless an Act of Parliament restricted or abolished such rights in clear and unambiguous terms.

From all of this, it follows that it would be simplistic to say that, prior to the entry into force of the HRA, a purely liberties-based approach obtained in the UK. It would be more accurate to say that the approach that applied reflected some features of both the liberties- and rights-based models. Rights were certainly recognized—and, as we have seen, courts were willing to take steps, principally through the interpretation of legislation, to uphold such rights. However, this could not fairly be described as a full implementation of the rights-based model, given that, first, the range of rights recognised by the courts as common law constitutional rights was relatively narrow, and second, the courts were ultimately powerless to protect such rights if legislation unambiguously interfered with or removed them.

Against this background, we can now turn to consider why the HRA was enacted. How was it intended to take the protection of rights in the UK beyond that which was already undertaken at common law? And has it succeeded in doing so?

3.3 The Human Rights Act 1998—an introduction

The HRA was a key element of the constitutional reform programme undertaken in the early years of the Labour administration that took office in 1997. It was intended to (and has) extended the protection of human rights in domestic law in two main respects.

3.3.1 The rights protected by the HRA

The range of rights offered protection by the HRA is substantially wider than the range of rights that had, by the time of its enactment, unambiguously been brought within the scope of the common law constitutional rights doctrine. The first effect, therefore, of the HRA was to broaden the scope of rights protected by UK courts.

The effect of the HRA is to give effect in UK law to certain of the rights set out in the European Convention on Human Rights (ECHR). The framers of the HRA did not therefore start out with a clean slate, choosing precisely which rights should

---

[22] *Anisminic Ltd v Foreign Compensation Commission* [1969] 2 AC 147.

be protected; rather, they adopted an off-the-shelf solution, in which they used an already-established set of rights. The ECHR is an international treaty—that is, an agreement between states that is binding upon them as a matter of international law. The principal undertaking made by the states that are party to the Convention is set out in Art 1, which says that they 'shall secure to everyone within their jurisdiction the rights and freedoms defined in Section I of this Convention'.[23] The ECHR took effect in 1950, and was drafted in the aftermath of—and as a direct response to—the horrors of the Second World War, during which Europe had witnessed human rights abuses (most obviously genocide) on an almost unimaginable scale.[24] A primary motivation lying behind the adoption of the ECHR was therefore a desire to guard against a repetition of such events by locking European governments into a legal regime for the protection of human rights.

Unlike many international treaties, the ECHR contains an institutional regime for the enforcement of the rights that it sets out. In particular, Art 19 provides for a court—the European Court of Human Rights (ECtHR)—the function of which is to 'ensure the observance of the engagements undertaken by the [states parties]' to the Convention. Claims alleging that a state party has violated relevant rights can be brought before the Court both by other states parties[25] and by individuals claiming to be victims of the alleged violation.[26] If the Court finds that there has been a violation, it has the power to 'afford just satisfaction to the injured party'[27]—for example, by ordering that the state concerned pays a sum of money to the victim. Moreover, the state parties have agreed 'to abide by the final judgment of the Court in any case to which they are parties'.[28] It should be noted at this point that the ECHR is legally and institutionally distinct from the European Union (EU).[29] Many more countries are parties to the ECHR than are member States of the EU, and the ECtHR is a separate institution from the Court of Justice of the European Union (CJEU), which, as we saw in Chapter 8, is concerned with the interpretation and application of EU law.

All of the above statements concerning the ECHR were as true before the enactment of the HRA as they are now; the UK has thus been bound by the ECHR as a matter of international law ever since it ratified it in 1950. Moreover, ever since the UK opted into the right of individual petition in 1965, individuals have been able to institute proceedings against it in the ECtHR. However, what they could not do, generally speaking, was to invoke the ECHR in *domestic* legal proceedings. This was one of the major factors that formed the impetus for enacting the HRA.[30]

---

[23] There are also several 'protocols' to the Convention; they are only binding upon those states that have specifically agreed to be bound by them.

[24] Simpson, *Human Rights and the End of Empire: Britain and the Genesis of the European Convention* (Oxford 2004).   [25] ECHR, Art 33.

[26] ECHR, Art 34.   [27] ECHR, Art 41.   [28] ECHR, Art 46(1).

[29] Albeit that Art 6(2) of the Treaty on European Union provides for the EU itself to become a party to the ECHR. Meanwhile, Art 6(3), in any event, makes the rights set out in the ECHR binding upon the institutions of the EU.

[30] Home Office, *Rights Brought Home: The Human Rights Bill* (Cm 3782 1997), [1.14].

What, then, are the rights that the HRA protects? The HRA empowers national courts to protect what it calls 'the Convention rights'. This means the rights set out in Arts 2–12 and 14 of the ECHR, along with those laid down in Arts 1–3 of the First Protocol to the Convention and in Art 1 of the Thirteenth Protocol. These rights are set out in Figure 19.2. From this, it will be apparent that the focus of the ECHR is on civil and political rights. It is thus centrally concerned with matters such as the physical liberty of the individual (which is most obviously protected by Art 5, but is also upheld by provisions such as Arts 2–4, and 8, which prohibit various sorts of interference with the person) and freedoms to live one's life without unwarranted interference in relation to such matters as expression, religion, and protest (Arts 9–11). In this way, the Convention focuses on those rights that are likely to uphold the *autonomy* of the individual, considerations of *equality* being secondary. This is apparent from the fact that the ECHR does not contain any general anti-discrimination provision: Art 14 is the closest it comes, but this only prohibits discrimination in relation to the enjoyment of the freedoms conferred by the other provisions of the Convention.[31] With the exception of the right to education, which is protected by Art 2 of the First Protocol, the ECHR does not extend to social rights (for example, there is no right to housing or to health care), and nor does it confer economic rights (such as a right to a decent standard of living or to employment).

3.3.2 The forms of protection afforded by the HRA

So much for the range of rights covered by the HRA—but what is the practical significance of a right falling within its scope? In order to answer this question, we need to consider—in some cases, only in outline for the time being—four key provisions contained in the HRA.

First, one of the ways in which the HRA seeks to protect the Convention rights is by making it more difficult in the first place for the UK Parliament to enact legislation that is inconsistent with those rights. To this end, s 19 of the HRA stipulates that, before a Bill's second reading, the Minister responsible for it must do one of two things: either he must make a *statement of compatibility*, saying that he believes the Bill to be compatible with the Convention rights, or he must explain why he thinks the Bill should be enacted even though he cannot undertake that it is compatible with the Convention rights. This system is intended to ensure that Parliament does not casually or unknowingly enact legislation that will breach the Convention rights: if a Minister finds himself unable to issue a statement of compatibility, this will draw Parliament's attention to the possibility that the Bill may be incompatible with one or more of the Convention rights, and will focus attention—both inside and beyond Parliament—on whether there are compelling reasons for enacting the legislation despite such putative incompatibility.

---

[31] A broader non-discrimination provision is contained in the Twelfth Protocol, but this has not been adopted by the UK. However, UK law, independently of the ECHR and HRA, contains extensive provision on discrimination: see Equalities Act 2010.

Provision	Right/ prohibition	Notes	
Article 2	Right to life	No infringement if killing relates to execution of lawfully imposed sentence (but note UK now signatory to Thirteenth Protocol—see below) or absolutely necessary use of force in relation to self-defence, quelling of disorder, or effecting lawful arrest/preventing escape of lawfully detained person	
Article 3	Prohibition of torture	Prohibits torture and inhuman or degrading treatment	
Article 4	Prohibition of slavery and forced labour	Prohibits slavery, servitude, and forced and compulsory labour	
Article 5	Right to liberty and security	Deprivation of liberty prohibited unless (i) in accordance with procedure prescribed by law, and (ii) for a legitimate purpose. Legitimate purposes include imprisonment of convicted criminals, trial of criminal offences, prevention of spreading of infectious diseases, deportation, extradition. Legal proceedings must be available whereby legality of detention can be determined.	
Article 6	Right to a fair trial	In all criminal proceedings, as well as in any proceedings determining civil rights and obligations, there must be a fair and public hearing within a reasonable time by an independent and impartial tribunal established by law. Additional rights in relation to criminal matters include presumption of innocence, suspect to be informed promptly of allegation, suspect to be given adequate time and facilities to prepare defence, suspect to be given free legal representation when interests of justice so require, opportunity to examine and cross-examine witnesses, access to interpreter if necessary.	
Article 7	No punishment without law	Essentially, a non-retrospectivity principle: prohibits finding someone guilty of an offence that was not specified at time of commission, prohibits imposition of heavier penalty than that applicable at time of commission.	
Article 8	Right to respect for private and family life	Applies to private life, family life, home, and correspondence	Articles 8–11 are all laid down according to a common format. The first paragraph of each Article states the matters to which the right relates. For example, Art 8(1) says: 'Everyone has the right to respect for his private and family life, his home and his correspondence.' The second paragraph sets out the circumstances in which it is lawful to do that which would otherwise be unlawful by virtue of the first paragraph. In relation to each Article, the requirements laid down in the second paragraph are that any restrictions must be (a) prescribed by (or, in relation to Art 8, 'in accordance with') law and (b) necessary in a democratic society for the advancement of (c) a legitimate objective. Such objectives include the prevention of disorder and crime, and the interests of national security.
Article 9	Freedom of thought, conscience, and religion	Includes freedom to change religion/ belief, and freedom to manifest religion/ belief through worship, teaching, practice, and observance	
Article 10	Freedom of expression	Includes freedom to hold opinions, and to receive and impart information and ideas; does not preclude state licensing of radio, television, and cinemas	
Article 11	Freedom of assembly and association	Includes right to form and join trade unions	

Figure 19.2 The 'Convention rights'

Article 12	Right to marry	Has been interpreted as applying only to marriage of opposite-sex couples. It therefore does not apply to gay couples, but does apply to couples that are opposite sex by virtue of one partner (or both partners) being transsexual.
Article 14	Prohibition of discrimination	Explicitly covers discrimination on grounds of sex, race, colour, language, religion, political or other opinion, national or social origin, association with a national minority, property, birth, or other status. Has been interpreted as applying to other matters, including sexual orientation. Only applies to discrimination in respect of access to other ECHR rights.
Article 1, First Protocol	Protection of property	Right to peaceful enjoyment of possessions. Deprivation permitted only if in public interest. Explicit provision for state to enforce such laws as it thinks necessary to control property use in public interest or to secure payment of taxes.
Article 2, First Protocol	Right to education	Does not require creation of educational provision; merely prohibits denial of access to such provision as exists. Where state assumes responsibility for education/teaching, parents' philosophical and religious convictions must be respected.
Article 3, First Protocol	Right to free elections	Free elections must be held at regular intervals, by secret ballot and under conditions allowing free expression of opinion in choice of legislature
Article 1, Thirteenth Protocol	Abolition of death penalty	Prohibits use of death penalty

Figure 19.2 (Continued)

There is, however, an obvious weakness in this system. For a variety of reasons (including incompetence, genuine misjudgement, and cynical political calculation), statements of compatibility may be issued in respect of Bills that later turn out to be incompatible with one or more of the Convention rights. For example, the Home Secretary made a statement of compatibility in respect of legislation, enacted in the wake of the 9/11 terrorist attacks, that provided for the indefinite detention of suspected foreign terrorists. Yet this legislation, as we saw in Chapter 1, was later held, both by the House of Lords in the UK and by the ECtHR, to be incompatible with Art 5 of the Convention.[32] Certainly, the incompatibility of that legislation with the ECHR was by no means clear-cut, and there was no evidence that the government deliberately made an incorrect statement of compatibility—but the general point remains: such statements of compatibility by themselves only offer limited constraints upon government.

Parliament does, however, have an additional, more independent, source of advice on the likely compatibility of Bills. The Joint Committee on Human Rights (JCHR) is a joint select committee of the House of Commons and the House of Lords that (with the assistance of expert legal advice) scrutinises all Bills and reports to Parliament on their

---

[32] *A v Secretary of State for the Home Department* [2004] UKHL 56, [2005] 2 AC 68; *A v UK* (2009) 49 EHRR 29.

human rights implications.[33] While it is far from being the case that Ministers inevitably give way when the JCHR identifies a potential incompatibility, the Committee is nevertheless highly regarded, and its reports often play an influential role when MPs and peers debate and propose amendments to Bills.

Second, s 6 of the HRA provides that *public authorities must act compatibly with the Convention rights* (unless primary legislation requires them to act incompatibly). This means, among other things, that the Convention rights have become grounds of judicial review: public bodies' acts and decisions can be quashed to the extent that they are incompatible with those rights. The implications of this were considered in Chapter 13 and need not be restated here.[34] It is sufficient to emphasise that the effect of s 6 has been to extend the courts' judicial review powers beyond those that they were prepared to assert prior to the HRA's entry into force. This is true in two senses. On the one hand, while, as we have seen, breach of common law constitutional rights was a ground of review, the Convention rights are *broader* in scope. On the other hand, judicial review under the HRA is *deeper* than it was beforehand: as we saw in Chapter 13, when Convention rights are involved, judicial review will be more intense, with proportionality, rather than *Wednesbury* reasonableness, being used to test the legality of any restrictions placed by public authorities upon individuals' rights.

Third, s 3 of the HRA requires courts, so far as is possible, to *read and give effect to legislation in a way that is compatible with the Convention rights*. As we will see when we consider this provision in more detail below, this is a very strong obligation that requires courts to go to considerable lengths in order to find a way of interpreting legislation compatibly with the Convention rights. This approach is not novel: we have already seen that, prior to the HRA's enactment, courts were willing to protect rights by interpretative means. The difference, however, is that the interpretative protection of rights is now triggered in a broader range of circumstances. Before the HRA entered into force, the courts would engage in such interpretation only in one of two scenarios. We have already encountered the first: it arose where the right in question fell within the relatively narrow category of common law constitutional rights. The other scenario arose when the right (not being a common law constitutional right) was one that was set out in the ECHR *and* the domestic legislation in question was ambiguous.[35] In contrast, under the HRA, the interpretative obligation arising under s 3 obtains in respect of all Convention rights (not only common law constitutional rights) and applies irrespective of whether the domestic legislation in question is ambiguous.

Fourth, the HRA's most novel device for protecting rights is found in s 4. This section provides that *when a legislative provision cannot be interpreted compatibly with a Convention right, certain courts may issue a 'declaration of incompatibility'*. The purpose of s 4 is to enable courts to issue a limited form of relief in respect of incompatible legislation, given that they are (by virtue both of the doctrine of parliamentary

---

[33] See further Feldman, 'Parliamentary Scrutiny of Legislation and Human Rights' [2002] PL 323.
[34] See Chapter 13, section 4.6.
[35] *R v Secretary of State for the Home Department, ex p Brind* [1991] 1 AC 696.

sovereignty and the explicit terms of the HRA) incapable of striking down or refusing to apply any provision in an Act of Parliament (or any subordinate legislation that has been lawfully adopted pursuant to an Act of Parliament that permits the enactment of legislation that is incompatible with Convention rights).[36] The courts had no equivalent power prior to the HRA's enactment.

Finally, a broader point should be noted. While the powers given by the HRA to the courts are important, courts are not the only means of overseeing and protecting human rights. As we have already noted, Parliament's JCHR performs an important role in scrutinising proposed legislation for its compliance with human rights. Meanwhile, whereas the HRA is principally concerned with giving courts powers to deal with human rights infractions that have occurred, the Equality and Human Rights Commission and the Northern Ireland Human Rights Commission seek to ensure (*inter alia*) that public bodies act in ways that, in the first place, are compliant with human rights standards.

3.4 Sections 3 and 4 of the HRA

Having set out the key provisions of the HRA in outline, we now turn to consider several of those provisions in more detail. We begin, in this section, with the two provisions lying at the heart of the Act: ss 3 and 4.

3.4.1 Introduction—the relationship between ss 3 and 4

Taken together, ss 3 and 4 provide a comprehensive regime for dealing with situations in which courts are faced with legislation that is potentially contrary to one or more of the Convention rights. They aim to confer upon the courts the maximum amount of power to uphold Convention rights that is consistent with the role of the courts under the UK constitution. This means, in effect, that what the courts can do is limited in two crucial ways. First, they can interpret legislation compatibly with the Convention rights only when this is 'possible': they are not permitted to cross the line, established by the separation of powers, between interpreting and legislating. The second constitutional inhibition that the scheme of the HRA reflects is the courts' general inability to disapply Acts of Parliament.[37] It is for this reason, as noted above, that the courts' power under s 4 is limited to declaring that legislation is incompatible with one or more of the Convention rights.

The relationship between ss 3 and 4 is therefore crucial. Neither stands alone: each is part of an integrated scheme of which the other is a crucial component. No case

---

[36] For simplicity, we refer in this paragraph to Acts of Parliament. In fact, s 4 actually refers to 'primary legislation'. The significance of this point is considered in section 3.4.6 below.

[37] We saw in Chapter 8 above that courts *can* disapply Acts of Parliament if they are incompatible with directly effective provisions of EU law. The basis of this power, and whether it is to be understood as an exception to, a denunciation of, or as compatible with, parliamentary sovereignty is considered in Chapter 8, section 4, above.

will arise in which the powers conferred by both sections is exercisable.[38] Either it is possible to interpret the legislation compatibly with the Convention rights under s 3—in which case, such an interpretation must be rendered—or it will be impossible to do so—in which case, a declaration may be issued under s 4. The criterion that determines into which category a given case falls is that of 'possibility': is it *possible* to interpret the provision compatibly with the relevant Convention right? This, as we will see, is a highly malleable concept, meaning that courts, in practice, have a good deal of discretion to decide whether to deal with a case under s 3 or s 4. In exercising that discretion, it is inevitable that courts are—and it is right that they should be—mindful of the implications of choosing one or other course.

Lord Irvine—who, as noted above, bears a large part of the responsibility for the HRA's enactment—underlined this point when he warned courts of the dangers of overreliance on either provision. On the one hand, he noted that stretching the concept of possibility, in order to fit cases within the s 3 category, would be constitutionally inappropriate: judges would be 'taking it upon themselves to rewrite legislation in order to render it consistent with the Convention, thereby excluding Parliament and the executive from the human rights enterprise'.[39] This would be problematic not least because ECHR-consistent interpretation under s 3 is not the only tool at the courts' disposal: they also have the option of issuing a declaration of incompatibility under s 4. But this does not mean that courts should rely too much on s 4 either. Irvine warned that if courts were to approach s 3 too narrowly, concluding too readily that legislation could not be interpreted consistently with the Convention rights and issuing s 4 declarations instead

> their ability interpretatively to guarantee Convention rights would be severely curtailed. Instead of reading municipal law in a way which gave effect to individuals' rights, the courts would tend to discover irreconcilable conflicts between UK law and the ECHR which would then require legislative correction.[40]

Indeed, overreliance on s 4 would substantially frustrate the purpose of the HRA, which was to enable domestic courts to deal with human rights matters. This follows because, as we explain below, a declaration of incompatibility has no legal effect upon the outcome of the case, meaning that the party whose human rights have been infringed, in practice, leaves court empty-handed.

3.4.2 Section 3—what is 'possible'?

Against this background, we turn to consider how the courts have approached s 3: when is it 'possible' to interpret legislation compatibly with the Convention rights, and when should a declaration of incompatibility instead be issued under s 4? In seeking

---

[38] Unless the case raises questions about the compatibility of two or more distinct legislative provisions.
[39] 'Activism and Restraint: Human Rights and the Interpretative Process' [1999] EHRLR 350, 367.
[40] Irvine at 367.

to answer this question, the decision of the House of Lords in *Ghaidan v Godin-Mendoza*[41] is a good starting point.

The claimant landlord wished to evict the defendant tenant from his property. If, however, the defendant was (as he contended) a 'statutory tenant' within the meaning of the Rent Act 1977, he would enjoy legal immunity from eviction except in limited circumstances. The case therefore hinged on whether the defendant was a statutory tenant. Whether he was such a tenant was governed by the Rent Act 1977, Sch 1, para 2, which, when *Ghaidan* was decided,[42] provided as follows:

> (1) The surviving spouse (if any) of the original tenant, if residing in the dwelling-house immediately before the death of the original tenant, shall after the death be the statutory tenant if and so long as he or she occupies the dwelling-house as his or her residence.
>
> (2) For the purposes of this paragraph, a person who was living with the original tenant as his or her wife or husband shall be treated as the spouse of the original tenant.

The question was whether these rules operated such that, upon the death of the defendant's partner—the 'original tenant' within the meaning of the foregoing provisions—a statutory tenancy was vested in the defendant. The defendant and his partner had lived together in the property concerned for 18 years before the latter's death, in a stable, monogamous relationship. As such, but for one crucial factor, the defendant would straightforwardly have satisfied the conditions for a statutory tenancy. The complication, however, was that the defendant and his partner had formed a same-sex couple. The House of Lords therefore had to decide whether, bearing in mind its obligation under s 3 of the HRA, the relevant provisions of the Rent Act should be read as applying to same-sex couples. In such cases, the courts, in effect, adopt a three-stage analysis.

The first question concerns *the natural meaning of the legislation*: what would the relevant provisions mean if the HRA were not to exist? In *Ghaidan*, the answer was clear. Throughout the provisions in question, gender-specific language was used: 'spouse', 'husband', 'wife'. Thus, as Lord Nicholls observed:

> On an ordinary reading of this language paragraph 2(2) draws a distinction between the position of a heterosexual couple living together in a house as husband and wife and a homosexual couple living together in a house. The survivor of a heterosexual couple may become a statutory tenant by succession, the survivor of a homosexual couple cannot.[43]

The second question is *whether, given its natural meaning, the legislation, when applied to the facts of the case, would produce an outcome that would infringe one or more of the Convention rights*. Clearly, if the relevant provisions of the Rent Act were to have been given their natural meaning in *Ghaidan*, the defendant would not have become a statutory tenant. Would this have involved a breach of the defendant's Convention

---

[41] [2004] UKHL 30, [2004] 2 AC 557.

[42] Paragraph 2 has since been amended: it now refers to 'civil partners' as well as 'spouses'.

[43] *Ghaidan* at [5].

rights? The House of Lords concluded, on the basis of Arts 8 and 14, that it would. Article 8, as Figure 19.2 shows, requires respect for, among other things, a person's home. Taken in isolation, this would not have assisted the defendant: Art 8 does not, by any means, impose a blanket prohibition upon landlords evicting tenants. Crucially, however, the landlord in *Ghaidan* would not have been able lawfully to evict the defendant if he had been asserting a statutory tenancy on the basis of an opposite-sex relationship. This factor made Art 14 relevant. As noted above, the effect of Art 14 is that the enjoyment of the other rights set out in the ECHR 'shall be secured without discrimination' on various grounds, including (according to the ECtHR's case law) sexual orientation.[44] It followed that the Rent Act, if applied to the defendant, would entail a breach of Art 14: he would have been accorded a lower degree of respect for his home simply because his claim was based on a same-sex, rather than an opposite-sex, relationship.

The third question (which only falls to be addressed if the second question is answered affirmatively) is *whether it is possible, pursuant to s 3 of the HRA, to read and give effect to the relevant provisions of domestic law in such a way as to produce an outcome that would be compatible with the relevant Convention rights*. It is at this point that the courts have to confront the precise nature of the obligation imposed upon them by s 3. They have to interpret UK law compatibly with the Convention rights '[s]o far as it is possible to do so'. This obligation, said Lord Nicholls in *Ghaidan*, is a very strong one. It is not to be understood as a narrow requirement that simply requires courts to resolve ambiguities;[45] rather, it is an 'unusual and far-reaching' obligation. Indeed, so unusual and far-reaching is it that it 'may require a court to depart from the unambiguous meaning the legislation would otherwise bear'. It might even require the court to 'depart from the intention of the Parliament which enacted the legislation'.[46] While this would (inevitably) involve frustrating Parliament's the intention when it passed the provision in question, it would fulfil its intention in enacting s 3 of the HRA. Importantly, Lord Nicholls said that Parliament, in enacting s 3, was not to be taken to have intended that whether ECHR-compliant interpretation is possible 'should depend critically upon the particular form of words adopted by the parliamentary draftsman in the statutory provision under consideration'. Such an approach 'would make the application of section 3 something of a semantic lottery'.[47] Lord Nicholls concluded that s 3 permits courts to read words into a statutory text in order to change its meaning so as to make it Convention-compliant.[48]

Yet Lord Nicholls did not consider the power conferred by s 3 to be an unlimited one. What, then, are the bounds of what is 'possible'? The answer, said Lord Nicholls, was that Parliament could not be taken to 'have intended that in the discharge of this extended interpretative function the courts should adopt a meaning inconsistent with a fundamental feature of legislation'. It follows that the one thing that courts may not

---

[44] *Da Silva Mouta v Portugal* (2001) 31 EHRR 4; *EB v France* (2008) 47 EHRR 21.
[45] *Ghaidan* at [29].   [46] *Ghaidan* at [30].
[47] *Ghaidan* at [31].   [48] *Ghaidan* at [32].

do under s 3 is to ascribe to a given provision a meaning that is inconsistent with the 'underlying thrust of the legislation being construed'.[49] Similarly, Lord Rodger said that the interpretation must 'go with the grain of the legislation'. The court must not ascribe a meaning to a provision that conflicts with the 'essential principles' of the legislation concerned: doing so, said Lord Rodger, would cross 'the boundary between interpretation and amendment of the statute', thereby taking the court beyond its proper role under s 3.[50]

Applying these principles in *Ghaidan*, the majority held that the thrust of the relevant parts of the Rent Act was to confer protection upon those who were the surviving partners of stable, close relationships. This meant that bringing same-sex partners within the scope of the protection afforded by the Act would not be improper. True to the principles that he had laid down earlier in his judgment, Lord Nicholls said: 'The precise form of words read in for this purpose is of no significance. It is their substantive effect which matters.'[51]

One of the five Law Lords in *Ghaidan* dissented. While Lord Millett was in general agreement with the principles laid down by Lord Nicholls,[52] his conclusion as to how they should be applied to the facts of the case differed. In essence, the disagreement between Lord Millett and the majority was about what the relevant fundamental features of the Act were. In seeking to identify these, Lord Millett looked in detail at the legislative history. He noted that when the relevant provision was originally enacted, it conferred protection only on women whose husbands had died. Later, an amendment extended protection to widowers. Later still, in recognition of the increasing incidence of extramarital cohabitation, protection was extended to those who were not married, but who had been living with the deceased tenant 'as his or her wife or husband'. This language, said Lord Millett, 'does not mean living together as lovers whether of the same or the opposite sex. It connotes persons who have openly set up home together as man and wife'.[53] Lord Millett concluded that the use of gender-specific language throughout all of the iterations of the relevant provisions indicated that a fundamental feature of the Act was that the protection that it conferred should extend only to opposite-sex couples. What ultimately distinguished Lord Millett's analysis, then, from that of the majority is that he placed more weight on the specific language used by Parliament in his attempt to identify the fundamental feature of the Act.

Q Did the House of Lords go too far in *Ghaidan*?[54] Are the principles set out by Lord Nicholls acceptable ones, or do they attach insufficient weight to what the legislation being interpreted actually says?

---

[49] *Ghaidan* at [33].   [50] *Ghaidan* at [121].
[51] *Ghaidan* at [35].   [52] *Ghaidan* at [67]–[68], *per* Lord Millett.   [53] *Ghaidan* at [92].
[54] For a further example of the courts using their s 3 power so as substantially to adapt the effect of legislation, see *R v A (No 2)* [2001] UKHL 25, [2002] 1 AC 45.

3.4.3 Section 3—three limiting factors

It should not be supposed from the discussion so far that courts are invariably prepared to do whatever is necessary under the guise of s 3 interpretation to render legislation ECHR-compliant. Three particular factors operate so as to constrain the extent to which courts are prepared to stretch statutory language in order to secure compatibility with the Convention.

First, as we have already seen, *the courts will not adopt an interpretation that conflicts with a fundamental feature of the legislation concerned* (albeit that, as in *Ghaidan*, there might be scope for disagreement about what the relevant fundamental feature is). *Anderson* is a good illustration of a case in which the court refused, on this ground, to render an ECHR-compatible interpretation.[55] The case concerned a challenge to the then-applicable regime governing the release from prison (on licence) of prisoners serving mandatory life sentences. The relevant domestic legislation provided that such prisoners could only be released if (i) the Parole Board so recommended; and (ii) the Home Secretary, after consulting with the Lord Chief Justice, accepted the Board's recommendation.[56] Within that scheme, it was, then, the Home Secretary who had the ultimate say: he could not release a prisoner unless the Parole Board agreed, but he could, in effect, veto the Parole Board by rejecting its recommendation. This, said the claimant, was inconsistent with ECHR, Art 6, which provides that criminal trials must be conducted 'by an independent and impartial tribunal established by law'. The House of Lords accepted in *Anderson* that if the domestic legislation were given its normal meaning, it would ascribe to the Home Secretary a sentencing function (since he would be instrumental in determining how long people serving such sentences should actually spend behind bars) and that this would be incompatible with Art 6.

The question was then whether the domestic legislation could be construed differently, so as to be consistent with Art 6. It was held that it could not. Securing compliance with Art 6 would require the Home Secretary to be written out of the picture (for example, by reading in an obligation on his part to abide by any recommendation of the Parole Board or the Lord Chief Justice, thereby reducing his role to a purely formal one). This, said Lord Bingham, 'would not be judicial interpretation but judicial vandalism: it would give the section an effect quite different from that which Parliament intended and would go well beyond any interpretative process sanctioned by section 3 of the 1998 Act'.[57] *Anderson* is not inconsistent with the principles laid down in *Ghaidan*; rather, it can be understood as an application of them: the House of Lords in *Anderson* took the view that a fundamental feature of the Act was that a politician should have the last word on the release of mandatory life sentence prisoners. As Lord Steyn put it, the 'plain legislative intent [was] to entrust the decision to the Home Secretary, who was intended to be free to follow or reject judicial advice'.[58]

---

[55] *R (Anderson) v Secretary of State for the Home Department* [2002] UKHL 46, [2003] 1 AC 83.
[56] Crime (Sentences) Act 1997, s 29 (since repealed).
[57] *Anderson* at [30].   [58] *Anderson* at [59].

Second, *Anderson* points towards a further factor that may operate so as to limit what courts are prepared to do under s 3. This factor is concerned with *the proper limits upon the courts' policymaking role.* In some situations, courts may be presented with binary choices: either interpretation X is adopted (in which case, the legislation is incompatible with the ECHR), or interpretation Y is preferred (which secures compliance with the Convention). *Ghaidan* was a case such as this: either the Rent Act did or did not cover same-sex partners. However, in other circumstances, the position may be more complex. While it might be clear that some feature of the legislation needs to be removed or changed, there may be several ways in which that could be achieved. This was the position in *Anderson*. The problem was obvious: the Home Secretary should play no part in release decisions. But, if he were to be written out of the picture, what alternative arrangement was to be put in place? Should the Parole Board have the last word? Or the Lord Chief Justice? Or someone else? In circumstances such as these, the courts are acutely aware that they risk crossing the line between interpreting and legislating. This suggests that, when securing an ECHR-compatible interpretation that would involve making significant policy choices, the court is likely to conclude that consistent interpretation is not possible within the meaning of s 3. In practice, these circumstances are more likely to arise when the feature of the Act at stake is a fundamental one, since ridding the Act of such a feature is liable to leave a bigger or more complicated gap that needs to be filled. As a result, the two limiting factors that we have identified—contradiction of a fundamental feature and the making of significant policy choices—are likely in many situations to coexist.

Third, situations may arise in which *the practical consequences of adopting an ECHR-compliant interpretation of the relevant provision would be so far-reaching that it would be inappropriate for the court to adopt such an interpretation.* This point arises most clearly from *Re S (Minors) (Care Order: Implementation of Care Plan)*.[59] The Court of Appeal was concerned with the regime contained in the Children Act 1989 concerning care orders—that is, court orders vesting parental responsibility for children in local authorities. The Court concluded that the Act made insufficient provision for circumstances in which a local authority failed properly to discharge its duties to children subject to care orders, and that this might result in a breach of Art 8. Having arrived at this view (which, for presently irrelevant reasons, the House of Lords[60] did not share), the Court of Appeal, purporting to use its power under s 3 of the HRA, set about designing a system whereby matters could be referred back to the courts if key 'milestones' within care plans were not achieved. The House of Lords held that, in doing so, the Court of Appeal had overstepped the mark: the 'judicial innovation' that it had sought to introduce 'passe[d] well beyond the boundary of interpretation', said Lord Nicholls (whose judgment commanded the unanimous support of the other Law Lords).[61] There were two reasons for this. The first was a familiar one: that

---

[59] [2001] EWCA Civ 757, [2001] 2 FLR 582.
[60] [2002] UKHL 10, [2002] 2 AC 291.
[61] *Re S*, HL, at [43].

it contradicted a 'cardinal principle' of the Children Act,[62] which indicated with 'complete clarity' that responsibility for children subject to care orders vested in local authorities, not courts.[63] There was, however, a further reason: the system fashioned by the Court of Appeal 'would not come free from additional administrative work and expense', and would potentially compromise local authorities' capacity to discharge their responsibilities to other children.[64] Lord Nicholls said that whether local authorities should be subjected to the sort of supervisory regime contemplated by the Court of Appeal was for 'decision by Parliament, not the courts', not least because it would be 'impossible for a court to attempt to evaluate these ramifications or assess what would be the views of Parliament if changes are needed'.[65]

One final point needs to be addressed in this section. Notwithstanding what has just been said about factors that limit the courts' capacity to render ECHR-compliant interpretations, it appears that those factors can be trumped, or at least rendered less compelling—such that their presence may not preclude a Convention-compatible interpretation—in certain circumstances. The circumstances in question appear to arise when the executive branch—which, in some guise, is inevitably involved in proceedings in which courts are considering whether to render an ECHR-consistent interpretation under s 3 or to issue a declaration of incompatibility under s 4[66]— concedes that the court's s 3 power should be exercised.

Consider, for example, *AF v Secretary of State for the Home Department (No 3)*.[67] At stake was legislation that specified that, when courts were determining the legality of 'control orders' imposed upon suspected terrorists, sensitive evidence against such suspects should be considered in proceedings from which they and their legal representatives were to be excluded.[68] The House of Lords accepted that, if given its natural meaning, the application of this provision would often produce results at odds with the right to a fair trial under ECHR, Art 6. The question then became whether the legislative provision in question should (under s 4 of the HRA) be declared to be incompatible with Art 6 or (under s 3) rendered compatible via interpretation. The House of Lords plumped for the latter approach: the provision was interpreted so as to equip courts with a discretion to act contrary to the rule requiring sensitive evidence to be withheld from suspects 'where to do so would be incompatible with the right of the controlled person to a fair trial'.[69] Importantly, for present purposes, the Home Secretary had specifically said that if the procedural regime were regarded as

---

[62] *Re S*, HL, at [23], *per* Lord Nicholls.   [63] *Re S*, HL, at [25].

[64] *Re S*, HL, at [43], *per* Lord Nicholls.

[65] *Re S*, HL, at [44]. See also *Bellinger v Bellinger* [2003] UKHL 21, [2003] 2 AC 467.

[66] The Crown has a right to intervene whenever the courts are considering whether to issue a s 4 declaration: HRA 1998, s 5.   [67] [2009] UKHL 28, [2009] 3 WLR 74.

[68] 'Control orders' are imposed under the Prevention of Terrorism Act 2005. They allow restrictions— including curfews, regular searches of homes, and bans on association with particular people and presence in particular places—to be imposed upon suspected terrorists.

[69] This formulation was adopted by Baroness Hale in an earlier case (*Secretary of State for the Home Department v MB* [2007] UKHL 46, [2008] 1 AC 440, [72]) and endorsed by the House of Lords in *AF (No 3)*.

problematic in Art 6 terms, she would prefer the court to deal with the matter under its s 3 power rather than by issuing a declaration under s 4. Lord Scott appeared to regard this factor as decisively important. He indicated that, but for the Home Secretary's concession, he would have regarded the level of detail in which Parliament had spelled out the relevant procedure to have evidenced an intention too clear to accommodate the sort of interpretation eventually adopted in the case.[70] This approach is highly suspect. Whatever else might be unclear or controversial about s 3, it is surely elementary that the tactical position adopted by one party in litigation (whether or not that party is a Minister of the Crown) should not be capable of affecting the meaning of an Act of Parliament. The ascription to such legislation of a meaning that is compatible with the ECHR either is or is not 'possible' within the meaning of s 3 of the HRA—a state of affairs that is logically incapable of being affected by the views of the executive.

3.4.4 Section 3–constitutional considerations

Strong views have been expressed by commentators about how far courts should press their power under s 3, and about the principles that should inform the exercise of that power.[71] One reason why there has been a good deal of controversy about s 3 is that it provides very little guidance about how the power it confers should be exercised. The fact that courts are only required to interpret legislation compatibly with the ECHR '[s]o far as it is possible to do so' clearly suggests that there is a limit as to how far they should go—but the precise nature of that limit is unclear from the text of the HRA. In the absence of textual guidance, the true extent of s 3 inevitably falls to be determined by reference to broader constitutional considerations. This point is clearly acknowledged by Allan.[72] He argues that there are two rival conceptions of constitutional thought in the UK: these he calls the 'constitution of will' and the 'constitution of reason'. Which of those two views we prefer will influence our view of what courts should do—and hence of the proper extent of their authority under s 3 of the HRA.

Adherents to the former view perceive the constitutional landscape to be a somewhat barren place: denuded of any rich set of inherent norms, the constitution of will is dominated by the intention of Parliament. The courts' primary responsibility, then, is to find the interpretation of legislation that best gives effect to that intention. Those who subscribe to an unreconstructed theory of parliamentary sovereignty

---

[70] *AF (No 3)* at [95]. See also *R (Hammond) v Secretary of State for the Home Department* [2005] UKHL 69, [2006] 1 AC 603, [17], in which Lord Bingham adopted an approach similar to that of Lord Scott in *AF (No 3)*.

[71] See, among other contributions, Marshall, 'The Lynchpin of Parliamentary Intention: Lost, Stolen, or Startled?' [2003] PL 236; Nicol, 'Statutory Interpretation and Human Rights after *Anderson*' [2004] PL 274; Kavanagh, 'Statutory Interpretation and Human Rights after *Anderson*: A More Contextual Approach' [2004] PL 537; Young, '*Ghaidan v Godin-Mendoza*: Avoiding the Deference Trap' [2005] PL 23; Kavanagh, 'Parliamentary Intent, Statutory Interpretation and the Human Rights Act 1998' (2006) 26 OJLS 179; Allan, 'Parliament's Will and the Justice of the Common Law: The HRA in Constitutional Perspective' (2006) 59 CLP 27.

[72] Allan, 'Parliament's Will and the Justice of the Common Law: The HRA in Constitutional Perspective' (2006) 59 CLP 27.

are likely to sympathise with this position. On this view, the requirement imposed under s 3 of the HRA is one that is alien to the pre-existing constitutional culture, and a relatively narrow view of s 3 is therefore likely to commend itself to adherents of the constitution of will. Marshall, for example, argues that a wide conception of the s 3 duty should be resisted, because it would be 'potentially damaging both to the authority of Parliament and the separation of the judicial and legislative functions'.[73]

Allan, in contrast, is an adherent of the constitution of reason, the first principle of which is that people should be 'treated by government in accordance with the standards of justice or fairness widely recognized as fundamental to political morality, without arbitrary exception or unjustified discrimination'.[74] On this view, the constitutional landscape is not a barren one dominated by parliamentary intention; rather, it is one that, independently of the HRA, is sympathetic to the norms underpinning many human rights—a view that is supported by the doctrine of common law constitutional rights that emerged before the HRA was contemplated.[75] As such, says Allan, the HRA was 'planted in fertile ground'.[76] Those who adhere to this view tend to be more comfortable with a wide reading of s 3, because such a reading is wholly consistent with what is regarded as the courts' proper role. This follows because, in the constitution of reason, the courts' primary responsibility is to protect fundamental constitutional values, including human rights: the will of Parliament, within this framework, is not an unimportant or irrelevant factor, but it is not necessarily the decisive one. For Allan, the notion that legislation may have some meaning independent of the context, including the constitutional context, in which it falls to be interpreted is therefore an ultimately empty one: meaning can only be ascribed to legislation through the process of judicial construction because it 'awaits integration into the tapestry of which it can only form a single thread'.[77] An illustration of how Allan's preferred approach translates into practice is furnished by his view that the House of Lords should have gone further than it did in *Anderson*: an 'appropriately robust' approach to the interpretation of the relevant legislation 'would have secured the essential requirements of the separation of powers' (and hence the claimant's right to be sentenced by an independent tribunal rather than a politician).[78]

3.4.5 Section 4—declarations of incompatibility

As foreshadowed above, rendering an ECHR-compatible interpretation is not the only tool at the courts' disposal when faced with legislation that, on its face, appears inconsistent with one or more of the Convention rights. Their other option is to issue a declaration of incompatibility under s 4. In this regard, six points should be noted.

First, *s 4 confers a discretionary power upon courts that only arises in certain circumstances*. The power is only exercisable if the court 'is satisfied that the provision is

---

[73] Marshall, 'The Lynchpin of Parliamentary Intention: Lost, Stolen, or Startled?' [2003] PL 236, 248.
[74] Allan at 31.   [75] See section 3.2 above.   [76] Allan at 31.   [77] Allan at 45.
[78] Allan at 49.

incompatible with a Convention right'.[79] This reflects the fact that, analytically speaking, the courts' powers under ss 3 and 4 arise in mutually exclusive circumstances. Either a provision in an Act of Parliament is (whether or not as the result of being interpreted pursuant to s 3) compatible with the Convention right in question (in which case, there can be no question of issuing a s 4 declaration), or the provision cannot, even by exercising the s 3 power, be rendered compatible with the ECHR (in which case, the possibility of a s 4 declaration arises). However, the fact that the s 4 power is exercisable does not mean that it has to be exercised. Whereas s 3 imposes a duty on the court, s 4 confers upon it a discretion. In practice, however, it would be exceptionally unusual for a court to decline to exercise its power under s 4.

Second, *only certain courts may issue a declaration under s 4*. These include the High Court and the Court of Appeal (in England and Wales, and in Northern Ireland), the High Court of Justiciary[80] and the Court of Session (in Scotland), the Supreme Court and the Judicial Committee of the Privy Council.[81] Courts such as magistrates courts' and county courts cannot issue declarations of incompatibility. The same is true of tribunals, including the Upper Tribunal—which is perhaps surprising, given that, as explained above, it possesses powers of judicial review. The Senior President of Tribunals has proposed that the Upper Tribunal be given the ability to issue declarations of incompatibility.[82]

Third, subject to one limited exception,[83] *a declaration of incompatibility has no legal effect*: under the HRA, such a declaration 'does not affect the validity, continuing operation or enforcement of the provision in respect of which it is given'.[84] This means that if the court issues a declaration of incompatibility, the legal position between the parties to the case is unaffected: the legal provision that is the subject of the declaration remains a fully operative part of the law, and the court must therefore go on to apply it, notwithstanding that this will involve a breach of one party's Convention rights. It would be unsurprising if this were to lead courts to prefer to resolve cases by means of s 3 whenever possible, by adopting a wide view of their power under that section. The use of the s 3 power means that the court is able to decide the case in a manner that is consistent with the relevant party's Convention rights (because, as a result of interpreting the provision concerned pursuant to s 3, it turns out that the applicable law is consistent with those rights). In contrast, the use of the s 4 power means that the relevant party loses the case (or at least loses the human rights point). If, for example, the House of Lords were to have relied on s 4 rather than s 3 in *Ghaidan*,[85] the defendant would not have counted as a statutory tenant and would thus have left court vulnerable to eviction. This may lead the courts, consciously or otherwise, to prefer to use

---

[79] HRA, s 4(2). This provision applies in respect of primary legislation. The position concerning subordinate legislation is considered later in this section.   [80] Except when sitting as a trial court.

[81] HRA, s 4(5).

[82] Senior President of Tribunals, *Third Implementation Review* (London 2009), annex B. On the Upper Tribunal, see further Chapter 17, section 3.4, above.

[83] The exception is explained in our fifth point below.   [84] HRA, s 4(6)(a).

[85] [2004] UKHL 30, [2004] 2 AC 557.

s 3 whenever possible. Indeed, Lord Steyn admitted as much in *Ghaidan*: the HRA's purpose of 'bringing rights home', he said, 'could only be effectively [achieved] if section 3(1) was the prime remedial measure, and section 4 a measure of last resort'.[86]

> **Q** Is it legitimate for courts to take into account the respective practical consequences of deciding a case under s 3 or s 4? Should, for example, courts be prepared to adopt a particularly strained interpretation under s 3, in order to be able to decide the case consistently with the relevant party's Convention rights, if (as in *Ghaidan*) applying ECHR-inconsistent law (albeit while declaring the incompatibility) would leave the party vulnerable to harsh treatment?

Fourth, *when a court issues a declaration of incompatibility, neither Parliament nor the executive is legally obliged to do anything in response.* Of course, legislation can be enacted to amend or replace the provisions found to be incompatible, but nothing in the HRA compels the taking of such action. This is a straightforward function of the fact that the HRA does not—and was not intended to—affect the orthodox doctrine of parliamentary sovereignty. But to conclude from this that the political branches are free to ignore declarations of incompatibility would be a mistake. We develop this point below.[87]

Fifth, if action is to be taken to amend or repeal provisions found to be incompatible with Convention rights, this can be done in one of two ways: either by passing an Act of Parliament or by issuing *a remedial order under s 10 of the HRA.* When a declaration is issued under s 4,[88] s 10 permits (but does not require) the government to enact secondary legislation amending (among other things) the Act of Parliament that was found to be incompatible. Section 10 thus confers a so-called 'Henry VIII' power[89] on the executive, enabling it, by means of secondary legislation, to amend ECHR-incompatible primary legislation. In practice, remedial orders are rarely used: most legislative provisions that have been the subject of declarations of incompatibility have been amended, replaced, or repealed via the enactment of fresh primary legislation.[90]

Sixth, it is clear from what has been said so far that *a judicial power to strike down or refuse to apply ECHR-incompatible primary legislation forms no part of the HRA scheme.* But this begs an important question. As we saw in Chapter 5, the normal principle is that when two Acts of Parliament conflict with one another, the more recent Act prevails over the earlier one, repealing it to the extent of the inconsistency. This, as we saw, is known as the doctrine of implied repeal. What happens, then, if legislation enacted prior to the HRA's enactment turns out to be incompatible with one of the

---

[86] *Ghaidan* at [46].   [87] See section 3.4.7 below.

[88] Or if the ECtHR has found UK law to be incompatible with the ECHR.

[89] See further Chapter 4, section 4.2.2, above.

[90] Ministry of Justice, *Responding to Human Rights Judgments: Government Response to the Joint Committee on Human Rights' Thirty-first Report of Session 2007–08* (Cm 7524 2009), p 41.

Convention rights? Is the pre-HRA provision impliedly repealed, meaning that it is simply invalid? If this were the case, then, in such circumstances, there would logically be no role for declarations of incompatibility: the pre-HRA provision would be invalid and unenforceable, and there would be no extant provision on which a declaration could meaningfully bite.

In fact, pre-HRA provisions that are incompatible with Convention rights are not impliedly repealed by the HRA—not because the HRA is immune from the effect of the doctrine, but because it is simply not relevant in the first place. The reason is as follows. The doctrine of implied repeal only operates when there is a conflict between the substance of two pieces of legislation. If, for example, an Act passed in 2011 were to say that 'everyone has the right to free speech', this would impliedly repeal a provision contained in a 2010 Act that restricted the right to free speech to an extent impermissible under the 2011 Act. Crucially, however, the HRA does not straightforwardly say that anyone has any rights; rather, it merely requires certain bodies to do certain things in relation to ECHR rights in certain circumstances. There is therefore no conflict, for the purposes of the doctrine of implied repeal, between the HRA and an earlier (or, for that matter, a later) provision that is incompatible with a Convention right. This is because the HRA does not make the Convention rights a substantive part of UK law; it merely requires (among other things) the courts to interpret legislation compatibly with them when this is possible. When it is not possible, the inconsistent legislation remains valid, because there is no substantive inconsistency between it and the HRA.[91]

3.4.6 Primary and subordinate legislation

Our focus so far has been on primary legislation. We now need to examine what is meant in the HRA by 'primary legislation' and how the principles set out above apply in relation to subordinate legislation.

The term 'primary legislation' is defined in s 21(1) of the HRA. Unsurprisingly, it includes Acts of Parliament. In contrast, legislation enacted under the authority of an Act of Parliament is subordinate legislation. For the time being, we focus on these senses of primary and subordinate legislation, although others are considered below. Within the HRA scheme, there is a crucial difference between 'primary' and 'subordinate' legislation. We saw above that, in respect of the former, courts have two options at their disposal: either the legislation is interpreted compatibly with Convention rights, or it can be declared incompatible. In relation to subordinate legislation, there are three possibilities (albeit that the courts cannot freely choose between them). These differences are apparent from Figures 19.3 and 19.4.

First, *subordinate legislation must be interpreted consistently with the Convention rights so far as this is possible.*[92] This is precisely the same interpretative obligation as

---

91 This also explains why the HRA is not itself impliedly repealed by subsequent legislation that is incompatible with Convention rights.   92 HRA, s 3(1).

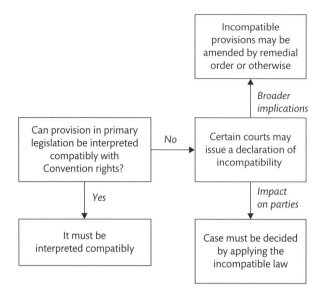

Figure 19.3 Sections 3 and 4—primary legislation

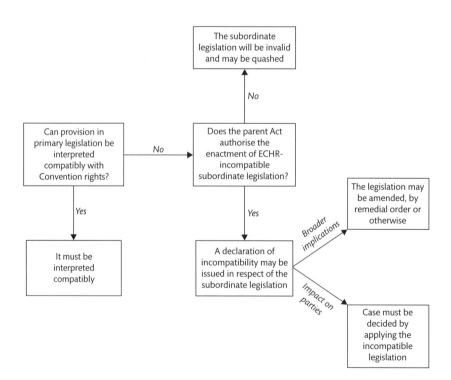

Figure 19.4 Sections 3 and 4—subordinate legislation

that under which the courts find themselves when they interpret primary legislation. Given the strength of that obligation, most cases concerning subordinate legislation, like most cases involving primary legislation, will be resolved at this stage.

If—and only if—subordinate legislation cannot be interpreted compatibly does the court turn to the second possibility—that is, *quashing it.* Whether this can actually be done turns on the proper interpretation of the legislation ('the parent Act') that purportedly authorised the subordinate legislation in question. Since the parent Act must itself be interpreted, so far as is possible, compatibly with the Convention rights, in most situations, it will turn out that the parent Act does not confer on the subordinate legislator any authority to enact subordinate legislation that is inconsistent with the Convention rights. It follows that subordinate legislation that cannot be read compatibly with those rights will normally be liable to be quashed.

The third possibility is that the *subordinate legislation may be neither compatible with the Convention rights nor* ultra vires *the parent Act.* This situation will only arise if the parent Act cannot, even following the application of s 3, be read as denying to the subordinate legislator the power to enact ECHR-incompatible provisions. In this scenario, a declaration of incompatibility may be made in respect of the incompatible subordinate legislation. This, in turn, would trigger the s 10 power to issue a remedial order in respect of the subordinate legislation (and, if necessary, the parent Act).

Three further points should be noted regarding the distinction between primary and subordinate legislation.

First, the HRA adopts, in one particularly significant respect, an unusually broad definition of primary legislation: s 21(1) states that, for the purposes of the HRA, *Orders in Council enacted under the royal prerogative are to be treated as primary, not subordinate, legislation.*[93] The practical effect of this is that such prerogative legislation cannot be quashed if found incompatible with Convention rights, albeit that, like an Act of Parliament, it can be the subject of a declaration of incompatibility under s 4. Categorising prerogative Orders in Council as primary legislation for HRA purposes is anomalous.[94] For present purposes, it is not necessary to get bogged down in the semantics of 'primary' and 'subordinate' legislation;[95] it is sufficient to point out that the general constitutional position of prerogative Orders in Council is inconsistent with that which they occupy in relation to the HRA. Orders in Council are not the constitutional equals of Acts of Parliament: the former, unlike the latter, can be quashed if they are unlawful. The normal principles of judicial review therefore apply: if, for example, a prerogative Order in Council is unreasonable, or made for an improper purpose, or adopted in breach of a legitimate expectation, it can be set aside by the courts. Any doubt that may have existed on this point was put to rest by the House of

---

[93] See further Chapter 4, section 4.3, above.

[94] Pontin and Billings, 'Prerogative Powers and the Human Rights Act: Elevating the Status of Orders in Council' [2001] PL 21.

[95] See generally McHarg, 'What is Delegated Legislation?' [2006] PL 539.

Lords in *Bancoult (No 2)*.[96] This position is entirely correct in principle. In constitutional theory, prerogative Orders in Council are acts of the Crown alone (meaning the executive), not of the Crown-in-Parliament, and are thus not cloaked by the doctrine of parliamentary sovereignty. And in constitutional practice, the prerogative is merely a tool in the hands of the executive. There is therefore no good reason why it should be immune from judicial review—and every reason why it should be. Against this background, it is highly anomalous that while the courts can quash prerogative Orders in Council if they fall foul of the normal principles of judicial review, they cannot do so if they contravene the Convention rights.

> **Q** Imagine that a prerogative Order in Council is enacted and that it is incompatible with a Convention right that covers the same ground as a common law constitutional right. It is clear that the Order in Council could not be quashed on the basis of its incompatibility with the Convention right—but could it be quashed on the ground of its incompatibility with the common law constitutional right?

Second, the enactment of subordinate legislation is simply a form of *administrative action*. There are, of course, other forms of such action: the formulation of policy, the making of decisions, and so on. These non-legislative forms of administrative action are, as we saw in Chapter 13, subject to judicial review, including on the ground that they are inconsistent with Convention rights. No question of a declaration of incompatibility arises in relation to such administrative action. Any administrative action that is inconsistent with Convention rights can be quashed unless the parent Act unequivocally authorises such action.

Third, *all legislation enacted by the devolved legislatures constitutes, for HRA purposes, subordinate legislation*.[97] This is important from the standpoint of one of our key themes—namely, the multilayered nature of governance in the UK. In particular, it means that the status of human rights differs significantly in relation to the devolved legislatures, on the one hand, and the UK Parliament, on the other hand. We have seen that the enactments of the latter cannot be quashed or otherwise set aside by the courts on the ground of incompatibility with Convention rights. The same is not, however, true of devolved legislation: such legislation is subject to full constitutional review in the sense that it may be quashed if found to be inconsistent with one or more of the Convention rights. In this sense, the ECHR, via the HRA and the devolution legislation, fulfils the role of a full constitutional Bill of Rights vis-à-vis the devolved legislatures: it constitutes an absolute brake on their power. On the face of it, this suggests that the HRA is a much more serious impediment to the exercise of legislative power by devolved legislatures than it is to the exercise of power by the UK Parliament. However, the reality, as we explain in the next section, is more complicated.

---

[96] *R (Bancoult) v Secretary of State for Foreign and Commonwealth Affairs (No 2)* [2008] UKHL 61, [2009] 1 AC 453.   [97] HRA, s 21(1).

3.4.7 **Legal and political constitutionalism**

We have already observed that a declaration of incompatibility under s 4 of the HRA does not impose any domestic legal obligation upon Parliament or the executive to amend a statute found by the court to be incompatible with Convention rights. On a purely legal analysis, then, the political branches retain a free hand.[98] This may seem to undercut our suggestion, made at the beginning of the chapter, that the HRA has been a principal driver of the shift from political to legal constitutionalism—but, for the reasons set out in this section, it does not.

Administrative bodies—a term that we use here to refer to all bodies incapable of enacting primary legislation—are now, to a very large extent, in practice locked into a legal requirement to comply with human rights. This follows both because they are, as we explain below,[99] generally obliged by s 6 of the HRA to act in conformity with the Convention rights, and because they are, by dint of s 3, in any event generally required to do so when exercising statutory powers. Of course, it is always open to administrative bodies—and in particular the UK executive, given its close relationship with (indeed, dominance of) the UK Parliament—to seek the enactment of legislation granting them powers to act contrary to Convention rights. Equally, an administrative body, were it to have an action struck down on Convention grounds, could seek the enactment of legislation reversing the effect of such a judicial decision. But none of these things is likely—and even if they were to happen, they would, given the intense demands on parliamentary time, be exceptional. Generally speaking, therefore, administrative bodies have no choice (if they wish to act lawfully) but to act compatibly with Convention rights.

The position is different in relation to those bodies, most obviously the UK Parliament, capable of enacting primary legislation.[100] Parliament is *legally* free to do as it pleases[101]—but this does not mean that it is *actually* free to do so. For several reasons, the HRA contributes to the existence of a *political* environment that is hostile to Parliament's using its unlimited *legal* powers in a way that undercuts the Convention rights. The net result of this is that while ongoing protection of human rights is ultimately contingent upon Parliament's political acquiescence—it could restrict or get rid of them if it were really to want to do so—such acquiescence is rendered more likely by the HRA. The legal constitution, in the form of the HRA, thus operates so as to limit the practical freedom of the political branches. What, then, are the features of the HRA that produce this effect?

---

98 Although the position is complicated by the UK's *international* legal obligations under the ECHR. This is considered below.   99 See section 3.5 below.

100 We saw above that the executive, by means of prerogative Orders in Council, is also able to enact primary legislation. However, such legislation may only be enacted within limited subject areas, and the executive's capacity to pass such legislation is not therefore a major exception to the general position set out in the previous paragraph.

101 This assumes that it is sovereign in the orthodox sense—although, as we saw in Chapter 5, the orthodox conception of sovereignty is increasingly questioned.

First, *the Act makes the enactment of ECHR-inconsistent legislation less likely in the first place.* As we saw above,[102] the effect of s 19 (along with the vital role played by the JCHR) is that ECHR-incompatible legislation is unlikely to be enacted either accidentally or covertly. Parliament's—and, by extension, the media's and the public's—attention will be drawn to provisions in Bills liable to be at odds with Convention rights. Of course, this does not make the enactment of such provisions legally impossible—but it is likely to make it politically more difficult. A government promoting such provisions will be required by its opponents, inside and beyond Parliament, to make a very clear case for enacting legislation that fails to respect the Convention rights. This point is buttressed by s 3 of the HRA. The net effect of that section is that a government intent on securing legislation that will produce effects contrary to Convention rights must persuade Parliament to make its intention to do so very clear. If it does not, there is a high degree of likelihood that the courts will, in discharge of their s 3 obligation, simply interpret the provision in a way that makes it compatible with Convention rights. The need clearly to spell out a desire to undercut such rights means that the enactment of such legislation cannot be achieved by sleight of hand.

Second, although, as we have seen, a declaration of incompatibility does not legally oblige anybody to do anything, such *a declaration is likely to be highly politically significant.* When the Human Rights Bill (as it then was) was being debated in Parliament, Lord Borrie said that the intention was 'surely…that government and Parliament will faithfully implement any declaratory judgment made by the [courts]'.[103] This view was endorsed by Lord Irvine, who said that the courts' powers should not be underestimated: a declaration of incompatibility, he said, 'will very probably to lead to the amendment of defective legislation', and that, in 'this *practical* sense, the Human Rights Act does introduce a *limited* form of constitutional review'.[104] Borrie and Irvine's expectations have been borne out in the decade or so since they were expressed. In a report published in July 2010, the government said that, of the 18 declarations of incompatibility made since the HRA entered into force,[105] steps had been taken to resolve the incompatibilities in 15 cases, while the government was considering how to respond in the remaining three cases.[106]

The figures tell an important part of the story concerning compliance, but it is equally noteworthy that the government has felt politically constrained to comply with declarations of incompatibility even in contexts in which it might have been tempted—and in which it might even have been politically expedient for it—to do

---

[102] See section 3.3.2 above.   [103] HL Deb, 3 November 1997, cols 1275–6.

[104] 'Sovereignty in Comparative Perspective: Constitutionalism in Britain and America' (2001) 76 NYULR 1, 19 (original emphasis).

[105] This figure excludes declarations that were made, but later set aside on appeal.

[106] Ministry of Justice, *Responding to Human Rights Judgments: Government Response to the Joint Committee on Human Rights' Fifteenth Report of Session 2009–10* (Cm 7892 2010). There has, however, been criticism of the length of time it sometimes takes for incompatibilities to be removed: JCHR, *Enhancing Parliament's Role in Relation to Human Rights Judgments* (HL 85 HC 455 2009–10).

otherwise. Consider, for example, the aftermath of the *Belmarsh* case concerning the extrajudicial detention of foreign terrorist suspects.[107] As we saw in Chapter 1, the House of Lords in *Belmarsh* held that the relevant provisions of the Anti-terrorism, Crime and Security Act 2001 were incompatible with ECHR, Art 5.[108] These provisions, it will be recalled, had been enacted in a climate of considerable fear in the immediate aftermath of the 9/11 attacks in the USA, and had in practice operated to the (admittedly very considerable) disadvantage of only a very small group of suspects. A substantial section of public opinion would undoubtedly have supported the government if it were to have decided to ignore the *Belmarsh* judgment and press on with the detention of the people concerned. And yet it did not. The then Home Secretary said that he 'accept[ed] the Law Lords' declaration of incompatibility',[109] and later stated that legislation introduced to replace the scheme condemned in *Belmarsh* was 'designed to meet the Law Lords' criticism that the previous legislation was both disproportionate and discriminatory'.[110] What this episode suggests is that, notwithstanding the absence of a strike-down power, the HRA is, to some extent, capable of curbing the worst excesses of majoritarianism even where the rights of an acutely unpopular and very small minority, such as suspected terrorists, are at stake.[111]

Third, while not compelling the taking of corrective action as a matter of domestic law, *declarations of incompatibility are not without relevance in terms of international law.* The ECHR—a treaty that is binding upon state parties as a matter of international law—requires the UK to 'secure to everyone within their jurisdiction' the Convention rights[112] and to abide by the judgments of the ECtHR.[113] It follows that a declaration of incompatibility by a UK court is strongly suggestive that the UK is in breach of its Art 1 obligation to secure the Convention rights. Of course, the government may take the view that the UK courts have got it wrong. But, if that were to happen, it is highly likely that the matter would be litigated in the ECtHR. In such circumstances, an applicant armed with a declaration of incompatibility would be in a very strong position to obtain a favourable judgment.[114] And such a judgment, unlike a declaration of incompatibility, would be *legally* binding.

---

[107] *A v Secretary of State for the Home Department* [2004] UKHL 56, [2005] 2 AC 68.

[108] This incompatibility was relatively obvious. The real issue in *Belmarsh* was whether the government had lawfully suspended the operation of Art 5—which, the House of Lords held, it had not.

[109] Charles Clarke, HC Deb, 26 January 2005, col 306.   [110] HC Deb, 22 February 2005, col 151.

[111] Nicol, 'Law and Politics after the Human Rights Act' [2006] PL 722, 741, argues that the 'control orders' system (on which, see section 3.4.3 above) that has replaced the detention regime condemned in *Belmarsh* involves a 'drastic, indeed unprecedented, curtailment of liberty, replacing the threat of *Belmarsh* incarceration for a minority with the threat of house arrest for everybody'. This may be so. However, the important point, for the purposes of the present discussion concerning the practical effects of declarations of incompatibility, is that the government felt (politically) compelled to introduce this change in an attempt to comply with the *Belmarsh* judgment.   [112] ECHR, Art 1.

[113] ECHR, Art 46.

[114] For example, in *A v UK* (2009) 49 EHRR 29, [182], the ECtHR, when addressing a point that the House of Lords had already considered, said that it would 'in principle follow the judgment of the House of Lords on the question of the proportionality of the applicants' detention, unless it can be shown that the national court misinterpreted the Convention or the Court's case-law or reached a conclusion which was manifestly

Taken in combination, the factors discussed in this section indicate that the Convention rights operate as real constraints upon the UK Parliament, notwithstanding that they do not technically constitute legal constraints in terms of domestic law. Two points may be made in conclusion.

First, for as long as the HRA (or something like it) is in force, it would be misguided to assume that Parliament, because it is sovereign, is free in political terms to legislate contrary to human rights. This does not represent any great insight: it has always been mistaken to assume that, just because it has legally unlimited powers, Parliament has the practical or political capacity to do whatever it wants.[115] The HRA, however, throws a particular set of constraints—the Convention rights—into sharp relief, and, as noted above, creates a political environment that makes it difficult for Parliament to remove or curtail them. In this way, while the security of human rights remains ultimately contingent upon the political constitution, the legal constitution, in the form of the HRA, now exerts an important influence upon its political counterpart. If a statute is declared incompatible with Convention rights by a court, then considerable political pressure will be placed upon the government to remedy that incompatibility. It is not inconceivable that a government might decide not to remedy such an incompatibility, but there would be a political price to pay and few politicians would wish to defend a law that had been declared incompatible with human rights by a court. The fact that the government did not take this course of action in response to the *Belmarsh* case, which concerned one of the most important and sensitive tasks of government—the protection of national security—illustrates just how seriously politicians take declarations of incompatibility.

Second, just as it would be wrong to underestimate the significance of the HRA, it would be mistaken to overestimate it. It is not a legally entrenched Bill of Rights; as an Act of Parliament, it can, like any other Act, be repealed. The factors considered above that encourage compliance with the HRA also suggest that more substantial interference, by way of amendment to or repeal of the HRA itself, would be far from straightforward in political terms. But just as repeal of the HRA is not legally impossible, so it is not politically impossible. Indeed, the HRA has had a very poor reception in some quarters, and there is a substantial strand of political opinion that holds that the courts should be stripped of the powers that they were given by the HRA in order that (as the argument runs) the interests of undeserving minorities should not be allowed to trump those of the wider public. We consider this issue below.[116] For the time being, we simply emphasise that, not being contained within an

unreasonable'. The amount of weight that the ECtHR is willing to attach to domestic courts' judgments may vary according to the circumstances, but this case demonstrates that the government is likely to face at least an uphill struggle if it chooses to take on an applicant who has already obtained a declaration of incompatibility in the domestic courts.

[115] For example, Dicey, *An Introduction to the Study of the Law of the Constitution* (London 1959), pp 70–85, recognised that *legal* sovereignty is, in fact, restricted by *practical* and *political* factors.

[116] See section 4.

entrenched constitution, neither the HRA nor the set of rights to which it gives effect are invulnerable to the chill winds of politics; it should not be assumed that either is sacrosanct.

> **Q** Does the HRA secure (or reflect) an appropriate balance between legal and political forms of constitutionalism? Would you prefer that a requirement to respect human rights be hard-wired into the constitution such that it could not be circumvented without going through a hard-to-comply-with procedure for amending the constitution itself?

3.4.8 Legislative discretion

We end our discussion of the implications of ss 3 and 4 of the HRA with the question of legislative discretion. In the light of the courts' powers under those provisions, what is the extent, if any, of the discretion enjoyed by the legislature on matters that touch upon human rights? At one level, there is a very simple answer to this question: legislatures capable of making primary legislation have complete discretion, because they are free, as a matter of domestic law, to enact provisions that are incompatible with Convention rights and to ignore any declarations of incompatibility made in respect of such provisions. On a deeper level, however, this answer is inadequate for two reasons: first, it does not address the position of administrative bodies and others that are unable to cloak their decisions and policies with the force of primary legislation; second—and more generally, given what was said in the previous section—it is pertinent to ask how much discretion primary legislators have if they wish to avoid judicial intervention (whether by means of a strained s 3 interpretation that may frustrate legislative intention, or a s 4 declaration of incompatibility).

In order to be clear about the question that is being asked, let us return to the facts of *Ghaidan*[117]—and let us assume, for the purposes of argument, that, in enacting the relevant provisions in the Rent Act 1977, Parliament had intended not to advantage surviving same-sex partners. To what extent, if any, does the HRA attribute to Parliament any latitude to make policy choices of this nature? We have already seen that courts defer, in appropriate circumstances, to decision-makers' views when judicially reviewing administrative measures on human rights grounds.[118] By analogy, there is scope for deference to the views of Parliament when courts are exercising their powers under ss 3 and 4, in recognition either of Parliament's democratic credentials or, where relevant, its relative institutional competence.

It is, however, important to be clear about the matters upon which deference can, and cannot, properly bite. Deference may be appropriate, in precisely the same way as in relation to administrative measures, when the court is determining whether, in the first place, the legislative provision in question (if it were given its natural meaning) would infringe a Convention right. If, for example, the question is whether a legislative

---

[117] [2004] UKHL 30, [2004] 2 AC 557.
[118] See Chapter 13, section 4.6.4, above.

restriction on a qualified right is necessary, the court might attach particular weight to Parliament's view (implicit in the statute) that the measure is necessary if, in the circumstances, Parliament is better equipped than the court to make such a judgement. Equally, if the question is whether a necessary restriction upon a qualified right is strictly proportionate, in the sense of being justified by the scale of the public-policy gains that it is liable to yield, the court may, in recognition of Parliament's democratic mandate, ascribe weight to Parliament's view as to the relative value to be attached to those factors.

However, Young points out that if the principles of deference operate in the normal way at this stage of the analysis, they must not, generally speaking, be permitted to operate subsequently. If, for example, having duly deferred to Parliament at the initial stage, the court concludes that the legislation, given its natural meaning, improperly restricts a Convention right, the question then becomes whether the legislation should be ascribed a different meaning (so as to render it compatible). Young argues that deference at this stage is generally inappropriate:

> To find a Convention-compatible interpretation impossible for the same reasons that have already been taken into account when ascertaining the scope of the Convention right runs the risk that courts will fail to fulfil their constitutional duty to protect Convention rights.[119]

However, Young goes on to point out that, as we have already observed,[120] *other* factors may deter the court from holding that an ECHR-compliant interpretation is possible. Most obviously, if the court would, in rendering such an interpretation, be forced to make a policy choice between various possible alternatives, it may well conclude that the constitutionally proper course is for it to refer the matter to the political branches by means of a s 4 declaration.

3.5 The scope of the Human Rights Act

3.5.1 Introduction

Our discussion so far has focused on the impact of the HRA on the interpretation of legislation. That discussion centred upon ss 3 and 4; two of the key provisions in the Act. We now turn our attention to a third such provision: s 6. Section 6(1) says: 'It is unlawful for a public authority to act in a way which is incompatible with a Convention right.'[121] On the face of it, this provision determines the range of circumstances in which the HRA is relevant: a distinction is drawn between bodies that constitute public authorities and those that do not; only the former are explicitly required by

---

[119] Young, '*Ghaidan v Godin-Mendoza*: Avoiding the Deference Trap' [2005] PL 23, 31.

[120] See section 3.4.3 above.

[121] Section 6(2) states that this duty does not apply if primary legislation means that the public authority could not have acted differently, or if the public authority was acting to give effect to provisions of, or made under, primary legislation that cannot be read compatibly with the Convention rights.

s 6(1) to abide by the Convention rights. Although, as we explain later in this section, the position is rather more subtle than this, s 6 is nevertheless of central importance to the reach of the Convention rights. This is evident from s 7, which is concerned with the making of legal claims under the HRA: proceedings under s 7 can be launched only by someone 'who claims that a public authority has acted (or proposes to act) in a way which is made unlawful by section 6(1)'.[122]

3.5.2 Functions of a public nature

The meaning of 'public authority', then, is key. That term is defined by s 6(3) and (5). As the House of Lords held in *Aston Cantlow*, the effect of those provisions is to establish two categories of public authority.[123] First, there are *core public authorities*—authorities that are bound by the Convention rights in all that they do. Then, there are what are often called *hybrid public authorities*. Two points should be noted here. First, any body 'certain of whose functions are functions of a public nature' will count as a hybrid public authority.[124] Second, however, such authorities will be bound by the HRA only when committing acts that are not 'private' acts.[125] The difference, then, is that core public authorities always have to respect Convention rights; everyone else has to do so only when performing public functions.

Although there is no definitive test, factors to be taken into account in determining whether something constitutes a core public authority include 'the possession of special powers, democratic accountability, public funding in whole or in part, an obligation to act only in the public interest, and a statutory constitution'.[126] In practice, the courts have had little difficulty in applying these tests, and have done so in a way that makes the category of core public authorities a decidedly narrow one limited to such bodies as government departments, local authorities, the police, and the armed forces.[127] If a given body is held not to constitute a core public authority, the issue then is whether the specific function in question is a public one, meaning that it is nevertheless, on the occasion in question, caught by the HRA. Here, the courts have encountered considerable difficulties, struggling to draw the line between public and private functions in a coherent way.

The leading case on what counts as a function of a public nature is *Aston Cantlow*. It concerned a dispute between a parochial church council[128] and the owners of a farm. The farm in question constituted 'rectorial property', which meant that the owners were liable to pay for all necessary repairs to the chancel of the church. It was argued

---

[122] HRA 1998, s 7(1).

[123] *Aston Cantlow and Wilmcote with Billesley Parochial Church Council v Wallbank* [2003] UKHL 37, [2004] 1 AC 546.   [124] HRA 1998, s 6(3)(b).

[125] HRA 1998, s 6(5).   [126] *Aston Cantlow* at [7], *per* Lord Nicholls.

[127] *Aston Cantlow* at [7], *per* Lord Nicholls.

[128] The role of a parochial church council is (according to Lord Nicholls, *Aston Cantlow* at [14]) 'to provide a formal means...whereby...members of the local church promote the mission of the Church and discharge financial responsibilities in respect of their own parish church, including responsibilities regarding maintenance of the fabric of the building'.

that if the church council were to enforce this liability, it would be acting inconsistently with the farm owners' property rights under the ECHR. However, this argument could only succeed if, in the first place, the church council were a public authority for the purposes of s 6 of the HRA. The House of Lords had no difficulty in holding that it was not a core public authority—but was it, when enforcing the liability in question, exercising a function of a public nature? In addressing this question, said Lord Nicholls, it was necessary to consider such factors as 'the extent to which in carrying out the relevant function the body is publicly funded, or is exercising statutory powers, or is taking the place of central government or local authorities, or is providing a public service'.[129] Against that background, it is unsurprising that the specific function in issue—namely, the enforcing of chancel repair liability—was not regarded as a public function. As Lord Hope put it: 'The nature of the act is to be found in the nature of the obligation which the [parochial church council] is seeking to enforce. It is seeking to enforce a civil debt. The function which it is performing has nothing to do with the responsibilities which are owed to the public by the State.'[130]

However, not all cases can be resolved as straightforwardly as this. Particularly difficult questions arise when the performance of a function is contracted out—a practice that, as we explained in Chapter 4, is now commonplace.[131] The way in which s 6 works means that something done in-house by a core public authority (which would therefore have to be done in a way that is compatible with Convention rights) might not count as a public function when performed by a body other than a core public authority. Craig argues that '[i]t is difficult to see why the nature of a function should alter if it is contracted out, rather than being performed in house [that is, by a core public authority]. If it is a public function when undertaken in house, it should equally be so when contracted out'.[132] Yet not all functions performed by core public authorities are necessarily public functions: everything that a core public authority does has to be done compatibly with Convention rights not because all of those things are public functions, but because they are all done by a core public authority. From this, it follows that when a core public authority contracts out a function, the contractor performing that function will not necessarily be bound by the HRA; rather, it will all depend on the answer to the question whether the function is a public one.[133] In some situations, the answer will be obvious. If a local authority (a core public authority) contracts out the cleaning of its offices to a company, the HRA will not apply: cleaning offices—even those of a core public authority—is not itself a public function. Equally obviously, if the Prison Service contracts out the running of a prison to a company, many of the functions performed by the latter will be public in nature, bearing in mind that it will, through its employees, be exercising coercive powers of the state.[134]

---

129 *Aston Cantlow* at [12].
130 *Aston Cantlow* at [64].   131 See Chapter 4, section 4.5, above.
132 'Contracting Out, the Human Rights Act and the Scope of Judicial Review' (2002) 118 LQR 551, 556.
133 See further Oliver, 'Functions of a Public Nature under the Human Rights Act' [2004] PL 329.
134 *YL v Birmingham City Council* [2007] UKHL 27, [2008] 1 AC 95, [63], *per* Baroness Hale.

But not all cases are as easy. Consider, for example, *YL v Birmingham City Council*.[135] In this case, the respondent local authority was required by the National Assistance Act 1948 to arrange the provision of residential care and accommodation for the appellant, an 84-year-old Alzheimer's sufferer—a duty that the council sought to discharge by entering into a contract with a company, Southern Cross Healthcare Ltd. The appellant was duly accommodated in a Southern Cross care home, largely at public expense. When the company later sought to terminate the contract, the appellant, whose relatives had allegedly behaved inappropriately during visits, argued that the resulting eviction would infringe the right to respect for her home under ECHR, Art 8. If this argument was to be capable of success, it first had to be established that Southern Cross was exercising a public function by accommodating and looking after the appellant. By a three–two majority, the House of Lords held that it was not.

For Lord Mance (with whom Lords Scott and Neuberger concurred), the key question was whether Southern Cross was undertaking a 'governmental' function. Close attention was paid to the text of the 1948 Act, and emphasis placed on the fact that the Council's statutory duty was to *make arrangements for the provision* of care and accommodation, whereas Southern Cross' contractual duty was to *make such provision*. Whatever the status of the former duty, it did not follow that the latter entailed what Lord Mance called 'an inherently governmental function'. In coming to this view, the majority judges were influenced (among other things) by the private and commercial motivation behind Southern Cross' operations, the undesirability (as it was perceived) of care home residents' rights differing according to whether they are private or state-placed clients, and Southern Cross' lack of any coercive or other statutory power. It followed that Southern Cross was not bound by the HRA.

The question that Lord Mance postulated—whether Southern Cross was performing a governmental function—was a sensible one (while 'public' and 'governmental' are not necessarily synonyms, the latter is an intelligible interpretation of the former in the present context). However, it is questionable whether the majority went about answering that question in the right way. In effect, they chose to examine matters at a micro-level—hence their concern with what Baroness Hale (dissenting) called the 'artificial and legalistic' distinction between the provision of care and the arrangement of such provision. Hence, too, Lord Neuberger's view that it is 'easier to invoke public funding to support the notion that a service is a function of "a public nature" where the funding effectively subsidises, in whole or in part, the cost of the service as a whole, rather than consisting of paying for the provision of that service to a specific person'.[136]

---

[135] [2007] UKHL 27, [2008] 1 AC 95.

[136] See further on this point *R (Weaver) v London and Quadrant Housing Trust* [2009] EWCA Civ 587, [2009] HRLR 29.

An alternative way of approaching this matter was suggested by the JCHR (and adopted by the minority in *YL*).[137] It involves examining the bigger picture. In particular, it acknowledges that few things are inherently public or private (or governmental or non-governmental): looking after vulnerable people, for example, is a function discharged primarily by families in some cultures, and primarily by the state in others. Against this background, the crucial question is whether, as Baroness Hale put it in her dissent in *YL*, the task in question is one 'for which the public, in the shape of the state, have assumed responsibility, at public expense if need be, and in the public interest'.[138] As Lord Bingham (also dissenting) observed, 'it can hardly be a matter of debate' that the 'British state has accepted a social welfare responsibility' as regards the provision of care and accommodation to those who (in the words of the 1948 Act) 'by reason of age, illness, disability or any other circumstances are in need of care and attention which is not otherwise available to them'.[139]

Following the judgment in *YL*, the JCHR registered its disapproval.[140] Parliament subsequently amended the law so that anyone providing accommodation, together with nursing or personal care, under (among other measures) the 1948 Act is to be taken in doing so to be performing functions of a public nature for the purpose of s 6(1) of the HRA.[141] This reversed the effect of the *YL* ruling in relation to care homes. Nonetheless, the general approach of the majority remains relevant to other contracting-out situations.

Q Do you prefer the view of the majority or the minority in *YL*? If the 'assumption of responsibility' test favoured by the minority were embraced, would this risk casting the HRA's net too wide? Would, for example, a contractor providing services (such as property maintenance) ancillary to the performance of a public function (for example, running a prison) be caught by the Act? Should it be?

3.5.3 **Other situations**

What if, as in *YL*, the relevant party is neither a core public authority nor performing a function of a public nature? Given that, in such circumstances, there is no duty under s 6 of the HRA to act in accordance with the Convention rights, does this mean that it is lawful to ride roughshod over them? Not necessarily. There are two sets of circumstances in which the Convention rights will be relevant even if the s 6 duty does not arise.

First, consider the *Ghaidan* case that was discussed earlier in the chapter[142]—a case between a landlord and a tenant. Clearly, neither was a core public authority; equally

---

[137] JCHR, *The Meaning of 'Public Authority' under the Human Rights Act* (HL 39 HC 382 2003–04).
[138] *YL* at [65].   [139] *YL* at [15].
[140] JCHR, *Legislative Scrutiny: Health and Social Care Bill* (HC 46 HL 303 2007–08).
[141] Health and Social Care Act 2008, s 145.
[142] See section 3.4.2 above.

clearly, in seeking to evict the tenant, the landlord was not performing a function of a public nature. And yet the landlord's freedom to evict the tenant was restricted, in effect, by the latter's Convention rights. How was this possible? The answer is as follows. In cases (such as *Ghaidan*) in which no one is under a s 6 duty, the Convention rights cannot operate as, in effect, a free-standing cause of action: in other words, it is not possible to launch proceedings against the other party on the straightforward basis that there has been a breach of Convention rights. However, if the relationship between the parties is governed in some relevant respect by legislation, then there may be scope for the Convention rights to impact upon that relationship. This is precisely what happened in *Ghaidan*. The landlord wanted to evict the tenant, but could only do so if the tenant was not a statutory tenant. But, as we know, the tenant was a statutory tenant—because when the relevant provisions of the Rent Act were interpreted in line with the defendant's Convention rights, the definition of 'statutory tenant' was stretched to include the category into which the defendant fell. It follows (with one exception) that whenever the relationship between the parties is governed by statute, the court must apply the statute in such a way as to secure compliance with relevant Convention rights. (The exception, of course, is that the court cannot do this when the legislation cannot be interpreted compatibly with relevant Convention rights.) All of this follows because the courts' s 3 interpretative obligation operates whether or not a public authority is involved in the proceedings.

Second, however, what if the relevant legal position between the parties is not governed by statute, meaning that s 3 is irrelevant? What if it is regulated by common law? Indeed, what if there simply is no relevant domestic law on the point? For example, should a newspaper publish an exposé of someone's private life in circumstances engaging no relevant statutory provisions, could the person concerned sue the newspaper—which is clearly not a public authority—on the ground that the publication involved a breach of the right to respect for private life contained in ECHR, Art 8?[143] Here, the position is murkier. Whereas s 3 imposes an explicit and strong obligation on the courts to apply legislation compatibly with the ECHR, the HRA contains no equivalent provision concerning the common law. A wide range of views has been expressed on the question of whether (and if so, to what extent) the Convention rights should be given 'horizontal effect'—that is, effect in disputes between private parties in circumstances to which s 3 has no application. Figure 19.5 summarises the views that have been expressed on this point. However, before considering their relative merits and the position adopted by the courts, it is necessary to say something about the background to this debate.

One of the main factors that has driven disagreement concerns the extent, if any, to which conferring horizontal effect on human rights is consistent with the classical liberal political philosophy from which much of human rights discourse itself

---

[143] We examine this specific question in Chapter 20 below. For the time being, we are concerned with the general question of whether Convention rights can have horizontal effect other than in circumstances in which such effect is, in effect, supplied, in the way set out in the previous paragraph, by s 3 of the HRA.

(1) Vertical effect only	(2) Common law development	(3) Application to all law	(4) Full horizontal effect
Human rights enforceable against public authorities, but not against private parties	Duty to develop and apply the law (including law applicable in horizontal cases) in the light of ECHR values and principles	All existing law (including common law) must be applied in a manner that gives effect to Convention rights	All cases must be decided compatibly with Convention rights, even if this involves courts inventing new causes of action

Figure 19.5 Horizontal effect?

originates.[144] The perceived difficulty is that, within the classical liberal tradition, individuals' freedom to do as they please should be jealously guarded. From this, two conclusions seem to follow. First, state power should be limited by reference to human rights: in this way, individuals' freedom will be secured against interferences by public bodies. Second, however, human rights should not themselves restrict individuals' liberty, because this would fly in the face of their very purpose. The difficulty, of course, is that if such rights are imbued with horizontal effect, they will necessarily end up restricting individuals' freedom: if X has a right to privacy, and if that right is horizontally enforceable against Y, it will be unlawful for Y to breach X's privacy in ways that, but for the horizontal enforceability of the right, may have been lawful.

While much of the discussion about whether Convention rights acquire horizontal effect under the HRA has inevitably focused upon the terms of the ECHR and the HRA, it is important to bear in mind that it has taken place against the philosophical background sketched above. It follows that when writers such as Buxton argue that Convention rights should only be effective vertically, against state bodies, they are buttressing the foregoing (interpretation of) the classical liberal position.[145] In advancing this view, Buxton argues that it chimes with the empirical context in which the ECHR was adopted. It was, he notes, specifically envisaged as a vehicle by which state power could be limited. Indeed, he points out that many of the rights are implicitly[146] or explicitly[147] addressed to the state—and, he says, *only* to the state—and that it is therefore meaningless to suppose that they could be enforced against individuals. Hence, says Buxton, even if the HRA were to make Convention rights enforceable against individuals, 'it would simply beat the air: because the content of those rights

---

[144]   See generally Hunt, 'The "Horizontal Effect" of the Human Rights Act' [1998] PL 423.

[145]   'The Human Rights Act and Private Law' (2000) 116 LQR 48.

[146]   For example, Art 6, which concerns the right to independent, fair, and impartial judicial (and sometimes administrative) proceedings, can only meaningfully be understood as applying to public bodies.

[147]   For example, in specifying when it may be lawful not to do that which Art 8(1) normally requires (namely, respecting private and family life, correspondence, and the home), Art 8(2) begins: 'There shall be no interference by a public authority with the exercise of this right except...'

does not impose obligations on private citizens'.[148] Buxton thus occupies the position lying at the far left of the spectrum depicted in Figure 19.5: in his view, the Convention rights are enforceable only vertically, against state bodies, and may, at most, have only a 'tangential effect on private law litigation'.[149]

At the other end of the spectrum, Wade argues that the HRA confers full horizontal effect on the Convention rights. His argument is a principally textual one—but one that is implicitly unsympathetic to the view that human rights should only ever protect, and should never restrict, individuals' freedom.[150] Wade observes that s 6(3) of the HRA says that 'courts and tribunals' constitute public authorities, meaning that they are required, by s 6(1), to act compatibly with the Convention rights. This, says Wade, obligates them to decide *all* cases—including purely horizontal ones—in accordance with those rights.[151] However, this argument is highly suspect, not least because, if accepted, it would undermine the very distinction between public and private functions that s 6 clearly sets out to erect.

Most commentators—along, as we shall see, with the courts—agree that a position between those advocated by Wade and Buxton is preferable. For example, Hunt—who adopts position (3) as shown in Figure 19.5—contends that, in applying all existing law, courts should do so compatibly with the ECHR.[152] This is close to, but does not go quite as far as, Wade's view. Because, for Hunt, s 6 applies only when courts are dealing with existing laws, it does not require them to invent new laws when that would be necessary in order to give full effect to Convention rights. If, for example, there is simply a gap in national law that leaves individuals without legal recourse in respect of ECHR-incompatible behaviour by other individuals, Hunt (in contrast to Wade) does not argue that courts should fill such a gap by developing a new cause of action. This approach, says Hunt, embraces the classical liberal view set out above, but does so in a nuanced way. Relationships, on Hunt's view, are purely private only when the law has not intervened to regulate them; human rights should not interfere with people's freedom to conduct such relationships as they see fit. But, Hunt contends, once the law has intervened to provide some form of regulation

> they have lost their truly private nature and the State, as the maker, the administrator, the interpreter and the applier of the law which governs those relationships, is bound to act in all those roles in a way which upholds and protects the rights made fundamental by the Constitution.[153]

Although this analysis arguably provides an elegant reconciliation of the classical liberal position with the recognition of (a degree of) horizontal effect, Phillipson—in adopting position (2)—argues that it is insufficiently sensitive to the terms of the HRA and so ascribes a greater degree of horizontal effect to human rights than is appropriate

---

[148] Buxton at 56.   [149] Buxton at 65.   [150] 'Horizons of Horizontality' (2000) 116 LQR 217.
[151] Wade at 217–18.   [152] Hunt, 'The "Horizontal Effect" of the Human Rights Act' [1998] PL 423.
[153] Hunt at 434–5, relying on the views of Kriegler J in the South African case of *Du Plessis v De Klerk* 1996 (3) SA 850.

under the Act.[154] Phillipson certainly does not go as far as Buxton: he rejects the view that the Convention rights simply have no meaning as against private parties. While some Convention rights, such as the right to a fair trial,[155] have no obvious application as against individuals, the substance of most of the rights is perfectly capable of such application: it is, for example, just as possible for a newspaper as for a public authority to deny someone respect for their private life.[156] However, Phillipson correctly points out that while this means that the Convention rights are *potentially capable* of full horizontal effect, they do not *in fact* have such effect. This is because the HRA does not actually incorporate the Convention rights: it merely gives them certain effects in domestic law.[157] One of those effects is that they are rendered enforceable against public authorities by virtue of the fact that s 6 obliges such authorities to act in accordance with the Convention rights. But, points out Phillipson, because individuals are placed under no equivalent obligation, 'it is clear that [Convention rights] can become in the private sphere at most legal values and principles, rather than the clear entitlements they are when exercised against public authorities'.[158] Ultimately, Phillipson's conclusion is that the best reading of the HRA is that, in horizontal cases, Convention rights are intended to have some effect, but not, for the reasons just considered, as much effect as Hunt favours. Thus, he says, 'the courts should apply and develop existing law in the light of the values represented by any applicable constitutional rights, in recognition that the actions of private individuals can produce similar or identical effects or harms to those of governmental bodies'.[159]

What position, then, have the courts adopted? This matter was considered in *Campbell v Mirror Group Newspapers Ltd*.[160] The case is considered in detail in the next chapter. For the time being, it suffices to say that it involved a claim brought against a newspaper in relation to the publication of allegedly private information; it therefore raised a question about the extent to which ECHR, Art 8 is enforceable against private parties. In addressing this question, Baroness Hale stated two principles. First, she said: 'The 1998 Act does not create any new cause of action between private persons.'[161] This means that the courts are not required to invent wholly new law in order to enable a private party to be sued for (what amounts in substance to) a breach of a Convention right. Second, however, she said that 'if there is a relevant cause of action applicable, the court as a public authority must act compatibly with both parties' Convention rights'.[162] A slightly more cautious note was struck by Lord Hoffmann. He said that while s 6 does not make Convention rights straightforwardly enforceable against private parties, the effect of the HRA is to emphasise the importance of certain norms. For example, in the context with which *Campbell* was concerned, Art 8 indicates that

---

[154] 'The Human Rights Act, "Horizontal Effect" and the Common Law: A Bang or a Whimper?' (1999) 62 MLR 824.   [155] See above.

[156] See further Beatson et al, *Human Rights: Judicial Protection in the United Kingdom* (London 2008), p 372.   [157] See section 3.3.2 above.

[158] Phillipson at 837.   [159] Phillipson at 830.   [160] [2004] UKHL 22, [2004] 2 AC 457.

[161] *Campbell* at [132].   [162] *Campbell* at [132].

'private information [is] something worth protecting as an aspect of human autonomy and dignity'.[163] Because, in this area, he could see 'no logical ground for saying that a person should have less protection against a private individual than he would have against the state',[164] Lord Hoffmann concluded that the values underlying Art 8 should 'have implications for the future development of the law'.[165]

On the face of it, Baroness Hale preferred Hunt's approach (all cases to be decided in accordance with Convention rights), whereas Lord Hoffmann preferred Phillipson's view (values underlying Convention rights to be allowed to influence the incremental development of the common law). However, this is perhaps too simplistic a reading of the case: a more nuanced reading suggests that the views of Baroness Hale and Lord Hoffmann represent complementary, rather than competing, approaches. The argument, advanced by Beatson et al, goes as follows.[166] Section 6 imposes an obligation[167] on courts to act compatibly with the Convention rights. This is not the same as (even though it may sometimes amount to) an obligation always to decide cases so as to ensure that parties' Convention rights are respected; rather, s 6 requires 'that a court must neither grant nor refuse relief' in a horizontal case where doing so would involve the *court's* acting incompatibly with a Convention right.[168] This means that the central question for the court is whether, 'if the result of a particular case would infringe a Convention right, this is properly attributable to the court' or to Parliament: 'The courts cannot be required to step outside their designated constitutional role in order to prevent or cure a breach of a Convention right.'[169]

On this approach, the courts are always (consistently with Lord Hoffmann's remarks in *Campbell*) at liberty to develop the common law, in the normal, incremental way, in a manner that is influenced by the values underpinning the Convention rights. But whether *their* obligation to act compatibly with Convention rights translates into a requirement to decide the case in a way that safeguards *the parties'* Convention rights depends on whether doing so would cross the line delimiting the courts' 'designated constitutional role'. That line will usually be crossed, as Baroness Hale indicated in *Campbell*, by the invention of a new cause of action. This is one way of understanding the relationship between two leading cases in this area. In *Campbell*, as we explain in the next chapter, the House of Lords was willing to extend existing common law principles concerning the confidentiality of private information so as to afford the claimant a remedy in relation to certain aspects of her claim. In contrast, *Wainwright* concerned the subjection of the claimants to a strip search by officials.[170] This was not something to which existing causes of action (such as trespass to the person) could be extended: if protection were to be afforded, a wholly new cause of action for breach

---

163   *Campbell* at [50].   164   *Campbell* at [50].

165   *Campbell* at [52]. See further Lord Hoffmann's judgment in *Wainwright v Home Office* [2003] UKHL 53, [2004] 2 AC 406.

166   Beatson et al, *Human Rights: Judicial Protection in the United Kingdom* (London 2008), pp 371–90.

167   Subject to the exceptions mentioned in section 3.5.1 above.   168   Beatson et al, p 375.

169   Beatson et al, p 380.   170   *Wainwright v Home Office* [2003] UKHL 53, [2004] 2 AC 406.

of privacy would be needed. The House of Lords declined to take such a step: in Lord Hoffmann's view, this 'is an area which requires a detailed approach which can be achieved only by legislation rather than the broad brush of common law principle'.[171] If we accept this analysis, such that courts are not required to create new causes of action, it does not follow that they must do everything that falls short of taking that step. In some circumstances, manipulating an existing cause of action so as to safe-guard Convention rights would constitute such a serious step, and involve such a significant policy choice, as to transgress the line that distinguishes the courts' role (of *developing* the common law) and Parliament's *legislative* role.

3.5.4 Who can enforce human rights claims?

The foregoing discussion was concerned with the range of parties upon which the HRA imposes obligations to act compatibly with Convention rights. The practical reach of the Act is also influenced by the obverse question: who can bring a claim for a breach of Convention rights? Article 34 of the ECHR says that only a 'victim' may bring a claim before the ECtHR. Similarly, s 7(1) of the HRA provides that only a 'victim' can bring a domestic claim alleging that a public authority has acted in a way that breaches its s 6(1) obligation to act compatibly with Convention rights—and, in applying this test, domestic courts are required by the HRA to adopt the same meaning of 'victim' as that which the ECtHR applies.[172]

Who, then, is a 'victim'? Clearly, someone who is actually affected by the conduct in question falls into this category. However, the ECtHR has not restricted victim status to such individuals. For example, the victim test is satisfied by someone who is an 'indirect victim'.[173] On this basis, the applicant in *Kurt v Turkey*,[174] was permitted to argue that *her son's* right to liberty under Art 5 had been violated when he was allegedly abducted and beaten by soldiers. The victim test is also satisfied if the person concerned can show that he or she is a 'potential victim'. If, for example, legislation exists that, if it were to be enforced against the individual concerned, would result in a breach of her Convention rights, this may be sufficient to establish victim status, notwithstanding that the legislation has not actually been enforced against her.[175] It follows that the victim test is rather broader than may at first appear. But it remains much more restrictive than the 'sufficient interest' test that applies to ordinary judicial review proceedings.[176] On the face of it, this means that domestic law now embodies two distinct standing tests: the liberal 'sufficient interest' test applies when a claimant wishes to allege that a public authority has acted contrary to the established principles of administrative law (for example, that it acted contrary to natural justice or *Wednesbury* unreasonably), while claimants seeking to establish a breach of Convention rights must bring

---

[171] *Wainwright* at [33].   [172] HRA 1998, s 7(7).

[173] See generally Feldman, 'Indirect Victims, Direct Injury: Recognising Relatives as Victims under the European Human Rights System' [2009] EHRLR 50.

[174] (1999) 27 EHRR 373. (The son had subsequently 'disappeared' and was therefore unable to bring the claim himself.)   [175] *Norris v Ireland* (1991) 13 EHRR 186.

[176] See Chapter 14, section 3.3, above.

themselves within the much narrower confines of the 'victim' criterion. This seems incoherent in principle (why have two distinct tests?) and unnecessarily complicated (for example, a claimant seeking judicial review on both 'traditional' and human rights grounds might be found to have standing in relation to the former, but not the latter).

However, for two reasons, a claimant seeking to bring a judicial review claim may be able to do so even if she is not a 'victim'. First, some human rights arguments can be made *without any reliance upon the HRA at all*. In such circumstances, the normal standing test, not the victim test, applies. For example, proceedings for breach of a common law constitutional right[177] can be brought without reference to the HRA, and so without having to establish victim status. Second, even if the right in question does not constitute a common law constitutional right, such that it is necessary to rely on the HRA, *it may not be necessary to rely on s 6*. Section 7 says that the claimant has to be a victim if she wishes to argue that a public authority has acted unlawfully under s 6 by failing to fulfil its obligation to act in accordance with the Convention rights. However, in cases involving the exercise by a public body of statutory power, it will be possible to argue that it has breached Convention rights, and has therefore acted unlawfully, without relying on s 6. This follows because, wholly independently of s 6, s 3 (as we have seen) requires legislation to be read compatibly with Convention rights. This means that (unless the legislation cannot be read in that way) public bodies' statutory powers will be read as excluding any legal authority to breach Convention rights. As a consequence, non-victims can argue that a public body has acted in a way made unlawful by s 3: the HRA does not say that, in order to make such an argument, the claimant must be a victim.[178]

4. The future

The HRA is one of the most significant pieces of constitutional reform undertaken in recent decades. But it has been a highly controversial piece of legislation. Some people strongly support it as an essential safeguard of basic rights. Others have criticised it for not going far enough, whether in terms of the strength of protection that it offers or the range of rights to which it applies. And still others—most volubly, certain sections of the popular press—have subjected the HRA to excoriating criticism, arguing, *inter alia*, that it gives judges too much power and produces perverse outcomes. As a result, there have, as we will see, been calls in some quarters for its repeal.

4.1 Dissatisfaction with the HRA

To the extent that there is dissatisfaction with the HRA, this can generally be attributed to a combination of two factors.

---

[177] See section 3.2 above.
[178] The House of Lords recognised the force of this reasoning in *R (Rusbridger) v Attorney-General* [2003] UKHL 38, [2004] 1 AC 357, [21].

The first is that there are serious misconceptions about the Act. For example, it is sometimes the case that media coverage confuses (or leads the public to confuse) an *assertion* of an entitlement arising under the HRA with the *existence* of such an entitlement. This, in turn, leads people wrongly to think that it is possible to derive wholly inappropriate rights from the Act. A classic example involved a convicted murderer who made a legal claim asserting that the prison authorities' refusal to supply him with access to certain forms of pornography constituted unlawful discrimination against homosexuals (contrary to Art 14) and inhuman and degrading treatment (contrary to Art 3).[179] Although this claim was dismissed by the courts at the initial stage, the mere fact that it had been made created a public perception that the HRA gave prisoners a right to hardcore pornography. In other situations, misguided assumptions by public authorities that the HRA requires them to do certain things leads to a wider perception that this is really so. For example, fried chicken was supplied by the police to a man who was evading arrest by sitting on the roof of a house. This was explained by a police spokesperson who said: 'He has been demanding various things and one was a KFC bargain bucket. Although he's a nuisance, we still have to look after his well-being and human rights.'[180] *The Sun* newspaper thus reported that a 'yob who spent all day on a roof lobbing bricks at cops was "rewarded" with a KFC takeaway...because of his human rights'.[181] As a government review correctly observed, the suspect had no human right requiring that he be supplied either with food in general or fried chicken in particular—but such episodes feed public perceptions that the HRA requires public bodies to do things that fly in the face of common sense, bringing it into disrepute.[182]

The fact that people think the HRA says and requires things that it actually does not is, of course, not a criticism of the Act per se. It is, however, noteworthy that this sort of reporting has found a receptive audience. While it is beyond the scope of this book to explore in any detail why this might be so, one suggestion may be ventured. In many countries, before a constitutional Bill of Rights is adopted, there is a good deal of public discussion about whether such a Bill is required and, if so, what rights it should protect. The HRA—which is, at least for the time being, the closest thing the UK has to a constitutional Bill of Rights—was not preceded by such a process. Although there was a great deal of discussion within legal circles, this did not impinge to any significant extent upon public discourse. The impression, among certain sections of the media and the public, that the HRA has been foisted upon them has been given further succour by the fact that it has been characterised as a European import, in that it gives effect to certain of the rights contained in the ECHR.[183] In the light of the tendency to conflate the ECHR and the EU, criticism of the former often piggybacks on

---

[179] Department for Constitutional Affairs, *Review of the Implementation of the Human Rights Act* (London 2006), p 30.   [180] 'KFC meal "ensures siege man's rights"', *The Daily Telegraph*, 7 June 2006.

[181] 'Finger-nickin good farce', *The Sun*, 7 June 2006.

[182] Department for Constitutional Affairs, p 31.

[183] This characterisation is, however, inaccurate. The UK was instrumental in the drafting of the ECHR, and it is therefore unsurprising that many of the rights that it safeguards are echoed in the common law.

'Euroscepticism' regarding the latter. This, in turn, is one of the factors that has given legs to the argument—that we address below—that the HRA should be modified or replaced with something specifically British.

The second source of dissatisfaction with the HRA has also contributed to that argument. The objection here is that the HRA strikes an inappropriate balance between the interests of rights-holders and wider society. There is, of course, room for legitimate disagreement about how that balance should be struck: for example, from a socialist, as opposed to a libertarian, perspective, the HRA may be criticised as placing too much emphasis on the interests of individuals and too little on the interests of the community. In a similar, but not identical, vein, it has been suggested that the HRA unacceptably gets in the way of public authorities doing things that would benefit the public generally. A particular strand within this discourse has focused on the perception that the HRA pays insufficient regard to the interests of the so-called law-abiding majority by ascribing undue weight to others' rights. Clearly, this view is informed in part by the sort of myths considered above—but it also rests, to some extent, on disapproval of decisions actually made by the courts under the HRA.

This has, on some occasions, resulted in surprising criticism of judges by senior politicians. When, in 2006, the High Court held that Afghan nationals who had hijacked a plane could not be deported because it would breach their right against torture under Art 3 of the ECHR, the then Prime Minister, Tony Blair, said that the ruling was 'an abuse of common-sense'.[184] On another occasion, in 2003, after losing a decision concerning asylum, the then Home Secretary, David Blunkett, said that he was 'fed up with having to deal with a situation where Parliament debates issues and the judges then overturn them',[185] while Blair reportedly considered 'new legislation to limit the role of judges in the interpretation of international human rights obligations and reassert the primacy of parliament'.[186] Although this plan (if indeed it existed) never came to fruition, the HRA has remained politically contentious; the central concern apparently being that out-of-touch, liberal judges are inappropriately restricting the government's ability to advance its conception of the public good. Unsurprisingly, a particular flashpoint has been the 'war on terror', in which context several of the government's preferred strategies have either been held by the courts to be incompatible with Convention rights[187] or largely neutered by being subject to an interpretation that upholds fundamental rights in a way that is at odds with what was most likely intended when the legislation was promoted by the government.[188]

---

[184] 'Reid pledge on Afghan hijackers', *The Independent*, 11 May 2006. The case was *R (S) v Secretary of State for the Home Department* [2006] EWHC Admin 1111, which was approved by the Court of Appeal: [2006] EWCA Civ 1157, [2006] INLR 575.

[185] 'Blair takes on judges over asylum', *The Daily Telegraph*, 20 February 2003.

[186] *The Daily Telegraph*.

[187] See, eg the discussion in Chapter 1 of the judicial condemnation in the *Belmarsh* case of the detention without trial of suspected foreign terrorists.

[188] See, eg the discussion in section 3.4.3 above of the way in which the House of Lords interpreted legislation setting out the procedure for 'control order proceedings'.

4.2 **The way forward**

Some of the arguments against the HRA described above are undoubtedly specious—but there is, as we noted at the beginning of this chapter, a genuine debate to be had about whether, and if so to what extent, courts should be charged with protecting individuals' human rights. If, as some argue, the approach adopted by the HRA is not the right one, what might be the way forward?

Here, the picture is complicated.[189] Even if it is felt that courts should have no involvement in enforcing human rights, and that questions about how to balance the interests of individuals against those of the wider community should only ever be undertaken by democratically accountable politicians, such a situation could not straightforwardly be achieved. Repealing the HRA would not, in itself, relieve public authorities in the UK of their obligations to act compatibly with the Convention rights. Those obligations would exist for as long as the UK remained a party to the ECHR—and they would continue to be enforceable judicially, albeit by the ECtHR rather than by domestic courts. It follows that, even if a radical critique of judicial protection of human rights were to be embraced, repealing the HRA would not constitute a sensible way forward unless withdrawal from the ECHR were in contemplation. Even taking that step would not be a panacea: the Convention rights are binding upon member States of the EU when they are implementing EU law, and, unless the UK were also to withdraw from the EU, it would, in those contexts, remain bound by the Convention even if it were formally to cease to be a party to it.

A less radical—but equally futile—option would be to adapt or replace the HRA so as to enhance the ability of public authorities to pursue their conception of the public interest. For example, in 2006, David Cameron, then the leader of the opposition, argued that a British Bill of Rights should be enacted (which, he later clarified, would replace the HRA[190]) so as to 'define the core values which give us our identity as a free nation' while facilitating a 'hard-nosed defence of security and freedom'.[191] A less-specific undertaking—to 'replace the Human Rights Act with a UK Bill of Rights'—was contained in the Conservatives' 2010 election manifesto.[192] In apparently similar vein, a government Consultation Paper in 2007 advocated 'explicit [legislative] recognition that human rights come with responsibilities and must be exercised in a way that respects the human rights of others'.[193] A moment's thought, however, indicates that approaches like this are just as problematic as outright repeal of the HRA. If, in effect, the protection afforded via domestic law to the Convention rights is to be watered down (for example, by making it easier for the public interest to prevail over such rights or by making their exercise contingent upon 'responsible'

---

[189] See generally Klug, '"Solidity or Wind?" What's on the Menu in the Bill of Rights Debate?' (2009) 80 Political Quarterly 420.   [190] Conservative Party media statement, 21 August 2007.

[191] 'Balancing freedom and security: A modern British Bill of Rights', speech to the Centre for Policy Studies, London, 26 June 2006.

[192] Conservative Party, *An Invitation to Join the Government of Britain* (London 2010), p 79.

[193] Ministry of Justice, *The Governance of Britain* (Cm 7170 2007), p 61.

behaviour), litigants will simply look to the ECtHR for relief for as long as the UK remains a party to the ECHR. This point was apparently taken by the Labour government in 2009: in a further Consultation Paper, it argued that people's 'responsibilities' should be articulated alongside their rights, but accepted that such a step should not involve making Convention rights conditional upon the fulfilment by individuals of their responsibilities.[194]

Ultimately, the position is very simple. If the UK is to remain a party to the ECHR—and withdrawal is, surely, unthinkable—little purpose would be served by repealing the HRA or otherwise constraining domestic courts' capacity to enforce the Convention rights. At most, this would simply reinstate the pre-HRA position, whereby it was often necessary to initiate proceedings against the UK in the ECtHR in order to vindicate Convention rights. It is, however, highly unlikely that repeal of the HRA would straightforwardly reinstate the situation that obtained before its enactment. While it would be rash to suggest that repeal would be without practical legal consequence, it would be equally misguided to assume that repeal of the HRA would result in the wholesale surgical removal from UK law of the Convention rights' influence. This is the case for five reasons.

First, repeal of the HRA would not accomplish removal of *common law constitutional rights*, which would therefore continue to be protected by the courts. Second, the *common law is not static*. The doctrine of common law constitutional rights developed over time. There is no reason to think that that process would not continue, nor that it *has* not continued since the HRA entered into force. It is, for example, far from fanciful to suggest that the common law may have absorbed at least some of the Convention rights, such that, upon repeal of the HRA, courts could continue to recognise and protect such rights. Third, it is highly unlikely that *proportionality*—one of the main techniques whereby Convention rights are protected—would vanish from domestic law if the HRA were to be repealed. Courts have already begun to use that doctrine in other contexts—most obviously when assessing the legality of government action that dashes a substantive legitimate expectation[195]—which suggests that it has become, or is in the process of becoming, an embedded feature of domestic law, rather than simply a feature of HRA cases. Fourth, independently of the doctrine of common law constitutional rights, *certain areas of the common law have been developed, thanks to the HRA, so as to be more closely aligned with Convention rights*. For example, as we explain in the next chapter, the extent to which the law of tort protects privacy has been considerably expanded. That new body of common law would not simply evaporate if the HRA was repealed. Fifth, the same point applies to *legislation the meaning of which has changed as a result of the HRA*. Legislation that has been reinterpreted pursuant to s 3 of the HRA in order to render it compatible with Convention rights would not simply revert to its pre-HRA meaning upon repeal

---

[194] Ministry of Justice, *Rights and Responsibilities: Developing Our Constitutional Framework* (Cm 7577 2009), [2.22].   [195] See Chapter 13, section 4.3.2, above.

of that enactment; rather, HRA-compatible interpretations would remain part of the body of precedent.[196]

Ultimately, then, a clear choice falls to be made between two options if reform is to be pursued. The first option would be to *water down the HRA*—for example, by limiting the courts' powers, extending the discretion of public bodies (as a matter of domestic law) to restrict rights in order to advance their perception of the common good, or even limiting the range of ECHR rights offered protection under national law. For the reasons set out above, such a step would be a retrograde—and, in some respects, a futile—one.

The second reform option could be described as an *ECHR-plus model*. This was advocated in a 2008 JCHR report in which the arguments for a Bill of Rights and Freedoms were set out.[197] Such legislation could, in a number of ways, confer greater protection on human rights than that which is presently provided by the HRA. The ECHR only sets a 'floor' of rights, beneath which state parties are not permitted to descend; a domestic Bill of Rights could therefore articulate some or all of the Convention rights in stricter form (for example, with more limited provision for qualification in the face of conflicting public interests). Moreover, said the JCHR, existing rights could be spelled out in more detail, and additional rights—for example, to jury trial, to fair administrative action, and of access to courts—could be covered.[198] The Committee also argued in favour of including social and economic rights, but suggested that they should be given a principally 'aspirational' status: the government would be placed under a statutory duty, resources permitting, to realise such rights, but they would not be straightforwardly enforceable in legal proceedings. Crucially, the JCHR noted that the drafting and enactment of a UK Bill of Rights would 'enable a national debate to take place about why it is needed and what should be in it, a debate which did not happen when the HRA was introduced'.[199]

The coalition government formed in the wake of the 2010 general election brought together two parties with contrasting policies on the HRA. The Conservatives, as noted above, were committed to repealing it in favour of a British Bill of Rights; the Liberal Democrats, however, promised to '[e]nsure that everyone has the same protections under the law by protecting the Human Rights Act'.[200] Following the election, the Conservative–Liberal Democrat coalition government agreed to establish a commission to look into this issue, but it seems clear that the Conservatives' plan to water down the protections contained in the HRA has sensibly been abandoned, in that

---

[196] The foregoing observations would apply in a scenario involving straightforward repeal of the HRA. It would, of course, be possible (at least on an orthodox view of parliamentary sovereignty) for the enactment of legislation to go further—eg restricting or abolishing common law rights, or requiring courts to ignore any precedent generated by virtue of the HRA.

[197] JCHR, *A Bill of Rights for the UK?* (HL 165 HC 150 2007–08).

[198] Of course, some of these rights already exist in practice: the law of judicial review, in effect, protects a right to fair administrative action, while the right of access to courts is recognised as a common law constitutional right.   [199] JCHR, HL 165 HC 150, [60].

[200] Liberal Democrats, *Manifesto 2010* (London 2010), p 94.

the Commission's brief is to propose a British Bill of Rights that will 'build on all our obligations under the ECHR', ensuring that 'these rights continue to be enshrined in British law'.[201]

> **Q** How, if at all, should the system for protecting human rights introduced by the HRA be changed?

5. Conclusions

The HRA has substantially enhanced the protection afforded to human rights in UK law. In doing so, it has contributed in a fundamental way to the shift from a more political to a more legal form of constitutionalism, and has become an important limitation upon the extensive powers of the executive branch. However, as the discussion in the previous section underlines, the HRA is not a constitutional Bill of Rights—that is, it does not form part of an entrenched constitution that enjoys a special legal status. As a result, the HRA is vulnerable to being amended or repealed just like any other piece of legislation. Just as the HRA was not the result of the sort of careful, inclusive discussion that often precedes the adoption of a constitutional Bill of Rights, so it can be done away with equally straightforwardly. It would, therefore, be mistaken to overemphasise the extent to which the HRA marks a transition to a newly legal form of constitutionalism in the UK. For as long as the UK lacks an entrenched constitution, the ultimate guarantee of human rights remains the political, not the legal, process. For those who think that it is undemocratic for judges to have the last word on the often politically or socially controversial issues raised by human rights adjudication, this is a good thing. For others, who doubt the capacity of the majority to stay its hand when perceptions of the public interest or naked electoral ambition invite the subjugation of vulnerable and unpopular minorities, it is a cause for grave concern.

Further reading

ALLAN, 'Parliament's Will and the Justice of the Common Law: The HRA in Constitutional Perspective' (2006) 59 CLP 27

BEATSON ET AL, *Human Rights: Judicial Protection in the United Kingdom* (London 2008)

CAMPBELL ET AL, *Sceptical Essays on Human Rights* (Oxford 2001)

---

[201] HM Government, *The Coalition: Our Programme for Government* (London 2010), p 11.

DEPARTMENT FOR CONSTITUTIONAL AFFAIRS, *Review of the Implementation of the Human Rights Act* (London 2006)

FELDMAN, *Civil Liberties and Human Rights in England and Wales* (Oxford 2002), ch 1

JOINT COMMITTEE ON HUMAN RIGHTS, *A Bill of Rights for the UK?* (HL 165 HC 150 2007–08)

JOINT COMMITTEE ON HUMAN RIGHTS, *The Human Rights Act: The DCA and Home Office Reviews* (HL 278 HC 1716 2005–06)

OLIVER, 'Functions of a Public Nature under the Human Rights Act' [2004] PL 329

Useful websites

http://www.equalityhumanrights.com
The website of the Equality and Human Rights Commission

http://www.echr.coe.int/echr
The website of the European Court of Human Rights

http://www.parliament.uk/business/committees/committees-a-z/joint-select/human
-rights-committee/
The website of the Joint Committee on Human Rights

http://www.nihrc.org
The website of the Northern Ireland Human Rights Commission

Freedom of Expression

20

1. Why freedom of expression matters

1.1 Introduction

The right to freedom of expression is often referred to simply as 'freedom of speech', although it is generally recognised as involving the protection not only of verbal communication, but also of images and sounds. A politician making a speech, a busker singing in a town centre, an artist exhibiting paintings, and a neo-Nazi wearing a swastika are all engaging in forms of expression. But, of course, a line has to be drawn somewhere: free speech may clash with, and might sometimes have to give way to, other rights and interests. The purpose of this chapter is to examine the nature of free speech. Where and how does the law draw the line between acceptable and unacceptable expression? Does the right to free speech encompass the right to publish pornography, including extreme forms thereof? Or to publicise the intimate details of celebrities' private lives? Or to make grotesquely racist comments? We examine these and other questions in the course of the chapter. But if we are to assess English law's response to them critically, it is necessary to start with a logically prior question: why protect free speech at all?

Gearty notes that 'in relatively stable societies'—the implication being that less stable ones may have other priorities—'restrictions on freedom of expression are regarded as the most serious conceivable breach of civil liberties'.[1] Raz regards this state of affairs as a 'puzzle': '[W]hy [free speech] deserves this importance is a mystery.'[2] Given that most people would place far greater value on other interests, such as having a job, why single out free speech as being worthy of especially vigilant legal protection? The significance of some rights is so obvious as to make it unnecessary to spell it out. This is often because of the self-evidently harmful consequences that would flow from the breach of such rights (for example, the right not to be tortured). But the harmful consequences of restricting speech may be less immediately obvious. It may be frustrating not to be allowed to say what you want to say, but surely that is far smaller a burden than spending weeks in a dungeon being tortured by state agents intent on

---

[1] Gearty, *Civil Liberties* (Oxford 2007), p 122.
[2] Raz, 'Free Expression and Personal Identification' (1991) 11 OJLS 303, 303.

extracting a confession? For this reason, free speech can appear somewhat esoteric, even elitist—something that is perhaps important to those who have the means and wherewithal to publish their views in newspapers, but largely irrelevant to the average person. However, there are two principal arguments that call this view into question, and which arguably provide the solution to Raz's puzzle.[3]

1.2 **Free speech and the status of individuals**

The US Supreme Court has said that 'the freedom to speak one's mind is…a good unto itself'.[4] In other words, freedom of expression is valuable for its own sake, judged from the perspective of the individual engaging in it, as well as being beneficial to wider society. This view is premised on the high value attached in liberal theory to the autonomy of the individual. On that view, the intrinsic worth of each person means that, as far as is possible and is consistent with respect for others' autonomy, he should be allowed to live his life as he wishes, and his status as an independent moral agent with his own personality, views, and preferences should be respected. Within that framework, freedom of expression assumes an important role in two senses.

First, autonomous individuals should be permitted to express themselves. As Sadurski notes, 'human communicative activities are crucial to our capacity for self-expression and self-fulfilment'.[5] Being able to communicate is important if people are to develop as individuals and to define themselves. As Barendt puts it: 'A right to express beliefs and political attitudes instantiates or reflects what it is to be human.'[6] To deny people the right to express themselves is to deny their humanity, given that '[t]he reflective mind, conscious of options and the possibilities for growth, distinguishes human beings from animals'.[7]

Second, autonomous individuals should be able to hear[8] and consider what *others* have to say.[9] Taken to its logical conclusion, this approach makes it illegitimate for the state to legislate paternalistically so as to restrict free speech. For example, legislation making it unlawful to say untrue things about people that would make others think badly of them would be inappropriate: autonomous, rational agents should be left to weigh up the credibility of what they hear and to decide how, if at all, to modify their behaviour and views in the light of it.

However, most legal systems recognise that, despite these arguments, the right of free speech should not be unlimited. Some forms of expression—spreading vicious lies about someone that risks ruining their private life or employment prospects, for example—may cause considerable harm; unless we regard the values discussed above as absolute, it is perfectly sensible—as is the case in most countries, including the

---

[3] For a more detailed examination of arguments in favour of free speech, see Barendt, *Freedom of Speech* (Oxford 2005), ch 1, and Raz (above).   [4] *Bose Corp v Consumers Union* (1984) 466 US 485, 503.
[5] *Freedom of Speech and Its Limits* (Dordrecht 1999), p 17.
[6] Barendt, *Freedom of Speech* (Oxford 2005), p 13.   [7] Barendt, p 13.   [8] Or read or see.
[9] See Scanlon, 'A Theory of Freedom of Expression' (1972) 1 Philosophy and Public Affairs 204.

United Kingdom—to contemplate restricting free speech in order to guard against such harmful consequences. But the significance of the arguments set out above is that they hold that the value of free speech should not be judged purely in terms of its consequences. Just because some speech has negative effects, such as offending or disconcerting others, does not *necessarily* mean that it should be prohibited; rather, the harm must be weighed against the good—and the good must include the intrinsic value of allowing individuals to express themselves.

1.3 Truth, democracy, and tolerance

The arguments just considered are often described collectively as 'non-consequentialist' arguments in that they focus upon freedom of speech as something that is valuable *for its own sake*. By contrast, 'consequentialist arguments' focus upon the beneficial social *consequences* that stem from affording people the freedom to say what they wish.

The first such argument concerns the so-called *marketplace of ideas*. In economic terms, free markets, in which everyone is free to buy and sell goods and services, are said by some to be valuable because, *inter alia*, they facilitate competition: good products succeed, poor ones fall by the wayside, and quality and value are driven up. For similar reasons, it has been suggested that there should be 'free trade in ideas'—'that the best test of truth is the power of the thought to get itself accepted in the competition of the market'.[10] On this view—which is most closely associated with John Stuart Mill[11]—an unfettered, or at least very broad, ability lawfully to advance opinions and make assertions is desirable.[12] Regulation or censorship—attempts by the state to predetermine the 'truth'—is considered both undesirable, because the state might get it wrong or present matters in a way that suits it, and unnecessary, because vigorous and unhindered public debate will ensure that bad ideas are not accepted, that good ideas are adopted and refined, and that false assertions are ignored in favour of true ones. There are, though, two main criticisms of the marketplace theory. It assumes, somewhat optimistically, that everyone is 'capable of making determinations that are both sophisticated and intricately rational if they are to separate truth from falsehood'.[13] And it overlooks the fact that just as markets in goods and services can be distorted (for example, by the existence of powerful monopolies), so the marketplace of ideas may also malfunction: people might, for example, be led to perceive as the 'truth' not the best ideas, but rather those that are advanced by those with the most persuasive communication skills—or the deepest pockets.[14]

---

[10] *Abrams v US* (1919) 250 US 616, 630, *per* Holmes J.   [11] *On Liberty*, ch 2.

[12] See, eg *Gertz v Robert Welch Inc* (1974) 418 US 323, 339–40.

[13] Ingber, 'The Marketplace of Ideas: A Legitimising Myth' [1984] Duke Law Journal 1, 7.

[14] We saw in Chapter 5, section 2.2.7, above that such concerns have resulted in the UK in limits on how much can be spent by political parties on election campaigns.

> **Q** In *Brandenburg v Ohio*,[15] the US Supreme Court held that a speech by the appellant, a member of a white supremacist group, advocating violence against blacks and Jews should attract the protection of the freedom of expression provisions in the US Constitution. A state law criminalising what the appellant had done was held unconstitutional. Do you think that the marketplace of ideas theory is capable of justifying this decision?

Second, it has been said that freedom of speech is the *'lifeblood of democracy'*.[16] Meiklejohn argued that a truly democratic system of government requires far more than regular elections. Those elections must be meaningful, in the sense that they must permit the people—on whose behalf the government will exercise power—to make an informed choice. And this requires that the people 'must try to understand the issues which, incident by incident, face the nation', passing judgement upon the choices made by politicians on their behalf.[17] This led him to the conclusion that the point of the free speech guarantee in the US Constitution was to prevent the making of laws 'abridg[ing] the freedom of a citizen's speech, press, peaceable assembly, or petition, whenever those activities are utilized for the governing of the nation'.[18]

Third, it has been argued that freedom of speech is a good thing because it promotes *tolerance*. This argument takes different forms, but its general thrust is that protecting free speech enables (indeed, requires) people to be exposed to a wide range of views, ideas, and values, and that such exposure will serve to promote a more tolerant, harmonious, broad-minded society.[19] It is, for example, likely that the increasing willingness of the mainstream media to acknowledge the existence and legitimacy of gay relationships and lifestyles has driven, as well as reflected, growing recognition that people should be able to live their lives according to their sexual orientation, free from legal or social interference.

1.4 **Free speech and our key themes**

We conclude this section by noting that freedom of speech is relevant to two of the key themes with which we are concerned in this book. The first is the importance of ensuing that the government can be held to account. For two reasons, free speech is imperative in this regard. Effective accountability is possible only if people have access to information about the decisions that the government has made, whether its policies are delivering their objectives, and whether mistakes have occurred. Free speech helps to ensure that such information is publicly available. In addition, people must be able to discuss such information freely and publicly—praising, blaming, criticizing, and demonstrating for or against the government as they see fit. As we know, there

---

[15] (1969) 395 US 444.
[16] *R v Secretary of State for the Home Department, ex p Simms* [2000] 2 AC 115, 126.
[17] 'The First Amendment is an Absolute' [1961] The Supreme Court Review 245, 255.
[18] Meiklejohn at 256.   [19] Raz, 'Free Expression and Personal Identification' (1991) 11 OJLS 303.

are a number of mechanisms in the British constitution that can be used to hold the government to account—but the raw power of public opinion freely expressed should not be underestimated.

The second key theme relevant to this chapter is the shift from a more political to a more legal form of constitutionalism. One of the principal engines of that change is the growing legal acknowledgement and enforcement of individual rights. The increasing recognition of freedom of speech as a legal right, traced in this chapter, forms part of that trend. That is not, however, to suggest that this renders political control of government unimportant—far from it. *Legal* protection of free speech means that *political* mechanisms of control can be more fully exploited by strengthening people's ability lawfully to speak out.

2. Article 10 of the European Convention on Human Rights

Freedom of speech existed in the UK long before it became a party to the European Convention on Human Rights (ECHR) and long before that instrument was given effect in national law by means of the Human Rights Act 1998 (HRA).[20] However, the fact that the ECHR does now have effect in domestic law means that Art 10—its free speech provision—forms a useful benchmark against which to assess the extent to which English law recognises and protects freedom of expression.

Article 10 follows the same structure as the other qualified rights.[21] Article 10(1) says that '[e]veryone has the right to freedom of expression' and that this 'shall include freedom to hold opinions and to receive and impart information and ideas without interference by public authority and regardless of frontiers'.[22] Article 10(2) then goes on to set out the circumstances in which it is legitimate to restrict freedom of speech:

> The exercise of these freedoms, since it carries with it duties and responsibilities, may be subject to such formalities, conditions, restrictions or penalties as are prescribed by law and are necessary in a democratic society, in the interests of national security, territorial integrity or public safety, for the prevention of disorder or crime, for the protection of health or morals, for the protection of the reputation or rights of others, for preventing the disclosure of information received in confidence, or for maintaining the authority and impartiality of the judiciary.

Two principal questions arise. The first concerns *what counts as expression*, since only freedom of 'expression' is protected by Art 10. Some guidance is given in the text: 'opinions', 'information', and 'ideas' are covered, although the use of the word 'include' indicates that this was intended to be a non-exhaustive list. Inevitably,

---

[20] On the ECHR and HRA generally, see Chapter 19 above.

[21] On qualified rights, see Chapter 19, section 3.4.8, above.

[22] A specific provision in Art 10(1) concerning broadcasters and certain others is considered in section 3.2 below.

therefore, difficult questions arise about the precise reach of Art 10. The European Court of Human Rights (ECtHR) has taken a generally broad approach to the category of things that are covered by Art 10(1), but it is not infinitely wide. Thus, while a film depicting hardcore pornography constitutes 'expression' for the purpose of Art 10(1),[23] certain forms of 'hate speech' do not: when white supremacists called blacks and foreign workers 'animals', that did not constitute expression within the meaning of Art 10(1).[24]

The second question is whether speech that constitutes expression and which is therefore *prima facie* protected by Art 10 may nevertheless be restricted under Art 10(2). This question—which involves the application of the proportionality test[25]—also raises difficult issues, because it requires courts to confront clashes between free speech and other important rights and interests. For example, media coverage of matters of general interest, such as criminal investigations, the doings of the rich and famous, and the conduct of the government bring into play tensions between, on the one hand, free speech and, on the other hand, the rights to a fair trial and to respect for private life, and interests such as national security. How we think such tensions should be resolved is necessarily coloured by the matters considered in the previous section. The importance that we attach to free speech—and the *reasons* why we think free speech is important—will inevitably affect how we think that right should be weighed up against other values. For example, drawing upon the arguments examined above concerning the significance of free speech to democracy, the ECtHR has held that it is especially important that political expression—especially in the context of an election campaign—should be respected, with the result that particularly weighty reasons are required if such speech is to be lawfully restricted.[26] By contrast, the Court accords less weight to commercial speech and advertising.[27]

3. Media freedom

3.1 Why start with the media?

With the foregoing points in mind, we begin our examination of English law—starting with several issues concerning the media. The reasons for doing so are twofold.

First, the media is uniquely situated to facilitate the exercise of freedom of expression. Although the Internet makes it easier than ever for ordinary people to reach a large audience, traditional forms of media—newspapers, radio, television—still offer the best prospects for wide exposure and influence. It is therefore unsurprising that

---

[23] *Hoare v UK* [1997] EHRLR 678 (although it was held that a national law banning the publication of such material could be justified under Art 10(2)).   [24] *Jersild v Denmark* (1995) 19 EHRR 1, 28.
[25] On which, see Chapter 13, section 4.6.2, above.   [26] *Bowman v UK* (1998) 26 EHRR 1, [42].
[27] *Jacubowski v Germany*, judgment of 23 June 1994, Series A, No 291-A, [26].

the role of the media is central to several of the justifications for free speech considered above: the media provides a public forum in which exchanges may take place in the marketplace of ideas; it has the capacity to promote tolerance and acceptance by exposing people to different views, ideas, and lifestyles; and it can facilitate the sort of public discourse necessary in a well-functioning democracy. The latter point is underlined by the apparently pivotal role played by the first ever televised debates between the leaders of the three main parties during the 2010 general election campaign.

Second, however, the media is, as we all know, far from perfect. For reasons such as proprietorial influence and the commercial need to attract readers, journalism is often somewhat distant from the paradigm described above. For all of its potential to do things that are socially beneficial, the media—which, for this reason, has been dubbed 'Janus-faced'[28]—also has the capacity to cause immense harm. Of course, the media's freedom of speech—and thus its capacity to use that freedom destructively—is subject to the same restrictions as everyone else's. But it might be thought that the media should be subject to additional regulation in recognition of its peculiarly powerful position. That view certainly prevails in the UK, and is legitimised by Art 10(1) of the ECHR, which says that the right to freedom of expression 'shall not prevent States from requiring the licensing of broadcasting, television or cinema enterprises'. In the next section, we consider three forms of media regulation.

3.2 Regulation of the media

3.2.1 Licensing–the need for prior permission

The default position in English law is that people do not need permission to do things: they are free to do whatever is not prohibited by law. But there are exceptions: a car can lawfully be driven only with prior authorisation in the form of a licence. Similarly, while people generally do not need prior permission to express views or convey information, certain forms of media do, since they are subject to licensing requirements. Broadly speaking, such arrangements may take one of two forms. Cinemas are subject to a system of *content-based licensing*, meaning that they must obtain advance permission from the relevant licensing authority—the local council[29]—in respect of each film that they wish to show. In the light of its content, the licensing authority may refuse permission for the film to be screened, or make such permission conditional upon certain cuts. Meanwhile, although television and radio broadcasters do not require state approval of each programme that they air, they are subject to an *activity-based licensing* system in that television and radio programmes (whatever their content) may lawfully be transmitted only by broadcasters holding appropriate licences.[30]

---

[28] Fenwick and Phillipson, *Media Freedom under the Human Rights Act* (Oxford 2006), p 2.

[29] Under the Cinemas Act 1985, local authorities are responsible for matters of this nature, although in practice they generally follow the recommendations of the British Board of Film Classification.

[30] Broadcasting Acts 1990 and 1996.

Both forms of licensing are clearly capable of being used in ways that restrict free speech. For example, a government might deny licences to prospective broadcasters that it thinks would be likely to make programmes exposing failures in government policy. Content-based licensing, on the other hand, constitutes a more granular form of control, but one that can also evidently be used to limit free speech, whether for reasons that are self-serving (for example, to deny permission for the publication or distribution of politically embarrassing material), or altruistic, but arguably paternalistic (for example, by prohibiting the showing of material that is considered offensive). In English law, however, two safeguards exist that make at least political manipulation of the licensing systems less likely. First, the bodies responsible for granting licences are public authorities within the meaning of the HRA, and as such are required to act compatibly with Art 10 of the ECHR. Second, television and radio licensing is carried out by the media regulator Ofcom, which is not under direct ministerial control.

3.2.2 **Additional duties and restrictions**

Media regulation may also take the form of imposing upon certain forms of media duties and restrictions that go beyond those to which everyone is subject under the general law. Under English law, this extra layer of legal regulation applies to television and radio (but not to newspapers), and consists principally in the requirements laid down in the Broadcasting Code.[31] The Code is issued by the regulatory body Ofcom under statutory authority.[32] Among other things, it prohibits the broadcasting of material 'that might seriously impair the physical, mental or moral development of people under eighteen', permits material—such as that of a sexual or violent nature—that may cause offence to be broadcast only if 'justified by the context', and requires broadcasters to avoid 'unjust or unfair treatment of individuals or organisations in programmes' and 'any unwarranted infringement of privacy in programmes and in connection with obtaining material included in programmes'. The Code also requires that 'news, in whatever form, must be reported with due accuracy and presented with due impartiality'—meaning, *inter alia*, that broadcasters are not at liberty to favour one party political view over another.[33] Much of the Code applies to the BBC as well as to commercial broadcasters, and to the extent that it does not, the BBC is under separate obligations that are at least as onerous.[34] Ofcom is required to ensure that the licences that it grants place broadcasters under a condition requiring observance of the Code.[35] In the event of a breach, Ofcom can impose fines and require the

---

[31] *The Ofcom Broadcasting Code* (London 2009).

[32] Broadcasting Act 1996, s 107; Communications Act 2003, ss 319–26.

[33] Special requirements apply in relation to elections: see Chapter 4, section 2.2.7, above.

[34] The BBC operates under a royal charter granted via an exercise of the royal prerogative. While it is covered by certain parts of the Broadcasting Code, some of its obligations derive instead from a 'framework agreement' issued pursuant to the charter. The BBC Trust, rather than Ofcom, is responsible for regulating the BBC in areas in which the Broadcasting Code does not apply to it. This arrangement is controversial because the Trust is regarded by some as lacking sufficient independence to discharge its regulatory functions adequately. [35] Communications Act 2003, ss 325–6.

broadcasting of a correction or a statement of its findings. In very serious cases, it can revoke broadcasters' licences.[36]

The preamble to the Broadcasting Code underlines the importance of freedom of expression, and it is clear that the restrictions that the Code places on broadcasters closely relate to the grounds on which, according to Art 10(2) of the ECHR, free speech may legitimately be curtailed. Fenwick and Phillipson argue that the Code 'strikes a balance between offence avoidance and the right of adult television audiences to receive a diverse range of broadcast expression',[37] but warn that the drafting of the Code and the likely reluctance of the courts to interfere with Ofcom's decisions (given its status as an expert regulator)[38] leaves it with considerable 'leeway to take a range of approaches in terms of liberality and the preservation of creative freedom'.[39]

> **Q** In the *Gaunt* case,[40] a radio presenter harangued an interviewee, calling him a 'Nazi' and an 'ignorant pig'. Ofcom ruled that this breached the provisions of its Code concerning the avoidance of offence to members of the public. On judicial review, the Administrative Court held that Ofcom's ruling was compatible with Art 10, even though the subject matter of the interview related to a matter of public concern and therefore constituted a form of 'political speech'. Do you think the Court was right to reach this conclusion?

3.2.3 Self-regulation

A sharp distinction exists between the regulatory regime applicable to television and radio broadcasters and the position of newspapers (and other print media).[41] That difference can be partly accounted for by the fact that there is (at least for now) a technical limit on the number of television and radio stations that can broadcast, but not on the number of newspapers that may be published. But that is an inadequate explanation:[42] as we have seen, the regulatory regime applicable to broadcasters limits not only their number, but also, via the Code, the content of their programmes—so why not regulate the content of newspapers in the same way? Why, for example, are newspapers free to support one political party over another, while broadcasters must ensure that their output is scrupulously balanced?

The explanation is partly historical: while the market has traditionally ensured that there exists a plurality of newspapers advancing a diverse range of views, it is less than 60 years since the UK had only one television channel. In that environment, the need for regulation of television was obvious. But does regulation remain necessary now that the average home receives dozens of channels? Received wisdom would say that it is—because broadcast, and particularly visual, media are significantly different from print media. The power of television images may be greater than that of still photos

---

[36] This does not apply to the BBC or Channel 4.
[37] Fenwick and Phillipson, *Media Freedom under the Human Rights Act* (Oxford 2006), p 605.
[38] See Chapter 13, section 4.6.4, above on deference in the face of expertise.
[39] Fenwick and Phillipson, p 606.   [40] *Gaunt v Ofcom* [2010] EWHC 1756 (Admin).
[41] See generally Barendt, *Broadcasting Law* (Oxford 1993), pp 3–10.   [42] Barendt, p 4.

or text in newspapers, and people may have less choice over their encounters with them: the US Supreme Court has observed that the broadcast media is 'uniquely pervasive' and that 'offensive, indecent material presented over the airwaves confronts the citizen not only in public, but also in the privacy of the home'.[43] This might, in turn, suggest that some form of regulation is appropriate in order to safeguard the interests—the autonomy—of those who do not wish to consume certain forms of material.[44] Regulation need not, however, mean prohibition: Ofcom's Broadcasting Code rightly recognises that the interests of those who do not wish to be offended might, for example, be adequately catered for by requiring broadcasters to provide advance warning of potentially offensive content.

Although not subject to statutory regulation, the press has adopted a system of *self-regulation* under the auspices of the Press Complaints Commission (PCC). There are two major differences between this system and that which applies to broadcasters. First, it is non-statutory and *voluntary*. Broadcasters have no choice about whether to submit to Ofcom, but newspapers can only be regulated by the PCC if they agree to it, and the PCC cannot legally enforce its decisions. This point, in itself, should not be overstated: the vast majority of newspapers and magazines do agree to PCC regulation and abide by its rulings, fearful that if the system of self-regulation is seen not to be effective, a statutory regulator may be imposed upon them. Second, the PCC system is *not independent*: seven of the seventeen members of the PCC board are senior newspaper editors, the PCC is funded by the industry, and the industry has considerable influence over the standards to which the PCC holds it. As one newspaper executive has put it, a great strength of self-regulation, as he saw it, 'is that the [PCC] Code has been produced by the editors and they have signed up to it: so there is no real pressure upon editors to break it'.[45] But of course that might be because the Code has been drafted so as not to prevent editors from doing certain things that they really wish to do. For example, the PCC Code of Practice imposes no requirements concerning taste and decency—an omission that the PCC has defended by saying that it is better for market forces to be left to curb journalistic excesses than for the PCC to act as a 'moral arbiter'.[46]

In 2009, the House of Commons Select Committee on Culture, Media and Sport published a major report on, *inter alia*, press standards and regulation.[47] It strongly criticised the PCC's response to a major scandal in which journalists had intercepted public figures' voicemails, saying that the Commission's report was 'simplistic and surprising'.[48] The Committee proposed reform of the PCC, including changing its name to the Press Complaints and Standards Commission (to underline its role as

---

[43] *FCC v Pacifica Foundation* 438 US 726 (1978), 749.

[44] See Dworkin, *A Matter of Principle* (London 1985), ch 17.

[45] Culture, Media and Sport Select Committee, *Self-Regulation of the Press* (HC 375 2006–07), [56].

[46] Statement online at **http://www.pcc.org.uk** (accessed 3 August 2010).

[47] House of Commons Culture, Media and Sport Committee, *Press Standards, Privacy and Libel* (HC 362 2009–10).   [48] House of Commons Culture, Media and Sport Committee, HC 362, [472].

a regulator), increasing non-industry membership of the Board, reducing industry influence over the Code, and imposing stronger penalties in appropriate cases, including fines and even suspending publication of offending newspapers and magazines for one issue.[49] Nevertheless, the Committee concluded that it was not necessary to move to a system of independent, statutory regulation of the press, thereby implicitly endorsing the view expressed in one of its earlier reports that statutory regulation 'would represent a very dangerous interference with the freedom of the press', such regulation being 'a hallmark of authoritarianism [that] risks undermining democracy'.[50]

> **Q** Can a convincing case be made for distinguishing between the broadcast and print media so as to justify statutory regulation of the former, but only self-regulation of the latter? If statutory regulation of the press would risk undermining democracy, why is the same not true of the existing regime of statutory regulation of television and radio?

Finally, in relation to the press, we should note that a limited amount of statutory regulation does exist in one particular area—namely, ownership. The need for the accurate presentation of news and free expression of opinions in newspapers, together with the need for 'a sufficient plurality of views in newspapers', are considerations that must be taken into account by the competition authorities when determining whether a merger between two companies should be disallowed on public interest grounds.[51] This is intended to ensure that no single publisher is able to achieve a stranglehold of newspaper ownership—something that would jeopardise the expression of a wide range of views.

3.2.4 The Internet

The growth of the Internet poses particular challenges for media regulation because it blurs two traditional boundaries.[52] First, even if *the distinction between broadcast and print media* is thought to make sense from a regulatory perspective, the Internet places it under considerable pressure: many websites combine the written word with audio and video, and so cannot be neatly categorised. It might be thought that each type of material should be regulated in the relevant way: that audio and video should be subject to the same regulation as television and radio, and that text should be treated analogously to newspapers and magazines. However, at present, the applicable regulatory regime is principally determined not by the type of material, but by the nature of the publisher. Thus broadcasters' websites are regulated by Ofcom, whereas newspapers' websites are subject only to self-regulation via the PCC. It is not obvious that this makes sense. Why, for example, should a podcast published via a newspaper

---

[49] House of Commons Culture, Media and Sport Committee, HC 362, ch 6.

[50] House of Commons Culture, Media and Sport Committee, *Self-Regulation of the Press* (HC 375 2006–07), [54].   [51] Enterprise Act 2002, s 58(2A)–(2B).

[52] See generally Rowbottom, 'Media Freedom and Political Debate in the Digital Era' (2006) 69 MLR 489.

website (and therefore subject to PCC regulation) be treated differently from a radio broadcast or, for that matter, a podcast published via the BBC website (both of which would be subject to the stricter terms of the Broadcasting Code[53])?

Second, the Internet calls into question *the distinction between media organisations and others.* As we noted at the beginning of this section, the particular influence wielded by the media is the standard justification for regulation. Yet in the age of the Internet, others can wield comparable influence. Anyone with Internet access can disseminate his views via websites and blogs—and, as Rowbottom notes: 'The "star" blogger that reaches a wide audience begins to blur with some characteristics of the established media.'[54] Meanwhile, websites such as Google might be thought today to be at least as influential as the broadcast media. These developments highlight dilemmas with which lawmakers will be increasingly confronted as the influence of new media eclipses that of the old. For now, though, the old dividing lines remain—at least as far as the regulatory system is concerned.

3.3 Contempt of court

3.3.1 Introduction

All media—broadcast and print—are subject to the law concerning *contempt of court,* a term that covers several distinct criminal offences that are committed by interfering in some way with judicial proceedings.[55] A person commits *civil contempt*—something on which we need not dwell here—by disregarding a court order, such as an injunction. In spite of the name, it is a criminal—indeed, an imprisonable—offence. *Criminal contempt* takes a number of different forms; here, we are concerned with three that bring into play the tension between the right to freedom of expression and other important rights and interests.

3.3.2 Scandalising the court

The offence known as *scandalising the court* is committed by publishing 'a scurrilous attack on the judiciary as a whole'—or on a particular judge—'which is calculated to undermine the authority of the courts and public confidence in the administration of justice'.[56] The publication must cause at least a real risk that public confidence will be undermined,[57] but the defendant need not have intended the publication to undermine confidence.[58] Of course, this involves a restriction of free speech—but one that is imposed for the purpose of 'maintaining the authority and impartiality of the judiciary', a legitimate purpose under Art 10(2) of the ECHR. That is not, of course, dispositive of the compatibility of the offence with Art 10; it must only generate liability

---

[53] Or equivalent provisions in the BBC framework agreement: cf n 34 above.
[54] Rowbottom at 503.
[55] See generally Eady and Smith, *Arlidge, Eady and Smith on Contempt* (London 2005).
[56] *Chokolingo v Attorney-General of Trinidad and Tobago* [1981] 1 WLR 106, 111, *per* Lord Diplock.
[57] *Ahnee v Director of Public Prosecutions* [1999] 2 AC 294, 306.   [58] *Ahnee* at 307.

when that is *necessary* for upholding judicial authority, and the restriction of free speech must be *proportionate* to that objective. But, in practice, the scope of potential liability for this species of contempt is limited. While imputing improper motives to judges and engaging in gratuitous verbal abuse—for example, calling a judge an 'impudent little man' who is 'a microcosm of conceit and empty-headedness'[59]—may attract liability, the courts have been careful to emphasise that reasoned criticism of judicial decisions will not.[60]

3.3.3 Prejudicial publications

According to Art 6 of the ECHR, everyone is entitled to a fair hearing whenever their civil rights and obligations or any criminal charge against them is being determined. The provision of a fair trial might, however, be made impossible, or at least substantially more difficult, if there is public discussion of the case—especially if such discussion is widely disseminated via the media. This issue arises in particular in relation to criminal trials involving a jury: while judges are trained to take into account only evidence that is relevant and admissible in the court proceedings, members of the public—of which juries are composed—are not. If information, speculation, or allegations that would be inadmissible in the trial comes to jurors' attention via the media, then there is a risk that they may be influenced by it and, hence, there is a risk of a miscarriage of justice. More generally, it has been noted that if the media were permitted to conduct 'pseudo-trials', this might have the effect of reducing public 'acceptance of the courts as the proper forum for the settlement of legal disputes'.[61] There is, then, a need to strike a balance between the rights to free speech and to a fair trial.

In 1979, the ECtHR held, in *Sunday Times v UK*,[62] that English law did not strike that balance acceptably. The House of Lords had upheld an injunction that had been granted to prevent the publication of a newspaper article on the ground that publication would have constituted contempt of court. The article concerned the drug thalidomide, which had been given to pregnant women and had caused birth defects. It was one of several articles intended to encourage the manufacturer—against which the victims had begun legal proceedings that had not yet reached trial—to agree to a generous out-of-court settlement. The ECtHR held that the injunction breached the right to free speech, and in doing so indicated that English law in this area was highly problematic. Whereas some of the Law Lords had formulated 'an absolute rule…to the effect that it was not permissible to prejudge issues in pending cases', Art 10 permitted interference with free speech only if it is 'necessary having regard to the facts and circumstances prevailing in the specific case'.[63] Bearing in mind, *inter alia*, the public importance of the matter in the *Sunday Times* case and the fact that a trial was

---

[59] *R v Gray* [1900] 2 QB 36; cf Miller, *Contempt of Court* (Oxford 2000), p 572.

[60] See, eg *R v Commissioner of Police of the Metropolis, ex p Blackburn (No 2)* [1968] 2 QB 150, 155, *per* Lord Denning MR. [61] *Sunday Times v UK* (1979–80) 2 EHRR 245, 278–9.

[62] (1979–80) 2 EHRR 245. [63] *Sunday Times v UK* at 280–1.

unlikely to take place in the short to medium term, the ECtHR held that the injunction was not 'necessary'.

In the wake of that judgment, the Contempt of Court Act 1981 was enacted in an attempt to recast English law in terms consistent with the Convention. In one sense, liability can arise under the Act *more* easily than under the common law offence that was at stake in the *Sunday Times* case: liability under the Act is strict, meaning that, unlike at common law, no intention to cause prejudice need be established.[64] (For this reason, the rule established by the Act is known as the 'strict liability rule'.) However, the Act contains a number of features that seek to safeguard free speech by ensuring that liability does not exceed that which is permitted by Art 10.

First, it imposes a *double hurdle* before there can be liability: the risk that the course of justice will be prejudiced must be 'substantial'—meaning 'not remote',[65] 'not insubstantial', or 'not minimal'[66]—and even if it is, liability will only arise if that risk is of 'serious' prejudice.[67] It follows that neither a remote chance of serious prejudice nor a strong chance of minor prejudice will do: there must be a *substantial* risk of *serious* prejudice. In *MGN v Attorney-General*,[68] the High Court said that the following questions should be considered when determining whether such a risk arises:

1. *How likely is it that the publication will come to the attention of a potential juror?* This will depend on such factors as the prominence and popularity of the publication, and on whether it is sold in the geographical area from which jurors are likely to be drawn.

2. *What would be the impact of the article on the average reader?* The more interesting the issue and the more sensational its presentation, the greater the likely impact.

3. *Crucially, what is likely to be the residual impact on a juror[69] at the time of the trial?* The more memorable the article, the more likely a juror is to be influenced by it—but this must be balanced against

    (i) the fact that the longer the gap between publication and trial, the more likely are memories to fade;

    (ii) the 'focusing effect' of the trial itself—of 'listening over a prolonged period to evidence in a case'; and

    (iii) the likely effect of the judge's directions (for example, telling the jury to disregard certain things they might have seen in the press).

---

[64] Contempt of Court Act 1981, s 1.

[65] *Attorney-General v English* [1983] 1 AC 116, 142, *per* Lord Diplock.

[66] *Attorney-General v News Group Newspapers plc* [1987] QB 1, 15.

[67] Contempt of Court Act 1981, s 2(2). Prior to the 1981 Act, it appears that a serious risk of *any* prejudice would be sufficient: see Eady and Smith, *Arlidge, Eady and Smith on Contempt* (London 2005), p 254.

[68] [1997] EMLR 284, 290–1.

[69] If the case is to be heard only by a judge, the double hurdle is unlikely to be cleared, given that judges are trained to disregard irrelevant information.

To this list of factors must be added the *content* of the information in the publication. If the material merely rehearses matter that is aired at the trial, it is hard to see how a juror might be prejudiced.[70] But some sorts of information plainly do have the capacity to prejudice jurors. This is true of information that is adverse to the defendant that would not be admissible at trial (for example, it is often impermissible to tell the jury about the defendant's previous convictions for fear that this might predispose them against him) and of comment (for example, an impressionable juror might be swayed by an opinion piece in a newspaper saying that the evidence clearly establishes the defendant's guilt and that no sensible juror could think otherwise).

Second, the strict liability rule only applies in relation to *legal proceedings that are 'active' at the time of publication*.[71] Criminal proceedings do not become active until one of certain 'initial steps' is taken, such as arrest or the issue of an arrest warrant, and cease to be active when the proceedings are concluded (most typically, when the defendant is acquitted or sentenced).[72] These rules are highly significant for two reasons. They create a *relatively narrow window* within which the strict liability rule operates: this helps to ensure that they represent a restriction on free speech that goes no further than is necessary. And the rules are *very clear*: this is important because it ensures that media organisations know where they stand and avoids a 'chilling effect' on free speech whereby uncertainty leads publishers to exercise greater self-restraint than is legally necessary. Even if proceedings are active, the accused will have a defence if he can show that, having taken all reasonable care, he did not know and had no reason to suspect that that was so.[73]

Third, s 5 of the Act says that when a publication constitutes 'a *discussion in good faith of public affairs or other matters of general public interest*', it is not to be treated as engaging the strict liability rule provided that 'the risk of impediment or prejudice to particular legal proceedings is merely incidental to the discussion'. Section 5 aims to ensure that responsible discussion of important matters is not precluded merely because legal proceedings that touch on the same issues are active, even if it causes a substantial risk of serious prejudice. It echoes one of the objections raised by the ECtHR to the injunction granted in the *Sunday Times* case—that matters do 'not cease to be a matter of public interest merely because they [form] the background to pending litigation'.[74] Section 5 was successfully invoked by the defendant in *Attorney-General v English*[75] who had published an article alleging, in condemnatory terms, that a practice had developed whereby doctors allowed or caused severely disabled newborn babies to die. Although the impetus for the article was the candidature in a by-election of a

---

[70] And, in any event, s 4(1) of the 1981 Act specifically says that, subject to certain limited exceptions, no liability will arise in relation to 'a fair and accurate report of legal proceedings held in public, published contemporaneously and in good faith'.

[71] Contempt of Court Act 1981, s 2(3).

[72] Contempt of Court Act 1981, Sch 1, paras 4–5. Different rules apply in relation to civil proceedings (see paras 12–14) and appellate proceedings (see paras 15–16).   [73] Contempt of Court Act 1981, s 3.

[74] *Sunday Times v UK* (1979–80) 2 EHRR 245, 280–2.   [75] [1983] 1 AC 116.

disabled person campaigning against that alleged practice, its publication coincided with the trial of a doctor who was said to have done that which the article condemned. Concluding that s 5 applied, the House Lords said that the test was whether the risk of prejudice that the article created was 'no more than an incidental consequence of expounding its main theme'. The Law Lords rejected the suggestion that s 5 allowed the newspaper to go no further than abstract discussion of the morality of the alleged practice: read in such a way, s 5 would inadequately safeguard free speech because it would limit the media to discussing hypothetical questions, resulting in articles 'devoid of any general public interest'.[76]

Having set out the main points concerning the strict liability rule under the 1981 Act, we conclude with three further observations about the law in this area.

The first is that *the strict liability rule is not exhaustive of the circumstances in which liability may arise* for publications that risk prejudicing legal proceedings. The effect of s 6(c) is that it remains an offence at common law to engage in conduct that is *intended* to impede or prejudice the administration of justice. This offence is, in one sense, wider than that created by the Act because there can be liability at common law when proceedings are 'pending or imminent' even if they are not 'active' within the meaning of the legislation.[77] However, the fact that the common law offence can be committed only if there is intention means that it is, in practice, a much narrower offence than the statutory offence.

Second, a substantial risk of serious prejudice—and thus liability—is much less likely in relation to *proceedings, such as appellate and most civil cases, not involving juries*. As Lord Parker CJ explained, although 'in no sense superhuman', a judge has 'by his training no difficulty in putting out of his mind matters which are not evidence in the case'.[78]

Third, we return to our original question: *whether English law now strikes the right balance been free speech and fair trials*. We saw that, in the *Sunday Times* case, the ECtHR held that English law gave too much weight to the latter and unduly restricted the former. Today, it is said by some that the pendulum has swung too far in the other direction: that the emphasis placed on media freedom is too great, such that it is difficult in some cases for a fair trial to be provided. Eady and Smith comment that 'trials have had to be abandoned, or convictions quashed, as a result of media coverage', but 'without necessarily any corresponding remedy or resort by means of the contempt jurisdiction against those responsible'.[79] Having said that, it does not automatically follow that a trial cannot go ahead just because there has been a publication creating a substantial risk of serious prejudice: remedial steps, such as relocating the trial (if media coverage has been limited to a particular geographical area) or delaying it

---

[76] *Attorney-General v English* at 143.
[77] *Attorney-General v News Group Newspapers plc* [1989] QB 110, 130, *per* Watkins LJ.
[78] *R v Duffy, ex p Nash* [1960] 2 QB 188, 198.
[79] Eady and Smith, *Arlidge, Eady and Smith on Contempt* (London 2005), p 89.

(to allow memories to fade), may be taken—although this may involve great cost and inconvenience.

3.3.4 Contempt in the face of the court

A number of forms of conduct, collectively referred to as *contempt in the face of the court*, constitute criminal contempt. Many of these do not have significant implications for freedom of speech and are therefore beyond the scope of this chapter. For example, although disturbing court proceedings—for example, by shouting slogans or singing songs[80]—can amount to criminal contempt, this represents a very modest restriction upon freedom of expression, and one for which there is an obviously sound justification.

Of greater interest to us is that a witness's refusal to answer a question can constitute contempt in the face of the court.[81] This has important free speech implications when the witness is a journalist being asked to reveal his sources. According to the ECtHR, Art 10 safeguards the media's 'vital role of "public watchdog"' by enabling it to impart 'information and ideas on matters of public interest' and by giving the public 'a right to receive them'.[82] But that process depends on a flow of information to journalists—and via them to the wider public—that risks drying up if sources cannot be sure that their identities will remain confidential.[83] Free speech therefore favours allowing journalists to refuse to name their sources. Section 10 of the Contempt of Court Act 1981 addresses this issue by stipulating that no offence is committed by a journalist who refuses to disclose his sources unless the court is satisfied 'that disclosure is necessary in the interests of justice or national security or for the prevention of disorder or crime'. This language largely mirrors that of Art 10—but in a series of cases, the courts applied s 10 in a way that appeared to place little weight on the interest in preserving sources' confidentiality.[84]

Palmer suggests that this might be because the 'harm to the public interest caused by a loss of free flow of information', although significant, 'cannot by definition be quantified',[85] whereas the competing interests served by disclosure may be more readily apparent. For example, the House of Lords held in *Morgan Grampian*[86] that a journalist should be required to identify his source in order that a company could identify the disloyal employee who had leaked sensitive and commercially damaging information. It was held that this would fall within the 'interests of justice'

---

[80] As in *Morris v Crown Office* [1970] 2 QB 114.

[81] See, eg *Attorney-General v Mulholland* [1963] 2 QB 477.

[82] *Sunday Times v UK (No 2)* (1992) 14 EHRR 229, [50]. This point was reiterated by the Grand Chamber of the ECtHR in *Sanoma Uitgevers BV v Netherlands* (2010) 51 EHRR 31.

[83] *Goodwin v UK* (1996) 22 EHRR 123, [39].

[84] See, eg *Secretary of State for Defence v Guardian Newspapers Ltd* [1985] AC 339; *X Ltd v Morgan Grampian (Publishers) Ltd* [1991] 1 AC 1; *Re an Inquiry under the Companies Securities (Insider Dealing) Act 1985* [1988] AC 660.

[85] 'Protecting Journalists' Sources: Section 10, Contempt of Court Act 1981' [1992] PL 61, 71.

[86] *X Ltd v Morgan Grampian (Publishers) Ltd* [1991] 1 AC 1.

exception under s 10, which, it was said, applied whenever the disclosure of sources was necessary to allow someone 'to exercise important legal rights and to protect themselves from serious legal wrongs whether or not resort to legal proceedings in a court of law will be necessary to attain these objectives'.[87] But the ECtHR later ruled in *Goodwin* that ordering disclosure in such circumstances constituted a breach of the Convention.[88] The House of Lords had, in effect, attached too much weight to the company's interests and, relatively speaking, too little to the competing interests served by maintaining sources' confidentiality. In subsequent cases, English courts have placed somewhat greater emphasis on the need to interpret s 10 pursuant to Art 10 and on the 'chilling effect' that orders for disclosure can have on press freedom.[89] For example, a disclosure order was refused in a case in which less draconian steps—such as the holding of an internal inquiry—had not been taken by a party wishing to identify the source of a leak, the 'necessity' of a court order not having been established in such circumstances.[90]

4. Defamation

4.1 Introduction

'Defamation' is the term used to describe two distinct, but closely related, legal wrongs—libel and slander—that can be committed by saying certain things that would tend to damage someone's reputation. There are some important differences between libel and slander—for example, the former concerns statements made in permanent form,[91] while the latter concerns oral statements—but it is sufficient for the purposes of this book to consider defamation generally, rather than libel and slander separately.[92] Our focus will be on whether English law appropriately strikes the balance called for by Art 10 between free speech and the protection of 'the reputation or rights of others'.

4.2 Ingredients of liability

The extent of the inroads made by the law of defamation into freedom of expression depends on the answers to two questions: when does something *prima facie* constitute defamation? And what defences are there to defamation claims? As to the former,

---

[87] *Morgan Grampian* at 43.

[88] *Goodwin v UK* (1996) 22 EHRR 123.

[89] *Ashworth Hospital Authority v MGN Ltd* [2002] UKHL 29, [2002] 1 WLR 2033.

[90] *John v Express Newspapers* [2000] 1 WLR 1931.

[91] For example, in writing. Libel also covers radio and television broadcasts: Broadcasting Act 1990, s 166.

[92] For more detailed discussion of defamation, see Deakin, Johnston, and Markesinis, *Markesinis and Deakin's Tort Law* (Oxford 2008), ch 21; Price and Duoddu, *Defamation: Law, Procedure and Practice* (London 2004).

there are three principal requirements. First, the statement must *refer to the claimant*, either explicitly or (judged on the basis of the inferences that an ordinary sensible person would draw from what has been said) implicitly.[93] Second, the statement must be *published*—that is, it must be issued to someone other than the claimant[94] or the defendant's spouse.[95] Third, the statement must be *defamatory*, meaning that it must be one that would tend to 'injure the reputation' of the claimant 'by exposing him to hatred, contempt or ridicule' or 'lower [him] in the estimation of right-thinking members of society'.[96] Recently, Tugendhat J suggested that the latter phrase, which has come to form the dominant test, is based on a misreading of the case in which it was originally advanced and makes it too easy to establish that a statement is defamatory. Tugendhat J instead proposed that the test should be whether the publication 'substantially affects in an adverse manner the attitude of other people towards [the claimant], or has a tendency so to do'.[97]

Allegations that someone has committed a criminal offence or has otherwise acted dishonestly or immorally will, in the normal course of things, be regarded as defamatory, but not all cases are as straightforward. Much depends on the views and attitudes that courts ascribe to 'right-thinking' or 'other' people—the obvious difficulty being that not everyone thinks the same way. For example, in *Byrne v Dean*,[98] the defendant published a poem indicating that the claimant had complained to the police about the unlawful presence of gambling machines on the premises of a club of which the claimant was a member. The claimant took exception, fearing that other members of the club, if they were to believe the allegation, would shun him, thinking him disloyal. The court, however, held that the statement was not capable of being defamatory—a conclusion to which it was led by considering the likely reaction of people generally (who would think it right to report illegal activity) rather than that subset of people (that is, club members) about whose views the claimant was concerned.

4.3 **Defences**

There are several possible defences to a defamation claim. The following have the effect of substantially reducing the inroads into freedom of expression that the law of defamation would otherwise make.

---

[93] *Morgan v Odhams Press Ltd* [1971] 1 WLR 1239.
[94] *Pullman v Walter Hill and Co Ltd* [1891] 1 QB 524, 527, *per* Lord Esher MR.
[95] *Wennhak v Morgan* (1888) LR 20 QBD 635.
[96] *Sim v Stretch* [1936] 2 All ER 1237, 1240, *per* Lord Atkin.
[97] *Thornton v Telegraph Media Group Ltd* [2010] EWHC 1414 (QB), [95], relying on Neill LJ in *Berkoff v Burchill* [1996] 4 All ER 1008, 1018.   [98] [1937] 1 KB 818.

4.3.1 **Truth**

Although the claimant does not have to establish the falsity of the statement complained of, proving the truth of the statement is a defence; for the defence to succeed, only the substantial truth of the 'sting', or thrust, of the allegation need be established.[99] It is obviously right, from a freedom of speech perspective, that it should not be unlawful to make true statements just because they are defamatory. If that were the case, it would, for example, be unlawful to accuse someone of being corrupt or dishonest—because such an allegation would lower right-thinking people's estimation of them—even if such an allegation were true. But should the burden lie with the claimant to establish that the statement is untrue, or is it preferable, as English law does, to place the burden of proving truth on the defendant? The difficulty with the latter approach is that it is likely to have a chilling effect on freedom of expression—as Lord Keith explained in *Derbyshire County Council v Times Newspapers Ltd*: 'Quite often the facts which would justify a defamatory publication are known to be true, but admissible evidence capable of proving those facts is not available. This may prevent the publication of matters which it is very desirable to make public.'[100]

> **Q** Would it be better to require the claimant to establish the falsity of the statement, or would this inadequately protect claimants' ability to safeguard their reputations?

4.3.2 **Comment**

Whereas truth is a defence in relation to allegations of *fact*, it is a defence to establish that a *comment* was an honest one made on a matter of public interest. This defence plays a very important part in ensuring that defamation law does not unduly restrict the sort of legitimate public debate that is highly prized in any free society and which lies close to the core of the sorts of speech protected by the right of freedom of expression.[101]

A number of requirements must be met if the defence is to be successfully pleaded.[102] First, the utterance in question must be a *comment* rather than a statement of fact. It has been said that what marks out comment is that it 'can reasonably be inferred to be a deduction, inference, conclusion, criticism, remark, observation, etc'.[103] This means that whether something is regarded as a comment or an allegation of fact may turn, in part, on how much information is given: 'To say that a man's conduct was dishonourable is not comment, it is a statement of fact. To say that he did certain specific things and that his conduct was dishonourable is a statement of fact coupled with a

---

[99] *Edwards v Bell* (1824) 1 Bing 403, 409, *per* Burrough J.

[100] [1993] AC 534, 548. For further discussion of this point, see House of Commons Culture, Media and Sport Committee, *Press Standards, Privacy and Libel* (HC 362 2009–10), [130]–[136]; English PEN/Index on Censorship, *Free Speech is Not for Sale* (London 2009).

[101] See, eg *Lingens v Austria* (1986) 8 EHRR 407, [42].

[102] These are usefully summarised in *Joseph v Spiller* [2010] UKSC 53, [2010] 3 WLR 1791, [83], *per* Lord Phillips.

[103] *Branson v Bower (No 2)* [2002] QB 737, [12], approving a dictum of Cussen J in *Clarke v Norton* [1910] VLR 494, 499.

comment.'[104] However, as Lord Phillips observed in *Joseph v Spiller*, this example is problematic, since a bald assertion of dishonourable conduct is not really a 'simple statement of fact'; rather, it is 'a comment coupled with an allegation of unspecified conduct upon which the comment is based'.[105] The key issue, then, is the amount of information that must accompany a statement if it is to be capable of being character- ised as a comment. It used to be said that there had to be an indication of sufficient facts to allow others to judge how well-founded the allegation was.[106] However, in *Joseph v Spiller*, the Supreme Court held that it is enough if the statement explicitly or implicitly indicates, in general terms, the facts on which it is based.

Second, those facts on which the comment is based must be *true* (or protected by privilege).[107]

Third, the comment must be on a matter of *public interest*—that is, something in which the public has a *legitimate* interest (for example, whether a government Minister has lied), rather than simply something in which people are interested (for example, celebrities' private lives).[108]

Fourth, it used to be said that the comment had to be a fair or reasonable one, but Eady J said in *Branson v Bower (No 2)*[109] that setting the threshold this high would have a 'chilling effect' on free speech, bearing in mind that the purpose of the defence 'is to allow citizens to express hard-hitting opinions on matters of public interest honestly without fear of being brought before the courts'. The better view now is that the com- ment must simply be 'one which could have been made by an *honest* person, however prejudiced he might be, and however exaggerated or obstinate his views'.[110]

Finally, the defence will fail if the claimant can show the defendant acted with '*malice*', meaning, in this context, that he did not actually hold the view that he expressed.[111]

4.3.3 Privilege

In situations attracting the defence of 'privilege', no legal wrong is committed by a person who makes a statement that would otherwise constitute unlawful defamation, whether or not any other defence is available. So, on privileged occasions, statements that cannot be shown to be true and comments not concerning matters of public interest are nevertheless not unlawful. The thinking behind this is that there are certain circumstances in which the public interest in free speech is so strong that the prospect of legal action for defamation—and, importantly, the likely chilling effect of that prospect—should be removed.

---

[104] *Myerson v Smith's Weekly* (1923) 24 SR (NSW) 20, 26, *per* Ferguson J. See also *Kemsley v Foot* [1952] AC 345, 356, *per* Lord Porter.   [105] Joseph v Spiller, [5].

[106] *Cheng v Tse Wai Chun* [2000] HKCFA 35, [2000] 3 HKLRD 418, [19], *per* Lord Nicholls.

[107] *London Artists Ltd v Littler Grade Organisation* [1969] 2 QB 375, 395. (Privilege is explained in sec- tion 4.3.3 below.)   [108] *London Artists* at 391.

[109] [2002] QB 737, [23]–[24].

[110] *Cheng v Tse Wai Chun*, [20]. This statement forms part of a passage that was subsequently endorsed in *Joseph v Spiller*, albeit that Lord Phillips described this requirement as an 'elusive' one.

[111] *Branson v Bower (No 2)* at [7].

In a number of circumstances, privilege is *absolute*, meaning that free speech is entirely unhindered by the law of defamation. These include statements made (for example, by judges or witnesses) in, or in relation to, proceedings before courts or tribunals;[112] fair and accurate contemporaneous reports of court proceedings;[113] and communications between government Ministers and between certain other office-holders (for example, military officers).[114] Statements made in,[115] and papers published by order of, Parliament[116] also attract absolute privilege. When prosecutions were brought in relation to alleged abuse of the parliamentary expenses system, the defendants argued that their expenses claims were covered by parliamentary privilege, thus immunising them against criminal proceedings. The Supreme Court rejected that argument. It held that the purpose of parliamentary privilege is to protect 'freedom of speech and debate in the Houses of Parliament', and that scrutiny in the courts of expenses claims would not inhibit 'any of the varied activities in which Members of Parliament indulge that bear in one way or another on their parliamentary duties'. The only thing that it would inhibit was 'the making of dishonest claims'.[117]

> **Q** Is it acceptable that some statements are wholly beyond the reach of the law of defamation? Does this give too *much* weight to free speech (and too little to the ability of people to protect their reputations)?

In certain other circumstances, privilege is *qualified*. Qualified privilege arises on 'an occasion where the person who makes a communication has an interest or a duty, legal, social, or moral, to make it to the person to whom it is made, and the person to whom it is so made has a corresponding interest or duty to receive it'.[118] Thus, for example, qualified privilege will arise when a company director alleges to the chairman that an employee was acting improperly (both have an interest in protecting the company)[119] and when a member of the public alleges to the police that someone has committed a criminal offence.[120] The difference between absolute and qualified privilege is that the latter defence (unlike the former) will fail if the claimant can show that the defendant acted maliciously—meaning, in this context, that the defendant makes a statement out of spite or in order to harm the claimant[121] or without a 'positive belief in its truth'.[122]

---

[112] See, eg *Royal Aquarium and Summer and Winter Garden Society Ltd v Parkinson* [1892] 1 QB 431.
[113] Defamation Act 1996, s 14.   [114] *Merricks v Nott-Bower* [1965] 1 QB 57, 68.
[115] Bill of Rights 1688, art 9.   [116] Parliamentary Papers Act 1840, s 1.
[117] *R v Chaytor* [2010] UKSC 52, [2010] 3 WLR 1707, [47]–[48], *per* Lord Phillips.
[118] *Adam v Ward* [1917] AC 309, 334, *per* Lord Atkinson.   [119] *Watt v Longsdon* [1930] 1 KB 130.
[120] *Reynolds v Times Newspapers Ltd* [2001] 2 AC 127, 194.
[121] *Cheng v Tse Wai Chun* [2000] HKCFA 35, [2000] 3 HKLRD 418, [55].
[122] *Reynolds* at 201, *per* Lord Nicholls.

For our purposes, a particularly important question is whether the media can use the defence of qualified privilege.[123] The reciprocal duty/interest requirements mean that the defence is not obviously well suited to situations in which statements are made to the world at large via newspapers, broadcasts, and so on. As a result, in *Sullivan v The New York Times*,[124] the US Supreme Court held that criticism of public officials (including elected politicians) in relation to their public conduct attracted qualified privilege as a category. This is a clearer test than the duty/interest one, thus helping to ensure that 'would-be critics of official conduct' are not 'deterred from voicing their criticism, even though it is believed to be true and even though it is, in fact, true, because of doubt whether it can be proved in court or fear of the expense of having to do so'.[125]

English courts have declined to adopt this approach: no categories of information have been marked out at common law as automatically attracting qualified privilege. But while the duty/interest test remains, it was significantly adapted in relation to media publications in *Reynolds v Times Newspapers Ltd*,[126] in which the Irish Prime Minister sued over an allegation in the *Sunday Times* that he had misled the Irish Parliament. The decision was noteworthy for the importance attached to media freedom. In his leading speech, Lord Nicholls noted the 'chilling effect' of the law of defamation, argued that '[a]t times people must be able to speak and write freely, uninhibited by the prospect of being sued for damages should they be mistaken or misinformed', and concluded that '[i]n the wider public interest, protection of reputation must then give way to a higher priority'.[127] But he said that the *Sullivan* test struck the wrong balance between protecting free speech and reputation: it gave the press too much latitude and encouraged irresponsible journalism. *Reynolds* therefore set out a defence, based on the established doctrine of qualified privilege, of 'responsible journalism'.

Under this approach, qualified privilege is likely to attach to a newspaper article on a matter of public interest provided that the decision to publish was a responsible one in all of the circumstances, irrespective of whether the information actually turns out to be true. Factors relevant to the assessment of responsibility include whether steps were taken to verify the information, whether comment was sought from the claimant, whether the article contained the gist of the claimant's side of the story, and whether the allegations are presented appropriately (for example, a responsible journalist would present in more circumspect terms allegations of the veracity of which he was less confident).[128] These requirements apply because (as it was put in a later case) 'there is no duty to publish and the public have no interest to read material which the publisher has not taken reasonable steps to verify'.[129] However, the precise extent to which it is neces-

---

123 See generally Loveland, *Political Libels* (Oxford 2000).

124 (1964) 376 US 254.

125 *Sullivan* at 279, *per* Brennan CJ.   126 [2001] 2 AC 127.

127 *Reynolds* at 192–3.   128 *Reynolds* at 205.

129 *Jameel v Wall Street Journal Europe Sprl* [2006] UKHL 44, [2007] 1 AC 359, [32], *per* Lord Bingham. Some judges, however, have said that the *Reynolds* defence is better thought of simply as a defence of responsible journalism that is conceptually distinct from qualified privilege. See, eg Lord Hofffmann in *Jameel* at [46].

sary to take such steps will depend on factors such as the seriousness of the allegations, and the importance and urgency of the story. Applying these criteria, the House of Lords upheld the Court of Appeal's decision that the *Sunday Times* story did *not* attract qualified privilege. The UK edition of the paper had omitted any mention of the claimant's 'considered explanation' of the allegations, the seriousness of which meant that the newspaper had fallen short of the required standard of responsible journalism.

> **Q** In *Reynolds*, the newspaper argued that failing to adopt a *Sullivan*-style rule would create uncertainty and would give courts 'an undesirable and invidious role as a censor'. Do you agree? Should the House of Lords have struck the balance between free speech and protection of reputation differently?

The House of Lords had cause to revisit the *Reynolds* defence in *Jameel*.[130] That case concerned an allegation published in a newspaper that the claimant's bank accounts were being monitored to prevent them from being used to channel funds to terrorists. The lower courts had held that no privilege attached to the article because, by publishing before contact had been successfully made with the claimant, the journalist had failed fully to comply with one of the factors said by Lord Nicholls in *Reynolds* to be relevant to assessing whether the standard of 'responsible journalism had been met'. But, said the House of Lords in *Jameel*, those factors 'are not tests which the publication has to pass'; rather, they are simply guidelines to be referred to in arrival at a rounded judgment about whether, in the circumstances, the journalist acted responsibly.[131] In the circumstances of the instant case—bearing in mind the importance of the matter and the fact that the claimant would, in any event, have been unaware if his accounts were monitored and would therefore have had little meaningful to say by way of response—it was held that privilege attached to the article notwithstanding the failure to speak to the claimant before publication.

Publication in 'old' forms of media, such as the printed versions of newspapers, is a one-off event: once the presses have rolled, the content of the newspaper cannot be changed (although it is, of course, possible to publish corrections in subsequent issues). In contrast, publication on the Internet is an ongoing affair in the sense that an article making what turn out to be unfounded allegations can be removed from the website concerned. It is therefore the case that even if the original publication of an article benefits from *Reynolds* qualified privilege, such privilege may be lost if a defamatory article remains on a website once it becomes apparent that the allegations in it are unfounded,[132] unless an appropriate warning is attached to it.[133]

Finally, it is worth noting that although, as we explained above, the defence of qualified privilege can be defeated by proof of malice on the part of the defendant, it is

---

[130] [2006] UKHL 44, [2007] 1 AC 359.　　[131] *Jameel* at [56], *per* Lord Hoffmann.

[132] *Flood v Times Newspapers Ltd* [2009] EWHC 2375 (QB) (upheld on this point by the Court of Appeal: [2010] EWCA Civ 804).

[133] *Loutchansky v Times Newspapers Ltd (No 2)* [2001] EWCA Civ 1805, [2002] QB 783.

unlikely that this proviso has any meaningful role to play in relation to the *Reynolds* defence: it is hard to see how someone might act both as a responsible journalist *and* with malice.[134]

4.4 **Reform**

There is anxiety in some quarters that English defamation law strikes the balance between reputation and free speech too far in favour of the former.[135] As a result, the government has signalled its intention to publish a draft Defamation Bill in 2011. That Bill may draw upon the following recommendations made by a Ministry of Justice working group prior to the 2010 election.[136] First, the working group suggested that the defence developed in *Reynolds* and *Jameel* should be placed on a statutory footing in order to clarify the law, and so reduce the chilling effect arguably caused at present by uncertainty about the scope of the defence. Second, the working group addressed the 'repeat publication rule',[137] which means, *inter alia*, that every time a webpage containing a defamatory statement is accessed, a fresh publication occurs.[138] This, in turn, means that a defamation claim may be brought many years after the original publication, thereby circumventing the normal one-year limitation period applicable to such claims. The ECtHR has held that this may breach Art 10.[139] Against this background, the working group proposed the introduction of a single publication rule that would remove the possibility of liability in respect of multiple publications of the same defamatory statement.

5. **Criminal offences**

There are several provisions in English law making it a criminal offence to say certain things. Criminalisation represents a particularly severe curb on free speech, and it is necessary to consider carefully whether such offences strike an acceptable balance between the policy interests that they exist to promote and freedom of expression.

---

[134] *Jameel* at [46], *per* Lord Hoffmann.

[135] See, eg English PEN/Index on Censorship, *Free Speech is Not for Sale* (London 2009); House of Commons Culture, Media and Sport Committee, *Press Standards, Privacy and Libel* (HC 362 2009–10). The need for reform was also acknowledged in *Joseph v Spiller* [2010] UKSC 53, [2010] 3 WLR 1791, [106]–[117]. However, free speech concerns cannot be accorded automatic priority, given that protection of reputation falls within the scope of the Art 8 right to respect for private life: *Pfeifer v Austria* (2009) 48 EHRR 8.

[136] Ministry of Justice, *Report of the Libel Working Group* (London 2010).

[137] *Duke of Brunswick v Harmer* (1849) 14 QB 185.

[138] *Loutchansky v Times Newspapers Ltd (No 2)* [2001] EWCA Civ 1805, [2002] QB 783; see further Law Commission, *Defamation and the Internet: A Preliminary Investigation* (London 2002).

[139] *Times Newspapers v UK* [2009] EMLR 14.

5.1 **Racial hatred**

Sections 18–23 of the Public Order Act 1986 create a series of criminal offences concerned with the incitement of 'racial hatred', meaning 'hatred against a group of persons defined by reference to colour, race, nationality (including citizenship) or ethnic or national origins'.[140] Offences are committed when

(i) the defendant uses words or behaviour, publishes or distributes written material, presents or directs a play, distributes, shows, or plays a recording of images or sounds, broadcasts a television or radio programme, or possesses (with a view to displaying or distributing) material; and

(ii) the words, behaviour, material, etc, is 'threatening, abusive or insulting'; and

(iii) either

(a) the defendant intends thereby to stir up racial hatred; or

(b) having regard to all of the circumstances, racial hatred is likely to be stirred up.

By singling out speech promoting racial hatred, these offences constitute restrictions on free speech that are not content-neutral. And because such restrictions amount to the censorship of particular views, they are treated with particular suspicion by proponents of free speech.[141] This does not mean that they are unjustifiable; rather, it means that they deserve a particularly close look. In terms of Art 10, it is arguable these offences may help to prevent crime (those amongst whom racial hatred has been stirred up are presumably more likely to act violently towards members of the relevant group) and to protect the 'rights of others' (that is, members of the groups concerned). It might also be felt that the value of the speech in question is so low, and the negative consequences of it (for example, feelings of victimisation, damage to race relations) so great, that content-based regulation is acceptable. That is certainly the view at which lawmakers in the UK, and in many other countries, have arrived.

> **Q** Do you agree with that view? Do any other groups—women, men, gays, lesbians, transsexuals, children, the aged—deserve similar protection? How would you draw the line?

5.2 **Religious hatred**

While it is hard to see what, if any, value racist speech might have—although even this fact would cut little ice with free speech purists—the position is more complicated in relation to religion. Saying that a particular religion (or all religion) is wrong, illogical, or harmful, or that adherents are misguided or unenlightened, is an exercise of

---

[140] Public Order Act 1986, s 17.
[141] See *RAV v City of St Paul, Minnesota* (1992) 505 US 377.

freedom of expression capable of constituting serious, legitimate debate and of making a significant social contribution. English law in this area has changed substantially in recent years. The offence of blasphemy—that is, of publishing matter that insults, offends, or vilifies 'the Deity of Christ or the Christian religion or some part of its doctrines', such as a poem depicting Jesus Christ as a promiscuous gay man[142]—has been abolished.[143] It was difficult, if not impossible, in a society characterised by a plurality of faiths to justify singling out one religion for such protection.[144]

However, a new set of offences concerning the stirring up of religious hatred was created by the Racial and Religious Hatred Act 2006 (which inserted new provisions into the Public Order Act 1986). Subject to certain differences set out below, those offences follow the same pattern as the racial hatred offences considered above. The enactment of the 2006 Act was deeply controversial, the main bone of contention being that it risked stifling free speech to an unacceptable degree—and thereby compromising the underlying principles that free speech serves. As Hare said: 'Government fails in its duty to treat us as autonomous and rational agents if it purports to prohibit speech on the basis that it might persuade us to hold what it considers to be dangerous or offensive convictions.'[145] Concerns of this nature led the new offences to be drawn more narrowly in three respects than the corresponding offences concerning racial hatred:

(i) the words, conduct, etc, must be 'threatening';[146]

(ii) the stirring up of religious hatred must be intended;[147] and

(iii) nothing in the relevant part of the Act is to be 'read or given effect in a way which prohibits or restricts discussion, criticism or expressions of antipathy, dislike, ridicule, insult or abuse of particular religions or the beliefs or practices of their adherents'.[148]

It seems highly likely that, drawn in these ways, the offences would pass muster before the ECtHR as consistent with Art 10, bearing in mind that the Court had been willing to uphold the less nuanced law of blasphemy against a free speech challenge.[149]

5.3 **Obscenity and indecency**

As already noted, it is well established that the right to free speech under Art 10 encompasses the right to *receive*, as well as to disseminate, information. Does this mean that a given person has, or should have, the right to access material that some

---

142 *R v Lemon* [1979] QB 10, 24, CA; see also *R v Lemon* [1979] AC 617, HL.

143 Criminal Justice and Immigration Act 2008, s 79(1).

144 See generally House of Lords Religious Offences Committee, *First Report* (HL 95 2002–03).

145 'Crosses, Crescents and Sacred Cows: Criminalising Incitement to Religious Hatred' [2006] PL 521, 532.   146 Rather than 'threatening, abusive or insulting' as in relation to racial hatred.

147 Whereas it is sufficient if racial hatred is likely to be stirred up, whether or not intended.

148 Public Order Act 1986, s 29J.

149 *Gay News Ltd and Lemon v United Kingdom* (1983) 5 EHRR 123; *Wingrove v United Kingdom* (1997) 24 EHRR 1.

might regard as obscene or indecent? We have seen that the ECtHR has, in practice, developed a hierarchy of forms of speech. If political speech is at the apex, pornography and the like are near the bottom. This does not mean that such forms of expression are unprotected—even hardcore pornography has been held to constitute 'expression'[150]—but it does mean that it will be easier for states to justify restrictions on the grounds specified in Art 10(2).

One of those grounds concerns the protection of the 'rights of others'. This undoubtedly permits the suppression of material the production or consumption of which causes involuntary harm. The most obvious example is images of children undergoing sexual abuse. While the taking of a photograph may not substantially enhance the harm caused by the abuse itself, in many situations, abuse occurs in order that photos can be taken; moreover, it is widely acknowledged that the circulation of such images amongst paedophiles stimulates demand for more, thus perpetuating cycles of abuse. No legitimate free speech objection can therefore be raised against legislation that criminalises the taking, distribution, and possession of indecent or pornographic images of children.[151]

> **Q** It is also a criminal offence to make or distribute indecent 'pseudo-photographs' of children (for example, images not of children actually undergoing abuse, but which have been digitally manipulated to convey that impression).[152] How might this restriction upon free speech be justified?

Beyond such situations, however, the suppression of obscene and indecent material becomes harder to reconcile with free speech considerations. If the production of the material does not harm those who appear in it,[153] what, if anything, can justify its suppression? Three possibilities arise. First, it might be argued that a wider conception of harm is appropriate. For example, many feminists have argued for the prohibition of pornography depicting women, contending that both those appearing in such photographs and women generally are harmed, *inter alia*, by being demeaned, rendering them more liable to discrimination and even abusive behaviour by men induced by pornography to view women as sex objects. Second, the 'rights of others' might be said to extend to a right not to be offended by certain forms of material—and while, in some contexts, such as political speech, the importance of the matter means that relatively little weight should be attached to any 'right' not to be offended, the position is arguably different in relation to material that has less intrinsic value. Third, it may be argued that considerations of morality demand that certain forms of

---

[150] *Hoare v UK* [1997] EHRLR 678.
[151] Protection of Children Act 1978, s 1; Coroners and Justice Act 2009, s 62.
[152] Protection of Children Act 1978, s 1.
[153] Or those subjected to similar treatment in the future thanks to the demand created by the earlier material.

obscene and indecent material should be unavailable or, at the very least, regulated. But such an argument raises questions about the autonomy of the individual: if my consumption of the material is not going to harm others, why should I not be permitted to run the risk of harming myself? This point notwithstanding, Art 10(2) does permit free speech to be limited when necessary in the interests of public morality, and it is in a combination of that rationale, the prevention of harm, and protection from offence that the justification for the English law of obscenity and indecency consists. Here, we focus on two aspects of it.

It is an offence to publish (whether or not for gain), or to have for publication for gain, an obscene article[154] unless publication 'is justified as being for the public good on the ground that it is in the interests of science, literature, art or learning, or of other objects of general concern'.[155] An obscene article is any form of reading or other visual matter or sound recording the effect of which is, if taken as a whole, such as to tend to deprave and corrupt persons who are likely, having regard to all relevant circumstances, to come into contact with it.[156] The paternalistic objective of this law, therefore, is to protect people from harming themselves through the consumption of obscene material, although liability is likely to be avoided if adequate steps are taken to ensure that the material does not come into contact with those most likely to be adversely affected by it. For example, if a particular item were likely to deprave or corrupt children, but not adults, publication in places unlikely to be accessed by children would not be unlawful. Of course, the extent to which this caveat renders this offence acceptable in free speech terms also depends on how susceptible to depravation and corruption courts think those *likely* to encounter the material are.[157] The ECtHR has held that states have a wide margin of appreciation in deciding what is necessary to protect public morality,[158] and it is therefore unlikely that the enforcement of the law in this area will fall foul of Art 10.

Whereas obscenity law is about preventing people from (supposedly) harming themselves, indecency law is about preventing people from being offended. The line between that which is indecent and that which is obscene is an uncertain one, but indecent material is regarded as *less* offensive. It has been suggested—in language the quaintness of which reflects the vintage of the case in which it was used—that '[f]or a male bather to enter the water nude in the presence of ladies would be indecent', but that directing 'the attention of a lady to a certain member of his body' would be obscene.[159] It is an offence at common law to outrage public decency (or to conspire to do so); in contrast with the obscenity offence considered above, no 'public good' defence applies. The offence of outraging public decency was held to have been com-

---

154 Obscene Publications Act 1959, s 2(1).
155 Obscene Publications Act 1959, s 4(1).   156 Obscene Publications Act 1959, s 1(1) and (2).
157 For example, in *DPP v Whyte* [1972] AC 849, sexually explicit material sold in an adult bookshop was held to be capable of depraving and corrupting its *adult* clientele.
158 *Handyside v UK* (1979–80) 1 EHRR 737.
159 *McGowan v Langmuir* 1931 JC 10, 13, *per* Lord Sands.

mitted in *R v Gibson*[160] by an artist who assembled, and a gallery owner who exhibited, earrings made from aborted human foetuses. The compatibility of this offence with Art 10 of the ECHR is questionable. That provision permits the limitation of free speech on, *inter alia*, public morality grounds—but as Lord Lane CJ put it in *Gibson*, the offence can be committed 'whether or not public morals are involved'.[161] Taking that fact together with the ECtHR's view that Art 10 includes the right to 'offend, shock or disturb',[162] Feldman concludes that 'the offence needs to be significantly refined if it is to survive challenge [on Art 10 grounds]'.[163]

6. Privacy

6.1 Introduction

Article 8 of the ECHR says that '[e]veryone has the right to respect for his private and family life, his home and his correspondence'.[164] The range of things protected by Art 8 is relatively wide: the ECtHR has found Art 8 to have been breached by, *inter alia*, the criminalisation of gay sex,[165] medical treatment carried out against a person's will,[166] and the long-term confiscation of the passport of a person with family and business ties in several countries.[167] Important though these aspects of privacy are, they do not engage freedom of speech, which is our concern in this chapter. Our focus is therefore a more particular one: on what might be called the right to *informational privacy*—that is, the individual's right to control the dissemination of information about himself. The desire to do so is instinctive, and is not confined to those with especially interesting or sordid lives—hence the possibility of allowing everyone but 'friends' to view only limited personal information on social networking websites. It is, for example, one thing for a nurse, doctor, or close relative to see a hospital patient in a vulnerable condition in his bed—but he might not want his photograph in the national newspapers.[168] Similarly, a person might want her counsellor, but not her colleagues, to know that she suffered abuse as a child. The protection of informational privacy serves to uphold the fundamental values of human dignity and autonomy: people are able to live more dignified, more fulfilled lives if they need not worry about all and sundry finding out about those parts of their lives that they would rather keep private.

---

[160] [1990] 2 QB 619.
[161] *R v Gibson* at 623.   [162] *Handyside v UK* (1979–80) 1 EHRR 737, 754.
[163] Feldman, *Civil Liberties and Human Rights in England and Wales* (Oxford 2002), p 935.
[164] The term 'right to privacy' will be used for concision.
[165] *Dudgeon v UK* (1982) 4 EHRR 149.
[166] *Storck v Germany* (2006) 43 EHRR 6.
[167] *İletmiş v Turkey* (Application 29871/96, judgment 6 December 2005).
[168] Precisely this happened in *Kaye v Robertson* [1991] FSR 62.

Legislation upholds specific aspects of informational privacy. The Data Protection Act 1998 imposes restrictions on the processing of certain personal information that is stored electronically or in a filing system,[169] while the Regulation of Investigatory Powers Act 2000 makes it a criminal offence—except in certain circumstances, such as on the authority of a Minister on national security grounds—intentionally to intercept postal communications or telecommunications. But outside of these specific contexts, to what extent does English law recognise and protect informational privacy? As we will see, this area of the law has developed rapidly in recent years under the influence of the ECHR. Both Arts 8 and 10 are qualified rights, and both can be limited (when necessary in a democratic society) 'for the protection of the rights of others'.[170] Thus one person's free speech can be restricted in the interests of another's privacy, and vice versa. When the HRA was being enacted, there was considerable concern—principally on the part of the media—that English courts would use Art 8 to fashion extensive new privacy laws that would drastically curtail freedom of expression.[171] As we examine the position now adopted in English law, we need to ask whether an acceptable balance has been struck between the protection of privacy and of free speech.

6.2 Background—breach of confidence

For a very long time, it was said, with some justification, that the law of privacy formed no part of English law. The case that could be said to prove that point was *Kaye*,[172] in which journalists entered the hospital room in which a well-known actor was recovering from brain surgery, taking photographs of and purporting to interview him. The Court of Appeal held that there was no legal basis on which publication of the photographs could be restrained, lamenting 'the failure of both the common law of England and statute to protect in an effective way the personal privacy of individual citizens'.[173] Few people would argue that this struck an appropriate balance between free speech and privacy.

There were, though, some circumstances in which the common law would provide a remedy in respect of the misuse of private information. Under the doctrine of breach of confidence, the unauthorised disclosure of information was unlawful if two conditions were met.[174] First, the information had to 'have the necessary quality

---

[169] As well as giving people certain rights to access information concerning themselves.

[170] Articles 8(2) and 10(2).

[171] This resulted in s 12 of the Human Rights Act 1998, which requires courts in certain circumstances to have 'particular regard' to freedom of expression. It is unclear, however, whether this has made any difference in practice.

[172] *Kaye v Robertson* [1991] FSR 62.   [173] *Kaye* at 70, *per* Bingham LJ.

[174] *Coco v AN Clark (Engineers) Ltd* [1969] RPC 41, 47.

of confidence about it',[175] meaning that it should not be widely available in the public domain.[176] Second, the information had to have been communicated 'on the basis that it is confidential'—the reason for judicial intervention being that it is 'unconscionable' for someone to reveal information obtained on such a basis.[177]

At one time, it was thought that this required a pre-existing relationship between the parties within which confidentiality was a given, or some form of agreement between the parties that the information would not be revealed. For example, in *Kaye*, the information contained in the photograph could not be said to be confidential (on a traditional understanding of the doctrine)[178] because there was no agreement to that effect between the claimant and the photographer. This seriously limited the capacity of breach of confidence to protect privacy: it was available when someone went back on an agreement to keep a secret, but could not touch situations in which the information was obtained in an underhand or otherwise unauthorised manner. However, in the 1980s and 1990s, the courts developed a more liberal approach in this regard. In the so-called *Spycatcher* case, Lord Goff said that information would be protected by the law of confidence when acquired by a person who 'has notice, or is held to have agreed, that the information is confidential'.[179] This meant that a duty of confidentiality could be imposed upon a passer-by who picked up 'an obviously confidential document...wafted by an electric fan out of a window into a crowded street'[180] or upon an intruder who took photos of a celebrity wedding at which it had been made crystal clear that no one but official photographers were to take photos.[181] This was a highly significant development that laid the foundation for the emergence, alongside breach of confidence, of what has been called a new tort of *misuse of private information*.[182]

6.3 **Misuse of private information**

The foundation of that new tort is *Campbell v Mirror Group Newspapers Ltd*,[183] in which the defendant newspaper had published an article concerning the treatment that model Naomi Campbell was receiving for drug addiction, together with a photograph

---

[175] *Saltman Engineering Co Ltd v Campbell Engineering Co Ltd* (1948) 65 RPC 203, 215, *per* Lord Greene MR.

[176] If, however, the information in question were only available to a limited subset of the public and additional harm would result to the claimant from further disclosure, such further disclosure might constitute a breach of confidence: *Attorney-General v Observer Ltd* [1990] 1 AC 109, 260, *per* Lord Keith.

[177] *Stephens v Avery* [1988] Ch 449, 456, *per* Sir Nicolas Browne-Wilkinson VC.

[178] Although that traditional understanding was arguably outdated by the time *Kaye* was decided: see Fenwick and Phillipson, 'Confidence and Privacy: A Re-Examination' [1996] CLJ 447, 453–5.

[179] *Attorney-General v Observer Ltd* at 281.

[180] *Attorney-General v Observer Ltd* at 281.

[181] *Douglas v Hello! Ltd (No 3)* [2005] EWCA Civ 595, [2006] QB 125.

[182] Although some judges still prefer talk of an extended concept of breach of confidence.

[183] [2004] UKHL 22 [2004] 2 AC 457. For more detailed discussion, see Moreham, 'Privacy and the Common Law: A Doctrinal and Theoretical Analysis' (2005) 121 LQR 628.

of her emerging from a meeting of Narcotics Anonymous. Five pieces of information were thereby conveyed:

(i)   The fact that Campbell was a drug addict.

(ii) The fact that she was receiving treatment for her addiction.

(iii) The fact that the treatment that she was receiving was provided by Narcotics Anonymous.

(iv) Details of the treatment.

(v)   The information contained in the photograph.

In holding that publication of items (iii)–(v) was unlawful, the House of Lords had to address several points that we consider in turn.

6.3.1 What is 'private' information?

While some of the information in *Campbell*—for example, item (iii)—might have counted as confidential under the *Spycatcher* test, some would clearly not. There is no sense in which the information contained in a photograph showing events occurring in a public place—Campbell was photographed in the street—can be regarded as confidential. But can it be regarded as private? Opinion was divided in *Campbell* about the test that should be used to identify private information. Lord Hope said 'the broad test is whether disclosure of the information about the individual ("A") would give substantial offence to A, assuming that A was placed in similar circumstances and was a person of ordinary sensibilities'.[184] However, the dominant test appears to be the one adopted by Lord Nicholls and Baroness Hale (and which was subsequently applied by the Court of Appeal in *Douglas (No 3)*[185]) that asks whether the defendant knows, or ought to know, that the claimant can reasonably expect his privacy to be respected. In any event, all five pieces of information in *Campbell* were held to be private.[186] A further point that should be noted here is that once information is widely available in the public domain, it can no longer be regarded as private—but the fact that someone has revealed information about one aspect of their private life does not mean that the rest of it is fair game as well.[187]

6.3.2 Public interest

Article 8 being a qualified right, the publication of private information may be lawful if necessary to uphold other recognised rights and interests—including, of course, free speech. It is therefore unsurprising that domestic law will not protect the privacy—just as it would not protect the confidentiality—of information when some conflicting and weightier legitimate interest points towards publication. Precisely this situation arose in *Campbell*. The Law Lords agreed that although all five pieces of information counted as private, there was a public interest justifying publication of items (i) and (ii) because

---

184 *Campbell* at [92].   185 *Douglas v Hello! Ltd (No 3)*, at [72].

186 Or confidential: see n 182 above.

187 *McKennitt v Ash* [2006] EWCA Civ 1714, [2008] QB 73, [53]–[55].

the claimant had previously denied using illegal drugs. Two of the judges went further, arguing that a margin of freedom should be extended to the media in recognition of the interest in free speech, and that the decision to publish the additional information in order to add colour to the story did not exceed that margin.[188] That point aside, the general principle, according to Lord Nicholls, was that 'where a public figure chooses to present a false image and make untrue pronouncements about his or her life, the press will normally be entitled to put the record straight'.[189]

In some circumstances, the public interest in such record-straightening is obvious. For example, if the Climate Change Minister makes a speech criticising non-essential long-haul air travel, there will be a public interest in revealing that he has booked a long weekend in Rio. Exposing him as a hypocrite on a matter directly relevant to his ministerial role is something that members of the electorate might legitimately wish to take into account in formulating an opinion about the government. But is the same really true of a model such as Naomi Campbell? Or a premiership footballer who was denied an injunction restraining publication of a story detailing his extramarital affairs?[190] Or a children's television presenter who could not prevent publication of a story about his use of a brothel?[191] In all of these cases, the courts have relied on, *inter alia*, the public interest in publication—but this arguably confuses those things that the public *is interested in* with situations in which there is a *legitimate* public interest in publication.[192] A more subtle approach—which appears to be more in line with ECtHR decisions[193]—was adopted in the more recent case of *Mosley v News Group Newspapers Ltd.*[194] It was held that there was no public interest in a newspaper publishing still and (via its website) moving images showing the president of the governing body of Formula 1 motor racing engaging in sadomasochistic sexual acts with prostitutes. None of the justifications for limiting privacy set down in Art 8(2) applied: 'titillation for its own sake' would not suffice.[195] Taken to its logical conclusion, the judge noted, this approach would have 'a profound effect on the tabloid and celebrity culture to which we have become accustomed in recent years'.[196]

Q It might be argued that requiring courts to draw the line between those things in which the public is *really* interested and those in which they are *legitimately entitled* to be interested concedes too much power to judges to set the parameters within which media freedom exists. Do you agree? How would you draw the line?

---

[188] *Campbell* at [28]–[29], *per* Lord Nicholls; [66], *per* Lord Hoffmann.   [189] *Campbell* at [24].
[190] *A v B plc* [2002] EWCA Civ 337, [2003] QB 195.
[191] *Theakston v MGN Ltd* [2002] EWHC 137, [2002] EMLR 22.
[192] See Phillipson 'Judicial Reasoning in Breach of Confidence Cases under the Human Rights Act: Not Taking Privacy Seriously?' [2003] EHRLR (supplement) 54.
[193] Such as *Von Hannover v Germany* (2005) 40 EHRR 1.
[194] [2008] EWHC 1777 (QB), [2008] EMLR 20.   [195] *Mosley* at [132].   [196] *Mosley* at [131].

6.3.3 **Public places and photographs**

Pictures—said to be 'worth a thousand words'—are capable of conveying more information, and with greater impact, than verbal descriptions; photographs may therefore constitute a graver invasion of privacy that is correspondingly harder to justify. It has even been suggested that every photograph is unique such that the publication of an unauthorised photograph might constitute a breach of privacy even if a substantially similar authorised version is already in the public domain.[197] Particular difficulties arise in relation to photographs taken in public places. It is initially hard to see how anyone can have a reasonable expectation of privacy if the event in question occurred in public, but in *Campbell*, the majority concluded that publishing photos of the claimant standing on the street outside the rehab centre was unlawful because it had increased the distress[198] or harm suffered by Campbell.[199] Baroness Hale sought to distinguish between a photo of Campbell 'pop[ping] out…for a bottle of milk' (publication of which would not damage her private life) and one of her coming out of a rehab centre.[200]

That reasoning does not provide a particularly clear basis on which to judge when the publication of photos taken in public places will entail a breach of privacy. The ECtHR decision in *Peck v UK*[201] is arguably more helpful in that regard. Late one night in a town centre, the applicant attempted to commit suicide using a kitchen knife. Images of the immediate aftermath were recorded by CCTV cameras operated by the local authority. Those images were disclosed to the media, and shown in newspapers and on television. Notwithstanding that these events had taken place in public, the ECtHR found that the disclosure constituted a breach of Art 8. It did so because 'the relevant moment was viewed to an extent which far exceeded any exposure to a passer-by or to security observation…and to a degree surpassing that which the applicant could possibly have foreseen'.[202] This provides a sensible and intelligible basis for dealing with situations that occur in public places (as well as those in which the information in question is already known to a limited class of people), the key question being whether the disclosure under challenge resulted in exposure going beyond that which the claimant could reasonably have expected.[203]

But what about someone who inevitably attracts the attention of the paparazzi? If the test is whether they have a reasonable expectation of privacy in public places, the answer is surely 'no': experience will, or ought, to have taught them that they will not be left alone. This issue arose in *Von Hannover*, which concerned the repeated publication of photos of a celebrity (who, despite her membership of Monaco's royal family, performed no official functions on behalf of that state) going about her daily business (for example, shopping and eating out).[204] The Court based its ruling that the applicant's

197 *Douglas v Hello! Ltd (No 3)* [2007] UKHL 21, [2008] 1 AC 1, [122], *per* Lord Hoffmann.
198 *Campbell* at [124], *per* Lord Hope.   199 *Campbell* at [157], *per* Baroness Hale.
200 *Campbell* at [154].   201 (2003) 36 EHRR 41.
202 *Peck v UK* at [62].   203 See further Moreham, 'Privacy in Public Places' [2006] CLJ 606.
204 *Von Hannover v Germany* (2005) 40 EHRR 1.

right to privacy had been breached on the fact that the media's conduct contravened her *legitimate* expectation that her privacy would be respected in relation to everyday aspects of her domestic life. This test appears to go further than *Campbell*[205] and *Peck* in that it permits aspects of a person's life to be characterised as private even if there is no *reasonable* expectation of privacy on account of long-standing press intrusion. Defining the range of things to which a legitimate expectation of privacy attaches is far from straightforward, but it is noteworthy that the ECtHR was influenced by the fact that (in its view) no public interest justified publication of the pictures. Logically, whether a public interest in publication exists is only relevant if the information is private—yet, in *Von Hannover*, the lack of public interest in publishing the photos in question appeared to influence the Court's conclusion that the information was, in the first place, private. While defining privacy by reference to the absence of legitimate public interest conflates what have hitherto been thought of as distinct parts of the analysis, this pragmatic approach reflects the fact that the concept of privacy is very difficult to define in the abstract.

7. Official secrecy

7.1 Breach of confidence

There are inevitably certain things that, if said publicly, would compromise the national interest and in relation to which it is therefore desirable for free speech to be curtailed. The doctrine of *breach of confidence* is capable, in some respects, of performing this function: if, for example, someone acquires information in circumstances in which they know, or ought to know, that it relates to state secrets, disclosure would constitute a breach of confidence. It was to this branch of the law that the government resorted when, in the so-called *Spycatcher* case, it wished to prevent a former MI5 officer from publishing memoirs alleging unlawful conduct on the part of other such officers. The government ultimately failed in that endeavour, the House of Lords holding that, in such cases, the Crown must be able to show that a remedy would serve the public interest, and that the book had become so widely available overseas that no such interest would be advanced by leaving in place injunctions that had been granted on an earlier occasion.[206] That episode formed an important part of the background to the enactment of the Official Secrets Act 1989.

---

[205] See, eg Baroness Hale's suggestion that it would be lawful to publish photos of Campbell popping out for a pint of milk: *Campbell* at [154].

[206] *Attorney-General v Observer Ltd* [1990] 1 AC 109.

7.2 **Official Secrets Acts**

The Official Secrets Acts distinguish between *spying* and *other disclosures* of sensitive information. The former is dealt with by s 1 of the 1911 Act, which says that a person commits a criminal offence if, *for any purpose prejudicial to the safety or interests of the State*, he

- enters, passes over, approaches, inspects, or is in the neighbourhood of a *prohibited place* (for example, a military or intelligence facility); or
- *prepares information* (sketches, plans, etc) that might be, or is meant to be, useful to an enemy; or
- *obtains or passes on information* that might be, or is meant to be, useful to an enemy.

It will be apparent that this section is sufficiently broadly drafted to cover conduct that would not normally be classed as espionage. Thus, in *Chandler v DPP*,[207] the House of Lords upheld the convictions of anti-nuclear protestors who approached an airbase with the intention of holding a sit-in on the runway.

More extensive provision concerning the disclosure of information is made by the Official Secrets Act 1989. As Figure 20.1 shows, ss 1–4 of the Act create criminal offences in respect of the disclosure of information concerning security and intelligence, defence, international relations, and crime and special investigation powers. The general structure of the offences is that a person to whom the Act applies commits an offence if (i) he or she discloses information of the relevant type, and (ii) that disclosure causes or is likely to cause certain consequences. As the table shows, there are limited defences—and no offence is committed under ss 1–4 if the disclosure is made with lawful authority, meaning in accordance with the person's official duty or pursuant to an official authorisation.[208] Section 5 creates a further offence concerning the passing on of information covered by ss 1–4 by people who receive such information in confidence or in breach of ss 1–4, but who are not otherwise covered by the Act.

Two points should be noted about the 1989 Act. First, as Figure 20.1 shows,[209] the s 1 offence concerning security and intelligence matters is different from—and more draconian than—the other offences in several respects. Most obviously, current and former security and intelligence officers and those notified that they are subject to the same rules ('notified persons') can incur liability under s 1 whether or not the disclosure in question causes, or is likely to cause, damage. It is at least arguable that the criminalisation of non-damaging disclosures does not constitute a necessary limitation upon free speech and that such a restriction would therefore fail to survive scrutiny under Art 10. This is compounded by the fact that, in respect of security and intelligence officers and notified persons, s 1 applies not only to sensitive material, but to *all* material encountered while

---

[207] [1964] AC 763.   [208] Official Secrets Act 1989, s 7.
[209] The table is intended to provide a general overview of the structure of the different offences, rather than an exhaustive account of them.

Section	Who can be liable?	What sort of material is covered?	What are the proscribed consequences of disclosure upon which liability depends?	What defences are there?
1: Security and intelligence	Current/former security/intelligence officers, anyone notified that he or she is subject to these rules	Anything concerning security/intelligence possessed as security/intelligence officer or obtained in course of work while notification in force	No consequences need be shown: all disclosures incur liability (unless defence applies)	Did not know and had no reason to believe material related to security/intelligence
2: Defence	Current/former Crown servants and government contractors	Material concerning security/intelligence possessed by virtue of position	Damages or likely to cause damage to work of security/intelligence services	1. As above 2. Did not know/had no reason to believe damage would result or be likely to result
	Current/former Crown servants and government contractors	Material possessed by virtue of position concerning defence (eg defence policy/strategy, organisation/deployment/readiness of armed forces)	Damages capability of armed forces, leads to loss of life or serious equipment damage, endangers interests of UK abroad, likely to have any of above effects	Did not know and had no reason to believe (i) material concerned defence, or (ii) disclosure would have proscribed consequence
3: International relations	Current/former Crown servants and government contractors	Material possessed by virtue of position that (i) concerns international relations, or (ii) is confidential material obtained from another state or international organization	Endangers interests of UK abroad, seriously obstructs promotion/protection of such interests, endangers safety of UK citizens abroad, likely to have any of above effects	Did not know and had no reason to believe (i) material covered by this section, or (ii) disclosure would have proscribed consequence
4: Crime and special investigation powers	Current/former Crown servants and government contractors	Material possessed by virtue of position the disclosure of which would have a proscribed consequence	Results in commission of offence, facilitates escape from legal custody, impedes prevention/detection of offences or apprehension/prosecution of suspects, likely to have any of above effects	Did not know and had no reason to believe disclosure would have any of first three proscribed consequences

Figure 20.1 Official Secrets Act 1989, ss 1–4

employed as such officers (or, in the case of notified persons, encountered in the course of their work while the notification is in force). Again, it is not clear that such an indiscriminate approach could be characterised as proportionate, as required by Art 10.

The second point—which applies to ss 1–4 generally, not only to s 1—is that it is not a defence to establish that the disclosure was in the public interest. This highly significant (and deliberate)[210] omission means that there is no room for weighing the positive and negative consequences of disclosure: once the prosecution establishes that disclosure had, or would be likely to have, a proscribed consequence, an even stronger public interest in favour of disclosure is irrelevant. The position is even starker in relation to security and intelligence officers and notified persons under s 1: disclosures that carry substantial benefits (for example, bringing to light unlawful or improper conduct) will be unlawful even if they cause no harm at all. Again, this raises questions about whether the Act meets the requirements of the ECHR, which permits only necessary and proportionate restrictions upon free speech.

This matter was considered by the House of Lords in *R v Shayler*,[211] in which the defendant—a former security officer charged with disclosing information in breach of the 1989 Act—sought to argue that a public interest defence should be read into the Act pursuant to s 3 of the HRA. The Law Lords disagreed. While they accepted that an absolute prohibition on disclosure would contravene Art 10, they held that the absence of a public interest defence did not render the prohibition absolute. That was because, as noted above, disclosures that would otherwise constitute offences under ss 1–4 are permitted if made with lawful authority. Their Lordships held that it was in this context that the HRA bit: those responsible for deciding whether to authorise disclosure are bound by Art 10 to do so (in the interests of free speech) unless withholding permission is a necessary and proportionate way of protecting national security. And if it were to be felt that the responsible person had not struck that balance appropriately, their decision would be open to judicial review on Art 10 grounds. The existence of the mechanism for seeking authorisation—and the duty of those operating it to respect Art 10—meant that the absence of a public interest defence did not make the 1989 Act incompatible with the ECHR.

> **Q** Do you agree with the House of Lords that the absence of a public interest defence is unproblematic in Art 10 terms?

8. Conclusions

So diverse are the situations considered in this chapter—a diversity that reflects the range of circumstances in which free speech questions arise—that it would be futile to attempt to provide a summary. Two points, though, can be made by way of conclusion.

---

[210] The government did not wish to be defeated under the Act by public interest arguments as in *Spycatcher*.   [211] [2002] UKHL 11, [2003] 1 AC 247.

Each relates, in different ways, to the subtlety of the right of free speech under the ECHR and, hence, of the developing body of English law in this area. First, the right of freedom of expression is not a monolithic concept: the question is not simply whether something constitutes 'speech' (and is thus protected) or not; rather, the courts—European and English—have developed a hierarchy of forms of free speech, with political speech at the apex. This reflects the underlying reasons, considered at the beginning of the chapter, for according respect to free speech, and the key role played by freedom of expression in a democracy. Second, however, even in its most compelling forms, free speech is a far from absolute right. It is one capable of clashing with—and, in appropriate fact situations, being eclipsed by—a range of other rights and interests, including the right to a fair trial, and the protection of reputation, privacy, and national security. In such circumstances, difficult questions arise about how the balance should be struck between the conflicting rights and interests that are in play; and it is inevitable that this places the courts in a powerful position. But that is surely a price worth paying if it helps to ensure that the extent to which we all enjoy free speech—the lifeblood of democracy—is not wholly within the gift of those democratic institutions the members of which might paradoxically be served by unduly limiting it.

Further reading

BARENDT, *Freedom of Speech* (Oxford 2005)

DEAKIN, JOHNSTON, AND MARKESINIS *Markesinis and Deakin's Tort Law* (Oxford 2008), ch 21

FELDMAN, *Civil Liberties and Human Rights in England and Wales* (Oxford 2002), pt IV

FENWICK AND PHILLIPSON, *Media Freedom under the Human Rights Act* (Oxford 2006)

HARE, 'Crosses, Crescents and Sacred Cows: Criminalising Incitement to Religious Hatred' [2006] PL 521, 532

MOREHAM, 'Privacy and the Common Law: A Doctrinal and Theoretical Analysis' (2005) 121 LQR 628

Freedom of Assembly

21

1. Introduction

1.1 Why freedom of assembly matters

We saw in the previous chapter that, for a number of reasons, freedom of expression is important. But it is one thing having the *right* to say what you want; having the *opportunity* to do so effectively is another. Even if there are no relevant legal restrictions on the *content* of the opinion or information that a given person wishes to convey, that fact will be relatively unimportant if, at the same time, the law prohibits the use of effective *means* of communication.

We are fortunate to live in an age in which technology, at least in the developed world, makes it easier than ever to communicate. Someone with a cause to promote or a view to express can do so by means of sending emails, establishing social networking groups, or setting up a website. And the Internet facilitates not only one-way communication; it also provides a way for like-minded individuals to organise and coordinate their efforts so as to maximise the impact of their message, whatever that might be. But, all of this notwithstanding, it is clear that physical forms of protest—marches through cities, gatherings in public places, and so on—remain a popular and effective mechanism for making people's views known. Indeed it has been said that the right to protest 'is a fundamental right in a democratic society and, like the right to freedom of expression, is one of the foundations of such a society'.[1]

The United Kingdom in recent years has witnessed several very large or otherwise high-profile protests. In 2000, hauliers protesting against rising fuel prices blockaded oil refineries, bringing the country to a virtual standstill by choking off the fuel supply. In 2002, nearly half a million people marched through central London to protest against a ban on hunting animals with dogs; in 2003, close to a million people in London (and hundreds of thousands more in towns and cities across the country) protested against the impending war in Iraq. More recently, in 2009, a major anti-globalisation protest took place in London during the G20 meeting of world leaders, the policing of which proved hugely controversial and included the use of tactics the

---

[1] *Rassemblement Jurassien et Unite Jurassienne v Switzerland* Application 8191/78 (1979) 17 DR 93, [3].

legality of which we consider later in this chapter. It is clear, then, that this type of protest remains highly significant. It constitutes an effective means by which to draw attention to issues, to shape public discourse, and to influence the political process.

The right to *freedom of assembly* is thus intimately connected with the right to *freedom of expression*: by facilitating effective forms of public protest, the former right provides a practical means by which the latter right can be exercised.[2] It follows that the *extent* of the right of freedom of assembly is important, since this impacts directly upon people's capacity to take part, in an effective way of their choosing, in debate about matters of public importance. Of course, people might 'assemble' for all sorts of reasons, including the purely social, but it is in relation to protest that the right to freedom of assembly assumes its greatest constitutional importance.

1.2 **Striking a balance**

We know from Chapters 19 and 20 that, in many matters concerning human rights, a balance falls to be struck between the rights of individuals and general public interest concerns. The interests of those who wish to sit, stand, shout, or wave banners in, or march through, towns and cities must be weighed against the interests of those who do not wish their daily lives to be disrupted by such conduct. As Williams noted in his seminal book on public order, the law in this area is a 'compromise' that 'seeks to balance the competing demands of freedom of speech and assembly on the one hand and the preservation of the Queen's Peace on the other'.[3] Where the balance lies will depend heavily on the context. For example, a large gathering in a park is obviously different from one that takes place on a motorway and causes traffic gridlock; a peaceful protest is clearly distinct from one that involves orchestrated property damage; different issues are raised by, on the one hand, protests that seek merely to communicate views and, on the other, 'direct action'—that is, conduct (for example, that of hunt saboteurs) that seeks to disrupt the activity that is the focus of the protest.[4] These pairs of contrasting examples are not intended to reflect our view of where the line between acceptable and unacceptable protest lies; they merely serve to highlight that a line inevitably has to be drawn somewhere.

Although, in this chapter, we need to consider the details of how English law regulates and restricts protest, our central concern, in keeping with a book on public law, is with the question of whether the law strikes the right balance between the competing sets of interests that arise in this sphere. In one sense, that is a largely subjective and political question: some people's ideological position would lead them to the view that the commission of property damage would be a wholly legitimate form of protest if it were to serve some greater good. For example, in 2007, environmental activists

---

[2] *Kuznetsov v Russia* (ECtHR, Application 10877/04), [23].
[3] *Keeping the Peace* (London 1967), p 9.
[4] See Fenwick and Phillipson, 'Direct Action, Convention Values and the Human Rights Act' (2001) 21 LS 535.

broke in and caused £30,000 of damage to a power station, but were acquitted at their subsequent criminal trial, having convinced the jury that they had a 'lawful excuse' for the action because it was intended to draw attention to and ultimately to prevent climate change.[5] However, the question of whether English law strikes the 'right' balance between the conflicting interests is a legal, as well as a subjective, one. Article 11 of the European Convention on Human Rights (ECHR) sets out the right of freedom of assembly; this provides a benchmark against which to measure English law—as well as, in the light of the Human Rights Act 1998 (HRA), a strong influence upon its interpretation, application and development. The ECHR will therefore be our reference point throughout this chapter as we explore the way in which English law balances the rights of protestors against the interests of other individuals and groups, and of society generally.

1.3 **Article 11**

Article 11 of the ECHR adheres to the two-part form common to many of the Convention rights. The first part provides that '[e]veryone has the right to freedom of peaceful assembly',[6] while Art 11(2) spells out the extent of the right in greater detail by indicating how freedom of assembly may legitimately be restricted:

> No restrictions shall be placed on the exercise of these rights other than such as are prescribed by law and are necessary in a democratic society in the interests of national security or public safety, for the prevention of disorder or crime, for the protection of health or morals or for the protection of the rights and freedoms of others. This Article shall not prevent the imposition of lawful restrictions on the exercise of these rights by members of the armed forces, of the police or of the administration of the State.

It follows that conduct will fall within the protective effect of Art 11 only if two conditions are met. The conduct must, in the first place, constitute 'peaceful assembly'. This has been held to cover 'both private meetings and meetings on public thoroughfares, as well as static meetings and public processions';[7] Art 11 evidently offers no protection to those who wish to engage in violent behaviour. Second, even peaceful assemblies will be unprotected by Art 11 to the extent that it is 'necessary in a democratic society' to restrict such assemblies for any of the purposes set out in Art 11(2). The thrust of Art 11, therefore, is that *peaceful assembly must be permitted except, and only to the extent, that its restriction is necessary.*

---

5 'Kingsnorth trial: Coal protesters cleared of criminal damage to chimney', *The Guardian*, 10 September 2008.

6 Article 11(1) also provides for 'freedom of association with others, including the right to form and to join trade unions'. In a sense, freedom of association is the institutional counterpart to freedom of assembly: the latter allows for the public communication of information and opinions, while the former is concerned with the right to form and join organisations (the purposes of which might include the communication of opinions and the advancement of members' interests).

7 *Kuznetsov v Russia* (ECtHR, Application 10877/04), [35].

The right to protest[8] is then a qualified right, meaning that it must yield in the face of more compelling legitimate interests. But it must be emphasised at the outset that the clash of rights and interests involved is often not merely two-dimensional (for example, between those who want to protest and those who do not wish to suffer the resulting disruption to everyday life), but multidimensional. At stake might be the rights and interests of the protestors themselves, those of counter-protestors (who wish publicly to express their disagreement with the position advocated by the 'original' protestors), those living and working nearby (whose lives might be disrupted by the protests), and wider society (bearing in mind, for example, the demands placed on the public purse by policing protests and the economic loss that might be caused by the disruption occasioned by protests).

> **Q** Should all of these interests be regarded as having equal value? For example, should the right of counter-protestors who wish to disrupt a demonstration be treated on an equal basis with the rights of the principal demonstrators? Should the inconvenience or offence that would be occasioned by a protest to members of the community be treated as factors capable of justifying restrictions upon or even the prohibition of a protest?

Courts, at both the national and European levels, have had to grapple with these complexities. One of the most difficult issues—that, as a result, has been the context in which many of the key principles have been teased out by the courts—relates to situations involving different groups of protestors holding opposing views. These situations can arise quite frequently; indeed, it is almost inevitable that protestors' views will not be met with universal acclaim—if everyone were in agreement, there would be no obvious need to protest—and will sometimes lead to confrontation with those holding differing opinions. Several principles can be extracted from the courts' decisions in such hard cases.

First, *it is unacceptable for the state to stand by and refuse to take any steps to safeguard legitimate protestors' interests against the unreasonable, threatening, or violent behaviour of others.* This is because the European Court of Human Rights (ECtHR) has held that Art 11 imposes not only a negative obligation on states *not to prohibit protests*,[9] but also a positive obligation *to facilitate peaceful protest.* In *Plattform 'Ärzte für das Leben' v Austria*,[10] when 500 counter-demonstrators interrupted (by using loudspeakers and throwing eggs) an open-air religious ceremony held by anti-abortionists, the anti-abortion protestors complained that the authorities had taken insufficient steps to prevent pro-abortion protestors from disrupting their demonstration. The Court held that the right to protest would be devalued if those with opposing

---

[8] The ECHR does not explicitly confer a right to protest; rather, this right is implicit in Art 11 read with Art 10. However, we use the term 'right to protest' in this chapter as convenient shorthand. See further Mead, 'The Right to Peaceful Protest under the European Convention on Human Rights: A Content Study of Strasbourg Case Law' [2007] EHRLR 345, 347–51.

[9] Except where this is necessary in the sense set out in Art 11(2).   [10] (1991) 13 EHRR 204.

views were effectively given an unlimited right to disrupt—and thus deter—such protests. At the very least, it followed that demonstrators should not have to fear 'physical violence by their opponents', and the state was therefore under a positive obligation 'to take reasonable and appropriate measures to enable lawful demonstrations to proceed peacefully'.[11] This might, for example, include taking steps to separate the 'original' protestors from those seeking to disrupt their protest. This does not, however, mean that states are obliged to provide an absolute guarantee that protestors will suffer no intimidation or disruption by others. Indeed, the ECtHR ultimately held that the Austrian authorities *had* taken all reasonable steps to protect the anti-abortionists' right to protest, and the fact that their ceremony had nevertheless been disrupted did not mean that the authorities had failed to do what was required of them.

Second, the fact that the state is not under an absolute obligation to facilitate peaceful protest means that, in certain circumstances, *it may be lawful for the authorities to close down such a protest if it is provoking, or seems likely to provoke, others into a violent response.* This is clearly the most efficient solution for authorities, such as the police, when faced with a small number of protestors stirring up an angry and potentially violent mob with opposing views. It used to be the case that English law permitted the authorities to pursue precisely this sort of strategy.[12] Similarly, the ECtHR has traditionally taken a relatively soft line when this sort of state action has been challenged, upholding decisions to target legitimate protestors rather than those threatening to react violently to the protestors' message.[13] However, there are signs that the ECtHR is now willing to look more closely at whether the targeting of legitimate protestors is a necessary and proportionate way of protecting public safety and others' interests.[14] It follows, as we will see, that Art 11 now imposes a qualified duty on the police and other public authorities to enable peaceful protests to continue by focusing their attention on those who are reacting, or who are threatening to react, violently.[15]

Third, what of *the rights of the counter-protestors themselves*? Naturally, Art 11 does not protect the rights of those who are acting violently, but what about situations involving opposing groups of legitimate protestors? In *Öllinger v Austria*,[16] two groups wished simultaneously to hold ceremonies in the same Salzburg cemetery: one commemorating Jews killed by the SS ('the Jewish ceremony') and the other commemorating SS soldiers killed during the Second World War ('the SS ceremony').[17] The SS ceremony had been held every year for 40 years, and the Jewish ceremony was

---

[11] *Plattform* at [32]–[34].   [12] *Duncan v Jones* [1936] 1 KB 218.

[13] See, eg *Chorherr v Austria* (1994) 17 EHRR 358.

[14] *Öllinger v Austria* (2008) 46 EHRR 38. See further Mead, 'Strasbourg Discovers the Right to Counter-Demonstrate: A Note on *Öllinger v Austria*' [2007] EHRLR 133.

[15] The qualification is that the legitimate protestors may be targeted—eg by being required to end or move their demonstration—if this is necessary and proportionate in the interests of public safety. This may be the case, for example, where police numbers are inadequate to deal with the baying mob.

[16] (2008) 46 EHRR 38.

[17] The SS, or *Schutzstaffel*, was a military force in Nazi Germany responsible for perpetrating many of the worst crimes against humanity during the Second World War, including the murder of approximately 12 million people, many of them Jews.

planned as a protest—a counter-demonstration—against it. Faced with this prospect, the Austrian authorities banned the Jewish ceremony, arguing that this was necessary to avoid a risk of disorder and conflict between the two groups, and in order to protect the rights of other people who simply wished to attend the cemetery. But what of the rights of those wishing to hold the Jewish ceremony? The Court noted that '[i]f every probability of tension and heated exchange between opposing groups during a dem-onstration was to warrant its prohibition, society would be faced with being deprived of the opportunity of hearing differing views'.[18] It went on to hold that, in the absence of clear evidence of likely violence, an absolute ban on the counter-demonstration was not a necessary or proportionate restriction on the rights of those wishing to hold the Jewish ceremony. This decision has been welcomed as one that recognises the import-ance to the political process of dissent—of allowing opposing points of view to be put forward in the interests of democratic decision-making.[19]

2. Domestic law

The balancing of the various interests set out above ends up, in some cases, as a matter for the courts. It is ultimately their responsibility to decide whether contested decisions properly accommodate the competing rights and interests of protestors, counter-protestors, property owners, passers-by, wider society, and so on. But, in the first instance, it is often the police that have to make decisions on such matters. The law does not simply instruct the police to permit protests, except to the extent that restrictions are necessary in the terms laid down by Art 11(2). Instead, there are extensive legislative and common law rules governing the police's powers to manage protests. Nearly all of this law came into existence long before the HRA placed the ECHR centre-stage. However, we know from Chapter 19 that the courts are under a duty to interpret and that the police, as a public authority, are under a duty to apply the law consistently with the Convention. As we will see, this has, in some instances, required significant changes to domestic law and practice.

Broadly speaking, English law in this sphere draws a distinction between *unacceptable conduct* and *potentially acceptable conduct*. Conduct of the former type is prohibited: it is impermissible in all circumstances, and engaging in it constitutes a criminal offence. Uncontroversially, into this category fall such things as riot and violent disorder. This sort of behaviour clearly does not constitute 'peaceful assem-bly' within the meaning of Art 11, and an absolute ban is therefore unproblematic in Convention terms. Behaviour that does not fall into the 'definitely unacceptable' cat-egory is potentially lawful—that is, it may, in principle, be lawfully undertaken—but is subject to regulation. For example, although generally lawful, such conduct might,

---

[18] *Öllinger v Austria* at [36].   [19] Mead at 142.

in *particular circumstances*, be prohibited (for example, because it is judged by the authorities that it would create an unacceptable risk of disorder) or those undertaking it might have *particular conditions* imposed upon them (for example, the size or duration of the protest might be limited).

As we consider domestic law, we will need to keep in mind two principal questions. First, is the distinction acceptably drawn between conduct that is absolutely prohibited and that which is, in principle, permitted, but subject to regulation? For example, English law *prima facie* criminalises behaviour that is 'insulting' and carried out 'within the hearing or sight of a person likely to be caused harassment, alarm or distress thereby'.[20] Is it right to place this sort of conduct on the 'prohibited' side of the line, or does this risk outlawing conduct that constitutes a legitimate form of protest? This raises important questions about whether one person's 'right' not to be offended should be allowed to trump someone else's right to protest. Second, even in relation to conduct falling on the 'in principle permissible' side of the line, is the regime of regulation supplied by English law an acceptable one? Does it strike the correct balance—whatever the 'correct' balance is—between the conflicting rights and interests that, we have already seen, are usually in play in cases of this type?

3. Prohibition of certain types of behaviour

3.1 Public Order Act 1986, ss 1–3

Part I of the Public Order Act 1986 criminalises a number of forms of behaviour.[21] As noted above, some of the prohibitions are wholly unsurprising and cannot be regarded as impinging upon legitimate protest. Into this category undoubtedly fall the offences under ss 1–3 of riot, violent disorder, and affray, all of which involve the intentional or reckless use or threat of unlawful violence such as to cause a person of reasonable firmness to fear for his personal safety. Riot, violent disorder, and affray are, then, very serious offences that carry maximum sentences on conviction of ten, five, and three years, respectively.

3.2 Public Order Act 1986, ss 4, 4A, and 5

Sections 4, 4A, and 5 respectively create offences concerning fear or provocation of violence; intentional harassment, alarm, or distress; and harassment, alarm, or distress. The ingredients of each of these offences, together with details of applicable defences, are set out in Figure 21.1. To assess whether ss 4, 4A, and 5 constitute

---

[20] Public Order Act 1986, s 5(1).

[21] As with all criminal offences, conviction is only possible if the prosecution establishes beyond reasonable doubt that all elements of the relevant offence have been committed.

	Prohibited behaviour	Mental requirement regarding behaviour	Effects of behaviour and mental requirement regarding effects of behaviour	Specific statutory defences
Section 4: Fear or provocation of violence	Use of threatening, abusive, or insulting words or behaviour towards another person; or distribution or display of writing, sign, or other visible representation that is threatening, abusive, or insulting	Intends words, behaviour, writing, sign, or other visible representation to be threatening, abusive, or insulting; or is aware that it may be threatening, abusive, or insulting	Intends victim to believe that immediate unlawful violence will occur; or intends to provoke such violence; or victim is likely to believe such violence will be used; or it is likely such violence will be provoked	
Section 4A: Intentional harassment, alarm, or distress	Actually causing harassment, alarm or distress by either using threatening, abusive, or insulting words or behaviour, or disorderly behaviour; or displaying any writing, sign, or other visible representation that is threatening, abusive, or insulting		Intends to cause harassment, alarm, or distress	Accused person was inside a dwelling and had no reason to believe that words, behaviour, writing, sign, or other visible representation would be seen or heard by anyone outside (no offence being committed if someone *inside* the building is harassed etc); or conduct was reasonable
Section 5: Harassment, alarm, or distress	Use of threatening, abusive, or insulting words or behaviour, or disorderly behaviour; or display of any writing, sign, or other visible representation that is threatening, abusive, or insulting	Intends words, behaviour, writing, sign, or other visible representation to be threatening, abusive or insulting; or intends behaviour to be disorderly; or is aware that behaviour may be disorderly	When the prohibited behaviour takes place, there must be someone within hearing or sight likely to be caused harassment, alarm, or distress either	No reason to believe anyone was within sight or hearing who was likely to be harassed, alarmed, or distressed Defences set out above in relation to s 4A also apply to s 5

Figure 21.1 Public Order Act 1986, ss 4, 4A, and 5

acceptable restrictions on the right of peaceful protest that are compatible with the requirements of the ECHR, it is necessary to address a number of issues that, although interconnected, we present separately for the purposes of exposition.

Engaging in *threatening, abusive, or insulting conduct* is not sufficient in itself to attract criminal liability under ss 4, 4A, or 5, but it is a prerequisite that is common to all three offences.[22] It stands to reason, then, that the more broadly the notion of threatening, abusive, or insulting conduct is understood, the greater the inroads into the right to protest. In *Brutus v Cozens*,[23] it was held that Parliament had intended the phrase 'insulting behaviour' to bear its 'ordinary meaning': 'an ordinary sensible man', said Lord Reid, 'knows an insult when he sees or hears it'. It followed, said his Lordship, that 'vigorous', 'distasteful', and 'unmannerly' speech was not necessarily insulting (or threatening or abusive).[24] Thus, when anti-apartheid protestors interrupted a Wimbledon tennis match by sitting on the court, Lord Reid, while willing to characterise their behaviour as 'deplorable', said that he could not see how it had been *insulting* to the spectators.[25] However, this decision notwithstanding, there have been occasions on which courts have arguably been too quick to characterise conduct as insulting and as therefore potentially attracting criminal liability. For example, in *Masterson v Holden*,[26] the conviction of a gay couple who had kissed in public was upheld,[27] Glidewell LJ opining that 'the display of such objectionable conduct in a public street may well be regarded by another person, particularly by a young woman, as conduct which insults her by suggesting that she is somebody who would find such conduct in public acceptable herself'.[28]

That case was decided in 1986, and it is (fortunately) hard to imagine it being decided the same way today, bearing in mind the sea change in social attitudes in the intervening period. It does, however, lead on to a further point. As noted above, engaging in threatening, abusive, or insulting conduct does not in itself constitute an offence under ss 4, 4A, or 5. In each case, there is a requirement concerning the *impact of the conduct on the audience*. Under s 4, the conduct must make it likely that unlawful violence will be anticipated or provoked, or such anticipation or provocation must be intended. Once this requirement is factored in, it becomes clear that s 4 does not make serious inroads into the right of legitimate protest—such protests are unlikely to have the effects, or to be accompanied by the intentions, proscribed by s 4. However, the 'effect' components of ss 4A and 5 are weaker: under s 4A, harassment, alarm, or distress must be caused (and intended), while under s 5, the conduct must be undertaken within the hearing or sight of someone likely to be caused harassment,

---

[22] Except that in relation to the ss 4A and 5 offences, liability may also arise if there is 'disorderly behaviour'.

[23] [1973] AC 854, 862. This case was concerned with s 5 of the Public Order Act 1936, but remains relevant to the interpretation of 'insulting behaviour' under the 1986 Act.   [24] [1973] AC 854, 862.

[25] Apartheid was the systematic policy of racial segregation and discrimination in force in South Africa from 1948 to 1991.   [26] [1986] 3 All ER 39.

[27] Under a different Act that also used the formulation 'threatening, abusive or insulting words or behaviour'.   [28] [1986] 3 All ER 39, 44.

alarm, or distress (whether or not intended). Depending on how these requirements are interpreted, ss 4A and 5 have the potential significantly to circumscribe lawful protest. Section 4A risks criminalising any protest that upsets sensitive—including unreasonably sensitive—people; s 5 risks allowing the police and the courts to criminalise conduct that they think is likely to upset people (witness Glidewell LJ's 'young woman' likely to be offended by a gay couple kissing[29]).

The essential question, then, is how we strike the balance between the interests of those who wish to speak out or otherwise act in a potentially controversial or provocative manner, and the interests of those who might be, and do not wish to be, troubled by such conduct. The ECHR, as we know, stipulates that the right to protest must be upheld except to the extent that its limitation is a necessary and proportionate way of safeguarding one of the competing interests recognised as legitimate in Arts 10(2) and 11(2). The challenge for UK courts, since the entry into force of the HRA, has been to interpret and apply the Public Order Act in a way that meets the requirements of the Convention. There are a number of ways in which this might be done: a particularly robust view might be taken of what is meant by 'threatening, abusive or insulting' or by 'harassed, alarmed or distressed', for example.

Alternatively, emphasis might be placed on the defence (shown in Figure 21.1) under ss 4A and 5 that the conduct was 'reasonable': a court might, for example, conclude that even if threatening, abusive, or insulting conduct causes or is likely to cause harassment, alarm, or distress, this is nevertheless reasonable if serving the end of legitimate protest. However, it has been argued that English courts have failed to take sufficient steps to reorientate English law[30] in the way required by the Convention—that they have placed too little weight on the right to protest and too much on the 'right' not to be offended.[31] For example, in *Norwood v DPP*,[32] Auld LJ said that once conduct had been shown to satisfy the requirements of s 5, it would, in most cases, follow that it was unreasonable—an analysis that has the potential largely to undercut the reasonableness defence. Meanwhile, in *Hammond v DPP*,[33] that defence did not avail a defendant who was convicted under s 5 for preaching in a busy town centre on (as he saw it) the immorality of same-sex relationships. And in *ProLife Alliance*,[34] the House of Lords held that broadcasters had acted lawfully by deciding that, on the grounds of its perceived offensiveness, they would not transmit a party election broadcast by an anti-abortion party that included graphic pictures of terminated foetuses.

---

[29] The couple in *Masterson v Holden* were not protesting, but shows of affection are perfectly capable of constituting a protest and (along with other forms of protest) have performed precisely that function in the context of campaigns for equal treatment of gays and lesbians in many societies.

[30] The 1986 Act applies in its entirety to England and Wales; parts of it also apply in the rest of the UK.

[31] Geddis, 'Free Speech Martyrs or Unreasonable Threats to Social Peace? "Insulting" Expression and Section 5 of the Public Order Act 1986' [2004] PL 853.

[32] [2003] EWHC 1564 (Admin).

[33] [2004] EWHC 69 (Admin).

[34] [2003] UKHL 23, [2004] 1 AC 185. This case did not concern the Public Order Act, but raised the same point about the balance between one person's right to put across his point of view in a manner of his choosing and another's 'right' not to be offended.

All of these decisions raise the question of whether the balance is being struck correctly—and as required by the ECHR—between those who wish to put forward their (perhaps unpalatable) views and those who do not wish to be offended by them. Ultimately, the choice is between what has been called a 'pro-civility' approach—one that emphasises the importance of respecting others' sensibilities and of preserving public decorum[35]—and one that places greater weight on free speech as a force for good and as something that people must therefore learn to tolerate, even when they disagree with the content or medium. In a strong endorsement of the latter approach, dissenting in *ProLife Alliance*, Lord Scott said that where a broadcast was factually accurate, not sensationalized, and relevant to an issue in an election, a refusal to transmit it would be incompatible with the ECHR: '[T]he public in a mature democracy', he said, 'are not entitled to be offended by the broadcasting of such a programme'.[36] Refusing to broadcast it, he said, would be 'inimical to the values of a democracy'—which, as the ECtHR has repeatedly said, include 'pluralism, tolerance and broad-mindedness',[37] and which mean that the right of freedom of expression (and thus the right to protest) must include the right to 'offend, shock or disturb'.[38] It is questionable whether, at least in the present context, English law has yet fully absorbed these Convention principles.

> **Q** Which of the two approaches set out above do you find preferable? How far (it at all) do you think Lord Scott's view should be taken? Should there be any legal recognition of a 'right' not to be offended?

3.3 Harassment

This is a convenient point at which to consider the Protection from Harassment Act 1997.[39] The Act sets out three forms of behaviour that constitute criminal offences.[40]

First, s 4(1) makes it an offence to (i) pursue a course of conduct that causes another person to fear, on at least two occasions, that violence will be used against him; (ii) provided that the perpetrator knows or ought to know that his conduct will cause violence to be feared on each occasion. Second, s 1(1) (read with s 2(1)) says that an offence is committed when a person (i) engages in a course of conduct that amounts to harassment of another person (ii) that he knows or ought to know amounts to harassment. Third, s 1(1A), read with s 2(1), says that an offence occurs when a

---

[35] Geddis at 869–70.   [36] [2003] UKHL 23, [2004] 1 AC 185, [98].

[37] *Handyside v UK* (1979–80) 1 EHRR 737, 754.   [38] *Handyside* at 754.

[39] The position set out here concerns England and Wales; different provision is made in ss 8–11 for Scotland.

[40] Under ss 3 and 3A, it is also possible in certain circumstances to obtain civil remedies—including injunctions—when prohibited harassment has occurred or is anticipated.

person (i) engages in a course of conduct that involves harassment of two or more persons (ii) that he knows or ought to know involves harassment and (iii) intends to persuade someone (whether or not it is one of the people actually being harassed) not to do something that he is entitled or required to do, or to do something that he is not obliged to do.

Do any of these provisions criminalise behaviour that might be regarded as a legitimate form of protest? The position is most straightforward in relation to s 4(1): it is difficult to argue that behaviour creating a fear of violence should be permitted as a form of legitimate, peaceful protest.[41] But what of the other two offences? The sort of behaviour criminalised by s 1(1) extends to conduct wholly unrelated to protest—it might, for example, involve one person stalking another. However, the Act does criminalise some types of behaviour that might be regarded as protest: for example, it would be an offence under the Act for an animal rights protestor to harass the managing director of a pharmaceutical company that tests its products on animals, perhaps hoping to persuade him to desist from doing so in the future.[42] And under s 1(1A) it would be an offence for protestors to harass employees of the company with a view to persuading them to leave the company or to refuse to perform their duties for it.[43]

Whether (and, if so, the extent to which) s 1(1) and (1A) of the 1997 Act criminalises behaviour that might be considered as legitimate forms of protest depends on two principal factors, the first being the meaning of 'harassment'. The Act does not define 'harassment' as such, but it says that it includes alarming or causing distress to a person.[44] This is not, on the face of it, a high hurdle, and it means that while the Act undoubtedly (and rightly) criminalises long-running hate campaigns that make people's lives intolerable, it also risks proscribing much more moderate forms of protest. The second factor to be borne in mind is that conduct that would otherwise constitute harassment is not unlawful if, in the particular circumstances, it was reasonable.[45] The courts are required by the HRA to construe the concepts of 'harassment' and 'reasonableness' in a manner consistent with the ECHR, which means striking an acceptable balance between the rights of protestors under Arts 10 and 11, and those of the people who are targeted by protestors.[46] However, as we saw above, the courts have been criticised for failing to attach sufficient weight to the right to protest when addressing analogous issues arising under the Public Order Act.

---

[41] This conclusion is reinforced by the fact that the fear of violence must be an objectively reasonable one: s 4(2).

[42] Provided that the protestor knew, or ought to have known, that his conduct amounted to harassment.

[43] Subject to the proviso in n 41.   [44] Section 7(2).   [45] Section 1(3).

[46] The most obvious right at stake for the latter group is the right to respect for private and family life under ECHR, Art 8. On the need to balance the interests of the parties, see further *Director of Public Prosecutions v Selvanayagam* The Times, 23 June 1999.

4. Statutory powers to regulate protests

4.1 Introduction

Even if a particular form of behaviour might not be a criminal offence, it may be potentially subject to an array of statutory powers of regulation. As we will see, the authorities have extensive powers to impose conditions on protests and even to ban certain forms of protest that, although not per se unlawful, are judged to pose unacceptable risks in the circumstances of the particular case.

The existence and extent of such powers is important to our inquiry into whether English law attaches sufficient weight to the right to protest. It is widely accepted that much of the value of freedom of expression lies in having the right to say not only *what* you want, but also to say it *how* and *where* you want to; otherwise, as Lord Neuberger MR has noted, free speech and the right to protest 'would be at risk of emasculation'.[47] ProLife Alliance, for example, wished to *show* images of aborted foetuses rather than merely to *describe* the effect on foetuses of termination procedures, because it felt that its point could be made more effectively in the former way.[48] Equally, the right to protest would be largely worthless if the authorities were to have an unfettered power to direct that protests could take place only in prescribed locations (a protest in a field in the middle of nowhere being unlikely to have the same impact as one conducted in a busy city centre) or to cap the number of protestors (three protestors are likely to be much less effective than 300,000). Yet it does not follow that the authorities should have *no* power to regulate protests: a sit-in on a busy road, although peaceful, is liable to bring an entire city to a standstill, and there is an obvious need, while recognising the protestors' rights, to give adequate weight to the interests of other people as well. It is against this background that we need to examine English law in this area.

4.2 Regulating public assemblies

Section 14 of the Public Order Act 1986 gives the police certain powers to regulate public assemblies. Three main points should be noted.

First, the way in which the Act defines the term 'public assembly' means that these powers only apply when three conditions are met: (i) the gathering must be of *two or more persons*, (ii) it must be in a *public place* (meaning a highway or any other place that the public may lawfully access), and (iii) it must take place wholly or partly in the *open air*.[49] If these requirements are satisfied, the regulatory powers contained in s 14 are in principle exercisable.

---

[47] *Hall v Mayor of London* [2010] EWCA Civ 817, [37]. [48] See section 3.2 above.
[49] Public Order Act 1986, s 16.

Second, the power to regulate public assemblies is only *triggered* in certain circumstances. The relevant police officer[50] must (taking into account the circumstances) reasonably believe either (i) that the assembly may result in serious public disorder, serious damage to property, or serious disruption to the life of the community; or (ii) that the organisers' purpose is to intimidate people in order to compel them not to do something that they have a right to do, or to do something that they have a right not to do.[51]

Third, if (and only if) at least one of those criteria is met, the relevant police officer may set *conditions* concerning the location of the assembly, its duration, and how many people may take part. Those conditions must go no further in terms of restricting the assembly than appear to the police officer to be necessary to prevent the feared outcomes mentioned in the previous paragraph.[52] It is a criminal offence to organise or take part in a public assembly and knowingly to fail to comply with such a condition (unless the failure arises due to circumstances beyond the relevant person's control).[53]

These powers are not particularly controversial viewed from the perspective of the right to protest. The conditions that must be met in order for the powers to be triggered are framed in robust terms—*serious* public disorder, and so on—and if a police officer were unreasonably to conclude that such conditions had been met, his decision would be open to challenge by means of judicial review. Equally, even when the power is triggered, the restrictions imposed must go no further than necessary. This is of a piece with Art 11, which permits freedom of assembly to be limited when (and to the extent) that this is necessary in the public interest.

4.3 **Prohibiting trespassory assemblies**

The power under s 14 does not extend to *banning* public assemblies. However, ss 14A–C allow steps to be taken to ban—that is, to criminalise the organisation of and participation in—'trespassory assemblies'. Clearly, outright prohibition of protest is a more draconian step than regulating the way in which a protest is conducted, and it follows that a power to prohibit assemblies *prima facie* makes greater inroads into the right to protest than does a power merely to regulate. To assess the extent to which ss 14A–C curtail the right to protest, we need to address two questions: when can the power to prohibit assemblies be exercised? And, when that power is used, what is its effect?

As to the former matter, the conditions circumscribing the use of the s 14A power of prohibition are tighter than those applying to the s 14 regulatory power. First, the s 14A power applies only to gatherings of *20 or more persons*.[54] Second, it only applies

---

[50] Being the most senior officer present at the protest or, if the power is being used before the start of the protest, the head of the relevant police force: s 14(2).   [51] Section 14(1).

[52] Section 14(1).   [53] Section 14(4) and (5).   [54] Section 14A(9).

to land in the open air to which the public has *no or only a limited right of access*;[55] this means that the s 14A power (unlike the s 14 power) does not extend to gatherings on common land to which the public has an unlimited right of access. Third, the head of the relevant police force must reasonably believe that the assembly is likely to be held *without the permission* of, or in *breach of terms* laid down by, the occupier of the land and that the assembly will result in *serious disruption to the life of the community* or *significant damage to land, a building, or a monument that is historically, architecturally, archaeologically, or scientifically important.*[56] Fourth, a s 14A prohibition may be imposed only with the *agreement of the Secretary of State* and (except in London) the *local authority.*[57]

What, then, are the practical consequences of a s 14A prohibition? The most important is that a person commits a criminal offence by taking part in or organising an assembly prohibited under s 14A.[58] However, it is important to bear in mind that s 14A orders only have the effect of prohibiting assemblies *to the extent that they constitute trespass.*[59] If the protestors have a right to be on the land or have the permission of the occupier of the land to be there, the s 14A order does not prohibit the protest: it only bites if, and to the extent that, the protestors exceed the limit of any right that they have (or of any permission that has been granted for them) to be present on the land. It follows that our inquiry into the extent to which the power to prohibit trespassory assemblies makes inroads into the right to protest must take account not only of the conditions limiting the imposition of such orders (considered in the previous paragraph), but also of the extent to which property law recognises a right on the part of protestors to be present on land. To the extent that such a right exists, the protestors' presence on the land in question will not constitute a trespass—meaning, in turn, that the protest cannot be banned under s 14A.

This issue has assumed particular prominence in relation to public highways (roads), which are owned not by 'the public', but (usually) by the Crown or by local authorities. Many demonstrations involve people being present on highways, and the question arises whether (and, if so, to what extent) it is possible to ban such demonstrations under s 14A. Not being the owners of highways, the public only avoid committing trespass when they use them to the extent to which they have a right to do so. In *Director of Public Prosecutions v Jones*,[60] a number of people were standing on a roadside verge near Stonehenge protesting against the authorities' policy of restricting access to the monument.[61] A s 14A order was in place and they were arrested for taking part in a prohibited trespassory assembly. In defence, they argued that they were not trespassing—that they had a right to be on a public highway for the purposes of peaceful protest—and that they had therefore done nothing prohibited by

---

[55] Section 14A(1).   [56] Section 14A(1).   [57] Section 14A(2)–(4).

[58] Section 14B(1) and (2).   [59] Section 14A(5).   [60] [1999] 2 AC 240.

[61] Particular controversy surrounds the extent to which those who attach religious or quasi-religious significance to the monument should have access to it at what they regard as significant times of the year, such as the summer solstice.

the order. Overturning the defendants' convictions, the House of Lords distinguished between two schools of thought concerning the extent of the individual's right to use the highway. The narrower—and, as it turned out, incorrect—view was that the public only had a right to 'pass and repass'—that is, to use highways for travel.[62] In *Jones*, Lord Irvine LC noted that this would produce 'surprising consequences'—for example, rendering trespassers people who stop to talk, children who play in the street, and political activists handing out leaflets.[63] The better view, he said, involved recognising that 'the public highway is a public place, on which all manner of reasonable activities may go on'.[64] It followed that 'there is a public right of peaceful assembly on the highway'.[65] This is not, of course, an unlimited right: the assembly must represent a *reasonable* use of the highway, and one that causes an unacceptable degree of inconvenience to others is unlikely to be reasonable.[66] However, the House of Lords had no difficulty in concluding that the conduct at stake in *Jones* was perfectly reasonable, that the defendants had not therefore exceeded their right to be present on the highway, and that they had not committed the offence of taking part in a prohibited trespassory assembly. Although the reasoning of some of the judges was not as bold as that of Lord Irvine, *Jones* is nevertheless widely regarded as a highly significant decision that is 'an important vindication of a fundamental civil liberty'.[67] As such, it means that the power to prohibit trespassory assemblies is a less draconian one than it first appears (and was probably intended) to be.

4.4 **Demonstrations near the Palace of Westminster**

Our discussion of the authorities' powers to regulate public assemblies cannot be allowed to conclude without mention of the issue of whether demonstrations should be allowed near Parliament. For centuries, people have, with varying degrees of success, organised demonstrations in Parliament Square just outside Parliament in order to protest against the government or a law being enacted by Parliament. Sections 132–138 of the Serious Organised Crime and Police Act 2005 made it a criminal offence to organise or participate in a demonstration within a kilometre of Parliament Square unless the prior permission of the police was obtained.[68] Although, following receipt of an application in the required form, such permission cannot be *withheld*, it can be made subject to extensive *conditions* as to, *inter alia*, the duration, size, and location of the demonstration. Failure to comply with such conditions is a criminal offence. This means that it is possible to criminalise protests at *particular locations*—such as

---

[62] See, eg *Harrison v Duke of Rutland* [1893] 1 QB 142, 158, per Kay LJ.

[63] *Director of Public Prosecutions v Jones* at 254.   [64] *Director of Public Prosecutions v Jones* at 254.

[65] *Director of Public Prosecutions v Jones* at 257.

[66] It should be noted in this regard that, separately from the Public Order Act 1986, obstruction of the highway is a criminal offence in its own right under the Highways Act 1980, s 137.

[67] Clayton, 'Reclaiming Public Ground: The Right to Peaceful Assembly' (2000) 63 MLR 252, 252.

[68] Further restrictions in relation to Parliament Square arise as a result of by-laws made under s 385 of the Greater London Authority Act 1999; see further *Mayor of London v Hall* [2010] EWCA Civ 817.

immediately outside the Palace of Westminster—by imposing conditions that the demonstration must occur at a venue other than that preferred by the protestor.

The legislation was enacted against the background of a long-running protest held in Parliament Square by a single person, Brian Haw, against government policy in relation to (and military action against) Iraq. Haw, it has been said,[69] was a 'primary target' of ss 132–138 of the 2005 Act.[70] Several people have been convicted under those provisions, including some who simply stood alone in Parliament Square reading out the names of British soldiers killed in Iraq.[71] Although the official rationale for the enactment of these provisions was the need to ensure security in the vicinity of Parliament, and although the preservation of national security is a legitimate reason under the ECHR for curtailing relevant rights, it is hard to see how the criminalisation of conduct of this type could be said to constitute a necessary and proportionate limitation of the right to protest. However, the High Court rejected the argument that the requirement to obtain prior authorisation for protests was inconsistent with the ECHR[72]—and although it remains open to protestors in individual cases to challenge the specific conditions imposed upon them, and although permission to hold protests cannot be withheld outright, the requirement of prior authorisation most likely has a chilling effect on the exercise of the right to protest. In 2008, in the face of significant opposition to the use made of the powers under ss 132–138 of the 2005 Act, the then government accepted that they imposed unnecessary restrictions on the right to protest and proposed their repeal, although this failed to happen prior to the 2010 general election. Following that election, the new government undertook to 'restore rights to non-violent protest',[73] and it seems likely that this will include modifying or repealing ss 132–138 of the 2005 Act. Nevertheless, this sorry episode serves as an important reminder of the sometimes irresistible temptation felt by those in authority to squash dissent that they regard as inconvenient, embarrassing, or just downright annoying.

4.5 **Regulating and prohibiting processions**

So far, we have been concerned with the regulation of *assemblies*. We turn now to *processions*. The essential distinction is that the former are stationary, while the latter are not. The legal regime for regulation of public processions is contained in ss 11–13 of the Public Order Act 1986, and differs in two key respects from that which applies to assemblies.

---

[69] Loveland, 'Public Protest in Parliament Square' [2007] EHRLR 251, 252.

[70] A legal wrangle then ensued in which Haw argued (ultimately unsuccessfully) that the Act had been drafted in a way that made it inapplicable to his case (*R (Haw) v Secretary of State for the Home Department* [2006] EWCA Civ 532, [2006] QB 780), but later successfully argued that the conditions imposed by the police on his demonstration were so vague as to be impossible to comply with ([2007] EWHC 1931 (Admin), [2008] 1 WLR 379). His conviction was therefore set aside—but not before 54 police officers had removed him from Parliament Square.

[71] Loveland at 264–5.   [72] *DPP v Blum* [2006] EWHC 3209 (Admin).

[73] HM Government, *The Coalition: Our Programme for Government* (London 2010), p 11.

First, whereas there is no requirement to give the police notice of an assembly,[74] *it is normally necessary to give the police advance notice of processions*—with details of date, time, route, and so on—that are intended to demonstrate support for, or opposition to, a particular view, to publicise a cause or campaign, or to mark or commemorate an event.[75] In terms of Art 11, such a requirement is in itself uncontentious: a procession in a public place (which almost inevitably means the highway) is liable to cause at least a degree of disruption, and requiring advance notice (which, in turn, allows the police to work out how to deal with the likely consequences of any disruption) is a proportionate restriction on the right of assembly that seeks to accommodate the interests of others. Organisers of processions commit a criminal offence if the procession goes ahead without such notice having been given, or if the timing or route of the procession differs from that specified in the notice given to the police.[76] However, the requirement to give advance notice does not apply if complying with it is not reasonably practicable or if the procession is one that is commonly or customarily held. The meaning of the latter exception was central to *Kay v Commissioner of Police of the Metropolis*.[77] The court was asked to determine whether the advance notification requirement applied to participants in mass cycle rides, known as 'Critical Mass', which had taken place in London every month for several years, departing from the same location each time, but taking a different and unplanned route (riders simply following whoever happened to be at the front). It was held that the advance notification requirement did not apply, and that no offence was therefore committed by failing to provide notice: the rides were 'commonly or customarily held', notwithstanding that they did not follow the same route each time, and were therefore exempt from the requirement to provide notice. A question left unanswered by *Kay* is what would happen if a different group were to wish to establish similar cycle rides (or other processions without a predetermined route). The police argued in *Kay* that it would be legally impossible to establish such processions: a *new* procession would (unlike the long-established Critical Mass rides) not be commonly or customarily held; it would therefore have to be notified to the police and the notification would have to include details of the route. Lord Phillips, *obiter*, said that he was 'unable to give section 11 this draconian effect', suggesting that another interpretation of s 11 would have to be found in such a case.[78]

Second, as with public assemblies, there is a power to impose conditions on public processions.[79] However, whereas there is no power to ban assemblies (unless they are trespassory assemblies), *there is a power to ban public processions*. The power can only be exercised if the head of the relevant police force reasonably believes that the

---

[74] Except those to be held in the vicinity of Parliament Square.   [75] Public Order Act 1986, s 11(1).
[76] Public Order Act 1986, s 11(7).   [77] [2008] UKHL 69, [2008] 1 WLR 2723.
[78] *Kay* at [24]. For example, the notification requirement does not apply when it is not reasonably practicable to give advance notice: Lord Phillips suggested that this exception might apply to a procession without a predetermined route.
[79] See Public Order Act 1986, s 12. The power to impose conditions on processions is very similar to that under s 14 concerning the imposition of conditions on assemblies, on which, see section 4.3 above.

imposition of conditions will be insufficient to prevent serious public disorder,[80] and the agreement of the Secretary of State and (outside London) the local authority is needed.[81] It is an offence for a person to organise or participate in a procession that he knows to be banned.[82] There is no explicit mention of the importance of the right to protest in the Public Order Act, but the effect of the HRA is that a procession may only be banned if this constitutes a necessary and proportionate restriction on that right. It is therefore incumbent upon those involved in making the decision to weigh the importance of the right to protest in the given circumstances against the risks that would be posed by allowing the procession to go ahead.

5. Common law powers to regulate protests

5.1 Introduction

We have seen that there exist extensive statutory powers to regulate, and in some circumstances prohibit, protests. There is, of course, room for legitimate disagreement about whether the relevant legislation attaches sufficient weight to the right to protest— but at least it can be said that, in the legislation considered above, Parliament has taken the trouble to set out in reasonably clear terms the powers (and, importantly, the *limits* of the powers) that the authorities have to manage public protests. It is therefore perhaps surprising that, alongside these statutory powers, the police also have a very broad common law power that can be used to manage, and even choke off, protest.

This is unsatisfactory on two grounds.[83] First, the common law power is, as we will see, ill defined.[84] As we saw in Chapters 1 and 2, legal certainty is a central requirement of the rule of law, and it is especially objectionable in an area concerning important rights that the extent of the police's powers should be uncertain. Second, the risk arises that the restrictions built into the authorities' statutory powers will be evaded by recourse to their wider common law powers.[85] These issues are of importance to the central concern of this chapter—namely, whether English law ascribes proper weight to the right to protest—but to explore them properly, we need to begin by explaining the nature of the common law power in question.

The common law power with which we are concerned in this section is *the power of police constables to take steps to prevent or stop a breach of the peace.* In order to understand the nature of this power—and hence in order to work out whether it is an acceptable limitation upon the right to protest—we need to examine three matters. First, what is a *breach of the peace*? Second, *in what circumstances* may the police step

---

[80] Section 13(1).   [81] Section 13(2)–(4).   [82] Section 13(7) and (8).
[83] See generally Stone, 'Breach of the Peace: The Case for Abolition' [2001] 2 Web JCLI.
[84] Williams, *Keeping the Peace* (London 1967), p 116.
[85] We will see, however, that the risk is now smaller because of the influence of the HRA.

in to deal with an ongoing or anticipated breach of the peace? And, third, when they do step in, *what exactly may the police do?*

5.2 What is a breach of the peace?

A 'breach of the peace' is something that disturbs 'the peace', or 'the Queen's peace', as it is sometimes rather quaintly known. This does not mean something that interferes with 'peace and quiet'; rather, it means something that interferes with the normal state of affairs in which members of the community live together peaceably. As Feldman puts it, 'peace', in this context, refers not to the 'absence of noise', but means the opposite of 'war'.[86] There has been a degree of uncertainty in the case law concerning the precise circumstances in which a 'breach of the peace' will occur. For example, it was suggested by Lord Denning MR, in a case in which protestors prevented a possible site for a nuclear power station from being surveyed, that there would be a breach of the peace 'whenever a person who is lawfully carrying out his work is unlawfully and physically prevented by another from doing it'.[87] However, it is now generally accepted that the correct definition of 'breach of the peace' is the narrower one set out in *R v Howell*.[88] Taking into account what was said in that case and what has been said in subsequent cases,[89] it can be stated that a breach of the peace arises whenever any of the following three things occurs or is likely to occur as a result of violence: (i) a person is injured, (ii) a person fears being injured, or (iii) a person's property is damaged in his presence. Breach of the peace is not itself an offence,[90] but it triggers police powers to intervene in relation to those who are causing the breach.

5.3 In what circumstances may the police intervene?

In the face of a breach of the peace, the police have a number of options at their disposal. We consider what those options are in the following section, but it may be helpful at this stage to say that they include arrest. Of course, there are many forms of conduct that constitute a breach of the peace that need not detain us. Dozens of such breaches are doubtless committed in most city centres at closing time on an average Saturday night as fights break out or threaten to break out. If the police arrest people engaging in such behaviour, this does not have the effect of curtailing the right to protest. It is also, of course, conceivable that conduct falling within the category of protest may constitute a breach of the peace—yet, on the face of it, it is hard to see why this should concern us. We noted above that the boundaries of *legitimate* protest are

---

[86] Feldman, *Civil Liberties and Human Rights in England and Wales* (Oxford 2002), p 1018.

[87] *R v Chief Constable of Devon and Cornwall, ex p Central Electricity Generating Board* [1982] QB 458, 471.   [88] [1982] QB 416.

[89] Including *Percy v Director of Public Prosecutions* [1995] 1 WLR 1382; *Steel v UK* (1999) 28 EHRR 603.

[90] Although, of course, it is entirely possible that conduct constituting a breach of the peace will also amount to a substantive criminal offence such as assault.

generally regarded as coterminous with those of *peaceful* protest. (It is, for example, only the right of *peaceful* protest that is protected by the ECHR.) Surely, then, the fact that the police have the power to intervene when a breach of the peace occurs—which means that *violence* is occurring or is likely to occur—cannot logically have the effect of restricting legitimate, *peaceful* protest?

The reality, though, is more complicated—particularly by the fact that a person may commit a breach of the peace even if he is not himself acting, or likely to act, violently. In *Percy*, Watkins LJ said that the conduct constituting a breach of the peace 'does not itself have to be disorderly'—or violent—'or a breach of the criminal law. It is sufficient if its natural consequence would, if persisted in, be to provoke others to violence, and so some actual danger to the peace is established'.[91] This means, *prima facie*, that it would be perfectly lawful for a police officer to arrest a protestor who was not himself acting or likely to act violently, but who was expressing views that were causing or likely to cause *others* to act violently. Precisely this happened in *Duncan v Jones*,[92] in which it was held that the police had acted lawfully and within the scope of their duty by requiring a protestor to desist. The protestor was not acting or threatening to act violently, but past experience suggested that others would act in such a manner because of the content of the protestor's views. In so holding, Lord Hewart CJ remarked that English law did 'not recognise any special right of public meeting for political or other purposes'.[93]

The law has moved on in this area since that case was decided in 1935. Allowing the police to target a peaceful protestor because of others' likely response is to give the mob a power of veto that is inconsistent with the right to protest now applicable under the ECHR, and with the allied responsibility of the state to facilitate peaceful protest.[94] Of particular note is *Redmond-Bate v Director of Public Prosecutions*,[95] in which Christian fundamentalist preachers who had attracted a crowd of over 100 people near a cathedral were arrested for breach of the peace and subsequently convicted by magistrates of a related offence. However, their appeal against conviction was allowed by the High Court. Sedley LJ, giving the only reasoned judgment, said that the '[f]reedom only to speak inoffensively is not worth having'. Free speech therefore includes 'the irritating, the contentious, the eccentric, the heretical, the unwelcome and the provocative'. In the later case of *Bibby v Chief Constable of Essex*,[96] Schiemann LJ emphasised that 'depriving of his liberty a citizen who is not at the time acting unlawfully' represents an 'extreme step' not to be lightly undertaken. It follows that the police may only arrest for breach of the peace someone who is not themselves acting or threatening to act violently if (i) the person is acting unreasonably, (ii) the natural consequence of his conduct is violence from a third party, and (iii) that

---

91 [1995] 1 WLR 1382, 1392.   92 [1936] 1 KB 218; cf *Beatty v Gillbanks* (1881–82) LR 9 QBD 308.

93 [1936] 1 KB 218, 222.

94 See discussion in section 1.3 above of *Plattform 'Ärzte für das Leben' v Austria*.

95 [2000] HRLR 249.   96 (2000) 164 JP 297, 302.

violence is not wholly unreasonable.[97] In practice, this means that a distinction falls to be drawn between situations in which the reactions of the audience are 'the voluntary acts of people who could not properly be regarded as objects of provocation' (in which case, they, but not the protestor, may be arrested for breach of the peace) and those in which the protestor's conduct is 'calculated to provoke violent and disorderly reaction' (in which case, the protestor can be arrested).[98] In a later case, Lord Brown emphasised that targeting the protestor, rather than those reacting or likely to react violently to what is being said, should be a measure of last resort for the police, their 'first duty' being to 'protect the rights of the innocent rather than to compel the innocent to cease exercising them'.[99] The foregoing is subject to the caveat that where the police reasonably believe that 'there are no other means whatsoever whereby a breach or imminent breach of the peace can be obviated, the lawful exercise by third parties of their rights may be curtailed'.[100]

5.4 **What can the police do?**

At common law, the police possess powers to arrest and detain people in order to prevent or stop a breach of the peace, as well as powers to take steps short of arrest and detention (for example, requiring people acting or threatening to act violently to move away from the place in which tensions are running high). The police are quite properly not required to wait until violence is taking place before exercising such powers, but when exactly may they intervene? Over the years, this has been a particular bone of contention between protestors and the authorities, the cause célèbre being the case of *Moss v McLachlin*,[101] which arose during the miners' strike of 1984–85. The police stopped 25 cars containing up to 80 striking miners at a motorway junction situated between 1.5 and 5 miles from four collieries at which the police feared the cars' occupants would become involved in violent confrontations. Forty miners refused to comply with police instructions not to proceed towards the collieries and were arrested. The miners subsequently argued that the police had had no right to interfere with their freedom of movement by, in effect, preventing them from entering a large exclusion zone around the collieries concerned. This argument, however, cut no ice in the High Court, which held that, in the circumstances—which included many other violent confrontations during the course of the strike—the police had been entitled to do as they had done. Giving the judgment of the Court, Skinner J said: 'Provided they honestly and reasonably form the opinion that there is a real risk of a breach of the peace in the sense that it is in close proximity both in place and time, then

---

[97] *Bibby* at 302–3.   [98] *Redmond-Bate* at 253.

[99] *R (Laporte) v Chief Constable of Gloucestershire Constabulary* [2006] UKHL 55, [2007] 2 AC 105, [124]. See also Lord Mance's comments at [148].

[100] *Austin v Commissioner of Police of the Metropolis* [2007] EWCA Civ 989, [2008] QB 660, [35], relying upon *obiter dicta* in *Laporte*.   [101] [1985] IRLR 76.

the conditions exist for reasonable preventative action including, if necessary, the measures taken in this case.'[102]

However, the law in this area has moved on, thanks in no small part to the HRA. *Laporte* is now the leading case.[103] It concerned three coachloads of people travelling from London towards an airbase at which they planned to participate in a protest against the war in Iraq. Fearing that among the occupants of the coaches were members of the 'Wombles', a group thought likely to attempt to gain unlawful access to the airbase, the police stopped the coaches 5 km by road (2 km in a straight line) from the airbase's perimeter fence. Having searched the coaches and formed the view that some, but not all, of their occupants were Wombles, the police did not arrest anyone for breach of the peace, but instead ordered the coaches and their occupants to turn back. Police outriders escorted the coaches to London to ensure that they did not attempt to return to the airbase and to prevent anyone from disembarking until arrival in London. These facts gave the court—which held that the police had acted unlawfully—an opportunity to clarify two key issues regarding the police's breach of the peace powers.

First, it was held that *only when a breach of the peace is imminent* may the police exercise such powers. In *Laporte*, the police conceded that, when they stopped the coaches and later ordered them back to London, they did not think a breach of the peace to be imminent. They accepted, that in those circumstances, they could not arrest anyone for breach of the peace, but contended that they could exercise less draconian powers such as turning the coaches back. This was based on remarks of Skinner J in *Moss v McLachlan* that '[t]he imminence or immediacy of the threat to the peace determines what action is reasonable'.[104] On this view, observed Lord Rodger in *Laporte*, 'a police officer would have the power—and duty—to take less drastic action (such as stopping cars), at an earlier stage than he would have the power and duty to take more serious action (such as arresting potential lawbreakers)'.[105] But this approach—which Lord Rodger said would 'weaken the long-standing safeguard against unnecessary and inappropriate interventions by the police'[106]—was rejected in *Laporte*, the court holding that *none* of the police's powers to prevent a breach of the peace becomes exercisable until such a breach is imminent (that is, 'on the point of happening').[107]

Second, as well as clarifying, and circumscribing, the circumstances in which the police may intervene *at all*, *Laporte* underlines the limits on what the police may do when they are allowed to intervene. In particular, the reasoning in *Laporte* is infused with the ECHR concept of proportionality. In the present context, that concept requires that the police only intervene when, and to the extent to which, it is necessary to do so to maintain public order. Although it was not necessary to decide this point (because it had already been held that *no* intervention was permissible in the

---

[102] *Moss v McLachlin* at [20].
[103] *R (Laporte) v Chief Constable of Gloucestershire Constabulary* [2006] UKHL 55, [2007] 2 AC 105.
[104] *Moss v McLachlin* at [39].   [105] *Laporte* at [63].   [106] *Laporte* at [66].
[107] *Laporte* at [39], *per* Lord Bingham.

absence of an imminent breach of the peace), it was said in *Laporte* that even if intervention were to have been permissible, the police would have been unable to show that their reaction had constituted a necessary and proportionate limitation of the right to protest. In the first place, they had intervened prematurely. While it would be unreasonable to require the police to stay their hand until the instant before the outbreak of violence, intervention at the early stage chosen by the police in *Laporte* was unnecessary: bearing in mind the extensive preparations that the police had made at the airbase, it had been unreasonable to assume that the people on the coach would have become involved in violent confrontations upon arrival. Moreover, the action taken by the police was unnecessarily draconian. Lord Rodger pointed out that the police had been unable to demonstrate the inadequacy of less drastic action such as allowing everyone to proceed to the airbase and arresting anyone who subsequently became, or threatened to become, violent, or arresting Wombles and letting everyone else go to the airbase.[108] It was therefore held that the police's 'general and indiscriminate' action was disproportionate and unlawful.[109] The position is different, however, if draconian action can be shown by the police to be necessary. In the *Austin* case—the House of Lords' decision in which is considered below—the Court of Appeal held that the detention for several hours of innocent third parties was lawful because, in the exceptional circumstances of the case, nothing less drastic would have sufficed to prevent an imminent breach of the peace.[110]

> **Q** Do you think that the court got it right in *Laporte*, or might it be argued that the decision places the police under an unacceptable duty to make fine judgements in the heat of the moment rather than (as in the case of the court) with the benefit of hindsight?

5.5 Breach of the peace and criminal liability

Although, as we have seen, people can be arrested for breach of the peace, it is not actually a criminal offence—but a breach of the peace is not itself unimportant. The fact that the police can take action against those committing or threatening imminently to commit a breach of the peace, including arresting them, means that it is a powerful tool for managing public order—and a potentially potent restriction on the right to protest. Nevertheless, it is not possible to charge someone with an offence of breaching the peace. If the police wish to press charges—thus raising the prospect of criminal liability and punishment, as distinct from the prevention or disruption of disorderly conduct—they must be charged with something that does constitute a criminal offence.[111]

---

[108] *Laporte* at [89].   [109] *Laporte* at [153]–[155], *per* Lord Mance.

[110] *Austin v Commissioner of Police of the Metropolis* [2007] EWCA Civ 989, [2008] QB 660. The House of Lords was not concerned with this aspect of the case on appeal.

[111] It is also possible for someone to be 'bound over' to keep the peace. This involves the court requiring the person to enter into an undertaking to pay a sum of money to the Crown if, within a stipulated period, he

One possibility—and an offence that is frequently pressed into service in this context—is the crime of resisting, or wilfully obstructing, a police constable in the execution of his duty.[112] Since one of the duties of a police constable is to maintain the peace, he may issue directions considered reasonably necessary to that end—and anyone who fails to obey them may commit the offence of obstruction. Feldman notes that this approach is 'regularly used to criminalise otherwise lawful behaviour in ways that interfere with freedom of expression and assembly'.[113] The extent to which this offence threatens to undermine the legality of legitimate protest principally depends upon how we draw the boundaries of a police constable's duty. The offence is not committed by anyone who fails to comply with instructions issued to them by a police constable; rather, it is only committed if, in the first place, those instructions are issued in pursuance of the constable's duty to maintain the peace. Importantly, under s 6 of the HRA, police constables, like all public authorities and officials, are required to act in accordance with the ECHR. It follows that a police constable will be acting *outside* the scope of his duty if he issues instructions that, if complied with, would entail unnecessary or disproportionate restrictions upon the right to protest. For example, applying the principles considered in the previous sections, if a police constable were to instruct someone to stop protesting when no breach of the peace was imminent, he would be acting outside the scope of his duty, and no criminal liability could arise. The upshot of all of this is that the extent to which protestors are at risk of committing the offence of obstruction is informed by the right to protest; the effect of the HRA is to preclude the criminalisation of activities that constitute legitimate exercises of the rights of freedom of speech and assembly.

5.6 **Evaluation**

It has, on occasion, been argued that the very existence of the police's breach of the peace powers is incompatible with the requirements of the ECHR. In particular, the Convention stipulates that any restriction upon the freedoms of expression and assembly must be 'prescribed by law'. The ECtHR has held that this means, *inter alia*, that any law imposing such restrictions, 'whether written or unwritten, [must] be sufficiently precise to allow the citizen—if need be, with appropriate advice—to foresee, to a degree that is reasonable in the circumstances, the consequences which a given action may entail'.[114] In fact, the ECtHR held in *Steel v UK*[115] that the law in this area *is* sufficiently precise—and several of the recent cases discussed above have provided significant clarification. Yet it has been argued that important issues remain uncertain, and that this is, at best, undesirable. For example, the definition of 'breach

---

or she breaches the peace. See generally Feldman, 'The King's Peace, the Royal Prerogative and Public Order: The Roots and Early Development of Binding Over Powers' [1988] CLJ 101.

112 Police Act 1996, s 89(2).

113 Feldman, *Civil Liberties and Human Rights in England and Wales* (Oxford 2002), p 1035.

114 *Steel v UK* (1999) 28 EHRR 603, [54].   115 (1999) 28 EHRR 603.

of the peace'—which refers, *inter alia*, to damage or harm to persons or property—does not clearly identify the severity of the required damage or harm. Similarly, while we know that a breach of the peace can occur if such damage or harm is likely, the case law does not clearly specify the degree of likelihood necessary to trigger a breach of the peace.[116]

Although perhaps undesirable, these areas of uncertainty are not, in themselves, knockout arguments for ridding English law of the notion of breach of the peace. However, they acquire additional potency when combined with a related point: that legislation confers upon the police extensive—and, in general, much more clearly defined—powers to manage public protests. As Stone observes: 'In the majority of situations in which a police officer might wish to use the breach of the peace power, there is an equivalent statutory power available.'[117] The risk that Stone perceives is that the existence of a 'catch-all' breach of the peace power will allow the police to intervene in a broader range of situations and to a greater extent than they can under their generally more tightly defined statutory powers. For example, in *Laporte*, Lord Bingham remarked that, in the Public Order Act 1986, Parliament had 'conferred carefully defined powers and imposed carefully defined duties' on the police: 'Offences were created and defences provided.' Resisting arguments on behalf of the police that their power to intervene in relation to breaches of the peace was constrained only by a vague notion of reasonableness, Lord Bingham said that he would find it 'surprising' if, alongside the police's closely defined statutory powers, there were to exist a common law power to control breaches of the peace 'bounded only by an uncertain and undefined condition of reasonableness'.[118]

Concerns about the breadth of the police's breach of the peace powers are potentially rendered less pressing by the fact that such powers now have to be exercised compatibly with the ECHR. But whether this is an adequate answer to criticisms such as Stone's depends on whether the courts are willing to give the relevant Convention rights sufficient bite. While several of the cases considered above are encouraging in this regard, we will see in the next section that it would be remiss to assume that the HRA has adequately curbed the breach of the peace doctrine.

5.7 **Article 5**

So far, our focus has been on the compatibility of English law with the provisions in Arts 10 and 11 of the ECHR, concerning freedom of speech and freedom of assembly. However, it is also necessary to consider the 'right to liberty and security of person' under Art 5. The most obvious way in which that right can be infringed is by imprisonment: someone locked in a prison cell does not enjoy liberty of the person in any meaningful sense. What is the relevance of this to the right to protest? Clearly, if

---

[116] Stone, 'Breach of the Peace: The Case for Abolition' [2001] 2 Web JCLI.
[117] [2001] 2 Web JCLI.
[118] *R (Laporte) v Chief Constable of Gloucestershire Constabulary* [2006] UKHL 55, [2007] 2 AC 105, [46].

'liberty' were simply to mean 'freedom of movement', in the sense of having the right to go wherever one wanted, then any power to control where protests can take place would constitute an infringement. However, the right to liberty is not as wide as that: a person is not deprived of his liberty simply because he is not permitted to enter or protest in a particular place. It follows that no difficulty in relation to Art 5 arises when the police exercise their powers under, for example, ss 11–14C of the Public Order Act 1986. However, this is without prejudice to the fact that there are ways more subtle than imprisonment—and which are relevant to the right to protest—in which the right to liberty may be infringed.

It is one thing to say that the right to liberty does not enable protestors to demonstrate wherever they desire—but what of a situation in which people engaged in a protest are forced to enter and remain in a particular location? The right to freedom of assembly is rendered largely worthless if protestors can lawfully be corralled by the authorities into a small area and required to remain there for several hours until a perceived threat of violence—whether from the protestors or from counter-demonstrators—has decayed. This tactic, known colloquially as 'kettling', has the effect of ghettoising protest: it prevents precisely the kind of interaction between protestors and the wider public that makes demonstrations worthwhile. It is a tactic that has been used by the police in attempts to control protests in which they anticipate serious violence or damage to property.[119] But those on the receiving end have argued that kettling constitutes an unlawful deprivation of liberty and should not therefore be used to restrict the right to protest.

That argument was considered in the case of *Austin v Commissioner of Police of the Metropolis*.[120] The police had good reason—on the basis of intelligence and past events—to expect that, on May Day 2001, serious public disorder would occur in central London spearheaded by up to 1,000 hardcore anti-capitalism protestors. Literature circulated by the organisers included incitement to looting and violence. Earlier in the day than the police had expected, demonstrators descended upon Oxford Circus, and it was decided that, in order to prevent injury to passers-by and damage to property, the protestors should be contained by placing an absolute cordon around them under breach of the peace powers. As a result, 3,000 people—including many who had done nothing wrong and who had no intention of doing anything violent or otherwise unlawful, some of whom were merely passers-by caught up in the melée—were penned into Oxford Circus and prevented from leaving for seven hours. Although the police sought to release people as soon as possible—and indeed did release 400 people who appeared to have nothing to do with the demonstration—the delay in releasing the majority resulted from the violent conduct of a large minority of the crowd, some of whom threw missiles at the police. Faced with such a difficult situation, the question was whether the police had acted lawfully by responding as they did—in particular, had the protestors' right to liberty under Art 5 been infringed?

---

[119] For discussion of 'kettling', see HMIC, *Adapting to Protest* (London 2009).
[120] [2009] UKHL 5, [2009] 1 AC 564.

Article 5 begins by saying that '[e]veryone has the right to liberty' and that, in general, '[n]o-one shall be deprived of his liberty'. It then goes on to set out particular circumstances in which it is lawful to deprive someone of their liberty. It follows that when courts decide issues arising under Art 5, they ought to ask themselves two questions, as follows:

(i) *Has the claimant been deprived of her liberty?* (Clearly, if no deprivation of liberty has occurred, there can have been no breach of Art 5.)

(ii) *If so, is that action rendered lawful by virtue of falling within one of the particular circumstances in which deprivation of liberty is permissible under Art 5?* (Those circumstances include lawful detention after conviction by a competent court or for the purpose of preventing the spread of infectious diseases.)

In *Austin*, it might have been expected that the court would say, in answer to the first question, that there had been a deprivation of liberty. If it had done so, it is likely that, in answering the second question, it would have been forced to say that the deprivation was unlawful. This is because the circumstances set out in Art 5 in which deprivation of liberty is permissible do not clearly extend to the maintenance of public order. However, in the event, the absence of any clear basis in Art 5 for deprivation of liberty on public order grounds proved irrelevant, because the court held that, in the first place, seven hours' detention in Oxford Circus did not amount to deprivation of liberty. Two factors underpinned that conclusion.

First, the court noted that there could be 'no room for argument' in relation to 'close confinement in a prison cell': this was the paradigm example of deprivation of liberty.[121] But away from that paradigm, the position is less clear: there is a "grey zone' where it is extremely difficult to draw the line'.[122] Factors relevant to drawing that line include 'the specific situation of the individual', 'the context in which the restriction of liberty occurs', and the extent to which it deviates from the paradigm of imprisonment.[123] It was also considered significant that a separate provision of the ECHR[124]—but one that has no application to the UK because it has not ratified the provision in question—guarantees freedom of movement, the existence of which tended to suggest that a restriction upon *movement* should not automatically be equated to a deprivation of *liberty*.[125]

Second, and, it seems, decisively, it was held that the fact that the police were acting for what the court, quite uncontroversially, regarded as a legitimate purpose—that is, attempting to prevent serious violence and disorder—prevented the containment of the protestors in Oxford Circus from amounting to a deprivation

---

[121] *Austin* at [18], *per* Lord Hope.

[122] *Guzzardi v Italy* (1981) 3 EHRR 333, 387, *per* Judge Matscher.

[123] *R (Laporte) v Chief Constable of Gloucestershire Constabulary* [2006] UKHL 55, [2007] 2 AC 105, [21].   [124] Protocol 4, Art 2.

[125] *Laporte* at [16], *per* Lord Hope; [43], *per* Lord Walker.

of liberty. It was therefore irrelevant that maintaining public order is not a legitimate reason under Art 5 for depriving someone of her liberty: no such deprivation had, on the Law Lords' analysis, taken place. This conclusion, it has been persuasively argued, was based on a misunderstanding of ECtHR case law.[126] In *Saadi v UK*,[127] the ECtHR said that if detention is arbitrary—for example, if the deprivation goes on for longer than is necessary or is imposed in bad faith—then it will automatically be contrary to Art 5. What it meant by this was that even if a given deprivation of liberty is *prima facie* lawful because it falls within the permissible circumstances set out in Art 5, it will be rendered unlawful if the decision to detain the person concerned is an arbitrary one. The leap of logic taken by the House of Lords in *Austin* was to reason that if arbitrariness can make unlawful that which would otherwise be a lawful deprivation of liberty, the absence of arbitrariness—that is, the existence of a good reason, such as preventing public disorder—can prevent something from counting in the first place as a deprivation of liberty. As Feldman has noted, this amounts to supposing that Art 5 'guarantees only freedom from *arbitrary* deprivation of liberty'—but, as he goes on to explain: 'It does not. It guarantees freedom from deprivation of liberty, save in the specific circumstances listed in the Article, and even then only if the action is non-arbitrary.'[128] The better view is that whether detention is arbitrary is relevant only to question (ii)—whether a deprivation is lawful by virtue of falling within one of the permissible circumstances—and is, on this analysis, irrelevant to the prior question whether a deprivation has, in the first place, occurred. As Mead points out, the 'rightful place' for consideration of questions of proportionality, or fair balance, is in assessing the legality of a limitation of a qualified right, not in determining the logically prior issue 'whether an article is engaged at all on the facts'.[129]

The practical effect of *Austin* is to make deprivation of liberty lawful if it strikes a fair balance between the interests of the protestors and the need to maintain public order even though no mention is made of this in Art 5. This might be regarded as an entirely sensible outcome, but the risk is that it might represent the thin end of the wedge. As Feldman puts it, while the Law Lords' intentions might be considered good—they were seeking to strike a balance between the interests of individuals and the wider community—'the road to hell is paved with good intentions', and it is possible to imagine such reasoning 'being applied in other contexts to reduce other fundamental and absolute rights almost to vanishing point'.[130] Fenwick, meanwhile, argues that *Austin* 'fuel[s] once again the argument that abolition of the breach of the peace doctrine, at least in relation to public protest, is overdue'.[131]

---

[126] Feldman, 'Containment, Deprivation of Liberty and Breach of the Peace' [2009] CLJ 243; Mead, 'Of Kettles, Cordons and Crowd Control: *Austin v Commissioner of Police for the Metropolis* and the Meaning of "Deprivation of liberty"' [2009] EHRLR 376.   [127] (2008) 47 EHRR 427.

[128] Feldman at 243–4.   [129] Mead at 385.   [130] Feldman, at 244.

[131] 'Marginalising Human Rights: Breach of the Peace, "Kettling", the Human Rights Act and Public Protest' [2009] PL 737, 757.

Q In *Austin*, Lord Neuberger said it would be 'very odd' if the police could not, without breaching Art 5, act as they had done so as to prevent serious violence and disorder.[132] Do you think that it was acceptable for the Law Lords to fill the perceived lacuna in Art 5—that is, the absence of a public order justification for deprivation of liberty—by treating the police's motivation as relevant to whether there was a deprivation in the first place?

6. Conclusions

For the reasons considered at the beginning of this chapter, freedom of association—and, in particular, the right to protest—is important. It is clear that the right is, in practice, recognised in English law to a significant extent. But, as we have seen, it is equally clear that the right to protest is circumscribed—in some senses, quite heavily—by the law. An important influence in this area, and an important yardstick against which English law falls to be measured, is the ECHR. It is apparent that since that measure was made effective in domestic law by the HRA, there has, in general, been greater recognition of the right to protest. Decisions such as *Jones* (in which the legitimacy of protesting on public highways was recognised), *Laporte* (in which it was made clear that the police must exercise their breach of the peace powers in a way that imposes only necessary and proportionate restrictions on the right to protest), and *Redmond-Bate* and *Bibby* (in which it was held that those powers cannot normally be exercised against peaceful protestors), have all served, under the influence of the HRA, to solidify and extend the right to protest in English law. Equally, however, there are areas in which English law does not yet appear to be on all fours with the requirements of the ECHR. The *Austin* decision, considered in the previous section, is arguably the starkest and most recent example, but into this category also fall the cases considered earlier in the chapter concerning the extent to which protestors' freedom of speech should yield in the face of the 'right' of others not to be offended.

Further reading

GEDDIS, 'Free Speech Martyrs or Unreasonable Threats to Social Peace? "Insulting" Expression and Section 5 of the Public Order Act 1986' [2004] PL 853

FELDMAN, *Civil Liberties and Human Rights in England and Wales* (Oxford 2002), ch 18

FENWICK, 'Marginalising Human Rights: Breach of the Peace, "kettling", the Human Rights Act and Public Protest' [2009] PL 737

MEAD, *The New Law of Peaceful Protest* (Oxford 2010)

WILLIAMS, *Keeping the Peace* (London 1967)

---

[132] *Austin v Commissioner of Police of the Metropolis* [2009] UKHL 5, [2009] 1 AC 564, [64].

Index

Introductory Note

References such as "178–9" indicate (not necessarily continuous) discussion of a topic across a range of pages. Wherever possible in the case of topics with many references, these have either been divided into sub-topics or only the most significant discussions of the topic are listed. Because the entire work is about 'public law', the use of this term (and certain others which occur constantly throughout the book) as an entry point has been minimized. Information will be found under the corresponding detailed topics.